Accounting Trends & Techniques

FIFTY-EIGHTH EDITION 2004

Fifty-eighth annual cumulative survey of the accounting aspects of the annual reports of 600 industrial, merchandising, technology, and service corporations. The reports analyzed are those with fiscal years ended not later than February 1, 2004.

Edited by

Yury Iofe
Senior Editor
Accounting and Auditing Publications

Matthew C. Calderisi, CPA
Managing Editor

03362368

1 2 3 4 5 6 7 8 9 0 AAP 0 9 8 7 6 5 4

ISSN 1531-4340

ISBN 0-87051-604-3

Notice to readers: This book is a publication of the staff of the American Institute of Certified Public
Accountants and is not to be regarded as an official pronouncement of the Institute.

Acknowledgments

Special acknowledgment and sincere thanks are due to the following individuals for their technical assistance in the analysis of the financial reports:

Matthew C. Calderisi, CPA
J. Richard Chaplin, CPA
Constance J. Crawford, CPA
Nickole Forbes, CPA
William A. Godla, CPA
Kathleen V. Karatas, CPA
Gene P. Leporiere, CPA

Toni Monier, CPA
Debra K. Ramnarace, CPA
Gene Ratin, CPA
Richard V. Rikert
Edward W. Swanson, CPA
Anthony E. Tarallo, CPA
Karen Venturini, CPA

In addition, special acknowledgment and sincere thanks are also due to the following individuals for their assistance in the preparation of the manuscript:

J. Richard Chaplin, CPA

Toni Monier, CPA

Edward W. Swanson, CPA

Anthony E. Tarallo, CPA

Preface

Accounting Trends & Techniques—2004, Fifty-Eighth Edition (the current edition), is a compilation of data obtained by a survey of 600 annual reports to stockholders undertaken for the purpose of analyzing the accounting information disclosed in such reports. The annual reports surveyed were those of selected industrial, merchandising, technology, and service companies for fiscal periods ending between February 22, 2003 and February 1, 2004.

Significant accounting trends, as revealed by a comparison of current survey findings with those of prior years, are highlighted in numerous comparative tabulations throughout this publication. These tables show trends in such diverse accounting matters as financial statement format and terminology and the accounting treatment of transactions and events reflected in the financial statements.

Accounting techniques are illustrated by excerpts from the annual reports of the survey companies. References (in the form of a listing of company reference numbers—see the following paragraph) to additional illustrations of an accounting technique may be requested from the American Institute of Certified Public Accountants by contacting **Yury Iofe,** Senior Editor, at:

Harborside Financial Center
201 Plaza Three, Jersey City, NJ 07311-3881
Telephone: (201) 938-3491
Fax: (201) 938-3780
E-mail: yiofe@aicpa.org

Each of the 600 survey companies included in the current edition has been assigned a company reference number which is used for reference in the discussion of pertinent information. Companies not included from the prior edition were eliminated because of a business combination with another company or a delisting by the SEC. The identification numbers of the eliminated companies have not been reused. Over the years, company reference numbers 601 through 1094 have been assigned to the replacement companies. In the current edition, company reference numbers 1095 through 1115 have been assigned to additional replacement companies. The 600 companies in the current edition are listed in the *Appendix of 600 Companies* both alphabetically and by company reference number.

With the appointment of the Public Company Accounting Oversight Board (PCAOB) by the Securities and Exchange Commission, the PCAOB was given responsibility of oversight over the audit of public companies. The Sarbanes-Oxley Act of 2002 authorized the PCAOB to establish auditing and related professional practice standards to be followed by public accounting firms registered with the PCAOB. On a transitional basis, the PCAOB adopted as interim standards, the generally accepted auditing standards described in the AICPA Auditing Standards Board's Statement on Auditing Standards No. 95, *Generally Accepted Auditing Standards*, in existence on April 16, 2003. Subsequently in 2004, the PCAOB issued Auditing Standard (AS) No. 1, *References in Auditors' Reports to the Standards of the Public Company Accounting Oversight Board*, and AS No. 2, *An Audit of Internal Control Over Financial Reporting Performed in Connection With an Audit of Financial Statements*. Although *AS No. 1* and *AS No. 2* did not yet apply to any of the company annual reports surveyed in this edition, a discussion of the reporting implications of *AS No. 1* and *AS No. 2* and illustrative exhibits of the required auditor and management reports can be found in Section 7.

We would appreciate your feedback! We hope the additions described above are informative and useful. However, we urge you to give us your comments regarding the content of this publication, suggested improvements for future editions, and any other feedback. Please direct your comments to **Yury Iofe** at the above address or phone numbers. All comments will be considered and kept strictly confidential.

Robert Durak, CPA, Senior Manager—Accounting & Auditing Publications
AMERICAN INSTITUTE OF CERTIFIED PUBLIC ACCOUNTANTS

Order/technical information:

Accounting Trends & Techniques: (201) 938-3491
AICPA Technical Hotline: (888) 777-7077, option 5
AICPA Member Satisfaction (order department): (888) 777-7077, option 1

TABLE OF CONTENTS

Section 1: General

COMPANIES SELECTED FOR SURVEY

1.01 This section is concerned with general information about the 600 companies selected for the survey and with certain accounting information usually disclosed in notes accompanying the basic financial statements.

1.02 All 600 companies included in the survey are registered with the Securities and Exchange Commission (SEC). Many of the survey companies have securities traded on one of the major stock exchanges—80% on the New York and 2% on the American. The remaining 18% were traded on "over-the-counter" exchanges. Table 1-1 presents an industry classification of the 600 survey companies.

1.03 Each year, companies are selected from the latest Fortune 1000 listing to replace those companies that were deleted from the survey (see the *Appendix of 600 Companies* for a comprehensive listing of the 600 companies as well as those that were added and removed in this edition). Companies are deleted from the survey when they have either been acquired, have become privately held (and are, therefore, no longer registered with the SEC), or have ceased operations.

1.04

TABLE 1-1: INDUSTRY CLASSIFICATIONS

	2003	2002
Advertising, marketing	4	4
Aerospace	17	17
Apparel	14	14
Beverages	10	9
Building materials, glass	8	9
Chemicals	29	29
Computer and data services	17	16
Computer peripherals	8	7
Computer software	9	9
Computers, office equipment	11	11
Diversified outsourcing services	8	7
Electronics, electrical equipment	42	41
Engineering, construction	11	11
Entertainment	6	6
Food	24	27
Food and drug stores	15	13
Food services	6	6
Forest and paper products	20	19
Furniture	12	10
General merchandisers	11	10
Health care	10	9
Hotels, casinos, resorts	8	8
Industrial and farm equipment	35	34
Medical products and equipment	13	12
Metal products	21	21
Metals	14	17
Mining, crude-oil production	13	13
Miscellaneous	9	11
Motor vehicles and parts	17	17
Network communications	6	6
Petroleum refining	13	13
Pharmaceuticals	10	10
Publishing, printing	20	20
Rubber and plastic products	6	6
Scientific, photographic, and control equipment	20	20
Semiconductors	14	14
Soaps, cosmetics	8	8
Specially retailers	17	18
Telecommunications	15	18
Temporary help	5	5
Textiles	5	6
Tobacco	6	6
Toys, sporting goods	2	2
Transportation equipment	4	4
Trucking, truck leasing	5	5
Waste management	3	3
Wholesalers	19	19
Total Companies	**600**	**600**

Accounting Trends & Techniques

1.05 Table 1-2 indicates the relative size of the survey companies as measured by dollar amount of revenue.

1.06

TABLE 1-2: REVENUE OF SURVEY COMPANIES

	2003	2002	2001	2000
Less than $100,000,000.............	23	23	18	25
Between $100,000,000 and $500,000,000.........................	41	44	50	53
Between $500,000,000 and $1,000,000,000......................	52	55	41	43
Between $1,000,000,000 and $2,000,000,000......................	110	128	123	110
	226	**250**	**232**	**231**
Between $2,000,000,000 and $3,000,000,000......................	77	64	77	N/C*
Between $3,000,000,000 and $4,000,000,000......................	42	46	44	N/C*
Between $4,000,000,000 and $5,000,000,000......................	43	40	41	N/C*
Between $5,000,000,000 and $10,000,000,000....................	91	84	80	N/C*
More than $10,000,000,000.......	121	116	126	N/C*
	374	**350**	**368**	**369**
Total Companies.......................	**600**	**600**	**600**	**600**

* N/C = Not compiled. Line item was not included in the table for the year shown.

INFORMATION REQUIRED BY RULE 14a-3 TO BE INCLUDED IN ANNUAL REPORTS TO STOCKHOLDERS

1.07 Rule 14a-3, *Information to Be Furnished to Security Holders*, of the Securities Exchange Act of 1934, states that annual reports furnished to stockholders in connection with the annual meetings of stockholders should include audited financial statements—balance sheets as of the 2 most recent fiscal years, and statements of income and of cash flows for each of the 3 most recent fiscal years. *Rule 14a-3* also states that the following information, as specified in Securities and Exchange Commission (SEC) Regulation S-K, *Standard Instructions for Filling Forms Under the Securities Act of 1933, Securities Exchange Act of 1934 and Energy Policy and Conservation Act of 1975*, should be included in the annual report to stockholders:

1. Selected quarterly financial data.
2. Disagreements with accountants on accounting and financial disclosure.
3. Summary of selected financial data for last 5 years.
4. Description of business activities.
5. Segment information.
6. Listing of company directors and executive officers.
7. Market price of Company's common stock for each quarterly period within the two most recent fiscal years.
8. Management's discussion and analysis of financial condition and results of operations.
9. Quantitative and qualitative disclosures about market risk.

1.08 Examples of items 1, 3, 8, and 9 follow. Included with the item 8 examples are excerpts from management's discussion and analysis as to forward looking information, liquidity and capital resources, and environmental matters.

1.09 Examples of segment information disclosures are presented under "Segment Information" in this section.

Quarterly Financial Data

1.10

L.B. FOSTER COMPANY (DEC)

NOTES TO CONSOLIDATED FINANCIAL STATEMENTS

Note 21. Quarterly Financial Information (Unaudited)

Quarterly financial information for the years ended December 31, 2003 and 2002 is presented below:

(In thousands, except per share amounts)	First Quarter[1]	Second Quarter	Third Quarter[2]	Fourth Quarter	Total
			2003		
Net sales	$59,519	$75,796	$75,802	$53,149	$264,266
Gross profit	$ 6,933	$ 9,196	$ 9,541	$ 6,062	$ 31,732
Income (loss) from continuing operations	$ 64	$ 1,123	$ 1,379	$ (403)	$ 2,163
(Loss) income from discontinued operations	$ (230)	$ (37)	$ 1,546	$ (2)	$ 1,277
Net (loss) income	$ (166)	$ 1,086	$ 2,925	$ (405)	$ 3,440
Basic (loss) earnings per common share:					
From continuing operations	$ 0.01	$ 0.12	$ 0.14	$ (0.04)	$ 0.23
From discontinued operations	$ (0.02)	$ —	$ 0.16	$ —	$ 0.13
Basic (loss) earnings per common share	$ (0.02)	$ 0.11	$ 0.30	$ (0.04)	$ 0.36
Diluted (loss) earnings per common share:					
From continuing operations	$ 0.01	$ 0.12	$ 0.14	$ (0.04)	$ 0.22
From discontinued operations	$ (0.02)	$ —	$ 0.16	$ —	$ 0.13
Diluted (loss) earnings per common share	$ (0.02)	$ 0.11	$ 0.30	$ (0.04)	$ 0.35

[1] Discontinued operations results include the finalized sale of certain assets and liabilities and charges taken primarily related to severance and a lease termination of the Foster Technologies subsidiary.

[2] The results from discontinued operations include the release of a $1,594,000 valuation allowance against foreign net operating losses that will be utilized as a result of the liquidation of the Foster Technologies subsidiary.

(continued)

	2002				
(In thousands, except per share amounts)	First Quarter[1]	Second Quarter	Third Quarter[2][3]	Fourth Quarter[4][5][6]	Total
Net sales	$63,173	$70,806	$66,965	$57,006	$257,950
Gross profit	$ 6,795	$ 8,700	$ 8,344	$ 5,628	$ 29,467
Income (loss) from continuing operations	$ 28	$ 1,063	$ (2,445)	$ (3,675)	$ (5,029)
Loss from discontinued operations	$ (317)	$ (332)	$ (302)	$ (1,054)	$ (2,005)
Cumulative effect of change in accounting principle	$ (4,390)	$ —	$ —	$ —	$ (4,390)
Net (loss) income	$ (4,679)	$ 731	$ (2,747)	$ (4,729)	$ (11,424)
Basic and diluted (loss) earnings per common share:					
From continuing operations	$ —	$ 0.11	$ (0.26)	$ (0.39)	$ (0.53)
From discontinued operations	$ (0.03)	$ (0.03)	$ (0.03)	$ (0.11)	$ (0.21)
From cumulative effect of change in accounting principle	$ (0.46)	$ —	$ —	$ —	$ (0.46)
Basic and diluted (loss) earnings per common share	$ (0.50)	$ 0.08	$ (0.29)	$ (0.50)	$ (1.20)

[1] During the third quarter of 2002, the Company completed its goodwill impairment testing required by the adoption of Statement of Financial Accounting Standards No. 142 "Goodwill and Other Intangible Assets" and recorded a $4,390,000 non-cash charge. In accordance with this standard, this charge was recognized as the cumulative effect of a change in accounting principle as of the date of adoption, January 1, 2002 and accordingly, previously recorded amounts were restated to reflect the adoption of this standard.

[2] Includes a non-cash charge of $2,260,000 related to the mark-to-market accounting for derivative instruments as a result of the Company entering into a new credit agreement late in the third quarter, which discontinued the hedging relationship of the Company's interest rate collars with the underlying debt instrument.

[3] Includes a $1,793,000 "other than temporary" impairment charge related to the Company's equity investment in its principal specialty trackwork supplier.

[4] Includes a $5,050,000 write-down of uncollectible advances made to the Company's principal specialty trackwork supplier and the remaining $100,000 balance in its equity investment.

[5] Includes a $765,000 charge for depreciation expense that had been suspended while the Company's Newport, KY pipe-coating assets were classified as held for resale.

[6] During the fourth quarter, the Company committed to a plan to sell the assets related to its rail signaling business and recorded a $660,000 impairment loss to adjust the assets to their expected realizable value. Accordingly, this business was reclassified as a discontinued operation and prior periods' continuing operations were restated by the amount reflected as discontinued operations.

1.11

THE NEW YORK TIMES COMPANY (DEC)

QUARTERLY INFORMATION (UNAUDITED)

(In thousands, except per share data)	2003 Quarters				
	First	Second	Third	Fourth	Year
Revenues	$783,740	$801,891	$759,287	$882,282	$3,227,200
Costs and expenses	661,445	671,834	666,550	687,821	2,687,650
Operating profit	122,295	130,057	92,737	194,461	539,550
Net (loss)/income from joint ventures	(6,212)	694	130	(2,835)	(8,223)
Interest expense, net	11,802	11,484	11,138	10,333	44,757
Other income	9,527	1,250	1,250	1,250	13,277
Income before income taxes and minority interest	113,808	120,517	82,979	182,543	499,847
Income taxes	44,946	47,606	32,779	72,431	197,762
Minority interest in net (income)/loss of subsidiaries	(16)	(82)	(80)	748	570
Net income	$ 68,846	$ 72,829	$ 50,120	$110,860	$ 302,655
Average number of common shares outstanding					
Basic	151,845	150,730	149,305	149,262	150,285
Diluted	154,598	153,403	151,606	151,775	152,840
Basic earnings per share	$ .45	$ .48	$ .34	$ .74	$ 2.01
Diluted earnings per share	$ .45	$ .47	$ .33	$ .73	$ 1.98
Dividends per share	$ .135	$ .145	$ .145	$ .145	$ .57

(In thousands, except per share data)	2002 Quarters				
	First	Second	Third	Fourth	Year
Revenues	$737,097	$772,211	$729,501	$840,198	$3,079,007
Costs and expenses	638,566	630,483	617,128	647,962	2,534,139
Operating profit	98,531	141,728	112,373	192,236	544,868
Net income/(loss) from joint ventures	241	(1,941)	(4,852)	(5,778)	(12,330)
Interest expense, net	10,555	11,600	11,747	11,533	45,435
Other income	1,250	1,250	1,250	1,250	5,000
Income before income taxes and minority interest	89,467	129,437	97,024	176,175	492,103
Income taxes	34,895	50,486	37,844	68,730	191,955
Minority interest in net (income)/loss of subsidiaries	(102)	(190)	(166)	57	(401)
Net income	$ 54,470	$ 78,761	$ 59,014	$107,502	$ 299,747
Average number of common shares outstanding					
Basic	151,104	151,789	151,668	151,691	151,563
Diluted	154,249	155,555	154,699	154,732	154,805
Basic earnings per share	$ .36	$ .52	$ .39	$ .71	$ 1.98
Diluted earnings per share	$ .35	$ .51	$ .38	$ .69	$ 1.94
Dividends per share	$ .125	$ .135	$ .135	$ .135	$ .53

Selected Information for Five Years

1.12

STANDEX INTERNATIONAL CORPORATION (JUN)

SELECTED FINANCIAL DATA

Selected financial data for the five years ended June 30, 2003
is as follows:

(In thousands)	2003	2002	2001	2000	1999
Summary of operations					
Net sales					
Industrial group	$332,855	$317,743	$327,836	$365,129	$356,393
Food service group	141,867	135,308	143,075	139,633	148,131
Consumer group	99,814	110,150	115,615	115,276	114,023
Total	574,536	563,201	586,526	620,038	618,547
Gross profit	185,483	185,908	195,636	205,205	205,609
Operating income					
Industrial group	35,057	33,419	37,610	47,146	42,764
Food service group	10,455	9,802	13,627	11,409	17,201
Consumer group	2,014	7,114	9,680	9,594	8,707
Restructuring	(5,580)	—	—	(5,408)	1,016
Other, net	(1,306)	—	—	—	—
Corporate	(12,979)	(11,342)	(8,057)	(10,157)	(9,652)
Total	27,661	38,993	52,860	52,584	60,036
Interest expense	6,956	8,546	10,998	10,571	10,492
Other, net	146	(161)	200	608	533
Gain on stock received	—	—	—	2,711	—
Provision for income taxes	7,014	9,657	17,399	18,602	19,264
Income from continuing operations	13,837	20,629	24,663	26,730	30,813
Income/(loss) from discontinued operations	312	(232)	234	973	548
Cumulative effect of accounting change	—	(3,779)	—	—	—
Net income	$ 14,149	$ 16,618	$ 24,897	$ 27,703	$ 31,361
Per share data					
Basic					
Income from continuing operations	$ 1.15	$ 1.70	$ 2.03	$ 2.11	$ 2.38
Income/(loss) from discontinued operations	0.02	(0.02)	0.02	0.08	0.04
Cumulative effect of change in accounting principle	—	(0.31)	—	—	—
Total	$ 1.17	$ 1.37	$ 2.05	$ 2.19	$ 2.42
Diluted					
Income from continuing operations	$ 1.14	$ 1.68	$ 2.00	$ 2.09	$ 2.37
Income/(loss) from discontinued operations	0.02	(0.02)	0.02	0.08	0.04
Cumulative effect of change in accounting principle	—	(0.31)	—	—	—
Total	$ 1.16	$ 1.35	$ 2.02	$ 2.17	$ 2.41
Dividends paid	$ 0.84	$ 0.84	$ 0.83	$ 0.79	$ 0.76
Balance sheet and cash flow					
Total assets	$422,480	$406,039	$424,264	$424,200	$410,042
Accounts receivable	91,714	93,219	98,470	104,431	97,871
Inventories	82,530	92,931	102,674	112,201	120,172
Accounts payable	41,241	35,209	33,554	36,495	35,975
Net working capital	133,003	150,941	167,590	180,137	182,068
Change in net working capital	(17,938)	(16,649)	(12,547)	(1,931)	(1,665)

(continued)

ATT-SEC 1.12

(In thousands)	2003	2002	2001	2000	1999
Long-term debt	$109,019	$ 50,087	$153,019	$153,436	$148,111
Short-term debt	910	82,221	2,532	2,357	3,963
Total debt	109,929	132,308	155,551	155,793	152,074
Less cash	11,509	8,092	8,955	10,438	5,909
Net debt	98,420	124,216	146,596	145,355	146,165
Shareholders' equity	161,922	178,432	172,174	164,814	162,301
Total capitalization	$260,342	$302,648	$318,770	$310,169	$308,466
Depreciation	$ 13,551	$ 13,492	$ 14,221	$ 14,018	$ 14,589
Capital expenditures	7,882	9,883	13,754	22,518	15,702
Cash flow from continuing operations	50,618	42,466	40,811	41,684	33,830
Key statistics					
Gross profit margin	32.28%	33.01%	33.36%	33.10%	33.24%
Operating income margin	4.81	6.92	9.01	8.48	9.71
Net debt to total capital ratio	37.80	41.04	45.99	46.86	47.38

1.13

UNITED STATES STEEL CORPORATION (DEC)

FIVE-YEAR FINANCIAL SUMMARY

(Dollars in millions, except as noted)	2003	2002	2001[a]	2000[a]	1999[a]
Revenues and other income					
Revenues by product:					
Sheet & semi-finished steel products	$ 6,382	$4,048	$3,163	$3,288	$3,433
Plate & tin mill products	1,035	1,057	1,273	977	919
Tubular products	556	554	755	754	221
Raw materials (coal, coke & iron ore)	389	502	485	626	549
Other[b]	966	788	610	445	414
Income (loss) from investees	(11)	33	64	(8)	(89)
Net gains on disposal of assets	85	29	22	46	21
Other income	56	43	3	4	2
Total revenues and other income	$9,458	$7,054	$6,375	$6,132	$5,470
Income (loss) from operations					
Segment income (loss):					
Flat-rolled	$ (54)	$ (84)	$ (596)	$ (65)	$ 70
USSE	203	110	123	2	—
Tubular	(25)	(6)	74	68	(60)
Real estate	50	50	63	65	48
Straightline	(70)	(45)	(19)	—	—
Total reportable segments	104	25	(355)	70	58
Other businesses	(35)	33	(62)	(32)	(4)
Items not allocated to segments	(799)	70	12	66	96
Total income (loss) from operations	(730)	128	(405)	104	150
Net interest and other financial costs	130	115	141	105	74
Income tax provision (benefit)	(454)	(48)	(328)	20	25
Net income (loss) before extraordinary item and cumulative effect					
of change in accounting principle[c]	(406)	61	(218)	(21)	44
Per common share—basic & diluted (in dollars)	(4.09)	.62	(2.45)	(.24)	.49
Net income (loss)	(463)	61	(218)	(21)	44
Per common share—basic & diluted (in dollars)	(4.64)	.62	(2.45)	(.24)	.49

(continued)

(Dollars in millions, except as noted)	2003	2002	2001[a]	2000[a]	1999[a]
Balance sheet position at year-end					
Current assets	$ 3,107	$ 2,440	$ 2,073	$ 2,717	$ 1,981
Net property, plant & equipment	3,415	2,978	3,084	2,739	2,516
Total assets	7,838	7,977	8,337	8,711	7,525
Short-term debt	43	26	32	209	13
Other current liabilities	2,087	1,346	1,226	1,182	1,271
Long-term debt	1,890	1,408	1,434	2,236	902
Employee benefits	2,382	2,601	2,008	1,767	2,245
Preferred securities	226	—	—	249	249
Stockholder's equity	1,093	2,027	2,506[a]	1,919[a]	2,056[a]
Cash flow data					
Net cash from operating activities	$ 577	$ 279	$ 669[d]	$ (627)	$ (80)
Capital expenditures	316	258	287	244	287
Dividends paid	35	19	57[a]	97[a]	97[a]
Employee data					
Total employment costs	$ 2,221[e]	$ 1,744	$ 1,581[f]	$ 1,197[g]	$ 1,148
Average domestic employment costs (dollars per hour)	41.51[e]	37.90	33.88	28.70	28.35
Average number of domestic employees	23,245	20,351	21,078	19,353	19,266
Average number of USSE employees	25,038[h]	15,900	16,083	16,256	—
Number of pensioners at year-end	87,576	88,030	91,003	94,339	97,102[i]
Stockholder data at year-end[j]					
Common shares outstanding (millions)	103.7	102.5	89.2	88.8	88.4
Registered shareholders (in thousands)	44.6	50.0	52.4	50.3	55.6
Market price of common stock	$ 35.02	$ 13.12	$ 18.11	$ 18.00	$ 33.00

[a] See Note 1 of the Notes to Financial Statements for discussion of the basis of presentation and the 2001 Separation from Marathon.

[b] Includes revenue from the sale of steel production by-products; transportation services; steel mill products distribution; the management of mineral resources; the management and development of real estate; and engineering and consulting services.

[c] See Note 12 of the Notes to Financial Statements for the basis of calculating earnings per share.

[d] Includes $819 million of tax settlements with Marathon. See the Statement of Cash Flows.

[e] Includes National Steel Corporation and USSB from dates of acquisition on May 20, 2003 and September 12, 2003, respectively, excluding $623 million of workforce restructuring charges.

[f] Includes East Chicago Tin and Transtar, Inc. subsidiaries from dates of acquisition, March 1, 2001 and March 23, 2001, respectively.

[g] Includes USSK from date of acquisition on November 24, 2000.

[h] Includes USSB from date of acquisition on September 12, 2003.

[i] Includes approximately 8,000 surviving spouse beneficiaries added to the U. S. Steel pension plan in 1999.

[j] Stockholder data prior to December 31, 2001, pertains to USX-U. S. Steel Group common stock.

Management's Discussion and Analysis of Financial Condition and Results of Operations

1.14

APPLIED INDUSTRIAL TECHNOLOGIES, INC. (JUN)

MANAGEMENT'S DISCUSSION AND ANALYSIS OF FINANCIAL CONDITION AND RESULTS OF OPERATIONS

Year Ended June 30, 2003 vs. 2002

Net sales in 2003 were $1.46 billion or slightly above (1%) the prior year's sales. This increase was primarily due to the acquisition of Industrial Equipment Co. Ltd. (IECO), and having one additional business day during the year. The sales product mix for the year was 84.8% industrial products and 15.1% fluid power products compared to 85.0% industrial and 14.8% fluid power in the prior year. Same store sales were slightly above (.4%) the prior year. While there was a reduction of 25 facilities in the U.S., Canada and Mexico, these were offset by the acquisition of 16 IECO facilities in Western Canada. At June 30, 2003, the Company had a total of 440 operating facilities versus 449 at June 30, 2002. Industrial production in the United States continues to be depressed. Our industry tends to lag slightly behind the manufacturing sector which continues to perform at or below the prior year levels reflected in the Manufacturing Capacity Utilization Index as published monthly by the Federal Reserve Board. The Company does not expect inflation or deflation to have a material impact on future revenues.

Despite relatively flat sales, the Company improved its gross profit margins (net sales less cost of sales) to 25.9% from 25.3% in 2002. Improved purchasing practices, improved pricing, training, systems and the growth of our catalog business contributed to this increase. The Company expects fiscal 2004 gross margin levels to be in the 25.5% to 26% range as anticipated improvements in pricing and shipping charges to customers are expected to offset a decline in supplier purchasing allowances and rebates.

Selling, distribution and administrative expense ("SD&A") consists of employee compensation, benefits and other expenses associated with purchasing, warehousing, supply chain management and providing marketing and distribution of the Company's products as well as costs associated with a variety of administrative functions, such as legal, treasury, accounting, tax and facility related expenses. SD&A increased 2.4% compared to the prior year, and increased slightly as a percent of sales to 23.4% from 23.1% in 2002. The increase was primarily due to the IECO acquisition, higher compensation and benefit costs and related payroll taxes based on improved profitability. These additional costs were partially offset by approximately $3.2 million of gains on sales of unneeded real estate and a decrease in bad debt expense due to fewer customer bankruptcies during fiscal 2003.

Operating income increased to $36.3 million in 2003 from $30.8 million in 2002. As a percent of sales, operating income increased to 2.5% in 2003 from 2.1% in 2002. The $5.4 million increase in operating income was due primarily to the improved gross profit margin factors noted above.

Interest expense – net for 2003 decreased $1.4 million, or 21.4%, compared with the prior year primarily from a decrease in average borrowings of $26.5 million related to strong cash flows from operations and lower interest rates.

Other, net represents certain non-operating items of income and expense. During the year, the Company recorded a charge of $2.1 million to provide for its share of net loss and other reserves associated with the Company's iSource Performance Materials LLC ("iSource") affiliate. The Company owns 49% of iSource, a certified minority-owned distributor of standard-use industrial specialty and general maintenance items requiring special shipping and handling. Offsetting the impact of this charge was the receipt of insurance proceeds of $2.1 million for the settlement of a fiscal 2000 property casualty claim.

Income tax expense as a percentage of income before taxes was 35.9% for the year ended June 30, 2003 and 37.9% for the year ended June 30, 2002. This decrease related to a change in the tax law that reduces the Company's taxable income beginning in fiscal 2003. Specifically, the Company can now take a tax deduction for cash dividends paid on Company stock to participant 401(k) plan accounts. Another factor that contributed to the rate decrease was a reduction in effective state, local and foreign tax rates, primarily due to the implementation of various tax planning initiatives. We expect our overall tax rate for fiscal 2004 to be slightly below the fiscal 2003 rate based on current tax laws and regulations.

Net income for the fiscal year ended June 30, 2003, increased $5.1 million or 34.4% from prior years' income before the cumulative effect of accounting change. Net income per share increased 35.5% to $1.03 in 2003 from $.76 in 2002 before the cumulative effect of the accounting change primarily due to the factors described above and a decrease in the average shares attributable to company repurchases.

The number of Company associates was 4,384 at June 30, 2003 and 4,508 at June 30, 2002.

Year Ended June 30, 2002 vs. 2001

Net sales in 2002 decreased to $1.45 billion or 11% below the $1.63 billion generated in 2001. This decrease was primarily due to the slowdown in U.S. industrial activity. Sectors hardest hit by the slowdown include the industrial machinery and equipment, durable goods and electronic equipment industries, all more than 20% below prior year sales levels. These sales decreases were partially offset by stronger sales in the food products and automotive sectors.

Gross margin for the year increased slightly from 25.2% in 2001 to 25.3% in 2002. The 2002 margin was higher than in the prior year due to improved buying practices and increased sales through catalog channels which improved the profitability of our product mix.

Selling, distribution and administrative expenses were approximately $19.4 million lower than in the prior year. The decreased amounts were due to lower incentive and employee benefit expenses attributable to the lower sales volumes, better overall expense management and additional operational efficiencies. SD&A as a percentage of sales was 23.1% in 2002 versus 21.8% in 2001. The increase in SD&A as a percent of sales was due to the lower overall sales noted above.

Operating income decreased to $30.8 million in 2002 from $55.0 million in 2001. As a percent of sales, operating income decreased to 2.1% in 2002 from 3.4% in 2001. The $24.2 million decline in operating income was due to the sales decrease noted above.

Interest expense, net for 2002, decreased $2.4 million or 26.0% compared with the prior year primarily as a result of a decrease in average borrowings related to strong cash flows from operations and lower interest rates.

Income tax expense as a percentage of income before income taxes decreased to 37.9% in 2002 from 38.1% in 2001. The decrease in the effective tax rate resulted from a reduction in the impact of non-deductible items offset somewhat by higher effective state and local income tax rates.

Net income before the cumulative effect of accounting change for the fiscal year ended June 30, 2002, decreased $13.3 million or 47.4% from the prior year. Net income per share before the cumulative effect of the accounting change decreased 46.1% to $.76 in 2002 from $1.41 in 2001 primarily due to the factors described above.

In connection with the adoption of Statement of Financial Accounting Standard ("SFAS") 142, "Goodwill and Other Intangible Assets," the Company recorded a non-cash impairment charge totaling $12.1 million, after tax, or $.63 per share as a change in accounting principle effective July 1, 2001. This charge wrote-off all of the remaining goodwill relating to the Company's fluid power business (see Notes 1 and 4 to the Consolidated Financial Statements).

The number of associates was 4,508 at June 30, 2002 and 4,789 at June 30, 2001.

Liquidity and Capital Resources

The Company generated $67.3 million of cash from operating activities in 2003 and $68.9 million in 2002.

Cash flow from operations depends primarily upon generating operating income, controlling investment in inventories and receivables, and managing the timing of payments to suppliers. The Company has continued to monitor and control its investments in inventories by taking advantage of various vendor purchasing programs and through the use of system enhancements to improve inventory tracking. The Company has continued to improve its collection of accounts receivable through improved billing systems and collection efforts. During the year ended June 30, 2003, inventories decreased approximately $10.4 million, exclusive of the additional $4.2 million of inventory acquired as part of the acquisition of certain assets of IECO. Net of the IECO acquisition, accounts receivable decreased $8.0 million due to improved collections and systems. Accrued expenses increased $15.7 million due to increased personnel compensation and benefit costs.

Cash used by investing activities of $16.3 million for the year ended June 30, 2003 consisted primarily of property purchases of approximately $12.8 million, and the expenditure for the purchase of IECO. The major components of our property and equipment purchases related to our NetPC project which converted all service center order entry equipment from old "green screen" terminals to Internet capable workstations. Additional purchases were made to enhance our AppliedACCESS® Web site and expand our electronic catalog content. The Company also realized proceeds of approximately $7.5 million from property sales, which generated gains of $3.2 million, primarily related to the disposal of unneeded real estate.

For fiscal 2004, our property purchases are expected to be in the $14 million to $15 million range which includes a $7.5 million buyout of properties currently being leased. These include our Ft. Worth distribution center and 3 service centers, all of which were originally constructed for the company under a lease facility 7 years ago (see discussion in Note 11). Depreciation for fiscal 2004 is expected to be in the range of $13 to $15 million.

Cash used in financing activities was approximately $19.0 million in fiscal 2003 and $51.1 million in fiscal 2002. During fiscal 2002, the Company had net repayments under revolving credit agreements of $21.4 million. Additionally, scheduled long-term debt repayments in fiscal 2002 were double the amounts paid in fiscal 2003. The next scheduled principal repayment on our long-term debt is in December 2007.

The following table shows the Company's approximate obligations and commitments to make future payments under contractual obligations as of June 30, 2003 (in thousands):

	Total	Period Less Than 1 Yr.	Period 2–3 Yrs.	Period 4–5 Yrs.	Period Over 5 Yrs.
Operating leases	$ 75,246	$17,496	$21,365	$12,542	$23,843
Long-term debt	75,000			50,000	25,000
Total contractual cash obligations	$150,246	$17,496	$21,365	$62,542	$48,843

The Company also used approximately $9.9 million to repurchase 581 thousand shares during the year for an average price of $17 per share compared to $14.3 million for 817 thousand shares in fiscal 2002.

In July 2003, the Board of Directors increased the authorization to purchase shares of the Company's common stock to 1.0 million shares. These purchases are being made to fund employee benefit programs, equity award programs, and future business acquisitions. These purchases are made in open market and negotiated transactions, from time to time, depending upon market conditions.

In fiscal 2003, the Company continued its practice of paying cash dividends each quarter. As in the last four fiscal years, the Company's dividend was 12 cents per share per quarter. The amount of the dividend paid is recommended quarterly by management and approved by the Company's Board of Directors based on financial performance, cash flow and payout guidelines consistent with other industrial companies.

Capital resources are obtained from income retained in the business, borrowings under the Company's lines of credit, revolving credit agreement and long-term debt facilities and from operating lease arrangements.

See Note 6 to the Consolidated Financial Statements for details regarding the outstanding debt amounts as of June 30, 2003. The Company had no short-term borrowings in fiscal 2003. The average long-term borrowings in fiscal 2003 were $76.4 million compared to the average combined short-term and long-term borrowings of $103.0 million in fiscal 2002. The weighted average interest rate on short-term borrowings in the prior year was 3.7%. The weighted average interest on borrowings under our long-term debt agreements, net of the benefits from interest rate swaps was 5.9% in 2003 and 5.5% in 2002, respectively. The increase in the weighted average interest rate was due to lower benefits from interest rate swap agreements in fiscal 2003 versus fiscal 2002. The effect of the swap agreements was to decrease interest expense by $880 thousand in 2003 and approximately $1.4 million in 2002. These settlement gains are being amortized as a reduction in interest expense of approximately $800 thousand per year over the remaining life of the notes through December 2007.

The Company manages interest rate risk through the use of a combination of fixed rate long-term debt, variable rate borrowings under its committed revolving credit agreement and interest rate swaps. At June 30, 2003, the Company has no variable rate debt or interest rate swaps outstanding. See Note 7 "Risk Management Activities" for additional discussion on the Company's derivative activities.

The Company's working capital at June 30, 2003 was $259.4 million compared to $250.6 million at June 30, 2002. The current ratio was 2.8 and 2.9 at June 30, 2003 and 2002, respectively. The increase in working capital is due to the increase of cash generated from our operating results and from the reduction of receivables and inventories.

The Company has a committed revolving credit agreement expiring in November 2003 with a group of banks. This agreement provides for unsecured borrowings of up to $150.0 million. The Company is currently exploring options to replace this facility and expects to have a replacement facility in place before the current facility expires. The Company had no borrowings outstanding under this facility at June 30, 2003. The Company also has a $10.0 million short-term uncommitted line of credit with a commercial bank that expires October 2003. The Company had no borrowings outstanding under this facility at June 30, 2003. Unused lines under these facilities, net of outstanding letters of credit, totaling $153.0 million are available to fund future acquisitions or other capital and operating requirements. An additional long-term financing shelf facility is in place enabling the Company to borrow up to $100.0 million at its discretion with terms up to twelve years. The Company has no outstanding borrowings under this facility at June 30, 2003.

The aggregate annual maturities of long-term debt are $50.0 million in fiscal 2008 and $25.0 million in fiscal 2011.

Management expects that cash provided from operations, available lines of credit, long-term debt and the use of operating leases will be sufficient to finance normal working capital needs, acquisitions, investments in properties, facilities and equipment and the purchase of additional Company common stock. Management also believes that additional long-term debt and line of credit financing could be obtained based on the Company's credit standing and financial strength.

Critical Accounting Policies

The preparation of financial statements and related disclosures in conformity with accounting principles generally accepted in the United States of America requires management to make judgments, assumptions and estimates at a specific point in time that affect the amounts reported in the Consolidated Financial Statements and disclosed in the accompanying notes. Note 1 to the Consolidated Financial Statements describes the significant accounting policies and methods used in preparation of the Consolidated Financial Statements. Estimates are used for, but not limited to, determining the net carrying value of trade receivables, inventories, goodwill, other intangible assets and recording self-insurance liabilities. Actual results could differ from these estimates. The following critical accounting policies are impacted significantly by judgments, assumptions and estimates used in the preparation of the Consolidated Financial Statements.

Allowances for Slow-Moving and Obsolete Inventories

The Company identifies slow moving or obsolete inventories and estimates appropriate loss provisions related thereto. Historically, these loss provisions have not been significant, as the majority of the Company's inventories are not highly susceptible to obsolescence and are eligible for credit under various supplier return programs. While the Company has no reason to believe its inventory return privileges and programs will be discontinued in the future, its risk of loss associated with obsolete or slow moving inventories would increase if such were to occur.

Allowances for Doubtful Accounts

The Company evaluates the collectibility of accounts receivable based on a combination of factors. Initially, the Company estimates an allowance for doubtful accounts as a percentage of net sales based on historical bad debt experience. This initial estimate is periodically adjusted when the Company becomes aware of a specific customer's inability to meet its financial obligations (e.g., bankruptcy filing) or as a result of changes in the overall aging of accounts receivable. While the Company has a large customer base that is diverse as to industry and geography, a general economic downturn in any of the industry segments in which the Company operates could result in higher than expected customer defaults, and, therefore, the need to revise estimates for bad debts.

Goodwill Accounting

The Company adopted Statement of Financial Accounting Standard ("SFAS") No. 142, "Goodwill and Other Intangible Assets," effective July 1, 2001. Goodwill is no longer amortized but rather is evaluated for impairment. The Company has elected to do annual tests for indications of goodwill impairment as of January 1 of each year. The Company utilizes discounted cash flow models and relevant market multiples for comparable businesses to determine fair value used in the goodwill impairment evaluation. Management's estimates of fair value are based upon factors such as projected future sales, price increases, and other uncertain elements requiring significant judgments. While the Company uses available information to prepare its estimates and to perform impairment evaluations, actual results could differ significantly,

resulting in future impairment and losses related to recorded goodwill balances.

Supplier Purchasing Programs

The Company enters into agreements with certain suppliers providing for inventory purchase rebates. The Company's inventory purchase rebate arrangements are unique to each supplier and are generally annual programs ending at either the Company's June 30th year end or the supplier's year end. Rebates are received in the form of cash or credits against future purchases upon attainment of specified purchase volumes and are received monthly, quarterly or annually based upon actual purchases for such period. The supplier rebates are a specified percentage of the Company's net purchases based upon achieving specific purchasing volume levels. These percentages can increase or decrease based on changes in the volume of purchases.

The Company accrues for the receipt of these inventory purchase rebates based upon actual cumulative purchases of inventory. The percentage level utilized is based upon the estimated total volume of purchases we expect to achieve during the life of the program. Each supplier program is analyzed, reviewed and reconciled each quarter as information becomes available to determine the appropriateness of the amount estimated to be received. Differences between our estimates and actual rebates subsequently received have not been material.

All rebates under these supplier purchasing programs are recognized under the Company's LIFO inventory accounting method as a reduction of cost of sales when the inventories representing these purchases are sold and recorded as cost of sales. The Company's accounting for rebates is in accordance with guidance issued by the FASB in EITF 02-16, "Accounting by a Customer (Including a Reseller) for Certain Consideration Received from a Vendor." While management believes the Company will continue to receive inventory purchase rebates, there can be no assurance that suppliers will continue to provide comparable amounts of rebates in the future.

Self-Insurance Liabilities

The Company has insurance programs to cover workers' compensation, business, automobile, general and product liability risks. The insurance programs have self-insured retention to $350 thousand per claim. On an annual basis, an independent actuarial firm is hired to determine the adequacy of estimated liabilities. The Company accrues estimated losses based on actuarial models and assumptions as well as the Company's historical loss experience. Although management believes that the estimated liabilities for self insurance are adequate, the estimates described above may not be indicative of current and future losses. In addition, the actuarial calculations used to estimate self insurance liabilities are based on numerous assumptions, some of which are subjective. The Company will continue to adjust its estimated liabilities for self insurance, as deemed necessary, in the event that future loss experience differs from historical loss patterns.

Guarantees and Other Off-Balance Sheet Arrangements

In December 2002, the Financial Accounting Standards Board issued Interpretation No. (FIN) 45, "Guarantor's Accounting and Disclosure Requirements". FIN 45 requires the disclosure of any guarantees in place at December 31, 2002 and the recognition of a liability for any guarantees entered into or modified after that date. The Company is a guarantor in three arrangements entered into prior to December 31, 2002 that require disclosure under FIN 45 as follows:

- The Company has a construction and lease facility under which a distribution center and several service centers were constructed by the lessor and leased to the Company under operating lease arrangements. These leases expire in September 2003 and permit the Company to purchase the facilities for $7.5 million. If the Company did not exercise this option, residual value guarantee provisions obligated the Company to compensate the lessor for up to $6.0 million at lease termination depending on the properties' market values at that time. Due to the nature of the guarantee, the Company has not recorded any liability on the financial statements. In July 2003, the Company exercised its option to purchase the facilities effective September 2003.

- In connection with the construction and lease of its corporate headquarters facility, the Company has guaranteed repayment of a total of approximately $5.7 million of taxable development revenue bonds issued by Cuyahoga County and the Cleveland-Cuyahoga County Port Authority. These bonds were issued with a 20-year term and are scheduled to mature in March 2016. Any default, as defined in the guarantee agreements, would obligate Applied for the full amount of the outstanding bonds through maturity. Due to the nature of the guarantee, the Company has not recorded any liability on the financial statements.

- The Company also has guaranteed, under an agreement scheduled to expire in December 2003, a related entity's repayment of borrowings under a line of credit. This guarantee was entered into to induce a financial institution to provide a line of credit for a joint venture, iSource Performance Materials L.L.C. (iSource), of which the Company is a minority owner. iSource is a certified minority-owned distributor of standard-use industrial specialty and general maintenance items requiring special shipping and handling. Any default, as defined in the guarantee agreement, will obligate the Company for any unpaid balance under the line of credit up to a maximum of $3.0 million.

In the event of a default and subsequent payout under any or all of these guarantees, the Company maintains the right to pursue all legal options available to mitigate its exposure.

New Accounting Pronouncements

The Company adopted SFAS 144 "Accounting for Impairment or Disposals of Long-Lived Assets" and SFAS 146, "Accounting for Costs Associated with Exit or Disposal Activities" as of July 1, 2002. The adoption of these statements did not have a material impact on the consolidated statements.

In December 2002, the Financial Accounting Standards Board issued SFAS 148, "Accounting for Stock-Based Compensation—Transition and Disclosure." The impact of this statement on the Company's current accounting policies was to amend the disclosure requirements of SFAS 123, "Accounting for Stock-Based Compensation" and require additional disclosure in the Company's quarterly financial statements. The Company adopted SFAS 148 effective January 1, 2003 (see Note 1).

In January 2003, the Financial Accounting Standards Board issued FIN 46, "Consolidation of Variable Interest Entities." As disclosed above, the Company is a minority owner in iSource and has guaranteed iSource's line of credit debt up to $3.0 million. iSource maintains assets of approximately $3.7 million. The Company's purchases currently account for more than 90% of iSource's sales and the Company is considered the primary beneficiary of iSource's operations. Accordingly, iSource's financial statements will be consolidated with the Company's beginning in July 2003 in accordance with the effective date of FIN 46. It is expected that the effect on the Company's consolidated financial statements will be immaterial.

Other Matters

In October 2002, the Company acquired certain assets of Industrial Equipment Co., Ltd. (IECO), a Canadian distributor of industrial products, for approximately $11.5 million. This acquisition was paid for from existing cash balances. The results of the acquired business operations are not material for periods represented. The acquired operations are reported in our service center based distribution segment from the acquisition date. The business contributed $12.2 million in sales from the date of acquisition through June 30, 2003. Sales and operating results to date have met Company expectations.

Cautionary Statement Under Private Securities Litigation Reform Act

This Annual Report to Shareholders, including Management's Discussion and Analysis, contains statements that are forward-looking, based on management's current expectations about the future. Forward-looking statements are often identified by qualifiers, such as "expect," "believe," "intend," "will," and similar expressions. The Company intends that the forward-looking statements be subject to the safe harbors established in the Private Securities Litigation Reform Act of 1995 and by the Securities and Exchange Commission in its rules, regulations and releases.

Readers are cautioned not to place undue reliance on any forward-looking statements. All forward-looking statements are based on current expectations regarding important risk factors. Accordingly, actual results may differ materially from those expressed in the forward-looking statements, and the making of such statements should not be regarded as a representation by the Company or any other person that the results expressed in the statements will be achieved. In addition, the Company undertakes no obligation publicly to update or revise any forward-looking statements, whether because of new information or events, or otherwise.

Important risk factors include, but are not limited to, the following: changes in the economy or in specific customer industry sectors; reduction in manufacturing capacity in our targeted geographic markets due to consolidation in customer industries and the transfer of manufacturing capacity to foreign countries; changes in interest rates; changes in customer procurement policies and practices; changes in product manufacturer sales policies and practices; the availability of products and labor; changes in operating expenses; the effect of price increases or decreases; the variability and timing of business opportunities including acquisitions, alliances, customer agreements and supplier authorizations; the Company's ability to realize the anticipated benefits of acquisitions and other business strategies; the incurrence of debt and contingent liabilities in connection with acquisitions; changes in accounting policies and practices; the effect of organizational changes within the Company; the emergence of new competitors, including firms with greater financial resources than the Company; risks and uncertainties associated with the Company's expansion into foreign markets, including inflation rates, recessions, and foreign currency exchange rates; adverse results in significant litigation matters; adverse regulation and legislation; and the occurrence of extraordinary events (including prolonged labor disputes, natural events and acts of God, fires, floods and accidents).

Quantitative and Qualitative Disclosures About Market Risk

We have evaluated the Company's exposure to various market risk factors, including but not limited to, interest rate, foreign currency exchange and commodity price risks. The Company is primarily affected by market risk exposure through the effect of changes in interest rates. The Company manages interest rate risk through the use of a combination of fixed rate long-term debt, variable rate borrowings under its committed revolving credit agreement and interest rate swaps. There were no variable rate borrowings under its committed revolving credit agreement and no interest rate swap agreements outstanding at June 30, 2003. All the Company's outstanding debt is currently at fixed interest rates at June 30, 2003.

The Company mitigates its foreign currency exposure from the Canadian dollar through the use of cross currency swap agreements as well as foreign-currency denominated debt. Hedging of the U.S. dollar denominated debt used to fund a substantial portion of the Company's net investment in its Canadian operations is accomplished through the use of cross currency swaps. Any gain or loss on the hedging instrument offsets the gain or loss on the underlying debt. Translation exposures with regard to our Mexican subsidiary are not hedged, as our Mexican activity is not material at this time. The impact on the Company's future earnings from exposure to changes in foreign currency exchange rates is expected to be immaterial.

1.15

COSTCO WHOLESALE CORPORATION (AUG)

MANAGEMENT'S DISCUSSION AND ANALYSIS OF FINANCIAL CONDITION AND RESULTS OF OPERATIONS

Certain statements contained in this document constitute forward-looking statements within the meaning of the Private Securities Litigation Reform Act of 1995. For these purposes, forward-looking statements are statements that address activities, events, conditions or developments that the Company expects or anticipates may occur in the future. Such forward-looking statements involve risks and uncertainties that may cause actual events, results or performance to differ materially from those indicated by such statements. These risks and uncertainties include, but are not limited to, domestic and international economic conditions including exchange rates, the effects of competition and regulation, conditions affecting the acquisition, development, ownership or use of real estate, actions of vendors, rising costs associated with employees (including health care and workers' compensation costs), consumer and small business debt levels and spending patterns, and other risks identified from time to time in the Company's public statements and reports filed with the Securities and Exchange Commission.

Comparison of Fiscal 2003 (52 Weeks) and Fiscal 2002 (52 Weeks) (Dollars in Thousands, Except Earnings Per Share)

Net income for fiscal 2003 increased 3% to $721,000, or $1.53 per diluted share, from $699,983, or $1.48 per diluted share during fiscal year 2002.

Net sales increased 10% to $41,692,699 in fiscal 2003 from $37,993,093 in fiscal 2002. Approximately 55% of the increase was due to an increase in comparable warehouse sales, that is sales in warehouses open for at least a year, and approximately 45% of the increase was due to opening a net of 23 new warehouses (29 opened, 6 closed) during fiscal 2003 and a net of 29 new warehouses (35 opened, 6 closed) during fiscal 2002, a portion of which is not included in comparable warehouse sales. With the exception of gasoline, which accounted for a comparable sales increase of approximately 70 basis points, changes in prices of merchandise did not materially contribute to sales increases. In addition, due to the weaker US dollar, translation of foreign sales into US dollars contributed to the increase in sales, accounting for a comparable sales increase of approximately one percent year-over-year. Comparable sales increased at a 5% annual rate in fiscal 2003 compared to a 6% annual rate during fiscal 2002.

Membership fees and other revenue increased 11% to $852,853, or 2.05% of net sales, in fiscal 2003 from $769,406 or 2.03% of net sales, in fiscal 2002. This increase was primarily due to additional membership sign-ups at the 23 new warehouses opened in fiscal 2003, and increased penetration of the Company's Executive Membership. Overall, member renewal rates remained consistent with the prior year, currently at 86%.

Gross margin (defined as net sales minus merchandise costs) increased 11% to $4,457,316, or 10.69% of net sales, in fiscal 2003 from $4,009,972, or 10.55% of net sales, in fiscal 2002. The increase in gross margin as a percentage of net sales reflects merchandise gross margin improvement within the Company's ancillary warehouse businesses and international operations accounting for increases of 15 and 8 basis points, respectively. Additionally, increased rewards related to the Executive Membership Two-Percent Reward Program reduced gross margin by 7 basis points. The gross margin figures reflect accounting for most U.S. merchandise inventories on the last-in, first-out (LIFO) method. The effect of the LIFO adjustment for fiscal 2003 was to increase gross margin by $19,650, compared to a gross margin increase of $13,500 in fiscal 2002. If all inventories had been valued using the first-in, first-out (FIFO) method, inventories would have been lower by $19,500 at August 31, 2003 and higher by $150 at September 1, 2002.

Selling, general and administrative expenses as a percent of net sales increased to 9.83% during fiscal 2003 from 9.41% during fiscal 2002. The increase in selling, general and administrative expenses as a percent of net sales was primarily due to increases in healthcare, workers' compensation (primarily in the state of California) and salary costs within the Company's domestic operations. International expenses also increased, accounting for approximately 7 basis points of the 42 basis points year-over-year increase.

Preopening expenses totaled $36,643, or 0.09% of net sales, during fiscal 2003 and $51,257, or 0.13% of net sales, during fiscal 2002. During fiscal 2003, the Company opened 29 new warehouses (including 5 relocations) compared to 35 new warehouses (including 6 relocations) during fiscal 2002. Pre-opening expenses also include costs related to remodels and expanded ancillary operations at existing warehouses, as well as expanded international operations.

The provision for impaired assets and closing costs was $19,500 in fiscal 2003 compared to $21,050 in fiscal 2002. The provision includes costs related to impairment of long-lived assets, future lease obligations of warehouses that have been relocated to new facilities and any losses or gains resulting from the sale of real property. The provision for fiscal 2003 included charges of $11,836 for warehouse closing expenses, $4,697 for impairment of long-lived assets and $2,967 for net losses on the sale of real property. The fiscal 2002 provision included charges of $13,683 for warehouse closing expenses and $7,765 for Canadian administrative reorganization, which were offset by $398 of net gains on the sale of real property. At August 31, 2003 the reserve for warehouse closing costs was $8,609, of which $7,833 related to lease obligations. This compares to a reserve for warehouse closing costs of $11,845 at September 1, 2002, of which $10,395 related to lease obligations.

Interest expense totaled $36,920 in fiscal 2003, and $29,096 in fiscal 2002. Interest expense in fiscal 2003 includes interest on the $3\frac{1}{2}$% Zero Coupon Notes, $7\frac{1}{8}$% and $5\frac{1}{2}$% Senior Notes and on balances outstanding under the Company's bank credit facilities and promissory notes. The increase is primarily related to the reduction in interest capitalized related to warehouse construction, as the overall cost of projects under construction was lower than in fiscal 2002. The increase was also attributed to the Company's issuance of $300,000 $5\frac{1}{2}$% Senior Notes in March 2002, which were simultaneously swapped to a floating interest rate. This increase was partially offset by an interest rate reduction in the Company's $300,000 $7\frac{1}{8}$% Senior Notes, resulting from interest rate swap agreements entered into effective November 13, 2001, converting the interest rate from fixed to floating, and to the fact that the Company had little interest expense related to borrowings under its commercial paper program in fiscal 2003.

Interest income and other totaled $38,525 in fiscal 2003, compared to $35,745 in fiscal 2002. The increase primarily reflects greater interest earned on higher cash and cash equivalents balances on hand throughout fiscal 2003, as compared to fiscal 2002, which was partially offset by an increase in the expense to record the minority interest in earnings of foreign subsidiaries.

The effective income tax rate on earnings was 37.75% in fiscal 2003 and 38.50% in fiscal 2002. The decrease in the effective income tax rate, year-over-year, is primarily attributable to lower statutory income tax rates for foreign operations.

Comparison of Fiscal 2002 (52 Weeks) and Fiscal 2001 (52 Weeks) (Dollars in Thousands, Except Earnings Per Share)

Net income for fiscal 2002 increased 16% to $699,983, or $1.48 per diluted share, from $602,089, or $1.29 per diluted share during fiscal year 2001.

Net sales increased 11% to $37,993,093 in fiscal 2002 from $34,137,021 in fiscal 2001. This increase was due to higher sales at existing locations opened price to fiscal 2001; increased sales at the 32 new warehouses opened (39 opened, 7 closed) during fiscal 2001; and first year sales at the 29 new warehouses opened (35 opened, 6 closed) during fiscal 2002. Changes in prices did not materially impact sales levels.

Comparable sales, that is sales in warehouses open for at least a year, increased at a 6% annual rate in fiscal 2002 compared to a 4% annual rate during fiscal 2001.

Membership fees and other revenue increased 17% to $769,406, or 2.03% of net sales, in fiscal 2002 from $660,016, or 1.93% of net sales, in fiscal 2001. This increase was primarily due to the increase in membership fees across all member categories—beginning with renewals on October 1, 2000, averaging approximately five dollars per member; additional membership sign-ups at the 29 new warehouses opened in fiscal 2002; and increased penetration of the Company's Executive Membership. Overall, member renewal rates remained consistent with the prior year, currently at 86%.

Gross margin (defined as net sales minus merchandise costs) increased 13% to $4,009,972, or 10.55% of net sales, in fiscal 2002 from $3,538,881, or 10.37% of net sales, in fiscal 2001. The increase in gross margin as a percentage of net sales reflects merchandise gross margin improvement within the Company's core merchandising business, with fresh foods and foods and sundries categories being the primary contributors. Additionally, a reduction in the LIFO reserve, improved purchasing resulting from expanded depot operations and improved international operations had a positive effect on margins, while increased costs related to the Executive Membership Two-Percent Reward Program had a negative impact. The gross margin figures reflect accounting for most U.S. merchandise inventories on the last-in, first-out (LIFO) method. The effect of the LIFO adjustment for fiscal 2002 was to increase gross margin by $13,500, compared to a gross margin decrease of $5,500 in fiscal 2001. If all inventories had been valued using the first-in, first-out (FIFO) method, inventories would have been higher by $150 at September 1, 2002 and $13,650 at September 2, 2001.

Selling, general and administrative expenses as a percent of net sales increased to 9.41% during fiscal 2002 from 9.17% during fiscal 2001. The increase in selling, general and administrative expenses as a percent of net sales was primarily due to higher expense ratios at new warehouses, where such expense ratios to sales are typically higher than at more mature warehouses; and also due to increases in salary, healthcare and workers' compensation costs.

Preopening expenses totaled $51,257, or 0.13% of net sales, during fiscal 2002 and $59,571, or 0.17% of net sales, during fiscal 2001. During fiscal 2002, the Company opened 35 new warehouses (including relocations) compared to 39 new warehouses (including relocations) during fiscal 2001. Pre-opening expenses also include costs related to remodels and expanded ancillary operations at existing warehouses, as well as expanded international operations.

The provision for impaired assets and closing costs was $21,050 in fiscal 2002 compared to $18,000 in fiscal 2001. The fiscal 2002 provision included charges of $7,765 for the Canadian administrative reorganization (See "Item 7—Management's Discussion and Analysis of Financial Condition and Results of Operations"—Liquidity and Capital Resources) and $13,683 for warehouse closing expenses which were offset by net gains on the sale of real property totaling $398. The fiscal 2001 provision included charges of $19,000 for the Canadian administrative reorganization, $15,231 for the impairment of long-lived assets and $2,412 for warehouse closing expense, which were offset by $18,643 of gains on the sale of real property. At September 1, 2002, the reserve for warehouse closing costs was $11,845, of which $10,395 related to future lease obligations. This compares to a reserve for warehouse closing costs of $15,434 at September 1, 2001, of which $6,538 related to future lease obligations. The increase in future lease obligation is attributable to leased warehouses constituting a larger percentage of the closed locations. (See Part II, "Item 8—Financial Statements"—Notes to Consolidated Financial Statements—Note 1).

Interest expense totaled $29,096 in fiscal 2002, and $32,024 in fiscal 2001. The decrease is primarily attributable to the retirement in April 2001 of a $140,000 unsecured note payable to banks and to the interest rate reduction on the Company's $300,000 $7\frac{1}{8}$% Senior Notes, resulting from interest rate swap agreements entered into effective November 13, 2001, converting the interest rate from fixed to floating. This decrease in interest expense was partially offset by a reduction in interest capitalized related to warehouse construction, as the Company had fewer construction projects in progress during the fiscal 2002 period, and the weighted average capitalized interest rate was lower than in fiscal 2001. The decrease in interest expense was also offset by the issuance of the $300,000 $5\frac{1}{2}$% Senior Notes issued in March, 2002, and simultaneously swapped to floating, and increased interest expense related to the Zero Coupon subordinated notes as accrued interest is accreted into principal.

Interest income and other totaled $35,745 in fiscal 2002, compared to $43,238 in fiscal 2001. The decrease primarily reflects lower interest income due to lower interest rates and lower daily cash and short-term investment balances on hand throughout fiscal 2002, as compared to fiscal 2001. This was partially offset by increased year-over-year earnings in Costco Mexico, the Company's 50%-owned joint venture.

The effective income tax rate on earnings was 38.5% in fiscal 2002 and 40% in fiscal 2001. The decrease in the effective income tax rate, year-over-year, is primarily attributable to lower statutory rates for foreign operations, the effect of which is expected, substantially, to continue to impact the effective tax rate on a prospective basis.

Liquidity and Capital Resources (Dollars in Thousands)

Expansion Plans

Costco's primary requirement for capital is the financing of the land, building and equipment costs for new warehouses plus the costs of initial warehouse operations and working capital requirements, as well as additional capital for international expansion through investments in foreign subsidiaries and joint ventures.

While there can be no assurance that current expectations will be realized, and plans are subject to change upon further review, it is management's current intention to spend an aggregate of approximately $900,000 to $1,000,000 during fiscal 2004 in the United States and Canada for real estate, construction, remodeling and equipment for warehouse clubs and related operations; and approximately $75,000 to $125,000 for international expansion, including the United Kingdom, Asia, Mexico and other potential ventures. These expenditures will be financed with a combination of cash provided from operations, the use of cash and cash equivalents and short-term investments, short-term borrowings under the Company's commercial paper program and other financing sources as required.

Expansion plans for the United States and Canada during fiscal 2004 are to open approximately 25 new warehouse clubs, including two relocations to larger and better-located warehouses. The Company expects to continue its review of expansion plans in its international operations in existing markets including the United Kingdom and in Asia along with other international markets. Costco and its Mexico-based joint venture partner, Controladora Comercial Mexicana, each own a 50% interest in Costco Mexico. As of August 31, 2003, Costco Mexico operated 21 warehouses in Mexico and planned to open two new warehouse clubs during fiscal 2004.

Reorganization of Canadian Administrative Operations

On January 17, 2001, the Company announced plans to reorganize and consolidate the administration of its operations in Canada. Total costs related to the reorganization were $26,765 pre-tax, of which $7,765 pre-tax ($4,775 after-tax, or $.01 per diluted share) was expensed in fiscal 2002 and $19,000 pre-tax ($11,400 after-tax, or $.02 per diluted share) was expensed in fiscal 2001 and reported as part of the provision for impaired assets and closing costs. These costs consisted primarily of employee severance, implementation and consolidation of support systems and employee relocation. The reorganization was completed in the first quarter of fiscal 2002.

Bank Credit Facilities and Commercial Paper Programs (All Amounts Stated in Thousands of US Dollars)

The Company has in place a $500,000 commercial paper program supported by a $300,000 bank credit facility with a group of ten banks, of which $150,000 expires on November 9, 2004 and $150,000 expires on November 15, 2005. At August 31, 2003, no amounts were outstanding under the commercial paper program and no amounts were outstanding under the credit facility.

A wholly owned Canadian subsidiary has a $144,000 commercial paper program supported by a $43,000 bank credit facility with a Canadian bank, which expires in March 2004. At August 31, 2003, no amounts were outstanding under the Canadian commercial paper program or the bank credit facility.

The Company has agreed to limit the combined amount outstanding under the U.S. and Canadian commercial paper programs to the $343,000 combined amounts of the supporting bank credit facilities.

The Company's wholly-owned Japanese subsidiary has a short-term ¥3 billion ($25,782) bank line of credit, which expires in November 2004. At August 31, 2003, no amounts were outstanding under the line of credit.

The Company's UK subsidiary has a £60 million ($94,842) bank revolving credit facility and a £20 million ($31,614) bank overdraft facility, both expiring in February 2007. At August 31, 2003, $47,421 was outstanding under the revolving credit facility with an applicable interest rate of 4.413% and no amounts were outstanding under the bank overdraft facility.

Letters of Credit

The Company has letter of credit facilities (for commercial and standby letters of credit), totaling approximately $369,000. The outstanding commitments under these facilities at August 31, 2003 totaled approximately $125,000, including approximately $44,000 in standby letters of credit.

Contractual Obligations

The Company's commitment to make future payments under long-term contractual obligations was as follows, as of August 31, 2003.

| Contractual Obligations | Total | Payments Due by Period | | | |
		Less Than 1 Year	1 to 3 Years	4 to 5 Years	After 5 Years
Long-term debt [1]	$1,702,618[2]	$ 44,368	$361,542	$379,528	$ 917,180[2]
Capital lease obligations	12,116	6,427	2,250	1,115	2,324
Operating leases	1,405,262[3]	85,862	173,996	162,101	983,303
Total	$3,119,996	$136,657	$537,788	$542,744	$1,902,807

[1] Amounts include contractual interest payments.
[2] The amount includes interest accreted to maturity for the Company's Zero Coupon $3\frac{1}{2}$% Convertible Subordinated Notes due August 2017, totaling $851,860. The consolidated balance sheet as of August 31, 2003 reflects the current balance outstanding of $524,735.
[3] Operating lease obligations have been reduced by $142,975 to reflect sub-lease income.

Financing Activities

In April 2003, the Company's wholly-owned Japanese subsidiary issued promissory notes bearing interest at 0.92% in the aggregate amount of approximately $34,376, through a private placement. Interest is payable semi-annually and principal is due on April 26, 2010.

In November 2002, the Company's wholly-owned Japanese subsidiary issued promissory notes bearing interest at 0.88% in the aggregate amount of approximately $25,782, through a private placement. Interest is payable semi-annually and principal is due on November 7, 2009.

In March 2002, the Company issued $300,000 of $5\frac{1}{2}$% Senior Notes due March 15, 2007. Interest is payable semi-annually. Simultaneous with the issuance of the Senior Notes, the Company entered into interest rate swap agreements converting the interest from fixed to floating.

In February 1996, the Company filed with the Securities and Exchange Commission a shelf registration statement for $500,000 of senior debt securities. On October 23, 2001, additional debt securities of $100,000 were registered, bringing the total amount of debt registered under the shelf registration to $600,000. The $300,000 of $5\frac{1}{2}$% Senior Notes issued in March 2002 reduced the amount of registered securities available for future issuance to $300,000.

Derivatives

The Company has limited involvement with derivative financial instruments and uses them only to manage well-defined interest rate and foreign exchange risks. Forward foreign exchange contracts are used to hedge the impact of fluctuations of foreign exchange on inventory purchases and typically have very short terms. The aggregate amount of foreign exchange contracts outstanding at August 31, 2003 was not material. The only significant derivative instruments the Company holds are interest rate swaps, which the Company uses to manage the interest rate risk associated with its borrowings and to manage for Company's mix of fixed and variable-rate debt. As of August 31, 2003, the Company had "fixed-to-floating" interest rate swaps with an aggregate notional amount of $600,000 and an aggregate fair value of $34,204, which is recorded in other assets. These swaps were entered into effective November 13, 2001, and March 25, 2002, and are designated and qualify as fair value hedges of the Company's $300,000 $7\frac{1}{8}$% Senior Notes and the Company's $300,000 $5\frac{1}{2}$% Senior Notes, respectively. As the terms of the swaps match those of the underlying hedged debt, the changes in the fair value of these swaps are offset by corresponding changes in the carrying amount of the hedged debt, and result in no net earnings impact.

Financial Position and Cash Flows

Working capital totaled $700,431 at August 31, 2003, compared to $180,806 at September 1, 2002. The increase of $519,625 was primarily due to an increase in cash and cash equivalents of $739,921, an increase in receivables of $81,229 and a reduction in short-term borrowing of $56,353, which was offset by increases in accrued salaries and benefits and in other current liabilities of $144,334 and $141,381, respectively, and a decrease in net inventory levels (inventories less accounts payable) of $34,844.

Net cash provided by operating activities totaled $1,507,208 in fiscal 2003, compared to $1,018,243 in fiscal 2002. The increase of $488,965 is primarily a result of a decrease in the change in net inventories (inventories less accounts payable) of $256,288; an increase in the change in the aggregation of receivables, other current assets, deferred income and accrued and other current liabilities of $102,284, an increase in the change in deferred income taxes of $56,514 and an increase in depreciation and amortization of $49,521 between fiscal 2003 and fiscal 2002.

Net cash used in investing activities totaled $790,588 in fiscal 2003, compared to $1,033,815 in fiscal 2002, a decrease of $243,227. This decrease is primarily a result of a reduction in the acquisition of property and equipment and the construction of facilities for new and remodeled warehouses of $227,940 and an increase in the proceeds received from the sale of property and equipment between fiscal 2003 and fiscal 2002 of $18,980.

Net cash used in financing activities totaled $1,428 in fiscal 2003 compared to cash provided by financing activities of $217,828 in fiscal 2002, a decrease of $219,256. The decrease in cash provided by financing activities primarily resulted from a decrease in net proceeds from the issuance of long-term debt of $240,576 and a reduction in proceeds from the exercise of stock options of $32,104 offset by a decrease in repayments of short-term borrowings of $41,031 between fiscal 2003 and fiscal 2002.

Stock Repurchase Program

On November 30, 2001, the Company's Board of Directors approved a stock repurchase program, authorizing the repurchase of up to $500,000 of Costco Common Stock through November 30, 2004. Under the program, the Company can repurchase shares at any time in the open market or in private transactions as market conditions warrant. The repurchased shares would constitute authorized, but non-issued shares and would be used for general corporate purposes, including stock option grants under stock option programs. To date, no shares have been repurchased under this program.

Additional Equity Investments in Subsidiary Subsequent to Year-End

Subsequent to the Company's fiscal year end, the Company, on October 3, 2003 acquired from Carrefour Nederland B.V. its 20% equity interest in Costco Wholesale UK Limited for cash of approximately $95,000, bringing Costco's ownership in Costco Wholesale UK Limited to 100%.

Critical Accounting Policies

The preparation of the Company's financial statements requires that management make estimates and judgments that affect the financial position and results of operations. Management continues to review its accounting policies and evaluate its estimates, including those related to merchandise inventory, impairment of long-lived assets and warehouse closing costs and insurance/self-insurance liabilities. The Company bases its estimates on historical experience and on other assumptions that management believes to be reasonable under the present circumstances.

Merchandise Inventories

Merchandise inventories are valued at the lower of cost or market as determined primarily by the retail method of accounting and are stated using the last-in, first-out (LIFO) method for substantially all U.S. merchandise inventories. Merchandise inventories for all foreign operations are primarily valued by the retail method of accounting, and are stated using the first-in, first-out (FIFO) method. The Company believes the LIFO method more fairly presents the results of operations by more closely matching current costs with current revenues. The Company records an adjustment each quarter for the expected annual effect of inflation, and these estimates are adjusted to actual results determined at year-end. The Company considers in its calculation of the LIFO cost the estimated net realizable value of inventory in those inventory pools where deflation exists and records a write down of inventory where estimated net realizable value is less than LIFO inventory.

The Company provides for estimated inventory losses between physical inventory counts on the basis of a percentage of sales. The provision is adjusted periodically to reflect the trend of the actual physical inventory count results, which generally occur in the second and fourth fiscal quarters.

Inventory cost, where appropriate, is reduced by estimates of vendor rebates earned when those rebates are deemed to be probable and reasonably estimable. Other consideration received from vendors is generally recorded as a reduction of merchandise costs upon completion of contractual milestones, terms of agreement, or other systematic and rational approach.

Impairment of Long-Lived Assets and Warehouse Closing Costs

The Company periodically evaluates its long-lived assets for indicators of impairment. Management's judgments are based on market and operational conditions at the present time. Future events could cause management to conclude that impairment factors exist, requiring an adjustment of these assets to their then-current fair market value.

The Company provides estimates for warehouse closing costs when it is appropriate to do so based on accounting principles generally accepted in the United States. Future circumstances may result in the Company's actual future closing costs or the amount recognized upon the sale of the property to differ substantially from the original estimates.

Insurance/Self Insurance Liabilities

The Company uses a combination of insurance and self-insurance mechanisms to provide for the potential liabilities for workers' compensation, general liability, property insurance, director and officers' liability, vehicle liability and employee health care benefits. Liabilities associated with the risks that are retained by the Company are estimated, in part, by considering historical claims experience and outside expertise, demographic factors, severity factors and other acturial assumptions. The estimated accruals for these liabilities could be significantly affected if future occurrences and claims differ from these assumptions and historical trends.

Recent Accounting Pronouncements

In June 2001, the Financial Accounting Standards Board (FASB) issued Statement of Financial Accounting Standards No. 143 (SFAS No. 143), "Accounting for Asset Retirement Obligations," which provides the accounting requirements for retirement obligations associated with tangible long-lived assets. SFAS No. 143 requires entities to record the fair value of a liability for an asset retirement obligation in the period in which it is incurred. SFAS No. 143 was effective for the Company's 2003 fiscal year. The adoption of SFAS No. 143 did not have a material impact on the Company's consolidated results of operations, financial position or cash flows.

In August 2001, the FASB issued SFAS No. 144, "Accounting for the Impairment or Disposal of Long-Lived Assets," effective for the Company's 2003 fiscal year. This Statement supersedes FASB Statement No. 121, "Accounting for the Impairment of Long-Lived Assets and for Long-Lived Assets to Be Disposed Of" and other related accounting guidance. The adoption of SFAS No. 144 did not have a material impact on the Company's consolidated results of operations, financial position, or cash flows.

In June 2002, the FASB issued SFAS No. 146, "Accounting for Costs Associated with Exit or Disposal Activities." This statement addresses financial accounting and reporting of costs associated with exit or disposal activities and nullifies Emerging Issues Task Force (EITF) Issue No. 94-3, "Liability Recognition for Certain Employee Termination Benefits and Other Costs to Exit an Activity (Including Certain Costs Incurred in a Restructuring)." This statement requires that a liability for a cost associated with an exit or disposal activity should be recognized at fair value when the liability is incurred. SFAS No. 146 was effective for the Company's 2003 fiscal year. The adoption of SFAS No. 146 did not have a material impact on the Company's consolidated results of operations, financial position or cash flows, other than to impact the timing of charges related to future warehouse relocations.

In December 2002, the FASB issued SFAS No. 148, "Accounting for Stock-Based Compensation—Transition and Disclosure," which provides guidance for transition to the fair value based method of accounting for stock-based employee compensation and the required financial statement disclosure. Effective September 3, 2002 the Company adopted the fair value based method of accounting for stock-based compensation. See Note (1) and Note (5) of the Company's consolidated financial statements.

In November 2002, the FASB issued FASB Interpretation No. 45, "Guarantor's Accounting and Disclosure Requirements for Guarantees, Including Indirect Guarantees of Indebtedness of Others." This interpretation established financial statement disclosure requirements for companies that enter into or modify certain types of guarantees subsequent to December 31, 2002. Beginning in calendar 2003, the standard requires that companies record the fair value of certain types of guarantees as a liability in the financial statements. The adoption of this interpretation did not have a material impact on the Company's results of operations, consolidated financial position or cash flows.

In January 2003, the FASB issued FASB Interpretation No. 46, "Consolidation of Variable Interest Entities." In general, a variable interest entity is a corporation, partnership, trust, or any other legal structure used for bussiness purposes that either does not have equity investors with voting rights or has equity investors that do not provide sufficient financial resources for the entity to support its activities. Interpretation No. 46 requires a variable interest entity to be consolidated by a company if that company is subject to a majority of the risk of loss from the variable interest entity's activities or entitled to receive a majority of the entity's residual returns or both. The consolidation requirements of Interpretation No. 46 apply immediately to variable interest entities created after January 31, 2003. The consolidation requirements apply to older entities in the first fiscal year or interim period beginning after June 15, 2003. Certain of the disclosure requirements apply in all financial statements issued after January 31, 2003, regardless of when the variable interest entity was established. The adoption of this interpretation did not have a material impact on the Company's consolidated results of operations, financial position or cash flows.

In November 2002, the EITF reached a consensus on EITF 00-21, "Revenue Arrangements with Multiple Deliverables," with respect to determining when and how to allocate revenue from sales with multiple deliverables. The EITF 00-21 consensus provides a framework for determining when and how to allocate revenue from sales with multiple deliverables based on a determination of whether the multiple deliverables qualify to be accounted for as separate units of accounting. The consensus is effective prospectively for arrangements entered into in fiscal periods beginning after June 15, 2003. The adoption of this consensus did not have a material impact on the Company's consolidated results of operations, financial position or cash flows.

In November 2002, the EITF reached consensus on certain issues discussed in EITF 02-16, "Accounting by a Customer (Including a Reseller) for Certain Consideration Received from a Vendor," with respect to determining how a reseller should characterize consideration received from a vendor and when to recognize and how to measure that consideration in its income statement. Requirements for recognizing volume-based rebates are effective for arrangements entered into or modified after November 21, 2002, and resellers with other supplier payments should generally apply the new rules prospectively for agreements entered into or modified after December 31, 2002. The adoption of this consensus did not have a material impact on the Company's consolidated results of operations, financial position or cash flows in fiscal 2003. However, the Company does expect the adoption of this consensus to impact interim quarterly financial information, commencing with the first quarter of fiscal 2004, as the application of the consensus will result in a change in the timing for the recognition of some vendor allowances for certain agreements entered into subsequent to December 31, 2002.

Quantitative and Qualitative Disclosure of Market Risk

The Company is exposed to financial market risk resulting from changes in interest and currency rates. As a policy, the Company does not engage in speculative or leveraged transactions, nor hold or issue financial instruments for trading purposes.

The nature and amount of the Company's long and short-term debt can be expected to vary as a result of future business requirements, market conditions and other factors. As of August 31, 2003, the Company's fixed rate long-term debt includes its $851,860 principal amount at maturity Zero Coupon Subordinated Notes and additional notes and capital lease obligations totaling $137,761. The Company's debt also includes $300,000 $7\frac{1}{8}$% Senior Notes and $300,000 $5\frac{1}{2}$% Senior Notes. The Company has entered into "fixed-to-floating" interest rate swaps on the Senior Notes, effectively converting these fixed interest rate securities to variable rate securities. Fluctuations in interest rates may affect the fair value of the fixed rate debt and may affect the interest expense related to the variable rate debt.

The Company holds interest-bearing instruments that are classified as cash and cash equivalents. As these investments are of a short-term nature, if interest rates were to increase or decrease immediately, there is no material risk of a valuation adjustment related to these instruments. In addition, changes in interest rates would not likely have a material impact on interest income.

Most foreign currency transactions have been conducted in local currencies, limiting the Company's exposure to changes in currency rates. The Company periodically enters into forward foreign exchange contracts to hedge the impact of fluctuations in foreign currency rates on inventory purchases. The fair value of foreign exchange contracts outstanding at August 31, 2003 was not material to the Company's results of operations or its financial position.

Change in Accountants

On May 13, 2002, the Audit Committee of Costco Wholesale Corporation's Board of Directors engaged KPMG LLP as the Company's firm of independent auditors for 2002. The information required by this item is incorporated herein by reference to Costco's Form 8-K filed on May 17, 2002 and the related Form 8-K/A filed on May 30, 2002.

Controls and Procedures

We carried out an evaluation as of August 31, 2003, under the supervision and with the participation of the Company's management, including our Chief Executive Officer and Chief Financial Officer, of the effectiveness of the design and operation of our disclosure controls and procedures pursuant to Exchange Act Rule 13a-14 and 15d-14. Based upon that evaluation, the Chief Executive Officer and the Chief Financial Officer concluded that our disclosure controls and procedures are effective to timely alert them to any material information relating to the Company (including its consolidated subsidiaries) that must be included in our periodic Securities and Exchange Commission filings. There have been no significant changes in the Company's internal controls or in other factors that could significantly affect internal controls subsequent to their evaluation.

The Company intends to review and evaluate the design and effectiveness of its disclosure controls and procedures on an ongoing basis and to improve its controls and procedures over time and to correct any deficiencies that may be discovered in the future in order to ensure that senior management has timely access to all material financial and non-financial information concerning the Company's business. While management believes that the present design of the Company's disclosure controls and procedures is effective to achieve these results, future events affecting the Company's business may cause management to modify its disclosure controls and procedures.

Forward Looking Information Excerpts

1.16

DARDEN RESTAURANTS, INC. (MAY)

FORWARD-LOOKING STATEMENTS

Certain statements included in this report and other materials filed or to be filed by us with the SEC (as well as information included in oral or written statements made or to be made by us) may contain statements that are forward-looking within the meaning of Section 27A of the Securities Act of 1933, as amended, and Section 21E of the Securities Exchange Act of 1934, as amended. Words or phrases such as "believe," "plan," "will," "expect," "intend," "estimate," and "project," and similar expressions are intended to identify forward-looking statements. All of these statements, and any other statements in this report that are not historical facts, are forward-looking. Examples of forward-looking

statements include, but are not limited to, projections regarding expected casual dining sales growth; the ability of the casual dining segment to weather economic downturns; demographic trends; our expansion plans, capital expenditures, and business development activities; and our long-term goals of increasing market share, expanding margins on incremental sales, and earnings growth. These forward-looking statements are based on assumptions concerning important factors, risks, and uncertainties that could significantly affect anticipated results in the future and, accordingly, could cause the actual results to differ materially from those expressed in the forward-looking statements.

These factors, risks, and uncertainties include, but are not limited to:

- the highly competitive nature of the restaurant industry, especially pricing, service, location, personnel, and type and quality of food;
- economic, market, and other conditions, including a protracted economic slowdown or worsening economy, industry-wide cost pressures, weak consumer demand, changes in consumer preferences, demographic trends, weather conditions, construction costs, and the cost and availability of borrowed funds;
- the price and availability of food, labor, utilities, insurance and media, and other costs, including seafood costs, employee benefits, workers' compensation insurance, and the general impact of inflation;
- unfavorable publicity relating to food safety or other concerns, including litigation alleging poor food quality, food-borne illness, or personal injury;
- the availability of desirable restaurant locations;
- government regulations, including those relating to zoning, land use, environmental matters, and liquor licenses; and
- growth plans, including real estate development and construction activities, the issuance and renewal of licenses and permits for restaurant development, and the availability of funds to finance growth.

1.17

SPRINT CORPORATION (DEC)

FORWARD-LOOKING INFORMATION

Sprint includes certain estimates, projections and other forward-looking statements in its reports and in other publicly available material. Statements regarding expectations, including performance assumptions and estimates relating to capital requirements, as well as other statements that are not historical facts, are forward-looking statements.

These statements reflect management's judgments based on currently available information and involve a number of risks and uncertainties that could cause actual results to differ materially from those in the forward-looking statements. With respect to these forward-looking statements, management has made assumptions regarding, among other things, customer and network usage, customer growth and retention, pricing, operating costs and the economic environment.

Future performance cannot be ensured. Actual results may differ materially from those in the forward-looking statements. Some factors that could cause actual results to differ include:

- extent and duration of any economic downturn;
- the effects of vigorous competition in the markets in which Sprint operates;
- the costs and business risks associated with providing new services and entering new markets;
- adverse change in the ratings afforded our debt securities by ratings agencies;
- the ability of our wireless operations and the global markets division to continue to grow a significant market presence;
- the ability of Sprint's wireless operations to continue to improve profitability;
- the ability of the global markets division and the local division to improve cash flow generation;
- the effects of mergers and consolidations in the telecommunications industry and unexpeceted announcements or developments from others in the telecommunications industry;
- the uncertainties related to the outcome of bankruptcies affecting the telecommunications industry;
- the impact of financial difficulties of third-party affiliates on Sprint's wireless network coverage;
- the uncertainties related to Sprint's investments in networks, systems, and other businesses;
- the uncertainties related to the implementation of Sprint's business strategies, including our initiative to realign services to enhance the focus on business and consumer customers;
- the impact of new, emerging and competing technologies on Sprint's business;
- unexpected results of litigation filed against Sprint;
- the impact of wireless local number portability (WLNP) on Sprint's wireless operation's growth and churn rates, revenues and expenses;
- the possibility of one or more of the markets in which Sprint competes being impacted by changes in political or other factors such as monetary policy, legal and regulatory changes, including the impact of the Telecommunications Act of 1996 (Telecom Act), or other external factors over which Sprint has no control; and
- other risks referenced from time to time in Sprint's filings with the Securities and Exchange Commission (SEC).

The words "estimate," "project," "intend," "expect," "believe," "target," and similar expressions are intended to identify forward-looking statements. Forward-looking statements are found throughout Management's Discussion and Analysis. The reader should not place undue reliance on forward-looking statements, which speak only as of the date of this report. Sprint is not obligated to publicly release any revisions to forward-looking statements to reflect events after the date of this report or unforeseen events. Sprint provides a detailed discussion of risk factors in various SEC filings, and you are encouraged to review these filings.

Liquidity and Capital Resources Excerpt

1.18

YUM! BRANDS, INC. (DEC)

LIQUIDITY AND CAPITAL RESOURCES

Operating in the QSR industry allows us to generate substantial cash flows from the operations of our company stores and from our franchise operations, which require a limited YUM investment. In each of the last two fiscal years, net cash provided by operating activities has exceeded $1 billion. These cash flows have allowed us to fund our discretionary spending, while at the same time reducing our long-term debt balances. We expect these levels of net cash provided by operating activities to continue in the foreseeable future. Our discretionary spending includes capital spending for new restaurants, acquisitions of restaurants from franchisees and repurchases of shares of our common stock. Though a decline in revenues could adversely impact our cash flows from operations, we believe our operating cash flows, our ability to reduce discretionary spending, and our borrowing capacity will allow us to meet our cash requirements in 2004 and beyond.

Our primary bank credit agreement comprises a senior unsecured Revolving Credit Facility (the "Credit Facility") which matures on June 25, 2005. On December 26, 2003, we voluntarily reduced our maximum borrowings under the Credit Facility from $1.2 billion to $1.0 billion. At December 27, 2003, our unused Credit Facility totaled $737 million, net of outstanding letters of credit of $263 million. There were no borrowings outstanding under the Credit Facility at December 27, 2003. Our Credit Facility contains financial covenants relating to maintenance of leverage and fixed charge coverage ratios. The Credit Facility also contains affirmative and negative covenants including, among other things, limitations on certain additional indebtedness, guarantees of indebtedness, level of cash dividends, aggregate non-U.S. investment and certain other transactions as defined in the agreement. We were in compliance with all covenants at December 27, 2003, and do not anticipate that the covenants will impact our ability to borrow under our Credit Facility for its remaining term.

The remainder of our long-term debt primarily comprises senior unsecured notes. Amounts outstanding under senior unsecured notes were $1.85 billion at December 27, 2003. The first of these notes, in the amount of $350 million, matures in 2005. We currently anticipate that out net cash provided by operating activities will permit us to make a significant portion of this $350 million payment without borrowing additional amounts.

We estimate that capital spending will be approximately $770 million and refranchising proceeds will be approximately $100 million in 2004. In November 2003, our Board of Directors authorized a new $300 million share repurchase program. At December 27, 2003, we had remaining capacity to repurchase, through May 21, 2005, up to $294 million of our outstanding Common Stock (excluding applicable transaction fees) under this program.

In addition to any discretionary spending we may choose to make, significant contractual obligations and payments as of December 27, 2003 included:

	Total	Less Than 1 Year	1–3 Years	3–5 Years	More Than 5 Years
Long-term debt[a]	$1,930	$ 1	$ 553	$254	$1,122
Capital leases[b]	192	15	29	26	122
Operating leases[b]	2,484	320	540	431	1,193
Purchase obligations[c]	162	124	26	7	5
Other long-term liabilities reflected on our consolidated balance sheet under GAAP	31	—	17	5	9
Total contractual obligations	$4,799	$460	$1,165	$723	$2,451

[a] Excludes a fair value adjustment of $29 million included in debt related to interest rate swaps that hedge the fair value of a portion of our debt. See Note 14.

[b] These obligations, which are shown on a nominal basis, relate to approximately 5,900 restaurants. See Note 15.

[c] Purchase obligations include agreements to purchase goods or services that are enforceable and legally binding on us and that specify all significant terms, including: fixed or minimum quantities to be purchased; fixed, minimum or variable price provisions; and the approximate timing of the transaction. We have excluded agreements that are cancelable without penalty. Purchase obligations rate primarily to purchase of property, plant and equipment as well as marketing, information technology, maintenance, consulting and other agreements.

We have not included obligations under our pension and postretirement benefit plans in the contractual obligations table. Our funding policy regarding our funded pension plan is to contribute amounts necessary to satisfy minimum pension funding requirements plus such additional amounts from time to time as are determined to be appropriate to improve the plan's funded status. The pension plan's funded status is affected by many factors including discount rates and the performance of plan assets. We are not required to make minimum pension funding payments in 2004, but we may make discretionary contributions during the year based on our estimate of the plan's expected September 30, 2004 funded status. During 2003, we made voluntary pension contributions of $130 million to our funded plan, none of which represented minimum funding requirements. Our postretirement plan is not required to be funded in advance, but is pay as you go. We made postretirement benefit payments of $4 million in 2003.

Also excluded from the contractual obligations table are payments we may make for employee health and property and casualty losses for which we are self-insured. The majority of our recorded liability for self-insured employee health and property and casualty losses represents estimated reserves for incurred claims that have yet to be filed or settled.

Environmental Matters Excerpt

1.19

FREEPORT-MCMORAN COPPER & GOLD INC. (DEC)

ENVIRONMENTAL MATTERS

We believe that we conduct our Indonesian operations pursuant to applicable permits and that we comply in all material respects with applicable Indonesian environmental laws, rules and regulations. We have had three independent environmental audits conducted by internationally recognized environmental consulting and auditing firms. Audits were completed in 1996 by Dames & Moore, in 1999 by Montgomery Watson, and in 2002 by SGS International Certification Services Indonesia, a member of the Société

Générale de Surveillance group. The 2002 audit found that the overall approach to practical management of environmental issues at PT Freeport Indonesia is considered to be very sound. There were no audit findings requiring corrective action.

In connection with obtaining our environmental approvals from the Indonesian government, we committed to performing a one-time environmental risk assessment on the impacts of our tailings management plan. We completed this extensive environmental risk assessment with more than 90 scientific studies conducted over four years and submitted it to the Indonesian government in December 2002. We developed the risk assessment study with input from an independent review panel, which included representatives from the Indonesian government, academia and non-governmental organizations. The risks that we identified during this process were in line with our impact projections of the tailings management program contained in our environmental approval documents.

We will determine our ultimate reclamation and closure activities based on applicable laws and regulations and our assessment of appropriate remedial activities in the circumstances after consultation with governmental authorities, affected local residents and other affected parties. As of December 31, 2003, we estimated aggregate reclamation and closure obligations on an undiscounted basis to be approximately $130 million for PT Freeport Indonesia, $17 million for Atlantic Copper and $11 million for PT Smelting. Estimates of the ultimate reclamation and closure costs we will incur in the future involve complex issues requiring integrated assessments over a period of many years and are subject to revision over time, and actual costs may vary from our estimates. Some reclamation costs will be incurred during mining activities, while most closure costs and the remaining reclamation costs will be incurred at the end of the Grasberg open-pit mining operations and at the end of all mining activities, which are currently estimated to continue for more than 30 years.

In 1996, we began contributing to a cash fund ($5.0 million balance at December 31, 2003) designed to accumulate at least $100 million by the end of our Indonesian mining activities. We plan to use this fund, including accrued interest, to pay mine closure and reclamation costs. Any costs in excess of the $100 million fund would be funded by operational cash flow or other sources. Future changes in regulations could require us to incur additional costs which would be charged against future operations. Estimates involving environmental matters are by their nature imprecise and can be expected to be revised over time because of changes in government regulations, operations, technology and inflation.

The cost of complying with environmental laws is a fundamental cost of our business. We incurred aggregate environmental capital expenditures and other environmental costs totaling $72.1 million in 2003, $62.6 million in 2002 and $78.2 million in 2001, including tailings management levee maintenance and mine reclamation. In 2004, we expect to incur approximately $11 million of aggregate environmental capital expenditures and $43 million of other environmental costs. These environmental expenditures are part of our overall 2004 operating budget.

Market Risk Information Excerpts

1.20

ITT INDUSTRIES, INC. (DEC)

MARKET RISK EXPOSURES

The Company, in the normal course of doing business, is exposed to the risks associated with changes in interest rates, currency exchange rates, and commodity prices. To limit the risks from such fluctuations, the Company enters into various hedging transactions that have been authorized pursuant to the Company's policies and procedures. See Note 1, "Accounting Policies," and Note 18, "Financial Instruments," in the Notes to Consolidated Financial Statements.

To manage exposure to interest rate movements and to reduce its borrowing costs, the Company has borrowed in several currencies and from various sources. The Company has several fixed to floating interest rate swap agreements for a notional amount of $336.8 million. As a result of the swaps, the interest expense on substantially all of the Company's long-term debt is calculated on a variable, rather than fixed rate, basis. Terms of the agreements match the terms of the fixed debt and reference the three-month LIBOR. The carrying value of these swaps at December 31, 2003 and 2002 was $81.6 million and $97.0 million, including $4.0 million of accrued interest in each period.

At December 31, 2003 and 2002, the Company's short-term and long-term debt obligations were $602.4 million and $791.8 million, respectively. In addition, the Company's cash balances at December 31, 2003 and 2002 were $414.2 million and $202.2 million, respectively. Based on these positions and the Company's overall exposure to interest rates, changes of 13 and 15 basis points (equivalent to 10% of the Company's weighted average short-term interest rates, including the rates associated with the Company's interest rate swaps, at December 31, 2003 and 2002, respectively) on the Company's cash and marketable securities and on its floating rate debt obligations and related interest rate derivatives would have a $0.1 million and $0.8 million effect on the Company's pretax earnings for the years ended December 31, 2003 and 2002, respectively. Increases of 74 and 78 basis points in long-term interest rates (equivalent to 10% of the Company's weighted average long-term interest rates at

December 31, 2003 and 2002, respectively) would have a $0.6 million and $0.5 million reduction in the fair value of the Company's fixed rate debt for the years ended December 31, 2003 and 2002, respectively.

The multinational operations of the Company are exposed to foreign currency exchange rate risk. The Company utilizes foreign currency denominated forward contracts to hedge against adverse changes in foreign exchange rates. Such contracts generally have durations of less than one year. The Company has utilized foreign currency denominated derivative instruments to selectively hedge certain transactions in foreign countries. During 2003, the Company's largest exposures to foreign exchange rates existed primarily with the Euro, Swedish Krona, and British Pound against the U.S. Dollar. At December 31, 2003, the Company had seven foreign currency derivative contracts outstanding for a total notional amount of $81.1 million. A 10% depreciation of the Euro against all other currencies related to the Company's foreign currency derivatives, held as of December 31, 2003, would cause a net reduction of $2.5 million on the fair value of such instruments. During 2002, the Company's largest exposures to foreign exchange rates existed primarily with the Euro, Swedish Krona, and British Pound against the U.S. Dollar. At December 31, 2002, the Company had nine foreign currency derivatives outstanding for a total notional amount of $109.1 million. A 10% depreciation of the Euro against all other currencies related to the Company's foreign currency derivatives, held as of December 31, 2002, would cause a net reduction of $4.3 million on the fair value of such instruments. During 2001, the Company's largest exposures to foreign exchange rates exist primarily with the Euro, Swedish Krona, and British Pound against the U.S. Dollar. At December 31, 2001, the Company had seven foreign currency derivatives outstanding for a total notional amount of $50.3 million. A 10% depreciation of the Euro against all other currencies related to the Company's foreign currency derivatives contracts held as of December 31, 2001, would cause a net reduction of $1.2 million on the fair value of such instruments. The Company uses derivative instruments to hedge exposures and, as such, the quantification of the Company's market risk for foreign exchange financial instruments does not account for the offsetting impact of the Company's underlying investment and transactional positions.

1.21

RUSSELL CORPORATION (DEC)

QUANTITATIVE AND QUALITATIVE DISCLOSURES ABOUT MARKET RISKS

We are exposed to market risks relating to fluctuations in interest rates, currency exchange rates and commodity prices. Our financial risk management objectives are to minimize the potential impact of interest rate, foreign exchange rate and commodity price fluctuations on our earnings, cash flows and equity. To manage these risks, we may use various financial instruments, including interest rate swap agreements, commodity futures contracts and forward currency exchange contracts. We only use traded instruments with major financial institutions as the counterparties to minimize the risk of credit loss. Refer to Notes 1 and 4 of the consolidated financial statements for a more complete description of our accounting policies and the extent of our use of such instruments.

The following analyses present the sensitivity of the market value, earnings and cash flows of our significant financial instruments to hypothetical changes in interest rates, exchange rates and commodity prices as if these changes had occurred at January 3, 2004. The range of changes chosen for these analyses reflects our view of changes that are reasonably possible over a one-year period. Market values are the present values of projected future cash flows based on the interest rate assumptions or quoted market prices where available. These forward-looking disclosures are selective in nature and only address the potential impacts from financial instruments. They do not include other potential effects which could impact our business as a result of changes in interest rates, exchange rates or commodity prices.

Interest Rate and Debt Sensitivity Analysis

At January 3, 2004, our outstanding debt totaled $281.4 million, which consisted of fixed-rate debt of $250.0 million and variable-rate debt of $31.4 million. Based on our 2003 average outstanding borrowings under our variable-rate debt, a one-percentage point increase in interest rates would negatively impact our annual pre-tax earnings and cash flows by approximately $0.9 million. A one-percentage point increase in market interest rates would decrease the fair market value of our fixed-rate debt at January 3, 2004, by approximately $5.4 million. Changes in the fair value of our fixed rate debt will not have any impact on us unless we repurchase the debt in the open market.

Currency Exchange Rate Sensitivity

We have foreign currency exposures related to buying, selling and financing in currencies other than our functional currencies. We also have foreign currency exposure related to foreign denominated revenues and costs translated into U.S. dollars. These exposures are primarily concentrated in the Euro, British pound sterling and Mexican peso. We enter into foreign currency forward contracts to manage the risk associated with doing business in foreign currencies. Our policy is to hedge currency exposures of firm commitments and anticipated transactions denominated in non-functional currencies to protect against the possibility of diminished cash flow and adverse impacts on earnings. A ten-percentage point adverse change in the foreign currency spot rates would decrease the fair market value of our foreign currency forward contracts held at January 3, 2004, by $6.2 million. Changes in the fair value of our foreign currency forward contracts will not have any impact on our results of operations unless these contracts are deemed to be ineffective at hedging currency exposures of anticipated transactions. We generally view our net investments in foreign subsidiaries that have a functional currency other than the U.S. dollar as long-term. As a result, we generally do not hedge these net investments.

Commodity Price Sensitivity

The availability and price of cotton is subject to wide fluctuations due to unpredictable factors such as weather conditions, governmental regulations, economic climate or other unforeseen circumstances. We are purchasing yarn primarily from Frontier Yarns, Frontier Spinning Mills, Inc. and other third parties, and our yarn pricing will continue to be directly impacted by the price of cotton. We did not have any outstanding cotton futures contracts at January 3, 2004.

SEGMENT INFORMATION

1.22 Statement of Financial Accounting Standards (SFAS) No. 131, *Disclosures about Segments of an Enterprise and Related Information*, supersedes SFAS No. 14, *Financial Reporting for Segments of a Business Enterprise,* in reporting information about a public business enterprise's operating segments. Operating segments are components of an enterprise about which separate financial information is available that is evaluated regularly by the chief operating decision maker in deciding how to allocate resources and in assessing performance.

1.23 *SFAS No. 131* requires that a public business enterprise report a measure of segment profit or loss, certain specific revenue and expense items, and segment assets. It requires reconciliations of total segment revenues, total segment profit or loss, total segment assets, and other amounts disclosed for segments to corresponding amounts in the enterprise's general-purpose financial statements. It requires that all public business enterprises report information about the revenues derived from the enterprise's products or services (or groups of similar products and services), about the countries in which the enterprise earns revenues and holds assets, and about major customers regardless of whether that information is used in making operating decisions. However, this Statement does not require an enterprise to report information that is not prepared for internal use if reporting it would be impracticable. In addition to *SFAS No. 131*, SFAS No. 142, *Goodwill and Other Intangible Assets*, requires that entities which report segment information shall provide information about the changes in the carrying amount of goodwill during the period for each reportable segment.

1.24   Table 1-3 shows the type of segment information most frequently presented as an integral part of the financial statements of the survey companies. Examples of segment information disclosures follow.

1.25

TABLE 1-3: SEGMENT INFORMATION

| | Number of Companies | | | |
	2003	2002	2001	2000
Industry segments				
Revenue	420	404	412	345
Operating income or loss	318	310	311	299
Identifiable assets	378	389	400	371
Depreciation expense	395	406	402	398
Capital expenditures	354	367	373	356
Geographic area				
Revenue	323	296	295	282
Operating income or loss	68	48	66	58
Identifiable assets	89	82	85	92
Depreciation expense	40	37	36	42
Capital expenditures	35	34	35	38
Export sales	37	33	43	37
Sales to major customers	178	137	138	104

1.26

THE BLACK & DECKER CORPORATION (DEC)

NOTES TO CONSOLIDATED FINANCIAL STATEMENTS

Note 1 (In Part): Summary of Accounting Policies

Goodwill and Other Intangible Assets (In Part)
The changes in the carrying amount of goodwill for the year ended December 31, 2003, by segment in millions of dollars, are as follows:

	Power Tools & Accessories	Hardware & Home Improvement	Fastening & Assembly Systems
Goodwill at January 1	$25.8	$363.9	$268.7
Acquisitions	—	94.4	—
Currency translation adjustment	—	3	18.6
Goodwill at December 31	$25.8	$458.6	$287.3

Note 17: Business Segments and Geographic Information

The Corporation has elected to organize its businesses based principally upon products and services. In certain instances where a business does not have a local presence in a particular country or geographic region, however, the Corporation has assigned responsibility for sales of that business's products to one of its other businesses with a presence in that country or region.

The Corporation operates in three reportable business segments: Power Tools and Accessories, Hardware and Home Improvement, and Fastening and Assembly Systems. The Power Tools and Accessories segment has worldwide responsibility for the manufacture and sale of consumer and professional power tools and accessories, electric cleaning and lighting products, and electric lawn and garden tools, as well as for product service. In addition, the Power Tools and Accessories segment has responsibility for the sale of security hardware to customers in Mexico, Central America, the Caribbean, and South America; for the sale of plumbing products to customers outside the United States and Canada; and for sales of household products. The Hardware and Home Improvement segment has worldwide responsibility for the manufacture and sale of security hardware (except for the sale of security hardware in Mexico, Central America, the Caribbean, and South America). On September 30, 2003, the Corporation acquired Baldwin Hardware Corporation and Weiser Lock Corporation. These acquired businesses are included in the Hardware and Home Improvement segment. The Hardware and Home Improvement segment also has responsibility for the manufacture of plumbing products and for the sale of plumbing products to customers in the United States and Canada. The Fastening and Assembly Systems segment has worldwide responsibility for the manufacture and sale of fastening and assembly systems.

Sales, segment profit, depreciation and amortization, and capital expenditures set forth in the following tables exclude the results of the discontinued European security hardware business, as more fully described in Note 3.

Business Segments

| (Millions of dollars) | Reportable Business Segments | | | | | | |
Year Ended December 31, 2003	Power Tools & Accessories	Hardware & Home Improvement	Fastening & Assembly Systems	Total	Currency Translation Adjustments	Corporate, Adjustments, & Eliminations	Consolidated
Sales to unaffiliated customers	$3,114.9	$715.7	$514.2	$4,344.8	$137.9	$ —	$4,482.7
Segment profit (loss) (for consolidated, operating income before restructuring and exit costs)	350.9	92.8	73.9	517.6	14.3	(71.6)	460.3
Depreciation and amortization	80.5	24.4	15.0	119.9	2.8	10.7	133.4
Income from equity method investees	21.3	—	—	21.3	—	(2.1)	19.2
Capital expenditures	68.2	17.1	13.4	98.7	3.0	.8	102.5
Segment assets (for consolidated, total assets)	1,516.7	594.4	312.1	2,423.2	177.7	1,621.6	4,222.5
Investment in equity method investees	10.8	—	.1	10.9	—	(1.7)	9.2
Year Ended December 31, 2002							
Sales to unaffiliated customers	$3,156.2	$659.3	$513.3	$4,328.8	$(37.0)	$ —	$4,291.8
Segment profit (loss) (for consolidated, operating income before restructuring and exit costs)	354.7	47.4	74.7	476.8	(3.9)	(58.3)	414.6
Depreciation and amortization	80.1	25.5	14.2	119.8	(.7)	3.3	122.4
Income from equity method investees	20.8	—	—	20.8	—	3.0	23.8
Capital expenditures	70.8	9.0	13.9	93.7	(.2)	.8	94.3
Segment assets (for consolidated, total assets)	1,595.8	357.6	317.0	2,270.4	35.7	1,824.4	4,130.5
Investment in equity method investees	25.4	—	.1	25.5	—	(1.7)	23.8
Year Ended December 31, 2001							
Sales to unaffiliated customers	$3,059.5	$658.3	$489.5	$4,207.3	$(67.4)	$ —	$4,139.9
Segment profit (loss) (for consolidated, operating income before restructuring and exit costs)	250.9	47.8	71.0	369.7	(1.3)	(30.4)	338.0
Depreciation and amortization	87.0	28.7	14.5	130.2	(1.5)	23.6	152.3
Income from equity method investees	13.2	—	—	13.2	—	2.1	15.3
Capital expenditures	86.0	29.7	15.7	131.4	(.8)	.8	131.4
Segment assets (for consolidated, total assets)	1,605.0	452.1	302.7	2,359.8	(66.2)	1,720.6	4,014.2
Investment in equity method investees	36.7	—	.1	36.8	(.2)	(2.7)	33.9

The profitability measure employed by the Corporation and its chief operating decision maker for making decisions about allocating resources to segments and assessing segment performance is segment profit (for the Corporation on a consolidated basis, operating income before restructuring and exit costs). In general, segments follow the same accounting policies as those described in Note 1, except with respect to foreign currency translation and except as further indicated below. The financial statements of a segment's operating units located outside of the United States, except those units operating in highly inflationary economies, are generally measured using the local currency as the functional currency. For these units located outside of the United States, segment assets and elements of segment profit are translated using budgeted rates of exchange. Budgeted rates of exchange are established annually and, once established, all prior period segment data is restated to reflect the current year's budgeted rates of exchange. The amounts included in the preceding table under the captions "Reportable Business Segments", and "Corporate, Adjustments, & Eliminations" are reflected at the Corporation's budgeted rates of exchange for 2003. The amounts included in the preceding table under the caption "Currency Translation Adjustments" represent the difference between consolidated amounts determined using those budgeted rates of exchange and those determined based upon the rates of exchange applicable under accounting principles generally accepted in the United States.

Segment profit excludes interest income and expense, non-operating income and expense, adjustments to eliminate intercompany profit in inventory, income tax expense, and, for 2001, goodwill amortization (except for the amortization of goodwill associated with certain acquisitions made by the Power Tools and Accessories and Fastening and Assembly Systems segments). In addition, segment profit excludes restructuring and exit costs. In determining segment profit, expenses relating to pension and other postretirement benefits are based solely upon estimated service costs. Corporate expenses, as well as certain centrally managed expenses, are allocated to each reportable segment based upon budgeted amounts. While sales and transfers between segments are accounted for at cost plus a reasonable profit, the effects of intersegment sales are excluded from the computation of segment profit. Intercompany profit in inventory is excluded from segment assets and is recognized as a reduction of cost of goods sold by the selling segment when the related inventory is sold to an unaffiliated customer. Because the Corporation compensates the management of its various businesses on, among other factors, segment profit, the Corporation may elect to record certain segment-related expense items of an unusual or non-recurring nature in consolidation rather than reflect such items in segment profit. In addition, certain segment-related items of income or expense may be recorded in consolidation in one period and transferred to the various segments in a later period.

Segment assets exclude assets of discontinued operations, pension and tax assets, intercompany profit in inventory, intercompany receivables, and goodwill associated with the Corporation's acquisition of Emhart Corporation in 1989.

Amounts in the preceding table under the caption "Corporate, Adjustments & Eliminations" on the lines entitled "Depreciation and amortization" represent depreciation of Corporate property and, for 2001, goodwill amortization (except for the amortization of goodwill associated with certain acquisitions made by the Power Tools and Accessories and

Fastening and Assembly Systems segments). The reconciliation of segment profit to consolidated earnings from continuing operations before income taxes for each year, in millions of dollars, is as follows:

	2003	2002	2001
Segment profit for total reportable business segments	$517.6	$476.8	$369.7
Items excluded from segment profit:			
Adjustment of budgeted foreign exchange rates to actual rates	14.3	(3.9)	(1.3)
Depreciation of corporate property and amortization of certain goodwill	(1.1)	(1.3)	(23.6)
Adjustment to businesses' postretirement benefit expenses booked in consolidation	15.4	38.3	42.6
Other adjustments booked in consolidation directly related to reportable business segments	(15.0)	(8.4)	(.7)
Amounts allocated to businesses in arriving at segment profit in excess of (less than) corporate center operating expenses, eliminations, and other amounts identified above	(70.9)	(86.9)	(48.7)
Operating income before restructuring and exit costs	460.3	414.6	338.0
Restructuring and exit costs	31.6	46.6	99.7
Operating income	428.7	368.0	238.3
Interest expense, net of interest income	35.2	57.8	84.3
Other expense	2.6	4.8	8.2
Earnings from continuing operations before income taxes	$390.9	$305.4	$145.8

The reconciliation of segment assets to consolidated total assets at the end of each year, in millions of dollars, is as follows:

	2003	2002	2001
Segment assets for total reportable business segments	$2,423.2	$2,270.4	$2,359.8
Items excluded from segment assets:			
Adjustment of budgeted foreign exchange rates to actual rates	177.7	35.7	(66.2)
Goodwill	633.3	604.2	598.0
Pension assets	42.2	36.9	406.1
Other corporate assets	946.1	1,183.3	716.5
	$4,222.5	$4,130.5	$4,014.2

Other Corporate assets principally consist of cash and cash equivalents, tax assets, property, assets of discontinued operations, and other assets.

Sales to The Home Depot, a customer of the Power Tools and Accessories and Hardware and Home Improvement segments, accounted for $779.4 million, $857.9 million, and $841.6 million of the Corporation's consolidated sales for the years ended December 31, 2003, 2002, and 2001, respectively. Sales to Lowe's Home Improvement Warehouse (Lowe's), a customer of the Power Tools and Accessories and Hardware and Home Improvement segments, accounted for $545.3 million and $467.5 million of the Corporation's consolidated sales for the years ended December 31, 2003 and 2002, respectively. Sales to Lowe's for the year ended December 31, 2001, did not exceed 10% of the Corporation's consolidated sales.

The composition of the Corporation's sales by product group for each year, in millions of dollars, is set forth below:

	2003	2002	2001
Consumer and professional power tools and product service	$2,360.1	$2,308.4	$2,227.2
Consumer and professional accessories	348.6	317.8	311.1
Electric lawn and garden products	313.8	285.4	279.3
Electric cleaning and lighting products	138.6	157.6	122.8
Household products	40.5	36.8	45.1
Security hardware	526.0	461.0	425.6
Plumbing products	218.7	221.6	252.3
Fastening and assembly systems	536.4	503.2	476.5
	$4,482.7	$4,291.8	$4,139.9

The Corporation markets its products and services in over 100 countries and has manufacturing sites in 10 countries. Other than in the United States, the Corporation does not conduct business in any country in which its sales in that country exceed 10% of consolidated sales. Sales are attributed to countries based on the location of customers. The composition of the Corporation's sales to unaffiliated customers between those in the United States and those in other locations for each year, in millions of dollars, is set forth below:

	2003	2002	2001
United States	$2,836.9	$2,824.0	$2,715.6
Canada	162.6	138.6	136.5
North America	2,999.5	2,962.6	2,852.1
Europe	1,107.2	986.8	950.2
Other	376.0	342.4	337.6
	$4,482.7	$4,291.8	$4,139.9

The composition of the Corporation's property, plant, and equipment between those in the United States and those in other countries as of the end of each year, in millions of dollars, is set forth below:

	2003	2002	2001
United States	$340.0	$362.0	$406.3
Mexico	109.0	78.6	74.4
United Kingdom	47.3	72.1	72.0
Other countries	163.9	116.9	109.8
	$660.2	$629.6	$662.5

1.27

CAMPBELL SOUP COMPANY (JUL)

NOTES TO CONSOLIDATED FINANCIAL STATEMENTS (Dollars in millions)

3 (In Part): Goodwill and Intangible Assets

Changes in the carrying amount for goodwill for the period ended August 3, 2003 are as follows:

	North America Soup and Away From Home	North America Sauces and Beverages	Biscuits and Confectionery	International Soup and Sauces	Total
Balance at July 28, 2002	$336	$365	$339	$541	$1,581
Goodwill acquired	—	—	92	11	103
Impairment losses	(48)	—	—	—	(48)
Foreign currency translation adjustment	10	—	93	64	167
Balance at August 3, 2003	$298	$365	$524	$616	$1,803

4 Business and Geographic Segment Information

Campbell Soup Company, together with its consolidated subsidiaries, is a global manufacturer and marketer of high quality, branded convenience food products. Through 2001, the company was organized and reported the results of operations in three business segments: Soup and Sauces, Biscuits and Confectionery, and Away From Home.

Beginning in 2002, the company changed its organizational structure such that operations are managed and reported in four segments: North America Soup and Away From Home, North America Sauces and Beverages, Biscuits and Confectionery, and International Soup and Sauces. Segment financial information has been modified for all periods in order to conform to the new structure. In addition, Net sales reflect the reclassifications related to the adoption of the new accounting standard as discussed in Note 1.

The North America Soup and Away From Home segment comprises the retail soup and Away From Home business in the U.S. and Canada. The U.S. retail business includes the *Campbell's* brand condensed and ready-to-serve soups and *Swanson* broths. The segment includes the company's total business in Canada, which comprises the *Habitant* and *Campbell's* soups, *Prego* pasta sauce and *V8* juices. The Away From Home operations represent the distribution of products such as *Campbell's* soups, *Campbell's* specialty entrees, beverage products, other prepared foods and *Pepperidge Farm* products through various food service channels in North America. The North America Sauces and Beverages segment includes *Prego* pasta sauces, *Pace* Mexican sauces, *Franco-American* canned pastas and gravies, *V8* vegetable juices, *V8 Splash* juice beverages, *Campbell's* tomato juice, as well as the total of all business in Mexico and other Latin American and Caribbean countries. The Biscuits and Confectionery segment includes all retail sales of *Pepperidge Farm* cookies, crackers, breads and frozen products in North America, *Arnott's* biscuits and crackers in Australia and Asia Pacific, Arnott's Snackfoods salty snacks in Australia, and *Godiva* chocolates worldwide. The International Soup and Sauces segment comprises operations outside of North America, including *Erasco* and *Heisse Tasse* soups in Germany, *Liebig* and *Royco* soups and *Lesieur* sauces in France, *Campbell's* and *Batchelors* soups, *Oxo* stock cubes and *Homepride* sauces in the United Kingdom, *Devos Lemmens* mayonnaise and cold sauces and *Campbell's* and *Royco* soups in Belgium, *Bla Band* soups in Sweden, and *McDonnells* and *Erin* soups in Ireland. In Asia Pacific, operations include *Campbell's* soups and stock and *Swanson* broths across the region.

Accounting policies for measuring segment assets and earnings before interest and taxes are substantially consistent with those described in Note 1. The company evaluates segment performance before interest and taxes, excluding certain non-recurring charges. The North America Soup and Away From Home and North America Sauces and Beverages segments operate under an integrated supply chain organization, sharing substantially all manufacturing, warehouse, distribution and sales activities. Accordingly, assets have been allocated between the two segments based on various measures, for example, budgeted production hours for fixed assets and depreciation.

The company's largest customer, Wal-Mart Stores, Inc. and its affiliates, accounted for approximately 12% of consolidated net sales during 2003 and 2002. All of the company's segments sold products to Wal-Mart Stores, Inc. or its affiliates.

Segment financial information for 2003 reflects the adoption of SFAS No. 142 as discussed in Note 3. Operating Segment results for 2002 and 2001 have been adjusted to reflect the pro forma impact of amortization eliminated under the standard. Amortization expense of $70 and $54 for 2002 and 2001, respectively, has been eliminated from the prior period results.

Information about operations by business segment, reflecting the reclassifications described in Note 1, is as follows:

Business Segments

2003	Net Sales	Earnings Before Interest and Taxes[3]	Depreciation and Amortization	Capital Expenditures	Segment Assets
North America Soup and Away From Home	$2,606	$ 632	$ 62	$ 71	$1,237
North America Sauces and Beverages	1,246	289	34	42	1,213
Biscuits and Confectionery	1,774	212	85	115	1,680
International Soup and Sauces	1,052	128	30	34	1,775
Corporate and eliminations[1]	—	(156)	32	21	300
Total	$6,678	$1,105	$243	$283	$6,205

2002	Net Sales	Earnings Before Interest and Taxes[3]	Depreciation and Amortization	Capital Expenditures	Segment Assets
North America Soup and Away From Home	$2,524	$ 634	$ 58	$ 75	$1,263
North America Sauces and Beverages	1,182	257	32	47	1,228
Biscuits and Confectionery	1,507	186	90	100	1,276
International Soup and Sauces	920	120	27	28	1,632
Corporate and eliminations[1]	–	(143)	42	19	322
Total	$6,133	$1,054	$249	$269	$5,721

2001	Net Sales[2]	Earnings Before Interest and Taxes[3]	Depreciation and Amortization	Capital Expenditures	Segment Assets
North America Soup and Away From Home	$2,532	$ 784	$ 57	$ 59	$1,248
North America Sauces and Beverages	1,161	316	32	33	1,243
Biscuits and Confectionery	1,446	208	76	77	1,249
International Soup and Sauces	632	63	20	21	1,519
Corporate and eliminations[1]	—	(123)	27	10	668
Total	$5,771	$1,248	$212	$200	$5,927

[1] Represents unallocated corporate expenses and unallocated assets, including corporate offices, deferred income taxes and prepaid pension assets.

[2] In the fourth quarter of 2001, the company adopted new guidance on the classification of shipping and handling costs. Shipping and handling costs of $207 for 2001 were reclassified, from Net sales to Cost of products sold. In the first quarter of 2002, the company adopted new accounting standards related to the income statement classification of certain consumer and trade sales promotion expenses, such as coupon redemption costs, cooperative advertising programs and in-store display incentives. As a result, the reclassifications, recorded in 2002, reduced Net sales by $893 for 2001. See Note 1 for further discussion.

[3] Contributions to earnings before interest and taxes by the Biscuits and Confectionery segment include the effect of costs of $1 in 2003, $20 in 2002, and $15 in 2001 associated with the Australian manufacturing reconfiguration.

Geographic Area Information

Information about operations in different geographic areas is as follows:

Net Sales[1]	2003	2002	2001
United States	$4,549	$4,339	$4,313
Europe	969	843	558
Australia/Asia Pacific	779	554	517
Other countries	492	502	455
Adjustments and eliminations	(111)	(105)	(72)
Consolidated	$6,678	$6,133	$5,771

Earnings Before Interest and Taxes	2003	2002	2001
United States	$ 965	$ 913	$1.137
Europe	126	92	53
Australia/Asia Pacific	93	41	46
Other countries	77	81	81
Segment earnings before interest and taxes	1,261	1,127	1,317
Unallocated corporate expenses	(156)	(143)	(123)
Consolidated	$1,105	$ 984	$1,194

Identifiable Assets	2003	2002	2001
United States	$2,774	$2,797	$2,737
Europe	1,718	1,586	1,472
Australia/Asia Pacific	1,100	725	717
Other countries	313	288	293
Corporate	300	325	708
Consolidated	$6,205	$5,721	$5,927

[1] In the fourth quarter of 2001, the company adopted new guidance on the classification of shipping and handling costs. Shipping and handling costs of $207 for 2001 were reclassified from Net sales to Cost of products sold. In the first quarter of 2002, the company adopted new accounting standards related to the income statement classification of certain consumer and trade sales promotion expenses, such as coupon redemption costs, cooperative advertising programs and in-store display incentives. As a result, the reclassifications, recorded in 2002, reduced Net sales $893 for 2001. See Note 1 for further discussion.

Transfers between geographic areas are recorded at cost plus markup or at market. Identifiable assets are those assets, including goodwill, which are identified with the operations in each geographic region. The restructuring charges in 2002 and 2001 were allocated to Australia/Asia Pacific.

1.28

DOW JONES & COMPANY, INC. (DEC)

NOTES TO FINANCIAL STATEMENTS

Note 6 (In Part): Goodwill and Intangibles

Goodwill balances by reportable segment were as follows:

(In thousands)	Print Publishing	Electronic Publishing	Community Newspapers	Total
Goodwill, net of accumulated amortization at December 31, 2001	$16,471	$2,649	$ 56,402	$ 75,522
Acquisitions		1,824	5,454	7,278
Sale of ONI properties			(26,549)	(26,549)
Goodwill, net of accumulated amortization at December 31, 2002	$16,471	$4,473	$ 35,307	$ 56,251
Acquisitions	16,932	3,427	76,710	97,069
Goodwill, net of accumulated amortization at December 31, 2003	$33,403	$7,900	$112,017	$153,320

Note 14. Business Segments

The Company reports the results of its operations in three segments: print publishing, electronic publishing and community newspapers. In addition, the Company reports certain administrative activities under the corporate segment.

Print publishing, which is largely comprised of the global operations of The Wall Street Journal, produces business and financial content world-wide. This content is published primarily in the U.S., Europe, Asia and Latin America editions of The Wall Street Journal and on U.S. television through a licensing arrangement with CNBC. The Company manages the global Journal operations as one segment as their products comprise the global Journal brand, and there are significant interrelationships within the editions including global management, shared news flows and workforce and a global advertising customer base and pricing. U.S. television, which represents a licensing agreement with NBC to provide branding, news content and on-air expertise to CNBC, is a further extension of the Journal brand and the content it produces. The Company also includes the operations of Barron's within print publishing instead of reporting them separately because of its relative immateriality to the Company's results on a consolidated basis and because it shares similarities with the global Journal operations.

Print publishing accounted for approximately 60% of 2003 revenues, while the electronic publishing and community newspapers segments each accounted for about 20%. The Company's overall performance is largely dependent on the operating performance of the global Wall Street Journal (including its extended U.S. television brand and content).

Electronic publishing, whose products provide business and financial news and information to customers via electronic dissemination and are expected to have similar long-term economic characteristics, includes the operations of Dow Jones Newswires, Consumer Electronic Publishing and Dow Jones Indexes/Ventures. Consumer Electronic Publishing includes the results of WSJ.com and its related vertical sites as well as the Company's licensing/business development and radio/audio businesses. Revenues in the electronic publishing segment are mainly subscription based. The community newspapers segment publishes 15 daily newspapers, 12 Sunday papers and more than 30 weeklies and shoppers in nine states in the U.S.

Management evaluates the performance of its segments exclusive of restructuring charges and September 11 related items. See Note 3 for a further discussion of these items.

The Company's operations by business segment and geographic area were as follows:

(In thousands)

Financial Data by Business Segment	2003	2002	2001
Revenues[1]			
Print publishing	$ 915,468	$ 948,870	$1,106,934
Electronic publishing	322,032	309,491	317,986
Community newspapers:			
Comparable operations[2]	282,236	278,638	273,331
Divested/newly-acquired operations	28,749	22,174	74,832
Total	310,985	300,812	348,163
Consolidated revenues	$1,548,485	$1,559,173	$1,773,083
Income before income taxes and minority interests[3]			
Print publishing	$ 8,079	$ (8,058)	$ 91,468
Electronic publshing	67,871	60,863	45,717
Community newspapers:			
Comparable operations[2]	73,954	74,000	66,037
Divested/newly-acquired operations	7,039	5,255	19,110
Total	80,993	79,255	85,147
Corporate	(32,438)	(33,167)	(38,914)
Segment operating income	124,505	98,893	183,418
Restructuring charges and September 11 related items, net[3]	18,408	(23,810)	(73,219)
Consolidated operating income	142,913	75,083	110,199
Equity in earnings (losses) of associated companies	2,869	(488)	(17,181)
Gain on sale of businesses		197,925	
Gain on non-monetary exchange of equity holdings	18,699		
Gain on resolution of telerate sale loss contingencies	59,821		
Contract guarantee, net	(9,523)	(11,878)	17,136
Write-down of investments			(8,827)
Other, net	6,079	(3,112)	(1,639)
Income before income taxes and minority interests	$ 220,858	$ 257,530	$ 99,688
Depreciation and amortization expense			
Print publishing	$ 67,054	$ 71,568	$ 65,668
Electronic publishing	26,263	25,374	22,421
Community newspapers:			
Comparable operations[2]	10,375	11,069	12,699
Divested/newly-acquired operations	1,675	681	3,751
Total	12,050	11,750	16,450
Corporate	647	1,046	1,174
Consolidated depreciation and amortization expense	$ 106,014	$ 109,738	$ 105,713
Assets at December 31			
Print publishing	$ 714,811	$ 762,071	$ 823,861
Electronic publishing	156,220	157,789	148,963
Community newspapers	305,821	159,247	218,805
Segment assets	1,176,852	1,079,107	1,191,629
Cash and investments	127,302	128,552	106,711
Consolidated assets	$1,304,154	$1,207,659	$1,298,340
Capital expenditures			
Print publishing	$ 30,409	$ 55,723	$ 91,628
Electronic publishing	11,571	16,136	29,139
Community newspapers	13,961	5,794	7,992
Consolidated capital expenditures	$ 55,941	$ 77,653	$ 128,759

(continued)

(In thousands)

Financial Data by Geographic Area	2003	2002	2001
Revenues			
United States	$1,417,854	$1,418,355	$1,604,455
International	130,631	140,818	168,628
Consolidated revenues	$1,548,485	$1,559,173	$1,773,083
Plant, property and equipment, net of accumulated depreciation			
United States	$ 678,550	$ 707,360	$ 744,943
International	10,734	13,341	16,406
Consolidated plant, property and equipment, net	$ 689,284	$ 720,701	$ 761,349
Goodwill and intangible assets, net of accumulated amortization			
United States	$ 181,763	$ 44,735	$ 65,112
International	41,681	18,295	16,471
Consolidated goodwill and intangible assets, net	$ 223,444	$ 63,030	$ 81,583

Notes:
[1] Revenues shown represent revenues from external customers. Transactions between segments are not significant.
[2] Amounts in 2002 have been reclassified between comparable and divested/newly-acquired operations to conform with comparable operations in 2003.
[3] Restructuring charges and September 11 related items, net are not included in segment expenses as management evaluates segment results exclusive of these items. For information purposes, restructuring and September 11 related items allocable to each segment were as follows:

(In thousands)	2003	2002	2001
Print publishing	$17,422	$(16,794)	$(49,447)
Electronic publishing	951	(6,521)	(18,796)
Community newspapers			(321)
Corporate	35	(495)	(4,655)
Total restructuring charges and September 11 related items, net	$18,408	$(23,810)	$(73,219)

1.29

THE DUN & BRADSTREET CORPORATION (DEC)

NOTES TO CONSOLIDATED FINANCIAL STATEMENTS

Note 14. Segment Information

The operating segments reported below are our segments for which separate financial information is available and upon which operating results are evaluated on a timley basis to assess performance and to allocate resources. We report our business on a geographical basis—with two operating segments, North America and International. Our product lines are Risk Management Solutions, Sales & Marketing Solutions, Supply Management Solutions and E-Business Solutions. We reclassify Receivable Management Services and all other divested businesses as "Receivable Management Services and Other Divested Businesses" (see Note 3). The accounting policies of our segments are the same as those described in Note 1. Inter-segment sales are immaterial and no single customer accounted for 10% or more of our total revenues. For management reporting purposes, we evaluate business segment performance before restructuring charges, certain other items we do not consider to reflect our underlying business performance and non-operating income or expenses. Additionally, transition costs, which are period costs such as consulting fees, costs of temporary employees, relocation costs and stay bonuses incurred to implement our Financial Flexibility program, are not allocated to our business segments.

(In millions)	2003	2002	2001
Operating revenues:			
North America	$ 960.1	$ 912.1	$ 909.8
International	426.3	363.5	394.8
Consolidated total	$1,386.4	$1,275.6	$1,304.6
Operating income (loss):			
North America	$ 329.9	$ 313.1	$ 295.8
International	59.9	43.5	23.3
Total divisions	389.8	356.6	319.1
All other[1]	(98.0)	(100.7)	(95.5)
Consolidated total	291.8	255.9	223.6
Non-operating income (expense) — net	(11.4)	(16.7)	30.0
Income before provision for income taxes	$ 280.4	$ 239.2	$ 253.6
Depreciation and amortization:[2]			
North America	$ 41.1	$ 57.7	$ 56.9
International	19.6	23.9	33.1
Total divisions	60.7	81.6	90.0
All other	3.3	2.6	4.5
Consolidated total	$ 64.0	$ 84.2	$ 94.5
Capital expenditures:			
North America	$ 7.7	$ 10.6	$ 10.7
International	3.3	5.2	4.9
Total divisions	11.0	15.8	15.6
All other	—	—	0.6
Consolidated total	$ 11.0	$ 15.8	$ 16.2
Additions to computer software and other intangibles:			
North America	$ 16.5	$ 29.8	$ 30.0
International	2.8	7.7	4.4
Total divisions	19.3	37.5	34.4
All other	—	0.2	2.6
Consolidated total	$ 19.3	$ 37.7	$ 37.0
Assets:			
North America	$ 456.8	$ 366.0	$ 387.7
International	541.1	493.1	473.7
Total divisions	997.9	859.1	861.4
All other (primarily domestic pensions and taxes)	626.8	668.6	601.2
Consolidated total	$1,624.7	$1,527.7	$1,462.6
Goodwill:			
North America	$ 118.0	$ 51.6	$ 45.9
International	138.9	131.7	93.7
Consolidated total	$ 256.9	$ 183.3	$ 139.6

(continued)

(In millions)	2003	2002	2001
Supplemental geographic and product line information:			
Long-lived assets:			
North America	$ 642.8	$ 534.8	$ 531.5
International	167.5	267.8	252.9
Consolidated total	$ 810.3	$ 802.6	$ 784.4
Product line revenues:			
North America:			
Risk management solutions	$ 603.6	$ 594.3	$ 586.9
Sales & marketing solutions	294.1	289.1	257.1
Supply management solutions	33.4	28.7	26.4
E-Business solutions	29.0	—	—
Total North America core	960.1	912.1	870.4
Receivable management services and other divested businesses	—	—	39.4
Total North America	960.1	912.1	909.8
International:			
Risk management solutions	339.0	283.2	274.0
Sales & marketing solutions	72.2	65.4	71.0
Supply management solutions	11.8	8.8	3.3
Total international core	423.0	357.4	348.3
Receivable management services and other divested businesses	3.3	6.1	46.5
Total international	426.3	363.5	394.8
Consolidated total:			
Risk management solutions	942.6	877.5	860.9
Sales & marketing solutions	366.3	354.5	328.1
Supply management solutions	45.2	37.5	29.7
E-Business solutions	29.0	—	—
Consolidated total core	1,383.1	1,269.5	1,218.7
Receivable management services and other divested businesses	3.3	6.1	85.9
Consolidated total	$1,386.4	$1,275.6	$1,304.6

[1] The following table itemizes "All Other":

	2003	2002	2001
Operating income (loss):			
Corporate costs	$(44.5)	$ (38.4)	$(31.6)
Transition costs (costs to implement our financial flexibility program)	(22.3)	(31.4)	(28.4)
Restructuring expense—net	(17.4)	(30.9)	(28.8)
Loss on High Wycombe building sale	(13.8)	—	—
Reorganization costs	—	—	7.0
Asset write-offs for World Trade Center attack	—	—	(1.0)
Other asset impairments	—	—	(6.2)
Murray Hill facility impairment	—	—	(6.5)
Total "all other"	$(98.0)	$(100.7)	$(95.5)

[2] Includes depreciation and amortization of Property, Plant and Equipment, Computer Software, Goodwill (prior to 2002) and Other Intangibles.

1.30

THE GILLETTE COMPANY (DEC)

NOTES TO CONSOLIDATED FINANCIAL STATEMENTS

5 (In Part): Supplemental Balance Sheet Information

Goodwill and Intangible Assets (In Part)
Total goodwill by segment follows.

(Millions)	2003	2002
Blades & Razors	$ 140	$140
Duracell	632	571
Oral Care	191	191
Braun	60	60
Personal Care	—	—
Total	$1,023	$962

14. Operating Segments and Related Information

The following table presents certain operating segment information.

(Millions)	Blades & Razors	Duracell	Oral Care	Braun	Personal Care	All Other	Total
2003							
Net sales	$3,869	$2,015	$1,327	$1,177	$864	$ —	$9,252
Profit from operations	1,426	348	218	49	73	(111)	2,003
Identifiable assets	3,099	2,754	1,269	1,224	470	1,139	9,955
Capital expenditures	203	46	77	51	29	2	408
Depreciation	243	113	81	81	29	10	557
2002							
Net sales	$3,435	$1,898	$1,248	$1,056	$816	$ —	$8,453
Profit from operations	1,299	233	222	75	51	(71)	1,809
Identifiable assets	3,170	2,741	1,112	1,047	520	1,273	9,863
Capital expenditures	168	67	69	57	40	4	405
Depreciation	225	82	73	66	26	8	480
2001							
Net sales	$3,200	$1,953	$1,149	$ 981	$801	$ —	$8,084
Profit from operations	1,141	217	240	98	68	(266)	1,498
Identifiable assets	3,195	2,932	994	945	515	1,388	9,969
Capital expenditures	222	162	92	69	49	30	624
Depreciation	197	78	53	53	26	46	453

Each operating segment is individually managed and has separate financial results that are reviewed by the Company's chief operating decision-maker. Each segment contains closely related products that are unique to the particular segment. There were no changes to the composition of segments in 2003.

The Blades & Razors segment consists of blades and razors. The Duracell segment consists of consumer batteries. Oral Care contains manual and power oral care products. The Braun segment contains male and female hair removal, household and hair care appliances, and personal diagnostic devices, including ear thermometers and blood pressure monitors. The Personal Care segment includes shave preparations, skin care products and antiperspirants/deodorants.

Profit from operations is net sales less cost of sales and selling, general and administrative expenses. In calculating profit from operations for individual operating segments, administrative expenses incurred at the operating level that are common to more than one segment, and headquarters expenses of an operational nature, are allocated on a net sales basis. All intercompany transactions, primarily merchandise transfers, have been eliminated.

Profit from operations in the All Other column includes all unallocated income/expense items, as well as the $30 million gain on the sale of Vaniqa and the $9 million total recovery to the 2001 and 2000 restructuring reserves in 2002, and the $172 million charge for restructuring and asset impairment in 2001.

Identifiable assets in the All Other column includes financial instruments managed by the Corporate Treasury Department, nonqualified benefit and compensation trusts, corporate fixed assets, deferred income tax assets, and net assets of discontinued operations. Capital expenditures in the All Other column are primarily related to research and development initiatives.

The Company's largest customer, Wal-Mart Stores, Inc. and its affiliates, accounted for 13% of net sales in 2003, and 12% of net sales in both 2002 and 2001. These sales occurred primarily in the United States and were across all product segments.

Net sales by geographic area follow.

(Millions)	2003	2002	2001
Foreign	$5,804	$5,171	$4,839
United States	3,448	3,282	3,245
	$9,252	$8,453	$8,084

Net property, plant and equipment by geographic area follows.

(Millions)	2003	2002	2001
Germany	$ 692	$ 606	$ 508
Other foreign	1,145	1,057	1,013
Total foreign	1,837	1,663	1,521
United States	1,805	1,902	2,027
	$3,642	$3,565	$3,548

1.31

QUANTUM CORPORATION (MAR)

NOTES TO CONSOLIDATED FINANCIAL STATEMENTS

Note 24. Business Segment and Geographic Information

Quantum's reportable segments are DLTG and SSG. These reportable segments are each managed separately as they distribute and, in the case of SSG, manufacture distinct products with different production processes. DLTG consists of tape drives and media. SSG consists of tape automation systems and service, and includes disk based backup products. Quantum directly markets its products to computer manufacturers and through a broad range of distributors, resellers and systems integrators.

The accounting policies of the reportable segments are the same as those described in the summary of significant accounting policies. Quantum evaluates segment performance based on operating income (loss) excluding infrequent or unusual items.

Quantum does not allocate interest and other income, interest expense, or taxes to operating segments. Additionally, Quantum does not allocate all assets by operating segment, only those assets included in the table below:

(In thousands)	2003			2002			2001		
	DLTG	SSG	Total	DLTG	SSG	Total	DLTG	SSG	Total
Total revenue	$680,032	$227,112	$907,144	$837,548	$233,298	$1,070,846	$1,090,444	$353,097	$1,443,541
Inter-segment revenue	(36,335)	—	(36,335)	(41,171)	—	(41,171)	(97,426)	—	(97,426)
Revenue from external customers	643,697	227,112	870,809	796,377	233,298	1,029,675	993,018	353,097	1,346,115
Cost of revenue	437,481	166,165	603,646	497,426	154,644	652,070	505,723	227,852	733,575
Gross margin	206,216	60,947	267,163	298,951	78,654	377,605	487,295	125,245	612,540
Research and development	75,309	36,617	111,926	83,080	28,371	111,451	83,826	33,010	116,836
Sales and marketing	45,295	55,159	100,454	61,966	48,767	110,733	65,390	52,900	118,290
General and administrative	44,756	26,510	71,266	66,421	47,120	113,541	38,382	29,661	68,043
Total operating expenses	165,360	118,286	283,646	211,467	124,258	335,725	187,598	115,571	303,169
Operating income (loss)	$ 40,856	$(57,339)	$ (16,483)	$ 87,484	$(45,604)	$ 41,880	$ 299,697	$ 9,674	$ 309,371
Goodwill impairment			58,689					—	—
Special charges			24,200			72,856			—
Purchased in-process research and development			7,802			13,200			—
Reported income (loss) from operations			$(107,174)			$ (44,176)			$ 309,371

(In thousands)	March 31, 2003			March 31, 2002			March 31, 2001		
	DLTG	SSG	Total	DLTG	SSG	Total	DLTG	SSG	Total
Accounts receivable, net	$91,415	$42,345	$133,760	$94,351	$ 55,073	$149,424	$139,150	$ 69,252	$208,402
Inventories	22,131	44,174	66,305	71,410	27,391	98,801	94,410	29,960	124,370
Service inventories	35,760	13,344	49,104	37,096	11,191	48,287	27,383	9,166	36,549
Property, plant and equipment, net	42,010	12,512	54,522	57,942	18,463	76,405	65,404	26,418	91,822
Goodwill and intangibles, net	39,861	80,499	120,360	—	200,122	200,122	—	174,833	174,833

Product Information

Revenue for reportable segments is comprised of the following:

(In thousands)	2003	2002	2001
Tape drives	$336,005	$ 445,381	$ 754,404
Tape media	157,374	182,851	114,067
Tape royalties	186,653	209,316	221,973
DLTG	680,032	837,548	1,090,444
SSG	227,112	233,298	353,097
Inter-group elimination*	(36,335)	(41,171)	(97,426)
	$870,809	$1,029,675	$1,346,115

* Represents inter-group sales of tape drives for incorporation into tape automation systems, for which the sales are included in storage solutions revenue.

Geographic and Customer Information

Revenue and long-lived assets (property, plant and equipment and goodwill and intangible assets) by region was as follows (revenue is attributed to regions based on the location of customers):

(In thousands)	2003		2002		2001	
	Revenue	Long-Lived Assets	Revenue	Long-Lived Assets	Revenue	Long-Lived Assets
United States	$527,523	$157,648	$ 608,188	$212,158	$ 871,535	$231,750
Europe	202,758	9,348	260,083	52,218	311,254	1,572
Asia Pacific	139,124	7,886	160,039	12,151	160,225	1,932
Latin America	1,404	—	1,365	—	3,101	—
	$870,809	$174,882	$1,029,675	$276,527	$1,346,115	$235,254

One customer accounted for 10% or more of Quantum's revenue in all of the fiscal years presented. Revenue from this customer represented $193.0 million, $292.5 million and $408.8 million of Quantum's revenue in fiscal years 2003, 2002, and 2001, respectively.

NATURAL BUSINESS YEAR

1.32 A natural business year is the period of 12 consecutive months which ends when the business activities of an entity have reached the lowest point in their annual cycle. In many instances, the natural business year of a company ends December 31.

1.33 Table 1-4 summarizes, by the month in which a fiscal year ends, the fiscal year endings of the survey companies. For tabulation purposes, if a fiscal year ended in the first week of a month, the fiscal year was considered to have ended in the preceding month.

1.34 For 2003, 160 survey companies were on a 52–53 week fiscal year. During 2003, 5 survey companies changed the date of their fiscal year end. Examples of fiscal year end changes and of fiscal year definitions follow.

1.35

TABLE 1-4: MONTH OF FISCAL YEAR END

	2003	2002	2001	2000
January	30	31	32	30
February	9	9	10	11
March	16	16	16	15
April	8	7	8	8
May	18	21	18	16
June	49	49	48	48
July	8	8	8	11
August	14	14	15	15
September	42	42	38	40
October	17	16	19	19
November	13	13	15	15
Subtotal	**224**	**226**	**227**	**228**
December	376	374	373	372
Total Companies	**600**	**600**	**600**	**600**

Change in Date of Fiscal Year End

1.36

MONSANTO COMPANY

Statement of Consolidated Operations

	Eight Months Ended Aug. 31, 2003	2002	Year Ended Dec. 31, 2001	2000

Statement of Consolidated Financial Position

	As of Aug. 31, 2003	2002	As of Dec. 31, 2001

Statement of Consolidated Cash Flows

	Eight Months Ended Aug. 31, 2003	2002	Year Ended Dec. 31, 2001	2000

NOTES TO CONSOLIDATED FINANCIAL STATEMENTS

Note 1 (In Part): Background and Basis of Presentation

In July 2003, Monsanto's board of directors approved a change to Monsanto's fiscal year end from December 31 to August 31. This change aligns the company's fiscal year more closely to the seasonal nature of its business. Accordingly, the company is presenting audited financial statements for the eight months ended Aug. 31, 2003 (the transition period). For comparative purposes, unaudited condensed results of operations data for the comparable period of the prior year is presented in Note 4—Change in Fiscal Year End. The Statement of Consolidated Operations for the 12 months ended Dec. 31, 2002, 2001, and 2000 will be referenced as calendar year 2002, calendar year 2001, and calendar year 2000, respectively. The Statement of Consolidated Financial Position is presented for Dec. 31, 2002 (year-end 2002), and Dec. 31, 2001 (year-end 2001).

Note 4. Change in Fiscal Year End

As discussed in Note 1—Background and Basis of Presentation—the company's fiscal year end has changed from December 31 to August 31. Accordingly, the company is presenting audited financial statements for the eight months ended Aug. 31, 2003, the transition period, in this Form 10-K. The following table provides certain unaudited financial information for the same period of the prior year.

	Eight Months Ended Aug. 31,	
(Dollars in millions, except per share amounts)	2003	2002[1]
Net sales	$3,373	$3,110
Gross profit	1,577	1,442
Income (loss) before income taxes and cumulative effect of accounting change	(38)	50
Income tax provision (benefit)	(27)	13
Income (loss) before cumulative effect of accounting change	(11)	37
Cumulative effect of a change in accounting principle, net of tax benefit of $7 in 2003 and $162 in 2002	(12)	(1,822)
Net loss	$ (23)	$(1,785)
Basic earnings (loss) per share		
Income (loss) before cumulative effect of accounting change	$ (0.04)	$ 0.14
Cumulative effect of accounting change	(0.05)	(7.00)
Net loss	$ (0.09)	$ (6.86)
Diluted earnings (loss) per share		
Income (loss) before cumulative effect of accounting change	$ (0.04)	$ 0.14
Cumulative effect of accounting change	(0.05)	(6.92)
Net loss	$ (0.09)	$ (6.78)

[1] Unaudited.

1.37

TENET HEALTHCARE CORPORATION

Consolidated Balance Sheets

		December 31	
	May 31, 2002	2002	2003

Consolidated Statements of Operations

Years Ended May 31		Seven Months Ended December 31,	Years Ended December 31	
2001	2002	2002	2002	2003
			(Unaudited)	

Consolidated Statements of Cash Flows

Years Ended May 31		Seven Months Ended December 31,	Years Ended December 31	
2001	2002	2002	2002	2003
			(Unaudited)	

NOTES TO CONSOLIDATED FINANCIAL STATEMENTS

Note 1 (In Part): Basis of Presentation

On March 18, 2003, our board of directors approved a change in our fiscal year. Instead of a fiscal year ending on May 31, we now have a fiscal year that coincides with the calendar year. As a result of this change, effective December 31, 2002, our audited consolidated statements of operations, changes in shareholders' equity and cash flows presented herein include the two previous fiscal years ended May 31, 2001 and 2002, the seven-month transition period ended December 31, 2002, and the year ended December 31, 2003. For comparative purposes only, we include unaudited information for the year ended December 31, 2002.

Definition of Fiscal Year

1.38

LEVI STRAUSS & CO.

NOTES TO CONSOLIDATED FINANCIAL STATEMENTS

Note 1 (In Part): Significant Accounting Policies

Basis of Presentation and Principles of Consolidation (In Part)
The Company's fiscal year consists of 52 or 53 weeks, ending on the last Sunday of November in each year. The 2003 fiscal year consisted of 53 weeks ended November 30, 2003. The 2002 and 2001 fiscal years consisted of 52 weeks ended November 24, 2002 and November 25, 2001, respectively. All amounts herein, unless otherwise indicated, are in thousands. The fiscal year end for certain foreign subsidiaries is fixed at November 30 due to certain local statutory requirements and does not include 53 weeks in 2003. All references to years relate to fiscal years rather than calendar years.

1.39

MARSH SUPERMARKETS, INC.

NOTES TO CONSOLIDATED FINANCIAL STATEMENTS

Note 1 (In Part): Significant Accounting Policies

Fiscal Year
The Company's fiscal year ends on Saturday of the thirteenth week of each calendar year. All references to "2003", "2002" and "2001" relate to the fiscal years ended March 29, 2003, March 30, 2002, and March 31, 2001, respectively.

1.40

PATHMARK STORES, INC.

NOTES TO CONSOLIDATED FINANCIAL STATEMENTS

Note 1 (In Part): Significant Accounting Policies

Fiscal Year

The Company's fiscal year, which ends on the Saturday nearest to January 31 of the following calendar year. The Company's fiscal 2003 consisted of 52-week period ended January 31, 2004, fiscal 2002 consisted of the 52-week period ended February 1, 2003 and fiscal 2001 consisted of the 52-week period ended February 2, 2002. Normally, each fiscal year consists of 52 weeks, but every five or six years the fiscal year consists of 53 weeks.

COMPARATIVE FINANCIAL STATEMENTS

1.41   *Rule 14a-3* requires that annual reports to stockholders should include comparative balance sheets, and statements of income and of cash flows for each of the 3 most recent fiscal years. All of the survey companies are registered with the SEC and conformed to the aforementioned requirements of *Rule 14a-3*.

1.42   In their annual reports, the survey companies usually present an income statement as the first financial statement. For 2003, 333 survey companies presented an income statement first followed by a balance sheet; 208 survey companies presented a balance sheet first followed by an income statement; 21 survey companies presented an income statement first followed by a statement of cash flows; and 18 survey companies presented an income statement first combined with a statement of comprehensive income or followed by a separate statement of comprehensive income.

1.43   Prior to 1986, the financial statements, with rare exception, were presented on consecutive pages. Beginning in 1986 certain survey companies did not present their financial statements on consecutive pages but interspersed the Management's Discussion and Analysis of Financial Condition and Results of Operations among the financial statements by having comments discussing the content of a financial statement follow the presentation of a financial statement. Such interspersed material was not covered by an auditor's report and was not presented in lieu of notes. For 2003, 3 survey companies did not present their financial statements on consecutive pages.

ROUNDING OF AMOUNTS

1.44   Table 1-5 shows that most of the survey companies state financial statement amounts in either thousands or millions of dollars.

1.45

TABLE 1-5: ROUNDING OF AMOUNTS

	2003	2002	2001	2000
To nearest dollar...............................	21	21	20	23
To nearest thousands dollars:				
Omitting 000.................................	322	336	334	335
Presenting 000............................	5	4	4	4
To nearest million dollars..................	252	239	242	238
Total Companies.............................	**600**	**600**	**600**	**600**

NOTES TO FINANCIAL STATEMENTS

1.46   SEC Regulations S-X, *Accounting Rules—Form and Content of Financial Statements*, and *S-K*, and Statement on Auditing Standards (SAS) No. 32, *Adequacy of Disclosure in Financial Statements*, state the need for adequate disclosure in financial statements. Normally the financial statements alone cannot present all information necessary for adequate disclosure without considering appended notes which disclose information of the sort listed below:

Changes in accounting principles.

Retroactive adjustments.

Long-term lease agreements.

Assets subject to lien.

Preferred stock data.

Pension and retirement plans.

Restrictions on the availability of retained earnings for cash dividend purposes.

Contingencies and commitments.

Depreciation and depletion policies.

Stock option or stock purchase plans.

Consolidation policies.

Computation of earnings per share.

Subsequent events.

Quarterly data.

Segment information.

Financial instruments.

1.47   Table 1-6 summarizes the manner in which financial statements refer to notes. Notes on specific topics are illustrated in this publication in the sections dealing with such topics.

1.48

TABLE 1-6: NOTES TO FINANCIAL STATEMENTS

	2003	2002	2001	2000
General reference only......................	509	514	475	448
General and direct references...........	91	85	124	151
Direct reference only.........................	0	1	1	1
Total Companies.............................	**600**	**600**	**600**	**600**

DISCLOSURE OF ACCOUNTING POLICIES

1.49 Accounting Principles Board (APB) Opinion No. 22, *Disclosure of Accounting Policies*, requires that the significant accounting policies of an entity be presented as an integral part of the financial statements of the entity. *APB Opinion No. 22* sets forth guidelines as to the content and format of disclosures of accounting policies. *APB Opinion No. 22* states that the preferable format is to present a Summary of Significant Accounting Policies preceding notes to financial statements or as the initial note. During 2003, 474 survey companies presented the Summary of Significant Accounting Policies as either the first footnote or as a separate presentation following the last financial statement and preceding the footnotes. Of the remainder, most survey companies presented the Summary of Significant Accounting Policies as the second footnote following a footnote which described the nature of operations.

1.50 Table 1-7 shows the nature of information frequently disclosed in summaries of accounting policies and the number of survey companies disclosing such information. Examples of summaries of accounting policies follows.

1.51

TABLE 1-7: DISCLOSURE OF ACCOUNTING POLICIES

	Number of Companies			
	2003	2002	2001	2000
Revenue recognition	587	584	574	555
Consolidation policy	572	576	587	581
Use of estimates	571	576	577	576
Stock-based compensation	567	483	335	318
Property	562	556	543	552
Impairment	561	540	533	428
Depreciation methods	552	567	584	581
Cash equivalents	551	537	543	518
Inventory pricing	518	522	523	538
Amortization of intangibles	512	509	495	481
Financial instruments	505	487	450	423
Interperiod tax allocation	464	444	418	404
Translation of foreign currency	441	420	407	398
Earnings per share calculation	402	386	383	407
Nature of operations	325	361	329	313
Advertising costs	271	250	227	197
Research and development costs	213	206	186	180
Credit risk concentrations	189	178	167	173
Fiscal years	176	181	175	178
Employee benefits	172	167	133	164
Environmental costs	138	133	131	139
Capitalization of interest	92	89	87	89

1.52

ACUITY BRANDS, INC. (AUG)

NOTES TO CONSOLIDATED FINANCIAL STATEMENTS
(Dollar amounts in thousands, except share and per-share data and as indicated)

Note 2. Summary of Significant Accounting Policies

Principles of Consolidation

The *Consolidated Financial Statements* include the accounts of Acuity Brands and its wholly-owned subsidiaries after elimination of significant intercompany transactions and accounts.

Revenue Recognition and Product Warranty

Acuity Brands records revenue as products are shipped and title passes. A provision for estimated returns, allowances, and warranty costs is recorded when products are shipped based on historical experience.

Use of Estimates

The preparation of financial statements in conformity with accounting principles generally accepted in the United States requires management to make estimates and assumptions, which include estimates of NSI costs allocated to Acuity Brands, that affect the reported amounts of assets and liabilities, the disclosure of contingent assets and liabilities at the date of the financial statements, and the reported amounts of revenue and expense during the reporting period. Actual results could differ from those estimates.

Cash and Cash Equivalents

Cash in excess of daily requirements is invested in time deposits and marketable securities and is included in the accompanying balance sheets at fair value. Acuity Brands considers time deposits and marketable securities purchased with an original maturity of three months or less to be cash equivalents.

Concentrations of Credit Risk

Concentrations of credit risk with respect to receivables, which are unsecured, are generally limited due to the wide variety of customers and markets using Acuity Brands' products, as well as their dispersion across many different geographic areas. As of August 31, 2003, receivables from The Home Depot were approximately $40.2 million. No other single customer accounted for more than ten percent of consolidated receivables at August 31, 2003.

Reclassifications

Certain prior period amounts have been reclassified to conform to current year presentation.

Inventories

Inventories are valued at the lower of cost (on a first-in, first-out basis) or market and consist of the following:

	2003	2002
Raw materials and supplies	$ 74,091	$ 97,036
Work in progress	22,201	19,884
Finished goods	104,932	108,659
	201,224	225,579
Less: reserves	(12,425)	(8,637)
	$188,799	$216,942

Goodwill and Other Intangibles

In July 2001, the Financial Accounting Standards Board ("FASB") issued Statement of Financial Accounting Standards ("SFAS") No. 142, *Goodwill and Other Intangible Assets*. SFAS No. 142 required companies to cease amortizing goodwill that existed at June 30, 2001 and established a new method for testing goodwill for impairment on an annual basis (or an interim basis if an event occurs that might reduce the fair value of a reporting unit below its carrying value). Any goodwill resulting from acquisitions completed after June 30, 2001 will not be amortized. SFAS No. 142 also required that an identifiable intangible asset which is determined to have an indefinite useful economic life not be amortized, but be separately tested for impairment using a fair-value-based approach. The Company adopted SFAS No. 142 effective September 1, 2001 resulting in a decrease in amortization expense of approximately $12.1 million during the year ended August 31, 2002 when compared to the year ended August 31, 2001.

Summarized information for the Company's acquired intangible assets is as follows:

	August 31, 2003		August 31, 2002	
	Gross Carrying Amount	Accumulated Amortization	Gross Carrying Amount	Accumulated Amortization
Amortized intangible assets:				
Trade names and trademarks	$13,030	$ (1,782)	$13,030	$ (1,347)
Distribution network	53,000	(7,216)	53,000	(5,448)
Other	17,080	(9,283)	17,076	(8,295)
Total	$83,110	$(18,281)	$83,106	$(15,090)
Unamortized intangible assets:				
Trade names	$65,014		$65,014	

The Company amortizes trade names with definite lives, trademarks, and the distribution network over their estimated useful lives of 30 years. Other amortized intangible assets consist primarily of patented technology and restrictive covenant agreements, which are amortized over their estimated useful lives of 12 years and 3 years, respectively. The Company recorded amortization expense of $3.2 million and $4.3 million related to intangible assets with definite lives during fiscal 2003 and fiscal 2002, respectively. Projected amortization expense is approximately $3.2 million in each of the next five years.

The changes in the carrying amount of goodwill during the period are summarized as follows:

	ABL	ASP	Total
Balance as of August 31, 2002	$314,103	$30,115	$344,218
Sale of business	—	(230)	(230)
Currency translation adjustments	1,093	595	1,688
Balance as of August 31, 2003	$315,196	$30,480	$345,676

ABL and ASP each test goodwill and intangible assets with indefinite useful lives for impairment on an annual basis, as required by SFAS No. 142, using a combination of valuation techniques including the expected present value of future cash flows, a market multiple approach, and a comparable transaction approach. This analysis did not result in an impairment during fiscal 2003 or 2002.

Prior to the adoption of SFAS No. 142, $3,460 of goodwill associated with a 1969 acquisition was not amortized. Remaining amounts of goodwill ($327,903 at August 31, 2001) were amortized over estimated useful lives ranging from 10 years to 40 years. Had the Company accounted for goodwill and intangibles with indefinite useful lives consistent with the provisions of SFAS No. 142 in prior periods, the Company's net income would have been affected as follows:

	2003	2002	2001
Reported net income	$47,782	$52,024	$40,503
Add back: Goodwill amortization	—	—	9,891
Add back: Trade name amortization	—	—	990
Adjusted net income	$47,782	$52,024	$51,384
Basic earnings per share*:			
Reported net income	$ 1.15	$ 1.26	$ 0.99
Add back: Goodwill amortization	—	—	0.24
Add back: Trade name amortization	—	—	0.03
Adjusted net income	$ 1.15	$ 1.26	$ 1.26

* Earnings per share for the years ended August 31, 2002 and 2001 are pro forma. See Note 5 for additional information.

The Company is required to test its goodwill and intangibles with indefinite useful lives for impairment on a periodic basis, which could have an adverse effect on the Company's *Consolidated Financial Statements* if these assets are deemed impaired.

Other Long-Term Assets

Other long-term assets consisted of the following:

	2003	2002
Long term investments [1]	$25,805	$28,677
Prepaid pension costs	—	12,693
Intangible pension asset	1,654	1,580
Note receivable, net	1,052	2,165
Debt issue costs	2,038	2,385
Miscellaneous	1,041	1,530
	$31,590	$49,030

[1] Long term investments—The Company maintains certain investments that generate returns that offset changes in certain liabilities related to deferred compensation arrangements. The investments primarily consist of marketable equity securities and fixed income securities, are stated at fair value, and are classified as trading in accordance with SFAS No. 115, *Accounting for Certain Investments in Debt and Equity Securities*. Realized and unrealized gains and losses are included in the *Consolidated Statements of Income* and generally offset the change in the deferred compensation liability.

Other Long-Term Liabilities

Other long-term liabilities consisted of the following:

	2003	2002
Accrued pension liability	$40,245	$15,622
Postretirement benefits other than pensions [1]	54,602	56,380
Director stock unit plan	1,605	970
Postemployment benefit obligation [2]	430	497
Miscellaneous	807	1,099
	$97,689	$74,568

[1] Postretirement benefits other than pensions—The Company maintains several non-qualified retirement plans for the benefit of eligible employees, primarily deferred compensation plans. The deferred compensation plans provide for elective deferrals of an eligible employee's compensation and, in some cases, matching contributions by the Company. In addition, one plan provides for an automatic contribution by the Company of three percent of an eligible employee's compensation. Deferred compensation associated with these plans, together with the Company's contributions and accumulated earnings, is generally distributable in cash pursuant to the terms of the plans, either after specified periods of time or after retirement. The Company maintains life insurance policies on certain current and former officers and other key employees as a means of satisfying a portion of these obligations.

[2] Postemployment benefit obligation—SFAS No. 112, *Employers' Accounting for Postemployment Benefits*, requires the accrual of the estimated cost of benefits provided by an employer to former or inactive employees after employment but before retirement. Acuity Brands' accrual relates primarily to the liability for life insurance coverage for certain eligible employees.

Earnings Per Share

Earnings per share data for periods prior to fiscal 2003 has not been presented since the businesses that comprise Acuity Brands were wholly-owned subsidiaries of NSI, or businesses thereof, during a portion of or for all of the periods presented and were recapitalized as part of the Distribution.

Pro Forma Earnings Per Share (Unaudited)

Pro forma basic earnings per share is calculated as net income divided by the pro forma weighted average number of common shares outstanding. Pro forma weighted average shares outstanding has been computed by applying the distribution ratio of one share of Acuity Brands common stock to the historical NSI weighted average shares outstanding for the same period presented. Pro forma earnings per share information is unaudited and has been presented for the years ended August 31, 2002 and 2001 only.

Shipping and Handling Fees and Costs

In September 2000, the Emerging Issues Task Force issued EITF 00-10, *Accounting for Shipping and Handling Fees and Costs*. EITF 00-10 requires shipping and handling fees billed to customers to be classified as revenue and shipping and handling costs to be either classified as cost of sales or disclosed in the notes to the financial statements. The Company includes shipping and handling fees billed to customers in *Net sales*. Shipping and handling costs associated with inbound freight are generally recorded in *Cost of products sold*. Other shipping and handling costs are included in *Selling, distribution, and administrative expenses* and totaled $120.4 million, $114.1 million, and $114.6 million in fiscal 2003, 2002, and 2001, respectively.

Stock-Based Compensation

The Company issues stock options to employees and directors under certain of its benefit plans. Under all stock option plans, the options expire no later than 10 years from the date of grant and have an exercise price equal to the fair market value of the Company's stock on the date of grant. The Company accounts for the employee and director plans under the Accounting Principles Board Opinion No. 25, *Accounting for Stock Issued to Employees* and related interpretations. Accordingly, no compensation expense has been recognized for these stock option plans in the *Consolidated Financial Statements*.

Acuity Brands has adopted the disclosure provisions of SFAS No. 148, *Accounting for Stock-Based Compensation—Transition and Disclosure an Amendment to FASB Statement No. 123*. The Company expects to begin using the fair value approach to account for stock-based compensation, in accordance with the prospective method as prescribed by SFAS No. 148, beginning in the first quarter of fiscal 2004. Had compensation cost for the Company's stock option plans been determined based on the fair value at the grant date for awards during fiscal 2003 and fiscal 2002, consistent with the recognition provisions of SFAS No. 123, the Company's net income and earnings per share would have been impacted as follows:

	2003	2002[1]
Net income, as reported	$47,782	$52,024
Less: Compensation expense related to the employee stock purchase plan, net of tax	287	201
Less: Stock-based compensation determined under fair value based method for stock option awards, net of tax	2,326	2,541
Pro forma net income	$45,169	$49,282
Earnings per share:		
Basic earnings per share—as reported	$ 1.15	$ 1.26
Basic earnings per share—pro forma	$ 1.09	$ 1.19
Diluted earnings per share—as reported	$ 1.15	n/a
Diluted earnings per share—pro forma	$ 1.08	n/a

[1] Weighted average shares outstanding for the year ended August 31, 2002 has been computed by applying the distribution ratio of one share of Acuity Brands common stock to the historical NSI weighted average shares outstanding for the same period presented.

The above pro-forma calculations only include the effects of options granted subsequent to the Distribution. Accordingly, the pro forma effect of applying SFAS No. 123 may not be representative of the effect on reported net income in future years because options vest over several years and varying amounts of awards are generally made each year.

The following weighted average assumptions were used to estimate the fair value of stock options granted in the fiscal year:

	2003	2002
Dividend yield	4.4%	4.3%
Expected volatility	43.8%	34.0%
Risk-free interest rate	3.0%	5.2%
Expected life of options	8 years	10 years

Depreciation

For financial reporting purposes, depreciation is determined principally on a straight-line basis using estimated useful lives of plant and equipment (20 to 40 years for buildings and 3 to 15 years for machinery and equipment) while accelerated depreciation methods are used for income tax purposes. Leasehold improvements are amortized over the life of the lease or the useful life of the improvement whichever is shorter.

Research and Development

Research and development costs are expensed as incurred. Research and development expenses amounted to $27.4 million, $22.0 million, and $15.6 million during fiscal years 2003, 2002, and 2001, respectively.

Advertising

Advertising costs are expensed as incurred and were $16.3 million, $18.1 million, and $13.8 million during fiscal years 2003, 2002, and 2001, respectively.

Foreign Currency Translation

The functional currency for the foreign operations of Acuity Brands is the local currency. The translation of foreign currencies into U.S. dollars is performed for balance sheet accounts using exchange rates in effect at the balance sheet dates and for revenue and expense accounts using a weighted average exchange rate during the year. The gains or losses resulting from the translation are included in *Accumulated Other Comprehensive Income (Loss) Items* in the *Consolidated Statements of Stockholders' Equity and Comprehensive Income* and are excluded from net income.

Gains or losses resulting from foreign currency transactions are included in *Miscellaneous (income) expense, net* in the *Consolidated Statements of Income* and were insignificant in fiscal years 2003, 2002, and 2001.

Interest Expense, Net

Interest expense, net, is comprised primarily of interest expense on long-term debt, revolving credit facility borrowings, and short-term secured borrowings partially offset by interest income on cash and cash equivalents.

The following table summarizes the components of interest expense, net:

	2003	2002	2001
Interest expense	$37,804	$41,196	$49,421
Interest income	(421)	(506)	(624)
Interest expense, net	$37,383	$40,690	$48,797

Miscellaneous (Income) Expense, Net

Miscellaneous (income) expense, net, is comprised primarily of gains or losses resulting from the sale of assets and gains or losses on foreign currency transactions. Additionally, during 2001, *Miscellaneous (income) expense, net*, includes a charge of approximately $3.1 million related to the early termination of a purchase contract.

Accounting Standards Adopted in Fiscal 2003

In June 2001, the FASB issued SFAS No. 143, *Accounting for Retirement Obligations*. This statement addresses financial accounting and reporting for obligations associated with the retirement of tangible long-lived assets and the associated asset retirement costs. It applies to legal obligations associated with the retirement of a long-lived asset, except for certain obligations of lessees. A legal obligation is an obligation that a party is required to settle as a result of an existing or enacted law, statute, ordinance, or written or oral contract or by legal construction of a contract under the doctrine of promissory estoppel. This statement amends FASB Statement No. 19, *Financial Accounting and Reporting by Oil and Gas Producing Companies*. SFAS No. 143 requires that the fair value of a liability for an asset retirement obligation be recognized in the period in which it is incurred if a reasonable estimate of fair value can be made. The associated asset retirement costs are capitalized as part of the carrying amount of the long-lived asset. This statement is effective for financial statements issued for fiscal years beginning after June 15, 2002. Acuity Brands adopted this statement effective September 1, 2002. Adoption of this statement did not have a significant effect on the Company's consolidated results of operations or financial position.

In August 2001, the FASB issued SFAS No. 144, *Accounting for the Impairment or Disposal of Long-Lived Assets*. SFAS No. 144 supersedes SFAS No. 121, *Accounting for the Impairment of Long-Lived Assets and for Long-Lived Assets to be Disposed Of* and supersedes the provisions of APB Opinion No. 30, *Reporting the Results of Operations—Reporting the Effects of Disposal of a Segment of a Business, and Extraordinary, Unusual and Infrequently Occurring Events and Transactions* with regard to reporting the effects of a disposal of a segment of a business. SFAS No. 144 provides a single accounting model for long-lived assets to be disposed of and significantly changes the criteria required to classify an asset as held-for-sale. Under SFAS No. 144, more dispositions will qualify for discontinued operations treatment in the income statement and expected future operating losses from discontinued operations will be displayed in discontinued operations in the period in which the losses are incurred. SFAS No. 144 is effective for all fiscal years beginning after December 15, 2001. Acuity Brands adopted this statement effective September 1, 2002. Adoption of this statement did not have a significant effect on the Company's consolidated results of operations or financial position.

In June 2002, the FASB issued SFAS No. 146, *Accounting for Costs Associated with Exit or Disposal Activities*. SFAS No. 146 addresses financial accounting and reporting for costs associated with exit or disposal activities and nullifies Emerging Issues Task Force Issue No. 94-3, *Liability Recognition for Certain Employee Termination Benefits and Other Costs to Exit an Activity (including Certain Costs Incurred in a Restructuring)*. The principal difference between SFAS No. 146 and Issue No. 94-3 relates to the requirements for recognition of a liability for a cost associated with an exit or disposal activity. SFAS No. 146 requires that a liability for a cost associated with an exit or disposal activity be recognized when the liability is incurred. SFAS No. 146 also establishes that fair value is the objective for initial measurement of the liability. SFAS No. 146 is effective for exit or disposal activities that are initiated after December 31, 2002. Acuity Brands adopted SFAS No. 146 effective September 1, 2002. Adoption of this statement did not have a significant effect on the Company's consolidated results of operations or financial position.

In November 2002, the FASB issued FASB Interpretation No. 45 ("FIN No. 45"), *Guarantor's Accounting and Disclosure Requirements for Guarantees, Including Indirect Guarantees of Indebtedness of Others*. FIN No. 45 elaborates on the disclosures to be made by a guarantor in its interim and annual financial statements about its obligations under certain guarantees that it has issued. It also clarifies that a guarantor is required to recognize, at the inception of the guarantee, a liability for the fair value of the obligation undertaken in issuing the guarantee. This interpretation does not prescribe a specific approach for subsequently measuring the guarantor's recognized liability over the term of the related guaranty. This interpretation also supersedes and incorporates the guidance in FASB Interpretation No. 34, *Disclosure of Indirect Guarantees of Indebtedness of Others*. The initial recognition and measurement provisions of FIN No. 45 are applicable on a prospective basis to guarantees issued or modified after December 31, 2002. The disclosure requirements of FIN No. 45, including those related to product warranties, are effective for financial statements for interim or annual periods ending after December 15, 2002. Acuity Brands adopted FIN No. 45 effective December 1, 2002. Adoption of this interpretation did not have a significant effect on the Company's consolidated results of operations or financial position.

Accounting Standards Yet to Be Adopted

On December 31, 2002, the FASB issued SFAS No. 148, *Accounting for Stock-Based Compensation—Transition and Disclosure-an Amendment of FASB Statement No. 123*, SFAS No. 148 amends SFAS No. 123, *Accounting for Stock-Based Compensation*, to provide alternative methods of transition to the fair value method of accounting for stock-based employee compensation. The alternative methods include the prospective method, the modified prospective method, and the retroactive restatement method. The prospective method requires application of the recognition provisions of SFAS No. 123 for awards granted after the beginning of the fiscal year in which the adoption is made. Acuity Brands expects to adopt the prospective method for transitioning to the fair value method of accounting for stock-based employee compensation as prescribed by SFAS No. 123 during the first quarter of fiscal 2004. SFAS No. 148 also amends the disclosure provision of SFAS No. 123 to require prominent disclosure of the effects of an entity's accounting policy with respect to stock-based employee compensation on reported net income and earnings per share in annual and interim financial statements, regardless of the method used to account for stock-based employee compensation. The annual disclosure requirements of SFAS No. 148 are effective for all fiscal years ending after December 15, 2002. See Note 5 of *Notes to Consolidated Financial Statements* for further information. The Company expects to incur incremental expense of approximately $7.2 million related to its stock-based plans in fiscal 2004, including approximately $4.3 million in connection with the adoption of SFAS No. 123 on a prospective basis.

In January 2003, the FASB issued FIN No. 46, *Consolidation of Variable Interest Entities—An Interpretation of Accounting Research Bulletin No. 51*. FIN No. 46 requires the consolidation of entities in which an enterprise absorbs a majority of the entity's expected losses, receives a majority of the entity's expected residual returns, or both, as a result of ownership, contractual interests or other financial interests in the entity. FIN No. 46 is effective for all new variable interest entities created or acquired after January 31, 2003. For variable interest entities created or acquired prior to February 1, 2003, the provisions of FIN No. 46 must be applied during the first interim or annual period beginning after December 15, 2003. Acuity Brands will adopt FIN No. 46 effective in fiscal 2004. Adoption of this interpretation is not expected to have a significant effect on the Company's consolidated results of operations or financial position.

1.53

CLEVELAND-CLIFFS INC (DEC)

NOTES TO CONSOLIDATED FINANCIAL STATEMENTS

Accounting Policies

Business

The Company is the largest supplier of iron ore pellets to integrated steel companies in North America. The Company manages and owns interests in North American mines and owns ancillary companies providing transportation and other services to the mines.

Basis of Consolidation

The consolidated financial statements include the accounts of the Company and its majority—owned subsidiaries ("Company"), including:

- Tilden Mining Company LC. ("Tilden") in Michigan; consolidated since January 31, 2002, when the Company increased its ownership from 40 percent to 85 percent;
- Empire Iron Mining Partnership ("Empire") in Michigan; consolidated effective December 31, 2002, when the Company increased its ownership from 46.7 percent to 79 percent;
- 100 percent of Wabush Iron Co. Limited ("Wabush Iron"); consolidated since August 29, 2002 when Acme Steel Company rejected its interest in Wabush Iron; Wabush Iron owns 26.83 percent interest in the Wabush Mines Joint Venture ("Wabush") in Canada; and
- United Taconite LLC ("United Taconite") in Minnesota; consolidated since December 1, 2003, when the Company acquired a 70 percent ownership interest; (see Note 1—"Operations and Customers—United Taconite").

Intercompany accounts are eliminated in consolidation. "Other Investments" includes Wabush Iron's equity interest in certain Wabush Mines related entities, which the Company does not control. The Company's equity interest in Hibbing Taconite Company ("Hibbing"), an unincorporated joint venture in Minnesota, which the Company does not control, was a net liability, and accordingly, was classified as "Payables to associated companies." Cliffs and Associates Limited ("CAL") results are included in "Discontinued Operation" in the Statement of Consolidated Operations. See Note 3—"Discontinued Operation."

Revenue Recognition

Revenue is recognized on sales of products when title has transferred, and on services when performed. Revenue from product sales includes reimbursement for freight charges ($59.2 million–2003; $38.7 million–2002; $17.8 million–2001) paid on behalf of customers and cost reimbursement of $79.1 million in 2003 and $36.9 million in 2002 from minority interest partners for their contractual share of mine costs. Royalties and management fees revenue from venture participants is recognized on production.

Business Risk

The major business risk faced by the Company, as it increases its merchant position, is lower customer consumption of iron ore from the Company's mines which may result from competition from other iron are suppliers; increased use of iron ore substitutes, including imported semi-finished steel; customers rationalization or financial failure, or decreased North American steel production, resulting from increased imports or lower steel consumption. The Company's sales are concentrated with a relatively few number of customers. Unmitigated loss of sales would have a greater impact on operating results and cash flow than revenue, due to the high level of fixed costs in the iron ore mining business in the near term and the high cost to idle or close mines. In the event of a venture participant's failure to perform, remaining solvent venturers, including the Company, may be required to assume and record additional material obligations. The premature closure of a mine due to the loss of a significant customer or the failure of a venturer would accelerate substantial employment and mine shutdown costs. See Note 1—"Operations and Customers".

Use of Estimates

The preparation of financial statements, in conformity with accounting principles generally accepted in the United States, requires management to make estimates and assumptions that affect the reported amounts of assets and liabilities and disclosure of contingent assets and liabilities at the date of the financial statements and the reported amounts of revenues and expenses during the reporting period. Actual results could differ from estimates.

Cash Equivalents

The Company considers investments in highly liquid debt instruments with an initial maturity of three months or less to be cash equivalents.

Derivative Financial Instruments

In the normal course of business, the Company enters into forward contracts for the purchase of commodities, primarily natural gas, which are used in its operations. Such contracts are in quantities expected to be delivered and used in the production process and are not intended for resale or speculative purposes.

Inventories

Product inventories are stated at the lower of cost or market. Cost of iron ore inventories is determined using the last-in, first-out ("LIFO") method. The excess of current cost over LIFO cost of iron ore inventories was $13.1 million and $6.5 million at December 31, 2003 and 2002, respectively. At December 31, 2003 and 2002, the Company had approximately 2.3 million tons and 2.5 million tons, respectively, at the lower lakes to service customers. The Company maintains ownership until title has transferred, usually when payment is made. The Company tracks the movement of the inventory and has the right to verify the quantities on hand. Supplies and other inventories reflect the average cost method.

Iron Ore Reserves

The Company reviews the iron ore reserves based on current expectations of revenues and costs, which are subject to change. Iron ore reserves include only proven and probable quantities of ore which can be economically mined and processed utilizing existing technology. Asset retirement obligations reflect remaining economic iron ore reserves.

Properties

Properties are stated at cost. Depreciation of plant and equipment is computed principally by straight-line methods based on estimated useful lives, not to exceed the estimated economic iron ore reserves. Depreciation is provided over the following estimated useful lives:

Buildings	45 Years
Mining Equipment	10 to 20 Years
Processing Equipment	15 to 45 Years
Information Technology	2 to 7 Years

Depreciation is not adjusted when operations are temporarily idled.

Asset Impairment

The Company monitors conditions that may affect the carrying value of its long-lived and intangible assets when events and circumstances indicate that the carrying value of the assets may be impaired. The Company determines impairment based on the asset's ability to generate cash flow greater than the carrying value of the asset, using an undiscounted probability-weighted analysis. If projected undiscounted cash flows are less than the carrying value of the asset, the asset is adjusted to its fair value. See Note 1—"Operations and Customers" and Note 3—"Discontinued Operation."

Repairs and Maintenance

The cost of power plant major overhauls is amortized over the estimated useful life, which is the period until the next scheduled overhaul, generally 5 years. All other planned and unplanned repairs and maintenance costs are expensed during the year incurred.

Income Taxes

Income taxes are based on income (loss) for financial reporting purposes and reflect a current tax liability (asset) for the estimated taxes payable (recoverable) in the current year tax return and changes in deferred taxes. Deferred tax assets or liabilities are determined based on differences between financial reporting and tax bases of assets and liabilities and are measured using enacted tax laws and rates. A valuation allowance is provided on deferred tax assets if it is determined that it is more likely than not that the asset will not be realized.

Environmental Remediation Costs

The Company has a formal code of environmental protection and restoration. The Company's obligations for known environmental problems at active and closed mining operations, and other sites have been recognized based on estimates of the cost of investigation and remediation at each site. If the cost can only be estimated as a range of possible amounts with no specific amount being most likely, the minimum of the range is accrued. Costs of future expenditures are not discounted to their present value. Potential insurance recoveries have not been reflected in the determination of the liabilities.

Stock Compensation

Effective January 1, 2003, the Company adopted the fair value method, which is considered the preferable accounting method, of recording stock-based employee compensation as contained in Statement of Financial Accounting Standards ("SFAS") No. 123, "Accounting for Stock-Based Compensation." As prescribed in SFAS No. 148, "Accounting for Stock-Based Compensation—Transition and Disclosure," the Company elected to use the "prospective method." The prospective method requires expense to be recognized for all awards granted, modified or settled beginning in the year of adoption. Historically, the Company applied the intrinsic method as provided in Accounting Principles Board Opinion No. 25, "Accounting for Stock Issued to Employees" and related interpretations and accordingly, no compensation cost had been recognized for stock options in prior years.

As a result of adopting the fair value method for stock compensation, all future awards will be expensed over the stock options vesting period. The adoption did not have a significant financial effect in 2003.

The following illustrates the pro forma effect on net income and earnings per share as if the Company had applied the fair value recognition provisions of SFAS No. 123 to all awards unvested in each period:

	Pro Forma		
(In millions)	2003	2002	2001
Net loss as reported	$(32.7)	$(188.3)	$(22.9)
Stock-based employee compensation:			
Plus expense included in reported results	6.0	2.0	.1
Less fair value-based expense	(3.8)	(2.7)	(1.0)
Pro forma net loss	$(30.5)	$(189.0)	$(23.8)
Loss per share:			
Basic—as reported	$(3.19)	$(18.62)	$(2.27)
Basic—pro forma	$(2.97)	$(18.69)	$(2.36)
Diluted—as reported	$(3.19)	$(18.62)	$(2.27)
Diluted—pro forma	$(2.97)	$(18.69)	$(2.36)

The market value of restricted stock awards and performance shares is charged to expense over the vesting period.

Research and Development Costs

Research and development costs, principally relating to the Mesabi Nugget project at the Northshore mine in Minnesota, are expensed as incurred. Mesabi Nugget project costs of $1.6 million, $1.9 million and $.1 million in 2003, 2002 and 2001, respectively, were included in "Other expenses."

Income Per Common Share

Basic income per common share is calculated on the average number of common shares outstanding during each period. Diluted income per common share is based on the average number of common shares outstanding during each period, adjusted for the effect of outstanding stock options, restricted stock and performance shares.

Reclassifications

Certain prior year amounts have been reclassified to conform to current year classifications.

Accounting and Disclosure Changes

In December 2003, the FASB modified SFAS Statement No. 132 (originally issued in February 1998), "Employers' Disclosures about Pensions and Other Post-retirement Benefits," to improve financial statement disclosures for defined benefit plans. The change replaces the existing SFAS disclosure requirements for pensions. The standard requires that companies provide more details about their plan assets, benefit obligations, cash flows, benefit costs and other relevant information. The guidance is effective for fiscal years ending after December 15, 2003. Accordingly, the Company's December 31, 2003, footnote disclosure regarding its pension and other postretirement benefits has been updated to conform to the requirements of SFAS No. 132R. See Note 8—"Retirement Related Benefits".

In May 2003, the FASB issued SFAS No. 150, "Accounting for Certain Financial Instruments with Characteristics of both Liabilities and Equity," to establish standards for how an issuer classifies and measures certain financial instruments with characteristics of both liabilities and equity. SFAS No. 150 requires an issuer to classify a financial instrument that is within its scope as a liability, or an asset, which may have previously been classified as equity. The Company adopted SFAS No. 150 effective June 30, 2003, as required. The adoption of this Statement did not have an impact on the Company's consolidated financial statements.

In January 2003 (as revised December 2003), the FASB issued Interpretation No. 46, "Consolidation of Variable Interest Entities" ("FIN 46"). FIN 46 clarifies the application of Accounting Research Bulletin No. 51, "Consolidated Financial Statements," for certain entities in which equity investors do not have the characteristics of a controlling financial interest or do not have sufficient equity at risk for the entity to finance its activities without additional subordinated financial support from other parties. FIN 46 requires that variable interest entities, as defined, should be consolidated by the primary beneficiary, which is defined as the entity that is expected to absorb the majority of the expected losses, receive the majority of the gains or both. FIN 46 requires that companies disclose certain information about a variable interest entity created prior to February 1, 2003 if it is reasonably possible that the enterprise will be required to consolidated that entity. The application of FIN 46, which was previously required on July 1, 2003 for entities created prior to February 1, 2003 and immediately for any variable interest entities created subsequent to January 31, 2003, has been deferred until years ending after December 31, 2003, except for those companies which previously issued financial statements implementing the provisions of FIN 46. The Company has evaluated its unconsolidated entities and does not believe that any entity in which it has an interest, but does not currently consolidate, meets the requirements for a variable interest entity to be consolidated.

In June 2002, the FASB issued SFAS No. 146, "Accounting for Costs Associated with Exit or Disposal Activities," when the liability is incurred and not as a result of an entity's commitment to an exit plan. The statement is effective for exit or disposal activities initiated after December 31, 2002. In 2003, and in accordance with SFAS No. 146 provisions, the Company recorded a charge of $8.7 million relating to the Company's staff reduction program. See Note 2— "Restructuring."

Effective January 1, 2002, the Company implemented SFAS No. 143, "Accounting for Asset Retirement Obligations" which addresses financial accounting and reporting for obligations associated with the retirement of tangible long-lived assets and the related asset retirement costs. The statement requires that the fair value of a liability for an asset retirement obligation be recognized in the period in which it is incurred and capitalized as part of the carrying amount of the long-lived asset. When a liability is initially recorded, the entity capitalizes the cost by increasing the carrying value of the related long-lived asset. Over time, the liability is accreted to its present value each period, and the capitalized cost is depreciated over the useful life of the related asset. Upon settlement of the liability, a gain or loss is recorded. The cumulative effect of this accounting change related to prior years was a one-time non-cash charge to income of $13.4 million (net of $3.3 million recorded under the Company's previous mine closure accrual method) recognized as of January 1, 2002. The net effect of the change was $1.9 million of additional expense in year 2002 results. The pro forma effect of this change, as if it had been made for 2001, would be to decrease net income by $8 million. See Note 5—"Environmental and Mine Closure Obligations."

In October 2001, the FASB issued SFAS No. 144, "Accounting for the Impairment or Disposal of Long-Lived Assets" which supersedes SFAS No. 121, "Accounting for the Impairment of Long-Lived Assets and for Long-Lived Assets to be Disposed Of." Although retaining many of the provisions of SFAS No. 121, SFAS No. 144 establishes a uniform accounting model for long-lived assets to be disposed. The Company's adoption of this statement in the first quarter of 2002 did not have a significant impact.

In July 2001, the FASB issued SFAS No. 142, "Goodwill and Other Intangible Assets." SFAS No. 142 requires testing of goodwill and intangible assets with indefinite lives for impairment rather than amortizing them. The adoption of this statement in the first quarter of 2002 did not have a significant impact on the Company's financial results.

Effective January 1, 2001, the Company changed its method of accounting for investment gains and losses on pension assets for the calculation of net periodic pension cost. Previously, the Company utilized a method that deferred and amortized realized and unrealized gains and losses over five years for most pension plans. Under the new accounting method, the market value of plan assets reflects realized and unrealized gains and losses from current year performance in the following year. The Company believes the new method results in improved financial reporting because the method more closely reflects the fair value of its pension assets at the date of reporting. The cumulative effect of this accounting change related to prior years was a one-time non-cash credit to income of $9.3 million ($14.3 million pre-tax) recognized as of January 1, 2001.

ATT-SEC 1.53

1.54

DIEBOLD, INCORPORATED (DEC)

NOTES TO CONSOLIDATED FINANCIAL STATEMENTS
(Dollars in thousands, except per share amounts and as noted)

Note 1 Summary of Significant Accounting Policies

Principles of Consolidation

The Consolidated Financial Statements include the accounts of the company and its wholly and majority owned subsidiaries. All significant intercompany accounts and transactions have been eliminated.

Statements of Cash Flows

For the purpose of the Consolidated Statements of Cash Flows, the company considers all highly liquid investments with maturities of three months or less at the time of purchase to be cash equivalents.

International Operations

The financial statements of the company's international operations are measured using local currencies as their functional currencies, with the exception of Venezuela, Mexico, Argentina and Ecuador, which are measured using the U.S. dollar as their functional currency. The company translates the assets and liabilities of its non-U.S. subsidiaries at the exchange rates in effect at year-end and the results of operations at the average rate throughout the year. The translation adjustments are recorded directly as a separate component of shareholders' equity, while transaction gains (losses) are included in net income. Sales to customers outside the United States approximated 36.9 percent of net sales in 2003, 37.1 percent of net sales in 2002 and 43.3 percent of net sales in 2001.

Financial Instruments

The carrying amount of financial instruments, including cash and cash equivalents, trade receivables and accounts payable, approximated their fair value as of December 31, 2003 and 2002 because of the relatively short maturity of these instruments.

Revenue Recognition

The company enters into contracts to sell its products and services.

Product

Product revenue consists of financial self-service, security and election equipment sales. The majority of financial self-service and security product sales agreements contain standard terms and conditions. Sales agreements pertaining to election equipment sales contain multiple deliverables and custom terms and conditions. Financial self-service and security product revenue is recognized in accordance with the terms of the contract. If customer acceptance occurs at time of delivery to a customer designated warehouse and the customer has assumed risk of loss, product revenue is recognized at time of delivery. If customer acceptance does not occur until after delivery, product revenue is delayed until customer acceptance is obtained.

Service

Service revenue primarily consists of billed work, service contract and product installation revenue related to either one-time or ongoing maintenance of financial self-service, security, and election equipment. Revenue related to billed work is recognized upon completion of the service provided. Revenue on service contracts is recognized ratably over the contract period. The financial self-service installation revenue relative to these contracts is recognized upon customer acceptance of the respective equipment.

Election Systems

Election systems revenue consists of election equipment, software, training, support, installation and maintenance. The election equipment and software components are included in product revenue. The training, support, installation and maintenance components are included in service revenue. The election systems contracts contain multiple deliverable elements and custom terms and conditions. As a result, significant analysis is required to determine the appropriate revenue recognition for each contract, including whether the deliverables specified in a multiple element arrangement should be treated as separate units of accounting for revenue recognition purposes and, if so, how the price should be allocated among the deliverable elements and when to recognize revenue for each element. The company recognizes revenue for delivered elements only when the fair values of undelivered elements are known, uncertainties regarding customer acceptance are resolved and there are no customer-negotiated refund or return rights affecting the revenue recognized for delivered elements. Some contracts may contain discounts and, as such, revenue is recognized using the relative fair value method of allocation of revenue to the product and service components of contracts.

Trade Receivables

The concentration of credit risk in the company's trade receivables with respect to financial and government sectors is substantially mitigated by the company's credit evaluation process and the geographical dispersion of sales transactions from a large number of individual customers. The company maintains allowances for potential credit losses, and such losses have been minimal and within management's expectations. The allowance for doubtful accounts is estimated based on various factors including revenue, historical credit losses and current trends.

Inventories

Domestic inventories are valued at the lower of cost or market applied on a first-in, first-out basis, and foreign inventories are valued using the average cost method. With the development of new products, the company also rationalizes its product offerings and will write down discontinued product to the lower of cost or net realizable value.

Depreciation and Amortization

Depreciation of property, plant and equipment is computed using the straight-line method for financial statement purposes. Accelerated methods of depreciation are used for federal income tax purposes. Amortization of leasehold improvements is based upon the shorter of original terms of the lease or life of the improvement.

Research, Development and Engineering

Total research, development and engineering costs charged to expense were $60,451, $56,693 and $58,321 in 2003, 2002 and 2001, respectively.

Advertising Costs

Advertising costs are expensed as incurred. Total advertising costs charged to expense were $12,086, $12,227 and $12,930 in 2003, 2002 and 2001, respectively.

Other Assets

Other assets consist primarily of pension assets, computer software, customer demonstration equipment, deferred tooling, investment in service contracts, retained interest in DCCF, finance receivables and certain other assets. Where applicable, these assets are stated at cost and, if applicable, are amortized ratably over a period of three to five years.

Goodwill

Goodwill is the cost in excess of the net assets of acquired businesses. These assets are stated at cost and, effective January 1, 2002, are no longer amortized, but evaluated at least annually for impairment, in accordance with SFAS No. 142, *Goodwill and Other Intangible Assets*. SFAS No. 142 establishes accounting and reporting standards for acquired goodwill and other intangible assets in that goodwill and other intangible assets that have indefinite useful lives will not be amortized but rather will be tested at least annually for impairment. Intangible assets that have finite useful lives will continue to be amortized over their useful lives. The year ended 2001 earnings per share of $0.93 included goodwill amortization of $10,287, net of tax. Amortization expense related to goodwill was $15,354 for the year ended December 31, 2001. Had goodwill amortization not been recorded in the year ended December 31, 2001, net income would have increased to $77,180; and net income per share to $1.08 on a diluted basis.

Under SFAS No. 142, the company is required to test all existing goodwill for impairment on a "reporting unit" basis. The reporting units were determined on a geographical basis that combines two or more component-level reporting units with similar economic characteristics within a single reporting unit. A fair value approach is used to test goodwill for impairment. An impairment charge is recognized for the amount, if any, by which the carrying amount of goodwill exceeds its implied fair value. Fair values of reporting units and the related implied fair values of their respective goodwill were established using discounted cash flows. When available and as appropriate, comparative market multiples were used to corroborate results of the discounted cash flows.

In June 2002, the company completed the transitional goodwill impairment test in accordance with SFAS No. 142, which resulted in a noncash charge of $38,859 ($33,147 after tax, or $0.46 per share) and is reported in the caption "Cumulative effect of a change in accounting principle" for the year ended December 31, 2002. All of the charge related to the company's businesses in Latin America and Brazil. The primary factor that resulted in the impairment charge was the difficult economic environment in those markets. No impairment charge was appropriate under previous goodwill impairment standards, which were based on undiscounted cash flows. The company performed annual impairment tests as of November 30, 2003 and 2002 resulting in no impairment.

The changes in carrying amount of goodwill for the years ended December 31, 2003 and 2002 are as follows:

	DNA	DI	ES & Other	Total
Balance at January 1, 2002	$25,503	$250,182	$ —	$275,685
Transitional impairment loss	—	(38,859)	—	(38,859)
Goodwill of acquired businesses	306	1,474	41,029	42,809
Currency translation adjustment	11	(11,040)	—	(11,029)
Balance at December 31, 2002	$25,820	$201,757	$41,029	$268,606
Goodwill of acquired businesses	844	17,020	5,589	23,453
Currency translation adjustment	264	39,323	—	39,587
Balance at December 31, 2003	$26,928	$258,100	$46,618	$331,646

Deferred Income

Deferred income is largely related to service contracts and deferred installation revenue. Service contract revenue is recognized for customer service collections in advance of the period in which the service will be performed and is recognized in income on a straight-line basis over the contract period.

Stock-Based Compensation

Compensation cost is measured on the date of grant only if the current market price of the underlying stock exceeds the exercise price. The company provides pro forma net income and pro forma net earnings per share disclosures for employee stock option grants made in 1995 and subsequent years as if the fair value based method had been applied in accordance with SFAS No. 123, *Accounting for Stock Based Compensation*.

In the following chart, the company provides net income and basic earnings per share reduced by the pro forma amounts calculating compensation cost for the company's fixed stock option plan under the fair value method. The fair value of each option grant was estimated on the date of grant using the Black-Scholes option-pricing model with the following assumptions for 2003, 2002 and 2001, respectively: risk-free interest rate of 2.8, 4.2 and 4.9 percent; dividend yield of 1.8, 1.9 and 1.7 percent; volatility of 41, 42 and 41 percent; and average expected lives of six years for management and four years for executive management and nonemployee directors. The company's stock options are accounted for in accordance with Accounting Principles Board Opinion No. 25, *Accounting for Stock Issued to Employees*. As a result, no compensation expense has been recognized in the "as reported" amounts listed in the table below.

	2003	2002	2001
Net income			
As reported	$174,776	$99,154	$66,893
Pro forma	$170,776	$95,956	$64,598
Earnings per share			
As reported			
Basic	$ 2.41	$ 1.38	$ 0.94
Diluted	$ 2.40	$ 1.37	$ 0.93
Pro forma			
Basic	$ 2.36	$ 1.33	$ 0.90
Diluted	$ 2.34	$ 1.33	$ 0.90
Weighted-average fair value of options granted during the year	$ 12	$ 13	$ 11

Taxes on Income

Deferred taxes are provided on an asset and liability method whereby deferred tax assets are recognized for deductible temporary differences and operating loss carryforwards and deferred tax liabilities are recognized for taxable temporary differences. Temporary differences are the differences between the reported amounts of assets and liabilities and their tax basis. Deferred tax assets are reduced by a valuation allowance when, in the opinion of management, it is more likely than not that some portion or all of the deferred tax assets will not be realized. Deferred tax assets and liabilities are adjusted for the effects of changes in tax laws and rates on the date of enactment.

Earning Per Share

Basic earnings per share are computed by dividing income available to common shareholders by the weighted-average number of common shares outstanding for the period. Diluted earnings per share reflect the potential dilution that could occur if common stock equivalents were exercised and then shared in the earnings of the company.

Comprehensive Income (Loss)

The company displays comprehensive income (loss) in the Consolidated Statements of Shareholders' Equity and accumulated other comprehensive loss separately from retained earnings and additional capital in the Consolidated Balance Sheets and Statements of Shareholders' Equity. Items considered to be other comprehensive income (loss) include adjustments made for foreign currency translation (under SFAS No. 52), pensions (under SFAS No. 87) and unrealized holding gains and losses on available-for-sale securities (under SFAS

No. 115). Accumulated other comprehensive loss consists of the following:

	2003	2002	2001
Translation adjustment	$(35,810)	$ (94,104)	$(54,813)
Pensions less accumulated taxes of $(3,159), $(2,829) and $(1,207), respectively	(7,245)	(6,635)	(3,623)
Unrealized losses on investment securities less accumulated taxes of $0, $550 and $533, respectively	—	(1,674)	(2,010)
	$(43,055)	$(102,413)	$(60,446)

Translation adjustments are not booked net of tax. Those adjustments are accounted for under the indefinite reversal criterion of APB Opinion 23, *Accounting for Income Taxes—Special Areas*.

Use of Estimates in Preparation of Consolidated Financial Statements

The preparation of the Consolidated Financial Statements in conformity with accounting principles generally accepted in the United States of America requires management to make estimates and assumptions that affect the reported amounts of assets and liabilities and disclosure of contingent assets and liabilities at the date of the Consolidated Financial Statements and the reported amounts of revenues and expenses during the reporting period. Actual results could differ from those estimates.

Reclassifications

The company has reclassified the presentation of certain prior-year information to conform to the current presentation.

1.55

LAND O'LAKES, INC. (DEC)

NOTES TO CONSOLIDATED FINANCIAL STATEMENTS ($ in thousands in tables)

1. Summary of Significant Accounting Policies

Nature of Operations

Land O'Lakes, Inc. is a diversified, farmer-owned food and agricultural cooperative serving agricultural producers throughout the United States. Land O'Lakes procures 13 billion pounds of member milk annually, markets more than 300 dairy products and provides member cooperatives, farmers and ranchers with an extensive line of agricultural supplies (including feed, seed, crop nutrients and crop protection products) and services.

Revenue Recognition

Sales are recognized upon shipment of product to the customer.

Statement Presentation

The consolidated financial statements include the accounts of Land O'Lakes, Inc. and wholly-owned and majority-owned subsidiaries and limited liability companies ("Land O'Lakes" or the "Company"). Intercompany transactions and balances have been eliminated. Certain reclassifications have been made to the 2002 and 2001 consolidated financial statements to conform to the 2003 presentation.

Cash and Short-Term Investments

Cash and short-term investments include short-term, highly liquid investments with original maturities of three months or less.

Inventories

Inventories are valued at the lower of cost or market. Cost is determined on a first-in, first-out or average cost basis.

Derivative Commodity Instruments

The Company uses derivative commodity instruments, primarily futures contracts, to reduce the exposure to changes in commodity prices. These contracts are not designated as hedges under Statement of Financial Accounting Standards ("SFAS") No. 133, "Accounting for Derivative Instruments and Hedging Activities." The futures contracts are marked to market each month and gains and losses are recognized in earnings.

Investments

Investments in other cooperatives are stated at cost plus unredeemed patronage refunds received, or estimated to be received, in the form of capital stock and other equities. Estimated patronage refunds are not recognized for tax purposes until notices of allocation are received. The equity method of accounting is used for investments in other companies in which Land O'Lakes voting interest is 20 to 50 percent. Investments in less than 20 percent-owned companies are stated at cost.

Property, Plant and Equipment

Property, plant and equipment are stated at cost. Depreciation is calculated using the straight-line method over the estimated useful life (10 to 30 years for land improvements and buildings and building equipment, 5 to 10 years for machinery and equipment and 3 to 5 years for software) of the respective assets in accordance with the straight-line method. Accelerated methods of depreciation are used for income tax purposes.

Goodwill and Other Intangible Assets

Goodwill represents the excess of the purchase price of an acquired entity over the amounts assigned to assets acquired and liabilities assumed. Upon adoption of the remaining provisions of SFAS No. 142, "Goodwill and Other Intangible Assets," on January 1, 2002, the Company no longer amortizes goodwill except for goodwill related to the acquisition of cooperatives and the formation of joint ventures.

Other intangible assets consist primarily of trademarks, patents and agreements not to compete. Certain trademarks are not amortized because they have indefinite lives. The remaining other intangible assets are amortized using the straight-line method over the estimated useful lives, ranging from 2 to 15 years.

Recoverability of Long-Lived Assets

The test for goodwill impairment is a two-step process and is performed on at least an annual basis. The first step is a comparison of the fair value of the reporting unit with its carrying amount, including goodwill. If this step reflects impairment, then the loss would be measured as the excess of recorded goodwill over its implied fair value. Implied fair value is the excess of fair value of the reporting unit over the fair value of all identified assets and liabilities. The Company assesses the recoverability of other long-lived assets annually or whenever events or changes in circumstance indicate that expected future undiscounted cash flows might not be sufficient to support the carrying amount of an asset. The Company deems an asset to be impaired if a forecast of undiscounted future operating cash flows is less than its carrying amount. If an asset is determined to be impaired, the loss is measured as the amount by which the carrying value of the asset exceeds its fair value.

Income Taxes

Land O'Lakes is a non-exempt agricultural cooperative and is taxed on all non-member earnings and any member earnings not paid or allocated to members by qualified written notices of allocation as that term is used in section 1388(c) of the Internal Revenue Code. The Company files a consolidated tax return with its fully taxable subsidiaries.

The Company established deferred income tax assets and liabilities based on the difference between the financial and income tax carrying values of assets and liabilities using existing tax rates.

Advertising and Promotion Costs

Advertising and promotion costs are expensed as incurred. Advertising and promotion costs were $52.1 million, $53.9 million and $48.8 million in 2003, 2002 and 2001, respectively.

Research and Development

Expenditures for research and development are charged to administrative expense in the year incurred. Total research and development expenses were $29.0 million, $33.3 million and $23.8 million in 2003, 2002 and 2001, respectively.

Recent Accounting Pronouncements

On January 17, 2003, the Financial Accounting Standards Board ("FASB") issued Interpretation No. 46, "Consolidation of Variable Interest Entities, an Interpretation of ARB 51," ("FIN 46"). The primary objectives of FIN 46 are to provide guidance on the identification and consolidation of variable interest entities, or VIEs, which are entities for which control is achieved through means other than through voting rights. As permitted by the Interpretation, the Company early-adopted FIN 46 as of July 1, 2003 and began consolidating its joint venture interest in MoArk LLC ("MoArk"), an egg production and marketing company. FIN 46 was revised in December 2003 and is effective for the Company on January 1, 2005. The revision is not expected to have a significant impact on the Company.

In May 2003, the FASB issued Statement of Financial Accounting Standards 150, "Accounting for Certain Financial Instruments with Characteristics of Both Liabilities and Equity." The statement establishes standards for how an issuer classifies and measures certain financial instruments with characteristics of both liabilities and equity. It requires that an issuer classify a financial instrument that is within its scope as a liability (or an asset in some circumstances). The statement is effective for the Company as of January 1, 2004. The Company has evaluated the standard and has determined that it will not have an impact on its consolidated financial statements.

In December 2003, the FASB revised Statement of Financial Accounting Standards 132, "Employers' Disclosures about Pensions and Other Postretirement Benefits." The statement revises the disclosures about pension and other postretirement benefit plans. It requires additional disclosure regarding changes in benefit obligations and fair value of plan assets. The statement was effective for the Company as of December 31, 2003.

On January 12, 2004, the FASB issued FASB Staff Position 106-1, "Accounting and Disclosure Requirements Related to the Medicare Prescription Drug, Improvement and Modernization Act of 2003" (the "Act"). The position permits a sponsor of a postretirement health care plan that provides a prescription drug benefit to make a one-time election to defer accounting for the effects of the Act. Regardless of whether a sponsor elects that deferral, the position requires certain disclosures pending further consideration of the underlying accounting issues. The position is effective for the Company as of December 31, 2003.

Accounting Estimates

The preparation of financial statements in conformity with accounting principles generally accepted in the United States of America requires management to make estimates and assumptions that affect the reported amounts of assets and liabilities and disclosure of contingent assets and liabilities at the date of the financial statements and the reported amounts of revenues and expenses during the reporting period. Actual results could differ from those estimates.

ACCOUNTING CHANGES

1.56 APB Opinion No. 20, *Accounting Changes*, "defines various types of accounting changes and establishes guides for determining the manner of reporting each type." Table 1-8 lists the accounting changes disclosed in the annual reports of the survey companies. As shown in Table 1-8, most of the accounting changes disclosed by the survey companies were changes made to conform to requirements stated in authoritative pronouncements.

1.57 Examples of accounting change disclosures follow.

1.58

TABLE 1-8: ACCOUNTING CHANGES

	Number of Companies			
	2003	2002	2001	2000
Consolidation of variable interest entities	200	N/C*	N/C*	N/C*
Financial instruments with liability and equity characteristics	188	N/C*	N/C*	N/C*
Cost of exit or disposal activities	181	18	N/C*	N/C*
Guarantees	172	N/C*	N/C*	N/C*
Derivatives and hedging activities	158	29	342	6
Asset retirement obligation	125	7	N/C*	N/C*
Stock compensation	122	16	5	5
Impairment or disposal of long-lived assets	68	156	N/C*	N/C*
Gains or losses from debt extinguishments	59	54	N/C*	N/C*
Goodwill and other intangibles	57	465	19	N/C*
Accounting for revenue with multiple deliveries	33	N/C*	N/C*	N/C*
Accounting for customer consideration from vendor	30	N/C*	N/C*	N/C*
Revenue recognition	13	6	60	68
Business combinations	8	54	73	N/C*
Inventories	3	5	3	9
Depreciable lives	1	5	3	3
Shipping and handling	1	2	38	20
Other	44	89	41	86

* N/C = Not compiled. Line item was not included in the table for the year shown.

Consolidation of Variable Interest Entities

1.59

CUMMINS INC. (DEC)

NOTES TO CONSOLIDATED FINANCIAL STATEMENTS

Note 1 (In Part): Summary of Significant Accounting Policies

Principles of Consolidation

Our *Consolidated Financial Statements* include the accounts of all majority-owned subsidiaries where our ownership is more than 50 percent of common stock except for majority-owned subsidiaries that are considered Variable Interest Entities (VIEs) where we are not deemed the primary beneficiary. Our *Consolidated Financial Statements* also include the accounts of any VIEs where we are deemed the primary beneficiary, regardless of our ownership percentage. All significant intercompany balances and transactions with consolidated subsidiaries are eliminated in our *Consolidated Financial Statements*. Where our ownership interest is less than 100 percent, the minority ownership interests are reported in our *Consolidated Statements of Financial Position* as a liability. The minority ownership interest of our earnings or loss, net of tax, is classified as "Minority interests in earnings of consolidated subsidiaries" in our *Consolidated Statements of Earnings*.

Recently Adopted Accounting Pronouncements (In Part)

In January 2003, the FASB issued FASB Interpretation No. 46, "Consolidation of Variable Interest Entities", an Interpretation of Accounting Research Bulletin No. 51, "Consolidated Financial Statements." In December 2003, the FASB issued FIN 46R, a revised version of FIN 46 (referred to herein as FIN 46). The Company has adopted the provisions of FIN 46 as it relates to certain entities previously considered to be Special Purpose Entities (SPEs) under generally accepted accounting principles and for new entities created on or after February 1, 2003. The Company has not yet adopted FIN 46 for all other entities. See Note 2 for a full description of the impact of the partial adoption of FIN 46 and a description of the entities for which FIN 46 has not yet been adopted.

Note 2. Variable Interest Entities

FIN 46 provides guidance related to evaluating, identifying and reporting of variable interest entities (VIEs), including entities commonly referred to as SPEs. FIN 46 requires the consolidation of certain VIEs if a company is deemed to be the primary beneficiary, defined in FIN 46 as the entity that holds the majority of variable interests in the VIE. We adopted FIN 46 as of December 31, 2003, for entities previously considered to be SPEs under generally accepted accounting principles and for new entities created on or after February 1, 2003. For all other entities, we are required to adopt FIN 46 as of March 28, 2004 (the end of our first fiscal quarter in 2004). The adoption of FIN 46 required us to consolidate one VIE that was previously not consolidated, and required us to deconsolidate one VIE that was previously consolidated in our *Consolidated Financial Statements*. These VIEs and the impact of the adoption of FIN 46 on our *Consolidated Financial Statements* are discussed in more detail below.

During 2001, we entered into a sale/leaseback transaction with a financial institution with regard to certain heavy-duty engine manufacturing equipment. The accounting for the original sale/leaseback transaction is discussed in Note 18. The financial institution created a grantor trust to act as the lessor in the arrangement. The financial institution owns 100 percent of the equity in the trust. The grantor trust has no assets other than the equipment and its rights to the lease agreement with us. On the initial sale, we received $125 million from the financial institution which was financed with $99 million of non-recourse debt and $26 million of equity. Our obligations to the grantor trust consist of the payments due under the lease and a $9 million guarantee of the residual value of the equipment. In addition, we have a fixed price purchase option that is exercisable on January 14, 2009, for approximately $35 million. We have determined that the grantor trust is a VIE under FIN 46 and due primarily to the existence of the residual value guarantee, we determined that we are the primary beneficiary of the VIE. As a result, we have consolidated the grantor trust as of December 31, 2003, even though we own none of its equity. In accordance with the transition provisions of FIN 46, we have recorded the assets and liabilities of the trust at the amounts for which the assets and liabilities would have been carried in the *Consolidated Financial Statements* had the VIE been consolidated since its inception. The impact of the consolidation of this VIE on our December 31, 2003, balance sheet (without regard to the tax impact) was to:

- Increase "Property, plant and equipment" by $92 million, which represents the value of the equipment at December 31, 2003, had it continued to be depreciated from the date of the original sale to the grantor trust. The property serves as collateral on the non-recourse debt discussed below and is not available to satisfy any of our other obligations.
- Increase Long-term debt" (including the current portion) by $90 million, which represents the balance of the $99 million non-recourse debt as of December 31, 2003. The terms of the non-recourse debt are discussed in Note 8.
- Increase "Minority interests" by $28 million, which represents the current equity interest of the equity holder in the VIE. In addition to our obligations under the non-recourse notes, we also have obligations for fixed payments to the equity holder in the grantor trust totaling approximately $21 million, almost all of which is due in 2009 and beyond.
- Decrease "Current liabilities" by $20 million, which represents the reversal of the deferred gain originally recorded on this transaction and the reversal of the accrued rent expense recorded during the first two years of the lease, offset by the accrual of interest due on the non-recourse debt.

The net effect of the above entries was to record a charge for the "Cumulative effect of change in accounting principle" of $6 million, before the related tax effects of $2 million.

In June 2001, Cummins Capital Trust I (the "Trust"), a Delaware business trust and our wholly-owned subsidiary, issued 6 million shares of 7 percent convertible quarterly income preferred securities ("Preferred Securities"). The total proceeds from the issuance of the Preferred Securities by the Trust were invested in $309 million aggregate principal amount of 7% convertible subordinated debentures (the "Debentures") that we issued. The Debentures are the sole assets of the Trust. This transaction is more fully discussed in Note 9. The Trust qualifies as a VIE under FIN 46. We have determined that we are not the primary beneficiary of the Trust and as a result have deconsolidated the Trust as of December 31, 2003. As a result of the deconsolidation of the Trust, we no longer report the Preferred Securities as an obligation in our *Consolidated Financial Statements*; rather, we now report the Debentures as an obligation, and have included the Debentures in "Long-term debt" in our *Consolidated Statements of Financial Position* as of December 31, 2003. The deconsolidation had no impact in 2003 on our *Consolidated Statements of Earnings* as there was no cumulative effect from this change. In 2004, rather than reporting the preferred dividends on the Preferred Securities, we will report interest expense associated with the Debentures resulting in an increase in interest expense.

In addition to the VIEs discussed above, we have investments in numerous businesses currently accounted for under the equity method that are potential VIEs under FIN 46. These businesses primarily consist of investments in certain of our North American distributors, investments in our numerous engine business joint ventures, and other joint venture investments. In addition, we guarantee the obligations of two U.S. distributors where we do not currently own an interest. We are required to adopt FIN 46 for these entities as of the end of our first fiscal quarter in 2004. We are in the process of performing an analysis to determine the proper reporting treatment under FIN 46 for each of these entities, and it is possible that some of them will meet the scope exception provisions in paragraph 4 of FIN 46. Our joint venture investments are further discussed in Note 5, which also includes summarized financial data related to the investments in total. In almost all cases, our maximum potential loss related to our joint venture investments is limited to the amount of our investment in and advances to these entities ($339 million at December 31, 2003) as we have no contractual requirements to fund losses of these entities. In limited circumstances, we also provide debt guarantees for certain joint ventures which are described in Note 19. We also have an obligation to fund certain working capital requirements of Consolidated Diesel Corporation as more fully discussed in Note 5. Our guarantee arrangements with the two U.S. distributors where we do not own an interest are described in Note 19. Our maximum potential loss related to these distributors is limited to the amount of our debt guarantee. As of December 31, 2003, these distributors have total revenues of $188 million, total assets of $101 million and total debt of $67 million (of which $54 million is under our guarantee and our guarantee is limited to $25 million).

Note 9. Convertible Preferred Securities of Subsidiary Trust and Junior Subordinated Convertible Debentures

In June 2001, Cummins Capital Trust I (the "Trust"), a Delaware business trust and our wholly-owned subsidiary, issued 6 million shares of 7% convertible quarterly income preferred securities ("Preferred Securities"), to qualified institutional buyers for net proceeds of $291 million. The Preferred Securities represent an undivided beneficial ownership interest in the assets of the Trust. The total proceeds from the issuance of the Preferred Securities by the Trust were invested in $309 million aggregate principal amount of 7% convertible subordinated debentures (the "Debentures") that we issued. The Debentures are the sole assets of the Trust. As discussed in Note 2, the Trust is no longer consolidated due to the adoption of FIN 46. The debentures are included in "Long-term debt" in our *Statement of Financial Position*.

Holders of the Preferred Securities are entitled to receive preferential cumulative cash dividends at an annual rate of 7% of the $50 per share liquidation value. In addition, we are accreting the difference between the liquidation amount and the original proceeds received as additional interest expense to the mandatory redemption date. The distribution rate and payment dates for the Preferred Securities correspond to the interest rate and payment dates for the Debentures. We may defer interest payments on the Debentures for a period not to exceed 20 consecutive quarters. If a deferral is made, the Trust will defer distributions on the Preferred Securities for a corresponding period but will continue to accrue for the distribution. We guarantee, on a subordinated basis, distributions and other payments due on the Preferred Securities, to the extent the Trust has available assets and subject to certain other restrictions (the "Guarantee"). The Guarantee, when taken together with our obligations under the Debentures, the indenture pursuant to which the Debentures were issued, and the obligations under the Trust Agreement, provides a full and unconditional guarantee of amounts due on the Preferred Securities.

The Debentures are redeemable for cash, at our option, in whole or in part, on or after June 15, 2006. The debentures are also redeemable under certain circumstances pursuant to a federal tax event, at par, plus accrued and unpaid interest. Upon any redemption of the Debentures, the Trust will redeem a like aggregate liquidation amount of Preferred Securities. The Preferred Securities do not have a stated maturity date, however, they are subject to mandatory redemption upon maturity of the Debentures on June 15, 2031, or upon earlier redemption or upon the occurrence of an event of default.

Each Preferred Security and the related Debenture are convertible at any time prior to the close of business on June 13, 2031, at the option of the holder into shares of our common stock at the rate of 1.0519 shares per Preferred Security (equivalent to a conversion price of $47.53 per share of Cummins Inc. common stock). The Trust will convert Debentures only upon notice of conversion by a holder of Preferred Securities.

1.60

NVR, INC. (DEC)

NOTES TO CONSOLIDATED FINANCIAL STATEMENTS (Dollars in thousands)

1 (In Part): Summary of Significant Accounting Policies

Principles of Consolidation

The accompanying consolidated financial statements include the accounts of NVR, Inc. ("NVR" or the "Company"), its wholly owned subsidiaries, certain partially owned entities, and variable interest entities of which the Company has determined that it is the primary beneficiary. All significant intercompany transactions have been eliminated in consolidation.

Recent Accounting Pronouncements (In Part)

In January 2003, the FASB issued Interpretation No. 46 ("FIN 46"), *Consolidation of Variable Interest Entities*. FIN 46 requires the primary beneficiary of a variable interest entity to consolidate that entity. The primary beneficiary of a variable interest entity is the party that absorbs a majority of the variable interest entity's expected losses, receives a majority of the entity's expected residual returns, or both, as a result of ownership, contractual or other financial interests in the entity. Prior to the issuance of FIN 46, an enterprise generally consolidated an entity when the enterprise had a controlling financial interest in the entity through ownership of a majority voting interest. Upon adoption, FIN 46 applied immediately to variable interest entities created after January 31, 2003. In December 2003, FASB revised FIN 46, deferring the application of the provisions of FIN 46 for an interest held in a variable interest entity or potential variable interest entity until the end of the first interim or annual period ending after March 15, 2004, if the public entity has not issued financial statements reporting that variable interest entity in accordance with FIN 46. See footnote 3 for further discussion of NVR's application of FIN 46.

3. Consolidation of Variable Interest Entities

NVR's Finished Lot Acquisition Strategy

NVR does not engage in the land development business. Instead, the Company acquires finished building lots at market prices from various development entities under fixed price purchase agreements that require deposits that may be forfeited in NVR fails to perform under the agreement. The deposits required under the purchase agreements are in the form of cash or letters of credit in varying amounts and represent a percentage, typically ranging up to 10% of the aggregate purchase price of the finished lots.

This lot acquisition strategy reduces the financial requirements and risks associated with direct land ownership and land development. NVR may, at its option, choose for any reason and at any time not to perform under these purchase agreements by delivering notice of its intent not to acquire the finished lots under contract. NVR's sole legal obligation and economic loss for failure to perform under these purchase agreements is limited to the amount of the deposit pursuant to the liquidating damage provision contained within the purchase agreement. NVR does not have any financial guarantees or completion obligations and does not guarantee specific performance under these purchase agreements.

Adoption of FIN 46

In January 2003, the Financial Accounting Standards Board ("FASB") issued Interpretation No. 46 ("FIN 46"), *Consolidation of Variable Interest Entities*. FIN 46 requires the primary beneficiary of a variable interest entity to consolidate that entity. The primary beneficiary of a variable interest entity is the party that absorbs a majority of the variable interest entity's expected losses, receives a majority of the entity's expected residual returns, or both, as a result of ownership, contractual or other financial interests in the entity. Prior to the issuance of FIN 46, an enterprise generally consolidated an entity when the enterprise had a controlling financial interest in the entity through ownership of a majority voting interest. In December 2003, FASB revised FIN 46, deferring the application of the provisions of FIN 46 for an interest held in a VIE or potential VIE until the end of the first interim or annual period ending after March 15, 2004 if the public entity has not issued financial statements reporting that VIE in accordance with FIN 46.

During the period from February 1, 2003 through September 30, 2003, NVR entered into fixed price purchase agreements with an aggregate purchase price of approximately $900,000, by making or committing to make deposits of approximately $80,000. The Company has evaluated all fixed price purchase agreements entered into during that period and determined that it is the primary beneficiary of certain of the variable interest entities with which it has entered into purchase agreements. NVR estimated the current fair value of the land underlying these purchase agreements and consolidated that amount and a related liability. The liability represents the difference between the estimated current fair value of the land under contact and the Company's related deposits. The effect of the consolidation at December 31, 2003 was the inclusion on the balance sheet of $12,807 to Inventory Not Owned, Consolidated Per FIN 46 with a corresponding inclusion of $12,071 to Liabilities Related To Inventory Not Owned, Consolidated Per FIN 46. NVR does not have access to the financial records of the development entities with which it enters into fixed price purchase agreements, and as

a result was unable to consolidate the variable interest entities' results of operations or cash flows. The Company has deferred implementation of FIN 46 on all other fixed price lot purchase agreements until the first quarter of 2004 as permitted under revised FIN 46.

Financial Instruments With Liability and Equity Characteristics

1.61

BAXTER INTERNATIONAL INC. (DEC)

NOTES TO CONSOLIDATED FINANCIAL STATEMENTS

Note 1 (In Part): Summary of Significant Accounting Policies

Changes in Accounting Principles (In Part)

The company adopted three new accounting standards during the three-year period ended December 31, 2003 which resulted in charges to earnings for the cumulative effect of changes in accounting principles. In 2003, the company adopted Statement of Financial Accounting Standards (SFAS) No. 150, "Accounting for Certain Financial Instruments with Characteristics of both Liabilities and Equity" (SFAS No. 150), and Financial Accounting Standards Board (FASB) Interpretation No. 46, "Consolidation of Variable Interest Entities" (FIN 46), with cumulative effect net-of-tax charges to earnings totaling $17 million. In 2001 the company adopted SFAS No. 133, "Accounting for Derivative Instruments and Hedging Activities" and its amendments (SFAS No. 133), with a cumulative effect net-of-tax charge to earnings of $52 million.

●　　●　　●　　●　　●　　●

SFAS No. 150

SFAS No. 150, which was effective July 1, 2003, requires that certain financial instruments, which previously had been classified as equity, be classified as liabilities. This new standard was applied to the company's equity forward agreements outstanding on that date. As a result, on July 1, 2003, the company recognized a $571 million liability relating to these agreements (representing the net present value of the redemption amounts on that date), reduced stockholders' equity by $561 million (representing the value of the underlying shares at the contract inception dates), and recorded the difference of $10 million as a cumulative effect of a change in accounting principle. Other than for the impact of adoption, SFAS No. 150 did not have a material impact on the company's consolidated financial statements. The company settled these equity forward agreements, which are further discussed in Note 6, during the third quarter of 2003.

Note 6 (In Part): Financial Instruments and Risk Management

Equity Forward Agreements

In order to partially offset the potentially dilutive effect of employee stock options, the company had periodically entered into forward agreements with independent third parties related to the company's common stock. The forward agreements, which had a fair value of zero at inception, required the company to purchase its common stock from the counterparties on specified future dates and at specified prices. At December 31, 2002 the company had outstanding forward agreements related to 15 million shares, which had maturity dates in 2003, and exercise prices ranging from $33 to $52 per share, with a weighted-average exercise price of $49 per share. During 2003, the company did not enter into any additional equity forward agreements, and settled all of its outstanding agreements. The settlement of the equity forward agreements did not have a material impact on the company's diluted EPS. The company physically settled agreements related to 15 million, 22 million and 9 million shares of Baxter common stock in 2003, 2002 and 2001, respectively. Such common stock repurchases totaled $714 million, $1.14 billion and $288 million in 2003, 2002 and 2001, respectively. Management does not intend to enter into equity forward agreements in the future.

Note 8 (In Part): Common and Preferred Stock

Stock Repurchase Programs

As authorized by the board of directors, from time to time the company repurchases its stock on the open market to optimize its capital structure depending upon its cash flows, net debt level and current market conditions. As further discussed in Note 6, the company has also periodically repurchased its stock from counterparty financial institutions in conjunction with the settlement of its equity forward agreements. As of December 31, 2003, $243 million was remaining under the board of directors' October 2002 authorization. No open-market repurchases were made in 2003. Total stock repurchases (including those associated with the settlement of equity forward agreements) were $714 million, $1,169 million, and $288 million in 2003, 2002 and 2001, respectively.

1.62

NEXTEL COMMUNICATIONS, INC. (DEC)

NOTES TO CONSOLIDATED FINANCIAL STATEMENTS

1 (In Part): Summary of Operations and Significant Accounting Policies

New Accounting Pronouncements (In Part)

SFAS No. 150

In May 2003, the FASB issued SFAS No. 150, "Accounting for Certain Financial Instruments with Characteristics of both Liabilities and Equity." This statement establishes standards for how an issuer classifies and measures certain financial instruments with characteristics of both liabilities and equity. It requires the issuer to classify a financial instrument that is within the scope of the standard as a liability if such financial instrument embodies an obligation of the issuer. The adoption of SFAS No. 150 required us to reclassify and account for our series D and series E mandatorily redeemable preferred stock as liabilities effective July 1, 2003 prospectively, as these mandatorily redeemable financial instruments embodied an unconditional obligation that required us to

redeem the instrument at a specified date and/or upon an event certain to occur. As discussed in note 6, we redeemed all outstanding shares of our series D preferred stock in July 2003 and all outstanding shares of our series E preferred stock in August 2003. We have not reclassified the series D and series E preferred stock balances and related amounts for dividends and gains (losses) on retirement for periods prior to July 1, 2003. Accordingly, the implementation of SFAS No. 150 did not have a material impact on our financial position or results of operations. The balance sheet classification of our zero coupon convertible preferred stock does not change under SFAS No. 150 because it is convertible into a fixed number of shares of our class A common stock.

6 (In Part): Long-Term Debt, Capital Lease and Finance Obligations and Mandatorily Redeemable Preferred Stock

Mandatorily Redeemable Preferred Stock

(Dollars in millions)	Balance December 31, 2002	Book and Principal Value of Retirements	Dividends and Accretion	Balance December 31, 2003
Series D exchangeable preferred stock mandatorily redeemable 2009, 13% cumulative annual dividend; 470,753 and 0 shares issued; 470,742 and 0 shares outstanding; stated at liquidation value	$ 471	$ 471	$ —	$ —
Series E exchangeable preferred stock mandatorily redeemable 2010, 11.125% cumulative annual dividend; 447,796 and 0 shares issued; 447,782 and 0 shares outstanding; stated at liquidation value	454	461	7	—
Zero coupon convertible preferred stock mandatorily redeemable 2013, no dividend; convertible into 4,779,386 shares of class A common stock; 245,245 shares issued and outstanding, stated at accreted liquidation preference value at 9.25% compounded quarterly	90	—	9	99
	$1,015	$ 932	$ 16	$ 99

Series D Preferred Stock

Shares of our series D exchangeable preferred stock due 2009 had a liquidation preference of $1,000 per share. Dividends on the series D preferred stock accrued at an annual rate of 13% of the liquidation preference, were cumulative from the date of issuance and were payable quarterly in cash. These shares of preferred stock were retired in 2003.

Series E Preferred Stock

Shares of our series E exchangeable preferred stock due 2010 had a liquidation preference of $1,000 per share. Dividends on the series E preferred stock accrued at an annual rate of 11.125% of the liquidation preference, were cumulative from the date of issuance and were payable quarterly in cash or, on or prior to February 15, 2003 at our option, in additional shares of series E preferred stock. These shares of preferred stock were retired in 2003.

Zero Coupon Preferred Stock

No dividends are payable with respect to the zero coupon convertible preferred stock due 2013; however, the liquidation preference accretes from the initial liquidation preference of $253.675 per share at issuance date at an annual rate of 9.25% compounded quarterly to a liquidation preference of $1,000 per share at maturity in 2013. The zero coupon preferred stock is convertible at the option of the holders prior to redemption or maturity into our class A common stock at a conversion rate of 19.4882 shares of our class A common stock for each share of zero coupon preferred stock, subject to adjustment upon the occurrence of specified events. We may choose to redeem some or all of the preferred stock starting December 23, 2005, and the preferred stock may be tendered by the holders for acquisition by us on December 23, 2005 and 2008. The zero coupon preferred stock is mandatorily redeemable on December 23, 2013 at the fully accreted liquidation preference of $1,000 per share. We may elect, subject to the satisfaction of specified requirements, to pay any redemption or tender price with our class A common stock.

Preferred Stock Retirements

For the year ended December 31, 2003, we purchased and retired a total of $932 million in aggregate face amount of our outstanding mandatorily redeemable preferred stock in exchange for about $972 million in cash. As a result, we recognized a $48 million loss in the statement of operations, representing the excess of the purchase price over the carrying value of the purchased and retired preferred stock and the write-off of unamortized financing costs. Pursuant to SFAS No. 150, the losses associated with our third quarter 2003 series D and series E preferred stock retirements are included in other income (expense) in the statement of operations. Additional information regarding our adoption of SFAS No. 150 can be found in note 1.

For the year ended December 31, 2002, we purchased and retired a total of $1,258 million in aggregate face amount at maturity of our outstanding mandatorily redeemable preferred stock in exchange for 74.8 million shares of class A common stock valued at $601 million and about $177 million in cash. As a result, we recognized a $485 million gain in paid-in capital, representing the excess of the carrying value over the purchase price of the purchased and retired preferred stock and the write-off of unamortized financing costs.

Cost of Exit or Disposal Activities

1.63

ARKANSAS BEST CORPORATION (DEC)

NOTES TO CONSOLIDATED FINANCIAL STATEMENTS

Note B (In Part): Accounting Policies

Exit or Disposal Activities

On January 1, 2003, the Company adopted Statement of Financial Accounting Standards No. 146 ("FAS 146"), *Accounting for Costs Associated with Exit or Disposal Activities.* As prescribed by FAS 146, liabilities for costs associated with the exit or disposal activity are recognized when the liability is incurred. See Note D regarding the sale and exit of Clipper's LTL division in 2003. The adoption of FAS 146 did not have a material impact upon the Company's financial statements or related disclosures.

Note D—Sale and Exit of Clipper's LTL Business

On December 31, 2003, Clipper Express Company closed the sale of all customer and vendor lists related to Clipper's LTL freight business to Hercules Forwarding Inc. of Vernon, California for $2.7 million in cash, resulting in a pre-tax gain of $2.5 million. This gain is reported below the operating income line. Total costs incurred with the exit of this business unit amounted to $1.2 million and include severance pay, software and fixed asset abandonment and certain operating leases. These exit costs are reported above the operating income line. No additional costs relating to the exit of this business are expected to be incurred. The impact of the gain was $1.5 million, net of taxes, or $0.06 per diluted common share and the impact of the exit costs was $0.7 million, net of taxes, or $0.03 per diluted common share.

1.64

ELKCORP (JUN)

NOTES TO CONSOLIDATED FINANCIAL STATEMENTS

Summary of Significant Accounting Policies (In Part)

New Accounting Standards (In Part)

In July 2002, the FASB issued SFAS No. 146, "Accounting for Costs Associated with Exit or Disposal Activities." SFAS No. 146 requires companies to recognize costs associated with exit or disposal activities when they are incurred rather than at a date of a commitment to an exit or disposal plan. SFAS No. 146 is to be applied prospectively to exit or disposal activities after December 31, 2002. In August 2003, the company relocated its corporate office to new leased space. In accordance with SFAS No. 146, total unexpired lease costs of $653,000 on its previous leased space will be recorded to expense through March 2004.

Guarantees

1.65

FIRST DATA CORPORATION (DEC)

NOTES TO CONSOLIDATED FINANCIAL STATEMENTS

Note 1 (In Part): Summary of Significant Accounting Policies

Reserve for Merchant Credit Losses and Check Guarantees
With respect to the merchant acquiring business, the Company's merchant customers (or those of its unconsolidated alliances) have the liability for any charges properly reversed by the cardholder. In the event, however, that the Company is not able to collect such amounts from the merchants, due to merchant fraud, insolvency, bankruptcy or another reason, the Company may be liable for any such reversed charges. The Company's risk in this area primarily relates to situations where the cardholder has purchased goods or services to be delivered in the future such as airline tickets.

During 2003, the Company adopted Financial Accounting Standards Board ("FASB") Interpretation No. 45, "Guarantor's Accounting and Disclosure Requirements for Guarantees, Including Indirect Guarantees of Indebtedness of Others" ("FIN 45"). Under FIN 45, the Company's obligation to stand ready to perform is minimal. The Company requires cash deposits, guarantees, letters of credit or other types of collateral by certain merchants to minimize its obligation. As of December 31, 2003 and December 31, 2002, the Company and its unconsolidated alliances had cash collateral of $503.7 million and $367.3 million, respectively. Collateral in the form of letters of credit amounted to $193.8 million and $73.7 million at December 31, 2003 and December 31, 2002, respectively. Collateral held by the Company is classified within "settlement obligations" on the Company's Consolidated Balance Sheet. The Company also utilizes a number of systems and procedures to manage merchant risk. Despite these efforts, the Company historically has experienced some level of losses due to merchant defaults.

The Company's contingent obligation under FIN 45 relates to imprecision in its estimates of required collateral and a provision for this obligation is recorded based on recent history of credit losses. The provision for this obligation is based primarily on historical experience and other relevant factors such as economic downturns or increases in merchant fraud. For the years ended December 31, 2003, 2002, and 2001 the Company and its unconsolidated alliances incurred aggregate merchant credit losses of $40.7 million, $39.8 million and $67.6 million, respectively, on total dollar volumes processed of $664.7 billion, $547.8 billion and $485.6 billion, respectively. Merchant credit losses attributable to the Company and its consolidated subsidiaries amounted to $32.1 million, $28.1 million and $15.9 million for the years ended December 31, 2003, 2002, and 2001, respectively. Such amounts are included in "cost of services" in the Company's Consolidated Statements of Income.

The reserve recorded on the Company's Consolidated Balance Sheets only relates to the business conducted by its consolidated subsidiaries. The reserve for unconsolidated alliances is recorded only in the alliances' financial statements. The Company has not recorded any reserve for estimated losses in excess of reserves recorded by the unconsolidated alliances nor has the Company identified needs to do so. At December 31, 2003 and 2002, the Company and its consolidated and unconsolidated alliances had aggregate merchant credit loss reserves of $27.3 million and $27.2 million, respectively. The foregoing disclosure presents merchant credit loss reserves in the aggregate without regard to whether the reserves relate to merchant contracts held by entities consolidated by the Company or alliances accounted for under the equity method. The amount of reserves attributable to entities consolidated by the Company were $19.4 million and $17.9 million at December 31, 2003 and 2002, respectively.

The credit loss reserves, both for the unconsolidated alliances and the Company, are comprised of amounts for known losses and a provision for losses incurred but not reported ("IBNR"). These reserves are primarily determined by performing a historical analysis of chargeback loss experience. Other factors are considered that could affect that experience in the future. Such items include the general economy and economic challenges in a specific industry (such as the travel industry after September 11, 2001) or those affecting certain types of clients. Once these factors are considered, the Company or the unconsolidated alliance establishes a rate (percentage) that is calculated by dividing the expected chargeback (credit) losses by dollar volume processed. This rate is then applied against the dollar volume processed each month and charged against earnings. The resulting reserve balance is then compared to requirements for known losses and estimates for IBNR items. Historically, this estimation process has proven to be materially accurate and the Company believes the recorded reserve approximates the fair value of the contingent obligation under FIN 45.

The majority of the TeleCheck Services, Inc. ("TeleCheck") business involves the guarantee of checks received by merchants for a period of 90 days from the check date. If the check is returned, TeleCheck is required to purchase the check from the merchant at its face value and pursue collection from the check writer. A provision for estimated check returns, net of anticipated recoveries, is recorded at the transaction inception based on recent history. At December 31, 2003 and 2002, the Company had accrued warranty and accrued recovery balances of $18.8 million and $59.5 million, and $22.9 million and $56.0 million, respectively. Accrued warranties are included in "accounts payable and other liabilities" and accrued recoveries are included in "accounts receivable" in the Consolidated Balance Sheets.

The adoption of FIN 45 resulted in the Company establishing an incremental liability (and deferring revenue) for the fair value of the check guarantee. The liability is relieved and revenue is recognized when the check clears, is presented to TeleCheck, or the guarantee period expires. The majority of the guarantees are typically settled within 10 days of the transaction and virtually all guarantees are settled within 30 days. An incremental liability of $5.2 million was recorded during the first quarter of 2003 and its balance was approximately $4.2 million at December 31, 2003. The aggregate face value of all checks guaranteed during the years ended December 31, 2003, 2002 and 2001 was $24.5 billion, $23.7 billion and $21.8 billion, of which $297.9 million, $287.7 million and $295.8 million, respectively, were returned to merchants and presented to TeleCheck. The net impact on operating income from warranty losses, net of recoveries from check writers was $64.3 million, $77.5 million and $75.8 million for the years ended December 31, 2003, 2002 and 2001, respectively. The maximum potential future payments under the guarantees was approximately $1.5 billion at December 31, 2003.

Derivatives and Hedging Activities

1.66

KELLOGG COMPANY (DEC)

NOTES TO CONSOLIDATED FINANCIAL STATEMENTS

Note 1 (In Part): Accounting Policies

Derivatives and Hedging Transactions

The Company adopted SFAS No. 133 "Accounting for Derivative Instruments and Hedging Activities" on January 1, 2001. This statement requires all derivative Instruments to be recorded on the balance sheet at fair value and establishes criteria for designation and effectiveness of hedging relationships. Upon adoption, the Company reported a charge to earnings of $1.0 million (net of tax benefit of $.6 million) and a charge to other comprehensive income of $14.9 million (net of tax benefit of $8.6 million) in order to recognize the fair value of derivative instruments as either assets or liabilities on the balance sheet. The charge to earnings relates to the component of the derivative instruments' net loss that has been excluded from the assessment of hedge effectiveness. Refer to Note 12 for further information.

During April 2003, the FASB issued SFAS No. 149 "Amendment of Statement 133 on Derivative Instruments and Hedging Activities." This statement amends and clarifies financial accounting and reporting guidance for derivative instruments and hedging activities, resulting primarily from decisions reached by the FASB Derivatives Implementation Group subsequent to the original issuance of SFAS No. 133. This Statement is generally effective prospectively for contracts and hedging relationships entered into after June 30, 2003. The adoption of SFAS No. 149 has had minimal impact on the Company, except that cash flows associated with certain derivatives are now being classified in the financing rather than the operating section of the cash flow statement. Such derivatives are generally limited to net investment hedges and those used by the Company to reduce volatility in the translation of foreign currency earnings to U.S. Dollars. The impact of this classification change during 2003 was insignificant.

Asset Retirement Obligation

1.67

AIR PRODUCTS AND CHEMICALS, INC. (SEP)

NOTES TO THE FINANCIAL STATEMENTS
(Millions of dollars)

2 (In Part): New Accounting Standards

Standards Adopted 2003 (In Part)

The company adopted SFAS No. 143, "Accounting for Asset Retirement Obligations," on 1 October 2002. The Statement requires that the fair value of a liability for an asset retirement obligation be recognized in the period in which it is incurred. The liability is measured at discounted fair value and is adjusted to its present value in subsequent periods as accretion expense is recorded. The corresponding asset retirement costs are capitalized as part of the carrying amount of the related long-lived asset and depreciated over the asset's useful life. The company's asset retirement obligations are primarily associated with Gases on-site long-term supply contracts under which the company has built a facility on land leased from the customer and is obligated to remove the facility at the end of the contract term. At 1 October 2002, the company recognized transition amounts for existing asset retirement obligation liabilities, associated capitalizable costs and accumulated depreciation. An after-tax transition charge of $2.9 was recorded as the cumulative effect of an accounting change. The ongoing expense on an annual basis resulting from the initial adoption of SFAS No. 143 is approximately $1.

Stock Compensation

1.68

TARGET CORPORATION (JAN)

NOTES TO CONSOLIDATED FINANCIAL STATEMENTS

Summary of Accounting Policies (In Part)

Stock-Based Compensation

In 2003, we adopted Statement of Financial Accounting Standards (SFAS) No. 123, "Accounting for Stock-Based Compensation," in accordance with the prospective transition method prescribed in SFAS No. 148, "Accounting for Stock-Based Compensation—Transition and Disclosure" and began recognizing compensation expense for stock options granted during the year. Compensation expense is reflected in selling, general and administrative expenses. Prior to 2003, we accounted for stock option awards under the intrinsic value method prescribed in Accounting Principles Board (APB) No. 25, "Accounting for Stock Issued to Employees" which resulted in no compensation expense because the exercise price of the stock options was equal to the fair market value of the underlying stock on the grant date. The pro forma impact of accounting for those awards at fair value is disclosed on page 35.

Stock Option Plans (In Part)

In the first quarter of 2003, we adopted SFAS No. 123 in accordance with the prospective transition method prescribed in SFAS No. 148. The adoption of this method increased compensation expense by less than $.01 per share in 2003. The requirements of SFAS No. 123 and SFAS No. 148 are discussed in Management's Discussion and Analysis on page 24.

Awards granted in fiscal year 2002 and earlier will continue to be accounted for under the intrinsic value method prescribed in APB No. 25. No compensation expense related to options was recognized because the exercise price of our employee stock options equaled the market price of the underlying stock on the grant date. The expense related

to the intrinsic value of performance-based and restricted stock awards issued was not significant to 2003 net earnings, cash flows or financial position. The pro forma impact of accounting for those awards at fair value will continue to be disclosed until the last of those awards vest in January of 2007. If we had elected to recognize compensation cost based on the fair value of the awards at the grant date, net earnings would have been the pro forma amounts shown below.

(Millions, except per share data)	Pro Forma Earnings		
	2003	2002	2001
Net earnings—as reported	$1,841	$1,654	$1,368
Stock-based employee compensation expense included in reported net earnings, net of tax	3	—	—
Stock-based employee compensation expense determined under fair value based method, net of tax	(35)	(31)	(28)
Net earnings—pro forma	$1,809	$1,623	$1,340
Earnings per share:			
Basic—as reported	$ 2.02	$ 1.82	$ 1.52
Basic—pro forma	$ 1.99	$ 1.79	$ 1.49
Diluted—as reported	$ 2.01	$ 1.81	$ 1.50
Diluted—pro forma	$ 1.97	$ 1.78	$ 1.47

The Black-Scholes model was used to estimate the fair value of the options at grant date based on the following assumptions:

	2003	2002	2001
Dividend yield	.8%	8%	6%
Volatility	29%	35%	30%
Risk-free interest rate	3.0%	3.0%	4.3%
Expected life in years	5.0	5.0	5.0
Weighted average fair value at grant date	$11.04	$10.07	$13.09

1.69

WAL-MART STORES, INC. (JAN)

NOTES TO CONSOLIDATED FINANCIAL STATEMENTS

1 (In Part): Summary of Significant Accounting Policies

New Accounting Pronouncements (In Part)

The Company has various stock option compensation plans for Associates. Beginning on February 1, 2003, the Company adopted the recognition and measurement provisions of FASB Statement No. 123, "Accounting and Disclosure of Stock-Based Compensation" ("FAS 123"). Under FAS 123, compensation expense is recognized based on the fair value of stock options granted. As a result of the accounting change, all prior periods presented have been restated to reflect the compensation cost that would have been recognized had the recognition provisions of FAS 123 been applied to all awards granted to employees. Prior to the adoption of FAS 123, the Company followed Accounting Principles Board Opinion No. 25, "Accounting for Stock Issued to Employees" ("APB 25"), and related interpretations to account for its employee stock options. Because the exercise price of the Company's employee stock options equals the market price of the underlying stock on the date of the grant in most cases, no significant compensation expense related to options was recognized under APB 25. The adoption of the fair value method in 2003 resulted in a reduction of retained earnings of $348 million, an increase in paid-in capital of $472 million and an increase in deferred tax assets of $124 million. Following the provisions of FAS 123, fiscal 2004, 2003 and 2002 include a reduction of net income of $102 million, $84 million and $79 million, respectively, or $0.02 in each fiscal year.

The fair value of stock options was estimated at the date of grant using the Black-Scholes option valuation model which was developed for use in estimating the fair value of traded options, which have no vesting restrictions and are fully transferable. Option valuation methods require the input of highly subjective assumptions, including the expected stock price volatility. The fair value of these options was estimated at the date of the grant based on the following assumptions:

	2004	2003	2002
Dividend yield	1.0%	0.7%	0.7%
Volatility	32.3%	32.1%	36.5%
Risk-free interest rate	2.8%	3.2%	4.6%
Expected life in years	4.5%	4.6	5.2
Weighted average fair value of options at grant date	$ 15.83	$ 15.67	$ 20.27

7 (In Part): Stock Option Plans

On February 1, 2003, the Company adopted the expense recognition provisions of FASB Statement No. 123. "Accounting and Disclosure of Stock-Based Compensation" ("FAS 123"). Under FAS 123, compensation expense is recognized based on the fair value of stock options granted. As a result, all prior periods presented have been restated to reflect the compensation cost that would have been recognized had the recognition provisions of FAS 123 been applied to all awards granted to employees since February 1, 1995. Following the provisions of FAS 123, the 12 months ended January 31, 2004, 2003 and 2002 include $102 million, $84 million and $79 million, respectively, of after-tax stock option expense, which is approximately $0.02 per share in each fiscal year.

Impairment or Disposal of Long-Lived Assets

1.70

MCKESSON CORPORATION (MAR)

FINANCIAL NOTES

1 (In Part): Significant Accounting Policies

New Accounting Pronouncements (In Part)

In August 2001, the FASB issued SFAS No. 144, "Accounting for the Impairment or Disposal of Long-Lived Assets," that replaces SFAS No. 121, "Accounting for the Impairment of Long-Lived Assets and for Long-Lived Assets to Be Disposed Of." SFAS No. 144 requires that long-lived assets to be disposed of by sale, including those of discontinued operations, be measured at the lower of carrying amount or fair value less cost to sell. Discontinued operations are no longer measured at net realizable value or include amounts for operating losses that have not yet been incurred. SFAS No. 144 also broadens the reporting of discontinued operations to include all components of an entity with operations that can be distinguished from the rest of the entity and that will be eliminated from the ongoing operations in a disposal transaction. We adopted SFAS No. 144 as of April 1, 2002. As a result of this new standard, in 2003, we classified a disposition of a business as a discontinued operation (see Financial Note 3).

3. Discontinued Operations and Other Divestitures

In September 2002, we sold the net assets of a marketing fulfillment business which was previously included in our Pharmaceutical Solutions segment. Net proceeds from the sale of this business were $4.5 million. The disposition resulted in an after-tax loss of $3.7 million or $0.01 per diluted share. The net assets and results of operations of this business have been presented as a discontinued operation and, as a result, prior year amounts have been reclassified.

In 2000, we sold our wholly-owned subsidiary, McKesson Water Products Company (the "Water Products business"). to Group Dan one for approximately $1.1 billion in cash. Fiscal 2003 and 2001 results include adjustments to the gain on discontinued operations for the Water Products business.

Results of discontinued operations were as follows:

(In millions)	2003	2002	2001
Revenues	$ 8.4	$17.9	$19.0
Discontinued operations before income taxes	$(4.5)	$ (4.9)	$ (8.2)
Income taxes	1.5	1.7	3.2
Discontinued operations	(3.0)	(3.2)	(5.0)
Loss on sale of business, net of tax of $2.3	(3.7)	—	—
Loss on discontinued operations	$(6.7)	$ (3.2)	$ (5.0)

Assets and liabilities of our discontinued operations were $7.3 million and $3.6 million at March 31, 2002, and $8.0 million and $3.4 million at March 31, 2001.

In 2002, we sold three businesses, Abaton.com, Inc., Amysis Managed Care Systems, Inc. and ProDental Corporation. Two of these businesses were from our Information Solutions segment and one was from our Pharmaceutical Solutions segment. Net proceeds from the sale of these businesses were $0.2 million, resulting in a pre-tax loss of $22.0 million and an after-tax gain of $22.0 million. For accounting purposes, the net assets of one of these businesses were written down in 2001 in connection with the restructuring of our former iMcKesson segment. The tax benefit could not be recognized until 2002 when the sale of the business was completed. In addition, as SFAS No. 144 was not effective until 2003, the dispositions of these businesses were not treated as discontinued operations.

Gains or Losses From Debt Extinguishment

1.71

GEORGIA GULF CORPORATION (DEC)

Consolidated Statements of Income

(In thousands)	2003	2002	2001
Operating income	$ 69,698	$ 98,320	$ 30,354
Other income (expense):			
Interest expense	(38,195)	(49,739)	(57,500)
Cost related to early retirement of debt	(13,816)	—	—
Interest income	53	160	185
Income (loss) before income taxes	17,740	48,741	(26,961)
Provision (benefit) for income taxes	5,245	17,546	(14,918)
Net income (loss)	$ 12,495	$ 31,195	$(12,043)

NOTES TO CONSOLIDATED FINANCIAL STATEMENTS

2 (In Part): New Accounting Pronouncements

In April 2002, the FASB issued SFAS No. 145, "*Rescission of FASB Statements No. 4, 44 and 64, Amendment of FASB Statement No. 13, and Technical Corrections.*" The Statement rescinds SFAS No. 4, "*Reporting Gains and Losses from Extinguishment of Debt,*" and an amendment of that Statement, SFAS No. 64, "*Extinguishments of Debt Made to Satisfy Sinking-Fund Requirements.*" SFAS No. 145 recognizes that the use of debt extinguishment can be a part of the risk management strategy of a company and hence, the classification of all early extinguishment of debt as an extraordinary item may no longer be appropriate. In addition, the Statement amends SFAS No. 13, "*Accounting for Leases,*" to eliminate an inconsistency between the required accounting for sale-leaseback transactions and the required accounting for certain lease modifications that have economic effects that are similar to sale-leaseback transactions. Provisions of this Statement, as they relate to Statement No. 13, are to be effective for transactions occurring after May 15, 2002. Provisions that relate to Statement No. 4 are effective for fiscal years beginning after May 15, 2002. We adopted SFAS No. 145 on January 1, 2003, and accordingly, have recorded the cost related to early retirement of debt as a component of operating income in our 2003 consolidated statement of income (see note 9).

9 (In Part): Long-Term Debt

In December 2003, we retired $200.0 million of unsecured 10.375 percent notes, which were due November 2007. Interest on the notes was payable on May 1 and November 1 of each year. We financed the retirement of the notes by replacing our senior credit facility $134.3 million tranche C term loan with a $200.0 million tranche D term loan, issuing $100.0 million of senior unsecured 7.125 percent notes and increasing our permitted receivables transaction by $25.0 million. As a result of the note retirement, we incurred a $13.8 million charge to income from operations, which is comprised of a redemption premium and related professional fees of $10.8 million and a write-off of unamortized debt issuance cost of $3.0 million.

Goodwill and Other Intangibles

1.72

FEDDERS CORPORATION (AUG)

NOTES TO CONSOLIDATED FINANCIAL STATEMENTS
(Amounts in thousands, except per share data)

1 (In Part): Description of Business and Summary of Significant Accounting Policies

Goodwill and Other Intangible Assets

The Company records the excess purchase price of net tangible and intangible assets acquired over their estimated fair value as goodwill. The Company adopted the provisions of SFAS 142 as of September 1, 2002. Under SFAS 142, the Company is required to test goodwill for impairment at least annually. The Company has elected to perform its annual test for indications of goodwill impairment as of September 30 of each year. The Company identifies potential goodwill impairment by comparing the fair value of a reporting segment with its carrying amount, including goodwill. The Company determines fair value using a discounted cash flow and market-multiple approach. If the fair value of a reporting segment exceeds its carrying amount, goodwill of the reporting segment is not considered impaired. If the carrying amount of a segment exceeds its fair value, the amount of goodwill impairment loss, if any, must be measured. The Company measures the amount of goodwill impairment loss by comparing the implied fair value of reporting segment goodwill with the carrying amount of that goodwill. If the carrying amount of the segment goodwill exceeds the implied fair value of goodwill, an impairment loss is recognized as an operating expense.

The Company completed the transitional goodwill impairment test during the fourth quarter for fiscal 2003. The Company did not identify any impairment within its HVACR reporting segment but has recognized a non-cash goodwill impairment charge of $11.9 million within its Engineered Products reporting segment. The projected financial performance of the Engineered Products reporting segment was insufficient to support the related goodwill. As required, the transitional goodwill impairment charge was recorded as a cumulative effect of a change in accounting principle as of September 1, 2002. In accordance with SFAS No. 142, "Goodwill and Other Intangible Assets," the

Company ceased amortization of goodwill as of September 1, 2002. The following table presents the annual results of the Company on a comparable basis at August 31:

	2003	2002	2001
Net (loss) income:			
Reported net (loss) income applicable to common stockholders	$(3,728)	$ 8,009	$(22,453)
Goodwill amortization, net of tax	—	2,000	1,827
Adjusted net (loss) income applicable to common stockholders	$(3,728)	$10,009	$(20,626)
Basic net (loss) earnings per common share:			
Reported basic net (loss) earnings per common share	$ (0.12)	$ 0.25	$ (0.71)
Goodwill amortization	—	0.06	0.06
Adjusted basic net (loss) earnings per common share	$ (0.12)	$ 0.31	$ (0.65)
Diluted net (loss) earnings per common share:			
Reported diluted net (loss) earnings per common share	$ (0.12)	$ 0.25	$ (0.71)
Goodwill amortization	—	0.06	0.06
Adjusted diluted net (loss) earnings per common share	$ (0.12)	$ 0.31	$ (0.65)

Goodwill and Other Intangible Assets consist of the following at August 31:

	2003	2002
Goodwill	$78,630	$90,536
Gross other amortizable intangibles	$ 3,189	$ 2,787
Accumulated amortization	(1,401)	(1,231)
Other intangible assets	$ 1,788	$ 1,556

As of August 31, 2003 and 2002, the Company had goodwill of $70,133 reflected in its HVACR reportable segment. As of August 31, 2003 and 2002, the Company had goodwill of $8,497 and $20,403 in its Engineered Products reportable segment, respectively. Other intangible assets primarily include a right associated with a joint venture that is being amortized over 20 years. Amortization expense for the fiscal years ended August 31, 2003, 2002, and 2001 is $181, $215 and $187, respectively. Estimated amortization expense for other intangibles will be approximately $120 for each of the next five years and $1,188 thereafter.

CONSOLIDATION POLICIES

1.73   Accounting Research Bulletin (ARB) No. 51, *Consolidated Financial Statements*, states in part:

1. The purpose of consolidated statements is to present, primarily for the benefit of the shareholders and creditors of the parent company, the results of op-

erations and the financial position of a parent company and its subsidiaries essentially as if the group were a single company with one or more branches or divisions. There is a presumption that consolidated statements are more meaningful than separate statements and that they are usually necessary for a fair presentation when one of the companies in the group directly or indirectly has a controlling financial interest in the other companies.

5. Consolidated statements should disclose the consolidation policy which is being followed. In most cases, this can be made apparent by the headings or other information in the statements, but in other cases a footnote is required.

1.74   SFAS No. 94, *Consolidation of All Majority-Owned Subsidiaries*, amends *ARB No. 51* by requiring the consolidation of subsidiaries having nonhomogenous operations. Consequently, with rare exception, the survey companies consolidate nonhomogenous operations. Table 1-9 shows the nature of nonhomogenous operations consolidated by the survey companies.

1.75   *SFAS No. 131*, amends *SFAS No. 94* to eliminate the requirement to disclose additional information about subsidiaries that were not consolidated prior to the effective date of *SFAS No. 94*.

1.76   Financial Accounting Standards Board Interpretation (FIN) No. 46, *Consolidation of Variable Interest Entities*, clarifies the application of *ARB No. 51* to certain entities in which equity investors do not have the characteristics of a controlling financial interest or do not have sufficient equity at risk for the entity to finance its activities without additional subordinated financial support. *ARB No. 51* requires that consolidated financial statements include subsidiaries in which the company has a controlling financial interest, i.e., a majority voting interest. Application of the majority voting interest requirement to certain types of entities may not identify the party with a controlling financial interest because that interest may be achieved through other arrangements. Under *FIN No. 46*, a company shall consolidate a variable interest entity if that company has a variable interest that will absorb a majority of the entity's expected losses, receive a majority of the entity's expected residual returns, or both. In determining whether it is a primary beneficiary of a variable interest entity, a company shall treat variable interests in that same entity held by the company's related parties as its own interest.

1.77   Examples of consolidation practice disclosures follow.

1.78

TABLE 1-9: NONHOMOGENEOUS OPERATIONS— CONSOLIDATED

	Number of Companies			
	2003	2002	2001	2000
Credit	56	54	47	34
Leasing	14	9	8	5
Insurance	12	12	20	18
Real estate	7	3	5	4
Banks	1	2	5	5

1.79

AGCO CORPORATION (DEC)

NOTES TO CONSOLIDATED FINANCIAL STATEMENTS

1 (In Part): Operations and Summary of Significant Accounting Policies

Basis of Presentation (In Part)

The Consolidated Financial Statements represent the consolidation of all wholly-owned companies, majority-owned companies and joint ventures where the Company has been determined as the primary beneficiary under FASB Interpretation No. 46, "Consolidation of Variable Interest Entities," ("FIN 46"). The Company records investments in all other affiliate companies using the equity method of accounting. Other investments representing an ownership of less than 20% are recorded at cost. All significant intercompany balances and transactions have been eliminated in the consolidated financial statements.

Accounting Changes (In Part)

In January 2003, the FASB issued FIN 46, as revised in December 2003, which addresses the consolidation by business enterprises of variable interest entities, to which the usual condition of consolidating a controlling financial interest does not apply. FIN 46 requires an entity to assess its equity investments to determine if they are variable interest entities. As defined in FIN 46, variable interests are contractual, ownership or other interests in an entity that change with changes in the entity's net asset value. Variable interests in an entity may arise from financial instruments, service contracts, guarantees, leases or other arrangements with the variable interest entity. An entity that will absorb a majority of the variable interest entity's expected losses or expected residual returns, as defined in FIN 46, is considered the primary beneficiary of the variable interest entity. The primary beneficiary must include the variable interest entity's assets, liabilities and results of operations in its consolidated financial statements. FIN 46 is immediately effective for all variable interest entities created after January 31, 2003. For variable interest entities created prior to this date, the provisions of FIN 46 must be applied no later than the first interim period ending after March 15, 2004; however, all public companies must apply the unmodified provisions of FIN 46 to entities considered "special purpose entities" by the end of the first reporting period ending after December 15, 2003. The Company analyzed the provisions of FIN 46 as they relate to its current securitization facilities and special purpose entity related to these facilities, and concluded that that it did not believe the special purpose entity or its securitization facilities are impacted by this interpretation. In addition, the Company analyzed the provisions of FIN 46 as they relate to the accounting for its investments in joint ventures and determined that it is the primary beneficiary of one of its joint ventures, GIMA. GIMA was established in 1994 between the Company and Renault Agriculture S.A. ("Renault") to cooperate in the field of purchasing, design and manufacturing of components for agricultural tractors. Each party has a 50% ownership in the joint venture.

On July 1, 2003, the Company began consolidating the accounts of GIMA. Historically, the Company accounted for its investment in GIMA under the equity method. The consolidation of GIMA did not have a material impact on the results of operations or financial position of the Company.

1.80

ANHEUSER-BUSCH COMPANIES, INC. (DEC)

NOTES TO CONSOLIDATED FINANCIAL STATEMENTS

1 (In Part): Summary of Significant Accounting Principles and Policies

Principles of Consolidation

The consolidated financial statements include the company and all its subsidiaries. The company consolidates all majority-owned and controlled subsidiaries, uses the equity method of accounting for investments in which the company is able to exercise significant influence, and uses the cost method for all other investments. All significant intercompany transactions have been eliminated. Minority interests in the company's China subsidiary are not material.

1.81

COOPER TIRE & RUBBER COMPANY (DEC)

NOTES TO CONSOLIDATED FINANCIAL STATEMENTS (Dollar amounts in thousands)

Significant Accounting Policies (In Part)

Principles of Consolidation

The consolidated financial statements include the accounts of the Company and its subsidiaries. Acquired businesses are included in the consolidated financial statements from the dates of acquisition. All material intercompany accounts and transactions have been eliminated.

The equity method of accounting is followed for investments in 20 percent to 50 percent owned companies. The cost method is followed in those situations where the Company's ownership is less than 20 percent and the Company does not have the ability to exercise significant influence over the affiliate.

The Company's investment in Nishikawa Standard Company ("NISCO"), a 50 percent owned joint venture in the United States, is accounted for under the equity method. The Company's investment in NISCO at December 31, 2002 and 2003 was $29,086 and $22,603, respectively, and is included in Other assets in the accompanying consolidated balance sheets.

1.82

LENNAR CORPORATION (NOV)

NOTES TO CONSOLIDATED FINANCIAL STATEMENTS

1 (In Part): Summary of Significant Accounting Policies

Basis of Consolidation

The accompanying consolidated financial statements include the accounts of Lennar Corporation and all subsidiaries, partnerships and other entities (the "Company") in which the Company has a controlling interest and variable interest entities ("VIEs") created after January 31, 2003 in which the Company is deemed the primary beneficiary (see Note 15). The Company's investments in unconsolidated partnerships in which a significant, but less than controlling, interest is held and VIEs created after January 31, 2003 in which the Company is not deemed to be the primary beneficiary, are accounted for by the equity method. All significant intercompany transactions and balances have been eliminated in consolidation.

15. Consolidation of Variable Interest Entities

In January 2003, the FASB issued FIN 46, as further clarified and amended by the FASB's issuance of a revision to FIN 46 in December 2003, which requires the consolidation of entities in which an enterprise absorbs a majority of the entity's expected losses, receives a majority of the entity's expected residual returns, or both, as a result of ownership, contractual or other financial interests in the entity. Prior to the issuance of FIN 46, entities were generally consolidated by an enterprise when it had a controlling financial interest through ownership of a majority voting interest in the entity. FIN 46 applied immediately to variable interests created after January 31, 2003, and with respect to variable interests created before February 1, 2003, FIN 46 will apply in the Company's second quarter ending May 31, 2004, as deferred by the FASB in December 2003. Although the Company does not believe the full adoption of FIN 46 will have a material impact on net earnings, the Company cannot make any definitive determination until it completes its evaluation.

Partnerships

At November 30, 2003, the Company had investments in and advances to partnerships established to acquire and develop land for sale to the Company in connection with its homebuilding operations or for sale to third parties. The Company evaluated its partnership agreements entered into subsequent to January 31, 2003 under FIN 46. The Company determined that it is the primary beneficiary of one partnership that was created after January 31, 2003, and, accordingly, included the accounts of that partnership in the accompanying consolidated financial statements. No other partnerships created after January 31, 2003 were consolidated as the Company determined it was not the primary beneficiary, as defined under FIN 46. The Company is in the process of evaluating the remainder of its unconsolidated partnerships that may be deemed variable interest entities under the provisions of FIN 46. At November 30, 2003, the Company's estimated maximum exposure to loss with regard to unconsolidated partnerships was its recorded investment in these partnerships totaling $390.3 million in addition to the exposure under the guarantees discussed in Note 5.

Option Contracts

The Company evaluated its option contracts for land entered into subsequent to January 31, 2003 and determined it is the primary beneficiary of certain of these option contracts. Although the Company does not have legal title to the optioned land, under FIN 46, the Company, as the primary beneficiary, is required to consolidate the land under option at fair value (the exercise price). The effect of the consolidation was an increase of $45.2 million to consolidated inventory not owned with a corresponding increase to liabilities related to consolidated inventory not owned in the accompanying consolidated balance sheet as of November 30, 2003. To reflect the fair value of the inventory consolidated under FIN 46, the Company reclassified $4.1 million of related option deposits from land under development to consolidated inventory not owned. The liabilities related to consolidated inventory not owned represent the difference between the exercise price of the optioned land and the Company's deposits. The Company is in the process of evaluating the remainder of its option contracts that may be deemed issued by variable interest entities under the provisions of FIN 46. At November 30, 2003, the Company's exposure to loss represents its nonrefundable option deposits and/or letters of credit related to options with estimated aggregate exercise prices totaling approximately $3 billion.

1.83

MOTOROLA, INC. (DEC)

NOTES TO CONSOLIDATED FINANCIAL STATEMENTS

1 (In Part): Summary of Significant Accounting Policies

Principles of Consolidation

The consolidated financial statements include the accounts of the Company and all majority-owned subsidiaries. The Company's investments in non-controlled entities in which it has the ability to exercise significant influence over operating and financial policies are accounted for by the equity method. The Company's investments in other entities are accounted for using the cost method.

1.84

PEROT SYSTEMS CORPORATION (DEC)

NOTES TO CONSOLIDATED FINANCIAL STATEMENTS
(Dollars and shares in thousands)

1 (In Part): Summary of Significant Accounting Policies

Principles of Consolidation

Our consolidated financial statements include the accounts of Perot Systems Corporation and all domestic and foreign subsidiaries. All significant intercompany balances and transactions have been eliminated.

Effective December 31, 2003, we adopted the consolidation requirements of Financial Accounting Standards Board Interpretation No. 46, "Consolidation of Variable Interest Entities," an interpretation of Accounting Research Bulletin No. 51, "Consolidated Financial Statements," which requires consolidation of variable interest entities if we are subject to a majority of the risk of loss from the variable interest entity's activities or entitled to receive a majority of the entity's residual returns or both.

Our investments in companies in which we have the ability to exercise significant influence over operating and financial policies are accounted for by the equity method. Accordingly, our share of the earnings (losses) of these companies is included in consolidated net income. Investments in unconsolidated companies that are less than 20% owned, where we have no significant influence over operating and financial policies, are carried at cost. We periodically evaluate whether impairment losses must be recorded on each investment by comparing the projection of the undiscounted future operating cash flows to the carrying amount of the investment. If this evaluation indicates that future undiscounted operating cash flows are less than the carrying amount of the investments, the underlying assets are written down by charges to expense so that the carrying amount equals the future discounted cash flows.

As discussed in Note 4, "Acquisitions," prior to December 31, 2003, we accounted for our investment in HCL Perot Systems (HPS) using the equity method. In connection with our acquisition of HCL Technologies' shares in HPS, we consolidated all assets and liabilities of HPS on December 31, 2003, which we renamed Perot Systems TSI B.V. (TSI). As of December 31, 2003, we have no investments in unconsolidated companies.

4 (In Part): Acquisitions

Perot Systems TSI B.V.

In 1996, we entered into a joint venture with HCL. Technologies whereby we each owned 50% of HCL. Perot Systems B.V. (HPS), an information technology services company based in India. On December 19, 2003, we acquired HCL Technologies' shares in HPS, and changed the name of HPS to Perot Systems TSI B.V. (TSI). This transaction was accounted for as a step acquisition under the purchase method of accounting. TSI is an IT services firm specializing in business transformation and application outsourcing. TSI currently serves customers in the United Kingdom, Singapore, Switzerland, Luxembourg, Germany, India, Thailand, Malaysia, Japan, Australia and the United States. As a result of the acquisition, we expanded the geographical areas in which we provide services and broadened our customer base in our application development service offering.

Because of the late December 2003 closing of this acquisition, the post-acquisition results of operations of TSI were not material to our consolidated results of operations for 2003. Therefore, to simplify the process of consolidating TSI, we continued to account for TSI's results of operations using the equity method of accounting through December 31, 2003. The balance of our investment in TSI immediately prior to their consolidation was $29,495.

The additional cash consideration paid for HCL Technologies' interest in TSI was $99,372 (including acquisition costs and net of $12,143 of cash acquired). As of December 31, 2003, we consolidated the assets and liabilities of TSI. Accordingly, the TSI assets acquired and liabilities assumed are included in our consolidated balance sheets at December 31, 2003, and our equity interest in their operating results for 2003 is included in equity in earnings (loss) of unconsolidated affiliates in our consolidated statements of operations.

1.85

XEROX CORPORATION (DEC)

NOTES TO CONSOLIDATED FINANCIAL STATEMENTS
(Dollars in millions)

Note 1 (In Part): Summary of Significant Accounting Policies

Basis of Consolidation

The Consolidated Financial Statements include the accounts of Xerox Corporation and all of our controlled subsidiary companies. All significant intercompany accounts and transactions have been eliminated. Investments in business entities in which we do not have control, but we have the ability to exercise significant influence over operating and financial policies (generally 20 to 50 percent ownership), are accounted for using the equity method of accounting. Upon the sale of stock of a subsidiary, we recognize a gain or loss in our Consolidated Statements of Income equal to our proportionate share of the corresponding increase or decrease in that subsidiary's equity. Operating results of acquired businesses are included in the Consolidated Statements of Income from the date of acquisition and, for variable interest entities in which we are determined to be the primary beneficiary, from the date such determination is made.

Certain reclassifications of prior year amounts have been made to conform to the current year presentation.

New Accounting Standards and Accounting Changes (In Part)

Variable Interest Entities

In January 2003, the FASB issued Interpretation No. 46, "Consolidation of Variable Interest Entities, an interpretation of ARB 51" ("FIN 46"). The primary objectives of FIN 46 were to provide guidance on the identification of entities for which control is achieved through means other than through voting rights and how to determine when and which business enterprise should consolidate the variable interest entity ("VIE").

We adopted FIN 46 on July 1, 2003 and, as a result, we began consolidating our joint venture with De Lage Landen International BV ("DLL"), our vendor financing partnership in the Netherlands, effective July 1, 2003 as we were deemed to be the primary beneficiary of the joint venture's financial results. Prior to the adoption of FIN 46, we accounted for our investment with DLL under the equity method of accounting.

In December 2003, the FASB published a revision to FIN 46 ("FIN 46R"), in part, to clarify certain of its provisions. FIN 46R addressed substantive ownership provisions related to consolidation. As a result of FIN 46R, we were required to deconsolidate three of our subsidiary trusts—Capital Trust I, Capital Trust II and Capital LLC. These trusts had previously issued mandatorily redeemable preferred securities and entered into loan agreements with the Company having similar terms as the preferred securities. Specifically, FIN 46R resulted in the holders of the preferred securities being considered the primary beneficiaries of the trusts. As such, we were no longer permitted to consolidate these entities. We have therefore deconsolidated the three trusts and reflected our obligations to them within the balance sheet liability caption "Liability to subsidiary trusts issuing preferred securities." In addition to deconsolidating these subsidiary trusts, the interest on the loans, which was previously reported net of tax as a component of "Minorities' interests in earnings of subsidiaries" in our Consolidated Statements of Income, are now accounted for as interest expense within "Other expenses, net", with the tax effects presented within "Income taxes (benefits)." Accordingly, $145, $145 and $64 in interest expense on loans payable to the subsidiary trusts for the years ended December 31, 2003, 2002, and 2001, respectively, was reflected as non-financing interest expense. The related income tax effects were $56, $56 and $24, for the years ended December 31, 2003, 2002, and 2001, respectively. Financial statements for all periods presented have been revised to reflect this change. The adoption of this interpretation had no impact on the net income or earnings per share. In connection with the adoption of FIN 46R, we also reclassified prior periods for the effects of the consolidation of DLL. The impact of consolidating DLL was immaterial for all periods presented.

BUSINESS COMBINATIONS

1.86   SFAS No. 141, *Business Combinations*, issued in June 2001, supersedes APB Opinion No. 16, *Business Combinations*, as the authoritative pronouncement on business combinations. *SFAS No. 141* requires that the purchase method be used for all business combinations initiated after June 30, 2001. The provisions of *SFAS No. 141* apply to all business combinations accounted for using the purchase method for which the date of acquisition is July 1, 2001 or later. Paragraphs 51–58 set forth required disclosures for business combinations.

1.87   During 2003, 265 survey companies used the purchase method to account for a business combination.

1.88   The nature of information commonly disclosed for business combinations is listed in Table 1-10. Examples of disclosures made by survey companies for business

combinations accounted for by the purchase method and for the formation of jointly owned entities follow.

1.89

TABLE 1-10: BUSINESS COMBINATION DISCLOSURES

	2003	2002	2001
Method of payment:			
Cash only	164	196	N/C*
Cash and stock	31	44	N/C*
Stock only	13	22	N/C*
Other—described	21	13	N/C*
Intangible assets not subject to amortization	156	167	61
Intangible assets subject to amortization	105	124	131
Preliminary allocation of acquisition cost	63	80	N/C*
Supplemental pro forma information	43	85	76
Contingent payments	31	29	16
Purchased research and development costs	25	25	21

* N/C = Not compiled. Line item was not included in the table for the year shown.

Purchase Method

1.90

AUTOMATIC DATA PROCESSING, INC. (JUN)

NOTES TO CONSOLIDATED FINANCIAL STATEMENTS

Note 3. Acquisitions

Assets acquired and liabilities assumed in business combinations were recorded on the Company's Consolidated Balance Sheets as of the respective acquisition dates based upon their estimated fair values at such dates. The results of operations of businesses acquired by the Company have been included in the Company's Statements of Consolidated Earnings since their respective dates of acquisition. The excess of the purchase price over the estimated fair values of the underlying assets acquired and liabilities assumed was allocated to goodwill. In certain circumstances, the allocations of the excess purchase price are based upon preliminary estimates and assumptions. Accordingly, the allocations are subject to revision when the Company receives final information, including appraisals and other analyses. Revisions to the fair values, which may be significant, will be recorded by the Company as further adjustments to the purchase price allocations.

On June 20, 2003, the Company acquired all of the outstanding common and preferred stock of ProBusiness Services, Inc. (ProBusiness) for $17 per common share and $26 per preferred share. The transaction was consummated in cash of approximately $517 million, net of cash acquired, of which $351 million was paid as of June 30, 2003. The remaining $166 million will be paid to former ProBusiness shareholders as they tender their shares. ProBusiness Services, Inc. is a leading provider of comprehensive payroll and human resource processing solutions to larger employers within the United States. The acquisition resulted in approximately $417 million of goodwill. Intangible assets acquired of approximately $79.8 million consist of software, customer contracts and lists and other intangible assets which are being amortized over an average life of 8 years.

The Company also acquired ten additional businesses in fiscal 2003 for approximately $118 million, net of cash acquired. These acquisitions resulted in approximately $90 million of goodwill. Intangible assets acquired of approximately $27.9 million consist of software, customer contracts and lists and other intangible assets which are being amortized over an average life of 5 years.

In addition to goodwill recognized in these transactions noted above, ADP made contingent payments totaling $28 million (including $12 million in common stock), relating to previously consummated acquisitions. As of June 30, 2003, the Company has contingent consideration remaining for all transactions of approximately $138 million, which is payable over the next three years, subject to the acquired entity's achievement of specified revenue, earnings and/or development targets.

The Company purchased several businesses in fiscal 2002 and 2001 in the amount of $232 million (including $12 million in common stock) and $75 million, respectively, net of cash acquired.

The acquisitions discussed above for fiscal 2003, 2002 and 2001 were not material to the Company's operations, financial position or cash flows.

1.91

BOISE CASCADE CORPORATION (DEC)

NOTES TO CONSOLIDATED FINANCIAL STATEMENTS

2 OfficeMax Acquisition

On December 9, 2003, we completed our acquisition of OfficeMax, Inc. We acquired 100% of the voting equity interest. OfficeMax is now a subsidiary of Boise Cascade Corporation, and the results of OfficeMax operations after December 9, 2003, are included in our consolidated financial statements. OfficeMax is a retail distributor of office supplies and paper, technology products, and office furniture. Our OfficeMax superstores feature CopyMax® and FurnitureMax® in-store modules devoted to print-for-pay services and office furniture. OfficeMax has operations in the United States, Puerto Rico, the U.S. Virgin Islands, and a 51%-owned joint venture in Mexico.

Growing our distribution businesses has been a part of our long-term strategy for many years. The acquisition of OfficeMax is a major step in advancing that strategy. The acquisition more than doubles the size of our office products business. Combining OfficeMax's retail expertise and strong brand with our contract office product segment's strength in serving contract customers will allow the combined office products business to better serve our customers across all distribution channels, meeting the needs of every market segment. The acquisition creates opportunities for synergies that will come from offering more products and services across more customer segments, purchasing leverage from

increased scale, and reduced costs in logistics, marketing, and administration.

The aggregate consideration paid for the acquisition was as follows:

(Thousands)	
Fair value of Boise common stock issued	$ 808,172
Cash consideration for OfficeMax common shares exchanged	486,738
Transaction costs	20,000
	1,314,910
Debt assumed by Boise	81,627
	$1,396,537

We paid OfficeMax shareholders $1.3 billion for the acquisition, paying 60% of the purchase price in Boise common stock and 40% in cash. OfficeMax shareholders had the opportunity to elect to receive cash or stock for their OfficeMax shares. Each shareholder's election was subject to proration, depending on the elections of all OfficeMax shareholders. As a result of this proration, OfficeMax shareholders electing Boise stock received approximately .230419 share of Boise stock and $3.1746 in cash for each of their OfficeMax shares. Fractional shares were paid in cash. OfficeMax shareholders electing cash or who had no consideration preference, as well as those shareholders who made no effective election, received $9.333 in cash for each of their OfficeMax shares. After the proration, the $1.3 billion paid to OfficeMax shareholders consisted of $486.7 million in cash and the issuance of 27.3 million of Boise common shares valued at $808.2 million. The value of the common shares issued was determined based on the average market price of our common shares over a ten-day trading period before the acquisition closed on December 9, 2003.

The following table summarizes the estimated fair values of the assets acquired and liabilities assumed on December 9, 2003. The initial purchase price allocations may be adjusted within one year of the purchase date for changes in estimates of the fair value of assets acquired and liabilities assumed.

(Thousands)	December 9, 2003
Current assets	$1,288,346
Property and equipment	324,760
Goodwill	675,173
Intangible assets	191,800
Other assets	142,344
Assets acquired	2,622,423
Current liabilities	1,032,376
Long-term debt	81,627
Other liabilities	193,510
Liabilities assumed	1,307,513
Net assets acquired	$1,314,910

The excess of the purchase price over the fair values of assets acquired and liabilities assumed was allocated to goodwill. Goodwill of $607.7 million was recorded in our Boise Office Solutions, Retail, segment, and $67.5 million was recorded in our Boise Office Solutions, Contract, segment. Of the $675.2 million recorded in goodwill, $132.0 million is expected to be deductible as operating expenses for tax purposes.

The amount allocated to intangible assets was attributed to the following categories:

(Thousands)	
Trade names	$177,000
Noncompete agreements	12,600
Customer lists and relationships	2,200
	$191,800

The trade name assets represent the fair value of the OfficeMax name and other trade names. This asset has an indefinite life and is not amortized. All other intangible assets are amortized on a straight-line basis over their expected useful lives. Noncompete agreements are amortized over four to five years, and customer lists and relationships are amortized over three to five years. In addition to the above intangible assets, we also calculated the fair value of operating leases. A portion of the acquired lease portfolio represented favorable operating leases, compared with current market conditions, and a portion represented unfavorable operating leases, compared with current market conditions. The favorable leases totaled $98.6 million and, after considering renewal periods, have an estimated weighted average life of 23 years. The unfavorable leases totaled $113.1 million and have an estimated weighted average life of nine years. The net favorable and unfavorable leases are recorded in "Other long-term liabilities." Both the favorable and unfavorable leases are amortized on the straight-line basis over their respective weighted average lives.

The following table summarizes unaudited pro forma financial information assuming the OfficeMax acquisition had occurred on January 1, 2003 and 2002. OfficeMax's fiscal year ended on the Saturday prior to the last Wednesday in January. The unaudited pro forma financial information uses OfficeMax data for the months corresponding to Boise's December 31 year-end. This unaudited pro forma financial information does not necessarily represent what would have occurred if the transaction had taken place on the dates presented and should not be taken as representative of our future consolidated results of operations or financial position. We have not finalized our integration plans. Accordingly, this pro forma information does not include all costs related to the integration. When the costs are determined, they will either increase the amount of goodwill recorded or decrease net income, depending on the nature of the costs. We also expect to realize operating synergies. Synergies will come from offering more products and services across more customer segments, purchasing leverage from increased scale, and reduced costs in logistics, marketing, and administration. The pro forma information does not reflect these potential expenses and synergies.

(Thousands except per-share amounts)	2003	2002
Sales	$12,864,790	$12,185,675
Net income (loss) before cumulative effect of accounting changes	$ 2,327	$ (53,190)
Cumulative effect of accounting changes, net of income tax	(8,803)	—
Net loss	$ (6,476)	$ (53,190)
Net loss per common share		
Basic and diluted before cumulative effect of accounting changes	$ (.13)	$ (.78)
Cumulative effect of accounting changes, net of income tax	(.10)	—
Basic and diluted	$ (.23)	$ (.78)

1.92

EMC CORPORATION (DEC)

NOTES TO CONSOLIDATED FINANCIAL STATEMENTS

B (In Part): Business Acquisitions, Goodwill and Intangible Assets

Acquisition of LEGATO Systems, Inc.

In October 2003, we acquired all of the shares of outstanding common stock of LEGATO Systems, Inc. ("LEGATO"). LEGATO develops, markets and supports software products and services for information protection and recovery, hierarchal storage management, automated availability, e-mail and content management. We determined that the acquisition would expand our portfolio of open storage software, provide software-focused sales expertise, extensive channel partner relationships and strong service capabilities. The aggregate purchase price was approximately $1.4 billion, which consisted of $1.2 billion of our Common Stock, $141.5 million in fair value of our stock options and $15.2 million of transaction costs, which primarily consisted of fees paid for financial advisory, legal and accounting services. We issued approximately 106 million shares of our Common Stock, the fair value of which was based upon a five-day average of the closing price two days before and two days after the terms of the acquisition were agreed to and publicly announced. The fair value of our stock options issued to employees was estimated using a Black-Scholes option pricing model. The fair value of the stock options was estimated assuming no expected dividends and the following weighted-average assumptions:

Expected life (in years)	4.0
Expected volatility	60.0%
Risk free interest rate	2.0%

The intrinsic value allocated to the unvested options issued in the transaction that had yet to be earned as of the transaction date was approximately $40.8 million and has been recorded as deferred compensation in the purchase price allocation.

The consolidated financial statements include the results of LEGATO from the date of acquisition. The purchase price has been allocated based on estimated fair values as of the acquisition date. The purchase price allocation is preliminary and a final determination of required purchase accounting adjustments will be made upon the completion of our integration plans. The following represents the preliminary allocation of the purchase price (table in thousands):

Current assets	$ 81,998
Property, plant & equipment	29,922
Deferred income taxes	85,727
Goodwill	1,068,934
Intangible assets:	
Customer relationships (estimated useful life of 9 years)	110,120
Developed technology (estimated useful life of 5 years)	64,730
Tradenames and trademarks (estimated useful life of 5 years)	3,024
Non-competition agreements (estimated useful life of 2 years)	227
Acquired in-process R&D ("IPR&D")	19,640
Total intangible assets	197,741
Deferred compensation	40,818
Other long-term assets	2,299
Current liabilities	(134,737)
Long-term liabilities	(21,252)
Total purchase price	$1,351,450

In determining the purchase price allocation, we considered, among other factors, our intention to use the acquired assets, historical demand and estimates of future demand of LEGATO's products and services. The fair value of intangible assets was primarily based upon the income approach. The rate used to discount the net cash flows to their present values was based upon a weighted average cost of capital of 16%. The discount rate was determined after consideration of market rates of return on debt and equity capital, the weighted average return on invested capital and the risk associated with achieving forecast sales related to the technology and assets acquired from LEGATO.

The total weighted average amortization period for the intangible assets is 7.5 years. The intangible assets are being amortized based upon the pattern in which the economic benefits of the intangible assets are being utilized. None of the goodwill is deductible for income tax purposes. The $1.1 billion of goodwill is classified within our LEGATO products and services segment and information storage products segment in the amounts of $842.9 million and $226.0 million, respectively.

Of the $197.7 million of acquired intangible assets, $19.6 million was allocated to IPR&D and was written off at the date of acquisition because the IPR&D had no alternative uses and had not reached technological feasibility. The write-off is included in restructuring and other special charges in our statement of operations. Six IPR&D projects were identified relating to information protection software and content and messaging software. The projects relating to information protection software had a value of $16.3 million and the projects relating to content and messaging software had a value of $3.3 million. The value assigned to IPR&D was determined utilizing the income approach by determining cash flow projections relating to the projects. The stage of completion of each in process project was estimated to determine the discount rate to be applied to the valuation of the in process technology. Based upon the level of completion and the risk associated with in process technology, a discount rate of 50% was deemed appropriate for valuing IPR&D.

In connection with the LEGATO acquisition, we commenced integration activities which have resulted in involuntary terminations and lease and contract terminations. The liability for involuntary termination benefits covers approximately 100 employees, primarily in general and administrative and engineering functions. We expect to pay the remaining balance for involuntary termination benefits in 2004. The liability for lease and other contractual termination benefits will be paid over the remaining contract periods through 2011. We are working to finalize our integration plans which may result in additional involuntary terminations, lease and other contractual terminations and employee relocations. We will finalize our integration plans and related liabilities in 2004. Finalization of our plans may result in additional liabilities which will increase goodwill. The following summarizes the obligations recognized in connection with the LEGATO acquisition and activity to date (table in thousands):

Category	Obligation	Current Utilization	Ending Balance
Involuntary termination benefits	$ 2,700	$(1,363)	$ 1,337
Lease and other contractual terminations	29,084	(899)	28,185
Total	$31,784	$(2,262)	$29,522

Acquisition of Documentum, Inc.

In December 2003, we acquired all of the shares of outstanding common stock of Documentum, Inc. ("Documentum"). Documentum provides enterprise content management software, enabling organizations to organize and manage unstructured data. We determined that the acquisition would provide us the opportunity to expand our product offerings, enabling customers to implement a total information storage solution for managing unstructured content. Additionally, the acquisition expanded our software-focused sales expertise and provided strong service capabilities. The aggregate purchase price was approximately $1.8 billion, which consisted of $1.6 billion of Common Stock, $207.6 million in fair value of our stock options and $13.8 million of transaction costs, which primarily consisted of fees paid for financial advisory, legal and accounting services. We issued approximately 115 million shares of our Common Stock, the fair value of which was based upon a five-day average of the closing price two days before and two days after the terms of the acquisition were agreed to and publicly announced. The fair value of our stock options issued to employees was estimated using a Black-Scholes option pricing model. The fair value of the stock-options was estimated assuming no expected dividends and the following weighted-average assumptions:

Expected life (in years)	4.0
Expected volatility	60.0%
Risk free interest rate	2.0%

The intrinsic value allocated to the unvested options issued in the transaction that had yet to be earned as of the transaction date was approximately $27.2 million and has been recorded as deferred compensation in the purchase price allocation.

The consolidated financial statements include the results of Documentum from the date of acquisition. The purchase price has been allocated based on estimated fair values as of the acquisition date. The purchase price allocation is preliminary and a final determination of required purchase accounting adjustments will be made upon the completion of our integration plans. The following represents the preliminary allocation of the purchase price (table in thousands):

Current assets	$ 367,534
Property, plant & equipment	17,481
Goodwill	1,427,131
Intangible assets:	
Customer relationships (estimated useful life of	
12 years)	130,050
Developed technology (estimated useful life of 5 years)	97,440
Tradenames and trademarks (estimated useful life of	
5 years)	7,150
Acquired IPR&D	9,500
Total intangible assets	244,140
Deferred compensation	27,186
Other long-term assets	13,558
Current liabilities	(128,151)
Deferred income taxes	(10,603)
Long-term convertible debt	(129,966)
Long-term liabilities	(10,346)
Fair value of the convertible debt conversion feature	(26,284)
Total purchase price	$1,791,680

In determining the purchase price allocation, we considered, among other factors, our intention to use the acquired assets, historical demand and estimates of future demand of Documentum's products and services. The fair value of intangible assets was primarily based upon the income approach. The rate used to discount the net cash flows to their present values was based upon a weighted average cost of capital of 15%. The discount rate was determined after consideration of market rates of return on debt and equity capital, the weighted average return on invested capital and the risk associated with achieving forecasted sales related to the technology and assets acquired from Documentum.

The total weighted average amortization period for the intangible assets is 8.9 years. The intangible assets are being amortized based upon the pattern in which the economic benefits of the intangible assets are being utilized. None of the goodwill is deductible for income tax purposes. The $1.4 billion of goodwill is classified within our Documentum products and services segment, information storage products segment and LEGATO products and services segment in the amounts of $1,072.1 million, $268.0 million and $87.0 million, respectively.

Of the $244.1 million of acquired intangible assets, $9.5 million was allocated to IPR&D and was written off at the date of acquisition because the IPR&D had no alternative uses and had not reached technological feasibility. The write-off is included in restructuring and other special charges in our statement of operations. Four IPR&D projects were identified relating to content management and collaboration software. The value assigned to IPR&D was determined utilizing the income approach by determining cash flow projections relating to the projects. The stage of completion of each in process project was estimated to determine the discount rate to be applied to the valuation of the in process technology. Based upon the level of completion and the risk associated with in process technology, a discount rate of 40% was deemed appropriate for valuing IPR&D.

In connection with the Documentum acquisition, we commenced integration activities which have resulted in involuntary terminations and lease terminations. The liability for involuntary termination benefits covers approximately 30 employees, primarily in general and administrative functions. We expect to pay the remaining balance for involuntary termination benefits in 2004. The liability for leases will be paid over their remaining lease terms through 2008. We are working to finalize our integration plans which may result in additional involuntary terminations, lease and other contractual terminations and employee relocations. We will finalize our integration plans and related liabilities in 2004. Finalization of our plans may result in additional liabilities which will increase goodwill. The following summarizes the obligations recognized in connection with the Documentum acquisition and activity to date (table in thousands):

Category	Obligation	Current Utilization	Ending Balance
Involuntary termination			
benefits	$ 718	$ —	$ 718
Lease terminations	4,970	—	4,970
Total	$5,688	$ —	$5,688

The following pro forma information assumes the LEGATO and Documentum acquisitions occurred as of the beginning of each year presented. The pro forma results are not necessarily indicative of what actually would have occurred had the acquisition been in effect for the periods presented (table in thousands, except per share data):

	2003	2002
Revenue	$6,735,862	$5,975,523
Net income (loss)	393,919	(433,579)
Net income (loss) per weighted average		
share, basic	$ 0.16	$ (0.18)
Net income (loss) per weighted average		
share, diluted	$ 0.16	$ (0.18)

1.93

PAYCHEX, INC. (MAY)

NOTES TO CONSOLIDATED FINANCIAL STATEMENTS

Note B—Business Combinations

In fiscal 2003, the Company acquired two comprehensive payroll processors that service small- to medium-sized businesses throughout the United States. On September 20, 2002, Paychex acquired Advantage Payroll Services, Inc. ("Advantage") for $314.4 million in cash including the redemption of preferred stock and the repayment of outstanding debt of Advantage. On April 1, 2003, Paychex acquired InterPay, Inc. ("InterPay"), a wholly owned subsidiary of FleetBoston Financial Corporation ("Fleet"), for $181.7 million in cash.

These acquisitions provided Paychex with over 82,000 new clients. In addition, the integration of these companies allows Paychex to expand geographic coverage into areas that were previously not served by the Company and the opportunity to achieve economies of scale in providing services to its clients. Results of operations for Advantage and InterPay are included in the Consolidated Statements of Income since their respective acquisition dates.

Advantage has license agreements with 15 independently owned associate offices. The associate offices are responsible for selling and marketing Advantage services and performing certain operation functions. Advantage provides all centralized back-office payroll processing and tax filing services for the associate offices, including the billing and collection of processing fees and the collection and remittance of payroll and payroll tax funds pursuant to Advantage's service arrangement with associate customers. Commissions earned by the associate offices are based on the volume of payrolls processed. Revenue generated from customers as a result of these relationships and commissions paid to associates are included in the Consolidated Statements of Income as payroll service revenue and selling, general, and administrative expense, respectively.

Purchase Price Allocations

The cost to acquire Advantage and InterPay has been allocated to the assets acquired and liabilities assumed according to estimated fair values. The following table summarizes the estimated fair values of the assets acquired and liabilities assumed for Advantage and InterPay at the date of their acquisition.

(In thousands)	Advantage	InterPay	Total
Current assets	$ 7,781	$ 6,432	$ 14,213
Funds held for clients	180,905	154,785	335,690
Deferred tax asset, net	7,786	3,540	11,326
Property and equipment	8,086	3,225	11,311
Intangible assets	59,450	35,700	95,150
Goodwill	243,315	150,388	393,703
Accounts payable and accrued expenses	(12,276)	(17,566)	(29,842)
Client fund deposits	(180,669)	(154,785)	(335,454)
Total purchase price	$314,378	$181,719	$496,097

The amounts assigned to funds held for clients represent investments in marketable securities, primarily money markets and other cash equivalents as well as mutual funds and debt securities, which are classified as available-for-sale securities. These investments were recorded at fair value obtained from an independent pricing service as of the acquisition date. The amounts assigned to client fund deposit liability represent the cash collected from clients for payroll and tax payment obligations, which had not yet been remitted to the related client employees or tax agencies.

The amount assigned to intangible assets primarily represents client lists and license agreements with associate offices, and was based on an independent appraisal. The intangible assets will be amortized over periods ranging from 7 to 12 years using either accelerated or straight-line methods, based on the provisions of SFAS No. 142, "Goodwill and Other Intangible Assets."

In connection with the acquisitions of Advantage and InterPay, the Company recorded $10.7 million of severance and $6.5 million of redundant lease liabilities in the preliminary allocation of the purchase price under EITF 95-3, "Recognition of Liabilities in Connection with a Purchase Combination." Approximately $4.7 million was paid in fiscal 2003 for severance and redundant lease costs.

Prior to the April 1, 2003 acquisition, InterPay entered into various salary continuation agreements with certain former employees. These agreements provide for benefits to these retired employees, and in certain cases to their beneficiaries, for life or other designated periods through 2015. This long-term liability of $2.1 million at May 31, 2003 represents the estimated present value of the benefits earned under these agreements. The estimated payments for these agreements are approximately $300,000 a year.

The amount of goodwill allocated to the Advantage purchase price was $243.3 million, which is not deductible for tax purposes. The amount of the goodwill allocated to the InterPay purchase price was $150.4 million, which is expected to be fully deductible for tax purposes.

Pro Forma Financial Information

The following table sets forth the unaudited pro forma results of operations of the Company for the years ended May 31, 2003 and May 31, 2002, respectively. The unaudited pro forma financial information summarizes the results of operations for the periods indicated as if the Advantage and InterPay acquisitions had occurred at the beginning of each of the annual periods presented. The pro forma information contains the actual combined operating results of Paychex, Advantage, and InterPay, with the results prior to the acquisition date adjusted to include the pro forma impact of: the amortization of acquired intangible assets, the elimination of Advantage's interest expense and preferred stock dividends, and lower interest income as a result of the sale of available-for-sale securities to fund the two acquisitions. The Company realized a total of $10.5 million of gains related to the sale of corporate investments to fund the acquisitions. These gains are included in each pro forma period presented as if they occurred at the beginning of that period. These pro forma amounts do not purport to be indicative of the results that would have actually been obtained if the acquisitions occurred as of the beginning of each of the periods presented or that may be obtained in the future.

(Pro forma, unaudited, in thousands, except per share amounts)	2003	2002
Total revenues	$1,166,065	$1,073,711
Net income	$ 284,666	$ 265,062
Diluted earnings per share	$ .75	$ .70

Formation of Jointly Owned Companies

1.94

E. I. DU PONT DE NEMOURS AND COMPANY (DEC)

NOTES TO CONSOLIDATED FINANCIAL STATEMENTS
(Dollars in millions)

8. Gain on Sale of Interest by Subsidiary—Nonoperating

In April 2003, the company formed a majority-owned venture, The Solae Company, with Bunge Limited, comprised of the company's protein technologies business and Bunge's North American and European ingredients operations. As a result of this transaction, the company's ownership interest in the protein technologies business was reduced from 100 percent to 72 percent. The company recorded a non operating pretax gain of $62, as the fair market value of the businesses contributed by Bunge exceeded the net book value of the 28 percent ownership interest acquired by Bunge. See Note 27 for additional information.

27 (In Part): Investment Activities

2003 Acquisitions (In Part)

The Solae Company

In April 2003, the company formed a majority—owned venture, The Solae Company, with Bunge Limited, Comprised of the company's protein technologies business and Bunge's North American and European ingredients operations. The results of these Bunge operations have been included in the Consolidated Financial Statements since that date. The transaction was accounted for as an acquisition under SFAS No. 141, "Business Combinations," with Bunge contributing businesses with a fair value of $520. As a result of this transaction, the company's ownership interest in the protein technologies business was reduced from 100 percent to 72 percent. The company recorded a non operating pretax gain of $62 in 2003 as the fair market value of the businesses contributed by Bunge exceeded the net book value of the 28 percent ownership interest acquired by Bunge. See Note 8.

In May 2003, as part of the plan of formation, The Solae Company acquired approximately 82 percent of Bunge Limited's Brazilian ingredients operations for $256. The results of these Bunge operations have been included in the Consolidated Financial Statements since that date. Pursuant to a tender offer, The Solae Company acquired an additional 16 percent ownership interest for $42 in November 2003. The remaining shares were acquired for approximately $2 in December 2003. Acquisition related costs were $3. During the first three years of the venture. Bunge has an option to increase its ownership to 40 percent. Additional minority interest would be recorded should Bunge choose to exercise the option.

The following table summarizes the preliminary estimated fair values of the assets acquired and liabilities assumed at the date of acquisition. These estimates are subject to refinement.

Current assets	$143
Property, plant & equipment	301
Intangible assets	148
Goodwill	346
Other non-current assets	1
Total assets	939
Current liabilities	60
Long-term liabilities	56
Net assets	$823

The $148 of acquired intangible assets have a weighted-average useful life of approximately 11 years. This includes customer relationships of $96, (10-year weighted-average useful life), purchased technology of $48 (15-year weighted-average useful life), and other intangible assets of $4 (10-year weighted-average useful life).

$346 of goodwill was assigned to Agriculture & Nutrition and is non-deductible for tax purposes. Factors that contributed to a purchase price resulting in the recognition of goodwill included improved revenue and profit growth rates, an expanded geographic manufacturing base and product portfolio, and significant operating synergies.

CONTINGENCIES

1.95 SFAS No. 5, *Accounting for Contingencies*, defines a contingency as "an existing condition, situation or set of circumstances involving uncertainty as to possible gain or loss to an enterprise that will ultimately be resolved when one or more future events occur or fail to occur." Paragraphs 8–16 of *SFAS No. 5* set forth standards of financial accounting and reporting for loss contingencies. Paragraph 17 of *SFAS No. 5* states the accounting and reporting standards for gain contingencies. During 2003, 295 survey companies presented a caption for contingencies in the balance sheet. Table 1–11 lists the loss and gain contingencies disclosed in the annual reports of the survey companies.

1.96 Examples of contingency disclosures, except for tax carry forwards, follow. Examples of operating loss carry forwards are presented in section 3.

1.97

TABLE 1-11: CONTINGENCIES

	Number of Companies			
	2003	2002	2001	2000
Loss Contingencies				
Litigation...	506	514	461	468
Environmental..............................	245	261	249	249
Insurance.......................................	122	116	76	58
Government investigations..........	94	96	61	45
Possible tax assessments...........	76	54	44	47
Other—described.........................	49	76	69	47
Gain Contingencies				
Operating loss carryforward........	416	390	350	353
Tax credits and other tax credit carryforwards............................	178	166	128	122
Alternative minimum tax carryforward...............................	69	70	79	80
Capital loss carryforward.............	66	56	29	28
Plaintiff litigation...........................	37	41	25	29
Investment credit carryforward....	18	21	23	39
Other—described.........................	10	17	6	5

LOSS CONTINGENCIES

Litigation

1.98

AMAZON.COM,INC. (DEC)

NOTES TO CONSOLIDATED FINANCIAL STATEMENTS

Note 7 (In Part): Commitments and Contingencies

Legal Proceedings

A number of purported class action complaints were field by holders of our equity and debt securities against us, our directors, and certain of our senior officers during 2001, in the United States District Court for the Western District of Washington, alleging violations of the Securities Act of 1933 (the "1933 Act") and/or the 1934 Act. On August 1, 2003, plaintiffs in the 1934 Act cases field a second consolidated amended complaint alleging that we, together with certain of our officers and directors, made false or misleading statements during the period from October 29, 1998 through October 23, 2001 concerning our business, financial condition and results, inventories, future prospects, and strategic alliance transactions. The 1933 Act complaint alleges that the defendants made false or misleading statements in connection with our February 2000 offering of the 6.875% PEACS. The complaints seek recissionary and/or compensatory damages and injunctive relief against all defendants. We dispute the allegations of wrongdoing in these complaints and intend to vigorously defend ourselves in these matters.

On October 29, 2002, Gary Gerlinger, individually and on behalf of all other similarly situated consumers in the United States who, during the period from August 1, 2001 to the present, purchased books online from either Amazon.com or Borders.com, instituted an action against us and Borders in the United States District Court for the Northern District of California. The complaint alleges that the agreement pursuant to which an affiliate of Amazon.com operates Borders.com as a co-branded site violates federal anti-trust laws, California statutory law, and the common law of unjust enrichment. The complaint seeks injunctive relief, damages, including treble damages or statutory damages where applicable, attorneys' fees, costs, and disbursements, disgorgement of all sums obtained by allegedly wrongful acts, interest, and declaratory relief. We dispute the plaintiff's allegations of wrongdoing and intend to vigorously defend ourselves in this matter.

Beginning in March 2003, we were served with complaints filed in several different states by a private litigant purportedly on behalf of the state governments under various state False Claims Acts. The complaints allege that we (along with other companies with which we have commercial agreements) wrongfully failed to collect and remit sales and use taxes for sales of personal property to customers in those states and knowingly created records and statements falsely stating we were not required to collect or remit such taxes. The complaints seek injunctive relief, unpaid taxes, interest, attorneys' fees, civil penalties of up to $10,000 per violation, and treble or punitive damages under the various state false claims acts. It is possible that we have been or will be named in similar cases in other states as well. We do not believe that we are liable under existing laws and regulations for any failure to collect sales or other taxes relating to Internet sales and intend to vigorously defend ourselves in these matters.

On July 17, 2003, Pinpoint, Inc. filed a complaint for patent infringement in the United States District Court for the Northern District of Illinois against us and several other companies with which we have commercial agreements. The complaint alleges that our personalization technology infringes several patents obtained by Pinpoint and seeks injunctive relief, monetary damages in an amount no less than a reasonable royalty, prejudgment interest, and attorneys' fees against all defendants. We dispute the allegations of wrongdoing in this complaint and intend to vigorously defend ourselves in this matter.

On January 12, 2004, Soverain Software LLC filed a complaint against us for patent infringement in the United States District Court for the Eastern District of Texas. The complaint alleges that our website technology infringes several patents obtained by Soverain purporting to cover "Internet Server Access Control and Monitoring Systems" (U.S. Patent No. 5,708,780) and "Network Sales Systems" (U.S. Patent Nos. 5,715,314 and 5,909,492) and seeks injunctive relief, monetary damages in an amount no less than a reasonable royalty, treble damages for alleged willful infringement, prejudgment interest, and attorneys' fees. We dispute the allegations of wrongdoing in this complaint and intend to vigorously defend ourselves in this matter.

Depending on the amount and the timing, an unfavorable resolution of some or all of these matters could materially affect our business, future results of operations, financial position, or cash flows in a particular period.

1.99

AMKOR TECHNOLOGY, INC. (DEC)

NOTES TO CONSOLIDATED FINANCIAL STATEMENTS

21 (In Part): Commitments and Contingencies

Amkor is involved in various claims incidental to the conduct of our business. Based on consultation with legal counsel, we do not believe that any claims, either individually or in the aggregate, to which the company is a party will have a material adverse effect on our financial condition or results of operations.

•   •   •   •   •   •

Litigation

We are currently a party to various legal proceedings, including those noted below. While we currently believe that the ultimate outcome of these proceedings, individually and in the aggregate, will not have a material adverse effect on our financial position or overall trends in results of operations, litigation is subject to inherent uncertainties. If an unfavorable ruling were to occur, there exists the possibility of a material adverse impact on our net income in the period in which the ruling occurs. The estimate of the potential impact from the following legal proceedings on our financial position or overall results of operations could change in the future.

Epoxy Mold Compound Litigation

Recently, we have become party to an increased number of litigation matters relative to our historic levels. Much of our recent increase in litigation relates to an allegedly defective epoxy mold compound, formerly used in some of our products, which is alleged to be responsible for certain semiconductor chip failures. In the case of each of these matters, we believe we have meritorious defenses, as well as valid third-party claims against Sumitomo Bakelite Co., Ltd. ("Sumitomo Bakelite"), the manufacturer of the challenged epoxy product, should the epoxy mold compound be found to be defective. We cannot be certain, however, that we will be able to recover any amount from Sumitomo Bakelite if we are held liable in these matters, or that any adverse result would not have a material impact upon us. Moreover, other customers of ours have made inquiries about the epoxy mold compound, which was widely used in the semiconductor industry, and no assurance can be given that claims similar to those already asserted will not be made against us by other customers in the future.

Fujitsu Limited v. Cirrus Logic, Inc., et al.

On April 16, 2002, we were served with a third-party complaint in an action entitled *Fujitsu Limited v. Cirrus Logic, Inc.*, No. 02-CV-01627 JW, pending in the United States District Court for the Northern District of California, San Jose Division. In this action, Fujitsu Limited ("Fujitsu") alleges that semiconductor devices it purchased from Cirrus Logic, Inc. ("Cirrus Logic") are defective in that a certain epoxy mold compound used in the manufacture of the chip causes a short circuit which renders Fujitsu disk drive products inoperable. Cirrus Logic, in response, denied the allegations of the complaint, counterclaimed against Fujitsu for unpaid invoices,

and filed its third-party complaint against us alleging that any liability for chip defects should be assigned to us because we assembled the subject semiconductor devices. Upon receipt of Cirrus Logic's third-party complaint, we filed an answer denying all liability, and our own third-party complaint against Sumitomo Bakelite. Sumitomo Bakelite filed an answer denying liability. In June 2003, Fujitsu amended its complaint and added direct claims against us. In response, we filed an answer denying all liability to Fujitsu. Fujitsu has indicated that it may seek damages in excess of $100 million. Discovery is ongoing and a trial is currently scheduled to begin in the Northern District Court of California on January 31, 2005. In November 2003, Fujitsu filed an action against Cirrus Logic, Sumitomo Bakelite and us entitled *Fujitsu Limited v. Cirrus Logic, Inc., et al.*, No. 1-03-CV-009885, in the California Superior Court for the County of Santa Clara, based on facts and allegations substantially similar to those asserted in the Northern District Court of California. In December 2003, Cirrus Logic filed a cross-complaint against Sumitomo Bakelite and us in the Superior Court case, also based on facts and allegations substantially similar to those asserted in the Northern District Court case. By stipulation among the parties, Fujitsu and Cirrus Logic have stated their intent to stay the action pending in the Northern District Court of California in favor of the action pending in the Santa Clara Superior Court. Trial in the Superior Court action is currently scheduled to begin on January 31, 2005. Amkor intends to deny all liability, to file cross-claims against Sumitomo Bakelite, and to seek dismissal of all claims against it in due course.

Seagate Technology LLC v. Atmel Corporation, et al.

In March 2003, we were served with a cross-complaint in an action between Seagate Technology LLC ("Seagate") and Atmel Corporation ("Atmel") in the Superior Court of California, Santa Clara County. Atmel's cross-complaint seeks indemnification from us for any damages incurred from the claims by Seagate involving the allegedly defective epoxy mold compound manufactured by Sumitomo Bakelite. We have answered Atmel's cross-complaint, denying all liability, and have filed a cross-complaint against Sumitomo Bakelite. Atmel later amended its cross-complaint, including adding ChipPAC Inc. ("ChipPAC") as a cross-defendant. ChipPAC filed a cross-complaint against Sumitomo Bakelite and us. On January 27, 2004, the Superior Court sustained Sumitomo Bakelite's motion to dismiss Atmel's cross-complaint, granting Atmel 30 days to file an amended pleading. We filed a motion to dismiss ChipPAC's cross-complaint on February 13, 2004, and otherwise intend to deny all liability to ChipPAC. We also intend to deny all liability to Atmel and may seek the dismissal of Atmel's further amended cross-complaint upon receipt, if appropriate. All parties are currently conducting discovery and no trial date has been set.

Maxtor Corporation v. Koninklijke Philips Electronics N.V., et al.

In April 2003, we were served with a cross-complaint in an action between Maxtor Corporation ("Maxtor") and Koninklijke Philips Electronics ("Philips"). Philips' cross-complaint seeks indemnification from us for any damages incurred from the claims by Maxtor involving the allegedly defective epoxy mold compound manufactured by Sumitomo Bakelite. Philips subsequently filed a cross-complaint directly against Sumitomo Bakelite, alleging, among other things, that

Sumitomo Bakelite breached its contractual obligations to both us and Philips by supplying a defective mold compound resulting in the failure of certain Philips semiconductor devices. We have denied all liability in this matter and have also asserted a cross-complaint against Sumitomo Bakelite. Sumitomo Bakelite has denied any liability. The parties' discovery efforts are ongoing, including expert discovery. In December 2003, we filed a motion for summary judgment against Philips's cross-claims. The motion shall be heard March 30, 2004. The trial is scheduled to start on April 12, 2004.

Maxim Integrated Products, Inc. v. Amkor Technology, Inc., et al.

In August 2003, we were served with a complaint filed by Maxim Integrated Products, Inc. ("Maxim") against us, Sumitomo Bakelite and Sumitomo Plastics America, Inc. ("Sumitomo Plastics") in the Superior Court of California, Santa Clara County. The complaint seeks damages related to our use of Sumitomo Bakelite's epoxy mold compound in assembling Maxim's semiconductor packages. Both the Sumitomo defendants and we filed motions to dismiss Maxim's complaint in September 2003. In lieu of contesting those motions to dismiss, Maxim has indicated its intent to file an amended pleading. We intend to deny all liability to Maxim and to file cross-claims against Sumitomo Bakelite; we may file another motion to dismiss Maxim's amended complaint upon receipt, if appropriate. Discovery has not commenced and there is no trial date set.

Fairchild Semiconductor Corporation v. Sumitomo Bakelite Singapore Pte. Ltd, et al.

In September 2003, we were served with an amended complaint filed by Fairchild Semiconductor Corporation ("Fairchild") against us, Sumitomo Bakelite, Sumitomo Plastics and Sumitomo Bakelite Singapore Pte. Ltd. in the Superior Court of California, Santa Clara County. The amended complaint seeks damages related to our use of Sumitomo Bakelite's epoxy mold compound in assembling Fairchild's semiconductor packages. Both the Sumitomo defendants and we filed motions to dismiss Fairchild's amended complaint in October 2003. Fairchild filed a second amended complaint in January 2004. On February 11, 2004, we filed a motion to dismiss Fairchild's second amended complaint. We also intend to deny all liability and to file cross-claims against Sumitomo Bakelite. Discovery is ongoing and no trial date has been scheduled.

Other Litigation

On August 16, 2002, we filed a complaint against Motorola, Inc. in an action captioned Amkor Technology, Inc. v. Motorola, Inc., C.A. No. 02C-08-160 CHT, pending in the Superior Court of the State of Delaware in and for New Castle County. In this action, we were seeking declaratory judgment relating to a controversy between us and Motorola concerning: (i) the assignment by Citizen Watch Co., Ltd. ("Citizen") to us of a Patent License Agreement dated January 25, 1996 between Motorola and Citizen (the "License Agreement") and concurrent assignment by Citizen to us of Citizen's interest in U.S. Patents 5,241,133 and 5,216,278 (the "133 and 278 patents"); and (ii) our obligation to make certain payments pursuant to an immunity agreement (the "Immunity Agreement") dated June 30, 1993 between us and Motorola.

We and Motorola resolved the controversy with respect to all issues relating to the Immunity Agreement, and all claims and counterclaims filed by the parties in the case relating to the Immunity Agreement were dismissed or otherwise disposed of without further litigation. The claims relating to the License Agreement and the '133 and '278 Patents remained pending.

We and Motorola both filed motions for summary judgment on the remaining claims, and oral arguments were heard on September 3, 2003. On October 6, 2003, the Superior Court of Delaware ruled in favor of us and issued an Opinion and Order granting our motion for summary judgment and denying Motorola's motion for summary judgment. On October 22, 2003, Motorola filed an appeal in Supreme Court of Delaware. We believe we will prevail on the same merits in such appeal. In addition, should Motorola prevail at the appellate level, we believe we have recourse against Citizen. However, no assurance can be given that an adverse outcome in the case cannot occur, or that any adverse outcome would not have a material impact.

Alcatel Business Systems v. Amkor Technology, Inc., Anam Semiconductor, Inc.

On November 5, 1999, we agreed to sell certain semiconductor parts to Alcatel Microelectronics, N.V. ("AME"), a subsidiary of Alcatel S.A. The parts were manufactured for us by Anam Semiconductor, Inc. ("ASI"). AME transferred the parts to another Alcatel subsidiary, Alcatel Business Systems ("ABS"), which incorporated the parts into cellular phone products. In early 2001, a dispute arose as to whether the parts sold by us were defective. On March 18, 2002, ABS and its insurer filed suit against us and ASI in the Paris Commercial Court of France, claiming damages of 50 million Euros (approximately $62.8 million based on the spot exchange rate at December 31, 2003). We have denied all liability and intend to vigorously defend ourselves. Additionally, we have entered into a written agreement with ASI whereby ASI has agreed to indemnify us fully against any and all loss related to the claims of AME, ABS and ABS' insurer. The Paris Commercial Court commenced a special proceeding before a technical expert to report on the facts of the dispute. The report of the court-appointed expert was put forth on December 31, 2003. The report does not specifically allocate liability to any particular party. The next proceeding in this matter is expected in April 2004.

In response to the lawsuit, on May 22, 2002, we filed a petition to compel arbitration in the United States District Court for the Eastern District of Pennsylvania (the "Court") against ABS, AME and ABS' insurer, claiming that the dispute is subject to the arbitration clause of the November 5, 1999 agreement between us and AME. ABS and ABS' insurer have refused to arbitrate. In August 2003, the Court denied the motion of ABS and its insurer to dismiss our petition for arbitration. The Court also subsequently denied a motion for reconsideration filed by ABS. The Court has not yet set a date for final disposition of our petition.

1.100

QUINTILES TRANSNATIONAL CORP. (DEC)

NOTES TO CONSOLIDATED FINANCIAL STATEMENTS

16 (In Part): Commitments and Contingencies

On January 26, 2001, a purported class action lawsuit was filed in the State Court of Richmond County, Georgia, naming Novartis Pharmaceuticals Corp., Pharmed Inc., Debra Brown, Bruce I. Diamond and Quintiles Laboratories Limited, a subsidiary of the Company, on behalf of 185 Alzheimer's patients who participated in drug studies involving an experimental drug manufactured by defendant Novartis, and their surviving spouses. The complaint alleges claims for breach of fiduciary duty, civil conspiracy, unjust enrichment, misrepresentation, Georgia RICO violations, infliction of emotional distress, battery, negligence and loss of consortium as to class member spouses. The complaint seeks unspecified damages, plus costs and expenses, including attorneys' fees and experts' fees. On September 27, 2003, the parties entered into a settlement memorandum following a mediated settlement conference. The parties are in the process of preparing final settlement documents, which would memorialize payments by several defendants to individual study participants or their representatives. The Company believes that its contribution will be covered by insurance or, in the alternative, will not represent a material amount to the Company.

On January 22, 2002, Federal Insurance Company ("Federal") and Chubb Custom Insurance Company ("Chubb") filed suit against the Company, Quintiles Pacific, Inc. and Quintiles Laboratories Limited, two of the Company's subsidiaries, in the United States District Court for the Northern District of Georgia. In the suit, Chubb, the Company's primary commercial general liability carrier for coverage years 2000–2001 and 2001–2002, and Federal, the Company's excess liability carrier for coverage years 2000–2001 and 2001–2002, seek to rescind the policies issued to the Company based on an alleged misrepresentation by the Company on the policy application. Alternatively, Chubb and Federal seek a declaratory judgment that there is no coverage under the policies for some or all of the claims asserted against the Company and its subsidiaries in the class action lawsuit filed on January 26, 2001 and described above and, if one or more of such claims is determined to be covered, Chubb and Federal request an allocation of the defense costs between the claims they contend are covered and non-covered claims. The Company has filed an answer with counterclaims against Federal and Chubb in response to their complaint. Additionally, the Company has amended its pleadings to add AON Risk Services ("AON") as a counterclaim defendant, as an alternative to the Company's position that Federal and Chubb are liable under the policies. In order to preserve its rights, on March 27, 2003, the Company also filed a separate action against AON in the United States District Court for the Middle District of North Carolina. The Company believes the allegations made by Federal and Chubb are without merit and is defending this case vigorously.

In October 2002, seven purported class action lawsuits were filed in Superior Court, Durham County, North Carolina by certain of the Company's shareholders seeking to enjoin the consummation of the initial transaction proposed by Pharma Services Company (a company controlled by Dennis B. Gillings, Ph.D.) to acquire all the Company's outstanding shares for $11.25 per share in cash. All of the lawsuits were subsequently transferred to the North Carolina Business Court. The lawsuits named as defendants Dr. Gillings, other members of the Company's Board of Directors, the Company and, in some cases Pharma Services Company. The complaints alleged, among other things, a breach of fiduciary duties by the directors with respect to the proposal. The complaints sought to enjoin the transaction proposed by Pharma Services Company, and the plaintiffs sought to recover damages. On November 11, 2002, a Special Committee of the Company's Board of Directors announced its rejection of the proposal by Pharma Services Company and its intention to investigate strategic alternatives available to the Company for purposes of enhancing shareholder value, including the possibility of a sale of the Company and alternatives that would keep the Company independent and publicly owned. On January 6, 2003, the North Carolina Business Court entered a Case Management Order consolidating all seven lawsuits for all purposes and staying the lawsuits until March 29, 2003 or until the Company provided notice of a change-of-control transaction.

On March 28, 2003, the Court entered an Order Maintaining the Status Quo, which continued its prior Case Management Order in all respects until the earlier of a date selected by the Court or until the Company provided the notice contemplated by the Case Management Order. On April 10, 2003, the Company's Board of Directors approved the merger agreement with Pharma Services which provided for payment to the Company's shareholders of $14.50 per share in cash. On June 25, 2003, counsel for the parties signed a Memorandum of Understanding, in which they agreed upon the terms of a settlement of the litigation, which would include the dismissal with prejudice of all claims against all defendants including the Company and the Company's Board of Directors. On August 28, 2003, lead counsel for the plaintiffs and counsel for the defendants executed a formal Stipulation and Agreement of Compromise, Settlement and Release (the "Stipulation of Settlement"). On August 29, 2003, the Court entered an Order for Notice and Hearing on Settlement of Class Action ("Order for Notice") and a Notice of Pendency of Class Action, Preliminary and Proposed Class Action Certification, Proposed Settlement of Class Action, Settlement Hearing and Right to Appear (the "Class Notice"). The Class Notice set a hearing date of October 10, 2003 (the "Settlement Hearing") to determine whether the Court should approve the settlement as fair, adequate and in the best interest of the settlement class, end the action, and to consider other matters including a request by plaintiffs' counsel for attorneys' fees and reimbursement of costs, in an amount not to exceed a total of $450,000. In accordance with the terms of the Order of Notice, the Company mailed the Class Notice to the record holders of the Company's Common Stock and options, as of the record date of August 19, 2003. A special meeting of the shareholders was held on September 25, 2003, at which time the shareholders approved the proposed transaction and the merger was consummated. On October 10, 2003, the Court certified a class for purposes of the settlement, approved the settlement as fair and reasonable and entered an Order and Final Judgment dismissing the lawsuit with prejudice. The Court also awarded plaintiff's counsel $450,000 in attorneys' fees and costs, which have been paid pursuant to the terms of the settlement. No other payments are required from the Company or any other party under the terms of the settlement and the Court's Order.

On June 13, 2003, ENVOY and Federal filed suit against the Company, in the United States District Court for the Middle District of Tennessee. One or both plaintiffs in this case have alleged claims for breach of contract, contractual subrogation, equitable subrogation, and equitable contribution. Plaintiffs reached settlement in principle, in the amount of $11 million, of the case pending in the same court captioned In Re Envoy Corporation Securities Litigation, Case No. 3-98-0760 (the "Envoy Securities Litigation"). Plaintiffs claim that the Company is responsible for payment of the settlement amount and associated fees and costs in the Envoy Securities Litigation based on merger and settlement agreements between WebMD, ENVOY and the Company. The Company has filed a motion to dismiss the suit, and the plaintiffs have filed motions for summary judgment. These motions are pending before the court. All parties have agreed to a stay of discovery. The Company believes that the allegations made by ENVOY and Federal are without merit and intends to defend the case vigorously.

The Company also is party to other legal proceedings incidental to its business. While the Company's management currently believes that the ultimate outcome of these proceedings, individually and in the aggregate, will not have a material adverse effect on the Company's consolidated financial statements, litigation is subject to inherent uncertainties. Were an unfavorable ruling to occur, there exists the possibility of a material adverse impact on the results of operations for the period in which the ruling occurs.

Environmental Matters

1.101

THE DOW CHEMICAL COMPANY (DEC)

NOTES TO CONSOLIDATED FINANCIAL STATEMENTS
(Dollars in millions)

Note A (In Part): Summary of Significant Accounting Policies and Accounting Changes

Environmental Matters

Accruals for environmental matters are recorded when it is probable that a liability has been incurred and the amount of the liability can be reasonably estimated, based on current law and existing technologies. These accruals are adjusted periodically as assessment and remediation efforts progress or as additional technical or legal information becomes available. Accruals for environmental liabilities are included in the consolidated balance sheets as "Other noncurrent obligations" at undiscounted amounts. Accruals for related insurance or other third-party recoveries for environmental liabilities are recorded when it is probable that a recovery will be realized and are included in the consolidated balance sheets as "Accounts receivable—Other."

Environmental costs are capitalized if the costs extend the life of the property, increase its capacity, and/or mitigate or prevent contamination from future operations. Environmental costs are also capitalized in recognition of legal asset retirement obligations resulting from the acquisition, construction and/or normal operation of a long-lived asset. Costs related to environmental contamination treatment and cleanup are charged to expense. Estimated future incremental operations, maintenance and management costs directly related to remediation are accrued when such costs are probable and estimable.

Note J (In Part): Commitments and Contingent Liabilities

Environmental Matters

Accruals for environmental matters are recorded when it is probable that a liability has been incurred and the amount of the liability can be reasonably estimated, based on current law and existing technologies. The Company had accrued obligations of $394 at December 31, 2002, for environmental remediation and restoration costs, including $43 for the remediation of Superfund sites. At December 31, 2003, the Company had accrued obligations of $381 for environmental remediation and restoration costs, including $40 for the remediation of Superfund sites. This is management's best estimate of the costs for remediation and restoration with respect to environmental matters for which the Company has accrued liabilities, although the ultimate cost with respect to these particular matters could range up to twice that amount. Inherent uncertainties exist in these estimates primarily due to unknown conditions, changing governmental regulations and legal standards regarding liability, and evolving technologies for handling site remediation and restoration.

The following table summarizes the activity in the Company's accrued obligations for environmental matters for the years ended December 31, 2003 and 2002:

Accrued Obligations for Environmental Matters

	2003	2002
Balance at January 1	$394	$444
Additional accruals	68	52
Charges against reserve	(77)	(108)
Adjustments to reserve	(4)	6
Balance at December 31	$381	$394

The amounts charged to income on a pretax basis related to environmental remediation totaled $68 in 2003, $52 in 2002 and $47 in 2001. Capital expenditures for environmental protection were $132 in 2003. $147 in 2002 and $179 in 2001.

On June 12, 2003, the Michigan Department of Environmental Quality ("MDEQ") issued a Hazardous Waste Operating License to the Company's Midland, Michigan, manufacturing site, which included provisions requiring the Company to conduct an investigation to determine the nature and extent of off-site contamination in Midland area soils; Tittabawassee and Saginaw River sediment and floodplain soils; and Saginaw Bay. The operating license required the Company, by August 11, 2003, to propose a detailed Scope of Work for the off-site investigation, for review and approval by the MDEQ. Scope of Work documents were submitted to the MDEQ and were the subject of public comment. On December 12, 2003, MDEQ provided its formal response to the Company's August 11, 2003, Scope of Work documents in the form a Notice of Deficiency ("Notice") that required the Company respond to the Notice by February 17, 2004. The Company has accrued an obligation of $7 (included in the total accrued obligation of $381 at December 31, 2003) with respect to off-site investigation, based on the investigative work that the Company has proposed and has discussed with MDEQ since the submission of the Scope of Work documents.

It is the opinion of the Company's management that the possibility is remote that costs in excess of those accrued or disclosed will have a material adverse impact on the Company's consolidated financial statements.

1.102

GEORGIA-PACIFIC CORPORATION (DEC)

NOTES TO CONSOLIDATED FINANCIAL STATEMENTS

Note 1 (In Part): Summary of Significant Accounting Policies

Environmental and Legal Matters

We recognize a liability for environmental remediation and legal indemnification and defense costs when we believe it is probable a liability has been incurred and the amount can be reasonably estimated. The liabilities are developed based on currently available information and reflect the participation of other potentially responsible parties, depending on the parties' financial condition and probable contribution. The accruals are recorded at undiscounted amounts and are reflected as liabilities on the accompanying consolidated balance sheets. We also have insurance that covers losses on certain environmental claims and we record a receivable to the extent that the realization of the insurance is deemed probable. These receivables are recorded at undiscounted amounts and are reflected as assets in the accompanying consolidated balance sheets.

Environmental costs are generally capitalized when the costs improve the condition of the property or prevent or mitigate future contamination. All other costs are expensed.

Note 17 (In Part): Commitments and Contingencies

Environmental Matters

We are involved in environmental remediation activities at approximately 171 sites, both owned by us and owned by others, where we have been notified that we are or may be a potentially responsible party ("PRP") under the United States Comprehensive Environmental Response, Compensation and Liability Act ("CERCLA") or similar state "superfund" laws. Of the known sites in which we are involved, we estimate that approximately 40% are being investigated, approximately 20% are being remediated and approximately 40% are being monitored (an activity that occurs after either site investigation or remediation has been completed). The ultimate costs to us for the investigation, remediation and monitoring of many of these sites cannot be predicted with certainty, due to the often unknown nature and magnitude of the pollution or the necessary cleanup, the varying costs of alternative cleanup methods, the amount of time necessary to accomplish the cleanups, the evolving nature of cleanup technologies and governmental regulations, and the inability to determine our share of multiparty cleanups or the extent to which contribution will be available from other parties, all of which factors are taken into account to the extent possible in estimating our liabilities. We have established reserves for environmental remediation costs for these sites that we

believe are probable and reasonably able to be estimated. To the extent that we are aware of unasserted claims, consider them probable, and can estimate their potential costs, we include appropriate amounts in the reserves.

Based on analyses of currently available information and previous experience with respect to the cleanup of hazardous substances, we believe it is reasonably possible that costs associated with these sites may exceed current reserves by amounts that may prove insignificant or that could range, in the aggregate, up to approximately $129 million. This estimate of the range of reasonably possible additional costs is less certain than the estimates upon which reserves are based, and in order to establish the upper limit of this range, assumptions least favorable to us among the range of reasonably possible outcomes were used. In estimating both our current reserve for environmental remediation and the possible range of additional costs, we have not assumed we will bear the entire cost of remediation of every site to the exclusion of other known PRPs who may be jointly and severally liable. The ability of other PRPs to participate has been taken into account, based generally on their financial condition and probable contribution on a per-site basis.

Presented below is the activity in our environmental liability account for the last three years.

(In millions)	2003	2002	2001
Beginning balance	$306	$318	$121
(Income) expense in earnings:			
Related to previously existing matters	(64)	1	2
Related to new matters	1	13	15
Amounts related to acquisitions:			
Purchase price allocations	—	—	207
Reclassification of reserves for adoption of SFAS No. 143	(4)	—	—
Payments	(9)	(26)	(27)
Ending balance	$230	$306	$318

Kalamazoo River Superfund Site

We are currently implementing an Administrative Order by Consent ("AOC") entered into with the Michigan Department of Natural Resources and the United States Environmental Protection Agency ("United States EPA") regarding an investigation of the Kalamazoo River Superfund Site. The Kalamazoo River Superfund Site is comprised of 35 miles of the Kalamazoo River, three miles of Portage Creek and a number of operable units in the form of landfills, waste disposal areas and impoundments. We became a PRP for the site in December 1990 by signing the AOC. There are two other named PRPs at this time. The contaminant of concern is polychlorinated biphenyls ("PCBs") in the river sediments and residuals in the landfills and waste disposal areas.

A draft Remedial Investigation/Feasibility Study ("RI/FS") for the Kalamazoo River was submitted to the State of Michigan on October 30, 2000 by us and other PRPs. The draft RI/FS evaluated five remedial options ranging from no action to total dredging of the river and off-site disposal of the dredged materials. In February 2001, the PRPs, at the request of the State of Michigan, also evaluated 9 additional potential remedies. The cost for these remedial options ranges from $0 to $2.5 billion. The draft RI/FS recommends a remedy involving stabilization of over twenty miles of riverbank and long-term monitoring of the riverbed. The total cost for this remedy is approximately $73 million. It is unknown over what timeframe these costs will be paid out. The United States EPA has taken over management of the RI/FS and is evaluating the proposed remedy. We cannot predict what impact or change will result from the United States EPA's assuming management of the site.

We are paying 50% of the costs for the river portion of the RI/FS investigation based on an interim allocation. This 50% interim allocation includes the share assumed by Fort James prior to its acquisition by us. Several other companies have been identified by government agencies as PRPs, and all but one is believed to be financially viable. We are currently engaged in cost recovery litigation against two other parties, and have identified several more parties that may have some share of liability for the river.

As part of implementing the AOC, we have investigated the closure of two disposal areas which are contaminated with PCBs. The cost to remediate one of the disposal areas, the King Highway Landfill, was approximately $9 million. The remediation of that area is essentially complete and we are waiting for final approval of the closure from the State of Michigan A 30-year post-closure care period will begin upon receipt of closure approval, and over that period we will make expenditures accrued for post-closure care. We are solely responsible for closure and post-closure care of the King Highway Landfill.

It is anticipated that the cost for closure of the second disposal area, the Willow Boulevard/A Site landfill, will be approximately $8 million. The State of Michigan has drafted a new RI/FS for this landfill and we are in the process of preparing comments on that document. The new draft RI/FS evaluates the same remedies proposed by the PRPs. The decision as to the actual remedy will be made by the United States EPA after the RI/FS is finalized, which is expected to be this year. We believe the United States EPA will require a remedy for this landfill similar to the King Highway landfill closure. It is anticipated these costs will be paid out over the next five years, and costs for post-closure care for 30 years following certification of the closure. We are solely responsible for closure and post-closure care of the Willow Boulevard portion of the landfill, and are sharing investigation costs for the A Site portion of the landfill with Millennium Holdings on an equal basis. A final determination as to how closure and post-closure costs for the A Site will be allocated between us and Millennium Holdings has not been made; however, our share should not exceed 50%.

We have spent approximately $33 million on the Kalamazoo River Superfund Site through January 3, 2004 broken down as follows:

(In millions)

Site	
River	$19
King Highway	9
A Site	2
Willow Blvd	3
	$33

All of these amounts were charged to earnings.

The reserve for the Kalamazoo River Superfund Site is based on the assumption that the bank stabilization remedy will be selected as the final remedy by the United States EPA and the State of Michigan, and that the costs of the remedy will be shared by several other PRPs.

Fox River Site

The Fox River site in Wisconsin is comprised of 39 miles of the Fox River and Green Bay. The site was nominated by the United States EPA (but never finally designated) as a Superfund site due to contamination of the river by PCBs through wastewater discharged from the recycling of carbonless copy paper from 1953–1971. We became a PRP through our acquisition of Fort James.

In late July of 2003, the Wisconsin Department of Natural Resources ("WDNR") and the United States EPA issued a Record of Decision ("ROD") for Operable Units ("OU") 3, 4 and 5 of the Fox River. OU 3 is the section of the Fox River running downstream from Little Rapids to the De Pere dam, and Operable Unit 4 runs from the De Pere dam downstream to the mouth of the Fox River at Green Bay. Operable Unit 5 is Green Bay. The Fort James facility, which potentially discharged PCBs, is located in OU 4 approximately 3 miles downstream from the De Pere dam.

The ROD calls for the removal by dredging of all sediments in OUs 3 and 4 containing PCBs above one part per million. The amount of sediment estimated to contain PCBs above one part per million is 586,800 cubic yards in OU 3 and 5,880,000 cubic yards in OU 4. The ROD also calls for monitored natural recovery for OU 5. The ROD estimates the dredging remedy for OUs 3 and 4 and the monitored natural recovery for OU 5 will cost $324 million. However, the ROD does allow for capping as an alternative remedy to dredging in certain areas of OUs 3 and 4 if capping would be less costly than dredging and provide the same level of protection as dredging. The WDNR estimated that approximately 40% of the total volume of contaminated sediments in OUs 3 and 4 would be eligible for capping based upon the capping criteria defined in the ROD. The allowance for capping in the ROD represents a major change from the proposed remedial action plan issued by WDNR in 2001, which did not provide or allow for capping in any areas of OUs 3 and 4.

Six other companies have been identified by the governments as PRPs. Under an interim allocation agreement, we were paying 30% of costs incurred by the PRPs in analyzing and responding to all of the governmental documents which preceeded the issuance of the ROD. With the issuance of the ROD, we do not anticipate that the PRPs will be engaged in any further formal work as a group. We believe that all of the PRPs are liable for some portion of the costs of remediating OUs 4 and 5, and that our ultimate liability will be less than 30% of the total estimated cost of remediating the Fox River site.

Along with another PRP, we are negotiating the terms and conditions for an Administrative Order on Consent ("AOC") to prepare the remedial design for OUs 3, 4 and 5. We intend to finalize and AOC for this design work with the WDNR and the United States EPA shortly.

We have analyzed the remedial provisions selected in the ROD as well as the relevant facts impacting our potential liability. We believe that we will be able to utilize the capping remedy to the extent permitted by the ROD. We also believe we have established the geographic limitations on our potential liability, and can therefore limit our responsibility for the removal and capping of PCBs to the part of OU 4 immediately adjacent to and downstream from the Fort James facility in Green Bay, Wisconsin. We share liability for any appropriate monitoring in OU 5 with all of the PRPs. Based upon the change in the remedy and new information concerning this liability, we now believe it will not be necessary to utilize all of the reserve previously established for this site, and have reduced such reserve by approximately $66 million.

We have spent approximately $37 million from 1995 to January 3, 2004 on the Fox River site, some of which was spent by Fort James prior to its acquisition by us.

In 2002, we entered into an agreement with the WDNR and the United States Fish and Wildlife Service that would settle claims for natural resource damages under CERCLA, the Federal Water Pollution Control Act and state law for approximately $12 million, and to date have paid approximately $9 million of this amount. The agreement will be effective when entered by a Federal District Court in Wisconsin. The United States Department of Justice moved in March of 2003 for the agreement to be entered by that Court; the motion remains pending. The $12 million to be paid under this agreement is separate and apart from any costs related to remediation of the Fox River site.

In 1999 we and Chesapeake Corporation formed a joint venture to which a Chesapeake subsidiary, Wisconsin Tissue Mills, Inc., contributed tissue mills and other assets located along the Fox River. Wisconsin Tissue is one of the PRPs for the Fox River site. Chesapeake and Wisconsin Tissue specifically retained all liabilities arising from Wisconsin Tissue's status as a PRP, and indeminified the joint venture and us against these liabilities. In 2001, we (having acquired all of Chesapeake's interest) sold this joint venture to Svenska Cellulosa Aktiebolaget (publ) ("SCA") and indemnified SCA and the joint venture against all environmental liabilities (including all liabilities arising from the Fox River site for which Wisconsin Tissue is ultimately responsible) arising prior to the closing of the SCA sale. As part of the agreement pursuant to which we acquired Chesapeake's interest in the joint venture, Chesapeake specifically agreed that we would retain Chesapeake's prior indeminification for these liabilities.

Whatcom Waterway Superfund Site

The Whatcom Waterway is a Federal channel located adjacent to our pulp and paper mill in Bellingham, Washington. The State of Washington declared the Whatcom Waterway a Superfund site due to historical contamination of sediments with woody debris, phenolics and mercury. On March 6, 1995, the Washington Department of Ecology named us as a Potentially Liable Party ("PLP") in the case. The State is presently preparing to name other PLPs in the case.

We completed an RI/FS and identified a preferred remedial alternative comprised of a combination of dredging, capping and habitat restoration with a total estimated cost of $23 million. It is anticipated these costs will be paid out over the next 5 to 10 years. We have completed interim remedial action and habitat restoration of a portion of the site. Environmental monitoring of this portion of the site is ongoing. The reserve for the Whatcom Waterway site is based on the assumptions that the $23 million proposed remedy involving limited dredging and capping will be selected by the State of Washington as the final remedy and that the cost of the remedy will be shared among a small group of PLPs.

We have spent approximately $4 million through January 3, 2004 on the Whatcom Waterway site, all of which was charged to earnings.

1.103

PHELPS DODGE CORPORATION (DEC)

NOTES TO CONSOLIDATED FINANCIAL STATEMENTS
(Dollar amounts in tables stated in millions except as noted)

1 (In Part): Summary of Significant Accounting Policies

Environmental Expenditures

Environmental expenditures are expensed or capitalized depending upon their future economic benefits. Liabilities for such expenditures are recorded when it is probable that obligations have been incurred and the costs can be reasonably estimated. For closed facilities and closed portions of operating facilities with closure obligations, an environmental liability is accrued when a closure determination is made and approved by management, and when the environmental liability is considered to be probable. Environmental liabilities attributed to the Comprehensive Environmental Response, Compensation, and Liability Act (CERCLA) or analogous state programs are considered probable when a claim is asserted, or is probable of assertion, and we have been associated with the site. Other environmental remediation liabilities are considered probable based on the specific facts and circumstances. Our estimates of these costs are based upon available facts, existing technology and current laws and regulations, and are recorded on an undiscounted basis. Where the available information is sufficient to estimate the amount of liability, that estimates has been used. Where the information is only sufficient to establish a range of probable liability and no point within the range is more likely than any other, the lower end of the range has been used. The possibility of recovery of some of these costs from insurance companies or other parties exists; however, we do not recognize these recoveries in our financial statements until they become probable. We recognize insurance receivables for environmental remediation when a settlement is reached with the insurance carrier.

21 (In Part): Contingencies

Environmental

Phelps Dodge is subject to various federal, state and local environmental laws and regulations that govern emissions of air pollutants; discharges of water pollutants; and generation, handling, storage and disposal of hazardous substances, hazardous wastes and other toxic materials. The Company is also subject to potential liabilities arising under CERCLA or similar state laws that impose responsibility on persons who arranged for the disposal of hazardous substances, and on current and previous owners and operators of a facility for the cleanup of hazardous substances released from the facility into the environment. In addition, the Company is subject to potential liabilities under the Resource Conservation and Recovery Act (RCRA) and analogous state laws that require responsible parties to remediate releases of hazardous or solid waste constituents into the environment associated with past or present activities.

Phelps Dodge or its subsidiaries have been advised by EPA, the U.S. Forest Service and several state agencies that they may be liable under CERCLA or similar state laws and regulations for costs of responding to environmental and natural resource conditions at a number of sites that have been or are being investigated by EPA, the U.S. Forest service or states to determine whether releases of hazardous substances have occurred and, if so, to develop and implement remedial actions to address environmental and natural resource concerns.

Phelps Dodge has provided reserves for potential environmental obligations that management considers probable and for which reasonable estimates can be made. For closed facilities and closed portions of operating facilities with closure obligations, an environmental liability is considered probable and is accrued when a closure determination is made and approved by management. Environmental liabilities attributed to CERCLA or analogous state programs are considered probable when a claim is asserted, or is probable of assertion, and we have been associated with the site. Other environmental remediation liabilities are considered probable based upon specific facts and circumstances. Liability estimates are based on an evaluation of, among other factors, currently available facts, existing technology, presently enacted laws and regulations, Phelps Dodge's experience in remediation, other companies' remediation experience, Phelps Dodge's status as a potentially responsible party (PRP), and the ability of other PRPs to pay their allocated portions. Accordingly, total environmental reserves of $317.2 million and $305.9 million were recorded as of December 31, 2003 and 2002, respectively. The long-term portion of these reserves is included in other liabilities and deferred credits on the Consolidated Balance Sheet and amounted to $271.3 million and $261.7 million at December 31, 2003 and 2002, respectively.

The site currently considered to be the most significant is the Pinal Creek site near Miami, Arizona.

Pinal Creek Site

The Pinal Creek site was listed under the Arizona Department of Environmental Quality (ADEQ) Water Quality Assurance Revolving Fund program in 1989 for contamination in the shallow alluvial aquifers within the Pinal Creek drainage near Miami, Arizona. Since that time, environmental remediation has been performed by the members of the Pinal Creek Group (PCG), comprising Phelps Dodge Miami, Inc. (a wholly owned subsidiary of the Company) and two other companies. In 1998, the District Court approved a Consent Decree between the PCG members and the state of Arizona resolving all matters related to an enforcement action contemplated by the state of Arizona against the PCG members with respect to the groundwater matter. The Consent Decree committed Phelps Dodge Miami, Inc. and the other PCG members to complete the remediation work outlined in the Consent Decree. That work continues at this time pursuant to the Consent Decree and consistent with the National Contingency Plan prepared by EPA under CERCLA.

Phelps Dodge Miami, Inc. and the other members of the PCG are pursuing contribution litigation against three other parties involved with the site. At least two of the three defendants now have admitted direct liability as responsible parties. The first phase of the case has been assigned a trial date in August 2004. Phelps Dodge Miami, Inc. also asserted claims against certain past insurance carriers. As of November 2002, all of the carriers have settled or had their liability adjudicated. One carrier has appealed the judgment against it.

In addition, a dispute between one dissenting PCG member and Phelps Dodge Miami, Inc. and the other PCG member was filed in Superior Court in 2002. The litigation seeks a declaratory judgment on the dissenting member's contract liability under the PCG agreement. Trial for this matter is scheduled for mid-2004.

While significant recoveries may be achieved in the contribution litigation, the Company cannot reasonably estimate the amount and, therefore, has not taken potential recoveries into consideration in the recorded reserve.

Phelps Dodge Miami, Inc.'s share of the planned remediation work has a cost range for reasonably expected outcomes estimated to be from $110 million to $216 million. Approximately $113 million remained in the Company's Pinal Creek remediation reserve at December 31, 2003.

The sites that had the largest adjustments to their reserves were the Yonkers and American Zinc and Chemical sites.

Yonkers Site

In 1984, the Company sold a cable manufacturing facility located in Yonkers, New York. In 2000, the owner of the property entered into a consent order with the New York State Department of Environmental Conservation (NYSDEC) under which the owner committed to complete a remedial investigation and feasibility study. In December 2001, the Company entered into an Interim Agreement with the owner of the property regarding the owner's claim for indemnification from the Company for certain environmental liabilities at the facility. The owner submitted its feasibility study to NYSDEC in December 2003. The feasibility study recommends excavation of PCB-contaminated soil, either removal of PCB and lead contamination from, or demolition of PCB- and lead-contaminated buildings, and monitored natural recovery of PCB-contaminated sediments in the Hudson River. Based on the feasibility study, and taking into consideration the reasonably possible allocation percentages that could apply to the Company and the property owner, the Company's remedial costs may range from $20 million to $37 million, with a most likely point in the range of $20 million.

American Zinc and Chemical Site

In June 1999, Cyprus Amax, now a subsidiary of Phelps Dodge, received an information request from the Pennsylvania Department of Environmental Protection (PADEP) regarding the former American Zinc and Chemical (AZC) site in Langeloth, Pennsylvania. The AZC site consists primarily of a former zinc smelter facility operated until 1947 by the former American Zinc and Chemical Company and includes some or all of a contiguous, currently operating molybdenum refinery formerly owned by the Climax Molybdenum Company, which is indirectly owned by Cyprus Amax. The American Zinc and Chemical Company, which was dissolved in 1951, also was a subsidiary of a corporate predecessor to Cyprus Amax.

In discussions with Cyprus Amax in 2001 and early 2002, PADEP informally indicated that it expects Cyprus Amax to investigate and remediate negative environmental conditions at the AZC site, which predominate at and about the former zinc smelter facility. The Company's Form 10-K for the year ended December 31, 2002, indicated preliminary evaluations of the nature and extent of conditions at the site may range in cost from $18 million to $52 million. The Company reserved $20 million for possible remediation work at this site. Recently, an engineering evaluation and reasonable-cost analysis was performed to estimate the cost and feasibility of implementing the most likely remedial action that PADEP would accept based on effectiveness and implementability. To check the validity of the analysis, estimated site remedial costs were compared with costs from other environmental sites that have implemented similar remedial actions. In addition, a reasonable-cost analysis was performed on other possible remedial alternatives so a range of costs could be established for consideration. This analysis indicated that remediation of the site may range from $9 million to $43 million, with a most likely point in the range of $9 million. The most likely remedial action would include an additional site investigation study, implementating of storm water controls, constructing an engineered cap over 60 acres of slag and process waste, and long-term monitoring and operation and maintenance of the site. While the Company has reduced its reserve to $9 million for possible remediation work at the site, Cyprus Amax continues to believe and will continue to indicate to PADEP that the Company is not liable for the actions of its former subsidiary, American Zinc and Chemical Company, under existing federal and state environmental laws. To date, PADEP has not responded to Cyprus Amax's assertion that it is not liable.

Other

In 2003, the Company recognized charges of $28.4 million for environmental remediation. The two sites with significant changes were the Yonkers site (an increase of $16.7 million) and the AZC site (a decrease of $10.4 million). The remainder of environmental remediation charges was primarily at closed sites, none of which increased or decreased individually more than approximately $7 million.

At December 31, 2003, the cost range for reasonably possible outcomes for all reservable environmental remediation sites other than Pinal Creek, Yonkers and AZC was estimated to be from $133 million to $329 million, of which $175 million has been reserved. Work on these sites is expected to be substantially completed in the next several years, subject to inherent delays involved in the remediation process.

Phelps Dodge believes certain insurance policies partially cover the foregoing environmental liabilities; however, some of the insurance carriers have denied coverage. We presently are negotiating with the carriers over some of these disputes. Further, Phelps Dodge believes it has other potential claims for recovery from other third parties, including the United States Government and other PRPs. Neither insurance recoveries nor other claims or offsets are recognized unless such offsets are considered probable of realization. In 2003 and 2002, the Company recognized proceeds from settlements reached with several insurance companies on historic environmental liability claims of $0.5 million and $34.3 million, net of fees and expenses, respectively.

Phelps Dodge has a number of sites that are not the subject of an environmental reserve because it is not probable that a successful claim will be made against the Company for those sites, but for which there is a reasonably possible likelihood of an environmental remediation liability. At December 31, 2003, the cost range for reasonably possible outcomes for all such sites was estimated to be from $3 million to $17 million. The liabilities arising from potential environmental obligations that have not been reserved at this time may be material to the results of any single quarter or year in the future. Management, however, believes the liability arising from potential environmental obligations is not likely to have a material adverse effect on the Company's liquidity or financial position as such obligations could be satisfied over a period of years.

The following table summarizes environmental reserve activities for the years ended December 31:

	2003	2002	2001
Balance, beginning of year	$305.9	$311.2	$307.1
Additions to reserves*	54.6	18.3	37.1
Reductions in reserve estimate	(12.7)	(4.3)	(6.0)
Spending against reserves	(24.1)	(19.3)	(27.0)
Reclassification to asset retirement obligation**	(6.5)	—	—
Balance, end of year	$317.2	$305.9	$311.2

* 2003 included $13.5 million for our acquisition of Heiser's one-third interest in Chino Mines Company.

** Upon adoption of SFAS No. 143, reserves for certain matters ($6.5 million) required by reclamation rules or laws were reclassified to asset retirement obligations (previously classified as environmental reserves).

Insurance Coverage/Self-Insurance

1.104

FLOWERS FOODS, INC. (DEC)

NOTES TO CONSOLIDATED FINANCIAL STATEMENTS

Note 2 (In Part): Summary of Significant Accounting Policies

Self-Insurance Reserves

We are self-insured for various levels of general liability, workers' compensation and employee medical and dental coverage. Insurance reserves are calculated on an undiscounted basis based on actual claim data and estimates of incurred but not reported claims developed utilizing historical claim trends. Projected settlements and incurred but not reported claims are estimated based on pending claims, historical trends and data. Though the company does not expect them to do so, actual settlements and claims could differ materially from those estimated. Material differences in actual settlements and claims could have an adverse effect on our results of operations and financial condition.

Note 22 (In Part): Commitments and Contingencies

The company has recorded current liabilities of $11.5 million and $15.7 million related to self-insurance reserves at January 3, 2004 and December 28, 2002, respectively. The reserves include an estimate of expected settlements on pending claims, defense costs and a provision for claims incurred but not reported. These estimates are based on the company's assessment of potential liability using an analysis of available information with respect to pending claims, historical experience and current cost trends. The amount of the company's ultimate liability in respect of these matters may differ materially from these estimates.

Governmental Investigations

1.105

SYMBOL TECHNOLOGIES, INC. (DEC)

NOTES TO CONSOLIDATED FINANCIAL STATEMENTS

14 (In Part): Commitments and Contingencies

D (In Part): Legal Matters

We are a party to lawsuits in the normal course of business. Litigation in the normal course of business, as well as the lawsuits and investigations described below, can be expensive, lengthy and disruptive to normal business operations. Moreover, the results of complex legal proceedings and government investigations are difficult to predict. Unless otherwise specified, Symbol is currently unable to estimate, with reasonable certainty, the possible loss, or range of loss, if any, for the lawsuits and investigations described herein. An unfavorable resolution to any of the lawsuits or investigations described below could have a material adverse effect on Symbol's business, results of operations or financial condition.

Government Investigations

The Securities and Exchange Commission ("SEC") has issued a Formal Order Directing Private Investigation and Designating Officers to Take Testimony with respect to certain accounting matters, principally concerning the timing and amount of revenue recognized by Symbol during the period of January 1, 2000 through December 31, 2001 as well as the accounting for certain reserves, restructurings, certain option programs and several categories of cost of revenue and operating expenses. We are cooperating with the SEC, and have produced hundreds of thousands of documents and numerous witnesses in response to the SEC's inquiries. Symbol and approximately ten or more former employees have received so-called "Wells Notices" stating that the SEC Staff in the Northeast Regional Office is considering recommending to the Commission that it authorize civil actions against Symbol and the individuals involved alleging violations of various sections of the federal securities laws and regulations. Pursuant to an action against Symbol, the Commission may seek permanent injunctive relief and appropriate monetary relief, including a fine, from us.

The United States Attorney's Office for the Eastern District of New York (the "Eastern District") has commenced a related investigation. We are cooperating with that investigation, and have produced documents and witnesses in response to the Eastern District's inquiries. The Eastern District could file criminal charges against Symbol and seek to impose a fine upon us and other relief the Eastern District deems appropriate.

Any criminal and/or civil action or any negotiated resolution may involve, among other things, injunctive and equitable relief, including material fines, which could have a material adverse effect on our business, results of operations and financial condition.

In addition, as a result of the investigations, various governmental entities at the federal, state and municipal levels may conduct a review of our supply arrangements with them to determine whether we should be considered for debarment. If we are debarred, we would be prohibited for a specified period of time from entering into new supply arrangements with such government entities. In addition, after a government entity has debarred Symbol, other government entities are likely to act similarly, subject to applicable law. Governmental entities constitute an important customer group for Symbol, and debarment from governmental supply arrangements at a significant level could have an adverse effect on our business, results of operations and financial condition.

In March 2003, Robert Asti, Symbol's former Vice President—North America Sales & Services—Finance, who left Symbol in March 2001, pleaded guilty to two counts of securities fraud in connection with matters that are the subject of the Commission and the Eastern District investigations. These counts included allegations that Mr. Asti acted together with other unnamed high-ranking corporate executives at Symbol to, among other things, manufacture revenue through sham "round-trip" transactions. The Commission has also filed a civil complaint asserting similar allegations against Mr. Asti.

In June 2003, Robert Korkuc, Symbol's former Chief Accounting Officer, who left Symbol in March 2003, pleaded guilty to two counts of securities fraud in connection with matters that are the subject of the Commission and the Eastern District investigations. These counts included allegations that Mr. Korkuc acted with others at Symbol in a fraudulent scheme to inflate various measures of Symbol's financial performance. The Commission also has filed a civil complaint asserting similar allegations against Mr. Korkuc.

Symbol is attempting to negotiate a resolution with each of the Commission and the Eastern District to the mutual satisfaction of the parties involved. In either case, an agreement has not yet been reached and there is no guarantee that Symbol will be able to successfully negotiate a resolution.

1.106

TENET HEALTHCARE CORPORATION (DEC)

NOTES TO CONSOLIDATED FINANCIAL STATEMENTS

Note 15 (In Part): Claims and Lawsuits

We and our subsidiaries are subject to a significant number of claims and lawsuits. We also are the subject of federal and state agencies' heightened and coordinated civil and criminal investigations and enforcement efforts, and have received subpoenas and other requests for information relating to a variety of subjects. In the present environment, we expect these enforcement activities to take on additional importance, that government enforcement activities will intensify, and that additional matters concerning us and our subsidiaries may arise. We also expect similar and new claims and lawsuits to be brought against us from time to time.

The results of these claims and lawsuits cannot be predicted, and it is reasonably possible that the ultimate resolution of these claims and lawsuits, individually or in the aggregate, may have a material adverse effect on our business both in the near and long term, financial position, results of operations or cash flows. Although we defend ourselves vigorously against claims and lawsuits and cooperate with investigations, these matters (1) could require us to pay substantial damages or amounts in judgments or settlements, which individually or in the aggregate could exceed amounts, if any, that may be recovered under our insurance policies where coverage applies and is available, (2) cause us to incur substantial expenses, (3) require significant time and attention from our management, and (4) could cause us to close or sell hospitals or otherwise modify the way we conduct our business. We record reserves for claims and lawsuits when they are probable and reasonably estimable.

Currently pending legal proceedings and investigations that are not in the ordinary course of business are principally related to the subject matters set forth below. We undertake no obligation to update this disclosure for any new developments.

1. Physician Relationships

We and certain of our subsidiaries are under scrutiny with respect to our hospitals' relationships with physicians. We believe that all aspects of our relationships with physicians potentially are under review. Proceedings in this area may be criminal, civil or both. One indication of the level of scrutiny we are under in this area is that a federal grand jury in San Diego, California on July 17, 2003 returned an indictment accusing Alvarado Hospital Medical Center, Inc. and Tenet HealthSystem Hospitals, Inc. (both Tenet subsidiaries) of illegal use of physician relocation, recruitment and consulting agreements. (Tenet HealthSystem Hospitals, Inc. is the legal entity that was doing business as Alvarado Hospital Medical Center during some of the period of time covered by the indictment.) Relocation agreements with physicians also are the subject of a criminal investigation by the United States Attorney's Office in Los Angeles, California, which recently served on us and several of our subsidiaries administrative subpoenas seeking documents related to physician relocation agreements at certain Southern California hospitals owned by our subsidiaries, as well as summary information about physician relocation agreements related to all of our hospitals subsidiaries. In addition, physician relationships at several Southern California hospitals and in El Paso, Texas are the subject of ongoing federal investigations, and we are cooperating with the government regarding investigations into other matters, including coronary procedures and billing practices at three hospitals in Southern California. Also, federal government agencies are conducting an investigation into agreements with the Women's Cancer Center, a physician's group practicing in the field of gynecologic oncology, and certain physicians affiliated with that group. An administrative subpoena for documents from us and several of our hospital subsidiaries relating to that investigation was issued in April 2003. Further, in June 2003, the Florida Medicaid Fraud Control Unit issued an investigative subpoena to us seeking the production of employee personnel records and contracts with physicians, physician assistants, therapists and management companies from the Florida hospitals owned by our subsidiaries. Since such date, we have received additional requests for information from that unit. Additionally, we have entered into a Letter of Understanding outlining the broad terms of a proposed settlement of a *qui tam* lawsuit under the False Claims Act concerning physician employment contracts and Medicare claims, which was filed by a former employee in 1997 after his employment with one of our subsidiaries was terminated. We have adequately provided for the proposed settlement as of December 31, 2003, pursuant to the Letter of Understanding. Separately, the Department of Justice (DOJ) has been

investigating certain hospital billings to Medicare for inpatient stays reimbursed under the diagnosis-related group system from January 1, 1992 to June 30, 2000. The investigation has focused on the coding of the patients' post-discharge status. The investigation arose from the federal government's nationwide transfer-discharge initiative. In January 2004, we reached an understanding with attorneys at the DOJ to recommend settlement of all civil claims against us with respect to the transfer-discharge matter at substantially all Tenet hospitals, subject to further approval by the DOJ and negotiation of a definitive agreement. We have adequately provided for the proposed settlement of this matter as of December 31, 2003.

2. Pricing (In Part)

We and certain of our subsidiaries are currently subject to governmental investigations and civil lawsuits arising out of the pricing strategies implemented at facilities owned by our subsidiaries. In that regard, federal government agencies are investigating whether outlier payments made to certain hospitals owned by our subsidiaries were paid in accordance with Medicare laws and regulations, and whether we omitted material facts concerning our outlier revenue from our public filings. In addition, plaintiffs in California Tennessee, Louisiana, Florida, South Carolina and Pennsylvania have brought class action lawsuits against us and certain of our subsidiaries in courts in those states alleging that they paid unlawful or unfair prices for prescription drugs or medical products or procedures at hospitals or other medical facilities owned by our subsidiaries. While the specific allegations vary from case to case, the plaintiffs generally allege that we and our hospital subsidiaries have engaged in an unlawful scheme to inflate charges for medical services and procedures, pharmaceutical supplies and other products, and prescription drugs.

3. Securities and Shareholder Matters (In Part)

The Securities and Exchange Commission is conducting a formal investigation of us and certain of our current and former directors and officers with respect to whether the disclosures in our financial reports of Medicare outlier reimbursements and stop-loss payments under managed care contracts were misleading or otherwise inadequate, and includes whether there was any improper trading in our securities by our current and former directors and officers. The SEC has served a series of document requests and deposition subpoenas of current and former employees, and we are cooperating with the government with respect to the investigation.

4. Redding Medical Center, Inc. (In Part)

On August 4, 2003, following an investigation by federal government agencies regarding whether two physicians who had staff privileges at Redding Medical Center performed medically unnecessary invasive cardiac procedures at the hospital, we reached a settlement in the amount of $54 million with the United States and the State of California. This settlement resolves all civil and monetary administrative claims that the United States and the State of California may have had arising out of the performance of, and billing for, allegedly medically unnecessary cardiac procedures at Redding Medical Center from January 1, 1997 through December 31, 2002.

We have been informed by the U.S. Attorney's Office for the Eastern District of California that it will not initiate any criminal charges against us for the conduct covered by the settlement. The Office of the Inspector General (OIG) of the U.S. Department of Health and Human Services agreed to the settlement, but reserved the right to pursue possible administrative action later. On September 3, 2003, the OIG issued a notice of its intent to exclude Redding Medical Center from participation in the Medicare and Medicaid programs and other federal health care programs. On December 11, 2003, we announced that, as part of an agreement with the OIG, we would seek a buyer for Redding Medical Center. Pending the sale, the OIG exclusion proceeding has been stayed.

5. Medicare Coding

The Medicare coding practices at hospitals owned by our subsidiaries also are under increased scrutiny. The federal government in January 2003 filed a civil lawsuit against us and certain of our subsidiaries relating to hospital billings to Medicare for inpatient stays reimbursed pursuant to four particular diagnosis-related groups. The government in this lawsuit has alleged violations of the False Claims Act and various common law claims.

6. Other Matters (In Part)

We are subject to an investigation by the Finance Committee of the United States Senate concerning Redding Medical Center, Medicare outlier payments, patient care and other matters. In addition, we are one of 20 large health care systems in the United States that has received requests for documents and information as part of an investigation by the U.S. House of Representatives, Committee on Energy and Commerce, into hospital billing practices and their impact on the uninsured.

In connection with an investigation by the United States Attorney's Office in New Orleans, People's Health Network, a New Orleans health plan management services provider in which a Tenet subsidiary holds a 50% membership interest, and Memorial Medical Center, a New Orleans hospital owned by a Tenet subsidiary, have received requests for documents. The subpoenas cover the time period January 1, 1999 to the present and seek various People's Health Network-related corporate records, as well as information on patients who were admitted to a rehabilitation unit and members for whom inpatient rehabilitation services were ordered, recommended or requested, and subsequently denied. The subpoenas also seek documents related to payments to and contractual matters related to physicians and others, third-party reviews of denials of services, and certain medical staff committees and other medical staff entities.

Possible Tax Assessments

1.107

BRUNSWICK CORPORATION (DEC)

NOTES TO CONSOLIDATED FINANCIAL STATEMENTS

8 (In Part): Income Taxes

In 2003, the Company lowered its annual effective tax rate from 36.0 percent to 32.75 percent, due in part to the prepayment of the United States Tax Court matter discussed in *Note 9, Commitments and Contingencies.* As a result of the prepayment, the Company will no longer need to accrue interest costs associated with the United States Tax Court matter. These net after-tax interest costs were previously included in the income tax provision. Additionally, the Company generated higher foreign and state earnings in lower effective-tax-rate jurisdictions.

9 (In Part): Commitments and Contingencies

Legal and Environmental (In Part)

In February 2003, the United States Tax Court issued a ruling upholding the disallowance by the Internal Revenue Service (IRS) of capital losses and other expenses for 1990 and 1991 related to two partnership investments entered into by the Company. Although the Company has filed a notice of appeal of the Tax Court decision to the United States Court of Appeals for the District of Columbia, the Company is in settlement negotiations with the IRS to resolve this matter. The amount of tax and interest associated with the two partnership investments is approximately $135 million, consisting of $60 million in taxes due plus $75 million of interest, net of tax. The Company expects the $135 million to be reduced to approximately $50 million, consisting of $28 million in taxes due and $22 million in interest, net of tax, as a result of the settlement of a number of issues and favorable adjustments with the IRS on open tax years 1989 through 1994. In April 2003, the Company elected to pay the IRS $62 million (approximately $50 million after-tax) in connection with this matter while the appeal is pending and settlement negotiations are continuing. The payment was comprised of $28 million in taxes due and $34 million of pre-tax interest ($22 million after-tax). The Company elected to make this payment to avoid future interest costs. No penalties have been formally asserted by the IRS to date. The Company believes, based on currently available information, that any penalties and accrued interest would not have a material adverse effect on the Company's consolidated financial position or results of operations.

1.108

W. R. GRACE & CO. (DEC)

NOTES TO CONSOLIDATED FINANCIAL STATEMENTS

14 (In Part): Commitments and Contingent Liabilities

Tax Matters

Grace has received the examination report from the Internal Revenue Service (the "IRS") for tax periods 1993 through 1996 asserting, in the aggregate, approximately $114.0 million of proposed tax adjustments, including accrued interest. The most significant contested issue addressed in such report concerns corporate-owned life insurance ("COLI") policies and is discussed below. Other proposed IRS tax adjustments include Grace's tax position regarding research and development credits, the reporting of certain divestitures and other miscellaneous proposed adjustments. The tax audit for the 1993 through 1996 tax period was under the jurisdiction of the IRS Office of Appeals, where Grace filed a protest. The IRS Office of Appeals has returned the audit to the examination team for further review of the proposed adjustments as well as several affirmative tax claims raised by Grace. Grace's federal tax returns covering periods 1997 and forward are either under examination by the IRS or open for future examination. In addition, Grace will be required to report the additional taxable income (and the related accrued interest) resulting from IRS adjustments to state and local tax jurisdictions upon resolution of the Federal tax audits. Grace believes that the impact of probable tax return adjustments are adequately recognized as liabilities at December 31, 2003. Any cash payment as a result of such adjustment would be subject to Grace's Chapter 11 proceedings.

In 1988 and 1990, Grace acquired COLI policies on the lives of certain of its employees as part of a strategy to fund the cost of postretirement employee health care benefits and other long-term liabilities. COLI premiums have been funded in part by loans issued against the cash surrender value of the COLI policies. The IRS is challenging deductions on interest on loans secured by COLI policies for years prior to 1999. In 2000, Grace paid $21.2 million of tax and interest related to this issue for tax years 1990 through 1992. Subsequent to 1992, Grace deducted approximately $163.2 million in interest attributable to COLI policy loans. Although Grace continues to believe that the deductions were legitimate, the IRS has successfully challenged interest deductions claimed by other corporations with respect to broad-based COLI policies in three out of four litigated cases. Given the level of IRS success in COLI cases, Grace requested and was granted early referral to the IRS Office of Appeals for consideration of possible settlement alternatives of the COLI interest deduction issue.

On September 23, 2002, Grace filed a motion in its Chapter 11 proceeding requesting that the Bankruptcy Court authorize Grace to enter into a settlement agreement with the IRS with respect to Grace's COLI interest deductions. The tax years at issue are 1989 through 1998. Under the terms of the proposed settlement, the government would allow 20% of the aggregate amount of the COLI interest deductions and Grace would owe federal income tax and interest on the remaining 80%. Grace has accrued for the potential tax and interest liability related to the disallowance of all COLI interest deductions and continues to accrue interest as part of its quarterly income tax provision. On October 22, 2002, the Bankruptcy Court issued an order authorizing Grace to enter into settlement discussions with the IRS consistent with the aforementioned terms and further ordered that any final agreement would be subject to Bankruptcy Court approval. Grace is currently in negotiations with the IRS concerning the proposed settlement, and the possible termination of the COLI policies.

The IRS has assessed additional federal income tax withholding and Federal Insurance Contributions Act taxes plus interest and related penalties for calendar years 1993 through 1995 against a Grace subsidiary that formerly operated a temporary staffing business for nurses and other health care personnel. The assessments, aggregating $21.8 million, were made in connection with a meal and incidental expense per diem plan for traveling health care personnel, which was in effect through 1999, the year in which Grace sold the business. The IRS contends that certain per diem reimbursements should have been treated as wages subject to employment taxes and federal income tax withholding. Grace contends that its per diem and expense allowance plans were in accordance with statutory and regulatory requirements, as well as other published guidance from the IRS. The IRS has issued additional assessments aggregating $40.1 million for the 1996 through 1998 tax periods. The statute of limitations has expired with respect to the 1999 tax year. Grace has a right to indemnification for approximately 36% of any tax liability (including interest thereon) for the period from July, 1996 through December, 1998 from its former partner in the business. The matter is currently pending in the United States Court of Claims. Grace is currently in discussions with the Department of Justice concerning possible settlement options. Grace does not expect the resolution of this matter to have significant adverse impact on its Consolidated Financial Statements.

Accounting for Contingencies

Although the outcome of each of the matters discussed above cannot be predicted with certainty, Grace has assessed its risk and has made accounting estimates as required under U.S. generally accepted accounting principles. As a result of the Filing, claims related to certain of the items discussed above will be addressed as part of Grace's Chapter 11 proceedings. Accruals recorded for such contingencies have been included in "liabilities subject to compromise" on the accompanying Consolidated Balance Sheets. The amounts of these liabilities as ultimately determined through the Chapter 11 proceedings could be materially different from amounts recorded by Grace at December 31, 2003.

Guarantees

1.109

BRIGGS & STRATTON CORPORATION (JUN)

NOTES TO CONSOLIDATED FINANCIAL STATEMENTS

9) (In Part): Commitments and Contingencies

In October 1998, the Company joined seventeen other companies in guaranteeing a $17.9 million letter of credit issued as a guarantee of certain City of Milwaukee Revenue Bonds used to develop a residential rental property. The Revenue Bonds were issued on behalf of a not-for-profit organization established to manage the project and rental property post construction. The revenues from the rental property are used to fund operating expenses and all debt service requirements. The Company's share of the guarantee and the maximum exposure to the Company under the agreement is $1.8 million. The letter of credit and underlying guarantee expires August 15, 2008. Management believes the likelihood is remote that material payments will be required under this guarantee. Accordingly, no liability has been reflected in the accompanying Consolidated Balance Sheets related to this item.

GAIN CONTINGENCIES

Plaintiff Litigation

1.110

A. O. SMITH CORPORATION (DEC)

NOTES TO CONSOLIDATED FINANCIAL STATEMENTS

14 (In Part): Litigation and Insurance Matters

In 1999, a class action lawsuit was filed in the United States District Court, Western District of Missouri, by individuals on behalf of themselves and all persons throughout the United States who have owned or currently own a water heater manufactured by Rheem Manufacturing Company, A. O. Smith Corporation, Bradford White Company, American Water Heater Company, Lochinvar Corporation and State Industries, Inc. (the "water heater manufacturers") that contains a dip tube manufactured, designed, supplied, or sold by Perfection Corporation between August 1993 and October 1996. A dip tube is a plastic tube in a residential water heater that brings the cold water supply to the bottom area of the tank to be heated. The plaintiffs and the water heater manufacturers reached a settlement of this lawsuit which the Court approved in 2000. The water heater manufacturers paid the settlement, and all other legal actions brought against the water heater manufacturers related to dip tube claims have been dismissed as a result of the settlement of the class action.

Separately, the water heater manufacturers in late 1999 filed a direct action lawsuit in the Civil District Court for the Parish of Orleans, State of Louisiana, against Perfection Corporation and American Meter Company, the parent company

of Perfection, and their insurers. This lawsuit seeks (1) recovery of damages sustained by the water heater manufacturers related to the costs of the class action settlement and the handling of dip tube claims outside of and prior to the national class action settlement, (2) damages for the liability of the water heater manufacturers assumed by Perfection Corporation by contract and (3) personal injuries suffered by the water heater manufacturers as a result of the disparagement of their businesses. Also relating to the water heater manufacturers' recovery efforts, the insurers of Perfection Corporation have brought third-party claims against the water heater manufacturers in a state court action in Cook County, Illinois. This action has been stayed by order of the Court.

Perfection Corporation has also sued the water heater manufacturers in a separate action in Cook County, Illinois. The filing by Perfection Corporation is an attempt to preempt the Louisiana lawsuit. This action has been stayed by order of the Court.

As of December 31, 2003 and 2002, respectively, the company recorded a long-term receivable of $34.0 million (as detailed below) related to dip tube repair claims, administrative costs, legal fees, and related expenses.

(Dollars in millions)	
Claim payments	$22.3
Administrative costs	7.5
Legal fees	4.2
	$34.0

It is the company's expectation that all or a substantial portion of its costs will be recovered from Perfection Corporation, American Meter Company and their insurers, as well as the company's insurers. The water heater manufacturers have negotiated settlements with 11 insurers of Perfection Corporation and American Meter Company with the proceeds of the settlements being placed in escrow. Negotiating opportunities with Perfection Corporation, American Meter Company and the two remaining insurance company defendants in the lawsuit continues to be available. Management also believes the two defendant companies have the financial ability to pay a judgment. The company has initiated the claim process with the company's insurers and reasonably believes that, if necessary, coverage provisions would apply. Management also believes the two insurance companies have the financial ability to pay a judgment.

1.111

SCIENTIFIC-ATLANTA, INC. (JUN)

NOTES TO CONSOLIDATED FINANCIAL STATEMENTS

16 (In Part): Legal Proceedings

Gemstar-Related Legal Proceedings

We have filed several lawsuits as plaintiff against Gemstar-TV Guide International, Inc. and affiliated and/or related companies. Gemstar-TV Guide International, Inc. and/or its affiliated entities are referred to hereafter as "Gemstar."

Multi-District Proceedings

On December 3, 1998, we filed an action against Gemstar in the U.S. District Court in Atlanta, Georgia. The suit alleges that Gemstar has violated federal antitrust laws and has misused certain patents. We seek damages, an injunction and a declaration that eight Gemstar patents related to interactive program guides are invalid, unenforceable and not infringed by our products. On December 4, 1998, Gemstar filed a responsive action against us in the United States District Court in Los Angeles, California alleging infringement of two of the same patents involved in the Atlanta, Georgia suit filed by us on December 3, 1998. The suit asks for damages and injunctive relief. This case has been consolidated in the Atlanta action.

We have been granted summary judgment of non-infringement of five Gemstar patents in this action, U.S. Patent Nos. 5,508,815; 5,568,272; 4,751,578; 5,038,211; and 5,293,357. The parties have also filed a consent order to dismiss all claims of infringement and invalidity related to a sixth Gemstar patent in this action. U.S. Patent No. 4,963,994. On July 18, 2003 we filed motions for summary judgment of non-infringement in relation to all claims of two other patents-in-suit in this action, U.S. Patent Nos. 5,915,068 and 4,908,713. Based on prior rulings of the court, the parties have submitted a consent order granting summary judgment of non-infringement of the '713 patent by Scientific-Atlanta's Explorer line of set-top boxes; Gemstar's claims relating to our 8600x set-top boxes remain in issue.

On March 14, 2003, in the Atlanta antitrust action, Gemstar filed three Motions for Partial Summary Judgment of three of our antitrust claims. We filed responsive briefs to these motions on April 14, 2003. The judge has not yet ruled on these motions.

Scientific-Atlanta Patents Proceedings

On April 23, 1999, we filed a patent infringement action against Gemstar in U.S. District Court in Atlanta. On July 23, 1999, we filed a patent infringement action against Star-Sight Telecast, Inc., a subsidiary of Gemstar International Group Ltd., in the U.S. District Court in Atlanta. These suits allege that Gemstar and StarSight infringe three Scientific-Atlanta patents, U.S. Patent Nos. 4,885,775, 4,991,011, and 5,477,262, relating to interactive program guides, and seeks damages and injunctive relief. The parties have filed briefs supporting their proposed interpretations of the claims of the patents. A "Markman Hearing" on these motions has been held and we await a claim interpretation ruling by the judge.

International Trade Commission and Related Proceedings

On June 25, 1999, we filed an action against StarSight in the U.S. District Court in Atlanta, seeking a declaratory judgment of invalidity and non-infringement of two StarSight patents, U.S. Patent Nos. 4,706,121 and 5,479,268, which StarSight asserts are related to interactive program guides. Thereafter Gemstar sought to raise claims under these same patents in an investigation by the International Trade Commission (ITC) (described in more detail below). The District Court action involving these patents has now been stayed by agreement of the parties, pending the outcome of Gemstar's appeal of the Final Determination of the ITC.

On February 14, 2001, Gemstar initiated an investigation in the ITC under Section 337 of the Tariff Act of 1930 (the "Act") against Scientific-Atlanta, Pioneer Corporation and related entities, Echostar Communications Corporation and SCI Systems, Inc. The investigation was based on Gemstar's allegation that certain imported set-top boxes, including those manufactured by Scientific-Atlanta in Mexico, infringe certain Gemstar patents. Two of these patents have been in dispute between the parties in connection with the June 25, 1999 action in the federal court in Atlanta. Immediately prior to filing the 337 action, Gemstar filed separate actions against Scientific-Atlanta, Pioneer and Echostar in the federal court in Atlanta alleging infringement of certain of the patents claimed in the 337 action. Scientific-Atlanta moved to stay any proceedings in these actions pending the outcome of the 337 action.

On June 21, 2002, the Administrative Law Judge in the ITC action issued an Initial Determination finding in favor of Scientific-Atlanta as to non-infringement and unenforceability of Gemstar's patents. The Administrative Law Judge found that Scientific-Atlanta does not infringe the three Gemstar patents in suit; that one of the three patents in suit is unenforceable for failure to name an inventor; and that Gemstar had engaged in patent misuse rendering one of its patents unenforceable. On August 29, 2002 the full ITC determined not to review any issues regarding patent infringement or inventorship. By declining to review those issues, the ITC adopted the findings of the Initial Determination that Scientific-Atlanta's products do not infringe the patents in issue. The ITC determined to take no position on the issue of Gemstar's patent misuse. In light of these determinations, the ITC concluded that there is no violation of the Tariff Act of 1930 by Scientific-Atlanta. On March 6, 2003, Gemstar appealed the decision of the ITC to the Court of Appeals for the Federal Circuit. All briefs have been filed by all parties in the appeal and oral argument is scheduled for October 10, 2003.

In the cases involving our patents, we seek both damages and an injunction against the Gemstar defendants' deployment of infringing program guides. In the cases challenging the Gemstar defendants' patents, we seek an injunction against Gemstar's enforcement of these patents. In those cases where Gemstar's patents are at issue, they have sought damages and injunctive relief against us for infringement of certain of those patents. The party or parties prevailing on their patents in these actions could be entitled to damages measured either as actual lost profits or as a reasonable royalty for the past sale of infringing interactive program guides, and potentially a trebling of damages if the court determines that the losing party acted willfully. The prevailing party also may be entitled to an injunction against the future sale of infringing interactive program guides. Accordingly, an adverse judgment against either us or the Gemstar defendants could result in an injunction against the future sale by us or the Gemstar defendants of infringing interactive program guides and could cause the offending party to have to redesign their program guide to avoid infringement.

Contingent Receivables

1.112

CHESAPEAKE CORPORATION (DEC)

NOTES TO CONSOLIDATED FINANCIAL STATEMENTS

3 (In Part): Discontinued Operations

In the fourth quarter of 2000, we decided to sell the principal businesses that were included in our former Merchandising and Specialty Packaging segment and the remaining interest in our former Tissue segment, a 5 percent equity interest in Georgia-Pacific Tissue, LLC (the "Tissue JV"). These segments are accounted for as discontinued operations.

The businesses that made up the Merchandising and Specialty Packaging segment were:

- Consumer Promotions International, Inc. ("CPI"), which designed, manufactured and assembled permanent point-of-purchase displays, sold on October 15, 2001, to a management investment group.

• • • • • •

The consideration for these discontinued operations consisted of cash proceeds of approximately $427.1 million and promissory notes of approximately $42.6 million. During 2002, we received cash prepayments on these promissory notes of $24.9 million. As of December 28, 2003, there were remaining note balances of $16.9 million due from CPI that are collateralized by subordinated liens on substantially all of CPI's U.S. assets. In accordance with the terms of the CPI term note, the principal balance has been adjusted for the working capital settlement related to the sale and accrued interest. Included in the promissory notes was a $13.6 million performance note received from CPI which is payable based on the financial performance of CPI during the period from October 15, 2001, through October 10, 2006. The performance note has been fully reserved because payments due on it are contingent on future events which are not determinable at this time.

RISKS AND UNCERTAINTIES

1.113 Statement of Position (SOP) 94-6, *Disclosure of Certain Significant Risks and Uncertainties,* issued by the Accounting Standards Division of the American Institute of Certified Public Accountants (AICPA), requires reporting entities to disclose information about the nature of their operations, the use of estimates in preparing financial statements, certain significant estimates, and vulnerabilities due to certain concentrations.

1.114 Examples of disclosures made by the survey companies to conform to the requirements of *SOP 94-6* follow.

Nature of Operations

1.115

AMERADA HESS CORPORATION (DEC)

NOTES TO CONSOLIDATED FINANCIAL STATEMENTS

1 (In Part): Summary of Significant Accounting Policies

Nature of Business (In Part)

Amerada Hess Corporation and subsidiaries (the "Corporation") engage in the exploration for and the production, purchase, transportation and sale of crude oil and natural gas. These activities are conducted primarily in the United States, United Kingdom, Norway, Denmark, Equatorial Guinea and Algeria. The Corporation also has oil and gas activities in Azerbaijan, Gabon, Indonesia, Malaysia, Thailand and other countries. In addition, the Corporation manufactures, purchases, transports, trades and markets refined petroleum and other energy products. The Corporation owns 50% of HOVENSA L.L.C., a refinery joint venture in the United States Virgin Islands. An additional refining facility, terminals and retail gasoline stations are located on the East Coast of the United States.

1.116

AMPCO-PITTSBURGH CORPORATION (DEC)

NOTES TO CONSOLIDATED FINANCIAL STATEMENTS

Description of Business

Ampco-Pittsburgh Corporation (the Corporation) is in two business segments that manufacture and sell primarily custom-engineered equipment. The Forged and Cast Rolls segment, consisting of Union Electric Steel and Davy Roll, located in England, manufactures and sells forged hardened steel rolls and cast rolls (iron and steel) to the metals industry. The Air and Liquid Processing segment consists of Aerofin-heat exchange coils, Buffalo Air Handling-air handling systems, and Buffalo Pumps-centrifugal pumps, all of which sell to a variety of commercial and industrial users. The Corporation previously operated in a third segment, the Plastics Processing Machinery segment, which was sold in August 2003.

1.117

ANALOGIC CORPORATION (JUL)

NOTES TO CONSOLIDATED FINANCIAL STATEMENTS

1 (In Part): Summary of Business Operations and Significant Accounting Policies

Business Operations

Analogic Corporation and its subsidiaries ("Analogic" or the "Company") are engaged primarily in the design, manufacture and sale of high technology, high performance, high-precision data acquisition, conversion (analog/digital) and signal processing instruments and systems to customers that manufacture products for medical and industrial use. The Company is subject to risks common to companies in the medical instrumentation technology industry, including, but not limited to, development by its competitors of new technological innovations, dependence on key personnel, loss of any significant customer, protection of proprietary technology, and compliance with regulations of domestic and foreign regulatory authorities and agencies.

Use of Estimates

1.118

AK STEEL HOLDING CORPORATION (DEC)

NOTES TO CONSOLIDATED FINANCIAL STATEMENTS

1 (In Part): Summary of Significant Accounting Policies

Use of Estimates

The preparation of financial statements in conformity with accounting principles generally accepted in the United States of America requires the use of management estimates and assumptions that affect the amounts reported. These estimates are based on historical experience and information that is available to management about current events and actions the Company may take in the future. Significant items subject to estimates and assumptions include the carrying value of long-lived assets; valuation allowances for receivables, inventories and deferred income tax assets; legal and environmental liabilities; and assets and obligations related to employee benefit plans. There can be no assurance that actual results will not differ from these estimates.

1.119

THE DOW CHEMICAL COMPANY (DEC)

NOTES TO CONSOLIDATED FINANCIAL STATEMENTS

Note A (In Part): Summary of Significant Accounting Policies and Accounting Changes

Use of Estimates in Financial Statement Preparation

The preparation of financial statements in conformity with GAAP requires the use of estimates and assumptions that affect the reported amounts of assets and liabilities, the disclosure of contingent assets and liabilities at the date of the financial statements, and the reported amounts of revenues and expenses during the reporting period. The Company's consolidated financial statements include amounts that are based on management's best estimates and judgments. Actual results could differ from those estimates.

1.120

PALL CORPORATION (JUL)

NOTES TO CONSOLIDATED FINANCIAL STATEMENTS

Accounting Policies and Related Matters (In Part)

Presentation and Use of Estimates (In Part)

To prepare the Company's consolidated financial statements in accordance with accounting principles generally accepted in the United States of America, management is required to make assumptions that may affect the reported amounts of assets and liabilities and the disclosure of contingent assets and liabilities at the date of the consolidated financial statements and the reported amounts of revenue and expenses during the reporting period. Estimates are used for, but not limited to, inventory valuation; provisions for doubtful accounts; asset impairment; depreciable lives of fixed assets and useful lives of patents and amortizable intangibles; fair value of financial instruments; income tax assets and liabilities; pension valuations; restructuring and other charges; valuation of assets acquired and liabilities assumed in business combinations; and liabilities for environmental remediation. The Company is subject to uncertainties such as the impact of future events, economic, environmental and political factors, and changes in the business climate; therefore, actual results may differ from those estimates. Accordingly, the accounting estimates used in the preparation of the Company's consolidated financial statements will change as new events occur, as more experience is acquired, as additional information is obtained and as the Company's operating environment changes. Changes in estimates are made when circumstances warrant. Such changes and refinements in estimation methodologies are reflected in reported results of operations; if material, the effects of changes in estimates are disclosed in the notes to the consolidated financial statements.

1.121

SUN MICROSYSTEMS, INC. (JUN)

NOTES TO CONSOLIDATED FINANCIAL STATEMENTS

2 (In Part): Summary of Significant Accounting Policies

Basis of Presentation (In Part)

Our consolidated financial statements have been prepared in accordance with generally accepted accounting principles in the United States (US GAAP). The preparation of these financial statements requires us to make estimates and judgments that affect the reported amounts in the financial statements and accompanying notes. These estimates form the basis for judgments we make about the carrying values of assets and liabilities that are not readily apparent from other sources. We base our estimates and judgments on historical experience and on various other assumptions that we believe are reasonable under the circumstances. However, future events are subject to change and the best estimates and judgments routinely require adjustment. US GAAP requires us to make estimates and judgments in several areas, including those related to impairment of intangible assets and equity investments, revenue recognition, recoverability of inventory and accounts receivable, the fair value of derivative financial instruments, the recording of various accruals (including our accrual for restructuring charges), the useful lives of long-lived assets such as property and equipment, income taxes, warranty obligations and potential losses from contingencies and litigation. Actual results in these particular areas could differ from those estimates.

Significant Estimates

1.122

ADMINISTAFF, INC. (DEC)

NOTES TO CONSOLIDATED FINANCIAL STATEMENTS

1 (In Part): Accounting Policies

Revenue and Direct Cost Recognition

The Company accounts for its revenues in accordance with EITF 99-19, *Reporting Revenues Gross as a Principal Versus Net as an Agent.* The Company's revenues are derived from its gross billings, which are based on (i) the payroll cost of its worksite employees; and (ii) a markup computed as a percentage of the payroll cost. The gross billings are invoiced concurrently with each periodic payroll of its worksite employees. Revenues are recognized ratably over the payroll period as worksite employees perform their service at the client worksite. Revenues that have been recognized but not invoiced are included in unbilled accounts receivable on the Company's Consolidated Balance Sheets.

In determining the pricing of the markup component of the gross billings, the Company takes into consideration its estimates of the costs directly associated with its worksite employees, including payroll taxes, benefits and workers' compensation costs, plus an acceptable gross profit margin.

As a result, the Company's operating results are significantly impacted by the Company's ability to accurately estimate, control and manage its direct costs relative to the revenues derived from the markup component of the Company's gross billings.

Consistent with its revenue recognition policy, the Company's direct costs do not include the payroll cost of its worksite employees. The Company's direct costs associated with its revenue generating activities are comprised of all other costs related to its worksite employees, such as the employer portion of payroll-related taxes, employee benefit plan premiums and workers' compensation insurance costs.

1.123

POLYONE CORPORATION (DEC)

NOTES TO CONSOLIDATED FINANCIAL STATEMENTS

Note C (In Part): Summary of Significant Accounting Policies

Use of Estimates

The preparation of consolidated financial statements in conformity with generally accepted accounting principles requires management to make extensive use of certain estimates and assumptions that affect the reported amounts of assets and liabilities and disclosure of contingent assets and liabilities at the date of the consolidated financial statements, as well as the reported amounts of revenues and expenses during the reported periods. Significant estimates in these consolidated financial statements include restructuring and other non-recurring (credits) charges, purchase accounting reserves, allowances for doubtful accounts receivable, estimates of future cash flows associated with assets, asset impairments, useful lives for depreciation and amortization, loss contingencies, net realizable value of inventories, environmental liabilities, income taxes and tax valuation reserves, and the determination of discount and other rate assumptions for pension and post-retirement employee benefit expenses. Actual results could differ from these estimates.

Note O (In Part): Commitments and Related-Party Information

Environmental

PolyOne has been notified by federal and state environmental agencies and by private parties that it may be a potentially responsible party (PRP) in connection with several environmental sites. While government agencies frequently claim PRPs are jointly and severally liable at these sites, in PolyOne's experience, interim and final allocation of liability costs are generally made based on the relative contribution of waste. PolyOne believes that its potential continuing liability with respect to such sites will not have a material adverse effect on its consolidated financial position, results of operations or cash flows. In addition, PolyOne initiates corrective and preventive environmental projects of its own to ensure safe and lawful activities at its operations. PolyOne believes that compliance with current governmental regulations at all levels will not have a material adverse effect on its financial condition. Based on estimates prepared by our environmental engineers and consultants, PolyOne, at December 31, 2003, had accruals totaling $54.7 million to cover probable future environmental expenditures relating to previously contaminated sites. The accrual represents PolyOne's best estimate, net of estimated insurance recoveries, for the remaining probable remediation costs, based upon information and technology currently available and PolyOne's view of the most likely remedy. Depending upon the results of future testing, the ultimate remediation alternatives undertaken, changes in regulations, new information, newly discovered conditions and other factors, it is reasonably possible that PolyOne could incur additional costs in excess of the accrued amount at December 31, 2003. However, such additional costs, if any, cannot be currently estimated. PolyOne's estimate of the liability may be revised as new regulations or technologies are developed or additional information is obtained. PolyOne incurred environmental expense of $4.1 million in 2003, $3.5 million in 2002 and $3.7 million in 2001.

1.124

SPX CORPORATION (DEC)

NOTES TO CONSOLIDATED FINANCIAL STATEMENTS
(Dollar amounts in millions)

2) Use of Estimates

The preparation of our consolidated financial statements in conformity with GAAP requires us to make estimates and assumptions. These estimates and assumptions affect the reported amounts of assets and liabilities, the disclosure of contingent assets and liabilities at the date of the consolidated financial statements, and the reported amounts of revenues and expenses during the reporting period. We evaluate these estimates and judgments on an ongoing basis and base our estimates on experience, current and expected future conditions, third party evaluations and various other assumptions that we believe are reasonable under the circumstances. The results of these estimates form the basis for making judgments about the carrying values of assets and liabilities as well as identifying and assessing the accounting treatment with respect to commitments and contingencies. Actual results may differ from the estimates and assumptions used in the financial statements and related notes.

Listed below are certain significant estimates and assumptions used in the preparation of our financial statements. Certain other estimates and assumptions are further explained in the related Notes.

Allowance for Doubtful Accounts

We estimate losses for uncollectible accounts based on the aging of the accounts receivable and the evaluation of the likelihood of success in collecting the receivable. Summarized below is the activity for the allowance for doubtful accounts.

	2003	2002	2001
Allowance for doubtful accounts:			
Balance at beginning of year	$ 32.3	$ 26.3	$ 14.2
Acquisitions/divestitures, net	2.7	3.5	10.5
Provisions	16.0	17.3	17.4
Write offs, net of recoveries	(12.2)	(14.8)	(15.8)
Balance at end of year	$ 38.8	$ 32.3	$ 26.3

Inventory

We estimate losses for excess and or obsolete inventory based on the aging of the inventory and the evaluation of the likelihood of recovering the inventory costs based on anticipated demand and selling price.

Impairment of Long-Lived Assets and Intangibles Subject to Amortization

We continually review whether events and circumstances subsequent to the acquisition of any long-lived assets, or intangible assets subject to amortization, have occurred that indicate the remaining estimated useful lives of those assets may warrant revision or that the remaining balance of those assets may not be recoverable. If events and circumstances indicate that the long-lived assets should be reviewed for possible impairment, we use projections to assess whether future cash flows on a non-discounted basis related to the tested assets are likely to exceed the recorded carrying amount of those assets to determine if a write-down is appropriate. If we identify an impairment, we will report a loss to the extent that the carrying value of the impaired assets exceeds their fair values as determined by valuation techniques appropriate in the circumstances that could include the use of similar projections on a discounted basis.

In determining the estimated useful lives of definite lived intangibles, we consider the nature, competitive position, life cycle position, and historical and expected future operating cash flows of each acquired asset, as well as our commitment to support these assets through continued investment and legal infringement protection.

Goodwill and Indefinite-Lived Intangible Assets

We test goodwill and indefinite-lived intangible assets for impairment annually as of December 31 and continually review whether triggering events have occurred to determine whether the carrying value exceeds the implied value. The fair value of reporting units is based on discounted projected cash flows, but we also consider factors such as comparable industry price multiples. We employ cash flow projections that we believed to be reasonable under current and forecasted circumstances, the results of which form the basis for making judgments about the carrying values of the reported net assets of our reporting units. Many of our businesses closely follow changes in the industries and end-markets that they serve. Accordingly, we consider estimates and judgments that affect the future cash flow projections, including principal methods of competition including volume, price, service, product performance, and technical innovations, as well as estimates associated with cost improvement initiatives, capacity utilization, and assumptions for inflation and foreign currency changes. Actual results may differ from these estimates under different assumptions or conditions. See Note 8 for more information.

Accrued Expenses

We make estimates and judgments in establishing accruals as required under GAAP. Summarized in the table below are current accrued expenses at December 31, 2003 and 2002.

	2003	2002
Employee benefits	$264.5	$256.1
Warranty	81.2	64.2
Other (1)	480.9	469.0
	$826.6	$789.3

(1) Other is comprised of various items including legal and income taxes payable, none of which individually meet the threshold for separate disclosure.

Legal

It is our policy to accrue for estimated losses from legal actions or claims, including legal expenses, when events exist that make the realization of the losses or expenses probable and they can be reasonably estimated.

Environmental Remediation Costs

We expense costs incurred to investigate and remediate environmental issues unless they extend the economic useful life of related assets. We record liabilities and report expenses when it is probable that an obligation has been incurred and the amounts can be reasonably estimated. Our environmental accruals cover anticipated costs, including investigation, remediation, and operation and maintenance of clean-up sites. Our estimates are based primarily on investigations and remediation plans established by independent consultants, regulatory agencies and potentially responsible third-parties. We do not discount environmental obligations or reduce them by anticipated insurance recoveries.

Self-Insurance

We are primarily self-insured for workers' compensation, automobile, product, and general liability costs, and we believe that we maintain adequate accruals to cover our retained liability. Our accrual for self-insurance liability is determined by management and is based on claims filed and an estimate of claims incurred but not yet reported. Management considers a number of factors, including third-party actuary valuations, when making these determinations. We maintain third party stop-loss insurance policies to cover liability costs in excess of predetermined retained amounts.

Warranty

In the normal course of business, we issue product warranties for specific product lines and provide for the estimated future warranty cost in the period in which the sale is recorded. We provide for the estimate of warranty cost based on contract terms and historical warranty loss experience that is periodically adjusted for recent actual experience. Because warranty estimates are forecasts that are based on the best available information, claims costs may differ from amounts provided. In addition, due to the seasonal fluctuations at certain of our businesses, the timing of warranty provisions and the usage of warranty accruals can vary period to period. We make adjustments to initial obligations for warranties as changes in the obligations

become reasonably estimable. The following is an analysis of our product warranty accrual in 2003:

Balance at beginning of year	$ 64.2
Acquisitions/divestitures, net	15.6
Provisions	37.7
Usage	(36.3)
Balance at end of year	$ 81.2

Employee Benefit Plans

We have defined benefit plans that cover a significant portion of our salaried and hourly paid employees, including certain employees in foreign countries. For the year ended December 31, 2003, we had $4.9 of net pension benefit income derived from our defined benefit plans. We derive pension benefit income from an actuarial calculation based on the defined benefit plans' provisions and management's assumptions regarding discount rate, rate of increase in compensation levels and expected long-term rate of return on assets. Management determines the expected long-term rate of return on plan assets based upon historical actual asset returns and the expectations of asset returns over the expected period to fund participant benefits based on the current investment mix of our plans. Management sets the discount rate based on the yield of high quality fixed income investments, commonly defined as fixed income investments with at least a Moody's AA credit rating. The rate of increase in compensation levels is established based on management's expectations of current and foreseeable future increases in compensation. In addition, management also consults with independent actuaries in determining these assumptions.

1.125

UNIVERSAL HEALTH SERVICES, INC. (DEC)

NOTES TO CONSOLIDATED FINANCIAL STATEMENTS

1) (In Part): Business and Summary of Significant Accounting Policies

B) Revenue Recognition

We record revenues and the related receivables for health care services at the time the services are provided. We have agreements with third-party payors that provide for payments to us at amounts different from our established rates. Payment arrangements include prospectively determined rates per discharge, reimbursed costs, discounted charges, and per diem payments. We report net patient service revenue at the estimated net realizable amounts from patients, third-party payors, and others for services rendered, including estimated retroactive adjustments under reimbursement agreements with third-party payors. We accrued retroactive adjustments on an estimated basis in the period the related services are rendered and adjusted in future periods as final settlements are determined.

Medicare and Medicaid revenues represented 41%, 42% and 42% of our net revenues during 2003, 2002 and 2001, respectively. Revenues from managed care entities, including health maintenance organizations and managed Medicare and Medicaid programs accounted for 41%, 39% and 37% of our revenues during 2003, 2002 and 2001, respectively. Laws and regulations governing the Medicare and Medicaid programs are extremely complex and subject to interpretation and as a result, there is at least a reasonable possibility that recorded estimates will change by material amounts in the near term. The large majority of the revenues generated by the acute care hospitals owned by our France subsidiary are paid by the government based on predetermined rates established in May of each year and consist of a per diem payment and per procedure rate plus reimbursement for certain supplies.

We provide care to patients who meet certain financial or economic criteria without charge or at amounts substantially less than established rates. Because we do not pursue collection of amounts determined to qualify as charity care, they are not reported in net revenues or accounts receivable, net.

Vulnerability Due to Certain Concentrations

1.126

CHIQUITA BRANDS INTERNATIONAL, INC. (DEC)

NOTES TO CONSOLIDATED FINANCIAL STATEMENTS

Note 15 (In Part): Segment Information

The Company had previously reported two business segments prior to the 2003 third quarter, Fresh Produce and Processed Foods. The Fresh Produce segment included the sourcing, transportation, distribution and marketing of bananas, as well as a wide variety of other fresh fruits and vegetables. The Processed Foods segment consisted primarily of the Company's vegetable canning division, which accounted for more than 90% of the net sales in this segment and was sold in May 2003. As a result of the sale of CPF and the acquisition of Atlanta, the Company's internal reporting of the results of its business units has changed, and the Company determined that it had the following two reportable segments: Bananas and Other Fresh Produce.

• • • • • •

The Company's products are sold throughout the world and its principal production and processing operations are conducted in Central and South America. Chiquita's earnings are heavily dependent upon products grown and purchased in Central and South America. These activities, a significant factor in the economies of the countries where Chiquita produces bananas and related products, are subject to the risks that are inherent in operating in such foreign countries, including government regulation, currency restrictions and other restraints, risk of expropriation, risk of political instability and burdensome taxes. Certain of these operations are substantially dependent upon leases and other agreements with these governments.

The Company is also subject to a variety of government regulations in most countries where it markets bananas and other fresh products, including health, food safety, and customs requirements, import quotas and tariffs, currency exchange controls and taxes.

1.127

GENERAL MOTORS CORPORATION (DEC)

NOTES TO CONSOLIDATED FINANCIAL STATEMENTS

Note 1 (In Part): Significant Accounting Policies

Labor Force

GM, on a worldwide basis, has a concentration of its labor supply in employees working under union collective bargaining agreements, of which certain contracts expired in 2003.

The 2003 United Auto Workers (UAW) labor contract was ratified on October 6, 2003 covering a four-year term from 2003-2007. The contract included a $3,000 lump sum payment per UAW employee paid in October 2003, and a 3% performance bonus per UAW employee to be paid in October 2004. GM will amortize these payments over the 12-month period following the respective payment dates. UAW employees will receive a gross wage increase of 2% in 2005 and 3% in 2006. Active UAW employees were also granted pension benefit increases. There were no pension benefit increases granted to current retirees and surviving spouses. However, the contract does provide for four lump sum payments and two vehicle discount vouchers for current retirees and surviving spouses. The retiree lump sum payments and vehicle discount vouchers resulted in a charge to GM's 2003 fourth quarter cost of sales of approximately $1.2 billion ($725 million after tax).

1.128

NATIONAL PRESTO INDUSTRIES, INC. (DEC)

NOTES TO CONSOLIDATED FINANCIAL STATEMENTS

J. Concentrations

For the year ended December 31, 2003, one customer accounted for 33% of net sales. One customer accounted for 37% of net sales for the year ended December 31, 2002. Two customers accounted for 37% and 11% of net sales for the year ended December 31, 2001. The preceding concentrations related to housewares/small appliance sales.

The Company sources its housewares/small appliances from the Orient and as a result risks deliveries from the Orient being disrupted by labor or supply problems at the vendors, or transportation delays. As a consequence, products may not be available in sufficient quantities during the prime selling period. The Company has made and will continue to make every reasonable effort to prevent these problems; however, there is no assurance that its efforts will be totally effective. In addition, the Company's manufacturing contracts with its foreign suppliers contain provisions to share the impact of fluctuations in the exchange rate between the U.S. dollar and the Hong Kong dollar above and below a fixed range contained in the contracts. All transactions with the foreign suppliers were within the exchange rate range specified in the contracts during 2002 and 2003.

1.129

QUANTUM CORPORATION (MAR)

NOTES TO CONSOLIDATED FINANCIAL STATEMENTS

Note 2 (In Part): Summary of Significant Accounting Policies

*Concentration of Credit Risk and Allowances
for Doubtful Accounts*

Quantum performs ongoing credit evaluations of its customers' financial condition and generally requires no collateral from its customers. These evaluations require significant judgment and are based on multiple sources of information and analyze such factors as Quantum's historical bad debt experiences, industry and geographic concentrations of credit risk, current economic trends and changes in customer payment terms.

Quantum records allowances for estimated losses resulting from the inability of its customers to make required payments. When Quantum becomes aware that a specific customer is unable to meet its financial obligations, Quantum records a specific allowance to reflect the level of credit risk in the customer's outstanding receivable balance. In addition, Quantum records additional allowances based on certain percentages of its aged receivable balances. Quantum records its bad debt expenses as general and administrative expenses.

Sales to Quantum's top five customers in fiscal year 2003 represented 39% of revenue, compared to 45% of revenue in fiscal year 2002 and 48% of revenue in fiscal year 2001. Sales to Hewlett-Packard were 22% of revenue in fiscal year 2003, compared to combined sales to Hewlett-Packard and Compaq of 28% of revenue in fiscal year 2002 and 30% of revenue in fiscal year 2001. These sales concentrations do not include revenues from sales of Quantum's media that was sold directly to these customers by Quantum's licensees, for which Quantum earns royalty revenue, or revenues from sales of tape libraries sold directly to these customers by Quantum's other OEM tape drive customers.

Quantum invests its excess cash in deposits with major banks and in money market funds and short-term debt securities of companies with strong credit ratings from a variety of industries. These securities generally mature within 365 days and, therefore, bear minimal risk. Quantum has not experienced any material losses on these investments and limits the amount of credit exposure to any one issuer and to any one type of investment.

Risks and Uncertainties

As is typical in the information storage industry, a significant portion of Quantum's customer base is concentrated among a small number of OEMs. The loss of any one of Quantum's more significant customers, or a significant decrease in the sales volume with one of these significant customers, could have a material adverse effect on Quantum's results of operations and financial condition. Furthermore, if adverse general economic conditions were to continue or worsen, the resulting effect on Information Technology ("IT") spending could also have a material adverse effect on Quantum's results of operations and financial condition.

The merger of Hewlett-Packard and Compaq has significantly increased the concentration of Quantum's sales and dependency on a single customer. Quantum could be materially affected if Hewlett-Packard, which accounted for 22% of Quantum's revenue in fiscal year 2003, experiences a significant drop in its storage business revenue due to customer loss or integration issues following its merger with Compaq, or if Hewlett-Packard decided to significantly reduce or cancel its orders from Quantum. Quantum also faces future uncertainties since the combined Hewlett-Packard and Compaq owns a competing LTO brand of tape drive and media. This sales concentration does not include revenues from sales of Quantum's media that was sold directly to Hewlett-Packard by Quantum's licensees, for which Quantum earns royalty revenue, or revenues from sales of tape libraries sold directly to Hewlett-Packard by Quantum's other OEM tape drive customers.

A limited number of tape drive storage products make up a significant majority of Quantum's sales, and due to increasingly rapid technological change in the industry, Quantum's future operating results depend on its ability to develop and successfully introduce new products.

Quantum's main supplier of tape heads is located in China. Political instability, trade restrictions, the SARS health problem, changes in tariff or freight rates or currency fluctuations in China could result in increased costs and delays in shipment of Quantum's products and could materially and adversely impact its operating results.

Quantum has outsourced a significant portion of its manufacturing to contract manufacturers. This concentration presents risks of component shortages or other delays in customer deliveries, increased costs for products manufactured for Quantum and risks associated with unacceptable quality of the products.

Note 24 (In Part): Business Segment and
Geographic Information

Geographic and Customer Information

Revenue and long-lived assets (property, plant and equipment and goodwill and intangible assets) by region was as follows (revenue is attributed to regions based on the location of customers):

(In thousands)	2003		2002		2001	
	Revenue	Long-Lived Assets	Revenue	Long-Lived Assets	Revenue	Long-Lived Assets
United States	$527,523	$157,648	$ 608,188	$212,158	$ 871,535	$231,750
Europe	202,758	9,348	260,083	52,218	311,254	1,572
Asia Pacific	139,124	7,886	160,039	12,151	160,225	1,932
Latin America	1,404	—	1,365	—	3,101	—
	$870,809	$174,882	$1,029,675	$276,527	$1,346,115	$235,254

One customer accounted for 10% or more of Quantum's revenue in all of the fiscal years presented. Revenue from this customer represented $193.0 million, $292.5 million and $408.8 million of Quantum's revenue in fiscal years 2003, 2002, and 2001, respectively.

1.130

SPARTON CORPORATION (JUN)

NOTES TO FINANCIAL STATEMENTS

11. Business, Geographic, and Sales Concentration

The Company operates in one business segment, electronic contract manufacturing services (EMS).

Sales to individual customers in excess of 10% were as follows:

Customer	2003	2002	2001
A	16%	16%	20%
B	11	*	*
C	*	*	10

(*) denotes sales were below 10% of total.

Total direct sales on prime contracts to U.S. governments agencies were $27,729,000 in fiscal 2003, $38,826,000 in fiscal 2002 and $27,997,000 in fiscal 2001.

The Company's net sales were made to customers in the following countries:

	2003	2002	2001
United States	$136,252,000	$129,633,000	$167,407,000
Canada	18,158,000	3,684,000	8,535,000
Other foreign countries[1]	15,451,000	16,355,000	11,678,000
Consolidated total	$169,861,000	$149,672,000	$187,620,000

[1] No single country accounted for 10% or more of export sales in the fiscal years ended 2003, 2002, or 2001.

Sales of anti-submarine warfare (ASW) devices and related engineering contract services for the years 2003-2001 contributed approximately 29%, 35%, and 18%, respectively, to total sales. Intercompany sales were not significant in any of these years.

Long-lived assets of the Company located outside of the United States are immaterial.

COMMITMENTS

1.131 Paragraph 18 of *SFAS No. 5* requires the disclosure of commitments such as those for capital expenditures or an obligation to restrict dividends. Table 1-12 lists the various commitments disclosed in the annual reports of the survey companies.

1.132 Examples of commitment disclosures follow.

1.133

TABLE 1-12: COMMITMENTS

	Number of Companies			
	2003	2002	2001	2000
Debt covenant restrictions	406	388	375	376
Purchase agreements	218	196	157	124
Capital expenditures	62	66	69	72
Additional payments related to acquisitions	38	41	45	20
Employment contracts	31	32	30	31
Sales agreements	24	35	18	20
Licensing agreements	23	25	23	17
Other—described	66	80	68	58

Debt Covenant Restrictions

1.134

GANNETT CO., INC. (DEC)

NOTES TO CONSOLIDATED FINANCIAL STATEMENTS

Note 5 (In Part): Long-Term Debt

The current revolving credit agreements contain restrictive provisions that require the maintenance of net worth of at least $2.5 billion and an interest coverage ratio of 3:1. At Dec. 28, 2003, and Dec. 29, 2002, net worth was $8.4 billion and $6.9 billion, respectively. The interest coverage ratio for the year ended Dec. 28, 2003, was 15:1.

1.135

GEORGIA-PACIFIC CORPORATION (DEC)

NOTES TO CONSOLIDATED FINANCIAL STATEMENTS

Note 9 (In Part): Indebtedness

The indentures associated with the $500 million and $1.5 billion senior notes offerings completed on June 3, 2003 and January 30, 2003, respectively, allow Georgia-Pacific and any restricted subsidiary (as defined in the indentures) of Georgia-Pacific to incur any debt so long as we meet a fixed charges coverage ratio of 2.00 to 1.00 (as defined in the indentures). In addition, we can incur other items of permitted debt (as defined in the indentures) without being in compliance with the fixed charge coverage ratio. The senior notes indentures allow us to make restricted payments, including making restricted investments, if certain conditions are met. We can, however, make permitted payments and permitted investments without complying with such conditions. These offerings also contain various non-financial covenants. We were in compliance with these debt covenants as of January 3, 2004.

•   •   •   •   •   •

Our borrowing arrangements contain a number of financial and non-financial covenants, which restrict our activities. The more significant financial covenants are discussed below. In addition, certain agreements contain cross-default provisions. At January 3, 2004, we were in compliance with the covenants of these agreements.

Covenants in the Multi-Year Revolving Credit Facility require a maximum leverage ratio (as defined) of 67.50% on January 3, 2004 and 65.00% on April 3, 2004 and thereafter. These covenants also require a minimum interest coverage ratio (as defined) of 2.25 to 1.00 on January 3, 2004; 2.50 to 1.00 on April 3, 2004; 2.75 to 1.00 on July 3, 2004; and 3.00 to 1.00 on October 2, 2004 and thereafter. In addition, the covenants require a minimum net worth (as defined) that changes quarterly, and a maximum debt level of $12,538 million, which changes quarterly, should our leverage ratio exceed 65.00%. We were in compliance with these debt covenants as of January 3, 2004, with a leverage ratio of 61.27%, an interest coverage ratio of 2.75 to 1.00, a

debt level (as defined) of $10,480 million and an adjusted net worth surplus (as defined) as shown below:

(In millions)	January 3, 2004
Adjusted net worth:	
Net worth	$5,394
Goodwill write-offs	757
Minimum pension liability adjustment	473
Adjusted net worth	6,624
Required net worth:	
80% of net worth as of the credit agreement closing date	4,650
50% of net income from fourth quarter 2000 through 2003*	208
Proceeds of capital stock or equity interest from fourth quarter 2000 through 2003	1,118
The Timber Company net worth	(329)
Required net worth	5,647
Adjusted net worth surplus	$ 977

* Does not include quarters with net losses.

On November 19, 2002, we amended our minimum net worth covenant in our Multi-Year Revolving Credit Facility, and a similar covenant in other borrowing agreements, to include the minimum pension liability adjustment described in Note 14 in our adjusted net worth calculation.

Our continued compliance with these restrictive covenants is dependent on a number of factors, many of which are outside of our control. Should events occur that result in non-compliance, we believe there are remedies available that are acceptable to our lenders and us.

1.136

HUGHES SUPPLY, INC. (JAN)

NOTES TO CONSOLIDATED FINANCIAL STATEMENTS

Note 7 (In Part): Total Debt

Other

Our debt agreements contain covenants that require that we, among other things, maintain certain financial ratios and minimum net worth levels. The covenants also restrict our activities regarding investments, liens, borrowing and leasing, and payment of dividends other than stock. Under the dividend covenant, approximately $155.4 million was available at January 30, 2004 for payment of dividends. At January 30, 2004, we were in compliance with all financial and other covenants.

1.137

IKON OFFICE SOLUTIONS, INC. (SEP)

NOTES TO CONSOLIDATED FINANCIAL STATEMENTS

5 (In Part): Notes Payable and Long-Term Debt

The Credit Facility contains affirmative and negative covenants, including limitations on certain fundamental changes, investments and acquisitions, mergers, certain transactions with affiliates, creation of liens, asset transfers, payment of dividends, intercompany loans and certain restricted payments. The Credit Facility does not affect our ability to continue to securitize lease receivables. Cash dividends may be paid on common stock subject to certain limitations. The Credit Facility also contains certain financial covenants including: (i) corporate leverage ratio; (ii) consolidated interest expense ratio; (iii) consolidated asset test ratios; and (iv) limitations on capital expenditures. The Credit Facility contains default provisions customary for facilities of this type. In order to provide certain additional financial flexibility under the corporate leverage ratio, the covenant was modified during the third quarter of 2003 as follows: (i) at September 30, 2003, 3.75 to 1.00; (ii) at December 31, 2003, 3.60 to 1.00; (iii) at March 31, 2004, 3.40 to 1.00 and (iv) at June 30, 2004 and as of the last day of each quarterly period thereafter, 3.00 to 1.00. This covenant measures a ratio of the Company's corporate non-finance subsidiary debt to business earnings (excluding financing income and interest expense associated with our financing operations). As of September 30, 2003, the corporate leverage ratio was 3.41 to 1.00. Failure to be in compliance with any material provision of the Credit Facility, including, without limitation, the financial covenants described above, could have a material adverse effect on our liquidity, financial position and results of operations.

1.138

POTLATCH CORPORATION (DEC)

NOTES TO CONSOLIDATED FINANCIAL STATEMENTS

Note 8 (In Part): Debt

Both the agreement governing our bank credit facility and the indenture governing our $250 million 10% senior subordinated notes contain certain covenants that, among other things, restrict our ability and our subsidiaries' ability to create liens, merge or consolidate, dispose of assets, incur indebtedness and guarantees, pay dividends, repurchase or redeem capital stock and indebtedness, make certain investments or acquisitions, enter into certain transactions with affiliates, make capital expenditures, or change the nature of our business. The bank credit facility also contains financial maintenance covenants establishing a maximum funded indebtedness to capitalization ratio, a minimum consolidated net worth requirement, and a minimum interest coverage ratio. Events of default under the bank credit facility and the indenture include, but are not limited to, payment defaults, covenant defaults, breaches of representations and

warranties, cross defaults to certain other material agreements and indebtedness, bankruptcy and other insolvency events, material adverse judgments, actual or asserted invalidity of security interests or loan documentation, and certain change of control events involving our company. As of December 31, 2003, we were in compliance with the covenants of our bank credit facility and the $250 million 10% senior subordinated notes.

Purchase Agreements

1.139

AIRGAS, INC. (MAR)

NOTES TO CONSOLIDATED FINANCIAL STATEMENTS

Note 21 (In Part): Commitments and Contingencies

c) Supply Agreements

The Company purchases industrial, medical and specialty gases pursuant to requirements contracts from national and regional producers of industrial gases. In February 2002, the Company entered into a 15-year take-or-pay supply agreement under which Air Products and Chemical ("Air Products") will supply at least 35% of the Company's bulk liquid nitrogen, oxygen and argon requirements. Additionally, the Company will purchase helium from Air Products under the terms of the supply agreement. Based on fiscal 2003 results, the Air Products supply agreement represents approximately $40 million in annual liquid bulk gas purchases. Effective December 1, 2002, the Company entered into a 3-year take-or-pay supply agreement with BOC Gases to purchase liquid nitrogen, oxygen and argon. Under the BOC Gases agreement, BOC Gases will reserve specified production volumes at certain plants and the Company will purchase at least 75% of those volumes. At the conclusion of the initial 3-year term of the BOC agreement, the Company may elect to extend it for an additional 3-year term. Purchases under the BOC Gases supply agreement are anticipated to be approximately $10 million annually. Both the Air Products and BOC Gases supply agreements contain market pricing subject to certain economic indices and market analysis. In addition, the Company is a party to other long-term supply agreements primarily for the purchase of liquid carbon dioxide, representing approximately $15 million, or 24% of the Company's annual carbon dioxide requirements. The Company believes the minimum product purchases under the agreements are well within the Company's normal product purchases.

1.140

NEXTEL COMMUNICATIONS, INC. (DEC)

NOTES TO CONSOLIDATED FINANCIAL STATEMENTS

10 (In Part): Commitments and Contingencies

Other Commitments

We are a party to service and other contracts in connection with conducting our business. Minimum amounts due under some of the more significant agreements are $683 million in 2004, $466 million in 2005, $391 million in 2006, $256 million in 2007, $221 million in 2008 and $420 million thereafter. Amounts actually paid under some of these agreements will likely be higher due to variable components of these agreements. The more significant variable components that determine the ultimate obligation owed include such items as hours contracted, subscribers and interest rates, and other factors. We also have committed, subject to certain conditions which may not be met, to pay up to about $334 million for spectrum acquisitions, including $195 million for the pending acquisition of certain FCC licenses, interests in certain FCC licenses and other network assets of WorldCom and Nucentrix, and leasing agreements entered into and outstanding as of December 31, 2003. In addition, we are party to various arrangements that are conditional in nature and obligate us to make payments only upon the occurrence of certain events, such as the delivery of functioning software or a product. In addition, significant amounts expected to be paid to Motorola for infrastructure, handsets and related services are not included above due to the uncertainty surrounding the timing and extent of these payments and because minimum contractual amounts under our agreements with Motorola are not significant. See note 13 with respect to amounts paid to Motorola in 2003, 2002 and 2001.

1.141

REPUBLIC SERVICES, INC. (DEC)

NOTES TO CONSOLIDATED FINANCIAL STATEMENTS
(All tables in millions)

12 (In Part): Commitments and Contingencies

Unconditional Purchase Commitments

Future minimum payments under unconditional purchase commitments at December 31, 2003 are as follows:

Year Ending December 31,	
2004	$29.9
2005	12.4
2006	11.6
2007	3.6
2008	2.7
Thereafter	17.0
	$77.2

Unconditional purchase commitments consist primarily of long-term disposal agreements that require the Company to dispose of a minimal number of tons at third party facilities.

1.142

VF CORPORATION (DEC)

NOTES TO CONSOLIDATED FINANCIAL STATEMENTS

Note S (In Part): Commitments

VF in the ordinary course of business enters into purchase commitments for raw materials, sewing labor and finished products. These agreements, typically ranging from 2 to 6 months in duration, require total payments of $507.3 million in 2004. VF also enters into advertising commitments and service and maintenance agreements for its management information systems. Future minimum payments under these agreements are $50.0 million, $9.6 million, $4.0 million, $1.8 million and $0.4 million for the years 2004 through 2008, respectively.

The trustee of the Employee Stock Ownership Plan may require VF to redeem Series B Convertible Preferred Stock held in participant accounts, and to pay each participant the value of their account, upon retirement or withdrawal from the ESOP. The amounts of these redemptions vary based on the conversion value of the Preferred Stock. Since 2002, no redemption payments have been required as the ESOP trustee has converted shares of Series B Convertible Preferred Stock for withdrawing participants into shares of Common Stock.

Capital Expenditures

1.143

ANALOGIC CORPORATION (JUL)

NOTES TO CONSOLIDATED FINANCIAL STATEMENTS
(In thousands)

9 (In Part): Commitments and Guarantees

During the third quarter of fiscal 2003, the Company commenced the construction of a 100,000 square foot addition to its headquarters building in Peabody, Massachusetts. This two-story addition will enable the Company to further consolidate its existing Massachusetts operations and to expand production capacity for its medical and security imaging system business. The building including fit-up is estimated to cost approximately $12,500 and will be financed by internally generated cash.

1.144

PRAXAIR, INC. (DEC)

NOTES TO CONSOLIDATED FINANCIAL STATEMENTS

Note 20 (In Part): Commitments and Contingencies

The following table sets forth Praxair's material commitments and contractual obligations as of December 31, 2003 excluding debt, leases, OPEB and long-term pension obligations:

(Millions of dollars)

Expiring Through December 31,	Unconditional Purchase Obligations	Construction Commitments	Guarantees and Other
2004	$108	$197	$121
2005	67	25	4
2006	49	—	—
2007	41	—	—
2008	33	—	4
Thereafter	118	—	—
	$416	$222	$129

•   •   •   •   •   •

Construction commitments of $222 million represent outstanding commitments to customers or suppliers to complete authorized construction projects as of December 31, 2003. A significant portion of Praxair's capital spending is related to the construction of new production facilities to satisfy customer commitments which may take a year or more to complete.

Additional Payments Related to Acquisitions

1.145

CLEAR CHANNEL COMMUNICATIONS, INC. (DEC)

NOTES TO CONSOLIDATED FINANCIAL STATEMENTS

Note C (In Part): Business Acquisitions

2003 Acquisitions

During 2003 the Company acquired 16 radio stations in ten markets for $45.9 million in cash. The Company also acquired 727 outdoor display faces in eight domestic markets and 1,906 display faces in four international markets for a total of $28.3 million in cash. The Company's outdoor segment also acquired investments in nonconsolidated affiliates for a total of $10.7 million in cash and acquired an additional 10% interest in a subsidiary for $5.1 million in cash. The Company's live entertainment segment made cash payments of $2.8 million during the year ended December 31, 2003, primarily related to various earn-outs and deferred purchase price consideration on prior year acquisitions. Also, the Company's national representation business acquired new contracts for a total of $42.6 million, of which $12.6 million was paid in cash during the year ended December 31, 2003 and $30.0 million was recorded as a liability at December 31, 2003.

Note G (In Part): Commitments and Contingencies

Various acquisition agreements include deferred consideration payments including future contingent payments based on the financial performance of the acquired companies, generally over a one to five year period. Contingent payments involving the financial performance of the acquired companies are typically based on the acquired company meeting certain EBITDA targets as defined in the agreement. The contingent payment amounts are generally calculated based on predetermined multiples of the achieved EBITDA not to exceed a predetermined maximum payment. At December 31, 2003, the Company believes its maximum aggregate contingency, which is subject to the financial performance of the acquired companies, is approximately $51.6 million. In addition, certain acquisition agreements include deferred consideration payments based on performance requirements by the seller, generally over a one to five year period. Contingent payments based on performance requirements by the seller typically involve the completion of a development or obtaining appropriate permits that enable the Company to construct additional advertising displays. At December 31, 2003, the Company believes its maximum aggregate contingency, which is subject to performance requirements by the seller, is approximately $28.2 million. As the contingencies have not been met or resolved as of December 31, 2003, these amounts are not recorded. If future payments are made, amounts will be recorded as additional purchase price.

1.146

MASCO CORPORATION (DEC)

NOTES TO CONSOLIDATED FINANCIAL STATEMENTS

C (In Part): Acquisitions

Certain recent purchase agreements provide for the payment of additional consideration in either cash or common stock, contingent upon whether certain conditions are met, including the operating performance of the acquired business and the price of the Company's common stock. Common shares that are contingently issuable at December 31, 2003 have been included in the computation of diluted earnings per common share for 2003. The Company also paid an additional $182 million of acquisition-related consideration, including amounts to satisfy share price guarantees, contingent consideration and other purchase price adjustments, in 2003, relating to previously acquired companies.

T (In Part): Other Commitments and Contingencies

Acquisition-Related Commitments

The Company, as part of certain recent acquisition agreements, provides for the payment of additional consideration in either cash or Company common stock, contingent upon whether certain conditions are met, including the operating performance of the acquired business and the price of the Company's common stock.

Stock Price Guarantees

Stock price guarantees as of December 31, 2003 are summarized as follows, in millions, except per share data:

Shares Issued		Minimum Stock Price Guarantee	Settlement Options (A)		Maturity Date
# of Shares	Issue Price		Shares	Cash	
17	$25.21	$31.20	2	$62	7/31/04
1	$30.00	$40.00	1	20	12/31/04–4/30/05
18			3	$82	

(A) Amounts computed based on the ten-day average of the high and low Company common stock prices ending December 31, 2003 of $27.50. Shares contingently issuable under these guarantees are included in the calculation of diluted earnings per common share.

Contingent Purchase Price

As part of certain recent acquisition agreements, the Company has additional consideration payable in cash of approximately $40 million contingent on the operating performance of the acquired businesses.

As part of the acquisition agreement, certain minority shareholders of Hansgrohe AG hold an option expiring in December 2007 to require the Company to purchase additional shares in Hansgrohe either with cash or common stock. The option value is based on Hansgrohe's operating results and, if exercised at December 31, 2003, would have approximated $21 million; if the option were settled in stock, the common shares to be issued at December 31, 2003 would have approximated 824,000.

The Company continues to guarantee the value of 1.6 million shares of Company common stock at a stock price of $40 per share related to a 2001 divestiture (through June 2004). The liability for this guarantee, which approximated $20 million and $30 million at December 31, 2003 and 2002, respectively, has been recorded in accrued liabilities and is marked to market each reporting period.

Employment Contracts

1.147

CONSTELLATION BRANDS, INC. (FEB)

NOTES TO CONSOLIDATED FINANCIAL STATEMENTS

14 (In Part): Commitments and Contingencies

Employment Contracts

The Company has employment contracts with certain of its executive officers and certain other management personnel with automatic one year renewals unless terminated by either party. These agreements provide for minimum salaries, as adjusted for annual increases, and may include incentive bonuses based upon attainment of specified management goals. In addition, these agreements provide for severance payments in the event of specified termination of employment. As of February 28, 2003, the aggregate commitment for future compensation and severance, excluding incentive bonuses, was $5.1 million, none of which was accruable at that date.

Sales Agreement

1.148

CABOT CORPORATION (SEP)

NOTES TO CONSOLIDATED FINANCIAL STATEMENTS

Note A (In Part): Significant Accounting Policies

Revenue Recognition (In Part)

Under certain multi-year supply contracts with declining prices and minimum volumes, Cabot recognizes revenue based on the estimated average selling price over the contract lives. During fiscal 2003, Cabot deferred approximately $8 million of revenue related to certain supply agreements representing the difference between the billed price and the estimated average selling price over the life of the contracts. The deferred revenue will be recognized over the remaining life of the contracts, based on an estimated average selling price of the contracted minimum volumes, extending through 2006.

Note U (In Part): Commitments & Contingencies

Other Long-Term Commitments (In Part)

During 2001, Cabot entered into long-term supply agreements with certain Supermetals customers. The contracts provide such customers with agreed upon amounts of product at agreed upon prices. These supply agreements are with four customers and expire in the periods from 2005 through 2006. The supply agreements contributed approximately $290 million and $220 million of revenue in 2003 and 2002.

Licensing Agreement

1.149

JDS UNIPHASE CORPORATION (JUN)

NOTES TO CONSOLIDATED FINANCIAL STATEMENTS

Note 20. Patent License

During the three months ended December 31, 2002, the Company determined that a payment on a patent dispute was probable and estimable. As a result, the Company accrued $8.3 million in connection with the dispute and included the amount under "Selling, general and administrative" expense.

During the three months ended March 31, 2003, the Company finalized a royalty-bearing patent license agreement and determined that its total liabilities were $19.2 million as of March 31, 2003. Therefore, the Company accrued an additional $10.9 million in connection with the patent license agreement. Of this amount, $2.2 million was recorded as prepaid royalty expense which will be amortized to "Cost of sales" through December 2004, and $8.7 million was recorded as royalty expense under "Cost of sales" for the three months ended March 31, 2003. In addition, the Company reclassified the previously recorded $8.3 million of "Selling, general and administrative" expense to royalty expense under "Cost of sales." Total royalty expense recorded in fiscal 2003 in connection with the patent license was $17.3 million.

In connection with this patent license agreement, the Company will incur additional minimum royalty obligations of $15.6 million to maintain the license over the next five years.

Divestiture Agreement

1.150

FIRST DATA CORPORATION (DEC)

NOTES TO CONSOLIDATED FINANCIAL STATEMENTS

Note 12 (In Part): Commitments and Contingencies

On April 2, 2003, FDC and Concord announced a proposed merger of the companies. On October 23, 2003, the United States Department of Justice ("DOJ"), along with District of Columbia and eight states, filed a lawsuit against FDC and Concord in United States District Court for the District of Columbia, seeking a permanent injunction against the merger of the two companies. On December 14, 2003, the Company and Concord entered into an agreement with the DOJ, the eight states and the District of Columbia on terms that will allow the companies to complete their proposed merger. The agreement calls for the Company to divest its 64% ownership of NYCE within 150 days after the Court's signing of the Hold Separate Stipulation and Order or entry of a final judgment, whichever is later, to an acquirer acceptable to the DOJ. The time period may be extended for up to 90 days. If NYCE is not divested within that time period, the DOJ may apply for the appointment of a trustee selected by the DOJ to effect the divestiture of NYCE. The Company also is required to hold

NYCE as a separate unit pending the divestiture. Following divestiture, the Company may not reacquire any ownership interest in NYCE for 10 years from the date of the final judgment. In meetings held on October 28, 2003 the shareholders of FDC and the shareholders of Concord each approved the merger of the two companies. A new meeting of the shareholders of Concord is scheduled for February 26, 2004 to approve the revised terms of the merger agreement. Consummation of the merger remains subject to approval of the Concord shareholders.

FINANCIAL INSTRUMENTS

1.151   The Financial Accounting Standards Board (FASB) has issued several statements concerning financial instruments. SFAS No. 107, *Disclosures about Fair Value of Financial Instruments,* requires reporting entities to disclose the fair value of financial instruments, and as amended by SFAS No. 133, *Accounting for Derivative Instruments and Hedging Activities,* includes the disclosure requirements of credit risk concentrations from SFAS No. 105, *Disclosure of Information about Financial Instruments with Off-Balance-Sheet Risk and Financial Instruments with Concentrations of Credit Risk.* In addition to amending *SFAS No. 107, SFAS No. 133* supersedes *SFAS No. 105* and SFAS No. 119, *Disclosure about Derivative Financial Instruments and Fair Value of Financial Instruments. SFAS No. 133* establishes accounting and reporting standards for derivative instruments, including certain derivative instruments embedded in other contracts (collectively referred to as derivatives), and for hedging activities. The Statement requires that an entity recognize all derivatives as either assets or liabilities in the statement of financial position and measure those instruments at fair value. SFAS No. 138, *Accounting for Certain Derivative Instruments and Certain Hedging Activities,* which amended *SFAS No. 133,* addresses implementation issues for certain derivative Instruments and Certain Hedging activities. SFAS No. 149, *Amendment of Statement 133 on Derivative Instruments and Hedging Activities,* amends and clarifies *SFAS No. 133* in connection with implementation issues and the definition of a derivative. SFAS No. 150, *Accounting for Certain Financial Instruments with Characteristics of both Liabilities and Equity,* requires that an issuer classify certain financial instruments with characteristics of both liabilities and equity as liabilities. Prior to *SFAS No. 150,* many of these freestanding financial instruments were classified as equity.

1.152   Table 1-13 lists the frequencies of the various types of financial instruments of the survey companies. 322 survey companies entered into interest rate swaps. 298 survey companies entered into forward foreign currency contracts, options, or foreign exchange contracts. Swaps, futures, forward contracts, or options were common types of commodity contracts reported by the survey companies. 107 survey companies entered into these types of contracts. The most frequent bases used by the survey companies to estimate fair value were broker quotes or market quotes.

1.153   Examples of fair value disclosure for financial instruments and of disclosures for concentration of credit risk follow.

1.154

TABLE 1-13: FINANCIAL INSTRUMENTS

| | Number of Companies | | | |
	2003	2002	2001	2000
Interest rate contracts	335	341	315	259
Foreign currency contracts	312	308	329	304
Commodity contracts	112	109	119	97
Guarantees/indemnifications:				
Debt	227	226	136	123
Lease payments	75	55	35	33
Environmental	73	N/C*	N/C*	N/C*
Contract performance	58	54	35	15
Tax	34	N/C*	N/C*	N/C*
Support agreements	21	24	7	9
Other	97	30	28	39
Letters of credit	304	263	205	182
Sale of receivables with recourse	33	20	25	45

* N/C = Not compiled. Line item was not included in the table for the year shown.

DERIVATIVE FINANCIAL INSTRUMENTS

1.155

ALCOA INC. (DEC)

NOTES TO THE CONSOLIDATED FINANCIAL STATEMENTS
(Dollars in millions)

A (In Part): Summary of Significant Accounting Policies

Derivatives and Hedging

Effective January 1, 2001, Alcoa adopted SFAS No. 133, "Accounting for Derivative Instruments and Hedging Activities," as amended. The fair values of all outstanding derivative instruments are recorded on the Consolidated Balance Sheet in other current and noncurrent assets and liabilities. The transition adjustment on January 1, 2001 resulted in a net charge of $4 (after tax and minority interests), which was recorded in other comprehensive income.

Derivatives are held as part of a formally documented risk management (hedging) program. All derivatives are straightforward and are held for purposes other than trading. Alcoa measures hedge effectiveness by formally assessing, at least quarterly, the historical and probable future high correlation of changes in the fair value or expected future cash flows of the hedged item. The ineffective portions are recorded in other income or expense in the current period. If the hedging relationship ceases to be highly effective or it becomes probable that an expected transaction will no longer occur, gains or losses on the derivative are recorded in other income or expense.

Changes in the fair value of derivatives are recorded in current earnings along with the change in the fair value of the underlying hedged item if the derivative is designated as a fair value hedge or in other comprehensive income if the derivative is designated as a cash flow hedge. If no hedging relationship is designated, the derivative is marked to market through earnings.

Cash flows from financial instruments are recognized in the Statement of Consolidated Cash Flows in a manner consistent with the underlying transactions.

W (In Part): Other Financial Instruments and Derivatives

Derivatives

Alcoa uses derivative financial instruments for purposes other than trading. Details of the fair value gains (losses) of the significant instruments follow.

	2003	2002
Aluminum	$ 70	$(14)
Interest rates	(74)	80
Foreign currency	(6)	57
Other commodities	73	51

Fair Value Hedges

Aluminum

Customers often require Alcoa to enter into forward-dated, fixed-price commitments. These commitments expose Alcoa to the risk of fluctuating aluminum prices between the time the order is committed and the time that the order is shipped. Alcoa's aluminum commodity risk management policy is to manage, through the use of futures contracts, the aluminum price risk associated with a portion of its fixed-price firm commitments. These contracts cover known exposures, generally within three years.

Interest Rates

Alcoa uses interest rate swaps to help maintain a strategic balance between fixed- and floating-rate debt and to manage overall financing costs. The company has entered into pay floating, receive fixed interest rate swaps to effectively convert the interest rate from fixed to floating on $4,150 of debt, through 2013.

Currencies

Aluminio uses cross-currency interest rate swaps that effectively convert its U.S. dollar denominated debt into Brazilian reais debt at local interest rates.

Hedges of these existing assets, liabilities, and firm commitments qualify as "fair value" hedges. As a result, the fair values of derivatives and changes in the fair values of the underlying hedged items are reported in the Consolidated Balance Sheet. Changes in the fair values of these derivatives and underlying hedged items generally offset and are recorded each period in sales, cost of goods sold, interest expense, or other income, consistent with the underlying hedged item. There were no transactions that ceased to qualify as a fair value hedge in 2003.

Cash Flow Hedges

Interest Rates

Alcoa also uses interest rate swaps to establish fixed interest rates on anticipated borrowings between June 2005 and June 2006. The anticipated borrowings have a high probability of occurrence because the proceeds will be used to fund debt maturities and anticipated capital expenditures.

Alcoa has $1,000 of interest rate swaps outstanding that will establish fixed interest rates on anticipated borrowings of $500 of debt through 2016 and $500 of debt through 2036.

Currencies

Alcoa is subject to exposure from fluctuations in foreign currencies. Foreign currency exchange contracts may be used from time to time to hedge the variability in cash flows from the forecasted payment or receipt of currencies other than the functional currency. Alcoa's foreign currency contracts were principally used to purchase Australian dollars, Brazilian reais, and Mexican pesos. The U.S. dollar notional amount of all foreign currency contracts was $203 and $798 as of December 31, 2003 and 2002, respectively.

Commodities

Alcoa anticipates the continued requirement to purchase aluminum and other commodities such as natural gas, fuel oil, and electricity for its operations. Alcoa enters into futures contracts to reduce volatility in the price of these commodities.

For these cash flow hedge transactions, the fair values of the derivatives are recorded on the Consolidated Balance Sheet. The effective portions of the changes in the fair values of these derivatives are recorded in other comprehensive income and are reclassified to sales, cost of goods sold, or interest expense in the period in which earnings are impacted by the hedged items or in the period that the transaction no longer qualifies as a cash flow hedge. There were no transaction that ceased to qualify as a cash flow hedge in 2003. These contracts cover periods commensurate with known or expected exposures, generally within three years. Assuming market rates remain constant with the rates at December 31, 2003, $33 of the $66 gain included in other comprehensive income is expected to be recognized in earnings over the next 12 months.

Alcoa is exposed to credit loss in the event of nonperformance by counterparties on the above instruments, as well as credit or performance risk with respect to its hedged customers' commitments. Although nonperformance is possible, Alcoa does not anticipate nonperformance by any of these parties. Contracts are with creditworthy counterparties and are further supported by cash, treasury bills, or irrevocable letters of credit issued by carefully chosen banks. In addition, various master netting arrangements are in place with counterparties to facilitate settlement of gains and losses on these contracts.

1.156

THE CLOROX COMPANY (JUN)

NOTES TO CONSOLIDATED FINANCIAL STATEMENTS
(Millions of dollars)

1 (In Part): Significant Accounting Policies

Derivative Instruments

Effective July 1, 2000, the Company adopted SFAS No. 133 "Accounting for Derivative Instruments and Hedging Activi-

ties," as amended by SFAS No. 138, "Accounting for Certain Derivative Instruments and Certain Hedging Activities." SFAS No. 133, as amended, established accounting and reporting standards for derivative instruments, including certain derivative instruments embedded in other contracts, and for hedging activities. The statement requires that an entity recognize all derivatives as either assets or liabilities in the balance sheet and measure those instruments at fair value. The effect of this new standard was a reduction of fiscal year 2001 net earnings of $2 (net of tax benefit of $1), which was recognized as a cumulative effect of a change in accounting principle and an increase in fiscal year 2001 accumulated other comprehensive income of $10 (net of tax benefit of $7). The ongoing effects are dependent on future market conditions and the Company's hedging activities.

The use of derivative instruments, principally swap, forward and option contracts, is limited to non-trading purposes and includes management of interest rate movements, foreign currency exposure and commodity price exposure. Most interest rate swaps and commodity purchase and foreign exchange contracts are designated as fair-value or cash-flow hedges of fixed and variable rate debt obligations, raw material purchase obligations, or foreign currency denominated debt instruments, based on certain hedge criteria. The criteria used to determine if hedge accounting treatment is appropriate are (a) the designation of the hedge to an underlying exposure, (b) whether overall risk is being reduced and (c) if there is correlation between the value of the derivative instrument and the underlying obligation. Changes in the fair value of such derivatives are recorded as either assets or liabilities in the balance sheet with an offset to current earnings or other comprehensive income, depending on whether the derivative is designated as a hedge transaction and the type of hedge transaction. For fair-value hedge transactions, changes in fair value of the derivative and changes in the fair value of the item being hedged are recorded in earnings. For cash-flow hedge transactions, changes in fair value of derivatives are reported as a component of other comprehensive income and are recognized in the period or periods during which the hedge transaction effects earnings. The Company also has contracts with no hedging designations. In fiscal year 2002, the Company elected to discontinue hedge accounting treatment for certain of its foreign exchange contracts that are considered immaterial. The financial statement impact of this change was insignificant. These contracts are accounted for by adjusting the carrying amount of the contracts to market and recognizing any gain or loss in other (income) expense, net.

The Company uses several different methodologies to estimate the fair value of its derivative contracts. The estimated fair values of the Company's interest rate swaps, certain commodity derivative contracts and foreign exchange contracts are based on quoted market prices, traded exchange market prices or broker price quotations and represent the estimated amounts that the Company would pay or receive to terminate the contracts. The estimated fair values of the Company's resin commodity contracts were previously determined using valuation models with forward resin market price curves provided by market makers. Starting in fiscal year 2002, the Company began using forward resin market price curves provided by other external sources because of a lack of available market quotations. Factors used to determine the fair value of the resin forward curve are based on resin market information, which reflects many economic factors, including technology, labor, material and capital costs, capacity, and supply and demand.

11. Fair Value of Financial Instruments

The Company's derivative financial instruments are recorded at fair value in the consolidated balance sheets as assets (liabilities) at June 30 as follows:

	2003	2002
Current assets:		
Foreign exchange contracts	$ 1	$ 2
Commodity purchase contracts	—	1
Other assets:		
Interest rate swaps	39	15
Commodity purchase contracts	2	—
Current liabilities:		
Interest rate swaps	2	—
Foreign exchange contracts	—	(3)
Long-term debt:		
Interest rate swaps	—	(6)
Foreign exchange contracts	—	(1)
Other long-term obligations—commodity option contracts	—	(9)

The Company utilizes derivative instruments, principally swap, forward and option contracts to enhance its ability to manage the risks associated with fluctuations in interest rates, foreign currencies, and commodity prices, which exist as part of the Company's ongoing business operations. These contracts hedge transactions and balances for periods consistent with the related exposures and do not constitute investments independent of these exposures.

The Company has policies with restrictions on the use of derivatives, including a prohibition of the use of any leveraged instrument. Derivative contracts are entered into with several major creditworthy institutions, thereby minimizing the risk of credit loss. Exposure to counterparty credit risk is considered low because these agreements have been entered into with major credit-worthy institutions with strong credit ratings, and they are expected to perform fully under the terms of the agreements.

Most of the Company's derivative instruments are designated as fair-value or cash-flow hedges of fixed and variable rate debt obligations, foreign currency-denominated debt instruments, or raw material purchase obligations. All hedges accorded hedge accounting treatment are considered highly effective. At June 30, 2003 and 2002, the Company also had certain foreign currency-related derivative contracts with no specific hedging designations. These contracts, which have been entered into to manage a portion of the Company's foreign exchange risk, are accounted for by adjusting the carrying amount of the contracts to market value and recognizing any gain or loss in other (income) expense.

The Company uses interest rate swap agreements to manage interest rate exposure and to achieve a desired proportion of variable and fixed rate debt. As of June 30, 2003, the Company also had preferred interest transferable securities, which is a Euro Dollar (EUR) denominated financing arrangement that expired in July 2003. The Company manages its interest rate and Euro Dollar risks from these securities through a series of swaps with notional amounts totaling $200. This interest rate swap effectively converts the Company's 5.8% fixed Euro Dollar obligation to a floating U.S. Dollar rate of 90-day LIBOR. In addition, the Company effectively pays a 4.5% fixed rate and receives a 4.6% Euro rate with its currency swap position. The estimated amount of existing pre-tax gains for these swap agreements in accumulated other comprehensive net losses at June 30, 2003 was reclassified into earnings in July 2003 was $2.

The Company uses foreign exchange contracts, including forward, swap and option contracts, to hedge existing foreign exchange exposures. Foreign currency contracts require the Company, at a future date, to either buy or sell foreign currency in exchange for U.S. Dollars and other currencies. Such currency contracts existed at June 30, 2003 and 2002 for Canadian dollars and certain other currencies. Contracts outstanding as of June 30, 2003 will mature over the next fiscal year.

The Company also uses commodity futures and swap contracts to fix the price of a portion of its raw material requirements. Contract maturities, which extend to fiscal year 2006, are matched to the length of the raw material purchase contracts and contract gains and losses are reflected as adjustments to the cost of the raw materials. The estimated amount of existing pre-tax net losses for commodity contracts in accumulated other comprehensive net losses that is expected to be reclassified into earnings during the year ended June 30, 2004 is less than $1.

The notional and estimated fair values of the Company's derivative instruments are summarized below as of June 30:

	2003		2002	
	Notional	Fair Value	Notional	Fair Value
Derivative Instruments				
Debt-related contracts	$400	$41	$400	$ 8
Foreign exchange contracts	259	—	393	(1)
Commodity purchase contracts	125	2	90	1
Commodity option contracts	—	—	35	(9)

The carrying values of cash, short-term investments, accounts and notes receivable, accounts payable and other derivative instruments approximate their fair values at June 30, 2003 and 2002. The Company has used market information for similar instruments and applied judgment in estimating fair values. See Note 10 for fair values of notes and loans payable and long-term debt.

1.157

THE GILLETTE COMPANY (DEC)

NOTES TO CONSOLIDATED FINANCIAL STATEMENTS

2 (In Part): Summary of Significant Accounting Policies

Financial Instruments

Cash and cash equivalents, trade receivables, investments, accounts payable, loans payable, and all derivative instruments are carried at fair value. The fair values of cash equivalents, trade receivables, accounts payable, and loans payable approximate cost. The fair value of investments is based on quoted market prices. The estimated fair values of derivative instruments are calculated based on market rates. These values represent the estimated amounts the Company would receive or pay to terminate agreements, taking into consideration current market rates and the current credit-worthiness of the counterparties. The fair value of long-term debt, including the current portion, is estimated based on quoted market prices or rates currently offered to the Company for debt of the same remaining maturities.

7 (In Part): Financial Instruments and Risk Management Activities

The estimated fair values of the Company's financial instruments are summarized below.

(Millions)	2003 Carrying Amount/ Fair Value	2002 Carrying Amount/ Fair Value
Long-term investments	$ 177	$ 161
Long-term debt, including current portion	(3,195)	(2,984)
Derivative instruments		
Currency forwards hedging net investments	(2)	(4)
Interest rate swaps	67	108
Forward rate agreements	—	(2)
Commodity swaps	4	(2)
Other currency forwards and swaps		
Assets	159	70
Liabilities	(17)	(17)
Equity contracts	4	3

The Company is subject to market risks, such as changes in currency and interest rates that arise from normal business operations. The Company regularly assesses these risks and has established business strategies to provide natural offsets, supplemented by the use of derivative financial instruments to protect against the adverse effects of these and other market risks. The Company has established clear policies, procedures, and internal controls governing the use of derivatives and does not use them for trading, investment, or other speculative purposes.

The Company uses derivative contracts to efficiently structure its debt in the desired currencies and mix of fixed to floating interest rates. Forward contracts effectively convert U.S. dollar commercial paper borrowings into non-U.S. dollar obligations, primarily in currencies with low interest rates. At December 31, 2003, the Company had forward contracts designated as hedges of the currency changes on the Company's foreign net investments with fair values of $2 million recorded in accrued liabilities. Currency effects of the net investment hedges are reflected as a component of foreign currency translation in accumulated other comprehensive loss and produced a $6 million aftertax loss, a $5 million aftertax loss, and a $53 million aftertax gain for the years ended December 31, 2003, 2002, and 2001, respectively. Interest effects of these hedges are reported in interest expense.

The Company uses primarily floating rate debt in order to match interest costs to the impact of inflation on earnings. The Company manages its mix of fixed to floating rate debt by entering into interest rate swaps and forward rate agreements. At December 31, 2003 and 2002, the Company had

interest rate swaps designated as fair value hedges with fair values of $67 million and $108 million, respectively, recored in other current assets and other assets These swaps effectively convert certain fixed rate debt into variable rate debt. The terms of the swaps match the terms of the underlying debt. The changes in the fair values of both the swaps and the debt are recored as equal and offsetting gains and losses in interest expense. The Company recored a $1 million hedge ineffectiveness gain in interest expense in 2003. There was no impact on earnings due to hedge ineffectiveness for the years ended December 31, 2002 and 2001.

At December 31, 2002, the Company had forward rate agreements designated as cash flow hedges with fair values of $2 million recorded in accrued liabilities, effectively fixing certain variable interest payments. After tax net losses of $2 million ($3 million pretax), $4 million ($7 million pretax), and $9 million ($14 million pretax) were recorded in other comprehensive loss during the years ended December 31, 2003, 2002, and 2001, respectively. Ineffective amounts had no impact on earnings for the years ended December 31, 2003, 2002, and 2001.

The Company also enters into commodity swaps to fix the price of certain forecasted purchases of raw material used in the manufacturing process. At December 31, 2003, the Company has swaps designated as cash flow hedges with fair values of $4 million recorded in other current assets. At December 31, 2002, the Company had swaps designated as cash flow hedges with fair values of $2 million recorded in accrued liabilities. Changes in fair values are included in other comprehensive loss to the extent effective and are charged to cost of sales in the period during which the hedged transaction affects earnings. Aftertax net gains of $4 million ($7 million pretax) and aftertax net losses of $2 million ($3 million pretax) were recorded in other comprehensive loss in the years ended December 31, 2003 and 2002, respectively. During the year ended December 31, 2001, total aftertax losses recorded in other comprehensive loss were $6 million ($9 million pretax), including the cumulative effect of change in accounting principle upon adoption of SFAS 133. Remaining pretax gains of $4 million included in accumulated other comprehensive loss will be credited to earnings in 2004. Ineffective amounts had no material impact on earnings for the years ended December 31, 2003, 2002, and 2001.

Most of the Company's transactional exchange exposure is managed through centralized cash management. The Company hedges net residual transactional exchange exposures, principally foreign denominated debt and intercompany balances, through forward contracts and currency swaps that were recorded at their net fair value of $142 million and $53 million at December 31, 2003 and 2002, respectively. Changes in fair value are recorded in nonoperating charges (income) and offset gains and losses resulting from the underlying exposures.

The Company also uses derivatives to hedge equity-linked employee compensation. The Company fixes the cost of certain employee compensation expenses linked to its stock price by entering into equity swap and option contracts. These contracts were recorded in other assets at their fair values of $4 million and $3 million at December 31, 2003 and 2002, respectively. Changes in fair value are recorded in profit from operations and offset the changes in the value of the underlying liabilities.

Several major international financial institutions are counterparties to the Company's financial instruments. It is

Company practice to monitor the financial standing of the counterparties and to limit the amount of exposure with any one institution. The Company may be exposed to credit loss in the event of nonperformance by the counterparties to these contracts, but does not anticipate such noneperformance.

1.158

H. J. HEINZ COMPANY (APR)

NOTES TO CONSOLIDATED FINANCIAL STATEMENTS

1 (In Part): Significant Accounting Policies

Financial Instruments

The Company's financial instruments consist primarily of cash and cash equivalents, short-term and long-term debt, swaps, forward contracts, commodity futures, and option contracts. The carrying values for the Company's financial instruments approximate fair value with the exception at times of long-term debt. As of April 30, 2003 and May 1, 2002, the fair value of debt obligations approximated the recorded value. As a policy, the Company does not engage in speculative or leveraged transactions, nor does the Company hold or issue financial instruments for trading purposes.

The Company uses derivative financial instruments for the purpose of hedging currency, price, and interest rate exposures, which exist as part of ongoing business operations. The Company carries derivative instruments on the balance sheet at fair value, determined by reference to quoted market prices. Interest rate swaps designated as fair value hedges are presented as a component of other non-current assets. All other derivatives are included in receivables or accounts payable, based on the instrument's fair value. The accounting for changes in the fair value of a derivative instrument depends on whether it has been designated and qualifies as part of a hedging relationship and, if so, the reason for holding it. The cash flows related to derivative instruments are classified in the consolidated statements of cash flows within operating activities as a component of other items, net.

13. Derivative Financial Instruments and Hedging Activities

The Company operates internationally, with manufacturing and sales facilities in various locations around the world, and utilizes certain derivative and non-derivative financial instruments to manage its foreign currency, commodity price, and interest rate exposures.

Foreign Currency Hedging

The Company uses forward contracts and to a lesser extent, option contracts to mitigate its foreign currency exchange rate exposure due to forecasted purchases of raw materials and sales of finished goods, and future settlement of foreign currency denominated assets and liabilities. Derivatives used to hedge forecasted transactions and specific cash flows associated with foreign currency denominated financial assets and liabilities which meet the criteria for hedge accounting are designated as cash flow hedges. Consequently, the effective portion of gains and losses is deferred as a component of accumulated other comprehensive loss and is recognized in earnings at the time the hedged item affects earnings, in the same line item as the underlying hedged item.

The Company uses certain foreign currency debt instruments as net investment hedges of foreign operations. Losses of $41.9 million (net of income taxes of $23.5 million), $2.4 million (net of income taxes of $1.4 million) and $0.2 million (net of income taxes of $0.1 million), which represented effective hedges of net investments, were reported as a component of accumulated other comprehensive loss within unrealized translation adjustment for the years ended April 30, 2003, May 1, 2002, and May 2, 2001, respectively.

Commodity Price Hedging

The Company uses commodity futures, swaps and option contracts in order to reduce price risk associated with forecasted purchases of raw materials such as corn, soybean oil, and soybean meal. Commodity price risk arises due to factors such as weather conditions, government regulations, economic climate and other unforeseen circumstances. Derivatives used to hedge forecasted commodity purchases that meet the criteria for hedge accounting are designated as cash flow hedges. Consequently, the effective portion of changes in the fair value of these derivatives is deferred as a component of accumulated other comprehensive loss and is recognized as part of cost of products sold at the time the hedged item affects earnings.

Interest Rate Hedging

The Company uses interest rate swaps to manage interest rate exposure. These derivatives may be designated as cash flow hedges or fair value hedges depending on the nature of the risk being hedged. Derivatives used to hedge risk associated with changes in the fair value of certain fixed rate debt obligations are designated as fair value hedges. Consequently, changes in the fair value of these derivatives, along with changes in the fair value of the hedged debt obligations that are attributable to the hedged risk, are recognized in current period earnings.

Hedge Ineffectiveness

Hedge ineffectiveness related to cash flow hedges, which is reported in current period earnings as other income and expense, was a net loss of $0.8 million, $0.3 million, and $0.6 million for the years ended April 30, 2003, May 1, 2002, and May 2, 2001, respectively. The Company excludes the time value component of option contracts from the assessment of hedge effectiveness.

Deferred Hedging Gains and Losses

As of April 30, 2003, the Company is hedging forecasted transactions for periods not exceeding 24 months. During the next 12 months, the Company expects $6.2 million of net deferred gain reported in accumulated other comprehensive loss to be reclassified to earnings. Net deferred losses reclassified to earnings because the hedged transaction was no longer expected to occur totaled $0.6 million for the year ended April 30, 2003 and were not significant for the years ended May 1, 2002 and May 2, 2001.

Other Activities

The Company enters into certain derivative contracts in accordance with its risk management strategy that do not meet the criteria for hedge accounting. Although these derivatives do not qualify as hedges, they have the economic impact of largely mitigating foreign currency, commodity price or interest rate exposures. These derivative financial instruments are accounted for on a full mark to market basis through current earnings even though they were not acquired for trading purposes.

At April 30, 2003, the notional amount outstanding of currency exchange, commodity, and interest rate derivative contracts was $715 million, $21 million, and $2.95 billion, respectively. At May 1, 2002, the notional amount outstanding of currency exchange, commodity, and interest rate derivative contracts was $845 million, $31 million, and $2.05 billion, respectively. The fair value of derivative financial instruments was a net asset of $300 million and $24 million at April 30, 2003 and May 1, 2002, respectively.

Concentration of Credit Risk

Counterparties to currency exchange and interest rate derivatives consist of larger major international financial institutions. The Company continually monitors its positions and the credit ratings of the counterparties involved and, by policy, limits the amount of credit exposure to any one party. While the Company may be exposed to potential losses due to the credit risk of non-performance by these counterparties, losses are not anticipated. During Fiscal 2003, no single customer represented more than 10% of the Company's sales.

1.159

HONEYWELL INTERNATIONAL INC. (DEC)

NOTES TO FINANCIAL STATEMENTS

Note 1 (In Part): Summary of Significant Accounting Policies

Derivative Financial Instruments

Derivative financial instruments are accounted for under Statement of Financial Accounting Standards No. 133, "Accounting for Derivative Instruments and Hedging Activities," as amended (SFAS No. 133) Under SFAS No. 133, all derivatives are recorded on the balance sheet as assets or liabilities and measured at fair value. For derivatives designated as hedges of the fair value of assets of liabilities, the changes in fair values of both the derivatives and the hedged items are recorded in current earnings. For derivatives designated as cash flow hedges, the effective portion of the changes in fair value of the derivatives are recorded in Accumulated Other Nonowner Changes and subsequently recognized in earnings when the hedged items impact income. Changes in the fair value of derivatives not designated as hedges and the ineffective portion of cash flow hedges are recorded in current earnings.

Note 17—Financial Instruments

As a result of our global operating and financing activities, we are exposed to market risks from changes in interest and foreign currency exchange rates and commodity prices, which may adversely affect our operating results and financial position. We minimize our risks from interest and foreign currency exchange rate and commodity price fluctuations through our normal operating and financing activities and, when deemed appropriate, through the use of derivative financial instruments.

Credit and Market Risk

Financial instruments, including derivatives, expose us to counterparty credit risk for nonperformance and to market risk related to changes in interest or currency exchange rates. We manage our exposure to counterparty credit risk through specific minimum credit standards, diversification of counterparties, and procedures to monitor concentrations of credit risk. Our counterparties are substantial investment and commercial banks with significant experience using such derivative instruments. We monitor the impact of market risk on the fair value and cash flows of our derivative and other financial instruments considering reasonably possible changes in interest and currency exchange rates and restrict the use of derivative financial instruments to hedging activities. We do not use derivative financial instruments for trading or other speculative purposes and do not use leveraged derivative financial instruments.

We continually monitor the creditworthiness of our customers to which we grant credit terms in the normal course of business. While concentrations of credit risk associated with our trade accounts and notes receivable are considered minima due to our diverse customer base, a significant portion of our customer are in the commercial air transport industry (aircraft manufacturers and airlines) accounting for approximately 12 percent of our consolidated sales in 2003. Following the abrupt downturn in the aviation industry after the terrorist attacks on September 11, 2001 and the already weak economy, we modified terms and conditions of our credit sales to mitigate or eliminate concentrations of credit risk with any single customer. Our sales are not materially dependent on a single customer or a small group of customers.

Foreign Currency Risk Management

We conduct our business on a multinational basis in a wide variety of foreign currencies. Our exposure to market risk for changes in foreign currency exchange rates arises from international financing activities between subsidiaries, foreign currency denominated monetary assets and liabilities and anticipated transactions arising from international trade. Our objective is to preserve the economic value of cash flows in non-functional currencies. We attempt to have all transaction exposures hedged with natural offsets to the fullest extent possible and, once these opportunities have been exhausted, through foreign currency forward and option agreements with third parties. Our principal currency exposures relate to the Euro, the British pound, the Canadian dollar, and the U.S. dollar.

We hedge monetary assets and liabilities denominated in foreign currencies. Prior to conversion into U.S dollars, these assets and liabilities are remeasured at spot exchange rates in effect on the balance sheet date. The effects of changes in spot rates are recognized in earnings and included in Other (Income) Expense. We hedge our exposure to changes in foreign exchange rates principally with forward contracts. Forward contracts are marked-to-market with the resulting gains and losses similarly recognized in earnings offsetting the gains and losses on the foreign currency denominated monetary assets and liabilities being hedged.

We partially hedge forecasted 2004 sales and purchases denominated in foreign currencies with currency forward contracts. When the dollar strengthens against foreign currencies, the decline in value of forecasted foreign currency cash inflows (sales) or outflows (purchases) is partially offset by the recognition of gains (sales) and losses (purchases), respectively, in the value of the forward contracts designated as hedges. Conversely, when the dollar weakens against foreign currencies, the increase in value of forecasted foreign currency cash inflows (sales) or outflows (purchases) is partially offset by the recognition of losses (sales) and gains (purchases), respectively in the value of the forward contracts designated as hedges. Market value gains and losses on these contracts are recognized in earnings when the hedged transaction is recognized. All open forward contracts mature by December 31, 2004.

At December 31, 2003 and 2002, we had contracts with notional amounts of $641 and $1,203 million, respectively, to exchange foreign currencies, principally in the Euro countries and Great Britain.

Commodity Price Risk Management

Our exposure to market risk for commodity prices arises from changes in our cost of production. We mitigate our exposure to commodity price risk through the use of long-term, firm-price contracts with our suppliers and forward commodity purchase agreements with third parties hedging anticipated purchases of several commodities (principally natural gas). Forward commodity purchase agreements are marked-to-market, with the resulting gains and losses recognized in earnings when the hedged transaction is recognized.

Interest Rate Risk Management

We use a combination of financial instruments, including medium-term and short-term financing, variable-rate commercial paper, and interest rate swaps to manage the interest rate mix of our total debt portfolio and related overall cost of borrowing. At December 31, 2003 and 2002, interest rate swap agreements designated as fair value hedges effectively changed $1,189 and $1,132 million, respectively, of fixed rate debt at an average rate of 6.45 and 6.51 percent, respectively, to LIBOR based floating rate debt. Our interest rate swaps mature through 2007.

Fair Value of Financial Instruments

The carrying value of cash and cash equivalents, trade accounts and notes receivables, payable, commercial paper and short-term borrowings contained in the Consolidated Balance Sheet approximates fair value. Summarized below are the carrying values and fair values of our other financial instruments at December 31, 2003 and 2002. The fair values are based on the quoted market prices for the issues (if traded), current rates offered to us for debt of the same remaining maturity and characteristics, or other valuation techniques, as appropriate.

	2003		2002	
(Dollars in millions)	Carrying Value	Fair Value	Carrying Value	Fair Value
Assets				
Long-term receivables	$ 388	$ 369	$ 464	$ 443
Interest rate swap agreements	67	67	76	76
Foreign currency exchange contracts	12	12	8	8
Forward commodity contracts	18	18	5	5
Liabilities				
Long-term debt and related current maturities (excluding capitalized leases)	$(4,992)	$(5,508)	$(4.812)	$(5.261)
Foreign currency exchange contracts	(11)	(11)	(16)	(16)

OFF-BALANCE-SHEET FINANCIAL INSTRUMENTS

Financial Guarantees

1.160

CHAMPION ENTERPRISES, INC. (DEC)

NOTES TO CONSOLIDATED FINANCIAL STATEMENTS

Note 13 (In Part): Contingent Liabilities

At January 3, 2004 the Company was contingently obligated for approximately $67.2 million under letters of credit, primarily comprised of $14.1 million to support insurance reserves, $18.4 million to support long-term debt, $27.7 million to secure surety bonds and $5.0 million to support an independent floor plan facility. Champion was also contingently obligated for $34.1 million under surety bonds, generally to support insurance and license and service bonding requirements. Approximately $37.6 million of the letters of credit and $20.8 million of the surety bonds support insurance reserves and debt that are reflected as liabilities in the consolidated balance sheet.

At January 3, 2004 certain of the Company's subsidiaries were guarantors $5.6 million of debt of unconsolidated subsidiaries, none of which was reflected in the consolidated balance sheet. These guarantees are several or joint and several and are related to indebtedness of certain manufactured housing community developments which are collateralized by the properties being developed.

The Company has provided various representations, warranties and other standard indemnifications in the ordinary course of its business, in agreements to acquire and sell business assets and in financing arrangements. The Company is subject to various legal proceedings and claims, which arise in the ordinary course of its business.

Management believes the ultimate liability with respect to these contingent obligations will not have a material effect on the Company's financial position, results of operations or cash flows.

1.161

EASTMAN CHEMICAL COMPANY (DEC)

NOTES TO CONSOLIDATED FINANCIAL STATEMENTS

Note 10 (In Part): Commitments

Guarantees

In November 2002, the Financial Accounting Standards Board ("FASB") issued FASB Interpretation No. 45 ("FIN 45"), "Guarantor's Accounting and Disclosure Requirements for Guarantees, Including Indirect Guarantees of Indebtedness, of Others," on interpretation of FASB Statement No. 5, 57 and 107 and Rescission of FASB Interpretation No. 34. FIN 45 clarifies the requirements of SFAS No. 5, "Accounting for Contingencies," relating to the guarantor's accounting for, and disclosure of, the issuance of certain types of guarantees. The Company has adopted the disclosure requirements of the interpretation as of December 31, 2002. Disclosure about each group of similar guarantees are provided below and summarized in the following table:

(Dollars in millions)	
Obligations of equity affiliates	$131
Residual value guarantees	93
Total	$224

Obligations of Equity Affiliates

Eastman has long-term commitments relating to joint ventures as described in Note 5 to the Company's consolidated financial statements. The Company guarantees up to $131 million of the principal amount of the joint ventures' third-party borrowings, but believes, based on current facts and circumstances and the structure of the ventures, that the likelihood of a payment pursuant to such guarantees is remote.

Residual Value Guarantees

If certain operating leases are terminated by the Company, it guarantees a portion of the residual value loss, if any, incurred by the lessors in disposing of the related assets. Under these operating leases, the residual value guarantees at December 31, 2003, totaled $93 million and consisted primarily of leases for railcars, company aircraft, and other equipment. The Company believes, based on current facts and circumstances, that a material payment pursuant to such guarantees is remote.

Equity Investment Guarantees

In addition, the Company has committed to funding obligations related to certain venture capital investments. If required, the Company's commitment could total $26 million over the next five years.

Other Guarantees

Guarantees and claims arise during the ordinary course of business from relationships with suppliers, customers, and nonconsolidated affiliates when the Company undertakes an obligation to guarantee the performance of others if specified triggering events occur. Nonperformance under a contract could trigger an obligation of the Company. These potential claims include actions based upon alleged exposures to products, intellectual property and environmental matters, and other indemnifications. The ultimate effect on future financial results is not subject to reasonable estimation because considerable uncertainly exists as to the final outcome of these claims. However, while the ultimate liabilities resulting from such claims may be significant to results of operations in the period recognized, management does not anticipate they will have a material adverse effect on the Company's consolidated financial position or liquidity.

1.162

KELLOGG COMPANY (DEC)

NOTES TO CONSOLIDATED FINANCIAL STATEMENTS

Note 1 (In Part): Accounting Policies

Guarantees

With respect to guarantees entered into or modified after December 31, 2002, the Company has applied guidance contained in FASB Interpretation No. 45 "Guarantor's Accounting and Disclosure Requirements for Guarantees, Including Indirect Guarantees of Indebtedness of Others." This interpretation clarifies the requirement for recognition of a liability by a guarantor at the inception of the guarantee, based on the fair value of the non-contingent obligation to perform. Application of this guidance did not have a significant impact on the Company's 2003 financial results.

Note 6 (In Part): Leases and Other Commitments

The Company's Keebler subsidiary is guarantor on loans to independent contractors for the purchase of DSD route franchises. At year-end 2003, there were total loans outstanding of $15.2 million to 413 franchisees. All loans are variable rate with a term of 10 years. Related to this arrangement, the Company has established with a financial institution a one-year renewable loan facility up to $17.0 million with a five-year term-out and servicing arrangement. The Company has the right to revoke and resell the route franchises in the event of default or any other breach of contract by franchisees. Revocations are infrequent. The Company's maximum potential future payments under these guarantees are limited to the outstanding loan principal balance plus unpaid interest. In accordance with FASB Interpretation No. 45 (refer to Note 1), we have recognized the fair value of guarantees associated with new loans to DSD route franchisees issued beginning in 2003. These amounts are insignificant.

The Company has provided various standard indemnifications in agreements to sell business assets and lease facilities over the past several years, related primarily to pre-existing tax, environmental, and employee benefit obligations. Certain of these indemnifications are limited by agreement in either amount and/or term and others are unlimited. The Company has also provided various "hold harmless" provisions within certain service type agreements. Because the Company is not currently aware of any actual exposures associated with these indemnifications, management is unable to estimate the maximum potential future payments to be made.

At December 27, 2003, the Company had not recorded any liability related to these indemnifications.

1.163

SARA LEE CORPORATION (JUN)

NOTES TO FINANCIAL STATEMENTS
(Dollars in millions)

Leases (In Part)

Contingent Lease Obligation

The corporation is contingently liable for leases on property operated by others. At June 28, 2003, the maximum potential amount of future payments the corporation could be required to make, if all of the current operators default on the rental arrangements, is $169. The minimum annual rentals under these leases is $22 in 2004, $21 in 2005, $21 in 2006, $18 in 2007, $16 in 2008 and $71 thereafter. Substantially all of these amounts relate to a number of retail store leases operated by Coach, Inc. Coach, Inc. is contractually obligated to provide the corporation, on an annual basis, with a standby letter of credit equal to the next year's rental obligations. The letter of credit in place at the close of 2003 was $19. This obligation to provide a letter of credit expires when the corporation's contingent lease obligation is substantially extinguished. The corporation has not recognized a liability for the contingent obligation on the Coach, Inc. leases.

Guarantees

In November 2002, the FASB issued Interpretation No. 45, "Guarantor's Accounting and Disclosure Requirements for Guarantees, Including Indirect Guarantees of Indebtedness of Others" (FIN 45). FIN 45 requires that guarantees issued or modified after December 31, 2002 be recorded at fair value, which is different from past practice, which was generally to record a liability only when a loss is probable and reasonably estimable. FIN 45 also requires the corporation to disclose certain types of guarantees, even if the likelihood of having to perform under the guarantee is remote.

The corporation is a party to a variety of agreements under which it may be obligated to indemnify a third party with respect to certain matters. Typically, these obligations arise as a result of contracts entered into by the corporation, under which the corporation agrees to indemnify a third party against losses arising from a breach of representations and covenants related to such matters as title to assets sold, the collectibility of receivables, specified environmental matters, lease obligations assumed and certain tax matters. In each of these circumstances, payment by the corporation is conditioned on the other party making a claim pursuant to the procedures specified in the contract. These procedures allow the corporation to challenge the other party's claims. In addition, the corporation's obligations under these agreements may be limited in terms of time and/or amount, and in some cases the corporation may have recourse against third parties for certain payments made by the corporation. It is not possible to predict the maximum potential amount of future payments under certain of these agreements, due to the conditional nature of the corporation's obligations and the

unique facts and circumstances involved in each particular agreement. Historically, payments made by the corporation under these agreements have not had a material effect on the corporation's business, financial condition or results of operations. The corporations believes taht if it were to incur a loss in any of these matters, such loss would not have a material effect on the corporation's business, financial condition or results of operations.

The material guarantees, within the scope of FIN 45, for which the maximum potential amount of future payments can be determined, are as follows:

- As is more completely described in the Sale of Accounts Receivable note on page 61 of this document, the corporation retains the risk of credit loss on $250 of receivables that have been sold. The fair value of the guarantee issued on the collection of these amounts is $15.
- The corporation is contingently liable for leases on property operated by others. At June 28, 2003, the maximum potential amount the corporation could be required to make if all the current operators default is $169. This contingent obligation is more completely described on page 60 of this document.
- The corporation has guaranteed the payment of certain third-party debt. The maximum potential amount of future payments that the corporation could be required to make, in the event that these third parties default on their debt obligations, is $32. At the present time, the corporation does not believe it is probable that any of these third parties will default on the amount subject to guarantee.

1.164

UNITED STATES STEEL CORPORATION (DEC)

NOTES TO CONSOLIDATED FINANCIAL STATEMENTS

31 (In Part): Contingencies and Commitments

Environmental and Other Indemnifications

Throughout its history, U. S. Steel has sold numerous properties and businesses and has provided various indemnifications with respect to many of the assets that were sold. These indemnifications have been associated with the condition of the property, the approved use, certain representations and warranties, matters of title and environmental matters. While the vast majority of indemnifications have not covered environmental issues, there have been a few transactions in which U. S. Steel indemnified the buyer for non-compliance with past, current and future environmental laws related to existing conditions; however, most recent indemnifications are of a limited nature only applying to non-compliance with past and/or current laws. Some indemnifications only run for a specified period of time after the transactions close and others run indefinitely. The amount of potential environmental liability associated with these transactions is not estimable due to the nature and extent of the unknown conditions related to the properties sold. Aside from the environmental liabilities already recorded as a result of these transactions due to specific environmental remediation cases (included in the $131 million of accrued liabilities for remediation discussed above), there are no other known environmental liabilities related to these transactions.

Guarantees

Guarantees of the liabilities of unconsolidated entities of U.S. Steel totaled $28 million at December 31, 2003, including $5 million related to an equity interest acquired as part of the National asset purchase, and $27 million at December 31, 2002. In the event that any defaults of guaranteed liabilities occur, U. S. Steel has access to its interest in the assets of the investees to reduce potential losses resulting from these guarantees. As of December 31, 2003, the largest guarantee for a single such entity was $14 million, which represents the maximum exposure to loss under a guarantee of debt service payments of an equity investee. No liability has been recorded for these guarantees.

Letters of Credit

1.165

INTERACTIVECORP (DEC)

NOTES TO CONSOLIDATED FINANCIAL STATEMENTS

Note 8 (In Part): Commitments

The Company also has funding commitments that could potentially require its performance in the event of demands by third parties or contingent events, such as under lines of credit extended or under guarantees of debt, as follows (in thousands):

| | Total Amounts Committed | Amount of Commitment Expiration Per Period | | |
		Less Than 1 Year	1–3 Years	3–5 Years
Letters of credit	$ 49,328	$46,649	$ 2,679	$ —
Purchase obligations	59,595	29,458	22,962	7,175
Guarantees	51,079	6,398	44,371	310
Total commercial commitments	$160,002	$82,505	$70,012	$7,485

The letters of credit are primarily extended to certain hotel properties to secure payment for the potential purchase of hotel rooms as well as for inventory purchases by HSN. There have been no claims made against any letters of credit. Purchase obligations are defined as agreements to purchase goods or services that are enforceable and legally binding and that specify all significant terms, including: fixed or minimum quantities to be purchased; fixed, minimum or variable pricing provisions; and the approximate timing of the transaction. The purchase obligations primarily relate to two national telecommunications contracts with certain vendors related to data transmission lines and telephones. The guarantees primarily relate to guarantees to the U.K. Civil Aviation Authority for the potential non-delivery of travel sold in the U.K. market

as agents are required to be bonded in the U.K. in the event that tour operators cannot fulfill their obligations.

Note 18. Financial Instruments

The additional disclosure below of the estimated fair value of financial instruments has been determined by the Company using available market information and appropriate valuation methodologies when available. The Company's financial instruments include letters of credit and bank guarantees. These commitments are in place to facilitate the commercial operations of certain IAC's subsidiaries.

(In thousands)	2003 Carrying Amount	2003 Fair Value	2002 Carrying Amount	2002 Fair Value
Cash and cash equivalents	$ 899,062	$ 899,062	$ 1,998,114	$ 1,998,114
Restricted cash	31,356	31,356	40,696	40,696
Long-term investments	2,855,032	2,855,032	3,010,712	3,010,712
Long-term obligations	(1,122,947)	(1,231,204)	(1,236,102)	(1,280,611)
Derivative contracts	(10,124)	(10,124)	—	—
Letters of credit	—	49,328	—	38,947
Bank guarantees	—	51,079	—	30,142

Sale of Receivables With Recourse

1.166

DILLARD'S, INC. (JAN)

NOTES TO CONSOLIDATED FINANCIAL STATEMENTS

14. Fair Value Disclosures

The estimated fair values of financial instruments which are presented herein have been determined by the Company using available market information and appropriate valuation methodologies. However, considerable judgment is required in interpreting market data to develop estimates of fair value. Accordingly, the estimates presented herein are not necessarily indicative of amounts the Company could realize in a current market exchange.

The fair value of trade accounts receivable is determined by discounting the estimated future cash flows at current market rates, after consideration of credit risks and servicing costs using historical rates. The fair value of the Company's long-term debt and Guaranteed Preferred Beneficial Interests in the Company's Subordinated Debentures is based on market prices or dealer quotes (for publicly traded unsecured notes) and on discounted future cash flows using current interest rates for financial instruments with similar characteristics and maturity (for bank notes and mortgage notes).

The fair value of the Company's cash and cash equivalents and trade accounts receivable approximates their carrying values at January 31, 2004 and February 1, 2003 due to the short-term maturities of these instruments. The fair value of the Company's long-term debt at January 31, 2004 and February 1, 2003 was $2.06 billion and $2.24 billion, respectively. The carrying value of the Company's long-term debt at January 31, 2004 and February 1, 2003 was $2.02 billion and $2.33 billion, respectively. The fair value of the Guaranteed Preferred Beneficial Interests in the Company's Subordinated Debentures at January 31, 2004 and February 1, 2003 was $526 million and $473 million, respectively. The carrying value of the Guaranteed Preferred Beneficial Interests in the Company's Subordinated Debentures at January 31, 2004 and February 1, 2003 was $532 million.

15. Securitizations of Assets

As part of its credit card securitizations, the Company transfers credit card receivable balances to a Trust in exchange for certificates representing undivided interests in such receivables. The Trust securitizes balances by issuing certificates representing undivided interests in the Trust's receivables to outside investors. In each securitization, the Company retains certain subordinated interests that serve as a credit enhancement to outside investors and expose the Trust assets to possible credit losses on receivables sold to outside investors. The investors and the Trust have no recourse against the Company beyond Trust assets. In order to maintain the committed level of securitized assets, the Trust reinvests cash collections on securitized accounts in additional balances. The Company also receives annual servicing fees as compensation for servicing the outstanding balances.

Currently, all borrowings under the Company's receivable financing conduit are recorded on balance sheet. The Company had $400 million of long-term debt outstanding under this agreement on the consolidated balance sheet as of January 31, 2004 and February 1, 2003. Prior to May 2002, the Company accounted for securitizations of credit card receivables as sales of receivables, thus off balance sheet. Since May 2002, future transfers no longer meet sale treatment, and interest paid to outside investors is recorded in interest expense instead of other revenue. The Company reclassified $11.3 million for the twelve months ended February 2, 2002 to conform to current period classification. Accordingly, as a result of this decision, the Company recorded an income statement charge of $5.4 million related to the amortization of the beneficial interests recognized up front on the off-balance-sheet financing for the twelve months ended February 1, 2003. This charge was included in Service Charges, Interest and Other Income.

At January 31, 2004 and February 1, 2003, the Company had $50.0 million and $0 outstanding, respectively, in short-term borrowings under its accounts receivable conduit facilities related to seasonal financing needs. Remaining available short-term borrowings under these conduit facilities at January 31, 2004 were $450.0 million.

1.167

TECUMSEH PRODUCTS COMPANY (DEC)

NOTES TO CONSOLIDATED FINANCIAL STATEMENTS

Note 12 (In Part): Guarantees and Warranties

A portion of export accounts receivable at the Company's Brazilian subsidiary are sold with recourse. Brazilian export receivables sold at December 31, 2003 and December 31,

2002 were $64.5 million and $41.2 million, respectively. The Company estimates the fair value of the contingent liability related to these receivables to be $0.1 million, which is included in operating income and allowance for doubtful accounts.

DISCLOSURES OF FAIR VALUE

1.168

ABBOTT LABORATORIES (DEC)

NOTES TO CONSOLIDATED FINANCIAL STATEMENTS
(Dollars in thousands, except where indicated)

Note 1 (In Part): Summary of Significant Accounting Policies

Cash, Cash Equivalents and Investment Securities

Cash equivalents consist of time deposits and certificates of deposit with original maturities of three months or less. Investments in marketable equity securities are classified as available-for-sale and are recorded at fair value with any unrealized holding gains or losses, net of tax, included in Accumulated other comprehensive income (loss). Investments in equity securities that are not traded on public stock exchanges are recorded at cost. Abbott monitors equity investments for other than temporary declines in fair value and charges impairment losses to income when an other than temporary decline in estimated value occurs. Investments in debt securities are classified as held-to-maturity, as management has both the intent and ability to hold these securities to maturity, and are reported at cost, net of any unamortized premium or discount. Income relating to these securities is reported as a component of interest income.

Note 3. Investment Securities

The following is a summary of investment securities at December 31:

	2003	2002	2001
Current investment securities			
Time deposits and certificates of deposit	$291,297	$120,000	$ 20,000
Other, primarily debt obligations issued or guaranteed by various governments or government agencies	—	141,677	36,162
Total	$291,297	$261,677	$ 56,162
Long-term investment securities			
Equity securities	$381,053	$222,667	$343,115
Time deposits and certificates of deposit	9,729	—	100,000
Corporate debt obligations	—	—	70,000
Debt obligations issued or guaranteed by various governments or governments agencies	15,575	28,112	134,099
Total	$406,357	$250,779	$647,214

Of the investment securities listed above, $15,575, $247,998, and $323,974 were held at December 31, 2003, 2002, and 2001, respectively, by subsidiaries operating in Puerto Rico under tax incentive grants expiring in 2015 and 2020.

Abbott reviews the carrying value of investments in equity securities each quarter to determine whether an other than temporary decline in market value exists. Abbott considers factors affecting the investee, factors affecting the industry the investee operates in, and general equity market trends. Abbott considers the length of time an investment's market value has been below carrying value and the near-term prospects for recovery to carrying value. When Abbott determines that an other than temporary decline has occurred, the investment is written down with a charge to Other (income) expense, net.

Gross unrealized holding gains (losses) on current and long-term held-to-maturity investment securities totaled $1,400 and $(2,200), respectively, at December 31, 2003; $1,500 and $(8,500), respectively, at December 31, 2002; and $2,000 and $(17,200), respectively, at December 31, 2001. Gross unrealized holding gains (losses) on available-for-sale equity securities totaled $162,700 and $(4,000), respectively, at December 31, 2003; $24,400 and $(9,200), respectively, at December 31, 2002; and $57,000 and $(1,800), respectively, at December 31, 2001. For current and long-term held-to-maturity securities and available-for-sale equity securities, the adjusted cost basis of the investments have been above the market value for less than one year as of December 31, 2003.

Note 4. Financial Instruments and Derivatives

Certain Abbott foreign subsidiaries enter into foreign currency forward exchange contracts to manage exposures to changes in foreign exchange rates for anticipated intercompany purchases by those subsidiaries whose functional currencies are not the U.S. dollar. These contracts, totaling $602 million, $857 million and $571 million at December 31, 2003, 2002 and 2001, are designated as cash flow hedges of the variability of the cash flows due to changes in foreign exchange rates. Abbott records the contracts at fair value, resulting in credits of $3.6 million and $11.4 million to Accumulated other comprehensive income (loss) in 2003 and 2001, respectively, and a $28.8 million charge to Accumulated other comprehensive income (loss) in 2002. No hedge ineffectiveness was recorded in income in 2003, 2002 or 2001. Accumulated gains and losses as of December 31, 2003 will be included in Cost of products sold at the time the products are sold, generally through the end of 2004.

Abbott is a party to interest rate hedge contracts totaling $3.25 billion to manage its exposure to changes in the fair value of $3.25 billion of fixed-rate debt due in July 2004 and 2006. These contracts are designated as fair value hedges of the variability of the fair value of fixed-rate debt due to changes in the long-term benchmark interest rates. The effect of the hedge is to change a fixed-rate interest obligation to a variable rate for that portion of the debt. Abbott records the contracts at fair value and adjusts the carrying amount of the fixed-rate debt by an offsetting amount. No hedge ineffectiveness was recorded in income in 2003, 2002 and 2001.

Abbott enters into foreign currency forward exchange contracts to manage currency exposures for foreign currency denominated third-party trade payables and receivables, and for intercompany loans and trade accounts payable where the receivable or payable is denominated in a currency other than the functional currency of the entity. For intercompany loans, the contracts require Abbott to sell foreign currencies, primarily European currencies and Japanese yen, in exchange for primarily U.S. dollars and other European currencies. For intercompany and trade payables and receivables, the currency exposures are primarily the U.S. dollar, European currencies and Japanese yen. These contracts are recorded at fair value, with the resulting gains or losses reflected in income as Net foreign exchange (gain) loss. At December 31, 2003, 2002, and 2001, Abbott held $3.0 billion, $1.9 billion, and $3.1 billion, respectively, of such foreign currency exchange contracts.

The carrying values and fair values of certain financial instruments as of December 31 are shown in the table below. The carrying values of all other financial instruments approximate their estimated fair values. Fair value is the quoted market price of the instrument held or the quoted market price of a similar instrument. The counter parties to financial instruments consist of select major international financial institutions. Abbott does not expect any losses from nonperformance by these counter parties.

	2003		2002		2001	
(Dollars in millions)	Carrying Value	Fair Value	Carrying Value	Fair Value	Carrying Value	Fair Value
Investment securities:						
Current	$ 291.3	$ 291.3	$ 261.7	$ 259.4	$ 56.2	$ 56.2
Long-term:						
Held-to-maturity debt securities	25.3	24.5	28.1	23.4	304.1	288.9
Available-for-sale equity securities	381.1	381.1	222.7	222.7	343.1	343.1
Total long-term debt	(5,161.6)	(5,407.2)	(4,495.1)	(4,640.4)	(4,337.9)	(4,453.2)
Foreign currency forward exchange contracts:						
(Payable) position	(33.3)	(33.3)	(34.3)	(34.3)	(38.7)	(38.7)
Receivable position	3.0	3.0	16.5	16.5	16.0	16.0
Interest rate hedge contracts	128.7	128.7	160.2	160.2	21.8	21.8

Note 13. Debt and Lines of Credit

The following is a summary of long-term debt at December 31:

	2003	2002	2001
5.6% debentures, due 2003	$ —	$ —	$ 200,000
5.125% debentures, due 2004	—	1,650,000	1,650,000
6.8% debentures, due 2005	150,000	150,000	150,000
5.625% debentures, due 2006	1,600,000	1,600,000	1,600,000
6.4% debentures, due 2006	250,000	250,000	250,000
0.77% Yen notes, due 2007	91,324	—	—
6.0% debentures, due 2008	200,000	200,000	200,000
5.4% debentures, due 2008	200,000	200,000	200,000
1.05% Yen notes, due 2008	456,621	—	—
1.51% Yen notes, due 2010	136,986	—	—
1.95% Yen notes, due 2013	228,311	—	—
Other, including fair market value adjustments relating to interest rate hedge contracts designated as fair value hedges	139,087	223,973	85,493
Total, net of current maturities	3,452,329	4,273,973	4,335,493
Current maturities of long-term debt, including fair market value adjustments relating to interest rate hedge contracts designated as fair value hedges	1,709,265	221,111	2,379
Total carrying amount	$5,161,594	$4,495,084	$4,337,872

Principal payments required on long-term debt outstanding at December 31, 2003, are $1,656,772 in 2004, $154,587 in 2005, $1,854,275 in 2006, $91,994 in 2007, $858,189 in 2008, and $417,053 thereafter.

At December 31, 2003, Abbott had $3,000,000 of unused lines of credit, which support commercial paper borrowing arrangements. Related compensating balances, which are subject to withdrawal by Abbott at its option, and commitment fees are not material. Abbott's weighted average interest rate on short-term borrowings was 1.1% at December 31, 2003 and 2002 and 1.9% at December 31, 2001.

1.169

BAUSCH & LOMB INCORPORATED (DEC)

NOTES TO FINANCIAL STATEMENTS
(Dollar amounts in millions)

Note 1 (In Part): Accounting Policies

Derivative Financial Instruments and Hedging Activity
Effective January 1, 2001, the Company adopted SFAS No. 133, *Accounting for Derivative Instruments and Hedging Activities,* as amended by SFAS No. 138, *Accounting for Certain Derivative Instruments and Certain Hedging Activities, an amendment of SFAS No. 133,* collectively referred to as SFAS No. 133. SFAS No. 133 requires that all derivative instruments be recorded on the balance sheet at their respective fair values. Changes in the fair value of derivatives are recorded each period in current income or other comprehensive income, depending on their designation as a hedge of a particular exposure.

The Company enters into financial derivative instruments only for the purpose of minimizing risk and thereby protecting income. Derivative instruments utilized as part of the Company's risk management strategy may include interest rate swaps, locks and caps, and forward foreign exchange contracts and options. All derivatives are recognized on the balance sheet at fair value. The Company does not employ leveraged derivative instruments, nor does it enter into derivative instruments for trading or speculative purposes.

Upon entering into a derivative contract, the Company may designate, as appropriate, the derivative as a fair value hedge, cash flow hedge, foreign currency hedge or hedge of a net investment in a foreign operation. At inception, the Company formally documents the relationship between the hedging instrument and underlying hedged item, as well as risk management objective and strategy. Specifically, this procedure will link the hedging instrument to recognized assets or liabilities on the balance sheet or to explicit firm commitments or forecasted transactions. In addition, the Company assesses, both at inception and on an ongoing basis, whether the derivative used in a hedging transaction is highly effective in offsetting changes in the fair value or cash flow of the respective hedged item. When it is determined that a derivative is no longer highly effective as a hedge, the Company will discontinue hedge accounting prospectively.

In using derivative instruments, the Company is exposed to credit risk. The Company's derivative instrument counterparties are high quality investment or commercial banks with significant experience with such instruments. The Company manages exposure to counterparty risk by requiring specific minimum credit standards and diversification of counterparties.

The Company will generally enter into interest rate swap agreements to limit its exposure to interest rate movements within the parameters of its interest rate hedging policy. This allows for interest rate exposures from floating-rate assets to be offset by a substantially similar amount of floating-rate liabilities. When appropriate, interest rate derivatives may be used to readjust this natural hedge position.

Fair value hedges may be employed by the Company to hedge changes in the fair value of recognized financial assets or liabilities or unrecognized firm commitments. This is usually accomplished by entering into interest rate swaps converting fixed-rate long-term investments or debt to a floating rate. Changes in the fair value of the derivative instrument and the hedged item attributable to the hedged risk are recognized in income, and will generally offset each other. The Company attempts to structure fair value hedges so as to qualify for the shortcut method of hedge effectiveness analysis, thereby assuming no ineffectiveness in the hedge relationship. Specifically, the Company seeks to ensure that the critical terms of the interest rate swap and the hedged item are identical, the swap value is zero at inception, settlement calculations are consistent throughout the term of the swap and no floors or caps exist on the swap variable rate. In the event it is determined that the hedging relationship no longer qualifies as an effective fair value hedge, the derivative will continue to be carried on the balance sheet at its fair value, with changes in fair value recorded in income. Upon termination of a derivative in an effective fair value hedge, any associated gain or loss will be an adjustment to income over the remaining life of the hedged item, if any.

The Company may implement cash flow hedges to protect itself from fluctuation in cash flows associated with recognized variable-rate assets or liabilities or forecasted transactions. This may be accomplished by entering into interest rate swaps converting the hedged item from a variable rate to a fixed rate. Changes in the fair value of the hedging derivative are initially recorded in other comprehensive income, then recognized in income in the same period(s) in which the hedged transaction affects income. The Company attempts to structure cash flow hedges such that all the critical terms of the derivative match the hedged item, thereby assuming no ineffectiveness in the hedge relationship at inception. Specifically, the Company seeks to ensure that the critical terms of the interest rate swap and the hedged item are identical, the swap value is zero at inception, settlement calculations are consistent throughout the term of the swap, no floors or caps exist on the swap variable rate, and variable rate repricing dates and indexes are comparable. The Company performs and documents an assessment of hedge effectiveness on an ongoing basis throughout the hedge period. In the event it is determined that the hedging relationship no longer qualifies as an effective cash flow hedge, the derivative will continue to be carried on the balance sheet at its fair value, with changes in fair value recorded in income. If hedge accounting is discontinued because it becomes probable a forecasted transaction will not occur, the derivative will continue to be carried on the balance sheet at its fair value, with changes in fair value recorded in income, and any amounts previously recorded in other comprehensive income will immediately be recorded in income.

The Company principally uses forward foreign exchange contracts to hedge foreign exchange exposures. The portfolio of contracts is adjusted at least monthly to reflect changes in exposure positions, as they become known. When possible and practical, the Company matches the maturity of the hedging instrument to that of the underlying exposure. Net settlements are generally made at contract maturity based on rates agreed to at contract inception.

The Company will enter into foreign currency derivatives to protect itself from variability in cash flows associated with recognized foreign currency denominated assets or liabilities or forecasted transactions. Changes in the fair value of the hedging derivative are initially recorded in other comprehensive income, then recognized in income in the same period(s) in which the hedged transaction affects income.

The Company has numerous investments in foreign subsidiaries, and the net assets of these subsidiaries are exposed to currency exchange rate volatility. To hedge this exposure the Company may utilize forward foreign exchange contracts, generally with maturities of approximately three months. Net investment hedges are implemented for material subsidiaries on a selective basis. The effective portion of the change in fair value of the hedging instrument is reported in the same manner as the translation adjustment for the hedged subsidiary; that is, reported in the cumulative translation adjustment section of other comprehensive income. The fair value of the derivative attributable to changes between the forward rate and spot rate is excluded from the measure of hedge effectiveness and that difference is reported in income over the life of the contract. Quarterly, the Company evaluates its hedges of net investments in foreign subsidiaries for effectiveness and adjusts the value of hedge instruments or redesignates the hedging relationship accordingly.

The Company enters into forward foreign exchange contracts, with terms normally lasting less than six months, to hedge against foreign currency transaction gains and losses on foreign currency denominated assets and liabilities based on changes in foreign currency spot rates. Although allowable, a hedging relationship for this risk has not been designated, as designation will not achieve different financial reporting results. Forward foreign exchange contracts within this category are carried on the balance sheet at fair value, with changes in fair value recorded in income.

Note 17. Financial Instruments

The carrying amount of cash, cash equivalents and notes payable approximates fair value, as maturities are less than one year in duration. The Company's remaining financial instruments consisted of the following:

	2003		2002	
	Carrying Value	Fair Value	Carrying Value	Fair Value
Non-derivatives				
Other investments	$ 6.1	$ 6.1	$ 7.1	$ 7.1
Long-term debt, including current portion	(847.0)	(897.4)	(842.7)	(825.9)
Derivatives held for purposes other than trading				
Foreign exchange instruments				
Other current assets	$ 8.0	$ 8.0	$ 6.3	$ 6.3
Accrued liabilities	(6.9)	(6.9)	(18.4)	(18.4)
Net foreign exchange instruments	$ 1.1	$ 1.1	$ (12.1)	$ (12.1)
Interest rate instruments				
Other current assets	$ 0.6	$ 0.6	$ —	$ —
Accrued liabilities	—	—	(4.9)	(4.9)
Net interest rate instruments	$ 0.6	$ 0.6	$ (4.9)	$ (4.9)

Fair value of other investments was determined based on contract terms and an evaluation of expected cash flows and investment risk. Fair value of long-term debt was estimated using either quoted market prices for the same or similar issues or current rates offered to the Company for debt with similar maturities. The fair value of foreign exchange and interest rate instruments was determined using a model that estimates fair value at market rates, or was based upon quoted market prices for similar instruments with similar maturities.

The Company enters into forward foreign exchange contracts primarily to hedge foreign currency transactions and equity investments in non-U.S. subsidiaries. At December 27, 2003 and at December 28, 2002, the Company hedged aggregate exposures of $408.5 and $910.2, respectively, by entering into forward foreign exchange contracts requiring the purchase or sale of U.S. and foreign currencies. The Company selectively hedges firm commitments that represent both a right and an obligation, mainly for committed purchase orders for foreign-sourced inventory.

At December 27, 2003 and at December 28, 2002, the Company was party to interest rate instruments that had aggregate notional amounts of $50.0.

Counterparties to the financial instruments discussed above expose the Company to credit risks to the extent of non-performance. The credit ratings of the counterparties, which consist of a diversified group of major financial institutions, are regularly monitored and thus credit loss arising from counterparty non-performance is not anticipated.

1.170

HERSHEY FOODS CORPORATION (DEC)

NOTES TO CONSOLIDATED FINANCIAL STATEMENTS

1 (In Part): Summary of Significant Accounting Policies

Cash Equivalents

Cash equivalents consist of highly liquid debt instruments, time deposits and money market funds with original maturities of three months or less. The fair value of cash and cash equivalents approximates the carrying amount.

Commodities Futures Contracts

In connection with the purchasing of cocoa, sugar, corn sweeteners, natural gas, fuel oil and certain dairy products for anticipated manufacturing requirements and to hedge transportation costs, the Company enters into commodities futures contracts as deemed appropriate to reduce the effect of price fluctuations.

In June 1998, the FASB issued Statement of Financial Accounting Standards No. 133, *Accounting for Derivative Instruments and Hedging Activities.* Subsequently, the FASB issued Statement No. 137, *Accounting for Derivative Instruments and Hedging Activities—Deferral of the Effective Date of FASB Statement No. 133, an amendment of FASB Statement No. 133,* Statement No. 138, *Accounting for Certain Derivative Instruments and Certain Hedging Activities, an amendment of FASB Statement No. 133, and Statement No. 149, Amendment of Statement 133 on Derivative Instruments and Hedging Activities* (collectively referred to as "SFAS No. 133, as amended"). SFAS No. 133, as amended, establishes accounting and reporting standards requiring that every derivative instrument be recorded on the balance sheet as either an asset or liability measured at its fair value. SFAS No. 133, as amended, requires that changes in the derivative's fair value be recognized currently in earnings unless specific hedge accounting criteria are met. Special accounting for qualifying hedges allows a derivative's gains and losses to offset related results on the hedged item in the income statement, to the extent effective, and requires that a company must formally document, designate and assess the effectiveness of transactions that receive hedge accounting.

The Company adopted SFAS No. 133, as amended, as of January 1, 2001. SFAS No. 133, as amended, provides that the effective portion of the gain or loss on a derivative instrument designated and qualifying as a cash flow hedging instrument be reported as a component of other comprehensive income and be reclassified into earnings in the same period or periods during which the transaction affects earnings. The remaining gain or loss on the derivative instrument, if any, must be recognized currently in earnings. For a derivative designated as hedging the exposure to changes in the fair value of a recognized asset or liability or a firm commitment (referred to as a fair value hedge), the gain or loss must be recognized in earnings in the period of change together with the offsetting loss or gain on the hedged item attributable to the risk being hedged. The effect of that accounting is to reflect in earnings the extent to which the hedge is not effective in achieving offsetting changes in fair value. All derivative instruments currently utilized by the Company, including commodities futures contracts, are designated and accounted for as cash flow hedges, except for fixed to variable interest rate swaps which are designated and accounted for as fair value hedges of the underlying long-term debt. Additional information with regard to accounting policies associated with derivative instruments is contained in Note 7, Derivative Instruments and Hedging Activities.

7. Derivative Instruments and Hedging Activities

The Company adopted SFAS No. 133, as amended, as of January 1, 2001. SFAS No. 133, as amended, requires the Company to recognize all derivative instruments as either assets or liabilities in the balance sheet at fair value. The accounting for the change in fair value of the derivative depends on whether the instrument qualifies for and has been designated as a hedging relationship and on the type of hedging relationship. There are three types of hedging relationships: a cash flow hedge, a fair value hedge and a hedge of foreign currency exposure of a net investment in a foreign operation. The designation is based upon the exposure being hedged. All derivative instruments currently utilized by the Company are designated and accounted for as cash flow hedges, except for fixed to variable interest rate swaps which are designated and accounted for as fair value hedges of the underlying long-term debt.

• • • • • •

Interest Rate Swaps

In order to minimize its financing costs and to manage interest rate exposure, the Company, from time to time, enters into interest rate swap agreements. In October 2003, the Company entered into interest rate swap agreements to effectively convert interest payments on long-term debt from fixed to variable rates. Interest payments on $200.0 million of 6.7% Notes due in October 2005 and $150.0 million of 6.95% Notes due in March 2007 were converted from the respective fixed rates to variable rates based on the London Interbank Offered Rate ("LIBOR"). The interest rate swap agreements qualify as fair value hedges and the notional amounts, interest rates and terms of the swap agreements are consistent with the underlying long-term debt they are intended to hedge. Therefore, there is no hedge ineffectiveness. Under SFAS No. 133, as amended, gains and losses on the fixed to variable interest rate swaps are recorded currently in earnings and the fair value is recorded as an asset or liability on the Consolidated Balance Sheets. The corresponding gain or loss on the underlying long-term debt is also recorded currently in earnings and an adjustment to the carrying value of the underlying long-term debt is recorded in the Consolidated Balance Sheets. The fair value of the fixed to variable interest rate swaps, an asset of $2.2 million, was included in other assets on the Consolidated Balance Sheets as of December 31, 2003. The corresponding increase to long-term debt was $2.2 million as of December 31, 2003.

In February 2001, the Company entered into interest rate swap agreements that effectively converted variable-interest-rate payments on certain leases from a variable to a fixed rate. Payments on leases associated with the financing of construction of a warehouse and distribution facility near Hershey, Pennsylvania for $61.7 million and the financing of the purchase of a warehouse and distribution facility near Atlanta, Georgia for $18.2 million are variable based on LIBOR. Such variable payments are forecasted transactions as defined by SFAS No. 133, as amended. The interest rate swap agreements effectively converted the variable-interest-rate payments on the leases from LIBOR to a fixed rate of 6.1%. Future changes in LIBOR are offset by changes in the value of the interest rate swap agreements, resulting in interest expense at the fixed rate of 6.1%.

As previously discussed in Note 2, Cumulative Effect of Accounting Change, the Company adopted Interpretation No. 46 as of June 30, 2003, resulting in the consolidation of the Company's three off-balance sheet arrangements with SPTs for the leasing of certain warehouse and distribution facilities. The consolidation of those entities resulted in the recording of long-term debt of $59.4 million and $17.5 million associated with the warehouse and distribution facilities near Hershey and Atlanta, respectively, corresponding to the aforementioned interest rate swap agreements. As of June 30, 2003, the Company designated a new hedging relationship contemporaneous with the discontinuance of the pre-existing hedging relationship due to the consolidation of the two corresponding SPTs. Prospectively, beginning on June 30, 2003, the interest rate differential on the interest rate swap agreements was classified as an adjustment to interest expense.

The vriable to fixed interest rate swap agreements qualify as cash flow hedges and the notional amounts, interest rates and terms of the swap agreements are consistent with the underlying lease agreements they are intended to hedge and, therefore, there is no hedge ineffectiveness. Gains and losses on the interest rate swap agreements are included in other comprehensive income and are recognized in cost of sales in the same period as the hedged interest payments affect earnings. The fair value of variable to fixed interest rate swap agreements was a liability of $5.2 million and $7.1 million as a December 31, 2003 and 2002, respectively, and was included on the Consolidated Balance Sheets as other long-term liabilities, with the offset reflected in accumulated other comprehensive income (loss), net of income taxes.

Cash flows from interest rate swap agreements are classified as net cash provided from operating activities on the Consolidated Statements of Cash Flows. The Company's risk related to the interest rate swap agreements is limited to the cost of replacing the agreements at prevailing market rates.

Foreign Exchange Forward Contracts and Options

The Company enters into foreign exchange forward contracts to hedge transactions primarily related to firm commitments to purchase equipment, certain raw materials and finished goods denominated in foreign currencies, and to hedge payment of intercompany transactions with its non-domestic subsidiaries. These contracts reduce currency risk from exchange rate movements. Foreign currency price risks are hedged generally for periods from 3 to 24 months.

Foreign exchange forward contracts and options are intended to be and are effective as hedges of firm, identifiable, foreign currency commitments. Since there is a direct relationship between the foreign currency derivatives and the foreign currency denomination of the transactions, foreign currency derivatives are highly effective in hedging cash flows related to transactions denominated in the corresponding foreign currencies. These contracts meet the criteria for cash flow hedge accounting treatment and, accordingly, gains and losses are included in other comprehensive income and are recognized in cost of sales or selling, marketing and administrative expense in the same period that the hedged items affect earnings. In entering into these contracts the Company has assumed the risk that might arise from the possible inability of counterparties to meet the terms of their contracts.

The Company does not expect any significant losses as a result of counterparty defaults.

The fair value of foreign exchange forward contracts and options was estimated by obtaining quotes for future contracts with similar terms, adjusted where necessary for maturity differences. The fair value of foreign exchange forward contracts and options was an asset of $1.6 million and $3.1 million as of December 31, 2003 and 2002, respectively, included on the Consolidated Balance Sheets as other current assets with the offset reflected in accumulated other comprehensive income (loss), net of income taxes. Cash flows from foreign exchange forward contracts and options designated as hedges of foreign currency price risks associated with the purchase of equipment are classified as net cash flows (used by) provided from investing activities on the Consolidated Statements of Cash Flows. Cash flows from other foreign exchange forward contracts are classified as net cash provided from operating activities.

Commodities Futures Contracts

In connection with the purchasing of cocoa, sugar, corn sweeteners, natural gas, fuel oil and certain dairy products for anticipated manufacturing requirements and to hedge transportation costs, the Company enters into commodities futures contracts as deemed appropriate to reduce the effect of price fluctuations. Commodity price risks are hedged generally for periods from 3 to 24 months. Commodities futures contracts meet the hedge criteria and are accounted for as cash flow hedges. Accordingly, gains and losses are included in other comprehensive income and are recognized ratably in cost of sales in the same period that the hedged raw material manufacturing requirements are recorded in cost of sales.

In order to qualify as a hedge of commodity price risk, it must be demonstrated that the changes in fair value of the commodities futures contracts are highly effective in hedging price risks associated with commodity purchases for manufacturing requirements and with transportation costs. The assessment of hedge effectiveness for commodities futures is performed on a quarterly basis by calculating the change in switch values relative to open commodities futures contracts being held and the number of futures contracts needed to price raw material purchases for anticipated manufacturing requirements and to hedge transportation costs. Tracking changes in basis differentials as discussed below also monitors effectiveness. The prices of commodities futures contracts reflect delivery to the same locations where the Company takes delivery of the physical commodities and, therefore, there is no ineffectiveness resulting from differences in location between the derivative and the hedged item. Commodities futures contracts have been deemed to be highly effective in hedging price risks associated with corresponding raw material purchases for manufacturing requirements and transportation costs.

Because of the rollover strategy used for commodities futures contracts, which is required by futures market conditions, some ineffectiveness may result in hedging forecasted manufacturing requirements as futures contracts are switched from nearby contract positions to contract positions which are required to fix the price of raw material purchases for manufacturing requirements. Hedge ineffectiveness may also result from variability in basis differentials associated with the purchase of raw materials for manufacturing requirements. Hedge ineffectiveness is measured on a quarterly basis and the ineffective portion of gains or losses on commodities futures is recorded currently in cost of sales in accordance with SFAS No. 133, as amended.

Exchange traded futures contracts are used to fix the price of physical forward purchase contracts. Cash transfers reflecting changes in the value of futures contracts (unrealized gains and losses) are made on a daily basis and are included in accumulated other comprehensive income (loss), net of income taxes, on the Consolidated Balance Sheets. Such cash transfers will be offset by higher or lower cash requirements for payment of invoice prices of raw materials, energy requirements and transportation costs in the future. Cash flows from commodities futures contracts are classified as net cash provided from operating activities on the Consolidated Statements of Cash Flows. Futures contracts being held in excess of the amount required to fix the price of unpriced physical forward contracts are effective as hedges of anticipated manufacturing requirements for each commodity. Physical commodity forward purchase contracts meet the SFAS No. 133, as amended, definition of "normal purchases and sales" and, therefore, are not considered derivative instruments.

The net after-tax impact of cash flow hedging derivatives on comprehensive income (loss) reflected a $20.2 million loss in 2003, a $106.7 million gain in 2002 and a $7.8 million loss in 2001. Net gains and losses on cash flow hedging derivatives were primarily associated with commodities futures contracts. Reclassification adjustments from accumulated other comprehensive income (loss) to income, for gains or losses on cash flow hedging derivatives, were reflected in cost of sales. Reclassification of gains of $51.9 million and $17.9 million for 2003 and 2002, respectively, and losses of $19.3 million for 2001 were associated with commodities futures contracts. Gains on commodities futures contracts recognized in cost of sales as a result of hedge ineffectiveness were approximately $.4 million, $1.5 million and $1.7 million before tax for the years ended December 31, 2003, 2002 and 2001, respectively. No gains or losses on cash flow hedging derivatives were reclassified from accumulated other comprehensive income (loss) into income as a result of the discontinuance of a hedge because it became probable that a hedged forecasted transaction would not occur. There were no components of gains or losses on cash flow hedging derivatives that were recognized in income because such components were excluded from the assessment of hedge effectiveness. As of December 31, 2003, the amount of net after-tax gains on cash flow hedging derivatives, including foreign exchange forward contracts and options, interest rate swap agreements and commodities futures contracts, expected to be reclassified into earnings in the next twelve months was approximately $28.3 million, which was primarily associated with commodities futures contracts.

9. Financial Instruments

The carrying amounts of financial instruments including cash and cash equivalents, accounts receivable, accounts payable and short-term debt approximated fair value as of December 31, 2003 and 2002, because of the relatively short maturity of these instruments. The carrying value of long-term debt, including the current portion, was $969.0 million as of December 31, 2003, compared to a fair value of $1,100.9 million based on quoted market prices for the same or similar debt issues. The carrying value of long-term debt, including the current portion, was $868.8 million as of December 31, 2002, compared to a fair value of $1,005.9 million.

As of December 31, 2003, the Company had foreign exchange forward contracts and options maturing in 2004 and 2005 to purchase $57.7 million in foreign currency, primarily Canadian dollars, and to sell $18.0 million in foreign currency, primarily Japanese yen, at contracted forward rates.

As of December 31, 2002, the Company had foreign exchange forward contracts maturing in 2003 and 2004 to purchase $45.1 million in foreign currency, primarily British sterling and euros, and to sell $17.2 million in foreign currency, primarily Japanese yen, at contracted forward rates.

The fair value of foreign exchange forward contracts and options is estimated by obtaining quotes for future contracts with similar terms, adjusted where necessary for maturity differences. The fair value of foreign exchange forward contracts and options included in prepaid expenses and other current assets was $1.6 million and $3.1 million as of December 31, 2003 and 2002, respectively. The Company does not hold or issue financial instruments for trading purposes.

In order to minimize its financing costs and to manage interest rate exposure, the Company, from time to time, enters into interest rate swap agreements. In October 2003, the Company entered into interest rate swap agreements to effectively convert interest payments on long-term debt from fixed to variable rates. Interest payments on $200.0 million of 6.7% Notes due in October 2005 and $150.0 million of 6.95% Notes due in March 2007 were converted from the respective fixed rates to variable rates based on LIBOR. In February 2001, the Company entered into interest rate swap agreements that effectively converted variable-interest-rate payments on certain leases from a variable to a fixed rate of 6.1%. The fair value of fixed to variable interest rate swap agreements was an asset of $2.2 million as of December 31, 2003 and the fair value of variable to fixed interest rate swaps was a liability of $5.2 million and $7.1 million as of December 31, 2003 and 2002, respectively.

1.171

YUM! BRANDS, INC. (DEC)

NOTES TO CONSOLIDATED FINANCIAL STATEMENTS
(Tabular amounts in millions)

Note 2 (In Part): Summary of Significant Accounting Policies

Guarantees

The Company has adopted Financial Accounting Standards Board ("FASB") Interpretation No. 45, "Guarantor's Accounting and Disclosure Requirements for Guarantees, Including Indirect Guarantees of Indebtedness to Others, an interpretation of FASB Statements No. 5, 57 and 107 and a rescission of FASB Interpretation No. 34" ("FIN 45"). FIN 45 elaborates on the disclosures to be made by a guarantor in its interim and annual financial statements about its obligations under guarantees issued. FIN 45 also clarifies that a guarantor is required to recognize, at inception of a guarantee, a liability for the fair value of certain obligations undertaken. The initial recognition and measurement provisions were applicable to certain guarantees issued or modified after December 31, 2002. While the nature of our business results in the issuance of certain guarantees from time to time, the adoption of FIN 45 did not have a material impact on our Consolidated Financial Statements for the year ended December 27, 2003.

We have also issued guarantees as a result of assigning our interest in obligations under operating leases as a condition to the refranchising of certain Company restaurants. Such guarantees are subject to the requirements of SFAS No. 145, "Rescission of FASB Statements No. 4, 44, and 64, Amendment of FASB Statement No. 13, and Technical Corrections" ("SFAS 145"). We recognize a liability for the fair value of such lease guarantees under SFAS 145 at their inception, with the related expense being included in refranchising gains (losses).

Derivative Financial Instruments

Our policy prohibits the use of derivative instruments for trading purposes, and we have procedures in place to monitor and control their use. Our use of derivative instruments has included interest rate swaps and collars, treasury locks and foreign currency forward contracts. In addition, on a limited basis we utilize commodity futures and options contracts. Our interest rate and foreign currency derivative contracts are entered into with financial institutions while our commodity derivative contracts are exchange traded.

We account for derivative financial instruments in accordance with SFAS No. 133, "Accounting for Derivative Instruments and Hedging Activities" ("SFAS 133") as amended by SFAS No. 149, "Amendment of Statement 133 on Derivative Instruments and Hedging Activities ("SFAS 149"). SFAS 133 requires that all derivative instruments be recorded on the Consolidated Balance Sheet at fair value. The accounting for changes in the fair value (i.e., gains or losses) of a derivative instrument is dependent upon whether the derivative has been designated and qualifies as part of a hedging relationship and further, on the type of hedging relationship. For derivative instruments that are designated and qualify as a fair value hedge, the gain or loss on the derivative instrument as well as the offsetting gain or loss on the hedged item attributable to the hedged risk are recognized in the results of operations. For derivative instruments that are designated and qualify as a cash flow hedge, the effective portion of the gain or loss on the derivative instrument is reported as a component of other comprehensive income (loss) and reclassified into earnings in the same period or periods during which the hedged transaction affects earnings. Any ineffective portion of the gain or loss on the derivative instrument is recorded in the results of operations immediately. For derivative instruments not designated as hedging instruments, the gain or loss is recognized in the results of operations immediately. See Note 16 for a discussion of our use of derivative instruments, management of credit risk inherent in derivative instruments and fair value information related to debt and interest rate swaps.

Note 14 (In Part): Short-Term Borrowings and Long-Term Debt

	2003	2002
Short-term borrowings		
Current maturities of long-term debt	$ 10	$ 12
International lines of credit	—	115
Other	—	19
	$ 10	$ 146
Long-term debt		
Senior, unsecured revolving credit facility, expires June 2005	$ —	$ 153
Senior, unsecured notes, due May 2005	351	351
Senior, unsecured notes, due April 2006	200	200
Senior, unsecured notes, due May 2008	251	251
Senior, unsecured notes, due April 2011	645	645
Senior, unsecured notes, due July 2012	398	398
Capital lease obligations (See Note 15)	112	99
Other, due through 2010 (6%–12%)	80	170
	2,037	2,267
Less current maturities of long-term debt	(10)	(12)
Long-term debt excluding SFAS 133 adjustment	2,027	2,255
Derivative instrument adjustment under SFAS 133 (See Note 16)	29	44
Long-term debt including SFAS 133 adjustment	$2,056	$2,299

Our primary bank credit agreement comprises a senior unsecured Revolving Credit Facility (the "Credit Facility") which matures on June 25, 2005. On December 26, 2003, we voluntarily reduced our maximum borrowings under the Credit Facility from $1.2 billion to $1.0 billion. The Credit Facility is unconditionally guaranteed by our principal domestic subsidiaries and contains financial covenants relating to maintenance of leverage and fixed charge coverage ratios. The Credit Facility also contains affirmative and negative covenants including, among other things, limitations on certain additional indebtedness, guarantees of indebtedness, level of cash dividends, aggregate non-U.S. investment and certain other transactions as defined in the agreement. We were in compliance with all debt covenants at December 27, 2003.

Under the terms of the Credit Facility, we may borrow up to the maximum borrowing limit less outstanding letters of credit. At December 27, 2003, our unused Credit Facility totaled $737 million, net of outstanding letters of credit of $263 million. There were no borrowings outstanding under the Credit Facility at the end of the year. The interest rate for borrowings under the Credit Facility ranges from 1.0% to 2.0% over the London Interbank Offered Rate ("LIBOR") or 0.00% to 0.65% over an Alternate Base Rate, which is the greater of the Prime Rate or the Federal Funds Effective Rate plus 0.50%. The exact spread over LIBOR or the Alternate Base Rate, as applicable, will depend upon our performance under specified financial criteria. Interest on any outstanding borrowings under the Credit Facility is payable at least quarterly. In 2003, 2002 and 2001, we expensed facility fees of approximately $6 million, $5 million and $4 million, respectively. At December 28, 2002, the weighted average contractual interest rate on borrowings outstanding under the Credit Facility was 2.6%.

Note 16 (In Part): Financial Instruments

Derivative Instruments

Interest Rates

We enter into interest rate swaps and forward rate agreements with the objective of reducing our exposure to interest rate risk and lowering interest expense for a portion of our debt. Under the contracts, we agree with other parties to exchange, at specified intervals, the difference between variable rate and fixed rate amounts calculated on a notional principal amount. At December 27, 2003 and December 28, 2002, we had outstanding pay-variable interest rate swaps with notional amounts of $350 million. These swaps have reset dates and floating rate indices which match those of our underlying fixed-rate debt and have been designated as fair value hedges of a portion of that debt. As the swaps qualify for the short-cut method under SFAS 133 no ineffectiveness has been recorded. The fair value of these swaps as of December 27, 2003 and December 28, 2002 was approximately $31 million and $48 million, respectively, and has been included in other assets. The portion of this fair value which has not yet been recognized as a reduction to interest expense (approximately $29 million and $44 million at December 27, 2003 and December 28, 2002, respectively) has been included in long-term debt.

During 2002, we entered into treasury locks with notional amounts totaling $250 million. These treasury locks were entered into to hedge the risk of changes in future interest payments attributable to changes in the benchmark interest rate prior to issuance of additional fixed-rate debt. These locks were designated and effective in offsetting the variability in cash flows associated with the future interest payments on a portion of the 2012 Notes. Thus, the insignificant loss at which these treasury locks were settled will be recognized as an increase to interest on the debt through 2012.

Foreign Exchange

We enter into foreign currency forward contracts with the objective of reducing our exposure to cash flow volatility arising from foreign currency fluctuations associated with certain foreign currency denominated financial instruments, the majority of which are intercompany short-term receivables and payables. The notional amount, maturity date, and currency of these contracts match those of the underlying receivables or payables. For those foreign currency exchange forward contracts that we have designated as cash flow hedges, we measure ineffectiveness by comparing the cumulative change in the forward contract with the cumulative change in the hedged item. No significant ineffectiveness was recognized in 2003 or 2002 for those foreign currency forward contracts designated as cash flow hedges.

Commodities

We also utilize on a limited basis commodity futures and options contracts to mitigate our exposure to commodity price fluctuations over the next twelve months. Those contracts have not been designated as hedges under SFAS 133. Commodity future and options contracts entered into for the fiscal years ended December 27, 2003 and December 28, 2002 did not significantly impact the Consolidated Financial Statements.

•   •   •   •   •   •

Fair Value

At December 27, 2003 and December 28, 2002, the fair values of cash and cash equivalents, short-term investments, accounts receivable, and accounts payable approximated carrying value because of the short-term nature of these instruments. The fair value of notes receivable approximates carrying value after consideration of recorded allowances.

The carrying amounts and fair values of our other financial instruments subject to fair value disclosures are as follows:

	2003		2002	
	Carrying Amount	Fair Value	Carrying Amount	Fair Value
Debt				
Short-term borrowings and long-term debt, excluding capital leases and the derivative instrument adjustments	$1,925	$2,181	$2,302	$2,470
Debt-related derivative instruments: Open contracts in a net asset position	31	31	48	48
Foreign currency-related derivative instruments: Open contracts in a net asset (liability) position	—	—	(1)	(1)
Lease guarantees	8	37	4	42
Guarantees supporting financial arrangements of certain franchisees, unconsolidated affiliates and other third parties	8	10	16	17
Letters of credit	—	3	—	3

We estimated the fair value of debt, debt-related derivative instruments, foreign currency-related derivative instruments, guarantees and letters of credit using market quotes and calculations based on market rates.

Note 24 (In Part): Guarantees, Commitments and Contingencies

Lease Guarantees and Contingencies

As a result of (a) assigning our interest in obligations under real estate leases as a condition to the refranchising of certain Company restaurants; (b) contributing certain Company restaurants to unconsolidated affiliates; and (c) guaranteeing certain other leases, we are frequently contingently liable on lease agreements. These leases have varying terms, the latest of which expires in 2030. As of December 27, 2003 and December 28, 2002, the potential amount of undiscounted payments we could be required to make in the event of nonpayment by the primary lessee was $411 million and $426 million, respectively. The present values of these potential payments discounted at our pre-tax cost of debt at December 27, 2003 and December 28, 2002, were $326 million and $310 million, respectively. Our franchisees are the primary lessees under the vast majority of these leases. We generally have cross-default provisions with these franchisees that would put them in default of their franchise agreement in the event of non-payment under the lease. We believe these cross-default provisions significantly reduce the risk that we will be required to make payments under these leases. Accordingly, the liability recorded for our exposure under such leases at December 27, 2003 and December 28, 2002, was not material.

Guarantees Supporting Financial Arrangements of Certain Franchisees, Unconsolidated Affiliates and Other Third Parties

At December 27, 2003 and December 28, 2002, we had provided approximately $32 million of partial guarantees of two loan pools related primarily to the Company's historical refranchising programs and, to a lesser extent, franchisee development of new restaurants. In support of one of these guarantees, we have posted $32 million of letters of credit. We also provide a standby letter of credit of $23 million under which we could potentially be required to fund a portion of one of the franchisee loan pools. The total loans outstanding under these loan pools were approximately $123 million at December 27, 2003. Any funding under the guarantees or letters of credit would be secured by the franchisee loans and any related collateral. We believe that we have appropriately provided for our estimated probable exposures under these contingent liabilities. These provisions were primarily charged to refranchising (gains) losses. New loans are not currently being added to either loan pool.

We have guaranteed certain lines of credit and loans of unconsolidated affiliates totaling $28 million and $26 million at December 27, 2003 and December 28, 2002, respectively. Our unconsolidated affiliates had total revenues of over $1.5 billion for the year ended December 27, 2003 and assets and debt of approximately $858 million and $41 million, respectively, at December 27, 2003.

We have also guaranteed certain lines of credit, loans and letters of credit of third parties totaling $8 million and $15 million at December 27, 2003 and December 28, 2002, respectively. If all such lines of credit and letters of credit were fully drawn the maximum contingent liability under these arrangements would be approximately $25 million as of December 27, 2003 and $27 million as of December 28, 2002.

We have varying levels of recourse provisions and collateral that mitigate the risk of loss related to our guarantees of these financial arrangements of unconsolidated affiliates and other third parties. Accordingly, our recorded liability as of December 27, 2003 and December 28, 2002 is not significant.

CONCENTRATIONS OF CREDIT RISK

1.172

KLA-TENCOR CORPORATION (JUN)

NOTES TO CONSOLIDATED FINANCIAL STATEMENTS

Note 1 (In Part): Summary of Significant Accounting Policies

Concentration of Credit Risk

Financial instruments that potentially subject KLA-Tencor to significant concentrations of credit risk consist principally of cash equivalents, short-term and non-current marketable securities, trade accounts receivable and derivative financial instruments used in hedging activities. KLA-Tencor invests in a variety of financial instruments, such as, but not limited to, certificates of deposit, corporate and municipal bonds, U.S. Treasury and agency securities, equity securities and, by policy, limits the amount of credit exposure with any one financial institution or commercial issuer. KLA-Tencor has not experienced any material credit losses on its investments.

A majority of KLA-Tencor's trade receivables are derived from sales to large multinational semiconductor manufacturers located throughout the world. Concentration of credit risk with respect ot trade receivables is considered to be limited due to its customer base and the diversity of its geographic sales areas. KLA-Tencor performs ongoing credit evaluations of its customers' financial condition and generally requires no collateral to secure accounts receivable. KLA-Tencor maintains a provision for potential credit losses based upon expected collectibility of all accounts receivable. In addition, KLA-Tencor may utilize letters of credit or non-recourse factoring to mitigate credit risk when considered appropriate.

KLA-Tencor is exposed to credit loss in the event of nonperformance by counterparties on the foreign exchange contracts used in hedging activities. These counterparties are large international financial institutions and to date, no such counterparty has failed to meet its financial obligations to us. KLA-Tencor does not anticipate nonperformance by these counterparties.

1.173

MCDERMOTT INTERNATIONAL, INC. (DEC)

NOTES TO CONSOLIDATED FINANCIAL STATEMENTS

Note 13. Financial Instruments With Concentrations of Credit Risk

Our Marine Construction Services segment's principal customers are businesses in the offshore oil, natural gas and hydrocarbon processing industries and other marine construction companies. The primary customer of our Government Operations segment is the U.S. Government (including its contractors). These concentrations of customers may impact our overall exposure to credit risk, either positively or negatively, in that our customers may be similarly affected by changes in economic or other conditions. In addition, we and many of our customers operate worldwide and are therefore exposed to risks associated with the economic and political forces of various countries and geographic areas. Approximately 58% of our trade receivables are due from foreign customers. We generally do not obtain any collateral for our receivables.

We believe that our provision for possible losses on uncollectible accounts receivable is adequate for our credit loss exposure. At December 31, 2003 and 2002, the allowance for possible losses we deducted from accounts receivable-trade on the accompanying balance sheet was $1.3 million and $1.6 million, respectively.

1.174

MONSANTO COMPANY (AUG)

NOTES TO CONSOLIDATED FINANCIAL STATEMENTS

Note 13 (In Part): Financial Instruments

Credit Risk Management

Monsanto invests its excess cash in deposits with major banks throughout the world and in high-quality short-term debt instruments. Such investments are made only in instruments issued or enhanced by high-quality institutions. As of Aug. 31, 2003, the company had no financial instruments that represented a significant concentration of credit risk. Limited amounts are invested in any single institution to minimize risk. The company has not incurred any credit risk losses related to those investments.

The company sells a broad range of agricultural products to a diverse group of customers throughout the world. In the United States, the company makes substantial sales to a relatively few large wholesale customers. The company's agricultural products business is highly seasonal, and it is subject to weather conditions that affect commodity prices and seed yields. Credit limits, ongoing credit evaluation, and account monitoring procedures are used to minimize the risk of loss. Collateral is secured when it is deemed appropriate by the company. For example, during the transition period, calendar year 2002, and calendar year 2001, in order to reduce credit exposure in Latin America, the company collected payments on certain customer accounts in grain.

Monsanto regularly evaluates its business practices to minimize its credit risk. As a result, the company improved its prepayment program and one of its marketing programs. In calendar year 2001, the U.S. prepayment program was modified. The change allowed the company to net customer prepayments as a legal offset against the customer's current outstanding balance during the transition period, calendar year 2002, and calendar year 2001. In calender year 2001, the company also modified one of its U.S. marketing programs, so that any amounts payable to a customer are first applied to the customer's receivable account.

1.175

WESTERN DIGITAL CORPORATION (JUN)

NOTES TO CONSOLIDATED FINANCIAL STATEMENTS

Note 1 (In Part): Organization and Summary of Significant Accounting Policies

Concentration of Credit Risk

The Company designs, develops, manufactures and markets hard drives to personal computer manufacturers, resellers and retailers throughout the world. The Company performs ongoing credit evaluations of its customers' financial condition and generally requires no collateral. The Company maintains reserves for potential credit losses, and such losses have historically been within management's expectations. At June 27, 2003 and June 28, 2002, the Company had reserves for potential credit losses of $5.2 million and $7.6 million, respectively. The Company also has cash equivalent policies that limit the amount of credit exposure to any one financial institution or investment instrument, and require that investments be made only with financial institutions or in investment instruments evaluated as highly credit-worthy.

SUBSEQUENT EVENTS

1.176 Events or transactions which occur subsequent to the balance sheet date but prior to the issuance of the financial statements and which have a material effect on the financial statements should be either recorded or disclosed in the financial statements. SAS No. 1, section 560, *Subsequent Events*, as amended by SAS No. 12, *Inquiry of a Client's Lawyer Concerning Litigation, Claims, and Assessments*, sets forth criteria for the proper treatment of subsequent events. Table 1-14 lists the subsequent events disclosed in the financial statements of the survey companies.

1.177 Examples of subsequent event disclosures follow.

1.178

TABLE 1-14: SUBSEQUENT EVENTS

	Number of Companies			
	2003	2002	2001	2000
Business combinations pending or effected..	83	67	72	63
Debt incurred, reduced or refinanced......................................	64	76	83	72
Discontinued operations....................	59	68	50	33
Litigation..	29	38	30	31
Capital stock issued or purchased...	27	18	20	16
Employee benefits.............................	11	8	12	4
Stock splits or dividends...................	11	3	7	5
Reorganization/bankruptcy..............	8	6	11	N/C*
Stock purchase rights........................	0	3	5	2
Other—described..............................	63	68	76	84

* N/C = Not compiled. Line item was not included in the table for the year shown.

Business Combinations

1.179

HILLENBRAND INDUSTRIES, INC. (SEP)

NOTES TO CONSOLIDATED FINANCIAL STATEMENTS

16. Subsequent Events

On October 20, 2003, Hill-Rom acquired Advanced Respiratory, Inc., a privately held manufacturer and distributor of non-invasive airway clearance products and systems. The acquisition of Advanced Respiratory fits well with Hill-Rom's existing pulmonary expertise, expands the Company's home-care product line, offers good growth potential and is aimed at allowing Hill-Rom to leverage its clinical sales force. The purchase price for the acquisition was $83 million, subject to certain working capital adjustments at the date of close not to exceed $12 million, with additional contingent payments not to exceed $20 million. The additional contingent purchase price is dependent upon Advanced Respiratory achieving certain net revenue targets over the next two years. The Company is currently still in the process of performing its allocation of purchase price, but goodwill associated with the transaction is expected to approximate between $50 and $55 million. Any required contingency payments would further increase goodwill at the time the net revenue targets are achieved. For the fiscal year ended June 30, 2003, Advanced Respiratory reported net revenues of approximately $45 million and income before income taxes of nearly $5 million.

In addition, on October 30, 2003, the Company announced a definitive agreement to acquire Mediq, Inc. (Mediq), a privately held company in the medical equipment outsourcing and asset management business. The acquisition of Mediq is subject to regulatory clearance and is expected to close before the end of January 2004. This acquisition will expand Hill-Rom's product and service offerings, strengthen after-sales service capabilities and allow increased leverage of Hill-Rom's global service center network. The purchase price for Mediq will approximate $330 million. Over the past twelve months, Mediq had approximately $165 million in revenues and approximately $53 million in EBITDA. The Company expects that upon consummation of the acquisition it could realize approximately $15 million in cost synergies over the course of its integration.

1.180

OXFORD INDUSTRIES, INC. (MAY)

NOTES TO CONSOLIDATED FINANCIAL STATEMENTS

Note 0. Subsequent Events

On June 13, 2003, we acquired all of the common stock of Viewpoint International, Inc. The transaction is valued at up to $325 million consisting of $240 million in cash, $10 million in Oxford common stock and up to $75 million in contingent payments, subject to the achievement by Viewpoint of certain performance targets. Viewpoint owns the Tommy Bahama lifestyle brand that is used to market a wide array of products and services including apparel, footwear, accessories, home furnishings and restaurants. Viewpoint also produces two additional collections under the Tommy Bahama label, Indigo Palms and Island Soft. It also operates over 30 Tommy Bahama retail locations across the country, six of which are retail/restaurant compounds.

We also entered into a new $275 million senior secured revolving credit facility, which has a five-year term and bears interest, at our option, at rates determined from time to time based upon (1) the higher of the federal funds rate or the applicable prime rate plus a spread or (2) LIBOR plus a spread. Borrowings under the new senior secured revolving credit facility are subject to a borrowing base calculation based on our inventories, real property and accounts receivable.

In connection with the completion of the Viewpoint acquision, the net proceeds from our $200 million senior notes offering were released from escrow. We used the net proceeds from our senior notes offering, together with limited borrowings under our new senior secured revolving credit facility and cash on hand, to finance the cash portion of the purchase price for the Viewpoint acquisition.

We also terminated the accounts receivable securitization facility in June 2003, in connection with the new senior revolving credit facility.

1.181

QUANEX CORPORATION (OCT)

NOTES TO CONSOLIDATED FINANCIAL STATEMENTS

19. Subsequent Events

On September 30, 2003 the Company announced that it signed a definitive purchase agreement with North Star Steel, a subsidiary of Cargill, Incorporated, to purchase the net assets of North Star's Monroe, Michigan based manufacturing facility in a cash transaction. The Company expects to close the transaction during its fiscal quarter ending January 31, 2004. North Star Steel-Monroe, located in Monroe, Michigan, is a scrap-based mini-mill producer of special bar quality and engineered steel bars primarily serving the light vehicle and heavy-duty truck markets. The facility, with revenues of approximately $175 million, can produce over 500,000 tons of bars in diameters from 0.5625″ to 3.25″. The facility employs approximately 380 employees. The operation will become part of Quanex's vehicular products segment and will be renamed MACSTEEL Monroe.

On November 21, 2003 the Company announced that it had signed a definitive purchase agreement to purchase the stock of TruSeal Technologies, Inc., in a cash transaction. The Company expects to close the transaction during its fiscal quarter ending January 31, 2004. TruSeal, headquartered in Beachwood, Ohio, manufactures and markets a full line of patented, flexible insulating glass spacer systems and sealants for wood, vinyl and aluminum windows. The product separates and seals glass within the window frame and acts as a thermal barrier to conserve energy. TruSeal's revenue for calendar year 2003 is expected to be approximately $80 million and they employ about 300 employees. The operation will become part of Quanex's building products segment.

These acquisitions will be financed through borrowings under the Company's existing Bank Agreement as amended on December 19, 2003.

Debt Incurred, Reduced, or Refinanced

1.182

CIENA CORPORATION (OCT)

NOTES TO CONSOLIDATED FINANCIAL STATEMENTS

17) Subsequent Events

On November 18, 2003, CIENA announced a full redemption of all of the outstanding ONI 5.00% convertible subordinated notes due October 15, 2005. The principal amount of the notes outstanding is $48.3 million. On the redemption date of December 19, 2003, CIENA will pay holders 102% of the outstanding principal amount of the notes plus accrued interest.

1.183

KNAPE & VOGT MANUFACTURING COMPANY (JUN)

NOTES TO CONSOLIDATED FINANCIAL STATEMENTS

17. Subsequent Events

In August 2003, the Company's Board of Directors approved a resolution to refinance the Company's revolving bank loan with a new lending institution. A commitment has been signed with the lender. The agreement calls for a $35 million unsecured revolving credit facility (including a $2.5 million sub limit for letters of credit) and matures on November 1, 2006. Interest on the revolving credit facility will be payable at prime or LIBOR rates plus a spread of up to .25 or 1.25%, respectively, based upon certain ratios.

1.184

MILACRON INC. (DEC)

NOTES TO CONSOLIDATED FINANCIAL STATEMENTS

Subsequent Events

On March 12, 2004, the company entered into a definitive agreement whereby Glencore Finance AG and Mizuho International plc purchased $100 million in aggregate principal amount of the company's new exchangeable debt securities. The proceeds from this transaction, together with existing cash balances, were used to repay the $8^3/_8$% Notes due March 15, 2004. The securities the company issued were

$30 million of 20% Secured Step-Up Series A Notes due 2007 and $70 million of 20% Secured Step-Up Series B Notes due 2007. The $30 million of Series A Notes are convertible into shares of the company's common stock at a conversion price of $2.00 per share and initially bear a combination of cash and pay-in-kind interest at a total rate of 20% per annum. The $70 million of Series B Notes initially bear a combination of cash and pay-in-kind interest at a total rate of 20% per annum. Both the Series A Notes and the Series B Notes are exchangeable for a new series of the company's convertible preferred stock with a cumulative dividend rate of 6%. Upon receipt of shareholder approval of both (i) the authorization of additional shares of the company's common stock and (ii) the issuance of the new series of convertible preferred stock convertible into such common stock and for which the Series A Notes and the Series B Notes may be exchanged, the interest rate applicable to both the Series A Notes and the Series B Notes will be retroactively reset to 6% per annum from the date of issuance, payable in cash. Following receipt of shareholder approval, as soon as a condition requiring the execution of a refinancing of the €115 million of $7^5/_8$% Eurobonds due in April 2005 is satisfied or waived, all Series A Notes and Series B Notes (and any common stock into which any Series A Notes had been converted) will be exchanged for shares of the new series of convertible preferred stock. If shareholder approval is not obtained on or before July 29, 2004, the Series A Notes and Series B Notes will be in default and will remain outstanding until March 15, 2007 with an initial interest rate of 20% from the date of issuance, increasing to 24% over time, and any common stock into which any Series A Notes had previously been converted will be exchanged for shares of the company's currently authorized, but unissued, serial preference stock with a 24% cumulative dividend rate.

Following exchange of the Series A Notes and the Series B Notes for convertible preferred stock, the holders of the convertible preferred stock would collectively own approximately between 40% and 60% of the company's fully diluted equity (on an as-converted basis), depending on whether the company exercises an option to redeem a portion of the convertible preferred stock with the proceeds from a rights offering to its existing shareholders. After seven years, the convertible preferred stock would automatically be converted into common stock at a conversion price of $2.00 per share but may be converted prior to that time at the option of the holders. The conversion price would be subject to reset to $1.75 per share at the end of the second quarter of 2005 if a test based on the company's financial performance for 2004 is not satisfied. In addition, as part of the transaction the company has agreed to issue to holders of the convertible preferred stock contingent warrants to purchase an aggregate of one million shares of the company's common stock, subject to receiving shareholder approval to increase its authorized common stock, which contingent warrants will be exercisable only if a test based on the company's financial performance for 2005 is not satisfied. Assuming that the company does not conduct a rights offering to its existing shareholders, and both the conversion price of the convertible preferred stock is reset to $1.75 and the contingent warrants are exercised, the holders of the convertible preferred stock would own approximately 62.5% of the company's fully diluted equity (on an as converted basis).

The events contemplated by the agreement with Glencore Finance AG and Mizuho International plc could result in an "ownership change" of the company for tax purposes. Were this to occur, the timing of the company's utilization of tax loss carryforwards and other tax attributes could be substantially delayed. Accordingly, this could affect income tax expense and cash income taxes in future years.

If the company does not obtain shareholder approval of both the authorization of additional shares of its common stock and the issuance of the new series of convertible preferred stock convertible into such common stock on or before July 29, 2004, its liquidity will be materially impaired as the Series A Notes and the Series B Notes will go into default and the interest rates thereon will become significantly higher. If shareholder approval has not been obtained on or before July 29, 2004, the interest payable on the Series A Notes and the Series B Notes will no longer be eligible for retroactive reset to 6%. Instead, interest on the Series A Notes and the Series B Notes will be payable in arrears (a) on September 15, 2004 in cash at a rate of 12% per annum and in additional Series A Notes or Series B Notes, as applicable, at a rate of 8% per annum, (b) on March 15, 2005 in cash at a rate of 16% per annum and in additional Series A Notes or Series B Notes, as applicable, at a rate of 8% per annum, (c) on September 15, 2005 in cash at a rate of 20% per annum and in additional Series A Notes or Series B Notes, as applicable, at a rate of 4% per annum, and (d) on March 15, 2006, and through to maturity on March 15, 2007, in cash at a rate of 24% per annum.

Pursuant to the definitive agreement with Glencore Finance AG and Mizuho International plc, the company has agreed to use its commercially reasonable efforts to cause a number of persons selected by holders of the Series A Notes, acting together, to be appointed or elected to a number of directorships on the company's board of directors in proportion to the percentage of the company's fully diluted equity represented by the number of shares of common stock into which the Series A Notes may be converted, rounded up to the nearest whole number.

On March 12, 2004, the company also reached a separate agreement with Credit Suisse First Boston for a $140 million credit facility having a term of approximately one year. At close, extensions of credit under the facility in an aggregate amount of $84 million were utilized to repay and terminate the company's existing revolving credit facility and its existing receivables purchase program.

This new credit facility consists of a $65 million revolving A facility, with a $25 million subfacility for letters of credit, and a $75 million term loan B facility. The company and certain of its wholly-owned domestic subsidiaries are joint and several borrowers under the new credit facility and the entire new credit facility is secured by first priority liens on substantially all assets of the company and its domestic subsidiaries and includes pledges of stock of various wholly-owned domestic subsidiaries and certain foreign subsidiaries.

Availability under the revolving A facility is limited by a borrowing base calculated based upon specified percentages of eligible receivables and eligible inventory, a $10 million minimum availability covenant (resulting in aggregate availability of no more than $55 million) and other reserve requirements. In addition, the borrowing base is subject to the customary ability of the administrative agent for the lenders to reduce advance rates, impose or change collateral value limitations, establish reserves and declare certain collateral ineligible from time to time in its reasonable discretion, any of which could reduce the company's borrowing availability under the revolving A facility at any time. At March 12, 2004, additional availability under the revolving A facility was approximately $20 million, after taking into account the minimum availability and existing reserve requirements.

With the exception of $4 million of domestic cash that may be held by the company outside the control of the administrative agent, all proceeds of the company's domestic accounts receivable and other domestic collateral are subject to a daily cash "sweep." Under the terms of the new credit facility, these proceeds are deposited in lockbox accounts under the control of the administrative agent and then transferred to blocked accounts under the control of the administrative agent. Each business day, the funds in the blocked accounts will be applied to pay down any outstanding borrowings under the revolving A facility. As a result, the company's liquidity is likely to be dependent on its ability to continue to make borrowings under the new credit facility. If the company is unable to satisfy the conditions to borrowing under the new credit facility, which include, among other things, conditions related to the continued accuracy of its representations and warranties and the absence of any unmatured or matured defaults, or any material adverse change in its business or financial condition, without a waiver the company would lose access to this important source of liquidity and its financial condition would be materially impaired.

The company has the ability to prepay the revolving A facility, in whole or in part, at any time without penalty. The company has the option to prepay the term loan B facility at any time, subject to a 2% prepayment fee on the principal amount prepaid, as follows: (i) in whole, to the extent concurrently therewith or prior thereto all revolving A loans have been repaid in full and all commitments under the revolving A facility have been terminated, or (ii) in whole or in part, if availability under the revolving A facility exceeds $10 million and no event of default exists. Prepayments of term loan B loans permanently reduce the company's availability under the new credit facility. The company is also required to make prepayments in connection with, among other things, asset sales and casualty events and in connection with the issuance of debt or equity, tax refunds, proceeds from other "corporate events" and other extraordinary receipts. Additionally, there are limitations placed on the amounts that can be paid to the holders of the $7^5/_8$% Eurobonds due April 2005 without causing a prepayment event.

The new credit facility includes a number of affirmative and negative covenants, including, but not limited to, negative covenants limiting the ability of the company and its subsidiaries to incur additional debt, incur liens, make capital expenditures, issue or sell capital stock and make restricted payments (including a prohibition on the ability to make cash interest or dividend payments on debt or equity securities issued pursuant to the terms of the definitive agreement entered into on March 12, 2004 among the company, Mizuho International plc and Glencore Finance AG, unless availability under the revolving A facility exceeds $25 million before taking into account minimum availability requirements). The new credit facility also includes a financial covenant that requires the company to achieve specified minimum levels of monthly cumulative EBITDA (earnings before interest, taxes, depreciation and amortization) adjusted to exclude certain restructuring costs and certain other items, each as specified in the financing agreement.

The new credit facility is subject to various events of default, including an event of default if the company does not obtain shareholder approval of both the authorization of additional shares of its common stock and the issuance of a new series of convertible preferred stock convertible into such common stock on or before July 29, 2004.

Borrowings under the new credit facility will bear interest, at the company's option, based upon either (i) a LIBOR rate plus the applicable margin (as defined below) or (ii) a reference rate plus the applicable margin (as defined below). The "applicable margin", with respect to revolver A LIBOR loans, is 3.25% per annum, and with respect to revolver A reference rate loans, is 1.5% per annum. The "applicable margin", with respect to term loan B LIBOR loans, is 10.5% per annum, and with respect to term loan B reference rate loans, is 8.00% per annum. In no event will the interest rate of (a) revolver A LIBOR loans be less than 4.75% and (b) revolver A reference rate loans be less than 5.5%. In no event will the interest rate of term loan B LIBOR loans or term loan B reference rate loans be less than 12%.

After giving effect to the repayment and termination of the existing revolving credit facility and the accounts receivable liquidity facility and repayment of the senior U.S. notes, the company's current cash balance was approximately $60 million at March 15, 2004.

Discontinued Operations

1.185

AVAYA INC. (SEP)

NOTES TO CONSOLIDATED FINANCIAL STATEMENTS

20 (In Part): Subsequent Events

Sale of Connectivity Solutions

In October 2003, the Company agreed to sell certain assets and liabilities of the Connectivity Solutions segment to CommScope, Inc. ("CommScope"). Under the terms of the agreement, the Company will receive a purchase price of $263 million, subject to adjustment, consisting of approximately $210 million of cash, a note in the amount of $18 million that is convertible into CommScope common stock one year after the closing, and CommScope common stock having a market value, at the time of the agreement, of $35 million. In addition, CommScope assumed approximately $75 million of primarily employee-related liabilities of Connectivity Solutions. The waiting period applicable to the sale under the Hart-Scott Rodino Antitrust Improvements Act, as amended, has expired. We expect the sale to close no later than the second quarter of fiscal 2004. Because the products offered by Connectivity Solutions do not fit strategically with the rest of the Company's product portfolio, the Company believes the sale will enable it to strengthen its focus on its core products offerings.

Listed below are the major classes of assets and liabilities as of September 30, 2003 that are included as part of the disposal group:

($ in millions)

Assets	
Receivables	$ 68
Inventory	142
Property, plant and equipment, net	179
Other assets	13
Total assets	$402

Liabilities	
Accounts payable	$ 54
Payroll and benefit obligation	31
Other liabilities	24
Total liabilities	$109

The final carrying values of the assets and liabilities to be transferred to Commscope will be determined upon the closing date, with the exception of the benefit obligations noted below.

Based upon an actuarial calculation using data as of September 30, 2003, the Company estimates that it will recognize a pension and postretirement curtailment loss of approximately $26 million upon the closing of the transaction and a settlement loss of approximately $37 million upon the transfer of pension and postretirement benefit assets and liabilities to Commscope. The estimated curtailment and settlement losses are subject to change based upon intervening events that may occur up to the closing date and the date on which the pension and postretirement benefit assets and liabilities are transferred, respectively. These losses will be recorded as a loss from discontinued operations. Additionally, these losses will increase the benefit obligation being transferred to Commscope by approximately $52 million and will remove an intangible asset of approximately $11 million that relates to unrecognized prior service costs associated with the benefit obligation which is included in other assets in the table above.

On October 30, 2003, in exchange for the International Brotherhood of Electrical Worker's agreement to withdraw numerous pending and threatened grievances and arbitration demands against the Company in connection with the Connectivity Solutions business, the Company agreed to provide a one-time payment of five thousand dollars to certain employees and offer an enhanced retirement incentive for those employees who are pension eligible as of December 2, 2003. The settlement agreement is contingent upon the closing of the sale of Connectivity Solutions to CommScope. Total payments, excluding the retirement incentive offer, are not expected to exceed $7 million. The Company expects to take a one-time charge in the first quarter of fiscal 2004 of approximately $4 million related to the acceptance by 124 employees of the retirement incentive offer.

1.186

EASTMAN KODAK COMPANY (DEC)

NOTES TO FINANCIAL STATEMENTS

Note 25 (In Part): Subsequent Events

On February 9, 2004, the Company announced its intent to sell the assets and business of the Remote Sensing Systems operation, including the stock of Kodak's wholly owned subsidiary, Research Systems, Inc., collectively known as RSS, to ITT Industries for $725 million in cash, RSS, a leading provider of specialized imaging solutions to the aerospace and defense community, is part of the Company's commercial & government systems' operation within the Commercial Imaging segment and its customers include NASA, other U.S. government agencies, and aerospace and defense companies. Kodak's RSS operation had sales in 2003 of approximately $425 million. The sale of RSS is expected to result in an after-tax gain of approximately $390 million (unaudited). The after-tax gain excludes the potential impacts from any settlement or cutailment gains or losses that may be incurred in connection with the Company's pension and postretirement benefit plans, as these amounts are not currently determinable. The Company is currently evaluating whether the sale of RSS will be accounted for as a discontinued operation beginning in the first quarter of 2004 in accordance with SFAS No. 144.

Litigation

1.187

POLO RALPH LAUREN CORPORATION (MAR)

NOTES TO CONSOLIDATED FINANCIAL STATEMENTS

20. Subsequent Events

On June 3, 2003, Jones filed a lawsuit against us in the Supreme Court of the State of New York alleging among other things that we breached our agreements with Jones with respect to the "Lauren" trademark by asserting our rights pursuant to the Cross Default and Term Extension Agreement and that we induced Ms. Jackwyn Nemerov, the former President of Jones, to breach the non-compete and confidentiality clauses in Ms. Nemerov's employment agreement with Jones. Jones has indicated that it will treat the Lauren license agreements as terminated as of December 31, 2003. Jones is seeking compensatory damages of $550.0 million as well as punitive damages and to enforce the provisions of Ms. Nemerov's agreement. If Jones' lawsuit were to be determined adversely to us, it could have a material adverse effect on our results of operations and financial condition; however, we believe that the lawsuit is without merit and that we will prevail. Also on June 3, 2003, we filed a lawsuit against Jones in the Supreme Court of the State of New York seeking among other things an injunction and a declaratory judgment that the Lauren license agreements terminate as of December 31, 2003 pursuant to the terms of the Cross Default and Term Extension Agreement. The Company is preparing to

begin production and marketing of the Lauren and Ralph lines with shipments beginning in January 2004.

Capital Stock Issued or Purchased

1.188

ARROW ELECTRONICS, INC. (DEC)

NOTES TO CONSOLIDATED FINANCIAL STATEMENTS

19 (In Part): Subsequent Events

In February 2004, the company sold 13,800,000 shares of common stock in an underwritten public offering, including 1,800,000 shares of common stock subject to a customary over-allotment option exercised by the underwriters.

The net proceeds from this offering of approximately $313,000,000, including the shares purchased pursuant to the over-allotment option, will be used to redeem the company's outstanding 8.7% senior notes due in 2005 (principal amount of $208,500,000) and for general corporate purposes, which may include the redemption or repurchase of other outstanding indebtedness from time to time. Until the redemption of the 8.7% senior notes, the net proceeds will be maintained as cash and short-term investments.

Employee Benefits

1.189

SEARS, ROEBUCK AND CO. (DEC)

NOTES TO CONSOLIDATED FINANCIAL STATEMENTS

Note 9 (In Part): Benefit Plans

Subsequent Event

Subsequent to the sale of its domestic Credit and Financial Products business, the Company initiated a project to review its domestic employee retirement benefits cost structure and programs. The Company assessed its retirement benefits programs in the context of comparable programs in the retail industry. As a result of this review, the Company concluded that its current retirement benefit package is not comparable with its retail peers nor is it consistent with the needs of the typical associate. As such, in January 2004, the Company announced a series of benefit plan changes which included the enhancement of the Company's 401(k) defined contribution plan and the phasing out of participation in its domestic pension plan. Associates hired in 2004 and those under the age of 40 as of December 31, 2004, will receive an increased Company-matching contribution to the 401(k) plan of 110%, but will no longer earn additional pension benefits effective January 1, 2005. Pension benefits continue to accrue for associates age 40 and older as of December 31, 2004, unless they elect to participate in the enhanced 401(k) defined contribution plan. In addition, the Company eliminated its retiree medical insurance contribution for associates hired in 2004 and those under the age of 40 as of December 31, 2004, and capped the contribution at the 2004 level for associates age 40 and older.

In connection with the domestic pension and postretirement plan changes discussed above, the Company believes that it would be preferable to change its accounting methods which under SFAS No's. 87 and 106 delay recognition of past events. Therefore, in the first quarter of 2004 the Company changed its method for determining the market-related value of plan assets used in determining the expected return-on-assets component of annual net pension costs and its method for recognizing gains and losses for both its domestic pension and postretirement benefit plans. Under the previous accounting method, the market-related value of the domestic pension plan assets was determined by averaging the value of equity assets over a five-year period. The new method recognizes equity assets at fair value. Further, under its previous accounting method, all unrecognized gains and losses in excess of the 10 percent corridor were amortized over the expected working lifetime of active employees (approximately 10 years). Under the new methodology, the portion of the total gain or loss outside the 10 percent corridor will be immediately recognized. As a result of this accounting change, the Company will record an after-tax charge of approximately $840 million in the first quarter of 2004 for the cumulative effect of the change in accounting. The charge represents the recognition of unamortized experience losses at the beginning of 2004 in accordance with the new methods.

Stock Splits/Dividends

1.190

JOHNSON CONTROLS, INC. (SEP)

NOTES TO CONSOLIDATED STATEMENTS

19. Subsequent Event (Unaudited)

On November 19, 2003, the Company's Board of Directors declared a two-for-one stock split of the common stock payable January 2, 2004 to shareholders of record on December 12, 2003. This stock split will result in the issuance of approximately 90.6 million additional shares of common stock and will be accounted for by the transfer of approximately $15.1 million from capital in excess of par value to common stock. Pro forma earnings per share amounts on

a post-split basis for the years ended September 30, 2003, 2002 and 2001 would be as follows:

Year Ended September 30,	2003	2002	2001 Adjusted**	As Reported
Earnings per share Basic				
As reported	$7.56	$6.71	$6.14	$5.41
Pro forma*	$3.78	$3.35	$3.07	$2.71
Diluted				
As reported	$7.20	$6.35	$5.79	$5.11
Pro forma*	$3.60	$3.18	$2.89	$2.55

* Pro forma amounts are unaudited and reflect the impact of the two-for-one stock split.

** The adjusted information is presented as if SFAS No. 142, "Goodwill and Other intangible Assets," had been adopted October 1, 2000. Results have been adjusted to exclude goodwill amortization expense of $70.8 million and the related income tax effect.

Information presented in the Consolidated Financial Statements, related notes and Five Year Summary have not been restated to reflect the two-for-one stock split.

Reorganization/Bankruptcy

1.191

INTERNATIONAL MULTIFOODS CORPORATION (FEB)

NOTES TO CONSOLIDATED FINANCIAL STATEMENTS

Note 18 (In Part): Subsequent Events

On April 1, 2003, we announced that we are taking actions to reduce the cost structured and improve the financial performance of our Canadian Foods and Foodservice Products businesses. This includes reorganizing our Canadian Foods business to reduce selling and administrative expenses and reducing production at our Foodservice Products plant in Sedalia, Missouri. These actions will result in a net reduction of approximately 100 full-time positions. We currently expect to recognize an unusual pre-tax charge of up to $3.5 million in the first quarter of fiscal 2004 and an annual pre-tax benefit of approximately $2 million from these actions, half of which will be recognized in fiscal 2004.

Sales Contract Terminated

1.192

GOODRICH CORPORATION (DEC)

NOTES TO CONSOLIDATED FINANCIAL STATEMENTS

Note W. Subsequent Event

On February 16, 2004 the Company was notified by Pratt & Whitney, a United Technologies Company, that it will not have requirements for original equipment PW4000 engine nacelle components after the Company completes delivery of 45 shipsets (2 units per shipset) through early 2005. The Company had originally forecasted 90 shipsets to be delivered through 2009. As a result of this action, the total estimated revenue associated with this contract has been significantly reduced and anticipated cost reductions related to future deliveries under this contract will not occur.

The notice of termination is considered a Type 1 subsequent event under generally accepted accounting principles, the effects of which must be reflected in the Company's 2003 financial statements. As a result, the Company recorded a pre-tax charge of $15.1 million, as of December 31, 2003 related to this contract. The charge includes impairment of excess over average inventory of $7.0 million and $8.1 million for forward losses relating to the reduction in forecasted contract revenue and the increase in costs.

Release of Commitments

1.193

UNITED TECHNOLOGIES CORPORATION (DEC)

NOTES TO CONSOLIDATED FINANCIAL STATEMENTS

Note 18 (In Part): Subsequent Events (Unaudited)

In January 2004, the Corporation received a $250 million payment from DaimlerChrysler. In consideration for this payment, the Corporation has released DaimlerChrysler from certain commitments previously made in support of MTU Aero Engines GmbH. The Corporation expects to use this first quarter gain for additional cost reduction actions across the businesses.

RELATED PARTY TRANSACTIONS

1.194 SFAS No. 57, *Related Party Disclosures*, specifies the nature of information which should be disclosed in financial statements about related party transactions. In 2003, 256 survey companies disclosed related party transactions. Examples of related party disclosures follow.

Sale of Receivables to Subsidiary

1.195

POLYONE CORPORATION (DEC)

NOTES TO CONSOLIDATED FINANCIAL STATEMENTS

Note C (In Part): Summary of Significant Accounting Policies

Sale of Accounts Receivable

PolyOne follows the provisions of SFAS No. 140, "Accounting for Transfers and Servicing of Financial Assets and Extinguishment of Liabilities," and as such, trade accounts receivable sold are removed from the balance sheet at the time of sale.

Note J—Sale of Accounts Receivable

Accounts receivable consist of the following:

(In millions)	2003	2002
Trade accounts receivable	$134.9	$114.2
Retained interest in securitized accounts receivable	137.9	56.5
Allowance for doubtful accounts	(9.3)	(9.6)
	$263.5	$161.1

Through May 6, 2003, PolyOne participated in a receivables sale facility that provided up to $250 million in liquidity through the sale of certain domestic trade accounts receivable at a cost similar to high-grade commercial paper. As part of the May 6, 2003 debt refinancing, previously discussed in Note H, PolyOne terminated the former facility and entered into a new receivables sale facility.

Under the terms of the new facility, PolyOne continues to sell its accounts receivable through its wholly owned, bankruptcy remote subsidiary to Investors who, in turn, purchase and receive ownership and security interests in those receivables. As collections reduce accounts receivable included in the pool, PolyOne sells new receivables. PolyOne has the risk of credit loss on the receivables and, accordingly the full amount of the allowance for doubtful accounts has been retained on the Consolidated Balance Sheets. At December 31, 2003, accounts receivable totaling $208.6 million were sold by PolyOne to PFC, and are thereby included as a reduction of trade accounts receivable within accounts receivable on the PolyOne Consolidated Balance Sheet. PFC in turn sells to certain purchasers an undivided interest in PolyOne's accounts receivable and realizes proceeds of up to $225.0 million, with the maximum amount of proceeds that PFC may receive under the facility currently limited to 85% of the then-current amount of the accounts receivable sold to PFC. At December 31, 2003, PFC had sold undivided interests in account receivable totaling $70.7 million. PolyOne retains an interest in the $137.9 million difference between the amount of trade receivables sold by PolyOne to PFC and the undivided interests sold by PFC. This interest retained by PolyOne is thereby included in accounts receivable on the PolyOne Consolidated Balance Sheet at December 31, 2003. The new receivables sale facility also makes available up to $50.0 million for the issuance of standby letters of credit as a sub-limit within the $225.0 million limit under the facility. Continued availability of the securitization program is conditioned upon compliance with covenants, related primarily to operation of the securitization, set forth in the related agreements. PolyOne is currently in compliance with all such covenants. The securitization agreement does not contain any credit rating downgrade triggers pursuant to which the program could be terminated.

Under this new arrangement, PolyOne receives the remaining proceeds from collection of the receivables after deduction for the aggregate yield payable on the undivided interests in the receivables sold by PFC, a servicer's fee, an unused commitment fee (between 0.5% and 0.75% depending upon the amount of the unused portion of the facility), fees for any outstanding letters of credit, and an administration and monitoring fee ($150,000 per annum).

Under this new arrangement, PolyOne continues to service the underlying accounts receivable and receives a service fee of 1% per annum on the average daily amount of the outstanding interests in its receivables. The net discount and other costs of the receivables sale facility are included in other expenses, net in the Consolidated Statements of Operations.

Transaction Between Reporting Entity and Investee

1.196

THE COCA-COLA COMPANY (DEC)

NOTES TO CONSOLIDATED FINANCIAL STATEMENTS

Note 2 (In Part): Bottling Investments

Coca-Cola Enterprises Inc.
Coca-Cola Enterprises Inc. ("CCE") is the world's largest marketer, distributor and producer of bottle and can nonalcoholic beverages, operating in eight countries. On December 31, 2003, our Company owned approximately 37 percent of the outstanding common stock of CCE.

•   •   •   •   •   •

A summary of our significant transactions with CCE is as follows (in millions):

	2003	2002	2001
Net concentrate and syrup sales to CCE	$4,681	$4,306	$3,852
CCE purchases of sweeteners through our company	311	325	295
Cash payments made by us directly to CCE	862	837	606
Cash payments made by us directly to CCE customers	214	204	282
Local media and marketing program reimbursements	221	264	252

Cash payments made by us directly to CCE represent support of certain marketing activities and our participation with them in cooperative advertising and other marketing. Cash payments made by us directly to CCE's customers represent support of certain marketing activities and programs. Pursuant to cooperative advertising and trade agreements with CCE, we received funds from CCE for local media and marketing program expense reimbursements.

In 2002, our Company entered into a multi-year Sales Growth Initiative ("SGI") agreement with CCE to support profitable growth of our brands in its territories. Total cash support paid by our Company under the SGI agreement was $150 million in 2002. This amount is included in the total support of certain marketing activities and our participation with them in cooperative advertising and other marketing programs noted above.

The entire SGI agreement may be terminated by either party by providing six months written notice to the other party; provided, however, that once an annual plan has been agreed upon by both companies, such termination shall not be effective until the end of the applicable plan year. In addition, during the first three quarters of any year, either party may cancel for ensuing quarters the sales volume growth targets and cash support funding provisions of the agreement for that year by providing 10 days' notice prior to the end of such quarter. Upon such quarterly cancellation, all other provisions of the agreement will remain in full force and effect. Volume growth funding is paid to CCE equally over the four quarters of the program year within 30 days after the beginning of each quarter. Our Company recognizes a charge as sales volume growth is attained by CCE. Such amounts are included as allowance deductions in net operating revenues.

The agreement provides for refunds of funding advances should CCE fail to attain specified minimum sales volume growth targets. Accordingly, should CCE not attain specified minimum cumulative sales volume growth targets in the ensuing quarters of a given year, amounts recognized to date for that year would be subject to refund.

In 2002, our Company agreed with CCE to modify the terms of the SGI agreement relating to 2003 and beyond. Under the amended agreement, funding for 2003, anticipated to be $250 million under the original agreement, was revised to $200 million. The 2003 amount paid to CCE was $161 million. This $39 million difference was due to a shortfall of 39 million unit cases below the sales volume growth target for 2003. The new amendment requires an additional $275 million in funding to CCE over the next eight years (2004–2011) and significantly reduces the annual reductions in funding that were a part of the original agreement. In addition, the amendment provides for each company to retain all cost savings it generates from future system efficiency initiatives. The previous agreement called for an equal sharing between our Company and CCE of combined proceeds above set targets.

Our Company previously entered into programs with CCE designed to help it develop cold-drink infrastructure. Under these programs, our Company paid CCE for a portion of the cost of developing the infrastructure necessary to support accelerated placements of cold-drink equipment. These payments support a common objective of increased sales of Coca-Cola beverages from increased availability and consumption in the cold-drink channel. In connection with these programs, CCE agrees to:

1) purchase and place specified numbers of venders/coolers or cold-drink equipment each year through 2008;
2) maintain the equipment in service, with certain exceptions, for a period of at least 12 years after placement;
3) maintain and stock the equipment in accordance with specified standards; and

4) report to our Company minimum average annual unit case sales volume throughout the economic life of the equipment.

CCE must achieve minimum average unit case sales volume for a 12-year period following the placement of equipment. These minimum average unit case sales volume levels ensure adequate gross profit from sales of concentrate to fully recover the capitalized costs plus a return on the Company's investment. Should CCE fail to purchase the specified numbers of venders/coolers or cold-drink equipment for any calendar year through 2008, the parties agree to mutually develop a reasonable solution. Should no mutually agreeable solution be developed, or in the event that CCE otherwise breaches any material obligation under the contracts and such breach is not remedied within a stated period, then CCE would be required to repay a portion of the support funding as determined by our Company. No repayments by CCE have ever been made under these programs. Our Company paid or committed to pay $3 million in 2002 and $159 million in 2001 to CCE in connection with these infrastructure programs. These payments are recorded in prepaid expenses and other assets and in noncurrent other assets and amortized as deductions in net operating revenues over the 10-year period following the placement of the equipment. Our carrying values for these infrastructure programs with CCE were approximately $829 million as of December 31, 2003 and $879 million as of December 31, 2002. Effective 2002 and thereafter, the Company has no further commitments under these programs.

As of January 1, 2001, CCE changed its method of accounting for infrastructure development payments received from the Company. Prior to this change, CCE recognized these payments as offsets to incremental expenses of the programs in the periods in which they were incurred. CCE now recognizes the infrastructure development payments received from the Company as income when obligations under the contracts are performed. Because the Company eliminates the financial effect of significant intercompany transactions (including transactions with equity method investees), this change in accounting method had no impact on the financial statements of our Company.

Other Equity Investments (In Part)

Net sales to equity investees other than CCE, the majority of which are located outside the United States, were $4.0 billion in 2003, $3.2 billion in 2002 and $3.7 billion in 2001. Total support payments, primarily marketing, made to equity investees other than CCE were approximately $511 million, $488 million and $636 million for 2003, 2002 and 2001, respectively.

Effective May 6, 2003, one of our Company's equity method investees, Coca-Cola FEMSA, S.A. de C.V. ("Coca-Cola FEMSA") consummated a merger with another of the Company's equity method investees, Panamerican Beverages, Inc. ("Panamco"). Our Company received new Coca-Cola FEMSA shares in exchange for all Panamco shares previously held by the Company. Our Company's ownership interest in Coca-Cola FEMSA increased from 30 percent to approximately 40 percent as a result of this merger. This exchange of shares was treated as a nonmonetary exchange of similar productive assets, and no gain was recorded by our Company as a result of this merger.

In connection with the merger, Coca-Cola FEMSA management initiated steps to streamline and integrate operations. This process included the closing of various distribution centers and manufacturing plants. Furthermore, due to the challenging economic conditions and an uncertain political situation in Venezuela, certain intangible assets were determined to be impaired and written down to their fair market value. During 2003, our Company recorded a noncash charge of $102 million primarily related to our proportionate share of these matters. This charge is included in the line item equity income—net.

In December 2003, the Company issued a stand-by line of credit ot Coca-Cola FEMSA.

In July 2003, we made a convertible loan of approximately $133 million to The Coca-Cola Bottling Company of Egypt ("TCCBCE"). The loan is convertible into preferred shares of TCCBCE upon receipt of governmental approvals. Additionally, upon certain defaults under either the loan agreement or the terms of the preferred shares, we have the ability to convet the loan or the preferred shares into common shares. At December 31, 2003, our Company owned approximately 42 percent of the common shares of TCCBCE.

Effective October 1, 2003, the Company and all of its bottling partners in Japan created a nationally integrated supply chain management company to centralize procurement, production and logistics operations for the entire Coca-Cola system in Japan. As a result of the creation of this supply chain management company in Japan, a portion of our Company's business has essentially been converted from a finished product business model to a concentrate business model, thus reducing our net operating revenues and cost of goods sold. The formation of this entity included the sale of Company inventory and leasing of certain Company assets to this new entity on October 1, 2003, as well as our recording of a liability for certain contractual obligations to Japanese bottlers. Such amounts were not material to the Company's results of operations.

1.197

KNIGHT-RIDDER, INC. (DEC)

NOTES TO CONSOLIDATED FINANCIAL STATEMENTS

Note 8 Related Party Transactions

We have regular transactions in the normal course of business with CareerBuilder, LLC, and Classified Ventures, LLC. At December 28, 2003, we owned 33.3% of CareerBuilder and 20.5% of Classified Ventures. In 2003, we recorded $31.0 million in sales related to CareerBuilder and $10.3 million related to Classified Ventures. We also had expenses related to services provided by CareerBuilder and Classified Ventures of $2.9 million and $6.4 million respectively. During 2002, we recorded $26.4 million in sales related to CareerBuilder and $7.1 million related to Classified Ventures. The expenses recorded related to services provided by CareerBuilder and Classified Ventures were $3.0 million and $5.2 million. The transactions with CareerBuilder and Classified Ventures are negotiated at arm's length.

We have ongoing purchase commitments with SP and Ponderay, our two newsprint mill partnership investments. These future commitments are for the purchase of a minimum of $42.5 million and $13.8 million of newsprint in 2004 with SP and Ponderay, respectively, at current market prices. We also have a sales commitment with DN to supply them with 50% of their newsprint requirements, which in 2004 will be approximately $27.4 million. We have the resources necessary to fulfill these commitments in 2004.

Transaction Between Reporting Entity and Major Stockholder

1.198

THE PEPSI BOTTLING GROUP, INC. (DEC)

NOTES TO CONSOLIDATED FINANCIAL STATEMENTS
(Tabular dollars in millions)

Note 1 (In Part): Basis of Presentation

PepsiCo, Inc. ("PepsiCo") owns 106,011,358 shares of our common stock, consisting of 105,911,358 shares of common stock and 100,000 shares of Class B common stock. All shares of Class B common stock that have been authorized have been issued to PepsiCo. At December 27, 2003, PepsiCo owned approximately 40.6% of our outstanding common stock and 100% of our outstanding Class B common stock, together representing approximately 45.8% of the voting power of all classes of our voting stock, In addition, PepsiCo owns 6.8% of the equity of Bottling Group, LLC, our principal operating subsidiary. We fully consolidate the results of Bottling Group, LLC and present PepsiCo's share as minority interest in our Consolidated Financial Statements.

Note 14 (In Part): Related Party Transactions

PepsiCo is considered a related party due to the nature of our franchisee relationship and its ownership interest in our company. The most significant agreements that govern our relationship with PepsiCo consist of:

1) The master bottling agreement for cola beverages bearing the "PEPSI-COLA" and "PEPSI" trademarks in the United States; master bottling agreements and distribution agreements for non-cola products in the United States, including MOUNTAIN DEW; and a master fountain syrup agreement in the United States;

2) Agreements similar to the master bottling agreement and the non-cola agreements for each country in which we operate, including Canada, Spain, Russia, Greece, Turkey and Mexico, as well as a fountain syrup agreement for Canada, similar to the master syrup agreement;

3) A shared services agreement whereby PepsiCo provides us or we provide PepsiCo with certain support, including information technology maintenance, procurement of raw materials, shared space, employee benefit administration, credit and collection, and international tax and accounting services. The amounts paid or received under this contract are equal to the actual costs incurred by the company providing the services. During 2001, a PepsiCo affiliate provided casualty insurance to us; and

4) Transition agreements that provide certain indemnities to the parties, and provide for the allocation of tax and other assets, liabilities, and obligations arising from periods prior to the initial public offering. Under our tax separation agreement, PepsiCo maintains full control and absolute discretion for any combined or consolidated tax filings for tax periods ended on or before the initial public offering.

Additionally, we review our annual marketing, advertising, management and financial plans each year with PepsiCo for its approval. If we fail to submit these plans, or if we fail to carry them out in all material respects, PepsiCo can terminate our beverage agreements. If our beverage agreements with PepsiCo are terminated for this or for any other reason, it would have a material adverse effect on our business and financial results.

Bottler Incentives and Other Arrangements

We share a business objective with PepsiCo of increasing the availability and consumption of Pepsi-Cola beverages. Accordingly, PepsiCo, at its discretion, provides us with various forms of bottler incentives to promote its beverages. These incentives are mutually agreed-upon between us and PepsiCo and cover a variety of initiatives, including direct marketplace support, capital equipment funding and advertising support. Based on the objectives of the programs and initiatives, we record bottler incentives as an adjustment to net revenues, cost of sales or selling, delivery and administrative expenses. Beginning in 2003, due to the adoption of Emerging Issues Task Force ("EITF") Issue No. 02-16, "Accounting by a Customer (Including a Reseller) for Certain Consideration Received from a Vendor," we have changed our accounting methodology for the way we record bottler incentives. See Note 2-Summary of Significant Accounting Policies for a discussion on the change in classification of these bottler incentives.

Bottler incentives received from PepsiCo, including media costs shared by PepsiCo, were $646 million, $560 million and $554 million for 2003, 2002 and 2001, respectively. Changes in our bottler incentives and funding levels could materially affect our business and financial results.

Purchases of Concentrate and Finished Product

We purchase concentrate from PepsiCo, which is the critical flavor ingredient used in the production of carbonated soft drinks and other ready-to-drink beverages. PepsiCo determines the price of concentrate annually at its discretion. We also pay a royalty fee to PepsiCo for the Aquafina trademark. Amounts paid or payable to PepsiCo and its affiliates for concentrate and royalty fees were $1,971 million, $1,699 million and $1,584 million in 2003, 2002 and 2001, respectively.

We also produce or distribute other products and purchase finished goods and concentrate through various arrangements with PepsiCo or PepsiCo joint ventures. During 2003, 2002 and 2001, total amounts paid or payable to PepsiCo or PepsiCo joint ventures for these transactions were $556 million, $464 million and $375 million, respectively.

We provide manufacturing services to PepsiCo and PepsiCo affiliates in connection with the production of certain finished beverage products. During 2003, 2002 and 2001, total amounts paid or payable by PepsiCo for these transactions were $6 million, $10 million and $32 million, respectively.

Fountain Service Fee

We manufacture and distribute fountain products and provide fountain equipment service to PepsiCo customers in some territories in accordance with the Pepsi beverage agreements. Amounts received from PepsiCo for these transactions are offset by the cost to provide these services and are reflected in our Consolidated Statements of Operations in selling, delivery and administrative expenses. Net amounts paid or payable by PepsiCo to us for these service were approximately $200 million, $200 million and $185 million, in 2003, 2002 and 2001, respectively.

Other Transactions

Prior to 2002, Hillbrook Insurance Company, Inc., a subsidiary of PepsiCo, provided insurance and risk management services to us pursuant to a contractual agreement. Total premiums paid to Hillbrook Insurance Company, Inc. during 2001 were $58 million.

We provide and receive various services from PepsiCo and PepsiCo affiliates pursuant to a shared services agreement and other arrangements, including information technology maintenance, procurement of raw materials, shared space, employee benefit administration, credit and collection, and international tax and accounting services. Total net expenses incurred were approximately $62 million, $57 million and $133 million during 2003, 2002 and 2001, respectively.

We purchase snack food products from Frito-Lay, Inc., a subsidiary of PepsiCo, for sale and distribution in all of Russia except Moscow. Amounts paid or payable to PepsiCo and its affiliates for snack food products were $51 million, $44 million and $27 million in 2003, 2002 and 2001, respectively.

Under tax sharing arrangements we have with PepsiCo, we received $7 million, $3 million and $4 million in tax-related benefits from PepsiCo in 2003, 2002 and 2001, respectively.

The Consolidated Statements of Operations include the following income (expense) amounts as a result of transactions with PepsiCo and its affiliates:

	2003	2002	2001
Net revenues:			
Bottler incentives	$ 21	$ 257	$ 262
Cost of sales:			
Purchases of concentrate and finished products, and Aquafina royalty fees	$(2,527)	$(2,163)	$(1,959)
Bottler incentives	527	—	—
Manufacturing and distribution service reimbursements	6	10	32
	$(1,994)	$(2,153)	$(1,927)
Selling, delivery and administrative expenses:			
Bottler incentives	$ 98	$ 303	$ 292
Fountain service fee	200	200	185
Frito-Lay purchases	(51)	(44)	(27)
Insurance fees	—	—	(58)
Shared services	(62)	(57)	(133)
	$ 185	$ 402	$ 259
Income tax expense	$ 7	$ 3	$ 4

We are not required to pay any minimum fees to PepsiCo, nor are we obligated to PepsiCo under any minimum purchase requirements.

As part of our acquisition in Turkey (see Note 16), PBG paid PepsiCo $8 million for its share of Fruko Mesrubar Sanayii A.S. and related entities in 2002. In addition, we sold certain brands to PepsiCo from the net assets acquired for $16 million in 2002.

As part of our acquisition of Gemex (see Note 16), PepsiCo received $297 million in 2002 for the tender of its shares for its 34.4% ownership in the outstanding capital stock of Gemex. In addition, PepsiCo made a payment to us for $17 million in 2002, to facilitate the purchase and ensure a smooth ownership transition of Gemex.

We paid PepsiCo $3 million, $10 million and $9 million during 2003, 2002 and 2001, respectively, for distribution rights relating to the SoBe brand in certain PBG-owned territories in the U.S. and Canada.

In connection with PBG's acquistion of Pepsi-Cola Bottling of Northern California in 2001, PBG paid $10 million to PepsiCo for its equity interest in Northern California.

Bottling Group, LLC will distribute pro rata to PepsiCo and PBG, based upon membership interest, sufficient cash such that aggregate cash distributed to us will enable us to pay our income taxes and interest on our $1 billion 7.0% senior notes due 2029. PepsiCo's pro rata cash distribution during 2003, 2002 and 2001 from Bottling Group, LLC was $7 million, $11 million and $16 million, respectively.

The $1.3 billion of 5.63% senior notes and the $1.0 billion of 5.38% senior notes issued on February 9, 1999, by our subsidiary Bottling Group, LLC, are guaranteed by PepsiCo. In addition, the $1.0 billion of 4.63% senior notes issued on November 15, 2002, also by Bottling Group, LLC, were guaranteed by PepsiCo starting in February 2004 in accordance with the terms set forth in the related indenture.

Amounts payable to PepsiCo and its affiliates were $20 million and $26 million at December 27, 2003, and December 28, 2002, respectively. Such amounts are recorded within accounts payable and other current liabilities in our Consolidated Balance Sheets.

Transaction Between Reporting Entity and Officer/Director

1.199

EQUIFAX INC. (DEC)

NOTES TO CONSOLIDATED FINANCIAL STATEMENTS

12. Related Party Transactions

We maintain lending, foreign exchange, debt underwriting, cash management, trust, investment managment, derivative counter-party, and shareholder services relationships with Sun Trust Banks, Inc. ("SunTrust") whom we consider a related party due to (a) Phillip Humann, a member of our board of directors, currently is the Chairman, President, and Chief Executive Officer of SunTrust, and (b) William Dahlberg and Larry Prince, members of our board of directors, are also directors of SunTrust. We paid $2.4 million and $3.3 million SunTrust for these services in 2003 and 2002, respectively.

We also provide credit management services to SunTrust, as a customer, from whom we received $2.9 million and $2.5 million, respectively, during the years 2003 and 2002, and had $0.2 million and $0.1 million of corresponding outstanding receivables with, as of December 31, 2003 and 2002, respectively. The relationships are described more fully below:

- The revolving credit agreement is composed of a $305.0 million multi-year portion which expires on October 4, 2004 and a $160.0 million 364-day portion which expires on September 30, 2004. Total borrowings outstanding under the 364-day and multi-year portion of this facility were $21.8 million at December 31, 2002 and $137.1 million at December 31, 2003.
- As of December 31, 2002 and December 31, 2003, SunTrust provided Equifax Inc. a $100.0 million committed portion of our $465.0 million U.S. revolving credit agreement. SunTrust's total commitment of $100.0 million at December 31, 2002 and December 31, 2003 was allocated 65.6% (S65.6 million) to the multi-year portion and 34.4% ($34.4 million) to the 364-day portion. Total borrowings outstanding under SunTrust's 364-day and multi-year portions of this facility were $4.7 million at December 31, 2002 and $29.5 million at December 31, 2003.
- Additionally, SunTrust extends financing in the form of an amortizing term loan to a leveraged real estate limited partnership which owns Equifax's Atlanta data center located in Alpharetta, Georgia. Equifax Inc. is the primary operating lease tenant in the data center. An unrelated bank leasing company is the equity owner of this partnership. Although this term loan is considered to be non-recourse financing to Equifax Inc., SunTrust is dependent on the operating lease payments made by Equifax Inc. to the partnership to service interest expense and amortize principal on the term loan's debt. The term loan is fully amortized in 2012. As of December 31, 2002 and December 31, 2003, $26.6 million and $24.3 million, respectively, were outstanding under the term loan.
- SunTrust also provides the $29.0 million synthetic lease facility related to our Atlanta corporate headquarters building. As of December 31, 2002 and December 31, 2003, the amount of this facility was $29.0 million.
- SunTrust provides investment management services for Equifax Inc.'s U.S. defined benefits plan (USRIP) through two of its subsidiaries, Trusco Capital and the Lighthouse Group. As of December 31, 2002 and December 31, 2003, a total of $30.2 million and $37.6 million, respectively, of USRIP assets were managed by these two subsidiaries of SunTrust.
- During 2002 and 2003, SunTrust was the counterparty on $90.0 million, notional value, of interest rate swaps with Equifax Inc.

Bank of America, N.A. ("B of A"). through its various subsidiaries, provides Equifax Inc. and our subsidiaries cash management, foreign exchange, lending, and debt underwriting services. We consider B of A a related party because Jacquelyn Ward, a member of our board of directors, is also a director of B of A. We paid $0.8 million and $2.0 million, to B of A for these services in 2003 and 2002, respectively. We also provide credit management services to B of A, as a customer, from whom we received $15.3 million and $11.2 million, respectively, during the years 2003 and 2002, and had $1.7 million and $1.6 million of corresponding outstanding receiv-

ables with, as of December 31, 2003 and 2002, respectively. The relationships are described more fully below:

- As of December 31, 2002 and December 31, 2003, B of A served as the Administrative Agent on Equifax Inc.'s $465.0 million revolving credit agreement, and provided Equifax Inc. a $100.0 million committed portion of that facility. B of A's total commitment of $100.0 million at December 31, 2002 and December 31, 2003 was allocated 65.6% ($65.6 million) to the multi-year portion and 34.4% ($34.4 million) to the 364-day portion. Total borrowings outstanding under B of A's 364-day and multi-year portions of this facility were $4.7 million at December 31, 2002 and $29.5 million at December 31, 2003.
- B of A also extends an uncommitted $25.0 million working capital line of credit to Equifax Inc. The facility is cancelable at the discretion of either party. The uncommitted working capital line, at December 31, 2002 and December 31, 2003, had outstanding balances of $3.4 million and $5.4 million, respectively.
- During December 31, 2002 and December 31, 2003, B of A was the counterparty on $124.0 million, notional value, of interest rate swaps with Equifax Inc.

We have maintained a cross-services arrangement with Intersections, Inc. ("Intersections"), whom we consider a related party because our Chief Financial Officer, Don Heroman, is a member of Intersections board of directors. We provide to, and purchase from, Intersections, consumer direct services (primarily identity theft protection products) and credit management services (primarily credit files and portfolio reviews). Fees received from Intersections for services delivered and sold were $6.8 million and $4.6 million, respectively for the years 2003 and 2002. Fees paid for services purchased from Intersections, were $4.3 million and $0.1 million, respectively, for the years 2003 and 2002. We had $1.2 million and $1.4 million in outstanding accounts receivable from intersections, respectively, at December 31, 2003 and 2002. We had no outstanding accounts payable due to Intersections at December 31, 2003 or 2002.

1.200

MERRIMAC INDUSTRIES, INC. (DEC)

NOTES TO CONSOLIDATED FINANCIAL STATEMENTS

14. Related Party Transactions

In May 1998, the Company sold 22,000 shares of Common Stock to Mason N. Carter, Chairman, President and Chief Executive Officer of the Company, at a price of $11.60 per share, which approximated the average closing price of the Company's Common Stock during the first quarter of 1998. The Company lent Mr. Carter $255,000 in connection with the purchase of these shares and combined that loan with a prior loan to Mr. Carter in the amount of $105,000. The resulting total principal amount of $360,000 was payable May 4, 2003 and bore interest at a variable interest rate based on the prime rate of the Company's lending bank. This loan was further amended on July 29, 2002. Accrued interest of $40,000 was added to the principal, bringing the new principal amount of the loan to $400,000, the due date was extended to May 4,

2006, and interest (at the same rate as was previously applicable) is now payable monthly. Mr. Carter has pledged 33,000 shares of Common Stock as security for this loan, which is a full-recourse loan.

On August 31, 2000, in connection with an amendment of Mr. Carter's employment agreement, the Company loaned Mr. Carter an additional $280,000. Interest on the loan varies and is based on the prime rate of the Company's lending bank, payable in accordance with Mr. Carter's employment agreement. Each year the Company is required to forgive 20% of the amount due under this loan and the accrued interest thereon. During 2003, the Company forgave $56,000 of principal and $7,000 of accrued interest and paid a tax gross-up benefit of $8,300. During 2002, the Company forgave $56,000 of principal and $12,000 of accrued interest and paid $10,700 for a tax gross-up benefit. During 2001, the Company forgave $56,000 of principal and $23,000 of accrued interest and paid a tax gross-up benefit of $11,000.

During fiscal years 2003, 2002 and 2001, respectively, the Company's General Counsel, KMZ Rosenman, was paid $359,000, $372,000 and $288,000 for providing legal services to the Company. A director of the Company is Counsel to the firm of KMZ Rosenman but does not share in any fees paid by the Company to the law firm.

During fiscal years 2003, 2002 and 2001, the Company retained Career Consultants, Inc. and SK Associates to perform executive searches and to provide outplacement services to the Company. The Company paid an aggregate of $40,000, $24,000 and $117,000 to these companies during 2003, 2002 and 2001, respectively. A director of the Company is the Chairman and Chief Executive Officer of each of these companies.

During fiscal years 2003, 2002 and 2001, respectively, a director of the Company was paid $12,000, $36,000 and $40,300 for providing financial-related consulting services to the Company.

During each of fiscal years 2003, 2002 and 2001, a director of the Company was paid $36,000 for providing technology-related consulting services to the Company.

During fiscal years 2003 and 2002, respectively, DuPont Electronic Technologies, a stockholder, was paid $109,000 and $36,000 for providing technological and marketing related personnel and services on a costsharing basis to the Company.

Each director who is not an employee of the Company receives a monthly director's fee of $1,500, plus an additional $500 for each meeting of the Board and of any Committees of the Board attended. The directors are also reimbursed for reasonable travel expenses incurred in attending Board and Committee meetings. In addition, pursuant to the 2001 Stock Option Plan, each non-employee director is granted an immediately exercisable option to purchase 2,500 shares of the Common Stock of the Company on the date of each Annual Meeting of Stockholders. Each such grant is priced at the fair market value of the Common Stock on the date of such grant. On June 24, 2003, non-qualified stock options to purchase an aggregate of 20,000 shares were issued to eight directors at an exercise price of $3.10 per share.

Transaction Between Reporting Entity and Special Purpose Entity

1.201

CENDANT CORPORATION (DEC)

NOTES TO CONSOLIDATED FINANCIAL STATEMENTS
(Unless otherwise noted, all amounts are in millions)

16 (In Part): Debt Under Management and Mortgage Programs and Borrowing Arrangements

Debt under management and mortgage programs (including related party debt due to AESOP Funding) consisted of:

	2003	2002
Asset-backed debt:		
Vehicle rental program		
AESOP Funding	$ 5,644	$ 4,029
Other	651	2,053
Vehicle management program	3,118	3,058
Mortgage program		
Bishop's Gate	1,651	—
Other	—	871
Timeshare program		
Sierra	774	—
Other	335	145
Relocation program		
Apple Ridge	400	—
Other	—	80
	12,573	10,236
Unsecured debt:		
Term notes	1,916	1,421
Commercial paper	164	866
Bank loans	—	107
Other	132	117
	2,212	2,511
Total debt under management and mortgage programs	$14,785	$12,747

Asset-Backed Debt

Vehicle Rental Program

AESOP Funding

AESOP Funding was established by the Company as a bankruptcy remote special purpose limited liability company that issues private placement notes and uses the proceeds from such issuances to make loans to a wholly-owned subsidiary of the Company, AESOP Leasing LP ("AESOP Leasing") on a continuing basis. AESOP Leasing uses these proceeds to acquire or finance the acquisition of vehicles used in the Company's rental car operations. Prior to December 31, 2003, both AESOP Funding and AESOP Leasing were consolidated by the Company and, as such, the intercompany transactions between these two entities were eliminated causing only the third-party debt issued by AESOP Funding and the vehicles purchased by AESOP Leasing to be presented within the Company's Consolidated Financial Statements. However, in connection with the adoption of FIN 46R, the Company determined that it was not the primary beneficiary of AESOP Funding. Accordingly, the Company deconsolidated AESOP Funding on December 31, 2003. As a result, AESOP Leasing's obligation to AESOP Funding is reflected as related party debt on the Company's Consolidated Balance Sheet as of December 31, 2003. The Company also recorded an asset within vehicle-related, net assets under management and mortgage programs on its Consolidated Balance Sheet at December 31, 2003, which represented the equity issued by AESOP Funding to the Company. The vehicles purchased by AESOP Leasing remain on the Company's Consolidated Balance Sheet as AESOP Leasing continues to be consolidated by the Company. Such vehicles, which approximate $5.5 billion, collateralize the debt issued by AESOP Funding and are not available to pay the general obligations of the Company.

The business activities of AESOP Funding are limited primarily to issuing indebtedness and using the proceeds thereof to make loans to AESOP Leasing for the purpose of acquiring or financing the acquisition of vehicles to be leased to the Company's rental car subsidiary and pledging its assets to secure the indebtedness. As the deconsolidation of AESOP Funding occurred on December 31, 2003, the income statement and cash flow activity of the Company were not impacted for 2003. Beginning on January 1, 2004, the results of operations and cash flows of AESOP Funding will no longer be reflected within the Company's Consolidated Financial Statements.

Borrowings under the AESOP Funding program primarily represent floating rate term notes with a weighted average interest rate of 3% for both 2003 and 2002.

Vehicle Management Program

Borrowings under the Company's vehicle management program primarily represent amounts issued under a domestic financing facility that provides for the issuance of variable rate term notes to unrelated third parties ($2.7 billion) and the issuance of preferred membership interests to an unconsolidated related party ($408 million). The variable rate term notes and preferred membership interests were issued to support the acquisition of vehicles used in the Company's fleet leasing operations. The debt issued is collateralized by the leased vehicles purchased, which are not available to pay the general obligations of the Company. The titles to all the vehicles collateralizing the debt issued under this program are held in a bankruptcy remote trust and the Company acts as a servicer of all such vehicles. The bankruptcy remote trust also acts as lessor under both operating and financing lease agreements. The debt issued under this program primarily represents floating rate term notes for which the weighted average interest rate was 2% for both 2003 and 2002.

Mortgage Program

Bishop's Gate

Bishop's Gate is a bankruptcy remote SPE that is utilized to warehouse mortgage loans originated by the Company's mortgage business prior to their sale into the secondary market, which is customary practice in the mortgage industry. The debt issued by Bishop's Gate is collateralized by $149 million of cash and approximately $1.6 billion of underlying mortgage loans, which are serviced by the Company and recorded within mortgage loans held for sale on the Company's Consolidated Balance Sheet as of December 31,

2003. Prior to the adoption of FIN 46, sales of mortgage loans to Bishop's Gate were treated as off-balance sheet sales. The activities of Bishop's Gate are limited to (i) purchasing mortgage loans from the Company's mortgage subsidiary, (ii) issuring commercial paper or other debt instruments and/or borrowing under a liquidity agreement to effect such purchases, (iii) entering into interest rate swaps to hedge interest rate risk and certain non-credit related market risk on the purchased mortgage loans, (iv) selling and securitizing the acquired mortgage loans to third parties and (v) engaging in certain related transactions. The assets of Bishop's Gate are not available to pay the general obligations of the Company. The debt issued under Bishop's Gate primarily represents term notes for which the weighted average interest rate was 2% for 2003.

Timeshare Program

Sierra Receivables Funding Entities

The Sierra Receivables Funding entities (the "Sierra entities") are bankruptcy remote SPEs that are utilized to securitize timeshare receivables generated from the sale of vacation ownership interests by the Company's timeshare businesses. The debt issued by the Sierra entities is collateralized by $63 million of cash and $957 million of underlying timeshare receivables, which are serviced by the Company and recorded within timeshare-related assets under management and mortgage programs on the Company's Consolidated Balance Sheet as of December 31, 2003. Prior to September 1, 2003, sales of timeshare receivables to the Sierra entities were treated as off-balance sheet sales, as these entities were structured as bankruptcy remote QSPEs and, therefore, excluded from the scope of FIN 46. However, on September 1, 2003, the underlying structures of the Sierra entities were amended in a manner that resulted in these entities no longer meeting the criteria to qualify as QSPEs pursuant to SFAS No. 140. Consequently, the Company began consolidating the account balances and activities of the Sierra entities on September 1, 2003 pursuant to FIN 46. The activities of the Sierra entities are limited to (i) purchasing timeshare receivables from the Company's timeshare subsidiaries, (ii) issuing debt securities and/or borrowing under a conduit facility to effect such purchases and (iii) entering into derivatives to hedge interest rate exposure. The assets of the Sierra entities are not available to pay the general obligations of the Company. The debt issued under the Sierra entities primarily represents fixed rate term notes for which the weighted average interest rate was 3% for 2003.

Relocation Program

Apple Ridge Funding LLC

Apple Ridge Funding LLC ("Apple Ridge") is a bankruptcy remote SPE that is utilized to securitize relocation receivables generated from advancing funds to clients of the Company's relocation business. The debt issued by Apple Ridge is collateralized by cash and underlying relocation receivables aggregating $519 million, which are serviced by the Company and recorded on the Company's Consolidated Balance Sheet as of December 31, 2003. Prior to November 26, 2003, sales of relocation receivables to Apple Ridge were treated as off-balance sheet sales, as this entity was structured as a bankruptcy remote QSPE and, therefore, excluded from the scope of FIN 46. However, on November 26, 2003, the underlying structure of Apple Ridge was amended in a manner that resulted in it no longer meeting the criteria to qualify as a QSPE pursuant to SFAS No. 140. Consequently, the Company began consolidating the account balances and activities of Apple Ridge on November 26, 2003 pursuant to FIN 46. Prior to consolidation, the Company recognized gains upon the sale of relocation receivable to Apple Ridge. However, such gains were not material for the period January 1, 2003 through November 25, 2003 and for the years ended December 31, 2002 and 2001. The activities of Apple Ridge are limited to (i) purchasing relocation receivables from the Company's relocation subsidiary, (ii) issuing debt securities and/or borrowing under a conduit facility to effect such purchases and (iii) entering into, terminating or modifying certain derivative transactions. The assets of Apple Ridge are not available to pay the general obligations of the Company. The debt issued under Apple Ridge represents a floating rate term note for which the weighted average interest rate was 1% for 2003.

1.202

VIAD CORP (DEC)

NOTES TO CONSOLIDATED FINANCIAL STATEMENTS

Note 1 (In Part): Summary of Significant Accounting Policies

Principles of Consolidation (In Part)

Viad's Payment Services segment participates in various trust arrangements (special-purpose entities) related to structured investments within its investment portfolio, official check processing agreements with financial institutions, and the sale of certain receivables. Certain structured investments owned by Viad represent beneficial interests in grantor trusts or other similar entities. These trusts typically contain an investment grade security, generally a U.S Treasury strip, and an investment in the residual interest in a collateralized debt obligation, or in some cases, a limited partnership interest. For certain of these trusts, Payment Services owns the majority of the beneficial interests, and therefore, consolidates those trusts by recording and accounting for the assets of the trust separately in Viad's consolidated financial statements.

In connection with its PrimeLink business, the Payment Services segment has established separate trust entities and processes that provide certain financial institution customers additional assurance of the Company's ability to clear their official checks. The assets, liabilities, revenues and expenses associated with these arrangements are consolidated in Viad's financial statements. Additionally, the Payment Services segment has an agreement to sell, on a periodic basis, undivided percentage ownership interests in certain receivables primarily from its money order agents. These receivables are sold to a commercial paper conduit and represent a small percentage of the total assets in such conduit. Viad's rights and obligations are limited to the receivables transferred, and are accounted for as a sales transaction under SFAS No. 140, "Accounting for Transfers and Servicing of Financial Assets and Extinguishments of Liabilities." The assets and liabilities associated with the conduit, including the sold receivables, are not recorded or consolidated in Viad's financial statements.

Consolidated Tax Return

1.203

SPRINT CORPORATION (DEC)

NOTES TO CONSOLIDATED FINANCIAL STATEMENTS

1 (In Part): Summary of Significant Accounting Policies

Intergroup Transactions and Allocations (In Part)

Allocation of Federal and State Income Taxes

Sprint files a consolidated federal income tax return and certain state income tax returns which include FON Group and PCS Group results. Sprint adopted a tax sharing agreement which provided for the allocation of income taxes between the two groups. The FON Group's income taxes are calculated as if it files returns which exclude the PCS Group. The PCS Group's income taxes reflect the PCS Group's incremental cumulative impact on Sprint's consolidated income taxes. Intergroup tax payments are satisfied on the date Sprint's related tax payment is due to or the refund is received from the applicable tax authority.

The original tax sharing agreement applied to tax years ending on or before December 31, 2001. In December 2001, Sprint adopted a continuation of this tax sharing arrangement except for the elimination of certain provisions addressing certain types of acquisitions or restructurings, which never became operable under the original agreement.

14 (In Part): Income Taxes

Income tax expense (benefit) allocated to continuing operations consists of the following:

(Millions) 2003	Sprint Corporation Consolidated	Sprint FON Group	Sprint PCS Group
Current income tax expense (benefit)			
Federal	$(672)	$ 418	$(1,090)
State	21	56	(35)
Total current	(651)	474	(1,125)
Deferred income tax expense (benefit)			
Federal	453	(271)	724
State	(58)	(63)	5
Total deferred	395	(334)	729
Total	$(256)	$ 140	$ (396)

2002			
Current income tax expense (benefit)			
Federal	$(599)	$(243)	$ (356)
State	(3)	(9)	6
Total current	(602)	(252)	(350)
Deferred income tax expense (benefit)			
Federal	544	602	(58)
State	12	58	(46)
Total deferred	556	660	(104)
Foreign income tax expense (benefit)	8	—	8
Total	$ (38)	$ 408	$ (446)

2001			
Current income tax expense (benefit)			
Federal	$ (94)	$ 99	$ (193)
State	57	50	7
Total current	(37)	149	(186)
Deferred income tax expense (benefit)			
Federal	(552)	(182)	(370)
State	(135)	(48)	(87)
Total deferred	(687)	(230)	(457)
Total	$(724)	$ (81)	$ (643)

The differences that caused Sprint's effective income tax rates to vary from the 35% federal statutory rate for income taxes related to continuing operations were as follows:

(Millions) 2003	Sprint Corporation Consolidated	Sprint FON Group	Sprint PCS Group
Income tax expense (benefit) at the federal statutory rate	$(218)	$ 152	$(370)
Effect of:			
State income taxes, net of federal income tax effect	(25)	(5)	(20)
Credit for research activities	(27)	(18)	(9)
Other, net	14	11	3
Income tax expense (benefit)	$(256)	$ 140	$(396)
Effective income tax rate	41.1%	32.2%	37.5%

2002			
Income tax expense (benefit) at the federal statutory rate	$ 151	$ 509	$(358)
Effect of:			
State income taxes, net of federal income tax effect	6	32	(26)
Equity in losses of foreign joint ventures	(55)	2	(57)
Decrease in valuation allowance for previous investment write downs	(130)	(130)	—
Other, net	(10)	(5)	(5)
Income tax expense (benefit)	$ (38)	$ 408	$(446)
Effective income tax rate	(8.8)%	28.0%	43.6%

2001			
Income tax expense (benefit) at the federal statutory rate	$(798)	$(133)	$(665)
Effect of:			
State income taxes, net of federal income tax effect	(51)	1	(52)
Equity in losses of foreign joint ventures	40	1	39
Write down of equity method investment	57	57	—
Goodwill amortization	44	6	38
Other, net	(16)	(13)	(3)
Income tax expense (benefit)	$(724)	$ (81)	$(643)
Effective income tax rate	31.8%	21.4%	33.8%

Income tax expense (benefit) allocated to other items was as follows:

(Millions) 2003	Sprint Corporation Consolidated	Sprint FON Group	Sprint PCS Group
Discontinued operations	$ 820	$ 820	$ —
Cumulative effect of change in accounting principle	(162)	(162)	—
Additional minimum pension liability[1]	(12)	(2)	(10)
Gains (losses) on securities[1]	27	27	—
Gains (losses) on qualifying cash flow hedges[1]	(23)	(23)	—
Stock ownership, purchase and option arrangements[2]	(4)	(3)	(1)
2002			
Discontinued operations	$ 97	$ 97	$ —
Additional minimum pension liability[1]	(444)	(431)	(13)
Gains (losses) on securities[1]	(18)	(18)	—
Gains (losses) on qualifying cash flow hedges[1]	9	9	—
Stock ownership, purchase and option arrangements[2]	(1)	(2)	1
2001			
Discontinued operations	$ 98	$ 98	$ —
Gains (losses) on securities[1]	(4)	(11)	—
Stock ownership, purchase and option arrangements[2]	(17)	(9)	(8)

[1] These amounts have been recorded directly to "Shareholders' equity—Accumulated other comprehensive income (loss)" on the Consolidated Balance Sheets.

[2] These amounts have been recorded directly to "Shareholders' equity—Capital in excess of par or stated value" on the Consolidated Balance Sheets.

Sprint recognizes deferred income taxes for the temporary differences between the carrying amounts of its assets and liabilities for financial statement purposes and their tax bases. The sources of the differences that give rise to the deferred income tax assets and liabilities at year-end 2003 and 2002, along with the income tax effect of each, were as follows:

(Millions)	Sprint Corporation Consolidated 2003 Deferred Income Tax		Sprint FON Group 2003 Deferred Income Tax		Sprint PCS Group 2003 Deferred Income Tax	
	Assets	Liabilities	Assets	Liabilities	Assets	Liabilities
Property, plant and equipment	$ —	$4,726	$ —	$2,550	$ —	$2,176
Intangibles	—	571	—	24	—	547
Postretirement and other benefits	834	—	811	—	23	—
Reserves and allowances	202	—	29	—	173	—
Operating loss carryforwards	2,583	—	269	—	2,314	—
Tax credit carryforwards	398	—	79	—	319	—
Other, net	138	—	58	—	80	—
	4,155	5,297	1,246	2,574	2,909	2,723
Loss valuation allowance	620	—	279	—	341	
Total	$3,535	$5,297	$ 967	$2,574	$2,568	$2,723

(Millions)	Sprint Corporation Consolidated 2002 Deferred Income Tax		Sprint FON Group 2002 Deferred Income Tax		Sprint PCS Group 2002 Deferred Income Tax	
	Assets	Liabilities	Assets	Liabilities	Assets	Liabilities
Property, plant and equipment	$ —	$4,465	$ —	$2,344	$ —	$2,121
Intangibles	—	936	—	465	—	471
Postretirement and other benefits	810	—	797	—	13	—
Reserves and allowances	248	—	55	—	193	—
Operating loss carryforwards	3,196	—	271	—	2,925	—
Tax credit carryforwards	288	—	—	—	288	—
Other, net	213	—	120	—	93	—
	4,755	5,401	1,243	2,809	3,512	2,592
Less valuation allowance	573	—	217	—	356	—
Total	$4,182	$5,401	$1,026	$2,809	$3,156	$2,592

●   ●   ●   ●   ●   ●

In 1999, Sprint acquired approximately $193 million of potential tax benefits related to net operating loss carryforwards in the acquisitions of the broadband fixed wireless companies. In 1998, Sprint acquired approximately $229 million of potential tax benefits related to net operating loss carryforwards in the PCS Restructuring. The benefits from the acquisitions and PCS Restructuring are subject to certain realization restrictions under various tax laws. A valuation allowance was provided for the total of these benefits. If these benefits are subsequently recognized, they will reduce goodwill or intangibles resulting from the application of the purchase method of accounting for these transactions.

In connection with the PCS Restructuring, the PCS Group is required to reimburse the FON Group and the Cable Partners for net operating loss and tax credit carryforward benefits generated before the PCS Restructuring if realization by the PCS Group produces a cash benefit that would not otherwise have been realized. The reimbursement will equal 60% of the net cash benefit received by the PCS Group and will be made to the FON Group in cash and to the Cable Partners in shares of Sprint stock. The carryforward benefits subject to this requirement total $259 million, which includes the $229 million acquired in the PCS Restructuring.

Tax Sharing Agreement

1.204

FMC CORPORATION (DEC)

NOTES TO CONSOLIDATED FINANCIAL STATEMENTS

Note 17 (In Part): Related-Party Transactions

FMC and Technologies entered into a tax sharing agreement wherein each company is obligated for those taxes associated with their respective business, generally determined as if each company filed its own consolidated, combined or unitary tax returns for any period where Technologies is included in the consolidated, combined or unitary tax return of FMC or its subsidiaries. If, within thirty months following the spin-off, Technologies breaches any representations in the tax sharing agreement relating to the favorable ruling FMC received from the IRS regarding the tax-free nature of the spin-off; takes or fails to take any action that causes such representations to be untrue; engages in a sale of substantially all of its assets; undergoes a change of control; or, discontinues the conduct of its business, the spin-off may be taxable to us. In the event the spin-off is determined to be taxable to us as a result of any of the foregoing. Technologies will be required to indemnify us for any resulting taxes, which would likely be material to our liquidity, results of operations and financial condition.

INFLATION ACCOUNTING

1.205   Effective for financial reports issued after December 2,1986, SFAS No. 89, *Financial Reporting and Changing Prices*, states that companies previously required to disclose current cost information are no longer required to disclose such information.

1.206   Many of the survey companies include comments about inflation in Management's Discussion and Analysis of Financial Condition and Results of Operations. Examples of such comments follow.

1.207

METTLER-TOLEDO INTERNATIONAL INC. (DEC)

INFLATION

Inflation can affect the costs of goods and services that we use. The competitive environment in which we operate limits somewhat our ability to recover higher costs through increased selling prices. Moreover, there may be differences in inflation rates between countries in which we incur the major portion of our costs and other countries in which we sell products, which may limit our ability to recover increased costs. We remain committed to operations in China and Eastern Europe, which have experienced inflationary conditions. To date, inflationary conditions have not had a material effect on our operating results. However, as our presence in China and Eastern Europe increases, these inflationary conditions could have a greater impact on our operating results.

1.208

PHELPS DODGE CORPORATION (DEC)

INFLATION

The principal impact of general inflation upon our financial results has been on implied unit cost of copper production, especially supply costs, at our mining and industrial operations. It is important to note, however, that there is generally no correlation between the selling price of our principal product, copper, and the rate of inflation or deflation.

Section 2: Balance Sheet

BALANCE SHEET TITLE

2.01   Table 2-1 summarizes the titles used to describe the statement of assets, liabilities and stockholders' equity.

2.02

TABLE 2-1: BALANCE SHEET TITLE

	2003	2002	2001	2000
Balance Sheet	574	574	573	571
Statement of Financial Position	24	24	25	27
Statement of Financial Condition	2	2	2	2
Total Companies	**600**	**600**	**600**	**600**

BALANCE SHEET FORMAT

2.03   Table 2-2 summarizes the different balance sheet formats used by the survey companies. Balance sheet formats include the account form, the report form, and the financial position form. The account form shows total assets on the left-hand side equal to the sum of liabilities and stockholders' equity on the right-hand side. The report form shows a downward sequence of either total assets minus total liabilities equal to stockholders' equity or total assets equal to total liabilities plus stockholders' equity. The financial position form, a variation of the report form, shows noncurrent assets added to and noncurrent liabilities deducted from working capital to arrive at a balance equal to stockholders' equity.

2.04   Effective for fiscal years ending after December 15, 1988, Statement of Financial Accounting Standards (SFAS) No. 94, *Consolidation of All Majority-Owned Subsidiaries*, requires that companies consolidate subsidiaries having non-homogeneous operations. This requirement resulted in certain survey companies presenting an unclassified balance sheet (15 companies in 2003) or a balance sheet classified as to industrial operations but showing assets and liabilities of nonhomogeneous operations as segregated amounts (7 companies in 2003). Prior to the effective date of *SFAS No. 94*, the survey companies with rare exception, presented classified balance sheets.

2.05   Occasionally, the survey companies disclose reclassifications of balance sheet amounts. Examples of a reclassification follow.

2.06

TABLE 2-2: BALANCE SHEET FORMAT

	2003	2002	2001	2000
Report form	506	507	494	502
Account form	94	92	105	97
Financial position form	0	1	1	1
Total Companies	**600**	**600**	**600**	**600**

Reclassifications

2.07

THE CLOROX COMPANY (JUN)

NOTES TO CONSOLIDATED FINANCIAL STATEMENTS (Millions of dollars)

1 (In Part): Significant Accounting Policies

Reclassifications

Certain reclassifications have been made to all periods presented in the consolidated financial statements to conform to the current year presentation, including the reclassification of the Company's Brazilian business as a discontinued operation (see Note 3) and the reclassification of capitalized software development costs from other assets to property, plant and equipment (approximately $89 at June 30, 2002). Assets for the Brazil business and other pending asset dispositions of $6 and $51 as of June 30, 2003 and June 30, 2002, respectively, have been reclassified to assets held for sale. The Company also reclassified $119 of deferred taxes related to foreign currency translation adjustments from other assets to deferred income taxes in the June 30, 2002 balance sheet, and $20 of investments held in two trust accounts from other liabilities to other assets as of June 30, 2003 as described in Notes 17 and 18.

2.08

STEWART & STEVENSON SERVICES, INC. (JAN)

NOTES TO CONSOLIDATED FINANCIAL STATEMENTS

Note 1 (In Part): Summary of Significant Accounting Policies

Reclassifications

The accompanying consolidated financial statements for prior fiscal years contain certain reclassifications to conform with the presentation used in Fiscal 2003. These reclassifications of prior fiscal year balances include $31.8 million of rental equipment (net of $20.2 million accumulated depreciation) which was removed from inventories and included in property, plant and equipment in the consolidated balance sheets.

CASH AND CASH EQUIVALENTS

2.09 Cash is commonly considered to consist of currency and demand deposits. SFAS No. 95, *Statement of Cash Flows*, defines cash equivalents as "short-term, highly liquid investments" that will mature within three months or less after being acquired by the holder. 466 survey companies stated explicitly that the carrying amount of cash and cash equivalents approximated fair value.

2.10 Table 2-3 lists the balance sheet captions used by the survey companies to describe cash and cash equivalents. As indicated in Table 2-3, the most frequently used caption is cash and cash equivalents. Examples of cash and cash equivalents presentations and disclosures follow.

2.11

TABLE 2-3: CASH AND CASH EQUIVALENTS— BALANCE SHEET CAPTIONS

	2003	2002	2001	2000
Cash..............................	35	35	35	53
Cash and cash equivalents.............	498	501	496	473
Cash and equivalents......................	33	32	32	37
Cash includes certificates of deposit or time deposits..............	1	2	4	7
Cash combined with marketable securities.................	21	25	27	27
No amount for cash........................	12	5	6	3
Total Companies........................	**600**	**600**	**600**	**600**

2.12

ALLERGAN, INC. (DEC)

(In millions)	2003	2002
Current assets		
Cash and equivalents	$507.6	$ 774.0
Trade receivables, net	220.1	220.6
Inventories	76.3	70.4
Other current assets	124.2	135.2
Total current assets	$928.2	$1,200.2

NOTES TO CONSOLIDATED FINANCIAL STATEMENTS

Note 1 (In Part): Summary of Significant Accounting Policies

Cash and Equivalents

The Company considers cash in banks, repurchase agreements, commercial paper and deposits with financial institutions with maturities of three months or less and that can be liquidated without prior notice or penalty, to be cash and equivalents.

Note 12 (In Part): Financial Instruments

Fair Value of Financial Instruments (In Part)

At December 31, 2003 and 2002, the Company's financial instruments included cash and equivalents, trade receivables, investments, accounts payable, borrowings and foreign exchange forward and option contracts. The carrying amount of cash and equivalents, trade receivables and accounts payable approximates fair value due to the short-term maturities of these instruments. The fair value of marketable equity investments, notes payable, long-term debt and foreign currency contracts were estimated based on quoted market prices at year-end. The fair value of non-marketable equity investments which represent investments in start-up technology companies or partnerships that invest in start-up technology companies, are estimated based on the fair value and other information provided by these ventures.

The carrying amount and estimated fair value of the Company's financial instruments at December 31 were as follows (in millions):

	2003		2002	
	Carrying Amount	Fair Value	Carrying Amount	Fair Value
Cash and equivalents	$507.6	$507.6	$774.0	$774.0
Non-current investments:				
Marketable equity	3.7	3.7	1.1	1.1
Non-marketable equity	2.9	3.4	3.2	3.2
Notes receivable	2.4	2.4	4.7	4.7
Notes payable	24.4	24.4	89.7	89.7
Long-term debt	66.0	74.0	25.4	29.9
Long-term convertible notes, net of discount	507.3	611.1	501.0	546.1

2.13

ANALOG DEVICES, INC. (OCT)

(Thousands)	2003	2002
Current assets		
Cash and cash equivalents	$ 517,874	$1,613,753
Short-term investments	1,598,869	1,284,270
Accounts receivable less allowances of $10,059 ($15,506 in 2002)	294,781	228,338
Inventories	287,502	306,391
Deferred tax assets	144,249	152,552
Prepaid expenses and other current assets	42,441	38,921
Total current assets	$2,885,716	$3,624,225

NOTES TO CONSOLIDATED FINANCIAL STATEMENTS
(All tabular amounts in thousands)

2 (In Part): Summary of Significant Accounting Policies

b. Cash, Cash Equivalents and Short-Term Investments

Cash and cash equivalents are highly liquid investments with insignificant interest rate risk and maturities of three months or less at the time of acquisition. The Company's investments, which generally have maturities between three and twelve months at time of acquisition, are considered short-term. Cash, cash equivalents and short-term investments consist primarily of corporate obligations such as commercial paper and corporate bonds, but also include government agency notes, certificates of deposit, bank time deposits and institutional money market funds.

The Company classifies its investments in readily marketable debt and equity securities as "held-to-maturity," "available-for-sale" or "trading" at the time of purchase. There were no transfers between investment classifications in any of the periods presented. Held-to-maturity securities, which are carried at amortized cost, include only those securities the Company has the positive intent and ability to hold to maturity. Securities, such as bank time deposits, which by their nature are typically held to maturity, are classified as such. The Company's other readily marketable investments are classified as available-for-sale. Available-for-sale securities are carried at fair value with unrealized gains and losses, net of related tax, if any, reported as a separate component of stockholders' equity. Realized gains and losses, as well as interest, and dividends on all securities, are included in earnings.

Substantially all of the Company's short-term investments have contractual maturities of twelve months or less at time of acquisition. Because of the short term to maturity, and hence relative price insensitivity to changes in market interest rates, amortized cost approximates fair value for all of these securities. No realized gains or losses were recorded during fiscal 2003, 2002 or 2001. Unrealized losses of $3.9 million, net of tax of $2.1 million, were recorded in fiscal 2002. Unrealized gains and losses were not material in fiscal 2003 or fiscal 2001.

There were no cash equivalents or short-term investments classified as trading at November 1, 2003 and November 2, 2002. Cash equivalents and short-term investments classified as held-to-maturity were $162 million and $130 million at November 1, 2003 and November 2, 2002, respectively and were comprised solely of Euro time deposits. The components of the Company's available-for-sale securities as of November 1, 2003 and November 2, 2002 were as follows:

	2003	2002
Corporate obligations	$1,783,969	$2,588,483
U.S. government agency and municipal	105,000	98,200
Institutional money market funds	11,396	42,111
Bankers' acceptances	—	5,352
Total available-for-sale securities	$1,900,365	$2,734,146

Cash balances included in cash and cash equivalents were $54 million and $34 million at November 1, 2003 and November 2, 2002, respectively.

j. (In Part): Fair Values of Financial Instruments

The following estimated fair value amounts have been determined by the Company using available market information and appropriate valuation methodologies. However, considerable judgment is required in interpreting market data to develop the estimates of fair value. Accordingly, the estimates presented herein are not necessarily indicative of the amounts that the Company could realize in a current market exchange.

	2003		2002	
	Carrying Amount	Fair Value	Carrying Amount	Fair Value
Assets:				
Cash and cash equivalents	$ 517,874	$ 517,874	$1,613,753	$1,613,753
Short-term investments	1,598,869	1,598,869	1,284,270	1,284,270
Deferred compensation investments	304,008	304,008	277,595	277,595
Other investments	37,565	37,565	2,010	2,010

The following methods and assumptions were used by the Company in estimating its fair value disclosures for financial instruments:

Cash, Cash Equivalents and Short-Term Investments

The carrying amounts of these items are a reasonable estimate of their fair value due to the short term to maturity and readily available market for these types of investments.

2.14

ARVINMERITOR, INC. (SEP)

(In millions)	2003	2002
Current assets		
Cash and cash equivalents	$ 103	$ 56
Receivables (less allowance for doubtful accounts: 2003, $24; 2002, $18)	1,327	1,251
Inventories	543	458
Other current assets	266	211
Total current assets	$2,239	$1,976

NOTES TO CONSOLIDATED FINANCIAL STATEMENTS

15 (In Part): Financial Instruments

The company's financial instruments include cash and cash equivalents, marketable securities, short-term debt, long-term debt, interest rate swaps, and foreign exchange contracts. The company uses derivatives for hedging and non-trading purposes in order to manage its interest rate and foreign exchange rate exposures. The company's interest rate swap agreements are discussed in Note 14.

Fair Value

Fair values of financial instruments are summarized as follows (in millions):

	2003		2002	
	Carrying Value	Fair Value	Carrying Value	Fair Value
Cash and cash equivalents	$ 103	$ 103	$ 56	$ 56
Marketable securities	17	17	—	—
Interest rate swaps—asset	46	46	48	48
Short-term debt	20	20	15	15
Long-term debt	1,541	1,533	1,474	1,473

Cash and Cash Equivalents

All highly liquid investments purchased with maturity of three months or less are considered to be cash equivalents. The carrying value approximates fair value because of the short maturity of these instruments.

MARKETABLE SECURITIES

2.15 SFAS No. 115, *Accounting for Certain Investments in Debt and Equity Securities*, is the authoritative pronouncement on accounting for and reporting investments in equity securities that have readily determinable fair value and all investments in debt securities. Paragraphs 19–22 of *SFAS No. 115*, as amended by SFAS No. 133, *Accounting for Derivative Instruments and Hedging Activities*, state the disclosure requirements for such investments.

2.16 By definition, investments in debt and equity securities are financial instruments. For investments subject to *SFAS No. 115* requirements, SFAS No. 107, *Disclosure about Fair Value of Financial Instruments*, as amended by *SFAS No. 133*, requires disclosure of both the fair value and the bases for estimating the fair value of marketable securities unless it is not practicable to estimate that value. 245 survey companies made 252 fair value disclosures. 108 of those disclosures used market or broker quotes of the investments in debt and equity securities to determine fair value. 15 of those disclosures estimated fair value using other valuation methods. 170 disclosures presented carrying amounts which approximated fair value of marketable securities. In addition there were 71 disclosures in which carrying value was compared to fair value in an exposition or a table.

2.17 *SFAS No. 115* requires that certain debt and equity securities be classified into one of three categories: held-to-maturity, available-for-sale, or trading securities. Investments in debt securities that the enterprise has the positive intent and ability to hold to maturity are classified as held-to-maturity and reported at amortized cost in the statement of financial position. Securities that are bought and held principally for the purpose of selling them in the near term (thus held for only a short period of time) are classified as trading securities and reported at fair value. Trading generally reflects active and frequent buying and selling, and trading securities are generally used to generate profit on short-term differences in price. Investments not classified as either held-to-maturity or trading securities are classified as available-for-sale securities and reported at fair value. 132 survey companies identified their marketable securities as available-for-sale.

2.18 Statement of Financial Accounting Concepts (SFAC) No. 7, *Using Cash Flow Information and Present Value in Accounting Measurements*, was issued in February 2000. It provides a framework for using future cash flows and present value as the basis for accounting measurements of fair value of an asset or a liability at initial recognition or fresh-start measurements and for future-cash-flow-based amortization techniques, such as interest method amortization. Fresh-start measurements are measurements in periods following initial recognition that establish a new carrying amount unrelated to previous amounts and accounting conventions. Reporting certain marketable securities at fair value under *SFAS No. 115* is an example of a fresh-start measurement.

2.19 When observable marketplace-determined values are not available, discounted cash flows are often used to estimate fair value. Accounting applications of present value typically use a single set of estimated cash flows and a risk-adjusted discount rate. *SFAC No. 7* introduces the expected cash flow approach, which differs from the traditional approach by focusing on explicit assumptions about the range of possible cash outcomes and their respective probabilities.

2.20 While *SFAC No. 7* does not require modification of any existing pronouncements, its concepts may be used to determine fair value. This Standard will be used in developing future accounting standards. No data on the use of expected cash flow approach or discounted cash flow applications were compiled.

2.21 The FASB's Emerging Issues Task Force (EITF) Issue No. 03-1, *The Meaning of Other-Than-Temporary Impairment and Its Application to Certain Investments*, should be used to determine when certain investments are considered impaired, whether that impairment is other than temporary, and the measurement and recognition of an impairment loss. *EITF Issue No. 03-1* also provides guidance on accounting considerations subsequent to the recognition of an other-than-temporary impairment and requires certain disclosures about unrealized losses that have not been recognized as other-than-temporary impairments.

2.22 Table 2-4 lists the balance sheet carrying bases for investments in debt and equity securities presented as current assets. Examples of presentations and disclosures for such investments follow.

2.23

TABLE 2-4: MARKETABLE SECURITIES—BASES

| | Number of Companies | | | |
	2003	2002	2001	2000
Market/fair value........................	175	168	163	136
Cost..	48	54	52	46
Lower of cost or market..............	0	1	2	0

Available-for-Sale Securities

2.24

CUMMINS INC. (DEC)

($ millions)	2003	2002
Current assets		
Cash and cash equivalents	$ 108	$ 224
Marketable securities	87	74
Receivables, net	772	676
Receivables from related parties	157	129
Inventories	733	641
Other current assets	273	238
Total current assets	$2,130	$1,982

NOTES TO CONSOLIDATED FINANCIAL STATEMENTS

Note 1 (In Part): Summary of Significant Accounting Policies

Marketable Securities

We classify our investments in marketable securities as "available-for-sale" or "held-to-maturity" in accordance with the provisions of Statement of Financial Accounting Standards No. 115, "Accounting for Certain Investments in Debt and Equity Securities" (SFAS 115). We do not have any investments classified as "trading." Investments that we intend to hold for more than one year are classified as long-term investments.

Available-for-sale securities are carried at fair value with the unrealized gain or loss, net of tax, reported in other comprehensive income. Held-to-maturity securities are recorded at amortized cost. Unrealized losses considered to be "other-than-temporary" are recognized currently in earnings. The cost of securities sold is based on the specific identification method. The fair value of most investment securities is determined by currently available market prices. Where quoted market prices are not available, we use the market price of similar types of securities that are traded in the market to estimate fair value. See Note 3 for a detailed description of our investments in marketable securities.

Note 3. Marketable Securities

The following is a summary of marketable securities at December 31:

($ millions)	2003 Cost	2003 Gross Unrealized Gains	2003 Est. Fair Value	2002 Cost	2002 Gross Unrealized Gains	2002 Est. Fair Value
Available-for-sale:						
Debt mutual funds	$50	$2	$52	$44	$2	$46
Government debt securities—non-U.S.	8	—	8	8	1	9
Corporate debt securities	16	1	17	14	—	14
Equity securities and other	6	5	11	5	—	5
Held-to-maturity:						
Commercial paper and other	9	—	9	5	—	5
Total marketable securities	$89	$8	$97	$76	$3	$79
Current	$84	$3	$87	$71	$3	$74
Non-current	5	5	10	5	—	5

Proceeds from sales of available-for-sale securities were $139 million, $59 million and $19 million in 2003, 2002 and 2001, respectively. Purchases of available-for-sale securities were $141 million, $95 million and $39 million in 2003, 2002 and 2001, respectively. Gross realized gains from the sale of available-for-sale securities were $4 million, $1 million and $2 million in 2003, 2002 and 2001, respectively. Gross realized losses from the sale of available-for-sale securities were $1 million in 2003 and not material in 2002 and 2001. During the fourth quarter of 2002, we recorded a $4 million charge related to an "other-than-temporary" impairment of an investment in equity securities.

The commercial paper and other investments mature during 2004. The fair value of available-for-sale investments in debt securities by contractual maturity at December 31, 2003, is as follows:

($ millions)

Maturity Date	Fair Value
1 year or less	$ 3
1–5 years	12
5–10 years	4
After 10 years	6
Total	$25

2.25

INTUIT INC. (JUL)

(In thousands)	2002	2003
Current assets:		
Cash and cash equivalents	$ 408,948	$ 170,043
Short-term investments	815,342	1,036,758
Marketable securities	16,791	865
Customer deposits	300,409	306,007
Accounts receivable, net of allowance for doubtful accounts of $5,696 and $5,409, respectively	51,999	88,156
Income taxes receivable	2,187	—
Deferred income taxes	67,799	34,824
Prepaid expenses and other current assets	49,581	32,217
Amounts due from discontinued operations entities	241,616	—
Total current assets	$1,954,672	$1,668,870

NOTES TO CONSOLIDATED FINANCIAL STATEMENTS

1 (In Part): Summary of Significant Accounting Policies

Cash Equivalents and Short-Term Investments

We consider highly liquid investments with maturities of three months or less at the date of purchase to be cash equivalents. Cash equivalents consist primarily of money market funds in all periods presented. Short-term investments consist of available-for-sale debt securities that we carry at fair value. We include unrealized gains and losses on short-term investments, net of tax, in stockholders' equity. Available-for-sale debt securities are classified as current assets based upon our intent and ability to use any and all of these securities as necessary to satisfy the significant short-term liquidity requirements that may arise from the highly seasonal and cyclical nature of our businesses. Because of our significant business seasonality, cash flow requirements may fluctuate dramatically from quarter to quarter and require us to use a significant amount of the short-term investments held as available-for-sale securities. See Note 2.

Marketable Securities and Other Long-Term Investments (In Part)

We classify our marketable securities as available-for-sale, carry them at fair value and include unrealized gains and losses on them, net of tax, in stockholders' equity. We use the specific identification method to account for gains and losses on marketable equity securities. We include realized gains and losses and declines in value judged to be other-than-temporary on available-for-sale securities in gains (losses) on marketable securities and other investments, net on our statement of operations. Our other long-term investments consist primarily of equity investments in privately held companies and are stated at cost, adjusted for declines in fair value that are considered other-than-temporary.

2. Short-Term Investments

As discussed in Note 1, "*Concentration of Credit Risk and Significant Customers and Suppliers,*" our portfolio of short-term investments consists primarily of investment-grade securities. Except for direct obligations of the United States government and money market or cash management funds, we diversify our short-term investments by limiting our holdings with any individual issuer to a maximum of $5.0 million in each of our three managed portfolios.

The following schedule summarizes the estimated fair value of our short-term investments at the dates indicated:

(In thousands)	2002	2003
Corporate notes	$ 24,405	$ 50,471
Municipal bonds	780,914	931,374
U.S. government securities	10,023	54,913
	$815,342	$1,036,758

The following table summarizes the estimated fair value of our available-for-sale debt securities held in short-term investments classified by the stated maturity date of the security:

(In thousands)	2002	2003
Due within one year	$230,716	$ 241,110
Due within two years	141,942	270,900
Due within three years	—	3,088
Due after three years	442,684	521,660
	$815,342	$1,036,758

Realized gains and losses from the sale of short-term investments were not material for fiscal 2001, 2002 and 2003.

2.26

PACCAR INC. (DEC)

(Millions of dollars)	2003	2002
Current assets		
Cash and cash equivalents	$1,323.2	$ 738.1
Trade and other receivables, net of allowance for losses (2003—$14.9 and 2002—$25.9)	479.1	404.7
Marketable debt securities	377.1	535.3
Inventories	334.5	310.6
Deferred taxes and other current assets	85.0	112.9
Total current assets	$2,598.9	$2,101.6

NOTES TO CONSOLIDATED FINANCIAL STATEMENTS (Currencies in millions)

B (In Part): Investments in Marketable Securities

The Company's investments in marketable securities are classified as available-for-sale. These investments are stated at fair value with any unrealized holding gains or losses, net of tax, included as a component of stockholders' equity until realized. Gross realized gains and losses on marketable debt securities were $5.1 and $.7 respectively for the year ended December 31, 2003. Gross realized gains and losses on marketable debt securities were not significant in 2002 and 2001. Unrealized losses are charged against net earnings when a decline in fair value is determined to be other than temporary.

The cost of debt securities available-for-sale is adjusted for amortization of premiums and accretion of discounts to maturity. Amortization of premiums, accretion of discounts, interest and dividend income and realized gains and losses are included in investment income. The cost of securities sold is based on the specific identification method.

Marketable debt securities at December 31, 2003, were as follows:

	Amortized Cost	Fair Value
U.S. government securities	$ 24.2	$ 24.5
Tax-exempt securities	347.8	352.6
	$372.0	$377.1

Marketable debt securities at December 31, 2002, were as follows:

	Amortized Cost	Fair Value
U.S. government securities	$135.5	$137.9
Tax-exempt securities	367.6	376.1
Other debt securities	21.2	21.3
	$524.3	$535.3

The contractual maturities of debt securities at December 31, 2003, were as follows:

Maturities	Amortized Cost	Fair Value
Within one year	$ 50.2	$ 50.3
One to five years	321.8	326.8
	$372.0	$377.1

N (In Part): Fair Values of Financial Instruments

The following methods and assumptions were used by the Company in determining its fair value disclosures for financial instruments:

Marketable Debt and Equity Securities

Amounts are carried at fair value. Fair values are based on quoted market prices (see Note B).

2.27

WYETH (DEC)

(In thousands)	2003	2002
Cash and cash equivalents	$ 6,069,794	$ 2,943,604
Marketable securities	1,110,297	1,003,275
Amgen investment	—	1,509,947
Accounts receivable less allowances (2003—$149,795 and 2002—$132,342)	2,529,613	2,379,819
Inventories	2,412,184	1,992,724
Other current assets including deferred taxes	2,840,354	1,776,330
Total current assets	$14,962,242	$11,605,699

NOTES TO CONSOLIDATED FINANCIAL STATEMENTS

1 (In Part): Summary of Significant Accounting Policies

Marketable Securities

The Company has marketable debt and equity securities, which are classified as either available-for-sale or held-to-maturity, depending on management's investment intentions relating to these securities. Available-for-sale securities are marked-to-market based on quoted market values of the securities, with the unrealized gains and losses, net of tax, reported as a component of *Accumulated other comprehensive loss*. Realized gains and losses on sales of available-for-sale securities are computed based upon initial cost adjusted for any other-than-temporary declines in fair value. Investments categorized as held-to-maturity are carried at amortized cost because the Company has both the intent and ability to hold these investments until they mature. Impairment losses are charged to income for other-than-temporary declines in fair value. Premiums and discounts are amortized or accreted into earnings over the life of the related available-for-sale or held-to-maturity security. Dividend and interest income is recognized when earned. The Company owns no investments that are considered to be trading securities.

4. Marketable Securities

The cost, gross unrealized gains (losses) and fair value of available-for-sale and held-to-maturity securities by major security type at December 31, 2003 and 2002 were as follows:

(In thousands)

At December 31, 2003	Cost	Gross Unrealized Gains	Gross Unrealized (Losses)	Fair Value
Available-for-sale:				
U.S. Treasury securities	$ 152,851	$ 44	$ (23)	$ 152,872
Commercial paper	42,964	4	(4)	42,964
Certificates of deposit	63,643	22	(27)	63,638
Corporate debt securities	212,198	252	(32)	212,418
Other debt securities	4,296	—	(11)	4,285
Equity securities	21,078	13,158	(188)	34,048
Institutional fixed income fund	522,847	16,868	—	539,715
Total available-for-sale	1,019,877	30,348	(285)	1,049,940
Held-to-maturity:				
Commercial paper	60,107	—	—	60,107
Certificates of deposit	250	—	—	250
Total held-to-maturity	60,357	—	—	60,357
	$1,080,234	$30,348	$(285)	$1,110,297

(In thousands)

At December 31, 2002	Cost	Gross Unrealized Gains	Gross Unrealized (Losses)	Fair Value
Available-for-sale:				
U.S. Treasury securities	$105,583	$ 615	$ (15)	$ 106,183
Commercial paper	57,397	—	—	57,397
Certificates of deposit	29,218	77	—	29,295
Corporate debt securities	214,127	1,202	(388)	214,941
Other debt securities	9,702	150	—	9,852
Institutional fixed income fund	510,574	16,312	—	526,886
Total available-for-sale	926,601	18,356	(403)	944,554
Held-to-maturity:				
Time/term deposits	30,002	—	—	30,002
U.S. Treasury securities	1,996	—	—	1,996
Commercial paper	10,473	—	—	10,473
Certificates of deposit	15,251	—	—	15,251
Other debt securities	999	—	—	999
Total held-to-maturity	58,721	—	—	58,721
	$985,322	$18,356	$(403)	$1,003,275

The contractual maturities of debt securities classified as available-for-sale at December 31, 2003 were as follows:

(In thousands)	Cost	Fair Value
Available-for-sale:		
Due within one year	$276,522	$276,578
Due after one year through five years	190,696	190,872
Due after five years through 10 years	—	—
Due after 10 years	8,734	8,727
	$475,952	$476,177

All held-to-maturity debt securities are due within one year and had aggregate fair values of $60.4 million at December 31, 2003.

Held-to-Maturity Securities

2.28

HECLA MINING COMPANY (DEC)

(In thousands)	2003	2002
Current assets:		
Cash and cash equivalents	$105,387	$19,542
Short-term investments	18,003	—
Accounts and notes receivable	16,318	10,154
Inventories	16,936	14,758
Deferred income taxes	1,427	2,700
Other current assets	3,174	1,780
Total current assets	$161,245	$48,934

NOTES TO CONSOLIDATED FINANCIAL STATEMENTS

Note 1 (In Part): Summary of Significant Accounting Policies

D. Investments

At December 31, 2003, short-term investments included certificates of deposit and held-to-maturity securities, as it is management's intent and we have the ability to hold the securities to maturity. Held-to-maturity securities are stated at amortized cost, which approximates market, and include government and corporate obligations rated A or higher.

Marketable equity securities are categorized as available for sale and carried at quoted market value. Realized gains and losses on the sale of securities are recognized on a specific identification basis. Unrealized gains and losses are included as a component of accumulated other comprehensive loss, net of related deferred income taxes, unless a permanent impairment in value has occurred, which is then charged to operations. At December 31, 2003 and 2002, these investments are recorded as noncurrent assets.

Restricted cash and investments primarily represent investments in money market funds and bonds of U.S. government agencies. These investments are restricted primarily for reclamation funding or surety bonds.

Note 2 (In Part): Restricted Cash and Investments

Short-Term Investments

At December 31, 2003, short-term investments included certificates of deposit and held-to-maturity securities, which are carried at amortized cost. Due to the short-term nature of these investments, the amortized cost approximates fair market value. All of these investments mature during 2004 and consisted of the following at December 31, 2003 (in thousands):

Certificates of deposit	$ 3,094
United States government and federal agency securities	5,616
Municipal securities	6,091
Corporate bonds	3,202
	$18,003

2.29

QUALCOMM INCORPORATED (SEP)

(In thousands)	2003	2002
Current assets:		
Cash and cash equivalents	$2,045,094	$1,406,704
Marketable securities	2,516,003	1,411,178
Accounts receivable, net	483,793	536,950
Finance receivables, net	5,795	388,396
Inventories, net	110,351	88,094
Deferred tax assets	611,536	122
Other current assets	176,192	109,322
Total current assets	$5,948,764	$3,940,766

NOTES TO CONSOLIDATED FINANCIAL STATEMENTS

Note 1 (In Part): The Company and Its Significant Accounting Policies

Marketable Securities

Management determines the appropriate classification of marketable securities at the time of purchase and reevaluates such designation as of each balance sheet date. Held-to-maturity securities are carried at amortized cost, which approximates fair value. Available-for-sale securities and trading securities are stated at fair value as determined by the most recently traded price of each security at the balance sheet date. The net unrealized gains or losses on available-for-sale securities are reported as a component of comprehensive income (loss), net of tax. Unrealized gains or losses on trading securities are reported in investment income (expense). The specific identification method is used to compute the realized gains and losses on debt and equity securities.

The Company regularly monitors and evaluates the realizable value of its marketable securities. When assessing marketable securities for other-than-temporary declines in value, the Company considers such factors as, among other things, how significant the decline in value is as a percentage of the original cost, how long the market value of the investment has been less than its original cost, the performance of the investee's stock price in relation to the stock price of its competitors within the industry and the market in general, analyst recommendations, any news that has been released specific to the investee and the outlook for the overall industry in which the investee operates. The Company also reviews the financial statements of the investee to determine if the investee is experiencing financial difficulties and considers new products/services that the investee may have forthcoming that will improve its operating results. If events and circumstances indicate that a decline in the value of these assets has occurred and is other than temporary, the Company records a charge to investment income (expense).

Note 2. Marketable Securities

Marketable securities were comprised as follows (in thousands):

	Current		Noncurrent	
	2003	2002	2003	2002
Held-to-maturity:				
Certificates of deposit	$ 5,073	$ 76,153	$ —	$ —
Commercial paper	—	—	—	6,200
Federal agencies	489	—	129,988	—
Corporate medium-term notes	161,416	97,669	70,111	89,418
	166,978	173,822	200,099	95,618
Available-for-sale:				
Federal agencies	346,056	270,896	—	—
U.S. government securities	349,398	238,286	—	—
Corporate medium-term notes	1,117,968	300,648	22,099	14,121
Mortgage and asset-backed securities	485,859	290,702	—	—
Non-investment grade debt securities	39,316	6,558	458,768	245,075
Equity securities	10,428	130,266	129,688	24,956
	2,349,025	1,237,356	610,555	284,152
Trading:				
Corporate convertible bonds	—	—	—	1,860
	—	—	—	1,860
	$2,516,003	$1,411,178	$810,654	$381,630

As of September 30, 2003, the contractual maturities of debt securities were as follows (in thousands):

	Years to Maturity					
	Less Than One Year	One to Five Years	Five to Ten Years	Greater Than Ten Years	No Single Maturity Date	Total
Held-to-maturity	$166,978	$ 200,099	$ —	$ —	$ —	$ 367,077
Available-for-sale	187,571	1,702,214	428,331	16,816	484,532	2,819,464
	$354,549	$1,902,313	$428,331	$16,816	$484,532	$3,186,541

Securities with no single maturity date include mortgage-backed securities and asset-backed securities.

Trading Securities

2.30

INTEL CORPORATION (DEC)

(In millions)	2003	2002
Current assets:		
Cash and cash equivalents	$ 7,971	$ 7,404
Short-term investments	5,568	3,382
Trading assets	2,625	1,801
Accounts receivable, net of allowance for		
doubtful accounts of $55 ($57 in 2002)	2,960	2,574
Inventories	2,519	2,276
Deferred tax assets	969	1,136
Other current assets	270	352
Total current assets	$22,882	$18,925

NOTES TO CONSOLIDATED FINANCIAL STATEMENTS

Note 2 (In Part): Accounting Policies

Investments (In Part)

Trading Assets

Trading assets are stated at fair value, with gains or losses resulting from changes in fair value recognized currently in earnings. The company elects to classify as trading assets a portion of its marketable debt securities. For these debt securities, gains or losses from changes in fair value due to interest rate and currency market fluctuations, offset by losses or gains on related derivatives, are included in interest and other, net. A portion of the company's marketable equity securities may from time to time be classified as trading assets, if the company no longer deems the investments to be strategic in nature at the time of trading asset designation, and has the ability and intent to mitigate equity market risk through sale or the use of derivative instruments. For these marketable equity securities, gains or losses from changes in fair value, primarily offset by losses or gains on related derivative instruments, are included in gains (losses) on equity securities, net. Also included in trading assets is a marketable equity portfolio held to generate returns that seek to offset changes in liabilities related to the equity market risk of certain deferred compensation arrangements. Gains or losses from changes in fair value of these equity securities, offset by losses or gains on the related liabilities, are included in interest and other, net. The company also uses fixed income investments and derivative instruments to seek to offset the remaining portion of the changes in the compensation liabilities.

Note 6 (In Part): Investments

Trading Assets

Trading assets outstanding at fiscal year-ends were as follows:

(In millions)	2003		2002	
	Net Unrealized Gains	Estimated Fair Value	Net Unrealized Gains (Losses)	Estimated Fair Value
Debt instruments	$174	$2,321	$ 64	$1,460
Equity securities	—	—	63	98
Equity securities offsetting deferred compensation	60	304	(1)	243
Total trading assets	$234	$2,625	$126	$1,801

Net holding gains (losses) on fixed income debt instruments classified as trading assets were $208 million in 2003, $79 million in 2002 and $(21) million in 2001. Net holding gains (losses) on the related derivatives were $(192) million in 2003, $(75) million in 2002 and $21 million in 2001. These amounts were included in interest and other, net in the consolidated statements of income.

Net holding gains on equity security trading assets were $77 million in 2003, $57 million in 2002 and $72 million in 2001. The $57 million net gain in 2002 includes a gain of $120 million that resulted from the designation of formerly restricted equity investments as trading assets as they became marketable. The cumulative difference between their cost and fair market value at the time they became marketable was recorded as a gain in 2002. Net holding gains (losses) on the related derivatives were $(84) million in 2003, $110 million in 2002 and $18 million in 2001. These gains and losses were included within losses on equity securities, net in the consolidated statements of income.

Certain equity securities within the trading asset portfolio are maintained to generate returns that seek to offset changes in liabilities related to the equity market risk of certain deferred compensation arrangements. These deferred compensation liabilities were $427 million in 2003 and $336 million in 2002, and are included in other accrued liabilities on the consolidated balance sheets. Net holding gains (losses) on equity securities offsetting deferred compensation arrangements were $52 million in 2003, $(64) million in 2002 and $(45) million in 2001, and were included within interest and other, net in the consolidated statements of income.

CURRENT RECEIVABLES

2.31 As stated in paragraph 13 of *SFAS No. 107*, as amended by *SFAS No. 133*, fair value disclosure is not required for trade receivables when the carrying amount of the trade receivable approximates its fair value. 315 survey companies made 317 fair value disclosures. 305 disclosures presented carrying amounts which approximated fair value of trade receivables.

2.32 Effective for fiscal years beginning after December 15, 2001, Statement of Position (SOP) 01-6, *Accounting by Certain Entities (Including Entities With Trade Receivables) That Lend to or Finance the Activities of Others*, issued by Accounting Standards Division of the American Institute of Certified Public Accountants (AICPA) requires that loans or trade receivables may be presented on the balance sheet as aggregate amounts. However, such receivables held for sale should be a separate balance-sheet category. Major categories of loans or trade receivables should be presented separately either in the balance sheet or in the notes to the financial statements. The allowance for credit losses, the allowance for doubtful accounts, and, as applicable, any unearned income, any unamortized premium and discounts, and any net unamortized deferred fees and costs, should be disclosed in the financial statements.

2.33 Table 2-5 summarizes both the descriptive titles used in the balance sheet to describe trade receivables, and the types of receivables, other than trade receivables, which the survey companies most frequently presented as current assets. Examples of presentations and disclosures for current receivables follow.

2.34

TABLE 2-5: CURRENT RECEIVABLES

	2003	2002	2001	2000
Trade Receivable Captions:				
Accounts receivable...........................	283	289	285	294
Receivables......................................	137	127	134	131
Trade accounts receivable..............	112	117	117	108
Accounts and notes receivable.........	52	51	51	61
No caption for current receivables....	16	16	13	6
Total Companies.............................	**600**	**600**	**600**	**600**
		Number of Companies		
Receivables Other Than Trade Receivables:				
Tax refund claims.............................	67	69	50	48
Investees...	41	45	39	35
Contracts...	36	35	35	36
Retained interest in sold receivables...................................	25	29	14	7
Finance..	24	26	26	24
Insurance claims..............................	15	6	7	3
Installment notes or accounts...........	8	8	5	2
Employees.......................................	2	4	3	1

RECEIVABLES OTHER THAN TRADE RECEIVABLES

Tax Refund Claims

2.35

THE BOEING COMPANY (DEC)

(Dollars in millions)	2003	2002
Cash and cash equivalents	$ 4,633	$ 2,333
Accounts receivable	4,515	5,007
Current portion of customer and commercial financing	857	1,289
Income taxes receivable	199	—
Deferred income taxes	1,716	2,042
Inventories, net of advances, progress billings and reserves	5,338	6,184
Total current assets	$17,258	$16,855

NOTES TO CONSOLIDATED FINANCIAL STATEMENTS (Dollars in millions)

Note 6 (In Part): Income Taxes

Of the deferred tax asset for net operating loss and credit carryovers, $61 expires in years ending from December 31, 2004 through December 31, 2023 and $15 may be carried over indefinitely. Income taxes have been settled with the IRS for all years through 1981, and IRS examinations have been completed through 1997. During 2003, a partial settlement was reached with the IRS for the years 1992–1997 and we received a refund of taxes and related interest of $1,095 (of which $397 represents interest). Also, in January and February 2004, we received federal tax refunds and a notice of approved refund totaling $145 (of which $40 represents interest). The refunds related to a settlement of the 1996 tax year and the 1997 partial tax year for McDonnell Douglas Corporation, which we merged with on August 1, 1997. The notice of approved refund related to the 1985 tax year. These events resulted in a $727 increase in net earnings for the year ended December 31, 2003. We believe adequate provision has been made for all outstanding issues for all open years.

2.36

ROBERT HALF INTERNATIONAL INC. (DEC)

(In thousands)	2003	2002
Cash and cash equivalents	$376,523	$316,927
Accounts receivable, less allowances of $13,608 and $12,578	242,348	225,721
Deferred income taxes and other current assets	79,748	102,849
Total current assets	$698,619	$645,497

NOTES TO CONSOLIDATED FINANCIAL STATEMENTS

Note C—Deferred Income Taxes and Other Current Assets

Deferred income taxes and other current assets consisted of the following (in thousands):

	2003	2002
Deferred income taxes	$27,102	$ 28,893
Deposits in trusts for employee benefits and retirement plans	31,238	29,707
Income taxes receivable	4,048	24,094
Other	17,360	20,155
	$79,748	$102,849

Receivables From Affiliates

2.37

AMERON INTERNATIONAL CORPORATION (NOV)

(Dollars in thousands)	2003	2002
Current assets		
Cash and cash equivalents	$ 20,390	$ 10,360
Receivables, less allowances of $8,168 in 2003 and $6,652 in 2002	155,629	131,283
Inventories	91,371	88,020
Deferred income taxes	19,241	16,528
Prepaid expenses and other current assets	8,882	6,671
Total current assets	$295,513	$252,862

NOTES TO CONSOLIDATED FINANCIAL STATEMENTS

Note 3. Receivables

Receivables were as follows at November 30:

(In thousands)	2003	2002
Trade	$153,041	$127,874
Joint ventures	2,461	2,653
Other	8,295	7,408
Allowances	(8,168)	(6,652)
	$155,629	$131,283

The Company's provision for bad debts was $3,071,000 in 2003, $1,300,000 in 2002, and $1,738,000 in 2001. Trade receivables included unbilled receivables related to the percentage-of-completion method of revenue recognition of $25,371,000 and $11,928,000 at November 30, 2003 and 2002, respectively.

2.38

FORTUNE BRANDS, INC. (DEC)

(In millions)	2003	2002
Current assets		
Cash and cash equivalents	$ 104.6	$ 15.4
Accounts receivable from customers less allowances for discounts, doubtful accounts and returns, 2003 $63.5; 2002 $65.8	860.5	741.7
Accounts receivable from related parties	112.9	103.4
Inventories		
Bulk whiskey	231.4	200.5
Other raw materials, supplies and work in process	281.2	247.0
Finished products	443.6	388.3
Total inventories	956.2	835.8
Other current assets	247.4	206.8
Total current assets	$2,281.6	$1,903.1

NOTES TO CONSOLIDATED FINANCIAL STATEMENTS

21. Related Party Transactions

Future Brands LLC

In 2001, the Company's spirits and wine business completed transactions with V&S Vin & Sprit AB (V&S) creating the Future Brands joint venture, which distributes both companies' spirits brands in the United States and provides related selling and invoicing services. Future Brands receives a commission from the partners for services provided. As part of forming this joint venture, JBBCo. has, in the event of default of Future Brands, a continuing obligation to satisfy any financial obligations of Future Brands that may arise in the event that Future Brands fails to fulfill its operating obligations and which results in a claim. These financial obligations include, but are not limited to, making payments to suppliers, employees and other parties with which Future Brands has contracts. At December 31, 2003 and 2002, JBBCo. did not

have any outstanding obligations as a result of this arrangement.

JBBCo.'s balances related to Future Brands included the following:

(In millions)	2003	2002	2001
Accounts receivable (invoicing by future brands on behalf of JBBCo.)	$73.5	$68.8	$92.0
Investment	8.2	11.7	9.4
Accounts payable (commissions)	14.4	15.6	23.7
Accrued liabilities	24.7	29.1	4.5

Maxxium Worldwide B. V.

In 1999, the spirits and wine business formed an international sales and distribution joint venture named Maxxium Worldwide B. V. (Maxxium) to distribute and sell spirits and wine in key markets outside the United States. The joint venture partners include Remy-Cointreau, Highland Distillers and V&S. JBBCo. records sales at the time spirits are sold to third parties rather than at the time of shipment to Maxxium. As a result of forming this joint venture, the Company has guaranteed certain credit facilities and bank loans entered into by Maxxium up to an amount totaling $79 million, of which $69 million was outstanding as of December 31, 2003. At December 31, 2002, the guarantees totaled $66 million, of which $57 million was outstanding. JBBW has executed a Shareholder Loan Facility (Loan Facility) with Maxxium amounting to $19 million. There were no amounts outstanding under the Loan Facility as of either December 31, 2003 or December 31, 2002. The Loan Facility expires June 30, 2006.

JBBCo.'s balances related to Maxxium included the following:

(In millions)	2003	2002	2001
Accounts receivable	$39.4	$34.6	$39.5
Investment	66.7	64.3	63.0
Accounts payable (expense reimbursement)	16.0	12.3	6.1

Contracts

2.39

GENERAL DYNAMICS CORPORATION (DEC)

(Dollars in millions)	2003	2002
Current assets:		
Cash and equivalents	$ 860	$ 328
Accounts receivable	1,378	1,074
Contracts in process	2,548	1,914
Inventories	1,160	1,405
Other current assets	448	377
Total current assets	$6,394	$5,098

NOTES TO CONSOLIDATED FINANCIAL STATEMENTS
(Dollars in millions)

A (In Part): Summary of Significant Accounting Policies

Accounts Receivable and Contracts in Process
Accounts receivable represent only amounts billed and currently due from customers. Recoverable costs and accrued profit related to long-term defense contracts and programs on which revenue has been recognized, but billings have not yet been presented to the customer (unbilled receivables) are included in contracts in process.

F. Contracts in Process

Contracts in process represent costs and accrued profit related to defense contracts and programs and consisted of the following:

	2003	2002
Contract costs and estimated profits	$17,700	$15,301
Other contract costs	749	711
	18,449	16,012
Less advances and progress payments	15,901	14,098
	$ 2,548	$ 1,914

Contract costs include production costs and related overhead, such as G&A expenses, as well as contract recoveries for such matters as contract changes, negotiated settlements and claims for unanticipated contract costs, which totaled $21 as of December 31, 2003, and $29 as of December 31, 2002. The company records revenue associated with these matters as either income or as an offset against a potential loss only when recovery can be reliably estimated and realization is probable. Other contract costs represent amounts required to be recorded under GAAP that are not currently allocable to contracts, such as a portion of the company's estimated workers' compensation, other insurance-related assessments, retirement benefits and environmental expenses. These costs will become allocable to contracts when they are paid. The company expects to recover these costs through ongoing business, including both existing backlog and probable follow-on contracts. This business base includes numerous contracts for which the company is the sole source or one of two suppliers on long-term defense programs. If the level of backlog in the future does not support the continued deferral of these costs, the profitability of the company's remaining contracts could be adversely affected.

Retained Interest in Sold Receivables

2.40

UNITED STATIONERS INC. (DEC)

(Dollars in thousands)	2003	2002
Current assets:		
Cash and cash equivalents	$ 10,307	$ 17,426
Accounts receivable, less allowance for doubtful accounts of $11,811 in 2003 and $16,445 in 2002	195,433	158,374
Retained interest in receivables sold, less allowance for doubtful accounts of $3,758 in 2003 and $2,058 in 2002	153,722	191,641
Inventories	539,919	572,498
Other current assets	25,943	26,958
Total current assets	$925,324	$966,897

NOTES TO CONSOLIDATED FINANCIAL STATEMENTS

2 (In Part): Summary of Significant Accounting Policies

Valuation of Accounts Receivable
The Company makes judgments as to the collectability of accounts receivable based on historical trends and future expectations. Management estimates an allowance for doubtful accounts, which represents the collectability of trade accounts receivable. This allowance adjusts gross trade accounts receivable downward to its estimated net realizable value. To determine the allowance for sales returns, management uses historical trends to estimate future period product returns. To determine the allowance for doubtful accounts, management reviews specific customer risks and the Company's accounts receivable aging.

6. Receivables Securitization Program

General
On March 28, 2003, USSC replaced its then existing $160 million Receivables Securitization Program with a new third-party receivables securitization program with Bank One, NA, as trustee (the "2003 Receivables Securitization Program"). Under this $225 million program, USSC sells, on a revolving basis, its eligible trade accounts receivable (except for certain excluded accounts receivable, which initially includes all accounts receivable of Lagasse, Canada and foreign subsidiaries) to the Receivables Company. The Receivables Company, in turn, ultimately transfers the eligible trade accounts receivable to a trust. The trustee then sells investment certificates, which represent an undivided interest in the pool of accounts receivable owned by the trust, to third-party investors. Affiliates of Bank One and PNC Bank act as funding agents. The funding agents provide standby liquidity funding to support the sale of the accounts receivable by the Receivables Company under 364-day liquidity facilities. The 2003 Receivables Securitization Program provides for the possibility of other liquidity facilities that may be provided by other commercial banks rated at least A-1/P-1.

The Company utilizes this program to fund its cash requirements more cost effectively than under the 2003 Credit Agreement. Standby liquidity funding is committed for only 364 days and must be renewed before maturity in order for the program to continue. The program contains certain covenants and requirements, including criteria relating to the quality of receivables within the pool of receivables. If the covenants or requirements were compromised, funding from the program could be restricted or suspended, or its costs could increase. In such a circumstance, or if the standby liquidity funding were not renewed, the Company could require replacement liquidity. As discussed above, the Company's 2003 Credit Agreement is an existing alternate liquidity source. The Company believes that, if so required, it also could access other liquidity sources to replace funding from the program.

Financial Statement Presentation

The Receivables Securitization Program is accounted for as a sale in accordance with FASB Statement No. 140 "*Accounting for Transfers and Servicing of Financial Assets and Extinguishments of Liabilities*." Trade accounts receivable sold under this Program are excluded from accounts receivable in the Consolidated Financial Statements. At December 31, 2003, the Company sold $150 million of interests in trade accounts receivable, compared with $105 million at December 31, 2002. Accordingly, trade accounts receivable of $150 million as of December 31, 2003 and $105 million as of December 31, 2002 are excluded from the Consolidated Financial Statements. As discussed further below, the Company retains an interest in the master trust based on funding levels determined by the Receivables Company. The Company's retained interest in the master trust is included in the Consolidated Financial Statements under the caption, "Retained interest in receivables sold, net." For further information on the Company's retained interest in the master trust, see the caption "Retained Interest" included herein below.

The Company recognizes certain costs and/or losses related to the Receivables Securitization Program. Costs related to this program vary on a daily basis and generally are related to certain short-term interest rates. The annual interest rate on the certificates issued under the Receivables Securitization Program during 2003 ranged between 0.9% and 1.6%. Losses recognized on the sale of accounts receivable, which represent the financial cost of funding under the program, totaled approximately $3.5 million and $1.9 million for 2003 and 2002, respectively. Proceeds from the collections under this revolving agreement were $3.4 billion for 2003, compared with $3.1 billion for 2002. All costs and/or losses related to the Receivables Securitization Program are included in the Consolidated Financial Statements of Income under the caption "Other Expense, net."

The Company has maintained the responsibility for servicing the sold trade accounts receivable and those transferred to the master trust. No servicing asset or liability has been recorded because the fees the Company receives for servicing the receivables approximate the related costs.

Retained Interest

The Receivables Company determines the level of funding achieved by the sale of trade accounts receivable, subject to a maximum amount. It retains a residual interest in the eligible receivables transferred to the trust, such that amounts payable in respect of such residual interest will be distributed to the Receivables Company upon payment in full of all amounts owed by the Receivables Company to the trust (and by the trust to its investors). The Company's net

retained interest on $303.7 million and $296.6 million of trade receivables in the master trust as of December 31, 2003 and 2002 was $153.7 million and $191.6 million, respectively. The Company's retained interest in the master trust is included in the Consolidated Financial Statements under the caption, "Retained interest in receivables sold, net."

The Company measures the fair value of its retained interest throughout the term of the Receivables Securitization Program using a present value model incorporating the following two key economic assumptions: (1) an average collection cycle of approximately 40 days; and (2) an assumed discount rate of 5% per annum. In addition, the Company estimates and records an allowance for doubtful accounts related to the Company's retained interest. Considering the above noted economic factors and estimates of doubtful accounts, the book value of the Company's retained interest approximates fair value. A 10% and 20% adverse change in the assumed discount rate or average collection cycle would not have a material impact on the Company's financial position or results of operations. Accounts receivable sold to the master trust that were written off during 2003 and 2002 were not material.

Finance Receivables

2.41

HARLEY-DAVIDSON, INC. (DEC)

(In thousands)	2003	2002
Current assets:		
Cash and cash equivalents	$ 812,449	$ 280,928
Marketable securities	510,211	514,800
Accounts receivable, net	112,406	108,694
Current portion of finance receivables, net	1,001,990	855,771
Inventories	207,726	218,156
Deferred income taxes	51,156	41,430
Prepaid expenses & other current assets	33,189	46,807
Total current assets	$2,729,127	$2,066,586
Finance receivables, net	$ 735,859	$ 589,809

NOTES TO CONSOLIDATED FINANCIAL STATEMENTS

No. 1 (In Part): Summary of Significant Accounting Policies

Finance Receivables Credit Losses

The provision for credit losses on finance receivables is charged to earnings in amounts sufficient to maintain the allowance for uncollectible accounts at a level HDFS believes is adequate to cover the losses of principal and accrued interest in the existing portfolio. HDFS' periodic evaluation of the adequacy of the allowance is generally based on HDFS' past loan loss experience, known and inherent risks in the portfolio, and current economic conditions. HDFS' wholesale and other large loan charge-off policy is based on a loan-by-loan review which considers the specific borrower's ability to repay and the estimated value of any collateral.

Retail loans are generally charged-off at 120 days contractually past due. All finance receivables accrue interest until either collected or charged-off. Accordingly, as of

December 31, 2003 and 2002, all finance receivables were accounted for as interest earning receivables.

Generally, it is HDFS' policy not to change the terms and conditions of finance receivables. The restructuring of retail and wholesale finance receivables may occasionally be required by judicial proceedings, primarily in situations involving bankruptcy. Total restructured finance receivables are not significant.

Repossessed inventory is recorded at net realizable value and is reclassified from finance receivables to other assets with any related loss charged against the allowance for credit losses. Repossessed inventory is $2.0 million and $0.9 million at December 31, 2003 and 2002, respectively.

Finance Receivable Securitizations

HDFS sells retail motorcycle loans through securitization transactions. Under the terms of securitization transactions, HDFS sells retail loans to a securitization trust. The securitization trust issues notes to investors, with various maturities and interest rates, secured by future collections of purchased retail loans. The proceeds from the issuance of the asset-backed securities are utilized by the securitization trust to purchase retail loans from HDFS.

Upon sale of the retail loans to the securitization trust, HDFS receives cash and also retains interest-only strip receivables, servicing rights, and cash reserve account deposits, collectively referred to as "investment in retained securitization interests." The investment in retained securitization interests is included with finance receivables in the consolidated balance sheets.

Interest-only strip receivables equal the present value of projected cash flows arising from retail loans sold to the securitization trust less contracted payment obligations due to securitization trust investors. Key assumptions in determining the present value of projected cash flows are prepayments, credit losses, and discount rate. Servicing rights entitle HDFS to service retail loans sold to the securitization trust for a fee. The servicing fee is considered adequate compensation for the services provided and is therefore recorded as earned and is included in financial services income.

Reserve account deposits held by the securitization trust represent interest-earning cash deposits collateralizing trust securities. The funds are not available for use by HDFS until the reserve account balances exceed thresholds specified in the securitization agreement.

Gains on current year securitizations on the sale of the retail loans are recognized in the period in which the sale occurs and depend on the original carrying amount of the transferred retail loans, allocated between the assets sold and the retained interests based on their relative fair value at the date of transfer.

Investments in retained securitization interests are recorded at fair value and are periodically reviewed for impairment. Market quotes of fair value are generally not available for retained interests, therefore HDFS estimates fair value based on the present value of future expected cash flows using HDFS' best estimates of key assumptions for credit losses, prepayments, and discount rate commensurate with the risks involved. Unrealized gains and losses on investments in retained securitization interests are recorded in other comprehensive income and, as of December 31, 2003 and 2002 were $59.1 million and $49.6 million, or $38.3 million and $32.1 million net of taxes, respectively.

HDFS does not guarantee securities issued by the securitization trusts or projected cash flows from the retail loans purchased from HDFS. Recourse against HDFS related to securitization transactions is limited to the respective investment in retained securitization interests excluding servicing rights.

HDFS utilizes a two-step process to transfer retail loans to a securitization trust. Loans are initially transferred to a special purpose, bankruptcy-remote, wholly-owned subsidiary which in turn sells the retail loans to the securitization trust. HDFS has surrendered control of retail loans sold to the securitization trust. Securitization transactions have been structured such that: a.) transferred assets have been isolated from HDFS by being put presumptively beyond the reach of HDFS and its creditors, even in bankruptcy or other receivership, b.) each holder of a beneficial interest in the securitization trust has the right to pledge or exchange their interest, and c.) HDFS does not maintain effective control over the transferred assets through either (1) an agreement that both entitles and obligates HDFS to repurchase or redeem the transferred assets before their maturity other than for breaches of representations and warranties relating to the transferred assets or (2) the ability to unilaterally cause the holder to return specific assets, other than through a customary cleanup call.

Activities of the securitization trust are limited to acquiring retail loans, issuing asset-backed securities and making payments on securities to investors. Securitization trusts have a limited life and generally terminate upon final distribution of amounts owed to the investors in the asset-backed securities. Historically, the life of securitization trusts purchasing retail loans from HDFS has approximated four years.

Due to the overall structure of the securitization transaction, the nature of the assets held by the securitization trust and the limited nature of its activities, the securitization trusts are considered QSPEs. Accordingly, gain on sale is recognized upon transfer of retail loans to a QSPE and assets and liabilities of the QSPEs are not consolidated in the financial statements of HDFS. See Note 3 to the consolidated financial statements for further discussion of HDFS' securitization program.

No. 3 Harley-Davidson Financial Services Inc.

HDFS is engaged in the business of financing and servicing wholesale inventory receivables and retail loans, primarily for the purchase of motorcycles. HDFS is responsible for all credit and collection activities for the Motorcycles segment's domestic dealer receivables and many of its European dealer receivables. Prior to August 2002, HDFS offered wholesale financing to the Company's European motorcycle dealers through a joint venture with Transamerica Distribution Finance. In August 2002, HDFS terminated the joint venture relationship and began directly servicing the wholesale financing needs of many of the Company's European dealers.

Additionally, HDFS is an agency for certain unaffiliated insurance carriers providing property/casualty insurance and extended service contracts to motorcycle owners. HDFS conducts business in the United States, Canada and Europe.

The condensed statements of operations relating to the Financial Services segment, for the years ended December 31, were as follows:

(In thousands)	2003	2002	2001
Interest income	$ 87,048	$ 76,078	$ 76,201
Gain on current year securitizations	82,221	56,139	45,037
Servicing fee income	24,317	18,571	13,284
Insurance commissions	44,847	36,055	28,744
Income on investment in retained securitization interests	32,181	18,776	14,559
Other income	8,845	5,881	3,720
Financial services income	279,459	211,500	181,545
Interest expense	17,635	15,149	24,707
Provision for credit losses	4,076	6,167	22,178
Operating expenses	89,875	85,957	73,387
Financial services expense	111,586	107,273	120,272
Operating income from financial services	$167,873	$104,227	$ 61,273

Interest income includes approximately $9.2 million, $8.4 million, and $9.3 million of interest on wholesale finance receivables paid by HDMC to HDFS in 2003, 2002 and 2001, respectively. This interest is paid on behalf of HDMC's independent dealers as an incentive to purchase inventory during winter months. Included in other income is approximately $5.1 million, $3.6 million, and $1.9 million of fees HDMC paid to HDFS for credit and collection activities on receivables purchased from HDMC during 2003, 2002, and 2001, respectively. The transactions described above, between the Motorcycles and Financial Services segments are not eliminated; however, the net effect had no impact on consolidated net income.

Finance Receivables

Finance receivables owned by HDFS at December 31, for the past five years were as follows:

(In thousands)	2003	2002	2001	2000	1999
Wholesale					
United States	$ 690,662	$ 574,489	$ 527,513	$414,713	$314,266
Europe	91,987	91,137	—	—	—
Canada	59,171	42,236	40,793	42,213	43,786
Total wholesale	841,820	707,862	568,306	456,926	358,052
Retail					
United States	580,191	509,094	291,796	168,960	189,540
Canada	92,740	60,921	52,241	49,574	38,893
Total retail	672,931	570,015	344,037	218,534	228,433
Retail revolving charge	—	—	—	—	149,818
	1,514,751	1,277,877	912,343	675,460	736,303
Less: allowance for credit losses	31,311	31,045	28,684	10,947	13,945
	1,483,440	1,246,832	883,659	664,513	722,358
Investment in retained securitization interests	254,409	198,748	152,097	100,437	73,481
	$1,737,849	$1,445,580	$1,035,756	$764,950	$795,839

Finance receivables include wholesale loans to dealers and retail loans to consumers. Wholesale loans to dealers are generally secured by financed inventory or property. Retail loans consist of secured promissory notes and installment loans. HDFS either holds titles or liens on titles to vehicles financed by promissory notes and installment loans.

Wholesale finance receivables are originated in the U.S., Canada, and Europe. HDFS began originating European receivables in August 2002, assuming business formerly served by HDFS' European joint venture.

As of December 31, 2003 and 2002, approximately 10% of gross outstanding finance receivables were originated in Canada and 10% were originated in California, respectively.

At December 31, 2003 and 2002, unused lines of credit extended to HDFS' wholesale finance customers totaled $588 million and $314 million respectively. Approved but unfunded retail finance loans totaled $289 million and $237 million at December 31, 2003 and 2002 respectively.

Wholesale finance receivables are related primarily to motorcycles and related parts and accessories sales and are generally contractually due within one year. Retail finance receivables are primarily related to sales of motorcycles and aircraft. On December 31, 2003, contractual maturities of finance receivables were as follows:

(In thousands)	United States	Europe	Canada	Total
2004	$ 742,336	$91,987	$ 70,610	$ 904,933
2005	61,724	—	12,281	74,005
2006	67,926	—	13,762	81,688
2007	72,623	—	15,422	88,045
2008	81,136	—	17,282	98,418
Thereafter	245,108	—	22,554	267,662
Total	$1,270,853	$91,987	$151,911	$1,514,751

As of December 31, 2003, all finance receivables due after one year were at fixed interest rates.

The allowance for credit losses is comprised of individual components relating to wholesale and retail finance receivables. Changes in the allowance for credit losses for the years ended December 31 are as follows:

(In thousands)	2003	2002	2001
Balance at beginning of year	$31,045	$28,684	$10,947
Provision for finance credit losses	4,076	6,167	22,178
Charge-offs	(3,810)	(3,806)	(4,441)
Balance at end of year	$31,311	$31,045	$28,684

At December 31, 2003, 2002 and 2001, the carrying value of retail and wholesale finance receivables contractually past due 90 days or more were as follows:

(In thousands)	2003	2002	2001
United States	$2,012	$1,724	$2,262
Canada	639	523	365
Europe	4,126	5,307	—
Total	$6,777	$7,554	$2,627

Securitization Transactions

During 2003, 2002 and 2001, the Company sold $1.7 billion, $1.3 billion, and $1.0 billion, respectively, of retail motorcycle loans through securitization transactions utilizing QSPE's

(see Note 1 to the consolidated financial statements). The Company retains interest-only strip receivables, servicing rights, and cash reserve account deposits, collectively referred to as investment in retained securitization interest. In conjunction with these and prior sales, HDFS has assets of $254.4 million and $198.7 million representing retained securitization interests at December 31, 2003 and 2002, respectively. The Company receives annual servicing fees approximating one percent of the outstanding balance. HDFS serviced $2.6 billion and $2.0 billion of retail loans as of December 31, 2003 and 2002, respectively.

The Company's retained securitization interests, excluding servicing rights, are subordinate to the interests of securitization trust investors. Investors and securitization trusts have no recourse to the Company's other assets. Recourse is limited to the Company's rights to future cash flow on retained securitization interests, excluding servicing rights and cash reserve account deposits. Key assumptions in the valuation of the investment in retained securitization interests and in calculating the gain on current year securitizations are credit losses, prepayments and discount rate.

Key assumptions used to calculate gain on current year securitizations, at the date of the transaction, for securitizations completed in 2003, 2002 and 2001 were:

	2003	2002	2001
Prepayment speed (single monthly mortality)	2.50%	2.50%	2.50%
Weighted-average life (in years)	1.93	1.95	1.93
Expected cumulative net credit losses	2.60%	2.38%	2.13%
Residual cash flows discount rate	12.00%	12.00%	12.00%

Key assumptions used to value the investment in retained securitization interests as of December 31, 2003 and 2002 were:

	2003	2002
Prepayment speed (single monthly mortality)	2.50%	2.50%
Weighted-average life (in years)	1.97	1.97
Expected cumulative net credit losses	2.48%	2.24%
Residual cash flows discount rate	12.00%	12.00%

Detailed below for all retained securitization interests at December 31, 2003 and 2002 is the sensitivity of the fair value to immediate 10 percent and 20 percent adverse changes in the weighted average key assumptions (dollars in thousands):

	2003	2002
Carrying amount/fair value of retained interests	$254,409	$198,748
Weighted-average life (in years)	1.97	1.97
Prepayment speed assumption (monthly rate)	2.50%	2.50%
Impact on fair value of 10% adverse change	$ (7,300)	$ (7,200)
Impact on fair value of 20% adverse change	$ (14,200)	$ (14,000)
Expected cumulative net credit losses	2.48%	2.24%
Impact on fair value of 10% adverse change	$ (11,100)	$ (7,300)
Impact on fair value of 20% adverse change	$ (22,300)	$ (14,600)
Residual cash flows discount rate (annual)	12.00%	12.00%
Impact on fair value of 10% adverse change	$ (4,600)	$ (3,400)
Impact on fair value of 20% adverse change	$ (9,000)	$ (6,700)

These sensitivities are hypothetical and should not be considered to be predictive of future performance. Changes in fair value generally cannot be extrapolated because the relationship of change in assumption to change in fair value may not be linear. Also, in this table, the effect of a variation in a particular assumption on the fair value of the retained interest is calculated independently from any change in another assumption. In reality, changes in one factor may contribute to changes in another, which may magnify or counteract the sensitivities. Furthermore, the estimated fair values as disclosed should not be considered indicative of future earnings on these assets.

Expected cumulative net credit losses are a key assumption in the valuation of retained securitization interests. Weighted average expected net credit losses for all active securitizations as of December 31, 2003, 2002, and 2001 were 2.48%, 2.24% and 2.05%, respectively. The table below summarizes expected cumulative net credit losses by year of securitization, expressed as a percentage of the original balance of loans securitized, as of December 31, 2003, 2002 and 2001, for all securitizations completed during the years noted.

Expected Cumulative Net Credit Losses (%) as of:	Loans Securitized in				
	2003	2002	2001	2000	1999
December 31, 2003	2.60%	2.39%	2.25%	2.37%	2.15%
December 31, 2002	—	2.38	2.13	2.06	2.05
December 31, 2001	—	—	2.13	1.95	1.94

The table below provides information regarding certain cash flows received from and paid to all motorcycle loan securitization trusts during the years ended December 31, 2003 and 2002:

(In thousands)	2003	2002
Proceeds from new securitizations	$1,724,060	$1,246,262
Servicing fees received	23,789	17,984
Other cash flows received on retained interests	144,343	105,216
10% clean-up call repurchase option	(31,779)	(21,416)

Managed retail motorcycle loans consist of all retail motorcycle installment loans serviced by HDFS including those held by securitization trusts and those held by HDFS. As of December 31, 2003 and 2002 managed retail motorcycle loans totaled $3.0 billion and $2.4 billion, respectively, of which $2.6 billion and $2.0 billion, respectively, are securitized. The principal amount of motorcycle managed loans 60 days or more past due was $40.7 million and $39.6 million at December 31, 2003 and 2002, respectively. Managed loans 60 days or more past due exclude loans reclassified as repossessed inventory. Credit losses, net of recoveries, of the motorcycle managed loans were $27.0 million and $15.8 million during 2003 and 2002, respectively.

Insurance Claims

2.42

ARVINMERITOR, INC. (SEP)

(In millions)	2003	2002
Current assets		
Cash and cash equivalents	$ 103	$ 56
Receivables (less allowance for doubtful accounts: 2003, $24; 2002, $18)	1,327	1,251
Inventories	543	458
Other current assets	266	211
Total current assets	$2,239	$1,976

NOTES TO CONSOLIDATED FINANCIAL STATEMENTS

9 (In Part): Other Current Assets

Other Current Assets are summarized as follows (in millions):

	2003	2002
Current deferred income taxes	$124	$116
Customer reimbursable tooling and engineering	74	33
Asbestos-related recoveries (see Note 21)	13	20
Prepaid and other	55	42
Other current assets	$266	$211

21 (In Part): Contingencies

Asbestos

Maremont Corporation ("Maremont", a subsidiary of the company) and many other companies are defendants in suits brought by individuals claiming personal injuries as a result of exposure to asbestos-containing products. Maremont manufactured friction products containing asbestos from 1953 through 1977, when it sold its friction product business. Arvin Industries, Inc. ("Arvin") acquired Maremont in 1986. Maremont's asbestos-related reserves and corresponding asbestos-related recoveries are summarized as follows (in millions):

	2003	2002
Unbilled committed settlements	$ 4	$ 9
Pending claims	72	50
Shortfall and other	6	7
Total asbestos-related reserves	$82	$66
Asbestos-related recoveries	$76	$59

A portion of the asbestos-related recoveries and reserves are included in Other Current Assets and Liabilities, with the majority of the amounts recorded in Other Noncurrent Assets and Liabilities.

The unbilled committed settlements reserve relates to committed settlements that Maremont agreed to pay when Maremont participated in the Center for Claims Resolution (CCR). Maremont shared in the payments of defense and indemnity costs of asbestos-related claims with other CCR members. The CCR handled the resolution and processing of asbestos claims on behalf of its members until February 1, 2001, when it was reorganized and discontinued negotiating shared settlements. There were no significant billings to insurance companies related to committed settlements in fiscal 2003. A 2003 review of CCR files indicated that Maremont was not named as a defendant in certain previously recorded unbilled settlements. Accordingly, the unbilled settlements and asbestos related recoveries were reduced by $5 million.

Upon dissolution of the CCR in February 2001, Maremont began handling asbestos-related claims through its own defense counsel and is committed to examining the merits of each asbestos-related claim. Maremont had approximately 63,000 and 37,500 pending asbestos-related claims at September 30, 2003 and 2002, respectively. Although Maremont has been named in these cases, in the cases where actual injury has been alleged very few claimants have established that a Maremont product caused their injuries. For purposes of establishing reserves for pending asbestos-related claims, Maremont estimates its defense and indemnity costs based on the history and nature of filed claims to date and Maremont's experience. As of September 30, 2003 and 2002, Maremont used experience factors for estimating indemnity and litigation liabilities using data on actual experience in resolving claims since February 2001 and its assessment of the nature of the claims. Billings to insurance companies for indemnity and defense costs of resolved cases were $15 million in fiscal 2003.

Several former members of the CCR have filed for bankruptcy protection, and these members have failed, or may fail, to pay certain financial obligations with respect to settlements that were reached while they were CCR members. Maremont is subject to claims for payment of a portion of these defaulted member shares (shortfall). In an effort to resolve the affected settlements, Maremont has entered into negotiations with plaintiffs' attorneys, and an estimate of Maremont's obligation for the shortfall is included in the total asbestos-related reserves. In addition, Maremont and its insurers are engaged in legal proceedings to determine whether existing insurance coverage should reimburse any potential liability related to this issue. Payments by the company related to shortfall and other were $1 million in fiscal 2003.

Maremont has insurance that reimburses a substantial portion of the costs incurred defending against asbestos-related claims. The coverage also reimburses Maremont for any indemnity paid on those claims. The coverage is provided by several insurance carriers based on the insurance agreements in place. Based on its assessment of the history and nature of filed claims to date, and of Maremont's insurance carriers, management believes that existing insurance coverage is adequate to cover substantially all costs relating to pending asbestos-related claims.

The amounts recorded for the asbestos-related reserves and recoveries from insurance companies are based upon assumptions and estimates derived from currently known facts. All such estimates of liabilities for asbestos-related claims are subject to considerable uncertainty because such liabilities are influenced by variables that are difficult to predict. If the assumptions with respect to the nature of pending claims, the cost to resolve claims and the amount of available insurance prove to be incorrect, the actual amount of Maremont's liability for asbestos-related claims, and the effect on the company, could differ materially from current estimates.

Maremont has not recorded reserves for unknown claims that may be asserted against it in the future. Maremont does not have sufficient information to make a reasonable estimate of its potential liability for asbestos-related claims that may be asserted against it in the future.

Installment Receivables

2.43

COMPUTER ASSOCIATES INTERNATIONAL, INC. (MAR)

(Dollars in millions)	2003	2002
Current assets		
Cash and cash equivalents	$1,421	$1,093
Marketable securities	91	87
Trade and installment accounts receivable, net	1,854	1,825
Deferred income taxes	78	—
Other current assets	121	73
Total current assets	$3,565	$3,078
Installment accounts receivable, due after one year, net	$ 519	$1,566

NOTES TO CONSOLIDATED FINANCIAL STATEMENTS

Note 5—Trade and Installment Accounts Receivable

The Company uses installment license agreements as a standard business practice and has a history of successfully collecting primarily all amounts due under the original payment terms without making concessions on payments, software products, maintenance, or professional services. Net trade and installment accounts receivable is composed of the total committed amounts due from customers throughout the license term pursuant to such agreements. These accounts receivable balances exclude unamortized discounts based on imputed interest for the time value of money for license agreements under the prior business model, unearned revenue attributable to maintenance, deferred subscription revenue, unearned professional services contracted for in the license agreement, and allowances for doubtful accounts. Deferred subscription revenue represents the deferred license agreement fees recorded under the Company's Business Model, which will amortize into revenue over the respective license agreement term.

Trade and installment accounts receivable consist of the following:

(In millions)	2003	2002
Billed accounts receivable	$ 835	$ 1,011
Unbilled amounts due within the next 12 months—business model	1,284	790
Unbilled amounts due within the next 12 months—prior business model	1,020	1,535
Less: Allowance for doubtful accounts	(190)	(353)
Net amounts expected to be collected	2,949	2,983
Less: Unearned revenue—current	(1,095)	(1,158)
Net trade and installment accounts receivable—current	$ 1,854	$ 1,825
Unbilled amounts due beyond the next 12 months—business model	$ 1,210	$ 1,565
Unbilled amounts due beyond the next 12 months—prior business model	1,807	2,730
Less: Allowance for doubtful accounts	(85)	(60)
Net amounts expected to be collected	2,932	4,235
Less: Unearned revenue—noncurrent	(2,413)	(2,669)
Net installment accounts receivable—noncurrent	$ 519	$ 1,566

As of March 31, 2003 and 2002, unearned revenue—current consists of unamortized discounts of $185 million and $288 million, respectively; unearned maintenance of $189 million and $290 million, respectively; deferred subscription revenue of $688 million and $522 million, respectively; and unearned professional services of $33 million and $58 million, respectively.

As of March 31, 2003 and 2002, unearned revenue—noncurrent consists of unamortized discounts of $250 million and $417 million, respectively; unearned maintenance of $173 million and $333 million, respectively; and deferred subscription revenue of $1.990 billion and $1.919 billion, respectively.

Unbilled amounts under the Company's Business Model are generally collectible over one to five years. As of March 31, 2003, on a cumulative basis, approximately 51%, 85%, 93%, 96%, and 98% of amounts due from customers recorded under the Company's Business Model come due within fiscal years ended 2004 through 2008, respectively.

Unbilled amounts under the prior business model are generally collectible over three to six years. As of March 31, 2003, on a cumulative basis, approximately 36%, 61%, 75%, 83%, and 88% of amounts due from customers recorded under the prior business model come due within fiscal years ended 2004 through 2008, respectively.

The provision for doubtful accounts for the fiscal years ended March 31, 2003, 2002, and 2001 was $68 million, $233 million, and $235 million, respectively, and is included in the "SG&A" line item on the Consolidated Statements of Operations.

The Company's estimate of the fair value of net installment accounts receivable recorded under the prior business model approximates carrying value since it is net of discounts, unearned contractual obligations, and an allowance for doubtful accounts. The fair value of the unbilled amounts recorded under the Company's Business Model (unbilled amounts due less deferred subscription revenue) may have a fair value greater than that reported in the balance sheet. Currently, amounts due from customers under the Company's Business Model are offset by unearned revenue related to these license agreements, leaving no or minimal net carrying value on the balance sheet for such amounts. The fair value may actually exceed this carrying value but cannot be practically assessed since there is no existing market for a pool of customer receivables with such contractual commitments similar to that of the Company's. The actual fair value may not be known until these amounts are sold, securitized, or collected. Although these customer license agreements commit the customer to payment under a fixed schedule, the agreements are considered executory in nature due to the ongoing commitment to provide "unspecified future deliverables" as part of the agreement terms.

Grants Receivable

2.44

ATMEL CORPORATION (DEC)

(In thousands)	2003	2002
Current assets		
Cash and cash equivalents	$385,887	$ 346,371
Short-term investments	45,167	99,431
Accounts receivable, net of receivable reserves of $16,411 in 2003 and $22,415 in 2002	215,303	195,182
Inventories	268,074	276,069
Other current assets	54,198	107,672
Total current assets	$968,629	$1,024,725

NOTES TO CONSOLIDATED FINANCIAL STATEMENTS (In thousands)

Note 1 (In Part): Summary of Significant Accounting Policies

Grant Recognition

Atmel receives grants from certain government authorities for expanding operations or performing technical services. Grants are recognized as receivable at the time specified milestones have been met for receiving them. Grants are amortized as a reduction of expenses over the period the related obligations are fulfilled.

Note 3 (In Part): Balance Sheet Detail

Other current assets consist of the following:

	2003	2002
Income tax receivable	$ 6,624	$ 61,750
VAT receivable	26,616	25,249
Grants receivable	6,027	7,249
Other	14,931	13,424
Total	$54,198	$107,672

RECEIVABLES SOLD OR COLLATERALIZED

2.45 Table 2-6 shows that 2003 annual reports ot 155 survey companies disclosed either the sale of receivables or the pledging of receivables as collateral. Of those 155 survey companies, 12 disclosed a factoring agreement and 77 disclosed that the receivables were transferred to a special-purpose entity.

2.46 SFAS No. 125, *Accounting for Transfers and Servicing of Financial Assets and Extinguishment of Liabilities*, as amended by *SFAS No. 133* and as replaced by SFAS No. 140, *Accounting for Transfers and Servicing of Financial Assets and Extinguishment of Liabilities*, establishes criteria for determining whether a transfer of financial assets in exchange for cash or other consideration should be accounted for as a sale or as a pledge of collateral in a secured borrowing, *SFAS No. 140* revises the criteria for accounting for securitizations and other transfers of financial assets and collateral, and requires certain disclosures. The Standard carries over most of the provisions of *SFAS No. 125* without reconsideration. Additionally, *SFAS No. 140* requires a debtor to:

> (a) reclassify financial assets pledged as collateral and report those assets in its statement of financial position separately from other assets not so encumbered if the secured party has the right by contract or custom to sell or repledge the collateral, and
>
> (b) disclose assets pledged as collateral that have not been reclassified and separately reported in the statement of financial position.

Also, *SFAS No. 140* requires a secured party to disclose Information about collateral that it has accepted and is permitted by contract or custom to sell or repledge. The required disclosure includes the fair value at the end of the period of that collateral and the portion of that collateral that it has sold or repledged, and information about the sources and uses of that collateral. As issued, *SFAS No. 140* is effective for transfers and servicing of financial assets and extinguishments of liabilities occurring after March 31, 2001. In addition, with regard to recognition and reclassification of collateral and for disclosures relating to securitization transactions and collateral, the effective date is for fiscal years ending after December 15, 2000.

2.47 Financial statement presentation and reporting of the sale of receivables is set forth in paragraphs 13d and 13e of *SOP 01-6*. In addition to requiring disclosure of the amount of gains or losses on the sale of trade receivables, receivables held for sale should be presented as a separate category either in the balance sheet or in the notes to the financial statements. *SOP 01-6* is effective for fiscal years beginning after December 15, 2001.

2.48 Examples of disclosures made in the reports of the survey companies having sold or collateralized receivables follow.

2.49

TABLE 2-6: RECEIVABLES SOLD OR COLLATERALIZED

	2003	2002	2001	2000
Receivables sold				
With recourse.............................	23	24	21	23
With limited recourse.................	14	14	18	16
Without recourse........................	36	44	40	31
Recourse not discussed............	65	61	54	51
	138	143	133	121
Receivables used as collateral.......	17	17	27	27
	155	160	160	148
No reference to receivable sold or collateralized...............................	445	440	440	452
Total Companies...........................	**600**	**600**	**600**	**600**

Receivables Sold With Recourse

2.50

BRUNSWICK CORPORATION (DEC)

(In millions)	2003	2002
Current assets		
Cash and cash equivalents, at cost, which approximates market	$ 345.9	$ 351.4
Accounts and notes receivable, less allowances of $31.3 and $31.8	374.4	401.4
Inventories		
Finished goods	325.3	272.5
Work-in-process	205.7	201.6
Raw materials	92.8	72.8
Net inventories	623.8	546.9
Prepaid income taxes	302.3	305.1
Prepaid expenses and other	68.8	55.4
Current assets	$1,715.2	$1,660.2

NOTES TO CONSOLIDATED FINANCIAL STATEMENTS

7. Financial Services

In 2002, the Company established a joint venture, BAC, with Transamerica Commercial Finance Corporation (TCFC). Since BAC was established, GE Commercial Finance, the business-to-business financial services unit of General Electric Company, announced its intention to acquire the commercial finance business of Transamerica, including TCFC.

Under the terms of the joint venture agreement, BAC provides secured wholesale floor-plan financing to the Company's boat and engine dealers. BAC also purchases and services a portion of Mercury Marine's domestic accounts

receivable relating to its boatbuilder and dealer customers. Pursuant to the joint venture agreement, BAC reimbursed Mercury Marine $0.9 million in 2003 for the related credit, collection, and administrative costs incurred in connection with the servicing of such receivables.

In January of 2003, the Company invested $3.3 million as BAC began its operations, which represented a 15 percent ownership interest. On July 2, 2003, the Company contributed an additional $19.5 million to increase its equity interest in BAC to 49 percent as permitted by the terms of the joint venture agreement. BAC is not consolidated in the accompanying financial statements. The Company's investment in BAC is accounted for under the equity method and is recorded as a component of Investments in the Consolidated Balance Sheets. The Company records its share of income or loss based on its ownership percentage and is included in Other Income (Expense) in the Consolidated Statements of Income.

During the third quarter of 2003, the Company began to sell a significant portion of Mercury Marine's domestic accounts receivable to BAC. On July 2, 2003, the Company made its initial sale of receivables of $124.9 million to BAC for $124.1 million in cash, net of discount. The remaining receivables sold during 2003 were $376.3 million, for which the Company received $373.4 million in cash, net of discount. Total discounts of $3.7 million on the sale of such receivables were recorded as an expense in Other Income (Expense) in the Consolidated Statements of Income. The outstanding balance for receivables sold to BAC was $74.7 million at December 31, 2003. BAC will continue to purchase and service a significant portion of Mercury Marine's domestic accounts receivable on an ongoing basis.

The Company has a retained interest in $28.4 million of total accounts receivable sold at December 31, 2003, as a result of recourse provisions reported in *Note 9, Commitments and Contingencies*, in which the Company's maximum exposure is $14.9 million. In accordance with SFAS No. 140, "Accounting for Transfers and Servicing of Financial Assets and Extinguishments of Liabilities," the Company treats the sale of receivables in which the Company retains an interest as a secured obligation.

Under the terms of the joint venture agreement, the receivable portfolio is consolidated on TCFC's financial statements and is funded 85 percent through a loan from TCFC and 15 percent by a cash investment from both TCFC (51 percent) and the Company (49 percent). As a result of the monthly changes in BAC's receivable portfolio, the Company's contributed equity is adjusted monthly to maintain a 49 percent equity interest. The Company's investment in BAC at December 31, 2003, was $22.0 million.

Summarized financial data for BAC is presented as of December 31, as follows:

(In millions)

Statement of Income	2003
Revenues	$ 13.9
Interest and other expenses	$ 9.0
Net income before income taxes	$ 4.9

(In millions)

Balance Sheet	2003
Net finance receivables	$319.6
Other assets	$ 0.4
Total assets	$320.0
Notes payable and other liabilities	$276.0
Equity	$ 44.0
Total liabilities and equity	$320.0

9 (In Part): Commitments and Contingencies

Financial Commitments (In Part)

The Company has entered into arrangements with financial institutions in connection with customer financing programs. Under these arrangements, the Company has guaranteed customer obligations to the financial institutions in the event of customer default, generally subject to a maximum amount. The Company has also guaranteed customer payments to third parties that have purchased Company receivables, and, in certain instances, has guaranteed secured term financing for customers. In each type of arrangement, upon repurchase of the obligation, the Company often receives rights to the collateral securing the financing. The maximum potential liability associated with these customer financing arrangements was approximately $100 million and approximately $65 million at December 31, 2003 and 2002, respectively.

The Company has also entered into arrangements with third-party lenders where it has agreed, in the event of a default by the customer, to repurchase from the third-party lender Company products repossessed from the customer. These arrangements are typically subject to a maximum repurchase amount. The Company's risk under these arrangements is mitigated by the value of the products repurchased as part of the transaction. The maximum amount of collateral the Company could be required to purchase was approximately $185 million and approximately $183 million at December 31, 2003 and 2002, respectively.

Based on historical experience and current facts and circumstances, and in accordance with FIN 45, the Company has reserves to cover potential losses associated with these guarantee and repurchase obligations. Historical cash requirements and losses associated with these obligations have not been significant.

Receivables Sold With Limited Recourse

2.51

APPLIED MATERIALS, INC. (OCT)

(In thousands)	2002	2003
Current assets:		
Cash and cash equivalents	$1,284,791	$1,364,857
Short-term investments	3,644,735	4,128,349
Accounts receivable, less allowance for doubtful accounts of $2,075 at 2002 and $1,847 at 2003	1,046,016	912,875
Inventories	1,273,816	950,692
Deferred income taxes	565,936	782,823
Other current assets	257,499	231,177
Total current assets	$8,072,793	$8,370,773

NOTES TO CONSOLIDATED FINANCIAL STATEMENTS

Note 11 (In Part): Commitments and Contingencies

Accounts Receivables Sales

Applied has several agreements that allow it to sell accounts receivable from selected customers at a discount to various financial institutions. Receivable sales have the effect of increasing cash and reducing accounts receivable and days sales outstanding. Discounting fees were recorded in interest expense and were not material for fiscal 2001, 2002 or 2003. Accounts receivable sales under these agreements were $1.2 billion for fiscal 2001, $689 million for fiscal 2002 and $556 million for fiscal 2003. At October 26, 2003, $168 million of sold receivables remained outstanding under these agreements. A portion of these sold receivables is subject to certain limited recourse provisions. However, Applied has not experienced any losses under these recourse provisions.

Receivables Sold Without Recourse

2.52

INGRAM MICRO INC. (DEC)

(Dollars in 000s)	2003	2002
Current assets:		
Cash and cash equivalents	$ 279,587	$ 387,513
Accounts receivable:		
Trade accounts receivable	1,955,979	1,770,988
Retained interest in securitized receivables	499,923	583,918
Total accounts receivable (less allowances of $91,613 and $89,889)	2,455,902	2,354,906
Inventories	1,915,403	1,564,065
Other current assets	317,201	293,902
Total current assets	$4,968,093	$4,600,386

NOTES TO CONSOLIDATED FINANCIAL STATEMENTS
(Dollars in 000s)

Note 5—Accounts Receivable

The Company has a revolving accounts receivable securitization program in the U.S., which provides for the issuance of up to $700,000 in commercial paper secured by undivided interests in a pool of transferred receivables. In connection with this program, which expires in March 2005, most of the Company's U.S. trade accounts receivable are transferred without recourse to a trust in exchange for a beneficial interest in the total pool of trade receivables. In addition, the trust has issued $25,000 of fixed-rate, medium-term certificates, which expire in February 2004, and are also secured by undivided interests in the pool of transferred receivables. Sales of undivided interests to third parties under this program result in a reduction of total accounts receivable in the Company's consolidated balance sheet. The excess of the trade accounts receivable transferred over amounts sold to and held by third parties at any one point in time represents the Company's retained interest in the transferred accounts receivable and is shown in the Company's consolidated balance sheet as a separate caption under accounts receivable. Retained interests are carried at their fair market value, estimated as the net realizable value, which considers the relatively short liquidation period and includes an estimated provision for credit losses. At January 3, 2004 and December 28, 2002, the amount of undivided interests sold to and held by third parties totaled $60,000 and $75,000, respectively.

The Company also has certain other trade accounts receivable-based facilities in Canada and Europe, which provide up to approximately $321,000 of additional financing capacity, depending upon the level of trade accounts receivable eligible to be transferred or sold. Approximately $116,000 of this capacity expires in December 2004 with the balance expiring in 2007. At January 3, 2004 and December 28, 2002, there were no trade accounts receivable sold to and held by third parties under these programs.

The Company is required to comply with certain financial covenants under some of its financing facilities, including minimum tangible net worth, restrictions on funded debt, interest coverage and trade accounts receivable portfolio performance covenants. The Company is also restricted in the amount of dividends it can pay as well as the amount of common stock that it can repurchase annually. At January 3, 2004, the Company was in compliance with all covenants or other requirements set forth in its accounts receivable financing programs discussed above.

Losses in the amount of $10,206, $9,363 and $20,332 in 2003, 2002, and 2001, respectively, related to the sale of trade accounts receivable under these facilities are included in other expenses in the Company's consolidated statement of income.

2.53

VIACOM INC. (DEC)

(In millions)	2003	2002
Current assets:		
Cash and cash equivalents	$ 850.7	$ 631.4
Receivables, less allowances of $295.5 (2003) and $278.0 (2002)	4,336.3	3,721.0
Inventory	1,444.4	1,332.7
Deferred tax assets, net	69.0	238.6
Prepaid expenses	339.3	413.1
Other current assets	696.6	830.0
Total current assets	$7,736.3	$7,166.8

NOTES TO CONSOLIDATED FINANCIAL STATEMENTS
(Tabular dollars in millions)

8 (In Part): Bank Financing and Debt

Accounts Receivable Securitization Programs

As of December 31, 2003 and December 31, 2002, the Company had an aggregate of $1.0 billion and $981.9 million, respectively, outstanding under revolving receivable securitization programs. The programs result in the sale of receivables on a non-recourse basis to unrelated third parties on a one-year renewable basis, thereby reducing accounts receivable and debt on the Company's consolidated balance sheets. The Company enters into these arrangements because they provide an additional source of liquidity. Proceeds from the programs were used to reduce outstanding borrowings. The terms of the revolving securitization arrangements require that the receivable pools subject to the programs meet certain performance ratios. As of December 31, 2003, the Company was in compliance with the required ratios under the receivable securitization programs.

2.54

WEATHERFORD INTERNATIONAL LTD. (DEC)

(In thousands)	2003	2002
Current assets:		
Cash and cash equivalents	$ 56,082	$ 48,837
Accounts receivable, net of allowance for uncollectible accounts of $16,753 in 2003 and $18,088 in 2002	561,356	485,178
Inventories	642,114	547,744
Current deferred tax assets	86,605	84,963
Other current assets	89,867	92,517
	$1,436,024	$1,259,239

NOTES TO CONSOLIDATED FINANCIAL STATEMENTS

1 (In Part): Summary of Significant Accounting Policies

Accounts Receivable and Allowance for Uncollectible Accounts

Accounts receivable are stated at the historical carrying amount net of write-offs and allowance for uncollectible accounts. The Company establishes an allowance for uncollectible accounts receivable based on historical experience and any specific customer collection issues that the Company has identified. Uncollectible accounts receivable are written off when a settlement is reached for an amount that is less than the outstanding historical balance or when the Company has determined the balance will not be collected. As of December 31, 2003, $73.2 million of accounts receivable included in the Company's Consolidated Balance Sheet were owned by W1 Receivables, L.P. ("W1"), a wholly-owned subsidiary, and were subject to a security interest in favor of third party lenders under an accounts receivable securitization (See Note 8). These receivables will be available first and foremost to satisfy the claims of W1's creditors.

8. Asset Securitization

The Company has an agreement with a financial institution through December 2004 to sell, on a continuous basis, an undivided interest in a specific pool of U.S. accounts receivable of certain subsidiaries of the Company. Pursuant to this agreement, these subsidiaries continuously sell certain trade accounts receivable to a wholly-owned bankruptcy-remote subsidiary of the Company, W1. W1 was formed to purchase accounts receivable and, in turn, sell participating interests in such accounts receivable to a financial institution. The sale of participating interests is limited to a percentage of receivables sold to W1. Receivables are sold at a discount approximating the financial institution's financing costs of issuing commercial paper backed by the accounts receivable. In accordance with SFAS No. 140, *Accounting for Transfers and Servicing of Financial Assets and Extinguishments of Liabilities*, at the time a participating interest is sold, the related receivables are removed from the Consolidated Balance Sheets. In this transaction, the Company retains servicing responsibilities and a subordinated interest in the pool of receivables. There is no recourse against the Company for failure of debtors to pay when due on account of debtors' bankruptcy or inability to pay.

The Company is permitted to sell participating interests in trade accounts receivable up to $80.0 million under this agreement. In connection with the reorganization, the Company fully and unconditionally guaranteed certain domestic subsidiaries' performance obligations relating to the asset securitization. The Company incurred charges, in connection with the sale of receivables under the Asset Securitization, of $1.0 million, $2.2 million and $2.3 million for the years ended December 31, 2003, 2002 and 2001, respectively, which are included in Other Income (Expense) on the accompanying Consolidated Statements of Operations. The Company had received $75.0 million and $68.9 million for purchased interests and had a subordinated interest in the revolving pool of receivables of $73.2 million and $59.9 million as of December 31, 2003 and 2002, respectively.

W1's assets, including the accounts receivable held by it, are not available to satisfy claims of the Company's creditors and are subject to the prior claims of a financial institution.

Receivables Used as Collateral

2.55

COOPER TIRE & RUBBER COMPANY (DEC)

(Dollar amounts in thousands)	2002	2003
Current assets:		
Cash and cash equivalents	$ 44,748	$ 66,426
Accounts receivable, less allowances of $14,319 in 2002 and $12,569 in 2003	460,879	613,269
Inventories:		
Finished goods	181,219	158,416
Work in process	33,457	35,485
Raw materials and supplies	65,965	88,451
	280,641	282,352
Prepaid expenses, income taxes refundable and deferred income taxes	74,260	62,362
Total current assets	$860,528	$1,024,409

NOTES TO CONSOLIDATED FINANCIAL STATEMENTS (Dollar amounts in thousands)

Debt (In Part)

In August 2001 a Canadian subsidiary of the Company entered into a $125,000 loan agreement with Market Street Funding Corporation, an affiliated company of PNC Bank NA, which is secured by certain trade accounts receivable. At that time, $90,000 was advanced under the loan agreement with a maturity date of August 2006. In February 2003 the agreement was amended to add Liberty Street Funding Corp., an affiliate of The Bank of Nova Scotia, as an additional lender. Interest on the loan is at a floating rate, based on the average commercial paper rates of Market Street Funding Corporation.

ALLOWANCE FOR DOUBTFUL ACCOUNTS

2.56 Table 2-7 summarizes the captions used by the survey companies to describe an allowance for doubtful accounts. Accounting Principles Board (APB) Opinion No. 12, *Omnibus Opinion—1967*, states that such allowances should be deducted from the related receivables and appropriately disclosed.

2.57

TABLE 2-7: DOUBTFUL ACCOUNT CAPTIONS

	2003	2002	2001	2000
Allowance for doubtful accounts.....	327	286	283	274
Allowance...	154	173	169	164
Allowance for uncollectible accounts...............................	20	15	13	14
Allowance for losses........................	14	13	14	16
Reserve..	11	10	14	10
Reserve for doubtful accounts........	2	3	5	8
Other caption titles..........................	10	23	26	21
	538	523	524	507
Receivables shown net....................	21	28	25	34
No reference to doubtful accounts..	41	49	51	59
Total Companies...........................	**600**	**600**	**600**	**600**

INVENTORIES

2.58   Accounting Research Bulletin (ARB) No. 43, Chapter 4, *Inventory Pricing*, states that the "primary basis of accounting for inventories is cost . . ." but "a departure from the cost basis of pricing the inventory is required when the utility of the goods is no longer as great as its costs . . ." Approximately 83% of the survey companies use lower of cost or market, an acceptable basis for pricing inventories when circumstances require a departure from cost, to price all or a portion of their inventories.

2.59   Table 2-8 shows the captions frequently used to identify the nature of inventory items owned by the survey companies. 114 survey companies either had no inventory items or did not disclose details as to the nature of inventory items.

2.60   Table 2-9 summarizes the methods used by the survey companies to determine inventory costs and indicates the portion of inventory cost determined by LIFO. As indicated in Table 2-9, it is not uncommon for a company to use more than one method in determining the total cost of inventory. Methods of inventory cost determination classified as Other in Table 2-9 include specific identification and accumulated costs for contracts in process.

2.61   A number of survey companies made supplemental disclosures concerning inventories, including information about items such as valuation accounts, obsolescence, and the effects of using LIFO. 26 survey companies disclosed that certain LIFO inventory layers were reduced which increased net income due to the matching of older, lower historical costs with current sales dollars. 10 survey companies disclosed the effect of income from using LIFO rather than FIFO or average cost to determine inventory cost.

2.62   Valuation accounts are used to adjust an inventory cost. 126 survey companies disclosed that they have inventory valuation accounts. 77 companies disclosed that a valuation account was used to reduce inventories to a LIFO basis. 44 survey companies disclosed that a valuation account was used for inventory obsolescence.

2.63   Table 2-10 shows, by industry classification, the number of companies using LIFO and the percentage relationship of those companies using LIFO to the total number of companies in a particular industry classification in the current year.

2.64   Each year, companies are selected from the latest Fortune 1000 listing to replace those companies that were deleted from the survey (see the *Appendix of 600 Companies* for a comprehensive listing of the 600 companies as well as those that were added and removed in this edition). Companies are deleted from the survey when they have either been acquired, have become privately held (and are, therefore, no longer registered with the SEC), or have ceased operations.

2.65   The decrease in the number of survey companies using LIFO was caused in part by the fact that more companies deleted from the survey used LIFO than those companies selected as replacements. Two survey companies changed from the LIFO method to another method of determining inventory cost.

2.66   Examples of presentations and disclosures for inventories follow.

2.67

TABLE 2-8: INVENTORY CAPTIONS

	Number of Companies		
	2003	2002	2001
Finished goods...	348	339	341
Finished goods and work in process.......	27	30	36
Work in process.......................................	249	278	269
Work in process and raw materials.........	60	29	38
Raw materials..	216	193	203
Raw materials and supplies/parts...........	113	117	111
Supplies and/or materials........................	83	89	84

2.68

TABLE 2-9: INVENTORY COST DETERMINATION

	Number of Companies			
	2003	2002	2001	2000
Methods				
First-in first-out (FIFO).....................	384	380	382	386
Last-in first-out (LIFO).....................	251	255	265	283
Average cost....................................	167	165	180	180
Other..	31	28	46	38
Use of LIFO				
All inventories.................................	26	17	17	23
50% or more of inventories.............	120	121	130	148
Less than 50% of inventories..........	77	88	88	82
Not determinable..............................	28	29	30	30
Companies Using LIFO.............	**251**	**255**	**265**	**283**

2.69

TABLE 2-10: INDUSTRY CLASSIFICATION OF COMPANIES USING LIFO

	2003 No.	2003 %[1]	2002 No.	2002 %[1]
Advertising, marketing......................	—	—	—	—
Aerospace.......................................	5	29	6	35
Apparel...	7	50	7	50
Beverages.......................................	4	40	4	44
Building materials, glass.................	6	75	6	67
Chemicals.......................................	24	83	24	83
Computer and data services...........	—	—	—	—
Computer peripherals......................	—	—	—	—
Computer software..........................	—	—	—	—
Computers, office equipment..........	1	9	1	9
Diversified outsourcing services.....	—	—	—	—
Electronics, electrical equipment....	12	29	12	29
Engineering, construction...............	1	9	1	9
Entertainment.................................	—	—	—	—
Food...	12	50	13	48
Food and drug stores......................	11	73	11	85
Food services.................................	—	—	—	—
Forest and paper products..............	16	80	15	79
Furniture...	8	67	8	80
General merchandisers...................	9	82	9	90
Health care.....................................	—	—	—	—
Hotels, casinos, resorts..................	—	—	—	—
Industrial and farm equipment........	26	74	25	74
Medical products and equipment....	4	31	4	33
Metal products................................	17	81	16	76
Metals..	12	86	13	76
Mining, crude-oil production............	3	23	3	23
Miscellaneous................................	2	22	3	27
Motor vehicles and parts................	10	59	10	59
Network communications................	—	—	—	—
Petroleum refining..........................	12	92	12	92
Pharmaceuticals.............................	4	40	4	40
Publishing, printing........................	11	55	12	60
Rubber and plastic products...........	5	83	5	83
Scientific, photographic, and control equipment......................	5	25	5	25
Semiconductors.............................	—	—	—	—
Soaps, cosmetics...........................	3	38	3	38
Specialty retailers..........................	5	29	6	33
Telecommunications.......................	—	—	—	—
Temporary help..............................	—	—	—	—
Textiles..	3	60	4	67
Tobacco..	3	50	3	50
Toys, sporting goods......................	—	—	—	—
Transportation equipment...............	2	50	2	50
Trucking, truck leasing...................	—	—	—	—
Waste management........................	—	—	—	—
Wholesalers...................................	8	42	8	44
Total Companies.........................	**251**	**42**	**255**	**43**

[1] This represents the percentage of survey companies that use LIFO in a particular industry classification. For example, 2003 data shows that 5 companies in the Aerospace industry use LIFO. Those 5 companies represent 29% of the total number of Aerospace companies surveyed.

First-In First-Out

2.70

BAUSCH & LOMB INCORPORATED (DEC)

(Dollar amounts in millions)	2003	2002
Cash and cash equivalents	$ 562.6	$ 465.1
Trade receivables, less allowances of $21.3 and $25.6, respectively	476.3	425.0
Inventories, net	207.3	208.5
Deferred income taxes	64.5	72.7
Other current assets	110.7	113.4
Total current assets	$1,421.4	$1,284.7

NOTES TO FINANCIAL STATEMENTS
(Dollar amounts in millions)

Note 1 (In Part): Accounting Policies

Inventories

Inventories are valued at the lower of cost or market using the first-in, first-out (FIFO) method. The Company provides estimated inventory allowances for excess, slow moving and obsolete inventory as well as inventory whose carrying value is in excess of net realizable value.

Note 6 (In Part): Supplemental Balance Sheet Information

	2003	2002
Inventories, net		
Raw materials and supplies	$ 42.6	$ 50.0
Work in process	19.3	21.3
Finished products	145.4	137.2
	$207.3	$208.5

2.71

BAXTER INTERNATIONAL INC. (DEC)

(In millions)	2003	2002
Current assets		
Cash and equivalents	$ 927	$1,169
Accounts and other current receivables	1,979	1,838
Inventories	2,101	1,745
Short-term deferred income taxes	140	125
Prepaid expenses and other	290	283
Total current assets	$5,437	$5,160

NOTES TO CONSOLIDATED FINANCIAL STATEMENTS

Note 1 (In Part): Summary of Significant Accounting Policy

Inventories

(In millions)	2003	2002
Raw materials	$ 568	$ 439
Work in process	731	511
Finished products	802	795
Total inventories	$2,101	$1,745

Inventories are stated at the lower of cost (first-in, first-out method) or market value. Market value for raw materials is based on replacement costs and, for other inventory classifications, on net realizable value. Reserves for excess and obsolete inventory were $121 million and $118 million at December 31, 2003 and 2002, respectively.

Last-In First-Out

2.72

AMCAST INDUSTRIAL CORPORATION (AUG)

($ in thousands)	2003	2002
Current assets		
Cash and cash equivalents	$ 5,697	$ 18,868
Accounts receivable	39,979	43,028
Inventories	19,004	27,796
Other current assets	5,338	3,941
Total current assets of continuing operations	70,018	93,633
Assets of discontinued operations	—	185,721
Total current assets	$70,018	$279,354

NOTES TO CONSOLIDATED FINANCIAL STATEMENTS
($ In thousands)

Accounting Policies (In Part)

Inventories

Inventories are valued at the lower of cost or market. The value of U.S. inventories is determined using the last-in, first-out method (LIFO). The value of foreign inventories, at the Company's Canadian facility, is determined using the first-in, first-out method (FIFO). Supplies and maintenance related materials, which are not a component of finished goods, but are utilized during manufacturing, are categorized as raw materials.

Inventory

The major components of inventories as of August 31 are:

	2003	2002
Finished products	$10,833	$19,429
Work in process	3,611	4,462
Raw materials and supplies	8,336	9,142
	22,780	33,033
Less amount to reduce certain inventories to LIFO value	(3,776)	(5,237)
Inventories	$19,004	$27,796

Inventory at the Company's Canadian facility is reported on the FIFO method and totaled $430 and $634 at August 31, 2003 and 2002, respectively. During 2003, inventory balances declined which resulted in liquidation of LIFO inventory layers carried at lower costs prevailing in prior years compared with the cost of current-year inventory additions. The effect of the inventory reduction decreased cost of sales by $1,461 and decreased the net loss by approximately $935, or $0.10 per share.

2.73

AMERADA HESS CORPORATION (DEC)

(Millions of dollars)	2003	2002
Current assets		
Cash and cash equivalents	$ 518	$ 197
Accounts receivable		
Trade	1,717	1,785
Other	185	187
Inventories	579	492
Other current assets	187	95
Total current assets	$3,186	$2,756

NOTES TO CONSOLIDATED FINANCIAL STATEMENTS

1 (In Part): Summary of Significant Accounting Policies

Inventories

Crude oil and refined product inventories are valued at the lower of average cost or market. For inventories valued at cost, the Corporation uses principally the last-in, first-out (LIFO) inventory method.

Inventories of materials and supplies are valued at the lower of average cost or market.

6. Inventories

Inventories at December 31 are as follows:

(Millions of dollars)	2003	2002
Crude oil and other charge stocks	$ 138	$ 99
Refined and other finished products	567	497
Less: LIFO adjustment	(293)	(261)
	412	335
Materials and supplies	167	157
Total	$ 579	$ 492

2.74

ASHLAND INC. (SEP)

(In millions)	2003	2002
Current assets		
Cash and cash equivalents	$ 223	$ 90
Accounts receivable (less allowances for doubtful accounts of $35 million in 2003 and $34 million in 2002)	1,135	1,056
Inventories—Note A	441	456
Deferred income taxes	142	119
Assets of discontinued operations held for sale	—	211
Other current assets	144	139
	$2,085	$2,071

NOTES TO CONSOLIDATED FINANCIAL STATEMENTS

Note A (In Part): Significant Accounting Policies

Inventories

(In millions)	2003	2002
Chemicals and plastics	$ 333	$ 335
Construction materials	67	68
Petroleum products	66	58
Other products	48	51
Supplies	5	5
Excess of replacement costs over LIFO carrying values	(78)	(61)
	$ 441	$ 456

Chemicals, plastics and petroleum products with a replacement cost of $279 million at September 30, 2003, and $294 million at September 30, 2002, are valued using the last-in, first-out (LIFO) method. The remaining inventories are stated generally at the lower of cost (using the first-in, first-out [FIFO] or average cost methods) or market.

2.75

OXFORD INDUSTRIES, INC. (MAY)

($ in thousands)	2003	2002
Current assets:		
Cash and cash equivalents	$ 24,091	$ 17,591
Receivables, less allowance for doubtful accounts of $3,505 in 2003 and $3,390 in 2002	110,304	103,198
Inventories	104,334	84,541
Prepaid expenses	12,631	9,754
Total current assets	$251,360	$215,084

NOTES TO CONSOLIDATED FINANCIAL STATEMENTS

Note A (In Part): Summary of Significant Accounting Policies

6. Inventories

For consolidated reporting purposes, inventories are principally stated at the lower of cost (last-in, first-out method, "LIFO") or market. For segment reporting purposes, inventories are principally stated at the lower of cost (first-in, first-out method, "FIFO") or market.

Note C. Inventories

The components of inventories are summarized as follows:

($ in thousands)	2003	2002
Finished goods	$ 64,695	$54,382
Work in process	11,981	11,681
Fabric	22,485	15,806
Trim and supplies	5,173	2,672
	$104,334	$84,541

The excess of replacement cost over the value of inventories based upon the LIFO method was $34,928,000 at May 30, 2003 and $35,212,000 at May 31, 2002.

During fiscal 2003, inventory quantities were reduced in certain pools, which resulted in a liquidation of LIFO inventory layers carried at lower costs which prevailed in prior years. The effect of the liquidation was to decrease cost of goods sold by approximately $69,251 and to increase net earnings by $42,000 or $0.01 per share basic. During fiscal 2002, the effect of the liquidation was to decrease cost of goods sold by approximately $750,272 and to increase net earnings by $459,000 or $0.06 per share basic.

Average Cost

2.76

MICROSOFT CORPORATION (JUN)

(In millions)	2002	2003
Current assets:		
Cash and equivalents	$ 3,016	$ 6,438
Short-term investments	35,636	42,610
Total cash and short-term investments	38,652	49,048
Accounts receivable, net	5,129	5,196
Inventories	673	640
Deferred income taxes	2,112	2,506
Other	2,010	1,583
Total current assets	$48,576	$58,973

NOTES TO FINANCIAL STATEMENTS

Note 1 (In Part): Accounting Policies

Inventories

Inventories are stated at the lower of cost or market, using the average cost method. Cost includes materials, labor, and manufacturing overhead related to the purchase and production of inventories.

Note 6—Inventories

(In millions)	2002	2003
Finished goods	$505	$393
Raw materials and work in process	168	247
Inventories	$673	$640

Production Cost

2.77

KAMAN CORPORATION (DEC)

(In thousands)	2003	2002
Current assets		
Cash and cash equivalents	$ 7,130	$ 5,571
Accounts receivable	193,243	195,857
Inventories	178,952	164,715
Income taxes receivable	1,043	5,192
Deferred income taxes	26,026	28,450
Other current assets	12,457	14,460
Total current assets	$418,851	$414,245

NOTES TO CONSOLIDATED FINANCIAL STATEMENTS
(In thousands)

Summary of Significant Accounting Policies (In Part)

Inventories

Inventory of merchandise for resale is stated at cost (using the average costing method) or market, whichever is lower. Contracts and work in process and finished goods are valued at production cost represented by material, labor and overhead, including general and administrative expenses where applicable. Contracts and work in process and finished goods are not recorded in excess of net realizable values.

Inventories

Inventories are comprised as follows:

	2003	2002
Merchandise for resale	$ 94,042	$ 95,056
Contracts in process:		
U.S. government	21,127	13,348
Commercial	15,895	16,694
Other work in process (including certain general stock materials)	23,103	31,875
Finished goods	24,785	7,742
Total	$178,952	$164,715

Included above in other work in process and finished goods at December 31, 2003 and 2002 is K-MAX inventory of $33,437 and $25,181, respectively.

The aggregate amounts of general and administrative costs incurred in the Aerospace segment and allocated to contracts in process during 2003, 2002 and 2001 were $34,793, $51,845 and $49,816, respectively.

The estimated amounts of general and administrative costs remaining in contracts in process at December 31, 2003 and 2002 amount to $4,118 and $4,222, respectively, and are based on the ratio of such allocated costs to total costs incurred.

PREPAID EXPENSES

2.78 Table 2-11 summarizes the number of survey companies disclosing, either on the balance sheet or in the notes to financial statements, an amount for prepaid expenses. Rarely is the nature of prepaid expenses disclosed. Examples of items identified as prepaid expenses follow.

2.79

TABLE 2-11: PREPAID EXPENSES

	Number of Companies			
	2003	2002	2001	2000
Prepaid expenses.............................	104	98	100	98
Prepaid expenses and other current assets...................................	195	199	182	182
Prepaid expenses and deferred taxes...................................	7	6	7	9
Prepaid expenses and other receivables................................	3	4	2	2
Prepaid expenses and advances......	—	3	9	14
Employee benefits............................	7	9	14	3
Advertising costs..............................	16	12	10	5
Other captions indicating prepaid expenses......................................	19	15	20	29

2.80

GOLDEN ENTERPRISES, INC. (MAY)

	2003	2002
Current assets		
Cash and cash equivalents	$ 1,278,333	$ 302,478
Receivables:		
Trade accounts	7,835,874	9,014,850
Other	299,142	931,911
	8,135,016	9,946,761
Less: Allowance for doubtful accounts	196,100	196,100
	7,938,916	9,750,661
Notes receivable, current	42,253	45,918
	7,981,169	9,796,579
Inventories:		
Raw materials	1,496,992	1,605,640
Finished goods	2,289,145	3,604,482
	3,786,137	5,210,122
Prepaid expenses	3,645,298	4,031,037
Total current assets	$16,690,937	$19,340,216

NOTES TO CONSOLIDATED FINANCIAL STATEMENTS

Note 4—Prepaid Expenses

At May 31, prepaid expenses consist of the following:

	2003	2002
Prepaid slotting fees	$ 333,799	$1,001,087
Other prepaid expenses	3,311,499	3,029,950
	$3,645,298	$4,031,037

2.81

REPUBLIC SERVICES, INC. (DEC)

(In millions)	2003	2002
Current assets:		
Cash and cash equivalents	$119.2	$141.5
Accounts receivable, less allowance for doubtful accounts of $19.0 at December 31, 2003 and 2002	248.9	238.6
Prepaid expenses and other current assets	182.1	63.0
Deferred tax assets	5.8	9.2
Total current assets	$556.0	$452.3

NOTES TO CONSOLIDATED FINANCIAL STATEMENTS (All tables in millions)

2 (In Part): Summary of Significant Accounting Policies

Prepaid Expenses and Other Current Assets

A summary of prepaid expenses and other current assets is as follows:

	2003	2002
Inventory	$ 17.7	$16.6
Prepaid expenses	20.5	19.3
Other non-trade receivables	27.9	14.2
Income taxes receivable	87.6	10.4
Note receivable	23.0	—
Other assets	5.4	2.5
	$182.1	$63.0

OTHER CURRENT ASSETS

2.82   Table 2-12 summarizes the nature of accounts (other than cash, marketable securities, inventories, and prepaid expense) appearing in the current asset section of the balance sheets of the survey companies. Examples of such other current asset captions follow.

2.83

TABLE 2-12: OTHER CURRENT ASSET CAPTIONS

	Number of Companies			
	2003	2002	2001	2000
Nature of Asset				
Deferred income taxes......................	387	399	403	359
Property held for sale........................	67	62	47	38
Derivatives..	34	23	33	3
Unbilled costs....................................	13	10	7	8
Advances or deposits........................	10	15	9	4
Other—identified................................	50	49	60	59

Deferred Taxes

2.84

ARVINMERITOR, INC. (SEP)

(In millions)	2003	2002
Current assets		
Cash and cash equivalents	$ 103	$ 56
Receivables (less allowance for doubtful accounts: 2003, $24; 2002, $18)	1,327	1,251
Inventories	543	458
Other current assets	266	211
Total current assets	$2,239	$1,976

NOTES TO CONSOLIDATED FINANCIAL STATEMENTS

9 (In Part): Other Current Assets

Other Current Assets are summarized as follows (in millions):

	2003	2002
Current deferred income taxes (see Note 20)	$124	$116
Customer reimbursable tooling and engineering	74	33
Asbestos-related recoveries	13	20
Prepaid and other	55	42
Other current assets	$266	$211

20 (In Part): Income Taxes

Net deferred income tax assets included in Other Current Assets in the consolidated balance sheet consist of the tax effects of temporary differences related to the following (in millions):

	2003	2002
Compensation and benefits	$ 54	$ 49
Product warranties	27	29
Inventories	18	19
Receivables	7	10
Restructuring costs	3	3
Other, net	15	6
Current deferred income taxes—asset	$124	$116

Net deferred income tax assets included in Other Assets in the consolidated balance sheet consist of the tax effects of temporary differences related to the following (in millions):

	2003	2002
Retiree medical liability	$ 90	$ 95
Loss and tax credit carryforwards	258	212
Pension liability	76	21
Taxes on undistributed income	(53)	(32)
Property	(68)	(83)
Intangible assets	29	(7)
Other, net	(17)	(8)
Subtotal	315	198
Valuation allowance	(32)	(11)
Long-term deferred income taxes—asset	$283	$187

Management believes it is more likely than not that current and long-term deferred tax assets will reduce future income tax payments. Significant factors considered by management in its determination of the probability of the realization of the deferred tax benefits include: (a) historical operating results, (b) expectations of future earnings and (c) the extended period of time over which the retirement medical and pension liabilities will be paid. The increase in the long-term deferred tax asset associated with intangible assets was primarily driven by a restructuring of certain Brazilian operations, which resulted in a benefit to the company's fiscal 2003 effective tax rate of 14.5%. The valuation allowance represents the amount of tax benefits related to net operating loss and tax credit carryforwards, which management believes are not likely to be realized. The carryforward periods for $186 million of net operating losses and tax credit carryforwards expire between fiscal 2004 and 2022. The carryforward period for the remaining net operating losses and tax credits is indefinite.

2.85

CENDANT CORPORATION (DEC)

(In millions)	2003	2002
Current assets:		
Cash and cash equivalents	$ 840	$ 126
Restricted cash	448	307
Receivables (net of allowance for doubtful accounts of $160 and $136)	1,671	1,457
Deferred income taxes	455	334
Other current assets	1,064	1,108
Total current assets	$4,478	$3,332

NOTES TO CONSOLIDATED FINANCIAL STATEMENTS
(Unless otherwise noted, all amounts are in millions)

11 (In Part): Income Taxes

Current and non-current deferred income tax assets and liabilities are comprised of the following:

	2003	2002
Current deferred income tax assets:		
Litigation settlement and related liabilities	$ 42	$ 18
Accrued liabilities and deferred income	416	280
Provision for doubtful accounts	85	73
Acquisition and integration-related liabilities	17	44
Other	—	20
Current deferred income tax assets	560	435
Current deferred income tax liabilities:		
Insurance retention refund	20	20
Franchise acquisition costs	14	21
Prepaid expenses	66	60
Other	5	—
Current deferred income tax liabilities	105	101
Current net deferred income tax asset	$ 455	$ 334
Non-current deferred income tax assets:		
Net operating loss carryforwards	$ 816	$1,051
State net operating loss carryforwards	287	360
Capital loss carryforward	33	103
Acquisition and integration-related liabilities	195	258
Accrued liabilities and deferred income	—	64
Other	78	—
Valuation allowance(*)	(370)	(392)
Non-current deferred income tax assets	1,039	1,444
Non-current deferred income tax liabilities:		
Depreciation and amortization	233	311
Accrued liabilities and deferred income	138	—
Other	—	18
Non-current deferred income tax liabilities	371	329
Non-current net deferred income tax asset	$ 668	$1,115

(*) The valuation allowance of $370 million at December 31, 2003 relates to $124 million for the net deferred tax assets associated with Trilegiant and to deferred tax assets for federal net operating loss carryforwards, state net operating loss carryforwards and capital loss carryforwards of $1 million, $231 million and $14 million, respectively. The valuation allowance will be reduced when and if the Company determines that the deferred income tax assets are more likely than not to be realized.

Deferred income tax liabilities related to management and mortgage programs are comprised of the following:

	2003	2002
Unamortized mortgage servicing rights	$ 426	$ 392
Depreciation and amortization	625	575
Other	41	50
Deferred income tax liability under management and mortgage programs	$1,092	$1,017

As of December 31, 2003, the Company had federal net operating loss carryforwards of approximately $2.3 billion, which primarily expire in 2020 and 2022. Additionally, the Company has alternative minimum tax credit carryforwards of $128 million.

No provision has been made for U.S. federal deferred income taxes on approximately $811 million of accumulated and undistributed earnings of foreign subsidiaries at December 31, 2003 since it is the present intention of management to reinvest the undistributed earnings indefinitely in those foreign operations. The determination of the amount of unrecognized U.S. federal deferred income tax liability for unremitted earnings is not practicable.

2.86

STRYKER CORPORATION (DEC)

(In millions)	2003	2002
Current assets		
Cash and cash equivalents	$ 65.9	$ 37.8
Accounts receivable, less allowance of $48.9 ($43.7 in 2002)	498.6	406.7
Inventories	467.9	426.5
Deferred income taxes	307.2	227.5
Prepaid expenses and other current assets	58.0	52.8
Total current assets	$1,397.6	$1,151.3

NOTES TO CONSOLIDATED FINANCIAL STATEMENTS
(In millions)

Note 1 (In Part): Significant Accounting Policies

Income Taxes

The Company accounts for income taxes using the liability method. Under this method, deferred income tax assets and liabilities are determined based on differences between financial reporting and tax bases of assets and liabilities and are measured using the enacted tax rates in effect for the years in which the differences are expected to reverse. Deferred income tax expense (credit) represents the change in net deferred tax assets and liabilities during the year.

Note 11 (In Part): Income Taxes

Deferred income taxes reflect the net tax effects of temporary differences between the carrying amounts of assets and liabilities for financial reporting purposes and the amounts used for income tax purposes. The tax effect of significant temporary differences, which comprise the Company's deferred income tax assets and liabilities, is as follows:

	2003	2002
Deferred income tax assets:		
Inventories	$202.7	$137.9
Accounts receivable and other assets	13.3	16.1
Other accrued expenses	51.4	49.1
Depreciation and amortization	22.8	41.8
State taxes	12.7	7.8
Net operating loss carryforwards	10.9	22.4
Other	19.5	14.2
Total deferred tax assets	333.3	289.3
Deferred tax liabilities:		
Depreciation and amortization	(73.3)	(55.0)
Other accrued expenses	(7.0)	(7.3)
Interest rate swaps	—	(1.1)
Other	(12.1)	(11.8)
Total deferred tax liabilities	(92.4)	(75.2)
Total net deferred tax assets	$240.9	$214.1

Net operating loss carryforwards totaling approximately $31.5 at December 31, 2003 are available to reduce future taxable earnings of certain foreign subsidiaries. A significant portion of these carryforwards may be carried forward indefinitely.

Deferred tax assets and liabilities are included in the consolidated balance sheets as follows:

	2003	2002
Current assets—deferred income taxes	$307.2	$227.5
Noncurrent assets—deferred income taxes	26.1	61.8
Current liabilities—accrued expenses and other liabilities	(37.6)	(28.7)
Noncurrent liabilities—other liabilities	(54.8)	(46.5)
Total net deferred tax assets	$240.9	$214.1

No provision has been made for United States federal and state income taxes or foreign taxes that may result from future remittances of the undistributed earnings ($988.8 at December 31, 2003) of foreign subsidiaries because it is expected that such earnings will be reinvested overseas indefinitely. Determination of the amount of any unrecognized deferred income tax liability on these unremitted earnings is not practicable.

Total income taxes paid, net of refunds received, were $189.5 in 2003, $112.1 in 2002 and $63.0 in 2001.

Property Held for Sale

2.87

SCHLUMBERGER LIMITED (DEC)

(In thousands)	2003	2002
Current assets		
Cash	$ 234,192	$ 168,110
Short-term investments	2,874,781	1,567,906
Receivables less allowance for doubtful accounts (2003—$128,199; 2002—$172,871)	2,568,425	3,489,406
Inventories	796,559	1,043,057
Deferred taxes	315,350	435,887
Other current assets	341,973	481,074
Assets held for sale	3,237,841	—
	$10,369,121	$7,185,440

NOTES TO CONSOLIDATED FINANCIAL STATEMENTS

1 (In Part): Business Description

On September 22, 2003, Schlumberger announced the signing of an agreement with Atos Origin for the sale of the SchlumbergerSema business. The sale closed on January 29, 2004.

6. Sale of SchlumbergerSema to Atos Origin

On September 22, 2003, Schlumberger announced the signing of an agreement with Atos Origin for the sale of the SchlumbergerSema business.

On January 29, 2004 the sale transaction was completed. As consideration for the transaction, Schlumberger received €443 million ($550 million) in cash which included a working capital adjustment, and 19.3 million shares of common stock of Atos with a value of €1.02 billion ($1.275 billion), which represented approximately 29% of the outstanding common shares of Atos Origin after the transaction was completed. Schlumberger expects the result of the sale will be a gain which will be recorded as part of *Discontinued Operations* in the first quarter of 2004.

On February 2, 2004 Schlumberger sold 9.6 million of the Atos Origin shares for a net consideration of €500 million ($625 million). As a result of this sale, Schlumberger's investment was reduced to approximately 15% of the outstanding common shares of Atos Origin. Schlumberger will account for the remaining investment in Atos Origin on the cost method.

11. Assets Held for Sale and Liabilities Held for Sale

On September 22, 2003, Schlumberger announced the signing of an agreement, with Atos Origin, for the sale of its SchlumbergerSema business. On January 29, 2004 the sale transaction was completed. In accordance with generally accepted accounting principles, the assets and liabilities which will be eliminated from the Schlumberger *Consolidated Balance Sheet* subsequent to the sale have been aggregated and presented on the *Consolidated Balance Sheet* at December 31, 2003 as *Assets held for sale* ($3.24 billion) and *Liabilities held for sale* ($1.22 billion).

An analysis of the Assets and Liabilities held for sale is as follows:

(Stated in millions)	
Assets held for sale	
Receivables	$ 978
Inventories	37
Other current assets	159
Fixed assets	481
Goodwill	1,334
Intangible assets	158
Deferred taxes	35
Other assets	56
	$3,238
Liabilities held for sale	
Accounts payable and accrued liabilities	$1,066
Liability for taxes on income	14
Other liabilities	133
Minority interest	5
	$1,218

2.88

WYNDHAM INTERNATIONAL, INC. (DEC)

(In thousands)	2003	2002
Current assets:		
Cash and cash equivalents	$ 62,441	$ 37,239
Restricted cash	130,457	143,839
Accounts receivable, net of allowance for doubtful accounts of $4,489 in 2003 and $5,172 in 2002	71,077	100,529
Inventories	13,680	15,488
Prepaid expenses and other assets	10,564	10,008
Assets held for sale, net of accumulated depreciation of $119,868 in 2003 and $28,526 in 2002	238,330	77,256
Total current assets	$526,549	$384,359

NOTES TO CONSOLIDATED FINANCIAL STATEMENTS
(Dollars in thousands)

2 (In Part): Summary of Significant Accounting Policies

Investment in Real Estate and Related Improvements (In Part)

The Company periodically reviews the carrying value of each property to determine if events and circumstances exist indicating that the assets might be impaired. If facts or circumstances support the possibility of impairment, the Company will prepare projections of undiscounted cash flows, without interest charges, of the specific property, to determine if the amounts estimated to be generated by those assets are less than the carrying amounts of those assets. If impairment is indicated, an adjustment will be made to the carrying amount based on the difference between the fair value and the carrying amount of the asset. When management identifies an asset held for sale, the Company estimates the net selling price of such asset. If the net selling price of the asset is less than the carrying amount of the asset, a reserve for loss is established. Depreciation is no longer recorded once management has identified an asset held for sale. Net selling price is estimated as the amount at which the asset could be bought or sold (fair value) less costs to sell. Fair value is determined at prevailing market conditions, appraisals or current estimated net sales proceeds from pending offers, if appropriate. The Company recorded impairment of $163,363, $38,013 and $24,159 for the years ended December 31, 2003, 2002 and 2001, respectively.

3 (In Part): Investment in Real Estate and Related Improvements and Assets Held for Sale

Investment in real estate and related improvements and assets held for sale consists of the following:

	2003			2002		
	Investment in Real Estate Held for Use	Assets Held for Sale	Total	Investment in Real Estate Held for Use	Assets Held for Sale	Total
Land	$ 288,106	$ 38,521	$ 326,627	$ 344,168	$ 23,978	$ 368,146
Land held for development	28,647	—	28,647	31,127	—	31,127
Buildings and improvements	2,867,596	252,538	3,120,134	3,324,568	84,743	3,409,311
Furniture, fixtures and equipment	641,294	77,777	719,071	861,411	28,099	889,510
Renovations in progress	14,944	767	15,711	29,135	408	29,543
	3,840,587	369,603	4,210,190	4,590,409	137,228	4,727,637
Less: impairment	—	(11,405)	(11,405)	—	(37,851)	(37,851)
Less: accumulated depreciation	(901,779)	(119,868)	(1,021,647)	(978,953)	(28,526)	(1,007,479)
Equity investment held for sale	—	—	—	—	6,405	6,405
	$2,938,808	$ 238,330	$ 3,177,138	$3,611,456	$ 77,256	$ 3,688,712

Management classifies certain assets as held for sale based on management having the authority and intent of entering into commitments for sale transactions expected to close in the next twelve months. At December 31, 2003, certain assets were classified as held for sale. At December 31, 2003 and 2002, the impairment for assets held for sale totaled $11,405 and $37,851, respectively. The assets held for sale had income from operations of $24,500 and $6,106 for the years ended December 31, 2003 and 2002, respectively, net of amounts owned by third party limited partners.

The Company continues to evaluate the assets in its total portfolio as well as to pursue an orderly disposition of its held for sale assets. There can be no assurance if or when sales will be completed or whether such sales will be completed on terms that will enable the Company to realize the full carrying value of such assets.

Derivatives

2.89

NOBLE ENERGY, INC. (DEC)

(In thousands)	2003	2002
Current assets:		
Cash and cash equivalents	$ 62,374	$ 15,442
Accounts receivable—trade, net	303,822	232,924
Derivative financial instruments	56,058	10,271
Materials and supplies inventories	11,083	10,663
Other current assets	23,805	41,074
Assets held for sale	21,245	—
Total current assets	$478,387	$310,374

NOTES TO CONSOLIDATED FINANCIAL STATEMENTS

Note 1 (In Part): Summary of Significant Accounting Policies

Derivative Financial Instruments and Hedging Activities

The Company, from time to time, uses various derivative instruments in connection with anticipated crude oil and natural gas sales to minimize the impact of product price fluctuations. Such instruments include fixed price hedges, variable to fixed price swaps, costless collars and other contractual arrangements. Although these derivative instruments expose the Company to credit risk, the Company monitors the creditworthiness of its counterparties and believes that losses from nonperformance are unlikely to occur. Hedging gains and losses related to the Company's crude oil and natural gas production are recorded in oil and gas sales and royalties.

The FASB issued SFAS No. 133, "Accounting for Derivative Instruments and Hedging Activities," in June 1998. The statement established accounting and reporting standards requiring every derivative instrument (including certain derivative instruments embedded in other contracts) to be recorded on the balance sheet as either an asset or liability measured at its fair value. The statement requires that changes in the derivative's fair value be recognized currently in earnings unless specific hedge accounting criteria are met wherein gains and losses are reflected in shareholders' equity as AOCI until the hedged item is recognized. Special accounting for qualifying hedges allows a derivative's gains and losses to offset related results on the hedged item on the statements of operations, and requires that a company formally document, designate and assess the effectiveness of transactions that receive hedge accounting.

The Company adopted SFAS No. 133 effective January 1, 2001. The adoption of this statement did not have a material impact on the Company's results of operations or financial position, as of the date of adoption. At December 31, 2003, the Company recorded crude oil and natural gas hedge receivables and liabilities of $56.1 million and $67.6 million, respectively, and other comprehensive loss, net of tax, of $7.6 million related to the Company's derivative contracts.

Note 2 (In Part): Fair Value of Financial Instruments

The following methods and assumptions were used to estimate the fair value of each class of financial instruments. The fair value of a financial instrument is the amount at which the instrument could be exchanged in a current transaction between two willing parties.

Crude Oil and Natural Gas Derivative Financial Instruments

The fair value of crude oil and natural gas derivative instruments is the estimated amount the Company would receive or pay to terminate the agreements at the reporting date taking into account creditworthiness of the counterparties.

Note 8 (In Part): Derivatives Instruments and Hedging Activities

Cash Flow Hedges

The Company, from time to time, uses various derivative instruments in connection with anticipated crude oil and natural gas sales to minimize the impact of product price fluctuations. Such instruments include fixed price hedges, variable to fixed price swaps, costless collars and other contractual arrangements. Although these derivative instruments expose the Company to credit risk, the Company takes reasonable steps to protect itself from nonperformance by its counterparties including periodic assessment of necessary provisions for bad debt allowance; however, the Company is not able to predict sudden changes in its counterparties' creditworthiness. The Company accounts for its derivative instruments under SFAS No. 133, "Accounting for Derivative Instruments and Hedging Activities," as amended, and has elected to designate its derivative instruments as cash flow hedges. Derivative instruments designated as cash flow hedges are reflected at fair value on the Company's consolidated balance sheets. Changes in fair value, to the extent the hedge is effective, are reported in AOCI until the forecasted transaction occurs. Gains and losses from such derivative instruments related to the Company's crude oil and natural gas production and which qualify for hedge accounting treatment are recorded in oil and gas sales and royalties on the Company's consolidated statements of operations upon sale of the associated products. Hedge effectiveness is assessed at least quarterly based on total changes in the derivative's fair value. Any ineffective portion of the derivative instrument's change in fair value is recognized immediately in other income.

During 2003, 2002 and 2001, the Company entered into various crude oil and natural gas fixed price swaps, costless collars and costless collar combinations related to its crude oil and natural gas production. The tables below depict the various transactions.

Natural Gas	2003	2002	2001
Hedge MMBTUpd	190,038	170,274	16,947
Fixed price range			$5.23–$5.41
Floor price range	$3.25–$3.80	$2.00–$3.50	$3.25–$5.00
Ceiling price range	$4.00–$5.25	$2.45–$5.10	$4.60–$6.25
Percent of daily production	56%	50%	5%

Crude Oil	2003	2002	2001
Hedge Bpd	15,793	5,247	126
Fixed price			$27.81
Floor price range	$23.00–$27.00	$23.00–$24.00	
Ceiling price range	$27.20–$35.05	$29.30–$30.10	
Percent of daily production	44%	18%	.5%

During 2003, 2002 and 2001, the Company included a reduction of $67.5 million and gains of $5.9 million and $5.1 million, respectively, related to its cash flow hedges in oil and gas sales and royalties. During 2003, 2002 and 2001, no gains or losses were reclassified into earnings as a result of the discontinuance of hedge accounting treatment. During 2003, the Company recorded $.5 million of ineffectiveness related to its cash flow hedges. No ineffectiveness was recorded for 2002 and 2001.

In 2001, the Company only had financial derivatives in the fourth quarter. Of these fourth quarter derivatives, 25,000 MMBTU of natural gas per day was terminated early. Amounts in AOCI were reclassified into earnings in the same periods during which the hedged forecasted transaction affected earnings, resulting in an increase in oil and gas sales and royalties of $6.3 million during the fourth quarter of 2001. As a result, the Company recognized an additional $.70 per MMBTU on the 25,000 MMBTU of natural gas per day in 2001.

As of December 31, 2003, the Company had entered into costless collars related to its natural gas and crude oil production to support the Company's investment program as follows:

Production Period	Natural Gas MMBTUpd	Price Per MMBTU Floor-Ceiling	Crude Oil Bopd	Price Per Bbl Floor-Ceiling
1Q2004	120,000	$4.81–$7.77	15,000	$25.33–$31.53
2Q2004	120,000	$4.06–$5.95	15,000	$24.83–$31.22
3Q2004	120,000	$4.19–$5.99	15,000	$25.00–$31.13
4Q2004	120,000	$4.19–$6.42	5,000	$24.00–$30.00

The contracts entitle the Company (floating price payor) to receive settlement from the counterparty (fixed price payor) for each calculation period in amounts, if any, by which the settlement price for the last scheduled NYMEX trading day applicable for each calculation period is less than the floor price. The Company would pay the counterparty if the settlement price for the last scheduled NYMEX trading day applicable for each calculation period is more than the ceiling price. The amount payable by the floating price payor, if the floating price is above the ceiling price, is the product of the notional quantity per calculation period and the excess, if any, of the floating price over the ceiling price in respect of each calculation period. The amount payable by the fixed price payor, if the floating price is below the floor price, is the product of the notional quantity per calculation period and the excess, if any, of the floor price over the floating price in respect of each calculation period.

Other Derivative Financial Instruments

In addition to the derivative instruments pertaining to the Company's production as described above, NEMI, from time to time, employs various derivative instruments in connection with its purchases and sales of third-party production to lock in profits or limit exposure to natural gas price risk. Most of the purchases made by NEMI are on an index basis; however, purchasers in the markets in which NEMI sells often require fixed or NYMEX-related pricing. NEMI may use a derivative to convert the fixed or NYMEX sale to an index basis thereby determining the margin and minimizing the risk of price volatility.

NEMI records gains and losses on derivative instruments using mark-to-market accounting. Under this accounting method, the changes in the market value of outstanding financial instruments are recognized as gains or losses in the period of change. NEMI recorded a loss of $.2 million, a gain of $.9 million and a loss of $.5 million in GMP proceeds during 2003, 2002 and 2001, respectively, related to derivative instruments.

Receivables/Payables Related to Crude Oil and Natural Gas Derivative Financial Instruments

At December 31, 2003, the Company's consolidated balance sheet included a receivable of $56.1 million and a payable of $67.6 million related to crude oil and natural gas derivative financial instruments. At December 31, 2002, the Company's consolidated balance sheet included a receivable of $10.3 million and a payable of $32.3 million related to crude oil and natural gas derivative financial instruments.

During 2003, the Company had contracts with Enron North America Corporation ("ENA") that resulted in gains of $6.9 million (net of allowance) included in GMP proceeds. In addition, as of December 31, 2003, the Company had NYMEX-related transactions with ENA totaling 149 contracts with a mark-to-market receivable value of $1.8 million. For additional discussion of ENA matters, see "Note 10—Commitments and Contingencies" of this Form 10-K.

Interest Rate Lock

The Company occasionally enters into forward contracts or swap agreements to hedge exposure to interest rate risk. Changes in fair value of interest rate swaps or interest rate "locks" used as cash flow hedges are reported in AOCI, to the extent the hedge is effective, until the forecasted transaction occurs, at which time they are recorded as adjustments to interest expense. At December 31, 2003, the Company's consolidated balance sheet included a payable of $4.0 million related to an outstanding interest rate lock. The amount of deferred loss included in AOCI at December 31, 2003 was $2.6 million, net of tax.

Unbilled Costs

2.90

PEERLESS MFG. CO. (JUN)

(Dollars in thousands)	2003	2002
Current assets:		
Cash and cash equivalents	$ 6,680	$ 1,386
Short-term investments	309	307
Accounts receivable—principally trade	17,547	25,506
Inventories	3,218	3,671
Costs and earnings in excess of billings on uncompleted contracts	7,715	9,218
Deferred income taxes	1,445	933
Other current assets	1,098	725
Total current assets	$38,012	$41,746

NOTES TO CONSOLIDATED FINANCIAL STATEMENTS
(Dollars in thousands)

Note A (In Part): Nature of Operations and Summary of Significant Accounting Policies

Revenue Recognition

The Company provides products under long-term, generally fixed-priced, contracts that may extend up to 18 months, or longer, in duration. In connection with these contracts, the Company follows the guidance contained in AICPA Statement of Position ("SOP") 81-1, "Accounting for Performance of Construction-Type and Certain Production-Type Contracts." SOP 81-1 requires the use of percentage-of-completion accounting for long-term contracts that contain enforceable rights regarding services to be provided and received by the contracting parties, consideration to be exchanged, and the manner and terms of settlement, assuming reasonably dependable estimates of revenues and expenses can be made. The percentage-of-completion methodology generally results in the recognition of reasonably consistent profit margins over the life of a contract. Amounts recognized in revenue are calculated using the percentage of construction cost completed, generally on a cumulative cost to total cost basis. Cumulative revenues recognized may be less or greater than cumulative costs and profits billed at any point in time during a contract's term. The resulting difference is recognized as "costs and earnings in excess of billings on uncompleted contracts" or "billings in excess of costs and earnings on uncompleted contracts."

The completed contract method is applied to relatively short-term contracts where the financial statement presentation does not vary materially from the presentation under the percentage-of-completion method. Revenues under the completed contract method are recognized upon shipment of the product.

Note F. Costs and Estimated Earnings on Uncompleted Contracts

The components of uncompleted contracts are as follows:

	2003	2002
Costs incured on uncompleted contracts and estimated earnings	$ 28,333	$ 42,371
Less billings to date	(22,645)	(37,384)
	$ 5,688	$ 4,987

The components of uncompleted contracts are reflected in the balance sheets at June 30, 2003 and 2002 as follows:

	2003	2002
Costs and earnings in excess billings on uncompleted contracts	$ 7,715	$ 9,218
Billings in excess of costs and earnings on uncompleted contracts	(2,027)	(4,231)
	$ 5,688	$ 4,987

Advances/Deposits

2.91

UNIVERSAL CORPORATION (JUN)

(In thousands)	2003	2002
Current		
Cash and cash equivalents	$ 44,659	$ 58,003
Accounts receivable	370,784	301,197
Advances to suppliers	115,928	53,684
Accounts receivable—unconsolidated affiliates	7,595	5,647
Inventories—at lower of cost or market:		
Tobacco	529,736	453,417
Lumber and building products	140,647	80,848
Agri-products	82,527	83,634
Other	30,377	32,103
Prepaid income taxes	12,375	6,297
Deferred income taxes	6,168	5,945
Other current assets	34,201	24,262
Total current assets	$1,374,997	$1,105,037

NOTES TO CONSOLIDATED FINANCIAL STATEMENTS

Note 1 (In Part): Summary of Significant Accounting Policies

Advances to Suppliers

The Company provides agronomy services and crop advances of, or for, seed, fertilizer, and other supplies. These advances are short term in nature and are repaid upon delivery of tobacco to the Company.

PROPERTY, PLANT, AND EQUIPMENT

2.92 Property, Plant, and Equipment are the long-lived, physical assets of the firm acquired for use in the firm's normal business operations and not intended for resale by the firm. These assets are usually valued at historical cost. SFAS No. 34, *Capitalization of Interest Cost*, establishes standards of financial accounting and reporting for capitalizing interest cost as part of the historical cost of acquiring certain assets such as plant assets that a firm constructs for its own use. In 2003, 121 survey companies disclosed that interest costs were capitalized during the period.

2.93 SOP No. 98-1, *Accounting for the Costs of Computer Software Developed or Obtained for Internal Use*, provides guidance on accounting for the costs of internal-use computer software other than software used in research and development activities. Under *SOP No. 98-1*, certain computer software costs should be capitalized and amortized over their estimated useful lives. Accounting for computer software costs is also addressed by SFAS No. 86, *Accounting for the Costs of Computer Software to be Sold, Leased or Otherwise Marketed*. Under *SFAS No. 86*, certain computer software production costs incurred subsequent to establishing technological feasibility should be capitalized and amortized on a product-by-product basis. Presentations of capitalized computer software costs by survey companies vary. Examples of capitalized software cost disclosures are included here and in the Other Noncurrent Asset section.

2.94 Paragraph 5 of *APB Opinion No. 12* states:

Because of the significant effects on financial position and results of operations of the depreciation method or methods used, the following disclosures should be made in the financial statements or in notes thereto:
a. Depreciation expense for the period,
b. Balance of major classes of depreciable assets, by nature or function, at the balance sheet date,
c. Accumulated depreciation, either by major classes of depreciable assets or in total, at the balance sheet date, and
d. A general description of the method or methods used in computing depreciation with respect to major classes of depreciable assets.

2.95 Tables 2-13 and 2-14 show the assets classified as Property, Plant, and Equipment by the survey companies. Table 2-15 summarizes the descriptive captions used to describe the accumulated allowance for depreciation.

2.96 Examples of Property, Plant, and Equipment disclosures follow.

2.97

TABLE 2-13: LAND CAPTIONS

	2003	2002	2001	2000
Land..	342	335	343	347
Land and improvements....................	132	124	127	133
Land and buildings..........................	55	54	55	46
Land combined with other identified assets..	7	12	10	9
No caption with term land.................	47	52	49	42
	583	577	584	577
Lines of business classification.........	17	23	16	23
Total Companies.............................	**600**	**600**	**600**	**600**

2.98

TABLE 2-14: DEPRECIABLE ASSET CAPTIONS

	2003	2002	2001	2000
Buildings				
Buildings................................	195	191	201	211
Buildings and improvement..................	256	254	248	239
Building and land or equipment............	73	72	75	77
Buildings combined with other identified assets.............................	14	16	15	20
No caption with term buildings.............	49	54	49	37
	587	587	588	584
Line of business classification..............	13	13	12	16
Total Companies...............................	**600**	**600**	**600**	**600**
	Number of Companies			
Other Depreciable Asset Captions				
Machinery and/or equipment...............	387	385	396	412
Machinery and/or equipment combined with other assets.............	113	129	131	109
Construction in progress......................	274	272	282	271
Leasehold improvements....................	131	131	116	111
Lease assets......................................	66	56	62	50
Automobiles, marine equipment etc.....	84	92	72	96
Furniture and fixtures.........................	107	100	87	85
Computer equipment...........................	38	43	43	N/C*
Software..	58	49	40	N/C*
Assets leased to others......................	21	19	13	14

* N/C = Not compiled. Line item was not included in table for year shown.

2.99

TABLE 2-15: ACCUMULATED DEPRECIATION

	2003	2002	2001	2000
Accumulated depreciation................	336	326	322	328
Accumulated depreciation and amortization.....................................	193	200	195	196
Accumulated depreciation, amortization and depletion...........	16	20	20	20
Accumulated depreciation and depletion...	7	7	9	7
Allowance for depreciation...............	20	23	25	27
Allowance for depreciation and amortization.....................................	6	6	6	8
Other captions..................................	22	18	23	14
Total Companies............................	**600**	**600**	**600**	**600**

2.100

ALBERTSON'S, INC. (JAN)

(In millions)	2004	2003
Total current assets	$ 4,419	$ 4,268
Land, buildings and equipment, net	9,145	9,029
Goodwill	1,400	1,399
Intangibles, net	130	214
Other assets	300	301
Total assets	$15,394	$15,211

NOTES TO CONSOLIDATED FINANCIAL STATEMENTS

2 (In Part): Summary of Significant Accounting Policies

Capitalization, Depreciation and Amortization

Land, buildings and equipment are recorded at cost. Depreciation is provided on the straight-line method over the estimated useful life of the asset. Estimated useful lives are generally as follows: buildings and improvements—10 to 35 years; fixtures and equipment—3 to 8 years; software—3 to 5 years; leasehold improvements—10 to 25 years; intangibles—3 to 10 years; and assets held under capitalized leases—20 to 30 years.

The costs of major remodeling and improvements on leased stores are capitalized as leasehold improvements and amortized on the straight-line method over the shorter of the life of the applicable lease or the useful life of the asset. Assets under capital leases are recorded at the lower of the fair market value of the asset or the present value of future minimum lease payments and amortized on the straight-line method over the lease term.

Beneficial lease rights and lease liabilities are recorded on purchased leases based on differences between contractual rents under the respective lease agreements and prevailing market rents at the date of the acquisition of the lease. Beneficial lease rights and lease liabilities are amortized over the lease term using the straight-line method.

Impairment of Long Lived Assets and Closed Store Reserves

The Company assesses long-lived assets for indicators of impairment based on operational performance. When events or changes in circumstances indicate that the carrying value of an asset or an asset group may not be recoverable, the asset's fair value is compared to its carrying value. Impairment losses are recognized as the amount by which the carrying amounts of the assets exceed their fair values. Asset fair values are determined by internal real estate specialists or by independent quotes. These estimates can be significantly impacted by changes in real estate market conditions, the economic environment and inflation.

For properties that are closed and are under long-term lease agreements, the present value of any remaining liability under the lease, discounted using credit risk-free rates and net of expected sublease recovery, is recognized as a liability and expensed. The value of any equipment and leasehold improvements related to a closed store is reduced to reflect net recoverable values. Internal real estate specialists estimate the subtenant income, future cash flows and asset recovery values based on their historical experience and knowledge of (1) the market in which the store to be closed is located, (2) the results of the Company's previous efforts to dispose of similar assets and (3) the current economic conditions. The actual cost of disposition for these leases and related assets is affected by specific real estate markets, the economic environment and inflation.

11. Land, Buildings and Equipment

Land, buildings and equipment, net, consisted of the following:

	2004	2003
Land	$ 1,936	$ 1,939
Buildings	5,978	5,713
Fixtures and equipment	5,928	5,561
Leasehold improvements	1,728	1,619
Capitalized leases	420	355
	15,990	15,187
Accumulated depreciation	(6,735)	(6,060)
Accumulated amortization on capital leases	(110)	(98)
	$ 9,145	$ 9,029

Depreciation expense was $931, $901 and $869 for 2003, 2002 and 2001. Amortization expense of capital leases was $18, $18 and $19 for 2003, 2002 and 2001, respectively.

2.101

ARDEN GROUP, INC. (DEC)

(In thousands)	2003	2002
Total current assets	$130,982	$ 80,286
Property held for resale or sublease	51	51
Property, plant and equipment, net	45,637	52,454
Deferred income taxes	7,010	2,066
Other assets	3,292	4,114
Total assets	$186,972	$138,971

NOTES TO CONSOLIDATED FINANCIAL STATEMENTS

1 (In Part): Accounting Policies

Property, Plant and Equipment

Property, plant and equipment is recorded at cost. Depreciation is provided on the straight-line method over the estimated useful lives of individual assets or classes of assets as follows:

Buildings and improvements	5 to 15 years
Store fixtures and office equipment	3 to 8 years
Transportation equipment	2 to 5 years
Machinery and equipment	3 to 10 years

Improvements to leased properties are amortized over their estimated useful lives or lease period, whichever is shorter. Leasehold interests are amortized over the initial lease term.

Leased property meeting certain capital lease criteria is capitalized and the present value of the related lease payments is recorded as a liability. Amortization of capitalized leased assets is computed on the straight-line method over the shorter of the estimated useful life or the initial lease term.

Normal repairs and maintenance are expensed as incurred. Expenditures which materially increase values, change capacities or extend useful lives are capitalized. Replacements are capitalized and the property, plant and equipment accounts are relieved of the items being replaced. The related costs and accumulated depreciation of disposed assets are eliminated and any gain or loss on disposition is included in income.

Impairment of Long-Lived Assets

The Company monitors the carrying value of long-lived assets for potential impairment each quarter whenever events or changes in circumstances indicate the carrying value of an asset may not be recoverable. Impairment is determined by comparing projected undiscounted cash flows to be generated by the asset to its carrying value. If impairment is identified, a loss would be recorded equal to the excess of the asset's net book value over the asset's fair value.

6. Property, Plant and Equipment

(In thousands)	2003	2002
Land	$ 8,584	$ 8,110
Buildings and improvements	9,693	9,693
Store fixtures and office equipment	36,065	35,417
Transportation equipment	2,664	2,796
Machinery and equipment	1,236	1,001
Leasehold improvements	39,206	42,153
Leasehold interests	4,538	4,538
Assets under capital leases	3,058	3,058
Assets under construction	488	1,410
	105,532	108,176
Accumulated depreciation and amortization	(59,895)	(55,722)
	$ 45,637	$ 52,454

As of January 3, 2004, approximately $19,258,000 of property, plant and equipment (at cost) was fully depreciated and is still being used in operations. As of January 3, 2004, the Company has recorded $2,636,000 in accumulated amortization for assets under capital lease.

In the fourth quarter of Fiscal 2003, the Company recorded a $4,311,000 pre-tax impairment on long-lived assets related to its Pasadena retail store. Sales at Pasadena have been below management's expectations since the store's initial opening in September 2001. During the fourth quarter of 2003, a labor dispute in the Company's trade area temporarily resulted in improved sales at Pasadena, however, sales remain at levels below management's expectations and are anticipated to decline significantly from strike levels at the conclusion of the labor dispute. The impairment charge, a component of delivery, selling, general and administrative expenses, reflects the difference between the carrying value of the Pasadena assets and the estimated fair value, which was based on the discounted future cash flows using a risk-free interest rate.

2.102

BRIGGS & STRATTON CORPORATION (JUN)

(In thousands)	2003	2002
Total current assets	$ 807,147	$ 675,507
Goodwill	159,756	161,030
Investments	44,175	46,889
Prepaid pension	74,005	60,343
Deferred loan costs, net	8,314	10,506
Other long-term assets, net	11,012	7,111
Plant and equipment:		
Land and land improvements	15,938	16,356
Buildings	156,823	153,043
Machinery and equipment	689,100	691,334
Construction in progress	14,803	18,902
	876,664	879,635
Less—accumulated depreciation	505,880	484,420
Total plant and equipment, net	370,784	395,215
	$1,475,193	$1,356,601

NOTES TO CONSOLIDATED FINANCIAL STATEMENTS

2 (In Part): Summary of Significant Accounting Policies

Plant and Equipment and Depreciation

Plant and equipment are stated at cost and depreciation is computed using the straight-line method at rates based upon the estimated useful lives of the assets (20–30 years for land improvements, 20–50 years for buildings and 8–16 years for machinery and equipment).

Expenditures for repairs and maintenance are charged to expense as incurred. Expenditures for major renewals and betterments, which significantly extend the useful lives of existing plant and equipment, are capitalized and depreciated. Upon retirement or disposition of plant and equipment, the cost and related accumulated depreciation are removed from the accounts and any resulting gain or loss is recognized in other income.

Impairment of Long-Lived Assets

Property, plant and equipment and other long-term assets are reviewed for impairment whenever events or changes in circumstances indicate that the carrying amount may not be recoverable. If the sum of the expected undiscounted cash flows is less than the carrying value of the related asset or group of assets, a loss is recognized for the difference between the fair value and carrying value of the asset or group of assets. There were no adjustments to the carrying value of long-lived assets in fiscal 2003, 2002 or 2001.

2.103

NOBLE ENERGY, INC. (DEC)

(In thousands)	2003	2002
Total current assets	$ 478,387	$ 310,374
Property, plant and equipment, at cost:		
Oil and gas mineral interests, equipment and facilities (successful efforts method of accounting)	3,875,598	4,285,508
Other	49,389	48,507
	3,924,987	4,334,015
Accumulated depreciation, depletion and amortization	(1,825,246)	(2,194,230)
Total property, plant and equipment, net	2,099,741	2,139,785
Investment in unconsolidated subsidiaries	227,669	234,668
Other assets	36,852	45,188
Total assets	$ 2,842,649	$ 2,730,015

NOTES TO CONSOLIDATED FINANCIAL STATEMENTS

Note 1 (In Part): Summary of Significant Accounting Policies

Property, Plant and Equipment

The Company accounts for its crude oil and natural gas properties under the successful efforts method of accounting. Under this method, costs to acquire mineral interests in crude oil and natural gas properties, to drill and equip exploratory wells that find proved reserves and to drill and equip development wells are capitalized, Capitalized costs of producing crude oil and natural gas properties are amortized to operations by the unit-of-production method based on proved developed crude oil and natural gas reserves on a property-by-property basis as estimated by Company engineers. The total asset retirement obligations of $199.3 million consist of $175.9 million for the United States and $23.4 million for the North Sea and are included in future production and development costs for purposes of estimating the future net revenues relating to the Company's proved reserves. Upon sale or retirement of depreciable or depletable property, the cost and related accumulated DD&A are eliminated from the accounts and the resulting gain or loss is recognized.

Individually significant unproved crude oil and natural gas properties are periodically assessed for impairment of value and a loss is recognized at the time of impairment by providing an impairment allowance. Other unproved properties are amortized on a composite method based on the Company's experience of successful drilling and average holding period. Geological and geophysical costs, delay rentals and costs to drill exploratory wells that do not find proved reserves are expensed. Repairs and maintenance are expensed as incurred.

In accordance with SFAS No. 144, "Accounting for the Impairment or Disposal of Long-Lived Assets," the Company reviews oil and gas properties and other long-lived assets for impairment when events and circumstances indicate a decline in the recoverability of the carrying value of such properties, such as a downward revision of the reserve estimates or commodity prices. The Company estimates the future cash flows expected in connection with the properties and compares such future cash flows to the carrying amount of the properties to determine if the carrying amount is recoverable. When the carrying amounts of the properties exceed their estimated undiscounted future cash flows, the carrying amount of the properties is written down to their fair value as determined by discounting its estimated future cash flows. The factors used to determine fair value include, but are not limited to, estimates of proved reserves, future commodity prices and timing of future production, future capital expenditures and a discount rate commensurate with the risk-free interest rate reflective of the lives remaining for the respective oil and gas properties.

The Company recognized $31.9 million of impairments in 2003, primarily related to a reserve revision on the East Cameron 338 field in the Gulf of Mexico after recompletion and remediation activities produced less-than-expected results. An analysis of the performance response of the field resulted in a reduction in proved reserves of 2.2 MMBoe (unaudited).

2.104

PAYCHEX, INC. (MAY)

(In thousands)	2003	2002
Total current assets	$3,032,642	$2,814,574
Other assets	7,057	7,895
Property and equipment, net	159,039	121,566
Intangible assets, net	98,342	9,040
Goodwill	393,703	—
Total assets	$3,690,783	$2,953,075

NOTES TO CONSOLIDATED FINANCIAL STATEMENTS

Note A (In Part): Significant Accounting Policies

Property and Equipment, Net

Property and equipment is stated at cost, less accumulated depreciation and amortization. Depreciation is based on the estimated useful lives of property and equipment using the straight-line method. The estimated useful lives of depreciable assets are generally 10 to 35 years for buildings and improvements, 2 to 15 years for data processing equipment, 3 to 5 years for software, 7 years for furniture and fixtures, and 2 to 10 years for leasehold improvements. The Company reviews the carrying value of property and equipment, including capitalized software, for impairment when events or changes in circumstances indicate that the carrying value of such assets may not be recoverable.

Software Development and Enhancements

Expenditures for major software purchases and software developed for internal use are capitalized and depreciated using the straight-line method over the estimated useful lives of the related assets, which are generally 3 to 5 years. For software developed for internal use, all external direct costs for materials and services and certain payroll and related fringe benefit costs are capitalized in accordance with Statement of Position (SOP) 98-1, "Accounting for the Costs of Computer Software Developed or Obtained for Internal Use."

Note E—Property and Equipment, Net

The components of property and equipment, net are as follows:

(In thousands)	2003	2002
Land and improvements	$ 4,205	$ 3,155
Buildings and improvements	65,634	37,909
Data processing equipment	107,694	78,488
Software	46,901	33,204
Furniture, fixtures, and equipment	90,265	81,959
Leasehold improvements	17,425	15,995
Construction in progress	4,978	22,761
	337,102	273,471
Less: Accumulated depreciation and amortization	178,063	151,905
Property and equipment, net	$159,039	$121,566

Construction in progress at May 31, 2002 primarily represents purchases of data processing equipment and software and related building improvements for the Company's data center, which was placed in service during the second quarter of fiscal 2003.

Depreciation expense was $33,918,000, $27,020,000, and $24,406,000 for fiscal years 2003, 2002, and 2001, respectively.

INVESTMENTS

2.105 APB Opinion No. 18, *The Equity Method of Accounting for investments in Common Stock*, stipulates that the equity method should be used to account for investments in corporate joint ventures and certain other companies when an investor has "the ability to exercise significant influence over operating and financial policies of an investee even though the investor holds 50% or less of the voting stock." *APB Opinion No. 18* considers an investor to have the ability to exercise significant influence when it owns 20% or more of the voting stock of an investee. Financial Accounting Standards Board (FASB) Interpretation No. 35, *Criteria for Applying the Equity Method of Accounting for Investments in Common Stock*, issued to clarify the criteria for applying the equity method of accounting to 50% or less owned companies, lists circumstances under which, despite 20% ownership, an investor may not be able to exercise significant influence.

2.106 In addition to investments accounted for by the equity method, many survey companies disclosed investments in equity and debt securities subject to the requirements of *SFAS No. 115*. This Statement is the authoritative pronouncement on accounting for and reporting investments in equity securities that have readily determinable fair value and all Investments in debt securities. Paragraphs 19–22 of *SFAS No. 115*, as amended by *SFAS No. 133*, state the disclosure requirements for such investments. SFAS No. 115 does not apply to investments accounted for by the equity method.

2.107 For investments subject to *SFAS No. 115* requirements, *SFAS No. 107*, as amended by *SFAS No. 133*, requires disclosure of both the fair value and the bases for estimating the fair value of investments unless it is not practicable to estimate that value. 195 survey companies made 220 fair value disclosures. 111 of those disclosures used market or broker quotes of the investments to determine fair value. 32 of those disclosures stated that either discounted cash flows or market prices of similar instruments were used to estimate fair value. 11 of those disclosures estimated fair value using other valuation methods. 103 disclosures presented carrying amounts which approximated fair value of investments. In addition, there were 80 disclosures in which carrying value was compared to fair value in an exposition or a table. 2 disclosures stated it was not practicable to estimate fair value.

2.108 *SFAC No. 7* provides a framework for using future cash flows and present value as the basis for accounting measurements of fair value of an asset or a liability at initial recognition or fresh-start measurements and for future-cash-flow-based amortization techniques, such as interest method amortization. Fresh-start measurements are measurements in periods following initial recognition that establish a new carrying amount unrelated to previous amounts and accounting conventions. Reporting certain marketable securities at fair value under *SFAS No. 115* is an example of a fresh-start measurement.

2.109 When observable marketplace-determined values are not available, discounted cash flows are often used to estimate fair value. Accounting applications of present value typically use a single set of estimated cash flows and a risk-adjusted discount rate. This Statement introduces the expected cash flow approach, which differs from the traditional approach by focusing on explicit assumptions about the range of possible cash outcomes and their respective probabilities.

2.110 While *SFAC No. 7* does not require modification of any existing pronouncements, its concepts may be used to determine fair value. This Standard will be used in developing future accounting standards. No data on the use of expected cash flow approach in discounted cash flow applications were compiled.

2.111 The FASB's Emerging Issues Task Force (EITF) Issue No. 03-1, *The Meaning of Other-Than-Temporary Impairment and Its Application to Certain Investments*, should be used to determine when certain investments are considered impaired, whether that impairment is other than temporary, and the measurement and recognition of an impairment loss. *EITF Issue No. 03-1* also provides guidance on accounting considerations subsequent to the recognition of an other-than-temporary impairment and requires certain disclosures about unrealized losses that have not been recognized as other-than-temporary impairments.

2.112 Table 2-16 lists the balance sheet carrying bases for investments presented as noncurrent assets.

2.113 Table 2-17 lists descriptions of investments presented as non-current investments. Examples of presentations and disclosures for such investments follow.

2.114

TABLE 2-16: INVESTMENTS—CARRYING BASES

	Number of Companies			
	2003	**2002**	**2001**	**2000**
Equity	290	304	308	261
Fair value	153	142	133	101
Cost	129	101	109	89
Lower of cost or market	3	4	4	2

2.115

TABLE 2-17: INVESTMENTS—DESCRIPTION

	Number of Companies			
	2003	2002	2001	2000
Common stock	246	235	237	219
Marketable equity securities	114	121	114	90
Joint ventures	71	59	81	N/C*
Debt	59	49	47	46
Leases	15	10	7	5
Preferred stock	14	11	14	11
Real estate	11	11	10	14
Other	21	30	24	37
No details	18	16	22	35

* N/C = Not compiled. Line item was not included in table for year shown.

Equity Method

2.116

CONOCOPHILLIPS (DEC)

Consolidated Balance Sheet

(Millions of dollars)	2003	2002
Total current assets	$11,192	$10,903
Investments and long-term receivables	7,258	6,821
Net properties, plants and equipment	47,428	43,030
Goodwill	15,084	14,444
Intangibles	1,085	1,119
Other assets	408	519
Total assets	$82,455	$76,836

Consolidated Income Statement

(Millions of dollars)	2003	2002	2001
Revenues			
Sales and other operating revenues	$104,196	$ 56,748	$ 24,892
Equity in earnings of affiliates	542	261	41
Other income	359	192	97
Total revenues	105,097	57,201	25,030
Costs and expenses			
Purchased crude oil and products	67,424	37,823	13,708
Production and operating expenses	7,208	4,698	2,643
Selling, general and administrative expenses	2,166	1,950	613
Exploration expenses	601	592	306
Depreciation, depletion and amortization	3,485	2,223	1,344
Property impairments	252	177	26
Taxes other than income taxes	14,679	6,937	2,740
Accretion on discounted liabilities	145	22	7
Interest and debt expense	844	566	338
Foreign currency transaction (gains) losses	(36)	24	11
Minority interests and preferred dividend requirements of capital trusts	20	48	53
Total costs and expenses	96,788	55,060	21,789
Income from continuing operations before income taxes and subsidiary equity transactions	8,309	2,141	3,241
Gain on subsidiary equity transactions	28	—	—
Income from continuing operations before income taxes	$ 8,337	$ 2,141	$ 3,241

NOTES TO CONSOLIDATED FINANCIAL STATEMENTS

Note 1 (In Part): Accounting Policies

Consolidation Principles and Investments

Consolidation decisions are based on the risk, rewards and voting rights associated with our interest in an entity. Entities that are determined to be Variable Interest Entities (VIEs), as defined by Financial Accounting Standards Board (FASB) Interpretation No. 46, as revised, (FIN 46) will be consolidated if we are the primary beneficiary of that entity. For entities that are not VIEs under FIN 46, we consolidate majority-owned, controlled subsidiaries. The equity method is used to account for investments in affiliates in which we exert significant influence, generally having a 20 to 50 percent ownership interest. We also use the equity method for our 50.1 percent and 57.1 percent non-controlling interests in Petrozuata C.A. and Hamaca Holding LLC, respectively, located in Venezuela because the minority shareholders have substantive participating rights, under which all substantive operating decisions (e.g., annual budgets, major financings, selection of senior operating management, etc.) require joint approvals. The cost method is used when we do not have significant influence. Undivided interests in oil and gas joint ventures, pipelines, natural gas plants, certain transportation assets and Canadian Syncrude mining operations are consolidated on a proportionate basis. Other securities and investments, excluding marketable securities, are generally carried at cost.

Note 7—Subsidiary Equity Transactions

ConocoPhillips, through various affiliates, and its unaffiliated co-venturers received final approvals from authorities in June 2003 to proceed with the natural gas development phase of the Bayu-Undan project in the Timor Sea. The natural gas development phase of the project includes a pipeline from the offshore Bayu-Undan field to Darwin, Australia, and a liquefied natural gas facility, also located in Darwin. The pipeline portion of the project is owned and operated by an unincorporated joint venture, while the liquefied natural gas facility is owned and operated by Darwin LNG Pty Ltd (DLNG). Both of these entities are consolidated subsidiaries of ConocoPhillips.

In June 2003, as part of a broad Bayu-Undan ownership interest re-alignment with co-venturers, these entities issued equity and sold interests to the co-venturers (as described below), which resulted in a gain of $28 million before-tax, $25 million after-tax, in 2003. This non-operating gain is shown in the consolidated statement of income in the line item entitled "Gain on subsidiary equity transactions."

DLNG

DLNG issued 118.9 million shares of stock, valued at 1 Australian dollar per share, to co-venturers for 118.9 million Australian dollars ($76.2 million U.S. dollars), reducing our ownership interest in DLNG from 100 percent to 56.72 percent. The transaction resulted in a before-tax gain of $21 million in the consolidated financial statements. Deferred income taxes were not recognized because this was an issuance of common stock and therefore not taxable.

Unincorporated Pipeline Joint Venture

The co-venturers purchased pro-rata interests in the pipeline assets held by ConocoPhillips Pipeline Australia Pty Ltd for $26.6 million U.S. dollars and contributed the purchased assets to the unincorporated joint venture, reducing our ownership interest from 100 percent to 56.72 percent. The transaction resulted in a before-tax gain of $7 million. A deferred tax liability of $1.3 million was recorded in connection with the transaction.

Note 9—Investments and Long-Term Receivables

Components of investments and long-term receivables at December 31 were:

(Millions of dollars)	2003	2002
Investments in and advances to affiliated companies	$6,258	$5,900
Long-term receivables	476	526
Other investments	524	395
	$7,258	$6,821

At December 31, 2003, retained earnings included $835 million related to the undistributed earnings of affiliated companies, and distributions received from affiliates were $496 million, $313 million and $163 million in 2003, 2002 and 2001, respectively.

Equity Investments

We own or owned investments in chemicals, heavy-oil projects, oil and gas transportation, coal mining and other industries. The affiliated companies for which we use the equity method of accounting include, among others, the following companies:

- Chevron Phillips Chemical Co. LLC (CPChem)—50 percent ownership interest—manufactures and markets petrochemicals and plastics;
- Duke Energy Field Services, LLC (DEFS)—30.3 percent ownership interest—owns and operates gas plants, gathering systems, storage facilities and fractionation plants;
- Hamaca Holding LLC—57.1 percent non-controlling ownership interest—currently building facilities to extract extra heavy crude oil from reserves in Eastern Venezuela;
- Merey Sweeney L.P. (MSLP)—50 percent ownership interest—processes heavy crude oil into intermediate products for the Sweeney, Texas, refinery;
- Petrovera Resources Limited—46.7 percent ownership interest—owns, operates and finances heavy-oil producing properties in Western Canada. On February 18, 2004, we sold our interest in this joint venture; and
- Petrozuata C.A.—50.1 percent non-controlling ownership interest—produces extra heavy crude oil and upgrades it into medium grade crude oil at Jose on the northern coast of Venezuela.

Summarized 100 percent financial information for equity-basis investments in affiliated companies, combined, was as follows:

(Millions of dollars)

2003	DEFS	CPChem	Other Equity Companies	Total
Revenues	$8,886	$7,018	$13,873	$29,777
Income before income taxes	268	12	1,753	2,033
Net income	214	7	1,274	1,495
Current assets	1,201	1,636	6,163	9,000
Noncurrent assets	5,313	4,606	23,776	33,695
Current liabilities	1,274	1,184	5,909	8,367
Noncurrent liabilities	2,376	1,298	7,629	11,303

2002				
Revenues	$5,992	$5,473	$ 5,378	$16,843
Income (loss) before income taxes	(37)	(24)	776	715
Net income (loss)	(47)	(30)	751	674
Current assets	1,182	1,561	5,783	8,526
Noncurrent assets	5,417	4,548	14,386	24,351
Current liabilities	1,504	1,051	5,046	7,601
Noncurrent liabilities	2,320	1,307	9,713	13,340

2001				
Revenues	$8,321	$6,010	$ 1,555	$15,886
Income (loss) before income taxes	367	(431)	607	543
Net income (loss)	364	(480)	414	298

Our share of income taxes incurred directly by the equity companies is reported in equity in earnings of affiliates, and as such is not included in income taxes in our consolidated financial statements.

Duke Energy Field Services, LLC

DEFS owns and operates gas plants, gathering systems, storage facilities and fractionation plants. At December 31, 2003, the book value of our common investment in DEFS was $212 million. Our 30.3 percent share of the net assets of DEFS was $831 million. This basis difference of $619 million is being amortized on a straight-line basis through 2014 consistent with the remaining estimated useful lives of DEFS' properties, plants and equipment. Included in net income for 2003, 2002 and 2001 was after-tax income of $36 million, $35 million and $36 million, respectively, representing the amortization of the basis difference.

DEFS supplies a substantial portion of its natural gas liquids to us and CPChem under a supply agreement that continues until December 31, 2014. This purchase commitment is on an "if-produced, will-purchase" basis so it has no fixed production schedule, but has been, and is expected to be, a relatively stable purchase pattern over the term of the contract. Natural gas liquids are purchased under this agreement at various published market index prices, less transportation and fractionation fees.

On December 31, 2003, DEFS redeemed the remaining $75 million of its preferred member interests. We received our 30.3 percent share, a $23 million distribution representing the return of our preferred member interests.

Chevron Phillips Chemical Company LLC

CPChem manufactures and markets petrochemicals and plastics. At December 31, 2003, the book value of our investment in CPChem was $1,917 million. Our 50 percent share of the total net assets of CPChem was $1,755 million. This basis difference of $162 million is being amortized through 2020, consistent with the remaining estimated useful lives of CPChem properties, plants and equipment.

We have multiple supply and purchase agreements in place with CPChem, ranging in initial terms from one to 99 years, with extension options. These agreements cover sales and purchases of refined products, solvents, and petrochemical and natural gas liquids feedstocks, as well as fuel oils and gases. Delivery quantities vary by product, and are generally on an "if-produced, will-purchase" basis. All products are purchased and sold under specified pricing formulas based on various published pricing indices, consistent with terms extended to third-party customers.

2.117

STANDARD COMMERCIAL CORPORATION (MAR)

Consolidated Balance Sheets

(In thousands)	2003	2002
Current assets	$ 538,953	$ 469,898
Property, plant and equipment	161,190	134,919
Investment in affiliates (Notes 1 and 6)	10,542	9,569
Goodwill	11,289	11,289
Other assets	26,326	24,967
Total assets	$ 748,300	$ 650,642

Consolidated Statements of Income and Comprehensive Income (Loss)

(In thousands)	2003	2002	2001
Sales	$993,716	$942,296	$1,067,966
Cost of sales:			
Materials, services and supplies	823,909	781,293	913,411
Interest	14,975	16,954	26,798
Gross profit	154,832	144,049	127,757
Selling, general and administrative expenses	89,090	78,133	80,487
Other interest expense	4,368	8,922	10,790
Other income/ (expense)—net	4,172	3,296	(882)
Income before income taxes	65,546	60,290	35,598
Income taxes	24,555	23,715	15,726
Income after income taxes	40,991	36,575	19,872
Minority interests	49	—	(644)
Equity in earnings/(loss) of affiliates (Note 6)	664	(356)	(62)
Income from continuing operations	$ 41,704	$ 36,219	$ 19,166

NOTES TO CONSOLIDATED FINANCIAL STATEMENTS

1 (In Part): Significant Accounting Policies

Consolidation

The accounts of all subsidiary companies are included in the consolidated financial statements and all intercompany transactions have been eliminated. Investments in affiliated companies are accounted for by the equity method of accounting.

6. Affiliated Companies

a) Net investment in affiliated companies are represented by the following:

(In thousands)	2003	2002
Net current assets	$ 10,270	$ 9,822
Property, plant and equipment	34,649	33,480
Other long-term liabilities	(16,309)	(17,026)
Interests of other shareholders	(18,325)	(16,936)
Company's interest	10,285	9,340
Goodwill	257	229
Net investments	$ 10,542	$ 9,569

b) The results of operations of affiliated companies were:

(In thousands)	2003	2002	2001
Sales	$149,749	$98,385	$92,043
Income before taxes	$ 2,929	$ 1,010	$ 2,089
Income taxes	1,725	1,032	845
Net income/(loss)	$ 1,204	$ (22)	$ 1,244
Company's share of equity in earnings	$ 664	$ (356)	$ (62)
Dividends received	$ 83	$ 52	$ 65

c) Balances with the unconsolidated affiliates are for the procurement of tobacco inventory as follows:

(In thousands)	2003	2002	2001
Purchases of tobacco	$ 49,745	$ 32,815	$ 42,311
Receivables from equity investees	14,589	13,462	9,529
Advances on purchases of tobacco	14,016	9,122	5,849
Payables to equity investees	367	—	1,466

The Company's significant affiliates and percentage of ownership at March 31, 2003 follow: Adams International Ltd., 49.0% (Thailand), Siam Tobacco Export Corporation Ltd., 49.0% (Thailand), Transcontinental Tobacco India Private Ltd. 49.0% (India), Stansum Leaf Tobacco Company Ltd., 50.0% (Kyrgyzstan), Jandakot Wool Washing Pty. Ltd., 24.9% (Australia), and Independent Wool Dumpers Pty Ltd., 16.8% (Australia). Audited financial statements of affiliates are obtained annually.

2.118

THE WASHINGTON POST COMPANY (DEC)

Consolidated Balance Sheets

(In thousands)	2003	2002
Total current assets	$ 495,836	$ 382,955
Property, plant and equipment		
Buildings	288,961	283,233
Machinery, equipment and fixtures	1,656,111	1,551,931
Leasehold improvements	102,753	85,720
	2,047,825	1,920,884
Less accumulated depreciation	(1,084,790)	(926,385)
	963,035	994,499
Land	32,234	34,530
Construction in progress	56,104	65,371
	1,051,373	1,094,400
Investments in marketable equity securities	245,335	214,780
Investments in affiliates	61,312	70,703
Goodwill, net	965,694	770,861
Indefinite-lived intangible assets, net	486,656	482,419
Amortized intangible assets, net	5,226	2,153
Prepaid pension cost	514,801	493,786
Deferred charges and other assets	75,325	71,837
	$ 3,901,558	$3,583,894

Consolidated Statements of Income

(In thousands)	2003	2002	2001
Operating revenues			
Advertising	$1,233,358	$1,226,834	$1,209,327
Circulation and subscriber	706,248	675,136	653,028
Education	838,077	621,125	493,271
Other	61,228	61,108	55,398
	2,838,911	2,584,203	2,411,024
Operating costs and expenses			
Operating	1,549,262	1,369,955	1,387,101
Selling, general and administrative	792,292	664,095	586,758
Gain on sale of land	(41,747)	—	—
Depreciation of property, plant and equipment	173,848	171,908	138,300
Amortization of goodwill and other intangibles	1,436	655	78,933
	2,475,091	2,206,613	2,191,092
Income from operations	363,820	377,590	219,932
Equity in losses of affiliates	(9,766)	(19,308)	(68,659)
Interest income	953	332	2,167
Interest expense	(27,804)	(33,819)	(49,640)
Other income (expense), net	55,385	28,873	283,739
Income before income taxes and cumulative effect of change in accounting principle	$ 382,588	$ 353,668	$ 387,539

NOTES TO CONSOLIDATED FINANCIAL STATEMENTS

A (In Part): Summary of Significant Accounting Policies

Investments in Affiliates

The Company uses the equity method of accounting for its investments in and earnings or losses of affiliates that it does not control but over which it does exert significant influence. The Company considers whether the fair values of any of its equity method investments have declined below their carrying value whenever adverse events or changes in circumstances indicate that recorded values may not be recoverable. If the Company considered any such decline to be other than temporary (based on various factors, including historical financial results, product development activities and the overall health of the affiliate's industry), a write-down would be recorded to estimated fair value.

C (In Part): Investments

Investments in Affiliates

The Company's investments in affiliates at December 28, 2003 and December 29, 2002 include the following (in thousands):

	2003	2002
BrassRing	$11,892	$13,658
Bowater Mersey Paper Company	48,559	42,519
International Herald Tribune	—	13,776
Los Angeles Times—Washington Post News Service	861	750
	$61,312	$70,703

At the end of 2003, the Company's investments in affiliates consisted of a 49.3 percent interest in BrassRing LLC, an internet-based hiring management company; a 49 percent interest in the common stock of Bowater Mersey Paper Company Limited, which owns and operates a newsprint mill in Nova Scotia; and a 50 percent common stock interest in the Los Angeles Times—Washington Post News Service, Inc. Summarized financial data for the affiliates operations are as follows (in thousands):

	2003	2002	2001
Financial position:			
Working capital	$ 11,108	$ 10,366	$ (8,767)
Property, plant and equipment	140,917	135,013	126,682
Total assets	214,658	235,208	246,321
Long-term debt	—	—	—
Net equity	149,584	138,723	125,211
Results of operations:			
Operating revenues	$174,505	$263,709	$317,389
Operating loss	(18,753)	(21,725)	(14,793)
Net loss	(20,164)	(36,326)	(157,409)

The following table summarizes the status and results of the Company's investments in affiliates (in thousands):

	2003	2002
Beginning investment	$ 70,703	$ 80,936
Additional investment	5,976	7,610
Equity in losses	(9,766)	(19,308)
Dividends and distributions received	(750)	(710)
Foreign currency translation	9,205	2,175
Sale of interest	(14,056)	—
Ending investment	$ 61,312	$ 70,703

In December 2001, BrassRing, Inc. was restructured and the Company's interest in BrassRing, Inc. was converted into an interest in the newly-formed BrassRing LLC. At December 30, 2001, the Company held a 39.7 percent interest in the BrassRing LLC common equity and a $14.9 million Subordinated Convertible Promissory Note ("Note") from BrassRing LLC. In February 2002, the Note was converted into Preferred Units, which are convertible at the Company's option to BrassRing LLC common equity. Assuming the conversion of the Preferred Units, the Company's common equity interest in BrassRing LLC would have been approximately 49.5 percent.

BrassRing accounted for $7.7 million of the 2003 equity in losses of affiliates, compared to $13.9 million in 2002 and $75.1 million in 2001. In 2001, BrassRing recorded a significant non-cash goodwill and other intangibles impairment charge primarily to reduce the carrying value of its career fair business. As a substantial portion of BrassRing's losses arose from goodwill and intangible amortization expense in 2001, the $75.1 million of equity in affiliate losses recorded by the Company in 2001 did not require significant funding by the Company.

On January 1, 2003, the Company sold its 50 percent interest in The International Herald Tribune newspaper for $65 million; the Company reported a $49.8 million pre-tax gain that is included in "Other income (expense), net" in the Consolidated Statements of Income.

Fair Value

2.119

EARTHLINK, INC. (DEC)

(In thousands)	2002	2003
Total current assets	$ 584,221	$ 500,577
Long-term investments in marketable securities	24,394	49,037
Other long-term assets	7,325	12,101
Property and equipment, net	168,877	108,810
Subscriber bases, net	118,354	38,264
Goodwill and other indefinite life intangible assets	120,382	118,231
Total assets	$ 1,023,553	$ 827,020

NOTES TO CONSOLIDATED FINANCIAL STATEMENTS

2 (In Part): Summary of Significant Accounting Policies

Investments (In Part)

Investments in marketable securities are accounted for in accordance with SFAS No. 115, "Accounting for Certain Investments in Debt and Equity Securities." All investments with original maturities greater than three months and with maturities less than one year from the balance sheet date are considered short-term investments. Investments with maturities greater than one year from the balance sheet date are considered long-term investments. The investments are of investment grade and include corporate bonds, asset-backed securities and government agency notes.

The Company has classified all short- and long-term investments in marketable securities as available-for-sale. Available-for-sale securities are carried at fair value, with any unrealized gains and losses, net of tax, included in unrealized gains (losses) on investments as a separate component of stockholders' equity. Realized gains and losses are included in interest income and other, net, in the Consolidated Statements of Operations and are determined on a specific identification basis.

6. Investments in Marketable Securities

Short- and long-term investments in marketable securities consist of debt securities classified as available-for-sale and have maturities greater than 90 days from the date of acquisition. The Company has invested primarily in U.S. corporate notes and asset-backed securities, all of which have a minimum investment rating of A, and government agency notes. The Company determines realized gains and losses on a specific identification basis. The realized gains and losses are included in interest income and other, net, in the accompanying Consolidated Statements of Operations. The following table summarizes proceeds received from the sale of available-for-sale securities and realized gains and losses from the sale of available-for-sale securities for the years ended December 31, 2001, 2002 and 2003:

(In thousands)	2001	2002	2003
Proceeds from the sale of investments	$ —	$62,696	$52,851
Realized gains from the sale of investments	—	371	336
Realized losses from the sale of investments	—	(324)	(10)

The following table summarizes unrealized gains and losses on the Company's investments in marketable securities based primarily on quoted market prices at December 31, 2002 and 2003:

	2002				2003			
(In thousands)	Amortized Cost	Gross Unrealized Losses	Gross Unrealized Gains	Estimated Fair Value	Amortized Cost	Gross Unrealized Losses	Gross Unrealized Gains	Estimated Fair Value
Less than 12 months								
U.S. corporate notes	$ 87,427	$(15)	$414	$ 87,826	$ 67,319	$ (42)	$ —	$ 67,277
Government agency notes	1,502	(12)	—	1,490	3,100	—	—	3,100
Asset-backed securities	19,542	—	120	19,662	18,786	(75)	—	18,711
	$108,471	$(27)	$534	$108,978	$ 89,205	$(117)	$ —	$ 89,088
12 months or longer								
U.S. corporate notes	$ 22,566	$(12)	$ 34	$ 22,588	$ 23,334	$ —	$ 11	$ 23,345
Government agency notes	—	—	—	—	20,250	—	6	20,256
Asset-backed securities	1,804	(2)	4	1,806	5,453	(17)	—	5,436
	$ 24,370	$(14)	$ 38	$ 24,394	$ 49,037	$ (17)	$ 17	$ 49,037
Total								
U.S. corporate notes	$109,993	$(27)	$448	$110,414	$ 90,653	$ (42)	$ 11	$ 90,622
Government agency notes	1,502	(12)	—	1,490	23,350	—	6	23,356
Asset-backed securities	21,346	(2)	124	21,468	24,239	(92)	—	24,147
	$132,841	$(41)	$572	$133,372	$138,242	$(134)	$ 17	$138,125

2.120

EBAY INC. (DEC)

Consolidated Balance Sheet

(In thousands)	2002	2003
Total current assets	$1,468,458	$2,145,882
Long-term investments	470,227	934,171
Restricted cash and investments	134,644	127,432
Property and equipment, net	218,028	601,785
Goodwill	1,456,024	1,719,311
Intangible assets, net	279,465	274,057
Other assets	13,380	17,496
	$4,040,226	$5,820,134

Consolidated Statement of Income

(In thousands)	2001	2002	2003
Income from operations	$ 140,426	$ 354,197	$ 629,241
Interest and other income, net	41,613	49,209	37,803
Interest expense	(2,851)	(1,492)	(4,314)
Impairment of certain equity investments	(16,245)	(3,781)	(1,230)
Income before cumulative effect of accounting change, income taxes and minority interests	162,943	398,133	661,500
Provision for income taxes	(80,009)	(145,946)	(206,738)
Minority interests	7,514	(2,296)	(7,578)
Income before cumulative effect of accounting change	$ 90,448	$ 249,891	$ 447,184

NOTES TO CONSOLIDATED FINANCIAL STATEMENTS

Note 1 (In Part): The Company and Summary of Significant Accounting Policies

Fair Value of Financial Instruments (In Part)

Short and long-term investments, which include marketable equity securities, municipal, government and corporate bonds, are classified as available-for-sale and reported at fair value using the specific identification method. Realized gains and losses are included in earnings and were immaterial in all periods presented. Unrealized gains and losses are excluded from earnings and reported as a component of other comprehensive income (loss), net of related estimated tax provisions or benefits. Additionally, we assess whether an other-than-temporary impairment loss on our investments has occurred due to declines in fair value or other market conditions. Declines in fair value that are considered other than temporary are recorded as an impairment of certain equity investments in the consolidated statement of income.

Note 5—Investments

At December 31, 2002 and 2003, short and long-term investments were classified as available-for-sale securities, except for restricted cash and investments, and are reported at fair value as follows (in thousands):

	2002			
	Gross Amortized Cost	Gross Unrealized Gains	Gross Unrealized Losses	Estimated Fair Value
Short-term investments:				
Municipal bonds and notes	$ 46,158	$ 157	$ —	$ 46,315
Government and agency securities	—	—	—	—
Time deposits and other	43,299	152	(76)	43,375
Total	$ 89,457	$ 309	$ (76)	$ 89,690
Long-term investments:				
Restricted cash and investments	$133,541	$1,103	$ —	$134,644
Municipal bonds and notes	388,535	2,320	—	390,855
Government and agency securities	35,232	281	(291)	35,222
Equity instruments	44,150	—	—	44,150
Total	$601,458	$3,704	$(291)	$604,871

	2003			
	Gross Amortized Cost	Gross Unrealized Gains	Gross Unrealized Losses	Estimated Fair Value
Short-term investments:				
Municipal bonds and notes	$ 8,065	$ —	$ —	$ 8,065
Corporate securities	223,400	2	(43)	223,359
Government and agency securities	60,419	259	—	60,678
Time deposits and other	48,474	—	—	48,474
Total	$ 340,358	$261	$ (43)	$ 340,576
Long-term investments:				
Restricted cash and investments	$ 127,544	$328	$ (440)	$ 127,432
Corporate securities	458,997	365	(491)	458,871
Government and agency securities	462,879	236	(2,067)	461,048
Equity instruments	14,252	—	—	14,252
Total	$1,063,672	$929	$(2,998)	$1,061,603

The following table summarizes the fair value and gross unrealized losses of our long-term investments, aggregated by type of investment instrument and length of time that individual securities have been in a continuous unrealized loss position, at December 31, 2003 (in thousands):

	Fair Value	Gross Unrealized Losses
Restricted cash and investments	$ 63,331	$ (440)
Corporate securities	431,689	(534)
Government and agency securities	340,863	(2,067)
Total	$835,883	$(3,041)

At December 31, 2003, our gross unrealized losses on investments were all in loss positions for less than 12 months.

Our investment portfolio consists of both corporate and government securities that have a maximum maturity of three years. The longer the duration of these securities, the more susceptible they are to changes in market interest rates and bond yields. As yields increase, those securities purchased with a lower yield-at-cost show a mark-to-market unrealized loss. All unrealized losses are due to changes in interest rates and bond yields. We expect to realize the full value of all these investments upon maturity or sale. The losses on these securities have an average duration of approximately 3.8 months.

The estimated fair value of short and long-term investments classified by date of contractual maturity at December 31, 2003 are as follows (in thousands):

	2003
Due within one year or less	$ 340,576
Due after one year through two years	286,581
Due after two years through three years	633,338
Due after three years through four years	—
Restricted cash and investments expiring in less than five years	127,432
Equity investments	14,252
	$1,402,179

During 2001, 2002 and 2003, we recorded impairment charges totaling $16.2 million, $3.8 million and $1.2 million, respectively, as a result of the deterioration of the financial condition of certain of our private and public equity investees that were considered to be other than temporary.

2.121

THE FAIRCHILD CORPORATION (JUN)

(In thousands)	2003	2002
Total current assets	$106,804	$341,916
Property, plant and equipment, net of accumulated depreciation of $26,081 and $22,228	126,574	119,757
Net noncurrent assets held for sale	312	9,928
Noncurrent assets of discontinued operations	125	384,145
Goodwill	10,821	17,438
Investments and advances, affiliated companies	7,136	3,261
Prepaid pension assets	59,892	64,693
Deferred loan costs	1,071	10,925
Long-term investments	61,486	5,360
Notes receivable	7,801	11,275
Deferred income tax assets	—	16,611
Other assets	8,527	6,809
Total assets	$390,549	$992,118

NOTES TO CONSOLIDATED FINANCIAL STATEMENTS (In thousands)

1 (In Part): Summary of Significant Accounting Policies

Restricted Cash and Investments

On June 30, 2003 and June 30, 2002, we had restricted cash and investments of $55,107 and $472, respectively, all of which are maintained as collateral for certain debt facilities, our interest rate contract and escrow arrangements. The restricted funds are invested in money market funds, U.S. government securities, or high investment grade corporate bonds. Restricted cash and investments are classified with short-term and long-term investments on June 30, 2003 and classified as short-term investments on June 30, 2002.

Investments

Management determines the appropriate classification of our investments at the time of acquisition and reevaluates such determination at each balance sheet date. Trading securities are carried at fair value, with unrealized holding gains and losses included in investment income (loss). Available-for-sale securities are carried at fair value, with unrealized holding gains and losses, net of tax, reported as a separate component of stockholders' equity. Investments in equity securities and limited partnerships that do not have readily determinable fair values are stated at cost and are categorized as other investments. Realized gains and losses are determined using the specific identification method based on the trade date of a transaction. Interest on corporate obligations, as well as dividends on preferred stock, are accrued at the balance sheet date. Investments in companies in which ownership interests range from 20 to 50 percent are accounted for using the equity method.

Fair Value of Financial Instruments (In Part)

The carrying amount reported in the consolidated balance sheets approximates the fair value for our cash and cash equivalents, investments, specified hedging agreements, short-term borrowings, current maturities of long-term debt, and all other variable rate debt (including borrowings under our credit agreements).

4. Cash Equivalents and Investments

Cash equivalents and investments at June 30, 2003 consist primarily of investments in United States government securities and investment grade corporate bonds, which are recorded at market value. Restricted cash equivalent investments are classified as short-term or long-term investments depending upon the length of the restriction period. Investments in common stock of public corporations are recorded at fair market value and classified as trading securities or available-for-sale securities. Other short-term investments and long-term investments do not have readily determinable fair values and consist primarily of investments in preferred and common shares of private companies and limited partnerships. A summary of the cash equivalents and investments held by us follows:

	Aggregate		Aggregate	
	Fair Value	Cost Basis	Fair Value	Cost Basis
Cash and cash equivalents:				
U.S. government securities	$ 10,829	$ 10,829	$ —	$ —
Money market and other cash funds	1,188	1,188	14,810	14,810
Total cash and cash equivalents	$ 12,017	$ 12,017	$14,810	$14,810
Short-term investments:				
U.S. government securities—restricted	$ 7,478	$ 7,478	$ —	$ —
Money market funds—restricted	—	—	472	472
Trading securities—corporate bonds	40,426	39,913	—	—
Trading securities—equity securities	388	607	355	574
Available-for-sale equity securities	56	199	84	200
Other investments	55	55	55	55
Total short-term investments	$ 48,403	$ 48,252	$ 966	$ 1,301
Long-term investments:				
U.S. government securities—restricted	$ 24,364	$ 24,364	$ —	$ —
Money market funds—restricted	220	220	—	—
Corporate bonds—restricted	23,045	23,033	—	—
Available-for-sale equity securities	9,571	9,215	1,074	3,329
Other investments	4,286	4,286	4,286	4,286
Total long-term investments	$ 61,486	$ 61,118	$ 5,360	$ 7,615
Total cash equivalents and investments	$121,906	$121,387	$21,136	$23,726

On June 30, 2003 and June 30, 2002, we had restricted investments of $55,107 and $472, respectively, all of which are maintained as collateral for certain debt facilities, our interest rate contract and escrow arrangements. The restricted funds are invested in money market funds, U.S. government securities, or high investment grade corporate bonds.

On June 30, 2003, we had gross unrealized holding gains from available-for-sale securities of $368 and gross unrealized losses from available-for-sale securities of $142. In 2003, we recognized $2,395 in realized loss on available-for-sale securities due to other than temporary declines in market value. On June 30, 2002, we had gross unrealized losses from availble-for-sale securities of $2,372. We use the specific identification method to determine the gross realized gains (losses) from sales of available-for-sale securities. Investment income (loss) is summarized as follows:

	2003	2002	2001
Gross realized gain from sales of available-for-sale securities	$ 633	$ 30	$10,732
Gross realized loss from sales of trading securities	—	(811)	—
Change in unrealized holding gain (loss) from trading securities	516	486	(668)
Gross realized loss from impairments	(2,395)	(2,296)	(2,376)
Dividend income	1,226	1,599	679
	$ (20)	$ (992)	$ 8,367

Cost

2.122

DATASCOPE CORP. (JUN)

(In thousands)	2003	2002
Total current assets	$177,516	$167,569
Property, plant and equipment, net	89,607	89,897
Long-term investments	36,827	30,525
Other assets	34,882	28,031
	$338,832	$316,022

NOTES TO CONSOLIDATED FINANCIAL STATEMENTS
(Dollars in thousands)

2 (In Part): Financial Instruments

The fair value of accounts receivable and payable are assumed to equal their carrying value because of their short maturity. Fair values of short-term investments are based upon quoted market prices, including accrued interest, and approximate their carrying values due to their short maturities. Fair values of long-term investments, which mature in years 2004 to 2013, are also based upon quoted market prices and include accrued interest. Investments in preferred stock are carried at cost and evaluated for impairment. We determined that our investment portfolio will be held-to-maturity and is therefore carried at amortized cost. Investments in preferred stock are accounted for under the provision of SFAS No. 115, "Accounting for Certain Investments in Debt and Equity Securities," or carried at cost, as appropriate.

As of June 30, 2003, investments were classified as follows:

| | Carrying Value | Gross Unrealized | | Fair Value |
		Gains	Losses	
Short term				
U.S. treasury securities	$27,878	$ 107	$ 1	$27,984
Short-term total	$27,878	$ 107	$ 1	$27,984
Long term				
U.S. treasury securities	$27,730	$1,099	$138	$28,691
AAA—rated corporate notes	2,097	294	—	2,391
Preferred stock	7,000	—	—	7,000
Long-term total	$36,827	$1,393	$138	$38,082
Totals	$64,705	$1,500	$139	$66,066

As of June 30, 2002, investments were classified as follows:

| | Carrying Value | Gross Unrealized | | Fair Value |
		Gains	Losses	
Short term				
U.S. treasury securities	$ 7,963	$ 2	$ —	$ 7,965
AAA—rated corporate notes	6,826	6	24	6,808
Tax-exempt securities	1,028	—	—	1,028
Short-term total	$15,817	$ 8	$24	$15,801
Long term				
U.S. treasury securities	$23,414	$252	$ 4	$23,662
AAA—rated corporate notes	2,111	30	—	2,141
Preferred stock	5,000	—	—	5,000
Long-term total	$30,525	$282	$ 4	$30,803
Totals	$46,342	$290	$28	$46,604

Since we hold all short- and long-term securities until maturity, such investments are subject to little market risk. We have not incurred losses related to these investments.

Contractual maturities of debt securities as of June 30, 2003 are as follows:

Held to Maturity	Carrying Value	Fair Value
Due within one year	$27,878	$27,984
Due after one year through five years	8,273	8,591
Due after five years through ten years	21,554	22,491
	$57,705	$59,066

NONCURRENT RECEIVABLES

2.123 ARB No. 43, Chapter 3A, *Current Assets and Current Liabilities*, states that the concept of current assets excludes "receivables arising from unusual transactions (such as the sale of capital assets, or loans or advances to affiliates, officers, or employees) which are not expected to be collected within twelve months."

2.124 *SFAS No. 107* defines noncurrent receivables as financial instruments. *SFAS No. 107*, as amended by *SFAS No. 133*, requires disclosure of both the fair value and the bases for estimating the fair value of noncurrent receivables unless it is not practicable to estimate that value. 61 survey companies made 73 fair value disclosures. 10 of those disclosures used market or broker quotes of the noncurrent receivables to determine fair value. 37 of those disclosures stated that either discounted cash flows or market prices of similar instruments were used to estimate fair value. 4 of those disclosures estimated fair value using other valuation methods. 41 disclosures presented carrying amounts which approximated fair value of noncurrent receivables. In addition, there were 25 disclosures in which carrying value was compared to fair value in an exposition or a table. One disclosure stated it was not practicable to estimate fair value.

2.125 *SFAC No. 7* provides a framework for using future cash flows and present value as the basis for accounting measurements of fair value of an asset or a liability at initial recognition or fresh-start measurements and for future-cash-flow-based amortization techniques, such as interest method amortization. Fresh-start measurements are measurements in periods following initial recognition that establish a new carrying amount unrelated to previous amounts and accounting conventions.

2.126 When observable marketplace-determined values are not available, discounted cash flows are often used to estimate fair value. Accounting applications of present value typically use a single set of estimated cash flows and a risk-adjusted discount rate. This Statement introduces the expected cash flow approach, which differs from the traditional approach by focusing on explicit assumptions about the range of possible cash outcomes and their respective probabilities.

2.127 While *SFAC No. 7* does not require modification of any existing pronouncements, its concepts may be used to determine fair value. This Standard will be used in developing future accounting standards. No data on the use of expected cash flow approach in discounted cash flow applications were compiled.

2.128 *SFAS No. 125*, as amended by *SFAS No. 133* and as replaced by *SFAS No. 140*, establishes criteria for determining whether a transfer of financial assets in exchange for cash or other consideration should be accounted for as a sale or as a pledge of collateral in a secured borrowing. This topic and the related examples are covered under the "Receivables Sold or Collateralized" part of this section.

2.129 Table 2-18 summarizes the balance sheet captions used to describe noncurrent receivables. Examples of noncurrent receivable presentations and disclosures follow.

2.130

TABLE 2-18: NONCURRENT RECEIVABLES

	2003	2002	2001	2000
Caption Title				
Long-term receivables....................	28	44	32	28
Notes receivable............................	21	25	30	24
Finance receivable.........................	22	17	16	12
Receivables from related party......	13	14	N/C*	N/C*
Insurance receivable......................	12	11	11	10
Other..	40	35	33	36
Receivables combined with other investments, deposits, etc.........	9	5	12	23
Total Presentations......................	**145**	**151**	**134**	**133**
Number of Companies				
Presenting noncurrent receivables................................	130	135	116	114
Not presenting noncurrent receivables................................	470	465	484	486
Total Companies..........................	**600**	**600**	**600**	**600**

* N/C = Not compiled. Line item was not included in the table for the year shown.

2.131

FEDDERS CORPORATION (AUG)

(Amounts in thousands)	2003	2002
Total current assets	$212,709	$166,911
Net property, plant and equipment	55,860	66,846
Deferred income taxes	8,224	2,867
Goodwill	78,630	90,536
Other intangible assets	1,788	1,556
Other assets	35,718	37,412
Total assets	$392,929	$366,128

NOTES TO CONSOLIDATED FINANCIAL STATEMENTS
(Amounts in thousands)

1 (In Part): Description of Business and Summary of Significant Accounting Policies

Other Assets

Other assets consist of the following at August 31:

	2003	2002
Note due from an executive officer (note 11)	$ 6,000	$ 6,000
Unamortized deferred finance costs, amortized over the life of the debt	2,413	3,112
Cash surrender value of life insurance	7,939	7,227
Supplemental retirement assets	7,389	8,858
Investment in unconsolidated joint ventures	9,979	9,784
Other	1,998	2,431
	$35,718	$37,412

11 (In Part): Pension Plans and Other Compensation Arrangements

In fiscal 2002, the Company entered into an employment agreement with an officer that has a term that extends through September 2006. The agreement provides for annual base and incentive compensation, a non-interest bearing, uncollateralized loan, which the Company expects to collect in six yearly installments over the six-year period following the officer's termination of employment (see note 1), a retirement contribution that vests over the life of the agreement and restricted stock, of which a portion vests in January 2004 and a portion vests in January 2007. The Company is amortizing the retirement contribution over the vesting period and the restricted stock, commencing on the date of grant, over the remaining life of the agreement.

2.132

HERMAN MILLER, INC. (MAY)

(In millions)	2003	2002
Total current assets	$413.5	$386.4
Property and equipment:		
Land and improvements	19.0	18.9
Buildings and improvements	125.7	133.7
Machinery and equipment	541.4	554.0
Construction in progress	10.9	12.8
	697.0	719.4
Less: accumulated depreciation	451.3	404.0
Net property and equipment	245.7	315.4
Notes receivable, less allowances of $4.4 in 2003, and $2.0 in 2002	4.6	6.9
Goodwill	39.1	39.1
Intangible assets, net	6.3	8.5
Deferred taxes	25.9	7.3
Other assets	32.4	24.4
Total assets	$767.5	$788.0

NOTES TO THE CONSOLIDATED FINANCIAL STATEMENTS

Significant Accounting and Reporting Policies (In Part)

Notes Receivable

The notes receivable are primarily from certain independent contract office furniture dealers. These notes are the result of dealers in transition either through a change in ownership or general financial difficulty. The notes are collateralized by the assets of the dealers and bear interest based on the prevailing prime rate. Recorded reserves are based on historical credit experience, collateralization levels and the specific identification of other potential collection problems. Interest income relating to these notes was $0.7 million, $0.8 million, and $2.2 million in 2003, 2002, and 2001, respectively.

Fair Value of Financial Instruments

The carrying amount of the company's financial instruments included in current assets and current liabilities approximates fair value due to their short-term nature. The fair value of the notes receivable is estimated by discounting expected future cash flows using current interest rates at which similar loans would be made to borrowers with similar credit ratings and remaining maturities. As of May 31, 2003, and June 1, 2002, the fair value of the notes receivable approximated the carrying value. The company intends to hold these notes to maturity and has recorded allowances to reflect the terms negotiated for carrying value purposes. As of May 31, 2003, the carrying value of the company's long-term debt including both current maturities and the fair value of the company's interest rate swap arrangement was $223.0 million with a corresponding fair market value of $256.8 million. At June 1, 2002, the carrying value and fair market value was $232.4 million and $233.7 million, respectively.

2.133

SNAP-ON INCORPORATED (DEC)

(Amounts in millions)	2003	2002
Total current assets	$1,131.7	$1,051.0
Property and equipment—net	328.6	330.2
Deferred income tax benefits	16.1	60.9
Goodwill	417.6	366.4
Other intangibles—net	69.5	65.7
Other assets	175.0	119.9
Total assets	$2,138.5	$1,994.1

NOTES TO CONSOLIDATED FINANCIAL STATEMENTS

Note 5. Accounts Receivable

Accounts receivable include trade accounts, installment and other receivables, including the current portion of dealer financing receivables. The components of Snap-on's current accounts receivable as of fiscal year-end 2003 and 2002 are as follows:

(Amounts in millions)	2003	2002
Trade accounts receivable	$501.8	$497.0
Installment receivables, net of unearned finance charges of $11.4 million and $8.1 million	55.1	41.4
Other accounts receivable	34.9	59.0
Total	591.8	597.4
Allowances for doubtful accounts	(45.0)	(41.2)
Total accounts receivable—net	$546.8	$556.2

The long-term portion of accounts receivable is classified in *Other assets* on the accompanying Consolidated Balance Sheets and is comprised of installment and other receivables, including dealer financing receivables, with payment terms that are due beyond one year. The components of Snap-on's long-term accounts receivable as of fiscal year-end 2003 and 2002 are as follows:

(Amounts in millions)	2003	2002
Installment receivables, net of unearned finance charges of $9.1 million and $7.9 million	$41.9	$37.3
Other long-term accounts receivable	19.8	20.5
Total	$61.7	$57.8

Note 11 (In Part): Financial Instruments

Fair Value of Financial Instruments (In Part)

SFAS No. 107, *Disclosures about Fair Value of Financial Instruments*, requires Snap-on to disclose the fair value of financial instruments for both on- and off-balance-sheet assets and liabilities for which it is practicable to estimate that value. The following methods and assumptions were used in estimating the fair value of financial instruments.

Installment Contracts

A discounted cash flow analysis was performed over the average life of a contract using a discount rate currently available to Snap-on adjusted for credit quality, cost and profit factors. As of January 3, 2004, and December 28, 2002, the fair value was approximately $114 million and $92 million, versus a book value of $97.0 million and $78.7 million.

INTANGIBLE ASSETS

2.134 APB Opinion No. 17, *Intangible Assets*, sets forth requirements as to accounting for intangible assets. *APB Opinion No. 17* stipulates that all intangible assets acquired after October 31, 1970 or recognized in business combinations initiated after October 31, 1970 be amortized over a period not to exceed 40 years and that "financial statements should disclose the method and period of amortization."

2.135 Effective for fiscal years beginning after December 15, 2001, SFAS No. 142, *Goodwill and Other Intangible Assets*, supersedes *APB Opinion No. 17* as to intangible assets acquired on or before June 30, 2001. For intangible assets acquired after June 30, 2001, *SFAS No. 142* is effective immediately. *APB Opinion No. 17* presumes that goodwill acquired as a result of a purchase method business combination and all other intangible assets are wasting assets subject to amortization. The Opinion also mandated an arbitrary ceiling of 40 years for that amortization. *SFAS No. 142* does not presume that all intangible assets are wasting assets. Instead, goodwill and intangible assets that have indefinite useful lives will not be subject to amortization, but rather will be tested at least annually for impairment. In addition, the Standard provides specific guidance on how to determine and measure goodwill impairment. Intangible assets that have finite useful lives will continue to be amortized over their useful lives, but without the constraint of an arbitrary ceiling. *SFAS No. 142* requires additional disclosures including information about carrying amounts of goodwill and other intangible assets, and estimates as to future intangible asset amortization expense.

2.136 Table 2-19 lists those intangible assets, amortized or not, which are most frequently disclosed by the survey companies. Data for 2000 is not presented because only data for intangible assets being amortized were complied for that year. Also, Table 2-19 does not include intangible pension assets recognized when an entity records a minimum pension liability in accordance with SFAS No. 87, *Employers' Accounting for Pensions*. In 2003, 133 survey companies disclosed an intangible pension asset.

2.137 Table 2-20 summarizes the amortization periods used by the survey companies to amortize intangible assets that have finite useful lives.

2.138 Examples of intangible asset presentations and disclosures follow.

2.139

TABLE 2-19: INTANGIBLE ASSETS

	Number of Companies			
	2003	**2002**	**2001**	**2000**
Goodwill recognized in a business combination	506	505	513	N/C*
Trademarks, brand names, copyrights	226	165	132	N/C*
Customer lists/relationships	157	121	52	N/C*
Patents, patent rights	136	130	73	N/C*
Technology	114	95	52	N/C*
Licenses, franchises, memberships	92	60	48	N/C*
Noncompete covenants	86	76	29	N/C*
Other—described	136	127	73	N/C*

* N/C = Not compiled. Line was not included in the table for the year shown.

2.140

TABLE 2-20: AMORTIZATION PERIOD—2003

			Number of Companies			
Period	Trademarks	Patents	Lists	Technology	Licenses	Noncompete
Exceeding 40..................	2	—	1	—	2	1
31–40.............................	4	1	2	1	2	0
21–30.............................	14	6	6	4	5	2
11–20.............................	27	33	33	18	12	10
Not exceeding 10..........	29	28	52	42	21	43
Legal/estimated life........	36	46	40	30	23	19
Other..............................	22	22	21	15	11	11

Goodwill

2.141

3M COMPANY (DEC)

(Dollars in millions)	2003	2002
Total current assets	$ 7,720	$ 6,059
Investments	218	238
Property, plant and equipment—net	5,609	5,621
Goodwill	2,419	1,898
Intangible assets	274	269
Other assets	1,360	1,244
Total assets	$17,600	$15,329

NOTES TO CONSOLIDATED FINANCIAL STATEMENTS

Note 1 (In Part): Significant Accounting Policies

Goodwill

Goodwill is the excess of cost of an acquired entity over the amounts assigned to assets acquired and liabilities assumed in a business combination. Effective January 1, 2002, with the adoption of SFAS No. 142, "Goodwill and Other Intangible Assets", goodwill is not amortized. Prior to January 1, 2002, goodwill was amortized on a straight-line basis, ranging from 5 to 40 years. Beginning January 1, 2002, goodwill is tested for impairment annually, and will be tested for impairment between annual tests if an event occurs or circumstances change that would indicate the carrying amount may be impaired. Impairment testing for goodwill is done at a reporting unit level. Reporting units are one level below the business segment level, but can be combined when reporting units within the same segment have similar economic characteristics. Under the criteria set forth by SFAS No. 142, 3M has 18 reporting units based on the current structure effective January 1, 2003. The vast majority of goodwill relates to and is assigned directly to a specific reporting unit. An impairment loss generally would be recognized when the carrying amount of the reporting unit's net assets exceeds the estimated fair value of the reporting unit. The estimated fair value of a reporting unit is determined using earnings for the reporting unit multiplied by a price/earnings ratio for comparable industry groups, or by using a discounted cash flow analysis. The Company completed its assessment of any potential impairment upon adoption of this standard and performs annual assessments. The Company has determined that no impairments exist. Prior to January 1, 2002, goodwill was tested for impairment in a manner consistent with property, plant and equipment and intangible assets with a definite life. See Note 3 to the Consolidated Financial Statements for goodwill and indefinite-lived intangible asset information, including supplemental consolidated statement of income information on both a reported and adjusted basis.

*Note 3 (In Part): Goodwill and Indefinite-Lived
Intangible Assets*

As discussed in Note 16 to the Consolidated Financial Statements, 3M realigned its business segments and began reporting under this new structure effective January 1, 2003. The business segment realignment resulted in certain changes in reporting units for 3M. Effective January 1, 2003, 3M has 18 reporting units under the criteria set forth by SFAS No. 142. SFAS No. 142 requires that goodwill be tested for impairment at least annually and when reporting units are changed. During the first quarter of 2003, the Company completed its assessment of any potential goodwill impairments under this new structure and determined that no impairments existed. In addition, the Company completed its annual goodwill impairment test in the fourth quarter of 2003 and determined that no goodwill was impaired.

Goodwill recorded in 2003 totaled $308 million, with $8 million expected to be fully deductible for tax purposes. The increase in the goodwill balance in 2003 primarily relates to the 2003 business combinations previously discussed and changes in foreign currency exchange rates during the period. The goodwill balance by business segment as of December 31, 2002, and December 31, 2003, follows:

	Goodwill			
(Millions)	Dec. 31, 2002 Balance	2003 Acquisition Activity	2003 Translation and Other	Dec. 31, 2003 Balance
Health care	$ 393	$ 56	$ 64	$ 513
Industrial	220	64	39	323
Display and graphics	824	65	14	903
Consumer and office	17	33	6	56
Safety, security and protection services	59	32	9	100
Electro and communications	380	38	76	494
Transportation	5	20	5	30
Total company	$1,898	$308	$213	$2,419

In accordance with SFAS No. 142, beginning January 1, 2002, 3M no longer amortizes goodwill and certain indefinite-lived intangible assets. Amortization expense by business segment relating to goodwill and indefinite-lived intangible assets for the year ended December 31, 2001, follows:

(Millions)	Amortization Expense 2001
Health care	$ 22
Industrial	6
Display and graphics	11
Consumer and office	2
Safety, security and protection services	3
Electro and communications	22
Transportation	1
Total company	$ 67
Income taxes	(12)
Minority interest	(4)
Amortization—net of income taxes and minority interest	$ 51

ATT-SEC 2.141

The impact of SFAS No. 142 on reported results for the year ended December 31 follows:

(Millions, except per share amounts)	Goodwill and Indefinite-Lived Tradenames		
	Supplemental Consolidated Statement of Income Information		
	2003	2002	2001
Reported net income	$2,403	$1,974	$1,430
Add back:			
Goodwill amortization—net	—	—	48
Indefinite-lived tradename amortization—net	—	—	3
Adjusted net income	$2,403	$1,974	$1,481
Earnings per share—basic			
Reported net income	$ 3.07	$ 2.53	$ 1.81
Add back:			
Goodwill and indefinite-lived tradename amortization—net	—	—	0.07
Adjusted net income	$ 3.07	$ 2.53	$ 1.88
Earnings per share—diluted			
Reported net income	$ 3.02	$ 2.50	$ 1.79
Add back:			
Goodwill and indefinite-lived tradename amortization—net	—	—	0.06
Adjusted net income	$ 3.02	$ 2.50	$ 1.85

2.142

JOHNSON & JOHNSON (DEC)

(Dollars in millions)	2003	2002
Total current assets	$22,995	$19,266
Marketable securities, non-current	84	121
Property, plant and equipment, net	9,846	8,710
Intangible assets, net (Notes 1 and 7)	11,539	9,246
Deferred taxes on income	692	236
Other assets	3,107	2,977
Total assets	$48,263	$40,556

NOTES TO CONSOLIDATED FINANCIAL STATEMENTS

1 (In Part): Summary of Significant Accounting Principles

Intangible Assets

In accordance with SFAS No. 142, no amortization was recorded for goodwill and/or intangible assets deemed to have indefinite lives for acquisitions completed after June 30, 2001. Further, effective at the beginning of fiscal year 2002 in accordance with SFAS No. 142, the Company discontinued the amortization relating to all existing goodwill and indefinite lived intangible assets. If SFAS No. 142 was effective for 2001, the effect would have been to reduce amortization expense by $141 million before tax. Intangible assets that have finite useful lives continue to be amortized over their useful lives. SFAS No. 142 requires that goodwill and non-amortizable intangible assets be assessed annually for impairment. The Company completed the annual impairment test for 2003 in the fiscal fourth quarter and no impairment was determined. Future impairment tests will be performed in the fiscal fourth quarter, annually.

7 Intangible Assets

At the end of 2003 and 2002, the gross and net amounts of intangible assets were:

(Dollars in millions)	2003	2002
Goodwill—gross	$ 6,085	$ 5,320
Less accumulated amortization	695	667
Goodwill—net	$ 5,390	$ 4,653
Trademarks (non-amortizable)—gross	$ 1,098	$ 1,021
Less accumulated amortization	136	138
Trademarks (non-amortizable)—net	$ 962	$ 883
Patents and trademarks—gross	$ 3,798	$ 2,016
Less accumulated amortization	818	534
Patents and trademarks—net	$ 2,980	$ 1,482
Other intangibles—gross	$ 3,187	$ 2,998
Less accumulated amortization	980	770
Other intangibles—net	$ 2,207	$ 2,228
Total intangible assets—gross	$14,168	$11,355
Less accumulated amortization	2,629	2,109
Total intangible assets—net	$11,539	$ 9,246

Goodwill as of December 28, 2003, as allocated by segments of business is as follows:

(Dollars in millions)	Consumer	Pharm	Med Dev and Diag	Total
Goodwill, net of accumulated amortization at December 29, 2002	$821	$244	$3,588	$4,653
Acquisitions	—	502	113	615
Translation & other	61	35	26	122
Goodwill at December 28, 2003	$882	$781	$3,727	$5,390

The weighted average amortization periods for patents and trademarks and other intangible assets are 16 years and 18 years, respectively. The amortization expense of amortizable intangible assets for the fiscal year ended December 28, 2003, was $454 million before tax and the estimated amortization expense for the five succeeding years approximates $485 million before tax, per year.

2.143

THE KROGER CO. (JAN)

(In millions)	2004	2003
Total current assets	$ 5,619	$ 5,566
Property, plant and equipment, net	11,178	10,548
Goodwill, net	3,134	3,575
Fair value interest rate hedges	6	110
Other assets	247	303
Total assets	$20,184	$20,102

NOTES TO CONSOLIDATED FINANCIAL STATEMENTS
(In millions)

1 (In Part): Accounting Policies

Goodwill

During 2001, goodwill was amortized on a straight-line basis over 40 years. Goodwill amortization expense totaled $103 in 2001. The Company adopted Statement of Financial Accounting Standards ("SFAS") No. 142 on February 3, 2002. Accordingly, goodwill was not amortized during 2002 and 2003. Instead, goodwill was reviewed for impairment during the first and fourth quarters of 2002, and also during the fourth quarter of 2003. Results of these impairment reviews are summarized in Note 5.

The Company reviews goodwill for impairment during the fourth quarter of each year, and also upon the occurrence of trigger events. The reviews are performed at the operating division level. Generally, fair value represents a multiple of earnings, or discounted projected future cash flows. Potential impairment is indicated when the carrying value of a division, including goodwill, exceeds its fair value. If potential for impairment exists, the fair value of a division is subsequently measured against the fair value of its underlying assets and liabilities, excluding goodwill, to estimate an implied fair value of the division's goodwill. Impairment loss is recognized for any excess of the carrying value of the division's goodwill over the implied fair value.

5. Goodwill, Net

As described in Note 1, the Company adopted SFAS No. 142 on February 3, 2002. The transitional impairment review required by SFAS No. 142 resulted in a $26 pre-tax non-cash loss to write off the jewelry store division goodwill based on its implied fair value. Impairment primarily resulted from the recent operating performance of the division and review of the division's projected future cash flows on a discounted basis, rather than on an undiscounted basis, as was the standard under SFAS No. 121, prior to adoption of SFAS No. 142. This loss was recorded as a cumulative effect of an accounting change, net of a $10 tax benefit, in the first quarter of 2002. No impairment resulted from the Company's annual evaluation of goodwill performed during the fourth quarter of 2002.

The annual evaluation performed during the fourth quarter of 2003 resulted in a $444 non-cash impairment charge related to the goodwill at the Company's Smith's division. This impairment charge, which is non-deductible for income tax purposes, adjusted the carrying value of the division's goodwill to its implied fair value. In 2003, the Smith's division experienced a substantial decline in operating performance when compared to prior year results and budgeted 2003 results.

Additionally, the Company has forecasted a further decline in the future operating performance of this division. The decline in expected performance reflects both investments in capital and targeted retail price reductions intended to maintain and grow market share and provide acceptable long-term return on capital. No impairment was indicated during this review for goodwill at other Company divisions.

The following table summarizes the changes in the Company's net goodwill balance during 2003 and 2002:

Balance at February 2, 2002	$3,594
Cumulative effect of an accounting change	(26)
Goodwill recorded	9
Reclassifications	(2)
Balance at February 1, 2003	$3,575
Goodwill impairment charge	(444)
Goodwill recorded	9
Purchase accounting adjustments in accordance with SFAS No. 141	(6)
Balance at January 31, 2004	$3,134

The following table adjusts net earnings, net earnings per basic common share and net earnings per diluted common share for the adoption of SFAS No. 142. This reflects the elimination of goodwill amortization, and its tax effect, in 2001, and the elimination of the cumulative effect of the accounting change, and its tax effect, in 2002.

	2003	2002	2001
Reported net earnings	$ 315	$1,205	$1,043
Add back:			
Goodwill amortization[1]	—	—	91
Cumulative effect of accounting change[1]	—	16	—
Adjusted net earnings	$ 315	$1,221	$1,134
Earnings per basic common share:			
Reported net earnings	$0.42	$ 1.55	$ 1.30
Add back:			
Goodwill amortization[1]	—	—	0.11
Cumulative effect of accounting change[1]	—	0.02	—
Adjusted net earnings	$0.42	$ 1.57	$ 1.41
Earnings per diluted common share:			
Reported net earnings	$0.42	$ 1.52	$ 1.26
Add back:			
Goodwill amortization[1]	—	—	0.11
Cumulative effect of accounting change[1]	—	0.02	—
Adjusted net earnings	$0.42	$ 1.54	$ 1.37

[1] Amounts are net of income tax benefits.

2.144

THE MCGRAW-HILL COMPANIES, INC. (DEC)

(In thousands)	2003	2002
Total current assets	$2,256,152	$1,674,307
Prepublication costs: (net of accumulated amortization: 2003—$1,037,142; 2002—$924,867)	463,635	534,835
Investments and other assets		
Investments in Rock-McGraw, Inc.— at equity	—	119,442
Prepaid pension expense	288,244	261,243
Other	215,732	205,243
Total investments and other assets	503,976	585,928
Property and equipment—at cost		
Land	13,658	13,252
Buildings and leasehold improvements	379,779	330,484
Equipment and furniture	737,989	728,217
Total property and equipment	1,131,426	1,071,953
Less—accumulated depreciation	664,098	640,493
Net property and equipment	467,328	431,460
Goodwill and other intangible assets (Notes 1 and 13)		
Goodwill—net	1,239,877	1,294,831
Copyrights—net	244,869	272,243
Other intangible assets—net	218,231	238,578
Net goodwill and other intangible assets	1,702,977	1,805,652
Total assets	$5,394,068	$5,032,182

NOTES TO CONSOLIDATED FINANCIAL STATEMENTS

1 (In Part): Accounting Policies

Goodwill and Other Intangible Assets

Goodwill represents the excess of purchase price and related costs over the value assigned to the net tangible and identifiable intangible assets of businesses acquired. As of December 31, 2003 and 2002, goodwill and other indefinite lived intangible assets that arose from acquisitions were $1.3 billion and $1.3 billion, respectively. On January 1, 2002, the Company adopted SFAS No. 142, "Goodwill and Other Intangible Assets." Under SFAS No. 142, goodwill and other intangible assets with indefinite lives are not amortized, but instead are tested for impairment annually, or if certain circumstances indicate a possible impairment may exist, in accordance with the provisions of SFAS No. 142. The Company evaluates the recoverability of goodwill and indefinite lived intangible assets using a two-step impairment test approach at the reporting unit level. In the first step the fair value for the reporting unit is compared to its book value including goodwill. In the case that the fair value of the reporting unit is less than the book value, a second step is performed which compares the implied fair value of the reporting unit's goodwill to the book value of the goodwill. The fair value for the goodwill is determined based on the difference between the fair values of the reporting units and the net fair values of the identifiable assets and liabilities of such reporting units. If the fair value of the goodwill is less than the book value, the difference is recognized as an impairment. SFAS No. 142 also requires that intangible assets with estimable useful lives be amortized over their respective estimated useful lives to the estimated residual values, and reviewed for impairment in accordance with SFAS No. 144, "Accounting for the Impairment or Disposal of Long-Lived Assets." See Note 13.

Beginning in January 2002, the Company did not amortize goodwill on its books in accordance with SFAS No. 142. Prior to the adoption of SFAS No. 142, goodwill was amortized on a straight-line basis over periods of up to 40 years. The amount of goodwill amortization recognized was $0 million, $0 million and $56.6 million for 2003, 2002 and 2001.

13. Goodwill and Intangible Assets

Effective as of January 1, 2002, the Company adopted Statement of Financial Accounting Standards (SFAS) No. 142, "Goodwill and Other Intangible Assets." Under SFAS No. 142, goodwill and other intangible assets with indefinite lives are no longer amortized but are reviewed annually or more frequently if impairment indicators arise. The Company performed the required transitional impairment review of goodwill as of January 1, 2002. For each of the reporting units, the estimated fair value was determined utilizing the expected present value of the future cash flows of the units. In all instances, the estimated fair value of the reporting units exceeded their book values and therefore no write-down of goodwill was required.

The following table reflects unaudited pro forma results of operations of the Company, giving effect to SFAS No. 142 as if it were adopted on January 1, 2001:

(In thousands except earnings per share)	2003	2002	2001
Net income as reported	$687,650	$576,760	$377,031
Add back: amortization expense net of tax	—	—	34,831
Pro forma net income	$687,650	$576,760	$411,862
Basic earnings per common share:			
As reported	$ 3.61	$ 2.99	$ 1.95
Pro forma	$ 3.61	$ 2.99	$ 2.12
Diluted earnings per common share:			
As reported	$ 3.58	$ 2.96	$ 1.92
Pro forma	$ 3.58	$ 2.96	$ 2.10

The following table summarizes the activity in goodwill for the periods indicated:

(In thousands)	2003	2002
Beginning balance	$1,294,831	$1,231,028
Net change from acquisitions and dispositions	(72,735)	9,088
Purchase price allocations	—	39,146
Other	17,781	15,569
Total	$1,239,877	$1,294,831

The following table summarizes net goodwill by segment:

(In thousands)	2003	2002
McGraw-Hill Education	$ 858,777	$ 913,624
Financial Services	287,405	288,236
Information and Media Services	93,695	92,971
Total	$1,239,877	$1,294,831

The following table summarizes the activity in goodwill for the periods indicated:

(In thousands)	2003	2002
McGraw-Hill Education		
Beginning balance	$913,624	$853,829
Additions/(dispositions)	(61,283)	15,271
Purchase price allocations	—	39,146
Other	6,436	5,378
Total	$858,777	$913,624
Financial Services		
Beginning balance	$288,236	$288,400
Additions/(dispositions)	(12,327)	(4,979)
Other	11,496	4,815
Total	$287,405	$288,236
Information and Media Services		
Beginning balance	$ 92,971	$ 88,799
Additions/(dispositions)	875	(1,204)
Other	(151)	5,376
Total	$ 93,695	$ 92,971

There were no material acquisitions or dispositions for the periods indicated both individually and in the aggregate, and therefore pro forma financial information is not required. Included in the McGraw-Hill Education segment's additions/dispositions is $61.3 million of goodwill impairment associated with the planned disposition of the juvenile retail publishing business.

Trademarks

2.145

CARPENTER TECHNOLOGY CORPORATION (JUN)

(In millions)	2003	2002
Total current assets	$ 369.3	$ 375.9
Property, plant and equipment, net	651.7	713.1
Prepaid pension cost	253.7	255.9
Goodwill	46.3	46.3
Trademarks and trade names, net	25.4	26.4
Other assets	53.5	61.9
Total assets	$1,399.9	$1,479.5

NOTES TO CONSOLIDATED FINANCIAL STATEMENTS

1 (In Part): Summary of Significant Accounting Policies

Trademarks and Tradenames

The cost of trademarks and tradenames are amortized on a straight-line basis over the 30 year estimated useful life of these finite-lived assets.

6 (In Part): Goodwill and Trademarks and Tradenames, Net

Trademarks and Tradenames, Net

(In millions)	2003	2002
Trademarks and tradenames, at cost	$32.0	$32.0
Less accumulated amortization	6.6	5.6
Trademarks and tradenames, net	$25.4	$26.4

Carpenter recorded $1.0 million of amortization expense in fiscal years 2003, 2002 and 2001. The estimated annual amortization expense for each of the succeeding five fiscal years is $1.0 million.

2.146

LA-Z-BOY INCORPORATED (APR)

(Amounts in thousands)	2003	2002
Total current assets	$ 679,494	$ 672,743
Property, plant and equipment, net	209,411	205,463
Goodwill	78,807	108,244
Trade names	71,144	116,772
Other long-term assets, less allowance of $6,481 in 2003 and $5,428 in 2002	84,210	58,605
Total assets	$1,123,066	$1,161,827

NOTES TO CONSOLIDATED FINANCIAL STATEMENTS

Note 1 (In Part): Accounting Policies

Goodwill and Tradenames

In prior fiscal years, goodwill and tradenames were amortized on a straight-line basis over 30 years from the date of acquisition. As of the beginning of fiscal 2003, we adopted SFAS No. 142, "Goodwill and Other Intangible Assets." Under this accounting standard, our goodwill and trade names are required to be reviewed at least annually for impairment. See Note 2 for additional information on our goodwill and trade names and the effect of adopting SFAS No. 142.

Note 2: Goodwill and Other Intangible Assets

Effective April 28, 2002, we adopted SFAS No. 142, "Goodwill and Other Intangible Assets." SFAS No. 142 eliminates the amortization of goodwill and indefinite-lived intangible assets and requires a review at least annually for impairment. We determined that our trade names are indefinite-lived assets, as defined by SFAS No. 142, and therefore not subject to amortization beginning in fiscal 2003.

In accordance with SFAS NO. 142, trade names were tested for impairment by comparing their fair value to their carrying values. The fair value for each trade name was established based upon a royalty savings approach. Additionally, goodwill was tested for impairment by comparing the fair value of our operating units to their carrying values. The fair value for each operating unit was established based upon a combination of the discounted cash flows and the projected profitability of the market in which the entity operates.

Using these procedures, we determined that, as of April 28, 2002, the carrying value of trade names exceeded their fair value creating an impairment loss of $48.3 million, all of which was attributable to the Casegoods segment, and the carrying value of goodwill exceeded its fair value creating an impairment loss of $29.4 million. Of the pre-tax impairment loss for goodwill, $17.1 million was attributable to the Upholstery segment and $12.3 million was attributable to the Casegoods segment. The after-tax effect of $59.8 million for these impairment losses was included in the "Cumulative effect of accounting change" in the consolidated statement of income. In the fourth quarter of fiscal 2003, we reevaluated the trade names and goodwill for impairment by comparing the fair values to the carrying values and determined that there was no additional impairment.

The tradenames and goodwill recorded in our April 27, 2002, financial statements, which included the $77.7 million described above, were supported by the undiscounted estimated future cash flow of the related operations in accordance with SFAS No. 121, "Accounting for the Impairment of Long-Lived Assets and for Long-Lived Assets to Be Disposed Of." SFAS No. 142 prescribes a different approach than SFAS No. 121, requiring the post-acquisition carrying amounts of goodwill and indefinite-lived intangible assets to be compared to their fair values. The impairments recognized in the first quarter of 2003 were the result of changing the impairment assessment model for our intangible assets from the undiscounted cash flows approach of SFAS No. 121 to the fair value approach prescribed by SFAS No. 142. Additionally, our impairment charges were consistent with the recent sales declines in our Casegoods segment.

Amortization expense for goodwill and trade names was $9.3 million ($7.5 million after tax) in fiscal 2002. Of this $9.3 million, $3.3 million was attributable to the Upholstery segment and $6.0 million was attributable to the Casegoods segment. Excluding the effect of amortization, our reported net income for fiscal 2002 would have been increased to $69.3 million from $61.8 million and our diluted net income per common share would have been increased to $1.13 from $1.01 per common share.

The following table summarizes changes to goodwill and trade names in fiscal 2003:

(Amounts in thousands)	Upholstery Group	Casegoods Group
Goodwill		
Balance as of 4/27/02	$ 70,265	$ 37,979
Effect of adopting SFAS No. 142	(17,062)	(12,349)
Dispositions	(26)	—
Balance at 4/26/03	$ 53,177	$ 25,630
Tradenames		
Balance as of 4/27/02	$ 14,255	$102,490
Effect of adopting SFAS No. 142	—	(48,291)
Acquisitions	2,690	—
Balance at 4/26/03	$ 16,945	$ 54,199

Customer Lists/Relationships

2.147

BARNES GROUP INC. (DEC)

(Dollars in thousands)	2003	2002
Total current assets	$312,100	$238,637
Deferred income taxes	22,790	22,610
Property, plant and equipment, net	154,088	159,440
Goodwill	220,118	164,594
Other intangible assets, net	61,923	16,702
Other assets	59,801	50,547
Total assets	$830,820	$652,530

NOTES TO CONSOLIDATED FINANCIAL STATEMENTS

5 (In Part): Goodwill and Other Intangible Assets

Acquired Intangible Assets

Other intangible assets at December 31 consisted of:

	Range of Life (Years)	2003		2002	
		Gross Amount	Accumulated Amortization	Gross Amount	Accumulated Amortization
Amortized intangible assets:					
Revenue sharing programs	Up to 30	$34,500	$ (48)	$ —	$ —
Customer lists/relationships	10	11,500	(1,037)	—	—
Patents, trademarks/trade names	5–30	11,128	(1,382)	9,806	(736)
Other	4.5–10	600	(295)	600	(173)
		57,728	(2,762)	10,406	(909)
Foreign currency translation		1,830	—	681	—
Unamortized intangible pension asset		5,127	—	6,524	—
Other intangible assets		$64,685	$(2,762)	$17,611	$(909)

Amortization of intangible assets for the year ending December 31, 2003 was $1,853. In each of the years 2004 through 2008, the estimated aggregated amortization expenses will be approximately $2,600.

During 2003, the Company entered into two RSP agreements with a major aerospace customer under which the Company will be the sole supplier of certain aftermarket parts. As consideration, the Company agreed to pay participation fees of $34,500, of which $17,500 was paid in 2003, with the remainder to be paid in two installments of $15,000 on April 1, 2004 and $2,000 on April 1, 2008. The Company has recorded the $34,500, participation fees as long-lived intangible assets which will be recognized as a reduction to sales over the life of the programs.

In connection with the acquisition of Kar, the Company recorded intangible assets including $11,500 related to customer lists/relationships and $800 related to trademarks and trade names. Trademarks acquired with the purchase of the nitrogen gas spring business were $4,459. Seeger-Orbis intangible assets acquired were $3,047 and consist of trademarks and patents. In 2003, patents increased $522 due to the recognition of a deferred tax liability. Intangible assets that were acquired with Spectrum were $2,300 and consist primarily of trademarks.

Patents

2.148

DOVER CORPORATION (DEC)

(In thousands)	2003	2002
Total current assets	$1,849,640	$1,604,695
Property, plant and equipment, net	717,875	676,196
Goodwill, net of amortization	1,844,701	1,627,865
Intangible assets, net of amortization	349,328	202,446
Other assets and deferred charges	208,069	167,516
Assets of discontinued operations	164,139	158,398
Total assets	$5,133,752	$4,437,116

NOTES TO CONSOLIDATED FINANCIAL STATEMENTS

1 (In Part): Description of Business and Summary of Significant Accounting Policies

Goodwill and Other Intangible Assets

As of January 1, 2002, the Company adopted Statement of Financial Accounting Standards ("SFAS") No. 142, "Goodwill and Other Intangible Assets". In accordance with the guidelines of this accounting principle, goodwill and indefinite-lived intangible assets are no longer amortized and are assessed for impairment on at least an annual basis. Refer to Note 6 for disclosure on the impact of the adoption. The Company has elected to test annually for goodwill impairment in the fourth quarter of the fiscal year. Goodwill of a reporting unit will also be tested for impairment between annual tests if a triggering event occurs, as defined by SFAS No. 142, that could potentially reduce the fair value of the reporting unit below its carrying value. Prior to 2002, the Company amortized goodwill over a period of principally 40 years.

6 (In Part): Goodwill and Other Intangible Assets

The following table provides the gross carrying value and accumulated amortization for each major class of intangible assets:

(In thousands)	2003 Gross Carrying Amount	2003 Accumulated Amortization	Average Life	2002 Gross Carrying Amount	2002 Accumulated Amortization
Trademarks	$ 22,870	$ 9,807	29	$ 21,736	$ 8,322
Patents	97,015	54,161	13	89,108	43,912
Customer intangibles	61,783	6,284	9	14,275	2,689
Unpatented technologies	68,141	21,561	9	58,092	11,248
Non-compete agreements	8,875	6,483	5	10,345	6,310
Drawings and manuals	6,177	2,237	5	5,999	1,704
Distributor relationships	38,300	383	25	—	—
Other	6,564	3,844	14	3,022	2,874
Total amortizable intangible assets	$309,725	$104,760	14	$202,577	$77,059
Total indefinite-lived trademarks	144,363	—		76,928	—
Total	$454,088	$104,760		$279,505	$77,059

The total intangible amortization expense for the twelve months ended December 31, 2003, 2002 and 2001 was $18.2 million, $17.8 million, and $18.6 million, respectively. The estimated amortization expense, based on current intangible balances, for the next five fiscal years beginning January 1, 2004 is as follows:

(In thousands)	
2004	$18,138
2005	$16,304
2006	$14,801
2007	$13,425
2008	$11,488

Technology

2.149

PFIZER INC (DEC)

(Millions)	2003	2002
Total current assets	$ 29,741	$ 24,781
Long-term investments and loans	6,142	5,161
Property, plant and equipment, less accumulated depreciation	18,287	10,712
Goodwill	22,306	1,200
Identifiable intangible assets, less accumulated amortization	36,350	921
Other assets, deferred taxes and deferred charges	3,949	3,581
Total assets	$116,775	$46,356

NOTES TO CONSOLIDATED FINANCIAL STATEMENTS

1 (In Part): Significant Accounting Policies

J. Depreciation, Amortization and Long-Lived Assets

Long-lived assets include:

- property, plant and equipment—These assets are recorded at original cost and increased by the cost of any significant improvements after purchase. We depreciate the cost evenly over the assets' estimated useful lives. For tax purposes, accelerated depreciation methods are used as allowed by tax laws.
- goodwill—Goodwill represents the difference between the purchase price of acquired business and the fair value of their net assets. Goodwill is not amortized.
- identifiable intangible assets—These assets are recorded at original cost. Intangible assets with finite lives are amortized evenly over their estimated useful lives. Intangible assets with indefinite lives are not amortized.

At least annually, we review all long-lived assets for impairment. When necessary, we record charges for impairments of long-lived assets for the amount by which the present value of future cash flows, or some other fair value measure, is less than the carrying value of these assets.

8 (In Part): Goodwill and Other Intangible Assets

B. Intangibles

The components of identifiable intangible assets follow:

(Millions of dollars)	Gross Carrying Amount		Accumulated Amortization	
	2003	2002	2003	2002
Amortized identifiable intangible assets:				
Developed technology rights	$32,289	$ 526	$(2,400)	$ (72)
Trademarks	147	133	(88)	(72)
License agreements	48	42	(13)	(25)
Patents	33	33	(27)	(24)
Noncompete agreements	50	48	(46)	(39)
Customer contracts	149	—	(25)	—
Other	355	78	(77)	(31)
Total amortized identifiable intangible assets	33,071	860	(2,676)	(263)
Unamortized identifiable intangible assets:				
Brands	5,308	—	—	—
License agreements	288	—	—	—
Trademarks	266	240	—	—
Pension asset	41	60	—	—
Other	52	24	—	—
Total unamortized intangible assets	5,955	324	—	—
Total identifiable intangible assets	$39,026	$1,184	$(2,676)	$(263)

Post-approval milestone payments made under our alliance agreements for the human pharmaceutical products, such as Rebif, Spiriva and Celebrex (prior to our acquisition of Pharmacia), are included in developed technology rights.

Total amortization expense for finite-lived intangible assets was $2,405 million in 2003, $60 million in 2002 and $54 million in 2001. Amortization expense for finite-lived intangible assets is recorded in various expenses, including *Cost of sales, Selling, informational and administrative expenses, Research and development expenses* and *Other (income)/deductions—net.*

The annual amortization expense expected for the years 2004 through 2008 is as follows:

(Millions of dollars)	2004	2005	2006	2007	2008
Amortization expense	$3,378	$3,372	$3,265	$3,113	$2,608

2.150

TEXAS INSTRUMENTS INCORPORATED (DEC)

(Millions of dollars)	2003	2002
Total current assets	$ 7,709	$ 6,126
Property, plant and equipment at cost	9,549	9,516
Less accumulated depreciation	(5,417)	(4,722)
Property, plant and equipment (net)	4,132	4,794
Long-term cash investments	1,335	1,130
Equity investments	265	808
Goodwill	693	638
Acquisition-related intangibles	169	185
Deferred income taxes	626	618
Other assets	581	380
Total assets	$15,510	$14,679

NOTES TO FINANCIAL STATEMENTS

Accounting Policies and Practices (In Part)

The company adopted SFAS No. 142, Goodwill and Other Intangible Assets, effective January 1, 2002. Under SFAS No. 142, goodwill is no longer amortized but is reviewed for impairment annually, or more frequently if certain indicators arise. The company completes its annual goodwill impairment tests as of October 1 of each year for all its reporting units. Based on an analysis of economic characteristics and how the company operates its business, the company has designated its business segments as its reporting units. As required by the Statement, intangible assets that do not meet the criteria for recognition apart from goodwill must be reclassified to goodwill. With the adoption of the Statement, the company ceased amortization of goodwill as of January 1, 2002, and reclassified $14 million (net of tax) of intangibles, primarily relating to acquired workforce intangibles, to goodwill. Fully amortized acquisition-related goodwill and intangible assets are written off against accumulated amortization.

Goodwill and Other Acquisition-Related Intangibles

(Millions of dollars)	Amortization Lives	2003	2002
Goodwill	No longer amortized	$693	$638
Developed and core technology	3–10 years	124	124
Other intangibles	2–10 years	45	61
Total		$862	$823

Other intangibles include items such as customer relationships. The balances shown are net of total accumulated amortization of $437 million and $391 million at year-end 2003 and 2002. The goodwill balances shown are net of total accumulated amortization of $230 million at year-end 2003 and 2002.

The company adopted SFAS No. 142, Goodwill and Other Intangible Assets, effective January 1, 2002. Under SFAS No. 142, goodwill is no longer amortized but reviewed for impairment annually, or more frequently if certain indicators arise.

As required by the Statement, intangible assets that do not meet the criteria for recognition apart from goodwill must be reclassified to goodwill. As a result of the company's analysis, $14 million (net of tax) of intangibles, primarily relating to acquired workforce intangibles, was transferred to goodwill as of January 1, 2002.

● ● ● ● ● ●

The following table reflects the components of amortized intangible assets, excluding goodwill (in millions of dollars):

Amortized Intangible Assets	2003 Gross Carrying Amount	2003 Accum. Amort.	2002 Gross Carrying Amount	2002 Accum. Amort.
Developed and core technology	$227	$103	$203	$ 79
Customer relationships	71	50	66	38
Non-compete agreements	60	42	57	35
Trademarks/Patents	14	10	16	8
Other	4	2	4	1
Total	$376	$207	$346	$161

In July 2003, TI acquired 100 percent of the equity of Radia Communications, Inc. (Radia) for a purchase price of approximately $133 million. The acquisition was made to further TI's development and product offerings in radio frequency (RF) semiconductor, subsystem, signal processing and networking technologies for 802.11 wireless local area networking multi-band/multi-mode radios. Goodwill of approximately $64 million was recognized as a result of the acquisition. The operations of Radia are included in the consolidated statements of operations from the date of acquisition. In connection with the acquisition, the company recorded a $23 million in-process research and development charge, which was recorded in research and development expense. The following table contains a summary of the intangible assets acquired (in millions of dollars):

Acquired Intangible Assets	Amount	Amortization Lives
Core technology	$28	5 years
Developed technology	4	3 years
Customer relationships	5	5 years
Non-compete agreements	3	3 years

In June 2002, TI acquired Condat AG, Berlin (Condat) for a purchase price of approximately $87 million. Goodwill of approximately $69 million was recognized as a result of the acquisition. The acquisition was made to further TI's development and product offerings in wireless chipset solutions, including protocol stack software for cellular phones. The operations of Condat are included in the consolidated statements of operations from the date of acquisition. The following table contains a summary of the intangibles acquired (in millions of dollars):

Acquired Intangible Assets	Amount	Amortization Lives
Developed technology	$26	5 years
Customer relationships	2	3 years
Non-compete agreements	2	3 years

Amortization of goodwill and other acquisition-related costs (including unearned compensation, a contra-stockholders' equity account) was $99 million, $115 million, and $229 million for 2003, 2002 and 2001. Of the total amortization, goodwill amortization was zero, zero and $97 million, with the remainder primarily related to developed technology.

The following table sets forth the estimated amortization of acquisition-related costs (including unearned compensation, a contra-stockholders' equity account) for the years ended December 31:

(Millions of dollars)	
2004	$68
2005	50
2006	40
2007	23
2008	7

Licenses and Franchises

2.151

IDT CORPORATION (JUL)

(In thousands)	2003	2002
Total current assets	$1,228,322	$1,312,166
Property, plant and equipment, net	286,807	279,410
Goodwill	41,651	34,411
Licenses and other intangibles, net	23,503	27,242
Investments	41,628	44,085
Restricted cash	23,064	—
Marketable securities	—	18,704
Other assets	87,367	61,644
Total assets	$1,732,342	$1,777,662

NOTES TO CONSOLIDATED FINANCIAL STATEMENTS

1 (In Part): Summary of Significant Accounting Policies

Goodwill and Other Intangibles

Goodwill is the excess of the acquisition cost of businesses over the fair value of the identifiable net assets acquired.

Effective August 1, 2001, the Company adopted SFAS No. 142, *Goodwill and Other Intangible Assets* and, as required, the Company no longer amortizes goodwill and other indefinite lived intangible assets. These assets are reviewed annually (or more frequently under various conditions) for impairment using a fair value approach. Intangible assets that do not have indefinite lives are amortized over their useful lives and reviewed for impairment in accordance with SFAS No. 144. Costs associated with obtaining the right to use trademarks and patents owned by third parties are capitalized and amortized on a straight-line basis over the term of the trademark licenses and patents. Licenses are amortized over 5 years using the straight-line method. Acquired core technology is amortized over 3 or 5 years. For additional information on the impact of adopting SFAS No. 142, see Note 5.

Prior to August 1, 2001, the Company generally amortized goodwill, licenses and other identifiable intangibles on a straight-line basis over their estimated useful life, not exceeding 40 years. The Company tested the carrying value of its acquired goodwill, licenses and other identifiable intangibles for impairment under SFAS No. 121, *Accounting for the Impairment of Long-Lived Assets and for Long-Lived Assets to Be Disposed Of*, whenever events of changes in circumstances indicated that the carrying value may not be recoverable. A determination of impairment (if any) was made based on estimates of future cash flows. In instances where goodwill was recorded for assets that were subject to impairment, the carrying amount of the goodwill was eliminated before any reduction was made to the carrying amounts of impaired long-lived assets.

5 (In Part): Goodwill, Licenses and Other Intangibles

The following disclosure presents certain information on the Company's licenses and other intangible assets. All licenses and other intangible assets are being amortized over their estimated useful lives, with no estimated residual values:

(In thousands)	Weighted Average Amortization Period	Gross Carrying Amount	Accumulated Amortization	Net Balance
As of July 31, 2003				
Amortized intangible assets:				
Licenses	5 years	$16,842	$ (5,329)	$11,513
Core technology, trademarks and patents	5 years	17,654	(5,664)	11,990
Total	5 years	$34,496	$(10,993)	$23,503
As of July 31, 2002				
Amortized intangible assets:				
Licenses	5 years	$23,994	$ (3,175)	$20,819
Core technology, trademarks and patents	5 years	7,544	(1,121)	6,423
Total	5 years	$31,538	$ (4,296)	$27,242

Licenses and other intangible assets amortization expense was $6.7 million, $4.9 million and $4.9 million for the years ended July 31, 2003, 2002 and 2001, respectively. The Company estimates that amortization expense of licenses and other intangible assets for each of the next five fiscal years ending July 31 will be approximately $4.7 million.

Covenants Not to Compete

2.152

THOR INDUSTRIES, INC. (JUL)

	2003	2002
Total current assets	$378,632,207	$291,238,354
Property, plant and equipment:		
Land	12,058,354	9,848,968
Buildings and improvements	55,541,971	37,249,824
Machinery and equipment	31,644,155	25,625,071
Total cost	99,244,480	72,723,863
Less accumulated depreciation	(25,829,440)	(20,882,575)
Net property, plant and equipment	73,415,040	51,841,288
Investments:		
Joint ventures	2,219,469	2,137,946
Investments available-for-sale	2,860,466	3,920,746
Total investments	5,079,935	6,058,692
Other assets:		
Goodwill	130,554,872	130,554,872
Noncompete agreements (note C)	3,739,589	4,454,408
Trademarks	8,669,642	8,669,642
Other	8,850,173	4,685,877
Total other assets	151,814,276	148,364,799
Total	$608,941,458	$497,503,133

NOTES TO THE CONSOLIDATED FINANCIAL STATEMENTS

A (In Part): Summary of Significant Accounting Policies

Other Assets

Other assets consist of goodwill, trademarks, and non-compete agreements. Non-compete agreements are amortized using the straight-line method over 5 to 10 years. Effective August 1, 2001 goodwill and trademarks are no longer amortized but are tested at least annually for impairment. Trademarks are not amortized because they have indefinite useful lives.

C (In Part): Goodwill and Other Intangible Assets

On August 1, 2001, the Company adopted SFAS No. 142, "Goodwill and Other Intangible Assets", which eliminated the amortization of goodwill and other intangibles with indefinite useful lives. In accordance with SFAS No. 142, goodwill will be tested for impairment at least annually and more frequently if an event occurs which indicates the goodwill may be impaired. On an annual basis, we test goodwill for impairment during the fourth quarter.

The components of other intangibles are as follows:

	2003		2002	
	Cost	Accumulated Amortization	Cost	Accumulated Amortization
Amortized intangible assets:				
Non-compete agreements	$14,073,367	$10,333,778	$14,073,367	$9,618,959

Aggregate amortization expense for non-compete agreements for the years ended, July 31, 2003, 2002 and 2001 were $714,818, $570,176, and $ 658,030 respectively. Noncompete agreements are amortized on a straight-line basis.

Estimated Amortization Expense

For the year ending July 2004	$714,819
For the year ending July 2005	$671,485
For the year ending July 2006	$584,818
For the year ending July 2007	$584,818
For the year ending July 2008	$584,818

Contracts

2.153

CINTAS CORPORATION (MAY)

(In thousands)	2003	2002
Total current assets	$ 877,544	$ 853,250
Property and equipment, at cost, net	777,432	778,402
Goodwill	721,855	678,598
Service contracts	144,899	158,529
Other assets	61,216	50,455
	$2,582,946	$2,519,234

NOTES TO CONSOLIDATED FINANCIAL STATEMENTS
(Amounts in thousands)

1 (In Part): Significant Accounting Policies

Service Contracts and Other Assets

Service contracts and other assets, which consist primarily of noncompete and consulting agreements obtained through the acquisition of businesses, are amortized by use of the straight-line method over the estimated lives of the agreements, which are generally five to ten years.

4 (In Part): Goodwill and Other Assets

As of June 1, 2001, Cintas adopted Statement of Financial Accounting Standards No. 142 (SFAS 142), *Goodwill and Other Intangible Assets*, which addresses the financial accounting and reporting standards for the acquisition of intangible assets outside of a business combination and for goodwill and other intangible assets subsequent to their acquisition. This accounting standard requires that goodwill be separately disclosed from other intangible assets in the balance sheet, and no longer be amortized, but tested for impairment on a periodic basis. The provisions of this accounting standard also require the completion of a transitional impairment test within six months of adoption, with any impairments identified treated as a cumulative effect of a change in accounting principle.

● ● ● ● ● ●

Information regarding Cintas' service contracts and other assets follows:

As of May 31, 2003	Carrying Amount	Accumulated Amortization	Net
Service contracts	$232,826	$87,927	$144,899
Noncompete and consulting agreements	$ 55,456	$38,990	$ 16,466
Other	46,401	1,651	44,750
Total	$101,857	$40,641	$ 61,216

As of May 31, 2002			
Service contracts	$226,023	$67,494	$158,529
Noncompete and consulting agreements	$ 61,742	$41,792	$ 19,950
Other	31,111	606	30,505
Total	$ 92,853	$42,398	$ 50,455

Amortization expense was $27,741, $18,810 and $21,850 for the years ended May 31, 2003, 2002 and 2001, respectively. Estimated amortization expense, excluding any future acquisitions, for each of the next five years is $25,106, $22,982, $20,357, $19,147 and $16,946, respectively.

OTHER NONCURRENT ASSETS

2.154 Table 2-21 summarizes the nature of assets (other than property, investments, noncurrent receivables, and intangible assets) classified as noncurrent assets on the balance sheet of the survey companies. Examples of other noncurrent asset presentations and disclosures, except assets leased to others, follow. Examples of assets leased to others are presented under "Lessor Leases" in the "Long-Term Leases" section.

2.155

TABLE 2-21: OTHER NONCURRENT ASSETS

	Number of Companies			
	2003	**2002**	**2001**	**2000**
Deferred income taxes...........	212	195	196	129
Prepaid pension costs...........	147	146	126	94
Software................................	124	128	105	84
Segregated cash or securities............................	61	69	49	34
Debt issue costs....................	57	64	53	49
Derivatives............................	54	61	34	4
Property held for sale.............	49	43	24	29
Cash surrender value of life insurance........................	31	33	32	18
Assets leased to others.........	11	16	10	9
Contracts...............................	8	13	9	8
Estimated insurance recoveries.........................	8	9	6	2
Assets of nonhomogeneous operations........................	3	6	12	7
Other identified noncurrent assets.................................	53	59	61	44

Deferred Income Taxes

2.156

H. B. FULLER COMPANY (NOV)

(In thousands)	2003	2002
Total current assets	$ 448,492	$408,874
Property, plant and equipment, net	348,653	354,964
Other assets	114,117	106,456
Goodwill	79,414	71,020
Other intangibles, net	16,912	20,125
Total assets	$1,007,588	$961,439

NOTES TO CONSOLIDATED FINANCIAL STATEMENTS
(In thousands)

1 (In Part): Nature of Business and Summary of Significant Accounting Policies

Income Taxes

The income tax provision is computed based on the pretax income included in the consolidated statement of income. The asset and liability approach is used to recognize deferred tax liabilities and assets for the expected future tax consequences of temporary differences between the carrying amounts and the tax bases of assets and liabilities. Enacted statutory tax rates applicable to future years are applied to differences between the financial statement carrying amounts and the tax basis of existing assets and liabilities. The effect on deferred taxes of a change in tax rates is recognized in income in the period that includes the enactment date. Valuation allowances are recorded to reduce deferred tax assets when it is more likely than not that a tax benefit will not be realized. See also Note 7.

4 (In Part): Supplemental Financial Statement Information

	2003	2002
Other assets		
Investment in trading securities	$ 23,639	$ 23,657
Investment in & advances to unconsolidated subsidiaries	31,373	31,699
Long-term deferred tax asset	9,122	13,660
Prepaid postretirement benefits	20,215	22,757
Prepaid pension costs	21,680	1,225
Other long-term assets	8,088	13,458
Total other assets	$114,117	$106,456

7 (In Part): Income Taxes

Deferred Income Tax Balances at Each Year-End Related to	2003	2002
Depreciation	$(34,171)	$(37,699)
Asset valuation allowances	2,127	2,236
Accrued expenses currently not deductible:		
Employee benefit costs	14,502	22,826
Product and other claims	2,935	2,733
Tax loss carryforwards	20,989	15,756
Other	9,388	9,825
	15,770	15,677
Valuation allowance	(11,433)	(7,912)
Net deferred tax assets	$ 4,337	$ 7,765

The differences between the change in the deferred tax assets in the balance sheet and the deferred tax provision is primarily due to minimum pension liability adjustments.

Net Deferred Taxes as Presented on the Consolidated Balance Sheet	2003	2002
Deferred tax assets:		
Current	$ 14,327	$ 16,742
Non-current	9,122	13,660
Deferred tax liabilities:		
Current	(1,964)	(1,830)
Non-current	(17,148)	(20,807)
Net deferred tax assets	$ 4,337	$ 7,765

Valuation allowances relate to foreign tax credit carry overs, tax loss carryforwards and other net deductible temporary differences in non-U.S. operations and U.S. state tax credit carry overs where the future potential benefits do not meet the more likely than not realization test. The increase in the valuation allowance during the year ended November 29, 2003, is primarily due to an increase in foreign tax loss carryforwards and state tax credit carryforwards, for which the company has currently determined that the future income tax benefits may not be realized.

U.S. income taxes have not been provided on approximately $93,327 of undistributed earnings of non-U.S. subsidiaries. The company plans to indefinitely reinvest these undistributed earnings. If any portion, however were to be distributed, the related U.S. tax liability may be reduced by foreign income taxes paid on those earnings plus any available foreign tax credit carry overs. Determination of the unrecognized deferred tax liability related to these undistributed earnings is not practicable.

While non-U.S. operations have been profitable overall, cumulative tax losses of $59,896 are carried as net operating losses in 16 different countries. These losses can be carried forward to offset income tax liability on future income in those countries. Cumulative losses of $41,528 can be carried forward indefinitely, while the remaining $18,368 must be used during the 2004–2009 period.

2.157

SCIENTIFIC-ATLANTA, INC. (JUN)

(In thousands)	2003	2002
Total current assets	$1,323,616	$1,308,394
Property, plant and equipment, at cost		
Land and improvements	22,139	21,943
Buildings and improvements	83,624	78,464
Machinery and equipment	219,647	241,420
	325,410	341,827
Less—accumulated depreciation and amortization	127,726	119,407
	197,684	222,420
Goodwill	235,248	195,645
Intangible assets	51,028	48,909
Non-current marketable securities	8,367	28,498
Deferred income taxes	38,200	29,861
Other assets	64,486	80,900
Total assets	$1,918,629	$1,914,627

NOTES TO CONSOLIDATED FINANCIAL STATEMENTS

1 (In Part): Summary of Significant Accounting Policies

Income Taxes

We provide for income taxes using the asset and liability method under which deferred income taxes are recognized for the estimated future tax effects attributable to temporary differences and carryforwards that result from events that have been recognized either in the financial statements or the income tax returns, but not both. The measurement of current and deferred income tax liabilities and assets is based on provisions of enacted tax laws. Valuation allowances are recognized if, based on the weight of available evidence, it is more likely than not that some portion of the deferred tax assets will not be realized.

11 (In Part): Income Taxes

The tax effect of significant temporary differences representing deferred tax assets and liabilities were as follows:

	2003	2002
Current deferred tax assets		
Expenses not currently deductible	$ 13,943	$ 27,518
Inventory valuation	22,562	15,891
Warranty reserves	4,336	3,103
Other	1,033	1,396
Current deferred tax assets	$ 41,874	$ 47,908
Non-current deferred tax assets		
Postretirement and post employment benefits	$ 41,717	$ 42,441
Accumulated comprehensive income items	—	121
Depreciation and amortization	—	2,963
Unrealized loss on investments	11,326	688
Warranty reserve	7,883	9,090
Foreign net operating losses and tax credits	21,684	15,077
Non-current deferred tax assets	$ 82,610	$ 70,380
Non-current deferred tax liabilities		
Income not currently recognized	$ (1,817)	$ (1,112)
Capitalized software	(2,670)	(3,505)
Accumulated comprehensive income items	(13,168)	—
Gain on sale of subsidiary stock	—	(7,876)
Purchased intangibles	(8,345)	12,949
Depreciation and amortization	(669)	—
Non-current deferred tax liabilities	$(26,669)	$(25,442)
Valuation allowances for foreign net operating losses	(17,741)	(15,077)
Net non-current deferred tax assets	$ 38,200	$ 29,861

Deferred tax assets are partially offset by valuation allowances of $17,741 and $15,077 at June 27, 2003 and June 28, 2002, respectively. These allowances relate to net operating losses generated by foreign subsidiaries we acquired. The allowances are required to reflect the net realizable value of the net operating loss carryforwards. Based on these subsidiaries' history of taxable earnings and our expectations for the future, we have determined that operating income and the reversal of future taxable temporary differences will more likely than not be insufficient to realize all of the foreign net operating loss carryforwards. These carryforwards have no expiration date.

Prepaid Pension Cost

2.158

FLUOR CORPORATION (DEC)

(In thousands)	2003	2002
Total current assets	$2,213,644	$1,924,092
Assets of discontinued operations	—	49,694
Property, plant and equipment		
Land	62,143	43,523
Buildings and improvements	271,045	158,422
Machinery and equipment	602,454	581,218
Construction in progress	2,061	2,721
	937,703	785,884
Less accumulated depreciation	368,223	318,864
Net property, plant and equipment	569,480	467,020
Other assets		
Goodwill	54,157	21,247
Investments	98,206	125,610
Deferred taxes	66,051	113,514
Pension assets	173,613	167,256
Other	274,331	273,718
Total other assets	666,358	701,345
	$3,449,482	$3,142,151

NOTES TO CONSOLIDATED FINANCIAL STATEMENTS

Retirement Benefits (In Part)

The following table sets forth the change in benefit obligation, plan assets and funded status of the company's defined benefit pension plans.

(In thousands)	2003	2002
Change in pension benefit obligation		
Benefit obligation at beginning of period	$600,261	$515,651
Service cost	33,634	33,928
Interest cost	38,358	33,988
Employee contributions	3,689	2,939
Currency translation	50,832	37,202
Actuarial loss	54,436	12,576
Benefits paid	(33,901)	(36,023)
Benefit obligation at end of period	$747,309	$600,261
Change in plan assets		
Fair value at beginning of period	$533,567	$503,839
Actual return (loss) on plan assets	89,333	(80,056)
Company contributions	52,458	110,468
Employee contributions	3,689	2,939
Currency translation	41,122	32,400
Benefits paid	(33,901)	(36,023)
Fair value at end of period	$686,268	$533,567
Funded status	$ (61,041)	$ (66,694)
Unrecognized net actuarial loss	245,924	247,805
Unrecognized prior service cost	(364)	(326)
Unrecognized net asset	(673)	(1,368)
Net amount recognized	$183,846	$179,417

The above table includes obligations and assets of certain discontinued operations for which the company retains responsibility.

Amounts recognized in the consolidated balance sheet as of December 31, 2003 and 2002 are as follows:

(In thousands)	2003	2002
Prepaid benefit cost	$173,613	$167,256
Accrued benefit cost	(27,935)	(28,862)
Accumulated other comprehensive income (loss)	38,168	41,023
Net amount recognized	$183,846	$179,417

2.159

PATHMARK STORES, INC. (JAN)

(In millions)	2004	2003
Total current assets	$ 330.6	$ 327.2
Property and equipment, net	584.5	604.5
Goodwill	434.0	434.0
Other noncurrent assets	171.8	156.9
Total assets	$1,520.9	$1,522.6

NOTES TO CONSOLIDATED FINANCIAL STATEMENTS

Note 6. Other Noncurrent Assets

Other noncurrent assets are comprised of the following (in millions):

	2004	2003
Funded pension plan assets	$133.5	$127.0
Capitalized software, net	26.0	14.0
Deferred financing costs, net	10.2	14.1
Other	2.1	1.8
Other noncurrent assets	$171.8	$156.9

Note 16 (In Part): Pension and Other Benefit Plans

Pension and Other Postretirement Benefits

The following table provides a reconciliation of benefit obligations, the funded plan assets and the funded status of the plans, accounted for on a calendar-year basis along with the amounts recognized in the consolidated balance sheets (in millions):

	Pension Benefits		Other Postretirement Benefits	
	2004	2003	2004	2003
Change in benefit obligations:				
Benefit obligations at beginning of year	$188.6	$176.9	$ 23.7	$ 24.7
Service cost (excluding expenses)	3.1	3.0	0.7	0.6
Interest cost	11.9	12.0	1.6	1.7
Plan amendments	—	0.6	—	—
Benefits and expenses paid	(11.0)	(7.7)	(1.1)	(0.9)
Actuarial experience losses (gains)	7.1	3.8	7.4	(2.4)
Retirement incentive program	2.1	—	0.4	—
Curtailment gain	—	—	(0.9)	—
Benefit obligations at end of year	$201.8	$188.6	$ 31.8	$ 23.7
Change in fair value of funded plan assets:				
Fair value of plan assets at beginning of year	$218.4	$240.5	$ —	$ —
Actual return on plan assets	41.5	(16.2)	—	—
Benefits and expenses paid	(9.2)	(5.9)	—	—
Fair value of plan assets at end of year	$250.7	$218.4	$ —	$ —
Reconciliation of funded status at end of year:				
Funded status (plan assets less benefit obligations)	$ 48.9	$ 29.8	$(31.8)	$(23.7)
Unrecognized prior service cost (benefit)	0.5	0.5	(0.6)	(0.6)
Unrecognized net actuarial losses	58.7	71.7	11.9	4.8
Prepaid (accrued) benefit cost	$108.1	$102.0	$(20.5)	$(19.5)
Amount recognized in the consolidated balance sheets:				
Other noncurrent assets	$133.5	$127.0	$ —	$ —
Accrued expenses and other current liabilities	(1.8)	(2.3)	(0.1)	—
Other noncurrent liabilities	(28.3)	(24.1)	(20.4)	(19.5)
Accumulated other comprehensive loss	4.7	1.4	—	—
Net amount recognized	$108.1	$102.0	$(20.5)	$(19.5)

Additional disclosures related to pension benefit obligations are as follows (in millions):

	2004		
	Qualified Pension Plan	Nonqualified Pension Plans	Total
Fair value of plan assets	$ 250.7	$ —	$ 250.7
Projected benefit obligations	(171.2)	(30.6)	(201.8)
Funded (unfunded) projected benefit obligations	79.5	(30.6)	48.9
Accumulated benefit obligations	(161.6)	(30.1)	(191.7)
Funded (unfunded) accumulated benefit obligations	89.1	(30.1)	59.0
Net asset (liability) recognized	133.5	(25.4)	108.1
Additional minimum pension liability	—	(4.7)	(4.7)

Software Development Costs

2.160

KIMBALL INTERNATIONAL, INC. (JUN)

(Amounts in thousands)	2003	2002
Total current assets	$338,427	$364,157
Property and equipment, net of accumulated depreciation of $351,430 and $347,463, respectively	198,981	236,176
Capitalized software, net of accumulated amortization of $29,128 and $28,049, respectively	42,376	38,968
Other assets	35,860	34,811
Total assets	$615,644	$674,112

NOTES TO CONSOLIDATED FINANCIAL STATEMENTS

Note 1 (In Part): Summary of Significant Accounting Policies

Capitalized Software

Internal-use software is stated at cost less accumulated amortization and is amortized using the straight-line method over its estimated useful life ranging from 2 to 7 years. Software assets are reviewed for impairment when events or circumstances indicate that the carrying value may not be recoverable over the remaining lives of the assets. During the software application development stage, capitalized costs include external consulting costs, cost of software licenses, and internal payroll and payroll-related costs for employees who are directly associated with a software project. Upgrades and enhancements are capitalized if they result in added functionality which enable the software to perform tasks it was previously incapable of performing. Software maintenance, training, data conversion and business process reengineering costs are expensed in the period in which they are incurred.

2.161

SYBASE, INC. (DEC)

(Dollars in thousands)	2003	2002
Total current assets	$ 644,482	$504,619
Long-term cash investments	103,296	92,173
Restricted long-term cash investments	3,400	—
Property, equipment and improvements, net	67,462	70,402
Deferred income taxes	58,506	46,295
Capitalized software, net	58,947	62,266
Goodwill	140,875	136,826
Other purchased intangibles, less accumulated amortization of $63,485 (2002—$46,227)	38,715	50,473
Other assets	35,673	29,695
Total assets	$1,151,356	$992,749

NOTES TO CONSOLIDATED FINANCIAL STATEMENTS

Note One (In Part): Summary of Significant Accounting Policies

Capitalized Software

The Company capitalizes software development costs in accordance with SFAS No. 86, "Accounting for Costs of Computer Software to be Sold, Leased or Otherwise Marketed," (SFAS 86), under which certain software development costs incurred subsequent to the establishment of technological feasibility may be capitalized and amortized over the estimated lives of the related products. The Company determines technological feasibility to be established upon the internal release of a working model or a detailed program design as specified by SFAS 86. Upon the general release of the product to customers, development costs for that product are amortized over periods not exceeding three years, based on the estimated economic life of the product. Capitalized software costs amounted to $214.7 million and $186.7 million, at December 31, 2003 and 2002, respectively, and related accumulated amortization was $155.8 million, and $124.5 million, respectively. Software amortization charges included in cost of license fees were $31.1 million, $24.0 million and $17.8 million for 2003, 2002, and 2001, respectively.

SFAS 86 also requires that the unamortized capitalized costs of a computer software product be compared to the net realizable value of such product at each reporting date. To the extent the unamortized capitalized cost exceeds the net realizable value of a software product based upon its estimated future gross revenues reduced by estimated future costs of completing and disposing of the product, the excess is written off. If the estimated future gross revenue associated with certain of the Company's software products were to be reduced, write-offs of capitalized software costs might be required.

Segregated Funds

2.162

FOSTER WHEELER LTD. (DEC)

(In thousands of dollars)	2003	2002
Total current assets	$1,174,376	$1,329,847
Land, buildings and equipment	622,729	769,680
Less accumulated depreciation	313,114	361,861
Net book value	309,615	407,819
Restricted cash	52,685	84,793
Notes and accounts receivable—long-term	6,776	21,944
Investment and advances	98,651	88,523
Goodwill, net	51,121	50,214
Other intangible assets, net	71,568	72,668
Prepaid pension cost and related benefit assets	7,240	26,567
Asbestos-related insurance recovery receivable	495,400	534,045
Other assets	182,151	156,279
Deferred income taxes	56,947	69,578
Total assets	$2,506,530	$2,842,277

NOTES TO CONSOLIDATED FINANCIAL STATEMENTS
(In thousands of dollars)

1 (In Part): Going Concern

As of December 26, 2003, the Company had aggregate indebtedness of approximately $1,000,000. The corporate debt must be funded primarily from distributions from foreign subsidiaries. As of December 26, 2003, the Company had cash and cash equivalents on hand, short-term investments, and restricted cash totaling $430,200 compared to $429,400 as of December 27, 2002. Of the $430,200 total at December 26, 2003, approximately $366,700 was held by foreign subsidiaries. The Company is sometimes required to cash collateralize bonding or certain bank facilities. The amount of restricted cash at December 26, 2003 was $52,700, of which $48,000 relates to the non-U.S. operations.

2 (In Part): Summary of Significant Accounting Policies

Restricted Cash

Restricted cash at December 26, 2003 consists of approximately $4,000 held primarily by special purpose entities and restricted for debt service payments, approximately $44,900 that was required to collateralize letters of credit and bank guarantees, and approximately $3,800 of client es-

crow funds. Domestic restricted cash totals approximately $4,700 which relates to funds held primarily by special purpose entities and restricted for debt service payments and client escrow funds. Foreign restricted cash totals approximately $48,000 and is comprised of cash collateralized letters of credit and bank guarantees and client escrow funds.

Debt Issue Costs

2.163

BRIGGS & STRATTON CORPORATION (JUN)

(In thousands)	2003	2002
Total current assets	$ 807,147	$ 675,507
Goodwill	159,756	161,030
Investments	44,175	46,889
Prepaid pension	74,005	60,343
Deferred loan costs, net	8,314	10,506
Other long-term assets, net	11,012	7,111
Plant and equipment:		
Land and land improvements	15,938	16,356
Buildings	156,823	153,043
Machinery and equipment	689,100	691,334
Construction in progress	14,803	18,902
	876,664	879,635
Less—accumulated depreciation	505,880	484,420
Total plant and equipment, net	370,784	395,215
	$1,475,193	$1,356,601

NOTES TO CONSOLIDATED FINANCIAL STATEMENTS

2 (In Part): Summary of Significant Accounting Policies

Deferred Loan Costs

Expenses associated with the issuance of debt instruments are capitalized and are being amortized over the terms of the respective financing arrangement using the straight-line method over periods ranging from five to ten years. Accumulated amortization amounted to $5.1 million as of June 29, 2003 and $2.9 million as of June 30, 2002.

Derivatives

2.164

THE CLOROX COMPANY (JUN)

(In millions)	2003	2002
Total current assets	$ 951	$1,044
Property, plant and equipment, net	1,072	992
Goodwill, net	730	728
Trademarks and other intangible assets, net	651	573
Other assets, net	248	187
Total assets	$3,652	$3,524

NOTES TO CONSOLIDATED FINANCIAL STATEMENTS
(Millions of dollars)

1 (In Part): Significant Accounting Policies

Derivative Instruments

Effective July 1, 2000, the Company adopted SFAS No. 133 "Accounting for Derivative Instruments and Hedging Activities," as amended by SFAS No. 138, "Accounting for Certain Derivative Instruments and Certain Hedging Activities." SFAS No. 133, as amended, establishes accounting and reporting standards for derivative instruments, including certain derivative instruments embedded in other contracts, and for hedging activities. The statement requires that an entity recognize all derivatives as either assets or liabilities in the balance sheet and measure those instruments at fair value. The effect of this new standard was a reduction of fiscal year 2001 net earnings of $2 (net of tax benefit of $1), which was recognized as a cumulative effect of a change in accounting principle and an increase in fiscal year 2001 accumulated other comprehensive income of $10 (net of tax benefit of $7). The ongoing effects are dependent on future market conditions and the Company's hedging activities.

The use of derivative instruments, principally swap, forward and option contracts, is limited to non-trading purposes and includes management of interest rate movements, foreign currency exposure and commodity price exposure. Most interest rate swaps and commodity purchase and foreign exchange contracts are designated as fair-value or cash-flow hedges of fixed and variable rate debt obligations, raw material purchase obligations, or foreign currency denominated debt instruments, based on certain hedge criteria. The criteria used to determine if hedge accounting treatment is appropriate are (a) the designation of the hedge to an underlying exposure, (b) whether overall risk is being reduced and (c) if there is correlation between the value of the derivative instrument and the underlying obligation. Changes in the fair value of such derivatives are recorded as either assets or liabilities in the balance sheet with an offset to current earnings or other comprehensive income, depending on whether the derivative is designated as a hedge transaction and the type of hedge transaction. For fair-value hedge transactions, changes in fair value of the derivative and changes in the fair value of the item being hedged are recorded in earnings. For cash-flow hedge transactions, changes in fair value of derivatives are reported as a component of other comprehensive income and are recognized in the period or periods during which the hedge transaction effects earnings. The Company also has contracts with no hedging designations. In fiscal year 2002, the Company elected to discontinue hedge accounting treatment for certain of its foreign exchange contracts that are considered immaterial. The financial statement impact of this change was insignificant. These contracts are accounted for by adjusting the carrying amount of the contracts to market and recognizing any gain or loss in other (income) expense, net.

The Company uses several different methodologies to estimate the fair value of its derivative contracts. The estimated fair values of the Company's interest rate swaps, certain commodity derivative contracts and foreign exchange contracts are based on quoted market prices, traded exchange market prices or broker price quotations and represent the estimated amounts that the Company would pay or receive to terminate the contracts. The estimated fair values of the Company's resin commodity contracts were previously determined using valuation models with forward resin market price curves provided by market makers. Starting in fiscal year 2002, the Company began using forward resin market price curves provided by other external sources because of a lack of available market quotations. Factors used to determine the fair value of the resin forward curve are based on resin market information, which reflects many economic factors, including technology, labor, material and capital costs, capacity, and supply and demand.

7 (In Part): Other Assets

Other assets at June 30 are comprised of the following:

	2003	2002
Equity investments in:		
Henkel Iberica, S.A. of Spain	$ 67	$ 65
Other entities	39	39
Investment in low income housing partnerships	46	44
Derivative contracts	41	15
Investment fund	14	15
Non-qualified retirement plan assets	22	—
Other	19	9
Total	$248	$187

11 (In Part): Fair Value of Financial Instruments

The Company's derivative financial instruments are recorded at fair value in the consolidated balance sheets as assets (liabilities) at June 30 as follows:

	2003	2002
Current assets:		
Foreign exchange contracts	$ 1	$ 2
Commodity purchase contracts	—	1
Other assets:		
Interest rate swaps	39	15
Commodity purchase contracts	2	—
Current liabilities:		
Interest rate swaps	2	—
Foreign exchange contracts	—	(3)
Long-term debt:		
Interest rate swaps	—	(6)
Foreign exchange contracts	—	(1)
Other long-term obligations—commodity option contracts	—	(9)

The Company utilizes derivative instruments, principally swap, forward and option contracts to enhance its ability to manage the risks associated with fluctuations in interest rates, foreign currencies, and commodity prices, which exist as part of the Company's ongoing business operations. These contracts hedge transactions and balances for periods consistent with the related exposures and do not constitute investments independent of these exposures.

The Company has policies with restrictions on the use of derivatives, including a prohibition of the use of any leveraged instrument. Derivative contracts are entered into with several major creditworthy institutions, thereby minimizing the risk of credit loss. Exposure to counterparty credit risk is considered low because these agreements have been entered into with major credit-worthy institutions with strong credit ratings, and they are expected to perform fully under the terms of the agreements.

Most of the Company's derivative instruments are designated as fair-value or cash-flow hedges of fixed and variable rate debt obligations, foreign currency-denominated debt instruments, or raw material purchase obligations. All hedges accorded hedge accounting treatment are considered highly effective. At June 30, 2003 and 2002, the Company also had certain foreign currency-related derivative contracts with no specific hedging designations. These contracts, which have been entered into to manage a portion of the Company's foreign exchange risk, are accounted for by adjusting the carrying amount of the contracts to market value and recognizing any gain or loss in other (income) expense.

The Company uses interest rate swap agreements to manage interest rate exposure and to achieve a desired proportion of variable and fixed rate debt. As of June 30, 2003, the Company also had preferred interest transferable securities, which is a Euro Dollar (EUR) denominated financing arrangement that expired in July 2003. The Company manages its interest rate and Euro Dollar risks from these securities through a series of swaps with notional amounts totaling $200. This interest rate swap effectively converts the Company's 5.8% fixed Euro Dollar obligation to a floating U.S. Dollar rate of 90-day LIBOR. In addition, the Company effectively pays a 4.5% fixed rate and receives a 4.6% Euro rate with its currency swap position. The estimated amount of existing pre-tax gains for these swap agreements in accumulated other comprehensive net losses at June 30, 2003 was reclassified into earnings in July 2003 was $2.

The Company uses foreign exchange contracts, including forward, swap and option contracts, to hedge existing foreign exchange exposures. Foreign currency contracts require the Company, at a future date, to either buy or sell foreign currency in exchange for U.S. Dollars and other currencies. Such currency contracts existed at June 30, 2003 and 2002 for Canadian dollars and certain other currencies. Contracts outstanding as of June 30, 2003 will mature over the next fiscal year.

The Company also uses commodity futures and swap contracts to fix the price of a portion of its raw material requirements. Contract maturities, which extend to fiscal year 2006, are matched to the length of the raw material purchase contracts and contract gains and losses are reflected as adjustments to the cost of the raw materials. The estimated amount of existing pre-tax net losses for commodity contracts in accumulated other comprehensive net losses that is expected to be reclassified into earnings during the year ended June 30, 2004 is less than $1.

The notional and estimated fair values of the Company's derivative instruments are summarized below as of June 30:

	2003		2002	
	Notional	Fair Value	Notional	Fair Value
Derivative Instruments				
Debt-related contracts	$400	$41	$400	$8
Foreign exchange contracts	259	—	393	(1)
Commodity purchase contracts	125	2	90	1
Commodity option contracts	—	—	35	(9)

The carrying values of cash, short-term investments, accounts and notes receivable, accounts payable and other derivative instruments approximate their fair values at June 30, 2003 and 2002. The Company has used market information for similar instruments and applied judgment in estimating fair values.

Property Held for Sale

2.165

GIANT INDUSTRIES, INC. (DEC)

(In thousands)	2003	2002
Total current assets	$259,402	$211,684
Property, plant and equipment	628,718	626,574
Less accumulated depreciation and amortization	(235,539)	(211,576)
	393,179	414,998
Goodwill	24,578	19,465
Assets held for sale	5,190	24,404
Other assets	25,005	31,735
Total assets	$707,354	$702,286

NOTES TO CONSOLIDATED FINANCIAL STATEMENTS

Note 1 (In Part): Organization and Significant Accounting Policies

Long-Lived Assets

On January 1, 2002, we adopted SFAS No. 144, "Accounting for the Impairment or Disposal of Long-Lived Assets." This Statement defines impairment as "the condition that exists when the carrying amount of a long-lived asset (asset group) is not recoverable and exceeds its fair value." The Statement provides for a single accounting model for the disposal of long-lived assets, whether previously held or newly acquired. Specific guidance is provided for recognition and measurement and reporting and disclosure for long-lived assets held and used, disposed of other than by sale, and disposed of by sale. This new standard had no impact on our financial position and results of operations at adoption, but we have reflected certain operations as discontinued operations in the years presented to comply with this statement.

In accordance with SFAS No. 144, we review the carrying values of our long-lived assets for possible impairment whenever events or changes in circumstances indicate that the carrying amount of assets to be held and used may not be recoverable. For assets to be disposed of, we report long-lived assets and certain identifiable intangibles at the lower of carrying amount or fair value less cost to sell. See Note 7 for information relating to the impairment of certain assets.

Note 7—Discontinued Operations, Asset Disposals, and Assets Held for Sale

The following table contains information regarding our discontinued operations, all of which are included in our retail group and include some service station/convenience stores and our travel center, which was sold on June 19, 2003.

(In thousands)	2003	2002	2001
Net revenues	$28,179	$63,776	$84,352
Net operating loss	$ (736)	$ (2,100)	$ (1,236)
Gain on disposal	$ 279	$ 6,463	$ —
Impairment and other write-downs	$ (233)	$ (1,310)	$ (1,203)
(Loss) earnings before income taxes	$ (690)	$ 3,053	$ (2,439)
Net (loss) earnings	$ (414)	$ 1,832	$ (1,464)
Allocated goodwill included in gain on disposal	$ 133	$ 308	$ —

Included in "Assets Held for Sale" in the accompanying Consolidated Balance Sheets are the following categories of assets.

(In thousands)	2003	2002
Operating retail units held for sale and included in discontinued operations:		
Property, plant and equipment	$ 330	$12,322
Inventories	106	558
	436	12,880
Vacant land—residential/commercial property	—	6,351
Closed retail units	3,158	2,376
Vacant land—industrial site	1,596	1,596
Vacant land—adjacent to retail units	—	1,201
	$5,190	$24,404

All of these assets are or were being marketed for sale at the direction of management. We expect to dispose of the remaining properties within the next 12 months. In 2003, certain properties were reclassified to property, plant and equipment because we were unable to dispose of them within 12 months. These properties included:
- nine closed retail units with a net book value of $1,219,000;
- vacant land—residential/commercial property with a net book value of $6,278,000; and
- vacant land—adjacent to retail units with a net book value of $1,189,000.

In addition, two closed retail units were added to assets held for sale, two were sold, one unit was written-off, and impairment write-downs of $796,000 were recorded relating of various other assets.

On June 19, 2003, we completed the sale of our travel center to Pilot Travel Centers LLC ("Pilot") and received net proceeds of approximately $5,820,000, plus an additional $491,000 for inventories. As a result of this transaction, we recorded a pre-tax loss of approximately $44,600, which included charges that were a direct result of the decision to sell the travel center. In connection with the sale, we entered into a long-term product supply agreement with Pilot. We will receive a supply agreement performance payment at the end of five years if there has been no material breach under the supply agreement and all requirements have been met for such payment.

On November 4, 2003 we sold our corporate headquarters building and approximately 8 acres of surrounding land. In connection with the sale, we entered into a ten-year agreement to lease back our corporate headquarters building. The gain on the sale of the property of approximately $924,000 has been deferred and is being amortized over the original lease term. The deferred gain is included in "Other Liabilities and Deferred Income" on our Consolidated Balance Sheet for December 31, 2003.

Cash Value of Life Insurance

2.166

W. R. GRACE & CO. (DEC)

(In millions)	2003	2002
Total current assets	$ 928.9	$ 830.3
Properties and equipment, net of accumulated depreciation and amortization of $1,216.9 (2002—$1,071.7)	656.6	622.2
Goodwill	85.2	65.2
Cash value of life insurance policies, net of policy loans	90.8	82.4
Deferred income taxes	587.1	574.1
Asbestos-related insurance expected to be realized after one year	269.4	282.6
Other assets	256.2	234.9
Total assets	$2,874.2	$2,691.7

NOTES TO CONSOLIDATED FINANCIAL STATEMENTS

11. Life Insurance

Grace is the beneficiary of life insurance policies on certain current and former employees with a net cash surrender value of $90.8 million and $82.4 million at December 31, 2003 and 2002, respectively. The policies were acquired to fund various employee benefit programs and other long-term liabilities and are structured to provide cash flow (primarily tax-free) over an extended number of years. The following table summarizes activity in these policies for 2003, 2002 and 2001:

(In millions)

Life Insurance—Activity Summary	2003	2002	2001
Earnings on policy assets	$ 38.7	$ 39.4	$ 40.3
Interest on policy loans	(33.1)	(34.7)	(34.9)
Premiums	2.4	2.4	2.5
Proceeds from policy loans	—	—	(48.7)
Policy loan repayments	3.1	5.1	15.0
Net investing activity	(2.7)	(5.4)	(2.9)
Change in net cash value	$ 8.4	$ 6.8	$ (28.7)
Gross cash value	$ 478.5	$ 471.3	$ 477.5
Principal—policy loans	(365.3)	(365.4)	(377.6)
Accrued interest—policy loans	(22.4)	(23.5)	(24.3)
Net cash value	$ 90.8	$ 82.4	$ 75.6
Insurance benefits in force	$2,213.1	$2,240.8	$2,291.0
Tax-free proceeds received	$ 11.9	$ 19.4	$ 18.0

Grace's financial statements display income statement activity and balance sheet amounts on a net basis, reflecting the contractual interdependency of policy assets and liabilities.

Contracts

2.167

HILTON HOTELS CORPORATION (DEC)

(In millions)	2002	2003
Total current assets	$ 630	$1,020
Investments, property and other assets		
Investments and notes receivable, net	490	558
Long-term receivable	325	—
Property and equipment, net	3,971	3,641
Management and franchise contracts, net	429	383
Leases, net	118	115
Brands	970	970
Goodwill	1,273	1,240
Other assets	142	251
Total investments, property and other assets	7,718	7,158
Total assets	$8,348	$8,178

NOTES TO CONSOLIDATED FINANCIAL STATEMENTS

Summary of Significant Accounting Policies (In Part)

Management and Franchise Contracts

Management and franchise contracts acquired in acquisitions that were accounted for as purchases are recorded at the estimated present value of net cash flow expected to be received over the lives of the contracts. This value is amortized using the straight-line method over the remaining contract lives. Costs incurred to acquire individual management and franchise contracts are amortized using the straight-line method over the life of the respective contract. Accumulated amortization of management and franchise contracts totaled $143 million and $185 million at December 31, 2002 and 2003, respectively.

Assets of Nonhomogeneous Operations

2.168

PACCAR INC. (DEC)

(Millions of dollars)	2003	2002
Total truck and other assets	$4,334.2	$3,590.2
Financial services		
Cash and cash equivalents	23.8	34.9
Finance and other receivables, net of allowance for losses (2003—$119.2 and 2002—$109.1)	4,994.9	4,659.2
Equipment on operating leases, net	471.0	310.9
Other assets	115.7	107.3
Total financial services assets	5,605.4	5,112.3
Total assets	$9,939.6	$8,702.5

NOTES TO CONSOLIDATED FINANCIAL STATEMENTS
(In millions)

A (In Part): Significant Accounting Policies

Description of Operations

PACCAR Inc (the Company of PACCAR) is a multinational company operating in two segments: (1) the manufacture and distribution of light-, medium- and heavy-duty commercial trucks and related aftermarket parts and (2) finance and leasing products and services provided to customers and dealers.

D. Finance and Other Receivables

Finance and other receivables are as follows:

	2003	2002
Retail notes and contracts	$2,901.1	$2,804.4
Wholesale financing	727.4	634.9
Direct financing leases	1,695.5	1,540.4
Interest and other receivables	71.2	63.3
	5,395.2	5,043.0
Less allowance for losses	(119.2)	(109.1)
	5,276.0	4,933.9
Unearned interest:		
Retail notes and contracts	(91.7)	(90.7)
Direct financing leases	(189.4)	(184.0)
	(281.1)	(274.7)
	$4,994.9	$4,659.2

The majority of the Company's customers are located in the United States, which represented 60% of total receivables at December 31, 2003, and 68% at December 31, 2002. Terms for substantially all finance and other receivables range up to 60 months. Repayment experience indicates some receivables will be paid prior to contract maturity, while others will be extended or renewed.

Annual payments due on retail notes and contracts beginning January 1, 2004, are $1,127.9, $786.1, $537.4, $309.9, $126.3 and $13.5 thereafter.

Annual minimum lease payments due on direct financing leases beginning January 1, 2004, are $491.1, $414.2, $324.5, $194.5, $95.3 and $46.3 thereafter. Estimated resid-

ual values included with direct financing leases amounted to $129.6 in 2003 and $114.6 in 2002.

E. Allowance for Losses

The provision for losses on net finance and other receivables is charged to income in an amount sufficient to maintain the allowance for losses at a level considered adequate to cover estimated credit losses. Receivables are charged to this allowance when, in the judgment of management, they are deemed uncollectible (generally upon repossession of the collateral).

The allowance for losses on Truck and Other and Financial Services receivables is summarized as follows:

	Truck and Other	Financial Services
Balance, December 31, 2000	$22.8	$104.6
Provision for losses	.4	86.5
Net losses, including translation	(1.5)	(86.4)
Balance, December 31, 2001	21.7	104.7
Provision for losses	2.1	53.2
Net losses	(.3)	(51.1)
Translation	2.4	2.3
Balance, December 31, 2002	25.9	109.1
Provision for losses	(8.6)	28.6
Net losses	(4.8)	(24.2)
Translation	2.4	5.7
Balance, December 31, 2003	$14.9	$119.2

The Company's customers are principally concentrated in the transportation industry. There are no significant concentrations of credit risk in terms of a single customer. Generally, Financial Services receivables are collateralized by financed equipment.

F (In Part): Equipment on Operating Leases

Financial Services

Equipment leased to customers under operating leases is recorded at cost and is depreciated on the straight-line basis to its estimated residual value. Estimated useful lives range from five to ten years.

	2003	2002
Transportation equipment	$607.8	$392.8
Less allowance for depreciation	(136.8)	(81.9)
	$471.0	$310.9

Original terms of operating leases generally average four years. Annual minimum lease payments due on operating leases beginning January 1, 2004, are $157.0, $109.3, $100.8, $43.5, $6.6 and $.2 thereafter.

Film and Television Costs

2.169

THE WALT DISNEY COMPANY (SEP)

(In millions)	2003	2002
Total current assets	$ 8,314	$ 7,849
Film and television costs	6,205	5,959
Investments	1,849	1,810
Parks, resorts and other property, at cost		
Attractions, buildings and equipment	19,499	18,917
Accumulated depreciation	(8,794)	(8,133)
	10,705	10,784
Projects in progress	1,076	1,148
Land	897	848
	12,678	12,780
Intangible assets, net	2,786	2,776
Goodwill	16,966	17,083
Other assets	1,190	1,788
Total assets	$49,988	$50,045

NOTES TO CONSOLIDATED FINANCIAL STATEMENTS

Note 2 (In Part): Summary of Significant Accounting Policies

Film and Television Costs

Film and television costs include capitalizable direct negative costs, production overhead, interest and development costs and are stated at the lower of cost, less accumulated amortization, or fair value. Acquired programming costs for the Company's television and cable/satellite networks are stated at the lower of cost, less accumulated amortization, or net realizable value. Acquired television broadcast program licenses and rights are recorded when the license period begins and the program is available for use. Marketing, distribution, and general and administrative costs are expensed as incurred.

Film and television production and participation costs are expensed based on the ratio of the current period's gross revenues to estimated remaining total gross revenues from all sources on an individual production basis. Television network series costs and multi-year sports rights are charged to expense based on the ratio of the current period's gross revenues to estimated remaining total gross revenues from such programs or straight-line, as appropriate. Estimated remaining gross revenue from all sources for film and television productions includes revenue that will be earned within ten years of the date of the initial theatrical release for film productions. For television network series, we include revenues that will be earned within 10 years of the delivery of the first episode, or if still in production, five years from the date of delivery of the most recent episode. For acquired film libraries, remaining revenues include amounts to be earned for up to 20 years from the date of acquisition. Television network and station rights for theatrical movies and other long-form programming are charged to expense primarily on an accelerated basis related to the usage of the programs. Development costs for projects that have been determined will not go into production or have not been set for production within three years are written-off.

Estimates of total gross revenues can change significantly due to a variety of factors, including the level of market acceptance of film and television products, advertising rates and subscriber fees. Accordingly, revenue estimates are reviewed periodically and amortization is adjusted, if necessary. Such adjustments could have a material effect on results of operations in future periods. The net realizable value of network television broadcast program licenses and rights is reviewed using a daypart methodology. A daypart is defined as an aggregation of programs broadcast during a particular time of day or programs of a similar type. The Company's dayparts are early morning, daytime, late night, primetime, news, children and sports (includes network and cable). The net realizable values of other cable programming are reviewed on an aggregated basis for each cable channel.

CURRENT LIABILITIES

2.170 ARB No. 43, Chapter 3A, *Current Assets and Current Liabilities,* as amended by SFAS No. 6, *Classification of Short-Term Obligations Expected to Be Refinanced,* and SFAS No. 78, *Classification of Obligations That Are Callable by the Creditor,* discusses, in paragraphs 7 and 8, the nature of current liabilities. Examples of the various types of current liabilities follow.

SHORT-TERM DEBT

2.171 Table 2-22 lists the captions used by the survey companies to describe short-term notes payable, loans payable and commercial paper. By definition, such short-term obligations are financial instruments.

2.172 *SFAS No. 107,* as amended by *SFAS No. 133,* requires disclosure of both the fair value and the bases for estimating the fair value of short-term notes payable, loans payable, and commercial paper unless it is not practicable to estimate that value. 234 survey companies made 243 fair value disclosures. 34 of those disclosures used market or broker quotes of the short-term debt to determine fair value. 24 of those disclosures stated that either discounted cash flows or market prices of similar instruments were used to estimate fair value. 3 of those disclosures estimated estimated fair value using other valuation methods. 210 disclosures presented carrying amounts which approximated fair value of short-term debt. In addition there were 36 disclosures in which carrying value was compared to fair value in an exposition or table. None of the disclosures stated it was not practicable to estimate fair value.

2.173 *SFAC No. 7* Provides a framework for using future cash flows and present value as the basis for accounting measurements of fair value of an asset or a liability at initial recognition or fresh-start measurements and for future-cash-flow-based amortization techniques, such as interest method amortization. Fresh-start measurements are measurements in periods following initial recognition that establish a new carrying amount unrelated to previous amounts and accounting conventions.

2.174 When observable marketplace-determined values are not available, discounted cash flows are often used to estimate fair value. Accounting applications of present value typically use a single set of estimated cash flows and a risk-adjusted discount rate. This Statement introduces the expected cash flow approach, which differs from the traditional approach by focusing on explicit assumptions about the range of possible cash outcomes and their respective probabilities.

2.175 While *SFAC No. 7* does not require modification of any existing pronouncements, its concepts my be used to determine fair value. This Standard will be used in developing future accounting standards. No data on the use of expected cash flow approach in discounted cash flow applications were compiled.

2.176 Examples of short-term debt presentations and disclosures follow.

2.177

TABLE 2-22: SHORT-TERM DEBT

	2003	2002	2001	2000
Description				
Notes or loans				
Payee indicated.............................	31	45	45	40
Payee not indicated.......................	100	112	131	140
Short-term debt or borrowings...........	145	148	142	144
Commercial paper............................	46	53	59	56
Other..	33	31	57	61
Total Presentations.....................	**355**	**389**	**434**	**441**
Number of Companies				
Showing short-term debt..................	308	321	361	382
Not showing short-term debt.............	292	279	239	218
Total Companies..............................	**600**	**600**	**600**	**600**

2.178

CHEVRONTEXACO CORPORATION (DEC)

(Millions of dollars)	2003	2002
Short-term debt	$ 1,703	$ 5,358
Accounts payable	8,675	8,455
Accrued liabilities	3,172	3,364
Federal and other taxes on income	1,392	1,626
Other taxes payable	1,169	1,073
Total current liabilities	$16,111	$19,876

NOTES TO THE CONSOLIDATED FINANCIAL STATEMENTS

Note 8 (In Part): Financial and Derivative Instruments

Fair Value

Fair values are derived either from quoted market prices or, if not available, the present value of the expected cash flows. The fair values reflect the cash that would have been received or paid if the instruments were settled at year-end.

Long-term debt of $7,229 and $7,296 had estimated fair values of $7,709 and $7,971 at December 31, 2003 and 2002, respectively.

Note 17. Short-Term Debt

	2003	2002
Commercial paper*	$4,078	$7,183
Notes payable to banks and others with originating terms of one year or less	190	713
Current maturities of long-term debt	863	740
Current maturities of long-term capital leases	71	45
Redeemable long-term obligations		
Long-term debt	487	487
Capital leases	299	300
Subtotal	5,988	9,468
Reclassified to long-term debt	(4,285)	(4,110)
Total short-term debt	$1,703	$5,358

* Weighted-average interest rates at December 31,2003 and 2002, were 1.01 percent and 1.47 percent, respectively including the effect of interest rate swaps.

Redeemable long-term obligations consist primarily of tax-exempt variable-rate put bonds that are included as current liabilities because they become redeemable at the option of the bondholders during the year following the balance sheet date.

The company periodically enters into interest rate swaps on a portion of its short-term debt. See Note 8 beginning on page FS-33 for information concerning the company's debt-related derivative activities.

At December 31, 2003, the company had $4,285 of committed credit facilities with banks worldwide, which permit the company to refinance short-term obligations on a long-term basis. The facilities support company's commercial paper borrowings. Interest on borrowings under the terms of specific agreements may be based on the London Interbank Offered Rate or bank prime rate. No amounts were outstanding under these credit agreements during 2003 or year-end.

At December 31, 2003 and 2002, the company classified $4,285 and $4,110, respectively, of short-term debt as long-term. Settlement of these obligations is not expected to require the use of working capital in 2004, as the company has both the intent and the ability to refinance this debt on a long-term basis.

2.179

WHIRLPOOL CORPORATION (DEC)

(Millions of dollars)	2003	2002
Current liabilities		
Notes payable	$ 260	$ 221
Accounts payable	1,944	1,631
Employee compensation	303	273
Deferred income taxes	48	100
Accrued expenses	701	664
Restructuring costs	45	122
Other current liabilities	269	283
Current maturities of long-term debt	19	211
Total current liabilities	$3,589	$3,505

NOTES TO CONSOLIDATED FINANCIAL STATEMENTS

8 (In Part): Financing Arrangements

Notes Payable and Debt (In Part)

At December 31, 2003, the Company had committed unsecured revolving lines of credit available from banks totaling $1.2 billion. The lines of credit are comprised of a committed $800 million credit agreement which expires in June 2006, and a committed $400 million 364-day credit agreement maturing in May 2004. These committed lines support the Company's commercial paper programs and other liquidity needs. The interest rate for borrowing under the credit agreements is generally based on the London Interbank Offered Rate plus a spread that reflects the Company's debt rating. The credit agreements require that the Company maintain a maximum debt to EBITDA ratio and a minimum interest coverage ratio. At December 31, 2003, the Company was in compliance with its financial covenants. The credit agreements provide the Company with access to adequate and competitive funding under usual or unusual market conditions. During 2003, there were no borrowings outstanding under these credit agreements.

Notes payable consist of the following:

(Millions of dollars)	2003	2002
Payable to banks	$170	$208
Commercial paper	90	13
Total notes payable	$260	$221

The fair value of the Company's notes payable approximates the carrying amount due to the short maturity of these obligations. The weighted average interest rate on notes payable was 3.8% and 5.7% at December 31, 2003 and 2002, respectively.

TRADE ACCOUNTS PAYABLE

2.180   All the survey companies disclosed the existence of amounts owed to trade creditors. As shown in Table 2-23, such amounts were usually described as *Accounts Payable* or *Trade Accounts Payable*.

2.181   As stated in paragraph 13 of *SFAS No. 107*, as amended by *SFAS No. 133*, fair value disclosure is not required for trade payables when the carrying amount of the trade payable approximates its fair value. 256 survey companies made 257 fair value disclosures. Carrying amount approximated fair value of trade payables for 254 disclosures.

2.182   Examples of trade accounts payable presentations follow.

2.183

TABLE 2-23: TRADE ACCOUNTS PAYABLE

	2003	2002	2001	2000
Accounts payable	466	454	453	451
Trade accounts payable	89	96	107	103
Accounts payable combined with accrued liabilities or accrued expenses	28	28	27	30
Other captions	17	22	13	16
Total Companies	**600**	**600**	**600**	**600**

2.184

THE BOEING COMPANY (DEC)

(Dollars in millions)	2003	2002
Accounts payable and other liabilities	$13,563	$13,739
Advances in excess of related costs	3,464	3,123
Income taxes payable	277	1,134
Short-term debt and current portion of long-term debt	1,144	1,814
Total current liabilities	$18,448	$19,810

NOTES TO CONSOLIDATED FINANCIAL STATEMENTS

Note 12 (In Part): Accounts Payable and Other Liabilities

Accounts payable and other liabilities at December 31 consisted of the following:

	2003	2002
Accounts payable	$ 3,822	$ 4,431
Accrued compensation and employee benefit costs	2,930	2,876
Pension liabilities	1,138	1,177
Product warranty liabilities	825	898
Lease and other deposits	316	280
Dividends payable	143	143
Other	4,389	3,934
	$13,563	$13,739

Accounts payable included $289 and $301 as of December 31, 2003 and 2002, attributable to checks written but not yet cleared by the bank.

Note 21 (In Part): Disclosures About Fair Value of Financial Instruments

As of December 31, 2003 and 2002, the carrying amount of accounts payable was $3,822 and $4,431 and the fair value of accounts payable was estimated to be $4,012 and $4,672. The higher fair value reflects a premium due to deferred payment for certain payables that will be collected over an extended period.

2.185

GENERAL MILLS, INC. (MAY)

(In millions)	2003	2002
Current liabilities:		
Accounts payable	$1,303	$1,217
Current portion of long-term debt	105	248
Notes payable	1,236	3,600
Other current liabilities	800	682
Total current liabilities	$3,444	$5,747

NOTES TO CONSOLIDATED FINANCIAL STATEMENTS

7 (In Part): Financial Instruments and Risk Management

The carrying amounts and fair values of our financial instruments (based on market quotes and interest rates at the balance sheet dates) were as follows:

	2003		2002	
(In millions)	Carrying Amount	Fair Value	Carrying Amount	Fair Value
Assets:				
Cash and cash equivalents	$ 703	$ 703	$ 975	$ 975
Receivables	980	980	1,010	1,010
Marketable securities	160	160	160	160
Liabilities:				
Accounts payable	1,303	1,303	1,217	1,217
Debt	8,857	9,569	9,439	9,507
Derivatives relating to:				
Debt	(446)	(446)	(435)	(435)
Commodities	4	4	9	9
Foreign currencies	(18)	(18)	(6)	(6)

EMPLOYEE-RELATED LIABILITIES

2.186   Table 2-24 shows the nature of employee related liabilities disclosed by the survey companies as current liabilities. Examples of employee related liability presentations and disclosures follow.

2.187

TABLE 2-24: EMPLOYEE-RELATED LIABILITIES

	2003	2002	2001	2000
Description				
Salaries, wages, payrolls, commissions	266	266	271	273
Compensation	222	218	203	193
Benefits	60	50	47	47
Pension or profit-sharing contributions	49	48	35	41
Compensated absences	14	14	17	14
Other	46	48	41	49
Total Presentations	**657**	**644**	**614**	**617**
Number of Companies				
Disclosing employee related liabilities	500	499	482	469
Not disclosing	100	101	118	131
Total Companies	**600**	**600**	**600**	**600**

2.188

HON INDUSTRIES INC. (DEC)

(Amounts in thousands)	2003	2002
Current liabilities		
Accounts payable and accrued expenses	$211,236	$252,145
Income taxes	5,958	3,740
Note payable and current maturities of long-term debt	26,658	41,298
Current maturities of other long-term obligations	1,964	1,497
Total current liabilities	$245,816	$298,680

NOTES TO CONSOLIDATED FINANCIAL STATEMENTS

Accounts Payable and Accrued Expenses

(In thousands)	2003	2002
Trade accounts payable	$ 44,295	$ 66,204
Compensation	22,803	20,686
Profit sharing and retirement expense	30,365	26,788
Vacation pay	13,745	14,095
Marketing expenses	44,795	59,224
Casualty self-insurance expense	9,385	10,973
Other accrued expenses	45,848	54,175
	$211,236	$252,145

2.189

NEWELL RUBBERMAID INC. (DEC)

(In millions)	2003	2002
Current liabilities:		
Notes payable	$ 21.9	$ 25.2
Accounts payable	777.4	686.6
Accrued compensation	131.1	153.5
Other accrued liabilities	996.3	1,165.4
Income taxes	81.8	159.7
Current portion of long-term debt	13.5	424.0
Total current liabilities	$2,022.0	$2,614.4

NOTES TO CONSOLIDATED FINANCIAL STATEMENTS

Footnote 4: Other Accrued Liabilities

Accrued liabilities included the following as of December 31, (in millions):

	2003	2002
Customer accruals	$191.5	$ 289.6
Accrued purchase accounting	12.2	119.0
Accrued self-insurance liability	85.7	91.5
Accrued restructuring	153.1	79.3
Accrued pension and other postemployment benefits	130.0	115.9
Accruals for inventory received, not invoiced	96.6	115.2
Accrued interest	26.1	63.4
Employee withholdings	25.0	24.4
Accrued contingencies	51.4	62.6
Other	224.7	204.5
Other accrued liabilities	$996.3	$1,165.4

Customer accruals are promotional allowances and rebates given to customers in exchange for their selling efforts. The self-insurance accrual is primarily casualty liabilities such as workers' compensation, general and product liability and auto liability and is estimated based upon historical loss experience.

INCOME TAX LIABILITY

2.190   Table 2-25 summarizes the descriptive balance sheet captions used to describe the current liability for income taxes.

2.191

TABLE 2-25: CURRENT INCOME TAX LIABILITY				
	2003	2002	2001	2000
Income taxes	318	296	285	303
Taxes—type not specified	59	47	45	45
Federal, state, and foreign income taxes	11	10	7	10
Federal and state income taxes	8	9	9	12
U.S. and foreign income taxes	8	4	6	7
Federal and foreign income taxes	2	5	5	3
Federal income taxes	2	5	4	3
Other captions	10	18	9	16
No current income tax liability	182	206	230	201
Total Companies	**600**	**600**	**600**	**600**

2.192

NORTHROP GRUMMAN CORPORATION (DEC)

(In millions)	2003	2002
Current liabilities		
Notes payable to banks	$ 10	$ 22
Current portion of long-term debt	461	203
Trade accounts payable	1,491	1,427
Accrued employees' compensation	995	1,018
Advances on contracts	1,285	1,066
Contract loss provisions	364	453
Income taxes payable	356	1,237
Other current liabilities	1,299	1,414
Liabilities of businesses held for sale	100	4,593
Total current liabilities	$6,361	$11,433

2.193

XEROX CORPORATION (DEC)

(In millions)	2003	2002
Short-term debt and current portion of long-term debt	$4,236	$4,377
Accounts payable	898	839
Accrued compensation and benefits costs	532	481
Unearned income	251	257
Other current liabilities	1,652	1,833
Total current liabilities	$7,569	$7,787

NOTES TO THE CONSOLIDATED FINANCIAL STATEMENTS
(Dollars in millions)

Note 9 (In Part): Supplementary Financial Information

The components of other current liabilities at December 31, 2003 and 2002 were as follows:

	2003	2002
Other current liabilities		
Income taxes payable	$ 264	$ 236
Other taxes payable	289	177
Interest payable	147	187
Restructuring reserves	180	286
Due to Fuji Xerox	111	117
Financial derivative instruments	51	70
Other	610	760
Total	$1,652	$1,833

CURRENT AMOUNT OF LONG-TERM DEBT

2.194 Table 2-26 summarizes the descriptive balance sheet captions used to describe the amount of long-term debt payable during the next year. *SFAS No. 107*, as amended by *SFAS No. 133*, requires disclosure of both the fair value and the bases for estimating the fair value of the current amount of long-term debt unless it is not practicable to estimate that value. 190 survey companies made 215 fair value disclosures. 80 of those disclosures used market or broker quotes of the current amount of long-term debt to determine fair value. 68 of those disclosures stated that either discounted cash flows or market prices of similar instruments were used to estimate fair value. 3 of those disclosures estimated fair value using other valuation methods. 113 disclosures presented carrying amounts which approximated fair value of current amount of long-term debt. In addition there were 48 disclosures in which carrying value was compared to fair value in an exposition or a table. One disclosure stated it was not practicable to estimate fair value.

2.195 *SFAC No. 7* provides a framework for using future cash flows and present value as the basis for accounting measurements of fair value of an asset or a liability at initial recognition or fresh-start measurements and for future-cash-flow-based amortization techniques, such as interest-method amortization. Fresh-start measurements are measurements in periods following initial recognition that establish a new carrying amount unrelated to previous amounts and accounting conventions.

2.196 When observable marketplace-determined values are not available, discounted cash flows are often used to estimate fair value. Accounting applications of present value typically use a single set of estimated cash flows and a risk-adjusted discount rate. This Statement introduces the expected cash flow approach, which differs from the traditional approach by focusing on explicit assumptions about the range of possible cash outcomes and their respective probabilities.

2.197 While *SFAC No. 7* does not require modification of any existing pronouncements, its concepts may be used to determine fair value. This Standard will be used in developing future accounting standards. No data on the use of expected cash flow approach in discounted cash flow applications were compiled.

2.198

TABLE 2-26: CURRENT AMOUNT OF LONG-TERM DEBT

	Number of Companies			
	2003	2002	2001	2000
Current portion of long-term debt..........	232	233	232	217
Current maturities of long-term debt.....	163	161	169	175
Current amount of long-term leases.....	34	36	36	29
Long-term debt due or payable within one year..............................	32	36	34	30
Current installment of long-term debt...	11	21	15	19
Other captions.................................	11	13	12	25

2.199

CONSTELLATION BRANDS, INC. (FEB)

(In thousands)	2003	2002
Current liabilities:		
Notes payable to banks	$ 2,623	$ 54,775
Current maturities of long-term debt	71,264	81,609
Accounts payable	171,073	153,433
Accrued excise taxes	36,421	60,238
Other accrued expenses and liabilities	303,827	245,155
Total current liabilities	$585,208	$595,210

NOTES TO CONSOLIDATED FINANCIAL STATEMENTS

1 (In Part): Summary of Significant Accounting Policies

Fair Value of Financial Instruments (In Part)

To meet the reporting requirements of Statement of Financial Accounting Standards No. 107, "Disclosures about Fair Value of Financial Instruments," the Company calculates the fair value of financial instruments using quoted market prices whenever available. When quoted market prices are not available, the Company uses standard pricing models for various types of financial instruments (such as forwards, options, swaps, etc.) which take into account the present value of estimated future cash flows.

The carrying amount and estimated fair value of the Company's financial instruments are summarized as follows:

(In thousands)	2003		2002	
	Carrying Amount	Fair Value	Carrying Amount	Fair Value
Assets:				
Cash and cash investments	$ 13,810	$ 13,810	$ 8,961	$ 8,961
Accounts receivable	$ 399,095	$ 399,095	$ 383,922	$ 383,922
Currency forward contracts	$ 35,132	$ 35,132	$ 6	$ 6
Liabilities:				
Notes payable to banks	$ 2,623	$ 2,623	$ 54,775	$ 54,775
Accounts payable	$ 171,073	$ 171,073	$ 153,433	$ 153,433
Long-term debt, including current portion	$1,262,895	$1,400,794	$1,374,792	$1,407,374
Currency forward contracts	$ —	$ —	$ 105	$ 105

The following methods and assumptions were used to estimate the fair value of each class of financial instruments:

Long-Term Debt

The senior credit facility is subject to variable interest rates which are frequently reset; accordingly, the carrying value of this debt approximates its fair value. The fair value of the remaining long-term debt, which is all fixed rate, is estimated by discounting cash flows using interest rates currently available for debt with similar terms and maturities.

9 (In Part): Borrowings

Borrowings consist of the following:

(In thousands)	2003			2002
	Current	Long-Term	Total	Total
Notes payable to banks:				
Senior credit facility—revolving credit loans	$ 2,000	$ —	$ 2,000	$ 50,000
Other	623	—	623	4,775
	$ 2,623	$ —	$ 2,623	$ 54,775
Long-term debt:				
Senior credit facility—term loans	$67,082	$ 78,281	$ 145,363	$ 281,292
Senior notes	—	643,229	643,229	619,205
Senior subordinated notes	—	450,000	450,000	450,000
Other long-term debt	4,182	20,121	24,303	24,295
	$71,264	$1,191,631	$1,262,895	$1,374,792

• • • • • •

Debt Payments

Prior to the payoff of the 2000 Credit Agreement principal payments required under long-term debt obligations (excluding unamortized discount) during the next five fiscal years and thereafter are as follows:

(In thousands)	
2004	$ 71,264
2005	82,777
2006	4,174
2007	203,918
2008	203,947
Thereafter	697,309
	$1,263,389

2.200

COOPER TIRE & RUBBER COMPANY (DEC)

(In thousands)	2002	2003
Current liabilties:		
Notes payable	$ 21,956	$ 2,770
Accounts payable	206,638	267,224
Accrued liabilities	189,662	197,169
Income taxes	1,326	6,549
Current portion of long-term debt	14,994	3,015
Total current liabilities	$434,576	$476,727

NOTES TO CONSOLIDATED FINANCIAL STATEMENTS
(Dollar amounts in thousands)

Debt (In Part)

The following table summarizes the long-term debt of the Company at December 31, 2002 and 2003:

	2002	2003
7.75% unsecured notes, aggregate principal payment due December 2009	$357,326	$353,905
8% unsecured notes, aggregate principal payment due December 2019	225,000	225,000
7.63% unsecured notes, aggregate principal payment due March 2027	189,900	189,900
6.55% unsecured notes due 2003	12,500	—
Canadian floating rate note due 2006	90,000	90,000
Capitalized leases and other	15,646	16,158
	890,372	874,963
Less current maturities	14,994	3,015
	$875,378	$871,948

The maturities of long-term debt through 2008 are as follows:

2004	$ 3,015
2005	2,101
2006	91,771
2007	1,057
2008	859

Fair Value of Financial Instruments (In Part)

The fair value of the Company's debt is computed using discounted cash flow analyses based on the Company's estimated current incremental borrowing rates. The carrying amounts and fair values of the Company's financial instruments as of December 31 are as follows:

	2002		2003	
	Carrying Amount	Fair Value	Carrying Amount	Fair Value
Cash and cash equivalents	$ 44,748	$ 44,748	$ 66,426	$ 66,426
Notes payable	(21,956)	(21,956)	(2,770)	(2,770)
Current portion of long-term debt	(14,994)	(15,394)	(3,015)	(3,015)
Long-term debt	(875,378)	(975,078)	(871,948)	(1,000,248)
Derivative financial instruments	6,911	6,911	(19,756)	(19,756)

OTHER CURRENT LIABILITIES

2.201   Table 2-27 summarizes other identified current liabilities. The most common types of other current liabilities are: liabilities related to discontinued operations, accrued interest, warranties and deferred revenue.

2.202

TABLE 2-27: OTHER CURRENT LIABILITIES

	Number of Companies			
	2003	2002	2001	2000
Costs related to discontinued operations/restructuring....	151	157	130	76
Interest	130	122	119	110
Deferred revenue	127	116	106	79
Warranties	126	104	71	60
Taxes other than federal income taxes	117	112	106	106
Insurance	89	76	58	56
Deferred taxes	69	61	46	47
Customer advances, deposits	64	60	68	58
Advertising	60	51	55	48
Dividends payable	56	52	58	58
Derivatives	52	45	37	6
Environmental costs	48	50	45	40
Rebates	40	21	14	12
Litigation	30	37	25	11
Due to affiliated companies...	22	20	20	16
Royalties	20	19	15	15
Billings on uncompleted contracts	19	18	15	14
Other—described	153	164	154	158

Costs Related to Discontinued Operations/Restructuring

2.203

CAESARS ENTERTAINMENT, INC. (DEC)

(Dollars in millions)	2003	2002
Accounts payable	$ 53	$ 52
Current maturities of long-term debt	1	325
Income taxes payable	5	4
Accrued expenses	570	602
Liabilities related to assets held for sale	46	36
Total current liabilities	$675	$1,019

NOTES TO CONSOLIDATED FINANCIAL STATEMENTS

Note 3. Discontinued Operations

In December 2003, the Company entered into a definitive agreement to sell the Las Vegas Hilton to an unrelated third party. The Company is to receive cash of approximately $280 million for the property, building, and equipment plus an amount for net working capital. The estimated selling price of the assets less costs to sell the Las Vegas Hilton exceeds the carrying value; therefore no gain or loss has been recognized as of December 31, 2003. This transaction is expected to be completed by the end of the second quarter of 2004 and is subject to customary closing conditions and regulatory approvals outlined in the purchase agreement.

The results of the Las Vegas Hilton are classified as discontinued operations in each period presented in the accompanying consolidated statements of operations. Consolidated interest expense has been allocated to the loss from discontinued operations based on the ratio of Las Vegas Hilton's net assets to the consolidated net assets. In accordance with generally accepted accounting principles, the assets of the Las Vegas Hilton are no longer being depreciated as a result of their designation of being assets held for sale. The assets and liabilities of the Las Vegas Hilton have been classified as "Assets Held for Sale" and "Liabilities Related to Assets Held for Sale" in the accompanying consolidated balance sheets.

Summary operating results for the discontinued operations of the Las Vegas Hilton are as follows:

(In millions)	2003	2002	2001
Net revenues	$214	$215	$ 228
Operating income (loss)	$ (6)	$ 2	$(136)
Interest expense	(6)	(6)	(6)
Income tax benefit	4	2	50
Loss from discontinued operations	$ (8)	$ (2)	$ (92)

The operating loss recorded for the year ended December 31, 2001 was the result of a $124 million asset write-down at the Las Vegas Hilton in accordance with SFAS No. 121, "Accounting for the Impairment of Long-Lived Assets and Long-Lived Assets to be Disposed Of." Due to the significant reduction in the operating performance and expected lower future results, management, with the assistance of an independent appraisal company, determined that the carrying value of the Las Vegas Hilton assets exceeded the fair value. Fair value was determined using a combination of future cash flow analysis and market/sales comparison analysis.

Assets held for sale and liabilities related to assets held for sale are as follows:

(In millions)	2003	2002
Cash and equivalents	$ 10	$ 12
Accounts receivable, net	22	12
Inventories, prepaids and other	6	6
Income taxes receivable	13	7
Deferred income taxes, net	32	39
Property and equipment, net	147	152
Total assets held for sale	$230	$228
Accounts payable	$ 2	$ 1
Accrued expenses	44	35
Total liabilities related to assets held for sale	$ 46	$ 36

2.204

MERISEL, INC. (DEC)

(In thousands)	2002	2003
Current liabilities:		
Accounts payable	$18,157	$13,883
Accrued liabilities	12,408	7,915
Total current liabilities	$30,565	$21,798

NOTES TO CONSOLIDATED FINANCIAL STATEMENTS

5 (In Part): Accounts Payable and Accrued Expenses

Accrued expenses consist of the following at December 31 (in thousands):

	2002	2003
Accrued liabilities:		
Restructuring accruals (see note 7)	$ 2,882	$1,929
Compensation and other benefit accruals	1,819	962
State and local sales taxes and other taxes	1,724	1,454
Other	5,983	3,570
Total accrued liabilities	$12,408	$7,915

7. Restructuring Charges

On December 14, 2000, the Company announced its plan to wind down virtually all of its U.S. distribution business (excluding software licensing). Pursuant to this plan, the Company recorded a restructuring charge of $6,672,000, of which $600,000 related to Optisel and has been reported as discontinued operations. Approximately $921,000 of the charge consists of severance costs and $5,151,000 related to lease termination and facility closures for all but two of the Company's United States locations.

During the third quarter of 2000, the Company announced plans that it would reduce its workforce by approximately 1,000 full-time positions. As a result, the Company recorded a restructuring charge of $10,964,000. Approximately $7,098,000 of the charge consists of termination benefits including severance pay and outplacement services to be provided to those employees that were involuntarily affected by the reduction in workforce. The charge also reflects approximately $3,866,000 of lease termination fees related to the planned closure of certain warehouses and offices.

During 2001 the Company adjusted the restructuring charges previously taken in relation to the wind-down of its U.S. distribution business (excluding software licensing) reducing the charge by $102,000. The adjustment is primarily due to $569,000 of favorable settlements reached with lessors of disposed facilities, net of $467,000 of additional charges related to severance costs associated with six employees.

During 2002 the Company recorded additional restructuring charges in relation to the wind-down of its U.S. distribution business (excluding software licensing) of $465,000. The adjustment is primarily due to $200,000 of additional charges related to facility lease costs and $265,000 of additional charges related to severance costs associated with four employees.

During 2003 the Company recorded additional restructuring charges in relation to the wind-down of its U.S. distribution business (excluding software licensing) of $650,000. The adjustment is due to $208,000 of additional charges related to severance costs associated with approximately ten employees and $442,000, primarily related to facility lease costs.

As of December 31, 2003, $1,929,000 of total restructuring costs had not been paid and was included in accrued liabilities in the accompanying consolidated balance sheets. Future payments of these liabilities are expected to be approximately $1,364,000 and $565,000 in 2004 and 2005, respectively. The following tables display the activity and balances of the restructuring reserve account from December 31, 2000 to December 31, 2003 (in thousands):

	December 31, 2002 Balance	Net Charges (Benefit)	Payments	December 31, 2003 Balance
Type of cost:				
Severance and related costs	$ 283	$ 208	$ (491)	$ 0
Facility, lease and other	2,599	442	(1,112)	1,929
Total	$ 2,882	$ 650	$(1,603)	$1,929

	December 31, 2001 Balance	Net Charges (Benefit)	Payments	December 31, 2002 Balance
Type of cost:				
Severance and related costs	$ 1,176	$ 265	$(1,158)	$ 283
Facility, lease and other	4,184	200	(1,785)	2,599
Total	$ 5,360	$ 465	$(2,943)	$2,882

	December 31, 2000 Balance	Net Charges (Benefit)	Payments	December 31, 2001 Balance
Type of cost:				
Severance and related costs	$ 5,443	$ 467	$(4,734)	$1,176
Facility, lease and other	7,929	(569)	(3,176)	4,184
Total	$13,372	$(102)	$(7,910)	$5,360

Interest

2.205

FREEPORT-MCMORAN COPPER & GOLD INC. (DEC)

(In thousands)	2003	2002
Current liabilities:		
Accounts payable and accrued liabilities	$311,948	$262,310
Current portion of long-term debt and short-term borrowings	152,396	77,112
Accrued interest payable	49,276	29,081
Accrued income taxes	43,134	81,319
Rio Tinto share of joint venture cash flows	39,693	51,297
Unearned customer receipts	35,335	36,754
Total current liabilities	$631,782	$537,873

Deferred Revenue

2.206

AMAZON.COM, INC. (DEC)

(In thousands)	2003	2002
Current liabilities:		
Accounts payable	$ 819,811	$ 618,128
Accrued expenses and other current liabilities	317,730	314,935
Unearned revenue	37,844	47,916
Interest payable	73,100	71,661
Current portion of long-term debt and other	4,216	13,318
Total current liabilities	$1,252,701	$1,065,958

NOTES TO CONSOLIDATED FINANCIAL STATEMENTS

Note 1 (In Part): Description of Business and Accounting Policies

Unearned Revenue

Unearned revenue is recorded when payments are received in advance of our service obligations and is amortized ratably over the service period.

Note 5—Unearned Revenue

During 2003 and 2002, activity in unearned revenue was as follows (in thousands):

Balance, December 31, 2001	$ 87,978
Cash received or accounts receivable	95,404
Amortization to revenue	(135,466)
Balance, December 31, 2002	47,916
Cash received or accounts receivable	101,774
Amortization to revenue	(111,846)
Balance, December 31, 2003	$ 37,844

All amounts recorded as accounts receivable, including amounts associated with unearned revenue, are legally due and contractually enforceable. At December 31, 2003 accounts receivable, net associated with unearned revenue was $2 million.

2.207

CIENA CORPORATION (OCT)

(In thousands)	2002	2003
Current liabilities:		
Accounts payable	$ 39,841	$ 44,402
Accrued liabilities	132,588	98,926
Restructuring liabilities	27,423	14,378
Unfavorable lease commitments	7,630	9,380
Income taxes payable	—	4,640
Deferred revenue	15,388	14,473
Other current obligations	948	—
Total current liabilities	$223,818	$186,199

NOTES TO CONSOLIDATED FINANCIAL STATEMENTS

1 (In Part): The Company and Significant Accounting Policies and Estimates

Revenue Recognition

CIENA recognizes product revenue in accordance with the terms of the sales contract and where collection is reasonably assured. For transactions where CIENA has yet to obtain customer acceptance, revenue is not recognized until the terms of acceptance are satisfied. Revenue for installation services is recognized as the services are performed unless the terms of the supply contract combine product acceptance with installation, in which case, revenue from installation services are recognized when the terms of acceptance are satisfied and installation is completed. Amounts received in excess of revenue recognized are included as deferred revenue in the accompanying balance sheet. For transactions involving the sale of software, revenue is recognized in accordance with Statement of Position No. 97-2 ("SOP 97-2"), "Software Revenue Recognition," including deferral of revenue recognition in instances where vendor specific objective evidence for undelivered elements is not determinable. For distributor sales where risks of ownership have not transferred, CIENA recognizes revenue when the product is shipped through to the end user.

Product Warranties

2.208

ROCKWELL COLLINS, INC. (SEP)

(In millions)	2003	2002
Current liabilities:		
Short-term debt	$ 42	$ 132
Accounts payable	198	211
Compensation and benefits	216	219
Income taxes payable	3	20
Product warranty costs	144	152
Other current liabilities	298	304
Total current liabilities	$901	$1,038

NOTES TO CONSOLIDATED FINANCIAL STATEMENTS

19 (In Part): Guarantees and Indemnifications

In November 2002, the FASB issued Interpretation No. 45, *Guarantor's Accounting and Disclosure Requirements for Guarantees, Including Indirect Guarantees of Indebtedness of Others* (FIN 45). FIN 45 expands the disclosure requirements related to certain guarantees, including product warranties, and requires the Company to recognize a liability for the fair value of all guarantees issued or modified after December 31, 2002. FIN 45 did not impact the Company's results of operations, financial position or cash flows, but did require additional disclosures for certain guarantees.

Product Warranty Costs

Reserves are recorded on the Statement of Financial Position to reflect the Company's contractual liabilities relating to warranty commitments to customers. Warranty coverage of various lengths and terms is provided to customers depending on standard offerings and negotiated contractual agreements. An estimate for warranty expense is recorded at the time of sale based on historical warranty return rates and repair costs.

Changes in the carrying amount of accrued product warranty costs for the year ended September 30, 2003 are summarized as follows:

(In millions)	
Balance at September 30, 2002	$152
Warranty costs incurred	(59)
Product warranty accrual	52
Pre-existing warranty adjustments	(1)
Balance at September 30, 2003	$144

Taxes Other Than Federal Income Taxes

2.209

ORACLE CORPORATION (MAY)

(In millions)	2003	2002
Current liabilities:		
Accounts payable	$ 228	$ 228
Current portion of long-term debt	153	—
Income taxes payable	891	1,091
Value added tax and sales tax payable	166	155
Accrued compensation and related benefits	454	458
Other accrued liabilities	857	787
Deferred revenues	1,409	1,241
Total current liabilities	$4,158	$3,960

Insurance

2.210

B J SERVICES COMPANY (SEP)

(In thousands)	2003	2002
Current liabilities:		
Accounts payable, trade	$220,031	$168,875
Short-term borrowings	5,888	3,522
Current portion of long-term debt	—	256
Accrued employee compensation and benefits	69,205	59,380
Income taxes	60,496	20,012
Taxes other than income	21,696	11,570
Accrued insurance	14,772	12,311
Other accrued liabilities	78,573	80,494
Total current liabilities	$470,661	$356,420

NOTES TO THE CONSOLIDATED FINANCIAL STATEMENTS

2 (In Part): Summary of Significant Accounting Policies

Self Insurance Accruals

The Company is self-insured for certain losses relating to workers' compensation, general liability, property damage and employee medical benefits for claims filed and claims incurred but not reported. The Company's liability is estimated on an actuarial undiscounted basis using individual case-based valuations and statistical analysis and is based upon judgment and historical experience, however, the final cost of many of these claims may not be known for five years or longer. Management reviews the reserve on a quarterly basis. At September 30, 2003 and September 30, 2002, self-insurance accruals totaled $14.8 million and $12.3 million, respectively.

Deferred Taxes

2.211

SMITH INTERNATIONAL, INC. (DEC)

(In thousands)	2003	2002
Current liabilities:		
Short-term borrowings and current portion of long-term debt	$ 89,747	$159,692
Accounts payable	310,754	256,069
Accrued payroll costs	73,723	49,946
Income taxes payable	69,301	43,936
Other	87,399	85,453
Total current liabilities	$630,924	$595,096

NOTES TO CONSOLIDATED FINANCIAL STATEMENTS
(All dollar amounts are expressed in thousands, unless otherwise noted)

1 (In Part): Summary of Significant Accounting Policies

Income Taxes

The Company accounts for income taxes using an asset and liability approach for financial accounting and income tax reporting based on enacted tax rates. Deferred tax assets are reduced by a valuation allowance when it is more likely than not that some portion, or all, of the deferred tax assets will not be realized.

10 (In Part): Income Taxes

The components of deferred taxes at December 31 are as follows:

	2003	2002
Deferred tax liabilities attributed to the excess of net book basis over remaining tax basis (principally depreciation):		
United States	$ (60,795)	$(50,727)
Non-United States	(46,517)	(38,225)
Total deferred tax liabilities	(107,312)	(88,952)
Deferred tax assets attributed to net operating loss and tax credit carryforwards:		
United States	—	2,088
Non-United States	16,039	21,817
Other deferred tax assets (principally accrued liabilities not deductible until paid and inventories):		
United States	49,400	41,868
Non-United States	6,243	2,249
Subtotal	71,682	68,022
Valuation allowance	(15,283)	(18,916)
Total deferred tax assets	56,399	49,106
Net deferred tax liabilities	$ (50,913)	$(39,846)
Balance sheet presentation:		
Deferred tax assets, net	$ 31,238	$ 25,403
Other assets	4,140	6,263
Other current liabilities	(6,226)	(6,833)
Deferred tax liabilities	(80,065)	(64,679)
Net deferred tax liabilities	$ (50,913)	$(39,846)

At December 31, 2003, the accompanying consolidated financial statements-include $16.0 million of deferred tax assets associated with operating loss carryforwards in tax jurisdictions outside the United States. Although the majority of these losses will carryforward indefinitely and are available to reduce future tax liabilities of the respective foreign entity, we do not currently believe the majority of these assets will be realized and have, accordingly, established a $15.3 million valuation reserve.

The valuation allowance as of December 31, 2002 totaled $18.9 million which consisted of established reserves for foreign operating loss carryforwards as well as amounts associated with certain recorded U.S. deferred tax assets. During 2003, the valuation allowance was reduced by $3.6 million as a result of changes in the anticipated realizability of U.S. deferred tax assets.

The Company has provided additional taxes for the anticipated repatriation of certain earnings of its non-U.S. subsidiaries. Undistributed earnings above the amounts upon which additional taxes have been provided, which approximated $108.6 million at December 31, 2003, are intended to be permanently invested by the Company. It is not practicable to determine the amount of applicable taxes that would be incurred if any of such earnings were repatriated.

Advances/Deposits

2.212

ALLTEL CORPORATION (DEC)

(Dollars in millions)	2003	2002
Current liabilities:		
Current maturities of long-term debt	$ 277.2	$ 494.7
Accounts payable	479.8	413.7
Advance payments and customer deposits	205.3	214.3
Accrued taxes	114.6	72.3
Accrued dividends	116.2	109.6
Accrued interest	107.1	123.8
Other current liabilities	192.5	171.8
Liabilities related to assets held for sale	—	190.5
Total current liabilities	$1,492.7	$1,790.7

Advertising

2.213

LIZ CLAIBORNE, INC. (DEC)

(Amounts in thousands)	2003	2002
Current liabilities:		
Short term borrowings	$ 18,915	$ 21,989
Accounts payable	227,125	225,032
Accrued expenses	251,286	283,458
Income taxes payable	29,316	26,241
Total current liabilities	$526,642	$556,720

NOTES TO CONSOLIDATED FINANCIAL STATEMENTS

Note 1 (In Part): Significant Accounting Policies

Advertising, Promotion and Marketing

All costs associated with advertising, promoting and marketing of Company products are expensed during the periods when the activities take place. Costs associated with cooperative advertising programs are expensed when the advertising is run. Advertising and promotion expenses were $131.0 million in 2003, $119.8 million in 2002 and $115.2 million in 2001. Marketing expenses, including in-store and other Company-sponsored activities, were $44.7 million in 2003, $41.9 million in 2002 and $40.5 million in 2001.

Note 8: Accrued Expenses

Accrued expenses consisted of the following:

(In thousands)	2003	2002
Payroll and bonuses	$ 43,233	$ 64,018
Taxes, other than taxes on income	5,643	12,210
Employee benefits	56,223	45,296
Advertising	28,561	25,049
Restructuring reserve	1,969	11,377
Accrued interest	11,551	9,582
Mark-to-market liability	14,973	4,369
Deferred royalty income	4,869	—
Additional purchase price payments	—	42,214
Other	84,264	69,343
	$251,286	$283,458

Dividends

2.214

BRISTOL-MYERS SQUIBB COMPANY (DEC)

(Dollars in millions)	2003	2002
Current liabilities:		
Short-term borrowings	$ 127	$1,379
Accounts payable	1,893	1,551
Accrued expenses	2,967	2,537
Accrued rebates and returns	950	883
U.S. and foreign income taxes payable	707	525
Dividends payable	543	542
Accrued litigation liabilities	267	600
Deferred revenue on consigned inventory	76	470
Total current liabilities	$7,530	$8,487

Derivatives

2.215

FLOWERS FOODS, INC. (DEC)

(Amounts in thousands)	2003	2002
Current liabilities:		
Current maturities of long-term debt	$ 5,286	$ 27,231
Accounts payable	81,293	82,827
Facility closing costs and severance	4,683	4,516
Liabilities related to assets to be disposed of—discontinued operations	—	2,553
Other accrued liabilities	71,870	100,151
	$163,132	$217,278

Note 8. Derivative Financial Instruments

The company enters into commodity derivatives, designated as cash flow hedges of existing or future exposure to changes in commodity prices. The company's primary raw materials are flour, sugar, shortening and dairy products, along with pulp and paper and petroleum-based packaging products. The company also enters into interest rate derivatives to hedge exposure to changes in interest rates.

As of January 3, 2004, the balance in accumulated other comprehensive income (loss) related to derivative transactions was $3.9 million. Of this total, approximately $4.0 million was related to fair value of instruments expiring in fiscal 2004 and $(0.1) million was related to deferred gains and losses on cash-flow hedge positions.

The company routinely transfers amounts from other comprehensive income ("OCI") to earnings as transactions for which cash flow hedges were held occur. Significant situations which do not routinely occur that could cause transfers from OCI to earnings are as follows: (i) an event that causes a hedge to be suddenly ineffective and significant enough that hedge accounting must be discontinued and (ii) cancellation of a forecasted transaction for which a derivative was held as a hedge or a significant and material reduction in volume used of a hedged ingredient such that the company is overhedged and must discontinue hedge accounting.

As of January 3, 2004, the company's hedge portfolio contained commodity derivatives with a fair value of $6.6 million, which is recorded in other current assets. The positions held in the portfolio are used to hedge economic exposure to changes in various raw material prices and effectively fix the price, or limit increases in prices, for a period of time extending into fiscal 2004. Under SFAS 133, these instruments are designated as cash-flow hedges. The effective portion of changes in fair value for these derivatives is recorded each period in other comprehensive income (loss), and any ineffective portion of the change in fair value is recorded to current period earnings in selling, marketing and administrative expenses. The company held no commodity derivatives at January 3, 2004 that do not qualify for hedge accounting under SFAS 133. During fiscal 2003, fiscal 2002 and fiscal 2001, $0.1 million, $0.4 million and $0.1 million, respectively was recorded as income to current earnings due to changes in fair value of these instruments.

In April 2001, the company entered into an interest rate swap transaction with a notional amount of $150.0 million, expiring on December 31, 2003, in order to effectively convert a designated portion of its borrowings under the facility to a fixed rate instrument. On December 26, 2002, that swap was amended to reduce the notional value to $105.0 million. In addition, the company entered into a new interest rate swap with a notional amount of $45.0 million, expiring on December 31, 2003, in order to effectively convert variable rate interest payments on a designated portion of its capital lease obligations to fixed rate payments. In accordance with SFAS 133, on January 30, 2003, the announcement date of the pending sale of the Mrs. Smith's Bakeries frozen dessert business, the company discontinued hedge accounting for these swaps, since the hedged debt and capital leases would be paid off and the swaps would be terminated at the close of the transaction. On April 24, 2003, at the close of the transaction, the interest rate swaps were terminated for cash, and the related balance in other accumulated comprehensive income of $3.3 million, net of income tax of $2.0 million, was reclassified to discontinued operations.

Additionally, on October 25, 2002, in connection with the acquisition of Ideal Baking Company, Inc. ("Ideal"), the company acquired two interest rate swaps with notional amounts of $1.7 million each, designated cash-flow hedges of the outstanding borrowings of the company.

The interest rate swap agreements result in the company paying or receiving the difference between the fixed and floating rates at specified intervals calculated based on the notional amounts. The interest rate differential to be paid or received is accrued as interest rates change and is recorded as interest expense. Under SFAS 133, these swap transactions are designated as cash-flow hedges. Accordingly, the effective portion of the change in the fair value of the swap transaction is recorded each period in other comprehensive income. The ineffective portion of the change in fair value is recorded to current period earnings in selling, marketing and administrative expenses. The fair value of the interest rate swaps on January 3, 2004 was a liability of $0.04 million, which was recorded in other accrued liabilities. During the fifty-three weeks ended January 3, 2004, interest expense was not materially impacted by periodic settlements of the swaps. However, $2.2 million of interest expense was recognized in discontinued operations during the fifty-three weeks ended January 3, 2004 as a result of periodic settlements of the swaps. Additionally, $0.5 million was recorded as a credit to discontinued operations resulting from the change in fair value of the swaps between January 30, 2003, when hedge accounting was discontinued, and April 24, 2003, when the swaps were terminated. An immaterial amount was recorded to current continuing earnings during the fifty-three weeks ended January 3, 2004.

The company's various commodity and ingredient purchasing agreements, which meet the normal purchases exception under SFAS 133, effectively commit the company to purchase approximately $47.8 million of raw materials at January 3, 2004. Of these commitments, approximately $46.5 million and $1.3 million are expected to be used in production in fiscal 2004 and 2005, respectively.

Note 10. Other Accrued Liabilities

Other accrued liabilities consist of:

(Amounts in thousands)	2003	2002
Employee compensation	$30,476	$ 27,533
Pension	17,000	11,000
Utilities	3,087	2,793
Fair value of derivative instruments	42	8,594
Insurance	11,888	16,098
Interest	19	4,039
Taxes	3,439	3,289
Non-compete agreements	1,905	2,165
Schwan indemnification	1,449	—
Arbitration award	—	11,375
Other	2,565	13,265
Total	$71,870	$100,151

Note 12. Fair Value of Financial Instruments

The carrying value of cash and cash equivalents, accounts and notes receivable and short-term debt approximates fair value, because of the short-term maturity of the instruments. Statement of Financial Accounting Standards No. 107, *"Disclosures about Fair Value of Financial Instruments"*, states that the appropriate interest rate that should be used to estimate the fair value of the distributor notes should be the current market rate at which similar loans would be made to distributors with similar credit ratings and for the same maturities. However, the company utilizes approximately 2,800 independent distributors all with varied financial histories and credit risks. Considering the diversity of credit risks among the independent distributors, the company has no method to accurately determine a market interest rate. The carrying value of the distributor notes at January 3, 2004 and December 28, 2002 were $81.3 million and $79.4 million, respectively, with an interest rate of 12%. The fair value of the company's long-term debt at January 3, 2004 approximates the recorded value due to the variable nature of the stated interest rates. The fair value of the company's outstanding derivative financial instruments based on valuation models using quoted market prices as of January 3, 2004 and December 28, 2002, was $6.5 million and $(7.6) million, respectively.

Environmental Costs

2.216

THE STANLEY WORKS (DEC)

(Millions of dollars)	2003	2002
Current liabilities		
Short-term borrowings	$ —	$140.1
Current maturities of long-term debt	157.7	8.6
Accounts payable	240.2	238.9
Accrued expenses	326.4	266.5
Liabilities held for sale	29.2	27.9
Total current liabilities	$753.5	$682.0

NOTES TO CONSOLIDATED FINANCIAL STATEMENTS

T (In Part): Contingencies

The Company is involved in various legal proceedings relating to environmental issues, employment, product liability and workers' compensation claims and other matters. The Company periodically reviews the status of these proceedings with both inside and outside counsel, as well as an actuary for risk insurance. Management believes that the ultimate disposition of these matters will not have a material adverse effect on operations or financial condition taken as a whole.

The Company recognizes liabilities for contingent exposures when analysis indicates it is both probable that an asset has been impaired or that a liability has been incurred and the amount of impairment or loss can reasonably be estimated. When a range of probable loss can be estimated, the Company accrues the most likely amount. In the event that no amount in the range of probable loss is considered most likely, the minimum loss in the range is accrued.

In the normal course of business, the Company is involved in various lawsuits and claims. In addition, the Company is a party to a number of proceedings before federal and state regulatory agencies relating to environmental remediation. Also, the Company, along with many other companies, has been named as a potentially responsible party (PRP) in a number of administrative proceedings for the remediation of various waste sites, including ten active Superfund sites. Current laws potentially impose joint and several liability upon each PRP. In assessing its potential liability at these sites, the Company has considered the following: the solvency of the other PRPs, whether responsibility is being disputed, the terms of existing agreements, experience at similar sites, and the fact that the Company's volumetric contribution at these sites is relatively small.

The Company's policy is to accrue environmental investigatory and remediation costs for identified sites when it is probable that a liability has been incurred and the amount of loss can be reasonably estimated. The amount of liability recorded is based on an evaluation of currently available facts with respect to each individual site and includes such factors as existing technology, presently enacted laws and regulations, and prior experience in remediation of contaminated sites. The liabilities recorded do not take into account any claims for recoveries from insurance or third parties. As assessments and remediation progress at individual sites, the amounts recorded are reviewed periodically and adjusted to reflect additional technical and legal information that becomes available. As of January 3, 2004 and December 28, 2002, the Company had reserves of $11.5 million and $16.7 million, respectively, primarily for remediation activities associated with Company-owned properties as well as for Superfund sites, for losses that are probable and estimable. Of this amount, $2.8 million is classified as current and $8.7 million as long-term. The range of environmental remediation costs that is reasonably possible is $11.5 million to $35.5 million which is subject to change in the near term. The Company may be liable for environmental remediation of sites it no longer owns. Liabilities have been recorded on those sites in accordance with policy.

The environmental liability for certain sites that have cash payments that are fixed or reliably determinable have been discounted using a rate in the range of 2.6% to 5.4%, depending on the timing of cash payments. The discounted and undiscounted amount of the liability relative to these sites is $6.4 million and $8.4 million, respectively, as of January 3, 2004 and $5.5 million and $7.7 million, respectively, as of December 28, 2002. The payments relative to these sites are expected to be $2.2 million in 2004, $0.7 million in 2005, $1.0 million in 2006, $0.3 million in 2007, $0.3 million in 2008 and $3.9 million thereafter.

The amount recorded for identified contingent liabilities is based on estimates. Amounts recorded are reviewed periodically and adjusted to reflect additional technical and legal information that becomes available. Actual costs to be incurred in future periods may vary from the estimates, given the inherent uncertainties in evaluating certain exposures. Subject to the imprecision in estimating future contingent liability costs, the Company does not expect that any sum it may have to pay in connection with these matters in excess of the amounts recorded will have a materially adverse effect on its financial position, results of operations or liquidity.

Rebates

2.217

ROCKWELL AUTOMATION, INC. (SEP)

(In millions)	2003	2002
Current liabilities		
Short-term debt	$ 9	$162
Accounts payable	327	325
Compensation and benefits	171	161
Income taxes payable	15	44
Other current liabilities	298	274
Total current liabilities	$820	$966

NOTES TO CONSOLIDATED FINANCIAL STATEMENTS

1 (In Part): Basis of Presentation and Accounting Policies

Revenue Recognition (In Part)

The Company records accruals for customer returns, rebates and incentives at the time of shipment based upon historical experience. Changes in such accruals may be required if future returns, rebates and incentives differ from historical experience. Rebates and incentives are recognized as a reduction of sales if distributed in cash or customer account credits. Rebates and incentives are recognized as cost of sales for products or services to be provided.

7. Other Current Liabilities

Other current liabilities are summarized as follows (in millions):

	2003	2002
Advance payments from customers and deferred revenue	$ 79	$ 73
Customer rebates and incentives	70	68
Unrealized losses on foreign exchange contracts	47	21
Product warranty costs	29	31
Taxes other than income taxes	25	28
Other	48	53
Other current liabilities	$298	$274

Litigation

2.218

PPG INDUSTRIES, INC. (DEC)

(Millions)	2003	2002
Current liabilities		
Short-term debt and current portion of long-term debt	$ 327	$ 352
Asbestos settlement (see note 13)	308	190
Accounts payable and accrued liabilities	1,504	1,378
Total current liabilities	$2,139	$1,920

NOTES

13 (In Part): Commitments and Contingent Liabilities

PPG is involved in a number of lawsuits and claims, both actual and potential, including some that it has asserted against others, in which substantial monetary damages are sought. These lawsuits and claims, the most significant of which are described below, relate to product liability, contract, patent, environmental, antitrust and other matters arising out of the conduct of PPG's business. To the extent that these lawsuits and claims involve personal injury and property damage, PPG believes it has adequate insurance; however, certain of PPG's insurers are contesting coverage with respect to some of these claims, and other insurers, as they had prior to the asbestos settlement described below, may contest coverage with respect to some of the asbestos claims if the settlement is not implemented. PPG's lawsuits and claims against others include claims against insurers and other third parties with respect to actual and contingent losses related to environmental, asbestos and other matters.

The result of any future litigation of such lawsuits and claims is inherently unpredictable. However, management believes that, in the aggregate, the outcome of all lawsuits and claims involving PPG, including asbestos-related claims in the event the settlement described below does not become effective, will not have a material effect on PPG's consolidated financial position or liquidity; however, any such outcome may be material to the results of operations of any particular period in which costs, if any, are recognized.

●   ●   ●   ●   ●   ●

For over thirty years, PPG has been a defendant in lawsuits involving claims alleging personal injury from exposure to asbestos. As of Dec. 31, 2003, PPG was one of many defendants in numerous asbestos-related lawsuits involving approximately 116,000 claims. Most of PPG's potential exposure relates to allegations by plaintiffs that PPG should be liable for injuries involving asbestos-containing thermal insulation products manufactured and distributed by Pittsburgh Corning Corporation (PC). PPG and Corning Incorporated are each 50% shareholders of PC. PPG has denied responsibility for, and has defended, all claims for any injuries caused by PC products.

On April 16, 2000, PC filed for Chapter 11 Bankruptcy in the U.S. Bankruptcy Court for the Western District of Pennsylvania located in Pittsburgh, Pa. Accordingly, in the first quarter of 2000, PPG recorded an aftertax charge of $35 million for the write-off of all of its investment in PC. As a consequence of the bankruptcy filing and various motions and orders in that proceeding, the asbestos litigation against PPG (as well as against PC) has been stayed and the filing of additional asbestos suits against them has been enjoined, until thirty days after the effective date of a confirmed plan of reorganization for PC substantially in accordance with the settlement arrangement among PPG and several other parties discussed below. The stay may be terminated if the Bankruptcy Court determines that such a plan will not be confirmed, or the settlement arrangement set forth below is not likely to be consummated.

On May 14, 2002, PPG announced that it had agreed with several other parties, including certain of its insurance carriers, the official committee representing asbestos claimants in the PC bankruptcy (ACC), and the legal representatives of future asbestos claimants appointed in the PC bankruptcy, on the terms of a settlement arrangement relating to asbestos claims against PPG and PC (the "PPG Settlement Arrangement").

On March 28, 2003, Corning Incorporated announced that it had separately reached its own arrangement with the representatives of asbestos claimants for the settlement of certain asbestos claims that might arise from PC products or operations (the "Corning Settlement Arrangement").

The terms of the PPG Settlement Arrangement and the Corning Settlement Arrangement have been incorporated into a bankruptcy reorganization plan for PC along with a disclosure statement describing the plan, which PC filed with the Bankruptcy Court on April 30, 2003. Amendments to the plan and disclosure statement were filed on Aug. 18 and Nov. 20, 2003. Creditors and other parties with an interest in the bankruptcy proceeding were entitled to file objections to the disclosure statement and the plan of reorganization, and a few parties filed objections. On Nov. 26, 2003, after considering objections to the second amended disclosure statement and plan of reorganization, the Bankruptcy Court entered an order approving it and directing that it be sent to creditors, including asbestos claimants, for voting. The Bankruptcy Court established March 2, 2004 as the deadline for receipt of votes. In order to approve the plan, at least two-thirds in amount and more than one-half in number of the allowed creditors in a given class must vote in favor of the plan, and for a plan to contain a channeling injunction for present and future asbestos claims under §524(g) of the Bankruptcy Code, as described below, seventy-five percent of the asbestos claimants voting must vote in favor of the plan. Assuming that the plan receives the requisite votes, the judge would conduct another hearing (which the judge has scheduled for May 3–7, 2004) regarding the fairness of the settlement, including whether the plan would be fair with respect to present and future claimants, whether such claimants would be treated in substantially the same manner, and whether the protection provided to PPG and its participating insurers would be fair in view of the assets they would convey to the asbestos settlement trust (Trust) to be established as part of the plan. At that hearing, creditors and other parties in interest could raise objections to the plan. Following that hearing, the Bankruptcy Court, after considering objections to the plan, would enter a confirmation order if all requirements to confirm a plan of reorganization under the Bankruptcy Code, including the requirements described above, have been satisfied; this order may be appealed to the U.S. District Court for the Western District of Pennsylvania. (The District Court may join the Bankruptcy Court in the confirmation order, in which case an appeal to the District Court would not be necessary). Assuming that the District Court approves the confirmation order, interested parties could appeal the order to the U.S. Third Circuit Court of Appeals and subsequently to the U.S. Supreme Court. The PPG Settlement Arrangement would not become effective until 30 days after the plan of reorganization was finally approved by an appropriate court order that was no longer subject to appeal (the "Effective Date").

If the PC plan of reorganization incorporating the terms of the PPG Settlement Arrangement were approved by the Bankruptcy Court and all legal requirements under the Bankruptcy Code or otherwise were satisfied, the Court would enter a channeling injunction under §524(g) and other provisions of the Bankruptcy Code, prohibiting present and future claimants from asserting bodily injury claims against

PPG or its subsidiaries or PC relating to the manufacture, distribution or sale of asbestos-containing products by PC or PPG or its subsidiaries. The injunction would also prohibit co-defendants in those cases from asserting claims against PPG or its subsidiaries for contribution, indemnification or other recovery. All such claims would have to be filed with the Trust and only paid from the assets of the Trust.

The channeling injunction would not extend to claims against PPG alleging injury caused by asbestos on premises owned, leased or occupied by PPG (so called "premises claims"), or claims alleging property damage resulting from asbestos. Approximately 9,000 of the 116,000 claims pending against PPG and its subsidiaries are premises claims. Many of PPG's premises claims have been resolved without payment from PPG. To date, PPG has paid about $7 million to settle approximately 1,100 premises claims, virtually all of which has been covered by PPG's insurers. There are no property damage claims pending against PPG or its subsidiaries. PPG believes that it has adequate insurance for the asbestos claims not covered by the channeling injunction and that any financial exposure resulting from such claims will not have a material effect on PPG's consolidated financial position, liquidity or results of operations.

PPG has no obligation to pay any amounts under the PPG Settlement Arrangement until the Effective Date. PPG and certain of its insurers (along with PC) would then make payments to the Trust, which would provide the sole source of payment for all present and future asbestos bodily injury claims against PPG, its subsidiaries or PC alleged to be caused by the manufacture, distribution or sale of asbestos products by these companies. PPG would convey the following assets to the Trust. First, PPG would convey the stock it owns in PC and Pittsburgh Corning Europe. Second, PPG would transfer 1,388,889 shares of PPG's common stock. Third, PPG would make aggregate cash payments to the Trust of approximately $998 million, payable according to a fixed payment schedule over 21 years, beginning on June 30, 2003, or, if later, the Effective Date. PPG would have the right, in its sole discretion, to prepay these cash payments to the Trust at any time at a discount rate of 5.5% per annum as of the prepayment date. Under the payment schedule, the amounts due June 30, 2003 and 2004 are $75 million and $98 million, respectively. In addition to the conveyance of these assets, PPG would pay $30 million in legal fees and expenses on behalf of the Trust to recover proceeds from certain historical insurance assets, including policies issued by certain insurance carriers that are not participating in the settlement, the rights to which would be assigned to the Trust by PPG.

PPG's participating historical insurance carriers would make cash payments to the Trust of approximately $1.7 billion between the Effective Date and 2023. These payments could also be prepaid to the Trust at any time at a discount rate of 5.5% per annum as of the prepayment date. In addition, as referenced above, PPG would assign to the Trust its rights, insofar as they relate to the asbestos claims to be resolved by the Trust, to the proceeds of policies issued by certain insurance carriers that are not participating in the PPG Settlement Arrangement and from the estates of insolvent insurers and state insurance guaranty funds.

PPG would grant asbestos releases to all participating insurers, subject to a coverage-in-place agreement with certain insurers for the continuing coverage of premises claims (discussed above). PPG would grant certain participating insurers full policy releases on primary policies and full product liability releases on excess coverage policies. PPG would also grant certain other participating excess insurers credit against their product liability coverage limits.

The following table summarizes the impact on our financial statements resulting from the initial charge in the second quarter of 2002 for the estimated cost of the PPG Settlement Arrangement which included the net present value as of Dec. 31, 2002, using a discount rate of 5.5%, of the aggregate cash payments of approximately $998 million to be made by PPG to the Trust. That amount also included the carrying value of PPG's stock in Pittsburgh Corning Europe, the fair value as of June 30, 2002 of 1,388,889 shares of PPG common stock and $30 million in legal fees of the Trust to be paid by PPG, which together with the first payment originally scheduled to be made to the Trust on June 30, 2003, were reflected in the current liability for PPG's asbestos settlement in the balance sheet as of June 30, 2002. The net present value of the remaining payments of $566 million was recorded in the noncurrent liability for asbestos settlement. The table also presents the impact of the subsequent changes in the estimated cost of the settlement due to the change in fair value of the stock to be transferred to the asbestos settlement trust and the equity forward instrument and the increase in the net present value of the future payments to be made to the trust.

(Millions)	Balance Sheet			
	Asbestos Settlement Liability		Equity Forward (Asset)	Pretax Charge
	Current	Long-Term		
Initial asbestos settlement charge	$206	$566	$ —	$772
Change in fair value:				
PPG stock	(16)	—	—	(16)
Equity forward instrument	—	—	(1)	(1)
Balance as of and activity for the year ended Dec. 31, 2002	190	566	(1)	$755
Change in fair value:				
PPG stock	20	—	—	20
Equity forward instrument	—	—	(14)	(14)
Accretion of asbestos liability	—	32	—	32
Reclassification	98	(98)	—	—
Balance as of and activity for the year ended Dec. 31, 2003	$308	$500	$(15)	$ 38

The fair value of the equity forward instrument is included as an other current asset as of Dec. 31, 2003 and Dec. 31, 2002 in the accompanying balance sheet. The amounts due June 30, 2003 and 2004 of $75 million and $98 million under the fixed payment schedule described above, are included in the current asbestos settlement liability in the accompanying balance sheet. The payment due June 30, 2005 of $91 million, and the net present value of the remaining payments is included in the long-term asbestos settlement in the accompanying balance sheet. It is expected that accretion expense associated with the asbestos liability will continue to be approximately $8 million per quarter through the end of 2004.

Because the filing of asbestos claims against the Company has been enjoined since April 2000, a significant number of additional claims may be filed against the Company if the Bankruptcy Court stay were to expire. If the PPG Settlement Arrangement is not implemented, for any reason, and the Bankruptcy Court stay expires, the Company intends to vigorously defend the pending and any future asbestos claims against it and its subsidiaries. The Company believes that it is not responsible for any injuries caused by PC products, which represent the preponderance of the pending bodily injury claims against it. Prior to 2000, PPG had never been found liable for any such claims, in numerous cases PPG had been dismissed on motions prior to trial, and aggregate settlements by PPG to date have been immaterial. In January 2000, in a trial in a state court in Texas involving six plaintiffs, the jury found PPG not liable. However, a week later in a separate trial also in a state court in Texas, another jury found PPG, for the first time, partly responsible for injuries to five plaintiffs alleged to be caused by PC products. PPG intends to appeal the adverse verdict in the event the settlement does not become effective. Although PPG has successfully defended asbestos claims brought against it in the past, in view of the number of claims, and the questionable verdicts and awards that other companies have experienced in asbestos litigation, the result of any future litigation of such claims is inherently unpredictable.

Billings in Excess of Uncompleted Contract Costs

2.219

MCDERMOTT INTERNATIONAL, INC. (DEC)

(In thousands)	2003	2002
Current liabilities:		
Notes payable and current maturities of long-term debt	$ 37,217	$ 55,577
Accounts payable	146,665	163,811
Accounts payable to The Babcock & Wilcox Company	42,137	32,379
Accrued employee benefits	69,923	60,897
Accrued liabilities—other	166,129	190,843
Accrued contract cost	69,928	53,335
Advance billings on contracts	176,105	329,031
U.S. and foreign income taxes payable	14,727	31,176
Total current liabilities	$722,831	$917,049

NOTES TO CONSOLIDATED FINANCIAL STATEMENTS

Note 1 (In Part): Summary of Significant Accounting Policies

Contracts and Revenue Recognition

We generally recognize contract revenues and related costs on a percentage-of-completion method for individual contracts or combinations of contracts based on work performed, man hours, or a cost-to-cost method, as applicable to the product or activity involved. Certain partnering contracts contain a risk-and-reward element, whereby a portion of total compensation is tied to the overall performance of the alliance partners. We include revenues and related costs so recorded, plus accumulated contract costs that exceed amounts invoiced to customers under the terms of the contracts, in contracts in progress. We include in advance billings on contracts billings that exceed accumulated contract costs and revenues and costs recognized under the percentage-of-completion method. Most long-term contracts contain provisions for progress payments. We expect to invoice customers for all unbilled revenues. We review contract price and cost estimates periodically as the work progresses and reflect adjustments proportionate to the percentage-of-completion in income in the period when those estimates are revised.

For contracts that we are unable to estimate the final profitability except to assure that no loss will ultimately be incurred, we recognize equal amounts of revenue and cost until the final results can be estimated more precisely. For first-of-a-kind in nature contracts, we will recognize revenue and cost equally and will only recognize gross margin when probable and reasonably estimable, which is generally when the contract is 70% complete. We define first-of-a-kind in nature contracts as those long-term construction contracts for projects that have never been attempted before or that contain such a level of risk and uncertainty that estimation of the final outcome is impractical except to assure that no loss will be incurred.

For all contracts including first-of-a-kind, if a current estimate of total contract cost indicates a loss on a contract, the projected loss is recognized in full when determined.

Variations from estimated contract performance could result in material adjustments to operating results for any fiscal quarter or year. We include claims for extra work or changes in scope of work to the extent of costs incurred in contract revenues when we believe collection is probable. At December 31, 2003 and 2002, we have included in accounts receivable approximately $19.5 million relating to commercial contract claims whose final settlement is subject to future determination through negotiations or other procedures that had not been completed.

(In thousands)	2003	2002
Included in contracts in progress:		
Costs incurred less costs of revenue recognized	$ 47,988	$ 44,391
Revenues recognized less billings to customers	21,497	102,945
Contracts in progress	$ 69,485	$ 147,336
Included in advance billings on contracts:		
Billings to customers less revenues recognized	$136,279	$ 477,073
Costs incurred less costs of revenue recognized	39,826	(148,042)
Advance billings on contracts	$176,105	$ 329,031

The following amounts represent retainages on contracts:

(In thousands)	2003	2002
Retainages expected to be collected in 2004	$28,407	$19,812
Retainages expected to be collected after one year	27,624	14,325
Total retainages	$56,031	$34,137

We have included in accounts receivable—trade retainages expected to be collected in 2004. Retainages expected to be collected after one year are included in other assets. Of the long-term retainages at December 31, 2003, we anticipate collecting $19.1 million in 2005, $7.9 million in 2006 and $0.6 million in 2007.

Asset Retirement Obligation

2.220

KERR-MCGEE CORPORATION (DEC)

(Millions of dollars)	2003	2002
Current liabilities		
Accounts payable	$ 735	$ 772
Long-term debt due within one year	574	106
Taxes on income	127	170
Taxes, other than income taxes	37	40
Accrued liabilities	759	520
Current liabilities associated with properties held for disposal	—	2
Total current liabilities	$2,232	$1,610

NOTES TO FINANCIAL STATEMENTS

1 (In Part): The Company and Significant Accounting Policies

Remediation, Restoration and Site Dismantlement Costs

As sites of environmental concern are identified, the company assesses the existing conditions, claims and assertions, generally related to former operations, and records an estimated undiscounted liability when environmental assessments and/or remedial efforts are probable and the associated costs can be reasonably estimated.

In June 2001, the FASB issued FAS 143, "Accounting for Asset Retirement Obligations." FAS 143 requires that an asset retirement obligation (ARO) associated with the retirement of a tangible long-lived asset be recognized as a liability in the period in which it is incurred or becomes determinable (as defined by the standard), with an associated increase in the carrying amount of the related long-lived asset. The cost of the tangible asset, including the initially recognized asset retirement cost, is depreciated over the useful life of the asset. The ARO is recorded at fair value, and accretion expense will be recognized over time as the discounted liability is accreted to its expected settlement value. The fair value of the ARO is measured using expected future cash outflows discounted at the company's credit-adjusted risk-free interest rate.

The company adopted FAS 143 on January 1, 2003, which resulted in an increase in net property of $108 million, an increase in abandonment liabilities of $161 million and a decrease in deferred income tax liabilities of $18 million. The net impact of these changes resulted in an after-tax charge to earnings of $35 million to recognize the cumulative effect of adopting the new accounting standard. In addition, accretion expense of $25 million was recorded during 2003. In accordance with the provisions of FAS 143, Kerr-McGee accrues an abandonment liability associated with its oil and gas wells and platforms when those assets are placed in service, rather than its past practice of accruing the expected abandonment costs on a unit-of-production basis over the productive life of the associated oil and gas field. No market risk premium has been included in the company's calculation of the ARO for oil and gas wells and platforms since no reliable estimate can be made by the company. Additionally, in January 2003, the company announced its plan to close the synthetic rutile plant in Mobile, Alabama, and closed the plant in June 2003. Since the plant had a determinate closure date, the company accrued an abandonment liability of $18 million as of January 1, 2003, associated with its plans to decommission the Mobile facility. Otherwise, the company has not recognized an asset retirement obligation associated with its operating chemical facilities, since there is either no legal obligation or the life of such facilities is indeterminate.

If the provisions of FAS 143 had been applied retroactively, pro forma net loss for 2002 would have been $492 million, with basic and diluted loss per share of $4.91. Pro forma net income for 2001 would have been $484 million, with basic and diluted earnings per share of $4.98 and $4.72, respectively.

7 (In Part): Accrued Liabilities

Accrued liabilities at year-end 2003 and 2002 are as follows:

(Millions of dollars)	2003	2002
Derivatives	$354	$135
Employee-related costs and benefits	141	103
Interest payable	109	105
Current environmental reserves	98	100
Asset retirement obligations (current portion)	20	—
Litigation reserves	5	43
North Sea royalties	—	13
Other	32	21
Total	$759	$520

13. Asset Retirement Obligations

As discussed in Note 1, the company adopted FAS 143 on January 1, 2003. At December 31, 2002, the comparable balance of $222 million reflected in the company's Consolidated Balance Sheet represents the non-current portion of the company's site dismantlement reserve prior to the adoption of FAS 143. A summary of the changes in asset retirement obligations since the date of adoption is included in the table below.

(Millions of dollars)	
January 1, 2003, balance upon adoption of FAS 143	$395
Obligations incurred	11
Accretion expense	25
Abandonment expenditures	(17)
Abandonment obligations settled through property divestitures	(15)
Changes in estimates, including timing	22
December 31, 2003	421
Less current asset retirement obligation	(20)
Non-current asset retirement obligation	$401

LONG-TERM DEBT

2.221   Table 2-28 summarizes the types of long-term debt most frequently disclosed by the survey companies.

2.222   Paragraph 10b of SFAS No. 47, *Disclosure of Long-Term Obligations*, requires that financial statements disclose for each of the five years following the date of the latest balance sheet presented the "aggregate amount of maturities and sinking fund requirements for all long-term borrowings." In addition, disclosure of terms and conditions provided in loan agreements, such as assets pledged as collateral, covenants to limit additional debt, maintain working capital, and restrict dividends, is required by paragraph 18 of SFAS No. 5, *Accounting for Contingencies*.

2.223   Paragraph 7 of *ARB 43, Chapter 3A*, as amended by SFAS No. 78, states that the current liability classification is intended to include long-term obligations that are or will be callable by the creditor either because the debtors' violation of a provision of the debt agreement at the balance sheet date makes the obligation callable or because the violation, if not cured within a specified grace period, will make the obligation callable. Such callable obligations shall be classified as current liabilities unless one of the following conditions is met:

a. The creditor has waived or subsequently lost the right to demand payment for more than one year (or operating cycle, if longer) from the balance sheet date.

b. For long-term obligations containing a grace period within which the debtor may cure the violation, it is probable that the violation will be cured within that period, thus preventing the obligation from becoming callable.

As part of long-term debt presentations there were 15 disclosures of covenant violations.

2.224   *SFAS No. 107*, as amended by *SFAS No. 133*, requires disclosure of both the fair value and the bases for estimating the fair value of long-term debt unless it is not practicable to estimate the value. 508 survey companies made 662 fair value disclosures. 268 of those disclosures used market or broker quotes of long-term debt to determine fair value. 300 of those disclosures stated that either discounted cash flows or market prices of similar instruments were used to estimate fair value. 13 of those disclosures estimated fair value using other valuation methods. 257 disclosures presented carrying amounts which approximated fair value of long-term debt. In addition there were 253 disclosures in which carrying value was compared to fair value in an exposition or a table. None of the disclosures stated it was not practicable to estimate fair value.

2.225   *SFAC No. 7* provides a framework for using future cash flows and present value as the basis for accounting measurements of fair value of an asset or a liability at initial recognition or fresh-start measurements and for future-cash-flow-based amortization techniques, such as interest method amortization. Fresh-start measurements are measurements in periods following initial recognition that establish a new carrying amount unrelated to previous amounts and accounting conventions.

2.226   When observable marketplace-determined values are not available, discounted cash flows are often used to estimate fair value. Accounting applications of present value typically use a single set of estimated cash flows and a risk-adjusted discount rate. This Statement introduces the expected cash flow approach, which differs from the traditional approach by focusing on explicit assumptions about the range of possible cash outcomes and their respective probabilities.

2.227 While *SFAC No. 7* does not require modification of any existing pronouncements, its concepts may be used to determine fair value. This Standard will be used in developing future accounting standards. No data on the use of expected cash flow approach in discounted cash flow applications were compiled.

2.228 Examples of long-term debt disclosures and presentations follow. Examples of long-term lease disclosures and presentations are presented under "Long-Term Leases" in this section.

2.229

TABLE 2-28: LONG-TERM DEBT

	Number of Companies			
	2003	**2002**	**2001**	**2000**
Unsecured				
Notes..................................	427	438	445	444
Debentures..........................	168	182	165	160
Foreign................................	82	86	101	81
Loans..................................	78	96	79	77
Commercial paper...............	59	60	85	104
Bonds..................................	31	30	25	N/C*
ESOP loans.........................	26	31	34	38
Collateralized				
Capitalized leases................	230	241	247	275
Notes or loans.....................	95	88	77	90
Mortgages...........................	50	53	55	54
Convertible				
Notes..................................	77	76	59	48
Debentures..........................	54	48	45	34

* N/C = Not compiled. Line item was not included in table for year shown.

Unsecured

2.230

NORTHROP GRUMMAN CORPORATION (DEC)

(In millions)	2003	2002
Total current liabilities	$6,361	$11,433
Long-term debt	5,410	9,398
Mandatorily redeemable preferred stock	350	350
Accrued retiree benefits	3,811	5,942
Deferred income taxes	509	—
Other long-term liabilities	770	742
Minority interest	13	139

NOTES TO CONSOLIDATED FINANCIAL STATEMENTS

10 (In Part): Fair Value of Financial Instruments

Carrying amounts and the related estimated fair values of the company's financial instruments at December 31 are as follows:

	2003		2002	
(In millions)	Carrying Amount	Fair Value	Carrying Amount	Fair Value
Cash and cash equivalents	$ 342	$ 342	$1,412	$ 1,412
Investment in Auto, at cost	170	—	—	—
Note receivable	499	482	—	—
Short-term notes payable	10	10	22	22
Long-term debt	5,871	6,508	9,601	10,179
Mandatorily redeemable preferred stock	350	436	350	432
Forward share sale agreements				
Liability portion	(13)	(13)	(228)	(237)
Hedge portion	13	13	205	205

Long-Term Debt

The fair value of the long-term debt was calculated based on interest rates available for debt with terms and due dates similar to the company's existing debt arrangements.

12. Notes Payable to Banks and Long-Term Debt

The company has available short-term credit lines in the form of money market facilities with several banks. The amount and conditions for borrowing under these credit lines depend on the availability and terms prevailing in the marketplace. No fees or compensating balances are required for these credit facilities.

TRW Debt Reduction

In connection with the acquisition of TRW, the company assumed various notes and debentures amounting to approximately $4.8 billion. In March 2003, the company's wholly owned subsidiary, Northrop Grumman Space & Mission. Systems Corp. (formerly TRW Inc.), commenced offers to purchase any or all of certain designated outstanding debt securities in a debt reduction plan substantially completed in the second quarter of 2003. In the first phase, approximately $2.4 billion in aggregate principal amount of outstanding debt securities were tendered and accepted for purchase, for a total purchase price of approximately $2.9 billion (including accrued and unpaid interest on the securities). In the second phase, the company purchased on the open market $658 million in aggregate principal amount for a total purchase price of $795 million (including accrued and unpaid interest on the securities). Cash proceeds from the sale of Auto were used to complete these transactions, which contributed to the reduction of total long-term debt to $5.9 billion at December 31, 2003, from $9.6 billion at December 31, 2002.

Notes and Debentures

In February 2001, Northrop Systems issued $1.5 billion of indebtedness pursuant to its senior debt indenture consisting of $750 million of 7.125 percent notes due 2011 and $750 million of 7.75 percent debentures due 2031.

Credit Facilities

In connection with the closing of the Litton acquisition, the company entered into unsecured senior credit facilities with lenders, which initially provided for borrowings of up to $5 billion (Credit Facilities) and replaced the company's previous credit agreement. The Credit Facilities consisted of a $2.5 billion 364-day revolving credit facility and a $2.5 billion five-year revolving credit facility. The 364-day revolving credit facility was terminated by the company in December 2001. At December 31, 2003, $2.5 billion was available under the five-year revolving credit facility. Borrowings under the Credit Facilities, together with the proceeds of the February 2001 issuance of notes and debentures, were used to finance the Litton acquisition and to pay related expenses, to retire and refinance a portion of the Litton debt, and to finance continuing operations. Borrowings under the Credit Facilities bear interest at various rates, including adjusted London Interbank Offered Rate (LIBOR), or an alternate base rate plus, in each case, an incremental margin based on the company's credit rating. The Credit Facilities also provide for a facility fee on the daily aggregate amount of commitments under the revolving facilities (whether or not utilized). The facility fee is also based on the company's credit rating level. The company's credit agreements contain various restrictive covenants relating to the payment of dividends, acquisition of the company's stock, minimum fixed charges, aggregate indebtedness for borrowed money, interest coverage, as well as customary covenants, representations and warranties, funding conditions and events of default. Under the most restrictive provisions of the Credit Facilities, the estimated amount available for common stock dividends, while maintaining financial agreement covenant compliance, was $208 million at December 31, 2003.

Equity Security Units

In November 2001, the company issued 6.9 million equity security units. Each equity security unit, issued at $100 per unit, initially consists of a contract to purchase shares of Northrop Grumman common stock on November 16, 2004, and a $100 senior note due 2006. The senior notes due 2006 are reported as long-term debt. The senior notes initially bear interest at 5.25 percent per annum, and each equity security unit also pays a contract adjustment payment of 2.0 percent per annum, for a combined yield on the equity security unit of 7.25 percent per annum. Each purchase contract, which is part of the equity security units, will obligate the holder thereof to purchase on November 16, 2004, for $100, the following number of shares of the company's common stock based on the average closing price of the company's common stock over the 20-day trading period ending on the third trading day immediately preceding November 16, 2004: (i) 0.9262 shares if the average closing price equals or exceeds $107.97, (ii) a number of shares having a value equal to $100 if the average closing price is less than $107.97 but greater than $88.50 and (iii) 1.1299 shares if the average closing price is less than or equal to $88.50. Prior to November 16, 2004, holders of equity security units have the opportunity to participate in a remarketing of the senior note component.

Long-term debt at December 31 consisted of the following:

(In millions)	2003	2002
Notes and debentures due 2004 to 2036, rates from 6.05% to 9.375%	$5,090	$8,772
Equity security unit notes due 2006, 7.25%	690	690
Other indebtedness due 2004 to 2024, rates from 7.0% to 8.5%	91	139
Total long-term debt	5,871	9,601
Less current portion	461	203
Long-term debt, net of current portion	$5,410	$9,398

Indentures underlying long-term debt issued by the company or its subsidiaries contain various restrictions with respect to the issuer, including one or more restrictions relating to limitations on liens, sale and leaseback arrangements, and funded debt of subsidiaries.

Maturities of long-term debt as of December 31, 2003, are as follows:

(In millions)	
2004	$ 461
2005	33
2006	1,211
2007	73
2008	108
Thereafter	3,885
Total principal payments	5,771
Premium on long-term debt, net of discount	100
Total long-term debt	$5,871

The premium on long-term debt primarily represents non-cash fair market value adjustments resulting from the acquisitions of Litton and TRW.

2.231

OCCIDENTAL PETROLEUM CORPORATION (DEC)

(In millions)	2003	2002
Total current liabilities	$2,526	$2,235
Long-term debt, net of current maturities and unamortized discount	3,993	3,997
Trust preferred securities	—	455
Deferred credits and other liabilities		
Deferred and other domestic and foreign income taxes	1,001	982
Other	2,407	2,228
	3,408	3,210
Contingent liabilities and commitments		
Minority interest	312	333

NOTES TO CONSOLIDATED FINANCIAL STATEMENTS

Note 6. Long-Term Debt and Trust Preferred Securities

Long-term debt and trust preferred securities consisted of the following:

(In millions)	2003	2002
Occidental Petroleum Corporation		
6.75% senior notes due 2012	$ 500	$ 500
7.65% senior notes due 2006(a)	476	485
6.4% senior notes due 2013, redeemed March 31, 2003	—	450
7.375% senior notes due 2008(a)	426	436
8.45% senior notes due 2029	350	350
5.875% senior notes due 2007(a)	318	323
9.25% senior debentures due 2019, putable August 1, 2004 at par(b)	300	300
4.25% medium-term notes due 2010	300	—
10.125% senior debentures due 2009(a)	280	276
7.2% senior debentures due 2028	200	200
4% medium-term notes due 2007(a)	178	175
6.5% senior notes due 2005(a)	161	164
8.75% medium-term notes due 2023	100	100
4.101% medium-term notes due 2007(a)	76	75
Medium-term notes due 2004 through 2008 (8.10% to 8.25% at December 31, 2003)	33	85
11.125% senior notes due 2010	12	12
	3,710	3,931
Subsidiary debt		
1.08% to 7.5% unsecured notes due 2006 through 2030	313	280
	4,023	4,211
Less:		
Unamortized discount, net	(7)	(8)
Current maturities	(23)	(206)
Total long-term debt	3,993	3,997
Trust preferred securities	453	455
Total	$4,446	$4,452

(a) Amounts include mark-to-market adjustments due to fair-value hedges.

(b) Amount is classified as non-current since Occidental does not expect debt holders to put the debt on August 1, 2004. If the debt were put to Occidental, it would refinance this amount on a long-term basis using available lines of long-term bank credit.

In January 1999, Occidental issued 21,000,000 shares of 8.16-percent Trust Originated Preferred Securities (trust preferred securities) to the public. Holders of the trust preferred securities are entitled to cumulative cash distributions at an annual rate of 8.16 percent of the liquidation amount of $25 per security. The trust preferred securities must be redeemed by January 20, 2039, but can be redeemed in whole, or in part, beginning January 20, 2004. Starting July 1, 2003, upon adoption of SFAS No. 150, the trust preferred securities are classified as a liability, and distributions on the trust preferred securities, which were previously recorded as minority interest on the statement of operations, are recorded as interest expense. On January 20, 2004, Occidental redeemed all of the trust preferred securities for par of $453 million plus accrued interest.

At March 31, 2003, Occidental redeemed its 6.4-percent senior notes due 2013 and recorded a pre-tax interest charge of $61 million. At December 31, 2003, Occidental had available lines of committed bank credit of approximately $1.5 billion. Bank fees on these committed lines of credit ranged from 0.100 percent to 0.225 percent.

At December 31, 2003, minimum principal payments on long-term debt subsequent to December 31, 2004 aggregated $3,913 million, of which $157 million is due in 2005, $496 million in 2006, $550 million in 2007, $405 million in 2008, $276 million in 2009 and $2,029 million thereafter. These amounts do not include the unamortized discount of $7 million and fair-value hedge mark-to-market gains of $87 million. Unamortized discount is generally being amortized to interest expense on the effective interest method over the lives of the related issuances.

At December 31, 2003, under the most restrictive covenants of certain financing agreements, the capacity for the payment of cash dividends and other distributions on, and for acquisitions of, Occidental's capital stock was approximately $5.2 billion, assuming that such dividends, distributions and acquisitions were made without incurring additional borrowings.

Occidental estimates the fair value of its long-term debt based on the quoted market prices for the same or similar issues or on the yields offered to Occidental for debt of similar rating and similar remaining maturities. The estimated fair value of Occidental's total debt, including trust preferred securities, at December 31, 2003 and 2002, was approximately $5.0 billion and $5.2 billion, respectively, compared with a carrying value of approximately $4.5 billion, and approximately $4.7 billion, respectively.

2.232

POTLATCH CORPORATION (DEC)

(Dollars in thousands)	2003	2002
Total current liabilities	$169,817	$247,116
Long-term debt (Notes 8 and 11)	618,278	622,645
Other long-term obligations	266,514	267,611
Deferred taxes	71,917	56,654

NOTES TO CONSOLIDATED FINANCIAL STATEMENTS

Note 8. Debt

(Dollars in thousands)	2003	2002
Revenue bonds fixed-rate 5.9% to 7.75% due 2003 through 2026	$170,265	$171,628
Debentures 6.95% due 2015	22,471	22,469
Credit sensitive debentures 9.125% due 2009	100,000	100,000
Medium-term notes fixed-rate 8.27% to 9.46% due 2006 through 2022	75,950	94,050
Senior subordinated notes 10% due 2011	250,000	250,000
Other notes	99	105
	618,785	638,252
Less current installments on long-term debt	507	15,607
Long-term debt	$618,278	$622,645

As a result of the Brainerd facility's sale in February 2003, we retired early $0.9 million of associated revenue bonds.

We repaid $15.0 million of our medium-term notes, which became due April 4, 2003, using the funds contained in an interest-bearing escrow account that were restricted to such use. In the fourth quarter of 2003, we retired $3.1 million of medium-term notes (which were due in 2018) through repurchase on the open market.

The interest rate payable on the 9.125% credit sensitive debentures is subject to adjustment in accordance with the table below if certain changes in the debt rating of the debentures occur. On January 30, 2003, S&P lowered its rating on our senior debt to BB+, causing the interest rate to increase from 9.425% to 12.5% effective that date.

Ratings		
Moody's	S&P	Applicable Rate(%)
Aaa	AAA	8.825
Aa1 to Aa3	AA+ to AA−	8.925
A1 to Baa2	A+ to BBB	9.125
Baa3	BBB−	9.425
Ba1	BB+	12.500
Ba2	BB	13.000
Ba3	BB−	13.500
B1 or lower	B+ or lower	14.000

Our current bank credit facility, which expires June 28, 2004, is comprised of a revolving line of credit of up to $150.0 million, including a $70.0 million subfacility for letters of credit, usage of which reduces availability under the revolving line of credit. Our obligations under the bank credit facility are secured by our accounts receivable and inventory. As of December 31, 2003, there were no borrowings outstanding under the revolving line of credit; however, approximately $14.7 million of the revolving line of credit was used to support outstanding letters of credit. At December 31, 2002, we had borrowed $40.0 million under the revolving line of credit, that was classified as "Notes payable" in the Balance Sheets. Prior to the expiration of our current bank credit facility, we expect to either extend the current credit facility or enter into a new credit facility.

Our 10% senior subordinated notes due 2011 are unsecured and are subordinated to our senior notes and our bank credit facility.

Both the agreement governing our bank credit facility and the indenture governing our $250 million 10% senior subordinated notes contain certain covenants that, among other things, restrict our ability and our subsidiaries' ability to create liens, merge or consolidate, dispose of assets, incur indebtedness and guarantees, pay dividends, repurchase or redeem capital stock and indebtedness, make certain investments or acquisitions, enter into certain transactions with affiliates, make capital expenditures, or change the nature of our business. The bank credit facility also contains financial maintenance covenants establishing a maximum funded indebtedness to capitalization ratio, a minimum consolidated net worth requirement, and a minimum interest coverage ratio. Events of default under the bank credit facility and the indenture include, but are not limited to, payment defaults, covenant defaults, breaches of representations and warranties, cross defaults to certain other material agreements and indebtedness, bankruptcy and other insolvency events, material adverse judgments, actual or asserted invalidity of security interests or loan documentation, and certain change of control events involving our company. As of December 31, 2003, we were in compliance with the covenants of our bank credit facility and the $250 million 10% senior subordinated notes.

Payments due on long-term debt during each of the five years subsequent to December 31, 2003, are as follows:

(Dollars in thousands)	
2004	$ 507
2005	1,508
2006	2,758
2007	6,559
2008	609

Note 11 (In Part): Financial Instruments

Estimated fair values of our financial instruments are as follows:

(Dollars in thousands)	2003		2002	
	Carrying Amount	Fair Value	Carrying Amount	Fair Value
Cash, restricted cash and short-term investments	$ 47,169	$ 47,169	$ 26,042	$ 26,042
Natural gas collars	112	112	—	—
Interest rate swap	2,386	2,386	6,446	6,446
Current notes payable	—	—	40,000	40,000
Long-term debt	618,785	651,905	638,252	659,818

For short-term investments and current notes payable, the carrying amount approximates fair value. The carrying amount and fair value of our interest rate swap and natural gas collars are based on current termination values. The fair value of our long-term debt is estimated based upon the quoted market prices for the same or similar debt issues. The amount of long-term debt for which there is no quoted market price is immaterial and the carrying amount approximates fair value.

2.233

TECUMSEH PRODUCTS COMPANY (DEC)

(Dollars in millions)	2003	2002
Total current liabilities	$ 434.6	$ 451.4
Long-term debt	327.6	298.2
Deferred income taxes	36.5	33.6
Other postretirement benefit liabilities	212.6	217.3
Product warranty and self-insured risks	24.4	21.3
Accrual for environmental matters	44.6	29.5
Pension liabilities	20.7	32.8
Total liabilities	$1,101.0	$1,084.1

NOTES TO CONSOLIDATED FINANCIAL STATEMENTS

Note 8. Debt

(In millions)	2003	2002
Short-term borrowings consist of the following:		
Borrowings by foreign subsidiaries under revolving credit agreements, advances on export receivables and overdraft arrangements with banks used in the normal course of business; weighted average interest rate of 7.4% in 2003 and 5.5% in 2002	$ 87.2	$ 35.6
Borrowings under a $125 million unsecured revolving credit facility with a consortium of banks, bearing interest at variable rates (2.16% at December 31, 2002)	—	75.0
Current maturities of long-term debt	2.4	2.0
Total short-term borrowings	$ 89.6	$112.6
Long-term debt consists of the following:		
Unsecured borrowings, primarily with banks, by foreign subsidiaries with weighted average interest rate of 8.7% in 2003 and 6.6% in 2002 and maturing in 2003 through 2012	$ 15.4	$ 37.7
Senior Guaranteed Notes, 4.66% fixed rate, maturing on March 5, 2008 through 2011	300.0	—
Unsecured bridge loan from a bank bearing interest at variable rates (2.06% at December 31, 2002)	—	250.0
Variable rate Industrial Development Revenue Bonds payable in quarterly installments from 2003 to 2021 (weighted average interest rate of 1.72% and 2.26% in 2003 and 2002, respectively)	11.8	12.5
	327.2	300.2
Plus: Unamortized net premiums	2.8	—
Less: Current maturities of long-term debt	(2.4)	(2.0)
Total long-term debt	$327.6	$298.2

On December 30, 2002, the Company acquired FASCO. The acquisition was financed with proceeds from $325.0 million in new bank borrowings and internal cash flows. Of $325.0 million in new borrowings, $250.0 million was from a six-month bridge loan and $75.0 million was from a new $125.0 million revolving credit facility. On March 5, 2003, the Company completed a private placement of $300 million Senior Guaranteed Notes due March 5, 2011. These notes bear interest at a fixed rate of 4.66%. Proceeds from the private placement were used to repay the $250 million bridge loan and pay down borrowings under the Company's revolving credit facility. On March 31, 2003, the remaining $25.0 million outstanding under the revolver was repaid from available cash resources.

Under the $125 million revolving credit facility, the Company may select among various interest rate arrangements. The facility has a three-year term, which may be extended annually with the consent of the participating banks. The facility had an applicable commitment fee rate of 17.5 basis points. The Company paid facility fees of $0.2 million in 2003, $0.1 million in 2002, and $0.1 million in 2001. As of December 31, 2003, the Company has $18.1 million of the facility committed to support letters of credit.

The Senior Guaranteed Notes and the revolving credit facility contain various operating and financial covenants. The more restrictive of these covenants require the Company to adhere to leverage and interest coverage ratios and limit aggregate new debt.

In addition, during the third quarter 2003, the Company entered into two pay variable, receive fixed interest rate swap agreements to lower the Company's overall borrowing costs. At December 31, 2003, long-term debt includes a net unamortized premium of $3.5 million, and the fair value

adjustment for the active interest rate swap agreements of $0.7 million. The active swap agreements have a total notional principal amount of $125.0 million with maturity terms that match the Company's Senior Guaranteed Notes. The variable interest payments are based upon 60 day LIBOR.

Scheduled maturities of long-term debt for each of the five years subsequent to December 31, 2003 are as follows:

(In millions)	
2004	$ 2.4
2005	8.6
2006	6.2
2007	61.4
2008	61.6
Thereafter	187.0
	$327.2

Interest paid was $15.3 million in 2003, $4.4 million in 2002, and $3.3 million in 2001.

Note 11 (In Part): Financial Instruments

The following table presents the carrying amounts and the estimated fair values of financial instruments at December 31, 2003 and 2002:

(In millions)	2003 Carrying Amount	2003 Fair Value	2002 Carrying Amount	2002 Fair Value
Cash and cash equivalents	$344.6	$344.6	$333.1	$333.1
Short-term borrowings	89.6	89.6	110.6	110.6
Long-term debt	327.6	326.6	300.2	300.2
Foreign currency contracts	0.6	0.6	(0.2)	(0.2)
Commodity contracts	—	2.7	—	1.1

The carrying amount of cash equivalents approximates fair value due to their liquidity and short-term maturities. The fair value of the Company's fixed interest rate debt reflects the difference between the contract rate and the prevailing rates as of the balance sheet date. The carrying value of the Company's variable interest rate debt approximates fair value. The fair values of foreign currency and commodity contracts reflect the differences between the contract prices and the forward prices available on the balance sheet date.

Collateralized

2.234

CVS CORPORATION (DEC)

(In millions)	2003	2002
Total current liabilities	$3,489.2	$3,105.9
Long-term debt	753.1	1,076.3
Deferred income taxes	41.6	—
Other long-term liabilities	237.4	266.1

NOTES TO CONSOLIDATED FINANCIAL STATEMENTS

1 (In Part): Significant Accounting Policies

Fair Value of Financial Instruments

As of January 3, 2004, the Company's financial instruments include cash and cash equivalents, accounts receivable, accounts payable and debt. Due to the short-term nature of these instruments, the Company's carrying value approximates fair value. The carrying amount of long-term debt was $1.1 billion and the estimated fair value was $1.1 billion as of January 3, 2004 and December 28, 2002. The fair value of long-term debt was estimated based on rates currently offered to the Company for debt with similar maturities. The Company also had outstanding letters of credit, which guaranteed foreign trade purchases, with a fair value of $6.5 million as of January 3, 2004, and $5.8 million as of December 28, 2002. The Company also has outstanding letters of credit associated with insurance programs with a fair value of $65.5 million as of January 3, 2004 and $53.1 million as of December 28, 2002. There were no investments in derivative financial instruments as of January 3, 2004 or December 28, 2002.

3—Borrowing and Credit Agreements

Following is a summary of the Company's borrowings as of the respective balance sheet dates:

(In millions)	2003	2002
Commercial paper	$ —	$ 4.8
5.5% senior notes due 2004	300.0	300.0
5.625% senior notes due 2006	300.0	300.0
3.875% senior notes due 2007	300.0	300.0
8.52% ESOP notes due 2008	163.2	194.4
Mortgage notes payable	12.2	13.0
Capital lease obligations	0.9	0.9
	1,076.3	1,113.1
Less:		
Short-term debt	—	(4.8)
Current portion of long-term debt	(323.2)	(32.0)
	$ 753.1	$1,076.3

In connection with our commercial paper program, the Company maintains a $650 million, five-year unsecured back-up credit facility, which expires on May 21, 2006 and a $600 million, 364-day unsecured back-up credit facility, which expires on May 17, 2004. The credit facilities allow for borrowings at various rates depending on the Company's public debt ratings and require the Company to pay a quarterly facility fee of 0.08%, regardless of usage. As of January 3, 2004, the Company had not borrowed against the credit facilities. There was no short-term debt outstanding as of January 3, 2004. The weighted average interest rate for short-term debt was 1.9% as of December 28, 2002.

In October 2002, the Company issued $300 million of 3.875% unsecured senior notes. The notes are due November 1, 2007, and pay interest semi-annually. The Company may redeem these notes at any time, in whole or in part, at a defined redemption price plus accrued interest. Net proceeds from the notes were used to repay outstanding commercial paper.

The Credit Facilities and unsecured senior notes contain customary restrictive financial and operating covenants. The covenants do not materially affect the Company's financial or operating flexibility.

The aggregate maturities of long-term debt for each of the five years subsequent to January 3, 2004 are $323.2 million in 2004, $27.9 million in 2005, $334.4 million in 2006, $341.7 million in 2007 and $45.8 million in 2008.

2.235

LABARGE, INC. (JUN)

(Amounts in thousands)	2003	2002
Total current liabilities	$21,826	$24,011
Other long-term liabilities	2,788	2,103
Other long-term liabilities of discontinued operations	—	1,361
Long-term debt	6,669	7,047

NOTES TO CONSOLIDATED FINANCIAL STATEMENTS

1 (In Part): Summary of Significant Accounting Policies

Fair Value of Financial Instruments

The Company considered the carrying amounts of cash and cash equivalents, accounts receivable and accounts payable to approximate fair value because of the short maturity of these financial instruments.

The Company has considered amounts outstanding under the term loan, and the Industrial Revenue Bonds and determined that carrying amounts recorded on the financial statement are consistent with the estimated fair value as of June 29, 2003.

9 (In Part): Short- and Long-Term Obligations

Short-term borrowings, long-term debt and the current maturities of long-term debt consist of the following:

(Dollars in thousands)	2003	2002
Short-term borrowings:		
Revolving credit agreement:		
Balance at year-end	$ —	$2,583
Interest rate at year-end	—	2.90%
Average amount of short-term borrowings outstanding during period	$ 256	$2,548
Average interest rate for fiscal year	3.38%	3.96%
Maximum short-term borrowings at any month-end	2,389	6,320
Senior long-term debt:		
Senior lender:		
Term loan	$6,251	$6,400
Other	813	925
Total senior long-term debt	7,064	7,325
Less current maturities	395	278
Long-term debt, less current maturities	$6,669	$7,047
Subordinated debt	$ —	$5,621

The average interest rate was computed by dividing the sum of daily interest costs by the sum of the daily borrowings for the respective periods.

Total cash payments for the interest in fiscal years 2003, 2002 and 2001 were $0.8 million, $1.2 million and $2.0 million, respectively.

Senior Lender

The Company has a credit facility with a bank that provides financing for the Company's headquarters building in St. Louis, Missouri, and provides working capital for its operations.

The following is a summary of the credit facility:

- A revolving credit facility up to $15.0 million, secured by substantially all the assets of the Company other than real estate, based on a borrowing base formula equal to the sum of 80% of eligible receivables, and 40% of eligible inventories, less outstanding letters of credit. As of June 29, 2003, net of letters of credit outstanding of $2.1 million, the maximum available was $12.9 million. The revolver borrowing at June 29, 2003 was $0. This credit facility matures on September 30, 2004.
- A $6.4 million term loan secured by the Company's head-quarters building in St. Louis, Missouri. The loan repayment schedule is based on a 25-year amortization and began in December 2002 with a balloon final payment due in October 2009. The current balance at June 29, 2003 was $6.3 million.
- Interest on the loans is at a percentage of prime or a stated rate over LIBOR based on certain ratios. For fiscal 2003, the average rate was approximately 2.4%.
- Covenants and performance criteria consist of Earnings Before Interest, Taxes, Depreciation and Amortization ("EBITDA") in relation to debt, EBITDA in relation to interest and tangible net worth. The Company is in compliance with its borrowing agreement covenants as of June 29, 2003.

Other Long-Term Debt

Industrial Revenue Bonds

In July 1998, the Company acquired tax-exempt Industrial Revenue Bond financing in the amount of $1.3 million. The debt is payable over 10 years with an interest rate of 5.28%. This funding was used to expand the Berryville, Arkansas facility. The outstanding balance at June 29, 2003 was $797,000.

The aggregate maturities of long-term obligations are as follows:

(Dollars in thousands)	
Fiscal year	
2004	$ 395
2005	403
2006	410
2007	418
2008	423
Thereafter	5,015
Total	$7,064

Convertible

2.236

STANDARD MOTOR PRODUCTS, INC. (DEC)

(In thousands)	2003	2002
Total current liabilities	$276,838	$187,677
Long-term debt (Notes 7 and 8)	114,757	93,191
Postretirement medical benefits and other accrued liabilities	36,848	30,414
Restructuring accrual	15,615	—
Accrued asbestos liabilities	24,426	25,595
Total liabilities	$468,484	$336,877

NOTES TO CONSOLIDATED FINANCIAL STATEMENTS

7 (In Part): Credit Facilities and Long-Term Debt

On July 26, 1999, we completed a public offering of convertible subordinated debentures amounting to $90 million. The convertible debentures carry an interest rate of 6.75%, payable semi-annually, and will mature on July 15, 2009. The convertible debentures are convertible into 2,796,120 shares of our common stock. We may, at our option, redeem some or all of the Debentures at any time on or after July 15, 2004, for a redemption price equal to the issuance price plus accrued interest. In addition, if a change in control, as defined, occurs at the Company, we will be required to make an offer to purchase the convertible debentures at a purchase price equal to 101% of their aggregate principal amount, plus accrued interest.

● ● ● ● ● ●

Long-term debt consists of:

(In thousands)	2003	2002
6.75% convertible subordinated debentures	$ 90,000	$90,000
Unsecured promissory note	15,125	—
Mortgage loan	9,824	—
Other	3,162	7,299
	118,111	97,299
Less current portion	3,354	4,108
Total non-current portion of long-term debt	$114,757	$93,191

Maturities of long-term debt during the five years ending December 31, 2004 through 2008 are $3.4 million, $0.6 million, $0.6 million, $0.6 million and $0.6 million, respectively.

16 (In Part): Fair Value of Financial Instruments

The following methods and assumptions were used to estimate the fair value of each class of financial instruments for which it is practicable to estimate that value:

Long-Term Debt

The fair value of our long-term debt is estimated based on quoted market prices or current rates offered to us for debt of the same remaining maturities.

Debt Covenant Violation

2.237

SOLECTRON CORPORATION (AUG)

NOTES TO CONSOLIDATED FINANCIAL STATEMENTS

Note 5. Lines of Credit

As of August 31, 2003, Solectron had available a $200 million revolving credit facility that expires on February 11, 2004, and a $250 million revolving credit facility that expires on February 14, 2005. Each of the revolving credit facilities is guaranteed by certain domestic subsidiaries and secured by the pledge of domestic accounts receivable, inventory and equipment,

the pledge of equity interests in certain subsidiaries and notes evidencing intercompany debt. Borrowings under the credit facilities bear interest, at Solectron's option, at the London Interbank offering rate (LIBOR) plus a margin of 1.75% based on Solectron's current senior unsecured debt ratings, or the higher of the Federal Funds Rate plus 1/2 of 1% or Bank of America N.A.'s publicly announced prime rate. As of August 31, 2003, there were no borrowings outstanding under these facilities. Solectron is subject to compliance with certain financial covenants set forth in these facilities including, but not limited to, capital expenditures, consolidated tangible net worth, cash interest coverage, leverage, liquidity, and minimum cash. Prior to the end of the fourth quarter, Solectron obtained waivers to the minimum cash interest coverage ratio covenants. As a result of these waivers, Solectron was in compliance with all applicable covenants as of August 31, 2003.

In addition, Solectron had $41 million in committed and $245 million in uncommitted foreign lines of credit and other bank facilities as of August 31, 2003 related to continuing operations. A committed line of credit obligates a lender to loan Solectron amounts under the credit facility as long the terms of the credit agreement are adhered to. An uncommitted line of credit is extended to us at the sole discretion of a lender. The interest rates range from the bank's prime lending rate to the bank's prime rate plus 2.0%. As of August 31, 2003, borrowings and guaranteed amounts were $18 million under committed and $51 million under uncommitted foreign lines of credit. Borrowings are payable on demand. The weighted-average interest rate was 5.4% for committed and 0.7% for uncommitted foreign lines of credit as of August 31, 2003.

CREDIT AGREEMENTS

2.238 As shown in Table 2-29, many of the survey companies disclosed the existence of loan commitments from the banks or insurance companies for future loans. Examples of such loan commitment disclosures follow:

2.239

TABLE 2-29: CREDIT AGREEMENTS

	2003	2002	2001	2000
Disclosing credit agreements	533	540	554	551
Not disclosing credit agreements	67	60	46	49
Total Companies	**600**	**600**	**600**	**600**

2.240

ADVANCED MICRO DEVICES, INC. (DEC)

NOTES TO CONSOLIDATED FINANCIAL STATEMENTS

Note 7 (In Part): Debt

Notes Payable

On July 7, 2003, the Company amended and restated its 1999 Loan and Security Agreement with a consortium of banks led by a domestic financial institution (the July 2003 Loan Agreement). The Company further amended the July 2003 Loan Agreement on October 3, 2003. The July 2003 Loan Agreement currently provides for a secured revolving line of credit of up to $125 million that expires in July 2007. The Company can borrow, subject to amounts set aside by the lenders, up to 85 percent of its eligible accounts receivable from OEMs and 50 percent of its eligible accounts receivable from distributors. The Company has to comply, among other things, with the following financial covenants if net domestic cash (as defined in the July 2003 Loan Agreement) declines below $125 million:

- restriction on its ability to pay cash dividends on its common stock;
- maintain an adjusted tangible net worth (as defined in the July 2003 Loan Agreement) as follows:

Measurement Date	Amount
December 31, 2003	$ 1.25 billion
Last day of each calendar quarter in 2004	$1.425 billion
Last day of each calendar quarter in 2005	$ 1.85 billion
March 31, 2006 and on the last day of each fiscal quarter thereafter	$ 2.0 billion

- achieve EBITDA (earnings before interest, taxes, depreciation and amortization) according to the following schedule:

Period	Amount
Four fiscal quarters ending December 31, 2003	$ 400 million
Four fiscal quarters ending March 31, 2004	$ 550 million
Four fiscal quarters ending June 30, 2004	$ 750 million
Four fiscal quarters ending September 30, 2004	$ 850 million
Four fiscal quarters ending December 31, 2004	$ 950 million
Four fiscal quarters ending March 31, 2005 and on each fiscal quarter thereafter	$1,050 million

As of December 28, 2003, net domestic cash, as defined, totaled $567 million and the preceding financial covenants were not applicable.

The Company's obligations under the July 2003 Loan Agreement are secured by all of its accounts receivable, inventory, general intangibles (excluding intellectual property) and the related proceeds, excluding FASL LLC's accounts receivable, inventory and general intangibles. As of December 28, 2003, no amount was outstanding under the July 2003 Loan Agreement.

Interest rates on foreign and short-term domestic borrowings are negotiated at the time of borrowing.

2.241

CLARCOR INC. (NOV)

NOTES TO CONSOLIDATED FINANCIAL STATEMENTS
(Dollars in thousands)

G (In Part): Long-Term Debt

Long-term debt at November 30, 2003 and 2002 consisted of the following:

	2003	2002
Multicurrency revolving credit agreements, interest payable at the end of each funding period at an adjusted LIBOR	$ —	$62,833
Promissory note, interest payable semi-annually at 6.69%	—	10,000
Industrial revenue bonds, at .85% to 1.75% interest rates	16,968	17,460
Other	619	811
	17,587	91,104
Less current portion	674	68,456
	$16,913	$22,648

•   •   •   •   •   •

In April 2003, the Company entered into a five-year multicurrency revolving credit agreement with a group of participating financial institutions under which it may borrow up to $165,000. This credit facility replaced a $185,000 agreement that was to expire in September 2003. The replacement agreement provides that loans may be made under a selection of currencies and rate formulas. The interest rate is based upon either a defined Base Rate or the London Interbank Offered Rate (LIBOR) plus or minus applicable margins. Facility fees and other fees on the entire loan commitment are payable for the duration of this facility. At November 30, 2003, there were no outstanding amounts under this agreement.

Borrowings under the credit facility are unsecured but are guaranteed by subsidiaries of the Company. The agreement related to this borrowing includes certain restrictive covenants that include maintaining minimum consolidated net worth, limiting new borrowings, maintaining a minimum interest coverage and restricting certain changes in ownership. The Company was in compliance with these covenants throughout fiscal year 2003. This agreement also includes a $40,000 letter of credit line subline, against which $14,095 in letters of credit had been issued at November 30, 2003.

At November 30, 2002, $62,833 was outstanding under the $185,000 revolving credit agreement and the related LIBOR, including the spread, was 1.97%. The amount outstanding at November 30, 2002 was classified as current debt as the credit agreement was to expire in 2003. This agreement also included a letter of credit facility, against which $12,743 in letters of credit had been issued as of November 30, 2002. Borrowings under the credit facility in place at November 30, 2002 were unsecured but were guaranteed by certain of the Company's subsidiaries. The Company was in compliance with restrictive covenants related to the borrowings under the credit facility throughout fiscal years 2003 and 2002.

2.242

THE DIXIE GROUP, INC. (DEC)

NOTES TO CONSOLIDATED FINANCIAL STATEMENTS
(Dollars in thousands)

Note H (In Part): Long-Term Debt and Credit Arrangements

Long-term debt consists of the following:

	2003	2002
Senior indebtedness		
Credit line borrowings	$ 7,000	$ 45,823
Term loans	25,000	35,243
Capital lease obligations	7,181	82
Other	—	292
Total senior indebtedness	39,181	81,440
Subordinated notes	—	35,714
Convertible subordinated debentures	29,737	32,237
Total long-term debt	68,918	149,391
Less current portion of long-term debt	(12,326)	(98,287)
Less current portion of capital lease obligations	(1,344)	(25)
Total long-term debt, less current portion	$ 55,248	$ 51,079

The Company is party to a senior revolving credit and term loan facility dated May 14, 2002 that matures on May 14, 2007. On March 14, 2003, the Company issued $37,000 of senior secured notes, amended its senior credit facility to reduce the revolving credit loan commitments to $90,000 and increased borrowing availability under the agreement's borrowing base formula by approximately $10,000, reissued the existing term loan at its outstanding balance, and added an additional $4,551 term loan, bringing the aggregate balance of the term loan portion of the facility to $38,333.

On November 12, 2003, proceeds from the sale of assets to Shaw Industries Group, Inc. were used to pay amounts then outstanding under the Company's senior secured notes and subordinated notes of $37,529 and $30,952, respectively. Additionally, the Company paid $66,096 of revolving credit and $8,679 of term loans under the Company's senior credit facility. The senior credit facility's revolving credit commitment was reduced to $40,000 in December 2003. The term loan is due in quarterly installments of $1,207 on February 1, 2004 and each quarter thereafter with the balance due in May 2007.

Interest rates available under the facility may be selected from a number of options that effectively allow for borrowing at rates ranging from the lender's prime rate plus 0.25% to the lender's prime rate plus 1.25% for base rate loans, or at rates ranging from LIBOR plus 2.5% to LIBOR plus 3.75% for LIBOR loans. The effective annual interest rate on borrowings under the revolving credit and term loan agreements was 6.73% for 2003 and 9.17% for 2002. The average interest rate on debt outstanding under these agreements was 9.36% at December 27, 2003 and 9.03% at December 28, 2002. Commitment fees, ranging from 0.375% to 0.50% per annum, are payable on the average daily unused balance of the revolving credit facility. The level of our accounts receivable and inventories limits borrowing availability under the revolving credit facility. The senior credit facility is secured by a first priority lien in substantially all of the Company's assets.

•　　•　　•　　•　　•　　•

The Company's senior credit agreement contains financial covenants relating to fixed charges, debt coverage and net worth and among other things, limit future acquisitions, capital expenditures, and the payment of dividends. The Company's revolving credit facility provides that the occurrence of any event or condition that has a Material Adverse Effect (as defined in the Agreement) shall constitute an Event of Default. The portion of the Company's revolving credit debt that is classified as long-term in the Company's balance sheet at December 27, 2003 and December 28, 2002 represents amounts that are not repaid through lockbox remittances. Because the assets sold in November 2003 and in early 2004 were classified as assets held for sale in the current asset section of our balance sheet, debt retired with the proceeds from the sales was classified in the current liability section of our balance sheet for the applicable periods. The unused borrowing capacity under the Company's credit facilities on December 27, 2003 was approximately $30,432.

2.243

PULTE HOMES, INC. (DEC)

NOTES TO CONSOLIDATED FINANCIAL STATEMENTS

5. Other Financing Arrangements

Corporate/Homebuilding
Effective October 1, 2003, Pulte Homes, Inc. replaced its $570 million revolving credit facility with an $850 million facility that includes the capacity to issue letters of credit up to $500 million. Borrowing availability on this line is reduced by the amount of letters of credit outstanding. This new credit facility expires October 1, 2008. The bank credit agreement contains restrictive covenants, the most restrictive of which requires the Company not to exceed a debt-to-total capitalization ratio as defined in the agreement of 50%. The following is a summary of aggregate borrowing information related to this facility ($000's omitted):

	2003	2002	2001
Available credit lines at year-end	$850,000	$570,000	$560,000
Unused credit lines at year-end	$693,000	$570,000	$450,000
Maximum amount outstanding at the end of any month	$ —	$245,000	$334,000
Average monthly indebtedness	$ 2,000	$ 92,000	$ 72,000
Range of interest rates during the year	2.08 to 4.25%	2.56 to 4.75%	2.65 to 6.81%
Weighted-average rate at year-end	2.22%	2.78%	3.79%

In addition, the Company's operating entity in Argentina entered into a $3 million revolving credit facility in October 2002 to provide an additional financial resource to support the operations. Pulte Homes, Inc. has guaranteed the credit facility. There was $2 million outstanding under this facility at December 31, 2003.

At December 31, 2003, other financing included limited recourse collateralized financing arrangements totaling $83.3 million. These financing arrangements have maturities ranging primarily from one to four years, a weighted average interest rate of 4.31%, are generally collateralized by certain land positions and have no recourse to any other assets. These arrangements have been classified as accrued and other liabilities in the Consolidated Balance Sheets.

Financial Services

Notes payable to banks (collateralized short-term debt) are secured by residential mortgage loans available-for-sale. The carrying amounts of such borrowings approximate fair value.

During 2003, Pulte Mortgage replaced and expanded its $175 million revolving credit facility with a $310 million facility and replaced its $325 million asset-backed commercial paper program with a $550 million program. The revolving credit facility expires in March 2005 and the asset-backed commercial paper program can be extended to August 2005. During the three years ended December 31, 2003, Pulte Mortgage provided compensating balances, in the form of escrows and other custodial funds, in order to further reduce interest rates. The bank credit agreements contain restrictive covenants, the most restrictive of which requires Pulte Mortgage to maintain a minimum tangible net worth of $30 million.

The following is aggregate borrowing information ($000's omitted):

	2003	2002	2001
Available credit lines at year-end	$860,000	$600,000	$450,000
Unused credit lines at year-end	$381,000	$ 41,000	$ 40,000
Maximum amount outstanding at the end of any month	$483,000	$559,000	$410,000
Average monthly indebtedness	$391,000	$290,000	$219,000
Range of interest rates during the year	0.45 to 2.31%	0.45 to 2.75%	0.45 to 9.18%
Weighted-average rate at year-end	1.59%	1.91%	2.35%

2.244

UNITED STATIONERS INC. (DEC)

NOTES TO CONSOLIDATED FINANCIAL STATEMENTS

8 (In Part): Long-Term Debt

United is a holding company and, as a result, its primary sources of funds are cash generated from operating activities of its operating subsidiary, USSC, and from borrowings by USSC. The 2003 Credit Agreement (as defined below) contains restrictions on the ability of USSC to transfer cash to United.

Long-term debt consisted of the following amounts (dollars in thousands):

	2003	2002
Revolver	$10,500	$ —
Tranche A term loan, due in installments until March 31, 2004	—	18,251
Tranche A-1 term loan, due in installments until June 30, 2005	—	78,125
8.375% Senior Subordinated Notes, due April 15, 2008	—	100,000
Industrial development bonds, at market-based interest rates, maturing in 2011	6,800	6,800
Industrial development bonds, at 66% to 78% of prime, maturing in 2004	—	8,000
Other long-term debt	24	73
Subtotal	17,324	211,249
Less—current maturities	(24)	(45,904)
Total	$17,300	$165,345

The Company has historically used both fixed-rate and variable or short-term rate debt. At December 31, 2003, 100% of the Company's outstanding debt and receivables sold under the Company's Receivables Securitization Program is priced at variable interest rates, compared to 32% of such outstanding amounts at December 31, 2002. The Company's variable rate debt is based primarily on the applicable prime rate or London InterBank Offered Rate ("LIBOR"). The prevailing prime rate was 4.0% at December 31, 2003 and 4.3% at December 31, 2002. The LIBOR rate as of December 31, 2003 was approximately 1.5% at both December 31, 2003 and 2002.

2003 Credit Agreement

In March 2003, the Company replaced its then existing senior secured credit facility (the "Prior Credit Agreement") by entering into a new Five-Year Revolving Credit Agreement (the "2003 Credit Agreement") dated as of March 21, 2003 by and among USSC, as borrower, United, as guarantor, the various lenders and Bank One, NA, as administrative agent. The 2003 Credit Agreement provides for a revolving credit facility with an aggregate committed principal amount of $275 million. USSC may, upon the terms and conditions of the 2003 Credit Agreement, seek additional commitments from its current or new lenders to increase the aggregate committed principal amount under the facility to a total amount of up to $325 million. As a result of the replacement of the Prior Credit Agreement, the Company recorded pre-tax charges of $0.8 million in the first quarter of 2003.

The 2003 Credit Agreement provides for the issuance of letters of credit for amounts totaling up to a sublimit of $90 million. It also provides a sublimit for swingline loans in an aggregate principal amount not to exceed $25 million at any one time outstanding. These amounts, as sublimits, do not increase the aggregate committed principal amount, and any undrawn issued letters of credit and all outstanding swingline loans under the facility reduce the remaining availability. The revolving credit facility matures on March 21, 2008.

Obligations of USSC under the 2003 Credit Agreement are guaranteed by United and certain of USSC's domestic subsidiaries. USSC's obligations under the 2003 Credit Agreement and the guarantors' obligations under the guaranty are secured by liens on substantially all assets, including accounts receivable, chattel paper, commercial tort claims, documents, equipment, fixtures, instruments, inventory, investment property, pledged deposits and all other tangible and intangible personal property (including proceeds) and certain real property, but excluding accounts receivable (and related credit support) subject to any accounts receivable securitization program permitted under the 2003 Credit Agreement. Also securing these obligations are first priority pledges of all of the capital stock of USSC and the domestic subsidiaries of USSC, other than TOP.

Loans outstanding under the 2003 Credit Agreement bear interest at a floating rate (based on the higher of either the prime rate or the federal funds rate plus 0.50%) plus a margin of 0% to 0.75% per annum, or at USSC's option, LIBOR (as it may be adjusted for reserves) plus a margin of 1.25% to 2.25% per annum, or a combination thereof. The margins applicable to floating rate and LIBOR loans are determined by reference to a pricing matrix based on the total leverage of United and its consolidated subsidiaries. Initial applicable margins are 0.50% and 2.00%, respectively.

The 2003 Credit Agreement contains representations and warranties, affirmative and negative covenants, and events of default customary for financings of this type.

Debt maturities under the 2003 Credit Agreement as of December 31, 2003, were as follows (dollars in thousands):

Year	Amount
2004	$ —
2005	—
2006	—
2007	—
2008	10,500
Later years	—
Total	$10,500

As of December 31, 2003 and 2002, the Company had outstanding letters of credit of $15.1 million and $21.9 million, respectively.

LONG-TERM LEASES

2.245   Standards for reporting leases on the financial statements of lessees and lessors are set forth in SFAS No. 13, *Accounting for Leases*, and in subsequently issued amendments and interpretations of *SFAS No. 13*.

2.246   Table 2-30, in addition to summarizing the number of survey companies reporting capitalized and/or noncapitalized lessee leases, shows the nature of information most frequently disclosed by the survey companies for capitalized and noncapitalized lessee leases. 65 survey companies reported lessor leases.

2.247   Examples of long-term lease presentations and disclosures follow.

2.248

TABLE 2-30: LONG-TERM LEASES

	Number of Companies			
	2003	2002	2001	2000
Information Disclosed as to Capitalized Leases				
Minimum lease payments......	131	122	112	114
Imputed interest....................	79	85	80	87
Leased assets by major classifications	30	43	44	35
Executory costs	8	7	7	8
Information Disclosed as to Noncapitalized Leases				
Rental expenses				
Basic..................................	564	563	548	531
Sublease...........................	63	59	62	46
Contingent........................	52	53	52	56
Minimum rental payments				
Schedule of.......................	547	543	528	518
Classified by major categories of property...	10	11	14	4
Number of Companies				
Noncapitalized leases only....	327	331	330	331
Capitalized and noncapitalized leases........	242	236	230	215
Capitalized leases only..........	6	4	6	12
No leases disclosed..............	25	29	34	42
Total Companies.................	**600**	**600**	**600**	**600**

Lessee—Capital Leases

2.249

KOHL'S CORPORATION (JAN)

(In thousands)	2004	2003
Current liabilities:		
Accounts payable	$ 532,599	$ 650,731
Accrued liabilities	441,902	359,842
Income taxes payable	135,327	142,150
Current portion of long-term debt and capital leases	12,529	355,464
Total current liabilities	1,122,357	1,508,187
Long-term debt and capital leases	1,075,973	1,058,784
Deferred income taxes	236,712	171,951
Other long-term liabilities	72,069	64,859

NOTES TO CONSOLIDATED FINANCIAL STATEMENTS

2 (In Part): Selected Balance Sheet Information

Property and equipment consist of the following:

(In thousands)	2004	2003
Land	$ 360,765	$ 283,302
Buildings and improvements	2,259,691	1,812,470
Store fixtures and equipment	1,062,956	904,561
Property under capital leases	88,840	58,982
Construction in progress	327,460	296,969
Total property and equipment	4,099,712	3,356,284
Less accumulated depreciation	775,469	616,994
	$3,324,243	$2,739,290

Depreciation expense for property and equipment, including property under capital leases, totaled $204,359,000, and $165,173,000 and $131,899,000 for fiscal 2003, 2002 and 2001, respectively.

4 (In Part): Debt

Long-term debt consists of the following:

	2004		2003	
(In thousands)	Weighted Average Effective Rate	Amount	Weighted Average Effective Rate	Amount
Notes and debentures:				
Senior debt				
Through 2004	6.57%	$ 10,000	6.57%	$ 20,000
2006	6.70%	100,000	6.70%	100,000
2011	6.59%	399,645	6.59%	399,595
2029	7.36%	197,687	7.36%	197,595
2033	6.05%	297,846	6.05%	297,772
Subordinated debt 2020		—	2.75%	343,271
Total notes and debentures	6.59%	1,005,178	5.62%	1,358,233
Capital lease obligations		81,936		54,493
Other		1,388		1,522
Less current portion		(12,529)		(355,464)
Long-term debt		$1,075,973		$1,058,784

5. Commitments

The Company leases certain property and equipment. Rent expense charged to operations was $248,766,000, $207,667,000 and $177,153,000 in fiscal 2003, 2002 and 2001, respectively. Rent expense includes contingent rents, based on sales, of $3,265,000, $4,025,000 and $3,901,000 in fiscal 2003, 2002 and 2001, respectively. In addition, many of the store leases obligate the Company to pay real estate taxes, insurance and maintenance costs, and contain multiple renewal options, exercisable at the Company's option, that generally range from two additional five-year periods to eight ten-year periods. These items are not included in the rent expenses listed above.

Property under capital leases consists of the following:

(In thousands)	2004	2003
Buildings and improvements	$87,543	$57,685
Equipment	1,297	1,297
Less accumulated amortization	16,788	14,282
	$72,052	$44,700

Amortization expense related to capital leases totaled $3,226,000, $1,864,000 and $1,800,000 for fiscal 2003, 2002 and 2001, respectively.

Future minimum lease payments at January 31, 2004, are as follows:

(In thousands)	Capital Leases	Operating Leases
Fiscal year:		
2004	$ 9,553	$ 286,452
2005	9,460	298,028
2006	9,464	291,801
2007	9,552	283,468
2008	9,815	281,114
Thereafter	125,119	3,440,169
	172,963	$4,881,032
Less amount representing interest	91,027	
Present value of minimum lease payments	$ 81,936	

Included in the operating lease schedule above is $1,039.1 million of minimum lease payments for stores that will open in 2004 and 2005.

The Company recorded capital leases totaling $33.0 million and $12.0 million during 2003 and 2002, respectively. As of January 31, 2003, the Company had entered into capital leases of approximately $22.7 million related to stores to be opened in 2004 and 2005 which had not been recorded as the related buildings are under construction.

2.250

NACCO INDUSTRIES, INC. (DEC)

(In millions)	2003	2002
Total current liabilities	$589.8	$545.5
Long-term debt—not guaranteed by the parent company	363.2	416.1
Self-insurance and other liabilities	249.3	258.7
Minority interest	.5	1.1

NOTES TO CONSOLIDATED FINANCIAL STATEMENTS
(Tabular amounts in millions, except percentage data)

Note 10 (In Part): Current and Long-Term Financing

Financing arrangements are obtained and maintained at the subsidiary level. NACCO has not guaranteed any borrowings of its subsidiaries.

The following table summarizes the Company's available and outstanding borrowings under revolving credit agreements and long-term debt.

	2003	2002
Total outstanding borrowings:		
Revolving credit agreements:		
NMHG	$ 17.1	$ 31.3
Housewares	34.8	57.6
NACoal	—	6.9
	51.9	95.8
Capital lease obligations and other term loans:		
NMHG	43.1	46.4
Housewares	.2	.3
NACoal	92.5	94.7
	135.8	141.4
Senior notes—NMHG	247.5	247.1
Total debt outstanding	$435.2	$484.3
Current portion of borrowings outstanding:		
NMHG	$ 37.6	$ 51.3
Housewares	16.2	—
NACoal	18.2	16.9
	$ 72.0	$ 68.2
Long-term portion of borrowings outstanding:		
NMHG	$270.1	$273.5
Housewares	18.8	57.9
NACoal	74.3	84.7
	$363.2	$416.1

Note 12—Leasing Arrangements

The Company leases certain office, manufacturing and warehouse facilities, retail stores and machinery and equipment under noncancellable capital and operating leases that expire at various dates through 2021. NMHG Retail also leases certain forklift trucks that are carried in its rental fleet or subleased to customers. Many leases include renewal and/or purchase options.

Future minimum capital and operating lease payments, at December 31, 2003, are:

	Capital Leases	Operating Leases
2004	$14.0	$ 81.0
2005	6.6	65.7
2006	3.3	52.4
2007	1.1	36.4
2008	.5	20.7
Subsequent to 2008	.4	30.1
Total minimum lease payments	25.9	$286.3
Amounts representing interest	2.6	
Present value of net minimum lease payments	23.3	
Current maturities	12.5	
Long-term capital lease obligation	$10.8	

Aggregate future minimum rentals to be received under noncancellable subleases of lift trucks as of December 31, 2003 are $169.3 million. Rental expense for all operating leases was $90.5 million, $71.8 million and $57.5 million for 2003, 2002 and 2001, respectively. The Company also recognized $74.5 million, $62.0 million and $45.5 million for 2003, 2002 and 2001, respectively, in rental income on subleases of equipment under operating leases in which it was the lessee. These subleases were primarily related to lift trucks, in which NMHG derives revenues in the ordinary course of business under rental agreements with its customers. The sublease rental income for these lift trucks is included in "Net sales" and the related rent expense is included in "Cost of sales" in the Consolidated Statements of Operations and Comprehensive Income (Loss) for each period.

Assets recorded under capital leases are included in property, plant and equipment and consist of the following:

	2003	2002
Plant and equipment	$77.4	$76.2
Less accumulated amortization	47.6	38.6
	$29.8	$37.6

Amortization of plant and equipment under capital leases is included in depreciation expense in each of the years ended December 31, 2003, 2002 and 2001.

During 2003, 2002 and 2001, capital lease obligations of $3.4 million, $15.6 million and $39.1 million, respectively, were incurred in connection with lease agreements to acquire plant and equipment, including $8.3 million related to the project mining subsidiaries in 2001.

2.251

TASTY BAKING COMPANY (DEC)

(In thousands)	2003	2002
Current liabilities:		
Current obligations under capital leases	$ 634	$ 176
Notes payable, banks	4,900	4,500
Accounts payable	9,261	6,074
Accrued payroll and employee benefits	6,013	6,480
Reserve for restructure	1,331	2,417
Other accrued liabilities	2,280	981
Total current liabilities	24,419	20,628
Long-term debt	8,000	9,000
Long-term obligations under capital leases, less current portion	4,705	3,486
Reserve for restructures, less current portion	1,044	3,568
Accrued pensions and other liabilities	19,938	15,669
Postretirement benefits other than pensions	16,718	16,684
Total liabilities	$74,824	$69,035

NOTES TO CONSOLIDATED FINANCIAL STATEMENTS (In thousands)

6. Obligations Under Capital Leases

Obligations under capital leases consist of the following:

	2003	2002
Capital lease obligation, with interest at 11%, payable in monthly installments of $47 through June 2014	$3,486	$3,654
Capital lease obligation, with interest at 5.9%, payable in monthly installments of $45 through October 2007	1,853	—
Industrial development mortgage, with interest at 8.5%, payable in monthly installments of $8 through January 2003	—	8
	5,339	3,662
Less current portion	634	176
	$4,705	$3,486

7 (In Part): Commitments and Contingencies

The company leases certain plant and distribution facilities, machinery and automotive equipment under noncancelable lease agreements. The company expects that in the normal course of business, leases that expire will be renewed or replaced by other leases. Included therein is a lease with the Trustees of the Tasty Baking Company Pension Plan for property contributed to the plan on December 1, 1960. The net annual rental is subject to adjustment every three years to provide fair market rental to the Pension Plan and accordingly, the net annual rental was adjusted effective July 1, 2002. The lease was renewed on July 1, 2002, for four additional three-year periods. In addition, the company has an option to purchase the property at any time at its then fair market value. Property, plant and equipment relating to capital leases was $8,310 at December 27, 2003 and $6,231 at December 28, 2002 with accumulated amortization of $2,303 and $2,042, respectively. Depreciation and amortization of assets recorded under capital leases was $261 in 2003 and $244 in 2002 and 2001.

The following is schedule of future minimum lease payments as of December 27, 2003:

	Capital Leases	Noncancelable Operating Leases
2004	$1,102	$1,307
2005	1,102	996
2006	1,102	753
2007	847	508
2008	561	411
Later years	3,085	151
Total minimum lease payments	$7,799	$4,126
Less interest portion of payments	2,460	
Present value of future minimum lease payments	$5,339	

2.252

TESORO PETROLEUM CORPORATION (DEC)

(Dollars in millions)	2003	2002
Total current liabilities	$ 687.0	$ 608.3
Deferred income taxes	179.2	128.7
Other liabilities	224.4	227.5
Debt	1,605.3	1,906.7

NOTES TO CONSOLIDATED FINANCIAL STATEMENTS

Note D (In Part): Divestitures

On December 31, 2002, we completed a sale/lease-back transaction for 30 of our retail stations located in Alaska, Hawaii, Idaho and Utah for cash proceeds of $40 million. We recognized a pretax loss on the sale of $4 million. The leases are for land, buildings and certain equipment and have an initial term of 17 years with four 5-year renewal options. The portion of the leases attributable to land is accounted for as an operating lease, while the portion attributable to buildings and equipment is accounted for as a capital lease.

Note F (In Part): Debt

Debt and Maturities

At December 31, 2003 and 2002, debt consisted of (in millions):

	2003	2002
Credit agreement—revolving credit facility	$ —	$ —
Senior secured term loans due 2008	199.0	—
8% senior secured notes due 2008 (net of unamortized discount of $3.3)	371.7	—
Senior secured credit facility—Tranche A term loan	—	194.2
Senior secured credit facility—Tranche B term loan	—	723.8
9 5/8 % senior subordinated notes due 2012	429.0	450.0
9 5/8 % senior subordinated notes due 2008	211.0	215.0
9% senior subordinated notes due 2008 (net of unamortized discount of $1.8 in 2003 and $2.1 in 2002)	295.7	297.9
Junior subordinated notes due 2012 (net of unamortized discount of $75.0 in 2003 and $83.0 in 2002)	75.0	67.0
Capital lease obligations and other	27.4	28.8
Total debt	1,608.8	1,976.7
Less current maturities	3.5	70.0
Debt, less current maturities	$1,605.3	$1,906.7

The aggregate maturities of Tesoro's debt for each of the five years following December 31, 2003 were: 2004—$3.5 million; 2005—$3.5 million; 2006—$3.4 million; 2007—$98.2 million; and 2008—$980.6 million. Gross borrowings and repayments under our revolving credit lines and interim facilities amounted to $1.0 billion, $624 million and $958 million in 2003, 2002 and 2001, respectively.

Capital Lease Obligations

Our capital lease obligations comprise primarily of 30 retail stations that we sold and leased-back in 2002 with initial terms of 17 years, with four 5-year renewal options (See Note D). We classified the portions of the leases attributable to land as operating leases, and we classified the portions attributable to depreciable buildings and equipment as capital leases. The combined present value of minimum lease payments totaled $22.9 million at December 31, 2003. Tesoro also has other capital leases for tugs and barges used to transport petroleum products, over varying terms ending in 2005 through 2009, in which the combined present value of minimum lease payments totaled $3.7 million at December 31, 2003.

At December 31, 2003 and 2002, the total cost of assets under capital leases was $34.7 million gross (accumulated amortization of $9.6 million) and $35.3 million gross (accumulated amortization of $7.6 million), respectively. Capital lease obligations included in debt totaled $27.4 million and $28.8 million at December 31, 2003 and 2002, respectively. We include amortization of the cost of assets under capital leases in depreciation and amortization.

Future minimum annual lease payments, including interest, as of December 31, 2003 for capital leases were (in millions):

2004	$ 4.2
2005	4.2
2006	3.9
2007	3.5
2008	3.4
Thereafter	35.1
Total minimum lease payments	54.3
Less amount representing interest	26.9
Capital lease obligations	$27.4

Lessee—Operating Leases

2.253

JONES APPAREL GROUP, INC. (DEC)

NOTES TO CONSOLIDATED FINANCIAL STATEMENTS

Commitments and Contingencies (In Part)

c) Leases

Total rent expense charged to operations for the years ended December 31, 2003, 2002 and 2001 was as follows.

(In millions)	2003	2002	2001
Minimum rent	$107.6	$100.8	$82.1
Contingent rent	1.1	1.1	1.1
Less: sublease rent	(6.4)	(5.6)	(4.4)
	$102.3	$ 96.3	$78.8

The following is a schedule of future minimum rental payments required under operating leases for the next five years:

(In millions)	
2004	$100.5
2005	85.8
2006	76.7
2007	65.2
2008	49.2
Later years	208.5
	$585.9

Certain of the leases provide for renewal options and the payment of real estate taxes and other occupancy costs. Future rental commitments for leases have not been reduced by minimum non-cancelable sublease rentals aggregating $47.2 million.

2.254

NORDSTROM, INC. (JAN)

NOTES TO CONSOLIDATED FINANCIAL STATEMENTS

Note 14: Leases

We lease land, buildings and equipment under noncancelable lease agreements with expiration dates ranging from 2004 to 2080. Certain leases include renewal provisions at our option. Most of the leases provide for additional rent payments based upon specific percentages of sales and require us to pay for certain common area maintenance and other costs.

	Fiscal Year		
	2003	2002	2001
Minimum rent:			
Store locations	$24,071	$19,609	$26,951
Offices, warehouses and equipment	23,158	27,610	20,144
Percentage rent:			
Store locations	7,920	7,776	8,047
Total rent expense	$55,149	$54,995	$55,142

Future minimum lease payments as of January 31, 2004 are as follows:

Year Ended January 31,	Capital Leases	Operating Leases
2005	$ 2,398	$ 73,265
2006	1,932	69,522
2007	1,564	65,216
2008	1,565	61,140
2009	1,565	58,332
Thereafter	7,167	390,731
Total minimum lease payments	16,191	$718,206
Less amount representing interest	4,704	
Present value of net minimum lease payments	$11,487	

2.255

RUDDICK CORPORATION (SEP)

NOTES TO CONSOLIDATED FINANCIAL STATEMENTS

Leases

The Company leases certain equipment under agreements expiring during the next 5 years. Harris Teeter leases most of its stores under leases that expire during the next 21 years. It is expected that such leases will be renewed by exercising options or replaced by leases of other properties. Most store leases provide for additional rentals based on sales, and certain store facilities are sublet under leases expiring during the next 14 years. Certain leases also contain rent escalation clauses (step rents) that require additional rental amounts in the later years of the term. Rent expense for leases with step rents is recognized on a straight-line basis over the minimum lease term. Rent expense for the fiscal years was as follows:

(In thousands)	2003	2002	2001
Minimum, net of sublease income	$65,333	$67,932	$73,816
Contingent	1,215	1,329	1,456
Total	$66,548	$69,261	$75,272

Future minimum lease commitments (excluding leases assigned or expected to be assigned—see below) and total minimum sublease rental income to be received under noncancelable subleases at September 28, 2003 were as follows:

(In thousands)	Operating Leases	Subleases	Capital Leases
2004	$ 63,832	$ (2,528)	$ 500
2005	63,073	(2,347)	464
2006	59,309	(2,270)	285
2007	54,934	(2,200)	285
2008	52,709	(1,906)	285
Later years	473,828	(14,260)	4,117
Total minimum lease obligations (receivables)	$767,685	$(25,511)	5,936
Amount representing interest			(2,892)
Present value of net minimum obligation (included with long-term debt)			$ 3,044

In connection with the closing of certain store locations, Harris Teeter has assigned leases to other merchants with recourse. These leases expire over the next 18 years and the future minimum lease payments of $102,093,000 over this period have been assumed by these merchants.

2.256

STEELCASE INC. (FEB)

NOTES TO CONSOLIDATED FINANCIAL STATEMENTS

16 (In Part): Financial Instruments, Concentrations of Credit Risk, Commitments, Guarantees and Contingencies

Lease Commitments

We lease certain sales offices, showrooms and equipment under non-cancelable operating leases that expire at various dates through 2018. During the normal course of business, we have entered into several sale-leaseback arrangements for certain equipment and facilities. In accordance with GAAP, these leases are accounted for as operating leases and any gains from the sale of the original properties were recorded as deferred gains and are amortized over the lease term. The deferred gains are included as a component of *Other Long-term Liabilities*, and amounted to $29.8 million as of February 28, 2003 and $32.9 million as of February 22, 2002.

(In millions)

Minimum Annual Rental Commitments Under Non-Cancelable Operating Leases	Amount
2004	$ 44.3
2005	37.7
2006	30.1
2007	23.3
2008	18.2
Thereafter	96.3
	$249.9

Rent expense under all operating leases approximated $55.9 million for 2003, $55.4 million for 2002 and $46.1 million for 2001.

As described in Note 2, we have leased aircraft under a synthetic lease structure that was put in place in May 2000. The synthetic lease structure provides us with access to funding at commercial rates. Under the accounting rules prior to FIN No. 46, the structure is defined as an operating lease. Under FIN No. 46 it is likely that the aircraft will be capitalized on our balance sheet, and the related obligation will be recorded as debt. If this occurs, the impact of this accounting change on the Consolidated Statements of Income will be an increase in depreciation and interest expense offset by the fact that the recording of rent expense will no longer be required. As required, we plan to implement FIN No. 46 in Q3 2004.

Lessor Leases

2.257

DANA CORPORATION (DEC)

(In millions)	2003	2002
Total current assets	$4,533	$4,118
Goodwill, net	558	568
Investments and other assets	1,694	1,484
Investments in leases	622	827
Property, plant and equipment, net	2,210	2,556
Total assets	$9,617	$9,553

NOTES TO CONSOLIDATED FINANCIAL STATEMENTS (In millions)

Note 1 (In Part): Summary of Significant Accounting Policies

Lease Financing

Lease financing consists of direct financing leases, leveraged leases and equipment on operating leases. Income on direct financing leases is recognized by a method which produces a constant periodic rate of return on the outstanding investment in the lease. Income on leveraged leases is recognized by a method which produces a constant rate of return on the outstanding net investment in the lease, net of the related deferred tax liability, in the years in which the net investment is positive. Initial direct costs are deferred and amortized using the interest method over the lease period. Equipment under operating leases is recorded at cost, net of accumulated depreciation. Income from operating leases is recognized ratably over the term of the leases.

Allowance for Losses on Lease Financing

Provisions for losses on lease financing receivables are determined based on loss experience and assessment of inherent risk. Adjustments are made to the allowance for losses to adjust the net investment in lease financing to an estimated collectible amount. Income recognition is generally discontinued on accounts which are contractually past due and where no payment activity has occurred within 120 days. Accounts are charged against the allowance for losses when determined to be uncollectible. Accounts where asset repossession has started as the primary means of recovery are classified within other assets at their estimated realizable value.

Note 16 (In Part): Composition of Certain Balance Sheet Amounts

The following items comprise the amounts indicated in the respective balance sheet captions:

	2003	2002
Investments in leases		
Leveraged leases	$588	$724
Direct financing leases	70	94
Property on operating leases, net of accumulated depreciation	1	60
Allowance for credit losses	(26)	(34)
	633	844
Less: Current portion	11	17
	$622	$827

The components of the net investment in leveraged leases are as follows:

	2003	2002
Rentals receivable	$ 4,310	$ 5,980
Residual values	429	778
Nonrecourse debt service	(3,622)	(5,200)
Unearned income	(528)	(833)
Deferred investment tax credit	(1)	(1)
	588	724
Less: Deferred taxes arising from leverage leases	441	466
	$ 147	$ 258

The components of the net investment in direct financing leases are as follows:

	2003	2002
Total minimum lease payments	$66	$ 98
Residual values	29	31
Deferred initial direct costs	1	2
	96	131
Less: Unearned income	26	37
	$70	$ 94

Total minimum lease payments receivable on direct financing leases as of December 31, 2003 are as follows:

Year ended December 31	
2004	$12
2005	10
2006	10
2007	10
2008	9
Later years	15
Total minimum lease payments receivable	$66

Total minimum lease payments receivable on operating leases as of December 31, 2003 were not material.

2.258

HEWLETT-PACKARD COMPANY (OCT)

(In millions)	2003	2002
Current assets:		
Cash and cash equivalents	$14,188	$11,192
Short-term investments	403	237
Accounts receivable, net of allowance for doubtful accounts of $347 and $410 as of October 31, 2003 and 2002, respectively	8,921	8,456
Financing receivables, net of allowance for doubtful accounts of $119 and $150 as of October 31, 2003 and 2002, respectively	2,965	3,453
Inventory	6,065	5,797
Other current assets	8,454	6,940
Total current assets	40,996	36,075
Property, plant and equipment, net of accumulated depreciation of $6,817 and $5,612 as of October 31, 2003 and 2002, respectively	6,482	6,924
Long-term financing receivables and other assets	7,980	7,758
Goodwill	14,894	15,089
Purchased intangible assets	4,356	4,864
Total assets	$74,708	$70,710

NOTES TO CONSOLIDATED FINANCIAL STATEMENTS

Note 1 (In Part): Summary of Significant Accounting Policies

Revenue Recognition (In Part)

Financing

HP recognizes revenue from the sale of equipment under sales-type leases and direct-financing leases as product revenue at the inception of the lease. HP earns associated financing interest income on an accrual basis under an effective interest method. HP ceases revenue recognition on delinquent accounts which are deemed to be delinquent based upon a number of factors, including customer credit history, number of days past due and the terms of the customer agreement. HP resumes revenue recognition and recognizes any associated deferred revenue when appropriate customer actions are taken to remove accounts from delinquent status. HP recognizes revenue from operating leases on an accrual basis as product revenue as the rental payments become due.

Property, Plant and Equipment

Property, plant and equipment is stated at cost less accumulated depreciation. Additions, improvements and major renewals are capitalized. Maintenance, repairs and minor renewals are expensed as incurred. Depreciation is provided using the straight-line or accelerated methods over the estimated useful lives of the assets. Estimated useful lives are 5 to 40 years for buildings and improvements and 3 to 10 years for machinery and equipment. Leasehold improvements are depreciated over the life of the lease or the asset, whichever is shorter. Equipment held for lease is depreciated over the initial term of the lease to the equipment's estimated residual value.

HP adopted the straight-line method of depreciation for all property, plant and equipment placed into service after April 30, 2002. Property, plant and equipment placed into service prior to May 1, 2002 continues to be depreciated using accelerated methods for buildings, improvements, and the majority of machinery and equipment and the straight-line method for leasehold improvements and leased equipment. HP believes this change allocates the costs of new property more appropriately in its financial results by better allocating costs of new property over the useful lives of these assets. In addition, the new method more closely conforms to the prevalent practices in the industries in which HP operates. The effect of this change was not material to HP's earnings or financial position for the years ended October 31, 2003 and 2002.

Note 6 (In Part): Balance Sheet Details

Balance sheet details were as follows at October 31, 2003 and 2002:

Long-Term Financing Receivables and Other Assets

(In millions)	2003	2002
Financing receivables	$2,698	$2,792
Deferred tax assets—long term	2,859	2,210
Other	2,423	2,756
	$7,980	$7,758

Note 8: Financing Receivables and Operating Leases

Financing receivables represent sales-type, direct-financing, and operating leases resulting from the marketing of HP's, and complementary third-party, products. These receivables typically have terms from two to five years and are usually collateralized by a security interest in the underlying assets. The components of net financing receivables, which are included in financing receivables and long-term financing receivables and other assets, were as follows at October 31, 2003 and 2002:

(In millions)	2003	2002
Minimum lease payments receivables	$ 5,902	$ 6,602
Allowance for doubtful accounts	(210)	(270)
Unguaranteed residual value	446	523
Unearned income	(475)	(610)
Financing receivables, net	5,663	6,245
Less current portion	(2,965)	(3,453)
Amounts due after one year, net	$ 2,698	$ 2,792

Scheduled maturities of HP's minimum lease payments receivable at October 31, 2003 and minimum future rentals on non-cancelable operating leases are as follows:

(In millions)	2004	2005	2006	2007	2008	Thereafter	Total
Scheduled maturities of HP's minimum lease payments receivable[1]	$3,097	$1,694	$781	$207	$115	$8	$5,902
Minimum future rentals on non-cancelable operating leases[1]	690	400	155	10	1	—	1,256

[1] Actual cash collections may differ due primarily to customer early buy-outs and refinancings.

Equipment leased to customers under operating leases was $2.1 billion at October 31, 2003 and $1.8 billion at October 31, 2002 and is included in machinery and equipment. Accumulated depreciation on equipment under lease was $1.2 billion at October 31, 2003 and $782 million at October 31, 2002.

OTHER NONCURRENT LIABILITIES

2.259   In addition to long-term debt, many of the survey companies presented captions for deferred taxes, minority interests, employee liabilities, estimated losses or expenses, and deferred credits. Table 2-31 summarizes the nature of such noncurrent liabilities and deferred credits. Examples of presentations and disclosures for noncurrent liabilities and deferred credits follow.

2.260

TABLE 2-31: OTHER NONCURRENT LIABILITIES

| | Number of Companies | | | |
	2003	2002	2001	2000
Deferred income taxes	376	370	392	390
Minority interest	146	160	159	151
Derivatives	95	93	39	12
Preferred securities of subsidiary trust	23	32	34	30
Liabilities of nonhomogeneous operations	4	6	10	4
Employee Liabilities				
Pension accruals	233	220	141	114
Benefits	209	221	191	195
Deferred compensation, bonus, etc.	64	55	52	45
Other—described	15	17	9	36
Estimated Losses or Expenses				
Environmental	63	67	54	45
Discontinued operations	54	54	21	13
Insurance	24	38	33	27
Warranties	22	22	10	6
Litigation	19	17	13	N/C*
Asset retirement obligation	19	1	N/C*	N/C*
Other—described	40	91	93	99
Deferred Credits				
Payments received prior to rendering service	58	34	33	9
Deferred profit on sales	26	34	33	9
Other—described	12	10	11	26

* N/C = Not compiled. Line item was not included in the table for the year shown.

Deferred Income Taxes

2.261

JABIL CIRCUIT, INC. (AUG)

(In thousands)	2003	2002
Total current liabilities	$1,263,218	$ 593,382
Notes payable, long-term debt and long-term lease obligations less current installments	297,018	354,668
Deferred income taxes (note 6)	19,223	41,323
Other liabilities	76,810	51,567
Total liabilities	$1,656,269	$1,040,940

NOTES TO CONSOLIDATED FINANCIAL STATEMENTS

1 (In Part): Description of Business and Summary of Significant Accounting Policies

i. Income Taxes

Deferred tax assets and liabilities are recognized for the future tax consequences attributable to differences between the financial statement carrying amounts of existing assets and liabilities and their respective tax basis. Deferred tax assets and liabilities are measured using enacted tax rates expected to apply to taxable income in the years in which those temporary differences are expected to be recovered or settled. The effect on deferred tax assets and liabilities of a change in the tax rate is recognized in income in the period that includes the enactment date of the rate change.

6 (In Part): Income Taxes

The Company currently intends to re-invest income from all of its foreign subsidiaries for the foreseeable future. The aggregate undistributed earnings of the Company's foreign subsidiaries for which no deferred tax liability has been recorded is approximately $345.2 million as of August 31, 2003. Determination of the amount of unrecognized deferred tax liability on these undistributed earnings is not practicable.

The tax effects of temporary differences that give rise to significant portions of the deferred tax assets and deferred tax liabilities are as follows (in thousands):

	2003	2002
Deferred tax assets:		
Net operating loss carryforward	$ 3,574	$ 2,854
Accounts receivable, principally due to allowance for doubtful accounts	2,751	1,734
Grant receivable	1,092	1,758
Inventories, principally due to costs capitalized for tax purposes pursuant to the Tax Reform Act of 1986	5,169	4,281
Compensated absences, principally due to accrual for financial reporting purposes	2,382	3,168
Accrued expenses, principally due to accrual for financial reporting purposes	23,761	7,551
Accrued UK interest, deductible when paid	4,107	3,331
Foreign currency translation gains and losses	3,508	—
Other	5,591	1,280
Total gross deferred tax assets	51,935	25,957
Less valuation allowance	(2,394)	(2,056)
Net deferred tax assets	$49,541	$23,901
Deferred tax liabilities:		
Intangible assets	$ 2,291	$ 3,340
Property, plant and equipment, principally due to differences in depreciation and amortization	30,718	40,611
Other	2,169	—
Deferred tax liabilities	$35,178	$43,951

Net current deferred tax assets were $33.6 million and $21.3 million at August 31, 2003 and August 31, 2002, respectively, and net noncurrent deferred tax liabilities were $19.2 million and $41.3 million at August 31, 2003 and August 31, 2002, respectively.

The net change in the total valuation allowance for years ended August 31, 2003 and 2002 was $338 thousand and ($46) thousand, respectively. In addition, at August 31, 2003, the Company has net operating loss carryforwards for federal, state and foreign income tax purposes of approximately $1.8 million, $0.3 million and $1.5 million, respectively, which are available to reduce future taxes, if any. These net operating loss carryforwards expire through the year 2019.

Based on the Company's historical operating income, management believes that it is more likely than not that the Company will realize the benefit of its net deferred tax assets.

2.262

JACUZZI BRANDS, INC. (SEP)

(In millions)	2003	2002
Total current liabilities	$ 306.7	$ 593.5
Long-term debt	451.4	516.9
Deferred income taxes	26.2	41.6
Asbestos claims	160.0	145.0
Other liabilities	136.8	131.2
Total liabilities	$1,081.1	$1,428.2

NOTES TO CONSOLIDATED FINANCIAL STATEMENTS

Note 2 (In Part): Accounting Policies

Income Taxes

Deferred tax assets and liabilities represent the tax effects, based on current law, of any temporary differences in the timing of when revenues and expenses are recognized for tax purposes and when they are recognized for financial statement purposes. The deferred tax assets are reviewed periodically for recoverability and valuation allowances are provided as necessary.

Note 8 (In Part): Income Taxes

We are able to carry back net operating losses in 2002 for which we had previously established a valuation allowance in 2001 as a result of a change in tax law under the Job Creation and Worker's Assistance Act of 2002. We had established the valuation allowance in 2001 to reflect the uncertainty of the future realization of losses recognized in connection with the 2001 Disposal Plan.

In August 2001, we recorded a deferred tax liability of $24.7 million for purchased intangibles, increasing the excess purchase price, and thus goodwill, by the same amount. The deferred tax liability is being reversed and a deferred tax benefit is being recognized over the amortization period of the intangible assets.

The components of deferred income tax assets and liabilities consisted of the following:

(In millions)	2003	2002
Deferred tax assets:		
Accruals and allowances	$ 36.3	$ 52.4
Post-employment benefits	8.2	7.9
Foreign tax credits	11.4	8.2
Expected benefit from Disposal Plans & capital loss carryforwards	70.1	42.8
Gross deferred tax assets	126.0	111.3
Valuation allowance	(79.8)	(65.9)
Total deferred tax assets	46.2	45.4
Deferred tax liabilities:		
Property, plant and equipment	5.9	10.6
Inventory	2.8	3.5
Net pension assets	12.2	13.4
Deductible goodwill	3.2	2.9
Purchased intangibles	24.2	24.2
Mark-to-market investments	8.2	—
Other	0.4	1.4
Total deferred tax liabilities	56.9	56.0
Net deferred tax liability	$ (10.7)	$ (10.6)

We have established a valuation allowance principally related to deferred tax assets resulting from the losses recognized in connection with the 2001 Disposal Plan, reflecting the uncertainty of the future realization of these assets.

● ● ● ● ● ●

At September 30, 2003, we had approximately $200.2 million in capital loss carryforwards for which we have established a valuation allowance. These capital losses expire in 2005 and 2007. We also have foreign tax credit carryforwards of $11.4 million, a substantial portion of which will expire in 2006.

The deferred tax balances have been classified in the balance sheet as follows:

(In millions)	2003	2002
Current assets	$ 18.3	$ 34.4
Current liabilities	(2.8)	(3.4)
Net current assets	15.5	31.0
Non-current assets	29.4	11.0
Non-current liabilities	(55.6)	(52.6)
Net non-current liabilities	(26.2)	(41.6)
Net deferred tax liability	$(10.7)	$(10.6)

Minority Interest

2.263

EBAY INC. (DEC)

(In thousands)	2002	2003
Total current liabilities	$386,224	$647,276
Long-term obligations	13,798	124,476
Deferred tax liabilities, net	27,625	79,238
Other liabilities	22,874	33,494
Minority interests	33,232	39,408
Total liabilities	$483,753	$923,892

NOTES TO CONSOLIDATED FINANCIAL STATEMENTS

Note 1 (In Part): The Company and Summary of Significant Accounting Policies

Principles of Consolidation and Basis of Presentation (In Part)

The accompanying financial statements are consolidated and include the financial statements of eBay and our majority-owned subsidiaries. All significant intercompany balances and transactions have been eliminated in consolidation.

The consolidated accounts include 100% of the assets and liabilities of these majority-owned subsidiaries and the ownership interests of minority investors are recorded as minority interests. Investments in entities where we hold more than a 20% but less than a 50% ownership interest and have the ability to significantly influence the operations of the investee are accounted for using the equity method of accounting and the investment balance is included in long term investments, while our share of the investees' operations is included in other income. As of December 31, 2003, we did not have any equity method investments. Investments in entities where we hold less than a 20% ownership interest or where we do not have the ability to significantly influence the operations of the investee are accounted for using the cost method of accounting and are included in long-term investments.

Consolidation of Variable Interest Entities

In accordance with the provisions of FIN 46, "Consolidation of Variable Interest Entities," we have included our San Jose corporate headquarters lease arrangement in our Consolidated Financial Statements effective July 1, 2003. Under this new accounting standard, our balance sheet at December 31, 2003 reflects additions for land and buildings totaling $126.4 million, lease obligations of $122.5 million and non-controlling minority interests of $3.9 million. Our consolidated income statement for year ended December 31, 2003, reflects the reclassification of lease payments on our San Jose corporate headquarters from operating expense to interest expense, beginning with quarters following our adoption of FIN 46 on July 1, 2003, a $5.4 million after-tax charge for cumulative depreciation for periods from lease inception through June 30, 2003, and incremental depreciation expense of approximately $400,000, net of tax, per quarter for the third and fourth quarters of 2003. We have adopted the provisions of FIN 46 prospectively from July 1, 2003, and as a result, prior periods have not been restated. The cumulative effect of the change in accounting principle arising from the adoption of FIN 46 has been reflected in net income in 2003.

2.264

GENERAL MILLS, INC. (MAY)

(In millions)	2003	2002
Total current liabilities	$ 3,444	$ 5,747
Long-term debt	7,516	5,591
Deferred income taxes	1,661	407
Other liabilities	1,131	1,066
Total liabilities	13,752	12,811
Minority interests	300	153

NOTES TO CONSOLIDATED FINANCIAL STATEMENTS

9. Minority Interests

In April 2002, the Company and certain of its wholly owned subsidiaries contributed assets with an aggregate fair market value of approximately $4 billion to another wholly owned subsidiary, General Mills Cereals, LLC (GMC), a limited liability company. GMC is a separate and distinct legal entity from the Company and its subsidiaries, and has separate assets, liabilities, businesses and operations. The contributed assets consist primarily of manufacturing assets and intellectual property associated with the production and retail sale of Big G ready-to-eat cereals, *Progresso* soups and *Old El Paso* products. In exchange for the contribution of these assets, GMC issued the managing membership interest and Class A and Class B preferred membership interests to wholly owned subsidiaries of the Company. The managing member directs the business activities and operations of GMC and has fiduciary responsibilities to GMC and its members. Other than rights to vote on certain matters, holders of the Class A and Class B interests have no right to direct the management of GMC.

In May 2002, GMC sold approximately 30 percent of the Class A interests to an unrelated third-party investor in exchange for $150 million. The Class A interests receive quarterly preferred distributions at a floating rate equal to the three-month LIBOR plus 90 basis points. The GMC limited liability company agreement requires that the rate of the preferred distributions for the Class A interests be reset by agreement between the third-party investors and GMC every five years, beginning in May 2007. If GMC and the investors fail to mutually agree on a new rate of preferred distributions, GMC must remarket the securities. Upon a failed remarketing, the rate over LIBOR will be increased by 75 basis points (up to a maximum total of 300 basis points following a scheduled reset date). In the event of four consecutive failed remarketings, the third-party investors can force a liquidation and winding up of GMC.

GMC has a scheduled duration of 20 years. However, GMC, through the managing member, may elect to redeem all of the Class A interests held by third-party investors at any time for an amount equal to the investors' capital accounts, plus an optional retirement premium if such retirement occurs prior to June 2007. Under certain circumstances, GMC also may be dissolved and liquidated earlier. Events requiring liquidation include, without limitation, the bankruptcy of GMC or its subsidiaries, failure to deliver the preferred quarterly return, failure to comply with portfolio requirements, breaches of certain covenants, and four consecutive failed attempts to remarket the Class A interests. In the event of a liquidation of GMC, the third-party investors that hold the Class A interests would be entitled to repayment from the proceeds of liquidation prior to the subsidiaries of the Company that are members of GMC. The managing member may avoid liquidation in most circumstances by exercising an option to purchase the preferred interests. An election to redeem the preferred membership interests could impact the Company's liquidity by requiring the Company to refinance the redemption price or liquidate a portion of GMC assets.

Currently, all of the Class B interests are held by a subsidiary of the Company. The Company may offer the Class B interests and the remaining, unsold Class A interests to third-party investors on terms and conditions to be determined.

For financial reporting purposes, the assets, liabilities, results of operations, and cash flows of GMC are included in the Company's consolidated financial statements. The third-party investor's Class A interest in GMC is reflected as a minority interest on the consolidated balance sheet of the Company, and the return to the third-party investor is reflected as interest expense in the Consolidated Statements of Earnings.

In fiscal 2003, General Mills Capital, Inc. (GM Capital), a wholly owned subsidiary, sold $150 million of its Series A preferred stock to an unrelated third-party investor. GM Capital regularly enters into transactions with the Company to purchase receivables of the Company. These receivables are included in the consolidated balance sheet and the $150 million purchase price for the Series A preferred stock is reflected as minority interest on the balance sheet. The proceeds from the issuance of the preferred stock were used to reduce short-term debt. The return to the third-party investor is reflected as interest expense in the Consolidated Statements of Earnings.

2.265

UNOCAL CORPORATION (DEC)

(Millions of dollars)	2003	2002
Total current liabilities	$2,085	$1,632
Long-term debt and capital leases	2,635	3,002
Deferred income taxes	704	593
Accrued abandonment, restoration and environmental liabilities	844	622
Other deferred credits and liabilities	960	902
Minority interests	39	275

NOTES TO THE CONSOLIDATED FINANCIAL STATEMENTS

Note 2 (In Part): Accounting Changes

FASB Interpretation No. 46

FASB Interpretation No. 46, "Consolidation of Variable Interest Entities ("VIE")" requires the consolidation of certain entities that generally lack sufficient equity to finance their own activity without support from others or where there is an absence of control by equity investors. Although this Interpretation was effective for new variable interest entities as of February 1, 2003, the Company did not participate in any new VIEs in 2003. Pursuant to the recognition requirements of FASB Interpretation No. 46, the Company consolidated in the third quarter of 2003 the long-term debt of an affiliate that operates geothermal steam-fired power plants in Indonesia. At December 31, 2003, the balance sheet includes $74 million related to this debt (see note 19 for further details). An additional $242 million, classified as minority interests as of June 30, 2003, related to a partnership interest in Spirit Energy 76 Development, L.P. ("Spirit LP"), would have been required to be consolidated as long-term debt under this Interpretation had it not been paid in July 2003. FASB Staff Position No. FIN 46-6, delayed mandatory adoption of this rule until December 31, 2003, and permitted adoption on an entity-by-entity basis.

In December 2003, the FASB issued FASB Interpretation No. 46 (revised December 2003) which clarifies the definition of a VIE and provides a scope exception for certain entities that meet the Statement's definition of a "business." The Company will adopt this Standard in the first quarter of 2004, which will result in the deconsolidation of the Unocal Capital Trust (see note 25 for further details). As a result, the $522 million obligation for the convertible preferred securities will be removed from the consolidated balance sheet and replaced by a non-current liability for the $538 million in 6-1/4% convertible junior subordinated debentures of Unocal payable to the Trust. The Company will also record its $16 million investment in the Trust on the consolidated balance sheet. The deconsolidation will not effect consolidated net earnings. Because of its complexities, the Company continues to review the revised Statement and may find additional material interests in entities which could require recognition or disclosure in the first quarter 2004 financial statements.

Note 18—Variable Interest Entities

Dayabumi Salak Pratama, Ltd. ("DSPL") is a variable interest entity formed for the purpose of building and operating a geothermal energy fueled power generating facility in

Indonesia. Under a long-term electricity sales contract, DSPL provides power to the Indonesian state-owned electricity company, PT. PLN (Persero) ("PLN"). Unocal Geothermal of Indonesia, Ltd. ("UGI") owns a 50 percent interest in DSPL and is under contract to administer DSPL operations. DSPL has no employees of its own. DSPL had loans and notes payable totaling $74 million at December 31, 2003. Neither UGI nor the Company has guaranteed DSPL's debt obligations, which are non-recourse. The Company consolidated DSPL commencing in the third quarter of 2003 in accordance with FASB Interpretation No. 46 (see note 2 for further details).

Note 23—Minority Interests

At December 31, 2003, the Company's minority interests on the consolidated balance sheet were $39 million, a decrease of $236 million from 2002. This decrease was primarily due to the payment of the limited partner's minority interest in Spirit LP in July 2003 for $252 million. Spirit LP was formed in 1999 when the Company contributed fixed-price overriding royalty interests, valued at $304 million, from its working interest shares in certain oil and gas producing properties in the Gulf of Mexico to the partnership. An unaffiliated investor contributed $250 million in cash to the partnership and received a priority allocation of profits and cash distributions.

At December 31, 2003, the $39 million reflected in minority interests included amounts relating to the outside interests of certain oil and gas, carbon, and real estate entities. Along with these entities, the amount in minority interests included the outside interest in DSPL, which was consolidated in the third quarter of 2003 as required by FASB Interpretation No. 46 (see notes 2 and 18 or further details).

Derivatives

2.266

JOHNSON CONTROLS, INC. (SEP)

(In millions)	2003	2002
Current liabilities	$5,584.1	$4,806.2
Long-term debt	1,776.6	1,826.6
Postretirement health and other benefits	167.8	170.5
Minority interests in equity of subsidiaries	221.8	189.0
Other noncurrent liabilities	1,115.7	673.3
Long-term liabilities	$3,281.9	$2,859.4

NOTES TO CONSOLIDATED STATEMENTS

Summary of Significant Accounting Policies (In Part)

Derivative Financial Instruments

The Company has written policies and procedures that place all financial instruments under the direction of corporate treasury and restrict all derivative transactions to those intended for hedging purposes. The use of financial instruments for trading purposes is strictly prohibited. The Company uses financial instruments to manage the market risk from changes in foreign exchange rates and interest rates.

The fair values of all derivatives are recorded in the Consolidated Statement of Financial Position. The change in a derivative's fair value is recorded each period in current earnings or accumulated other comprehensive income (OCI), depending on whether the derivative is designated as part of a hedge transaction and if so, the type of hedge transaction.

The Company hedges 70 to 90 percent of its known foreign exchange transactional exposures. The Company primarily enters into forward exchange contracts to reduce the earnings and cash flow impact of non-functional currency denominated receivables and payables. Gains and losses resulting from these contracts offset the foreign exchange gains or losses on the underlying assets and liabilities being hedged. The maturities of the forward exchange contracts generally coincide with the settlement dates of the related transactions. Gains and losses on these contracts are recorded in miscellaneous—net in the Consolidated Statement of Income and are recognized in the same period as gains and losses on the hedged items.

Cash Flow Hedges

The Company selectively hedges anticipated transactions that are subject to foreign exchange exposure, primarily using foreign currency exchange contracts. These instruments are designated as cash flow hedges in accordance with SFAS No. 133, "Accounting for Derivative Instruments and Hedging Activities," as amended by SFAS No. 137, No. 138 and No. 149 and are recorded in the Consolidated Statement of Financial Position at fair value. The effective portion of the contracts' gains or losses due to changes in fair value are initially recorded as a component of accumulated OCI and are subsequently reclassified into earnings when the hedged transactions, typically sales and costs related to sales, occur and affect earnings. These contracts are highly effective in hedging the variability in future cash flows attributable to changes in currency exchange rates. The Company also selectively uses interest rate swaps to modify its exposure to interest rate movements. These swaps also qualify as cash flow hedges, with changes in fair value recorded as a component of accumulated OCI. Interest expense is recorded in earnings at the fixed rate set forth in the swap agreement. At September 30, 2003, the Company had one interest rate swap outstanding designated as a cash flow hedge related to the Company's $250 million variable rate note associated with an October 2001 acquisition (see Note 11 to the Consolidated Financial Statements).

For the years ended September 30, 2003 and 2002, the net amounts recognized in earnings due to ineffectiveness and amounts excluded from the assessment of hedge effectiveness were not material. The amount reported as realized and unrealized gains/losses on derivatives in the accumulated OCI account within shareholders' equity represents the net gain/loss on derivatives designated as cash flow hedges. The majority of the balance at September 30, 2003 will be recognized within the subsequent 12 months as the anticipated transactions occur.

Fair Value Hedges

The Company had one interest rate swap outstanding at September 30, 2003 designated as a hedge of the fair value of a portion of a fixed-rate bond issued in connection with an October 2001 acquisition (see Note 11 to the Consolidated Financial Statements). Both the swap and the hedged portion of the debt are recorded in the Consolidated Statement of Financial Position. The change in fair value of the swap exactly offsets the change in fair value of the hedged debt, with no net impact on earnings.

Net Investment Hedges

The Company has cross-currency interest rate swaps and foreign currency-denominated debt obligations that are designated as hedges of the foreign currency exposure associated with its net investments in foreign operations. The currency effects of the debt obligations are reflected in the accumulated OCI account where they offset translation gains and losses recorded on the Company's net investments in Europe and Japan. The cross-currency interest rate swaps are recorded in the Consolidated Statement of Financial Position at fair value, with changes in value attributable to changes in foreign exchange rates recorded in the foreign currency translation adjustments component of accumulated OCI. Net interest payments or receipts from the interest rate swaps are recorded as adjustments to interest expense in earnings on a current basis. Net losses of approximately $70 million and $25 million associated with hedges of net investments in foreign operations were recorded in the accumulated OCI account for the periods ended September 30, 2003 and 2002, respectively.

11. Financial Instruments

The fair values of cash and cash equivalents, accounts receivable, shortterm debt and accounts payable approximate their carrying values. The fair value of long-term debt, which was $2,324 million and $1,958 million at September 30, 2003 and 2002, respectively, was determined using market interest rates and discounted future cash flows.

The Company selectively uses derivative instruments to reduce market risk associated with changes in foreign currency and interest rates. The use of derivatives is restricted to those intended for hedging purposes; the use of any derivative instrument for trading purposes is strictly prohibited. See the Summary of Significant Accounting Policies for additional information regarding the Company's objectives for holding certain derivative instruments, its strategies for achieving those objectives, and its risk management and accounting policies applicable to these instruments.

The Company has global operations and participates in the foreign exchange markets to minimize its risk of loss from fluctuations in currency exchange rates. The Company primarily uses foreign currency exchange contracts to hedge certain of its foreign currency exposure.

The Company selectively uses interest rate swaps to reduce market risk associated with changes in interest rates (cash flow or fair value hedges). In May 2002, the Company entered into two interest rate swaps. A four-and-a-half-year swap was entered into to hedge a protion of the Company's five percent notes maturing in the first quarter of fiscal 2007. Under the swap, the Company receives interest based on a fixed U.S. dollar rate of five percent and pays interest based on a floating three-month U.S. dollar LIBOR rate plus 14.75 basis points. A one-and-a-half-year swap was also entered into to hedge the Company's $250 million variable interest rate note maturing in the first quarter of fiscal 2004. Under the swap, the Company receives interest based on a floating three-month U.S. dollar LIBOR rate plus 60 basis

points and pays interest based on a fixed U.S. dollar rate of 3.88 percent.

The Company also selectively uses cross-currency interest rate swaps to hedge the foreign currency exposure associated with its net investment in certain foreign operations (net investment hedges). Under the swaps, the Company receives interest based on a variable U.S. dollar rate and pays interest based on variable yen and euro rates on the outstanding notional principal amounts in dollars, yen and euro, respectively.

The Company's derivative instruments are recorded at fair value in the Consolidated Statement of Financial Position as follows:

(In millions; U.S. dollar equivalents)	2003		2002	
	Notional Amount	Fair Value Asset (Liability)	Notional Amount	Fair Value Asset (Liability)
Other noncurrent assets				
Interest rate swaps	$ 150	$ 14	$ 250	$ 22
Other current liabilities				
Foreign currency exchange contracts	1,681	1	1,421	(2)
Other noncurrent liabilities				
Interest rate swaps	250	(4)	303	(8)
Cross-currency interest rate swaps	734	(106)	509	(30)

It is important to note that the Company's derivative instruments are hedges protecting against underlying changes in foreign currency and interest rates. Accordingly, the implied gains/losses associated with the fair values of foreign currency exchange contracts and cross-currency interest rate swaps would be offset by gains/losses on underlying payables, receivables and net investments in foreign subsidiaries. Similarly, implied gains/losses associated with interest rate swaps offset changes in interest rates and the fair value of long-term debt.

The fair values of interest rate and cross-currency interest rate swaps were determined using dealer quotes and market interest rates. The fair values of foreign currency exchange contracts were determined using market exchange rates.

Preferred Securities of Subsidiary Trust

2.267

MCKESSON CORPORATION (MAR)

(In millions)	2003	2002
Total current liabilities	$7,974.4	$7,588.3
Postretirement obligations and other noncurrent liabilities	363.5	312.7
Long-term debt	1,290.7	1,288.7
McKesson Corporation-obligated mandatorily redeemable preferred securities of subsidiary grantor trust whose sole assets are junior subordinated debentures of McKesson Corporation	196.3	196.1

FINANCIAL NOTES

12 (In Part): Financial Instruments and Hedging Activities

At March 31, 2003 and 2002 the carrying amounts of cash and cash equivalents, marketable securities, receivables, drafts and accounts payable, and other liabilities approximate their estimated fair values because of the short maturity of these financial instruments. The carrying amounts and estimated fair values of our long-term debt and convertible preferred securities were as follows:

(In millions)	2003 Carrying Amount	2003 Estimated Fair Value	2002 Carrying Amount	2002 Estimated Fair Value
Long-term debt, including current portion	$1,300.9	$1,482.6	$1,430.0	$1,465.9
Convertible preferred securities	196.3	189.5	196.1	220.0

The estimated fair values of our financial instruments were determined based on quoted market prices or market comparables. The estimated fair values may not be representative of actual values of the financial instruments that could have been realized or that will be realized in the future.

17. Convertible Preferred Securities

In February 1997, the McKesson Financing Trust, a business trust sponsored by the Company, issued four million shares of preferred securities to the public and 123,720 common securities to us, which are convertible at the holder's option into McKesson Corporation common stock. The proceeds of such issuances were invested by the trust in $206,186,000 aggregate principal amount of our 5% Convertible Junior Subordinated Debentures due 2027 (the "Debentures"). The Debentures represent the sole assets of the trust. The Debentures mature on June 1, 2027, bear interest at an annual rate of 5%, payable quarterly, and are currently redeemable by us at 102.0% of the principal amount.

Holders of the securities are entitled to cumulative cash distributions at an annual rate of 5% of the liquidation amount of $50 per security. Each preferred security is convertible at the rate of 1.3418 shares of McKesson Corporation common stock, subject to adjustment in certain circumstances. The preferred securities will be redeemed upon repayment of

the Debentures and are callable by us on or after March 4, 2000, in whole or in part, initially at 103.5% of the liquidation preference per share, and thereafter at prices declining at 0.5% per annum to 100% of the liquidation preference on and after March 4, 2007 plus, in each case, accumulated, accrued and unpaid distributions, if any, to the redemption date.

We have guaranteed, on a subordinated basis, distributions and other payments due on the preferred securities (the "Guarantee"). The Guarantee, when taken together with our obligations under the Debentures, and in the indenture pursuant to which the Debentures were issued, and our obligations under the Amended and Restated Declaration of Trust governing the subsidiary trust, provides a full and unconditional guarantee of amounts due on the preferred securities.

The Debentures and related trust investment in the Debentures have been eliminated in consolidation and the preferred securities reflected as outstanding in the consolidated financial statements.

Employee-Related Liabilities

2.268

ARVINMERITOR, INC. (SEP)

(In millions)	2003	2002
Total current liabilities	$1,878	$1,743
Long-term debt	1,541	1,474
Retirement benefits	683	512
Other liabilities	188	123
Minority interests	64	58

NOTES TO CONSOLIDATED FINANCIAL STATEMENTS

18 (In Part): Retirement Medical Plans

ArvinMeritor has retirement medical plans that cover the majority of its U.S. and certain non–U.S. employees and provide for medical payments to eligible employees and dependents upon retirement.

The company's retiree medical obligations are measured as of June 30. The following are the assumptions used in the measurement of the accumulated projected benefit obligation (APBO):

	2003	2002
Assumptions as of June 30		
Discount rate	6.00%	7.25%
Health care cost trend rate (weighted average)	8.00%	9.00%
Ultimate health care trend rate	5.00%	5.00%
Years to ultimate rate (2011)	7	8

The discount rate is used to calculate the present value of the APBO. This rate is determined based on high-quality fixed income investments that match the duration of expected retiree medical benefits. The company has typically used the corporate AA/Aa bond rate for this assumption. The health care cost trend rate represents the company's expected annual rates of change in the cost of health care benefits. The trend rate noted above represents a forward projection of health care costs as of the measurement date. The company's projection for fiscal 2004 is an increase in health care costs of 8.0 percent.

The APBO as of the June 30 measurement date is summarized as follows (in millions):

APBO	2003	2002
Retirees	$603	$502
Employees eligible to retire	17	17
Employees not eligible to retire	62	57
Total	$682	$576

The following reconciles the change in the APBO and the amounts included in the consolidated balance sheet (in millions):

	2003	2002
APBO—beginning of year	$ 576	$ 542
Service cost	4	4
Interest cost	40	38
Plan amendments	—	(36)
Actuarial losses	127	88
Benefit payments	(65)	(60)
APBO—end of year	682	576
Items not yet recognized in the balance sheet		
Plan amendments	34	40
Actuarial (losses)/gains:		
Discount rate	(138)	(60)
Health care cost trend rate	(35)	4
Demographic and other	(245)	(251)
Retiree medical liability	$ 298	$ 309

The increase in the APBO was driven primarily by actuarial losses. The actuarial losses resulted from the decrease in the discount rate assumption and unfavorable health care cost trend experience. The demographic and other actuarial losses relate to earlier than expected retirements due to certain plant closings and restructuring actions. In accordance with Statement of Financial Accounting Standards No. 106 (SFAS 106), "Employers' Accounting for Postretirement Benefits Other than Pensions", a portion of the actuarial losses is not subject to amortization. The actuarial losses that are subject to amortization are generally amortized over the average expected remaining service life, which is approximately 14 years. Union plan amendments are generally amortized over the contract period, or 3 years. In fiscal 2002, the company approved changes to certain retiree medical plans. These plan amendments were implemented in fiscal 2003 and were reflected in the APBO as of September 30, 2002.

The retiree medical liability is included in the consolidated balance sheet as follows (in millions):

	2003	2002
Current—included in compensation and benefits	$ 65	$ 60
Long-term—included in retirement benefits	233	249
Retiree medical liability	$298	$309

19 (In Part): Retirement Pension Plans

ArvinMeritor sponsors defined benefit pension plans that cover most of its U.S. employees and certain non-U.S. employees. Pension benefits for salaried employees are based on years of credited service and compensation. Pension benefits for hourly employees are based on years of service and specified benefit amounts. The company's funding policy provides that annual contributions to the pension trusts will be at least equal to the minimum amounts required by ERISA in the U.S. and the actuarial recommendations or statutory requirements in other countries.

Certain of the company's non-U.S. subsidiaries provide limited non-pension benefits to retirees in addition to government-sponsored programs. The cost of these programs is not significant to the company. Most retirees outside the U.S. are covered by government-sponsored and administered programs.

The company's pension obligations are measured as of June 30. The U.S. plans include a qualified and non-qualified pension plan. The Non-U.S. plans include plans primarily in the United Kingdom, Canada and Germany. The following are the assumptions used in the measurement of the projected benefit obligation (PBO) and net periodic pension expense:

	2003		2002	
	U.S.	Non U.S.	U.S.	Non U.S.
Assumptions as of June 30				
Discount rate	6.00%	5.50–6.25%	7.25%	6.00–6.75%
Assumed return on plan assets	8.50%	8.00–8.50%	8.50%	8.00–8.50%
Rate of compensation increase	3.75%	3.00–3.50%	4.25%	2.50–3.50%

The discount rate is used to calculate the present value of the PBO. The rate used reflects a rate of return on high-quality fixed income investments that match the duration of expected benefit payments. The company has typically used the corporate AA/Aa bond rate for this assumption. The assumed return on plan assets noted above represents a forward projection of the average rate of earnings expected on the pension assets.

This rate is used in the calculation of assumed rate of return on plan assets, a component of net periodic pension expense. The rate of compensation increase represents the long-term assumption for expected increases to salaries for pay-related plans. This rate was reduced in fiscal 2003 in the U.S. to 3.75% from 4.25% to reflect management's expectations of future compensation increases.

The following table reconciles the change in the PBO and the change in plan assets (in millions):

June 30 Measurement Date	2003			2002		
	U.S.	Non U.S.	Total	U.S.	Non U.S.	Total
PBO—beginning of year	$ 645	$ 431	$1,076	$ 596	$390	$ 986
Service cost	23	12	35	20	12	32
Interest cost	47	27	74	45	24	69
Participant contributions	—	3	3	—	3	3
Amendments	8	4	12	5	—	5
Actuarial loss	136	40	176	11	2	13
Divestitures	(4)	11	7	—	—	—
Benefit payments	(37)	(21)	(58)	(32)	(19)	(51)
Foreign currency rate changes	—	42	42	—	19	19
PBO—end of year	818	549	1,367	645	431	1,076
Change in plan assets						
Fair value of assets — beginning of year	386	341	727	398	372	770
Actual return (loss) on plan assets	10	(17)	(7)	(32)	(40)	(72)
Employer contributions	93	20	113	52	9	61
Participant contributions	—	3	3	—	3	3
Benefit payments	(37)	(21)	(58)	(32)	(19)	(51)
Foreign currency rate changes	—	28	28	—	16	16
Fair value of assets—end of year	452	354	806	386	341	727
Unfunded status	$(366)	$(195)	$ (561)	$(259)	$ (90)	$ (349)

The following reconciles the funded status with the amount included in the consolidated balance sheet (in millions):

June 30 Measurement Date	2003			2002		
	U.S.	Non U.S.	Total	U.S.	Non U.S.	Total
Unfunded status	$(366)	$(195)	$(561)	$(259)	$(90)	$(349)
Items not yet recognized in balance sheet:						
Actuarial losses	402	250	652	243	143	386
Prior service cost	8	12	20	2	12	14
Initial net asset	—	(4)	(4)	—	(6)	(6)
Sept. 2002 employer contribution	—	—	—	15	—	15
Net amount recognized	$ 44	$ 63	$ 107	$ 1	$ 59	$ 60

The increase in the PBO due to actuarial losses for fiscal 2003 and 2002 relates primarily to the reduction in the discount rate assumptions. In accordance with Statement of Financial Accounting Standards No. 87 (SFAS 87), "Employers' Accounting for Pensions," a portion of the actuarial losses is not subject to amortization. The actuarial losses that are subject to amortization are generally amortized over the expected remaining service life, which ranges from 12 to 18 years, depending on the plan. In addition, a significant impact on the funded status has been the underperformance of the pension assets for both fiscal 2003 and 2002. This was driven by worldwide financial market conditions. In accordance with SFAS 87, the company utilizes a market-related value of assets, which recognizes changes in the fair value of assets over a five-year period.

The increase in the unfunded status resulted in the company recording an additional minimum pension liability for both fiscal 2003 and 2002. SFAS 87 requires a company to record a minimum liability that is at least equal to the unfunded accumulated benefit obligation. The company recorded an additional minimum pension liability adjustment of $294 million and $116 million in fiscal 2003 and 2002, respectively. The additional minimum pension liability, net of a deferred tax asset, is charged to accumulated other comprehensive loss.

Amounts included in the consolidated balance sheet at September 30 are comprised of the following (in millions):

	2003			2002		
	U.S.	Non U.S.	Total	U.S.	Non U.S.	Total
Prepaid pension asset	$ —	$ 32	$ 32	$ —	$ 98	$ 98
Pension liability	(282)	(130)	(412)	(175)	(56)	(231)
Deferred tax asset on minimum pension liability	122	46	168	67	4	71
Accumulated other comprehensive loss	197	97	294	108	4	112
Intangible asset and other	7	13	20	1	6	7
Minority interest liability	—	5	5	—	3	3
Net amount recognized	$ 44	$ 63	$ 107	$ 1	$ 59	$ 60

The pension liability is included in Retirement Benefits in the consolidated balance sheet as follows (in millions):

	2003	2002
Pension liability	$412	$231
Retiree medical liability—long term (see note 18)	233	249
Other	38	32
Retirement benefits	$683	$512

In accordance with Statement of Financial Accounting Standard No. 132 "Employer's Disclosures about Pensions and Other Postretirement Benefits," the PBO, accumulated benefit obligation (ABO) and fair value of plan assets is required to be disclosed for all plans where the ABO is in excess of plan assets. The difference between the PBO and ABO is that the PBO includes projected compensation increases. Additional information is as follows (in millions):

	2003			2002		
	ABO Exceeds Assets	Assets Exceed ABO	Total	ABO Exceeds Assets	Assets Exceed ABO	Total
PBO	$1,331	$36	$1,367	$739	$337	$1,076
ABO	1,176	35	1,211	663	288	951
Plan assets	766	40	806	418	309	727

2.269

ELECTRONIC DATA SYSTEMS CORPORATION (DEC)

(In millions)	2003	2002
Total current liabilities	$7,473	$6,129
Deferred income taxes	—	51
Pension benefit liability	1,121	1,113
Long-term debt, less current portion	3,488	4,148
Minority interests and other long-term liabilities	484	417

NOTES TO CONSOLIDATED FINANCIAL STATEMENTS

Note 13 (In Part): Retirement Plans

The Company has several qualified and nonqualified pension plans (the "Plans") covering substantially all its employees. The majority of the Plans are noncontributory. In general, employees become fully vested upon attaining two to five years of service, and benefits are based on years of service and earnings. The actuarial cost method currently used is the projected unit credit cost method. The Company's U.S. funding policy is to contribute amounts that fall within the range of deductible contributions for U.S. federal income tax purposes.

The following tables provide a reconciliation of the changes in the Plans' benefit obligations and fair value of assets (using October 31, 2003 and 2002 measurement dates), and a statement of the funded status as of December 31, 2003 and 2002 (in millions):

	2003	2002
Reconciliation of benefit obligation		
Benefit obligation at beginning of year	$ 5,154	$ 3,943
Service cost	290	287
Interest cost	353	277
Plan amendments	(5)	—
Actuarial loss	372	161
Foreign currency exchange rate changes	384	213
Benefit payments	(157)	(88)
Curtailments	—	(22)
Settlements	—	(26)
Special termination benefit	20	—
Other	133	409
Benefit obligation at end of year	$ 6,544	$ 5,154
Reconciliation of fair value of plan assets		
Fair value of plan assets at beginning of year	$ 3,739	$ 3,585
Actual return on plan assets	702	(381)
Foreign currency exchange rate changes	259	124
Employer contributions	271	207
Benefit payments	(157)	(88)
Settlements	(1)	(26)
Other	84	318
Fair value of plan assets at end of year	$ 4,897	$ 3,739
Funded status		
Funded status at December 31	$(1,647)	$(1,415)
Unrecognized transition obligation	13	12
Unrecognized prior-service cost	(240)	(267)
Unrecognized net actuarial loss	1,542	1,541
Adjustments from October 31 to December 31	83	22
Net amount recognized on the consolidated balance sheets (as described below)	$ (249)	$ (107)

The following table summarizes the assets and liabilities reflected on the Company's balance sheets for pension benefits as of December 31, 2003 and 2002 (in millions):

	2003	2002
Prepaid benefit cost	$ 288	$ 283
Accrued benefit liability	(1,121)	(1,113)
Intangible asset	32	35
Accumulated other comprehensive income	552	688
Net amount recognized	$ (249)	$ (107)

The accumulated benefit obligation for all defined benefit pension plans was $5,697 million and $4,321 million at October 31, 2003 and 2002, respectively.

The Company has additional defined benefit retirement plans outside the U.S. not included in the tables above due to their individual insignificance. These plans collectively represent an additional benefit obligation of approximately $30 million and plan assets of approximately $20 million.

The projected benefit obligation, accumulated benefit obligation, and fair value of plan assets for the pension plans with accumulated benefit obligations in excess of plan assets were $6,055 million, $5,298 million, and $4,410 million, respectively, at December 31, 2003 and $4,714 million, $4,228 million, and $3,401 million, respectively, at December 31, 2002.

•   •   •   •   •   •

The Company recorded a special termination benefit of $20 million during 2003 related to contractual obligations to its former Chief Executive Officer. The Company recorded a curtailment gain of $18 million and a settlement loss of $4 million during 2002 related to the conversion of one of the international plans to a defined contribution plan. As a result of the termination of the Company's service contract with the U.K. Government's Inland Revenue department, the contract's workforce will transition to the new IT provider in July 2004. The pension liability associated with this workforce will also transition to the new provider, resulting in the recognition of a settlement loss of up to $75 million. The actual amount of the loss will be determined and recognized in the Company's statement of operations upon final settlement of the obligation, which is expected to occur in late 2004 or early 2005.

At December 31, 2003 and 2002, the Plans' assets consisted primarily of equity securities and, to a lesser extent, government obligations and other fixed income securities. The U.S. pension plan is a cash balance plan that uses a benefit formula based on years of service, age and earnings. Employees are allocated the current value of their retirement benefit in a hypothetical account. Monthly credits based upon age, years of service, compensation and interest are added to the account. Upon retirement, the value of the account balance is converted to an annuity. Effective January 1, 2000, the Company allowed employees to elect to direct up to 33% of their monthly credits to the EDS 401(k) Plan. The Company contributed $3 million, $6 million and $8 million to the EDS 401(k) Plan related to these elections during the years ended December 31, 2003, 2002 and 2001, respectively. These amounts are not included in net periodic pension cost shown in the table above.

The following table summarizes the weighted-average assumptions used in the determination of the Company's benefit obligation for the years ended December 31, 2003, 2002 and 2001:

	2003	2002	2001
Discount rate at October 31	6.0%	6.4%	6.4%
Rate of increase in compensation levels at October 31	3.3%	3.5%	3.5%

• • • • • •

Plan assets for the Company's U.S. pension plans comprise 55% of the total assets for all plans. The following table provides the weighted-average asset allocation of U.S. plan assets at December 31, 2003 and 2002, by asset category:

	2003	2002
Equity securities	87%	85%
Debt securities	8%	10%
Cash and cash equivalents	5%	4%
Real estate	—	—
Other	—	1%
Total	100%	100%

In determining pension expense recognized in its statements of operations, the Company utilizes an expected long-term rate of return that, over time, should approximate the actual long-term returns earned on pension plan assets. The Company derives the assumed long-term rate of return on assets based upon the historical return of actual plan assets and the historical long-term return on similar asset classes as well as anticipated future returns based upon the asset mix of the plans. Assumed rates of return are based upon a long-term view of the pension investment strategy, which is consistent with the average age of the Company's workforce and associated average periods until retirement. Accordingly, plan assets are weighted heavily towards equity investments. Equity investments, while susceptible to significant short-term fluctuations, have historically outperformed most other investment alternatives on a long-term basis. The Company utilizes an active management strategy through third-party investment managers to maximize asset returns. As of December 31, 2003, the weighted-average target asset allocation for all plans was 82% equity; 15% fixed income; 1% cash and cash equivalents; 1% real estate; and 1% other. The company expects to contribute $150 million to its U.S. pension plans during 2004, all of which are discretionary for statutory purposes.

Estimated benefit payments, which include amounts to be earned by active plan employees through expected future service for U.S. pension plans over the next ten years are: 2004–$81 million; 2005–$86 million; 2006–$92 million; 2007–$102 million; 2008–$114 million; and 2009 through 2013–$826 million.

2.270

R. J. REYNOLDS TOBACCO HOLDINGS, INC. (DEC)

(Dollars in millions)	2003	2002
Total current liabilities	$2,865	$3,427
Long-term debt (less current maturities)	1,671	1,755
Deferred income taxes	806	1,236
Long-term retirement benefits	1,034	1,176
Other noncurrent liabilities	244	341

NOTES TO CONSOLIDATED FINANCIAL STATEMENTS

Note 17 (In Part): Retirement Benefits

RJR and its subsidiaries sponsor a number of non-contributory defined benefit pension plans covering most employees, and also provide certain health and life insurance benefits for retired employees and their dependents. The changes in benefit obligations and plan assets, as well as the funded status of these plans at December 31 were:

	Pension Benefits		Postretirement Benefits	
	2003	2002	2003	2002
Change in benefit obligation:				
Obligation at beginning of year	$2,848	$2,529	$ 919	$ 740
Service cost	40	38	6	6
Interest cost	181	181	53	60
Actuarial loss	109	264	49	177
Plan amendments	6	5	(155)	—
Benefits paid	(204)	(194)	(63)	(71)
Settlements	(5)	(11)	—	—
Special termination benefits	71	34	—	—
Curtailment	10	2	5	7
Obligation at end of year	$3,056	$2,848	$ 814	$ 919
Change in plan assets:				
Fair value of plan assets at beginning of year	$1,915	$2,160	$ —	$ —
Actual return on plan assets	488	(240)	—	—
Employer contributions	112	200	63	71
Benefits paid	(204)	(194)	(63)	(71)
Settlements	(5)	(11)	—	—
Fair value of plan assets at end of year	$2,306	$1,915	$ —	$ —
Funded status:				
Funded status	$ (750)	$ (933)	$(814)	$(919)
Unrecognized transition asset	—	—	(3)	(9)
Unrecognized prior service cost	17	15	(133)	—
Unrecognized net actuarial loss	851	1,097	351	330
Net amount recognized	$118	$ 179	$(599)	$(598)
Amounts recognized in the consolidated balance sheets consist of:				
Accrued benefit—current liability	$ (116)	$ (100)	$ (58)	$ (82)
Accrued benefit—long-term liability	(493)	(660)	(541)	(516)
Intangible asset	17	16	—	—
Accumulated other comprehensive income	710	923	—	—
Net amount recognized	$ 118	$ 179	$(599)	$(598)

Weighted-average assumptions used to determine benefit obligations at December 31:

	2003	2002
Discount rate	6.15%	6.40%
Rate of compensation increase	5.00%	5.00%

The measurement date used for all plans was December 31, 2003.

As of December 31, 2003, all of the pension plans experienced accumulated benefit obligations in excess of plan assets, for which the projected benefit obligation, accumulated benefit obligation and fair value of plan assets were $3,056 million, $2,913 million and $2,306 million, respectively. As of December 31, 2002, all of the pension plans experienced accumulated benefit obligations in excess of plan assets, for which the projected benefit obligation, accumulated benefit obligation and fair value of plan assets were $2,848 million, $2,673 million and $1,915 million, respectively.

•   •   •   •   •   •

Plan assets are invested using a combination of active and passive investment strategies. Active strategies employ multiple investment management firms. Managers within each asset class cover a range of investment styles and approaches and are combined in a way that controls for capitalization, style biases (equity investments), and interest rate bets (fixed income investments) against related benchmark indices, while focusing primarily on issue selection as a means to add value. Risk is controlled through diversification among asset classes, managers, styles and securities. Risk is further controlled both at the manager and asset class level by assigning excess return and tracking error targets. Investment managers are monitored to evaluate performance against these benchmark indices and targets.

Allowable investment types include U.S. equity, non-U.S. equity, fixed income and hedge funds. The U.S. equity fund is composed of common stocks of large, medium and small companies, which are predominantly U.S. based. The non-U.S. equity fund includes equity securities issued by companies domiciled outside the U.S. and in depository receipts, which represent ownership of securities of non-U.S. companies. The fixed income fund includes fixed income securities issued or guaranteed by the U.S. government, and to a lesser extent by non-U.S. governments, or by their respective agencies and instrumentalities, mortgage backed securities, including collateralized mortgage obligations; corporate debt obligations and dollar-denominated obligations issued in the United States by non-U.S. banks and corporations (Yankee bonds). Up to 25% of the fixed income assets can be in debt securities that are below investment grade. The hedge funds invest as a limited partner in portfolios of primarily public securities, including equities and fixed income.

Futures are used to equitize cash held by investment managers in order to approach fully invested portfolio positions. Otherwise, a small number of investment managers employ limited use of derivatives, including futures contracts, options on futures and interest rate swaps in place of direct investment in securities to gain efficient exposure to markets. Derivatives are not used to leverage portfolios.

The target asset allocation is 45% U.S. equity investments, 20% non-U.S. equity investments, 25% fixed income investments and 10% hedge fund investments, with a rebalancing range of approximately plus or minus 5% around the target asset allocations.

RJR's pension plans weighted-average asset allocations at December 31, 2003, and 2002, by asset category were as follows:

	Plan Assets at December 31	
	2003	2002
Asset category		
U.S. equity securities	46%	42%
Non U.S. equity securities	22%	18%
Debt securities	21%	26%
Hedge funds	9%	12%
Other	2%	2%
Total	100%	100%

2.271

STEELCASE INC. (FEB)

(In millions)	2003	2002
Total current liabilities	$ 502.5	$ 673.1
Long-term liabilities:		
Long-term debt	294.2	433.6
Employee benefit plan obligations	237.8	248.3
Deferred income taxes	5.5	7.1
Other long-term liabilities	47.1	49.9
Total long-term liabilities	584.6	738.9
Total liabilities	$1,087.1	$1,412.0

NOTES TO CONSOLIDATED FINANCIAL STATEMENTS

11 (In Part): Employee Benefit Plan Obligations

(In millions)

Employee Benefit Plan Obligations	2003	2002
Defined contribution retirement plans	$ 17.5	$ 27.7
Post-retirement medical benefits	190.9	205.4
Defined benefit pension plans	36.1	25.2
Deferred compensation plans	32.9	41.0
	277.4	299.3
Current portion	39.6	51.0
Long-term portion	$237.8	$248.3

Defined Contribution Retirement Plans

Substantially all United States employees are covered under defined contribution retirement plans, primarily the Steelcase Inc. Retirement Plan (the "Retirement Plan"). Company contributions and 401 (k) pre-tax employee contributions fund the Retirement Plan. All contributions are made to a trust, which is held for the sole benefit of participants. The Retirement Plan requires minimum annual Company contributions of 5% of eligible annual compensation. Additional Company contributions for this plan are discretionary and declared by the Compensation Committee at the end of each fiscal year.

As of February 28, 2003, the Company-funded portion of the trust had net assets of approximately $1.1 billion.

Contributions for similar subsidiary plans are discretionary and declared by management. Total expense under all defined contribution retirement plans was $19.1 million for 2003, $24.8 million for 2002 and $51.8 million for 2001.

Post-Retirement Medical Benefits

Certain of our subsidiaries have unfunded post-retirement benefit plans that provide medical and life insurance benefits to retirees and eligible dependents. We accrue the cost of post-retirement insurance benefits during the service lives of employees based on actuarial calculations for each plan. These plans are unfunded, but we have purchased company owned life insurance policies with the intention of utilizing them as a future funding source for post-retirement medical benefits and other obligations (see Note 9).

During 2003, we adopted plan amendments limiting certain benefits. These plan amendments resulted in the establishment of a deferred actuarial gain that was to be amortized over the remaining service life of the affected plan participants. Due to the significant workforce reductions in 2003, curtailment accounting rules were triggered and we recognized a plan curtailment gain of $16.4 million.

Defined Benefit Pension Plans

Our defined benefit pension plans include various qualified domestic and foreign retirement plans as well as a non-qualified supplemental retirement plan that is limited to a select group of management or highly compensated employees. The funded status of our defined benefit pension plans is as follows:

| | 2003 | | | 2002 | | |
| | Qualified Plans | | Unqualified Supplemental Retirement Plan | Qualified Plans | | Unqualified Supplemental Retirement Plan |
(In millions)	Domestic	Foreign		Domestic	Foreign	
Plan assets	$11.3	$ 25.3	$ —	$13.7	$24.8	$ —
Projected benefit plan obligations	13.4	41.2	17.9	16.4	33.3	18.6
Funded status	$ (2.1)	$(15.9)	$(17.9)	$ (2.7)	$ (8.5)	$(18.6)
Accrued benefit plan obligations	$ (2.1)	$(16.5)	$(17.5)	$ —	$ (8.1)	$(17.1)

The following tables summarize the required disclosures related to our defined benefit pension and post-retirement plans.

Changes in Projected Benefit Obligations, Assets and Funded Status	Pension Plans		Post-Retirement Plans	
(In millions)	2003	2002	2003	2002
Change in benefit obligations:				
Projected benefit plan obligations, beginning of year	$ 68.3	$ 72.5	$ 271.5	$ 240.4
Service cost	2.4	3.3	4.5	6.2
Interest cost	4.3	4.2	15.3	17.6
Amendments	1.9	—	(57.2)	—
Net actuarial (gain) loss	2.2	(0.9)	25.6	16.4
Plan participants' contributions	0.1	0.1	5.7	3.6
Pension divestitures	(0.6)	(6.2)	—	—
Currency changes	4.7	(1.1)	0.3	(0.2)
Adjustment due to plan curtailment	(3.8)	—	(10.2)	—
Adjustment due to plan settlement	(1.2)	—	—	—
Benefits paid	(5.8)	(3.6)	(21.5)	(12.5)
Projected benefit plan obligations, end of year	72.5	68.3	234.0	271.5
Change in plan assets:				
Fair value of plan assets, beginning of year	38.5	38.5	—	—
Actual return on plan assets	(3.6)	(0.8)	—	—
Employer contributions	8.1	5.8	15.8	8.8
Plan participants' contributions	0.1	0.1	5.7	3.6
Pension divestitures	(0.1)	(0.6)	—	—
Currency changes	2.5	(0.7)	—	—
Adjustment due to plan settlement	(3.1)	—	—	—
Benefits paid	(5.8)	(3.8)	(21.5)	(12.4)
Fair value of plan assets, end of year	36.6	38.5	—	—
Funded status	(35.9)	(29.8)	(234.0)	(271.5)
Unrecognized prior service cost (gain)	1.0	2.7	(38.2)	(2.4)
Unrecognized transition (asset) obligation	—	0.2	—	1.0
Unrecognized net actuarial loss	11.4	4.6	81.3	67.5
Net amount recognized	$(23.5)	$(22.3)	$(190.9)	$(205.4)
Amounts recognized in the consolidated balance sheets:				
Accrued benefit plan obligations	$(36.1)	$(25.2)	$(190.9)	$(205.4)
Prepaid pension costs	5.3	3.1	—	—
Intangible assets	0.8	—	—	—
Accumulated other comprehensive income	6.5	(0.2)	—	—
Net amount recognized	$(23.5)	$(22.3)	$(190.9)	$(205.4)

●   ●   ●   ●   ●   ●

Deferred Compensation Plans

We also have deferred salaried obligations to certain employees in return for agreeing not to receive part of their compensation for a period of three to five years. This deferred compensation liability is unfunded, but we have purchased company owned life insurance policies, with the intention of utilizing them as a future funding source for the deferred compensation obligation and other obligations (see further discussion in Note 9). Deferred compensation expense approximated $4.7 million for 2003, $5.2 million for 2002 and $6.0 million for 2001.

Environmental Costs

2.272

ALLIANT TECHSYSTEMS INC. (MAR)

(Amounts in thousands)	2003	2002
Total current liabilities	$ 428,053	$ 355,257
Long-term debt	820,856	867,638
Deferred income tax liability	—	65,091
Post-retirement and post-employment benefits liability	234,037	235,639
Minimum pension liability	379,856	9,313
Other long-term liabilities	138,538	100,462
Total liabilities	$2,001,340	$1,633,400

NOTES TO THE CONSOLIDATED FINANCIAL STATEMENTS
(Amounts in thousands)

1(In Part): Summary of Significant Accounting Policies

Environmental Remediation and Compliance

Costs associated with environmental compliance and preventing future contamination that are estimable and probable are accrued and expensed, or capitalized as appropriate. Expected remediation and monitoring costs relating to the remediation of an existing condition caused by past operations, and which do not contribute to current or future revenue generation, are accrued and expensed in the period that such costs become estimable. Liabilities are recognized for remedial activities when they are probable and the remediation cost can be reasonably estimated.

The cost of each environmental liability is estimated by ATK's engineering, financial, and legal specialists based on current law and existing technologies. Such estimates are based primarily upon the estimated cost of investigation and remediation required and the likelihood that other potentially responsible parties ("PRPs") will be able to fulfill their commitments at the sites where ATK may be jointly and severally liable. ATK's estimates for environmental obligations are dependent on, and affected by, the nature and extent of historical information and physical data relating to a contaminated site, the complexity of the site, methods of remediation available, the technology that will be required, the outcome of discussions with regulatory agencies and other PRPs at multi-party sites, the number and financial viability of other PRPs, changes in environmental laws and regulations, future technological developments, and the timing of expenditures; accordingly, such estimates could change materially as ATK periodically evaluates and revises such estimates based on expenditures against established reserves and the availability of additional information.

6 (In Part): Other Accrued Liabilities

The major categories of other current and long-term accrued liabilities are as follows:

	2003	2002
Employee benefits and insurance	$ 40,037	$ 43,038
Interest	14,932	14,238
Warranty	12,463	13,387
Environmental remediation	6,251	4,347
Legal	1,838	3,882
Other	50,311	42,666
Total other accrued liabilities—current	$125,832	$121,558
Environmental remediation	$ 43,939	$ 44,354
Interest rate swaps	29,371	10,965
Supplemental employee retirement plan	24,431	22,400
Management deferred compensation plan	11,967	9,466
Legal	3,000	7,590
Other	25,830	5,687
Total other long-term liabilities	$138,538	$100,462

12 (In Part): Contingencies

Environmental Remediation

ATK's operations and ownership or use of real property are subject to a number of federal, state, and local environmental laws and regulations. At certain sites, there is known or potential contamination that ATK is required to investigate or remediate. ATK could incur substantial costs, including remediation costs, fines, and penalties, or third party property damage or personal injury claims, as a result of violations or liabilities of environmental laws or non-compliance with environmental permits.

The liability for environmental remediation represents management's best estimate of the present value of the probable and reasonably estimable costs related to known remediation obligations. The receivable represents the present value of the amount that ATK expects to recover, as discussed below. Both the liability and receivable have been discounted to reflect the present value of the expected future cash flows, using a discount rate, net of estimated inflation, of 3.5% as of March 31, 2003. This discount rate represents a decrease from 4.6% used as of March 31, 2002. The impact of the reduction in the rate during fiscal 2003 was an increase in the net liability of approximately $1,900, which was recognized in expense during the year. The following is a summary of the amounts recorded for environmental remediation:

	2003		2002	
	Liability	Receivable	Liability	Receivable
Amounts (payable) receivable	$(61,865)	$26,415	$(63,519)	$24,937
Unamortized discount	11,675	(3,821)	14,818	(4,458)
Present value amounts (payable) receivable	$(50,190)	$22,594	$(48,701)	$20,479

Of the $50,190 net liability, $6,251 is recorded within other current liabilities and $43,939 is recorded within other non-current liabilities. Of the $22,594 net receivable, $3,547 is recorded within other current assets and $19,047 is recorded within other non-current assets.

ATK expects that a portion of its environmental compliance and remediation costs will be recoverable under U.S. Government contracts. Some of the remediation costs that are not recoverable from the U.S. Government that are associated with facilities purchased in a business acquisition may be covered by various indemnification agreements. As part of its acquistion of the Hercules Aerospace Company, ATK assumed responsibility for environmental compliance at the facilities acquired from Hercules (the Hercules Facilities). ATK believes that a portion of the compliance and remediation costs associated with the Hercules Facilities will be recoverable under U.S. Government contracts, and that those environmental remediation costs not recoverable under these contracts will be covered by Hercules Incorporated (Hercules) under environmental agreements entered into in connection with the Hercules acquisition. Under these agreements, Hercules has agreed to indemnify ATK for environmental conditions relating to releases or hazardous waste activities occurring prior to ATK's purchase of the Hercules Facilities; fines relating to pre-acquisition environmental compliance; and environmental claims arising out of breaches of Hercules's representations and warranties. Hercules is not required to indemnify ATK for any individual claims below $50. Hercules is obligated to indemnify ATK for the lowest cost response of remediation required at the facility that is acceptable to the applicable regulatory agencies. ATK is not responsible for conducting any remedial activities with respect to the Kenvil, NJ facility or the Clearwater, FL facility. Hercules' environmental indemnity obligation relating to contamination on federal lands remains effective, provided that ATK gives notice of any claims related to federal lands on or before December 31, 2005.

Under the Thiokol purchase agreement, ATK generally assumed responsibility for environmental compliance at the acquired facilities. While ATK expects that a portion of the compliance and remediation costs associated with the acquired Thiokol Facilities will be recoverable under U.S. Government contracts, ATK has recorded an accrual to cover those environmental remediation costs at these facilities that will not be recovered through U.S. Government contracts. ATK is responsible for any costs not recovered through U.S. Government contracts at Thiokol Facilities up to $29,000; ATK and Alcoa have agreed to split evenly any amounts between $29,000 and $49,000, subject to ATK having appropriately notified Alcoa of any issues prior to January 30, 2004; and ATK is responsible for any payments in excess of $49,000.

With respect to the facilities purchased from Blount, Blount has agreed to indemnify ATK for certain compliance and remediation liabilities, to the extent those liabilities are related to pre-closing environmental conditions at or related to these facilities. Some other remediation costs are expected to be paid directly by a third party pursuant to an existing indemnification agreement with Blount. Blount's indemnification obligations relating to environmental matters, which extend for five years following closing, are capped at $30,000, less any other indemnification payments made for breaches of representations and warranties. The third party's obligations, which extend through November 4, 2007, are capped at approximately $125,000, less payments previously made.

ATK also has an indemnification agreement from The Boeing Company in connection with the facilities of ATK Gun Systems.

ATK cannot ensure that the U.S. Government, Hercules, Alcoa, Blount, or other third parties will reimburse it for any particular environmental costs or reimburse ATK in a timely manner or that any claims for indemnification will not be disputed. U.S. Government reimbursements for cleanups are financed out of a particular agency's operating budget and the ability of a particular governmental agency to make timely reimbursements for cleanup costs will be subject to national budgetary constraints. ATK's failure to obtain full or timely reimbursement from the U.S. Government, Hercules, Alcoa, Blount, or other third parties could have a material adverse effect on its operating results, financial condition, or cash flows. While ATK has environmental management programs in place to mitigate these risks, and environmental laws and regulations have not had a material adverse effect on ATK's operating results, financial condition, or cash flows in the past, it is difficult to predict whether they will have a material impact in the future.

At March 31, 2003, the aggregate undiscounted amounts payable for environmental remediation costs, net of expected recoveries, are estimated to be $2,799 in fiscal 2004, $1,134 in fiscal 2005, $928 in fiscal 2006, $3,597 in fiscal 2007, and $4,363 in fiscal 2008; estimated amounts payable thereafter total $22,629. Amounts payable/receivable in periods beyond fiscal 2004 have been classified as non-current on the March 31, 2003 balance sheet. As of March 31, 2003, the estimated discounted range of reasonably possible costs of environmental remediation was $50,190 to $89,637. ATK does not anticipate that resolution of the environmental contingencies in excess of amounts accrued, net of recoveries, will materially affect its future operating results, financial condition, or cash flows. There were no material insurance recoveries related to environmental remediations during fiscal 2003, 2002, or 2001.

Discontinued Operations

2.273

THE SERVICEMASTER COMPANY (DEC)

(In thousands)	2003	2002
Total current liabilities	$818,240	$839,064
Long-term debt	$785,490	$804,340
Long-term liabilities:		
Deferred taxes	276,000	312,500
Liabilities of discontinued operations	34,396	30,682
Other long-term obligations	125,474	109,343
Total long-term liabilities	$435,870	$452,525

NOTES TO CONSOLIDATED FINANCIAL STATEMENTS

Dispositions (In Part)

During the third quarter of 2003, the Company sold substantially all of the assets and related operational obligations of Trees, Inc., the utility line clearing operations of TruGreen LandCare, to an independent subsidiary of Asplundh Subsidiary Holdings, Inc., for approximately $20 million in cash. The impact of the sale was not material to the Company's consolidated financial statements for 2003.

2002 Dispositions

During the second quarter of 2002, the Company completed the sale of its ownership interest in five assisted living facilities. These properties were financed through an operating lease arrangement, whereby, the Company guaranteed a portion of the residual value of the properties. In the fourth quarter of 2001, a $13.5 million reserve was established representing the amount by which the residual value guarantees exceeded the value of bids to purchase the facilities at that time. The final sales price was significantly greater than these bid levels and the Company realized a gain of $3.6 million from the sale of the assisted living properties in 2002, which is included in operating income.

During the third quarter of 2002, the Company sold its remaining Terminix operations in the United Kingdom. The sale was not material to the Company's operating results. Related to this sale, the Company entered into a licensing agreement with the buyer for the use of the Terminix trade name in the United Kingdom. This agreement was valued at $6 million and accordingly, a like amount was allocated from the purchase price. The entire amount was recognized as income in the third quarter of 2002.

Portfolio Review and Dispositions in 2001

In October 2001, the Company's Board of Directors approved a series of strategic actions which were the culmination of an extensive portfolio review process that was initiated earlier in 2001. In the fourth quarter of 2001, the Company sold its Management Services business to ARAMARK Corporation for approximately $800 million and recorded an after-tax gain of $404 million. (A division of Management Services was not sold as part of this transaction and the Company recorded a $15 million loss upon disposition of this unit.) Also in the fourth quarter of 2001, the Company's Board of Directors approved the exit of non-strategic and underperforming

businesses including TruGreen LandCare Construction, Certified Systems Inc. (CSI), and certain Terminix operations in Europe. The Company sold its TruGreen LandCare Construction operations in certain markets to Environmental Industries, Inc. (EII) and EII managed the wind-down of commercial landscaping construction contracts in the remaining markets. In addition, the Company sold all of its customer contracts relating to the exit of CSI (the Company's professional employer organization) to AMS Staff Leasing, N.A., Inc. In the fourth quarter of 2001, the Company sold certain subsidiaries of its European pest control and property services operations.

In the fourth quarter of 2002, the purchaser of the Company's European pest control and property services operations made a claim for a purchase price adjustment (relating to the 2001 sale), relating to an alleged breach of certain conditions in the purchase agreement. In the course of responding to that claim, the Company discovered that personnel of the former operations had made unsupported monthly adjustments to certain accounts. The Company subsequently agreed to an adjustment to the purchase price consisting of an $8 million cash payment and the cancellation of a previously reserved note receivable of $7 million. An $8 million charge was recorded in 2002.

Reported "Discontinued operations" for all periods presented include the operating results of the sold and discontinued businesses noted above and the 2001 results include the gain from the sale of Management Services, net of losses from the disposition of other entities. The operating results and financial position of discontinued operations are as follows:

(In thousands, except per share data)

Operating Results	2003	2002	2001
Operating revenue	$65,057	$129,060	$2,356,010
Income (loss) from discontinued operations before income taxes	(3,482)	7,543	(20,009)
Provision (benefit) for income taxes	(1,375)	3,012	14,601
Income (loss) from discontinued operations	(2,107)	4,531	(34,610)
Gain (loss) on sale of businesses, net[1]	(605)	(4,840)	323,213
Income (loss) from discontinued operations	$ (2,712)	$ (309)	$ 288,603
Diluted earnings per share from discontinued operations	$ (0.01)	$ —	$ 0.97

[1] Net of income tax expense (benefit) of ($.4) million, ($3) million, and $218 million in 2003, 2002 and 2001, respectively.

Financial Position	2003	2002
Current assets	$ 5,273	$15,883
Property, plant and equipment	—	6,703
Total assets	$ 5,273	$22,586
Current liabilities	$14,380	$36,624
Long-term liabilities	34,396	30,682
Total liabilities	$48,776	$67,306

At December 31, 2003, the Company has certain assets on its financial statements relating to discontinued operations, primarily receivables. Management is actively collecting the outstanding receivables. The Company believes that the remaining assets are presented at their net realizable value.

The table below summarizes the activity during the twelve months ended December 31, 2003 for the remaining liabilities from the discontinued operations. The Company believes that the remaining reserves continue to be adequate and reasonable.

(In thousands)	Balance at Dec. 31, 2002	Cash Payments or Other	Income/(Expense)	Balance at Dec. 31, 2003
Remaining liabilities from discontinued operations				
LandCare Construction	$13,974	$ 6,822	$ —	$ 7,152
LandCare Utility line clearing business[1]	6,393	185	(2,803)	9,011
Certified Systems, Inc.	13,586	2,562	—	11,024
Management Services	1,569	1,286	—	283
International businesses	21,348	10,331	(1,000)	12,017
Other	10,436	1,147	—	9,289

[1] In September 2003, the Company sold the assets and related operational obligations of Trees, Inc., the utility line clearing operations of TruGreen LandCare. The Company retained certain liabilities and recorded accruals in connection with the sold operations.

Insurance

2.274

SAFEWAY INC. (DEC)

(In millions)	2003	2002
Total current liabilities	$ 3,464.3	$ 3,792.6
Long-term debt:		
Notes and debentures	6,404.0	7,009.9
Obligations under capital leases	668.3	602.7
Total long-term debt	7,072.3	7,612.6
Deferred income taxes	421.9	577.9
Accrued claims and other liabilities	493.9	436.6
Total liabilities	$11,452.4	$12,419.7

NOTES TO CONSOLIDATED FINANCIAL STATEMENTS

Note A (In Part): The Company and Significant Accounting Policies

Self-Insurance

The Company is primarily self-insured for workers' compensation, automobile and general liability costs. The self-insurance liability is determined actuarially, based on claims filed and an estimate of claims incurred but not yet reported, and is discounted using a risk-free rate of interest. The present value of such claims was calculated using a discount rate of 3.0% in 2003 and 4.0% in 2002. A summary of changes in Safeway's self-insurance liability is as follows (in millions):

	2003	2002	2001
Beginning balance	$ 340.6	$ 320.4	$ 299.1
Expense	235.2	166.5	149.1
Claim payments	(166.3)	(146.3)	(139.8)
Genuardi's acquisition	—	—	12.0
Ending balance	$ 409.5	$ 340.6	$ 320.4
Less: current portion	(124.7)	(119.5)	(102.1)
Long-term portion	$ 284.8	$ 221.1	$ 218.3

The current portion of the self-insurance liability is included in other accrued liabilities and the long-term portion is included in accrued claims and other liabilities in the consolidated balance sheets. The total undiscounted liability was $451.4 million at year-end 2003 and $388.6 million at year-end 2002.

Warranties

2.275

WHIRLPOOL CORPORATION (DEC)

(Millions of dollars)	2003	2002
Total current liabilities	$3,589	$3,505
Other liabilities		
Deferred income taxes	236	117
Pension benefits	298	358
Postemployment benefits	489	487
Product warranty	53	57
Other liabilities	198	198
Long-term debt	1,134	1,092
	$2,408	$2,309

NOTES TO CONSOLIDATED FINANCIAL STATEMENTS

9 (In Part): Guarantees, Commitments and Contingencies

Product warranty reserves are established in the same period that revenue from the sale of the related products is recognized. The amounts of those reserves are based on established terms and the Company's best estimate of the amounts necessary to settle future and existing claims on products sold as of the balance sheet date. The product warranty reserves increased in 2003 when compared to 2002 due to increased sales volume and final costs recognized in 2003 primarily related to final costs in connection with the 2001 recall (See Note 14).

The following represents a reconciliation of the changes in product warranty reserves for the periods presented:

(Millions of dollars)	2003	2002
Balance at January 1	$ 128	$ 108
Warranties issued during the period	262	228
Warranties acquired	—	7
Settlements made during the period	(248)	(214)
Other changes	6	(1)
Balance at December 31	$ 148	$ 128
Current portion	$ 95	$ 71
Non-current portion	53	57
Total	$ 148	$ 128

14) Product Recalls

In 2001, the Company announced a voluntary recall of 1.8 million microwave hood combination units sold under the *Whirlpool, KitchenAid*, and Sears *Kenmore* brands. The Company recognized product recall pre-tax charges of $221 million ($136 million after-tax) during 2001 and recorded these charges as separate components of operating profit. During 2002, the Company incurred additional charges of approximately $9 million ($6 million after-tax) for costs related to this recall. During 2003, the Company incurred an additional $16 million ($10 million after-tax) primarily related to final expenses in connection with the 2001 recall. Approximately $6 million of accrued product recall costs is reflected in other current liabilities in the balance sheet at December 31, 2003.

In 2002, the Company announced a voluntary recall of approximately 1.4 million dehumidifier units sold under the

Whirlpool, ComfortAire, and Sears *Kenmore* brands. The Company recognized a product recall pre-tax charge of $74 million ($45 million after-tax) during the fourth quarter of 2001 and recorded this charge as a separate component of operating profit.

The Company does not expect further liabilities related to these two product recalls.

Litigation

2.276

STANDARD MOTOR PRODUCTS, INC. (DEC)

(In thousands)	2003	2002
Total current liabilities	$276,838	$187,677
Long-term debt	114,757	93,191
Postretirement medical benefits and other accrued liabilities	36,848	30,414
Restructuring accrual	15,615	—
Accrued asbestos liabilities (Note 17)	24,426	25,595
Total liabilities	$468,484	$336,877

NOTES TO CONSOLIDATED FINANCIAL STATEMENTS

1 (In Part): Summary of Significant Accounting Policies

Use of Estimates

In conformity with generally accepted accounting principles, we have made a number of estimates and assumptions relating to the reporting of assets, liabilities, revenues and expenses, and the disclosure of contingent assets and liabilities to prepare these consolidated financial statements. Some of the more significant estimates include allowances for doubtful accounts, inventory valuation reserves, depreciation and amortization of long-lived assets, product liability, asbestos and litigation matters, deferred tax asset valuation allowance and sales return allowances. Actual results could differ from those estimates.

17 (In Part): Commitments and Contingencies

On January 28, 2000, a former significant customer of ours, which is currently undergoing a Chapter 7 liquidation in U.S. Bankruptcy Court, filed claims against a number of its former suppliers, including us. The claim against us alleged $0.5 million of preferential payments in the 90 days prior to the related Chapter 11 bankruptcy petition. The claim pertaining to the preferential payments was settled for an immaterial amount during the second quarter of 2002. In addition, this former customer seeks $9.4 million from us for a variety of claims including antitrust, breach of contract, breach of warranty and conversion. These latter claims arise out of allegations that this customer was entitled to various discounts, rebates and credits after it filed for bankruptcy. We have purchased insurance with respect to the actions. On August 22, 2002, the court dismissed the antitrust claims. On July 8, 2003, the remaining claims were settled without any material financial effect on our business, financial condition or results of operations.

In 1986, we acquired a brake business, which we subsequently sold in March 1998 and which is accounted for as a discontinued operation in the accompanying consolidated financial statements. When we originally acquired this brake business, we assumed future liabilities relating to any alleged exposure to asbestos-containing products manufactured by the seller of the acquired brake business. In accordance with the related purchase agreement, we agreed to assume the liabilities for all new claims filed on or after September 1, 2001. Our ultimate exposure will depend upon the number of claims filed against us on or after September 1, 2001 and the amounts paid for indemnity and defense thereof. At December 31, 2001, approximately 100 cases were outstanding for which we were responsible for any related liabilities. At December 31, 2002, the number of cases outstanding for which we were responsible for related liabilities increased to approximately 2,500, which include approximately 1,600 cases filed in December 2002 in Mississippi. We believe that these Mississippi cases filed against us in December 2002 were due in large part to potential plaintiffs accelerating the filing of their claims prior to the effective date of Mississippi's tort reform statue in January 2003, which statute eliminated the ability of plaintiffs to file consolidated cases. At December 31, 2003, approximately 3,300 cases were outstanding for which we were responsible for any related liabilities. Since inception in September 2001, the amounts paid for settled claims are $1.1 million. We do not have insurance coverage for the defense and indemnity costs associated with these claims.

In evaluating our potential asbestos-related liability, we have considered various factors including, among other things, an actuarial study performed by a leading actuarial firm with expertise in assessing asbestos-related liabilities, our settlement amounts and whether there are any codefendants, the jurisdiction in which lawsuits are filed, and the status and results of settlement discussions. Actuarial consultants with experience in assessing asbestos-related liabilities completed a study in September 2002 to estimate our potential claim liability. The methodology used to project asbestos-related liabilities and costs in the study considered: (1) historical data available from publicly available studies; (2) an analysis of our recent claims history to estimate likely filing rates for the remainder of 2002 through 2052; (3) an analysis of our currently pending claims; and (4) an analysis of our settlements to date in order to develop average settlement values. Based upon all the information considered by the actuarial firm, the actuarial study estimated an undiscounted liability for settlement payments, excluding legal costs, ranging from $27.3 million to $58 million for the period through 2052. Accordingly, based on the information contained in the actuarial study and all other available information considered by us, we recorded an after tax charge of $16.9 million as a loss from discontinued operation during the third quarter of 2002 to reflect such liability, excluding legal costs. We concluded that no amount within the range of settlement payments was more likely than any other and, therefore, recorded the low end of the range as the liability associated with future settlement payments through 2052 in our consolidated financial statements, in accordance with generally accepted accounting principles.

As is our accounting policy, the actuarial study was updated as of August 31, 2003 using methodologies consistent with the September 2002 study. The updated study has estimated an undiscounted liability for settlement payments, excluding legal costs, ranging from $27 to $71 million for the period through 2052. We continue to believe that no amount within the range was a better estimate after the updated

study, therefore, no adjustment was recorded as our consolidated balance sheet at September 30, 2003 reflects a total liability of approximately $27 million. Legal costs, which are expensed as incurred, are estimated to range from $21 to $28 million during the same period. We plan on performing a similar annual actuarial analysis during the third quarter of each year for the foreseeable future. Given the uncertainties associated with projecting such matters into the future, the short period of time that we have been responsible for defending these claims, and other factors outside our control, we can give no assurance that additional provisions will not be required. Management will continue to monitor the circumstances surrounding these potential liabilities in determining whether additional provisions may be necessary. At the present time, however, we do not believe that any additional provisions would be reasonably likely to have a material adverse effect on our liquidity or consolidated financial position.

We are involved in various other litigation and product liability matters arising in the ordinary course of business. Although the final outcome of any asbestos-related matters or any other litigation or product liability matter cannot be determined, based on our understanding and evaluation of the relevant facts and circumstances, it is our opinion that the final outcome of these matters will not have a material adverse effect on our business, financial condition or results of operations.

Asset Retirement Obligation

2.277

MURPHY OIL CORPORATION (DEC)

(Thousands of dollars)	2003	2002
Total current liabilities	$ 810,326	$717,892
Notes payable	1,061,410	788,554
Nonrecourse debt of a subsidiary	28,897	74,254
Deferred income taxes	421,700	327,771
Asset retirement obligations	252,397	160,543
Accrued major repair costs	20,513	52,980
Deferred credits and other liabilities	166,521	170,228

NOTES TO CONSOLIDATED FINANCIAL STATEMENTS

Note B (In Part): New Accounting Principles and Recent Accounting Pronouncements

One January 1, 2003, the Company adopted SFAS No. 143, Accounting for Asset Retirement Obligations, which requires the Company to record a liability equal to the fair value of the estimated cost to retire an asset. The asset retirement obligation (ARO) liability is recorded in the period in which the obligation meets the definition of a liability, which is generally when the asset is placed in service. When the ARO liability is initially recorded, the Company increases the carrying amount of the related long-lived asset by an amount equal to the original liability. The liability is accreted to its present value each period, and the capitalized cost is depreciated over the useful life of the related long-lived asset. Any difference between costs incurred upon settlement of an asset retirement obligation and the recorded liability will be recognized as a gain or loss in the Company's earnings. The ARO is based on a number of assumptions requiring professional judgment. The Company cannot predict the type of revisions to these assumptions that will be required in future periods due to the availability of additional information, including prices for oil field services, technological changes, governmental requirements and other factors. Upon adoption of SFAS No. 143, the Company recorded a charge of $6,993,000, net of $1,400,000 in income taxes, as the cumulative effect of a change in accounting principle. The noncash transition adjustment increased property, plant and equipment, accumulated depreciation, and asset retirement obligations by $142,894,000, $58,786,000, and $92,500,000, respectively.

The majority of the ARO recognized by the Company at December 31, 2003 related to the estimated costs to dismantle and abandon its producing oil and gas properties and related equipment. A portion of the transition adjustment and ARO related to its investment in retail gasoline stations. The Company did not record an ARO for its refining and certain of its marketing assets because sufficient information is presently not available to estimate a range of potential settlement dates for the obligation. These assets are consistently being upgraded and are expected to be operational into the foreseeable future. The obligation for these refining and marketing assets will be initially recognized in the period in which sufficient information exists to estimate the timing and amount of the obligation.

A reconciliation of the 2003 changes in the ARO liability is shown in the following table.

(Thousands of dollars)	2003
December 31, 2002	$160,543
Transition adjustment	92,500
Accretion expense	12,366
Liabilities incurred	28,210
Liabilities settled	(67,234)
Changes due to translation of foreign currencies	26,012
December 31, 2003	$252,397

Liabilities settled includes approximately $62,578,000 in noncash reductions of ARO associated with the sale of certain oil and gas producing properties.

Deferred Credits

2.278

ALCOA INC. (DEC)

(In millions)	2003	2002
Total current liabilities	$ 5,084	$ 4,459
Long-term debt, less amount due within one year	6,692	8,366
Accrued postretirement benefits	2,220	2,319
Other noncurrent liabilities and deferred credits (J)	3,389	2,867
Deferred income taxes	804	520
Liabilities of operations held for sale	107	59
Total liabilities	$18,296	$18,590

NOTES TO THE CONSOLIDATED FINANCIAL STATEMENTS
(Dollars in millions)

A (In Part): Summary of Significant Accounting Policies

Revenue Recognition

Alcoa recognizes revenue when title, ownership, and risk of loss pass to the customer, in accordance with the provisions of Staff Accounting Bulletin 101, "Revenue Recognition in Financial Statements."

Alcoa periodically enters into long-term supply contracts with alumina and aluminum customers and receives advance payments for product to be delivered in future periods. These advance payments are recorded as deferred revenue, and revenue is recognized as shipments are made and title, ownership, and risk of loss pass to the customer during the term of the contracts.

J. Other Noncurrent Liabilities and Deferred Credits

	2003	2002
Deferred alumina sales revenue	$ 187	$ 195
Deferred aluminum sales revenue	384	104
Environmental remediation	330	368
Deferred credits	108	89
Accrued pension benefit liability	1,580	1,547
Other noncurrent liabilities	800	564
	$3,389	$2,867

In 2003, Alcoa received a partial advance payment of $440 (approximately $70 was classified as current) related to a long-term aluminum supply contract with a customer. Each month for a six-year period, the customer will purchase and Alcoa is required to deliver 7,500 tons of aluminum at market prices. Aloca has deposited $7 into a cash collateral account to satisfy one month's delivery obligation under the aluminum supply contract.

2.279

CISCO SYSTEMS, INC. (JUL)

(In millions)	2003	2002
Total current liabilities	$8,294	$8,375
Deferred revenue	774	749
Total liabilities	$9,068	$9,124

NOTES TO CONSOLIDATED FINANCIAL STATEMENTS

2 (In Part): Summary of Significant Accounting Policies

Revenue Recognition

The Company recognizes product revenue when persuasive evidence of an arrangement exists, delivery has occurred, the fee is fixed or determinable, and collectibility is reasonably assured. In instances where the customer specifies final acceptance of the product, system, or solution, revenue is deferred until all acceptance criteria have been met. Service revenue is generally deferred and, in most cases, recognized ratably over the period during which the services are to be performed, which is typically from one to three years. Cash payments received in advance of product or service revenue are recorded as deferred revenue.

When a sale involves multiple elements, such as sales of products that include services, the entire fee from the arrangement is allocated to each respective element based on its relative fair value and recognized when revenue recognition criteria for each element are met. Fair value for each element is established based on the sales price charged when the same element is sold separately.

The Company makes sales to two-tier distribution channels and recognizes revenue to two-tier distributors based on a sell-through method utilizing information provided by its distributors. These distributors are given business terms to return a portion of inventory, receive credits for changes in selling prices, and participate in various cooperative marketing programs. The Company maintains estimated accruals and allowances for such exposures. The Company accrues for warranty costs, sales returns, and other allowances based on its historical experience.

5 (In Part): Balance Sheet and Cash Flow Details

The following tables provide details of selected balance sheet items (in millions):

	2003	2002
Deferred revenue:		
Service	$ 2,451	$ 2,207
Product	1,357	1,685
Total	3,808	3,892
Less, current portion	(3,034)	(3,143)
Non-current deferred revenue	$ 774	$ 749

2.280

MEREDITH CORPORATION (JUN)

(In thousands)	2003	2002
Total current liabilities	$297,199	$307,406
Long-term debt	375,000	385,000
Long-term broadcast rights payable	21,514	24,906
Unearned subscription revenues	122,275	91,270
Deferred income taxes	71,979	92,351
Other noncurrent liabilities	47,989	51,614
Total liabilities	$935,956	$952,547

NOTES TO CONSOLIDATED FINANCIAL STATEMENTS

1 (In Part): Organization and Summary of Significant Accounting Policies

k. Revenues

Revenues are recognized only when realized/realizable and earned, in accordance with accounting principles generally accepted in the United States of America (GAAP). Advertising revenues are recognized, net of agency commissions, when the underlying advertisements are published, defined as the issue's on-sale date, or aired by the broadcasting stations. Magazine advertising revenues totaled $383.1 million in fiscal 2003 ($325.5 million in fiscal 2002 and $352.5 million in fiscal 2001). Broadcasting advertising revenues were $265.5 million in fiscal 2003 ($247.2 million in fiscal 2002 and $263.3 million in fiscal 2001). Barter advertising revenues, and the offsetting expense, are recognized at the fair value of the advertising surrendered, as determined by similar cash transactions. Barter advertising revenues were not material in any period. Revenues from magazine subscriptions are deferred and recognized proportionately as products are delivered to subscribers. Revenues from magazine and book retail sales are recognized upon delivery, net of provisions for anticipated returns. The Company bases its estimates for returns on historical experience and has not experienced significant fluctuations between estimated and actual return experience. Revenues from integrated marketing and other custom programs are recognized when the products or services are delivered. In certain instances, revenues are recorded gross in accordance with GAAP although the Company receives cash for a lesser amount due to the netting of certain expenses.

Mandatorily Redeemable Preferred Stock

2.281

CABLEVISION SYSTEMS CORPORATION (DEC)

(Dollars in thousands)	2003	2002
Total current liabilities	$ 1,620,058	$ 1,630,385
Feature film and contract obligations, long-term	286,955	229,431
Deferred revenue	16,322	17,479
Deferred tax liability	289,055	245,021
Liabilities under derivative contracts	127,751	104,949
Other long-term liabilities	217,946	225,519
Bank debt, long-term	2,246,000	2,080,000
Collateralized indebtedness	1,617,620	1,234,106
Senior notes and debentures	3,692,699	3,691,772
Subordinated debentures	599,203	599,128
Notes payable	150,000	—
Capital lease obligations, long-term	69,220	71,231
Series H redeemable exchangeable preferred stock	434,181	—
Series M redeemable exchangeable preferred stock	1,110,113	—
Deficit investment in affiliates	41,111	19,933
Minority interests	580,766	626,571
Total liabilities	$13,099,000	$10,775,525
Preferred stock of CSC Holdings, Inc.	$ 80,001	$ 1,544,294

NOTES TO CONSOLIDATED FINANCIAL STATEMENTS
(Dollars in thousands, except per share amounts)

Note 1 (In Part): Summary of Significant Accounting Policies

Recently Issued Accounting Standards (In Part)

In May 2003, the FASB issued Statement 150, Accounting for Certain Financial Instruments with Characteristics of Both Liabilities and Equity. This Statement requires that certain instruments that were previously classified as equity on a company's statement of financial position now be classified as liabilities. As a result of adopting the Statement on July 1, 2003, liabilities increased $1,544,294 reflecting the reclassification of CSC Holdings' Series H and Series M Redeemable Preferred Stock and dividends of $87,258 were classified as interest expense for the year ended December 31, 2003. In addition, the Company currently consolidates a 60% majority-owned interest in a limited-life partnership. The estimated liquidation value of the 40% minority interest is approximately $1,128,900 as of December 31, 2003.

Note 10. Preferred Stock of CSC Holdings, Inc.

The following summarizes each series of CSC Holdings' preferred stock:

	2003		2002	
	Shares	Balance	Shares	Balance
Series A Preferred	80,001	$ 80,001	—	$ —
Series H Preferred	4,341,813	434,181	4,341,813	434,181
Series M Preferred	11,101,126	1,110,113	11,101,126	1,110,113
		$1,624,295		$1,544,294

In February 2003, Quadrangle Capital Partners LP, a private investment firm, invested $75,000 in CSC Holdings, in the form of 10% Series A Exchangeable Participating Preferred Stock convertible into Cablevision NY Group Class A common stock.

In connection with the issuance of the Series A preferred stock to Quadrangle, the Company entered into an agreement with Quadrangle which grants Quadrangle the right to require the Company to purchase the preferred stock ("put option") for cash or through the issuance of registered equity securities of the Company, at the Company's option. The exchange right and the put option have been accounted for as a derivative. Accordingly, the fair value of the exchange right and the put option has been reflected as a liability under derivative contracts in the accompanying consolidated balance sheet. The change in the fair value of $38,618 has been included in loss on derivative contracts in the accompanying consolidated statement of operations.

In October 2003, Quadrangle exercised its "put option" to require CSC Holdings to purchase all of its Series A Exchangeable Participating Preferred Stock. The terms of the agreement provide for the delivery of cash or registered equity securities of Cablevision in settlement of the put price. The Company is in discussions with Quadrangle as to the process for determining the put price.

In February 1996, CSC Holdings issued 6,500,000 depositary shares, representing 65,000 shares of 11-1/8% Series L Redeemable Exchangeable Preferred Stock (the "Series L Preferred Stock"), which were subsequently exchanged for Series M Redeemable Exchangeable Preferred Stock (the "Series M Preferred Stock") in August 1996 with terms identical to the Series L Preferred Stock. The depositary shares are exchangeable, in whole but not in part, at the option of CSC Holdings, for CSC Holdings' 11-1/8% Senior Subordinated Debentures due 2008. CSC Holdings is required to redeem the Series M Preferred Stock on April 1, 2008 at a redemption price equal to the liquidation preference of $10,000 per share plus accumulated and unpaid dividends. The Series M Preferred Stock is redeemable at various redemption prices beginning at 105.563% at any time on or after April 1, 2003, at the option of CSC Holdings, with accumulated and unpaid dividends thereon to the date of redemption. Before April 1, 2001, dividends could, at the option of CSC Holdings, be paid in cash or by issuing fully paid and nonassessable shares of Series M Preferred Stock with an aggregate liquidation preference equal to the amount of such dividends. On and after April 1, 2001, dividends must be paid in cash. CSC Holdings paid cash dividends on the Series M Preferred Stock of approximately $123,500 in each of 2003, 2002 and 2001.

In September 1995, CSC Holdings issued 2,500,000 shares of its $.01 par value 11-3/4% Series H Redeemable Exchangeable Preferred Stock (the "Series H Preferred Stock") with an aggregate liquidation preference of $100 per share. CSC Holdings is required to redeem the Series H Preferred Stock on October 1, 2007 at a redemption price per share equal to the liquidation preference of $100 per share, plus accrued and unpaid dividends thereon. The Series H Preferred Stock is redeemable at various redemption prices beginning at 105.875% at any time on or after October 1, 2002, at the option of CSC Holdings, with accumulated and unpaid dividends thereon to the date of redemption. Before October 1, 2000, dividends could, at the option of CSC Holdings, be paid in cash or by issuing fully paid and nonassessable shares of Series H Preferred Stock with an aggregate liquidation preference equal to the amount of such dividends. On and after October 1, 2000, dividends must be paid in cash. The terms of the Series H Preferred Stock permit CSC Holdings, at its option, to exchange the Series H Preferred Stock for CSC Holdings' 11-3/4% Senior Subordinated Debentures due 2007 in an aggregate principal amount equal to the aggregate liquidation preference of the shares of Series H Preferred Stock. CSC Holdings paid cash dividends on the Series H Preferred Stock of approximately $51,016 in each of 2003, 2002 and 2001, respectively.

In connection with the implementation of Statement 150 on July 1, 2003, the carrying value of CSC Holdings' Series H and Series M Redeemable Preferred Stock of $434,181 and $1,110,113, respectively, was classified as a liability. In addition, beginning July 1, 2003, dividends have been classified as interest expense, increasing interest expense by $87,258 for the year ended December 31, 2003. Prior to July 1, 2003, preferred stock dividend requirements of CSC Holdings are included in minority interests in the accompanying consolidated statements of operations.

2.282

PRIMEDIA INC. (DEC)

(Dollars in thousands)	2003	2002
Total current liabilities	$ 493,503	$ 552,951
Long-term debt	1,562,441	1,727,677
Shares subject to mandatory redemption	474,559	—
Deferred revenues	33,604	41,466
Deferred income taxes	61,364	49,500
Other non-current liabilities	23,905	23,359
Total liabilities	$2,649,376	$2,394,953
Commitments and contingencies		
Exchangeable preferred stock (aggregate liquidation and redemption value of $493,409 at December 31, 2002)	$ —	$ 484,465

2 (In Part): Summary of Significant Accounting Policies

$10.00 Series D Exchangeable Preferred Stock ("Series D Exchangeable Preferred Stock"), $9.20 Series F Exchangeable Preferred Stock ("Series F Exchangeable Preferred Stock"), and $8.625 Series H Exchangeable Preferred Stock ("Series H Exchangeable Preferred Stock")

The Series D Exchangeable Preferred Stock, Series F Exchangeable Preferred Stock and Series H Exchangeable Preferred Stock shall be referred to herein collectively as the "Exchangeable Preferred Stock." The Series D Exchangeable Preferred Stock, Series F Exchangeable Preferred Stock and Series H Exchangeable Preferred Stock are stated at redemption value and classified as long-term liabilities in accordance with SFAS 150, "Accounting for Certain Financial Instruments with Characteristics of both Liabilities and Equity" effective July 1, 2003. Dividends on the Series D Exchangeable Preferred Stock, Series F Exchangeable Preferred Stock and Series H Exchangeable Preferred Stock are classified as interest expense and the related issuance costs are classified as other assets on the consolidated balance sheet. Prior to July 1, 2003, the Series D Exchangeable Preferred Stock, Series F Exchangeable Preferred Stock and Series H Exchangeable Preferred Stock were stated at fair value on the date of issuance less issuance costs. The difference between their carrying values and their redemption values was being accreted (using the interest method) by periodic charges to additional paid-in capital (see Note 13).

Recent Accounting Pronouncements (In Part)

In 2002 and 2003 the Company adopted a series of accounting changes, as recommended by the FASB and EITF, that impact year-over-year comparisons of financial results. These changes are summarized below.

SFAS 150, "Accounting for Certain Financial Instruments With Characteristics of Both Liabilities and Equity"

Effective July 1, 2003, the Company prospectively adopted SFAS 150. SFAS 150 requires the Company to classify as long-term liabilities its Series D Exchangeable Preferred Stock, Series F Exchangeable Preferred Stock and Series H Exchangeable Preferred Stock and to classify dividends from this preferred stock as interest expense. As a result of the adoption by the Company of SFAS 150, the Series D Exchangeable Preferred Stock, Series F Exchangeable Preferred Stock and Series H Exchangeable Preferred Stock are now collectively described as "shares subject to mandatory redemption" on the accompanying consolidated balance sheet as of December 31, 2003. Dividends on these shares are now described as "interest on shares subject to mandatory redemption" and included in loss from continuing operations for the year ended December 31, 2003, whereas previously they were presented below net income (loss) as preferred stock dividends (see Note 13).

13. Shares Subject to Mandatory Redemption (the Company's Series D Exchangeable Preferred Stock, Series F Exchangeable Preferred Stock and Series H Exchangeable Preferred Stock)

The Company prospectively adopted SFAS 150 on July 1, 2003, which requires the Company to classify as long-term liabilities its Series D Exchangeable Preferred Stock, Series F Exchangeable Preferred Stock and Series H Exchangeable Preferred Stock ($474,559 at December 31, 2003). Such stock is now collectively described as "shares subject to mandatory redemption" on the accompanying consolidated balance sheet. Each series individually is legally known as Exchangeable Preferred Stock. Related issuance costs of $7,264 were required to be classified as other non-current assets on the accompanying consolidated balance sheet at December 31, 2003. These issuance costs were included in Exchangeable Preferred Stock at December 31, 2002. In addition, SFAS 150 requires that the related dividends on these shares be described as "interest on shares subject to mandatory redemption" and included in loss from continuing operations for the year ended December 31, 2003, whereas previously they were presented below net income (loss) as preferred stock dividends. The adoption of SFAS 150 increased the loss from continuing operations for the year ended December 31, 2003 by $22,547 which represents primarily interest on shares subject to mandatory redemption and amortization of issuance costs which are included in the amortization of deferred financing costs on the accompanying statement of consolidated operations. If SFAS 150 was adopted on July 1, 2002, and July 1, 2001, loss from continuing operations would have increased by $19,763 and $27,345, respectively, for the years ended December 31, 2002 and 2001. The 2002 increase to loss from continuing operations has been reduced by a net gain of $4,488 on exchanges of the preferred stock. This gain was included in additional paid-in capital on the accompanying consolidated balance sheet at December 31, 2002.

Shares subject to mandatory redemption consist of the following:

	2003	2002
$10.00 Series D Exchangeable Preferred Stock ($.01 par value, 2,000,000 shares authorized and 1,674,867 shares and 1,769,867 shares issued and outstanding at December 31, 2003 and 2002, respectively)	$167,487	$174,531
$9.20 Series F Exchangeable Preferred Stock ($.01 par value, 1,250,000 shares authorized and 953,328 shares and 1,023,328 shares issued and outstanding at December 31, 2003 and 2002, respectively)	95,333	99,984
$8.625 Series H Exchangeable Preferred Stock ($.01 par value, 2,500,000 shares authorized and 2,117,391 shares and 2,140,891 shares issued and outstanding at December 31, 2003 and 2002, respectively)	211,739	209,950
	$474,559	$484,465

$10.00 Series D Exchangeable Preferred Stock

Annual dividends of $10.00 per share on the Series D Exchangeable Preferred Stock are cumulative and payable quarterly, in cash. On or after February 1, 2001, the Series D Exchangeable Preferred Stock may be redeemed in whole or in part, at the option of the Company, at specified redemption prices plus accrued and unpaid dividends. The Company is required to redeem the Series D Exchangeable Preferred Stock on February 1, 2008 at a redemption price equal to the liquidation preference of $100 per share, plus accrued and unpaid dividends. The Series D Exchangeable Preferred Stock is exchangeable, in whole but not in part, at the option of the Company, on any scheduled dividend payment date, into 10% Class D Exchangeable Subordinated Exchange Debentures due 2008 provided the Company is in compliance with the terms of its bank credit facility agreement. The liquidation and redemption value at December 31, 2003 and 2002 was $167,487 and $176,987, respectively.

$9.20 Series F Exchangeable Preferred Stock

Annual dividends of $9.20 per share on the Series F Exchangeable Preferred Stock are cumulative and payable quarterly, in cash. The Company is required to redeem the Series F Exchangeable Preferred Stock on November 1, 2009 at a redemption price equal to the liquidation preference of $100 per share, plus accrued and unpaid dividends. The Series F Exchangeable Preferred Stock is exchangeable into 9.20% Class F Subordinated Exchange Debentures due 2009, in whole but not in part, at the option of the Company on any scheduled dividend payment date provided the Company is in compliance with the terms of its bank credit facility agreement. As of December 31, 2003 and 2002, the liquidation and redemption value of the Series F Exchangeable Preferred Stock was $95,333 and $102,333, respectively.

$8.625 Series H Exchangeable Preferred Stock

Annual dividends of $8.625 per share on the Series H Exchangeable Preferred Stock are cumulative and payable quarterly, in cash. On or after April 1, 2003, the Series H Exchangeable Preferred Stock may be redeemed in whole or in part, at the option of the Company, at prices ranging from 104.313% with annual reductions to 100% in 2006, plus accrued and unpaid dividends. The Company is required to redeem the Series H Exchangeable Preferred Stock on April 1, 2010 at a redemption price equal to the liquidation preference of $100 per share, plus accrued and unpaid dividends. The Series H Exchangeable Preferred Stock is exchangeable, in whole but not in part, at the option of the Company, on any scheduled dividend payment date into $8\frac{5}{8}$% Class H Subordinated Exchange Debentures due 2010 provided the Company is in compliance with the terms of its bank credit facility agreement. As of December 31, 2003 and 2002, the liquidation and redemption value of the Series H Exchangeable Preferred Stock was $211,739 and $214,089, respectively.

In the fourth quarter of 2002, the Company's Board of Directors authorized the exchange by the Company of up to $30,000 of Exchangeable Preferred Stock for common stock and the subsequent repurchase by the Company of the common stock issued in connection with the exchange transactions. In the second quarter of 2003, the Board of Directors increased this authorization to an aggregate of $50,000. A summary of these exchanges is presented below.

	Liquidation Value	Common Shares Issued	Common Share Repurchase Amount
Fourth quarter 2002 Series H Exchangeable Preferred Stock[1]	$ 6,150	2,860,465	$ 4,244
Second quarter 2003 Series D Exchangeable Preferred Stock	7,000	2,223,334	6,670
Series F Exchangeable Preferred Stock	7,000	2,124,166	6,372
Series H Exchangeable Preferred Stock	2,350	693,250	2,080
Fourth quarter 2003 Series D Exchangeable Preferred Stock	2,500	832,627	2,456
Total	$25,000	8,733,842	$21,822

[1] Repurchase of common stock settled during January 2003.

During the first quarter of 2002, the Board of Directors authorized the exchange by the Company of up to $100,000 of Exchangeable Preferred Stock for common stock. During May 2002, the Board of Directors increased this authorization to an aggregate of $165,000. A summary of these exchanges is presented below.

	Liquidation Value	Common Shares Issued
First quarter 2002 Series H Exchangeable Preferred Stock	$ 7,066	1,144,778
Second quarter 2002 Series D Exchangeable Preferred Stock	19,013	3,696,979
Series F Exchangeable Preferred Stock	22,667	4,385,222
Series H Exchangeable Preferred Stock	22,695	4,363,273
Fourth quarter 2002 Series D Exchangeable Preferred Stock	4,000	770,054
Total	$75,441	14,360,306

The exchange transactions described above were entered into by the Company with the holders of the Exchangeable Preferred Stock in privately negotiated transactions.

The Company recognized net gains of $959 and $32,788 on these exchanges for the years ended December 31, 2003 and 2002, respectively. Of these gains, $944 and $32,788 are included in additional paid-in capital on the Company's consolidated balance sheets as of December 31, 2003 and 2002, respectively and $15 is included in other, net on the Company's statement of consolidated operations for the year ended December 31, 2003 due to the adoption of SFAS 150 effective July 1, 2003.

The gains on these exchanges are net of the write-offs of unamortized issuance costs of $313 and $1,686 for the years ended December 31, 2003 and 2002, respectively. Of these costs, $284 and $1,686 are included in additional paid-in capital on the Company's consolidated balance sheet as of December 31, 2003 and 2002, respectively and $29 is included in other, net on the Company's statement of consolidated operations for the year ended December 31, 2003 due to the adoption of SFAS 150 effective July 1, 2003.

There were no such Exchangeable Preferred Stock exchanges in 2001.

RESERVES—USE OF THE TERM "RESERVE"

2.283 Prior to being superseded by the APB, the Committee on Terminology of the AICPA issued four terminology bulletins. In Accounting Terminology Bulletin No. 1, *Review and Resume*, the Committee recommended that the term *reserve* be applied only to amounts of retained earnings appropriated for general or specific purposes. In practice, the term *reserve*, with rare exceptions, is applied to amounts designated as valuation allowances deducted from assets or as accruals for estimated liabilities. Table 2-32 shows that the term *reserve* appears occasionally in the financial statements of the survey companies.

2.284

TABLE 2-32: USE OF TERM "RESERVE"

	Number of Companies			
	2003	2002	2001	2000
To describe deductions from assets for				
Reducing inventories to LIFO cost.....	26	23	33	20
Inventory obsolescence......................	14	19	15	N/C*
Doubtful accounts.............................	12	13	19	18
Accumulated depreciation.................	3	3	5	3
Other—described..............................	4	9	6	16
To describe accruals for				
Estimated expenses relating to property abandonments or discontinued operations.................	34	26	25	10
Environmental costs..........................	25	18	16	7
Insurance..	21	13	18	12
Litigation...	14	7	4	N/C*
Employee benefits or compensation..	3	3	2	2
Other—described..............................	40	20	16	17

* N/C = Not compiled. Line item was not included in table for year shown.

TITLE OF STOCKHOLDERS' EQUITY SECTION

2.285 Table 2-33 summarizes the titles used by the survey companies to identify the stockholders' equity section of the balance sheet.

2.286

TABLE 2-33: TITLE OF STOCKHOLDERS' EQUITY SECTION

	2003	2002	2001	2000
Stockholders' equity...................	294	299	292	286
Shareholders' equity.................	232	222	226	229
Shareowners' equity..................	21	20	21	25
Shareholders' investment..........	8	9	14	12
Common stockholders' equity....	6	5	5	6
Common shareholders' equity...	5	6	6	7
Term deficit or deficiency in title......................................	23	30	22	N/C*
Other or no title..........................	11	9	14	35
Total Companies....................	**600**	**600**	**600**	**600**

* N/C = Not compiled. Line item was not included in table for year shown.

CAPITAL STRUCTURES

2.287 Effective for periods ending after December 15, 1997, SFAS No. 129, *Disclosure of Information about Capital Structure*, states the disclosure requirements for the capital structure of an entity.

2.288 Table 2-34 summarizes the capital structures disclosed on the balance sheets of the survey companies.

2.289

TABLE 2-34: CAPITAL STRUCTURES

	2003	2002	2001	2000
Common Stock With:				
No preferred stock.............................	516	502	507	514
One class of preferred stock.............	73	81	80	71
Two classes of preferred stock..........	9	14	10	10
Three of more classes of preferred stock..	2	3	3	5
Total Companies........................	**600**	**600**	**600**	**600**
Companies included above with two or more classes of common stock	62	70	59	66

COMMON STOCK

2.290   Table 2-35 summarizes the reporting bases of common stock. As in prior years, the majority of the survey companies show common stock at par value.

2.291

TABLE 2-35: COMMON STOCK

	2003	2002	2001	2000
Par value stock shown at:				
Par value.................................	570	577	564	561
Amount in excess of par..............	17	21	29	10
Assigned per share amount.........	8	1	5	9
No par value stock shown at:				
Assigned per share amount.........	6	4	7	7
No assigned per share amount....	54	57	61	57
Issues Outstanding........................	**655**	**660**	**666**	**644**

PREFERRED STOCK

2.292   *SFAS No. 129* provides reporting and disclosure requirements for preferred stock. SFAS No. 150, *Accounting for Certain Financial Instruments with Characteristics of both Liabilities and Equity*, requires that an issuer classify certain financial instruments with characteristics of both liabilities and equity as liabilities. Prior to *SFAS No. 150*, many of these freestanding financial instruments were classified as equity. Some issuances of stock, such as mandatorily redeemable preferred stock, impose unconditional obligations requiring the issuer to transfer assets or issue its equity shares. *SFAS No. 150* requires an issuer to classify such financial instruments as liabilities. Examples of preferred stock issues within the scope of *SFAS No. 150* are included in the Other Noncurrent Liability section.

2.293   Table 2-36 summarizes the reporting bases of preferred stock. As with common stock, many of the survey companies present preferred stock at par value. Examples of preferred stock presentations and disclosures follow.

2.294

TABLE 2-36: PREFERRED STOCK

	Number of Companies			
	2003	2002	2001	2000
Par value stock shown at:				
Par value......................................	30	42	39	45
Liquidation or redemption value....	16	13	12	7
Fair value at issuance date...........	2	2	4	3
Assigned per share amount..........	1	3	4	5
Other...	2	4	5	6
No par value stock shown at:				
Liquidation or redemption value....	15	13	9	8
Assigned per share amount..........	9	8	7	5
Fair value at issuance date...........	—	1	1	1
No assigned per share amount.....	19	10	10	15
Number of Companies				
Preferred stock outstanding...............	88	93	89	88
No preferred stock outstanding.........	512	507	511	512
Total Companies.............................	**600**	**600**	**600**	**600**

Preferred Stock Extended at Par Value

2.295

HECLA MINING COMPANY (DEC)

(In thousands, except share data)	2003	2002
Shareholders' equity		
Preferred stock $0.25 par value, authorized 5,000,000 shares; issued 2003—464,777 shares and 2002—753,402 shares liquidation preference 2003—$28,932 and 2002—$44,262	$ 116	$ 188
Common stock, $0.25 par value, authorized 200,000,000 shares; issued 2003—115,543,695 shares and issued 2002—86,187,468 shares	28,886	21,547
Capital surplus	504,858	405,959
Accumulated deficit	(361,560)	(355,544)
Accumulated other comprehensive loss	(753)	(36)
Less stock held by grantor trust; 2002—20,442 common shares	—	(66)
Less treasury stock, at cost; 2003 and 2002—8,274 common shares	(118)	(118)
Total shareholders' equity	$ 171,429	$ 71,930

NOTES TO CONSOLIDATED FINANCIAL STATEMENTS

Note 10 (In Part): Shareholders' Equity

Preferred Stock

Our Charter authorizes us to issue 5,000,000 shares of preferred stock (Series A and B), par value $0.25 per share. The preferred stock is issuable in series with such voting rights, if any, designations, powers, preferences and other rights and such qualifications, limitations and restrictions as may be determined by our board of directors or a duly authorized committee thereof, without stockholder approval. The board may fix the number of shares constituting each series and increase or decrease the number of shares of any series. As of December 31, 2003, there were 464,777 shares of Series B Cumulative Convertible Preferred Stock outstanding. All of the shares of our Series B Preferred Stock are listed on the New York Stock Exchange under the symbol "HLPrB".

Ranking

The Series B preferred stock ranks senior to our common stock and any shares of Series A Preferred Shares issued pursuant to the Rights (as defined above) with respect to payment of dividends and amounts upon liquidation, dissolution or winding up.

While any shares of Series B preferred stock are outstanding, we may not authorize the creation or issue of any class or series of stock that ranks senior to the Series B preferred stock as to dividends or upon liquidation, dissolution or winding up without the consent of the holders of 66of the outstanding shares of Series B preferred stock and any other series of preferred stock ranking on a parity with the Series B preferred stock as to dividends and upon liquidation, dissolution or winding up (a "Parity Stock"), voting as a single class without regard to series.

Dividends

Series B preferred stockholders are entitled to receive, when, as and if declared by the board of directors out of our assets legally available therefore, cumulative cash dividends at the rate per annum of $3.50 per share of Series B preferred stock. Dividends on the Series B preferred stock are payable quarterly in arrears on October 1, January 1, April 1 and July 1 of each year (and, in the case of any undeclared and unpaid dividends, at such additional times and for such interim periods, if any, as determined by the board of directors), at such annual rate. Dividends are cumulative from the date of the original issuance of the Series B preferred stock, whether or not in any dividend period or periods we have assets legally available for the payment of such dividends. Accumulations of dividends on shares of Series B preferred stock do not bear interest.

Redemption

The Series B preferred stock is redeemable at our option, in whole or in part, at $50 per share, plus, in each case, all dividends undeclared and unpaid on the Series B preferred stock ($12.25 per share at January 2, 2004) up to the date fixed for redemption, upon giving notice as provided below.

Liquidation Preference

The Series B preferred stockholders are entitled to receive, in the event that we are liquidated, dissolved or wound up, whether voluntary or involuntary, $50 per share of Series B preferred stock plus an amount per share equal to all dividends undeclared and unpaid thereon to the date of final distribution to such holders (the "Liquidation Preference"), and no more. Until the Series B preferred stockholders have been paid the Liquidation Preference in full, no payment will be made to any holder of Junior Stock upon our liquidation, dissolution or winding up. The term "Junior Stock" means our common stock and any other class of our capital stock issued and outstanding that ranks junior as to the payment of dividends or amounts payable upon liquidation, dissolution and winding up to the Series B preferred stock. As of December 31, 2003, our preferred stock had a liquidation preference of $23.2 million, plus dividends in arrears of approximately $5.7 million.

Voting Rights

Except as indicated below, or except as otherwise from time to time required by applicable law, the Series B preferred stockholders have no voting rights and their consent is not required for taking any corporate action. When and if the Series B preferred stockholders are entitled to vote, each holder will be entitled to one vote per share.

Because we had not declared and paid six quarterly dividends on the Series B preferred stock, the Series B preferred stockholders, voting as a single class, elected two additional directors to the board to serve for three year terms at our annual meeting on May 10, 2002. The Series B preferred stockholders will have the right to elect two directors (never to total more than two) at subsequent annual meetings at which the three year terms expire if any cumulative dividends then remain unpaid.

Conversion Rights

Each share of Series B preferred stock is convertible, in whole or in part at the option of the holders thereof, into shares of common stock at a conversion price of $15.55 per share of common stock (equivalent to a conversion rate of 3.2154 shares of common stock for each share of Series B preferred stock). The right to convert shares of Series B preferred stock called for redemption will terminate at the close of business on the day preceding a redemption date (unless we default in payment of the redemption price).

In July 2002, we completed an offer to acquire all currently outstanding Series B preferred stock in exchange for newly issued shares of common stock. A total of 1,546,598 shares, or 67.2%, of the total number of Series B preferred shares outstanding were validly tendered and exchanged into 10,826,186 shares of our common stock. During the third quarter of 2002, we incurred a non-cash dividend of approximately $17.6 million related to the exchange offering. The $17.6 million dividend represents the difference between the value of the common stock issued in the exchange offer and the value of the shares that were issuable under the stated conversion terms of the Series B preferred stock. The non-cash dividend had no impact on our total shareholders' equity as the offset was an increase in common stock and surplus. Following the completed exchange offering, the total of cumulative preferred dividends was $23.3 million for the year ending December 31, 2002. The completed exchange offering eliminated $11.2 million of previously undeclared and unpaid preferred stock dividends.

During the fourth quarter of 2003, we entered into privately negotiated exchange agreements with holders of approximately 38% of our currently outstanding Series B preferred stock in exchange for shares of common stock. A total of 287,975 shares of the total number of Series B preferred shares were exchanged into 2,181,630 shares of our common stock. During the fourth quarter of 2003, we incurred a non-cash dividend of approximately $9.6 million related to the exchanges, which represents the difference between the value of the common stock issued and the value of the shares that were issuable under the stated conversion terms of the Series B preferred stock. Similar to the July 2002 exchange offer, the non-cash dividend had no impact on our total shareholders' equity. Following the exchanges, the total of cumulative preferred dividends was $12.2 million for the year ended December 31, 2003. Also during 2003, a total of 650 shares of Series B preferred stock were converted into 2,089 shares of our common stock at the election of the stock holders.

On January 9, 2004, we announced an exchange offer for the 464,777 remaining outstanding shares of our preferred stock at an exchange rate equal to $66.00, divided by the volume-weighted average of the reported sales price on the New York Stock Exchange of our common stock for the five trading days ending at the close of the second trading day prior to the expiration date of the exchange offer (not to exceed 8.25 common shares).

Preferred Stock Extended at Liquidating Value

2.296

UNITED RENTALS, INC. (DEC)

(In thousands, except share data)	2003	2002
Stockholders' equity:		
Preferred stock—$.01 par value, 5,000,000 shares authorized:		
Series C perpetual convertible preferred stock—$300,000 liquidation preference, 300,000 shares issued and outstanding	$ 3	$ 3
Series D perpetual convertible preferred stock—$150,000 liquidation preference, 150,000 shares issued and outstanding	2	2
Common stock—$.01 par value, 500,000,000 shares authorized, 77,150,277 shares issued and outstanding in 2003 and 76,657,521 in 2002	771	765
Additional paid-in capital	1,329,946	1,341,290
Deferred compensation	(25,646)	(52,988)
(Accumulated deficit) retained earnings	(189,300)	69,281
Accumulated other comprehensive income (loss)	25,099	(26,848)
Total stockholders' equity	$1,140,875	$1,331,505

NOTES TO CONSOLIDATED FINANCIAL STATEMENTS

2 (In Part): Summary of Significant Accounting Policies

Preferred Stock

The Company issued Series A Perpetual Convertible Preferred Stock ("Series A Preferred") and Series B Perpetual Convertible Preferred Stock ("Series B Preferred") in 1999 and included such preferred stock in stockholders' equity. In July 2001, the SEC issued guidance to all public companies as to when redeemable preferred stock may be classified as stockholders' equity. This guidance indicates that preferred stock that would be subject to redemption on the occurrence of an event outside the control of the issuer may not be classified as equity and that the probability of the event occurring is not a factor to be considered. Under this guidance, the Series A Preferred and Series B Preferred would not be included in stockholders' equity because this stock would be subject to mandatory redemption on a hostile change of control. On September 28, 2001, the Company entered into an agreement effecting the exchange of new Series C Perpetual Convertible Preferred Stock ("Series C Preferred") for the Series A Preferred and new Series D Perpetual Convertible Preferred Stock ("Series D Preferred") for the Series B Preferred (see Note 12). The Series C Preferred and Series D Preferred stock is not subject to mandatory redemption on a hostile change of control, and is classified as stockholders' equity under the SEC guidance.

The effect of the foregoing is that the Company's perpetual convertible preferred stock is classified as stockholders' equity as of September 28, 2001 and thereafter, but is classified outside of stockholders' equity for earlier dates. Accordingly, the Company has restated the 2000 balance sheet to show its $430.8 million of perpetual convertible preferred stock under "Series A and B Preferred Stock" rather than under "Stockholders' Equity." The Company has also made a corresponding change to the related Consolidated Statements of Stockholders' Equity. In all other respects, the financial statements remain unchanged, including total assets and liabilities, revenues, operating income, net income and earnings per share.

Impact of Recently Issued Accounting Standards (In Part)

In May 2003, the FASB issued SFAS No. 150, "Accounting for Certain Financial Instruments with Characteristics of both Liabilities and Equity," which establishes standards for how an issuer classifies and measures certain financial instruments with characteristics of both liabilities and equity. This standard requires that financial instruments falling within the scope of this standard be classified as liabilities. This standard is effective for financial instruments entered into or modified after May 31, 2003 and otherwise is effective with the first interim period beginning after June 15, 2003. The adoption of this standard did not have a material effect on the Company's statements of financial position or results of operations.

12. Series A, B, C and D Preferred Stock

Series A Preferred and Series B Preferred

The Company sold 300,000 shares of its Series A Preferred on January 7, 1999 and sold 150,000 shares of its Series B Preferred on September 30, 1999. On September 28, 2001, the Company entered into an agreement effecting (a) the exchange of the outstanding Series A Preferred for an equal number of shares of Series C Preferred and (b) the exchange of the outstanding Series B Preferred for an equal number of shares of Series D Preferred.

Series C Preferred and Series D Preferred

There are 300,000 shares of the Company's Series C Preferred outstanding and 150,000 shares of the Company's Series D Preferred outstanding. The Series D Preferred includes 105,252 shares designated as Class D–1 and 44,748 shares designated as Class D–2. The rights of the two classes of Series D Preferred are substantially the same, except that only the Class D–1 has the voting rights described below.

Principal terms of the Series C Preferred and Series D Preferred include the following (subject to the special provisions described below that will apply in the event of certain Non–Approved Change of Control transactions): (i) each share is entitled to a liquidation preference of $1,000 per share; (ii) at holder's option, each share of Series C Preferred is convertible into 40 shares of common stock subject to adjustment (representing a conversion price of $25 per share based on the liquidation preference) and each share of Series D Preferred is convertible into $33\frac{1}{3}$ shares of common stock subject to adjustment (representing a conversion price of $30 per share based on the liquidation preference); (iii) the holders of the Series C Preferred and Series D Preferred (on an as converted basis) and the holders of the common stock vote together as a single class on all matters (except that the Series C Preferred may vote as a separate class as described in the next clause); (iv) the holders of the Series C Preferred, voting separately as a single class, may elect two directors (subject to reduction to one, if the shares of Series C Preferred owned by specified holders cease to represent, on an as converted basis, at least eight million shares of common stock, and reduction to zero, if such shares of Series C Preferred cease to represent at least four million shares of common stock), (v) there are no stated dividends on the Series C Preferred or Series D Preferred, but the Series C Preferred and Series D Preferred, on an as converted basis, will participate in any dividends declared on the common stock, (vi) upon the occurrence of specified change of control transactions, other than a Non–Approved Change of Control (as defined below), the Company must offer to redeem the Series C Preferred and Series D Preferred at a price per share equal to the liquidation preference plus an amount equal to 6.25% of the liquidation preference compounded annually from the date of the issuance of the Series A Preferred, in the case of the Series C Preferred, and the date of the issuance of the Series B Preferred, in the case of the Series D Preferred, to the redemption date, (vii) if the Company issues for cash common stock (or a series of preferred stock convertible into common stock) and the price for the common stock is below the conversion price of the Series C Preferred, then the Company must offer to repurchase a specified portion of the outstanding Series C Preferred at the price per share set forth in the preceding clause, and (viii) if the Company issues for cash common stock (or a series of preferred stock convertible into common stock) for a price for the common stock below the conversion price of the Series D Preferred, then the Company must offer to repurchase a specified portion of the outstanding Series D Preferred at the price per share specified in the second preceding clause.

Special Rights of Series C Preferred and Series D Preferred Upon Non-Approved Change of Control

In general, a Non-Approved Change of Control transaction is a change of control transaction that the Board of Directors (the "Board") has disapproved and which the Board has not facilitated by such actions as weakening or eliminating the Company's Stockholder Rights Plan. If a Non-Approved Change of Control occurs, and the Board does not offer the holders of the Series C Preferred and Series D Preferred essentially the same redemption rights that apply to an Approved Change of Control transaction: (i) the holders of the Series C Preferred would elect a majority of the Board for a specified period, (ii) the holders of the Series C Preferred and Series D Preferred would be entitled to an additional 6.25% return on the liquidation preference, compounded annually from January 1999 for the Series C Preferred and from September 1999 for the Series D Preferred, (iii) after the holders of the common stock receive an amount equivalent to the liquidation preference, the holders of the Series C Preferred and Series D Preferred would share with the holders of the common stock, on an as converted basis, in any remaining amounts available for distribution, and (iv) the Series C Preferred and Series D Preferred would accrue dividends at a maximum annual rate, compounded annually, equal to 18% of the liquidation preference.

Preferred Stock Extended at Redemption Value

2.297

THE ESTÉE LAUDER COMPANIES INC. (JUN)

(In millions, except share data)	2003	2002
$6.50 cumulative redeemable preferred stock, at redemption value	$ 360.0	$ 360.0
Minority interest	12.3	10.2
Stockholders' equity		
Common stock, $.01 par value; 650,000,000 shares Class A authorized; shares issued: 133,616,710 in 2003 and 131,567,986 in 2002; 240,000,000 shares Class B authorized; shares issued and outstanding: 107,462,533 in 2003 and 108,412,533 in 2002	2.4	2.4
Paid-in capital	293.7	268.8
Retained earnings	1,613.6	1,363.7
Accumulated other comprehensive income (loss)	(53.1)	(92.5)
	1,856.6	1,542.4
Less: Treasury stock, at cost; 13,623,060 Class A shares at June 30, 2003 and 2,377,860 Class A shares at June 30, 2002	(433.0)	(80.5)
Total stockholders' equity	$1,423.6	$1,461.9

NOTES TO CONSOLIDATED FINANCIAL STATEMENTS

Note 2 (In Part): Summary of Significant Accounting Policies

Recently Issued Accounting Standards (In Part)

In May 2003, the Financial Accounting Standards Board ("FASB") issued SFAS No. 150, "Accounting for Certain Financial Instruments with Characteristics of both Liabilities and Equity" ("SFAS No. 150"). SFAS No. 150 established standards for classifying and measuring certain financial instruments with characteristics of both liabilities and equity. It specifically requires that mandatorily redeemable instruments, instruments with repurchase obligations which embody, are indexed to, or obligate the repurchase of, the issuer's own equity shares, and instruments with obligations to issue a variable number of the issuer's own equity shares, be classified as a liability. Initial and subsequent measurements of the instruments differ based on the characteristics of each instrument and as provided for in the statement. SFAS No. 150 is effective for all freestanding financial instruments entered into or modified after May 31, 2003 and otherwise became effective at the beginning of the first interim period beginning after June 15, 2003. The Company has adopted this statement effective for all instruments entered into or modified after May 31, 2003 and will adopt the statement for any existing financial instruments in the first quarter of fiscal 2004. Based on the provisions of this statement, beginning in fiscal 2004, the Company will be classifying the $6.50 Cumulative Redeemable Preferred Stock as a liability and the related dividends will be characterized as interest expense. Restatement of financial statements for earlier years presented is not permitted. The adoption of this statement will result in the inclusion of the dividends on the preferred stock (equal to $23.4 million per year) as interest expense. While the inclusion will impact net earnings, net earnings attributable to common stock and earnings per common share will be unaffected. Given that the dividends are not deductible for income tax purposes, the inclusion of the preferred stock dividends as interest expense will cause an increase in the Company's effective tax rate. The adoption of SFAS No. 150 will have no impact on the Company's financial condition.

Note 9 (In Part): Financial Instruments

Fair Value of Financial Instruments (In Part)

The following methods and assumptions were used to estimate the fair value of each class of financial instruments for which it is practicable to estimate that value:

Cumulative Redeemable Preferred Stock

The fair value of the cumulative redeemable preferred stock is estimated utilizing a cash flow analysis at a discount rate equal to rates available for debt with terms similar to the preferred stock.

Note 12—$6.50 Cumulative Redeemable Preferred Stock, at Redemption Value

As of June 30, 2003, the Company's authorized capital stock included 23.6 million shares of preferred stock, par value $.01 per share, of which 3.6 million shares are outstanding and designated as $6.50 Cumulative Redeemable Preferred Stock. The outstanding preferred stock was issued in June 1995 in exchange for nonvoting common stock of the Company owned by The Estée Lauder 1994 Trust.

Holders of the $6.50 Cumulative Redeemable Preferred Stock are entitled to receive cumulative cash dividends at a rate of $6.50 per annum per share payable in quarterly installments. Such dividends have preference over all other dividends of stock issued by the Company. Shares are subject to mandatory redemption on June 30, 2005 at a redemption price of $100 per share. Following such date and so long as such mandatory redemption obligations have not been discharged in full, no dividends may be paid or declared upon the Class A or Class B Common Stock, or on any other capital stock ranking junior to or in parity with such $6.50 Cumulative Redeemable Preferred Stock and no shares of Class A or Class B Common Stock or such junior or parity stock may be redeemed or acquired for any consideration by the Company. Under certain circumstances, the Company may redeem the stock, in whole or in part, prior to the mandatory redemption date. Holders of such stock may put such shares to the

Company at a price of $100 per share upon the occurrence of certain events.

The Company recorded the $6.50 Cumulative Redeemable Preferred Stock at its redemption value of $360.0 million and charged this amount, net of the par value of the shares of nonvoting common stock exchanged, to stockholders' equity in fiscal 1995.

Preferred Stock Extended at Fair Value at Issuance Date

2.298

PRIMEDIA INC. (DEC)

(Dollars in thousands, except per share amounts)	2003	2002
Shareholders' deficiency:		
Series J convertible preferred stock ($.01 par value, 1,319,093 shares and 1,166,324 shares issued and outstanding, aggregate liquidation and redemption values of $164,887 and $145,791 at December 31, 2003 and 2002, respectively)	$ 164,533	$ 145,351
Common stock ($.01 par value, 350,000,000 shares authorized at December 31, 2003 and 2002 and 268,333,049 and 267,505,223 shares issued at December 31, 2003 and 2002, respectively)	2,683	2,675
Additional paid-in capital (including warrants of $31,690 at December 31, 2003 and 2002)	2,345,152	2,336,091
Accumulated deficit	(3,447,710)	(3,445,083)
Accumulated other comprehensive loss	(176)	(247)
Unearned compensation	(175)	(4,730)
Common stock in treasury, at cost (8,610,491 shares and 8,639,775 shares at December 31, 2003 and 2002, respectively)	(77,562)	(77,855)
Total shareholders' deficiency	$(1,013,255)	$(1,043,798)

NOTES TO CONSOLIDATED FINANCIAL STATEMENTS
(Dollars in thousands, except per share amounts)

2 (In Part): Summary of Significant Accounting Policies

Series J Convertible Preferred Stock ("Series J Convertible Preferred Stock")

Series J Convertible Preferred Stock was stated at fair value on the date of issuance less issuance costs. The difference between its carrying value and its redemption value is being accreted (using the interest method) by periodic charges to additional paid-in capital. The accretion is deducted in the calculation of net loss applicable to common shareholders (see Note 14).

14. Series J Convertible Preferred Stock

As of December 31, 2003 and December 31, 2002, the Company had $164,533 and $145,351 of Series J Convertible Preferred Stock outstanding, respectively. These shares are convertible at the option of the holder after one year from the date of issuance, into approximately 23,600,000 shares of the Company's common stock at a conversion price of $7 per share, subject to adjustment. Dividends on the Series J Convertible Preferred Stock accrue quarterly, at an annual rate of 12.5%, and are payable quarterly in-kind. The Company paid dividends-in-kind of 152,769 and 135,076 shares of Series J Convertible Preferred Stock valued at $19,096 and $16,884

during the years ended December 31, 2003 and 2002, respectively. The Company has the option to redeem any or all of the shares of the Series J Convertible Preferred Stock at any time for cash at 100% of the liquidation preference of each share being redeemed. On any dividend payment date, the Company has the option to exchange, in whole but not in part, the Series J Convertible Preferred Stock into 12.5% Class J Subordinated Notes. The Company's ability to redeem or exchange the Series J Convertible Preferred Stock into debt is subject to the approval of a majority of the independent directors.

ADDITIONAL PAID-IN CAPITAL

2.299   Table 2-37 lists the balance sheet captions used to describe additional paid-in capital. Examples of descriptive captions for additional paid-in capital are shown in this section in connection with discussions of the other components of stockholders' equity.

2.300

**TABLE 2-37: ADDITIONAL PAID-IN CAPITAL—
                     CAPTION TITLE**

	2003	2002	2001	2000
Additional paid-in capital..................	313	305	293	281
Capital in excess of par or stated value...	111	113	118	123
Paid-in capital.................................	59	57	56	59
Additional capital, or other capital...	23	23	28	27
Capital surplus................................	17	17	17	20
Paid-in surplus................................	—	—	2	1
Other captions................................	12	14	13	11
	535	529	527	522
No additional paid-in capital account..	65	71	73	78
Total Companies..........................	**600**	**600**	**600**	**600**

RETAINED EARNINGS

2.301   Table 2-38 indicates that most of the survey companies use the term *retained earnings*. Examples of descriptive captions used for retained earnings are shown in connection with discussions of other components of stockholders' equity.

2.302

TABLE 2-38: RETAINED EARNINGS—CAPTION TITLE

	2003	2002	2001	2000
Retained earnings.........................	461	457	471	482
Retained earnings with additional words...	4	4	6	4
Earnings with additional words.....	24	24	22	27
Income with additional words.......	8	9	10	10
Earned surplus..............................	—	—	1	2
Retained earnings (deficit)............	23	36	31	26
Accumulated deficit.......................	78	68	56	49
Other...	2	2	3	—
Total Companies..........................	**600**	**600**	**600**	**600**

ACCUMULATED OTHER COMPREHENSIVE INCOME

2.303   SFAS No. 130, *Reporting Comprehensive Income*, requires that a separate caption for accumulated other comprehensive income be presented in the equity section of a balance sheet. Accumulated balances, by component, included in accumulated other comprehensive income must be disclosed either in the equity section of the balance sheet, or in a statement of changes of stockholders' equity, or in notes to the financial statements.

2.304   Table 2-39 summarizes the captions used to describe comprehensive income in the stockholders' equity section of the balance sheet.

2.305   Table 2-40 shows where accumulated component balances are presented.

2.306   Examples showing the disclosure of accumulated balances for other comprehensive income items follow.

2.307

**TABLE 2-39: ACCUMULATED OTHER
                     COMPREHENSIVE INCOME—
                     BALANCE SHEET CAPTION**

	2003	2002	2001	2000
Accumulated other comprehensive loss...................	245	304	262	155
Accumulated other comprehensive income (loss)....	160	116	91	120
Accumulated other comprehensive income.............	99	91	131	144
Accumulated other non-owner changes in equity.....................	7	5	5	3
Other captions.............................	13	10	13	16
	524	526	502	438
Accumulated balance by component presented...............	50	49	51	67
	574	575	553	505
No accumulated other comprehensive income.............	26	25	47	95
Total Companies.........................	**600**	**600**	**600**	**600**
	Number of Companies			
Accumulated Balances by Component Presented				
Cumulative translation adjustments..............................	47	35	44	93
Minimum pension liability adjustments..............................	39	31	21	31
Changes in fair value of derivatives................................	29	19	15	1
Unrealized losses/gains on certain investments...............	25	25	26	38

2.308

TABLE 2-40: ACCUMULATED OTHER COMPREHENSIVE INCOME— PRESENTATION OF COMPONENT BALANCES

	2003	2002	2001	2000
Notes to financial statements..........	278	215	186	128
Statement of changes in stockholders' equity....................	113	191	194	219
Stockholders' equity section of the balance sheet............................	50	49	51	60
Statement of comprehensive income..	8	7	4	1
Component balances not presented..................................	125	113	118	97
	574	575	553	505
No accumulated other comprehensive income...............	26	25	47	95
Total Companies..........................	**600**	**600**	**600**	**600**

Notes to Financial Statements

2.309

HERSHEY FOODS CORPORATION (DEC)

(In thousands of dollars)	2003	2002
Stockholders' equity:		
Preferred stock, shares issued: none in 2003 and 2002	$ —	$ —
Common stock, shares issued: 149,528,776 in 2003 and 149,528,564 in 2002	149,528	149,528
Class B common stock, shares issued: 30,422,096 in 2003 and 30,422,308 in 2002	30,422	30,422
Additional paid-in capital	4,034	593
Unearned ESOP compensation	(9,580)	(12,774)
Retained earnings	3,263,988	2,991,090
Treasury—common stock shares, at cost: 50,421,139 in 2003 and 45,730,735 in 2002	(2,147,441)	(1,808,227)
Accumulated other comprehensive (loss) income	(11,085)	21,071
Total stockholders' equity	$ 1,279,866	$ 1,371,703

1 (In Part): Summary of Significant Accounting Policies

Comprehensive Income

Comprehensive income (loss) is reported on the Consolidated Statements of Stockholders' Equity and accumulated other comprehensive income (loss) is reported on the Consolidated Balance Sheets. Additional information regarding comprehensive income is contained in Note 8, Comprehensive Income.

Results of operations for foreign entities are translated using the average exchange rates during the period. For foreign entities, assets and liabilities are translated to U.S. dollars using the exchange rates in effect at the balance sheet date. Resulting translation adjustments are recorded as a component of other comprehensive income (loss), "Foreign Currency Translation Adjustments."

A minimum pension liability adjustment is required when the actuarial present value of accumulated pension plan benefits exceeds plan assets and accrued pension liabilities, less allowable intangible assets. Minimum pension liability adjustments, net of income taxes, are recorded as a component of other comprehensive income (loss), "Minimum Pension Liability Adjustments."

Gains and losses on cash flow hedging derivatives, to the extent effective, are included in other comprehensive income (loss). Reclassification adjustments reflecting such gains and losses are ratably recorded in income in the same period as the hedged items affect earnings. Additional information with regard to accounting policies associated with derivative instruments is contained in Note 7, Derivative Instruments and Hedging Activities.

8. Comprehensive Income

A summary of the components of comprehensive income is as follows:

(In thousands of dollars)	2003	2002	2001
Net income	$457,584	$403,578	$207,156
Other comprehensive income (loss):			
Foreign currency translation adjustments	40,938	(16,530)	(6,745)
Minimum pension liability adjustments, net of tax	(942)	34,899	(34,219)
(Losses) gains on cash flow hedging derivatives, net of tax	(20,239)	106,748	(7,764)
Add: Reclassification adjustments, net of tax	(51,913)	(17,914)	19,312
Other comprehensive income (loss)	(32,156)	107,203	(29,416)
Comprehensive income	$425,428	$510,781	$177,740

Comprehensive income is included on the Consolidated Statements of Stockholders' Equity. The components of accumulated other comprehensive income (loss) as shown on the Consolidated Balance Sheets are as follows:

(In thousands of dollars)	Foreign Currency Translation Adjustments	Minimum Pension Liability Adjustments	Gains (Losses) on Cash Flow Hedging Derivatives	Accumulated Other Comprehensive Income (Loss)
Balance as of January 1, 2001	$(55,800)	$ (916)	$ —	$(56,716)
Transition adjustment (loss), net of a tax benefit of $41,756	—	—	(70,191)	(70,191)
Current period credit (charge), gross	(6,745)	(57,127)	99,565	35,693
Income tax benefit (expense)	—	22,908	(37,138)	(14,230)
Reclassification adjustment charge, gross	—	—	30,800	30,800
Income tax (expense)	—	—	(11,488)	(11,488)
Balance as of December 31, 2001	(62,545)	(35,135)	11,548	(86,132)
Current period (charge) credit, gross	(16,530)	58,261	168,463	210,194
Income tax (expense)	—	(23,362)	(61,715)	(85,077)
Reclassification adjustment (credit), gross	—	—	(28,300)	(28,300)
Income tax benefit	—	—	10,386	10,386
Balance as of December 31, 2002	(79,075)	(236)	100,382	21,071
Current period credit (charge), gross	40,938	(1,565)	(31,971)	7,402
Income tax benefit	—	623	11,732	12,355
Reclassification adjustment (credit), gross	—	—	(82,012)	(82,012)
Income tax benefit	—	—	30,099	30,099
Balance as of December 31, 2003	$(38,137)	$ (1,178)	$ 28,230	$(11,085)

2.310

PERKINELMER, INC. (DEC)

(In thousands except share and per share data)	2003	2002
Stockholders' equity:		
Preferred stock—$1 par value per share, authorized 1,000,000 shares; none issued or outstanding	$ —	$ —
Common stock—$1 par value per share, authorized 300,000,000 shares; issued 145,101,000 shares; and 126,909,000 and 125,854,000 shares outstanding in 2003 and 2002, respectively	145,101	145,101
Capital in excess of par value	681,550	679,929
Unearned compensation	(3,494)	(5,890)
Retained earnings	672,616	655,066
Accumulated other comprehensive income (loss)	30,908	(31,865)
Cost of shares held in treasury—18,192,000 shares and 19,247,000 shares in 2003 and 2002, respectively	(177,631)	(189,997)
Total stockholders' equity	$1,349,050	$1,252,344

NOTES TO CONSOLIDATED FINANCIAL STATEMENTS

*Note 1 (In Part): Nature of Operations and
Accounting Policies*

Comprehensive Income (Loss)

Comprehensive income (loss) is defined as net income or
loss and other changes in stockholders' equity from transactions and other events from sources other than stockholders.
Comprehensive income (loss) is reflected in the Consolidated
Statements of Stockholders' Equity.

Note 19 (In Part): Stockholders' Equity

Comprehensive Income

The components of accumulated other comprehensive (loss)
income, net of tax were as follows:

(In thousands)	Foreign Currency Translation Adjustment	Change in Minimum Liability of Pension	Unrealized Gains (Losses) on Derivative Instruments	Unrealized Gains (Losses) on Securities	Accumulated Other Comprehensive (Loss) Income
Balance, January 1, 2001	$(39,945)	$ —	$ —	$ 903	$(39,042)
Current year change	(20,976)	—	1,407	(2,329)	(21,898)
Balance, December 30, 2001	(60,921)	—	1,407	(1,426)	(60,940)
Current year change	34,350	(3,928)	(1,407)	60	29,075
Balance, December 29, 2002	(26,571)	(3,928)	—	(1,366)	(31,865)
Current year change	70,475	(9,110)	—	1,408	62,773
Balance, December 28, 2003	$ 43,904	$(13,038)	$ —	$ 42	$ 30,908

The tax effects related to each component of other comprehensive income (loss) were as follows:

(In thousands)	Tax Before Amount	(Provision) Benefit	After-Tax Amount
2003			
Foreign currency translation adjustments	$70,475	$ —	$70,475
Change in minimum liability of pension	(9,110)	—	(9,110)
Unrealized gains (losses) on securities	2,166	(758)	1,408
Other comprehensive income	$63,531	$ (758)	$62,773
2002			
Foreign currency translation adjustments	$34,350	$ —	$34,350
Change in minimum liability of pension	(5,611)	1,683	(3,928)
Unrealized losses on derivative instruments	(1,407)	—	(1,407)
Unrealized gains (losses) on securities	104	(44)	60
Reclassification adjustments	(869)	452	(417)
Other comprehensive income	$26,567	$2,091	$28,658

Statement of Changes in Stockholders' Equity

2.311

HARRIS CORPORATION (JUN)

Consolidated Statement of Comprehensive Income and Shareholders' Equity

| | | | | | Accumulated Other Comprehensive Income (Loss) | | | |
| | | | | | Net Unrealized Gain (Loss) From | | | |
(In millions except per share amounts)	Common Stock	Other Capital	Retained Earnings	Unearned Comp.	Marketable Securities	Hedging Derivatives	Currency Translation	Total
Balance at June 30, 2000	$69.0	$228.4	$864.1	$(3.2)	$ 232.5	$ —	$(16.5)	$1,374.3
Net income	—	—	21.4	—	—	—	—	21.4
Foreign currency translation	—	—	—	—	—	—	(12.0)	(12.0)
Net unrealized loss on hedging derivatives net of income taxes of $(0.6)	—	—	—	—	—	(1.0)	—	(1.0)
Net unrealized loss on securities net of income taxes of $(97.1)	—	—	—	—	(165.4)	—	—	(165.4)
Comprehensive loss								(157.0)
Shares issued under Stock Incentive Plan (80,245 shares)	0.1	1.9	—	—	—	—	—	2.0
Shares granted under Stock Incentive Plans (57,500 shares)	—	1.6	—	(1.6)	—	—	—	—
Compensation expense	—	—	—	1.1	—	—	—	1.1
Options granted in connection with the WavTrace acquisition (179,900 shares)	—	4.9	—	(3.7)	—	—	—	1.2
Termination and award of shares granted under Stock Incentive Plans (73,803 shares)	(0.1)	(3.7)	—	2.9	—	—	—	(0.9)
Purchase and retirement of common stock for treasury (3,175,800 shares)	(3.2)	(19.1)	(69.9)	—	—	—	—	(92.2)
Cash dividends ($.20 per share)	—	—	(13.3)	—	—	—	—	(13.3)
Balance at June 29, 2001	$65.8	$214.0	$802.3	$(4.5)	$ 67.1	$(1.0)	$(28.5)	$1,115.2

(continued)

| (In millions except per share amounts) | Common Stock | Other Capital | Retained Earnings | Unearned Comp. | Accumulated Other Comprehensive Income (Loss) | | | Total |
| | | | | | Net Unrealized Gain (Loss) From | | | |
					Marketable Securities	Hedging Derivatives	Currency Translation	
Balance at June 29, 2001	$65.8	$214.0	$802.3	$(4.5)	$ 67.1	$(1.0)	$(28.5)	$1,115.2
Net income	—	—	82.6	—	—	—	—	82.6
Foreign currency translation	—	—	—	—	—	—	5.7	5.7
Net unrealized gain on hedging derivatives net of income taxes of $0.7	—	—	—	—	—	1.1	—	1.1
Net unrealized loss on securities net of income taxes of $(31.9)	—	—	—	—	(54.3)	—	—	(54.3)
Comprehensive income								35.1
Shares issued under Stock Incentive Plan (458,719 shares)	0.5	8.9	—	—	—	—	—	9.4
Shares granted under Stock Incentive Plans (64,500 shares)	—	1.9	—	(1.9)	—	—	—	—
Compensation expense	—	—	—	3.6	—	—	—	3.6
Termination and award of shares granted under Stock Incentive Plans (26,782 shares)	—	(0.9)	—	0.7	—	—	—	(0.2)
Cash dividends ($.20 per share)	—	—	(13.2)	—	—	—	—	(13.2)
Balance at June 28, 2002	66.3	223.9	871.7	(2.1)	12.8	0.1	(22.8)	1,149.9
Net income	—	—	59.5	—	—	—	—	59.5
Foreign currency translation	—	—	—	—	—	—	9.8	9.8
Net unrealized gain on hedging derivatives net of income taxes of $(0.1)	—	—	—	—	—	(0.2)	—	(0.2)
Net unrealized loss on securities net of income taxes of $(7.4)	—	—	—	—	(12.7)	—	—	(12.7)
Comprehensive income								56.4
Shares issued under Stock Incentive Plan (112,975 shares)	0.1	2.2	—	—	—	—	—	2.3
Shares granted under Stock Incentive Plans (177,000 shares)	0.2	5.4	—	(5.6)	—	—	—	—
Compensation expense	—	—	—	2.5	—	—	—	2.5
Termination and award of shares granted under Stock Incentive Plans (23,783 shares)	—	(0.7)	—	—	—	—	—	(0.7)
Purchase and retirement of common stock for treasury (217,500 shares)	(0.2)	(1.1)	(4.7)	—	—	—	—	(6.0)
Cash dividends ($.32 per share)	—	—	(21.2)	—	—	—	—	(21.2)
Balance at June 27,2003	$66.4	$229.7	$905.3	$(5.2)	$ 0.1	$(0.1)	$(13.0)	$1,183.2

2.312

LEAR CORPORATION (DEC)

Consolidated Statements of Stockholders' Equity

(In millions except share data)	2003	2002	2001
Common stock			
Balance at beginning and end of period	$ 0.7	$ 0.7	$ 0.7
Additional paid-in capital			
Balance at beginning of period	$ 943.6	$ 888.3	$ 874.1
Stock options exercised	66.4	47.4	10.1
Tax benefit of stock options exercised	17.5	7.9	4.1
Settlement of stock-based compensation	0.2	—	—
Balance at end of period	$1,027.7	$ 943.6	$ 888.3
Notes receivable from sale of common stock			
Balance at beginning of period	$ —	$ (0.1)	$ (0.1)
Notes receivable payment received	—	0.1	—
Balance at end of period	$ —	$ —	$ (0.1)
Treasury stock			
Balance at beginning of period	$ (111.4)	$ (111.4)	$ (111.4)
Purchases of 31,800 shares at an average price of $34.07 per share	(1.1)	—	—
Issuance of 102,828 shares at an average price of $17.08 per share in settlement of stock-based compensation	1.7	—	—
Balance at end of period	$ (110.8)	$ (111.4)	$ (111.4)
Retained earnings			
Balance at beginning of period	$1,075.8	$1,062.8	$1,036.5
Net income	380.5	13.0	26.3
Dividends	(14.5)	—	—
Balance at end of period	$1,441.8	$1,075.8	$1,062.8
Accumulated other comprehensive loss			
Minimum pension liability			
Balance at beginning of period	$ (48.9)	$ (20.6)	$ (1.5)
Minimum pension liability adjustments	(13.3)	(28.3)	(19.1)
Balance at end of period	$ (62.2)	$ (48.9)	$ (20.6)
Derivative instruments and hedging activities			
Balance at beginning of period	$ (26.5)	$ (13.1)	$ —
Derivative instruments and hedging activities adjustments	12.8	(13.4)	(13.1)
Balance at end of period	$ (13.7)	$ (26.5)	$ (13.1)
Cumulative translation adjustments			
Balance at beginning of period	$ (187.5)	$ (255.1)	$ (198.1)
Cumulative translation adjustments	126.0	67.6	(57.0)
Balance at end of period	$ (61.5)	$ (187.5)	$ (255.1)
Deferred income tax asset			
Balance at beginning of period	$ 16.5	$ 7.6	$ 0.6
Deferred income tax asset adjustments	19.0	8.9	7.0
Balance at end of period	$ 35.5	$ 16.5	$ 7.6
Accumulated other comprehensive loss	$ (101.9)	$ (246.4)	$ (281.2)
Total stockholders' equity	$2,257.5	$1,662.3	$1,559.1

(continued)

ATT-SEC 2.312

(In millions except share data)	2003	2002	2001
Comprehensive income (loss)			
Net income	$ 380.5	$ 13.0	$ 26.3
Minimum pension liability adjustments	(13.3)	(28.3)	(19.1)
Derivative instruments and hedging activities adjustments	12.8	(13.4)	(13.1)
Cumulative translation adjustments	126.0	67.6	(57.0)
Deferred income tax asset adjustments	19.0	8.9	7.0
Comprehensive income (loss)	$ 525.0	$ 47.8	$ (55.9)

Equity Section of Balance Sheet

2.313

PEPSIAMERICAS, INC. (DEC)

(In millions)	2003	2002
Shareholders' equity:		
Preferred stock ($0.01 par value, 12.5 million shares authorized; no shares issued)	$ —	$ —
Common stock ($0.01 par value, 350 million shares authorized; 167.6 million shares issued—2003 and 2002)	1,534.5	1,538.7
Retained income	439.8	288.0
Unearned stock-based compensation	(8.2)	(8.6)
Accumulated other comprehensive loss:		
Cumulative translation adjustment	(0.4)	(9.2)
Net unrealized investment and cash flow hedging losses, net	—	(9.8)
Minimum pension liability adjustment	(29.0)	(27.9)
Accumulated other comprehensive loss	(29.4)	(46.9)
Treasury stock (23.8 million shares—2003 and 20 million shares—2002)	(371.6)	(322.6)
Total shareholders' equity	$1,565.1	$1,448.6

NOTES TO CONSOLIDATED FINANCIAL STATEMENTS

20. Other Comprehensive Income (Loss)

The components of accumulated other comprehensive income (loss) are as follows (in millions):

	Foreign Currency Translation	Net Unrealized Gains (Losses) in Investments	Net Unrealized Gains (Losses) on Derivatives	Minimum Pension Liability Adjustment	Other Comprehensive Income
As of fiscal year end 2000	$(30.3)	$ 1.6	$ —	$ —	$(28.7)
Other comprehensive income (loss)	5.2	(1.5)	(4.8)	(4.1)	(5.2)
As of fiscal year end 2001	(25.1)	0.1	(4.8)	(4.1)	(33.9)
Other comprehensive income (loss)	15.9	(5.0)	(0.1)	(23.8)	(13.0)
As of fiscal year end 2002	(9.2)	(4.9)	(4.9)	(27.9)	(46.9)
Other comprehensive income (loss)	8.8	2.5	7.3	(1.1)	17.5
As of fiscal year end 2003	$ (0.4)	$(2.4)	$ 2.4	$(29.0)	$(29.4)

Unrealized gains (losses) on derivatives in shown net of re-classifications into net income of $0.1 million, $(4.9) million, and $(0.7) million in fiscal year 2003, 2002 and 2001, respectively. In fiscal year 2001, $1.0 million was recorded associated with the adoption of SFAS No. 133, "Accounting for Derivative Instruments and Hedging Activities," as amended by SFAS Nos. 137 and 138.

Unrealized gains (losses) in investments is shown net of income tax (expense) benefit of $(1.5) million, $2.8 million, and $0.8 million in fiscal year 2003, 2002 and 2001, respectively. Unrealized gains (losses) on derivatives is shown net of income tax (expense) benefit of $(4.4) million, $(0.2) million, and $3.1 million in fiscal year 2003, 2002 and 2001, respectively. The minimum pension liability adjustment is shown net of income tax (expense) benefit of $0.2 million, $(15.1) million, and $(2.6) million at the end of fiscal year 2003, 2002 and 2001 respectively.

2.314

WM. WRIGLEY JR. COMPANY (DEC)

(In thousands of dollars and shares)	2003	2002
Stockholders' equity:		
Preferred stock—no par value		
Authorized: 20,000 shares		
Issued: none		
Common stock—no par value		
Common stock		
Authorized: 400,000 shares		
Issued: 2003—191,964 shares;		
2002—190,898 shares	$ 12,790	$ 12,719
Class B common stock—convertible		
Authorized: 80,000 shares		
Issued and outstanding: 2003—40,477		
shares; 2002—41,543 shares	2,706	2,777
Additional paid-in capital	8,342	4,209
Retained earnings	2,152,566	1,902,990
Common stock in treasury, at cost		
(2003—7,581 shares; 2002—		
7,385 shares)	(320,450)	(297,156)
Accumulated other comprehensive income:		
Foreign currency translation adjustment	(42,692)	(112,303)
Loss on derivative contracts	(1,902)	(853)
Unrealized holding gains on marketable		
equity securities	9,461	10,193
	(35,133)	(102,963)
Total stockholders' equity	$1,820,821	$1,522,576

TREASURY STOCK

2.315   APB Opinion No. 6, *Status of Accounting Research Bulletins*, discusses the balance sheet presentation of treasury stock. As shown in Table 2-41, the prevalent balance sheet presentation of treasury stock is to show the cost of treasury stock as a reduction of stockholders' equity.

2.316   Examples of treasury stock presentations follow.

2.317

TABLE 2-41:   TREASURY STOCK—BALANCE SHEET PRESENTATION

	2003	2002	2001	2000
Common Stock				
Cost of treasury stock shown as stockholders' equity deduction......	370	365	362	372
Cost of treasury stock deducted from stock of the same class................	14	16	10	12
Par or stated value of treasury stock deducted from issued stock of the same class....................................	12	14	19	. 23
Other..	2	1	6	3
Total Presentations....................	398	396	397	410
Preferred Stock				
Cost of treasury stock shown as stockholders' equity deduction......	2	1	2	3
Par or stated value of treasury stock deducted from issued stock of the same class....................................	—	2	1	1
Other..	2	2	2	2
Total Presentations....................	4	5	5	6
Number of Companies				
Disclosing treasury stock..................	399	397	396	410
Not disclosing treasury stock.............	201	203	204	190
Total Companies...........................	600	600	600	600

Cost of Treasury Stock Shown as Reduction of Stockholders' Equity

2.318

CDW CORPORATION (DEC)

(In thousands)	2003	2002
Shareholders' equity:		
Preferred shares, $1.00 par value; 5,000 shares authorized; none issued	$ —	$ —
Common shares, $.01 par value; 500,000 shares authorized; 90,903 and 89,669 shares issued, respectively	909	897
Paid-in capital	408,413	346,054
Retained earnings	956,867	806,548
Unearned compensation	(269)	(837)
Accumulated other comprehensive income	183	3
	1,366,103	1,152,665
Less cost of common shares in treasury; 7,561 shares and 5,708 shares, respectively	(304,919)	(228,595)
Total shareholders' equity	$1,061,184	$ 924,070

NOTES TO CONSOLIDATED FINANCIAL STATEMENTS

3 (In Part): Summary of Significant Accounting Policies

Treasury Shares

We intend to hold repurchased shares in treasury for general corporate purposes, including issuances under various employee stock option plans. We account for the treasury shares using the cost method.

18. Share Repurchase Programs

In January 2001, our Board of Directors authorized the purchase of up to 5,000,000 shares of our common stock. From January 2001 though September 2002, we purchased the 5,000,000 shares authorized to be repurchased at a total cost of $204.6 million (an average price of $40.92 per share).

In July 2002, our Board of Directors authorized a new share repurchase program of up to 2,500,000 shares of our common stock. These purchases may be made from time to time in both the open market and private transactions, as conditions warrant. This program will remain in effect through July 2004 unless earlier terminated by the Board or completed. Under this repurchase program, we purchased 1,852,424 shares of our common stock at a total cost of $76.3 million (an average price of $41.20 per share) during the year ended December 31, 2003. From July 2002 through December 31, 2003, we purchased a total of 2,360,800 shares of our common stock under this program at a total cost of $98.2 million (an average price of $41.59 per share).

In July 2003, our Board of Directors authorized a new share repurchase program of up to 2,500,000 shares of our common stock. These purchases may be made from time to time in both open market and private transactions, as conditions warrant. This new repurchase program is expected to remain in effect through July 2005, unless earlier terminated by the Board or completed. During the year ended December 31, 2003, no purchases were made under this new program.

Repurchased shares are held in treasury pending use for general corporate purposes, including issuances under various employee stock plans.

2.319

DELL INC. (JAN)

(In millions)	2004	2003
Stockholders' equity:		
Preferred stock and capital in excess of $.01 par value; shares issued and outstanding: none	$ —	$ —
Common stock and capital in excess of $0.1 par value; shares authorized: 7,000; shares issued: 2,721 and 2,681, respectively	6,823	6,018
Treasury stock, at cost; 165 and 102 shares, respectively	(6,539)	(4,539)
Retained earnings	6,131	3,486
Other comprehensive loss	(83)	(33)
Other	(52)	(59)
Total stockholders' equity	$ 6,280	$ 4,873

NOTES TO CONSOLIDATED FINANCIAL STATEMENTS

Note 1 (In Part): Description of Business and Summary of Significant Accounting Policies

Treasury Stock

Effective with the beginning of the second quarter of fiscal 2002, Dell began holding repurchased shares of its common stock as treasury stock. Prior to that date, Dell retired all such repurchased shares which were recorded as a reduction to retained earnings. Dell accounts for treasury stock under the cost method and includes treasury stock as a component of stockholders' equity.

Note 4 (In Part): Capitalization

Common Stock

Share Repurchase Program

Dell has a share repurchase program that authorizes the purchase of up to 1.25 billion shares of common stock to manage the dilution resulting from shares issued under Dell's employee stock plans. As of the end of fiscal 2004, Dell had cumulatively repurchased 1.1 billion shares for an aggregate cost of approximately $14 billion. During fiscal 2004, Dell repurchased 63 million shares of common stock for an aggregate cost of $2.0 billion.

Dell historically utilized equity instrument contracts to facilitate its repurchase of common stock; however, all remaining put and call contracts were settled in full during the fourth quarter of fiscal 2003.

Par Value of Treasury Stock Deducted From Issued Stock

2.320

WYETH (DEC)

(In thousands except share and per share amounts)	2003	2002
Stockholders' equity		
$2.00 convertible preferred stock, par value $2.50 per share; 5,000,000 shares authorized	$ 42	$ 46
Common stock, par value $0.33⅓ per share; 2,400,000,000 shares authorized (1,332,451,733 and 1,326,055,415 issued and outstanding, net of 89,930,211 and 96,276,705 treasury shares at par, for 2003 and 2002, respectively)	444,151	442,019
Additional paid-in capital	4,764,390	4,582,773
Retained earnings	4,112,285	3,286,645
Accumulated other comprehensive loss	(26,487)	(155,571)
Total stockholders' equity	$9,294,381	$8,155,912

NOTES TO CONSOLIDATED FINANCIAL STATEMENTS

11 (In Part): Capital Stock

The Company has a common stock repurchase program under which the Company is authorized to repurchase common shares. The Company made no repurchases during 2003 but did repurchase 2,000,000 shares in 2002. At December 31, 2003, the Company was authorized to repurchase 4,492,460 common shares in the future.

Treasury stock is accounted for using the par value method. Shares of common stock held in treasury at December 31, 2003 and 2002 were 89,930,211 and 96,276,705, respectively. The Company has not retired any shares held in treasury during 2003 and 2002.

OTHER ACCOUNTS SHOWN IN STOCKHOLDERS' EQUITY SECTION

2.321   Many of the survey companies present accounts other than Capital Stock, Additional Paid-In Capital, Retained Earnings, Accumulated Other Comprehensive Income, and Treasury Stock in the stockholders' equity section of the balance sheet. Other stockholders' equity accounts appearing on the balance sheets of the survey companies include, but are not limited to, guarantees of ESOP debt, unearned or deferred compensation related to employee stock award plans, and amounts owed to a company by employees for loans to buy company stock.

2.322   Table 2-42 shows the number of survey company balance sheets presenting other stockholders' equity accounts. Cumulative translation adjustments, unrealized losses/gains on certain investments, and a minimum pension liability adjustments are all *other comprehensive income*

items which are included in Table 2-39 under "Accumulated Balances by Component Presented."

2.323   236 survey companies disclosed that stock purchase rights have been distributed to common shareholders. The rights enable the holder to purchase additional equity in a company should an outside party acquire or tender for a substantial minority interest in the subject company. Such rights usually do not appear on the balance sheet.

2.324   Examples showing the presentation of other stockholders' equity accounts follow.

2.325

TABLE 2-42: OTHER STOCKHOLDERS' EQUITY ACCOUNTS

	Number of Companies			
	2003	2002	2001	2000
Unearned compensation.......	194	169	151	145
Guarantees of ESOP debt.....	26	32	32	37
Receivables from sale of stock.................................	23	25	25	22
Warrants.................................	23	17	20	19
Employee benefit trusts.........	18	20	20	25

Unearned Compensation Relating to Stock Award Plans

2.326

THE GILLETTE COMPANY (DEC)

(Millions, except per share amount)	2003	2002
Stockholders' equity		
Common stock, par value $1 per share Authorized: 2,320 shares Issued 2003—1,374 shares; 2002—1,370 shares	$1,374	$1,370
Additional paid-in capital	1,273	1,197
Earnings reinvested in the business	7,333	6,608
Accumulated other comprehensive loss	(1,088)	(1,523)
Treasury stock, at cost: 2003—367 shares; 2002—326 shares	(6,665)	(5,392)
Deferred stock-based compensation	(3)	—
Total stockholders' equity	$2,224	$2,260

NOTES TO CONSOLIDATED FINANCIAL STATEMENTS

13 (In Part): Stock Compensation Plan and Capital Stock

Other Stock-Based Compensation

Stock Appreciation Rights (SARs) were awarded to the Chairman and Chief Executive Officer (CEO) under an August 2003 amendment to his employment agreement and represented the right to the appreciation in 1 million shares of the Company's common stock for the period from June 19, 2003, through January 2, 2004. By its terms, the SARs were automatically converted into approximately 108,480 stock units valued at the fair market value of the Company's common stock on January 2, 2004, ($36.32) for a total value of $4 million. Of this, $1 million was earned and recorded as compensation cost in the Company's financial statements in the year ended December 31, 2003. The stock units earn dividend equivalent units and are subject to market risk until paid. Subject to contingencies, the stock units vest on January 19, 2005, and would be forfeited if the Chairman and CEO does not remain with the Company through the vesting date. The stock units are payable in cash, based upon the fair market value of the Company's common stock on their payment date, one year from the Chairman and CEO's retirement.

2.327

GUIDANT CORPORATION (DEC)

(In millions, except share data)	2003	2002
Shareholders' equity		
Preferred stock:		
Authorized shares: 50,000,000		
Issued shares: none	$ —	$ —
Common stock, no par value:		
Authorized shares: 1,000,000,000		
Issued shares: 312,129,000 (2003)		
308,992,000 (2002)	301.5	226.1
Additional paid-in capital	242.4	200.7
Retained earnings	2,258.9	2,002.3
Deferred cost, ESOP	(17.1)	(24.2)
Unearned compensation	(25.2)	—
Treasury stock, at cost:		
Shares: 3,158,000 (2003)		
2,388,000 (2002)	(171.2)	(92.0)
Accumulated other comprehensive income	124.0	8.9
Total shareholders' equity	$2,713.3	$2,321.8

NOTES TO CONSOLIDATED FINANCIAL STATEMENTS (In millions, except per share data)

Note 5 (In Part): Stock Plans

The Company may periodically grant nonqualified stock options and restricted stock grants to outside members of its Board of Directors and consultants and may grant incentive stock options, nonqualified stock options, performance shares and restricted stock grants to employees, including executive officers of the Company. Grants to employees are consistent with Guidant's commitment to recognize and re-

ward employees and enable them to participate as shareholders.

• • • • • •

In February 2003, Guidant's Board of Directors authorized the issuance of approximately 2.3 million restricted shares of common stock (US) and restricted stock units (outside the US) to over 2,000 employees. Restricted stock awards are expensed ratably over the vesting period. Restricted stock awards granted to certain executive officers were scheduled to vest over six years. Awards granted to other employees were scheduled to vest over three years. Grants may vest earlier upon a qualifying disability, death, retirement or change in control. This grant includes a performance element that allowed vesting to accelerate when certain Guidant share price performance measures were met. Specifically, 1/3 of the general grants vested upon achievement of 25%, 50% and 75% appreciation of the 60-day moving average stock price from the date of grant ($34.37 on February 18, 2003). Portions of the executive officer grants accelerated from six years to three years under this same performance measure. Guidant recorded $78.7 million of unearned compensation in conjunction with this grant, representing the fair value of restricted stock awards on the date of grant. Approximately two-thirds of the share price appreciation targets were achieved and expensed in 2003. The first performance measure was met in July 2003 and the second measure was met in December 2003. The final share price appreciation target was achieved in January 2004. Unearned compensation will be recognized as compensation expense ratably over the remaining vesting periods. The related compensation expense totaled $53.5 million for the year ended December 31, 2003.

Guarantees of ESOP Debt

2.328

ANHEUSER-BUSCH COMPANIES, INC. (DEC)

(In millions)	2003	2002
Total current liabilities	$ 1,857.2	$ 1,787.7
Postretirement benefits	470.4	474.2
Debt	7,285.4	6,603.2
Deferred income taxes	1,462.1	1,345.1
Other long-term liabilities	902.7	857.0
Shareholders equity:		
Common stock, $1.00 par value, authorized 1.6 billion shares	1,457.9	1,453.4
Capital in excess of par value	1,194.0	1,024.5
Retained earnings	13,935.4	12,544.0
Treasury stock, at cost	(12,939.0)	(11,008.6)
Accumulated other comprehensive loss	(890.3)	(870.7)
ESOP debt guarantee	(46.3)	(90.3)
Total shareholders equity	2,711.7	3,052.3
Commitments and contingencies	—	—
Total liabilities and shareholders equity	$ 14,689.5	$ 14,119.5

NOTES TO CONSOLIDATED FINANCIAL STATEMENTS

4 (In Part): Debt

The company uses SEC shelf registrations for debt issuance efficiency and flexibility, and currently has $1.1 billion in registered debt available for issuance. Gains or losses on debt redemptions (either individually or in the aggregate) were not material for any year presented.

Debt at December 31 consisted of the following (in millions):

	2003	2002
U.S. dollar notes due 2006 to 2023, interest rates from 4.375% to 7.5%	$2,929.9	$2,100.0
U.S. dollar debentures due 2009 to 2043, interest rates from 5.95% to 9.0%	2,950.0	3,150.0
EuroNotes due 2004 to 2006, interest rates from 4.51% to 6.5%	351.0	351.0
Medium-term notes due 2010, interest rate 5.625%	200.0	200.0
Commercial paper, interest rates of 1.00% and 1.24%, respectively, at year-end	526.4	412.9
Industrial revenue bonds due 2006 to 2038, interest rates from 4.6% to 7.4%	270.8	270.1
ESOP note guarantee due 2004, interest rate 8.25%	46.3	90.3
Miscellaneous items	33.5	48.0
Unamortized debt discounts	(22.5)	(19.1)
Total debt	$7,285.4	$6,603.2

6. Employee Stock Ownership Plans

In 1989, the company added Employee Stock Ownership Plans (ESOPs) to its existing Deferred Income Stock Purchase and Savings Plans (401(k) plans). Most regular employees are eligible for participation in the ESOPs. The ESOPs initially borrowed $500 million for a 15-year term at an interest rate of 8.25% and used the proceeds to buy approximately 45.4 million shares of common stock from the company at a then market price of $11.03 per share. ESOP shares are being allocated to participants over the 15-year period as contributions are made to the plans. The ESOPs purchased an additional 400,000 shares from the company using proceeds from the sale of spin-off-related Earthgrains shares in 1996. Of this 45.8 million total shares purchased, 44.9 million shares have been allocated to plan participants through December 31, 2003.

ESOP cash contributions and expense recorded during the year are determined by several factors, including the market price of Anheuser-Busch common stock, number of shares allocated to participants, debt service requirements, dividends on unallocated shares and the company's matching contribution. Over the 15-year life of the ESOPs, total expense recognized will equal total cash contributions made by the company for ESOP debt service. The company guarantees the ESOP debt. The guarantee expires when the ESOPs expire in March 2004. The company anticipates benefits expense in 2004 will increase by approximately $30 million compared to 2003, due to the expiration of the ESOPs.

ESOP expense is allocated to operating and interest expense based on the ratio of principal and interest payments on the underlying ESOP debt. Total ESOP expense for the three years ended December 31 is presented below (in millions):

	2003	2002	2001
Operating expense	$15.1	$13.3	$5.2
Interest expense	1.9	2.7	1.0
Total ESOP expense	$17.0	$16.0	$6.2

Cash contributions are made to the ESOPs in March and September to correspond with debt service requirements. A summary of cash contributions and dividends on unallocated ESOP shares for the three years ended December 31 is presented below (in millions):

	2003	2002	2001
Cash contributions	$10.2	$6.1	$1.3
Dividends	1.7	3.7	5.2

Receivables From Sale of Stock

2.329

UNIVERSAL FOREST PRODUCTS, INC. (DEC)

(In thousands except share data)	2003	2002
Shareholders' equity:		
Preferred stock, no par value; shares authorized 1,000,000; issued and outstanding, none	$ —	$ —
Common stock, no par value; shares authorized 40,000,000; issued and outstanding, 17,813,564 and 17,741,982 (Note J)	17,814	17,742
Additional paid-in capital (Note J)	85,189	82,139
Deferred stock compensation	1,477	1,434
Retained earnings	200,745	164,221
Accumulated other comprehensive earnings	1,396	299
	306,621	265,835
Employee stock notes receivable (Note J)	(1,872)	(1,401)
Total shareholders' equity	$304,749	$264,434

NOTES TO CONSOLIDATED FINANCIAL STATEMENTS

J. Employees' Stock Notes Receivable

Notes were obtained by us from certain officers for the purchase of our common stock. On April 30, 2002, we sold 12,555 shares of common stock to three officers in exchange for additional notes receivable totaling approximately $300,000. Interest on all of the outstanding notes range from fixed rates of five to eleven percent per annum and a variable rate of the prime rate less 10% (minimum 6%, maximum 12%). Each loan is evidenced by a promissory note from the participating officer and is secured by all of the shares purchased with the loan proceeds. As of August 1, 2002, we no longer issue notes to executive officers under this program.

On April 30, 2003, we sold 57,232 shares of common stock to employees in exchange for notes receivable totaling almost $900,000. Interest on these notes is fixed at 4.8% per annum. Each loan is evidenced by a promissory note from the participating employee and is secured by all of the shares purchased with the loan proceeds.

All loans are recourse loans. On December 27, 2003, payments on the notes are due as follows (in thousands):

2004	$ 193
2005	62
2006	124
2007	113
2008	82
Thereafter	1,298
	$1,872

Common Stock Warrants

2.330

PRIMEDIA INC. (DEC)

(Dollars in thousands, except per share amounts)	2003	2002
Shareholders' deficiency:		
Series J convertible preferred stock ($.01 par value, 1,319,093 shares and 1,166,324 shares issued and outstanding, aggregate liquidation and redemption values of $164,887 and $145,791 at December 31, 2003 and 2002, respectively)	$ 164,533	$ 145,351
Common stock ($.01 par value, 350,000,000 shares authorized at December 31, 2003 and 2002 and 268,333,049 and 267,505,223 shares issued at December 31, 2003 and 2002, respectively)	2,683	2,675
Additional paid-in capital (including warrants of $31,690 at December 31, 2003 and 2002)	2,345,152	2,336,091
Accumulated deficit	(3,447,710)	(3,445,083)
Accumulated other comprehensive loss	(176)	(247)
Unearned compensation	(175)	(4,730)
Common stock in treasury, at cost (8,610,491 shares and 8,639,775 shares at December 31, 2003 and 2002, respectively)	(77,562)	(77,855)
Total shareholders' deficiency	$(1,013,255)	$(1,043,798)

NOTES TO CONSOLIDATED FINANCIAL STATEMENTS
(Dollars in thousands, except per share amounts)

3 (In Part): Acquisitions

EMAP (In Part)
On August 24, 2001, the Company acquired the outstanding common stock of EMAP. The total consideration was $525,000, comprised of $515,000 in cash, including an estimate of working capital settlements of $10,000, and warrants to acquire 2,000,000 shares of the Company's common stock at $9 per share. The fair value of the warrants was approximately $10,000 and was determined using a Black Scholes pricing model. These warrants expire ten years from the date of issuance.

The Company financed the acquisition of EMAP by (1) issuing 1,000,000 shares of Series J Convertible Preferred Stock to KKR 1996 Fund L.P. ("KKR 1996 Fund") (an investment partnership created at the direction of Kohlberg Kravis Roberts & Co. L.P., ("KKR") a related party of the Company) for $125,000 and (2) drawing upon its revolving credit facility in an amount of approximately $265,000. In addition, KKR 1996 Fund purchased from the Company $125,000 of common stock and Series K Convertible Preferred Stock, both at a price per share equal to $4.70. This resulted in an additional 10,800,000 shares of common stock and 15,795,745 shares of Series K Convertible Preferred Stock. On September 27, 2001, all of the issued and outstanding shares of the Series K Convertible Preferred Stock were, in accordance with their terms, converted into 15,795,745 shares of the Company's common stock.

In connection with the equity financing by KKR 1996 Fund, the Company paid KKR 1996 Fund a commitment fee consisting of warrants to purchase 1,250,000 shares of common stock ("commitment warrants") of the Company at an exercise price of $7 per share, subject to adjustment, and a funding fee consisting of warrants to purchase an additional 2,620,000 shares of the Company's common stock ("funding warrants") at an exercise price of $7 per share, subject to adjustment. These warrants may be currently exercised and expire on the earlier of August 24, 2011 or upon a change in control, as defined therein. Based on the terms of the Series J Convertible Preferred Stock agreement, the Company was required to issue, and has issued, to KKR 1996 Fund additional warrants to purchase up to 4,000,000 shares of the Company's common stock at an exercise price of $7 per share, subject to adjustment. The Company ascribed a value of $6,389 to these warrants using the Black Scholes pricing model. These warrants expire on the earlier of ten years from the date of issuance or upon a change in control.

The 1,250,000 commitment warrants issued to KKR 1996 Fund represent a commitment fee related to the financing transaction as a whole. The Company valued these warrants at $5,622 using the Black Scholes pricing model and recorded them as a component of additional paid-in capital.

The Company attributed the 2,620,000 funding warrants to the issuance of the Series J Convertible Preferred Stock. The Company valued these warrants at $9,679 using the Black Scholes pricing model and has accordingly reduced the face value of the Series J Convertible Preferred Stock. The Company accreted the difference between the carrying value and the redemption value of the Series J Convertible Preferred Stock to additional paid-in capital using the effective interest method over a one year period as the earliest date at which the preferred stock was convertible was one year from the date of issuance. The accretion was deducted in the calculation of loss applicable to common shareholders.

15 (In Part): Common Stock

Other Transactions (In Part)

In August 2001, in connection with the EMAP financing, the Company paid KKR 1996 Fund a commitment fee consisting of warrants to purchase 1,250,000 shares of common stock of the Company at an exercise price of $7.00 per share and a funding fee consisting of warrants to purchase an additional 2,620,000 shares of the Company's stock at an exercise price of $7.00 per share. The Company also granted 4,000,000 warrants to the KKR 1996 Fund in 2001 and 2002. The grants were based on the length of time that the Series J Convertible Preferred Stock was outstanding. See Note 3 for further discussion.

Employee Benefit Trust

2.331

SNAP-ON INCORPORATED (DEC)

(Amounts in millions, except share data)	2003	2002
Shareholders' equity		
Preferred stock—authorized 15,000,000 shares of $1 par value; none outstanding	$ —	$ —
Common stock—authorized 250,000,000 shares of $1 par value; issued 66,956,246 and 66,897,506 shares	67.0	66.9
Additional paid-in capital	94.5	72.9
Retained earnings	1,084.7	1,064.2
Accumulated other comprehensive income (loss)	38.6	(123.8)
Grantor stock trust at fair market value—5,007,809 and 5,321,977 shares	(159.2)	(147.5)
Treasury stock at cost—3,774,764 and 3,326,462 shares	(114.7)	(102.3)
Total shareholders' equity	$1,010.9	$ 830.4

NOTES TO CONSOLIDATED FINANCIAL STATEMENTS

Note 16 (In Part): Capital Stock

Snap-on created a Grantor Stock Trust ("GST") in 1998 that was subsequently amended. In conjunction with the formation of the GST, Snap-on sold 7.1 million shares of treasury stock to the GST. The sale of these shares had no net impact on shareholders' equity or on Snap-on's Consolidated Statements of Earnings. The GST is a funding mechanism for certain benefit programs and compensation arrangements, including the 2001 Incentive Stock and Awards Plan and employee and dealer stock purchase plans. The Northern Trust Company, as trustee of the GST, votes the common stock held by the GST based on the terms set forth in the GST Agreement as amended. The GST is recorded as *Grantor stock trust at fair market value* on the accompanying Consolidated Balance Sheets. Shares owned by the GST are accounted for as a reduction to shareholders' equity until used in connection with employee benefits. Each period, the shares owned by the GST are valued at the closing market price, with corresponding changes in the GST balance reflected in additional paid-in capital. At January 3, 2004, the GST held 5,007,809 shares of common stock.

Stockholder Rights

2.332

UNIVERSAL CORPORATION (JUN)

NOTES TO CONSOLIDATED FINANCIAL STATEMENTS

Note 7. Share Purchase Rights Plan

In 1999, the Company distributed, as a dividend, one preferred share purchase right for each outstanding share of common stock. Each right entitles the shareholder to purchase 1/200 of a share of Series A Junior Participating Preferred Stock ("Preferred Stock") at an exercise price of $110, subject to adjustment. The rights will become exercisable only if a person or group acquires or announces a tender offer for 15% or more of the Company's outstanding shares of common stock. Under certain circumstances, the Board of Directors may reduce this threshold percentage to not less than 10%. If a person or group acquires the threshold percentage of common stock, each right will entitle the holder, other than the acquiring party, to buy shares of common stock or Preferred Stock having a market value of twice the exercise price. If the Company is acquired in a merger or other business combination, each right will entitle the holder, other than the acquiring person, to purchase securities of the surviving company having a market value equal to twice the exercise price of the rights. Following the acquisition by any person of more than the threshold percentage of the Company's outstanding common stock but less than 50% of such shares, the Company may exchange one share of common stock or 1/200 of a share of Preferred Stock for each right (other than rights held by such person). Until the rights become exercisable, they may be redeemed by the Company at a price of one cent per right. The rights expire on February 13, 2009.

Section 3: Income Statement

INCOME STATEMENT TITLE

3.01 Table 3-1 summarizes the key words used in statement of income titles. Many of the survey companies which used the term "operations" showed a net loss in one or more of the years presented in the statement of income.

3.02

TABLE 3-1: INCOME STATEMENT TITLE

	2003	2002	2001	2000
Operations	261	250	230	198
Income	242	242	259	284
Earnings	90	98	102	108
Other	7	10	9	10
Total Companies	**600**	**600**	**600**	**600**

INCOME STATEMENT FORMAT

3.03 Either a single-step form or a multi-step form is acceptable for preparing a statement of income. Table 3-2 shows that the survey companies presented a multi-step income statement more frequently than a single-step income statement.

3.04 Effective for fiscal years beginning after December 15, 1997, Statement of Financial Accounting Standards (SFAS) No. 130, *Reporting Comprehensive Income*, requires that comprehensive income and its components, as defined in the Statement, be reported in a financial statement. Comprehensive income and its components can be reported in an income statement, a separate statement of comprehensive income, or a statement of changes in stockholders' equity.

3.05 Examples of financial statement reporting comprehensive income and its components are presented in section 4.

3.06 Occasionally the survey companies disclosed reclassifications of income statement amounts. Examples of such reclassifications follow.

3.07

TABLE 3-2: INCOME STATEMENT FORMAT

	2003	2002	2001	2000
Single-Step Form				
Income tax shown as separate last item	133	156	153	134
Income tax listed among operating items	—	—	—	—
Multi-Step Form				
Costs deducted from sales to show gross margin	256	223	227	225
Costs and expenses deducted from sales to show operating income	211	221	220	241
Total Companies	**600**	**600**	**600**	**600**

Reclassification

3.08

OMNICOM GROUP INC. (DEC)

NOTES TO CONSOLIDATED FINANCIAL STATEMENTS

1 (In Part): Summary of Significant Accounting Policies

Reclassifications

Certain prior amounts have been reclassified to conform with the 2003 presentation. These reclassifications include changing the income statement line item from "Salary and related costs" to a new category entitled "Salary and service costs", and reallocating certain items previously shown in "Office and general expenses" to this new category. We have regrouped certain direct service costs such as freelance labor, travel, entertainment, reproduction, client service costs and other expenses from "Office and general expenses" into "Salary and service costs" in order to better segregate the expense items between those that are more closely related to directly serving clients versus those expenses, such as facilities, overhead, depreciation and other administrative expenses, which in nature are not directly related to servicing clients.

3.09

THE STANLEY WORKS (DEC)

NOTES TO CONSOLIDATED FINANCIAL STATEMENTS

A (In Part): Significant Accounting Policies

Reclassifications

Certain prior years' amounts have been reclassified to conform to the current year presentation. In addition the assets and liabilities of the discontinued operation have been reclassified as held for sale in the Consolidated Balance Sheets, and the earnings from discontinued operations have been reclassified within the Consolidated Statement of Operations.

In January 2002, the Company adopted EITF Issue No. 00-25, "Vendor Income Statement Characterization of Consideration to a Purchaser of the Vendor's Products or Services." EITF No. 00-25 requires the reclassification of certain customer promotional payments previously reported in SG&A expenses as a reduction of revenue, and prior periods must be restated for comparability of results. Net sales and SG&A expenses are $14.2 million lower for fiscal year 2001 than previously published amounts, reflecting reclassification of certain cooperative advertising expenses.

REVENUES AND GAINS

3.10 Paragraphs 78 and 82 of Financial Accounting Standards Board (FASB) Statement of Financial Accounting Concepts (SFAC) No. 6, *Elements of Financial Statements*, define revenues and gains.

> 78. Revenues are inflows or other enhancements of assets of an entity or settlements of its liabilities (or a combination of both) from delivering or producing goods, rendering services, or other activities that constitute the entity's ongoing major or central operations.
>
> 82. Gains are increases in equity (net assets) from peripheral or incidental transactions of an entity and from all other transactions and other events and circumstances affecting the entity except those that result from revenues or investments by owners.

3.11 Table 3-3 summarizes the descriptive income statement captions used by the survey companies to describe revenue. Gains most frequently disclosed by the survey companies are listed in Table 3-4. Excluded from Table 3-4 are segment disposals, gains shown after the caption for income taxes (Table 3-16), and extraordinary gains (Table 3-17).

3.12 Examples of revenues and gains follow.

3.13

TABLE 3-3: REVENUE CAPTION TITLE

	2003	2002	2001	2000
Net Sales				
Net sales	285	283	293	312
Net sales and operating revenues	7	11	8	13
Net sales combined with other items	5	3	4	—
Sales				
Sales	76	83	86	79
Sales and operating revenues	14	10	8	11
Sales and/or services	2	7	14	16
Sales combined with other items	6	3	4	11
Other Captions				
Revenue	204	198	180	145
Shipments, rentals, fees, etc	1	2	3	13
Total Companies	**600**	**600**	**600**	**600**

3.14

TABLE 3-4: GAINS

	Number of Companies			
	2003	2002	2001	2000
Interest	361	350	339	333
Sale of assets	199	187	182	94
Equity in earnings of investees	120	106	98	94
Liability accrual reduced	89	63	46	34
Foreign currency transactions	77	45	42	42
Dividends	53	66	58	57
Change in fair value of derivatives	49	25	28	2
Royalty, franchise and license fees	33	23	26	26
Litigation settlements	33	20	11	16
Rentals	22	17	14	13
Insurance recoveries	17	16	16	15
Debt extinguishment	13	3	N/C*	N/C*

*N/C = Not compiled. Line item was not included in the table for the year shown.

REVENUES

3.15

BANTA CORPORATION (DEC)

(Dollars in thousands)	2003	2002	2001
Net sales	$1,418,497	$1,366,457	$1,457,935
Cost of goods sold	1,113,113	1,062,968	1,159,822
Gross earnings	$ 305,384	$ 303,489	$ 298,113

NOTES TO CONSOLIDATED FINANCIAL STATEMENTS

Note 1 (In Part): Significant Accounting Policies

Revenue Recognition

Revenues are recognized when title and risk of loss transfers to the customer and the earnings process is complete. The Securities and Exchange Commission's Staff Accounting Bulletin (SAB) No. 101, "Revenue Recognition," provides guidance on the application of accounting principles generally accepted in the United States to selected revenue recognition issues. In addition, revenues in the supply-chain management segment are recognized in accordance with Emerging Issues Task Force (EITF) Issue No. 99-19, "Reporting Revenue Gross as a Principal versus Net as an Agent." Each major contract is evaluated based on various criteria, with management judgment required to assess the importance of each criterion in reaching the final decision. Revenue is recognized on a gross basis if the Corporation has the risks and rewards of ownership, latitude in establishing component vendors and pricing, and bears all credit risk. Revenues from contracts that do not meet these criteria are recognized on a net basis, recording only the portion that is related to services or products provided directly by the Corporation.

The Corporation records all shipping and handling fees billed to customers as revenue, and related costs as cost of goods sold, when incurred, in accordance with EITF 00-10 "Accounting for Shipping and Handling Fees and Costs."

3.16

BECKMAN COULTER, INC. (DEC)

(In millions)	2003	2002	2001
Sales	$2,192.5	$2,059.4	$1,984.0
Cost of sales	1,144.8	1,124.9	1,058.4
Gross profit	$1,047.7	$ 934.5	$ 925.6

NOTES TO CONSOLIDATED FINANCIAL STATEMENTS

1 (In Part): Nature of Business and Summary of Significant Accounting Policies

Revenue Recognition, Including Customer Leased Equipment

For products, revenue is recognized when risk of loss transfers, when persuasive evidence of an arrangement exists, the price to the buyer is fixed and determinable and collectibility is reasonably assured, except when a customer enters into an operating-type lease agreement, in which case revenue is recognized over the life of the lease. Under a sales-type lease agreement, revenue is recognized at the time of shipment with interest income recognized over the life of the lease. Service revenues on maintenance contracts are recognized ratably over the life of the service agreement or as service is performed, if not under contract. For those equipment sales that include multiple deliverables, such as installation, training, after-market supplies or service, revenue is allocated based on the relative fair values of the individual components as determined in accordance with EITF 00-21. Credit is extended based upon the evaluation of the

customer's financial condition and we generally do not require collateral.

3.17

EMCOR GROUP, INC. (DEC)

(In thousands)	2003	2002	2001
Revenues	$4,534,646	$3,968,051	$3,419,854
Cost of sales	4,052,192	3,485,417	3,028,031
Gross profit	$ 482,454	$ 482,634	$ 391,823

NOTES TO CONSOLIDATED FINANCIAL STATEMENTS

Note B (In Part): Summary of Significant Accounting Policies

Revenue Recognition

Revenues from long-term construction contracts are recognized on the percentage-of-completion method. Percentage-of-completion is measured principally by the percentage of costs incurred to date for each contract to the estimated total costs for such contract at completion. Certain of EMCOR's electrical contracting business units measure percentage-of-completion by the percentage of labor costs incurred to date for each contract to the estimated total labor costs for such contract. Revenues from services contracts are recognized as services are provided. There are two basic types of services contracts: (1) fixed price facilities services contracts which are signed in advance for maintenance, repair and retrofit work over periods typically ranging from one to three years (for which there may be EMCOR employees on the customer's site full time) and (2) services contracts which may or may not be signed in advance for similar maintenance, repair and retrofit work on an as needed basis (frequently referred to as time and material work). Fixed price services contracts are generally performed evenly over the contract period, and, accordingly, revenue is recognized on a pro-rata basis over the life of the contract. Revenues derived from other services contracts are recognized when the services are performed in accordance with Staff Accounting Bulletin No. 104, "Revenue Recognition, revised and updated." Expenses related to all services contracts are recognized as incurred.

Provisions for estimated losses on uncompleted long-term contracts are made in the period in which such losses are determined. In the case of customer change orders for uncompleted long-term construction contracts, estimated recoveries are included for work performed in forecasting ultimate profitability on certain contracts. Due to uncertainties inherent in the estimation process, it is reasonably possible that completion costs, including those arising from contract penalty provisions and final contract settlements, will be revised in the near-term. Such revisions to costs and income are recognized in the period in which the revisions are determined.

3.18

THE REYNOLDS AND REYNOLDS COMPANY (SEP)

(In thousands)	2003	2002	2001
Net sales and revenues			
Services	$ 624,795	$604,191	$ 600,681
Products	346,918	346,483	361,413
Financial services	36,532	41,709	41,918
Total net sales and revenues	1,008,245	992,383	1,004,012
Cost of sales			
Services	233,097	211,014	220,721
Products	201,641	192,077	203,933
Financial services	8,843	10,645	13,258
Total cost of sales	443,581	413,736	437,912
Gross profit	$ 564,664	$578,647	$ 566,100

NOTES TO CONSOLIDATED FINANCIAL STATEMENTS

1 (In Part): Summary of Significant Accounting Policies

Revenue Recognition

Automotive Solutions

Sales of computer hardware and business forms products are recorded when title passes upon shipment to customers. Revenues from software license fees are accounted for in accordance with American Institute of Certified Public Accountants (AICPA) Statement of Position (SOP) 97-2, "Software Revenue Recognition." The company recognizes revenue when (i) persuasive evidence of an arrangement exists; (ii) delivery has occurred or services have been rendered; (iii) the sales price is fixed or determinable; and (iv) collectibility is reasonably assured. Service revenues, which include computer hardware maintenance, software support, training, consulting and Web hosting are recorded ratably over the contract period or as services are performed. The application of SOP 97-2 requires judgment, including whether a software arrangement includes multiple elements (as defined in Emerging Issues Task Force (EITF) Issue No. 00-21, "Revenue Arrangements with Multiple Deliverables"), and if so, whether vendor-specific objective evidence of fair value exists for those elements. Software revenues which do not meet the criteria set forth in EITF Issue No. 00-3, "Application of AICPA SOP 97-2 to Arrangements That Include the Right to Use Software Stored on Another Entity's Hardware," are recorded ratably over the contract period as services are provided.

Financial Services

Financial Services revenues consist primarily of interest earned on financing the company's computer systems sales. Revenues are recognized over the lives of financing contracts, generally five years, using the interest method.

GAINS

Interest

3.19

TERADYNE, INC. (DEC)

(In thousands)	2003	2002	2001
Net revenue:			
Products	$1,115,888	$ 992,127	$1,233,728
Services	236,979	230,109	206,853
Total net revenue	1,352,867	1,222,236	1,440,581
Expenses:			
Cost of products	798,748	829,172	1,016,236
Cost of services	155,220	160,395	145,496
Total cost of revenue	953,968	989,567	1,161,732
Engineering and development	254,600	293,922	287,318
Selling and administrative	249,464	290,376	270,084
Restructuring and other charges	71,284	125,240	74,292
Goodwill impairment	—	78,936	—
Gain on sale of a business	—	—	(14,779)
	1,529,316	1,778,041	1,778,647
Loss from operations	(176,449)	(555,805)	(338,066)
Interest income	14,013	16,953	22,743
Interest expense	(20,883)	(21,783)	(4,091)
Other income and expense, net	(2,874)	(310)	(6,739)
Loss before income taxes	$ (186,193)	$ (560,945)	$ (326,153)

Sale of Assets

3.20

ARKANSAS BEST CORPORATION (DEC)

($ thousands)	2003	2002	2001
Operating revenues	$1,527,473	$1,422,297	$1,526,206
Operating expenses and costs	1,454,293	1,354,076	1,450,272
Operating income	73,180	68,221	75,934
Other income (expense)			
Net gains on sales of property and other	643	3,524	918
Gain on sale of G.I. Trucking Company	—	—	4,642
Gain on sale of Wingfoot	12,060	—	—
Gain on sale of Clipper LTL	2,535	—	—
IRS interest settlement	—	5,221	—
Fair value changes and payments on interest rate swap	(10,257)	—	—
Interest expense	(3,855)	(8,097)	(12,636)
Other, net	648	(238)	(2,139)
	1,774	410	(9,215)
Income before income taxes	$ 74,954	$ 68,631	$ 66,719

NOTES TO CONSOLIDATED FINANCIAL STATEMENTS

Note B (In Part): Accounting Policies

Impairment Assessment of Long-Lived Assets

Assets held for sale represent primarily ABF's nonoperating freight terminals and older revenue equipment that are no longer in service. Assets held for sale are carried at the lower of their carrying value or fair value less costs to sell. Write-downs to fair value less costs to sell are reported below the operating income line in gains or losses on sales of property, in the case of real property, or above the operating income line as gains or losses on sales of equipment, in the case of revenue or other equipment. Assets held for sale are expected to be disposed of by selling the properties or assets to a third party within the next 12 to 24 months.

Total assets held for sale at December 31, 2002 were $3.2 million. During 2003, additional assets of $9.1 million were identified and reclassified to assets held for sale. Non-operating terminals and revenue equipment carried at $3.1 million were sold for gains of $2.0 million, of which $1.7 million related to real estate and was reported below the operating line and $0.3 million was related to equipment and reported in operating income. During 2003, the Company recorded $1.0 million of losses from write-downs related to real estate moved into assets held for sale. These real estate losses were reported below the operating income line.

Note D—Sale and Exit of Clipper's LTL Business

On December 31, 2003, Clipper Express Company closed the sale of all customer and vendor lists related to Clipper's LTL freight business to Hercules Forwarding Inc. of Vernon, California for $2.7 million in cash, resulting in a pre-tax gain of $2.5 million. This gain is reported below the operating income line. Total costs incurred with the exit of this business unit amounted to $1.2 million and include severance pay, software and fixed asset abandonment and certain operating leases. These exit costs are reported above the operating income line. No additional costs relating to the exit of this business are expected to be incurred. The impact of the gain was $1.5 million, net of taxes, or $0.06 per diluted common share and the impact of the exit costs was $0.7 million, net of taxes, or $0.03 per diluted common share.

Note E—Sale of 19% Interest in Wingfoot

On March 19, 2003, the Company announced that it had notified The Goodyear Tire & Rubber Company ("Goodyear") of its intention to sell its 19.0% ownership interest in Wingfoot Commercial Tire Systems, LLC ("Wingfoot") to Goodyear for a cash price of $71.3 million. The transaction closed on April 28, 2003 and the Company recorded a pre-tax gain of $12.1 million ($8.4 million after tax, or $0.33 per diluted common share) during the second quarter of 2003. The Company used the proceeds to reduce the outstanding debt under its Credit Agreement.

Equity in Earnings of Investee

3.21

KB HOME (NOV)

(In thousands)	2003	2002	2001
Total revenues	$ 5,850,554	$ 5,030,816	$ 4,574,184
Construction:			
Revenues	$ 5,775,429	$ 4,938,894	$ 4,501,715
Construction and land costs	(4,479,019)	(3,890,243)	(3,612,936)
Selling, general and administrative expenses	(733,511)	(595,734)	(536,463)
Operating income	562,899	452,917	352,316
Interest income	3,000	4,173	3,559
Interest expense, net of amounts capitalized	(23,780)	(32,730)	(41,072)
Minority interests	(26,889)	(16,994)	(27,932)
Equity in pretax income of unconsolidated joint ventures	2,457	4,378	3,875
Construction pretax income	517,687	411,744	290,746
Mortgage banking:			
Revenues:			
Interest income	14,232	22,578	21,935
Other	60,893	69,344	50,534
	75,125	91,922	72,469
Expenses:			
Interest	(6,445)	(11,467)	(18,436)
General and administrative	(32,903)	(22,949)	(20,262)
Mortgage banking pretax income	35,777	57,506	33,771
Total pretax income	$ 553,464	$ 469,250	$ 324,517

NOTES TO CONSOLIDATED FINANCIAL STATEMENTS

Note (In Part): Summary of Significant Accounting Policies

Basis of Presentation

The consolidated financial statements include the accounts of the Company and all significant subsidiaries and joint ventures in which a controlling interest is held. All intercompany transactions have been eliminated. Investments in unconsolidated joint ventures in which the Company has less than a controlling interest are accounted for using the equity method.

Note 5: Investments in Unconsolidated Joint Ventures

The Company participates in a number of joint ventures in which it has less than a controlling interest. These joint ventures, which operate in certain markets in the United States and France where the Company's consolidated construction operations are located, are typically engaged in the development, construction and sale of residential properties and commercial projects. Combined condensed financial information concerning the Company's unconsolidated joint venture activities follows:

(In thousands)	2003	2002
Cash	$ 16,702	$ 13,627
Receivables	25,476	27,608
Inventories	139,569	86,949
Other assets	746	1,006
Total assets	$182,493	$129,190
Mortgages and notes payable	$ 55,869	$ 41,490
Other liabilities	48,152	32,145
Equity of:		
The Company	32,797	21,023
Others	45,675	34,532
Total liabilities and equity	$182,493	$129,190

The joint ventures finance land and inventory investments of the Company's operating subsidiaries through a variety of borrowing arrangements. The Company typically does not guarantee these financing arrangements.

(In thousands)	2003	2002	2001
Revenues	$ 47,454	$ 65,884	$ 82,122
Cost of sales	(32,469)	(45,490)	(56,969)
Other expenses, net	(8,129)	(10,715)	(18,668)
Total pretax income	$ 6,856	$ 9,679	$ 6,485
The Company's share of pretax income	$ 2,457	$ 4,378	$ 3,875

The Company's share of pretax income includes management fees earned from the unconsolidated joint ventures.

Liability Accruals Reduced

3.22

WORTHINGTON INDUSTRIES, INC. (MAY)

(In thousands)	2003	2002	2001
Net sales	$2,219,891	$1,744,961	$1,826,100
Cost of goods sold	1,916,990	1,480,184	1,581,178
Gross margin	302,901	264,777	244,922
Selling, general and administrative expense	182,692	165,885	173,264
Restructuring (credit) expense	(5,622)	64,575	6,474
Operating income	125,831	34,317	65,184
Other income (expense):			
Miscellaneous expense	(7,240)	(3,224)	(928)
Nonrecurring losses	(5,400)	(21,223)	—
Interest expense	(24,766)	(22,740)	(33,449)
Equity in net income of unconsolidated affiliates	29,973	23,110	25,201
Earnings before income taxes	$ 118,398	$ 10,240	$ 56,008

NOTES TO CONSOLIDATED FINANCIAL STATEMENTS

Note N—Restructuring Expense

During the quarter ended February 28, 2002, the Company announced a consolidation plan that affected each of the Company's business segments and resulted in the closure of six facilities and the restructuring of two others. As a result, the Company recorded a $64,575,000 pre-tax restructuring expense, which included a writedown to estimated fair value of certain property and equipment, severance and employee related costs, and other items. The severance and employee related costs were due to the elimination of approximately 542 administrative, production and other employee positions. As of May 31, 2003, 497 employees had been terminated, 43 others had either retired or left through normal attrition, and the Company had paid severance of $7,071,000. All six of the facilities to be closed have been closed, and their related assets have been transferred, sold or are being marketed. The restructuring of the other two facilities is complete.

During the quarter ended November 30, 2002, the Company recorded a favorable pre-tax adjustment of $5,622,000 to the restructuring charge mentioned above. This credit was the result of higher-than-estimated proceeds from the sale of real estate at the Company's former facility in Malvern, Pennsylvania, and the net reduction of previously established reserves, partially offset by estimated charges for the announced closure of three additional facilities discussed below.

The components of this adjustment are as follows:

(In thousands)	
Gain on sale of Malvern assets	$(4,965)
Reductions to other reserves	(3,637)
Charge for three additional facilities	2,980
Total	$(5,622)

The closure of three additional facilities was announced during the quarter ended November 30, 2002. Two facilities from the Metal Framing segment and one from the Pressure Cylinders segment were affected. The Metal Framing facilities in East Brunswick, New Jersey, and Atlanta, Georgia, were considered redundant following the July 31, 2002, acquisition of Unimast. See "Note Q—Acquisition" for more information. The other facility, located in Citronelle, Alabama, produced acetylene cylinders. The production of these cylinders has been partially transferred to another plant and partially out-sourced. The closure of these three facilities resulted in an additional $2,980,000 pre-tax restructuring charge. The re-structuring charge included a write-down to estimated fair value of certain equipment, property related costs, severance and employee related costs, and other items. The severance and employee related costs are due to the estimated elimi-nation of 69 administrative, production and other employee positions. As of May 31, 2003, 69 employees had been ter-minated and severance of $604,000 had been paid. All three were leased facilities. The Citronelle lease has been termi-nated and the other two are being marketed for sublease. This portion of the consolidation process should be substan-tially completed during calendar year 2003.

The progression of the restructuring charge is summarized as follows:

(In thousands)	Balance May 31, 2002	Payments	Charges to Net Earnings		Charges Against Assets	Balance May 31, 2003
			Adjustments	Additions		
Property and equipment	$48,090	$ (3,801)	$(9,766)	$1,846	$(31,782)	$ 4,587
Severance and employee related	10,404	(6,386)	1,835	817	—	6,670
Other	4,244	(258)	(671)	317	(3,632)	—
Total	$62,738	$(10,445)	$(8,602)	$2,980	$(35,414)	$11,257

Sales that were historically generated by the closed plants are anticipated to transfer to other Company facilities except for the sales from the Itu, Brazil, facility and sales related to the painted and coated products at the Malvern, Pennsylvania, facility. Net sales that will not be transferred were $9,090,000, $42,363,000 and $65,484,000 for fiscal 2003, fiscal 2002 and fiscal 2001, respectively. The related operating loss for these products was $659,000, $5,314,000 and $14,528,000 for fis-cal 2003, fiscal 2002 and fiscal 2001, respectively.

Foreign Currency Transactions

3.23

PEERLESS MFG. CO. (JUN)

(Dollars in thousands)	2003	2002	2001
Revenues	$69,170	$109,456	$78,159
Cost of goods sold	52,514	78,531	54,649
Gross profit	16,656	30,925	23,510
Operating expenses			
Sales and marketing	6,130	8,636	6,613
Engineering and project management	5,613	8,233	5,098
General and administrative	5,922	7,788	5,897
Restructuring expense	483	—	—
	18,148	24,657	17,608
Operating income (loss)	(1,492)	6,268	5,902
Other income (expense)			
Interest expense	—	(123)	(744)
Foreign exchange gain (loss)	146	84	(155)
Gain on sale of assets	473	267	—
Other, net	155	244	(128)
	774	472	(1,027)
Earnings (loss) before income taxes	$ (718)	$ 6,740	$ 4,875

NOTES TO CONSOLIDATED FINANCIAL STATEMENTS

Note A (In Part): Nature of Operations and Summary of Significant Accounting Policies

Foreign Currency

All balance sheet accounts of foreign operations are translated into U.S. dollars at the year-end rate of exchange and statements of operations items are translated at the weighted average exchange rates for the year. The resulting translation adjustments are made directly to a separate component of stockholders' equity. Gains and losses from foreign currency transactions, such as those resulting from the settlement of foreign receivables or payables, are included in the consolidated statements of operations.

Change in Fair Value of Derivatives

3.24

CHARTER COMMUNICATIONS, INC. (DEC)

(Dollars in millions)	2003	2002	2001
Revenues	$ 4,819	$ 4,566	$ 3,807
Costs and expenses:			
Operating (excluding depreciation and amortization)	1,952	1,807	1,486
Selling, general and administrative	940	963	826
Depreciation and amortization	1,479	1,439	2,693
Impairment of franchises	—	4,638	—
Gain on sale of system	(21)	—	—
Option compensation expense (income), net	4	5	(5)
Special charges, net	21	36	18
Unfavorable contracts and other settlements	(72)	—	—
	4,303	8,888	5,018
Income (loss) from operations	516	(4,322)	(1,211)
Other income and expenses:			
Interest expense, net	(1,557)	(1,503)	(1,310)
Gain (loss) on derivative instruments and hedging activities, net	65	(115)	(50)
Gain on debt exchange, net	267	—	—
Loss on equity investments	(3)	(3)	(54)
Other, net	(13)	(1)	(5)
	(1,241)	(1,622)	(1,419)
Loss before minority interest, income taxes and cumulative effect of accounting change	$ (725)	$(5,944)	$(2,630)

*NOTES TO CONSOLIDATED FINANCIAL STATEMENTS
(Dollars in millions)*

3 (In Part): Summary of Significant Accounting Policies

Derivative Financial Instruments

The Company accounts for derivative financial instruments in accordance with SFAS No. 133, *Accounting for Derivative Instruments and Hedging Activities*, as amended, which became effective for the Company on January 1, 2001. The Company uses interest rate risk management derivative instruments, such as interest rate swap agreements, interest rate cap agreements and interest rate collar agreements (collectively referred to herein as interest rate agreements) as required under the terms of the credit facilities of the Company's subsidiaries. The Company's policy is to manage interest costs using a mix of fixed and variable rate debt. Using interest rate swap agreements, the Company agrees to exchange, at specified intervals, the difference between fixed and variable interest amounts calculated by reference to an agreed-upon notional principal amount. Interest rate cap agreements are used to lock in a maximum interest rate should variable rates rise, but enable the Company to otherwise pay lower market rates. Interest rate collar agreements are used to limit exposure to and benefits from interest rate fluctuations on variable rate debt to within a certain range of rates. The Company does not hold or issue any derivative financial instruments for trading purposes.

14. Accounting for Derivative Instruments and Hedging Activities

The Company uses interest rate risk management derivative instruments, such as interest rate swap agreements and interest rate collar agreements (collectively referred to herein as interest rate agreements) as required under the terms of its credit facilities. The Company's policy is to manage interest costs using a mix of fixed and variable rate debt. Using interest rate swap agreements, the Company agrees to exchange, at specified intervals through 2007, the difference between fixed and variable interest amounts calculated by reference to an agreed-upon notional principal amount. Interest rate collar agreements are used to limit the Company's exposure to and benefits from interest rate fluctuations on variable rate debt to within a certain range of rates.

Effective January 1, 2001, the Company adopted SFAS No. 133. Interest rate agreements are recorded in the consolidated balance sheet at December 31, 2003 and 2002 as either an asset or liability measured at fair value. In connection with the adoption of SFAS No. 133, the Company recorded a loss of $10 million (approximately $24 million before minority interest effects) as the cumulative effect of change in accounting principle. The effect of adoption was to increase net loss and loss per share by $10 million and $0.04 per share, respectively, for the year ended December 31, 2001.

The Company does not hold or issue derivative instruments for trading purposes. The Company does however have certain interest rate derivative instruments that have been designated as cash flow hedging instruments. Such instruments are those that effectively convert variable interest payments on certain debt instruments into fixed payments. For qualifying hedges, SFAS No. 133 allows derivative gains and losses to offset related results on hedged items in the consolidated statement of operations. The Company has formally documented, designated and assessed the effectiveness of transactions that receive hedge accounting. For the years ended December 31, 2003, 2002 and 2001, net gain (loss) on derivative instruments and hedging activities includes gains of $8 million and losses of $14 million and $2 million, respectively, which represent cash flow hedge ineffectiveness on interest rate hedge agreements arising from differences between the critical terms of the agreements and the related hedged obligations. Changes in the fair value of interest rate agreements designated as hedging instruments of the variability of cash flows associated with floating-rate debt obligations are reported in accumulated other comprehensive loss. For the years ended December 31, 2003, 2002 and 2001, a gain of $48 million and losses of $65 million and $39 million, respectively, related to derivative instruments designated as cash flow hedges was recorded in accumulated other comprehensive loss and minority interest. The amounts are subsequently reclassified into interest expense as a yield adjustment in the same period in which the related interest on the floating-rate debt obligations affects earnings (losses).

Certain interest rate derivative instruments are not designated as hedges as they do not meet the effectiveness criteria specified by SFAS No. 133. However, management believes such instruments are closely correlated with the respective debt, thus managing associated risk. Interest rate derivative instruments not designated as hedges are marked to fair value with the impact recorded as gain (loss) on derivative instruments and hedging activities in the Company's statement of operations. For the years ended December 31, 2003, 2002 and 2001, net gain (loss) on derivative instruments and hedging activities includes gains of $57 million and losses of $101 million and $48 million, respectively, for interest rate derivative instruments not designated as hedges.

As of December 31, 2003, 2002 and 2001, the Company had outstanding $3.0 billion, $3.4 billion and $3.3 billion and $520 million, $520 million and $520 million, respectively, in notional amounts of interest rate swaps and collars, respectively. The notional amounts of interest rate instruments do not represent amounts exchanged by the parties and, thus, are not a measure of exposure to credit loss. The amounts exchanged are determined by reference to the notional amount and the other terms of the contracts.

15. Fair Value of Financial Instruments

The Company has estimated the fair value of its financial instruments as of December 31, 2003 and 2002 using available market information or other appropriate valuation methodologies. Considerable judgment, however, is required in interpreting market data to develop the estimates of fair value. Accordingly, the estimates presented in the accompanying consolidated financial statements are not necessarily indicative of the amounts the Company would realize in a current market exchange.

The carrying amounts of cash, receivables, payables and other current assets and liabilities approximate fair value because of the short maturity of those instruments. The Company is exposed to market price risk volatility with respect to investments in publicly traded and privately held entities.

The fair value of interest rate agreements represents the estimated amount the Company would receive or pay upon termination of the agreements. Management believes that the sellers of the interest rate agreements will be able to meet their obligations under the agreements. In addition, some of the interest rate agreements are with certain of the participating banks under the Company's credit facilities, thereby reducing the exposure to credit loss. The Company has policies regarding the financial stability and credit standing of major counterparties. Nonperformance by the counterparties is not anticipated nor would it have a material adverse effect on the Company's consolidated financial condition or results of operations.

The estimated fair value of the Company's notes, credit facilities and interest rate agreements at December 31, 2003 and 2002 are based on quoted market prices or a discounted cash flow analysis using the Company's incremental borrowing rate for similar types of borrowing arrangements and dealer quotations.

A summary of the carrying value and fair value of the Company's debt and related interest rate agreements at December 31, 2003 and 2002 is as follows:

	2003		2002	
	Carrying Value	Fair Value	Carrying Value	Fair Value
Debt				
Charter convertible notes	$ 774	$ 732	$1,383	$ 295
Charter Holdings debt	8,316	7,431	9,222	3,867
CCH II debt	1,601	1,680	—	—
CCO Holdings debt	500	510	—	—
Credit facilities	7,227	6,949	7,789	6,367
Other	229	238	277	212
Interest rate agreements				
Assets (liabilities)				
Swaps	(171)	(171)	(258)	(258)
Collars	(8)	(8)	(34)	(34)

The weighted average interest pay rate for the Company's interest rate swap agreements was 7.25% and 7.40% at December 31, 2003 and 2002, respectively. The Company's interest rate collar agreements are structured so that if LIBOR falls below 5.3%, the Company pays 6.7%. If the LIBOR rate is between 5.3% and 8.0%, the Company pays LIBOR. The LIBOR rate is capped at 8.0%, if LIBOR is between 8.0% and 9.9%. If the LIBOR rate rises above 9.9%, the cap is removed.

Royalty, Franchise and License Fees

3.25

YUM! BRANDS, INC. (DEC)

(In millions)	2003	2002	2001
Revenues			
Company sales	$7,441	$6,891	$6,138
Franchise and license fees	939	866	815
Total revenues	$8,380	$7,757	$6,953

NOTES TO CONSOLIDATED FINANCIAL STATEMENTS (Tabular amounts in millions)

Note 2 (In Part): Summary of Significant Accounting Policies

Franchise and License Operations
We execute franchise or license agreements for each unit which sets out the terms of our arrangement with the franchisee or licensee. Our franchise and license agreements typically require the franchisee or licensee to pay an initial, non-refundable fee and continuing fees based upon a percentage of sales. Subject to our approval and payment of a renewal fee, a franchisee may generally renew the franchise agreement upon its expiration.

We recognize initial fees as revenue when we have performed substantially all initial services required by the franchise or license agreement, which is generally upon the opening of a store. We recognize continuing fees as earned. We recognize renewal fees in income when a renewal agreement becomes effective. We include initial fees collected upon the sale of a restaurant to a franchisee in refranchising gains (losses). Fees for development rights are capitalized and amortized over the life of the development agreement.

We incur expenses that benefit both our franchise and license communities and their representative organizations and our company operated restaurants. These expenses, along with other costs of servicing of franchise and license agreements are charged to general and administrative expenses as incurred. Certain direct costs of our franchise and license operations are charged to franchise and license expenses. These costs include provisions for estimated uncollectible fees, franchise and license marketing funding, amortization expense for franchise related intangible assets and certain other direct incremental franchise and license support costs. Franchise and license expenses also includes rental income from subleasing restaurants to franchisees net of the related occupancy costs.

We monitor the financial condition of our franchisees and licensees and record provisions for estimated losses on receivables when we believe that our franchisees or licensees are unable to make their required payments. While we use the best information available in making our determination, the ultimate recovery of recorded receivables is also dependent upon future economic events and other conditions that may be beyond our control. Included in franchise and license expense in 2003 is a net benefit for uncollectible franchise and license receivables of $3 million as we were able to recover previously reserved receivables in excess of provisions made. Net provisions for uncollectible franchise and license receivables of $15 million and $24 million were included in franchise and license expense in 2002 and 2001, respectively.

Note 9—Franchise and License Fees

	2003	2002	2001
Initial fees, including renewal fees	$ 36	$ 33	$ 32
Initial franchise fees included in refranchising gains	(5)	(6)	(7)
	31	27	25
Continuing fees	908	839	790
	$939	$866	$815

Litigation Settlements

3.26

IDT CORPORATION (JUL)

(In thousands)	2003	2002	2001
Revenues	$1,834,547	$1,583,794	$1,230,950
Costs and expenses:			
Direct cost of revenues (exclusive of items shown below)	1,409,465	1,214,802	1,066,845
Selling, general and administrative	421,829	451,476	334,025
Depreciation and amortization	89,309	83,916	60,351
Settlement by Net2Phone of litigation	(58,034)	—	—
Non-cash compensation	32,286	16,440	3,082
Restructuring, severance and impairment charges	13,312	257,501	199,357
Total costs and expenses	1,908,167	2,024,135	1,663,660
Loss from operations	$ (73,620)	$ (440,341)	$ (432,710)

NOTES TO CONSOLIDATED FINANCIAL STATEMENTS

9 (In Part): Commitments and Contingencies

Net2Phone (In Part)

In August 2002, Net2Phone and its ADIR subsidiary consummated the settlement of their lawsuit in the United States District Court for the District of New Jersey against Cisco and a Cisco executive who had been a member of the board of directors of ADIR Technologies, Inc., Net2Phone's majority-owned subsidiary. The suit arose out of the relationships that had been created in connection with Cisco's and Net2Phone's original investments in ADIR and out of ADIR's subsequent purchase of NetSpeak, Inc. in August 2001. The parties settled the suit and all related claims against Cisco and the Cisco executive in exchange for: (i) the transfer, during the first quarter of fiscal 2003, to Net2Phone of Cisco's and Softbank Asia Infrastructure Fund's respective 11.5% and 7.0% interests in ADIR, and (ii) the payment by Cisco, during such quarter, of $19.5 million to Net2Phone and ADIR. As a result of this settlement, the Company recognized, for the quarter ended October 31, 2002, a gain of $58.4 million consisting of a $38.9 million reduction in minority interests as a result of the transfer of the ADIR shares and receipt of settlement proceeds of $19.5 million less $1.6 million of legal and other expenses related to the settlement that were recorded in fiscal 2002 and $0.4 million in compensation expense related directly to the settlement that was recorded during the three months ended January 31, 2003.

Rentals

3.27

THE FAIRCHILD CORPORATION (JUN)

(In thousands)	2003	2002	2001
Revenue:			
Net sales	$68,820	$76,531	$ 94,192
Rental revenue	8,699	7,159	7,498
	$77,519	$83,690	$101,690

NOTES TO CONSOLIDATED FINANCIAL STATEMENTS
(In thousands)

1 (In Part): Summary of Significant Accounting Policies

Revenue Recognition

Sales and related costs are recognized upon shipment of products and/or performance of services, when collection is probable. Sales and related cost of sales on long-term contracts are recognized as products are delivered and services performed, as determined by the percentage of completion method. Lease and rental revenue are recognized on a straight-line basis over the life of the lease. Shipping and handling amounts billed to customers are classified as revenues.

15 (In Part): Leases

Leasing Operations

Our real estate operations segment owns and operates a 451,000 square foot shopping center located in Farmingdale, New York and also owns and leases a 102,000 square foot building in Chatsworth, California and a 208,000 square foot manufacturing facility located in Fullerton, California. Rental revenue is recognized as lease payments are due from tenants, and the related costs are amortized over their estimated useful life. The future minimum lease payments to be received from non-cancelable operating leases on June 30, 2003 are $7,760 in 2004; $7,689 in 2005; $7,629 in 2006; $7,629 in 2007; $7,071 in 2008; and $38,222 thereafter. Certain tenants of the shopping center have options to extend their lease term by an additional 5 to 35 years. Rental property we have leased to third parties under operating leases consists of the following:

	2003	2002
Land and improvements	$27,727	$24,302
Buildings and improvements	59,249	57,349
Tenant improvements	11,365	9,121
Less: Accumulated depreciation	(8,841)	(5,915)
	$89,500	$84,857

The tenant leasing our building in Chatsworth, California has an option to purchase the property for $4.6 million.

Insurance Recoveries

3.28

QUANEX CORPORATION (OCT)

(In thousands)	2003	2002	2001
Net sales	$1,031,215	$994,387	$924,353
Costs and expenses:			
Cost of sales	867,782	812,949	769,328
Selling, general and administrative	53,572	54,408	54,202
Depreciation and amortization	46,066	43,730	43,507
Operating income	63,795	83,300	57,316
Other income (expense):			
Interest expense	(2,517)	(14,812)	(16,555)
Capitalized interest	—	1,879	1,666
Retired executive life insurance benefit	2,152	9,020	—
Other, net	2,393	2,227	3,195
Income before income taxes	$ 65,823	$ 81,614	$ 45,622

NOTES TO CONSOLIDATED FINANCIAL STATEMENTS

3. Executive Life Insurance Benefit

During the fiscal year ended October 31, 2003, a former executive of the Company, on whose life the Company held life insurance policies, died. As a result, the Company received life insurance proceeds totaling $6.4 million. Estimates of the cash surrender value of these life insurance policies amounting to $4.3 million were previously recognized in "Other assets" on the financial statements. The excess of the proceeds over the previously recorded cash surrender value amounting to $2.2 million was recognized as a non-taxable benefit on the income statement during the year ended October 31, 2003. The impact to the fiscal year ended October 31, 2003 basic and diluted earnings per share of this benefit was $0.13.

During the fiscal year ended October 31, 2002, another of the Company's former executives, on whose life it held life insurance policies, died. As a result, the Company received life insurance proceeds totaling $26.1 million. Estimates of the cash surrender value of these life insurance policies amounting to $15.9 million were previously recognized in "Other assets" on the financial statements. The excess of the proceeds over the previously recorded cash surrender value and the liability to the beneficiaries of the executive amounting to $9.0 million was recognized as a non-taxable benefit on the income statement during the period ended October 31, 2002. The impact on October 31, 2002 earnings per share of this benefit was $0.61 basic and $0.56 diluted.

Debt Extinguishment

3.29

WHX CORPORATION (DEC)

(In thousands)	2003	2002	2001
Net sales	$ 326,296	$386,393	$388,139
Cost of goods sold	265,001	318,104	318,670
Gross profit	61,295	68,289	69,469
Selling, general and administrative expenses	70,063	73,652	74,304
Pension—curtailment and special termination benefits	48,102	—	—
Goodwill impairment charge	89,000	—	—
Loss on disposal of assets	6,286	2,576	18
Restructuring charges	—	19,994	—
Income (loss) from operations	(152,156)	(27,933)	(4,853)
Other:			
Interest expense	19,166	27,257	46,969
Equity in loss of WPC	—	20,000	
Gain on disposition of WPC	534	—	
Gain on early retirement of debt	2,999	42,491	19,011
Gain on sale of interest in Wheeling-Downs	—	—	88,517
Other income (expense)	(222)	(3,412)	11,130
Income (loss) from continuing operations before taxes	$(168,011)	$ (36,111)	$ 66,836

NOTES TO CONSOLIDATED FINANCIAL STATEMENTS

Note 12 (In Part): Long-Term Debt

(In thousands)	2003	2002
Senior Notes due 2005, 10 1/2%	$ 92,820	$110,504
Handy & Harman Senior Secured Credit Facility	129,080	130,465
Other	7,500	8,737
	229,400	249,706
Less portion due within one year	40,056	—
Total long-term debt	$189,344	$249,706

WHX Corporation 10 1/2% Senior Notes Due 2005 (In Part)

The WHX 10 1/2% Senior Notes in the amount of $92.8 million are due on April 15, 2005. It is the Company's intention to refinance this obligation prior to its scheduled maturity; however there can be no assurance that such refinancing will be obtained. The Company's access to capital markets in the future to refinance such indebtedness may be limited. If the Company were unable to refinance this obligation, it would have a material adverse impact on the liquidity, financial position and capital resources of WHX and would impact the Company's ability to continue as a going concern. The financial statements do not reflect any adjustments related to this matter.

On April 7, 1998, WHX issued $350.0 million principal amount of 10 1/2% Senior Notes ("Notes"), which replaced privately placed notes of the same amount. Interest on the Notes is payable semi-annually on April 15 and October 15 of each year, commencing October 15, 1998. The Notes mature on April 15, 2005.

The Notes are redeemable at the option of WHX, in whole or in part, on or after April 15, 2002 at specified prices, plus accrued interest and liquidated damages, if any, thereon to the date of redemption.

• • • • • •

During 2001, the Company purchased and retired $36.4 million aggregate principal amount of the Notes in the open market resulting in a gain of $19.0 million.

During 2002, the Company purchased and retired $134.6 million aggregate principal amount of the Notes in the open market resulting in a gain of $42.5 million.

During 2003, the Company purchased and retired $17.7 million aggregate principal amount of the Notes in the open market resulting in a gain of $3.0 million.

Nonrecurring Gain

3.30

PILGRIM'S PRIDE CORPORATION (SEP)

(In thousands)	2003	2002	2001
Net sales	$2,619,345	$2,533,718	$2,214,712
Cost and expenses:			
Cost of sales	2,465,341	2,369,309	2,000,762
Non-recurring recoveries	(46,479)	(756)	—
Selling, general and administrative	136,870	135,261	119,408
	2,555,732	2,503,814	2,120,170
Operating income	$ 63,613	$ 29,904	$ 94,542

NOTES TO CONSOLIDATED FINANCIAL STATEMENTS

Note B (In Part): Significant Events

Non-recurring recoveries, which is a component of gross profit and operating income, include (1) reimbursements received from the U.S. Federal Government under a relief plan related to the avian influenza outbreak in Virginia on March 12, 2002 in the amount of $26.6 million in fiscal 2003 and (2) proceeds received from litigation initiated by the Company in antitrust lawsuits alleging a world-wide conspiracy to control production capacity and raise prices of vitamins and methionine. Proceeds received by the Company as successor to WLR Foods are recorded as Other Expense (Income); Miscellaneous, net.

The following table presents the impact of avian influenza federal compensation and the vitamin and the methionine litigation settlements on Non-recurring recoveries and Miscellaneous, net (in millions):

	2003			2002		
	Non-Recurring	Miscellaneous Net	Total	Non-Recurring	Miscellaneous Net	Total
Avian influenza	$26.6	$ —	$26.6	$ —	$ —	$ —
Vitamin	1.6	23.5	25.1	0.8	4.3	5.1
Methionine	18.3	12.5	30.8	—	—	—
Total	$46.5	$36.0	$82.5	$0.8	$4.3	$5.1

EXPENSES AND LOSSES

3.31 Paragraphs 80 and 83 of FASB *SFAC No. 6* define expenses and losses.

> 80. Expenses are outflows or other using up of assets or incurrences of liabilities (or a combination of both) from delivering or producing goods, rendering services, or carrying out other activities that constitute the entity's ongoing major or central operations.

> 83. Losses are decreases in equity (net assets) from peripheral or incidental transactions of an entity and from all other transactions and other events and circumstances affecting the entity except those that result from expenses of distributions to owners.

3.32 Table 3-5 reveals that most of the survey companies show a single caption and amount for cost of goods sold. Table 3-6 summarizes the nature of expenses, other than cost of goods sold. Excluded from Table 3-6 are rent (Table 2-30), employee benefits, depreciation (Table 3-13), and income taxes (Table 3-14). Table 3-7 lists losses most frequently disclosed by the survey companies. Excluded from Table 3-7 are losses shown after the caption for income taxes (Table 3-16), segment disposals, and extraordinary losses (Table 3-17).

3.33 Examples of expenses and losses follow.

3.34

TABLE 3-5: EXPENSES—COST OF GOODS SOLD CAPTIONS

	2003	2002	2001	2000
Single Amount				
Cost of sales	230	222	230	233
Cost of goods sold	95	89	93	95
Cost of products sold	74	73	83	93
Cost of revenues	38	33	35	30
Elements of cost	4	6	7	9
Other captions	102	110	99	84
	543	533	547	544
More than one amount	57	67	53	56
Total Companies	**600**	**600**	**600**	**600**

3.35

TABLE 3-6: EXPENSES—OTHER THAN COST OF GOODS SOLD

	Number of Companies			
	2003	2002	2001	2000
Selling, general and administrative	344	340	340	336
Selling and administrative	110	114	117	121
General and/or administrative	103	99	98	96
Selling	37	43	40	39
Interest	543	556	565	577
Research, development, engineering, etc.	302	284	289	300
Advertising	207	191	184	164
Shipping	59	61	51	28
Provision for doubtful accounts	54	64	66	35
Taxes other than income taxes	19	20	26	26
Exploration, dry holes, abandonments	14	17	14	20
Maintenance and repairs	10	9	9	10

3.36

TABLE 3-7: LOSSES

	Number of Companies			
	2003	2002	2001	2000
Restructuring of operations	219	263	285	154
Write-down of assets	205	214	232	159
Intangible asset amortization	205	214	188	139
Foreign currency transactions	82	91	84	68
Sale of assets	80	96	71	40
Impairment of intangibles	72	97	74	N/C*
Debt extinguishment	59	N/C*	N/C*	N/C*
Change in fair value of derivatives	55	42	48	6
Minority interests	54	62	55	48
Equity in losses of investees	50	74	60	44
Litigation settlements	47	43	38	23
Sale of receivables	32	31	31	23
Environmental cleanup	23	24	20	14
Purchased R&D	14	19	21	20
Merger costs	12	25	29	28
Royalties	9	20	11	6
Start-up costs	6	6	14	6
Distributions on preferred securities of subsidiary trust	4	6	4	10

*N/C = Not compiled. Line item was not included in the table for the year shown.

EXPENSES

Cost of Goods Sold

3.37

HEALTH NET, INC. (DEC)

(Amounts in thousands)	2003	2002	2001
Revenues			
Health plan services premiums	$ 9,093,219	$ 8,581,658	$ 8,575,012
Government contracts	1,865,773	1,498,689	1,339,066
Net investment income	59,332	65,210	78,785
Other income	46,378	49,201	70,282
Total revenues	11,064,702	10,194,758	10,063,145
Expenses			
Health plan services	7,516,838	7,161,520	7,243,645
Government contracts	1,789,523	1,452,968	1,324,648
General and administrative	912,531	856,169	874,504
Selling	233,519	197,751	186,143
Depreciation	55,903	61,832	61,073
Amortization	2,774	7,060	37,622
Interest	39,135	40,226	54,940
Asset impairments and restructuring charges	16,409	60,337	79,667
Net (gain)loss on sales of businesses and properties and assets held for sale	(18,901)	5,000	72,422
Total expenses	10,547,731	9,842,863	9,934,664
Income from continuing operations before income taxes and cumulative effect of a change in accounting principle	$ 516,971	$ 351,895	$ 128,481

NOTES TO CONSOLIDATED FINANCIAL STATEMENTS

Note 2 (In Part): Summary of Significant Accounting Policies

Health Care Services and Government Contract Expenses

The cost of health care services is recognized in the period in which services are provided and includes an estimate of the cost of services which have been incurred but not yet reported. Such costs include payments to primary care physicians, specialists, hospitals, outpatient care facilities and the costs associated with managing the extent of such care. We estimate the amount of the provision for service costs incurred but not reported using standard actuarial methodologies based upon historical data including the period between the date services are rendered and the date claims are received and paid, denied claim activity, expected medical cost inflation, seasonality patterns and changes in membership. The estimates for service costs incurred but not reported are made on an accrual basis and adjusted in future periods as required. Any adjustments to the prior period estimates are included in the current period. Such estimates are subject to the impact of changes in the regulatory environment and economic conditions. Given the inherent variability of such estimates, the actual liability could differ significantly from the amounts provided. While the ultimate amount of claims and losses paid are dependent on future developments, management is of the opinion that the recorded reserves are adequate to cover such costs. These estimated liabilities are reduced by estimated amounts recoverable from third parties for subrogation.

Our HMOs, primarily in California, generally contract with various medical groups to provide professional care to certain of their members on a capitated, or fixed per member per month fee basis. Capitation contracts generally include a provision for stop-loss and non-capitated services for which we are liable. Professional capitated contracts also generally contain provisions for shared risk, whereby the Company and the medical groups share in the variance between actual costs and predetermined goals. Additionally, we contract with certain hospitals to provide hospital care to enrolled members on a capitation basis. Our HMOs also contract with hospitals, physicians and other providers of health care, pursuant to discounted fee-for-service arrangements, hospital per diems, and case rates under which providers bill the HMOs for each individual service provided to enrollees.

We assess the profitability of contracts for providing health care services when operating results or forecasts indicate probable future losses. Contracts are grouped in a manner consistent with the method of determining premium rates. Losses are determined by comparing anticipated premiums to estimates for the total of health care related costs less reinsurance recoveries, if any, and the cost of maintaining the contracts. Losses, if any, are recognized in the period the loss is determined and are classified as Health Plan Services. We had no premium deficiency reserves as of December 31, 2003 or 2002.

3.38

SANMINA-SCI CORPORATION (SEP)

(In thousands)	2003	2002	2001
Net sales	$10,361,434	$8,761,630	$4,054,048
Cost of sales	9,898,964	8,386,929	3,512,579
Gross profit	$ 462,470	$ 374,701	$ 541,469

Research and Development

3.39

INTERNATIONAL BUSINESS MACHINES CORPORATION (DEC)

(Dollars in millions)	2003	2002	2001
Revenue			
Global services	$42,635	$36,360	$34,956
Hardware	28,239	27,456	30,593
Software	14,311	13,074	12,939
Global financing	2,826	3,232	3,426
Enterprise investments/other	1,120	1,064	1,153
Total revenue	89,131	81,186	83,067
Cost			
Global services	31,903	26,812	25,355
Hardware	20,401	20,020	21,231
Software	1,927	2,043	2,265
Global financing	1,248	1,416	1,693
Enterprise investments/other	634	611	634
Total cost	56,113	50,902	51,178
Gross profit	33,018	30,284	31,889
Expense and other income			
Selling, general and administrative	17,852	18,738	17,048
Research, development and engineering (Note R)	5,077	4,750	4,986
Intellectual property and custom development income	(1,168)	(1,100)	(1,476)
Other (income) and expense	238	227	(353)
Interest expense	145	145	234
Total expense and other income	22,144	22,760	20,439
Income from continuing operations before income taxes	$10,874	$ 7,524	$11,450

NOTES TO CONSOLIDATED FINANCIAL STATEMENTS

A (In Part): Significant Accounting Policies

Research, Development and Engineering

Research, development and engineering (RD&E) costs are expensed as incurred.

R. Research, Development and Engineering

RD&E expense was $5,077 million in 2003, $4,750 million in 2002 and $4,986 million in 2001.

The company incurred expense of $4,609 million in 2003, $4,247 million in 2002 and $4,321 million in 2001 for scientific research and the application of scientific advances to the development of new and improved products and their uses as well as services and their application. Of these amounts, software-related expense was $2,300 million, $1,974 million and $1,926 million in 2003, 2002 and 2001, respectively.

Included in the expense was a charge of $9 million and $4 million in 2003 and 2002, respectively, for acquired in-process R&D. There was no in-process R&D expense recorded in 2001.

Expense for product-related engineering was $468 million, $503 million and $665 million in 2003, 2002 and 2001, respectively.

3.40

TENNECO AUTOMOTIVE INC. (DEC)

(Millions)	2003	2002	2001
Revenues			
Net sales and operating revenues	$3,766	$3,459	$3,364
Costs and expenses			
Cost of sales (exclusive of depreciation shown below)	2,994	2,735	2,699
Engineering, research, and development	67	67	67
Selling, general, and administrative	364	351	353
Depreciation and amortization of other intangibles	163	144	137
Amortization of goodwill	—	—	16
	3,588	3,297	3,272
Other income (expense)			
Gain on sale of assets	—	10	3
Loss on sale of receivables	(2)	(2)	(5)
Other income (loss)	—	(1)	2
	(2)	7	—
Income before interest expense, income taxes, and minority interest	$ 176	$ 169	$ 92

NOTES TO FINANCIAL STATEMENTS

1 (In Part): Summary of Accounting Policies

Engineering, Research and Development

We expense engineering, research, and development costs as they are incurred. Engineering, research and development expenses were $67 million for 2003, 2002 and 2001, and are included in the income statement caption of the same name. Of these amounts, $9 million in 2003, and $6 million for both 2002 and 2001 relate to research and development, which includes the search, design, and development of a new unproven product or process. Additionally, $35 million, $36 million, and $37 million of engineering, research, and development expense for 2003, 2002, and 2001, respectively, relates to improvements and enhancements to existing products and processes. The remainder of the expenses in each year relate to engineering costs we incurred for application of existing products and processes to vehicle platforms. Further, our customers reimburse us for engineering, research, and development costs on some platforms when we prepare prototypes and incur costs before platform awards. Our engineering research and development expense for 2003, 2002, and 2001 has been reduced by $11 million, $13 million, and $16 million, respectively, for these reimbursements.

Advertising

3.41

BROWN-FORMAN CORPORATION (APR)

(In millions)	2001	2002	2003
Net sales	$2,195	$2,224	$2,378
Excise taxes	256	250	318
Cost of sales	786	841	878
Gross profit	1,153	1,133	1,182
Advertising expenses	294	298	321
Selling, general, and administrative expenses	488	475	487
Other expense (income), net	(3)	7	(4)
Operating income	$ 374	$ 353	$ 378

NOTES TO CONSOLIDATED FINANCIAL STATEMENTS
(Dollars expressed in millions)

1 (In Part): Accounting Policies

Advertising Costs

We expense most advertising costs as we incur them, but we capitalize and amortize certain direct-response advertising costs over periods not exceeding one year. Capitalized advertising costs totaled $12 and $9 as of April 30, 2002 and 2003, respectively.

Shipping

3.42

BOWATER INCORPORATED (DEC)

(In millions)	2003	2002	2001
Sales	$2,721.1	$2,581.1	$2,454.3
Cost of sales, excluding depreciation, amortization and cost of timber harvested	2,194.0	2,020.7	1,688.4
Depreciation, amortization and cost of timber harvested	339.0	340.5	321.3
Distribution costs	264.4	232.6	180.0
Selling and administrative expense	148.6	140.2	114.5
Impairment of assets	—	28.5	—
Net gain on sale of assets	124.0	85.7	163.3
Operating income (loss)	$ (100.9)	$ (95.7)	$ 313.4

NOTES TO CONSOLIDATED FINANCIAL STATEMENTS

Note 1 (In Part): Summary of Significant Accounting Policies

Distribution Costs

Bowater's shipping and handling costs are classified as distribution costs and presented separately on the Consolidated Statement of Operations, in accordance with the Emerging Issues Task Force ("EITF") issued EITF No. 00-10, "Accounting for Shipping and Handling Fees and Costs."

Provision for Doubtful Accounts

3.43

TEXTRON INC. (DEC)

(In millions)	2003	2002	2001
Revenues			
Manufacturing revenues	$9,287	$ 9,766	$11,295
Finance revenues	572	584	681
Total revenues	9,859	10,350	11,976
Costs, expenses and other			
Cost of sales	7,669	7,961	9,440
Selling and administrative	1,294	1,305	1,457
Interest, net	270	297	425
Provision for losses on finance receivables	81	111	69
Special charges	159	135	143
Gain on sale of businesses	(15)	(25)	(342)
Total costs, expenses and other	9,458	9,784	11,192
Income from continuing operations before income taxes and distributions on preferred securities of subsidiary trusts	$ 401	$ 566	$ 784

NOTES TO CONSOLIDATED FINANCIAL STATEMENTS

Note 1 (In Part): Summary of Significant Accounting Policies

Allowance for Losses on Finance Receivables

Provisions for losses on finance receivables are charged to income in amounts sufficient to maintain the allowance at a level considered adequate to cover losses in the existing receivable portfolio. Management evaluates the allowance by examining current delinquencies, the characteristics of the existing accounts, historical loss experience, the value of the underlying collateral and general economic conditions and trends. Finance receivables are charged off when they are deemed to be uncollectible. Finance receivables are written down to the fair value (less estimated costs to sell) of the related collateral at the earlier of the date the collateral is repossessed or when no payment has been received for six months, unless management deems the receivable collectible.

Note 3 (In Part): Finance Receivables and Securitizations

Finance Receivables

Textron Finance provides financial services primarily to the aircraft, golf, vacation interval resort, dealer floorplan and middle market industries under a variety of financing vehicles with various contractual maturities.

Installment contracts and finance leases have initial terms ranging from two to 20 years, and are primarily secured by the financed equipment. Finance leases include residual values expected to be realized at contractual maturity. Distribution finance and revolving loans generally mature within one to five years. Distribution finance receivables are generally secured by the inventory of the financed distributor, while revolving loans are secured by trade receivables, inventory, plant and equipment, and pools of vacation interval notes receivables, pools of residential and recreational land lots, and the underlying real property. Golf course mortgages

have initial terms ranging from five to seven years with amortization periods from 15 to 25 years. Resort mortgages generally represent construction and inventory loans with terms up to two years. Golf course and resort mortgages are secured by real property and are generally limited to 75% or less of the property's appraised market value at loan origination. Leveraged leases are secured by the ownership of the leased equipment and real property and have initial terms up to approximately 30 years.

At the end of fiscal 2003 and 2002, Textron Finance had nonaccrual finance receivables, excluding receivables with recourse to the Manufacturing group, totaling $152 million and $177 million, respectively. Of these respective amounts $99 million and $122 million were considered impaired, which excludes finance leases and homogeneous loan portfolios. The allowance for losses on finance receivables related to impaired loans was $18 million and $33 million at the end of fiscal 2003 and 2002, respectively. The average recorded investment in impaired loans during 2003 was $123 million, compared with $97 million in 2002. No interest income was recognized on these loans using the cash basis method.

• • • • • •

The activity in the allowance for credit losses on finance receivables was as follows:

(In millions)	2003	2002	2001
Balance at the beginning of the year	$ 145	$ 125	$ 116
Provision for losses	81	111	69
Charge-offs	(131)	(114)	(69)
Recoveries	14	11	8
Acquisitions and other	10	12	1
Balance at the end of the year	$ 119	$ 145	$ 125

Textron Finance manages and services finance receivables for a variety of investors, participants and third-party portfolio owners. The total managed and serviced finance receivable portfolio, including owned finance receivables, was $8.5 billion at the end of 2003 and $9.0 billion at the end of 2002. Managed receivables include owned finance receivables and finance receivables sold in securitizations and private transactions where Textron Finance has retained some element of credit risk and continues to service the portfolio.

At January 3, 2004, Textron Finance's receivables are primarily diversified geographically across the United States, along with 4% held in South America and 9% in other countries. The most significant collateral concentration was in general aviation aircraft, which accounted for 22% of managed receivables. Textron Finance also has industry concentrations in the golf and vacation interval industries, which each accounted for 15% and 14%, respectively, of managed receivables at January 3, 2004.

LOSSES

Restructuring of Operations

3.44

AIR PRODUCTS AND CHEMICALS, INC. (SEP)

(Millions of dollars)	2003	2002	2001
Sales	$6,297.3	$5,401.2	$5,857.8
Costs and expenses			
Cost of sales	4,613.1	3,815.7	4,216.4
Selling and administrative	832.6	704.3	698.7
Research and development	121.1	120.3	121.8
Other (income) expense, net	(26.5)	(37.1)	(31.5)
Global cost reduction plans, net	152.5	23.1	107.0
Operating income	$ 604.5	$ 774.9	$ 745.4

NOTES TO THE FINANCIAL STATEMENTS

2 (In Part): New Accounting Standards

Standards Adopted 2003 (In Part)

In August 2001, the FASB issued SFAS No. 144, "Accounting for the Impairment or Disposal of Long-Lived Assets." The Statement supersedes SFAS No. 121, "Accounting for the Impairment of Long-Lived Assets and for Long-Lived Assets to Be Disposed Of." The Statement also supersedes APB Opinion No. 30 provisions related to the accounting and reporting for the disposal of a segment of a business. This Statement establishes a single accounting model, based on the frame-work established in SFAS No. 121, for long-lived assets to be disposed of by sale. The Statement retains most of the requirements in SFAS No. 121 related to the recognition of impairment of long-lived assets to be held and used. Additionally, SFAS No. 144 broadens the definition of businesses that qualify for reporting as discontinued operations and changes the timing of recognizing losses on such operations. The company adopted this Statement as of 1 October 2002, with no material effect on the company's financial statements.

In June 2002, the FASB issued SFAS No. 146, "Accounting for Costs Associated with Exit or Disposal Activities." This Statement addresses the accounting for costs associated with disposal activities covered by SFAS No. 144, "Accounting for the Impairment or Disposal of Long-Lived Assets," and with exit (restructuring) activities previously covered by Emerging Issues Task Force (EITF) Issue No. 94-3, "Liability Recognition for Certain Employee Termination Benefits and Other Costs to Exit an Activity." This Statement nullifies EITF Issue No. 94-3 in its entirely and requires that a liability for all costs be recognized when the liability is incurred. Generally, the ability to accrue for termination benefits at the communication date of a plan in the form of a one-time benefit arrangement is limited. The cost of the termination benefits would be recognized over the future service period of the employees. This Statement does not change the accounting for termination benefits under ongoing benefit arrangement such as those included in the company's global cost reduction plans discussed in Note 3. The company adopted SFAS No. 146 as of 1 October 2002. The adoption of this Statement did not have an impact on the company's financial statements.

3. Global Cost Reduction Plans

2003 Plan

In 2003, the company recorded an expense of $152.7 for a global cost reduction plan (2003 Plan). This expense included $56.8 for severance and pension-related benefits and $95.9 for asset disposals and facility closures in the Gases and Chemicals segments.

During the third quarter of 2003, the company completed a capacity utilization analysis in several businesses in the Gases segment. To reduce capacity and costs, several facilities ceased operation as of 30 June 2003. An expense of $37.6 was recognized for the closure of these facilities, net of expected recovery from disposal. A decision was made to terminate several incomplete capacity expansion projects. An expense of $13.0 was recognized for the cost of terminating these projects, net of expected recovery from disposal and redeployment. An expense of $3.6 was also recognized for the planned sale of two real estate properties and the termination of several leases for small facilities. These expenses were principally in the North American merchant and tonnage businesses with a modest amount in the Electronics business.

The rationalization of excess capacity in certain products resulted in a decision to exit certain Chemical Intermediates operations. Late in the quarter ended 30 June 2003, the company decided to pursue the sale of its European methylamines and derivatives business. The company expects to complete the sale by 30 June 2004. Expected proceeds from the sale were determined and a loss was recognized for the difference between the carrying value of the assets and the expected net proceeds from the sale. Additional expenses for the closure of the methanol and ammonia plants in Pensacola, Florida, which made products for internal consumption, were also recognized. The total expense for these actions was $41.7.

In addition to the capacity reduction initiatives, the company continues to implement cost reduction and productivity-related efforts. The divestitures, the capacity reductions and the cost control initiatives will result in the elimination of 461 positions from the company. The company will complete the 2003 Plan by 30 June 2004. Approximately 30% of the position reductions relates to capacity rationalization and divestitures. An additional 40% relates to ongoing productivity efforts and balancing engineering resources with project activity and the remaining 30% relates to a reduction in the number of management positions.

The following table presents the detail of expenses by segment for the global cost reduction plan recorded in 2003:

	Severance	Pension	Other(A)	Total
Gases	$27.1	$10.9	$54.2	$ 92.2
Chemicals	14.4	2.0	41.7	58.1
Equipment	2.2	.2	—	2.4
Provision for 2003 Plan	$43.7	$13.1	$95.9	$152.7
Reversal of 2002 Plan	(.2)	—	—	(.2)
Net expense in 2003	$43.5	$13.1	$95.9	$152.5

(A) Asset impairments and related expenses are included in the other category.

2002 Plan

In 2002, the company recorded an expense of $30.8 for a global cost reduction plan (2002 Plan), including U.S. packaged gas divestiture-related reductions. This expense included $27.1 for severance and pension-related benefits and $3.7 for asset impairments related to the planned sale or closure of two small chemical facilities. The 2002 Plan included 333 position eliminations in the areas of manufacturing, engineering, distribution and overheads. The 2002 Plan was completed as expected in March 2003.

The following table presents the detail of expenses by segment for the global cost reduction plan recorded in 2002:

	Severance	Pension	Other[A]	Total
Gases	$15.6	$10.6	$ —	$26.2
Chemicals	.8	.1	3.7	4.6
Provision for 2002 Plan	$16.4	$10.7	$3.7	$30.8
Reversal of 2001 Plan	(7.1)	—	(.6)	(7.7)
Net expense in 2002	$ 9.3	$10.7	$3.1	$23.1

[A] Asset impairments and related expenses are included in the other category.

2001 Plan

In 2001, the company recorded an expense of $109.2 for a global cost reduction plan (2001 Plan). This expense included $79.6 for severance benefits and pension plan settlements and $29.6 for asset impairments and related restructuring charges. The 2001 Plan included 670 position eliminations in the areas of manufacturing, engineering, distribution and overheads. The company decided to divest several small facilities, which required a write-down of the net carrying value to the estimated net realizable value. The 2001 Plan was completed in 2002, with 644 positions eliminated and total expenses of $101.5 incurred. The balance of the accrual of $7.7 was reversed into income during 2002.

The following table presents the detail of expenses by segment for the global cost reduction plan recorded in 2001:

	Severance	Pension	Other[A]	Total
Gases	$47.0	$10.3	$11.8	$ 69.1
Chemicals	9.4	1.4	17.8	28.6
Equipment	1.2	.8	—	2.0
Corporate	—	9.5	—	9.5
Provision for 2001 Plan	$57.6	$22.0	$29.6	$109.2
Reversal of 2000 Plan	(2.2)	—	—	(2.2)
Net expense in 2001	$55.4	$22.0	$29.6	$107.0

[A] Asset impairments and related expenses are included in the other category.

Plan Accrual

The following table summarizes changes to the carrying amount of the accrual for global cost reduction plans:

Balance as of	Severance	Pension	Other[A]	Total
30 September 2000	$ 23.5	$ —	$ —	$ 23.5
Provision	57.6	22.0	29.6	109.2
Noncash expenses	—	(22.0)	(23.8)	(45.8)
Cash expenditures	(29.8)	—	(4.3)	(34.1)
Reverse 2000 Plan balance	(2.2)	—	—	(2.2)
30 September 2001	$ 49.1	$ —	$ 1.5	$ 50.6
Provision	16.4	10.7	3.7	30.8
Noncash expenses	—	(10.7)	(3.7)	(14.4)
Cash expenditures	(51.6)	—	(.9)	(52.5)
Reverse 2001 Plan balance	(7.1)	—	(.6)	(7.7)
30 September 2002	$ 6.8	$ —	$ —	$ 6.8
Provision	43.7	13.1	95.9	152.7
Noncash expenses	—	(13.1)	(90.1)	(103.2)
Cash expenditures	(11.7)	—	(1.7)	(13.4)
Reverse 2002 Plan balance	(.2)	—	—	(.2)
30 September 2003	$ 38.6	$ —	$ 4.1	$ 42.7

[A] Asset impairments and related expenses are included in the other category.

3.45

PITNEY BOWES INC. (DEC)

(Dollars in thousands)	2003	2002	2001
Revenue from			
Sales	$1,325,490	$1,309,342	$1,304,811
Rentals	859,783	828,096	784,368
Core financing	544,938	539,876	526,200
Non-core financing	109,696	139,867	150,347
Business services	1,119,146	1,010,912	820,934
Support services	617,800	581,665	535,814
Total revenue	4,576,853	4,409,758	4,122,474
Costs and expenses			
Cost of sales	611,620	593,163	611,230
Cost of rentals	171,119	174,303	150,585
Cost of core financing	141,028	145,075	154,955
Cost of non-core financing	39,017	46,500	45,330
Cost of business services	921,027	814,187	660,215
Cost of support services	323,279	297,275	264,652
Cost of meter transition—impairment	—	—	227,300
Cost of meter transition—additional depreciation	—	—	41,000
Capital services charges	—	213,182	—
Selling, general and administrative	1,219,873	1,186,205	1,105,500
Research and development	147,262	141,269	133,105
Restructuring charges	116,713	—	116,142
Other income	(117)	—	(338,097)
Interest expense	167,649	185,352	193,076
Interest income	(2,708)	(6,198)	(8,903)
Total costs and expenses	3,855,762	3,790,313	3,356,090
Income from continuing operations before income taxes	$ 721,091	$ 619,445	$ 766,384

NOTES TO CONSOLIDATED FINANCIAL STATEMENTS
(Dollars in thousands)

1 (In Part): Summary of Significant Accounting Policies

Restructuring Charges

In 2002, FAS No. 146, "Accounting for Costs Associated with Exit or Disposal Activities," was issued. This statement nullifies EITF No. 94-3, "Liability Recognition for Certain Employee Termination Benefits and Other Costs to Exit an Activity (including Certain Costs Incurred in a Restructuring)." FAS No. 146 requires that a liability for costs associated with an exit or disposal activity be recognized when the liability is incurred. The company adopted the provisions of FAS No. 146, which are effective for one-time benefit arrangements and exit or disposal activities initiated after December 31, 2002. The company accounts for ongoing benefit arrangements under FAS No. 112, "Employers' Accounting for Postemployment Benefits," which requires that a liability be recognized when the costs are probable and reasonably estimable. See Note 13 to the consolidated financial statements.

13 (In Part): Restructuring Charges

2003 Restructuring Plan

In January 2003, the company announced that it would undertake restructuring initiatives related to realigned infrastructure requirements and reduced manufacturing needs for digital equipment. The charges related to these restructuring initiatives will be recorded as the various initiatives take effect. See Note 1 to the consolidated financial statements for the company's accounting policy related to restructuring charges.

In connection with this plan, the company recorded pre-tax restructuring charges of $116.7 million for the year ended December 31, 2003. The pre-tax restructuring charges are composed of:

(Dollars in millions)	Restructuring Charges	Non-Cash Charges	Cash Payments	Balance at December 31, 2003
Severance and benefit costs	$ 81.0	$ —	$(53.5)	$27.5
Asset impairments	26.6	(26.6)	—	—
Other exit costs	9.1	—	(4.4)	4.7
	$116.7	$(26.6)	$(57.9)	$32.2

All restructuring charges, except for the asset impairments, will result in cash outflows. The severance and benefit costs relate to a reduction in workforce of approximately 1,438 employees worldwide at December 31, 2003 and expected future workforce reductions of approximately 1,000 employees. The workforce reductions relate to actions across several of the company's businesses resulting from infrastructure and process improvements and its continuing efforts to streamline operations, and include managerial, professional, clerical and technical roles. Approximately 65% of the workforce reductions are in the U.S. The majority of the international workforce reductions are in Europe and Canada. Asset impairments relate primarily to the write-down of property, plant and equipment, resulting from the closure or streamlining of certain facilities. During 2003, the company recorded an asset impairment of $23.8 million as a result of the company's decision to exit its Main Plant facility in Connecticut in connection with its product sourcing and real estate optimization strategy. The fair values of the impaired long-lived assets were determined primarily using probability weighted expected cash flows in accordance with FAS No. 144. Other exit costs relate primarily to lease termination costs, noncancelable lease payments, consolidation of excess facilities and other costs associated with exiting business activities.

Write-Down of Assets

3.46

JDS UNIPHASE CORPORATION (JUN)

(In millions)	2003	2002	2001
Net sales	$ 675.9	$ 1,098.2	$ 3,232.8
Cost of sales	620.5	1,171.1	2,306.7
Gross profit (loss)	55.4	(72.9)	926.1
Operating expenses:			
Research and development	153.7	254.8	325.9
Selling, general and administrative	267.3	382.9	818.1
Amortization of goodwill	—	937.5	4,945.9
Amortization of other intangibles	19.8	371.2	441.1
Acquired in-process research and development	0.4	25.3	393.2
Reduction of goodwill	225.7	4,360.8	49,699.5
Reduction of other long-lived assets	167.9	1,618.6	385.5
Restructuring charges	121.3	260.0	264.3
Total operating expenses	956.1	8,211.1	57,273.5
Loss from operations	(900.7)	(8,284.0)	(56,347.4)
Interest and other income, net	32.5	48.3	48.5
Gain (loss) on sale of subsidiaries' net assets	(2.2)	0.1	1,770.2
Gain (loss) on sale of investments	4.0	15.0	(559.1)
Reduction in fair value of investments	(45.4)	(225.8)	(522.1)
Loss on equity method investments	(8.5)	(54.6)	(883.9)
Loss before income taxes	$(920.3)	$(8,501.0)	$(56,493.8)

NOTES TO CONSOLIDATED FINANCIAL STATEMENTS

Note 1 (In Part): Description of Business and Summary of Significant Accounting Policies

Investments

The Company's investments in all debt securities and marketable equity securities are classified as available-for-sale investments and are recorded at fair value. The cost of securities sold is based on the specific identification method. Unrealized gains and losses are reported as a separate component of stockholders' equity. The Company also has certain minority investments in privately-held companies. These investments are generally carried at cost and are classified as long-term investments.

The Company accounts for investments in joint ventures, limited liability partnerships and other investments in 50% or less owned companies over which it has the ability to exercise significant influence using the equity method of accounting. The Company accounts for the increase or decrease of its proportionate share of net book value in equity basis investments from the investees' issuance of stock at a price above or below the net book value per share as a change to additional paid-in capital. Due to the limited availability of timely data, the Company records the adjustments to its equity basis investments in the quarter subsequent to the issued financial statements.

The Company periodically reviews these investments for impairment. In the event the carrying value of an investment exceeds its fair value and the decline in fair value is determined to be other-than-temporary, the Company writes down the value of the investment to its fair value. The Company generally believes an other-than-temporary decline occurs when the fair value of an investment is below the carrying value for two full consecutive quarters.

Impairment or Disposal of Long-Lived Assets (Plant and Equipment and Intangible Assets)

Long-Lived Assets Held and Used

The Company tests long-lived assets or asset groups for recoverability when events or changes in circumstances indicate that their carrying amount may not be recoverable. Circumstances which could trigger a review include, but are not limited to: significant decreases in the market price of the asset; significant adverse changes in the business climate or legal factors; accumulation of costs significantly in excess of the amount originally expected for the acquisition or construction of the asset; current period cash flow or operating losses combined with a history of losses or a forecast of continuing losses associated with the use of the asset; and current expectation that the asset will more likely than not be sold or disposed significantly before the end of its estimated useful life (see Note 12).

Recoverability is assessed based on the carrying amount of the asset and its fair value which is generally determined based on the sum of the undiscounted cash flows expected to result from the use and the eventual disposal of the asset, as well as specific appraisal in certain instances. An impairment loss is recognized when the carrying amount is not recoverable and exceeds fair value.

Long-Lived Assets Held for Sale

Long-lived assets are classified as held for sale when certain criteria are met, which include: management commitment to a plan to sell the assets; the availability of the assets for immediate sale in their present condition; whether an active program to locate buyers and other actions to sell the assets has been initiated; whether the sale of the assets is probable and their transfer is expected to qualify for recognition as a completed sale within one year; whether the assets are being marketed at reasonable prices in relation to their fair value; and how unlikely it is that significant changes will be made to the plan to sell the assets (see Note 12).

The Company measures long-lived assets to be disposed of by sale at the lower of carrying amount and fair value less cost to sell. Fair value is determined using quoted market prices or the anticipated cash flows discounted at a rate commensurate with the risk involved.

Recent Accounting Pronouncements (In Part)

SFAS No. 144

In August 2001, the FASB issued SFAS No. 144, which superseders SFAS No. 121, "Accounting for the Impairment of Long-Lived Assets and for Long-Lived Assets to Be Dis-

posed Of," and certain provisions of Accounting Principles Board ("APB") Opinion No. 30, "Reporting the Results of Operations—Reporting the Effects of Disposal of a Segment of a Business, and Extraordinary. Unusual and Infrequently Occurring Events and Transactions." SFAS No. 144 retains the fundamental provisions of SFAS No. 121 related to: (i) the recognition and measurement of the impairment of long-lived assets to be held and used, and (ii) the measurement of long-lived assets to be disposed by sale. It provides more guidance on estimating cash flows when performing recoverability tests, requires long-lived assets to be disposed of other than by sale to be classified as held and used until disposal, and establishes more restrictive criteria to classify long-lived assets as held for sale. In addition, SFAS No. 144 supersedes the accounting and reporting provisions of APB Opinion No. 30 for the disposal of a segment of a business. However, it retains the basic provisions of APB Opinion No. 30 to report discontinued operations separately from continuing operations and extends the reporting of a discontinued operation to a component of an entity.

The Company adopted SFAS No. 144 on July 1, 2002. Under SFAS No. 121, excluding asset write-downs associated with the Global Realignment Program, the Company recorded impairment charges of $5,979.4 million in fiscal 2002. During fiscal 2003, the Company recorded impairment charges of $167.9 million, under SFAS No. 144 (see Note 12).

Note 3 (In Part): Investments

Reductions in Fair Value of Investments

The Company regularly evaluates the carrying value of its investments. When the carrying value of an investment exceeds the fair value and the decline in fair value is deemed to be other-than-temporary, the Company writes down the value of the investment to its fair value. During fiscal 2003, 2002 and 2001, the Company recorded $45.4 million, $225.8 million and $522.1 million, respectively, of other-than-temporary reductions in fair value of the Company's available-for-sale and non-marketable equity investments. Details of the other-than-temporary reductions were as follows (in millions):

	2003	2002	2001
Available-for-sale investments:			
Nortel common stock	$ —	$187.3	$511.8
Other	—	9.6	10.3
Non-marketable equity investments:			
Adept Technology ("Adept")	25.0	—	—
Other	20.4	28.9	—
Total reductions in fair value of investments	$45.4	$225.8	$522.1

During fiscal 2002, the Company entered into an automation development alliance agreement with Adept. In connection with this alliance, the Company invested $25.0 million in Adept's convertible preferred stock. During fiscal 2003, the Company determined that the decline in fair value of its Adept investment was other-than-temporary and wrote the investment down to zero.

Should the fair value of the Company's investments continue to decline in future periods, the Company may be required to record additional charges if the decline is determined to be other-than-temporary.

Note 12 (In Part): Reduction of Other Long-Lived Assets

During fiscal 2003, the Company recorded $167.9 million of reductions in the carrying value of its long-lived assets in accordance with SFAS No. 144. During fiscal 2002 and fiscal 2001, the Company recorded $1,618.6 million and $385.5 million, respectively, of reductions in the carrying value of its long-lived assets in accordance with SFAS No. 121. These charges excluded asset write-downs associated with the Global Realignment Program (see Note 13). The following table summarizes the components of the reductions of other long-lived assets (in millions):

	2003	2002	2001
Assets held and used:			
Purchased intangibles (other than goodwill)	$ 68.6	$1,243.1	$375.3
Property, plant and equipment	79.1	375.5	10.2
Assets held for sale:			
Property, plant and equipment	20.2	—	—
Total reductions of other long-lived assets	$167.9	$1,618.6	$385.5

Fiscal 2003 Charges

Assets Held and Used

On July 1, 2002, the Company adopted SFAS No. 144, under which long-lived assets other than goodwill are tested for recoverability if certain events or changes in circumstances indicate that the carrying value may not be recoverable. The Company noted indicators during the first quarter of fiscal 2003 that the carrying value of its long-lived assets, including purchased intangibles recorded in connection with its various acquisitions and property, plant and equipment, may not be recoverable and performed an impairment review. The impairment review was performed pursuant to SFAS No. 144 because of the prolonged economic downturn affecting the Company's operations and revenue forecasts. As a result of the prolonged economic downturn, the Company's projected future revenue and cash flows for certain of the Company's asset groupings were revised downward in the first quarter of fiscal 2003. Therefore, the Company evaluated the recoverability of its long-lived assets and recorded impairment charges based on the amounts by which the carrying amounts of these assets exceeded their fair value. For purchased intangibles, fair value was determined based on discounted future cash flows for the operating entities that had separately identifiable cash flows. For tangible fixed assets, the Company valued these assets that were subject to impairment using specific appraisals.

The following table summarizes the write-downs of purchased intangibles and property, plant and equipment by acquisition for the first quarter of fiscal 2003 (in millions):

Acquired Entities	Purchased Intangibles	Property, Plant and Equipment
Datacom	$39.1	$15.6
Epitaxx	19.9	26.3
SDL	—	24.3
Scion	8.9	12.9
Other	0.7	—
Total	$68.6	$79.1

During the rest of fiscal 2003, the Company noted no impairment indicators in connection with its long-lived assets held and used, and accordingly, a test of recoverability of its long-lived assets was not required.

Assets Held for Sale

During the third quarter and fourth quarter of fiscal 2003, the Company classified certain property, plant and equipment intended to be disposed of within a twelve month period as assets held for sale. In accordance with SFAS No. 144, the Company recorded an impairment charge of $13.3 million, representing the amount by which their carrying value exceeds fair value less cost to sell. During the first quarter of fiscal 2003, the Company classified certain property and equipment as assets held for sale in connection with the sales of its SIFAM and Cronos subsidiaries and recorded total impairment charges of $6.9 million.

3.47

THE KROGER CO. (JAN)

(In millions)	2003	2002	2001
Sales	$53,791	$51,760	$50,098
Merchandise costs, including advertising, warehousing, and transportation, excluding items shown separately below	39,637	37,810	36,398
Operating, general and administrative	10,354	9,618	9,483
Rent	653	656	650
Depreciation and amortization	1,209	1,087	973
Goodwill amortization	—	—	103
Goodwill impairment charge	444	—	—
Asset impairment charges	120	—	91
Restructuring charges	—	15	37
Merger-related costs	—	1	4
Operating profit	$ 1,374	$ 2,573	$ 2,359

NOTES TO CONSOLIDATED FINANCIAL STATEMENTS

1 (In Part): Accounting Policies

Impairment of Long-Lived Assets

In accordance with SFAS No. 144, "Accounting for the Impairment or Disposal of Long-Lived Assets," the Company monitors the carrying value of long-lived assets for potential impairment each quarter based on whether certain trigger events have occurred. These events include current period losses combined with a history of losses or a projection of continuing losses or a significant decrease in the market value of an asset. When a trigger event occurs, an impairment calculation is performed, comparing projected undiscounted future cash flows, utilizing current cash flow information and expected growth rates related to specific stores, to the carrying value for those stores. If impairment is identified for long-lived assets to be held and used, discounted future cash flows are compared to the asset's current carrying value. Impairment is recorded when the carrying value exceeds the discounted cash flows. With respect to owned property and equipment held for disposal, the value of the property and equipment is adjusted to reflect recoverable values based on previous efforts to dispose of similar assets and current economic conditions. Impairment is recognized for the excess of the carrying value over the estimated fair market value, reduced by estimated direct costs of disposal.

The Company performs impairment reviews at both the division and corporate levels. Generally, for reviews performed by local divisional management, costs to reduce the carrying value of long-lived assets are reflected in the Consolidated Statements of Earnings as "Operating, general and administrative" expense. Cost to reduce the carrying value of long-lived assets that result from corporate-level strategic plans are separately identified in the Consolidated Statements of Earnings as "Asset impairment charges." Refer to Note 3 for a description of asset impairment charges recorded during 2003 and 2001.

3 (In Part): Asset Impairment Charges and Related Items

In accordance with its policy on impairment of long-lived assets, the Company identified impairment losses for both assets to be disposed of and assets to be held and used during 2003 and 2001. These losses, which are reflected in the

Consolidated Statements of Earnings as "Asset impairment charges," totaled $120 and $91, pre-tax, in 2003 and 2001, respectively. In both years, the impairment reviews were conducted as a consequence of a corporate-level strategic plan that coordinated the closings of several locations over a relatively short period of time. The 2001 charge related to investments by acquired companies in stores opened shortly after the Fred Meyer merger that did not perform as expected during 2000 and 2001. Based on those results and forecasts for 2002 and beyond, the Company performed an impairment review in the third quarter of 2001 that resulted in a pre-tax charge of $91. The 2003 charge related to locations whose operating performance deteriorated subsequent to the 2001 review. During the fourth quarter of 2003, the Company authorized closure of several stores throughout the country based on results for 2002 and 2003, as well as updated projections for 2004 and beyond. This event triggered an impairment review of stores slated for closure as well as several other under-performing locations in the fourth quarter of 2003. The review resulted in a pre-tax charge totaling $120. These charges are more fully described below. No corporate-level asset impairment charges were recorded in 2002.

Assets to Be Disposed Of

The impairment charges for assets to be disposed of related primarily to the carrying values of land, buildings, equipment and leasehold improvements for stores that have closed or have been approved for closure. The impairment charges were determined by estimating the fair values of the locations, less costs of disposal. Fair values were based on third party offers to purchase the assets, or market value for comparable properties, if available. As a result, pre-tax impairment charges related to assets to be disposed of were recognized, reducing the carrying value of fixed assets by $54 in 2003 and $37 in 2001.

Assets to Be Held and Used

The impairment charges for assets to be held and used related primarily to the carrying values of land, buildings, equipment and leasehold improvements for stores that will continue to be operated by the Company. Updated projections, based on revised operating plans, were used, on a gross basis, to determine whether the assets were impaired. Then, discounted cash flows were used to estimate the fair value of the assets for purposes of measuring the impairment charge. As a result, impairment charges related to assets to be held and used were recognized, reducing the carrying value of fixed assets by $66 in 2003 and $54 in 2001.

Intangible Asset Amortization

3.48

BOWNE & CO., INC. (DEC)

(In thousands)	2003	2002	2001
Revenue	$ 1,064,820	$1,003,326	$ 1,054,631
Expenses:			
Cost of revenue	(717,928)	(667,089)	(713,710)
Selling and administrative	(273,438)	(275,818)	(268,773)
Depreciation	(40,332)	(40,662)	(41,117)
Amortization	(3,621)	(2,017)	(8,001)
Restructuring charges, integration costs and asset impairment charges	(25,591)	(19,378)	(20,949)
Gain (loss) on sale of certain printing assets	—	15,369	(1,858)
Gain on sale of building	—	4,889	—
Purchased in-process research and development	—	—	(800)
	(1,060,910)	(984,706)	(1,055,208)
Operating income (loss)	$ 3,910	$ 18,620	$ (577)

NOTES TO CONSOLIDATED FINANCIAL STATEMENTS (In thousands)

Note 1 (In Part): Summary of Significant Accounting Policies

Intangible Assets

Prior to July 1, 2001, intangible assets acquired in business combinations accounted for by the purchase method of accounting were capitalized and amortized over their expected useful life as a non-cash charge. Acquisitions after June 30, 2001 were accounted for under SFAS No. 141, "Business Combinations" and SFAS No. 142, "Goodwill and Other Intangible Assets". Those standards require that certain identifiable intangible assets be amortized over their expected useful lives. Under the new standards, the portion of the purchase price allocated to goodwill and indefinite-lived intangible assets is not amortized but is subject to impairment testing at least annually.

Amounts allocated to identifiable intangible assets are amortized on a straight-line basis over their estimated useful lives as follows:

Customer relationships	5–15 years
Software license agreement	5 years
Covenants not-to-compete	5 years
Proprietary technology	3 years

The Company also has a non-amortizable intangible asset with a balance of $10.4 million and $7.2 million as of December 31, 2003 and 2002, respectively, related to a minimum pension liability on its defined benefit pension plan and SERP plan.

Note 7 (In Part): Goodwill and Intangible Assets

The gross amounts and accumulated amortization of identifiable intangible assets is as follows:

	2003		2002	
	Gross Amount	Accumulated Amortization	Gross Amount	Accumulated Amortization
Amortizable intangible assets:				
Customer lists	$35,423	$7,708	$34,068	$4,792
Software licenses and proprietary technology	1,760	596	1,617	242
Covenants not-to-compete	1,800	390	1,800	—
Unamortizable intangible assets:				
Trade name	1,900	—	1,900	—
Intangible asset related to minimum pension liability	10,383	—	7,222	—
	$51,266	$8,694	$46,607	$5,034

Amortization expense related to identifiable intangible assets was $3,621, $2,017 and $1,146 for the years ended December 31, 2003, 2002, and 2001, respectively. Estimated annual amortization expense for the years ended December 31, 2004 through December 31, 2008 is shown below:

2004	$3,580
2005	$3,548
2006	$3,380
2007	$3,148
2008	$2,653

3.49

E. I. DU PONT DE NEMOURS AND COMPANY (DEC)

(Dollars in millions)	2003	2002	2001
Net sales	$26,996	$24,006	$24,726
Other income	734	516	644
Total	27,730	24,522	25,370
Cost of goods sold and other operating charges	19,476	16,296	16,727
Selling, general and administrative expenses	2,995	2,699	2,925
Depreciation	1,355	1,297	1,320
Amortization of goodwill and other intangible assets (Note 15)	229	218	434
Research and development expense	1,349	1,264	1,588
Interest expense	347	359	590
Restructuring and asset impairment charges	(17)	290	1,078
Separation charges—Textiles & Interiors	1,620	—	—
Goodwill impairment—Textiles & Interiors	295	—	—
Gain on sale of DuPont Pharmaceuticals	—	(25)	(6,136)
Gain on sale of interest by subsidiary—nonoperating	(62)	—	—
Total	27,587	22,398	18,526
Income before income taxes and minority interests	$ 143	$ 2,124	$ 6,844

NOTES TO CONSOLIDATED FINANCIAL STATEMENTS
(Dollars in millions)

1 (In Part): Summary of Significant Accounting Policies

Goodwill and Other Intangible Assets

Effective January 1, 2002, the company no longer amortizes goodwill and indefinite-lived intangible assets. Goodwill and indefinite-lived intangible assets are tested for impairment at least annually, however, these tests are performed more frequently when events or changes in circumstances indicate the carrying value may not be recoverable. The company's fair value methodology is based on quoted market prices, if available. If quoted market prices are not available, an estimate of fair market value is made based on prices of similar assets or other valuation methodologies including present value techniques. Impairment losses are included in income from operations.

Definite-lived intangible assets, such as purchased technology, patents, and customer lists are amortized over their estimated useful lives, generally for periods ranging from 5 to 20 years. The company continually evaluates the reasonableness of the useful lives of these assets.

15 (In Part): Goodwill and Other Intangible Assets

Goodwill

Upon adoption of SFAS No. 142 on January 1, 2002, amortization of goodwill was discontinued.

Other Intangible Assets

The adoption of SFAS No. 142 established two broad categories of intangible assets: definite-lived intangible assets which are subject to amortization and indefinite-lived intangible assets which are not subject to amortization. The gross carrying amounts and accumulated amortization in total and by major class of other intangible assets are as follows:

	Gross	Accumulated Amortization	Net
2003			
Intangible assets subject to amortization (definite-lived)			
Purchased technology	$2,097	$ (856)	$1,241
Patents	150	(30)	120
Trademarks	74	(11)	63
Other[1]	540	(136)	404
	2,861	(1,033)	1,828
Intangible assets not subject to amortization (indefinite-lived)			
Trademarks/Tradenames	183	—	183
Pioneer germplasm[2]	975	—	975
	1,158	—	1,158
	$4,019	$(1,033)	$2,986
2002			
Intangible assets subject to amortization (definite-lived)			
Purchased technology	$2,378	$ (785)	$1,593
Patents	77	(22)	55
Trademarks	55	(9)	46
Other[1]	395	(126)	269
	2,905	(942)	1,963
Intangible assets not subject to amortization (indefinite-lived)			
Trademarks/Tradenames	171	—	171
Pioneer germplasm[2]	975	—	975
	1,146	—	1,146
	$4,051	$ (942)	$3,109

[1] Primarily consists of sales and grower networks, customer lists, marketing and manufacturing alliances, mineral rights and noncompetition agreements. Totals at December 31, 2003 include those intangibles obtained through the acquisitions of the remaining interest in Griffin LLC and DuPont Canada Inc., and the formation of The Solae Company.

[2] Pioneer germplasm is the pool of genetic source material and body of knowledge gained from the development and delivery stage of plant breeding. The company recognized germplasm as an intangible asset upon the acquisition of Pioneer Hi-Bred International, Inc. This intangible asset is expected to contribute to cash flows beyond the foreseeable future and there are no legal, regulatory, contractual, or other factors which limit its useful life. Prior to the adoption of SFAS No. 142, the company amortized germplasm on a straight-line basis over a period of forty years, the maximum period previously allowed under generally accepted accounting principles.

The aggregate amortization expense for definite-lived intangible assets was $229 for 2003, and is estimated to be $210, $206, $201, $174, and $156 for each of the next five years, respectively.

Foreign Currency Transactions

3.50

KERR-MCGEE CORPORATION (DEC)

(Millions of dollars)	2003	2002	2001
Revenues	$4,185	$3,646	$3,555
Costs and expenses			
Costs and operating expenses	1,668	1,456	1,264
Selling, general and administrative expenses	371	313	228
Shipping and handling expenses	140	125	111
Depreciation and depletion	745	814	747
Accretion expense	25	—	—
Impairments on assets held for use	14	652	76
Loss (gain) associated with assets held for sale	(45)	176	—
Exploration, including dry holes and amortization of undeveloped leases	354	273	210
Taxes, other than income taxes	98	104	114
Provision for environmental remediation and restoration net of reimbursements	62	80	82
Interest and debt expense	251	275	195
Total costs and expenses	3,683	4,268	3,027
	502	(622)	528
Other income (expense)	(59)	(35)	224
Income (loss) from continuing operations before income taxes	$ 443	$ (657)	$ 752

NOTES TO FINANCIAL STATEMENTS

1 (In Part): The Company and Significant Accounting Policies

Foreign Currencies

The U.S. dollar is considered the functional currency for each of the company's international operations, except for its European chemical operations. Foreign currency transaction gains or losses are recognized in the period incurred and are included in other income (expense) in the Consolidated Statement of Operations. The company recorded net foreign currency transaction gains (losses) of $(41) million, $(38) million and $3 million in 2003, 2002 and 2001, respectively.

The euro is the functional currency for the European chemical operations. Translation adjustments resulting from translating the functional currency financial statements into U.S. dollar equivalents are reported separately in accumulated other comprehensive income in the Consolidated Statement of Comprehensive Income and Stockholders' Equity.

15 Other Income (Expense)

Other income (expense) included the following during each of the years in the three-year period ended December 31, 2003:

(Millions of dollars)	2003	2002	2001
Gain (loss) on foreign currency exchange	$(41)	$(38)	$ 3
Loss from unconsolidated affiliates	(33)	(25)	(5)
Gain on sale of Devon stock	17	—	—
Derivatives and Devon stock revaluation	4	35	225
Interest income	5	5	10
Other	(11)	(12)	(9)
Total	$(59)	$(35)	$224

Sale of Assets

3.51

THE GOODYEAR TIRE & RUBBER COMPANY (DEC)

(Dollars in millions)	2003	2002	2001
Net sales	$15,119.0	$13,856.2	$14,162.5
Cost of goods sold	12,495.3	11,303.9	11,685.3
Selling, administrative and general expense	2,371.2	2,203.2	2,220.5
Rationalizations	291.5	5.5	210.3
Interest expense	296.3	241.7	297.1
Other (income) and expense (note 4)	267.3	56.8	40.8
Foreign currency exchange	40.2	(9.7)	10.0
Equity in (earnings) losses of affiliates	12.1	13.2	39.7
Minority interest in net income (loss) of subsidiaries	35.0	55.3	(3.3)
Loss before income taxes	$ (689.9)	$ (13.7)	$ (337.9)

NOTES TO FINANCIAL STATEMENTS

Note 4 (In Part): Other (Income) and Expense

(In millions)	2003	2002	2001
Asset sales	$ 21.5	$(28.0)	$(45.8)
Interest income	(25.9)	(18.8)	(13.5)
Financing fees and financial instruments	99.4	48.4	50.1
General and product liability—discontinued products	145.4	33.8	31.1
Miscellaneous	26.9	21.4	18.9
	$267.3	$ 56.8	$ 40.8

Other (Income) and Expense in 2003 included a loss of $17.6 million ($8.9 million after tax or $0.05 per share) on the sale of 20,833,000 shares of Sumitomo Rubber Industries, Ltd. ("SRI") in the second quarter. 2003 included a loss of $11.6 million ($11.2 million after tax or $0.07 per share) on the sale of assets in the Engineered Products, North American Tire and European Union Tire Segments. 2003 also included a gain of $7.7 million ($6.4 million after tax or $0.04 per share) resulting from the sale of land in the Asia Tire Segment and assets in the Latin American and European Union Tire Segments. During 2002, Goodyear recorded a gain of $28.0 million (as restated) ($23.7 million after tax or $0.14 per share (as restated)) resulting from the sale of land and buildings in the Latin American Tire, Engineered Products and European Union Tire Segments. 2002 also included the writeoff of a miscellaneous investment of $4.1 million ($4.1 million after tax or $0.02 per share). In 2001, Goodyear recorded a gain of $18.4 million (as restated) ($14.7 million after tax or $0.09 per share (as restated)) resulting from the sale of land and buildings in the European Union Tire Segment in the first quarter. Additionally, Goodyear recorded a gain of $27.4 million ($16.9 million after tax or $0.10 per share) resulting from the sale of the Specialty Chemical Business in the 2001 fourth quarter. Refer to Note 18 for further information on Business Segments.

Impairment of Intangibles

3.52

SUN MICROSYSTEMS, INC. (JUN)

(In millions)	2003	2002	2001
Net revenues			
Products	$ 7,793	$ 9,093	$15,015
Services	3,641	3,403	3,235
Total net revenues	11,434	12,496	18,250
Cost of sales			
Cost of sales-products	4,342	5,506	7,960
Cost of sales-services	2,150	2,074	2,080
Total cost of sales	6,492	7,580	10,040
Gross margin	4,942	4,916	8,210
Operating expenses			
Research and development	1,837	1,832	2,016
Selling, general and administrative	3,329	3,806	4,445
Restructuring charges	371	517	75
Impairment of goodwill and other intangible assets	2,125	6	1
Goodwill amortization	—	—	285
Purchased in-process research and development	4	3	77
Total operating expenses	7,666	6,164	6,899
Operating income (loss)	$(2,724)	$(1,248)	$ 1,311

NOTES TO CONSOLIDATED FINANCIAL STATEMENTS

2 (In Part): Summary of Significant Accounting Policies

Long-Lived Assets

Intangible Assets Other Than Goodwill

Sun reviews its long-lived assets (other than goodwill) for impairment whenever events or changes in circumstances indicate that the carrying amount of an asset may not be recoverable. We assess the recoverability of the long-lived assets (other than goodwill) by comparing the estimated undiscounted cash flows associated with the related asset or group of assets against their respective carrying amounts. The amount of an impairment, if any, is calculated based on the excess of the carrying amount over the fair value of those assets.

At June 30, 2003, we had Intangible Assets Other than Goodwill (Other Intangible Assets) with a net book value of approximately $114 million, net of accumulated amortization of $525 million, as compared with a net book value of $215 million, net of accumulated amortization of $429 million at June 30, 2002. These amounts include intangibles related to acquisitions with a net book value of $91 million, net of accumulated amortization of $326 million, as compared with a net book value of $104 million, net of accumulated amortization of $262 million at June 30, 2002. In addition, at June 30, 2003, Other Intangible Assets includes amounts related to a revenue generating technology license, acquired as part of the Strategic Alliance with AOL with a net book value of $23 million, net of accumulated amortization of $199 million, as compared with a net book value of $111 million, net of accumulated amortization of $167 million at June 30, 2002.

During the fiscal year ended June 30, 2003, Sun recognized an impairment expense related to Other Intangible Assets totaling $98 million, as compared with $6 million in fiscal 2002 and $1 million in fiscal 2001. The impairment charges in fiscal 2003, 2002 and 2001 pertained to the Product Group segment. These charges were based on a comparison of the fair value of the underlying intangible asset, calculated based on the discounted cash flows expected during its remaining useful life, to its carrying value. While our cash flow assumptions are consistent with the plans and estimates we are using to manage the underlying businesses, there is significant judgment in attributing cash flows to our Other Intangible Assets over their respective estimated useful lives. See Note 4.

Goodwill

We adopted Statement of Financial Accounting Standard No. 142 (SFAS 142), "Goodwill and Other Intangible Assets" on July 1, 2001. This standard requires that goodwill no longer be amortized, and instead, be tested for impairment on an annual basis (or whenever events occur which may indicate possible impairment). We perform the impairment analysis at one level below the operating segment level as defined in SFAS 142. This analysis requires management to make a series of critical assumptions to: (1) evaluate whether any impairment exists, and (2) measure the amount of impairment.

In testing for a potential impairment of goodwill, SFAS 142 requires us to: (1) allocate goodwill to the various Sun businesses to which the acquired goodwill relates; (2) estimate the fair value of those Sun businesses to which goodwill relates; and (3) determine the carrying value (book value) of those businesses, as some assets and liabilities related to those businesses, such as inventory and accounts receivable, are not held by those businesses but by functional departments (for example, our Global Sales Operations and Worldwide Operations organizations). Furthermore, if the estimated fair value is less than the carrying value for a particular business, then we are required to estimate the fair value of all identifiable assets and liabilities of the business, in a manner similar to a purchase price allocation for an acquired business. This requires independent valuations of certain internally generated and unrecognized intangible assets such as in-process research and development and developed and technology. Only after this process is completed, is the amount of goodwill impairment determined.

The process of evaluating the potential impairment of goodwill is highly subjective and requires significant judgment at many points during the analysis. In estimating the fair value of the businesses with recognized goodwill for the purposes of our annual or periodic analyses, we make estimates and judgments about the future cash flows of these businesses. Our cash flow forecasts are based on assumptions that are consistent with the plans and estimates we are using to manage the underlying businesses. In addition, we make certain judgments about allocating shared assets such as accounts receivable and inventory to the estimated balance sheet for those businesses. We also consider our market capitalization (adjusted for unallocated monetary assets such as cash, marketable debt securities and debt) on the date we perform the analysis.

Recent Pronouncements (In Part)

In October, 2001, the Financial Accounting Standard Board (FASB) issued Statement of Financial Accounting Standard No. 144 (SFAS 144), "Accounting for the Impairment or Disposal of Long-Lived Assets." SFAS 144 supersedes SFAS 121, "Accounting for the Impairment of Long-Lived Assets and for Long-Lived Assets to be disposed of." The primary objectives of SFAS 144 are to develop one accounting model based on the framework established in SFAS 121 for long-lived assets to be disposed of by sale, and to address significant implementation issues identified after the issuance of SFAS 121. We adopted SFAS 144 for our fiscal year beginning July 1, 2002; however, the adoption did not have a significant impact on our financial statements.

4 (In Part): Goodwill and Other Acquisition-Related Intangible Assets

Goodwill (In Part)

We adopted SFAS 142, "Goodwill and Other Intangible Assets," on July 1, 2001. This standard requires that goodwill no longer be amortized, and instead, be tested for impairment on an annual basis (or whenever events occur which may indicate possible impairment).

• • • • • •

Changes in the carrying amount of goodwill for the years ended June 30, 2003 and 2002, by reportable segment, are as follows (in millions):

	Product Group	Sun Services	Total
Balance as of June 30, 2001	$ 2,120	$ 6	$ 2,126
Goodwill reclassified on July 1, 2001	(3)	3	—
Workforce reclassified as goodwill	11	1	12
Goodwill acquired during the period	5	39	44
Goodwill reclassified during the period[1]	(17)	17	—
Balance as of June 30, 2002	2,116	66	2,182
Goodwill acquired during the period	151	20	171
Impairments	(2,027)	—	(2,027)
Balance as of June 30, 2003	$ 240	$86	$ 326

[1] We reclassified $17 million of goodwill during fiscal 2002 relating to our former i-Planet products business from the Products Group segment to the Sun Services segment because certain product support resources were moved into our Services business during fiscal 2002, as well as related revenues earned from those resources.

During fiscal 2003, we recognized an impairment expense of $2,125 million. As discussed further below, this impairment related to three different types of intangible assets: (1) goodwill ($2,027 million); (2) other acquisition-related intangible assets ($42 million); and (3) a revenue generating technology license ($56 million).

We perform the impairment analysis at one level below the operating segment level as defined in SFAS 142. This analysis requires management to make a series of critical assumptions to: (1) evaluate whether any impairment exists; and (2) measure the amount of impairment.

In October 2002, based on a combination of factors, particularly: (1) our current and projected operating results; (2) our decision to reduce our workforce and eliminate excess facility space; and (3) our then current market capitalization, we concluded there were sufficient indicators to require us to assess whether any portion of our recorded goodwill balance was impaired. As part of this analysis, SFAS 142 requires that

we estimate the fair value of our reporting units as compared with their estimated book value. If the estimated fair value of a reporting unit is less than the estimated book value, then an impairment is deemed to have occurred. In estimating the fair value of our reporting units, we primarily used the income approach (which utilizes forecasted discounted cash flows to estimate the fair value of the reporting unit) and the market approach (which estimates fair value based on market prices for comparable companies). We also considered Sun's total market capitalization as of October 17, 2002 (the date we concluded an analysis was required), and our average market capitalization for the 30 days prior to and subsequent to October 17, 2002 to adequately consider the impact of volatility on market capitalization on that day.

We conducted our fiscal 2002 annual analysis in the fourth quarter of fiscal 2002. We concluded at that time, that we did not have any impairment of goodwill based on our then forecasted discounted cash flows as well as our market capitalization. However, in October 2002, the estimated fair value of our reporting units decreased because our current forecasted discounted cash flows and market capitalization were lower than at the time of our previous analysis. Based on this analysis, we concluded that the goodwill in our Volume Systems and Network Storage reporting units was impaired. As required by SFAS 142, in measuring the amount of goodwill impairment, we made a hypothetical allocation of the estimated fair value of the reporting units to the tangible and intangible assets (other than goodwill) within these reporting units. Prior to this allocation of the assets to the reporting units, we assessed long-lived assets for impairment in accordance with SFAS 144. Based on this allocation, we concluded that all of the recorded goodwill in the Volume Systems reporting unit ($1,566 million) and the Network Storage reporting unit ($461 million) was impaired and needed to be expensed as a non-cash charge to continuing operations during the second quarter of fiscal 2003. Approximately $1,560 million and $360 million of the impairment related to goodwill acquired from our acquisitions of Cobalt Networks, Inc. and HighGround Systems, Inc., respectively.

In our fiscal 2003 annual analysis conducted in the fourth quarter of fiscal 2003, we concluded that we did not have any additional impairment of goodwill based on our then forecasted discounted cash flows as well as our market capitalization. Reporting units in our Product Group segment accounted for approximately 75% of the carrying value of our goodwill at June 30, 2003.

Other Acquisition-Related Intangible Assets (In Part)

Based on the same considerations outlined in the previous discussion on goodwill, in October 2002, we also concluded that sufficient indicators existed to require us to assess whether a portion of our other acquisition-related intangible assets was impaired. SFAS 144 is the authoritative standard on the accounting for the impairment of other intangible assets. This analysis differs from our goodwill analysis in that an impairment is only deemed to have occurred if the sum of the forecasted undiscounted future cash flows related to the asset are less than the carrying value of the intangible asset we are testing for impairment. If the forecasted cash flows are less than the carrying value, then we must write down the carrying value to its estimated fair value. As a result of our analysis, we recognized an impairment charge of $42 million in our Product Group segment to reduce our other acquisition-related intangible assets balance to its estimated fair value during fiscal 2003. All impairments of non-goodwill intangible assets were recognized before we made a hypothetical allocation of the estimated fair value of the reporting units to the tangible and intangible assets (other than goodwill) within each reporting unit tested for goodwill impairment, as required by SFAS 142. The estimated fair value of the other acquisition-related intangibles was determined using the income approach (discounted cash flows). Approximately $31 million and $11 million of the impairment related to intangible assets acquired in our acquisitions of Cobalt Networks, Inc. and HighGround Systems, Inc., respectively.

Information regarding our other acquisition-related intangible assets is as follows (in millions):

		2002							
	Gross Carrying Amount				**Accumulated Amortization**				**Net**
	6/30/01	Additions	Impairments/ Reclass	6/30/02	6/30/01	Additions	Impairments/ Reclass	6/30/02	6/30/02
Developed technology	$290	$18	$ —	$308	$(169)	$(55)	$—	$(224)	$ 84
Customer base	57	—	(6)	51	(19)	(15)	—	(34)	17
Acquired workforce and other	53	—	(46)	7	(27)	(2)	25	(4)	3
	$400	$18	$(52)	$366	$(215)	$(72)	$25	$(262)	$104

The impairments/reclass in gross carrying amount of $52 million consists of a $6 million impairment charge and a $46 million reclassification of assembled workforce intangible to goodwill due to the adoption of SFAS 142 as outlined above in the goodwill discussion.

	2003								Net
	Gross Carrying Amount				Accumulated Amortization				
	6/30/02	Additions	Impairments	6/30/03	6/30/02	Additions	Impairments	6/30/03	6/30/03
Developed technology	$308	$ 39	$(47)	$300	$(224)	$(46)	$14	$(256)	$44
Customer base	51	—	(8)	43	(34)	(8)	—	(42)	1
Acquired workforce and other	7	68	(1)	74	(4)	(24)	—	(28)	46
	$366	$107	$(56)	$417	$(262)	$(78)	$14	$(326)	$91

Revenue Generating Technology License

Based on the considerations outlined in the previous discussion on goodwill, in October 2002, we concluded that sufficient indicators existed to require us to perform an analysis in accordance with SFAS 144 to assess whether a portion of the technology license we acquired from America Online in fiscal 1999 was impaired. Based on our impairment analysis, we concluded that the carrying value of the intangible asset was impaired. Accordingly, we recognized a non-cash impairment expense of $56 million related to this technology license during fiscal 2003. As of June 30, 2003, this technology license had a carrying value of $23 million.

Debt Extinguishment

3.53

GEORGIA GULF CORPORATION (DEC)

(In thousand)	2003	2002	2001
Net sales	$1,444,483	$1,230,751	$1,205,896
Operating costs and expenses:			
Cost of sales	1,319,094	1,086,746	1,125,439
Selling, general and administrative expenses	55,691	45,685	44,665
Asset write-off and other related charges	—	—	5,438
Total operating costs and expenses	1,374,785	1,132,431	1,175,542
Operating income	69,698	98,320	30,354
Other income (expense):			
Interest expense	(38,195)	(49,739)	(57,500)
Cost related to early retirement of debt	(13,816)	—	—
Interest income	53	160	185
Income (loss) before income taxes	$ 17,740	$ 48,741	$ (26,961)

NOTES TO CONSOLIDATED FINANCIAL STATEMENTS

2 (In Part): New Accounting Pronouncements

In April 2002, the FASB issued SFAS No. 145, "*Rescission of FASB Statements No. 4, 44 and 64, Amendment of FASB Statement No. 13, and Technical Corrections.*" The Statement rescinds SFAS No. 4, "*Reporting Gains and Losses from Extinguishment of Debt,*" and an amendment of that Statement, SFAS No. 64, "*Extinguishments of Debt Made to Satisfy Sinking-Fund Requirements.*" SFAS No. 145 recognizes that the use of debt extinguishment can be a part of the risk management strategy of a company and hence, the classificatoion of all early extinguishment of debt as an extraordinary item may no longer be appropriate. In addition, the Statement amends SFAS No. 13, "*Accounting for Leases,*" to eliminate an inconsistency between the required accounting for sale-leaseback transactions and the required accounting for certain lease modifications that have economic effects that are similar to sale-leaseback transactions. Provisions of this Statement, as they relate to Statement No. 13, are to be effective for transactions occuring after May 15, 2002. Provisions that relate to Statement No. 4 are effective for fiscal years beginning after May 15, 2002. We adopted SFAS No. 145 on January 1, 2003, and accordingly, have recorded the cost related to early retirement of debt as a component of operating income in our 2003 consolidated statement of income (see note 9).

9 (In Part): Long-Term Debt

Long-term debt consisted of the following:

(In thousands)	2003	2002
Senior credit facility:		
Tranche C term loan	$ —	$149,780
Tranche D term loan	200,000	—
7.625% notes due 2005	100,000	100,000
7.125% notes due 2013	100,000	—
10.375% notes due 2007	—	200,000
Other	27,872	27,206
Total debt	427,872	476,986
Less current portion	1,000	600
Long-term debt	$426,872	$476,386

In December 2003, we retired $200.0 million of unsecured 10.375 percent notes, which were due November 2007. Interest on the notes was payable on May 1 and November 1 of each year. We financed the retirement of the notes by replacing our senior credit facility $134.3 million tranche C term loan with a $200.0 million tranche D term loan, issuing $100.0 million of senior unsecured 7.125 percent notes and increasing our permitted receivables transactions by $25.0 million. As a result of the note retirement, we incurred a $13.8 million charge to income from operations, which is comprised of a redemption premium and related professional fees of $10.8 million and a write-off of unamortized debt issuance cost of $3.0 million.

On December 3, 2003, we entered into an amended and restated credit agreement amending the senior credit agreement dated as of November 12, 1999, as amended by amendment no. 2 dated September 26, 2003. The amendment created a new $200.0 million tranche D term loan used to repay our existing $134.3 million tranche C term loan and to retire a portion of our $200.0 million 10.375 percent notes. The new tranche D term loan delays the required principal payments and matures December 2, 2010. The amendment also modified the applicable interest margin depending on our leverage ratio and increased the commitments under the revolving credit facility, which matures on November 12, 2005, by $20 million to $120 million.

On December 3, 2003, we also issued $100.0 million in principal amount of our unsecured 7.125 percent senior notes, which are due December 15, 2013. The proceeds of the notes were used to retire a portion of the $200.0 million 10.375 percent notes. Interest on the notes is payable June 15 and December 15 of each year. On or after December 15, 2008, we may redeem the notes in whole or in part, initially at 103.563 percent of their principal amount, and thereafter at prices declining annually to 100 percent on or after December 15, 2011.

Change in Fair Value of Derivatives

3.54

DIMON INCORPORATED (JUN)

(In thousands)	2003	2002	2001
Sales and other operating revenues	$1,271,683	$1,259,720	$1,400,955
Cost of goods and services sold	1,061,270	1,054,255	1,209,931
	210,413	205,465	191,024
Selling, administrative and general expenses	116,075	109,363	103,537
Restructuring recovery	—	—	(1,384)
Recovery from litigation settlements	—	—	(3,923)
Operating Income	94,338	96,102	92,794
Interest expense	46,887	47,877	53,574
Current charge derivative financial instruments	12,409	10,202	4,680
Income before income taxes, equity in net income (loss) of investee companies, cumulative effect of accounting changes and extraordinary item	$ 35,042	$ 38,023	$ 34,540

NOTES TO CONSOLIDATED FINANCIAL STATEMENTS
(In thousands)

Note A (In Part): Significant Accounting Policies

Accounting Pronouncements (In Part)

In June 1998, the Financial Accounting Standards Board (FASB) issued Statement of Financial Accounting Standards (SFAS) No. 133, "Accounting for Derivative instruments and Hedging Activities," which provided a comprehensive and consistent standard for the recognition and measurement of derivatives and hedging activities. In June 1999, the FASB issued SFAS No. 137, "Accounting for Derivative Instruments and Hedging Activities—Deferral of the Effective Date of SFAS No. 133," which delayed implementation of SFAS No. 133 until years beginning after June 15, 2000. In June 2000, the FASB issued SFAS No. 138, "Accounting for Certain Derivative Instruments and Certain Hedging Activities," which amended SFAS No. 133. Effective July 1, 2000, the Company adopted SFAS No. 133 as amended.

• • • • • •

In April 2003, FASB issued SFAS No. 149, "Amendment of Statement 133 on Derivative Instruments and Hedging Activities. "SFAS No. 149 amends and clarifies financial accounting and reporting for derivative instruments, including certain derivative instruments embedded in other contracts and for hedging activities under SFAS No. 133, "Accounting for Derivative Instruments and Hedging Activities." This Statement will become effective in fiscal 2004 for contracts entered into or modified after June 30, 2003. The Company will adopt the provisions under SFAS No. 149 beginning on July 1, 2003 and does not expect any material impact on its financial statements.

Note D (In Part): Derivative and Other Financial Instruments

Fair Value of Derivative Financial Instruments

Effective July 1, 2000, the Company adopted SFAS No. 133, "Accounting for Derivative instruments and Hedging Activities," As a result of adoption of SFAS No. 133, the Company recognizes all derivative financial instruments, such as interest rate swap contracts and foreign exchange contracts, in the consolidated financial statements at fair value regardless of the purpose or intent for holding the instrument. Changes in the fair value of derivative financial instruments are either recognized periodically in income or in shareholders' equity as a component of comprehensive income depending on whether the derivative financial instrument qualifies for hedge accounting, and if so, whether it qualifies as a fair value hedge or cash flow hedge. Changes in fair values of derivatives accounted for as fair value hedges are recorded in income along with the portions of the changes in the fair values of the hedged items that relate to the hedged risk(s). Changes in fair values of derivatives accounted for as cash flow hedges, to the extent they are effective as hedges, are recorded in other comprehensive income net of deferred taxes. Changes in fair values of derivatives not qualifying as hedges are reported in income.

The fair value estimates presented herein are based on information available to management and were determined using quoted market prices and the discounted value of future cash flows.

During the fiscal year ended June 30, 2003, accumulated other comprehensive income increased by $1,638, net of deferred taxes of $804 due to the reclassification of $418, net of taxes of $202, which was reclassified into earnings, primarily as cost of goods and services sold, due to the fulfillment of transactions. The remaining $1,220, net of tax of $602, was due to the issuance of new cash flow hedges during the year. During the fiscal year ended June 30, 2002, accumulated other comprehensive income decreased by $4,192, net of deferred taxes of $2,112, due to the reclassfication of net losses on derivative instruments to earnings. Of this amount, $994, net of taxes of $535, was reclassified into earnings as a result of the discontinuance of a cash flow hedge that had been deemed effective. During the fiscal year ended June 30, 2001, accumulated other comprehensive income decreased by $4,828, net of deferred taxes of $2,423, related specifically to accumulated unrealized net losses on forward contracts and interest rate swap agreements accounted for as cash flow hedges.

At June 30, 2003, the Company expects to reclassify approximately $1,002 of gains on derivative instruments, net of deferred taxes of $494, from accumulated other comprehensive income to earnings during the next twelve months due to the actual fulfillment of forecasted transactions. The Company is hedging its exposure to the variability of future cash flows for forecasted transactions over various time periods not exceeding ten years.

The carrying value and estimated fair value of the Company's long-term debt are $426, 122 and $449,522, respectively, as of June 30, 2003 and $403,339 and $402,977, respectively, as of June 30, 2002.

The counterparties to all of the Company's derivative financial instruments are a diverse group of major financial institutions with which the Company also has other financial relationships. These counterparties expose the Company to credit loss in the event of non-performance. If a counterparty fails to meet the terms of an agreement, the Company's exposure is limited to the net amount that would have been received, if any, over the agreement's remaining life. The Company does not anticipate non-performance by the counterparties, given their high credit ratings, and no material loss would be expected from non-performance by any one of such counterparties.

Fixed to Floating Rate Interest Swaps

Concurrent with the private issuance of $200 million principal amount of 9 5/8% Senior Notes on October 30, 2001, the Company entered into a derivative financial instrument to swap the entire $200 million notional amout of the Senior Notes to a floating interest rate equal to LIBOR plus 4.11%, set six months in arrears. Also, concurrent with the private issuance of $125 million principal amount of 7 3/4% Senior Notes on May 30, 2003, the Company entered into a derivative financial instrument to swap the entire $125 million notional amount of Senior Notes to a floating interest rate equal to LIBOR plus 3.69%, set six months in arrears. See also Note F to the "Notes to Consolidated Financial Statements."

The maturity, payment dates, and other fundamental terms of these derivative financial instruments match those of the related Senior Notes. In accordance with SFAS No. 133, these derivatives qualify for hedge accounting treatment. They are accounted for as fair value hedges. Changes in the fair value of these derivative financial instruments, as well as offsetting changes in the fair value of the Senior Notes, are being recognized in current period earnings. As of June 30, 2003 and 2002, the fair value of the debt increased the Senior Notes liability by $16,319 and decreased the liability by $3,638, respectively, with a corresponding change in the fair value of the derivative financial instruments reflected in Deferred Credits—Compensation and Other.

Floating to Fixed Rate Interest Swaps

Prior to the implementation of SFAS No. 133, the Company entered into multiple interest swaps to convert a portion of its worldwide debt portfolio from floating to fixed interest rates, to reduce its exposure to interest rate volatility. At June 30, 2003, the Company held instruments of this type with an aggregate notional value of $265 million, bearing interest at rates between 4.29% and 6.22% and with maturity dates ranging from September 15, 2003 to September 15, 2008. The implementation of SFAS No. 133 eliminated hedge accounting treatment for these instruments because they do not meet certain criteria. Accordingly, the Company is required to reflect the full amount of all changes in their fair value, without offset, in its current earnings. These fair value adjustments have caused substantial volatility in the Company's reported earnings. For the fiscal years ended June 30, 2003, 2002 and 2001, the Company recognized non-cash charges before income taxes of $12,409, $10,202 and $4,680, respectively, from the change in the fair value of these derivative financial instruments. With the recognition of each charge or credit relating to these instruments, a corresponding amount is recognized in Deferred Credits—Compensation and Other. At June 30, 2003, there was an aggregate credit of $27,884 relating to these instruments accumulated in this balance sheet classification, all of which will reverse through future earnings over the remaining life of the instruments.

Minority Interest

3.55

CHARTER COMMUNICATIONS, INC. (DEC)

(Dollars in millions)	2003	2002	2001
Revenues	$4,819	$ 4,566	$ 3,807
Costs and expenses			
Operating (excluding depreciation and amortization)	1,952	1,807	1,486
Selling, general and administrative	940	963	826
Depreciation and amortization	1,479	1,439	2,693
Impairment of franchises	—	4,638	—
Gain on sale of system	(21)	—	—
Option compensation expense (income), net	4	5	(5)
Special charges, net	21	36	18
Unfavorable contracts and other settlements	(72)	—	—
	4,303	8,888	5,018
Income (loss) from operations	516	(4,322)	(1,211)
Other income and expenses			
Interest expense, net	(1,557)	(1,503)	(1,310)
Gain (loss) on derivative instruments and hedging activities, net	65	(115)	(50)
Gain on debt exchange, net	267	—	—
Loss on equity investments	(3)	(3)	(54)
Other, net	(13)	(1)	(5)
	(1,241)	(1,622)	(1,419)
Loss before minority interest, income taxes and cumulative effect of accounting change	(725)	(5,944)	(2,630)
Minority interest	377	3,176	1,461
Loss before income taxes and cumulative effect of accounting change	$ (348)	$(2,768)	$(1,169)

NOTES TO CONSOLIDATED FINANCIAL STATEMENTS
(Dollars in millions)

3 (In Part): Summary of Significant Accounting Policies

Minority Interest

Minority interest on the consolidated balance sheets represents the portion of members' equity of Charter Holdco not owned by Charter, plus preferred membership interests in two indirect subsidiaries of Charter held by Mr. Paul G. Allen and certain sellers of the Helicon systems. Minority interest totaled $689 million and $1.0 billion as of December 31, 2003 and 2002, respectively, on the accompanying consolidated balance sheets. Gains or losses arising from issuances by Charter Holdco of its membership units are recorded as capital transactions thereby increasing or decreasing shareholders' equity and decreasing or increasing minority interest on the consolidated balance sheets. These losses totaled $1 million, $1 million and $253 million for the years ended December 31, 2003, 2002 and 2001, respectively, on the accompanying consolidated statements of changes in shareholders' equity. Operating losses are allocated to the minority owners based on their ownership percentage, thereby reducing the Company's net loss.

10. Minority Interest and Equity Interest of Charter Holdco

The Company is a holding company whose primary asset is a controlling equity interest in Charter Holdco, the indirect owner of the Company's cable systems and mirror notes that are payable by Charter Holdco to the Company which have the same principal amount and terms as those of Charter's convertible senior notes. Minority interest on the Company's consolidated balance sheets represents the ownership percentages of Charter Holdco not owned by the Company, or 54% of total members' equity of Charter Holdco, plus $694 million, $668 million and $655 million of preferred membership interests in CC VIII, LLC (CC VIII), an indirect subsidiary of Charter Holdco, as of December 31, 2003, 2002 and 2001, respectively. This preferred interest arises from the approximately $630 million of preferred membership units issued by CC VIII in connection with the Bresnan acquisition in February, 2000. As of December 31, 2003 and December 31, 2002, minority interest also includes $25 million of preferred interest in Charter Helicon, LLC issued in connection with the Helicon acquisition.

Members' equity of Charter Holdco was ($57) million, $662 million and $7.0 billion as of December 31, 2003, 2002 and 2001, respectively. Gains and losses arising from the issuance by Charter Holdco of its membership units are recorded as capital transactions, thereby increasing or decreasing shareholders' equity and decreasing or increasing minority interest on the accompanying consolidated balance sheets. Minority interest was 53.5% as of December 31, 2003, 2002 and 2001. Minority interest includes the proportionate share of changes in fair value of interest rate risk management derivative agreements. Such amounts are temporary as they are contractually scheduled to reverse over the life of the underlying instrument. Additionally, reported losses allocated to minority interest on the statement of operations will be limited to the extent of any remaining minority interest on the balance sheet related to Charter Holdco. Accordingly, commencing in 2004, the Company expects to absorb all, or substantially all, future losses before income taxes, since the minority interest in Charter Holdco was substantially elimi-

nated at December 31, 2003, subject to any changes in Charter Holdco's capital structure. Changes to minority interest consist of the following for the periods presented:

	Minority Interest
Balance, December 31, 2000	$ 4,571
Equity reclassified from redeemable securities (26,539,746 shares of Class A common stock)	1,096
Minority interest in loss of a subsidiary	(1,461)
Minority interest in change in accounting principle	(14)
Minority interest in income tax benefit	16
Changes in fair value of interest rate agreements	(22)
Gain on issuance of equity by Charter Holdco	253
Other	(5)
Balance, December 31, 2001	4,434
Minority interest in loss of a subsidiary	(3,176)
Minority interest in change in accounting principle	(306)
Minority interest in income tax benefit	132
Changes in fair value of interest rate agreements	(35)
Other	1
Balance, December 31, 2002	1,050
Minority interest in loss of a subsidiary	(377)
Minority interest in income tax benefit	(8)
Changes in fair value of interest rate agreements	25
Other	(1)
Balance, December 31, 2003	$ 689

Equity in Losses of Investee

3.56

W.W. GRAINGER, INC. (DEC)

(In thousands of dollars)	2003	2002	2001
Net sales	$4,667,014	$4,643,898	$4,754,317
Cost of merchandise sold	3,028,937	3,045,686	3,165,030
Gross profit	1,638,077	1,598,212	1,589,287
Warehousing, marketing and administrative expenses	1,251,380	1,206,996	1,211,644
Restructuring (credit) charge	(564)	(1,939)	39,070
Total operating expenses	1,250,816	1,205,057	1,250,714
Operating earnings	387,261	393,155	338,573
Other income (expense):			
Interest income	3,347	4,573	2,827
Interest expense	(6,015)	(6,163)	(10,674)
Equity in loss of unconsolidated entities—net	(2,288)	(3,025)	(7,205)
Write-down of investments in unconsolidated entities	(1,921)	—	—
Loss on liquidation of investment in unconsolidated entity	—	—	(20,123)
Unclassified—net	706	9,297	(6,118)
Total other income (expense)	(6,171)	4,682	(41,293)
Earnings before income taxes and cumulative effect of accounting change	$ 381,090	$ 397,837	$ 297,280

NOTES TO CONSOLIDATED FINANCIAL STATEMENTS

Note 1 (In Part): Background and Basis of Presentation

Investments in Unconsolidated Entities

For investments in which the Company owns or controls from 20% to 50% of the voting shares, the equity method of accounting is used. The Company also accounts for investments below 20% using the equity method when significant influence can be exercised over the operating and financial policies of the investee company. See Note 9 to the Consolidated Financial Statements.

Note 9—Investments in Unconsolidated Entities

In 2001, the Company wrote off its equity investment in Works.com. See Note 5 to the Consolidated Financial Statements. On February 1, 2002, the Company finalized an agreement creating the joint venture USI-AGI Prairies Inc. The joint venture was between Acklands and Uni-Select Inc. (Uni-Select), a Canadian company. The joint venture combined Uni-Select's Western Division with the automotive aftermarket division of Acklands, which operated as Bumper to Bumper. Acklands' contribution of net assets was approximately U.S.$14.6 million. Additionally, Acklands' carrying value of its investment in this joint venture includes U.S.$5.1 million of allocated goodwill. The Company has a 50% stake in the new entity, which Uni-Select manages. Net sales for the automotive aftermarket parts division of Acklands were approximately U.S.$33 million in 2001.

No gain or loss was recognized when this transaction was finalized. Through February 1, 2002, the results of the Company's automotive aftermarket parts division were consolidated with Acklands. Beginning February 2, 2002, the Company accounted for its joint venture investment using the equity method. In 2003, Acklands made a loan denominated in Canadian dollars to USI-AGI Prairies Inc., of U.S.$3.7 million bearing interest at market rates. The loan is due and payable on demand.

The Company also has investments in three Asian joint ventures, with ownership percentages ranging from 11% to 49%. The Company accounts for these joint ventures using the equity method of accounting. As start-up businesses, the time frame, or the ultimate ability, to achieve profitability is uncertain. Reaching profitability is also dependent upon the entities securing sufficient capital funding to support developmental activities. The losses reflect the start-up nature of these businesses. In the fourth quarter of 2003, the Company wrote off its investment in two of these Asian joint ventures due to their questionable market value and uncertainty regarding future profitability and capital funding.

The table below summarizes the activity of these investments.

(In thousands of dollars)	Investment Cost	Loan	Cumulative After-Tax Equity Income (Losses)	Divestiture/ Write-Down	Foreign Currency Translation Adjustment	Total
Balance at January 1, 2001	$34,693	$ —	$(10,855)	$ —	$ —	$ 23,838
Works.com	—	—	(4,608)	(17,621)	—	(22,229)
Other equity investments	5,764	—	(2,597)	—	—	3,167
Balance at December 31, 2001	40,457	—	(18,060)	(17,621)	—	4,776
USI-AGI Prairies Inc	20,580	—	970	—	(595)	20,955
Cash distribution from USI-AGI Prairies Inc	(8,959)	—	—	—	—	(8,959)
Other equity investments	3,211	—	(3,995)	—	—	(784)
Balance at December 31, 2002	55,289	—	(21,085)	(17,621)	(595)	15,988
USI-AGI Prairies Inc	—	3,706	1,442	—	2,802	7,950
Other equity investments	4,535	—	(3,730)	(1,921)	—	(1,116)
Balance at December 31, 2003	$59,824	$3,706	$(23,373)	$(19,542)	$2,207	$ 22,822

Litigation Settlement

3.57

YUM! BRANDS, INC. (DEC)

(In millions)	2003	2002	2001
Revenues			
Company sales	$ 7,441	$ 6,891	$ 6,138
Franchise and license fees	939	866	815
	8,380	7,757	6,953
Costs and expenses, net			
Company restaurants			
Food and paper	2,300	2,109	1,908
Payroll and employee benefits	2,024	1,875	1,666
Occupancy and other operating expenses	2,013	1,806	1,658
	6,337	5,790	5,232
General and administrative expenses	945	913	796
Franchise and license expenses	28	49	59
Facility actions	36	32	1
Other (income) expense	(41)	(30)	(23)
Wrench litigation	42	—	—
AmeriServe and other charges (credits)	(26)	(27)	(3)
Total costs and expenses, net	7,321	6,727	6,062
Operating profit	$ 1,059	$ 1,030	$ 891

NOTES TO CONSOLIDATED FINANCIAL STATEMENTS

Note 24 (In Part): Guarantees, Commitments and Contingencies

Litigation

We are subject to various claims and contingencies related to lawsuits, taxes, environmental and other matters arising out of the normal course of business. Like certain other large retail employers, the Company has been faced in certain states with allegations of purported class-wide wage and hour violations.

On August 29, 1997, a class action lawsuit against Taco Bell Corp., entitled *Bravo, et al. v. Taco Bell Corp.* ("Bravo"), was filed in the Circuit Court of the State of Oregon of the County of Multnomah. The lawsuit was filed by two former Taco Bell shift managers purporting to represent approximately 17,000 current and former hourly employees statewide. The lawsuit alleged violations of state wage and hour laws, principally involving unpaid wages including overtime, and rest and meal period violations, and sought an unspecified amount in damages. Under Oregon class action procedures, Taco Bell was allowed an opportunity to "cure" the unpaid wage and hour allegations by opening a claims process to all putative class members prior to certification of the class. In this cure process, Taco Bell paid out less than $1 million. On January 26, 1999, the Court certified a class of all current and former shift managers and crew members who claim one or more of the alleged violations. A Court-approved notice and claim form was mailed to approximately 14,500 class members on January 31, 2000. Trial began on January 4, 2001. On March 9, 2001, the jury reached verdicts on the substantive issues in this matter. A number of these verdicts were in favor of the Taco Bell position; however, certain issues were decided in favor of the plaintiffs. In April 2002, a jury trial to determine the damages of 93 of those claimants found that Taco Bell failed to pay for certain meal breaks and/or off-the-clock work for 86 of the 93 claimants. However, the total amount of hours awarded by the jury was substantially less than that sought by the claimants. In July and September 2002, the court ruled on several post-trial motions, including fixing the total number of potential claimants at 1,031 (including the 93 claimants for which damages had already been determined) and holding that claimants who prevail are entitled to prejudgment interest and penalty wages. The second damages trial for the remaining 938 claimants began on July 7, 2003. Before the trial concluded, the parties reached an agreement to settle this matter in full. The court granted final approval of the settlement on December 23, 2003 and final judgment of dismissal was entered on December 26, 2003. Payments to class counsel and eligible claimants were made in the first quarter of 2004. We have previously provided for the costs of this settlement as AmeriServe and other charges (credits).

On January 16, 1998, a lawsuit against Taco Bell Corp., entitled *Wrench LLC, Joseph Shields and Thomas Rinks v. Taco Bell Corp.*, was filed in the United States District Court for the Western District of Michigan. The lawsuit alleged that Taco Bell Corp. misappropriated certain ideas and concepts used in its advertising featuring a Chihuahua. The plaintiffs sought to recover monetary damages under several theories, including breach of implied-in-fact contract, idea misappropriation, conversion and unfair competition. On June 10, 1999, the District Court granted summary judgment in favor of Taco Bell Corp. Plaintiffs filed an appeal with the U.S. Court of Appeals for the Sixth Circuit (the "Court of Appeals"), and oral arguments were held on September 20, 2000. On July 6, 2001, the Court of Appeals reversed the District Court's judgment in favor of Taco Bell Corp. and remanded the case to the District Court. Taco Bell Corp. unsuccessfully petitioned the Court of Appeals for rehearing en banc, and its petition for writ of certiorari to the United States Supreme Court was denied on January 21, 2002. The case was returned to District Court for trial which began on May 14, 2003 and on June 4, 2003 the jury awarded $30 million to the plaintiffs. Subsequently, the plaintiffs' moved to amend the judgment to include pre-judgment interest and post-judgment interest and Taco Bell filed its post-trial motion for judgment as a matter of law or a new trial. On September 9, 2003, the District Court denied Taco Bell's motion and granted the plaintiff's motion to amend the judgment.

In view of the jury verdict and subsequent District Court ruling, we recorded a charge of $42 million in 2003. We continue to believe that the Wrench plaintiffs' claims are without merit and have appealed the verdict to the Sixth Circuit Court of Appeals. Post-judgment interest will continue to accrue during the appeal process.

On July 9, 2003 we filed suit against Taco Bell's former advertising agency in the United States District Court for the Central District of California seeking reimbursement for any final award that may be ultimately affirmed by the appeals courts and costs that we have incurred in defending this matter. We are also seeking reimbursement from our insurance carriers.

Sale of Receivables

3.58

AIRGAS, INC. (MAR)

(In thousands)	2003	2002	2001
Net sales	$ 1,786,964	$ 1,636,047	$ 1,628,901
Costs and expenses			
Cost of products sold (excluding depreciation expense)	850,316	818,753	847,200
Selling, distribution and administrative expenses	698,228	619,316	583,355
Depreciation	73,482	64,785	62,938
Amortization	6,362	8,160	23,816
Special charges, net	2,694	—	3,643
Total costs and expenses	1,631,082	1,511,014	1,520,952
Operating income	155,882	125,033	107,949
Interest expense, net	(46,375)	(47,013)	(60,207)
Discount on securitization of trade receivables (Note 12)	(3,326)	(4,846)	(1,303)
Other income (expense), net	(645)	1,382	242
Equity in earnings of unconsolidated affiliates	3,768	3,835	2,260
Earnings before income taxes and the cumulative effect of a change in accounting principle	$ 109,304	$ 78,391	$ 48,941

Note 12 Trade Receivables Securitization

The Company participates in a securitization agreement with two commercial banks to sell up to $175 million of qualifying trade receivables. The agreement was originally to expire in December 2003, but the agreement was extended to December 2005, and remains subject to additional renewal provisions contained in the agreement. During fiscal 2003, the Company sold, net of its retained interest, $1,879 million of trade receivables and remitted to bank conduits, pursuant to a servicing agreement, $1,720 million in collections on those receivables. The net proceeds were used to reduce borrowings under the Company's revolving credit facilities. The amount of outstanding receivables under the agreement was $159 million at March 31, 2003 and $134 million at March 31, 2002.

The transaction has been accounted for as a sale under the provisions of SFAS No. 140, *Accounting for Transfers and Servicing of Financial Assets and Extinguishments of Liabilities*. Under the securitization agreement, eligible trade receivables are sold to bank conduits through a bankruptcy-remote special purpose entity, which is consolidated for financial reporting purposes. The difference between the proceeds from the sale and the carrying value of the receivables is recognized as discount on securitization of trade receivables in the accompanying Consolidated Statements of Earnings and varies on a monthly basis depending on the amount of receivables sold and market rates. The Company retains a subordinated interest in the receivables sold, which is recorded at the receivables' previous carrying value. A subordinated retained interest of approximately $45 million and $41 million is included in trade receivables in the accompanying Consolidated Balance Sheets at March 31, 2003 and 2002, respectively. The Company's retained interest is generally collected within 60 days. On a monthly basis, management measures the fair value of the retained interest at management's best estimate of the undiscounted expected future cash collections on the transferred receivables. Changes in the fair value are recognized as bad debt expense. Actual cash collections may differ from these estimates and would directly affect the

fair value of the retained interest. In accordance with a servicing agreement, the Company will continue to service, administer and collect the trade receivables on behalf of the bank conduits. The servicing fees charged to the bank conduits approximate the costs of collections.

Environmental Clean-Up

3.59

W. R. GRACE & CO. (DEC)

(In millions)	2003	2002	2001
Net sales	$1,980.5	$1,819.7	$1,722.9
Other income	16.7	22.5	30.8
	1,997.2	1,842.2	1,753.7
Cost of goods sold, exclusive of depreciation and amortization shown separately below	1,289.8	1,148.1	1,076.3
Selling, general and administrative expenses, exclusive of net pension expense (income) shown separately below	365.6	345.1	343.6
Depreciation and amortization	102.9	94.9	89.2
Research and development expenses	52.0	51.5	49.5
Net pension expense (income)	52.7	19.5	(9.5)
Interest expense and related financing costs	15.6	20.0	37.1
Provision for environmental remediation	142.5	70.7	5.8
Provision for asbestos-related litigation	30.0	—	—
	2,051.1	1,749.8	1,592.0
(Loss) income before Chapter 11 expenses, income taxes, and minority interest	$ (53.9)	$ 92.4	$ 161.7

NOTES TO CONSOLIDATED FINANCIAL STATEMENTS

14 (In Part): Commitments and Contingent Liabilities

Environmental Remediation

General Matters and Discussion

Grace is subject to loss contingencies resulting from extensive and evolving federal, state, local and foreign environmental laws and regulations relating to the generation, storage, handling, discharge and disposition of hazardous wastes and other materials. Grace accrues for anticipated costs associated with investigative and remediation efforts where an assessment has indicated that a probable liability has been incurred and the cost can be reasonably estimated. These accruals do not take into account any discounting for the time value of money.

Grace's environmental liabilities are reassessed whenever circumstances become better defined or remediation efforts and their costs can be better estimated. These liabilities are evaluated based on currently available information, including the progress of remedial investigation at each site, the current status of discussions with regulatory authorities regarding the method and extent of remediation at each site, existing technology, prior experience in contaminated site remediation and the apportionment of costs among potentially responsible parties. Grace expects that the funding of environmental remediation activities will be affected by the Chapter 11 proceedings; any such effect could be material. Grace's environmental liabilities are included in "liabilities subject to compromise" as of December 31, 2003.

At December 31, 2003, Grace's estimated liability for environmental investigative and remediation costs totaled $332.4 million, as compared with $201.1 million at December 31, 2002. This liability covers both vermiculite and non-vermiculite related matters. The amount is based on funding and/or remediation agreements in place and Grace's best estimate of its cost for sites not subject to a formal remediation plan.

For the years ended December 31, 2003 and 2002, Grace recorded pre-tax charges of $142.5 million and $70.7 million, respectively, for environmental matters. Approximately

$180.0 million of the pre-tax charges for these two years were in connection with a cost recovery lawsuit brought by the U.S. government relating to Grace's former vermiculite mining near Libby, Montana, and Grace's evaluation of probable remediation costs at vermiculite processing sites currently or formerly operated by Grace, as described below. The remainder of the pre-tax charges were primarily attributable to the ongoing review of bankruptcy claims.

Cash expenditures charged against previously established reserves for the years ended December 31, 2003, 2002 and 2001 were $11.2 million, $20.8 million and $28.9 million, respectively.

Vermiculite Related Matters

From the 1920's until 1990, Grace and previous owners conducted vermiculite mining and related activities near Libby, Montana. The vermiculite ore that was mined contained varying amounts of asbestos as a contaminant, almost all of which was removed during processing. Expanded vermiculite from Libby was used in products such as fireproofing, insulation and potting soil. In November 1999, Region 8 of the Environmental Protection Agency ("EPA") began an investigation into alleged excessive levels of asbestos-related disease in the Libby population related to these former mining activities. This investigation led the EPA to undertake additional investigative activity and to carry out response actions in and around Libby. On March 30, 2001, the EPA filed a lawsuit in U.S. District Court for the District of Montana, Missoula Division (*United States v. W. R. Grace & Company et al.*) under the Comprehensive Environmental Response, Compensation and Liability Act for the recovery of costs allegedly incurred by the United States in response to the release or threatened release of asbestos in the Libby, Montana area relating to such former mining activities. These costs include cleaning and/or demolition of contaminated buildings, the excavation and removal of contaminated soil, health screening of Libby residents and former mine workers, and investigation and monitoring costs. In this action, the EPA also sought a declaration of Grace's liability that would be binding in future actions to recover further response costs.

In connection with its defense, Grace conducted its own investigation to determine whether the EPA's actions and cost claims were justified and reasonable. However, in December 2002, the District Court granted the United States' motion for partial summary judgment on a number of issues that limited Grace's ability to challenge the EPA's response actions. In January 2003, a trial was held on the remainder of the issues, which primarily involved the reasonableness and adequacy of documentation of the EPA's cost recovery claims through December 31, 2001. On August 28, 2003, the District Court issued a ruling in favor of the United States that requires Grace to reimburse the government for $54.5 million in costs expended through December 2001, and for all appropriate future costs to complete the clean-up. Grace has appealed the court's ruling.

As a result of such ruling, Grace recorded a pre-tax charge of $50.0 million in the third quarter of 2003. During the fourth quarter of 2003, Grace recorded a $70.0 million pre-tax charge for estimated remediation costs in and around Libby, Montana, and at vermiculite processing sites currently or formerly operated by Grace. Grace's estimated liability for vermiculite-related matters at December 31, 2003 and 2002 was $181.0 million and $62.7 million, respectively. Grace's estimate of expected costs is based on public comments regarding the EPA's spending plans, discussions of spending forecasts with EPA representatives, analysis of other information made available from the EPA, and evaluation of probable remediation costs at vermiculite processing sites. However, the EPA's cost estimates have changed regularly and increased substantially over the course of this clean-up. Consequently, Grace's estimate may change materially as more information becomes available. Grace's liability for this matter is included in "liabilities subject to compromise" as of December 31, 2003.

Non-Vermiculite Related Matters

At December 31, 2003 and 2002, Grace's estimated liability for remediation of sites not related to its former vermiculite mining and processing activities was $151.4 million and $138.4 million, respectively. This liability relates to Grace's current and former operations, including its share of liability for off-site disposal at facilities where it has been identified as a potentially responsible party. During the fourth quarter of 2003, Grace recorded a $20.0 million increase in its estimated environmental liability for non-vermiculite related sites as part of the Chapter 11 claims review process. Grace's revised estimated liability is based upon claims for which sufficient information was available. As Grace receives new information and continues its claims evaluation process, its estimated liability may change materially. Grace's liability for this matter is included in "liabilities subject to compromise" as of December 31, 2003.

Insurance Matters

Grace is a party to three environmental insurance coverage actions involving one primary and one excess insurance carrier regarding the applicability of the carriers' policies to Grace's environmental remediation costs. The outcome of such litigation, as well as the amounts of any recoveries that Grace may receive, is presently uncertain. Accordingly, Grace has not recorded a receivable with respect to such insurance coverage.

Purchased R&D

3.60

JOHNSON & JOHNSON (DEC)

(Dollars in millions)	2003	2002	2001
Sales to customers	$41,862	$36,298	$32,317
Cost of products sold	12,176	10,447	9,581
Gross profit	29,686	25,851	22,736
Selling, marketing and administrative expenses	14,131	12,216	11,260
Research expense	4,684	3,957	3,591
Purchased in-process research and development (Note 17)	918	189	105
Interest income	(177)	(256)	(456)
Interest expense, net of portion capitalized	207	160	153
Other (income) expense, net	(385)	294	185
	19,378	16,560	14,838
Earnings before provision for taxes on income	$10,308	$ 9,291	$ 7,898

NOTES TO CONSOLIDATED FINANCIAL STATEMENTS

17. Mergers, Acquisitions and Divestitures

Certain businesses were acquired for $2.8 billion in cash and $323 million of liabilities assumed during 2003. These acquisitions were accounted for by the purchase method and, accordingly, results of operations have been included in the accompanying consolidated financial statements from their respective dates of acquisition.

The 2003 acquisitions included: Link Spine Group, Inc., a privately owned corporation with exclusive worldwide rights to the CHARITÉ™ Artificial Disc; Scios Inc. a biopharmaceutical company with a marketed product for cardiovascular disease and research projects focused on auto-immune diseases; 3-Dimensional Pharmaceuticals, Inc., a company with a technology platform focused on the discovery and development of therapeutic small molecules; OraPharma, Inc., a specialty pharmaceutical company focused on the development and commercialization of unique oral therapeutics; and certain assets of Orquest, Inc., a privately held biotechnology company focused on developing biologically-based implants for orthopaedics and spine surgery.

The excess of purchase price over the estimated fair value of tangible assets acquired amounted to $1.8 billion and has been allocated to identifiable intangibles and goodwill. Approximately $918 million has been identified as the value of in-process research and development (IPR&D) primarily associated with the acquisition of Link Spine Group, Inc. and Scios Inc.

The IPR&D charge related to the Link Spine acquisition was $170 million and is associated with the CHARITÉ™ Artificial Disc. The CHARITÉ™ Artificial Disc is marketed in more than 30 countries outside the U.S., and a Premarket Approval Application was filed with U.S. Food and Drug Administration on February 17, 2004. The value of the IPR&D was calculated with the assistance of a third party appraiser using cash flow projections discounted for the risk inherent in such projects. A probability of success factor of 95% was used to reflect inherent clinical and regulatory risk. The discount rate was 19%. On a preliminary basis, the purchase price for the Link Spine acquisition was allocated to the tangible and identifiable intangible assets acquired and liabilities assumed based on their estimated fair values at the acquisition date. The excess of the purchase price over the fair values of assets and liabilities acquired was approximately $84 million and was allocated to goodwill. The Company expects that substantially all of the amount allocated to goodwill will not be deductible for tax purposes.

The IPR&D charge related to Scios was $730 million and is largely associated with its p-38 kinase inhibitor program. The value of the IPR&D was calculated with the assistance of a third party appraiser using cash flow projections discounted for the risk inherent in such projects using a 16% probability of success factor and a 9% discount rate. On a preliminary basis, the purchase price for the Scios Inc. acquisition was allocated to the tangible and identifiable intangible assets acquired and liabilities assumed based on their estimated fair values at the acquisition date. Identifiable intangible assets included patents and trademarks valued at approximately $1.5 billion. The excess of the purchase price over the fair values of assets and liabilities acquired was approximately $440 million and was allocated to goodwill. The Company expects that substantially all of the amount allocated to goodwill will not be deductible for tax purposes.

The remaining IPR&D was associated with Orquest, Inc., and 3-Dimensional Pharmaceuticals, Inc., with charges of $11 million and $7 million, respectively. In both cases the value of the IPR&D was calculated with the assistance of a third party appraiser.

Certain businesses were acquired for $478 million in cash and liabilities assumed of $72 million during 2002. These acquisitions were accounted for by the purchase method, and, accordingly, results of operations have been included in the accompanying consolidated financial statements from their respective dates of acquisition.

The 2002 acquisitions included Tibotec-Virco N.V., a privately-held biopharmaceutical company focused on developing anti-viral treatments; Micro Typing Systems, Inc., a manufacturer of reagents and supplier of distributed instruments known as the ID-Micro Typing System™ and Obtech Medical AG, a privately-held company that markets an adjustable gastric band for the treatment of morbid obesity.

The excess of purchase price over the estimated fair value of tangible assets of the acquired entities amounted to $325 million and has been allocated to identifiable intangibles and goodwill. Approximately $189 million has been identified as the value of IPR&D associated with the Tibotec-Virco N.V. and Obtech Medical AG acquisitions.

The IPR&D charge related to Tibotec-Virco N.V. was $150 million and is associated with two early stage HIV compounds. The value of the IPR&D was calculated with the assistance of a third party appraiser using cash flow projections discounted for the risk inherent in such projects using probability of success factors ranging from 30–33%. The discount rate was 9%.

The IPR&D charge related to Obtech Medical AG was $39 million and is associated with the development of the current Swedish Adjustable Gastric Band (SAGB) for use in the United States as well as development of a next generation technology platform. The value of the IPR&D was calculated with the assistance of a third party appraiser using cash flow projections discounted for the risk inherent in such projects using a 70% probability of success factor and a 20% discount rate.

Supplemental pro forma information for 2003 and 2002 per SFAS No. 141, *Business Combinations,* and SFAS No. 142, *Goodwill and Other Intangible Assets,* are not provided as the impact of the aforementioned acquisitions did not have a material effect on the Company's results of operations, cash flows or financial position.

On June 22, 2001, Johnson & Johnson and ALZA Corporation (ALZA) completed the merger between the two companies. This transaction was accounted for as a pooling-of-interests. ALZA had approximately 239 million shares outstanding (286 million on a fully diluted basis) that were exchanged for approximately 234 million shares of Johnson & Johnson common stock. On a diluted basis when adjusted for stock options and convertible debt, the total number of Johnson & Johnson shares issued was approximately 280 million. Holders of ALZA common stock received 0.98 of a share of Johnson & Johnson common stock, valued at $52.39 per share.

ALZA is a research-based pharmaceutical company with leading drug delivery technologies. The company applies its delivery technologies to develop pharmaceutical products with enhanced therapeutic value for Johnson & Johnson affiliate portfolios and for many of the world's leading pharmaceutical companies.

Certain businesses were acquired for $1.9 billion during 2001 ($0.6 billion in cash and liabilities assumed and 24.5 million shares of the Company's common stock issued from Treasury valued at $1.3 billion). These acquisitions were accounted for by the purchase method, and, accordingly, results of operations have been included in the accompanying consolidated financial statements from their respective dates of acquisition.

The 2001 acquisitions included Inverness Medical Technology Inc., the supplier of LifeScan's electrochemical products for blood glucose monitoring following the spin-off of the nondiabetes businesses; Heartport Inc., a company that develops and manufactures products for less invasive open chest and minimally invasive heart operations, including stopped heart and beating heart procedures; TERAMed Corporation, an earlystage medical device company that is developing endovascular stent-graft systems for the minimally invasive treatment of abdominal aortic aneurysms and peripheral occlusive disease; BabyCenter, L.L.C., an Internet content and commerce company devoted to supporting a community of expectant and new mothers; and the VIACTIV® product line, a chewable calcium supplement, from the Mead Johnson Nutritionals Division of Bristol-Myers Squibb.

Inverness Medical Technology was acquired to enhance control of the primary supplier of LifeScan blood glucose monitoring products and will allow for the achievement of operational synergies. The acquisition also provides key technology for the development of future products.

Approximately $105 million has been identified as the value of IPR&D associated with the Inverness Medical Technology and TERAMed Corporation acquisitions. The IPR&D charge is primarily related to Inverness projects for minimally invasive testing, continuous monitoring and insulin delivery. The value of the IPR&D was calculated with the assistance of a third party appraiser using cash flow projections discounted for the risk inherent in such projects using probability of success factors ranging from 25–40%. The discount rate used was 12%.

Divestitures in 2003, 2002 and 2001 did not have a material effect on the Company's results of operations, cash flows or financial position.

Merger Costs

3.61

THE J.M. SMUCKER COMPANY (APR)

(Dollars in thousands)	2003	2002	2001
Net sales	$1,311,744	$687,148	$651,242
Cost of products sold	854,407	462,157	443,948
Cost of products sold—restructuring	1,256	—	—
Gross profit	456,081	224,991	207,294
Selling, distribution, and administrative expenses	279,760	165,172	155,973
Merger and integration costs	10,511	5,031	—
Other restructuring costs	1,281	—	2,152
Operating income	$ 164,529	$ 54,788	$ 49,169

NOTES TO CONSOLIDATED FINANCIAL STATEMENTS

Note C (In Part): Merger

On June 1, 2002, the Company merged the *Jif* peanut butter and *Crisco* shortening and oils businesses of The Procter & Gamble Company (P&G) with and into the Company in a tax-free stock transaction. Under the terms of the agreement, P&G spun off its *Jif* and *Crisco* businesses to its shareholders and immediately thereafter those businesses were merged with and into the Company. P&G shareholders received one Company common share for every 50 P&G common shares that they held as of the record date for the distribution of the *Jif* and *Crisco* businesses to the P&G shareholders. The Company's shareholders received 0.9451 of a new Company common share for each Company common share that they held immediately prior to the merger. Approximately 26,000,000 common shares were issued to the P&G shareholders, valued at approximately $781,485,000 based on the average market price of the Company's common shares over the period from three days before to three days after the terms of the merger were announced. Upon completion of the merger, the Company had 49,531,376 common shares outstanding.

The conversion of the Company's common shares into new Company common shares has been treated in a manner similar to a reverse stock split. All per share data for all periods presented have been restated to reflect the effects of the conversion.

The merger and the combination of three brands—*Smucker's*, *Jif*, and *Crisco*—enhances the Company's strategic and market position. The merger was accounted for as a purchase business combination and for accounting purposes, the Company was the acquiring enterprise. Accordingly, the results of the *Jif* and *Crisco* operations are included in the Company's consolidated financial statements from the date of the merger. The aggregate purchase price was approximately $792,252,000 including $10,767,000 of capitalized acquisition related expenses. In addition, the Company incurred costs of $10,511,000 and $5,031,000 in fiscal 2003 and 2002, respectively, that were directly related to the merger and integration of *Jif* and *Crisco*. Due to the nature of these costs, they were expensed as incurred.

Nonrecurring/Unusual Losses

3.62

GENCORP INC. (NOV)

(Dollars in millions)	2003	2002	2001
Net sales	$1,192	$1,135	$1,486
Costs and expenses			
Cost of products sold	979	935	1,328
Selling, general and administrative	87	55	42
Depreciation and amortization	81	66	77
Interest expense	28	16	33
Other (income) expense, net	(5)	4	(22)
Restructuring charge	—	2	40
Unusual items, net	5	15	(199)
	1,175	1,093	1,299
Income before income taxes	$ 17	$ 42	$ 187

NOTES TO CONSOLIDATED FINANCIAL STATEMENTS

11 (In Part): Commitments and Contingencies

b (In Part): Legal Proceedings

Water Entity Cases

In October 1999 Aerojet was sued by American States Water Company (ASWC), a local water purveyor, for damages, including unspecified past costs, future damages and replacement water for contaminated drinking water wells near Aerojet's Sacramento site's manufacturing facility. *American States Water Company, et al. v. Aerojet-General Corporation, et al.,* Case No. 99AS05949, Sacramento County Superior Court. Weeks before the scheduled trial, Aerojet and ASWC initiated mediation to resolve the dispute. As a result, Aerojet and ASWC have entered into a Memorandum of Understanding (MOU) to settle this matter. The settlement agreement has not yet been finalized, but the trial court has ruled that the MOU is binding. The trial date was vacated. Any disputes arising in subsequent negotiations with respect to the settlement agreement are to be resolved by arbitration subject to the continuing jurisdiction of the trial court for enforcement or ancillary purposes.

Aerojet's recent agreement with the Sacramento County Water Agency (the County) in which Aerojet agreed to transfer all of its remediated groundwater to the County is anticipated to satisfy Aerojet's water replacement obligations in eastern Sacramento County. Subject to various provisions of the County agreement, including approval under California Environmental Quality Act, the County will assume Aerojet's responsibility for providing replacement water to ASWC and other impacted water purveyors up to the amount of remediated water Aerojet transfers to the County. Aerojet has also agreed to pay the County approximately $13 million over several years toward the cost of constructing a replacement water supply project. If the amount of Aerojet's transferred water is in excess of the replacement water provided to the impacted water purveyors, the County has committed to make such water available for the development of Aerojet's land in an amount equal to the excess.

In October 2002, Aerojet, along with approximately 65 other individual and corporate defendants, was served with four civil suits filed in the U.S. District Court for the Central District of California that seek recovery of costs allegedly incurred in response to the contamination present at the South El Monte Operable Unit (SEMOU) of the San Gabriel Valley Superfund site. The cases are denominated as follows: *The City of Monterey Park v. Aerojet-General Corporation, et al.,* (CV-02-5909 ABC (RCx)); *San Gabriel Basin Water Quality Authority v. Aerojet-General Corporation, et al.,* (CV-02-4565 ABC (RCx)); *San Gabriel Valley Water Company v. Aerojet-General Corporation, et al.,* (CV-02-6346 ABC (RCx)) *and Southern California Water Company v. Aerojet-General Corporation, et al.,* (CV-02-6340 ABC (RCx)). The cases have been coordinated for ease of administration by the court. The plaintiffs' claims are based upon allegations of discharges from a former site in the El Monte area, as more fully discussed below under the headings "San Gabriel Valley Basin, California—South El Monte Operable Unit." Aerojet is vigorously defending the actions as its investigations do not identify a credible connection between the contaminants identified by the water entities in the SEMOU and those detected at Aerojet's former facility located in El Monte, California, near the SEMOU (East Flair Drive site). Aerojet has notified its insurers of these claims. Discovery is ongoing and a trial is likely to be scheduled for early 2005. The EPA has retained the services of a professional mediator to assist the recipients of its Unilateral Administrative Order (UAO) for groundwater investigation and remediation to form a group and negotiate with the EPA and the water entities. The cost estimates to implement projects under the UAO prepared by EPA and the water entities range from $77 million to $127 million.

15 (In Part): Restructuring and Unusual Items

Charges associated with unusual items are summarized as follows:

(Dollars in millions)	2003	2002	2001
Aerospace and defense			
Unrecoverable portion of legal settlement with local water company	$ 5	$ —	$ —
Write-off of the Redmond, Washington operations in-process research and development	—	6	—
Aerojet sale of EIS business	—	6	(206)
Tax-related (customer reimbursements of tax recoveries)	—	—	9
	5	12	(197)
Corporate headquarters			
Environmental remediation insurance cost recovery	—	—	(2)
Reacquisition of AFC minority interest	—	2	—
Write-off of bank fees for Term Loan C repayment	—	1	—
	—	3	(2)
Net unusual expense (income)	$ 5	$ 15	$(199)

In 2003, Aerojet recorded unusual charges totaling $5 million representing the unrecoverable portion of an estimated legal settlement with a local water company related to contaminated wells. See *Water Entity Cases* in Note 11(b) for more information.

PENSIONS AND OTHER POSTRETIREMENT BENEFITS

3.63 SFAS No. 132, *Employers' Disclosures about Pensions and Other Postretirement Benefits,* states the disclosure requirements for pensions and other postretirement benefits. *SFAS No. 132* does not supersede SFAS No. 87, *Employers' Accounting for Pensions,* SFAS No. 88, *Employers' Accounting for Settlements and Curtailments and for Termination Benefits,* or SFAS No. 106, *Employers' Accounting for Postretirement Benefits Other Than Pensions,* with respect to the measurement or recognition of pensions and other postretirement benefits. In December 2003, the FASB issued SFAS No. 132 (Revised), *Employers' Disclosures about Pensions and Other Postretirement Benefits— Revised. SFAS No. 132 (Revised)* retains the disclosure requirements contained in *SFAS No. 132,* which it replaces. The revised Statement requires additional disclosures to those contained in the original *SFAS No. 132* about the assets, obligations, cash flows, investment strategy, and net periodic benefit cost of defined pension and postretirement plans. *SFAS No. 132 (Revised)* is effective for financial statements with fiscal years ending after December 15, 2003.

3.64 The disclosure requirements of *SFAS No. 132* include, but are not limited to, disclosing the actuarial assumption rates used in accounting for pensions and other postretirement benefits. *SFAS No. 132* also requires disclosure of the assumed health care cost trend rate for other post retirement benefits. Tables 3-8, 3-9 and 3-10 show the actuarial assumption rates used by the survey companies for the years 2000–2003 in accounting for pension benefits. Table 3-11 shows the health care cost trend rate used by the survey companies in 2003 to account for other postretirement benefits. As shown in Table 3-11, 334 survey companies disclosed the health care cost trend rate. Of those 334 survey companies, 305 disclosed one rate for all participants and 29 disclosed two rates—the rate for participants under age 65 and the rate for participants age 65 and over.

3.65 In addition to standardizing disclosure requirements, *SFAS No. 132* suggests a parallel format for presenting information about pensions and other postretirement benefits. Examples of such presentations follow.

3.66

TABLE 3-8: ASSUMED DISCOUNT RATE

%	2003	2002	2001	2000
4.5 or less	4	2	—	2
5	7	—	1	—
5.5	11	5	—	2
6	145	24	12	8
6.5	210	240	25	12
7	46	127	248	73
7.5	—	18	124	223
8	—	1	10	108
8.5	—	—	—	1
9	—	—	—	—
9.5	—	—	—	1
10	—	—	—	—
10.5	—	—	1	—
11 or greater	—	—	1	2
Not disclosed	7	5	6	7
Companies Disclosing Defined Benefit Plans	**430**	**422**	**428**	**439**

3.67

TABLE 3-9: ASSUMED RATE OF COMPENSATION INCREASE

%	2003	2002	2001	2000
4.5 or less	339	317	284	247
5	40	52	84	109
5.5	9	11	17	26
6	7	8	12	15
6.5	1	1	1	2
7	—	—	—	1
7.5	2	3	2	2
8	—	—	1	3
8.5	1	—	—	2
9	—	—	2	4
9.5	—	1	—	1
10	1	—	—	2
10.5	—	—	1	1
11 or greater	—	1	—	1
Not disclosed	30	28	24	23
Companies Disclosing Defined Benefit Plans	**430**	**422**	**428**	**439**

3.68

TABLE 3-10: EXPECTED RATE OF RETURN

%	2003	2002	2001	2000
4.5 or less	4	—	1	1
5	2	1	—	4
5.5	1	—	—	—
6	3	2	1	3
6.5	7	2	2	2
7	18	11	6	8
7.5	25	16	9	11
8	80	61	39	33
8.5	157	89	45	44
9	101	140	135	134
9.5	12	65	98	99
10	3	18	63	67
10.5	1	7	14	19
11 or greater	1	—	5	8
Not disclosed	15	10	10	6
Companies Disclosing Defined Benefit Plans	**430**	**422**	**428**	**439**

3.69

TABLE 3-11: HEALTH CARE COST TREND RATE—2003

%	All Participants	Participants Under Age 65	Participants Age 65 and Over
5.5 or less	10	—	—
6–6.5	5	—	—
7–7.5	9	2	—
8–8.5	29	11	2
9–9.5	68	9	4
10–10.5	96	3	7
11–11.5	51	1	11
12–12.5	20	3	3
13–13.5	8	—	1
14 or greater	3	—	1
Fixed amount (not subject to escalation)	6	—	—
Companies Disclosing Rate	**305**	**29**	**29**

Defined Benefit Plans

3.70

AETNA INC. (DEC)

NOTES TO CONSOLIDATED FINANCIAL STATEMENTS

2 (In Part): Summary of Significant Accounting Policies

New Accounting Standards (In Part)

Disclosures of Pension Plans and Other Post Employment Benefit Plans

In December 2003, the FASB issued a revision to FAS No. 132, *Employers' Disclosures about Pensions and Other Postretirement Benefits* ("FAS 132-R"). FAS 132-R retains the original disclosure provisions of FAS No. 132 and adds new disclosures about plan assets, investment strategy, plan obligations and cash flows. FAS 132-R is effective December 31, 2003. (Refer to Note 14 for additional information.)

14 (In Part): Benefit Plans

Defined Benefit Pension Plans

The Company's noncontributory defined benefit pension plans cover substantially all of its employees. Effective January 1, 1999, the Company, in conjunction with former Aetna, changed the formula from the previous final average pay formula to a cash balance formula, which will credit employees annually with an amount equal to a percentage of eligible pay based on age and years of service, as well as an interest credit based on individual account balances. The formula also provides for a transition period until December 31, 2006, which allows certain employees to receive vested benefits at the higher of the previous final average pay or cash balance formula. For employees hired after January 1, 2002, the Company changed the cash balance formula to provide greater initial credits and make the benefit less dependent on length of service. Existing employees will receive the larger of the pension credit under the previous formula or this new formula. These changes did not have a material effect on the Company's results of operations, liquidity or financial condition.

Components of the net periodic benefit income (cost) of the Company's noncontributory defined benefit pension plan for the years ended December 31, were as follows:

(Millions)	2003	2002	2001
Service cost	$ (74.8)	$ (74.3)	$ (82.0)
Interest cost	(258.5)	(259.9)	(263.8)
Expected return on plan assets	255.4	295.6	375.4
Amortization of prior service cost	(4.6)	(4.0)	(4.5)
Recognized net acturial gain (loss)	(76.0)	(6.9)	11.9
Net periodic benefit income (cost)	$(158.5)	$ (49.5)	$ 37.0

Weighted average assumptions used to determine net periodic benefit cost for the years ended December 31, were as follows:

	2003	2002	2001
Weighted average discount rate	6.75%	7.50%	7.75%
Expected return on plan assets	9.00%	9.25%	9.25%
Rate of compensation increase	3.75%	4.50%	4.75%

As of the measurement date (September 30), the status of the Company's defined benefit pension plans was as follows:

(Millions)	2003	2002
Projected benefit obligation, beginning of year	$3,945.7	$ 3,580.6
Service cost	74.8	74.3
Interest cost	258.6	259.9
Actuarial loss	268.0	261.2
Benefits paid	(244.2)	(230.3)
Projected benefit obligation, end of year	$4,302.9	$ 3,945.7
Fair value of plan assets, beginning of year	$2,943.2	$ 3,301.5
Actual return on plan assets	534.5	(246.3)
Employer contributions	261.0	118.3
Benefits paid	(244.2)	(230.3)
Fair value of plan assets, end of year	$3,494.5	$ 2,943.2
Fair value of plan assets less than projected benefit obligation	$ (808.4)	$(1,002.5)
Unrecognized net loss	1,136.5	1,230.7
Unrecognized prior service cost	40.8	41.5
Net amount recognized	$ 368.9	$ 269.7
Amounts recognized in the statement of financial position consist of:		
Accrued pension liability	$ (751.2)	$ (934.5)
Intangible asset	37.9	42.4
Accumulated other comprehensive income	1,082.2	1,161.8
Net amount recognized	$ 368.9	$ 269.7

Weighted average assumptions used to determine projected benefit obligations at September 30, were as follows:

	2003	2002
Weighted average discount rate	6.25%	6.75%
Rate of compensation increase	3.25%	3.75%

For 2003 and 2002, the Company's defined benefit plans had accumulated benefit obligations of approximately $4.3 billion and $3.9 billion, respectively.

The defined benefit pension plan asset allocation as of the measurement date (September 30) and the target asset allocation, presented as a percentage of total plan assets, were as follows:

	2003	2002	Target Allocation
Debt securities	26%	34%	20%–30%
Equity securities	66	56	60%–70%
Real estate/other	8	10	6%–15%
Total	100%	100%	

The Company's defined benefit plan invests in a diversified mix of traditional asset classes. Investments in U.S. and foreign equity securities, fixed income securities, real estate and cash are made to maximize long-term returns while recognizing the need for adequate liquidity to meet on-going benefit and administrative obligations. Risk tolerance of unexpected investment and actuarial outcomes is continually evaluated by understanding the pension plan's liability characteristics. This is performed through forecasting and assessing ranges of investment outcomes over short and long-term horizons, and by assessing the Company's financial condition and its future potential obligations from both the pension and general corporate requirements. Complementary investment styles, such as growth and value equity investing techniques, are utilized by multiple investment advisors to further improve portfolio and operational risk characteristics. Equity investments, both active and passively managed, are used primarily to increase overall plan returns. Real estate investments are viewed favorably for their diversification benefits and above-average dividend generation. Fixed income investments provide diversification benefits and liability hedging attributes that are desirable, especially in falling interest rate environments.

Asset allocations and investment performance is formally reviewed quarterly by the plan's Investment Oversight Committee. Forecasting of asset and liability growth is performed at least annually. More thorough analysis of assets and liabilities are also performed periodically.

The expected long-term rate of return is estimated based on many factors including the expected forecast for inflation, risk premiums for each asset class, expected asset allocation, current and future financial market conditions, and diversification and rebalancing strategies. Historical return patterns and correlations, consensus return forecasts and other relevant financial factors are analyzed to check for reasonability and appropriateness.

The Company does not have any regulatory contribution requirements for 2004, however the Company currently intends to make voluntary contributions to the defined benefit pension plan of $245 million in 2004.

3.71

OWENS-ILLINOIS, INC. (DEC)

NOTES TO CONSOLIDATED FINANCIAL STATEMENTS
(Tabular data in millions of dollars)

1 (In Part): Significant Accounting Policies

New Accounting Standards (In Part)

FAS No. 132 (Revised)

In December 2003, the Financial Accounting Standards Board issued FAS No. 132 (Revised) "Employers' Disclosure about Pensions and Other Postretirement Benefits". The revised statement requires additional disclosures to those in the original FAS No. 132 about the assets, obligations, cash flows, and net periodic benefit costs of defined benefit pension plans and other defined benefit postretirement plans. Except for certain disclosures for foreign pension plans and for benefit obligations, FAS No. 132 (Revised) was effective for financial statements with fiscal years ending after December 15, 2003 and has been adopted by the Company.

14 (In Part): Pension Benefit Plans

Net credits to results of operations for all of the Company's pension plans and certain deferred compensation arrangements amounted to $17.8 million in 2003, $72.5 million in 2002, and $83.4 million in 2001.

The Company has defined benefit pension plans covering substantially all employees located in the United States, the United Kingdom, Australia, and Canada. Benefits generally are based on compensation for salaried employees and on length of service for hourly employees. The Company's policy is to fund pension plans such that sufficient assets will be available to meet future benefit requirements. The following tables relate to the Company's principal defined benefit pension plans in the United States, the United Kingdom, Australia, and Canada.

The Company's defined benefit pension plans in the United States, the United Kingdom, Australia, and Canada use a December 31 measurement date.

The changes in the pension benefit obligations for the year were as follows (certain amounts from prior year have been reclassified to conform to current year presentation):

	2003	2002
Obligations at beginning of year	$2,752.4	$2,520.6
Change in benefit obligations		
Service cost	48.8	38.8
Interest cost	179.1	172.4
Actuarial loss, including effect of changing discount rates	211.4	165.3
Participant contributions	5.1	3.6
Benefit payments	(219.4)	(197.7)
Plan amendments	0.7	7.1
Foreign currency translation	110.6	41.5
Other	1.3	0.8
Net increase in benefit obligations	337.6	231.8
Obligations at end of year	$3,090.0	$2,752.4

The changes in the fair value of the pension plans' assets for the year were as follows:

	2003	2002
Fair value at beginning of year	$2,483.9	$2,744.0
Change in fair value		
Actual gain (loss) on plan assets	483.2	(113.7)
Benefit payments	(219.4)	(197.7)
Employer contributions	35.1	14.7
Participant contributions	5.1	3.6
Foreign currency translation	82.0	33.2
Other	—	(0.2)
Net increase (decrease) in fair value of assets	386.0	(260.1)
Fair value at end of year	$2,869.9	$2,483.9

The funded status of the pension plans at year end was as follows:

	2003	2002
Plan assets at fair value	$2,869.9	$2,483.9
Projected benefit obligations	3,090.0	2,752.4
Plan assets less than projected benefit obligations	(220.1)	(268.5)
Net unrecognized items		
Actuarial loss	1,157.7	1,143.7
Prior service cost	45.2	50.0
	1,202.9	1,193.7
Net amount recognized	$ 982.8	$ 925.2

The net amount recognized is included in the Consolidated Balance Sheets at December 31, 2003 and 2002 as follows:

	2003	2002
Prepaid pension	$967.1	$925.5
Accrued pension, included with other liabilities	(45.4)	(50.9)
Minimum pension liability, included with other liabilities	(107.3)	(92.2)
Intangible asset, included with deposits and other assets	12.4	12.1
Accumulated other comprehensive income	156.0	130.7
Net amount recognized	$982.8	$925.2

The accumulated benefit obligation for all defined benefit pension plans was $2,823.8 million and $2,530.1 million at December 31, 2003 and 2002, respectively.

The components of the net pension credit for the year were as follows:

	2003	2002	2001
Service cost	$ 48.8	$ 38.8	$ 36.6
Interest cost	179.1	172.4	169.3
Expected asset return	(275.1)	(303.4)	(311.0)
Amortization			
Prior service cost	6.8	7.6	7.6
Loss	10.5	1.1	0.5
Net amortization	17.3	8.7	8.1
Net credit	$ (29.9)	$ (83.5)	$ (97.0)

The following information is for plans with accumulated benefit obligations in excess of the fair value of plan assets at year end:

	2003	2002
Accumulated benefit obligations	$632.3	$513.5
Fair value of plan assets	479.9	372.4

The weighted average assumptions used to determine benefit obligations were as follows:

	2003	2002
Discount rate	6.10%	6.52%
Rate of compensation increase	4.71%	4.72%

The weighted average assumptions used to determine net periodic pension costs were as follows:

	2003	2002	2001
Discount rate	6.52%	6.95%	7.14%
Rate of compensation increase	4.72%	4.78%	4.82%
Expected long-term rate of return on assets	8.71%	9.64%	10.12%

Future benefits are assumed to increase in a manner consistent with past experience of the plans, which, to the extent benefits are based on compensation, includes assumed salary increases as presented above. Amortization included in net pension credits is based on the average remaining service of employees.

As of December 31, 2002, the Company recognized a minimum pension liability for the pension plan in the United Kingdom that was equal to the difference between the accumulated benefit obligation over plan assets. In addition to eliminating the prepaid pension asset, additional amounts were recognized as an intangible asset and a reduction of equity. Pursuant to this requirement, the Company recorded a minimum pension liability of $92.2 million, an intangible asset of $12.1 million, and accumulated other comprehensive loss of $130.7 million. As of December 31, 2003, the Company updated the minimum pension liability from the December 31, 2002 amounts. Pursuant to this requirement, the Company reduced the minimum pension liability by $1.2 million, reduced the intangible asset by $1.5 million, and increased accumulated other comprehensive income by $4.8 million.

As of December 31, 2003 and 2002, the Company recognized an additional minimum pension liability for the pension plan in Canada that was equal to the difference between the accumulated benefit obligation over plan assets in excess of accured pension cost. In addition to recording the additional minimum liability, additional amounts were recognized as an intangible asset and a reduction of equity. Pursuant to this requirement, the Company recorded, as of December 31, 2003, an additional minimum pension liability of $6.2 million, an intangible asset of $0.3 million, and accumulated other comprehensive loss of $5.8 million.

For 2003, the Company's weighted average expected long-term rate of return on assets was 8.71%. In developing this assumption, the Company evaluated input from its third party pension plan asset managers, including their review of asset class return expectations and long-term inflation assumptions. The Company also considered its historical 10-year average return (through December 31, 2002), which was in line with the expected long-term rate of return assumption for 2003.

The weighted average actual asset allocations and weighted average target allocation ranges by asset category for the Company's pension plan assets were as follows:

	Actual Allocation		Target Allocation Ranges
Asset Category	2003	2002	
Equity securites	68%	61%	58–68%
Debt securities	24%	30%	23–33%
Real estate	7%	8%	2–12%
Other	1%	1%	0–2%
Total	100%	100%	

It is the Company's policy to invest pension plan assets in a diversified portfolio consisting of an array of asset classes within the above target asset allocation ranges. The investment risk of the assets is limited by appropriate diversification both within and between asset classes. The assets for both the U.S. and non-U.S. plans are primarily invested in a broad mix of domestic and international equities, domestic and international bonds, and real estate, subject to the target asset allocation ranges. The assets are managed with a view to ensuring that sufficient liquidity will be available to meet expected cash flow requirements.

Plan assets at December 31, 2003 and 2002 included 14,423,621 shares of the Company's common stock, which amounted to $171.5 million or 6.0% of total plan assets as of December 31, 2003 and $210.3 million or 8.5% of total plan assets as of December 31, 2002.

The Company expects to contribute $33.9 million to its defined benefit pension plans in 2004.

The following estimated future benefit payments, which reflect expected future service, as appropriate, are expected to be paid in the years indicated:

Year(s)	Amount
2004	$ 206.4
2005	199.9
2006	203.2
2007	206.6
2008	213.1
2009–2013	1,167.2

3.72

R.J. REYNOLDS TOBACCO HOLDINGS, INC. (DEC)

NOTES TO CONSOLIDATED FINANCIAL STATEMENTS

Note 1 (In Part): Summary of Significant Accounting Policies

Pension and Postretirement

Gains or losses are annual changes in the amount of either the benefit obligation or the market-related value of plan assets resulting from experience different from that assumed or from changes in assumptions. The minimum amortization of unrecognized gains or losses, as described in SFAS No. 87, "Employers' Accounting for Pensions," is included in pension expense. Prior service costs, which are changes in benefit obligations due to plan amendments, are amortized on a straight-line basis over the average remaining service period for active employees. The market-related value of plan assets recognizes changes in fair value in a systematic and rational manner over five years. For further information and detailed disclosure in accordance with SFAS No. 132(R), "Employers' Disclosures about Pensions and Other Postretirement Benefits," see note 17 to consolidated financial statements.

Recently Adopted Accounting Pronouncements (In Part)

In December 2003, the FASB issued SFAS No. 132(R), which replaces SFAS No. 132, "Employers' Disclosures about Pensions and Other Postretirement Benefits." SFAS No. 132(R) does not change the measurement and recognition provisions of SFAS No. 87, SFAS No. 88, "Employers' Accounting for Settlements and Curtailments of Defined Benefit Pension Plans and for Termination Benefits," and SFAS No. 106, "Employers' Accounting for Postretirement Benefit Other Than Pensions," however, it includes additional disclosure provisions for annual reporting, including detailed plan asset information by category, expanded benefit obligation disclosure and key assumptions. In addition, interim disclosures related to the individual elements of plan costs and employer's current year contributions are required. See note 17 to consolidated financial statements for further information regarding RJR's pension and postretirement plans.

Note 17 (In Part): Retirement Benefits

RJR and its subsidiaries sponsor a number of noncontributory defined benefit pension plans covering most employees, and also provide certain health and life insurance benefits for retired employees and their dependents. The changes in benefit obligations and plan assets, as well as the funded status of these plans at December 31 were:

	Pension Benefits		Postretirement Benefits	
	2003	2002	2003	2002
Change in benefit obligation				
Obligation at beginning of year	$2,848	$2,529	$ 919	$ 740
Service cost	40	38	6	6
Interest cost	181	181	53	60
Actuarial loss	109	264	49	177
Plan amendments	6	5	(155)	—
Benefits paid	(204)	(194)	(63)	(71)
Settlements	(5)	(11)	—	—
Special termination benefits	71	34	—	—
Curtailment	10	2	5	7
Obligation at end of year	$3,056	$2,848	$ 814	$ 919
Change in plan assets				
Fair value of plan assets at beginning of year	$1,915	$2,160	$ —	$ —
Actual return on plan assets	488	(240)	—	—
Employer contributions	112	200	63	71
Benefits paid	(204)	(194)	(63)	(71)
Settlements	(5)	(11)	—	—
Fair value of plan assets at end of year	$2,306	$1,915	$ —	$ —
Funded status				
Funded status	$ (750)	$ (933)	$(814)	$(919)
Unrecognized transition asset	—	—	(3)	(9)
Unrecognized prior service cost	17	15	(133)	—
Unrecognized net actuarial loss	851	1,097	351	330
Net amount recognized	$ 118	$ 179	$(599)	$(598)
Amounts recognized in the consolidated balance sheets consist of				
Accured benefit—current liability	$ (116)	$ (100)	$ (58)	$ (82)
Accured benefit—long-term liability	(493)	(660)	(541)	(516)
Intangible asset	17	16	—	—
Accumulated other comprehensive income	710	923	—	—
Net amount recognized	$ 118	$ 179	$(599)	$(598)

Weighted-average assumptions used to determine benefit obligations at December 31:

	2003	2002
Discount rate	6.15%	6.40%
Rate of compensation increase	5.00%	5.00%

The measurement date used for all plans was December 31, 2003.

As of December 31, 2003, all of the pension plans experienced accumulated benefit obligations in excess of plan assets, for which the projected benefit obligation, accumulated benefit obligation and fair value of plan assets were $3,056 million, $2,913 million and $2,306 million, respectively. As of December 31, 2002, all of the pension plans experienced accumulated benefit obligations in excess of plan assets, for which the projected benefit obligation, accumulated benfit obligation and fair value of plan assets were $2,848 million, $2,673 million and $1,915 million, respectively.

	Pension Benefits			Postretirement Benefits		
	2003	2002	2001	2003	2002	2001
Components of total benefit cost (income)						
Service cost	$ 40	$ 38	$ 35	$ 6	$ 6	$ 6
Interest cost	181	181	179	53	60	54
Expected return on plan assets	(187)	(222)	(220)	—	—	—
Amortization of transition asset	—	—	—	(6)	(6)	(6)
Amortization of prior service cost	1	(2)	(3)	(10)	—	—
Amortization of net loss (gain)	51	4	2	27	16	9
Net periodic benefit cost (income)	86	(1)	(7)	70	76	63
Curtailment/special benefits	87	37	—	(6)	7	—
Settlements	—	3	4	—	—	—
Total benefit cost (income)	$ 173	$ 39	$ (3)	$ 64	$83	$63

Weighted-average assumptions used to determine net periodic benefit cost for years ended December 31:

	2003	2002	2001
Discount rate	6.40%/6.50%[1]	7.40%	7.50%
Expected long-term return on plan assets	9.00%	9.50%	9.50%
Rate of compensation increase	5.00%	5.00%	5.00%

[1] A discount rate of 6.40% was used for the period from January 1, 2003 to August 31, 2003, and adjusted to a discount rate of 6.50% for the period from August 31, 2003 to December 31, 2003 to reflect the impact of the 2003 restructuring plan.

The overall expected long-term rate of return on assets assumption is based on: (1) the target asset allocation for plan assets, (2) long-term capital markets forecasts for asset classes employed, and (3) active management excess return expectations to the extent asset classes are actively managed.

SFAS No. 87 permits the delayed recognition of pension fund gains and losses in ratable periods of up to five years. RJR uses a five-year period wherein pension fund gains and losses are reflected in the pension calculation at 20% per year, beginning the year after the gains or losses occur. Recent stock market increases have partially offset prior year declines, which in turn resulted in a reduction of additional minimum pension liabilities through a benefit of $213 mil-

lion, $137 million after tax, to other comprehensive income in 2003. Prior service costs are amortized on a straight-line basis over the average remaining service period of employees expected to receive benefits under the plan.

In connection with the 2003 and 2002 restructuring plans, curtailment and special termination benefits costs were $87 million and $37 million for pension benefits, respectively, and $(6) million and $7 million for postretirement benefits, respectively.

Plan assets are invested using a combination of active and passive investment strategies. Active strategies employ multiple investment management firms. Managers within each asset class cover a range of investment styles and approaches and are combined in a way that controls for capitalization, style biases (equity investments), and interest rate bets (fixed income investments) against related benchmark indices, while focusing primarily on issue selection as a means to add value. Risk is controlled through diversification among asset classes, managers, styles and securities. Risk is further controlled both at the manager and asset class level by assigning excess return and tracking error targets. Investment managers are monitored to evaluate performance against these benchmark indices and targets.

Allowable investment types include U.S. equity, non-U.S. equity, fixed income and hedge funds. The U.S. equity fund is composed of common stocks of large, medium and small companies, which are predominantly U.S. based. The non-U.S. equity fund includes equity securities issued by companies domiciled outside the U.S. and in depository receipts, which represent ownership of securities of non-U.S. companies. The fixed income fund includes fixed income securities issued or guaranteed by the U.S. government, and to a lesser extent by non-U.S. governments, or by their respective agencies and instrumentalities, mortgage backed securities, including collateralized mortgage obligations; corporate debt obligations and dollar-denominated obligations issued in the United States by non-U.S. banks and corporations (Yankee bonds). Up to 25% of the fixed income assets can be in debt securities that are below investment grade. The hedge funds invest as a limited partner in portfolios of primarily public securities, including equities and fixed income.

Futures are used to equitize cash held by investment managers in order to approach fully invested portfolio positions. Otherwise, a small number of investment managers employ limited use of derivatives, including futures contracts, options on futures and interest rate swaps in place of direct investment in securities to gain efficient exposure to markets. Derivatives are not used to leverage portfolios.

The target asset allocation is 45% U.S. equity investments, 20% non-U.S. equity investments, 25% fixed income investments and 10% hedge fund investments, with a rebalancing range of approximately plus or minus 5% around the target asset allocations.

RJR's pension plans weighted-average asset allocations at December 31, 2003, and 2002, by asset category were as follows:

	Plan Assets at December 31	
	2003	2002
Asset category		
U.S. equity securities	46%	42%
Non U.S. equity securities	22%	18%
Debt securities	21%	26%
Hedge funds	9%	12%
Other	2%	2%
Total	100%	100%

• • • • • •

RJR expects to contribute $116 million to its pension plans and $58 million to its post-retirement plan during 2004.

Year	Estimated Future Benefits Payments	
	Pension Benefits	Postretirement Benefits
2004	$ 219	$ 58
2005	326[1]	64
2006	262	66
2007	229	66
2008	223	66
2009–2013	1,107	323

[1] The increased pension benefits payments in 2005 include the assumption that a larger than normal portion of the employees downsized during the 2003 restructuring will request a lump sum payment of their retirement benefits at the end of their severance period.

Defined Contribution Plans

3.73

THE PROCTER & GAMBLE COMPANY (JUN)

NOTES TO CONSOLIDATED FINANCIAL STATEMENTS (Amounts in millions)

Note 9 (In Part): Postretirement Benefits and Employee Stock Ownership Plan

The Company offers various postretirement benefits to its employees.

Defined Contribution Retirement Plans

The most prevalent employee benefit plans offered are defined contribution plans, which cover substantially all employees in the United States as well as employees in certain other countries. These plans are fully funded.

Under the defined contribution plans, the Company generally makes annual contributions to participants' accounts based on individual base salaries and years of service. In the United States, the Company makes annual contributions to participants' accounts that do not exceed 15% of total participants' annual wages and salaries.

The Company maintains The Procter & Gamble Profit Sharing Trust (Trust) and Employee Stock Ownership Plan (ESOP) to provide funding for the U.S. defined contribution plan, as well as other retiree benefits. Operating details of the ESOP are provided at the end of this Note. The fair value of the ESOP Series A shares serves to reduce the Company's cash contribution required to fund the profit sharing plan contributions earned. Under the American Institute of Certified Public Accountants (AICPA) Statement of Position (SOP) 76-3, shares of the ESOP are allocated at original cost based on debt service requirements, net of advances made by the Company to the Trust.

Defined contribution expense pursuant to this plan was $286, $279 and $303 in 2003, 2002 and 2001, respectively, which approximates the amount funded by the Company.

Supplemental Retirement Plans

3.74

INTERNATIONAL BUSINESS MACHINES CORPORATION (DEC)

NOTES TO CONSOLIDATED FINANCIAL STATEMENTS

W (In Part): Retirement-Related Benefits

Defined Benefit and Defined Contribution Plans (In Part)

The company and its subsidiaries have defined benefit and defined contribution pension plans that cover substantially all regular employees, and supplemental retirement plans that cover certain executives.

U.S. Supplemental Executive Retention Plan

The company also has a non-qualified U.S. Supplemental Executive Retention Plan (SERP). The SERP, which is unfunded, provides defined benefit pension benefits in addition to the PPP to eligible executives based on average earnings, years of service and age at retirement. Effective July 1, 1999, the company adopted the SERP (which replaced the previous Supplemental Executive Retirement Plan). Some participants of the prior SERP will still be eligible for benefits under that plan, but will not be eligible for the new plan. The total cost of this plan for the years ended December 31, 2003, 2002 and 2001, was $25 million, $18 million and $23 million, respectively. These amounts are reflected in Cost of other defined benefit plans in the table below. At December 31, 2003 and 2002, the benefit obligation was $181 million and $130 million, respectively, and the amounts included in Retirement and nonpension postretirement benefit obligations in the Consolidated Statement of Financial Position at December 31, 2003 and 2002, were liabilities of $186 million and $165 million, respectively.

Cost/(Income) of Pension Plans

(Dollars in millions)	U.S. Plans			Non-U.S. Plans		
	2003	2002	2001	2003	2002	2001
Service cost	$ 576	$ 650	$ 647	$ 537	$ 505	$ 429
Interest cost	2,518	2,591	2,560	1,477	1,270	1,214
Expected return on plan assets	(3,703)	(4,121)	(4,202)	(2,228)	(2,132)	(2,062)
Amortization of transition assets	(144)	(144)	(143)	(15)	(12)	(10)
Amortization of prior service cost	61	61	52	17	28	28
Recognized actuarial losses/(gains)	—	—	—	101	33	(12)
Divestitures/settlement losses/(gains)	—	46	—	—	26	(12)
Net periodic pension income—U.S. Plan and material non-U.S. Plans	(692)	(917)	(1,086)	(111)	(282)	(425)
Cost of other defined benefit plans	132	124	141	100	58	54
Total net periodic pension income for all defined benefit plans	(560)	(793)	(945)	(11)	(224)	(371)
Cost of defined contribution plans	333	315	313	265	178	162
Total retirement plan (income)/cost recognized in the consolidated statement of earnings	$ (227)	$ (478)	$ (632)	$ 254	$ (46)	$ (209)

Multiemployer Plans

3.75

POTLATCH CORPORATION (DEC)

NOTES TO CONSOLIDATED FINANCIAL STATEMENTS

Note 12 (In Part): Savings, Pension and Other Postretirement Benefit Plans

Hourly employees at two of our manufacturing facilities participate in multi-employer defined benefit pension plans, the Paper, Allied-Industrial, Chemical and Energy Workers International Union (PACE) Pension Fund and the International Association of Machinist & Aerospace Workers (IAMA) National Pension Fund, to which we make contributions. We also make contributions to a trust fund established to provide retiree medical benefits for a portion of these employees, which is managed by PACE. Company contributions to these plans in 2003, 2002 and 2001 amounted to $7.7 million, $6.4 million and $6.1 million, respectively.

Amendment of Plan

3.76

ASHLAND INC. (SEP)

NOTES TO CONSOLIDATED FINANCIAL STATEMENTS

Note O (In Part): Employee Benefit Plans

Pension and Other Postretirement Plans

Ashland and its subsidiaries sponsor noncontributory pension plans that cover substantially all employees. For certain plans, half of the balances in employees' accounts under an employee stock ownership plan are coordinated with their pension benefits. Ashland's objective is to fully fund the accumulated benefit obligations of its qualified plans, and the level of its contributions is determined annually to achieve that objective over time. During 2003, Ashland contributed $61 million to its qualified pension plans, and an additional $50 million was contributed on October 1, 2003. Ashland funds the costs of its nonqualified pension plans as the benefits are paid.

Prior to July 1, 2003, benefits under Ashland's pension plans were generally based on employees' years of service and compensation during the years immediately preceding their retirement. Although certain changes were implemented on that date, the pension benefits of employees with at least ten years of service were not affected. As of July 1, 2003, the pension benefits of most other employees were converted to cash balance accounts. Such employees received an initial account balance equal to the present value of their accrued benefits under the previous plan on that date. Although individual plans have varying provisions, employees with cash balance accounts generally receive either fixed pay credits or variable pay credits ranging from 3% to 16% of pay based on their age plus vested service. Their accounts are also credited with interest based on the one-year U.S. Treasury rate plus 1%, subject to a minimum annual crediting rate of 4% and a maximum of 7%. Pension benefits for these employees will be based on the balances in their accounts upon retirement.

Ashland and its subsidiaries also sponsor healthcare and life insurance plans for eligible employees who retire or are disabled. Ashland's retiree life insurance plans are noncontributory, while Ashland shares the costs of providing healthcare coverage with its retired employees through premiums, deductibles and coinsurance provisions. Ashland funds its share of the costs of the postretirement benefit plans as the benefits are paid.

As of July 1, 2003, Ashland implemented changes in the way it will share the cost of healthcare coverage with future retirees. Those changes did not affect the previous cost-sharing program for retirees or for employees meeting certain qualifications (based on age and years of service) at that date. However, Ashland did amend that program to limit its annual per capita costs to an amount equivalent to base year per capita costs, plus annual increases of up to 1.5% per year for costs incurred after January 1, 2004. Under a previous amendment, base year costs were limited to the amounts incurred in 1992, plus annual increases of up to 4.5% per year thereafter. Premiums for retiree healthcare coverage are equivalent to the excess of the estimated per capita costs over the amounts borne by Ashland.

Employees not meeting the required qualifications were allocated notional accounts based on their age and years of service that can only be used to pay all or part of the premiums for retiree healthcare coverage. Such premiums represent the full costs of providing that coverage, without any subsidy from Ashland. The notional accounts are credited with interest based on the one-year U.S. Treasury rate plus 1%, subject to a minimum annual crediting rate of 4% and a maximum of 7%. Retirees will continue to have access to Ashland coverage after their notional accounts are exhausted, but they will be responsible for paying the full premiums.

Summaries of the changes in the benefit obligations and plan assets (primarily listed stocks and debt securities) and of the funded status of the plans follow. Pension benefit obligations under the qualified plans at September 30, 2003 were reduced by approximately $82 million, which represents the amount expected to be funded by the balances in the employees' accounts under an employee stock ownership plan.

| | Pension Benefits | | | | Other Postretirement Benefits | |
| | 2003 | | 2002 | | | |
(In millions)	Qualified Plans	Nonqualified Plans	Qualified Plans	Nonqualified Plans	2003	2002
Change in benefit obligations						
Benefit obligations at October 1	$ 874	$ 109	$ 715	$ 103	$ 361	$ 333
Service cost	42	1	42	1	11	12
Interest cost	58	7	52	7	22	23
Retiree contributions	—	—	—	—	12	8
Benefits paid	(33)	(4)	(30)	(4)	(33)	(33)
Plan amendments	(6)	—	—	—	(95)	—
Changes in assumptions	58	5	59	7	19	19
Other—net	9	(19)	36	(5)	(1)	(1)
Benefit obligations at September 30	$ 1,002	$ 99	$ 874	$ 109	$ 296	$ 361

(continued)

| (In millions) | Pension Benefits | | | | Other Postretirement Benefits | |
| | 2003 | | 2002 | | | |
	Qualified Plans	Nonqualified Plans	Qualified Plans	Nonqualified Plans	2003	2002
Change in plan assets						
Value of plan assets at October 1	$ 551		$ 518			
Actual return on plan assets	99		(42)			
Employer contributions	61		103			
Benefits paid	(33)		(30)			
Other	2		2			
Value of plan assets at September 30	$ 680		$ 551			
Funded status of the plans						
Unfunded accumulated obligation	$ 139	$ 90	$ 150	$ 98	$ 296	$ 361
Provision for future salary increases	183	9	173	11	—	—
Excess of obligations over plan assets	322	99	323	109	296	361
Unrecognized actuarial loss	(344)	(41)	(354)	(43)	(87)	(72)
Unrecognized prior service credit (cost)	3	—	(2)	—	100	15
Net liability recognized	$ (19)	$ 58	$ (33)	$ 66	$ 309	$ 304
Balance sheet liabilities (assets)						
Accrued benefit liabilities		$ 231		$ 250	$ 309	$ 304
Intangible assets		(1)		(2)	—	—
Accumulated other comprehensive loss		(191)		(215)	—	—
Net liability recognized		$ 39		$ 33	$ 309	$ 304
Assumptions as of September 30						
Discount rate		6.25%		6.75%	6.25%	6.75%
Salary adjustment rate		4.50		5.00	—	—

The following table details the components of pension and other postretirement benefit costs.

| (In millions) | Pension Benefits | | | Other Postretirement Benefits | | |
	2003	2002	2001	2003	2002	2001
Service cost	$ 43	$ 43	$ 37	$ 11	$ 12	$ 11
Interest cost	65	59	53	22	23	22
Expected return on plan assets (9%)	(51)	(47)	(48)	—	—	—
Other amortization and deferral	30	19	4	(7)	(6)	(6)
	$ 87	$ 74	$ 46	$ 26	$ 29	$ 27

The changes previously discussed in the postretirement benefit plans reduced Ashland's accrued obligations under those plans, and the reductions are being amortized to income. Such amortization reduced Ashland's costs for postretirement benefit costs by $10 million in 2003, $8 million in 2002 and $9 million in 2001. At September 30, 2003, the remaining unrecognized prior service credit resulting from the changes amounted to $100 million, and will reduce future costs by $15 million in 2004, $9 million in 2005 and about $8 million annually thereafter through 2014.

Special Termination Benefits

3.77

ANADARKO PETROLEUM CORPORATION (DEC)

NOTES TO CONSOLIDATED FINANCIAL STATEMENTS

20 (In Part): Pension Plans, Other Postretirement Benefits and Employee Savings Plans

Pension Plans and Other Postretirement Benefits (In Part)

The Company has defined benefit pension plans and supplemental pension plans that are noncontributory pension plans. The Company also has a foreign pension plan which is a contributory defined benefit pension plan. The Company also provides certain health care and life insurance benefits for retired employees. Health care benefits are funded by contributions from the Company and the retiree, with the retiree contributions adjusted according to the provisions of the Company's health care plans. The Company's retiree life insurance plan is noncontributory. The Company uses a December 31 measurement date for the majority of its plans.

In 2003, the Company made contributions of $61 million to its funded pension plans, $5 million to its unfunded pension plans and $9 million to its unfunded other postretirement benefit plans. Contributions to the funded plans increase the plan assets while contributions to unfunded plans are made to fund current period benefit payments. In 2004, the Company expects to contribute between $73 million and $78 million to its funded pension plans, $24 million to its unfunded pension plans and $9 million to its unfunded other postretirement benefit plans.

The following table sets forth the Company's pension and other postretirement benefits changes in benefit obligation, fair value of plan assets, funded status and amounts recognized in the financial statements as of December 31, 2003 and 2002.

(Millions)	Pension Benefits		Other Benefits	
	2003	2002	2003	2002
Change in benefit obligation				
Benefit obligation at beginning of year	$ 489	$ 417	$ 131	$ 123
Service cost	22	14	7	5
Interest cost	34	29	9	8
Plan amendments	21	—	(6)	(7)
Special termination benefits	3	—	—	—
Acturial loss	26	61	29	8
Foreign currency exchange rate change	8	—	—	—
Benefit payments	(44)	(32)	(9)	(6)
Benefit obligation at end of year	$ 559	$ 489	$ 161	$ 131
Change in plan assets				
Fair value of plan assets at beginning of year	$ 286	$ 338	$ —	$ —
Actual return on plan assets	58	(26)	—	—
Employer contributions	66	6	9	6
Foreign currency exchange rate change	9	—	—	—
Benefit payments	(44)	(32)	(9)	(6)
Fair value of plan assets at end of year	$ 375	$ 286	$ —	$ —
Funded status of the plan	$(184)	$(203)	$(161)	$(131)
Unrecognized actuarial loss	174	195	58	31
Unrecognized prior service cost	8	8	—	8
Unrecognized initial asset	—	(1)	—	—
Total recognized	$ (2)	$ (1)	$(103)	$ (92)
Total recognized amounts in the balance sheet consist of:				
Prepaid benefit cost	$ 21	$ 24	$ —	$ —
Accrued benefit liability	(123)	(155)	(103)	(92)
Intangible asset	10	11	—	—
Other comprehensive expense	90	119	—	—
Total recognized	$ (2)	$ (1)	$(103)	$ (92)

The accumulated benefit obligation for all defined benefit pension plans was $492 million and $427 million as of December 31, 2003 and 2002, respectively. The projected benefit obligation, accumulated benefit obligation and fair value of plan assets for the pension plans with accumulated benefit obligations in excess of plan assets were $530 million, $463 million and $332 million, respectively, as of December 31, 2003, and $467 million, $404 million and $251 million, respectively, as of December 31, 2002. The Company's benefit obligation under the unfunded pension plans are secured by the Anadarko Petroleum Corporation Executives and Directors Benefits Trust. See Note 11.

In December 2003, the Medicare Prescription Drug, Improvement and Modernization Act of 2003 (the Act) was signed into law. The Act introduces a prescription drug benefit under Medicare (Medicare Part D) as well as a federal subsidy to sponsors of retiree health care plans that provide a benefit that is at least actuarially equivalent to Medicare Part D. Under FASB Staff Position No. FAS 106-1, "Accounting and Disclosure Requirements Related to the Medicare Prescription Drug, Improvement and Modernization Act of 2003," the Company has made a one-time election to defer accounting for the effect of the Act for the year ended December 31, 2003. The accumulated projected benefit obligation and the net periodic benefit cost included in other benefits do not reflect the effects of the Act on the Plan. The authoritative guidance on the accounting for the federal subsidy is pending and, when issued, could require the Company to change previously reported information.

The following table sets forth the Company's pension and other postretirement benefit cost.

(Millions)	Pension Benefits			Other Benefits		
	2003	2002	2001	2003	2002	2001
Components of net periodic benefit cost						
Service cost	$ 22	$ 14	$ 11	$ 7	$ 5	$ 3
Interest cost	34	29	27	9	8	6
Expected return on plan assets	(30)	(31)	(28)	—	—	—
Settlements	17	—	—	—	—	—
Special termination benefits	3	—	—	—	—	—
Amortization values and deferrals	14	4	1	2	1	(1)
Net periodic benefit cost	$ 60	$ 16	$ 11	$18	$14	$ 8

As a result of the Company's cost reduction plan, a special termination benefit charge of $3 million was expensed to restructuring costs in 2003. As a result of executive retirements, a settlement charge of $17 million was expensed to administrative and general expense. The increase (decrease) in the Company's minimum liability included in other comprehensive income related to the pension plans was $(29) million, $115 million and $4 million for 2003, 2002 and 2001, respectively.

POSTEMPLOYMENT BENEFITS

3.78 SFAS No. 112, *Employers' Accounting for Postemployment Benefits*, requires that entities providing postemployment benefits to their employees accrue the cost of such benefits. *SFAS No. 112* does not require that the amount of postemployment benefits be disclosed. Accordingly, many of the survey companies make little or no disclosure about postemployment benefits in the years following the year of adopting *SFAS No. 112*.

3.79 An example of a disclosure for postemployment benefits follows.

3.80

GENERAL MOTORS CORPORATION (DEC)

NOTES TO CONSOLIDATED FINANCIAL STATEMENTS

Note 5: Postemployment Benefit Costs

GM records liabilities for termination and other postemployment benefits to be paid pursuant to the union or other contractual agreements in connection with closed plants in North America. GM reviews the adequacy and continuing need for these liabilities on an annual basis in conjunction with its year-end production and labor forecasts. Furthermore, GM reviews the reasonableness of these liabilities on a quarterly basis.

The liability for postemployment benefits as of December 31, 2003 totals approximately $384 million relating to nine plants and approximately 2,900 employees, with anticipated spending of approximately 96% over the next three years. The liability for postemployment benefits was $613 million relating to 11 plants and approximately 3,400 employees as of December 31, 2002. The liability for postemployment benefits was $626 million relating to 12 plants and approximately 5,800 employees as of December 31, 2001. The following table summarizes the activity from December 31, 2001 through December 31, 2003 for this liability (dollars in millions):

Balance at December 31, 2001	$ 626
Spending	(182)
Interest accretion	47
Additions	281
Adjustments	(159)
Balance at December 31, 2002	$ 613
Spending	(189)
Interest accretion	31
Additions	—
Adjustments	(71)
Balance at December 31, 2003	$ 384

In 2003, GM recognized adjustments of $71 million to reduce the liability balance of existing closed plants ($44 million after tax, or $0.08 per share of GM $1-2/3 par value common stock), recorded in cost of sales. The adjustments are primarily the result of the reversal of the remaining postemployment liabilities for employees at the Janesville, Wisconsin plant location, a reduction of the respective liabilities for employees at the Oklahoma City, Oklahoma, plant, and an increase of the liabilities at the Wilmington, Delaware, plant. The Janesville charge was established in 2002, relating to 772 employees impacted by the transfer of commercial truck production from Janesville to Flint, Michigan. The reversal is primarily due to earlier than anticipated retirements of 479 employees. The adjustments also include a reduction in the reserve for the Oklahoma City plant, as employees have been absorbed into the continuing workforce due to increased manpower requirements. The Wilimington plant reserve is increased to account for increased duration that employees will not be absorbed into the continuing workforce due to a change in the production plan.

In 2002, GM recognized postemployment benefit liabilities of $281 million ($174 million after tax, or $0.31 per share of GM $1-2/3 par value common stock) primarily related to the transfer of commercial truck production from Janesville to Flint. The Janesville charge related to 772 employees and was included in cost of sales. The adjustments of $159 million ($99 million after tax or $0.18 per share of GM $1-2/3 par value common stock), recorded in cost of sales, are primarily the result of a reversal of postemployment benefit liabilities for employees at the Spring Hill, Tennessee, plant. This reversal was recorded due to approximately 400 employees, who had been included in the planned production capacity reduction but were instead absorbed into the continuing workforce due to a change in the plan.

EMPLOYEE COMPENSATORY PLANS

3.81 Effective for fiscal years beginning after December 15, 1995, SFAS No. 123, *Accounting for Stock-Based Compensation*, establishes accounting and reporting standards for stock-based compensation plans. *SFAS No. 123* encourages entities to use a "fair value based method" in accounting for employee stock-based compensation plans but allows the "intrinsic value based method" prescribed by Accounting

Principles Board (APB) Opinion No. 25, *Accounting for Stock Issued to Employees. SFAS No. 123* amends *APB Opinion No. 25* to require pro forma disclosures of net income and earnings per share as if the "fair value based method" was used.

3.82 Effective for fiscal years ending after December 15, 2002, SFAS No. 148, *Accounting for Stock-Based Compensation—Transition and Disclosure*, amends *SFAS No. 123* to provide alternative methods of transition for a voluntary change to the fair value based method of accounting for stock-based employee compensation. In addition, *SFAS No. 148* amends the disclosure requirements of *SFAS No. 123* to require prominent disclosures in both annual and interim financial statements about the method of accounting for stock-based employee compensation and the effect of the method used on reported results.

3.83 Table 3-12 lists the types of employee compensatory plans disclosed by the survey companies. Compensatory plans may consist of stock awards or cash payments. The "stock award" caption in Table 3-12 represents restricted stock awards, performance awards, and bonuses paid by issuing stock.

3.84 Examples of employee compensatory plan disclosures follow.

3.85

TABLE 3-12: EMPLOYEE COMPENSATORY PLANS

	Number of Companies			
	2003	2002	2001	2000
Stock options	590	587	585	583
Savings/investment	358	339	324	263
Stock award	318	332	327	337
Stock purchase	189	189	188	150
Deferred compensation	108	93	78	68
Employee stock ownership	93	93	110	110
Profit-sharing	81	80	94	94
Incentive compensation	66	63	76	70

Stock Option Plans

3.86

CHESAPEAKE CORPORATION (DEC)

NOTES TO CONSOLIDATED FINANCIAL STATEMENTS

1 (In Part): Summary of Significant Accounting Policies

Restricted Stock

Accruals of compensation cost are made for restricted stock grants based on the best available estimate of the number of shares expected to vest. The compensation cost is recognized over the periods in which the related employee services are rendered.

Stock Options

Chesapeake uses the intrinsic-value-based method of accounting for our stock plans. Under the intrinsic-value-based method, compensation cost is the excess, if any, of the quoted market price of the stock at grant date over the amount an employee must pay to acquire the stock. Chesapeake generally grants stock options with an exercise price equal to the market value of the common stock on the date of grant.

The Black-Scholes option pricing model was used to estimate fair value as of the date of grant using the following assumptions:

	2003	2002	2001
Dividend yield	4.7%	3.1%	4.0%
Risk-free interest rates	3.4%	4.6%	4.4%
Volatility	45.8%	32.5%	30.7%
Expected option term (years)	5.5	5.5	5.0

Weighted-Average Fair Value of Options
Granted During the Year

2001	$5.58
2002	$7.65
2003	$5.51

Had the compensation cost for our stock option plans been determined based on the fair value at the grant date, rather than the intrinsic-value-method, our pro forma amounts would be as follows:

(In millions, except per share data)	2003	2002	2001
Stock-based compensation expense, net of tax, included in net income as reported	$ 1.6	$ 0.1	$ 0.3
Net income as reported	26.5	21.9	123.5
Pro forma stock-based compensation expense, net of tax	1.3	1.7	1.8
Pro forma net income	25.2	20.2	121.7
Earnings per share as reported:			
Basic	$1.74	$1.45	$ 8.18
Diluted	1.74	1.44	8.12
Pro forma:			
Basic	$1.66	$1.34	$ 8.06
Diluted	1.66	1.33	8.01

Pro forma disclosures for stock option accounting may not be representative of the effects on reported net income in future years.

12 (In Part): Stock Option and Award Plans

At December 28, 2003, Chesapeake had three stock compensation plans for employees and officers. All three plans have been approved by our shareholderes. Under the 1997 Incentive Plan, we may grant stock options, stock appreciation rights ("SARs"), stock awards, performance shares or stock units, and may make incentive awards to our key employees and officers. The options outstanding were awarded under our 1993 and 1997 Incentive Plans. Up to 2,610,405 additional shares may be issued pursuant to all of the stock option and award plans; however, the Board of Directors has stated that all future grants will be made only from those shares available under the 1997 Incentive Plan, which had 560,940 additional shares available for issuance at December 28, 2003. The stock compensation plans are administered by the Executive Compensation Committee of the Board of Directors.

Chesapeake has a Directors' Stock Option and Deferred Compensation Plan that provides for annual grants of stock options to nonemployee directors. Up to 289,250 additional shares may be issued pursuant to the Directors' Plan.

Stock Options

Stock options are generally granted with an exercise price equal to the marker value of the common stock on the date of the grant, expire 10 years from the date they are granted, and generally vest over a three-year service period.

The following schedule summarizes stock option activity for the three years ended December 28, 2003:

	Number of Stock Options	Weighted-Average Exercise Price
Outstanding, December 31, 2000	1,608,034	$29.41
Granted	405,500	21.91
Exercised	(68,410)	21.40
Forfeited/expired	(179,415)	29.45
Outstanding, December 30, 2001	1,765,709	27.91
Granted	287,500	28.09
Exercised	(17,350)	23.03
Forfeited/expired	(249,258)	26.32
Outstanding, December 29, 2002	1,786,601	28.21
Granted	111,500	17.89
Exercised	(32,266)	19.34
Forfeited/expired	(156,068)	27.53
Outstanding, December 28, 2003	1,709,767	$27.77
Exercisable:		
December 30, 2001	1,088,638	
December 29, 2002	1,237,965	
December 28, 2003	1,337,371	

Information about options outstanding at December 28, 2003, is summarized below:

	Options Outstanding			Options Exercisable	
Range of Exercise Prices	Number Outstanding	Weighted-Average Remaining Contractual Life (Years)	Weighted-Average Exercise Price	Number Exercisable	Weighted-Average Exercise Price
$15.38–$19.22	111,500	9.1	$17.89	0	$ 0
$19.23–$23.07	304,452	6.9	21.93	216,247	21.96
$23.08–$26.91	91,828	3.1	24.64	91,828	24.64
$26.92–$30.76	829,717	5.8	28.46	657,026	28.55
$30.77–$34.60	244,305	2.7	33.04	244,305	33.04
$34.61–$38.45	127,965	4.3	38.03	127,965	38.03
	1,709,767	5.5	$27.77	1,337,371	$28.95

Restricted Stock

In 2003, the Executive Compensation Committee of the Board of Directors made grants of performance-based restricted stock to Chesapeake's officers and certain managers for the 2003–2005 Cycle of the Long-Term Incentive Program under the 1997 Incentive Plan. The performance criteria established by the Executive Compensation Committee for vesting the restricted stock was the achievement of certain stock price targets of Chesapeake's common stock. If the performance targets are not achieved during the Cycle, the shares will be forfeited. On July 18, 2003, one of the performance targets was met when the average closing price of Chesapeake's common stock exceeded $22.00 for a 20-day period.

	2003
Outstanding grants at start of year	0
New shares granted	144,500
Shares forfeited	0
Shares vested	(48,162)
Outstanding grants at year-end	96,338

On December 31, 2003, 48,167 shares were issued when another performance target was met, as the average closing price of our common stock exceeded $26.00 for a 20-day period.

Stock Purchase Plans

Chesapeake has stock purchase plans for certain eligible salaried and hourly employees. Shares of Chesapeake common stock are purchased based on participant authorized payroll deductions and a company match of a portion of the employee contributions. At December 28, 2003, 412,391 shares remain available for issuance under these plans.

Stock-Based Compensation Expense

The charges to income from continuing operations before taxes for all stock-based employee compensation plans approximated $2.4 million in 2003, $0.2 million in 2002 and $0.5 million in 2001.

3.87

CLARCOR INC. (NOV)

NOTES TO CONSOLIDATED FINANCIAL STATEMENTS
(Dollars in thousands except per share data)

A (In Part): Accounting Policies

Stock-Based Compensation

In accordance with Statement of Financial Accounting Standards (SFAS) No. 123, "Accounting for Stock-Based Compensation," the Company accounts for stock-based compensation using the intrinsic value method as prescribed under Accounting Principles Board Opinion No. 25, "Ac-

counting for Stock Issued to Employees," and related Interpretations and provides the disclosure-only provisions of SFAS No. 123. In December 2002, the Financial Accounting Standards Board issued SFAS No. 148, "Accounting for Stock-Based Compensation—Transition and Disclosure," which amends SFAS No. 123, providing alternative methods of accounting and requiring more prominent and frequent disclosures of the effects of stock-based compensation under the fair value-based method.

If the Company had determined compensation expense for its stock-based compensation plans based on the fair value at the grant dates consistent with the method of SFAS No. 123 and SFAS No. 148, the Company's pro forma net earnings and basic and diluted earnings per share (EPS) would have been as follows. (See Note M.)

	2003	2002	2001
Net earnings, as reported	$54,552	$46,601	$41,893
Less total stock-based compensation expense under the fair value-based method, net of tax	(2,307)	(1,487)	(1,133)
Pro form net earnings	$52,245	$45,114	$40,760
Basic EPS, as reported	$ 2.17	$ 1.88	$ 1.71
Pro forma basic EPS	$ 2.08	$ 1.82	$ 1.66
Diluted EPS, as reported	$ 2.15	$ 1.85	$ 1.68
Pro forma diluted EPS	$ 2.06	$ 1.79	$ 1.64

M. Incentive Plan

In 1994, the shareholders of CLARCOR adopted the 1994 Incentive Plan, which allows the Company to grant stock options, restricted stock and performance awards to officers, directors and key employees. The 1994 Incentive Plan incorporates the various incentive plans in existence prior to March 1994.

The 1994 Incentive Plan, as amended on March 25, 2000, allows grants and awards of up to 1.5% of the outstanding common stock as of January 1 of each calendar year. In addition, the Compensation Committee of the Company's Board of Directors may approve an additional 1% of outstanding common stock to be awarded during any calendar year. Any portion that is not granted in a given year is available for future grants. After the close of fiscal year 2003, 312,316 shares were granted, including the restricted stock units discussed hereafter.

On March 24, 2003, the shareholders of CLARCOR approved the 2004 Incentive Plan, which replaces the 1994 Incentive Plan on its termination date of December 14, 2003. The 2004 Incentive Plan provides for similar types of awards and grants as were permitted by the 1994 Incentive Plan for up to 1,500,000 shares.

The following is a description and a summary of key provisions related to outstanding grants under the 1994 Incentive Plan.

Stock Options

Nonqualified stock options may, at the discretion of the Board of Directors, be granted at the fair market value at the date of grant or at an exercise price less than the fair market value at the date of grant. Options granted to key employees vest primarily 25% per year beginning at the end of the first year;

therefore, they become fully exercisable at the end of four years. Options granted to non-employee directors vest immediately. All options expire ten years from the date of grant unless otherwise terminated.

The following table summarizes the activity under the non-qualified stock option plans.

| | 2003 | | 2002 | | 2001 | |
	Shares	Weighted Average Exercise Price	Shares	Weighted Average Exercise Price	Shares	Weighted Average Exercise Price
Outstanding at beginning of year	2,046,268	$19.38	2,324,130	$16.83	2,286,026	$14.53
Granted at fair market value on dates of grants	509,721	33.66	356,925	28.19	449,366	19.93
Exercised/surrendered	(640,055)	17.90	(634,787)	15.00	(411,262)	14.15
Outstanding at end of year	1,915,934	$23.67	2,046,268	$19.38	2,324,130	$16.83
Options exercisable at end of year	1,349,040	$22.80	1,381,858	$18.52	1,531,152	$16.06

The following table summarizes information about the options at November 30, 2003.

| | Options Outstanding | | | Options Exercisable | |
Range of Exercise Prices	Number	Weighted Average Exercise Price	Weighted Average Remaining Life in Years	Number	Weighted Average Exercise Price
$12.58–$17.94	439,295	$16.18	4.32	322,706	$15.55
$18.38–$25.55	669,955	$19.10	5.79	562,287	$19.16
$27.50–$38.80	806,684	$31.55	7.28	464,047	$32.26

The weighted average fair value per option at the date of grant for options granted in 2003, 2002 and 2001 was $7.80, $7.87 and $5.12, respectively. The fair value of each option grant is estimated on the date of grant using the Black-Scholes option pricing model with the following weighted average assumptions by grant year. Adjustments for forfeitures are made as they occur.

	2003	2002	2001
Risk-free interest rate	3.87%	4.70%	5.53%
Expected dividend yield	1.58%	1.91%	2.50%
Expected volatility factor	23.00%	25.50%	25.50%
Expected option term (in years)	7.0	7.0	7.0

Restricted Stock Awards

During 2003, 2002, and 2001, respectively, the Company granted 22,645, 25,436 and 44,404 restricted units of Company common stock with a fair value of $32.30, $27.50 and $18.50 per share, the respective market price of the stock at the date granted. The restricted share units require no payment from the employee and compensation cost is recorded based on the market price on the grant date and is recorded equally over the vesting period of four years. During the vesting period, officers and key employees receive compensation equal to dividends declared on common shares. Upon vesting, the employee may elect to defer receipt of their shares. Subsequent to the end of fiscal year 2003, the Company granted 18,916 restricted stock units in December 2003 at the then-market price of $45.59.

Compensation expense related to restricted stock awards and long range performance stock awards totaled $569, $426 and $618 in 2003, 2002 and 2001, respectively. There have been no grants of long range shares or units since December 1999 and no future awards of long range performance shares or units are expected to be granted.

Directors' Restricted Stock Compensation

The amended 1994 Incentive Plan provides for grants of shares of common stock to all non-employee directors equal to a one-year annual retainer in lieu of cash. The directors' rights to the shares vest immediately on the date of grant. In 2003, 2002 and 2001, respectively, 7,176, 8,120 and 10,618 shares of Company common stock were issued under the amended plan. Compensation expense for the plan totaled $260 for each year 2003, 2002 and 2001.

3.88

SAUCONY, INC. (DEC)

*NOTES TO CONSOLIDATED FINANCIAL STATEMENTS
(In thousands and per share amounts)*

1 (In Part): Summary of Significant Accounting Policies

Stock-Based Compensation

The Company accounts for employee stock options and share awards under the intrinsic-value method prescribed by Accounting Principles Board Opinion No. 25, "Accounting for Stock Issued to Employees", "APB 25", as interpreted, with pro-forma disclosures of net earnings and earnings per share, as if the fair value method of accounting defined in Statement of Financial Accounting Standards No. 123, "SFAS 123". SFAS 123 establishes a fair value based method of accounting for stock-based employee compensation plans. Under the fair value method, compensation cost is measured at the grant date based on the value of the award and is recognized over the service period, which is usually the vesting period. Had the Company determined the stock-based compensation expense for the Company's stock options based upon the fair value at the grant date for stock option awards in 2003, 2002 and 2001, consistent with the provisions of SFAS 123, the Company's net income (loss) and net income (loss) per share would have been reduced to the pro forma amounts indicated below. Pro forma net income available to the Company's common stockholders is allocated among our two classes of common stock, Class A common stock and Class B common stock. The allocation among each class was based upon the two-class method. Under the two-class method, pro forma earnings per share for each class of common stock is determined according to dividends declared. Pro forma net income allocated to Class A common stockholders and Class B common stockholders and the calculation of pro forma basic and diluted earnings per share are as follows:

	2003		2002		2001	
	Basic	Diluted	Basic	Diluted	Basic	Diluted
Net income (loss):						
As reported	$ 8,488	$ 8,488	$ 5,243	$ 5,243	$ (940)	$ (940)
Add: Stock-based compensation expense included in reported net income (loss), net of related tax benefit	23	23	26	26	22	22
Less: Total stock-based compensation expense determined under the fair value based method for all awards, net of related tax benefit	(1,161)	(1,161)	(710)	(710)	(768)	(768)
Pro forma net income (loss)	$ 7,350	$ 7,350	$ 4,559	$ 4,559	$ (1,686)	$ (1,686)
Pro forma net income (loss) allocated:						
Class A common stock	$ 2,868	$ 2,743	$ 1,808	$ 1,784	$ (673)	$ (673)
Class B common stock	4,482	4,607	2,751	2,775	(1,013)	(1,013)
	$ 7,350	$ 7,350	$ 4,559	$ 4,559	$ (1,686)	$ (1,686)
Pro forma earnings per share:						
Class A common stock as reported	$ 1.31	$ 1.26	$ 0.81	$ 0.80	$ (0.15)	$ (0.15)
Add: Stock-based compensation expense included in reported net income (loss), net of related tax	0.00	0.00	0.00	0.00	0.00	0.00
Less: Total stock-based compensation expense determined under the fair value based method for all awards net of related tax benefit	(0.17)	(0.17)	(0.10)	(0.10)	(0.11)	(0.11)
Pro forma net income (loss) per share	$ 1.14	$ 1.09	$ 0.71	$ 0.70	$ (0.26)	$ (0.26)
Class B common stock as reported	$ 1.44	$ 1.38	$ 0.89	$ 0.88	$ (0.16)	$ (0.16)
Add: Stock-based compensation expense included in reported net income (loss), net of related tax	0.00	0.00	0.00	0.00	0.00	0.00
Less: Total stock-based compensation expense determined under the fair value based method for all awards, net of related tax benefit	(0.19)	(0.18)	(0.11)	(0.11)	(0.13)	(0.13)
Pro forma net income (loss) per share	$ 1.25	$ 1.20	$ 0.78	$ 0.77	$ (0.29)	$ (0.29)

ATT-SEC 3.88

See Note 13 for the weighted-average assumptions incorporated into the Black-Scholes option-pricing model, used to calculate the fair value stock-based employee compensation.

11. Stock Options and Stock Purchase Warrants

1993 Equity Incentive Plan

Under the Company's 1993 Equity Incentive Plan (Equity Incentive Plan), approved by the Company's stockholders on May 25, 1993, the Company may grant incentive stock options and restricted stock awards to officers, key employees and Directors of the Company. Outside consultants and advisors to the Company are eligible to receive non-statutory stock options and awards of restricted stock.

The Equity Incentive Plan is administered by the Board of Directors, which, at its sole discretion, grants options to purchase shares of Common Stock and makes awards of restricted stock. The purchase price per share of Common Stock shall be determined by the Board of Directors, provided, however, that in the case of incentive stock options, the purchase price may not be less than 100% of the fair market value of such stock at the time of grant of the option. The terms of option agreements are established by the Board of Directors, except in the case of incentive stock options, the term of which may not exceed ten years, or five years for certain principal stockholders. The vesting schedule is subject to the discretion of the Board of Directors.

Restricted stock awards granted under the Equity Incentive Plan entitle recipients to purchase shares of the Company's Common Stock subject to restrictions concerning the sale, transfer and other disposition of the shares issued until such shares are vested. The Board of Directors determines the purchase price, which may be less than the fair market value of the Common Stock, and the vesting schedule for such awards.

The Board of Directors has delegated its powers under the Equity Incentive Plan to the Compensation Committee of the Board of Directors. At January 2, 2004, a total of 1,900,000 shares, in the aggregate, of Class A Common Stock and Class B Common Stock have been reserved by the Company and may be issued under the Plan. The Equity Incentive Plan expires on April 7, 2003, at which time no further options or stock awards may be granted.

The following table summarizes the awards available for grant under the Company's 1993 Equity Incentive Plan for the three-year reporting period ended January 2, 2004:

	Shares
Shares available at January 5, 2001	870,913
Awards granted	(284,801)
Options expired or cancelled	72,465
Shares available at January 4, 2002	658,577
Awards granted	(160,000)
Options expired or cancelled	128,621
Share available at January 3, 2003	627,198
Awards granted	(157,750)
Options expired or cancelled	39,112
Shares available at January 2, 2004	508,560

The Equity Incentive Plan expired on April 7, 2003 and no further new awards may be made under the plan. However, awards outstanding under the plan remain outstanding in accordance with their terms.

2003 Equity Plan

On May 21, 2003 the Company's stockholders approved the 2003 Stock Incentive Plan (Stock Incentive Plan), which had been adopted by the Board of Directors on February 20, 2003. Under the Stock Incentive Plan Company may grant incentive stock options and restricted stock awards to officers, key employees and Directors of the Company. Outside consultants and advisors to the Company are eligible to receive non-statutory stock options and awards of restricted stock.

The Stock Incentive Plan is adminsitered by the Board of Directors, which, at its sole discretion, grants options to purchase shares of Common Stock and makes awards of restricted stock. The purchase price per share of Common Stock shall be determined by the Board of Directors, provided, however, that in the case of incentive stock options, the purchase price may not be less than 100% of the fair market value of such stock at the time of grant of the option. The terms of option agreements are established by the Board of Directors, except in the case of incentive stock options, the term of which may not exceed ten years, or five years for certain principal stockholders: The vesting schedule is subject to the discretion of the Board of Directors.

Restricted stock awards granted under the Stock Incentive Plan entitle recipients to purchase shares of the Company's Common Stock subject to restrictions concerning the sale, transfer and other disposition of the shares issued until such shares are vested. The Board of Directors determines the purchase price, which may be less than the fair market value of the Common Stock, and the vesting schedule for such awards.

The Board of Directors has delegated its powers under the Equity Incentive Plan to the Compensation Committee of the Board of Directors. At January 2, 2004, a total of 1,750,000 shares, in the aggregate, of Class A Common Stock and Class B Common Stock have been reserved by the Company and may be issued under the Plan. No award may be made under the Stock Incentive Plan after February 19, 2013.

The following table summarizes the awards available for grant under the Company's 2003 Equity Incentive Plan for the period ended January 2, 2004:

	Shares
Shares reserved	1,750,000
Awards granted	(602,785)
Options expired or cancelled	—
Shares available at January 2, 2004	1,147,215

The following table summarizes the Company's stock option activity for the periods ended January 4, 2002, January 3, 2003 and January 2, 2004:

	Shares	Weighted Average Exercise Price	Option Price Range
Outstanding at January 5, 2001	638,677	$ 9.59	$4.00–$19.88
Granted	284,801	$ 6.64	$4.50–$10.50
Exercised	(17,930)	$ 4.67	$4.00–$ 5.13
Forfeited	(65,465)	$ 7.63	$4.13–$14.63
Expired	(7,000)	$ 4.19	$4.00–$ 4.44
Outstanding at January 4, 2002	833,083	$ 8.89	$4.00–$19.88
Granted	160,000	$ 6.67	$5.90–$ 9.30
Exercised	(57,650)	$ 4.78	$4.00–$ 7.06
Forfeited	(96,771)	$ 9.45	$4.00–$14.69
Expired	(35,850)	$ 4.84	$4.44–$ 5.36
Outstanding at January 3, 2003	802,812	$ 8.85	$4.00–$19.88
Granted	760,535	$14.67	$5.50–$17.88
Exercised	(79,268)	$ 6.52	$4.13–$12.50
Forfeited	(37,212)	$11.39	$4.13–$19.88
Expired	(1,900)	$ 4.71	$4.44–$ 6.50
Outstanding at January 2, 2004	1,444,967	$11.98	$4.00–$17.88

Options exercisable for shares of the Company's Class A and Class B Common Stock as of January 4, 2002, January 3, 2003 and January 2, 2004 are as follows:

	Options Exercisable			Weighted Average Exercise Price	
	Class A Common Stock	Class B Common Stock	Total	Class A Common Stock	Class B Common Stock
January 4, 2002	—	396,209	396,209	—	$8.81
January 3, 2003	—	435,736	435,736	—	$9.30
January 2, 2004	—	513,123	513,123	—	$9.60

The following table summarizes information about stock options outstanding at January 2, 2004:

	Options Outstanding			Options Exercisable	
Range of Exercise Prices	Shares Outstanding at Jan. 2, 2004	Weighted Average Remaining Contractual Life (Years)	Weighted Average Exercise Price	Shares Exercisable at Jan. 2, 2004	Weighted Average Exercise Price
$ 4.00–$ 4.75	850	1.48	$ 4.44	850	$ 4.44
$ 5.13–$ 5.90	128,940	3.48	$ 5.51	83,460	$ 5.41
$ 6.00–$ 6.95	129,200	6.99	$ 6.30	71,933	$ 6.27
$ 7.01–$ 7.77	150,034	6.85	$ 7.15	100,283	$ 7.13
$ 8.06–$ 8.59	4,100	7.59	$ 8.31	1,050	$ 8.31
$ 9.30–$ 9.88	7,550	8.72	$ 9.39	1,300	$ 9.34
$10.00–$10.55	145,139	7.77	$10.26	300	$10.19
$11.25–$11.80	181,150	6.33	$11.38	139,900	$11.38
$12.13–$12.50	38,191	1.10	$12.13	22,881	$12.31
$13.34–$13.89	37,278	4.12	$13.52	14,566	$13.34
$14.00–$14.68	35,750	3.51	$14.60	24,600	$14.68
$16.16–$16.60	559,009	9.16	$16.24	40,000	$16.16
$17.13–$17.88	27,776	2.73	$17.47	12,000	$17.13
	1,444,967			513,123	

ATT-SEC 3.88

On March 12, 2001, the Company issued common stock purchase warrants to purchase, in the aggregate, 50,250 shares of the Company's Class B Common Stock at a per share price of $7.00 to five footwear suppliers. The stock purchase warrants vest in five equal annual installments, commencing on March 12, 2002 and expire on March 12, 2006. The stock purchase warrant grant was approved by the Company's Board of Directors on February 27, 2001. The warrants were issued for no cash consideration; but rather as an incentive to the recipients of the warrants to satisfy specific performance criteria which support the Company's financial and operating goals. On December 31, 2003, the Board of Directors amended the terms of the stock purchase warrants to provide that the warrants vesied in full as of December 31, 2003. The right to exercise the warrants is subject to the satisfaction of specific performance criteria by each of the recipients. See Note 13 for further discussion of the stock warrant fair value and annual stock-based compensation expense.

13. Accounting for Stock-Based Compensation

The Company has elected to continue to measure stock-based compensation expense using the intrinsic value method prescribed by Accouting Principles Board Opinion No. 25, "Accounting for Stock Issued to Employees", "APB 25." Accordingly, compensation cost for stock options and restricted stock awards is measured as the excess, if any, of the quoted market price of the Company's stock at the date of the grant over the exercise price an employee must pay to acquire the stock.

The Company recognizes stock-based compensation arising from the issuance of restricted stock warrants and below market options over the vesting period of the stock grant or option term. Stock-based compensation emounted to $0, $1 and $7 for 2003, 2002 and 2001, respectively.

The Company issued common stock purchase warrants to purchase, in the aggregate, 50,250 shares of the Company's Class B Common Stock at a per share price of $7.00 to five footwear suppliers. Fair value at date of grant for the warrants was $3.93 per share issuable upon exercise of each warrant. Amortization of stock-based compensation resulting from the stock purchase warrants amounted to $37, $42 and $31 for 2003, 2002 and 2001, respectively, and is recorded as a component of cost of goods sold. In addition, the Company recorded stock-based compensation expense of $566 and $44, respectively, in 2003 and 2002, to record additional stock-based compensation expense to reflect changes in the market value of our Class B Common Stock and is recorded as a component of cost of goods sold. The 2003 stock-based compensation expense includes $416 of stock-based compensation expense recorded as a result of accelerating the vesting on the common stock purchase warrants.

The weighted average fair value at date of grant for options granted in 2003, 2002 and 2001 was $7.53, $3.18 and $3.57 per share issuable upon exercise of each option, respectively. The weighted-average fair value of these options at the date of grant was estimated using the Black-Scholes option-pricing model with the following weighted-average assumptions for 2003, 2002 and 2001, respectively:

	2003	2002	2001
Weighted-average expected life (years)	5.0	3.3	3.5
Risk free interest rate	3.0%	3.7%	5.0%
Expected volatility	62.8%	67.3%	71.9%
Expected dividend yield	1.0%	0.0%	0.0%

3.89

THE SERVICEMASTER COMPANY (DEC)

NOTES TO CONSOLIDATED FINANCIAL STATEMENTS

Significant Accounting Policies (In Part)

Stock-Based Compensation

Beginning in 2003, the Company is accounting for employee stock options as compensation expense in accordance with SFAS 123, "Accounting for Stock-Based Compensation." SFAS 148, "Accounting for Stock-Based Compensation—Transition and Disclosure, an amendment of FASB Statement No. 123", provides alternative methods of transitioning to the fair-value based method of accounting for employee stock options as compensation expense. The Company is using the "prospective method" of SFAS 148 and is expensing the fair value of new employee option grants awarded subsequent to 2002.

Prior to 2003, the Company had accounted for employee share options under the intrinsic method of Accounting Principles Board Opinion 25, as permitted under GAAP. Had compensation expense for employee options been determined under the fair-value based method of SFAS 123 for all periods, proforma reported net income and net earnings per share would reflect the following:

(In thousands, except per share data)	2003	2002	2001
Net income (loss) as reported	$(224,687)	$156,994	$ 16,384
Add back: Stock-based compensation expense included in reported net income, net of related tax effects	609	—	—
Deduct: Stock-based compensation expense determined under fair value method, net of related tax effects	(6,179)	(7,576)	(7,613)
Proforma net income (loss)	$(230,257)	$149,418	$108,771
Basic earnings per share:			
As reported	$ (0.76)	$ 0.52	$ 0.39
Proforma	(0.78)	0.50	0.36
Diluted earnings per share:			
As reported	$ (0.76)	$ 0.51	$ 0.39
Proforma	(0.78)	0.49	0.36

Shareholders' Equity (In Part)

As of December 31, 2003, there were 44.9 million Company shares available for issuance upon the exercise of employee stock options outstanding and future grants. Stock options are issued at a price not less than the fair market value on the grant date and expire within ten years of the grant date. Certain options may permit the holder to pay the option exercise price by tendering Company shares that have been owned by the holder without restriction for an extended period. Share grants and restricted stock awards carry a vesting period and are restricted stock as to the sale or transfer of the shares. Shares of restricted stock are non-transferable and subject to forfeiture if the holder does not remain continuously employed by the Company during the vesting period, or if the restricted stock is subject to performance measures, if those performance measures are not attained. A holder of a restricted stock award has rights as a shareholder of the Company and the Company includes the vested and unvested portions of the restricted stock awards in shares outstanding in the denominator of its earnings per share calculations.

Beginning in 2003, the Company is accounting for employee stock options as compensation expense in accordance with SFAS 123, "Accounting for Stock-Based Compensation." SFAS 148, "Accounting for Stock-Based Compensation—Transition and Disclosure, an amendment of FASB Statment No. 123," provides alternative methods of transitioning to the fair-value based method of accounting for employee stock options as compensation expense. The Company is using the "prospective method" permitted under SFAS 148 and is expensing the fair value of new employee option grants awarded subsequent to 2002.

Prior to 2003, the Company accounted for employee share options under the intrinsic method of Accounting Principles Board Opinion 25, as permitted under GAAP. Accordingly, no compensation cost had been recognized in the accompanying financial statements in 2002 and 2001 related to these options. See the "Stock-Based Compensation" note in the "Significant Accounting Policies" section for the proforma net income and earnings per share under the fair-value based method of SFAS 123. In computing this proforma impact, the fair value of each option is estimated on the date of grant based on the Black-Scholes option pricing model with the following weighted-average assumptions in 2003, 2002 and 2001: risk-free interest rates of 3.6 percent, 4.5 percent and 4.8 percent, respectively; dividend yields of 4.2 percent 3.2 percent and 3.7 percent, respectively; and average expected lives of six to seven years. The options granted to employees in 2003, 2002 and 2001 have weighted-average fair values of $2.14, $3.51 and $2.41, respectively and vest ratably over five years. The Company has estimated the value of these options assuming a single weighted-average expected life for the entire award.

ATT-SEC 3.89

Options and grant transactions during the last three years are summarized below:

	Stock Options	Price Range[1]	Weighted Avg. Exercise Price	Share Grants/ Restricted Stock	Price Range
Total exercisable, December 31, 2000	12,208,351	$2.25–87.55	$12.37	—	—
Total outstanding, December 31, 2000	26,515,329	$2.25–87.55	$12.84	482,356	$ 2.86–7.96
Transactions during 2001					
Granted to employees	5,184,141	$9.10–12.52	$10.63	—	—
Exercised or vested	(864,418)	$2.25–11.41	$ 6.52	(171,518)	$ 2.86–7.96
Terminated or resigned	(1,503,167)	$2.25–87.55	$17.27	(210,319)	$ 2.86–7.96
Total exercisable, December 31, 2001	15,237,607	$2.25–77.56	$12.36	—	—
Total outstanding, December 31, 2001	29,331,885	$2.25–77.56	$12.40	100,519	$ 2.86–7.96
Transactions during 2002					
Granted to employees	4,939,141	$9.09–15.10	$13.08	179,000	$10.51–13.80
Exercised or vested	(1,586,248)	$2.25–14.55	$ 7.60	(46,632)	$ 2.86–7.96
Terminated or resigned	(871,439)	$5.14–73.53	$16.37	—	—
Total exercisable, December 31, 2002	18,089,830	$2.25–77.56	$13.05	—	—
Total outstanding, December 31, 2002	31,813,339	$2.25–77.56	$12.64	232,887	$ 2.86–13.80
Transactions during 2003					
Granted to employees	2,432,674	$8.40–11.21	$ 9.91	364,419	$ 9.50–11.97
Exercised or vested	(1,296,101)	$6.44–11.50	$ 7.70	(56,092)	$ 2.86–13.80
Terminated or resigned	(1,240,146)	$2.25–37.40	$13.49	(3,514)	$ 9.95
Total exercisable, December 31, 2003	20,346,581	$6.44–77.56	$13.16	—	—
Total outstanding, December 31, 2003	31,709,766	$6.44–77.56	$12.60	537,700	$ 3.03–13.80

[1] The options priced at $73.53 to $87.55 are options assumed by the Company as a result of business acquisitions.

Options outstanding at December 31, 2003:

Range of Exercise Prices	Number Outstanding at 12/31/03	Weighted Average Remaining Life	Weighted Average Exercise Price	Number Exercisable at 12/31/03	Weighted Average Exercise Price
$6.44–10.78	13,366,166	4.0 years	$ 9.63	7,407,729	$ 9.38
$10.80–15.94	12,072,574	5.0 years	$12.26	7,279,233	$11.88
$16.12–22.33	5,919,582	5.0 years	$18.18	5,308,175	$18.19
$27.20–77.56	351,444	3.0 years	$43.09	351,444	$43.09
$6.44–77.56	31,709,766	5.0 years	$12.60	20,346,581	$13.16

3.90

SMITHFIELD FOODS, INC. (APR)

NOTES TO CONSOLIDATED FINANCIAL STATEMENTS
(Dollars in millions, except per share data)

Note 6 (In Part): Shareholders' Equity

Stock Options
The Company's 1992 Stock Option Plan and its 1998 Stock Incentive Plan (collectively, the incentive plans) provide for the issuance of nonstatutory stock options to management and other key employees. Options were granted for periods not exceeding 10 years and exercisable five years after the date of grant at an exercise price of not less than 100% of the fair market value of the common stock on the date of grant. There are 11,000,000 shares reserved under the incentive plans. As of April 27, 2003, there were 3,473,000 shares available for grant under the incentive plans.

The following is a summary of stock option transactions for fiscal years 2001 through 2003:

	Number of Shares	Weighted Average Exercise Price
Outstanding at April 30, 2000	3,701,000	$ 8.34
Granted	1,480,000	13.22
Exercised	(849,000)	5.89
Canceled	(130,000)	11.42
Outstanding at April 29, 2001	4,202,000	10.46
Granted	1,845,000	18.99
Exercised	(341,000)	6.66
Canceled	(20,000)	13.22
Outstanding at April 28, 2002	5,686,000	13.45
Granted	140,000	21.00
Exercised	(112,600)	5.85
Canceled	(80,000)	13.22
Outstanding at April 27, 2003	5,633,400	$13.79

The following table summarizes information about stock options outstanding as of April 27, 2003:

Range of Exercise Price	Shares	Weighted Average Remaining Contractual Life (Years)	Weighted Average Exercise Price	Options Exercisable	
				Shares	Weighted Average Exercise Price
$ 5.76 to $ 7.65	1,148,400	1.0	$ 6.03	1,148,400	$ 6.03
8.23 to 9.39	210,000	4.5	8.57	140,000	8.23
13.12 to 14.59	2,230,000	6.2	13.46	340,000	13.21
15.81 to 16.34	60,000	4.8	16.03	60,000	16.03
18.20 to 21.84	1,985,000	8.2	19.13	—	—
$ 5.76 to $21.84	5,633,400	5.8	$13.79	1,688,400	$ 8.01

On April 29, 2002, the Company adopted the fair value method defined in SFAS No. 123, "Accounting for Stock-Based Compensation" (SFAS 123), which is in compliance with the provisions of SFAS No. 148, "Accounting for Stock-Based Compensation—Transition and Disclosure, an amendment to SFAS No. 123," issued December 2002, to account for the Company's stock option plans. The Company records compensation expense for stock options granted subsequent to April 28, 2002 based on the fair value as determined using the Black-Scholes option pricing model and weighted average assumptions. The impact of recording compensation expense for stock options granted was $0.2, or less than one cent per diluted share in fiscal 2003. The weighted average fair values of the option shares granted in fiscal 2003 was $7.76 per share. The expected option life, risk-free interest rate and the expected annual volatility and dividend yield used to calculate the value of the option shares granted in fiscal 2003 was 8.0 years, 4.3%, 35.0% and 0.0%, respectively.

Stock options granted prior to April 29, 2002 continue to be accounted for under Accounting Principles Board (APB) Opinion No. 25, "Accounting for Stock Issued to Employees" (APB 25). Under APB 25, no compensation expense is recorded. Had the Company used the fair value method to determine compensation expense for its stock options granted prior to April 29, 2002, net income and net income per basic and diluted share would have been as follows:

	2003	2002	2001
Net income, as reported	$26.3	$196.9	$223.5
Pro forma net income	22.6	193.9	221.7
Net income per share, as reported:			
Basic	$ .24	$ 1.82	$ 2.06
Diluted	.24	1.78	2.03
Pro forma net income per share:			
Basic	$ .21	$ 1.79	$ 2.05
Diluted	.21	1.76	2.01
Weighted average fair values of option shares granted		$ 9.00	$ 6.64
Expected option life		7.0 years	7.0 years
Risk-free interest rate		5.1%	6.3%
Expected annual volatility		35.0%	35.0%
Dividend yield		0.0%	0.0%

Savings/Investment Plans

3.91

DIEBOLD, INCORPORATED (DEC)

NOTES TO CONSOLIDATED FINANCIAL STATEMENTS (Dollars in thousands)

Note 12 (In Part): Benefit Plans

Retirement Savings Plan

The company offers an employee 401(k) Savings Plan (Savings Plan) to encourage eligible employees to save on a regular basis by payroll deductions, and to provide them with an opportunity to become shareholders of the company. Effective July 1, 2003, a new enhanced benefit to the Savings Plan became effective. All new salaried employees hired on or after July 1, 2003 are provided with an employer basic matching contribution in the amount of 100 percent of the first three percent of eligible pay and 50 percent of the next three percent of eligible pay. This new enhanced benefit is in lieu of participation in the pension plan for salaried employees. For employees hired prior to July 1, 2003, the company matched 60 percent of participating employees' first 3 percent of contributions and 30 percent of participating employees' second 3 percent of contributions. Total company match was $7,129, $6,813 and $6,100 in 2003, 2002 and 2001, respectively.

3.92

FMC CORPORATION (DEC)

NOTES TO CONSOLIDATED FINANCIAL STATEMENTS

Note 12 (In Part): Pensions and Other Postretirement Benefits

FMC Corporation Savings and Investment Plan

The FMC Corporation Savings and Investment Plan is a qualified salary-reduction plan under Section 401(k) of the Internal Revenue Code in which substantially all of our U.S. employees may participate by contributing a portion of their compensation. We match contributions up to specified percentages of each employee's compensation depending on how the employee allocates his or her contributions. Charges against income for the matching contributions, not of forfeitures were $6.2 million in 2003, $6.5 million in 2002, and $7.3 million in 2001.

3.93

HARMAN INTERNATIONAL INDUSTRIES, INCORPORATED (JUN)

NOTES TO CONSOLIDATED FINANCIAL STATEMENTS

12 (In Part): Postretirement Benefits

Under the Retirement Savings Plan, domestic employees may contribute up to 50.0% of their pretax compensation. Each division will make a safe harbor non-elective contribution in an amount equal to 3.0% of a participant's eligible contribution. With the approval of the Board of Directors, each division may make a matching contribution of up to 3.0% (50.0% on the first 6.0% of an employee's tax-deferred-contribution); and a profit sharing contribution. Profit sharing and matching contributions vest at a rate of 25.0% for each year of service with the employer, beginning with the second year of service. Expenses related to the Retirement Savings Plan for the years ended June 30, 2003, 2002 and 2001 totaled $12.7 million, $8.5 million and $6.7 million respectively.

Stock Award Plans

3.94

BECTON, DICKINSON AND COMPANY (SEP)

NOTES TO CONSOLIDATED FINANCIAL STATEMENTS

14 (In Part): Stock Plans

Other Stock Plans

The Company has a compensatory Stock Award Plan which allows for grants of common shares to certain key employees. Distribution of 25% or more of each award, as elected by the grantee, is deferred until after retirement or involuntary termination. Commencing on the first anniversary of a grant following retirement, the remainder is distributable in five equal annual installments. During 2003, 60,684 shares were distributed. No awards were granted in 2003, 2002, or 2001. At September 30, 2003, 2,260,389 shares were reserved for future issuance, of which awards for 159,001 shares have been granted.

The Company has a compensatory Restricted Stock Plan for Non-Employee Directors which reserves for issuance 300,000 shares of the Company's common stock. No restricted shares were issued in 2003, 2002, or 2001.

The Company has a Directors' Deferral Plan which provides a means to defer director compensation, from time to time, on a deferred stock or cash basis. As of September 30, 2003, 149,996 shares were held in trust, of which 9,049 shares represented Directors' compensation in 2003, in accordance with the provisions of the Plan. Under the Plan, which is unfunded, directors have an unsecured contractual commitment from the Company to pay directors the amounts due to them under the Plan.

The Company also has a Deferred Compensation Plan that allows certain highly-compensated employees, including executive officers, to defer salary and annual incentive awards. As of September 30, 2003, 165,100 shares were issuable under this plan.

3.95

BOISE CASCADE CORPORATION (DEC)

NOTES TO CONSOLIDATED FINANCIAL STATEMENTS

14 (In Part): Shareholders' Equity

2003 Director Stock Compensation Plan and Boise Incentive and Performance Plan

In February 2003, our board adopted the 2003 Director Stock Compensation Plan (the 2003 DSCP) and the 2003 Boise Incentive and Performance Plan (the 2003 Plan), which were approved by our shareholders in April 2003. The 2003 DSCP replaces our previous Director Stock Compensation Plan, which was approved by shareholders in 1992 and expired on January 1, 2003. A total of 75,000 shares of common stock are reserved for issuance under the 2003 DSCP. The provisions of the 2003 DSCP are substantially similar to the previous plan. The 2003 DSCP permits nonemployee directors to elect to receive grants of options to purchase shares of our common stock in lieu of cash compensation. The difference between the $2.50-per-share exercise price of 2003 DSCP options and the market value of the common stock subject to the options is intended to offset the cash compensation that participating directors elect not to receive. Options expire three years after the holder ceases to be a director.

The 2003 Plan was effective January 1, 2003, and replaces the Key Executive Performance Plan for Executive Officers, Key Executive Performance Plan for Key Executives/Key Managers, 1984 Key Executive Stock Option Plan (KESOP), Key Executive Performance Unit Plan (KEPUP), and Director Stock Option Plan (DSOP), which are discussed below. No further grants or awards will be made under the Key

Executive Performance Plans, KESOP, KEPUP, or DSOP after 2003. A total of 5,950,169 shares of common stock are reserved for issuance under the 2003 Plan. Our executive officers, key employees, and nonemployee directors are eligible to receive awards under the 2003 Plan at the discretion of the Executive Compensation Committee of the Board of Directors. Eight types of awards may be granted under the 2003 Plan, including (1) stock options, (2) stock appreciation rights, (3) restricted stock, (4) restricted stock units, (5) performance units, (6) performance shares, (7) annual incentive awards, and (8) stock bonus awards.

Restricted Stock and Restricted Stock Units

In 2003, we granted to employees 1.2 million shares of restricted stock and 0.1 million restricted stock units (collectively "restricted stock"). The weighted-average grant-date fair value of the restricted stock was $25.09. The restricted stock vests at the end of July 2006, provided, however, that if specific performance criteria are met, some or all of the restricted stock may vest earlier than July 2006, but generally no earlier than the end of January 2005. Based on a rise in Boise's stock price, 75% of the award may vest in January 2005, subject to other performance criteria, as applicable. Vesting of the remaining 25% of the award can accelerate if additional stock price targets are achieved in the future.

The restricted stock is issued and outstanding. However, because the stock is restricted, in accordance with the requirements of SFAS No. 123, no entries were made in our financial statements upon issuance of the award. We recognize compensation expense over the vesting period based on closing stock prices on the dates of grant. In 2003, we recognized $6.5 million of pretax compensation expense related to the restricted stock awards. As we recognize compensation expense, "Additional paid-in-capital" is increased in shareholders' equity. The restricted shares are not included as shares outstanding in the calculation of basic earnings per share but are included in the number of shares used to calculate diluted earnings per share. The restricted stock receives the same dividend as our common shares outstanding.

However, dividends on the restricted stock are not paid until the restrictions lapse and are recorded as dividends payable.

3.96

LOUISIANA-PACIFIC CORPORATION (DEC)

NOTES TO THE FINANCIAL STATEMENTS

10 (In Part): Stockholders' Equity

Performance-Contingent Stock Awards

LP has granted performance-contingent stock awards to senior executives as allowed under the current stock award plan. The awards entitle the participant to receive a number of shares of LP common stock determined by comparing LP's cumulative total stockholder return to the mean total stockholder return of five other forest products companies for the four-year period beginning in the year of the award. Awards were initially granted at a target share level. No awards have been granted since 2000. Depending on LP's four-year total stockholder return, the actual number of shares issued at the end of the four-year period could range from zero to 200 percent of this target. LP did not record any compensation expense related to these awards in 2002 or before based on the cumulative stockholders return for the applicable periods however due to the disability of one of the participants, LP was required to issue 23,102 shares in 2002 and recorded $0.2 million in expense. During 2003, due to LP's stockholder return compared to the mean total stockholder return of four other forest products, LP recorded compensation expense of $1.6 million. Subsequent to year-end, the Compensation Committee of the Board of Directors approved the stock award at the 200% level. LP issued fifty percent of these shares on an unrestricted basis in early 2004 with the remaining award being issued as restricted stock with a vesting period of two years.

Changes in performance-contingent stock awards were as follows:

	Number of Shares		
	2003	2002	2001
Target shares—awards outstanding at January 1	57,988	144,848	201,876
Target shares—awards granted	—	—	—
Target shares—awards issued	—	(23,012)	—
Target shares—awards cancelled or forfeited	(7,402)	(65,954)	(57,028)
Target shares—adjustment for dividends	7,744	2,106	—
Target shares—adjustment for performance	50,586	—	—
Target shares—awards outstanding at December 31	108,916	57,988	144,848

Stock Purchase Plans

3.97

RADIOSHACK CORPORATION (DEC)

NOTES TO CONSOLIDATED FINANCIAL STATEMENTS

Note 21. Company Stock Purchase Plan

Eligible employees may contribute 1% to 7% of their annual compensation to purchase our common stock at the monthly average daily closing price. We match 40%, 60% or 80% of the employee's contribution, depending on the employee's length of continuous participation in the Stock Purchase Plan. This match is also in the form of our common stock. Company contributions to the Stock Plan amounted to $15.4 million, $15.1 million and $15.4 million for the years ended December 31,2003, 2002 and 2001, respectively.

3.98

THE STANLEY WORKS (DEC)

NOTES TO CONSOLIDATED FINANCIAL STATEMENTS

A (In Part): Significant Accounting Policies

Stock-Based Compensation (In Part)

Employee Stock Purchase Plan compensation cost is recognized in the fourth quarter when the purchase price for the following fiscal year is established. The fair value of the employees' purchase rights under the Employee Stock Purchase Plan was estimated using the following assumptions for 2003, 2002 and 2001, respectively: dividend yield of 3.9%, 3.3% and 3.0% expected volatility of 25%, 30%, and 40%, risk-free interest rates of 1.2%, 1.9% and 2.0%; and expected lives of one year. The weighted average fair value of those purchase rights granted in 2003, 2002 and 2001 was $6.35, $7.50 and $8.48, respectively.

K (In Part): Capital Stock

Employee Stock Purchase Plan

The Employee Stock Purchase Plan enables substantially all employees in the United States, Canada and Belgium to subscribe at any time to purchase shares of common stock on a monthly basis at the lower of 85% of the fair market value of the shares on the first day of the plan year ($25.41 per share for fiscal year 2003 purchases) or 85% of the fair market value of the shares on the last business day of each month. A maximum of 6,000,000 shares are authorized for subscription. During 2003, 2002 and 2001 shares totaling 49,743, 119,853, and 273,784, respectively, were issued under the plan at average prices of $23.41, $31.42 and $17.32 per share, respectively.

Deferred Compensation Plans

3.99

LABARGE, INC. (JUN)

NOTES TO CONSOLIDATED FINANCIAL STATEMENTS

1 (In Part): Summary of Significant Accounting Policies

Employee Benefit Plans (In Part)

The Company offers a non-qualified deferred compensation program to certain key employees whereby they may defer a portion of annual compensation for payment upon retirement plus a guaranteed return. The program is unfunded; however, the Company purchases Company-owned life insurance contracts throught which the Company will recover a portion of its cost upon the death of the employee.

11 (In Part): Employee Benefit Plans

The Company has a deferred compensation plan for selected employees who, due to Internal Revenue Service guidelines, cannot take full advantage of the contributory savings plan. This plan, which is not required to be funded, allows eligible employees to defer portions of their current compensation and the Company guarantees an interest rate of between prime and prime plus 2%. To support the deferred compensation plan, the Company has elected to purchase Company-owned file insurance. The increase in the cash value of the life insurance policies exceeded the premiums paid by $115,000, $92,000 and $123,000 in fiscal years 2003, 2002 and 2001, respectively. The cash surrender value of the Company-owned life insurance related to deferred compensation is included in other assets along with other policies owned by the Company, and was $1.2 million, at June 29, 2003, compared with $1.3 million at June 30, 2002. The liability for the deferred compensation and interest thereon is in accured employee compensation and was $2.4 million at June 29, 2003 versus $2.1 million at June 30, 2002.

Employee Stock Ownership Plans

3.100

ANHEUSER-BUSCH COMPANIES, INC. (DEC)

NOTES TO CONSOLIDATED FINANCIAL STATEMENTS

6. Employee Stock Ownership Plans

In 1989, the company added Employee Stock Ownership Plans (ESOPs) to its existing Deferred Income Stock Purchase and Savings Plans (401(k) plans). Most regular employees are eligible for participation in the ESOPs. The ESOPs initially borrowed $500 million for a 15-year term at an interest rate of 8.25% and used the proceeds to buy approximately 45.4 million shares of common stock from the company at a then market price of $11.03 per share. ESOP shares are being allocated to participants over the 15-year period as contributions are made to the plans. The ESOPs purchased an additional 400,000 shares from the company using proceeds from the sale of spin-off-related Earthgrains shares in 1996. Of this 45.8 million total shares purchased, 44.9 million shares have been allocated to plan participants through December 31, 2003.

ESOP cash contributions and expense recorded during the year are determined by several factors, including the market price of Anheuser-Busch common stock, number of shares allocated to participants, debt service requirements, dividends on unallocated shares and the company's matching contribution. Over the 15-year life of the ESOPs, total expense recognized will equal total cash contributions made by the company for ESOP debt service. The company guarantees the ESOP debt. The guarantee expires when the ESOPs expire in March 2004. The company anticipates benefits expense in 2004 will increase by approximately $30 million compared to 2003, due to the expiration of the ESOPs.

ESOP expense is allocated to operating and interest expense based on the ratio of principal and interest payments on the underlying ESOP debt. Total ESOP expense for the three years ended December 31 is presented below (in millions):

	2003	2002	2001
Operating expense	$15.1	$13.3	$5.2
Interest expense	1.9	2.7	1.0
Total ESOP expense	$17.0	$16.0	$6.2

Cash contributions are made to the ESOPs in March and September to correspond with debt service requirements. A summary of cash contributions and dividends on unallocated ESOP shares for the three years ended December 31 is presented below (in millions):

	2003	2002	2001
Cash contributions	$10.2	$6.1	$1.3
Dividends	1.7	3.7	5.2

Profit Sharing Plans

3.101

KLA-TENCOR CORPORATION (JUN)

NOTES TO CONSOLIDATED FINANCIAL STATEMENTS

Note 7 (In Part): Employee Benefit Plans

KLA-Tencor has a profit sharing program for eligible employees, which distributes on a quarterly basis, a percentage of pretax profits. In addition, KLA-Tencor has an employee savings plan that qualifies as a deferred salary arrangement under Section 401(k) of the Internal Revenue Code. Starting fiscal year 2000, KLA-Tencor has matched up to a maximum of $1,000 or 50% of the first $2,000 of an eligible employee's contribution, with $500 of the amount funded from the profit sharing program. The total charge to operations under the profit sharing and 401(k) programs aggregated $10 million, $3 million and $57 million in fiscal years 2003, 2002 and 2001, respectively. KLA-Tencor has no defined benefit plans in the United States. In addition to the profit sharing plan and the

U.S. employee saving plan, several of KLA-Tencor's foreign subsidiaries have retirement plans for their full time employees, several of which are defined benefit plans.

Incentive Compensation Plans

3.102

NEXTEL COMMUNICATIONS, INC. (DEC)

NOTES TO CONSOLIDATED FINANCIAL STATEMENTS

12 (In Part): Stock and Employee Benefit Plans

Long-Term Incentive Plan

In 2002, we adopted a long-term incentive plan designed to reward key members of our management for achieving specific performance goals over a two-year period commencing January 1, 2002. This plan offers management the opportunity to receive a cash-based payment, or a combination of cash and stock-based payments at the discretion of the compensation committee of the board of directors. We recorded compensation expense related to the long-term incentive plan of $26 million in 2003 and $22 million in 2002. In 2003, we adopted a similar long-term incentive plan designed to reward key members of our management for achieving specific performance goals over a two-year period commencing January 1, 2004.

Phantom Share Agreement

3.103

PPG INDUSTRIES, INC. (DEC)

NOTES TO CONSOLIDATED FINANCIAL STATEMENTS

12 (In Part): Pensions and Other Postretirement Benefits

The Company has a deferred compensation plan for certain key managers which allows them to defer a portion of their compensation in a phantom PPG stock account or other phantom investment accounts. The amount deferred earns a return based on the investment options selected by the participant. The amount owed to participants is an unfunded and unsecured general obligation of the Company. Upon retirement, death, disability or termination of employment, the compensation deferred and related accumulated earnings are distributed in cash or in PPG stock, based on the accounts selected by the participant.

The plan provides participants with investment alternatives and the ability to transfer amounts between the phantom non-PPG stock investment accounts. To mitigate the impact on compensation expense of changes in the market value of the liability, the Company purchased a portfolio of marketable securities that mirror the phantom non-PPG stock investment accounts selected by the participants except the money market accounts. The changes in market value of these securities are also included in earnings. Trading will occur in this portfolio to align the securities held with the participant's phantom non-PPG stock investment accounts except the money market accounts.

The cost of the deferred compensation plan, comprised of dividend equivalents accrued on the phantom PPG stock account, investment income and the change in market value of the liability, was a loss in 2003 of $13 million, and income of $9 million and $6 million in 2002 and 2001, respectively. These amounts are included in "Selling, general and administrative" in the accompanying statement of income. The change in market value of the investment portfolio in 2003 was income of $13 million, and a loss of $10 million and $7 million in 2002 and 2001, respectively, and is also included in "Selling, general and administrative."

The Company's obligations under this plan, which are included in "Other liabilities" in the accompanying balance sheet, were $100 million and $84 million as of Dec. 31, 2003 and 2002, respectively, and the investments in marketable securities, which are included in "Investments" in the accompanying balance sheet, were $68 million and $53 million as of Dec. 31, 2003 and 2002, respectively.

DEPRECIATION EXPENSE

3.104 Paragraph 5 of APB Opinion No. 12, *Omnibus Opinion—1967*, stipulates that both the amount of depreciation expense and method or methods of depreciation should be disclosed in the financial statements or in notes thereto. Paragraph 5 of Accounting Research Bulletin (ARB) No. 43, Chapter 9C, *Emergency Facilities: Depreciation, Amortization, and Income Taxes*, defines depreciation accounting (the process of allocating the cost of productive facilities over the expected useful lives of the facilities) as a "system of accounting which aims to distribute the cost or other basic value of tangible capital assets, less salvage (if any), over the estimated useful life of the unit (which may be a group of assets) in a systematic and rational manner. It is a process of allocation, not of valuation."

3.105 Table 3-13 summarizes the methods of depreciation used to allocate the cost of productive facilities. Examples of depreciation expense disclosures follow.

3.106

TABLE 3-13: DEPRECIATION METHODS

	Number of Companies			
	2003	2002	2001	2000
Straight-line............................	580	579	579	576
Declining-balance..................	22	22	22	22
Sum-of-the-years'-digits........	5	5	6	7
Accelerated method—not specified............................	41	44	49	53
Units-of-production...............	30	32	32	34
Other.....................................	4	7	9	10

Straight-Line Method

3.107

ELECTRONIC ARTS INC. (MAR)

Consolidated Statements of Cash Flows

(In thousands)	2003	2002	2001
Operating activities			
Net income (loss)	$317,097	$101,509	$(11,082)
Adjustments to reconcile net income (loss) to net cash provided by operating activities			
Minority interest in consolidated joint venture	1,303	809	1,815
Equity in net income of affiliates	(5,467)	(2,999)	(820)
Gain on sale of affiliate	—	(200)	(214)
Depreciation and amortization	91,639	110,901	78,601
Non-cash restructuring and asset impairment charges	66,329	13,399	—
Other-than-temporary impairment of investments in affiliates	10,590	—	—
Loss on sale of fixed assets, net	527	331	1,992
Loss on marketable securities	706	96	—
Bad debt expense	7,058	9,361	7,541
Stock-based compensation	906	3,099	2,707
Charge for acquired in-process technology	—	—	2,719
Tax benefit from exercise of stock options	74,620	22,541	25,750

NOTES TO CONSOLIDATED FINANCIAL STATEMENTS

1 (In Part): Summary of Significant Accounting Policies

k) Property and Equipment

Property and equipment are stated at cost. Depreciation is calculated using the accelerated and straight-line methods over the following useful lives:

Buildings	20 to 25 years
Computer equipment and software	3 to 7 years
Furniture and equipment	3 to 7 years
Leasehold improvements	Lesser of the lease terms or the estimated useful lives of the improvements, generally 1 to 8 years

Under the provisions of SOP 98-1, *"Accounting for the Costs of Computer Software Developed or Obtained for Internal Use,"* the Company capitalizes costs associated with customized internal-use software systems that have reached the application stage and meet recoverability tests. Such capitalized costs include external direct costs utilized in developing or obtaining the applications and payroll and payroll-related expenses for employees who are directly associated with the applications. Capitalization of such costs begins when the preliminary project stage is complete and ceases at the point in which the project is substantially complete and ready for its intended purpose. Capitalized costs associated with internal-use software amounted to $87.4 million and $121.0 million at March 31, 2003 and 2002, respectively, and are being depreciated on a straight-line basis over each project's estimated useful life that ranges from four to seven years.

11) Property and Equipment

Property and equipment at March 31, 2003 and 2002 consisted of (in thousands):

	2003	2002
Computer equipment and software	$ 348,413	$ 319,893
Buildings	105,342	97,939
Land	49,078	44,911
Office equipment, furniture and fixtures	32,984	31,915
Leasehold improvements	23,957	15,463
Warehouse equipment and other	9,447	5,396
	569,221	515,517
Less accumulated depreciation and amortization	(306,969)	(206,690)
	$ 262,252	$ 308,827

Depreciation and amortization expenses associated with property and equipment amounted to $66.3 million, $67.6 million and $50.3 million for the fiscal years ended March 31, 2003, 2002 and 2001, respectively.

3.108

NVR, INC. (DEC)

Consolidated Statements of Cash Flows

(Dollars in thousands)	2003	2002	2001
Cash flows from operating activities			
Net income	$ 419,791	$ 331,470	$ 236,794
Adjustments to reconcile net income to net cash provided by operating activities			
Depreciation and amortization	8,427	7,657	15,162
Loss from extinguishment of debt	8,503	—	—
Gain on sales of loans	(59,095)	(48,424)	(37,663)
Deferred tax benefit	(3,429)	(21,669)	(6,277)
Mortgage loans closed	(1,982,900)	(1,846,843)	(1,604,615)
Proceeds from sales of mortgage loans	2,096,782	1,858,086	1,603,540
Gain on sales of mortgage servicing rights	(14)	(268)	(642)

NOTES TO CONSOLIDATED FINANCIAL STATEMENTS
(Dollars in thousands)

1 (In Part): Summary of Significant Accounting Policies

Property, Plant, and Equipment

Property, plant, and equipment are carried at cost less accumulated depreciation and amortization. Depreciation is based on the estimated useful lives of the assets using the straight-line method. Amortization of capital lease assets is included in depreciation expense. Model home furniture and fixtures are generally depreciated over a two year period, office facilities and other equipment are depreciated over a period from three to ten years, manufacturing facilities are depreciated over a period of from five to forty years and property under capital leases is depreciated in a manner consistent with the Company's depreciation policy for owned assets.

5. Property, Plant and Equipment, Net

	2003	2002
Homebuilding		
Office facilities and other	$ 7,109	$ 7,310
Model home furniture and fixtures	14,542	11,360
Manufacturing facilities	16,850	16,113
Property under capital leases	7,631	7,631
	46,132	42,414
Less: accumulated depreciation	(21,601)	(20,288)
	$ 24,531	$ 22,126
Mortgage banking		
Office facilities and other	$ 2,821	$ 2,673
Less: accumulated depreciation	(1,946)	(1,732)
	$ 875	$ 941

Certain property, plant and equipment listed above is collateral for certain debt of NVR.

Accelerated Methods

3.109

TEXAS INSTRUMENTS INCORPORATED (DEC)

Consolidated Statement of Cash Flows

(Millions of dollars)	2003	2002	2001
Cash flows from operating activities			
Net income (loss)	$1,198	$ (344)	$ (201)
Depreciation	1,429	1,574	1,599
Amortization of acquisition-related costs	99	115	229
Purchased in-process research and development	23	1	—
Write-downs of equity investments	42	808	80
Gains on sale of equity investments	(213)	(7)	(91)
Deferred income taxes	75	13	19

NOTES TO FINANCIAL STATEMENTS

Accounting Policies and Practices (In Part)

Property, plant and equipment are stated at cost and depreciated primarily on the 150 percent declining-balance method over their estimated useful lives. Fully depreciated assets are written off against accumulated depreciation. Acquisition-related costs are amortized on a straight-line basis over the estimated economic life of the assets. Capitalized software licenses are amortized on a straight-line basis over the term of the license. Reviews are regularly performed to determine whether facts or circumstances exist that indicate the carrying values of the company's fixed assets, intangible assets or capitalized software licenses are impaired. The company assesses the recoverability of its assets by comparing the projected undiscounted net cash flows associated with those assets to their respective carrying amounts. Impairment, if any, is based on the excess of the carrying amount over the fair value of those assets.

Property, Plant and Equipment at Cost

(Millions of dollars)	Depreciable Lives	2003	2002
Land		$ 100	$ 93
Buildings and improvements	5–40 years	2,917	2,891
Machinery and equipment	3–10 years	6,532	6,532
Total		$9,549	$9,516

Authorizations for property, plant and equipment expenditures in future years were approximately $595 million at December 31, 2003, and $225 million at December 31, 2002.

Units-of-Production Method

3.110

CUMMINS INC. (DEC)

Consolidated Statements of Cash Flows

($ millions)	2003	2002	2001
Cash flows from operating activities			
Net earnings (loss)	$ 50	$ 82	$(103)
Adjustments to reconcile net earnings (loss) to net cash flows from operating activities			
Cumulative effect of change in accounting principles	4	(3)	—
Loss on early retirement of debt	—	8	—
Depreciation and amortization	223	219	229
Restructuring asset impairment and other charges (credits)	—	(21)	66
Equity in (earnings) losses of investees	(54)	(9)	8
Minority interests in earnings of consolidated subsidiaries	14	16	15
Distributions from equity investees	17	10	2
Noncash compensation expense	24	19	10
Amortization of gain on terminated interest rate swaps	(7)	(4)	(2)
Translation and hedging activities	(18)	2	5

NOTES TO CONSOLIDATED FINANCIAL STATEMENTS

Note 1 (In Part): Summary of Significant Accounting Policies

Property, Plant and Equipment

We record property, plant and equipment at cost. We depreciate the cost of substantially all engine production equipment using a modified units-of-production method, which is based upon units produced subject to a minimum level. We depreciate the cost of all other equipment using the straight-line method with depreciable lives ranging from 20 to 40 years for buildings and 3 to 20 years for machinery, equipment and fixtures. We expense normal maintenance and repair costs as incurred. Depreciation expense totaled $183 million, $183 million and $184 million for the years ended December 31, 2003, 2002 and 2001, respectively. Details of our property, plant and equipment balance at December 31, 2003 and 2002 were as follows:

($ millions)	2003	2002
Land and buildings	$ 597	$ 580
Machinery, equipment and fixtures	2,470	2,303
Construction in process	54	69
	3,121	2,952
Less accumulated depreciation	(1,774)	(1,647)
Property, plant and equipment, net	$ 1,347	$ 1,305

Composite Method

3.111

CITIZENS COMMUNICATIONS COMPANY (DEC)

(In thousands)	2003	2002	2001
Revenue	$2,444,938	$2,669,332	$2,456,993
Operating expenses:			
Cost of services (exclusive of depreciation and amortization)	369,689	476,920	599,378
Other operating expenses	901,751	1,002,355	951,710
Depreciation and amortization	595,276	755,522	632,336
Reserve for (recovery of) telecommunications bankruptcies	(4,377)	10,880	21,200
Restructuring and other expenses	9,687	37,186	19,327
Loss on impairment	15,300	1,074,058	—
Total operating expenses	1,887,326	3,356,921	2,223,951
Operating income (loss)	$ 557,612	$ (687,589)	$ 233,042

NOTES TO CONSOLIDATED FINANCIAL STATEMENTS

1 (In Part): Description of Business and Summary of Significant Accounting Policies

e) Construction Costs and Maintenance Expense

Property, plant and equipment are stated at original cost or fair market value for our acquired properties, including capitalized interest for unregulated telecommunications businesses. Maintenance and repairs are charged to operating expenses as incurred. The book value, net of salvage, of routine property, plant and equipment dispositions is charged against accumulated depreciation for regulated operations.

Capitalized interest for unregulated construction activities amounted to $2,993,000, $7,390,000 and $5,675,000 for 2003, 2002 and 2001, respectively.

4) Property, Plant and Equipment

The components of property, plant and equipment at December 31, 2003 and 2002 are as follows:

(In thousands)	Estimated Useful Lives	2003	2002
Land	N/A	$ 21,650	$ 21,372
Buildings and leasehold improvements	30 to 41 years	354,855	349,781
General support	3 to 17 years	411,660	463,750
Central office/electronic circuit equipment	5 to 11 years	2,421,341	2,265,117
Cable and wire	15 to 55 years	2,843,510	2,731,302
Other	5 to 20 years	53,303	91,305
Construction work in progress		114,988	217,145
		6,221,307	6,139,772
Less: accumulated depreciation		(2,695,667)	(2,449,716)
Property, plant and equipment, net		$ 3,525,640	$ 3,690,056

Depreciation expense is principally based on the composite group method. Depreciation expense was $468,438,000, $630,113,000 and $488,957,000 for the years ended December 31, 2003, 2002 and 2001, respectively. Effective January 1, 2003, as a result of the adoption of SFAS No. 143, "Accounting for Asset Retirement Obligations," we ceased recognition of the cost of removal provision in depreciation expense and eliminated the cumulative cost of removal included in accumulated depreciation. In addition, we increased the average depreciable lives for certain of our equipment in our ILEC segment. As part of the preparation

and adoption of SFAS No. 143, we analyzed depreciation rates for the ILEC segment and compared them to industry averages and historical expense data. Based on this review, the Company identified certain assets for which the Company's analysis of historical/estimated lives indicated that the existing estimated depreciable life was shorter than such revised estimates. This change in estimate reduced depreciation expense by $38,882,000 or $0.09 per share for the year ended December 31, 2003.

We ceased to record depreciation expense on the gas assets held for sale effective October 1, 2000 and on the electric assets held for sale effective January 1, 2001. During 2002 and 2001, we recognized accelerated depreciation of $23,379,000 and $22,000,000 related to the change in useful lives of our accounting and human resource systems and our Plano, Texas office building, furniture and fixtures as a result of a restructuring.

Depletion

3.112

WAUSAU•MOSINEE PAPER CORPORATION (DEC)

Consolidated Statements of Cash Flows

(Dollar amounts in thousands)	2003	2002	2001
Cash flows from operating activities			
Net earnings	$15,863	$23,068	$ 8,913
Provision for depreciation, depletion, and amortization	60,823	60,624	60,948
Provision (credit) for losses on accounts receivable	(261)	307	1,339
Loss on property, plant, and equipment disposals	3,234	934	1,145
Compensation expense for stock option grants	39	37	3,085
Deferred income taxes	7,154	16,108	598

NOTES TO CONSOLIDATED FINANCIAL STATEMENTS

Note 1 (In Part): Description of the Business and Summary of Significant Accounting Policies

Property, Plant, and Equipment (In Part)

Timber and timberlands are stated at net depleted value. The Company capitalizes the cost of purchasing timberlands and reforestation costs. Interest and taxes related to timberlands are expensed as incurred. Reforestation costs include site preparation, planting, fertilizing, herbicide application, and thinning. Temporary logging roads are expensed while long-term logging roads are capitalized and amortized over the estimated useful lives of the roads, which is generally 15 to 20 years. Depletion is recorded as timber is harvested and included in inventory until conversion into saleable product. Depletion is calculated using the block and units-of-production methods. Under these methods, the capitalized costs of large land tracts are divided by the estimated volume of timber anticipated to be harvested on each tract. As the timber is harvested, depletion is either recorded as each block is harvested or as a percentage of each block is harvested.

Note 3 (In Part): Supplemental Balance Sheet Information

(Dollar amounts in thousands)	2003	2002
Property, plant, and equipment		
Buildings	$ 137,604	$ 136,412
Machinery and equipment	1,061,342	1,055,507
	1,198,946	1,191,919
Less: accumulated depreciation	(652,990)	(613,840)
Net depreciated value	545,956	578,079
Land	5,521	5,307
Timber and timberlands, net of depletion	5,818	5,821
Idle assets	98	98
Construction in progress	8,329	8,674
	$ 565,722	$ 597,979

INCOME TAXES

PRESENTATION OF INCOME TAXES

3.113 SFAS No. 109, *Accounting for Income Taxes*, is the authoritative pronouncement on accounting for and reporting income tax liabilities and expense. Paragraphs 41–49 of *SFAS No. 109* set forth standards for financial presentation and disclosure of income tax liabilities and expense.

3.114 Table 3-14 summarizes the descriptive captions used by the survey companies to identify income tax expense. Examples of income tax expense presentation and disclosure follow.

3.115

TABLE 3-14: INCOME TAX EXPENSE

Descriptive Terms	2003	2002	2001	2000
Income taxes.........................	585	583	575	580
Federal income taxes............	10	11	10	13
United States (U.S.) income taxes....................	1	1	1	1
	596	595	586	594
Other or no current year amount..............................	4	5	14	6
Total Companies.................	**600**	**600**	**600**	**600**

Expense Provision

3.116

DOVER CORPORATION (DEC)

(In thousands)	2003	2002	2001
Net sales	$4,413,296	$4,053,593	$4,223,245
Cost of sales	2,892,874	2,722,674	2,869,782
Gross profit	1,520,422	1,330,919	1,353,463
Selling and administrative expenses	1,076,664	996,209	1,039,581
Operating profit	443,758	334,710	313,882
Interest expense, net	62,166	64,787	75,218
All other (income) expense, net	9,700	6,554	(14,270)
Total	71,866	71,341	60,948
Earnings from continuing operations, before taxes on income	371,892	263,369	252,934
Federal and other taxes on income	86,676	55,523	74,698
Net earnings from continuing operations	$ 285,216	$ 207,846	$ 178,236

NOTES TO CONSOLIDATED FINANCIAL STATEMENTS

1 (In Part): Description of Business and Summary of Significant Accounting Policies

Income Taxes

The provision for income taxes on continuing operations includes federal, state, local and foreign taxes. Tax credits, primarily for research and experimentation and foreign earnings and export programs are recognized as a reduction of the provision for income taxes on continuing operations in the year in which they are available for tax purposes. Deferred taxes are provided on temporary differences between assets and liabilities for financial reporting and tax purposes as measured by enacted tax rates expected to apply when temporary differences are settled or realized. Future tax benefits are recognized to the extent that realization of those benefits is considered to be more likely than not. A valuation allowance is established for deferred tax assets for which realization is not assured. The Company has not provided for any residual U.S. income taxes on unremitted earnings of foreign subsidiaries as such earnings are intended to be indefinitely reinvested.

11. Taxes on Income

Total income taxes for the years ended December 31, 2003, 2002 and 2001 were allocated as follows:

(In thousands)	2003	2002	2001
Taxes on income from continuing operations	$86,676	$55,523	$74,698
Stockholders' equity, for compensation expense for tax purposes in excess of amounts recognized for financial reporting purposes	(3,513)	(2,597)	(2,345)
	$83,163	$52,926	$72,353

Income tax expense (benefit) is made up of the following components:

(In thousands)	2003	2002	2001
Current			
U.S. Federal	$ 3,572	$ 5,648	$27,380
State and local	3,397	327	4,777
Foreign	32,005	28,486	39,651
Total current—continuing	$38,974	$34,461	$71,808
Deferred			
U.S. Federal	$48,583	$19,487	$ 8,673
State and local	1,422	2,199	(1,726)
Foreign	(2,303)	(624)	(4,057)
Total deferred—continuing	47,702	21,062	2,890
Total expense—continuing	$86,676	$55,523	$74,698

Income taxes have been based on the following components of earnings before taxes on continuing income:

(In thousands)	2003	2002	2001
Domestic	$241,512	$202,504	$171,816
Foreign	130,380	60,865	81,118
	$371,892	$263,369	$252,934

The reasons for the difference between the effective rate and the U.S. Federal income statutory rate of 35% are as follows:

	2003	2002	2001
U.S. Federal income tax rate	35.0%	35.0%	35.0%
State and local taxes, net of Federal income tax benefit	1.9	0.6	0.8
Foreign operations tax effect	(4.3)	3.5	3.0
Subtotal	32.6	39.1	38.8
R&E tax credits	(1.3)	(2.5)	(2.5)
Foreign export program benefits	(3.0)	(4.3)	(5.0)
Foreign tax credits	—	(1.1)	(1.2)
Branch losses	(1.5)	(2.3)	(1.4)
Other, reflecting settlement of tax contingencies	(3.4)	—	—
Other, principally non-tax deductible items	0.4	0.8	2.8
Effective rate before reorganizations	23.8	29.7	31.5
Reorganization of entities and other	(0.5)	(8.6)	(2.0)
Effective rate from continuing operations	23.3%	21.1%	29.5%

The tax effects of temporary differences that give rise to significant portions of the deferred tax assets and deferred tax liabilities at December 31 of each year are as follows:

(In thousands)	2003	2002
Deferred tax assets:		
Accrued insurance	$ 4,885	$ 15,058
Accrued compensation, principally postretirement benefits, and other employee benefits	42,922	38,389
Accrued expenses, principally for disposition of businesses, interest and warranty	19,334	16,986
Long-term liabilities principally warranty, environmental and exit costs	12,038	12,427
Inventories, principally due to reserves for financial reporting purposes and capitalization for tax purposes	23,977	28,121
Net operating loss carryforwards	50,845	30,086
Accounts receivable, principally due to allowance for doubtful accounts	7,083	6,702
Other assets	3,809	5,182
Total gross deferred tax assets	164,893	152,951
Valuation allowance	(50,845)	(30,086)
Total deferred tax assets	$ 114,048	$ 122,865
Deferred tax liabilities:		
Accounts receivable	$ (20,355)	$ (21,439)
Plant and equipment, principally due to differences in depreciation	(22,562)	(9,527)
Intangible assets, principally due to different tax and financial reporting bases and amortization lives	(211,222)	(133,781)
Prepaid pension assets	(48,321)	(37,244)
Other liabilities	(947)	(368)
Total gross deferred tax liabilities	(303,407)	(202,359)
Net deferred tax liability	(189,359)	(79,494)
Net current deferred tax asset	44,547	56,554
Net non-current deferred tax liability	$(233,906)	$(136,048)

The Company has loss carryovers from continuing operations for federal and foreign purposes as of December 31, 2003 of $24.0 million and $289.4 million, respectively, and for 2002 federal and foreign loss carryovers of $298.2 and $177.0 million, respectively. The Company expects to utilize all of the $24.0 million federal losses in the 2000 and 2001 carryback period. The federal loss of $298.2 million from 2002 was carried back to 1999. The entire balance of the foreign losses is available to be carried forward, with $62.9 million of these beginning to expire during the years 2004 through 2010. The remaining $226.5 million of such losses can be carried forward indefinitely. The Company maintains a valuation allowance to reduce the deferred tax assets related to these carry forwards, as utilization of these losses is not assured.

The Company does not provide for U.S. federal income taxes or tax benefits on the undistributed earnings or losses of its international subsidiaries because such earnings are reinvested and, in the opinion of management, will continue to be reinvested indefinitely. At December 31, 2003 and 2002, the Company had not provided federal income taxes on earnings of approximately $223.2 million and $160.0 million, respectively, from its international subsidiaries. Should these earnings be distributed in the form of dividends or otherwise, the Company would be subject to both U.S. income taxes and withholding taxes in various international jurisdictions. These taxes will be partially offset by U.S. foreign tax credits. Determination of the related amount of unrecognized deferred U.S. income taxes is not practicable because of the complexities associated with this hypothetical calculation.

Dover is continuously undergoing examination of its federal income tax returns by the Internal Revenue Service (the "IRS"). The Company and the IRS have settled tax years through 1995. The Company expects to resolve open years (1996–1999) in the near future, all within the amounts paid and/or reserved for these liabilities. The IRS is currently examining the Company's 2000, 2001 and 2002 federal income tax returns. Additionally, the Company is routinely involved in state and local income tax audits, and on occasion, foreign jurisdiction tax audits.

3.117

THE NEW YORK TIMES COMPANY (DEC)

(In thousands)	2003	2002	2001
Revenues			
Advertising	$2,120,814	$2,048,815	$2,042,211
Circulation	885,767	825,208	759,674
Other	220,619	204,984	214,073
Total	3,227,200	3,079,007	3,015,958
Costs and expenses			
Production costs			
Raw materials	274,147	262,292	321,204
Wages and benefits	671,040	619,652	594,197
Other	483,608	470,688	477,675
Total	1,428,795	1,352,632	1,393,076
Selling, general and administrative expenses	1,258,855	1,181,507	1,248,479
Total	2,687,650	2,534,139	2,641,555
Operating profit	539,550	544,868	374,403
Net (loss)/income from joint ventures	(8,223)	(12,330)	7,472
Interest expense, net	44,757	45,435	47,199
Other income	13,277	5,000	5,000
Income from continuing operations before income taxes and minority interest	499,847	492,103	339,676
Income taxes	197,762	191,955	137,559
Minority interest in net loss/(income) of subsidiaries	570	(401)	105
Income from continuing operations	$ 302,655	$ 299,747	$ 202,222

NOTES TO CONSOLIDATED FINANCIAL STATEMENTS

1 (In Part): Summary of Significant Accounting Policies

Income Taxes

Income taxes are accounted for in accordance with FAS No. 109, Accounting for Income Taxes, which requires that deferred tax assets and liabilities be recognized using enacted tax rates for the effect of temporary differences between the book and tax basis of recorded assets and liabilities. In addition, the Company uses the deferral method of accounting for investment tax credits.

9. Income Taxes

Income tax expense for each of the years presented is determined in accordance with FAS 109. Reconciliations between the effective tax rate on income before income taxes and the federal statutory rate are presented below.

(In thousands)	2003 Amount	2003 % of Pretax	2002 Amount	2002 % of Pretax	2001 Amount	2001 % of Pretax
Tax at federal statutory rate	$170,300	35.0%	$170,486	35.0%	$117,136	35.0%
Increase (decrease)						
State and local taxes—net	25,423	5.2	15,646	3.2	11,663	3.5
Amortization of nondeductible intangible assets acquired	—	—	—	—	9,273	2.8
Other—net	(3,206)	(0.6)	3,873	0.8	(2,538)	(0.8)
Subtotal	192,517	39.6%	190,005	39.0%	135,534	40.5%
Tax effect of other income	5,245		1,950		2,025	
Income tax expense	197,762	39.6%	191,955	39.0%	137,559	40.5%
Income taxes in minority interest	(163)	(0.1)%	(315)	0%	73	0%
Income tax expense excluding income taxes in minority interest	$197,599	39.5%	$191,640	39.0%	$137,632	40.5%

The components of income tax expense as shown in the Consolidated Statements of Income are as follows:

(In thousands)	2003	2002	2001
Current tax expense			
Federal	$119,004	$103,334	$137,362
Foreign	525	—	—
State and local	24,697	1,940	47,022
Total current tax expense	144,226	105,274	184,384
Deferred tax expense/(benefit)			
Federal	41,550	64,180	(18,218)
Foreign	(3,348)	—	
State and local	15,334	22,501	(28,607)
Total deferred tax expense/(benefit)	53,536	86,681	(46,825)
Income tax expense	197,762	191,955	137,559
Income taxes in minority interest	(163)	(315)	73
Income tax expense excluding income taxes in minority interest	$197,599	$191,640	$137,632

Income tax benefits related to the exercise of stock options reduced current taxes payable and increased additional paid-in capital by $13.2 million in 2003, $27.0 million in 2002 and $30.6 million in 2001.

State tax operating loss carryforwards totaled $4.6 million as of December 28, 2003, and $8.7 million as of December 29, 2002. Such loss carryforwards expire in accordance with provisions of applicable tax laws and have remaining lives ranging from 3 to 13 years. Certain loss carryforwards are likely to expire unused. Accordingly, the Company has valuation allowances amounting to $2.2 million ($1.5 million net of federal benefit) as of December 28, 2003, and $5.3 million ($3.4 million net of federal benefit) as of December 29, 2002.

Foreign tax operating loss carryforwards totaled approximately $9 million in 2003. Such loss carryforwards expire in accordance with provisions of applicable tax laws and have primarily unlimited lives. A valuation allowance of $2.2 million has been established for certain of these losses. In connection with the acquisition of the IHT, the Company recorded deferred tax assets, including net operating losses, as part of purchase accounting. Subsequent recognition of the deferred tax asset relating to the valuation allowance would result in a reduction of goodwill recorded in connection with the acquisition.

Tax expense in 2003 decreased by $2.0 million ($3.1 million before federal income tax effect) due to a reduction in the valuation allowance attributable to state net operating tax loss benefits. Tax expense in 2002 increased by $1.7 million ($2.7 million before federal income tax effect) due to an increase in the valuation allowance attributable to state net operating loss tax benefits. Tax expense in 2001 was reduced by $0.2 million ($0.3 million before federal income tax effect) due to a reduction in the valuation allowance attributable to state net operating tax loss benefits.

The Company's intent is for foreign earnings of the IHT to be permanently reinvested. Since no foreign earnings currently exist, an incremental U.S. or foreign tax on repatriation of such earnings cannot be estimated.

The Company generated $16.0 million in investment tax credits in the state of New York in connection with the construction of its Flushing, NY facility in 1997. The Company has fully utilized the investment tax credit for state income tax purposes. For financial statement purposes, the Company has selected the deferral method of accounting for investment tax credits, and will amortize the tax benefit over the average useful life of the assets which ranges from 10 to 20 years.

The Internal Revenue Service has completed its examination of federal income tax returns through 2000. The Internal Revenue Service may audit the Company's federal income tax returns for years subsequent to 2000. Such audits are not expected to have a material effect on the Company's Consolidated Financial Statements.

The components of the net deferred tax assets and liabilities recognized in the Company's Consolidated Balance Sheets were as follows:

(In thousands)	2003	2002
Deferred tax assets:		
Retirement, post employment and deferred compensation plans	$236,441	$278,195
Accruals for other employee benefits, compensation, insurance and other	45,477	65,707
Accounts receivable allowances	6,690	7,613
Other	58,842	39,860
Gross deferred tax assets	347,450	391,375
Valuation allowance	(3,627)	(3,448)
Net deferred tax assets	343,823	387,927
Deferred tax liabilities:		
Property, plant and equipment	237,753	234,556
Intangible assets	110,449	113,950
Investments in joint ventures	36,416	16,289
Other	30,338	23,428
Gross deferred tax liabilities	414,956	388,223
Net deferred tax liability	$ 71,133	$ 296

Amounts recognized in the Consolidated Balance Sheets consist of:

	2003	2002
Deferred tax asset—current	$ 66,178	$ 73,528
Deferred tax asset—long term	3,025	—
Deferred tax liability—long term	140,336	73,824
Net deferred tax liability	$ 71,133	$ 296

As of December 28, 2003, and December 29, 2002, "Accumulated other comprehensive income/(loss), net of income taxes" in the Company's Consolidated Balance Sheets and for the years then ended in the Consolidated Statements of Stockholders' Equity was net of a deferred income tax asset of $68.6 million, and $79.4 million, respectively.

3.118

OFFICE DEPOT, INC. (DEC)

(In thousands)	2003	2002	2001
Sales	$12,358,566	$11,356,633	$11,082,112
Cost of goods sold and occupancy costs	8,484,420	8,022,663	7,940,067
Gross profit	3,874,146	3,333,970	3,142,045
Store and warehouse operating and selling expenses	2,802,240	2,338,128	2,331,013
General and administrative expenses	578,840	486,279	445,538
Other operating expenses	22,809	9,855	12,125
Operating profit	470,257	499,708	353,369
Other income (expense)			
Interest income	14,196	18,509	12,980
Interest expense	(54,805)	(46,195)	(43,339)
Miscellaneous income (expense), net	15,392	7,183	(9,057)
Earnings from continuing operations before income taxes and cumulative effect of accounting change	445,040	479,205	313,953
Income taxes	143,016	167,722	112,296
Earnings from continuing operations before cumulative effect of accounting change	$ 302,024	$ 311,483	$ 201,657

NOTES TO CONSOLIDATED FINANCIAL STATEMENTS

Note A (In Part): Summary of Significant Accounting Policies

Income Taxes

Income tax expense is recognized at applicable U.S. or international tax rates. Certain revenue and expense items may be recognized in one period for financial statement purposes and in a different period's income tax return. The tax effects of such differences are reported as deferred income taxes.

Essentially all earnings of foreign subsidiaries are expected to be reinvested in overseas expansion. Accordingly, no provision has been made for incremental U.S. taxes on undistributed earnings considered permanently invested. Cumulative undistributed earnings of our foreign subsidiaries for which no Federal income taxes have been provided was $1,046.2 million and $778.7 million as of December 27, 2003 and December 28, 2002, respectively.

Note H—Income Taxes

The income tax provision related to earnings from continuing operations consisted of the following:

(Dollars in thousands)	2003	2002	2001
Current			
Federal	$ 70,802	$114,420	$ 66,074
State	(3,753)	14,181	12,904
Foreign	42,915	29,127	33,122
Deferred	33,052	9,994	196
Total provision for income taxes	$143,016	$167,722	$112,296

The components of earnings from continuing operations before income taxes and cumulative effect of accounting change consisted of the following:

(Dollars in thousands)	2003	2002	2001
North America	$227,962	$352,645	$176,711
International	217,078	126,560	137,242
Total	$445,040	$479,205	$313,953

The tax-effected components of deferred income tax assets and liabilities consisted of the following:

(Dollars in thousands)	2003	2002
Self-insurance accruals	$ 24,348	$ 26,049
Inventory	22,976	34,125
Vacation pay and other accrued compensation	26,672	31,558
Reserve for bad debts	7,926	4,585
Reserve for facility closings	28,226	52,637
Acquisition and integration costs	11,821	4,934
Unrealized loss on investments	1,660	20,279
Foreign and state net operating loss carryforwards	156,903	86,281
State credit carryforwards net of Federal	7,015	—
Other items, net	50,515	39,545
Gross deferred tax assets	338,062	299,993
Valuation allowance	(156,903)	(86,281)
Deferred tax assets	181,159	213,712
Basis difference in fixed assets	42,940	86,433
Intangibles	44,949	3,356
Other items, net	20,560	1,730
Deferred tax liabilities	108,449	91,519
Net deferred tax assets	$ 72,710	$122,193

As of December 27, 2003, we had approximately $805 million of state and $372 million of foreign net operating loss carryforwards, of which approximately $126 million, $45 million tax effected, relate to the Guilbert acquisition. Of these carryforwards, approximately $15 million will expire in 2004, $126 million will carry over indefinitely, and the balance will expire between 2005 and 2023. The valuation allowance has been developed to reduce our deferred tax asset to an amount that is more likely than not to be realized, and is based upon the uncertainty of the realization of certain foreign and state deferred tax assets relating to net operating loss carryforwards. In addition to the net operating loss carryforward noted above, the deferred asset above includes approximately $17 million, consisting mainly of acquisition and integration related items, and the deferred tax liability above includes approximately $43 million, consisting mainly of basis differences in intangible assets related to the acquisition of Guilbert.

The following is a reconciliation of income taxes at the Federal statutory rate to the provision for income taxes:

(Dollars in thousands)	2003	2002	2001
Federal tax computed at the statutory rate	$155,764	$167,721	$109,945
State taxes, net of Federal benefit	4,136	8,526	13,333
Non-deductible goodwill	—	—	1,834
State credits	(10,400)	—	—
Foreign income taxed at rates other than Federal	(9,470)	(12,656)	(14,534)
Other items, net	2,986	4,131	1,718
Provision for income taxes	$143,016	$167,722	$112,296

Credit Provision

3.119

INTERNATIONAL PAPER COMPANY (DEC)

(In millions)	2003	2002	2001
Net sales	$25,179	$24,976	$26,363
Costs and expenses			
Cost of products sold	18,803	18,256	19,409
Selling and administrative expenses	1,980	2,046	2,279
Depreciation, amortization and cost of timber harvested	1,644	1,587	1,870
Distribution expenses	1,103	1,098	1,105
Taxes other than payroll and income taxes	247	249	265
Restructuring and other charges	298	695	1,117
Net (gains) losses on sales and impairments of businesses held for sale	32	(41)	629
Merger integration costs	—	—	42
Total costs and expenses	24,107	23,890	26,716
Reversals of reserves no longer required, net	40	68	17
Earnings (loss) before interest, income taxes, minority interest, extraordinary items and cumulative effect of accounting changes	1,112	1,154	(336)
Interest expense, net	766	783	929
Earnings (loss) before income taxes, minority interest, extraordinary items and cumulative effect of accounting changes	346	371	(1,265)
Income tax benefit	(92)	(54)	(270)
Minority interest expense, net of taxes	123	130	147
Earnings (loss) before extraordinary items and cumulative effect of accounting changes	$ 315	$ 295	$ (1,142)

NOTES TO CONSOLIDATED FINANCIAL STATEMENTS

Note 1 (In Part): Summary of Significant Accounting Policies

Income Taxes

International Paper uses the asset and liability method of accounting for income taxes whereby deferred income taxes are recorded for the future tax consequences attributable to differences between the financial statement and tax bases of assets and liabilities. Deferred tax assets and liabilities are measured using tax rates expected to apply to taxable income in the years in which those temporary differences are expected to be recovered or settled. Deferred tax assets and liabilities are revalued to reflect new tax rates in the periods rate changes are enacted.

Note 9: Income Taxes

The components of International Paper's earnings (loss) before income taxes, minority interest, extraordinary items and cumulative effect of accounting changes by taxing jurisdiction were:

(In millions)	2003	2002	2001
Earnings (loss)			
U.S.	$(249)	$ (73)	$(1,683)
Non-U.S.	595	444	418
	$ 346	$371	$(1,265)

The provision (benefit) for income taxes by taxing jurisdiction was:

(In millions)	2003	2002	2001
Current tax provision			
U.S. federal	$ 173	$ 175	$ 186
U.S. state and local	11	543	3
Non-U.S.	125	111	100
	$ 309	$ 340	$ 289
Deferred tax provision (benefit)			
U.S. federal	$(271)	$(231)	$(455)
U.S. state and local	(73)	(146)	(116)
Non-U.S.	(57)	(17)	12
	$(401)	$(394)	$(559)
Income tax provision (benefit)	$ (92)	$ (54)	$(270)

The Company's deferred income tax provision (benefit) includes a $1 million provision for the effect of changes in Non-U.S. and state tax rates.

International Paper made income tax payments, net of refunds, of $277 million, $295 million and $333 million in 2003, 2002 and 2001, respectively.

A reconciliation of income tax expense (benefit) using the statutory U.S. income tax rate compared with actual income tax expense (benefit) follows:

(In millions)	2003	2002	2001
Earnings (loss) before income taxes, minority interest, extraordinary items and cumulative effect of accounting changes	$346	$371	$(1,265)
Statutory U.S. income tax rate	35%	35%	35%
Tax expense (benefit) using statutory U.S. income tax rate	$121	$130	$ (443)
State and local income taxes	(41)	(60)	(73)
Non-U.S. tax rate differences	(95)	(50)	(19)
Permanent differences on sales of non-strategic assets	(1)	(70)	180
Nondeductible business expenses	22	13	12
Retirement plan dividends	(7)	—	—
Tax benefit on export sales	(12)	(4)	(4)
Minority interest	(52)	(43)	(70)
Goodwill amortization	—	—	55
Net U.S. tax on non-U.S. dividends	15	27	108
Tax credits	(56)	—	—
Other, net	14	3	(16)
Income tax benefit	$ (92)	$ (54)	$ (270)
Effective income tax rate	−27%	−15%	21%

The tax effects of significant temporary differences representing deferred tax assets and liabilities at December 31, 2003 and 2002, were as follows:

(In millions)	2003	2002
Deferred tax assets		
Postretirement benefit accruals	$ 372	$ 363
Prepaid pension costs	322	397
Alternative minimum and other tax credits	474	423
Net operating loss carryforwards	1,703	1,295
Compensation reserves	196	174
Legal reserves	147	174
Other	449	527
Gross deferred tax assets	3,663	3,353
Less: valuation allowance	(148)	(169)
Net deferred tax assets	$ 3,515	$ 3,184
Deferred tax liabilities		
Plants, properties, and equipment	$(2,867)	$(2,832)
Forestlands	(1,153)	(1,092)
Other	(264)	(253)
Total deferred tax liabilities	$(4,284)	$(4,177)
Net deferred tax liability	$ (769)	$ (993)

The valuation allowance for deferred tax assets as of January 1, 2003, was $169 million. The net change in the total valuation allowance for the year ended December 31, 2003, was a decrease of $21 million.

During 2003, International Paper recorded decreases totaling $123 million in the provision for income taxes for significant items occurring in 2003, including a $13 million reduction in the fourth quarter ($26 million before minority interest) for a favorable settlement with Australian tax authorities of net operating loss carry-forwards, a $60 million reduction in the third quarter reflecting a favorable revision of estimated tax accruals upon filing the 2002 federal income tax return and increased research and development credits, and a $50 million reduction in the second quarter reflecting a favorable tax audit settlement and benefits from an overseas tax program.

During the fourth quarter of 2002, International Paper completed a review of its deferred income tax accounts, including the effects of state tax credits and the taxability of the Company's operations in various state taxing jurisdictions. As a result of this review, the Company recorded a decrease of approximately $46 million in the income tax provision in the 2002 fourth quarter, reflecting the effect of the estimated state income tax effective rate applied to these deferred tax items.

International Paper has federal and non-U.S. net operating loss carryforwards that expire as follows: years 2004 through 2013—$176 million, years 2014 through 2023—$3.5 billion, and indefinite carryforwards—$704 million. International Paper has tax benefits from net operating loss carryforwards for state taxing jurisdictions of approximately $322 million that expire as follows: years 2004 through 2013—$74 million, and years 2014 through 2023—$248 million. International Paper also has federal and state tax credit carryforwards that expire as follows: years 2004 through 2013—$142 million, and indefinite carryforward—$387 million.

Deferred taxes are not provided for temporary differences of approximately $3.3 billion, $2.5 billion and $1.8 billion as of December 31, 2003, 2002 and 2001, respectively, representing earnings of non-U.S. subsidiaries that are intended to be permanently reinvested. Computation of the potential deferred tax liability associated with these undistributed earnings is not practicable.

3.120

STARWOOD HOTELS & RESORTS WORLDWIDE, INC. (DEC)

(In millions)	2003	2002	2001
Revenues			
Owned, leased and consolidated joint venture hotels	$3,085	$3,190	$3,301
Other hotel and leisure	694	618	592
	3,779	3,808	3,893
Other revenues from managed and franchised properties	851	780	740
	4,630	4,588	4,633
Costs and expenses			
Owned, leased and consolidated joint venture hotels	2,392	2,350	2,338
Selling, general, administrative and other	540	426	411
Restructuring and other special charges (credits), net	(9)	(7)	50
Depreciation	410	473	430
Amortization	19	15	88
	3,352	3,257	3,317
Other expenses from managed and franchised properties	851	780	740
	4,203	4,037	4,057
Operating income	427	551	576
Gain on sale of VOI notes receivable	15	16	12
Equity earnings from unconsolidated ventures, net	12	8	15
Interest expense, net of interest income of $5, $2 and $11	(282)	(323)	(354)
Gain (loss) on asset dispositions and impairments, net	(183)	3	(57)
Income (loss) from continuing operations before taxes and minority equity	(11)	255	192
Income tax benefit (expense)	113	(2)	(42)
Minority equity in net loss (income)	3	(2)	(3)
Income from continuing operations	$ 105	$ 251	$ 147

NOTES TO FINANCIAL STATEMENTS

Note 1 (In Part): Basis of Presentation

Income Taxes

The Company provides for income taxes in accordance with SFAS No. 109, "Accounting for Income Taxes". The objectives of accounting for income taxes are to recognize the amount of taxes payable or refundable for the current year and deferred tax liabilities and assets for the future tax consequences of events that have been recognized in an entity's financial statements or tax returns.

Deferred tax assets and liabilities are measured using enacted tax rates in effect for the year in which those temporary differences are expected to be recovered or settled. The effect on deferred tax assets and liabilities of a change in tax rates is recognized in earnings in the period when the new rate is enacted.

The Trust has elected to be treated as a REIT under the provisions of the Code. As a result, the Trust is not subject to federal income tax on its taxable income at corporate rates provided it distributes annually all of its taxable income to its shareholders and complies with certain other requirements.

Note 13. Income Taxes

Income tax data from continuing operations of the Company is as follows (in millions):

	2003	2002	2001
Pretax income (loss)			
U.S.	$ (64)	$169	$ 66
Foreign	53	86	126
	$ (11)	$255	$192
Provision (benefit) for income tax			
Current			
U.S. federal	$ 1	$(14)	$ 57
State and local	4	(3)	8
Foreign	48	69	63
	53	52	128
Deferred			
U.S. federal	$(108)	$ (32)	$ (91)
State and local	(14)	(4)	—
Foreign	(44)	(14)	5
	(166)	(50)	(86)
	$(113)	$ 2	$ 42

No provision has been made for U.S. taxes payable on undistributed foreign earnings amounting to approximately $814 million as of December 31, 2003, since these amounts are permanently reinvested.

Deferred income taxes represent the tax effect of the differences between the book and tax bases of assets and liabilities. Deferred tax assets (liabilities) include the following (in millions):

	2003	2002
Plant, property and equipment	$(527)	$(579)
Intangibles	(171)	(155)
Allowances for doubtful accounts and other reserves	137	180
Employee benefits	42	59
Deferred gain on ITT World Directories disposition	(551)	(551)
Net operating loss and tax credit carryforwards	372	318
Deferred income	(136)	(145)
Other	(47)	(58)
	(881)	(931)
Less valuation allowance	(17)	(55)
Deferred income taxes	$(898)	$(986)

At December 31, 2003, the Company had net operating loss and tax credit carryforwards of approximately $914 million and $33 million, respectively, for federal income tax purposes. Substantially all operating loss carryforwards, available to provide future tax benefits, expire between 2018 and 2023.

In February 1998, the Company disposed of ITT World Directories. Through December 31, 2003, the Company has recorded $551 million of income taxes relating to this transaction, which are included in deferred income taxes in the accompanying consolidated balance sheets. While the Company strongly believes this transaction was completed on a tax-deferred basis, this position is currently being challenged by the IRS. During 2002 the matter was transferred from the IRS Field Agent to IRS Appeals. To date, the Company has been unable to reach a satisfactory resolution of the matter with IRS Appeals. The Company expects to receive notification from IRS Appeals advising the Company of its rights to either pay the liability or elect to pursue the matter in litigation. Upon receiving this notification, the Company plans on electing to litigate the matter with the ultimate outcome unpredictable at this time. If this transaction were deemed fully taxable in 1998, then the Company's federal tax obligation would be approximately $499 million, plus interest, and would be partially offset by the Company's net operating loss discussed above. The Company plans to vigorously defend its position in this matter.

A reconciliation of the tax provision of the Company at the U.S. statutory rate to the provision for income tax as reported is as follows (in millions):

	2003	2002	2001
Tax provision (benefit) at U.S. statutory rate	$ (4)	$ 86	$ 66
U.S. state and local income taxes	(7)	(5)	5
Exempt trust income	(60)	(60)	(57)
Tax on repatriation of foreign earnings	12	15	13
Foreign tax rate differential	(1)	13	10
Non-deductible goodwill	—	—	16
Tax settlements	(36)	(30)	—
Basis difference on asset sales	(5)	—	—
Reduction of valuation allowance	(12)	(18)	(10)
Other	—	1	(1)
Provision for income tax (benefit)	$(113)	$ 2	$ 42

In 2003 the Company filed for tax amnesty in Italy for certain of its Italian subsidiaries related to the 1997–2001 tax years. As a result of these filings, the Company recognized a $2 million tax benefit, which represented the reversal of reserves associated with these tax years, net of the tax amnesty cost. In addition, the Company recognized a $26 million tax benefit for the reversal of a valuation allowance associated with a tax matter, which can no longer be contested as a result of the tax amnesty filings. Also in 2003, the Company recognized an $8 million tax benefit relating to the reduction of previously accrued taxes after an evaluation of the exposure items and the expiration of related statutes of limitation.

During 2002, the IRS completed its audits of various tax returns of the Company for tax periods dating back to 1993. As a result of the completion of these audits, the Company recorded a tax benefit in the fourth quarter of 2002 of approximately $30 million, which consists of $17 million in expected refunds offset by a $5 million reduction to the Company's net operating loss, and $18 million of reversals of accured income tax liabilities associated with these audit years, which are no longer deemed necessary.

No Provision

3.121

EARTHLINK, INC. (DEC)

(In thousands)	2001	2002	2003
Revenues:			
Narrowband access	$ 999,251	$1,037,829	$ 965,025
Broadband access	167,935	250,591	361,124
Web hosting	59,263	53,210	49,902
Content, commerce and advertising	18,479	15,791	25,879
Total revenues	1,244,928	1,357,421	1,401,930
Operating costs and expenses:			
Telecommunications service and equipment costs	509,514	543,981	519,149
Sales incentives	67,919	37,669	21,176
Total cost of revenues	577,433	581,650	540,325
Sales and marketing	327,951	373,481	382,965
Operations and customer support	339,490	324,555	297,045
General and administrative	127,849	123,379	127,664
Acquisition-related amortization	217,483	110,885	84,299
Facility exit costs	—	3,492	36,596
Intangible asset write-off	11,252	—	—
Total operating costs and expenses	1,601,458	1,517,442	1,468,894
Loss from operations	(356,530)	(160,021)	(66,964)
Write-off of equity investments in other companies	(10,000)	(650)	(202)
Interest income and other, net	25,469	12,638	4,972
Net loss	$ (341,061)	$ (148,033)	$ (62,194)

NOTES TO CONSOLIDATED FINANCIAL STATEMENTS

2 (In Part): Summary of Significant Accounting Policies

Income Taxes

Income taxes are accounted for under the liability method. Under this method, deferred tax assets and liabilities are recognized for operating loss carryforwards, tax credit carryforwards and the estimated future tax consequences attributable to differences between the financial statement carrying amounts of existing assets and liabilities and their respective tax bases. Deferred tax assets and liabilities are measured using enacted tax rates in effect for the year in which the temporary differences are expected to be recovered or settled. A valuation allowance is recorded to reduce the carrying amounts of deferred tax assets if there is uncertainty regarding their realization.

13. Income Taxes

The following table summarizes the significant differences between the U.S. federal statutory tax rate and the Company's effective tax rate for financial statement purposes for the years ended December 31, 2001, 2002 and 2003:

(In thousands)	2001	2002	2003
Federal income tax benefit at statutory rate	$(119,372)	$(51,812)	$(21,768)
State income taxes, net of federal benefit	(12,633)	(6,699)	(2,830)
Nondeductible goodwill, acquisition costs and other permanent items	13,389	—	(266)
Net change to valuation allowance	121,633	58,225	25,446
Other	(3,017)	286	(582)
	$ —	$ —	$ —

The Company acquired $49.4 million and $35.8 million of deferred tax assets, primarily related to net operating loss carryforwards, in conjunction with the acquisitions of Cidco in December 2001 and PeoplePC in July 2002, respectively. These additional deferred tax assets and liabilities impact the net change to the valuation allowance.

Deferred tax assets and liabilities include the following as of December 31, 2002 and 2003:

(In thousands)	2002	2003
Deferred tax assets		
Net operating loss carryforwards	$ 283,253	$ 263,607
Accrued liabilities and reserves	21,729	24,728
Subscriber base and other intangible assets	95,373	117,625
Depreciation and other	30,312	21,335
Total deferred tax assets	430,667	427,295
Valuation allowance	(430,667)	(427,295)
Net deferred taxes	$ —	$ —

At December 31, 2002 and 2003, the Company had net operating loss carryforwards for federal income tax purposes totaling approximately $671.9 million and $639.5 million, respectively, which begin to expire in 2010. At December 31, 2002 and 2003, the Company had net operating loss carryforwards for state income tax purposes totaling approximately $523.5 million and $404.7 million, respectively, which started to expire in 2002. The Company also had $35.5 million and $35.6 million of foreign net operating loss carryforwards at December 31, 2002 and 2003, respectively. Under the Tax Reform Act of 1986, the Company's ability to use its federal, state and foreign net operating loss carryforwards and federal and state tax credit carryforwards to reduce future taxable income and future taxes, respectively, is subject to restrictions attributable to equity transactions that have resulted in a change of ownership as defined in Internal Revenue Code Section 382. During the year ended December 31, 2003, the Company reduced the net operating loss carryforward deferred tax asset and the associated valuation allowance by $28.8 million based on an analysis of Section 382 limitations associated with acquired federal and state net operating loss carryforwards. As a result, the net operating loss carryforward amount at December 31, 2003 reflects the restriction on the Company's ability to use its federal and state net

operating loss carryforwards. The utilization of these carryforwards could be further restricted in future periods which could result in significant amounts of these carryforwards expiring prior to benefiting the Company. At December 31, 2002 and 2003, the net operating loss carryforwards include $75.2 million and $76.8 million, respectively, related to the exercise of employee stock options and warrants. Any benefit resulting from the utilization of this portion of the net operating loss carryforward will be credited directly to equity. The Company has provided a valuation allowance for its deferred tax assets, including net operating loss carryforwards, because of uncertainty regarding their realization.

OPERATING LOSS AND TAX CREDIT CARRYFORWARDS

3.122 Paragraph 48 of *SFAS No. 109* states that amounts and expiration dates of operating loss and tax credit carryforwards for tax purposes should be disclosed. Examples of operating loss and tax credit carryforward disclosures follow.

3.123

INTERNATIONAL MULTIFOODS CORPORATION (FEB)

NOTES TO CONSOLIDATED FINANCIAL STATEMENTS

Note 1 (In Part): Summary of Significant Accounting Policies

Income Taxes

Deferred tax assets and liabilities are recognized for the expected future tax consequences of temporary differences between the financial statement carrying amount and the tax basis of assets and liabilities.

Note 6 (In Part): Income Taxes

Temporary differences that gave rise to deferred tax assets and liabilities as of March 1, 2003, and March 2, 2002, were as follows:

| | 2003 | | 2002 | |
(In thousands)	Deferred Tax Assets	Deferred Tax Liabilities	Deferred Tax Assets	Deferred Tax Liabilities
Depreciation and amortization	$ 1,099	$37,153	$ 1,945	$40,574
Prepaid pension assets	—	32,128	—	28,425
Accrued expenses	20,750	1,429	19,718	561
Inventory valuation methods	1,485	—	1,557	—
Provision for losses on receivables	461	—	845	—
Deferred income	902	—	—	—
Loss carryforwards	47,997	—	11,738	—
Alternative minimum tax credit carryforward	2,615	—	2,615	—
Foreign tax credit carryforward	953	—	953	—
Other	3,025	240	3,665	1,569
Subtotal	79,287	70,950	43,036	71,129
Valuation allowance	(11,460)	—	(1,594)	—
Total deferred taxes	$ 67,827	$70,950	$41,442	$71,129

At March 1, 2003, we had a U.S. federal consolidated net operating loss carryforward of approximately $100 million that will expire in fiscal 2022 and 2023. Our foreign operations had a net operating loss carryforward of approximately $2.7 million that will expire in fiscal 2009 and 2010. We expect to fully utilize these operating loss carryforwards.

At March 1, 2003, we had a U.S. federal consolidated capital loss carryforward of approximately $15 million that will expire in fiscal 2008. Our foreign operations had a capital loss carryforward of approximately $1.5 million that has no expiration date. We have a valuation allowance of approximately $5.3 million and $0.6 million, respectively, for the U.S. and foreign capital loss carryforwards due to the uncertainty over our ability to utilize the capital losses. This represents an increase of approximately $5.3 million over fiscal 2002, and was recognized in discontinued operations.

We have approximately $1 million in U.S. foreign tax credit carryforwards that will expire by fiscal 2006. We have a valuation allowance for the entire $1 million carryforward due to uncertainty over our ability to utilize these credits.

We have U.S. state net operating loss carryforwards that will expire from fiscal 2004 to fiscal 2023. We have established a valuation allowance for approximately $4.6 million for certain of these U.S state net operating loss carryforwards, due to the uncertainty over our ability to utilize these operating loss carryforwards.

●　　●　　●　　●　　●　　●

No provision has been made for U.S. income taxes applicable to remittance of earnings from non-U.S. affiliates. It is not practicable to estimate the remaining deferred tax liability associated with temporary differences related to investments in non-U.S. affiliates. Earnings before income taxes from non-U.S. affiliates were $16.9 million in fiscal 2003, $ 21.6 million in fiscal 2002 and $26.9 million in fiscal 2001.

3.124

IOMEGA CORPORATION (DEC)

NOTES TO CONSOLIDATED FINANCIAL STATEMENTS

1 (In Part): Operations and Significant Accounting Policies

Income Taxes

The Company recognizes liabilities or assets for the deferred tax consequences of temporary differences between the tax bases of assets or liabilities and their reported amounts in the financial statements in accordance with SFAS No. 109, "Accounting for Income Taxes" ("SFAS 109"). These temporary differences will result in taxable or deductible amounts in future years when the reported amounts of the assets or liabilities are recovered or settled.

SFAS 109 requires that a valuation allowance be established when it is more likely than not that all or a portion of a deferred tax asset will not be realized. The Company evaluates the realizability of its net deferred tax assets on a quarterly basis and valuation allowances are provided, as necessary. During this evaluation, the Company reviews its forecasts of income in conjunction with other positive and negative evidence surrounding the realizability of its deferred

tax assets to determine if valuation allowance is needed. Adjustments to the valuation allowance will increase or decrease the Company's income tax provisions.

3 (In Part): Income Taxes

The realizability of the net deferred tax assets is evaluated quarterly in accordance with SFAS 109, which requires that a valuation allowance be established when it is more likely than not that all or a portion of a deferred tax asset will not be realized.

During 2003, the Company established an additional valuation allowance totaling $4.7 million for a portion of its U.S. deferred tax assets primarily related to state net operating loss carryforwards ("NOLs"). After considering its forecasts of taxable income in conjunction with other positive and negative evidence surrounding the realizability of its deferred tax assets, the Company concluded that a partial valuation allowance should be recorded against the net deferred tax assets in the fourth quarter of 2003.

During 2002, the Company's decision to sell its Penang Manufacturing Subsidiary necessitated the recording of a tax provision during the third quarter of 2002 for the Company's foreign earnings that were previously considered permanently invested in non-U.S. operations. This resulted in an additional deferred U.S. tax liability of $39.6 million. This provision was partially offset by the release of $12.8 million of valuation allowance for a net provision of $26.8 million in the third quarter of 2002. The release of the valuation allowance on the U.S. deferred tax assets resulted from the Company no longer being in a net deferred tax asset position. The resulting net deferred tax liability position was primarily due to the $39.6 million provision on the Company's foreign earnings that were previously considered permanently invested in non-U.S. operations.

During 2002, the Company recorded a $29.4 million decrease in the valuation allowance for net deferred tax assets which was comprised of the $12.8 million decrease in valuation allowance described above related to the sale of the Penang Manufacturing Subsidiary and a $16.6 million decrease resulting primarily from a reduction in net deferred tax assets associated with U.S. NOLs. The reduction in NOLs was primarily the result of the passage of the Job Creation and Worker Assistance Act of 2002, which allowed for a 5-year carryback and utilization of a portion of the Company's 2001 tax net operating loss.

During the third quarter of 2001, the Company established a U.S. valuation allowance totaling $28.7 million for a portion of its U.S. deferred tax assets. After considering its forecasts of taxable income in conjunction with the positive and negative evidence surrounding the realizability of its deferred tax assets, the Company concluded that a partial valuation allowance should be recorded against the net deferred tax assets in the third quarter of 2001. The remaining $0.5 million increase in the valuation allowance related to an increase in the foreign net deferred tax assets associated with foreign NOLs.

Deferred tax assets and liabilities are determined based on the differences between the financial reporting and tax bases of assets and liabilities. They are measured by applying the enacted tax rates and laws in effect for the years in which such differences are expected to reverse. The significant components of the Company's deferred tax assets and liabilities are as follows:

(In thousands)	2003	2002
Deferred tax assets (liabilities)		
Current deferred tax assets		
Trade receivable reserves	$ 5,193	$ 11,259
Inventory reserves	3,753	3,042
Accrued expense reserves	10,911	13,030
Other	53	242
Total current deferred tax assets	19,910	27,573
Non-current deferred tax assets		
Fixed asset reserves	370	1,185
Tax credit carryforwards	21,370	19,058
Accelerated depreciation and amortization	4,521	4,301
U.S. and foreign loss carryforwards	38,370	49,643
Other	1,466	884
Total non-current deferred tax assets	66,097	75,071
Total deferred tax assets	86,007	102,644
Non-current deferred tax liabilities		
Tax on unremitted foreign earnings	(73,569)	(109,988)
Purchased goodwill	(4,824)	(4,991)
	(78,393)	(114,979)
Current valuation allowance	(2,120)	—
Non-current valuation allowance	(17,780)	(15,199)
Net deferred tax liabilities	$(12,286)	$ (27,534)
As reported on the balance sheets		
Current deferred tax assets	$ 17,790	$ 27,573
Non-current deferred tax liabilities	$(30,076)	$ (55,107)

The following table summarizes U.S. and foreign loss and tax credit carryforwards as of December 31, 2003:

(In thousands)	Amount	Expiration Dates
U.S. and foreign loss deferred tax assets		
Federal NOLs	$16,595	2022 to 2023
State NOLs	9,281	2004 to 2022
Foreign NOLs	12,021	2004 to 2006
Capital losses	473	2006
	$38,370	
Tax credit deferred tax assets		
Foreign tax credits	$11,226	2005 to indefinite
Research credits	9,584	2007 to 2023
Alternative minimum tax credits	560	Indefinite
	$21,370	

At December 31, 2003, the Company had $16.6 million of deferred tax assets related to U.S. federal NOLs, which reflect a tax benefit of approximately $47 million in future U.S.

federal tax deductions. At December 31, 2003, the Company had $9.3 million of deferred tax assets related to state NOLs, which reflect a tax benefit of approximately $232 million in future state tax deductions. The difference in the amount of future federal and state tax deductions related to the NOLs is largely the result of differences between federal and state NOL carryback rules which have allowed the use of federal NOLs in instances where state NOLs could not be utilized.

Net deferred tax liabilities for the Company at December 31, 2003 were $12.3 million. As of December 31, 2003, deferred tax liabilities for estimated U.S. federal and state taxes of $73.6 million have been accrued on unremitted foreign earnings of $198.8 million. During the third quarter of 2002 taxes were provided on all earnings previously considered to be permanently invested in non-U.S. operations.

3.125

RYERSON TULL, INC. (DEC)

NOTES TO CONSOLIDATED FINANCIAL STATEMENTS

Statement of Accounting and Financial Policies (In Part)

Income Taxes

The Company records operating loss and tax credit carryforwards and the estimated effect of temporary differences between the tax basis of assets and liabilities and the reported amounts in the Consolidated Balance Sheet. The Company follows detailed guidelines in each tax jurisdiction when reviewing tax assets recorded on the balance sheet and provides for valuation allowances as required.

Note 11 (In Part): Income Taxes

The components of the deferred income tax assets and liabilities arising under FASB Statement No. 109 were as follows:

(Dollars in millions)	2003	2002
Deferred tax assets		
AMT tax credit carryforwards	$ 60	$ 56
FASB Statement No. 106 impact (post-retirement benefits other than pensions)	58	58
General business credit carryforwards	1	1
Federal net operating loss carryforwards	14	—
State net operating loss carryforwards	17	13
Bad debt allowances	4	4
Pension liability	37	49
Amortization (goodwill and purchase accounting adjustment)	13	15
Other deductible temporary differences	15	17
Less valuation allowances	(5)	(1)
	214	212
Deferred tax liabilities		
Fixed asset basis difference	47	48
Inventory basis difference	34	30
Other taxable temporary differences	1	2
	82	80
Net deferred tax asset	$132	$132

The Company had available at December 31, 2003, federal AMT credit carryforwards of approximately $60 million, which may be used indefinitely to reduce regular federal income taxes. The Company had available at December 31, 2003, federal net operating loss ("NOL") carryforwards of approximately $14 million which expire during the years 2022 and 2023. The Company also had other federal general business credit carryforwards for tax purposes of approximately $1 million, which expire during the years 2004 through 2009. The Company believes that it is more likely than not that all of its federal tax credits and NOL's will be realized.

At December 31, 2003, the deferred tax asset related to the Company's post-retirement benefits other than pensions ("FASB Statement No. 106 obligation") was $58 million. At December 31, 2003, the Company also had a deferred tax asset related to the Company's pension liability of $37 million. To the extent that future annual charges under FASB Statement No. 106 and the pension expense continue to exceed amounts deductible for tax purposes, this deferred tax asset will continue to grow. Thereafter, even if the Company should have a tax loss in any year in which the deductible amount would exceed the financial statement expense, the tax law provides for a 20-year carryforward period of that loss. Because of the long period that is available to realize these future tax benefits and the long-term nature of the related liabilities, these items are treated as having an indefinite reversal period and a valuation allowance for this deferred tax asset is not considered necessary.

The Company had $17 million of state NOL carryforwards available at December 31, 2003. The deferred tax asset for state NOL carryforwards as reviewed for recoverability based on historical taxable income, the expected reversals of existing temporary differences, tax planning strategies, and, most importantly, on projections of future taxable income. As a result of its analysis, the Company recorded an additional valuation allowance of $4.5 million in the current year as part of its income tax provision. The cumulative valuation allowance of $5.1 million as of December 31, 2003 relates to the NOL's for thirteen specific state and local jurisdictions. Ten of these jurisdictions have a 3–5 year carryforward period, and all of the NOL's associated with these ten jurisdictions have been included in the valuation allowance. In addition, a significant portion of the NOL's for an additional three jurisdictions have been included in the valuation allowance to the extent that the Company does not expect to be able to utilize all of these specific NOL's prior to their expiration in 2015–2023.

TAXES ON UNDISTRIBUTED EARNINGS

3.126 *SFAS No. 109* requires, except in certain specified situations, that undistributed earnings of a subsidiary included in consolidated income be accounted for as a temporary difference. If a deferred tax liability is not recognized, paragraph 44 of *SFAS No. 109* specifies what information should be disclosed. Examples of disclosures concerning undistributed earnings follow.

3.127

AMGEN INC. (DEC)

NOTES TO CONSOLIDATED FINANCIAL STATEMENTS

5 (In Part): Income Taxes

The Company does not provide for U.S. income taxes on undistributed earnings of its foreign operations that are intended to be permanently reinvested. At December 31, 2003, these earnings amounted to approximately $1,185 million. If these earnings were repatriated to the United States, the Company would be required to accrue and pay approximately $421 million of additional taxes based on the current tax rates in effect. For the years ended December 31, 2003 and 2002, the Company's total foreign profits before income taxes were approximately $956 million and $360 million, respectively. For the year ended December 31, 2001, foreign profits before income taxes were not material.

3.128

THE LUBRIZOL CORPORATION (DEC)

NOTES TO FINANCIAL STATEMENTS

Note 10 (In Part): Income Taxes

U.S. income taxes and foreign withholding taxes are not provided on undistributed earnings of foreign subsidiaries, which are considered to be indefinitely reinvested in the operations of such subsidiaries. The amount of these earnings was approximately $500.6 million at December 31, 2003. Determination of the net amount of unrecognized U.S. income tax with respect to these earnings is not practicable.

3.129

METRO-GOLDWYN-MAYER INC. (DEC)

NOTES TO CONSOLIDATED FINANCIAL STATEMENTS

Note 9 (In Part): Income Taxes

The Company has various foreign subsidiaries formed or acquired to produce or distribute motion pictures outside the United States. In the opinion of management, the earnings of these subsidiaries are not permanently invested outside the United States. Pursuant to APB Opinion No. 23, "Accounting For Income Taxes—Special Areas," tax expense has accordingly been provided for these unremitted earnings.

3.130

POLYONE CORPORATION (DEC)

NOTES TO CONSOLIDATED FINANCIAL STATEMENTS

Note Q (In Part): Income Taxes

PolyOne had provided for U.S. federal and foreign withholding tax on $22.0 million, or 9%, of foreign subsidiaries' undistributed earnings as of December 31, 2003. Regarding the undistributed earnings on which no federal and foreign withholding tax has been provided, earnings are intended to be re-invested indefinitely. It is not practicable to determine the amount of income tax liability that would result had such earnings actually been repatriated.

LONG-TERM CONTRACTS

3.131 Accounting and disclosure requirements for long-term contracts are discussed in ARB No. 43, Chapter 11, *Government Contracts*, ARB No. 45, *Long-Term Construction-Type Contracts*, and American Institute of Certified Public Accountants (AICPA) Statement of Position (SOP) 81-1, *Accounting for Performance of Construction-Type and Certain Production-Type Contracts.*

3.132 Table 3-15 shows that usually the percentage of completion method or a modification of this method, the units-of-delivery method is used to recognize revenue on long-term contracts. 17 companies used both of the aforementioned methods. Examples of disclosure for long-term contracts follow.

3.133

TABLE 3-15: METHOD OF ACCOUNTING FOR LONG-TERM CONTRACTS

	Number of Companies			
	2003	2002	2001	2000
Percentage-of-completion.....	78	82	80	71
Units-of-delivery....................	32	26	21	19
Completed contract................	9	5	3	5

3.134

THE BOEING COMPANY (DEC)

NOTES TO CONSOLIDATED FINANCIAL STATEMENTS (Dollars in millions)

Note 1 (In Part): Summary of Significant Accounting Policies

Revenue Recognition (In Part)

Contract Accounting
Contract accounting is used predominately by the segments within Integrated Defense Systems (IDS). The majority of business conducted in these segments is performed under contracts with the U.S. Government and foreign governments that extend over a number of years. Contract accounting involves a judgmental process of estimating the total sales and costs for each contract, which results in the development of estimated cost of sales percentages. For each sale contract, the amount reported as cost of sales is determined by applying the estimated cost of sales percentage to the amount of revenue recognized.

Sales related to contracts with fixed prices are recognized as deliveries are made, except for certain fixed-price contracts that require substantial performance over an extended period before deliveries begin, for which sales are recorded based on the attainment of performance milestones. Sales related to contracts in which we are reimbursed for costs incurred plus an agreed upon profit are recorded as costs are incurred. Contracts may contain provisions to earn incentive and award fees if targets are achieved. Incentive and award fees that can be reasonably estimated are recorded over the performance period of the contract. Incentive and award fees that cannot be reasonably estimated are recorded when awarded.

Program Accounting

We use program accounting to account for sales and cost of sales related to our 7-series commercial airplane programs. Program accounting is a method of accounting applicable to products manufactured for delivery under production-type contracts where profitability is realized over multiple contracts and years. Under program accounting, inventoriable production costs (including overhead), program tooling costs and warranty costs are accumulated and charged as cost of sales by program instead of by individual units or contracts. A program consists of the estimated number of units (accounting quantity) of a product to be produced in a continuing, long-term production effort for delivery under existing and anticipated contracts. To establish the relationship of sales to cost of sales, program accounting requires estimates of (a) the number of units to be produced and sold in a program, (b) the period over which the units can reasonably be expected to be produced, and (c) the units' expected sales prices, production costs, program tooling, and warranty costs for the total program.

We recognize sales for commercial airplane deliveries as each unit is completed and accepted by the customer. Sales recognized represent the price negotiated with the customer, adjusted by an escalation formula. The amount reported as cost of sales is determined by applying the estimated cost of sales percentage for the total remaining program to the amount of sales recognized for airplanes delivered and accepted by the customer during the quarter.

Note 7—Accounts Receivable

Accounts receivable at December 31 consisted of the following:

	2003	2002
U.S. Government contracts	$2,493	$2,860
Commercial and customers	866	1,478
Other	1,251	780
Less valuation allowance	(95)	(111)
	$4,515	$5,007

The following table summarizes our accounts receivable under U.S. Government contracts that were not billable or related to outstanding claims as of December 31:

	2003	2002
Unbillable		
Current	$287	$340
Expected to be collected after one year	289	482
	$576	$822
Claims		
Current	$ 2	$ 7
Expected to be collected after one year	23	31
	$ 25	$ 38

Unbillable receivables on U.S. Government contracts arise when the sales or revenues based on performance attainment, though appropriately recognized, cannot be billed yet under terms of the contract. Accounts receivable related to claims are items that we believe are earned, but are subject to uncertainty concerning their determination or ultimate realization.

As of December 31, 2003 and 2002, other accounts receivable included $602 and $474 of reinsurance receivables relating to Astro Ltd., a wholly-owned subsidiary, that operates as a captive insurance company. Currently, Astro Ltd. insures aviation liability, workers compensation, general liability, property, as well as various other smaller risk liability insurances.

As of December 31, 2003 and 2002, amounts due to us pending contract completion amounted to $68 and $195.

Note 8—Inventories

Inventories at December 31 consisted of the following:

	2003	2002
Long-term contracts in progress	$ 10,117	$ 9,790
Commercial aircraft programs	6,448	7,379
Commercial spare parts, used aircraft, general stock materials and other, net of reserves	2,707	2,713
	19,272	19,882
Less advances and progress billings	(13,934)	(13,698)
	$ 5,338	$ 6,184

As a normal course of our Commercial Airplanes segment production process, our inventory may include a small quantity of airplanes that are completed but unsold. As of December 31, 2003 the value of completed but unsold aircraft in inventory was insignificant. As of December 31, 2002 these aircraft were valued at $246. Inventory balances included $233 subject to claims or other uncertainties primarily relating to the A-12 program as of December 31, 2003 and 2002.

Commercial aircraft inventory production costs incurred on in-process and delivered units in excess of the estimated average cost of such units determined as described in Note 1 represent deferred production costs. As of December 31, 2003 and 2002, there were no significant excess deferred production costs or unamortized tooling costs not recoverable from existing firm orders for the 777 program. The deferred production costs and unamortized tooling included in the 777 program's inventory at December 31 are summarized in the following table:

	2003	2002
Deferred production costs	$837	$785
Unamortized tooling	582	709

During the years ended December 31, 2003 and 2002, we purchased $746 and $706 of used aircraft. Used aircraft in inventory totaled $819 and $506 as of December 31, 2003 and 2002.

When we are unable to immediately sell used aircraft, we may place the aircraft on operating leases, or finance the sale of new aircraft with a short-term note receivable. The net change in the carrying amount of aircraft on operating lease, or sales financed under a note receivable, totaled $144 and $139 as of December 31, 2003 and 2002, and resulted in a decrease to Inventory and an offsetting increase to Customer and commercial financing. These changes in the Consolidated Statements of Financial Position are non-cash transactions and, therefore, are not reflected in the Consolidated Statements of Cash Flows.

The U.S. Government is currently reviewing the USAF proposal for the purchase/lease combination of 100 767 Tankers. If approved, delivery of the pre-modified aircraft from Commercial Airplanes to IDS is scheduled to begin in 2004. In order to meet the USAF's proposed schedule for delivery of 100 767 Tankers, we have incurred significant development costs and inventoriable contract costs. These inventoriable costs are being deferred based on our assessment that it is probable the contract will be received. As of December 31, 2003, the Commercial aircraft programs and Long-term contracts in progress categories above contained $113 (Commercial Airplanes) and $35 (IDS) related to the USAF tanker inventoriable precontract costs.

3.135

GRIFFON CORPORATION (SEP)

NOTES TO CONSOLIDATED FINANCIAL STATEMENTS

1. (In Part): Summary of Significant Accounting Policies

Revenue Recognition

Sales are generally recorded as products are shipped and title and risk of ownership have passed to customers.

The Electronic Information and Communication Systems segment records sales and gross profits on its long-term contracts on a percentage-of-completion basis. The percentage of completion method is used for those construction-type contracts where the performance is anticipated to take more than one year. Contract claims are recognized in revenue to the extent of costs incurred when their amounts can be reliably estimated and realization is probable. The company determines sales and gross profits by relating costs incurred to current estimates of total manufacturing costs of such contracts. General and administrative expenses are expensed as incurred. Revisions in estimated profits are made in the period in which the circumstances requiring the revision become known. Provisions are made currently for anticipated losses on uncompleted contracts.

"Contract costs and recognized income not yet billed" consists of recoverable costs and accrued profit on long-term contracts for which billings had not been presented to the customers because the amounts were not billable at the balance sheet date, net of progress payments of $985,000 and $5,325,000 at September 30, 2003 and 2002, respectively. Amounts become billable when applicable contractual terms are met. Such terms vary, and include the achievement of specified milestones, product delivery and stipulated progress payments. Substantially all such amounts will be billed and collected within one year.

3.136

JOY GLOBAL INC. (OCT)

NOTES TO CONSOLIDATED FINANCIAL STATEMENTS

3 (In Part): Significant Accounting Policies

Revenue Recognition

Revenue is generally recognized upon shipment of products (when title and risk and reward of ownership are transferred to the customer), or upon completion of service provided. We recognize revenue on long-term contracts, such as the manufacture of mining shovels, draglines and roof support systems, using either the percentage-of-completion or completed contract methods. Percentage-of-completion sales and gross profits are recognized as work is performed based on the relationship between actual costs incurred and total estimated costs at completion. When using the percentage-of-completion method, sales and gross profit are adjusted prospectively for revisions in estimated total contract costs and contract values. Losses, if any, are recognized in full when identified. Provisions for warranty expense are based upon experience and recorded in the period that the related revenue is recognized.

We have life cycle management contracts with customers to supply parts and service for terms of 1 to 13 years. These contracts are set up based on the projected costs and revenues of servicing the respective machines over the specified contract terms. Revenue is recognized in the period in which parts are supplied or services provided.

8. Accounts Receivable

Consolidated accounts receivable consisted of the following:

(In thousands)	2003	2002
Trade receivables	$176,428	$158,669
Unbilled receivables (due within one year)	25,099	20,519
Allowance for doubtful accounts	(7,645)	(7,654)
	$193,882	$171,534

3.137

ROCKWELL COLLINS, INC. (SEP)

NOTES TO CONSOLIDATED FINANCIAL STATEMENTS

2 (In Part): Significant Accounting Policies

Revenue Recognition

The Company enters into sales arrangements that include multiple deliverables as defined in Emerging Issues Task Force (EITF) Issue No. 00-21, *Accounting for Revenue Arrangements with Multiple Deliverables*. Effective July 1, 2003, the Company identifies all goods and/or services that are to be delivered separately under a sales arrangement and allocates revenue to each deliverable based on fair value. In general, revenues are separated between hardware, maintenance services, and installation services. The allocated revenue for each deliverable is then recognized using appropriate revenue recognition methods.

The Company recognizes sales for most products or services when all of the following criteria are met: an agreement of sale exists, product delivery and acceptance has occurred or services have been rendered, pricing is fixed or determinable, and collection is reasonably assured.

Sales related to long-term separately priced product maintenance or warranty contracts are accounted for in accordance with the terms of the underlying agreements. Certain contracts are fixed price contracts with sales recognized ratably over the contractual life, while other contracts have a fixed hourly rate with sales recognized based on actual labor or flight hours incurred. The cost providing these services is expensed as incurred.

Sales related to certain other long-term contracts requiring development and delivery of products over several years are accounted for under the percentage-of-completion method of accounting under the American Institute of Certified Public Accountants' Statement of Position 81-1, *Accounting for Performance of Construction-Type and Certain Production-Type Contracts* (SOP 81-1). Sales and earnings under these contracts are recorded either as products are shipped under the units-of-delivery method (for production effort), or based on the ratio of actual costs incurred to total estimated costs expected to be incurred related to the contract under the cost-to-cost method (for development effort). Sales and costs related to profitable purchase options are included in estimates only when the options are exercised while sales and costs related to unprofitable purchase options are included in estimates when exercise is determined to be probable. Change orders are accounted for either as an integral part of the original contract or separately depending upon the nature and value of the item. Sales related to change orders are included in profit estimates only if they can be reliably estimated and collectibility is reasonably assured. Anticipated losses on contracts are recognized in full in the period in which losses become probable and estimable. Changes in estimates of profit or loss on contracts are included in earnings on a cumulative basis in the period the estimate is changed.

4. Receivables

Receivables are summarized as follows:

(In millions)	2003	2002
Billed	$ 460	$ 445
Unbilled	200	154
Less progress payments	(118)	(64)
Total	542	535
Less allowance for doubtful accounts	(17)	(16)
Receivables	$ 525	$ 519

Unbilled receivables principally represent sales recorded under the percentage-of-completion method of accounting that are billed to customers in accordance with applicable contract terms.

5. Inventories

Inventories are summarized as follows:

(In millions)	2003	2002
Finished goods	$155	$168
Work in process	215	211
Raw materials, parts, and supplies	322	333
Total	692	712
Less progress payments	(74)	(59)
Inventories	$618	$653

In accordance with industry practice, inventories include amounts which are not expected to be realized within one year. These amounts primarily relate to life-time buy inventory, which is inventory that is typically no longer being produced by the Company's vendors but for which multiple years of supply are purchased in order to meet production and service requirements over the life span of a product. Life-time buy inventory was $106 million and $86 million at September 30, 2003 and 2002, respectively.

DISCONTINUED OPERATIONS

3.138 APB Opinion No. 30, *Reporting the Results of Operations—Reporting the Effects of Disposal of a Segment of a Business, and Extraordinary, Unusual and Infrequently Occurring Events and Transactions*, addresses the financial accounting and reporting requirements for a segment of a business accounted for as a discontinued operation. Under *APB Opinion No. 30*, discontinued operations were reported separately from continuing operations.

3.139 Effective for fiscal years beginning after December 15, 2001, with early application encouraged, SFAS No. 144, *Accounting for the Impairment or Disposal of Long-Lived Assets*, supersedes the accounting and reporting provisions of *APB Opinion No. 30*. Paragraphs 41–44 of *SFAS No. 144* set forth the reporting for discontinued operations.

3.140 While retaining the basic provisions of APB Opinion No. 30 for the presentation of discontinued operations, the statement broadens the presentation to include a component

of an entity (rather than a segment of a business). A component of an entity comprises operations and cash flows that can be clearly distinguished, operationally and for financial reporting purposes, from the rest of the entity. A component of an entity may be a reportable segment or operating segment (as defined by SFAS No. 131, *Disclosures about Segments of an Enterprise and Related Information*), a reporting entity (as defined by SFAS No. 142, *Goodwill and Other Intangible Assets*), or an asset group (as defined by paragraph 4 of *SFAS No. 144*).

3.141 *SFAS No. 144* uses a single accounting model, based on the framework established in SFAS No. 121, *Accounting for Impairment of Long-Lived Assets and for Long-Lived Assets to be Disposed Of*, to account for all long-lived assets to be disposed of (by sale, abandonment, or a distribution to owners). This includes asset disposal groups meeting the criteria for presentation as a discontinued operation as specified in paragraph 43 of *SFAS No. 144*. A long-lived asset group classified as held for sale shall be measured at the lower of its carrying amount or fair value less cost to sell. Additionally, in accordance with paragraph 37 of *SFAS No. 144*, a loss shall be recognized for any write-down to fair value less cost to sell. A gain shall be recognized for any subsequent recovery of cost. Lastly, a gain or loss not previously recognized that results from the sale of the asset disposal group should be recognized at the date of sale. Therefore, discontinued operations are no longer measured on a net realizable value basis, and future operating losses are no longer recognized before they occur.

3.142 The conditions for determining whether discontinued operation treatment is appropriate and the required income statement presentation are stated in paragraphs 42 and 43 of *SFAS No. 144* as follows:

42. The results of operations of a component of an entity that either has been disposed of or is classified as held for sale shall be reported in discontinued operations in accordance with paragraph 43 if both of the following conditions are met: (a) the operations and cash flow of the component have been (or will be) eliminated from the ongoing operations of the enterprise as a result of the disposal transaction and (b) the entity will not have any significant continuing involvement in the operations of the component after the disposal transaction.

43. In a period in which a component of an entity either has been disposed of or is classified as held for sale, the income statement of a business enterprise for current and prior periods shall report the results of operations of the component, including any gain or loss recognized in accordance with paragraph 37, in discontinued operations. The results of operations of a component classified as held for sale shall be reported in discontinued operations in the period(s) in which they occur. The results of discontinued operations, less applicable income taxes (benefit), shall be reported as a separate component of income before extraordinary items and the cumulative effect of accounting changes (if applicable). For example, the results of discontinued

operations may be reported in the income statement of a business enterprise as follows:

Income from continuing operations before income taxes	$XXXX	
Provision for income taxes	XXX	
Income from continuing operations		$XXXX
Discontinued operations (Note—):		
Loss from operations of component X (including loss on disposal of $—)		$XXXX
Income tax benefit		XXXX
Loss on discontinued operations		XXXX
Net income		$XXXX

A gain or loss recognized on the disposal shall be disclosed either on the face of the income statement or in the notes to the financial statements.

3.143 Illustrations of transactions which should and should not be accounted for as business segment disposals are presented in FASB *Accounting Standards—Current Text*, Section I13, *Income Statement Presentation: Discontinued Operations*.

3.144 In 2003, 92 survey companies discontinued or planned to discontinue the operations of a component of an entity. 73 of the survey companies reported a gain or loss recognized on the disposal of a component of an entity. 45 of those survey companies presented the disposal gain or loss on the face of the income statement. Examples of discontinued operations accounted for separately from continuing operations follow.

Business Component Disposals

3.145

GENERAL MOTORS CORPORATION (DEC)

(Dollars in millions)	2003	2002	2001
Income from continuing operations before income taxes, equity income and minority interests	$ 2,981	$ 2,338	$ 2,454
Income tax expense	731	644	1,094
Equity income (loss) and minority interests	612	281	(138)
Income from continuing operations	2,862	1,975	1,222
(Loss) from discontinued operations (Note 2)	(219)	(239)	(621)
Gain on sale of discontinued operations	1,179	—	—
Net income	$ 3,822	$ 1,736	$ 601

NOTES TO CONSOLIDATED FINANCIAL STATEMENTS

Note 2. Discontinued Operations

On December 22, 2003 GM completed a series of transactions that resulted in the split-off of Hughes from GM and the simultaneous sale of GM's approximately 19.8% economic interest in Hughes to the News Corporation, Ltd. (News Corporation).

In the transactions, GM split off Hughes by distributing Hughes common stock to the holders of GM Class H common stock in exchange for all outstanding shares of GM Class H common stock. Simultaneously, GM sold its 19.8% economic interest in Hughes to News Corporation in exchange for cash and News Corporation Preferred American Depositary Shares (Preferred ADSs). All shares of GM Class H common stock were then cancelled. News Corporation then acquired from the former GM Class H common stockholders an additional 14.2% of the outstanding shares of Hughes common stock in exchange for News Corporation Preferred ADSs.

GM sold 80 percent of its 19.8% retained economic interest in Hughes to News Corporation for a total of approximately $3.1 billion in cash. GM sold the remaining 20% of its retained economic interest in Hughes to News Corporation for approximately 28.6 million News Corporation Preferred ADSs, valued at $819 million at December 22, 2003. Including Hughes' transaction expenses of approximately $90 million, GM recorded a net gain of $1.2 billion from the sale of GM's approximately 19.8% economic interest in Hughes, reported as gain on sale of discontinued operations in GM's Consolidated Statement of Income for 2003. In addition, as a result of the transactions, there was a net reduction to GM's stockholders' equity of approximately $7.0 billion.

All News Corporation Preferred ADSs were sold by GM in January 2004.

The financial data related to GM's investment in Hughes through December 22, 2003 is classified as discontinued operations for all periods presented. The financial data of Hughes reflect the historical results of operations and cash flows of the businesses that were considered part of the Hughes business segment of GM during each respective period, and the assets and liabilities of Hughes as of the respective dates.

Hughes' net sales included in discontinued operations were $9.8 billion, $9.5 billion, and $8.3 billion for 2003, 2002, and 2001, respectively, and Hughes' net losses from discontinued operations were $219 million, $239 million, and $621 million for 2003, 2002, and 2001, respectively.

The Hughes amounts reported as assets and liabilities of discontinued operations were as follows (in millions):

	2002
Current assets	$ 3,670
Property and equipment—net	1,558
Intangible assets	7,158
Other assets	6,267
Assets of discontinued operations	$18,653
Current liabilities	$ 3,177
Long-term debt	2,390
Other liabilities	2,389
Liabilities of discontinued operations	$ 7,956

3.146

MEDIA GENERAL, INC. (DEC)

(In thousands)	2003	2002	2001
Income from continuing operations before income taxes and cumulative effect of change in accounting principle	$ 93,846	$ 85,986	$ 28,603
Income taxes	34,800	33,944	12,170
Income from continuing operations before cumulative effect of change in accounting principle	59,046	52,042	16,433
Discontinued operations			
Income from discontinued operations (net of income taxes of $551 in 2003, $787 in 2002, and $852 in 2001)	964	1,377	1,491
Gain on sale of operations (net of income taxes of $3,860 in 2003 and $160 in 2001)	6,754	—	280
Cumulative effect of change in accounting principle (net of income tax benefit of $3,420 in 2003 and $12,188 in 2002)	(8,079)	(126,336)	—
Net income (loss)	$ 58,685	$ (72,917)	$ 18,204

NOTES TO CONSOLIDATED FINANCIAL STATEMENTS

Note 3 (In Part): Acquisitions, Dispositions and Discontinued Operations

In October 2003, the Company sold Media General Financial Services, Inc. (MGFS), a component of its Interactive Media Division, to CenterPoint Data, Inc. The Company recorded an after-tax gain of $6.8 million (net of income taxes of $3.9 million). The following results of MGFS have been presented as income from discontinued operations in the accompanying consolidated statements of operations:

(In thousands)	2003	2002	2001
Revenues	$ 3,854	$ 5,218	$ 5,556
Costs and expenses	2,339	3,054	3,213
Income before income taxes	1,515	2,164	2,343
Income taxes	551	787	852
Income from discontinued operations	$ 964	$ 1,377	$ 1,491

In September 2000 the Company sold Garden State Paper (GSP) to an affiliate of Enron North America Corporation; a favorable adjustment resulted in a gain of $280 thousand which was reported in discontinued operations in the third quarter of 2001.

3.147

UNOVA, INC. (DEC)

(Thousands of dollars)	2003	2002	2001
Earnings (loss) from continuing operations before income taxes	$ 1,331	$15,599	$(284,995)
Provision for income taxes	12,400	7,996	2,516
Earnings (loss) from continuing operations	(11,069)	7,603	(287,511)
Loss from discontinued operations, net of tax	(8,198)	(5,176)	(4,673)
Net earnings (loss)	$(19,267)	$ 2,427	$(292,184)

NOTES TO CONSOLIDATED FINANCIAL STATEMENTS

Note O: Loss From Discontinued Operations, Net of Tax

During the third quarter 2003, in conjunction with the consolidation plan described in Note G, the Company sold substantially all the assets and existing backlog of its Lamb Body & Assembly Systems division for approximately the book value of the divested assets. The Company received $12.8 million in 2003 and retained $9.9 million in accounts payable. The division meets the definition of a "component of and entity" and has been accounted for as a discontinued operation under Statement of Financial Accounting Standards No. 144, "Accounting for the Impairment or Disposal of Long-Lived Assets," ("SFAS No. 144"). The results of operations for this division have been classified as discontinued operations in all periods presented.

Sales and Service Revenue from discontinued operations was $32.7 million, $47.1 million and $100.5 million for the years ended December 31, 2003, 2002 and 2001, respectively. Losses from discontinued operations were $8.2 million for the year ended December 31, 2003, including a $3.1 million pretax loss on disposal. Losses from discontinued operations were $5.2 million and $4.7 million for the years ended December 31, 2002 and 2001, respectively. Losses from discontinued operations are net of tax benefits of $4.4 million, $2.8 million and $2.5 million for the years ended December 31, 2003, 2002 and 2001, respectively.

The Company's consolidated balance sheet as of December 31, 2003 includes $3.7 million in current assets, including $1.8 million of net property, plant and equipment classified as assets held for sale, and $7.0 million in current liabilities pertaining to discontinued operations. The Company's consolidated balance sheet as of December 31, 2002 includes $25.5 million in current assets, $6.3 million of net property, plant and equipment, and $12.0 million in current liabilities pertaining to discontinued operations.

Adjustment of Gain/Loss Reported in Prior Period

3.148

COHERENT, INC. (SEP)

(In thousands)	2003	2002	2001
Income (loss) from continuing operations before income taxes and minority interest	$(57,414)	$(97,582)	$ 43,182
Provision (benefit) for income taxes	(6,640)	(27,172)	15,156
Income (loss) from continuing operations before minority interest	(50,774)	(70,410)	28,026
Minority interest in subsidiaries' (earnings) losses	4,241	(427)	(541)
Income (loss) from continuing operations	(46,533)	(70,837)	27,485
Discontinued operations, net of income taxes (note 3)			
Gain on disposal of Medical segment	642	1,869	74,690
Income (loss) from discontinued Medical segment	—	—	(1,479)
Income (loss) before accounting changes	(45,891)	(68,968)	100,696
Cumulative effect of accounting change (net of income tax of $36)	—	—	54
Net income (loss)	$(45,891)	$(68,968)	$100,750

NOTES TO CONSOLIDATED FINANCIAL STATEMENTS

2 (In Part): Significant Accounting Policies

Discontinued Operations

On April 30, 2001, we completed the sale of our Medical segment to Lumenis, Ltd. (formerly ESC Medical Systems, Ltd.). The disposal of the Medical segment represents the disposal of a business segment under Accounting Principles Board Opinion No. 30, "Reporting the Results of Operations—Reporting the Effects of Disposal of a Segment of a Business, and Extraordinary, Unusual and Infrequently Occurring Events and Transactions" (APB 30). Accordingly, results of the operations of our Medical segment have been classified as discontinued (see Note 3).

3. Discontinued Operations

On February 25, 2001, we entered into a definitive agreement to sell our Medical segment to Lumenis, Ltd. (formerly ESC Medical Systems Ltd.). On April 30, 2001, we completed the sale of the Medical segment assets for cash of $100.0 million, notes receivable of $12.9 million and 5,432,099 shares of Lumenis common stock. We estimated the total value of this consideration to be $236.0 million as of the closing of the sale. The agreement provided additional cash consideration up to $6.0 million if the actual net tangible assets sold were more than a predetermined amount and a note receivable reduction if the actual net tangible assets sold were less than a predetermined amount. In fiscal 2001, we recognized a gain of $71.8 million (net of taxes of $44.7 million), inclusive of $12.6 million in stock compensation charges due to the acceleration of stock option vesting, on our sale of the Medical segment. In fiscal 2002, we reached a purchase price settlement with Lumenis, resulting in a gain of $1.9 million (net of income taxes of $1.2 million), which was included in our results of discontinued operations in fiscal 2002. In addition, the agreement provides a future earnout payment of up to $25.0 million based on the future sales of certain Medical laser and light-based products through December 31, 2004. In fiscal 2003, we recorded a net benefit of $0.6 million relating to the anticipated refund of prior year taxes.

The face value of the note received was $12.9 million, bearing interest at 5% payable semi-annually over its 18-month term and was due on October 30, 2002. At April 30, 2001, we recorded the note at its fair value of $11.6 million and amortized the discount to interest income over the term of the note. In October 2002, we renegotiated the terms of our note receivable from Lumenis (see Note 8). The Lumenis common stock received is unregistered and its trading is subject to restrictions under Rule 144 of the Securities Act of 1933 and other contractual restrictions as defined in the definitive agreement. At April 30, 2001, we estimated the value of the Lumenis stock at $124.4 million (see Note 6 concerning the subsequent writedown of this investment).

The results of the operations of the Medical segment have been classified as discontinued in the accompanying consolidated financial statements. Income from discontinued operations consisted of the following (in thousands):

	2003	2002	2001
Net sales	$ —	$ —	$109,219
Loss from operations prior to phase-out period	$ —	—	$ (1,672)
Benefit for income taxes	—	—	(193)
Loss from operations, net	—	—	(1,479)
Gain on disposal	47	3,099	116,576
Provision (benefit) for income taxes on gain	(595)	1,230	44,729
Operating income during phase-out period	—	—	3,888
Provision for income taxes on operating income in phase-out period	—	—	1,045
Gain on disposal, net	642	1,869	74,690
Income from discontinued operations, net	$ 642	$1,869	$ 73,211

CHARGES OR CREDITS SHOWN AFTER INCOME TAX CAPTION

3.149 Table 3-16 indicates the nature of charges or credits, other than extraordinary items, positioned on an income statement after the caption for income taxes applicable to income from continuing operations. An example of a charge/credit shown after the caption for income taxes applicable to income from continuing operations follows.

3.150

TABLE 3-16: CHARGES OR CREDITS SHOWN AFTER INCOME TAX CAPTION

| | Number of Companies | | | |
	2003	2002	2001	2000
Cumulative effect of accounting change	118	179	103	43
Minority interest	101	95	98	91
Equity in earnings or losses of investees	35	38	41	43
Distributions on trust preferred securities	5	4	4	8
Other	2	1	4	3

3.151

PHELPS DODGE CORPORATION (DEC)

(In millions)	2003	2002	2001
Income (loss) before taxes, minority interests, equity in net earnings (losses) of affiliated companies, extraordinary item and cumulative effect of accounting changes	$ 71.4	$(425.0)	$(246.6)
Benefit (provision) for taxes on income	(48.3)	114.9	(77.8)
Minority interests in consolidated subsidiaries	(7.7)	(7.8)	(4.8)
Equity in net earnings (losses) of affiliated companies	2.7	2.7	(0.3)
Income (loss) before extraordinary item and cumulative effect of accounting changes	18.1	(315.2)	(329.5)
Extraordinary gain on acquisition of partner's interest in Chino, net of taxes of $0 in 2003	68.3	—	—
Cumulative effect of accounting changes (net of tax of $(1.3), $10.1 and $0 in 2003, 2002 and 2001, respectively)	8.4	(22.9)	(2.0)
Net income (loss)	$ 94.8	$(338.1)	$(331.5)

EXTRAORDINARY ITEMS

3.152 *APB Opinion No. 30* defines extraordinary items as "events and transactions that are distinguished by their unusual nature and by the infrequency of their occurrence," and states that an event or transaction "should be presumed to be an ordinary and usual activity of the reporting entity, the effects of which should be included in income from operations, unless the evidence clearly supports its classification as an extraordinary item as defined in this Opinion." *APB Opinion No. 30* and related AICPA Accounting Interpretation, *Reporting the Results of Operations*, illustrate events and transactions which should and should not be classified as extraordinary items. These examples are reprinted in FASB *Accounting Standards—Current Text*, Section I17,

Income Statement Presentation: Extraordinary Items. SFAS No. 4, Reporting Gains and Losses From Extinguishment of Debt, specifies that material debt extinguishment gains and losses be classified as extraordinary items. Under *SFAS No. 4*, all gains and losses from extinguishment of debt were required to be aggregated and, if material, classified as an extraordinary item, net of related income tax effect. Effective for fiscal years beginning after May 15, 2002, SFAS No. 145, *Rescission of FASB Statements No. 4, 44, and 64, Amendment of FASB Statement No. 13, and Technical Corrections*, rescinds *SFAS No. 4*. Since the issuance of *SFAS No. 4*, the use of debt extinguishment has become part of the risk management strategy of many companies. *SFAS No. 145* stipulates that only debt extinguishments, which meet the criteria in *APB Opinion No. 30* for classification as extraordinary items, are classified as extraordinary.

3.153   Table 3-17 shows the nature of items classified as extraordinary by the survey companies. As shown in Table 3-17, many of the transactions classified as an extraordinary item in 2003 by the survey companies were debt extinguishments—3 at a gain, 1 at a loss. Examples of the presentation and disclosure of extraordinary items follow.

3.154

TABLE 3-17: EXTRAORDINARY ITEMS

	2003	2002	2001	2000
Nature				
Debt extinguishments............................	4	40	70	48
Other..	8	2	8	7
Total Extraordinary Items.................	**12**	**42**	**78**	**55**
Number of Companies				
Presenting extraordinary items............	12	42	78	55
Not presenting extraordinary items......	588	558	522	545
Total Companies.................................	**600**	**600**	**600**	**600**

Debt Extinguishments

3.155

ALLIANT TECHSYSTEMS INC. (MAR)

(Amounts in thousands)	2003	2002	2001
Income from continuing operations before income taxes	$211,231	$140,876	$103,394
Income tax provision	82,384	53,533	35,473
Minority interest expense, net of income taxes		1,240	
Income from continuing operations	128,847	86,103	67,921
Loss on disposal of discontinued operations, net of income taxes		(4,660)	
Income before extraordinary loss and cumulative effect of change in accounting principle	128,847	81,443	67,921
Extraordinary loss on early extinguishment of debt, net of income taxes	(8,390)	(12,116)	—
Cumulative effect of change in accounting prinicple, net of income taxes	3,830	—	—
Net income	$124,287	$ 69,327	$ 67,921

*NOTES TO CONSOLIDATED FINANCIAL STATEMENTS
(Amounts in thousands)*

7 (In Part): Long-Term Debt and Interest Rate Swaps

Also in May 2001, in connection with the acquisition of Thiokol, ATK entered into senior credit facilities totaling $1,050,000. The senior credit facilities consisted of a six-year revolving credit facility of $250,000, $300,000 six-year Tranche A term loans, and $500,000 eight-year Tranche B term loans. In May 2002, ATK restructured the senior credit facilities, repaying the Tranche B term loans and entering into new seven-year term loans, Tranche C, in the amount of $525,000. The additional debt incurred on the Tranche C term loans was used to finance the purchase of ATK Gun Systems and to cover the approximately $2,000 in debt issuance costs relating to this debt restructure. The debt issuance costs are being amortized to interest expense over the term of the Tranche C term loans. Through March 31, 2003, ATK had paid $100,000 on its Tranche C term loans, of which $95,037 represented prepayments. The senior credit facilities are secured by perfected first priority security interests, subject only to permitted liens, in substantially all of ATK's tangible and intangible assets, including the capital stock of certain of its subsidiaries and are guaranteed by its domestic subsidiaries. All of these guarantor subsidiaries are 100% owned by ATK. Interest charges on the Tranche C term loans are at the London Inter-Bank Offered Rate (LIBOR) plus a fixed rate of 2.25%. As of March 31, 2003, the interest rate on the Tranche C term loans was 7.3% per annum after taking into account the related interest rate swap agreements, which are discussed below. As of March 31, 2003, ATK had no borrowings against its $250,000 bank revolving credit facility and had outstanding letters of credit of $60,932, which reduced amounts available on the revolving facility to $189,068. Of this $189,068, $39,068 may be used exclusively for the issuance of letters of credit and $150,000 may be used for borrowings. Had ATK had an outstanding balance on the revolving credit loans, the interest rate would have been 3.7% per annum. ATK's weighted average interest rate on short-term borrowings was 5.0% during fiscal 2003 and 6.9% during fiscal 2002.

As a result of these financing activities, $8,390 (net of $5,364 in taxes) of debt issuance costs were written off as an extraordinary loss on early extinguishment of debt in fiscal 2003.

Asset Disposals

3.156

UNITED STATES STEEL CORPORATION (DEC)

(Dollars in millions)	2003	2002	2001
Income (loss) before income taxes, extraordinary loss and cumulative effect of change in accounting principle	$(860)	$ 13	$(546)
Income tax benefit	(454)	(48)	(328)
Income (loss) before extraordinary loss and cumulative effect of change in accounting principle	(406)	61	(218)
Extraordinary loss, net of tax (Note 3)	(52)	—	—
Cumulative effect of change in accounting principle, net of tax	(5)	—	—
Net income (loss)	$(463)	$ 61	$(218)

NOTES TO CONSOLIDATED FINANCIAL STATEMENTS

3. Divestiture

On June 30, 2003, U.S. Steel completed the sale of the coal mines and related assets of U. S. Steel Mining Company, LLC (Mining Sale) to PinnOak Resources, LLC (PinnOak), which is not affiliated with U. S. Steel. PinnOak acquired the Pinnacle No. 50 mine complex located near Pineville, West Virginia and the Oak Grove mine complex located near Birmingham, Alabama. In conjuction with the sale, U. S. Steel and PinnOak entered into a long-term coal supply agreement, which runs through December 31, 2006.

The gross proceeds from the sale were $55 million and resulted in a pretax gain on disposal of assets of $13 million in the second quarter of 2003. In addition, EITF 92-13, "Accounting for Estimated Payments in Connection with the Coal Industry Retiree Health Benefit Act of 1992" requires that enterprises no longer having operations in the coal industry must account for their entire obligation related to the multiemployer health care benefit plans created by the Act as a loss in accordance with SFAS No. 5, "Accounting for Contingencies." Accordingly, U. S. Steel recognized the present value of these obligations in the amount of $85 million, resulting in the recognition of an extraordinary loss of $52 million, net of tax of $33 million.

EARNINGS PER SHARE

3.157 Effective for periods ending after December 15, 1997, SFAS No. 128, *Earnings Per Share*, supersedes APB Opinion No. 15, *Earnings Per Share*. The reporting and disclosure requirements of *SFAS No. 128* are stated in paragraphs 36–42. Examples of earnings per share presentations follow.

3.158

IKON OFFICE SOLUTIONS, INC. (SEP)

(In thousands, except per share data)	2003	2002	2001
Income from continuing operations	$116,017	$150,334	$14,005
Discontinued operations, net of taxes of $942	—	—	1,200
Net income	$116,017	$150,334	$15,205
Basic earnings per common share			
Continuing operations	$ 0.80	$ 1.05	$ 0.10
Discontinued operations	—	—	0.01
Net income	$ 0.80	$ 1.05	$ 0.11
Diluted earnings per common share			
Continuing operations	$ 0.75	$ 0.99	$ 0.10
Discontinued operations	—	—	0.01
Net income	$ 0.75	$ 0.99	$ 0.11
Cash dividends per common share	$ 0.16	$ 0.16	$ 0.16

NOTES TO CONSOLIDATED FINANCIAL STATEMENTS

10. Earnings Per Common Share

The following table sets forth the computation of basic and diluted earnings per common share from continuing operations:

(In thousands, except per share data)	2003	2002	2001
Numerator			
Numerator for basic earnings per common share—income from continuing operations	$116,017	$150,334	$ 14,005
Effect of dilutive securities			
Interest expense on Convertible Notes, net of taxes of: 2003—$5,662 and 2002—$2,159	9,338	3,636	—
Numerator for diluted earnings per common share—income from continuing operations plus assumed conversion	$125,355	$153,970	$ 14,005
Denominator			
Denominator for basic earnings per common share—weighted average common shares	145,216	143,178	141,888
Effect of dilutive securities			
Convertible Notes	19,960	7,711	—
Employee stock options	304	3,725	2,272
Employee stock awards	2,322	470	248
Dilutive potential common shares	22,586	11,906	2,520
Denominator for diluted earnings per common share—adjusted weighted shares and assumed conversions	167,802	155,084	144,408
Basic earnings per common share from continuing operations	$ 0.80	$ 1.05	$ 0.10
Diluted earnings per common share from continuing operations	$ 0.75	$ 0.99	$ 0.10

We account for the effect of the Convertible Notes in the diluted earnings per common share calculation using the "if converted" method. Under that method, the Convertible Notes are assumed to be converted to shares (weighted for the number of days outstanding in the period) at a conversion price of $15.03, and interest expense, net of taxes, related to the Convertible Notes is added back to net income.

Options to purchase 8,098, 6,328 and 7,257 shares of common stock were outstanding during fiscal 2003, 2002 and 2001, respectively, but were not included in the computation of diluted earnings per share because the options' exercise prices were greater than the average market price of the common shares and, therefore, the effect would be antidilutive.

3.159

MPS GROUP, INC. (DEC)

(Dollar amounts in thousands except per share amounts)	2003	2002	2001
Income (loss) from continuing operations before cumulative effect of accounting change	$ 21,835	$ (14,002)	$ 2,303
Discontinued operations			
Income (loss) from discontinued operations (net of income taxes of $(1,289), $759, and $3,702, respectively)	(2,395)	1,410	6,040
Loss on disposition of discontinued operations (net of a $11,133 income tax benefit)	(20,675)	—	—
Income (loss) from operations before cumulative effect of accounting change	(1,235)	(12,592)	8,343
Cumulative effect of accounting change (net of a $112,953 income tax benefit)	—	(553,712)	—
Net income (loss)	$ (1,235)	$(566,304)	$ 8,343
Basic net income (loss) per common share			
Income (loss) from continuing operations before cumulative effect of accounting change	$ 0.21	$ (0.14)	$ 0.02
Income (loss) from discontinued operations, net of tax	(0.02)	0.01	0.06
Loss on disposition of discontinued operations, net of tax	(0.20)	—	—
Cumulative effect of accounting change, net of tax	—	(5.49)	—
Basic net income (loss) per common share	$ (0.01)	$ (5.62)	$ 0.09
Average common shares outstanding, basic	101,680	100,833	97,868
Diluted net income (loss) per common share			
Income (loss) from continuing operations before cumulative effect of accounting change	$ 0.21	$ (0.14)	$ 0.02
Income (loss) from discontinued operations, net of tax	(0.02)	0.01	0.06
Loss on disposition of discontinued operations, net of tax	(0.20)	—	—
Cumulative effect of accounting change, net of tax	—	(5.49)	—
Diluted net income (loss) per common share	$ (0.01)	$ (5.62)	$ 0.08
Average common shares outstanding, diluted	104,518	100,833	98,178

NOTES TO CONSOLIDATED FINANCIAL STATEMENTS

2 (In Part): Summary of Significant Accounting Policies

Net Income (Loss) Per Common Share

The consolidated financial statements include "basic" and "diluted" per share information. Basic per share information is calculated by dividing net income by the weighted average number of shares outstanding. Diluted per share information is calculated by also considering the impact of potential common stock on both net income and the weighted average number of shares outstanding. The weighted average number of shares used in the basic earnings per share computations were 101.7 million, 100.8 million, and 97.9 million in 2003, 2002 and 2001, respectively. The only difference in the computation of basic and diluted earnings per share is the inclusion of 2.8 million and 310,000 potential common shares in 2003 and 2001, respectively. As the Company was in loss position for 2002 from continuing operations, before the cumulative effect of an accounting change, the potential common shares for 2002 were excluded from the calculation of diluted earnings per share as the shares would have had an anti-dilutive effect. See Note 10 to the Consolidated Financial Statements.

10. Net Income Per Common Share

The calculation of basic net (loss) income per common share and diluted net (loss) income per common share is presented below:

(Dollar amounts in thousands except per share amounts)	2003	2002	2001
Basic income (loss) per common share computation			
Income (loss) from continuing operations before cumulative effect of accounting change	$ 21,835	$ (14,002)	$ 2,303
Income (loss) from discontinued operations, net of tax	(2,395)	1,410	6,040
Loss on disposition of discontinued operations, net of tax	(20,675)	—	—
Cumulative effect of accounting change, net of tax	—	(553,712)	—
Net income (loss)	$ (1,235)	$(566,304)	$ 8,343
Basic average common shares outstanding	101,680	100,833	97,868
Basic income (loss) per common share			
Income (loss) from continuing operations before cumulative effect of accounting change	$ 0.21	$ (0.14)	$ 0.02
Income (loss) from discontinued operations, net of tax	(0.02)	0.01	0.06
Loss on disposition of discontinued operations, net of tax	(0.20)	—	—
Cumulative effect of accounting change, net of tax	—	(5.49)	—
Basic net income (loss) per common share	$ (0.01)	$ (5.62)	$ 0.09
Diluted income (loss) per common share computation			
Income (loss) from continuing operations before cumulative effect of accounting change	$ 21,835	$ (14,002)	$ 2,303
Income (loss) from discontinued operations, net of tax	(2,395)	1,410	6,040
Loss on disposition of discontinued operations, net of tax	(20,675)	—	—
Cumulative effect of accounting change, net of tax	—	(553,712)	—
Net income (loss)	$ (1,235)	$(566,304)	$ 8,343
Basic average common shares outstanding	101,680	100,833	97,868
Incremental shares from assumed exercise of stock options	2,838	—	310
Diluted average common shares outstanding	104,518	100,833	98,178
Diluted income (loss) per common share			
Income (loss) from continuing operations before cumulative effect of accounting change	$ 0.21	$ (0.14)	$ 0.02
Income (loss) from discontinued operations, net of tax	(0.02)	0.01	0.06
Loss on disposition of discontinued operations, net of tax	(0.20)	—	—
Cumulative effect of accounting change, net of tax	—	(5.49)	—
Diluted net income (loss) per common share	$ (0.01)	$ (5.62)	$ 0.08

Options to purchase 1.6 million, 2.3 million, and 7.8 million shares of common stock that were outstanding during 2003, 2002, and 2001 respectively, were not included in the computation of diluted earnings per share as the exercise prices of these options were greater than the average market price of the common shares.

3.160

PHELPS DODGE CORPORATION (DEC)

(In millions except per share data)	2003	2002	2001
Income (loss) before extraordinary item and cumulative effect of accounting changes	$ 18.1	$(315.2)	$(329.5)
Extraordinary gain on acquisition of partner's interest in Chino, net of taxes of $0 in 2003	68.3	—	—
Cumulative effect of accounting changes (net of tax of $(1.3), $10.1 and $0 in 2003, 2002 and 2001, respectively)	8.4	(22.9)	(2.0)
Net income (loss)	94.8	(338.1)	(331.5)
Preferred stock dividends	(13.5)	(9.1)	—
Net income (loss) applicable to common shares	$ 81.3	$(347.2)	$(331.5)
Weighted average number of common shares outstanding—basic	88.8	84.1	78.5
Basic earnings (loss) per common share before extraordinary item and cumulative effect of accounting changes	$ 0.06	$ (3.86)	$ (4.19)
Extraordinary item	0.77	—	—
Cumulative effect of accounting changes	0.09	(0.27)	(0.03)
Basic earnings (loss) per common share	$ 0.92	$ (4.13)	$ (4.22)
Weighted average number of common shares outstanding—diluted*	89.4	84.1	78.5
Diluted earnings (loss) per common share before extraordinary item and cumulative effect of accounting changes	$ 0.06	$ (3.86)	$ (4.19)
Extraordinary item	0.76	—	—
Cumulative effect of accounting changes	0.09	(0.27)	(0.03)
Diluted earnings (loss) per common share	$ 0.91	$ (4.13)	$ (4.22)

* Diluted earnings (loss) per common share would have been anti-dilutive for the years ended December 31, 2003 and 2002, if based on fully diluted shares adjusted to reflect the conversion of mandatory convertible preferred shares to common shares. Diluted earnings (loss) per common share would have been anti-dilutive for the years ended December 31, 2002 and 2001, if based on fully diluted shares adjusted to reflect stock option exercises.

NOTES TO CONSOLIDATED FINANCIAL STATEMENTS
(Dollar amounts in tables stated in millions except as noted)

1 (In Part): Summary of Significant Accounting Policies

Earnings (Loss) Per Share

Basic earnings (loss) per share are computed by dividing income (loss) available to common shareholders by the weighted average number of common shares outstanding for the period. Diluted earnings (loss) per share are similar to basic earnings per share except that the denominator is increased to include the number of additional common shares that would have been outstanding if the potentially dilutive common shares had been issued, and the numerator excludes dividends. Restricted stock is unvested; accordingly, these shares are only included in the computation of diluted earnings per share as they are only contingent upon vesting.

	2003	2002	2001
Basic earnings (loss) per share computation			
Numerator:			
Net income (loss)	$ 94.8	$(338.1)	$(331.5)
Preferred stock dividends	(13.5)	(9.1)	—
Net income (loss) applicable to common shares	81.3	(347.2)	(331.5)
Denominator:			
Weighted average common shares outstanding	88.8	84.1	78.5
Basic earnings (loss) per common share	$ 0.92	$ (4.13)	$ (4.22)
Diluted earnings (loss) per share computation			
Numerator:			
Net income (loss)	$ 94.8	$(338.1)	$(331.5)
Preferred stock dividends	(13.5)	(9.1)	—
Net income (loss) applicable to common shares	81.3	(347.2)	(331.5)
Denominator:			
Weighted average common shares outstanding	88.8	84.1	78.5
Weighted average employee stock option*	0.4	—	—
Weighted average restricted stock issued to employees	0.2	—	—
Total weighted average common shares outstanding	89.4	84.1	78.5
Diluted earnings (loss) per common shares**	$ 0.91	$ (4.13)	$ (4.22)

* Additional common shares of 0.3 million and 0.2 million in 2002 and 2001, respectively, were anti-dilutive.

** If the conversion of mandatory convertible preferred shares to common shares of 4.7 million shares and 2.8 million shares for the years ended December 31, 2003 and 2002, respectively, were reflected, diluted earnings (loss) per common share of $1.01 and $(3.88), respectively, would have been anti-dilutive.

Stock options excluded from the computation of diluted earnings per share because option exercise prices exceeded the per share market value of our common stock were as follows:

	2003	2002	2001
Outstanding options	6.3	8.9	7.7
Average option exercise price	$61.27	$56.67	$61.91

3.161

RAYTHEON COMPANY (DEC)

(In millions except per share amounts)	2003	2002	2001
Income from continuing operations	$ 535	$ 756	$ 2
Loss from discontinued operations, net of tax	(170)	(887)	(757)
Income (loss) before accounting change	365	(131)	(755)
Cumulative effect of change in accounting principle, net of tax	—	(509)	—
Net income (loss)	$ 365	$ (640)	$ (755)
Earnings per share from continuing operations			
Basic	$1.30	$ 1.88	$ 0.01
Diluted	1.29	1.85	0.01
Earnings (loss) per share			
Basic	$0.88	$(1.59)	$(2.12)
Diluted	0.88	(1.57)	(2.09)

NOTES TO CONSOLIDATED FINANCIAL STATEMENTS

Note A (In Part): Accounting Policies

Impairment of Long-Lived Assets (In Part)

Effective January 1, 2002, the Company adopted Statement of Financial Accounting Standards No. 142, Goodwill and Other Intangible Assets (SFAS No. 142). This accounting standard addresses financial accounting and reporting for goodwill and other intangible assets and requires that goodwill amortization be discontinued and replaced with periodic tests of impairment. A two-step impairment test is used to first identify potential goodwill impairment and then measure the amount of goodwill impairment loss, if any.

In 2002, the Company recorded a goodwill impairment charge of $360 million related to its former Aircraft Integration Systems business (AIS) as a cumulative effect of change in accounting principle. The fair value of AIS was determined based upon the proceeds received by the Company in connection with the sale, as described in Note B, Discontinued Operations. Due to the non-deductibility of this goodwill, the Company did not record a tax benefit in connection with this impairment. Also in 2002, the Company completed the transitional review for potential goodwill impairment in accordance with SFAS No. 142 and recorded a goodwill impairment charge of $185 million pretax or $149 million after-tax, which represented all of the goodwill at Raytheon Aircraft, as a cumulative effect of change in accounting principle. The fair value of Raytheon Aircraft was determined using a discounted cash flow approach. The total goodwill impairment charge in 2002 was $545 million pretax, $509 million after-tax, or $1.25 per diluted share. The Company performs the annual impairment test in the fourth quarter of each year. There was no goodwill impairment associated with the annual impairment test performed in the fourth quarter of 2003 and 2002.

Note B (In Part): Discontinued Operations

In 2003, the total loss from discontinued operations was $261 million pretax, $170 million after-tax, or $0.41 per diluted share versus $1,013 million pretax, $887 million after-tax, or $2.17 per diluted share in 2002 and $1,138 million pretax, $757 million after-tax, or $2.10 per diluted share in 2001.

Note K (In Part): Stockholders' Equity

Basic earnings per share (EPS) is computed by dividing net income by the weighted-average shares outstanding during the period. Diluted EPS reflects the potential dilution that could occur if securities or other contracts to issue common stock were exercised or converted into common stock or resulted in the issuance of common stock that then shared in the earnings of the entity.

The weighted-average shares outstanding for basic and diluted EPS were as follows:

(In thousands)	2003	2002	2001
Average common shares outstanding for basic EPS	412,686	401,444	356,717
Dilutive effect of stock options, restricted stock, and equity security units	2,743	6,587	4,606
Shares for diluted EPS	415,429	408,031	361,323

Stock options to purchase 30.6 million, 23.7 million, and 20.5 million shares of common stock outstanding at December 31, 2003, 2002, and 2001, respectively, did not affect the computation of diluted EPS. The exercise prices for these options were greater than the average market price of the Company's common stock during the respective years.

Stock options to purchase 15.3 million, 17.9 million, and 15.5 million shares of common stock outstanding at December 31, 2003, 2002, and 2001, respectively, had exercise prices that were less than the average market price of the Company's common stock during the respective periods and are included in the dilutive effect of stock options and restricted stock in the table above.

3.162

SAUCONY, INC. (DEC)

(In thousands, except per share amounts)	2003	2002	2001
Net income (loss)	$8,488	$5,243	$ (940)
Earnings per share			
Basic			
Class A common stock	$ 1.31	$ 0.81	$(0.15)
Class B common stock	$ 1.44	$ 0.89	$(0.16)
Diluted			
Class A common stock	$ 1.26	$ 0.80	$(0.15)
Class B common stock	$ 1.38	$ 0.88	$(0.16)
Weighted-average shares outstanding			
Basic			
Class A common stock	2,521	2,563	2,567
Class B common stock	3,583	3,544	3,513
Total	6,104	6,107	6,080
Diluted			
Class A common stock	2,521	2,563	2,567
Class B common stock	3,850	3,623	3,513
Total	6,371	6,186	6,080
Cash dividends per share of common stock			
Class A common stock	$0.120	$0.000	$0.000
Class B common stock	$0.132	$0.000	$0.000

NOTES TO CONSOLIDATED FINANCIAL STATEMENTS
(In thousands, except per share amounts)

1 (In Part): Summary of Significant Accounting Policies

Earnings Per Share

The Company presents basic and diluted earnings per share using the two-class method. The two-class method is an earnings allocation formula that determines earnings per share for each class of common stock according to dividends declared and participation rights in undistributed earnings.

Basic earnings per share for the Company's Class A and Class B common stock is calculated by dividing net income by the weighted average number of shares of Class A and Class B common stock outstanding. Diluted earnings per share for the Company's Class A and Class B common stock is calculated similarly, except that the calculation includes the dilutive effect of the assumed exercise of options issuable under the Company's stock incentive plans and the assumed exercise of stock warrants.

Net income available to the Company's common stockholders is allocated among our two classes of common stock, Class A common stock and Class B common stock. The allocation among each class was based upon the two-class method. Under the two-class method, earnings per share for each class of common stock is presented. See Note 12 for the calculation of basic and diluted earnings per share under the two-class method.

12. Earnings Per Share

The following table sets forth the computation of basic earnings per common share and diluted earnings per common share for the years ended January 2, 2004, January 3, 2003 and January 4, 2002:

	2003		2002		2001	
	Basic	Diluted	Basic	Diluted	Basic	Diluted
Net income (loss) available for common shares and assumed conversions	$8,488	$8,488	$5,243	$5,243	$ (940)	$ (940)
Weighted-average common shares and equivalents outstanding						
Weighted-average shares outstanding	6,104	6,104	6,107	6,107	6,080	6,080
Effect of dilutive securities						
Stock options	—	245	—	76	—	—
Stock purchase warrants	—	22	—	3	—	—
	6,104	6,371	6,107	6,186	6,080	6,080
Net income (loss) allocated						
Class A common stock	$3,312	$3,168	$2,080	$2,052	$ (375)	$ (375)
Class B common stock	5,176	5,320	3,163	3,191	(565)	(565)
	$8,488	$8,488	$5,243	$5,243	$ (940)	$ (940)
Weighted-average common shares and equivalents outstanding						
Class A common stock	2,521	2,521	2,563	2,563	2,567	2,567
Class B common stock	3,583	3,850	3,544	3,623	3,513	3,513
	6,104	6,371	6,107	6,186	6,080	6,080
Earnings per share						
Class A common stock	$ 1.31	$ 1.26	$ 0.81	$ 0.80	$ (0.15)	$ (0.15)
Class B common stock	$ 1.44	$ 1.38	$ 0.89	$ 0.88	$ (0.16)	$ (0.16)

Options to purchase 336,000 and 312,000 shares of common stock were outstanding at January 2, 2004 and January 3, 2003, respectively, were not included in the computations of earnings per share since the options were anti-dilutive. Stock warrants to purchase 47,000 shares of common stock outstanding at January 3, 2003, were not included in the computation of earnings per share since the warrants were anti-dilutive.

Section 4: Comprehensive Income

PRESENTATION IN ANNUAL REPORT

4.01 Effective for fiscal years beginning after December 15, 1997, Statement of Financial Accounting Standards (SFAS) No. 130, *Reporting Comprehensive Income*, requires that a full set of general-purpose financial statements report comprehensive income and its components. Comprehensive income includes net income, foreign currency items, minimum pension liability adjustments, changes in the fair value of certain derivatives, and unrealized gains and losses on certain investments in debt and equity securities. If an entity has only net income, it is not required to report comprehensive income. *SFAS No. 130* encourages reporting comprehensive income in either a combined statement of income and comprehensive income or in a separate statement of comprehensive income.

4.02 *SFAS No. 130* also states that an enterprise shall disclose the amount of income tax expense or benefit allocated to each component of other comprehensive income (including reclassification adjustments), either on the face of the statement in which those components are displayed or in the notes thereto.

4.03 Table 4-1 shows the statement in which comprehensive income and the related tax effect was presented.

4.04

TABLE 4-1: COMPREHENSIVE INCOME—REPORTING STATEMENT

	2003	2002	2001	2000
Reporting format:				
Included in statement of changes in stockholders' equity	488	469	450	422
Separate statement of comprehensive income	69	68	78	65
Combined statement of income and comprehensive income	23	25	31	32
	580	**562**	**559**	**519**
No comprehensive income reported	20	38	41	81
Total Companies	**600**	**600**	**600**	**600**
Tax effect disclosure in any statement:				
Amount of tax effect allocated to some, but not all, components	111	114	102	47
Amount of tax effect allocated to each component	89	73	74	59
Total amount of tax effect	16	16	9	14
	216	**203**	**185**	**120**
Tax effect disclosure in notes:				
Amount of tax effect allocated to some, but not all, components	71	67	51	49
Amount of tax effect allocated to each component	75	66	68	75
Total amount of tax effect	16	29	15	6
	162	**162**	**134**	**130**
Tax effect not disclosed in any statement	202	197	240	269
	580	**562**	**559**	**519**
No comprehensive income reported	20	38	41	81
Total Companies	**600**	**600**	**600**	**600**

4.05   Table 4-2 summarizes the titles used to describe comprehensive income.

4.06   Examples of comprehensive income reported in a statement of changes in stockholders' equity, in a separate statement of comprehensive income, and in a combined statement of income and comprehensive income follow.

4.07

TABLE 4-2: COMPREHENSIVE INCOME—REPORTING STATEMENT TITLE

	2003	2002	2001	2000
Comprehensive income reported in a statement of income and comprehensive income, or in a statement of comprehensive income				
Comprehensive income....................	59	46	63	68
Comprehensive income (loss)..........	26	27	28	23
Comprehensive loss..........................	3	7	3	1
Comprehensive earnings.................	1	2	3	2
Other title...	3	11	5	3
	92	**93**	**102**	**97**
Comprehensive income reported in a statement of changes in stockholders' equity				
Statement title does not refer to comprehensive income.................	406	395	403	362
Statement title does refer to comprehensive income.................	82	74	54	60
	488	**469**	**457**	**422**
No comprehensive income reported.....	20	38	41	81
Total Companies...................................	**600**	**600**	**600**	**600**

Included in Statement of Changes in Stockholders' Equity

4.08

AMETEK, INC. (DEC)

Consolidated Statement of Stockholders' Equity

	2003		2002		2001	
(In thousands)	Comprehensive Income	Stockholders' Equity	Comprehensive Income	Stockholders' Equity	Comprehensive Income	Stockholders' Equity
Capital stock						
Preferred stock, $.01 par value		$ —		$ —		$ —
Common stock, $.01 par value						
Balance at the beginning of the year		339		334		334
Shares issued		6		5		—
Balance at the end of the year		345		339		334
Capital in excess of par value						
Balance at the beginning of the year		14,045		683		2,248
Employee stock option, savings and award plans, including tax benefits		19,149		13,362		(1,565)
Balance at the end of the year		33,194		14,045		683
Retained earnings						
Balance at the beginning of the year		464,731		388,929		330,696
Net income	$ 87,815	87,815	$83,698	83,698	$66,111	66,111
Cash dividends paid		(8,124)		(7,896)		(7,878)
Balance at the end of the year		544,422		464,731		388,929
Accumulated other comprehensive losses[1]						
Foreign currency translation:						
Balance at the beginning of the year		(22,429)		(32,891)		(30,467)
Translation adjustments	9,502	9,502	10,462	10,462	(2,424)	(2,424)
Balance at the end of the year		(12,927)		(22,429)		(32,891)
Minimum pension liability adjustment:						
Balance at the beginning of the year		(12,280)		(4,680)		(169)
Adjustments during the year	4,610	4,610	(7,600)	(7,600)	(4,511)	(4,511)
Balance at the end of the year		(7,670)		(12,280)		(4,680)
Valuation adjustments for marketable securities and other:						
Balance at the beginning of the year		(10)		548		471
(Increase) decrease in marketable securities[2]	1,411	1,411	(558)	(558)	77	77
Balance at the end of the year		1,401		(10)		548
Total other comprehensive income (loss) for the year	15,523		2,304		(6,858)	
Total comprehensive income for the year	$103,338		$86,002		$59,253	
Accumulated other comprehensive loss at the end of the year		(19,196)		(34,719)		(37,023)
Treasury stock						
Balance at the beginning of the year		(24,215)		(17,865)		(22,275)
Employee stock option, savings and award plans		428		996		16,038
Purchase of treasury stock		(5,848)		(7,346)		(11,628)
Balance at the end of the year		(29,635)		(24,215)		(17,865)
Total stockholders' equity		$529,130		$420,181		$335,058

[1] Amounts presented are net of tax based on an average tax rate of 35%, except for foreign currency translation adjustments, which are presented on a pretax basis.

[2] Includes reclassification adjustment for (losses) gains included in net income for 2003, 2002, and 2001 of $0.1 million, ($0.1) million, and $0.6 million, respectively.

4.09

FIRST DATA CORPORATION (DEC)

Consolidated Statements of Stockholders' Equity

(In millions)	Total	Comprehensive Income	Retained Earnings	Accumulated Other Comprehensive Income	Common Shares	Paid-In Capital	Treasury Stock Shares	Treasury Stock Cost
Balance, December 31, 2000	$3,727.7		$3,717.1	$ (18.9)	897.9	$2,297.2	(111.2)	$(2,267.7)
Comprehensive income								
Net income	871.9	$ 871.9	871.9					
Other comprehensive income:								
Unrealized gains on securities	4.9	4.9						
Unrealized losses on hedging activities	(69.1)	(69.1)						
Foreign currency translation adjustment	(27.2)	(27.2)						
Minimum pension liability adjustment	(33.0)	(33.0)						
Other comprehensive loss		(124.4)		(124.4)				
Comprehensive income		$ 747.5						
Purchase of treasury shares	(1,318.5)						(43.4)	(1,318.5)
Stock issued for compensation and benefit plans	339.9		(194.2)			94.9	15.8	439.2
Stock issued for business previously acquired	52.9					28.0	2.0	24.9
Cash dividends declared ($0.04 per share)	(29.6)		(29.6)					
Balance, December 31, 2001	3,519.9		4,365.2	(143.3)	897.9	2,420.1	(136.8)	(3,122.1)
Comprehensive income								
Net income	1,237.9	$1,237.9	1,237.9					
Other comprehensive income:								
Unrealized gains on securities	196.1	196.1						
Unrealized losses on hedging activities	(212.5)	(212.5)						
Foreign currency translation adjustment	34.0	34.0						
Minimum pension liability adjustment	(71.9)	(71.9)						
Other comprehensive loss		(54.3)		(54.3)				
Comprehensive income		$1,183.6						
Purchase of treasury shares	(849.1)						(22.9)	(849.1)
Stock issued for compensation and benefit plans	321.5		(195.5)			114.3	12.8	402.7
Stock issued for conversion of debt	33.3		7.9				1.8	25.4
Cash dividends declared ($0.07 per share)	(52.9)		(52.9)					
Balance, December 31, 2002	$4,156.3		$5,362.6	$(197.6)	897.9	$2,534.4	(145.1)	$(3,543.1)

(continued)

(In millions)	Total	Comprehensive Income	Retained Earnings	Accumulated Other Comprehensive Income	Common Shares	Paid-In Capital	Treasury Stock Shares	Treasury Stock Cost
Balance, December 31, 2002	$4,156.3		$5,362.6	$(197.6)	897.9	$2,534.4	(145.1)	$(3,543.1)
Comprehensive income								
Net income	1,408.7	$1,408.7	1,408.7					
Other comprehensive income:								
Unrealized losses on securities	(36.1)	(36.1)						
Unrealized gains on hedging activities	72.3	72.3						
Foreign currency translation adjustment	87.9	87.9						
Minimum pension liability adjustment	(26.7)	(26.7)						
Other comprehensive income		97.4		97.4				
Comprehensive income		$1,506.1						
Purchase of treasury shares	(1,825.0)						(46.5)	(1,825.0)
Stock issued for compensation and benefit plans	249.3		(121.4)			51.7	8.7	319.0
Stock issued for conversion of debt	16.7		4.0				0.9	12.7
Stock issued for conversion of warrants	2.6		(5.9)			(0.2)	0.6	8.7
Cash dividends declared ($0.08 per share)	(58.7)		(58.7)					
Balance, December 31, 2003	$4,047.3		$6,589.3	$(100.2)	897.9	$2,585.9	(181.4)	$(5,027.7)

4.10

THE TIMKEN COMPANY (DEC)

Consolidated Statement of Shareholders' Equity

(Thousands of dollars, except share data)	Total	Common Stock		Earnings Invested in the Business	Accumulated Other Comprehensive Loss	Treasury Stock
		Stated Capital	Other Paid-In Capital			
Balance at January 1, 2001	$1,004,682	$53,064	$256,873	$839,242	$ (84,913)	$(59,584)
Net loss	(41,666)			(41,666)		
Foreign currency translation adjustments (net of income tax of $963)	(15,914)				(15,914)	
Minimum pension liability adjustment (net of income tax of $61,892)	(122,520)				(122,520)	
Change in fair value of derivative financial instruments net of reclassifications	(1,191)				(1,191)	
Total comprehensive loss	(181,291)					
Dividends—$0.67 per share	(40,166)			(40,166)		
Purchase of 206,300 shares for treasury	(2,931)					(2,931)
Issuance of 97,225 shares from treasury	1,441		(450)			1,891
Balance at December 31, 2001	$ 781,735	$53,064	$256,423	$757,410	$(224,538)	$(60,624)
Net income	38,749			38,749		
Foreign currency translation adjustments (net of income tax of $2,843)	14,050				14,050	
Minimum pension liability adjustment (net of income tax of $147,303)	(254,318)				(254,318)	
Change in fair value of derivative financial instruments net of reclassifications	(871)				(871)	
Total comprehensive loss	(202,390)					
Dividends—$0.52 per share	(31,713)			(31,713)		
Issuance of 3,186,470 shares from treasury	57,747		(2,138)			59,885
Issuance of 369,290 shares from authorized	3,707		3,707			
Balance at December 31, 2002	$ 609,086	$53,064	$257,992	$764,446	$(465,677)	$ (739)
Net income	36,481			36,481		
Foreign currency translation adjustments (net of income tax of $1,638)	75,062				75,062	
Minimum pension liability adjustment (net of income tax of $19,164)	31,813				31,813	
Change in fair value of derivative financial instruments net of reclassifications	420				420	
Total comprehensive income	143,776					
Dividends—$0.52 per share	(42,078)			(42,078)		
Tax benefit from exercise of stock options	1,104		1,104			
Issuance of 29,473 shares from treasury	301		(262)			563
Issuance of 25,624,198 shares from authorized	377,438		377,438			
Balance at December 31, 2003	$1,089,627	$53,064	$636,272	$758,849	$(358,382)	$ (176)

Separate Statement of Comprehensive Income

4.11

OCCIDENTAL PETROLEUM CORPORATION (DEC)

Consolidated Statements of Comprehensive Income

(In millions)	2003	2002	2001
Net income	$1,527	$ 989	$1,154
Other comprehensive income (loss) items:			
Foreign currency translation adjustments[a]	38	5	(12)
Derivative mark-to-market adjustments[b]	2	(6)	(20)
Minimum pension liability adjustments[c]	13	(5)	(6)
Unrealized gains on securities[d]	24	65	2
Other comprehensive income (loss), net of tax	77	59	(36)
Comprehensive income	$1,604	$1,048	$1,118

[a] Net of tax of $15 million, $0 million and $0 million in 2003, 2002 and 2001, respectively.

[b] Net of tax of $1 million, $(5) million and $(11) million in 2003, 2002 and 2001, respectively.

[c] Net of tax of $7 million, $(3) million and $(3) million in 2003, 2002 and 2001, respectively.

[d] Net of tax of $13 million, $35 million and $0 million in 2003, 2002 and 2001, respectively.

4.12

TENNECO AUTOMOTIVE INC. (DEC)

Statements of Comprehensive Income (Loss)

(Millions)	2003 Accumulated Other Comprehensive Income (Loss)	2003 Comprehensive Income (Loss)	2002 Accumulated Other Comprehensive Income (Loss)	2002 Comprehensive Income (Loss)	2001 Accumulated Other Comprehensive Income (Loss)	2001 Comprehensive Income (Loss)
Net income (loss)		$ 27		$(187)		$(130)
Accumulated other comprehensive income (loss)						
Cumulative translation adjustment						
Balance January 1	$(273)		$(316)		$(237)	
Translation of foreign currency statements	130	130	43	43	(79)	(79)
Balance December 31	(143)		(273)		(316)	
Fair value of interest rate swaps						
Balance January 1	(4)		(17)		—	
Fair value adjustment	4	4	13	13	(17)	(17)
Balance December 31	—		(4)		(17)	
Additional minimum pension liability adjustment						
Balance January 1	(80)		(42)		(2)	
Additional minimum pension liability adjustment	(29)	(29)	(61)	(61)	(64)	(64)
Income tax benefit	11	11	23	23	24	24
Balance December 31	(98)		(80)		(42)	
Balance December 31	$(241)		$(357)		$(375)	
Other comprehensive income (loss)		116		18		(136)
Comprehensive income (loss)		$143		$(169)		$(266)

Combined Statement of Net Income and Comprehensive Income

4.13

FOSTER WHEELER LTD. (DEC)

Consolidated Statement of Operations and Comprehensive Loss

(In thousands of dollars)	2003	2002	2001
Revenues			
Operating revenues	$3,723,815	$3,519,177	$3,315,314
Other income (including interest: 2003—$10,130; 2002—$12,251; 2001—$9,060)	77,493	55,360	77,160
Total revenues and other income	3,801,308	3,574,537	3,392,474
Costs and expenses			
Cost of operating revenues	3,441,342	3,426,910	3,164,025
Selling, general and administrative expenses	199,949	226,524	225,392
Other deductions	168,455	193,156	126,495
Minority interest	5,715	4,981	5,043
Interest expense	77,354	66,418	68,734
Dividends on preferred security of subsidiary trust	18,130	16,610	15,750
Total costs and expenses	3,910,945	3,934,599	3,605,439
Loss before income taxes	(109,637)	(360,062)	(212,965)
Provision for income taxes	47,426	14,657	123,395
Net loss prior to cumulative effect of a change in accounting principle	(157,063)	(374,719)	(336,360)
Cumulative effect of a change in accounting principle for goodwill, net of $0 tax	—	(150,500)	—
Net loss	(157,063)	(525,219)	(336,360)
Other comprehensive income/(loss)			
Cumulative effect of prior years (to December 29, 2000) of a change in accounting principle for derivative instruments designated as cash flow hedges	—	—	6,300
Change in gain on derivative instruments designated as cash flow hedges	—	(3,834)	(2,466)
Foreign currency translation adjustment	6,762	22,241	(10,191)
Minimum pension liability adjustment net of tax provision/(benefits): 2003—$18,886; 2002—($73,400); 2001—$0	58,677	(226,011)	(36,770)
Comprehensive loss	$ (91,624)	$ (732,823)	$ (379,487)

4.14

THE STANDARD REGISTER COMPANY (DEC)

Consolidated Statements of Income and Comprehensive Income

(Dollars in thousands, except per share amounts)	2003	2002	2001
Revenue			
Products	$759,009	$ 842,144	$ 975,350
Services	157,325	185,939	212,247
Total revenue	916,334	1,028,083	1,187,597
Cost of sales			
Products	464,659	501,421	665,797
Services	111,817	120,007	115,797
Total cost of sales	576,476	621,428	781,594
Gross margin	339,858	406,655	406,003
Operating expenses			
Research and development	17,236	17,865	14,385
Selling, general and administrative	300,598	274,915	304,499
Depreciation and amortization	46,270	46,674	45,419
Asset impairments	15,910	—	41,512
Restructuring charges (reversals)	20,082	(1,837)	64,856
Total operating expenses	400,096	337,617	470,671
Income (loss) from operations	(60,238)	69,038	(64,668)
Other income (expense)			
Interest expense	(4,055)	(13,324)	(12,755)
Investment and other income (expense)	982	(605)	3,171
Total other expense	(3,073)	(13,929)	(9,584)
Income (loss) before income taxes	(63,311)	55,109	(74,252)
Income tax expense (benefit)	(24,244)	22,528	(30,931)
Net income (loss)	$ (39,067)	$ 32,581	$ (43,321)
Earnings (loss) per share			
Basic	$ (1.38)	$ 1.16	$ (1.57)
Diluted	$ (1.38)	$ 1.14	$ (1.57)
Net income (loss)	$ (39,067)	$ 32,581	$ (43,321)
Minimum pension liability adjustment, net of $4,135, $77,973, and $134 deferred income tax benefit	(6,135)	(115,676)	(199)
Deferred cost on interest rate swap, net of $(815), $(2,605), and $4,095 deferred income tax benefit (expense)	1,210	3,863	(6,075)
Available for sale securities	680	(680)	—
Deferred cost on forward contract, net of $30 and $(30) deferred income tax benefit (expense)	(45)	45	—
Cumulative translation adjustment	1,468	(23)	—
Comprehensive income (loss)	$ (41,889)	$ (79,890)	$ (49,595)

TAX EFFECT DISCLOSURE

4.15

COOPER INDUSTRIES, LTD. (DEC)

Consolidated Statements of Shareholders' Equity

(In millions)	Common Stock	Capital in Excess of Par Value	Retained Earnings	Treasury Stock	Unearned Employee Stock Ownership Plan Compensation	Accumulated Nonowner Changes in Equity	Total
Balance December 31, 2000	$ 615.0	$ 663.3	$2,225.0	$(1,470.0)	$(8.6)	$(120.5)	$1,904.2
Net income			231.3				231.3
Minimum pension liability adjustment						(0.7)	(0.7)
Translation adjustment						(6.3)	(6.3)
Change in fair value of derivatives						(0.3)	(0.3)
Net income and other nonowner changes in equity							224.0
Common stock dividends			(131.3)				(131.3)
Purchase of treasury shares				(42.0)			(42.0)
Stock issued under employee stock plans		(16.6)		74.4			57.8
ESOP shares allocated					8.6		8.6
Other activity		(0.7)		2.6			1.9
Balance December 31, 2001	615.0	646.0	2,325.0	(1,435.0)	—	(127.8)	2,023.2
Net income			213.7				213.7
Minimum pension liability adjustment						(33.4)	(33.4)
Translation adjustment						(4.4)	(4.4)
Change in fair value of derivatives						0.2	0.2
Net income and other nonowner changes in equity							176.1
Common stock dividends			(129.7)				(129.7)
Purchase of treasury shares				(37.9)			(37.9)
Subsidiary purchase of parent shares		(56.4)					(56.4)
Share conversion	(614.1)	(171.0)	(664.8)	1,449.9			—
Stock issued under employee stock plans		4.0		21.6			25.6
Other activity		0.1		1.4			1.5
Balance December 31, 2002	0.9	422.7	1,744.2	—	—	(165.4)	2,002.4
Net income			148.3				148.3
Minimum pension liability adjustment						(22.9)	(22.9)
Translation adjustment						26.2	26.2
Change in fair value of derivatives						(1.4)	(1.4)
Net income and other nonowner changes in equity							150.2
Common stock dividends			(129.7)				(129.7)
Stock-based compensation		7.1					7.1
Subsidiary purchase of parent shares		(5.5)					(5.5)
Stock issued under employee stock plans		92.0					92.0
Other activity		1.7					1.7
Balance December 31, 2003	$ 0.9	$ 518.0	$1,762.8	$ —	$ —	$(163.5)	$2,118.2

NOTES TO CONSOLIDATED FINANCIAL STATEMENTS

Note 11 (In Part): Accumulated Nonowner Changes in Equity

(In millions)	2003			2002			2001		
	Before Tax Amount	Tax (Expense) Benefit	Net Amount	Before Tax Amount	Tax (Expense) Benefit	Net Amount	Before Tax Amount	Tax (Expense) Benefit	Net Amount
Minimum pension liability adjustment	$(38.1)	$ 15.2	$(22.9)	$(55.7)	$22.3	$(33.4)	$ (1.1)	$ 0.4	$(0.7)
Change in fair value of derivatives	(4.7)	1.9	(2.8)	0.1	—	0.1	(1.0)	0.4	(0.6)
Reclassification to earnings	2.4	(1.0)	1.4	0.2	(0.1)	0.1	0.5	(0.2)	0.3
	(2.3)	0.9	(1.4)	0.3	(0.1)	0.2	(0.5)	0.2	(0.3)
Translation adjustment	40.2	(14.0)	26.2	(6.8)	2.4	(4.4)	(9.7)	3.4	(6.3)
Other nonowner changes in equity	$ (0.2)	$ 2.1	$ 1.9	$(62.2)	$24.6	$(37.6)	$(11.3)	$ 4.0	$(7.3)

4.16

MERCK & CO., INC. (DEC)

Consolidated Statement of Comprehensive Income

(In millions)	2003	2002	2001
Net income	$6,830.9	$7,149.5	$7,281.8
Other comprehensive income (loss)			
Net unrealized (loss) gain on derivatives, net of tax and net income realization	(21.3)	(20.0)	7.3
Net unrealized (loss) gain on investments net of tax and net income realization	(46.3)	73.1	11.1
Minimum pension liability, net of tax	231.9	(162.5)	(38.6)
	164.3	(109.4)	(20.2)
Comprehensive income	$6,995.2	$7,040.1	$7,261.6

NOTES TO CONSOLIDATED FINANCIAL STATEMENTS

17 (In Part): Comprehensive Income

Upon the adoption of FAS 133 on January 1, 2001, the Company recorded a favorable cumulative effect of accounting change of $45.5 million in Other comprehensive income (loss). This amount represented the mark to fair value of purchased local currency put options maturing throughout 2001, which hedged anticipated foreign currency denominated sales over that same period. At December 31, 2003, $30.4 million of deferred loss is associated with options maturing in the next 12 months, which hedge anticipated foreign currency denominated sales over that same period.

The components of Other comprehensive income (loss) are as follows:

(In millions)	Pretax	Tax	After Tax
Year ended December 31, 2003			
Net unrealized loss on derivatives	$ (87.6)	$ 35.9	$ (51.7)
Net loss realization	51.5	(21.1)	30.4
Derivatives	(36.1)	14.8	(21.3)
Net unrealized gain on investments	105.0	(33.8)	71.2
Net income realization	(114.3)	(3.2)	(117.5)
Investments	(9.3)	(37.0)	(46.3)
Minimum pension liability	424.5	(192.6)	231.9
	$ 379.1	$(214.8)	$ 164.3
Year ended December 31, 2002			
Net unrealized loss on derivatives	$ (31.8)	$ 13.0	$ (18.8)
Net income realization	(2.0)	0.8	(1.2)
Derivatives	(33.8)	13.8	(20.0)
Net unrealized gain on investments	128.6	24.5	153.1
Net income realization	(86.6)	6.6	(80.0)
Investments	42.0	31.1	73.1
Minimum pension liability	(263.2)	100.7	(162.5)
	$(255.0)	$ 145.6	$(109.4)
Year ended December 31, 2001			
Cumulative effect of accounting change	$ 76.9	$ (31.4)	$ 45.5
Net unrealized gain on derivatives	49.7	(20.3)	29.4
Net income realization	(114.3)	46.7	(67.6)
Derivatives	12.3	(5.0)	7.3
Net unrealized gain on investments	44.7	35.3	80.0
Net income realization	(73.7)	4.8	(68.9)
Investments	(29.0)	40.1	11.1
Minimum pension liability	(87.1)	48.5	(38.6)
	$(103.8)	$ 83.6	$ (20.2)

4.17

VF CORPORATION (DEC)

Consolidated Statements of Comprehensive Income

(In thousands)	2003	2002	2001
Net income (loss)	$397,933	$(154,543)	$137,830
Other comprehensive income (loss)			
Foreign currency translation			
Amount arising during year	89,000	40,693	(24,340)
Less income tax effect	(40,157)	(15,252)	6,317
Minimum pension liability adjustment			
Amount arising during year	(52,691)	(205,080)	(2,504)
Less income tax effect	20,335	78,239	851
Derivative financial instruments			
Amount arising during year	(14,492)	(15,802)	14,161
Less income tax effect	5,536	6,168	(5,693)
Reclassification to net income for (gains) losses realized	15,817	280	(7,151)
Less income tax effect	(6,042)	(107)	2,875
Unrealized gains and losses on marketable securities			
Amount arising during year	13,730	(3,184)	(952)
Less income tax effect	(5,369)	1,255	373
Reclassification to net income for (gains) losses realized	(1,613)	2,763	1,502
Less income tax effect	632	(1,074)	(604)
Comprehensive income (loss)	$422,619	$(265,644)	$122,665

COMPONENTS OF OTHER COMPREHENSIVE INCOME

4.18 *SFAS No. 130* requires that items included in other comprehensive income shall be classified based on their nature. For example, under existing pronouncements, other comprehensive income shall be classified separately into foreign currency items, minimum pension liability adjustments, changes in fair value of derivatives, and unrealized gains and losses on certain debt and equity securities.

4.19 *SFAS No. 130* also requires that adjustments shall be made to avoid double counting, in comprehensive income, items that are displayed as part of net income for a period that also had been displayed as part of other comprehensive income in that period or earlier periods. For example, gains on investment securities that were realized and included in net income of the current period, that also had been included in other comprehensive income as unrealized holding gains in the period in which they arose, must be deducted through other comprehensive income of the period in which they are included in net income to avoid including them in comprehensive income twice. These adjustments are called reclassification adjustments. An enterprise may display reclassification adjustments on the face of the financial statement in which comprehensive income is reported or it may disclose them in the notes to the financial statements.

4.20 Table 4-3 lists the components of other comprehensive income disclosed by survey companies in the statement used to present comprehensive income for the period reported.

4.21 Examples showing the presentation of components of other comprehensive income follow.

4.22

TABLE 4-3: OTHER COMPREHENSIVE INCOME—COMPONENTS

	2003	2002	2001	2000
Cumulative translation adjustments............................	477	468	462	455
Minimum pension liability adjustments............................	389	373	254	192
Changes in fair value of derivatives...............................	311	325	287	12
Unrealized losses/gains on certain investments................	268	268	273	224
Other..	2	4	4	27

Cumulative Translation Adjustments

4.23

BECTON, DICKINSON AND COMPANY (SEP)

Consolidated Statements of Comprehensive Income

(Thousands of dollars)	2003	2002	2001
Net income	$547,056	$479,982	$401,652
Other comprehensive income (loss), net of tax			
Foreign currency translation adjustments	207,107	16,472	(38,704)
Minimum pension liability adjustment	(9,248)	(77,661)	—
Unrealized gains (losses) on investments, net of amounts recognized	9,653	4,005	(3,616)
Unrealized losses on cash flow hedges, net of amounts realized	(5,499)	(380)	(4,013)
Other comprehensive income (loss), net of tax	202,013	(57,564)	(46,333)
Comprehensive income	$749,069	$422,418	$355,319

NOTES TO CONSOLIDATED FINANCIAL STATEMENTS
(Thousands of dollars)

1 (In Part): Summary of Significant Accounting Policies

Foreign Currency Translation

Generally, the net assets of foreign operations are translated into U.S. dollars using current exchange rates. The U.S. dollar results that arise from such translation, as well as exchange gains and losses on intercompany balances of a long-term investment nature, are included in the cumulative currency translation adjustments in Accumulated other comprehensive loss.

12 (In Part): Other Comprehensive Income (Loss)

The components of Accumulated other comprehensive loss are as follows:

	2003	2002
Foreign currency translation adjustments	$(156,193)	$(363,300)
Minimum pension liability adjustment	(86,909)	(77,661)
Unrealized gains on investments	9,721	68
Unrealized losses on cash flow hedges	(9,892)	(4,393)
	$(243,273)	$(445,286)

The income tax provision recorded in fiscal year 2003 and 2002 for the unrealized gains on investments was $6,700 and $2,800. The income tax benefits recorded in fiscal years 2003 and 2002 for cash flow hedges were $5,500 and $1,900, respectively. The income tax benefit amounts recorded in fiscal years 2003 and 2002 for the minimum pension liability adjustment was $300 and $52,600, respectively. Income taxes are generally not provided for translation adjustments.

4.24

INTERNATIONAL PAPER COMPANY (DEC)

Consolidated Statement of Common Shareholders' Equity

(In millions, except share amounts in thousands)	Common Stock Issued		Paid-In Capital	Retained Earnings	Accumulated Other Comprehensive Income (Loss)[1]	Treasury Stock		Total Common Shareholders' Equity
	Shares	Amount				Shares	Amount	
Balance, January 1, 2001	484,160	$484	$6,501	$ 6,308	$(1,142)	2,690	$117	$12,034
Issuance of stock for various plans	121	—	(36)	—	—	(1,727)	(76)	40
Repurchase of stock	—	—	—	—	—	1,730	64	(64)
Cash dividends—common stock ($1.00 per share)	—	—	—	(482)	—	—	—	(482)
Comprehensive income (loss):								
Net loss	—	—	—	(1,204)	—	—	—	(1,204)
Minimum pension liability adjustment (less tax benefit of $4)	—	—	—	—	(6)	—	—	(6)
Change in cumulative foreign currency translation adjustment (less tax benefit of $59)	—	—	—	—	(10)	—	—	(10)
Net losses on cash flow hedging derivatives:								
Net loss arising during the period (less tax benefit of $25)	—	—	—	—	(67)	—	—	(67)
Less: reclassification adjustment for losses included in net income (less tax benefit of $18)	—	—	—	—	50	—	—	50
Total comprehensive loss								(1,237)
Balance, December 31, 2001	484,281	484	6,465	4,622	(1,175)	2,693	105	10,291
Issuance of stock for various plans	479	1	28	—	—	(1,403)	(55)	84
Repurchase of stock	—	—	—	—	—	4,390	169	(169)
Cash dividends—common stock ($1.00 per share)	—	—	—	(482)	—	—	—	(482)
Comprehensive income (loss):								
Net loss	—	—	—	(880)	—	—	—	(880)
Minimum pension liability adjustment[2]:								
U.S. plans (less tax benefit of $964)	—	—	—	—	(1,543)	—	—	(1,543)
Non-U.S. plans (less tax benefit of $9)	—	—	—	—	(21)	—	—	(21)
Change in cumulative foreign currency translation adjustment (less tax expense of $2)	—	—	—	—	27	—	—	27
Net gains on cash flow hedging derivatives:								
Net gain arising during the period (less tax expense of $33)	—	—	—	—	71	—	—	71
Less: reclassification adjustment for gains included in net income (less tax expense of $3)	—	—	—	—	(4)	—	—	(4)
Total comprehensive loss								(2,350)
Balance, December 31, 2002	484,760	$485	$6,493	$ 3,260	$(2,645)	5,680	$219	$ 7,374

(continued)

(In millions, except share amounts in thousands)	Common Stock Issued		Paid-In Capital	Retained Earnings	Accumulated Other Comprehensive Income (Loss)[1]	Treasury Stock		Total Common Shareholders' Equity
	Shares	Amount				Shares	Amount	
Balance, December 31, 2002	484,760	$485	$6,493	$ 3,260	$(2,645)	5,680	$219	$ 7,374
Issuance of stock for various plans	402	—	7	—	—	(2,725)	(105)	112
Repurchase of stock	—	—	—	—	—	713	26	(26)
Cash dividends—common stock ($1.00 per share)	—	—	—	(480)	—	—	—	(480)
Comprehensive income (loss):								
Net income	—	—	—	302	—	—	—	302
Minimum pension liability adjustment:								
U.S. plans (less tax expense of $94)	—	—	—	—	150	—	—	150
Non-U.S. plans (less tax benefit of $2)	—	—	—	—	(4)	—	—	(4)
Change in cumulative foreign currency translation adjustment (less tax benefit of $51)	—	—	—	—	808	—	—	808
Net gains on cash flow hedging derivatives:								
Net gain arising during the period (less tax expense of $38)	—	—	—	—	66	—	—	66
Less: reclassification adjustment for gains included in net income (less tax expense of $36)	—	—	—	—	(65)	—	—	(65)
Total comprehensive income								1,257
Balance, December 31, 2003	485,162	$485	$6,500	$ 3,082	$(1,690)	3,668	$ 140	$ 8,237

[1] The cumulative foreign currency translation adjustment (in millions) was $(284), $(1,092) and $(1,119) at December 31, 2003, 2002 and 2001, respectively, and is included as a component of accumulated other comprehensive income (loss).

[2] This noncash equity reduction resulted from declines in pension fund asset market values and increases in computed fund liabilities due to lower interest rates.

NOTES TO CONSOLIDATED FINANCIAL STATEMENTS

Note 1 (In Part): Summary of Significant Accounting Policies

Translation of Financial Statements

Balance sheets of international operations are translated into U.S. dollars at year-end exchange rates, while statements of earnings are translated at average rates. Adjustments resulting from financial statement translations are included as cumulative translation adjustments in Accumulated other comprehensive income (loss) (OCI).

Minimum Pension Liability Adjustments

4.25

BRISTOL-MYERS SQUIBB COMPANY (DEC)

Consolidated Statement of Comprehensive Income

(Dollars in millions)	2003	2002	2001
Net earnings	$3,106	$2,137	$4,662
Other comprehensive income:			
Foreign currency translation, net of tax benefit of $25 in 2003, $53 in 2002 and $40 in 2001	233	161	160
Deferred (losses) on derivatives qualifying as hedges, net of tax benefit of $65 in 2003, $19 in 2002 and $37 in 2001	(171)	(25)	(62)
Minimum pension liability adjustment, net of tax benefit of $17 in 2003, $43 in 2002 and $3 in 2001	(36)	(89)	(5)
Available for sale securities, net of taxes of $13 in 2003	23	1	—
Total other comprehensive income	49	48	93
Comprehensive income	$3,155	$2,185	$4,755

NOTES TO CONSOLIDATED STATEMENTS

*Note 21 (In Part): Pension and Other Postretirement
Benefit Plans*

Changes in benefit obligations and plan assets for
December 31, 2003 and 2002, for the Company's defined
benefit and postretirement benefit plans, were:

	Pension Benefits		Other Benefits	
(Dollars in millions)	2003	2002	2003	2002
Benefit obligation at beginning of year	$4,172	$4,012	$ 717	$ 661
Service cost—benefits earned during the year	144	143	8	10
Interest cost on projected benefit obligation	275	275	46	46
Plan participants' contributions	3	1	4	4
Curtailments and settlements	(3)	(13)	—	—
Transfer from DuPont Pharmaceuticals	—	7	—	—
Actuarial loss	382	107	59	56
Plan amendments	38	16	(13)	—
Benefits paid	(344)	(420)	(65)	(60)
Exchange rate losses	88	44	2	—
Benefit obligation at end of year	$4,755	$4,172	$ 758	$ 717
Fair value of plan assets at beginning of year	$3,318	$3,557	$ 164	$ 168
Actual return on plan assets	707	(473)	41	(25)
Employer contribution	332	554	61	77
Plan participants' contributions	3	1	4	4
Settlements	(3)	(10)	—	—
Transfer from DuPont Pharmaceuticals	—	68	—	—
Transfer in	1	—	—	—
Benefits paid	(344)	(420)	(65)	(60)
Exchange rate gains	71	41	—	—
Fair value of plan assets at end of year	$4,085	$3,318	$ 205	$ 164
Funded status	$ (670)	$ (854)	$(553)	$(553)
Unamortized net obligation at adoption	10	9	—	—
Unrecognized prior service cost	94	95	(16)	(4)
Unrecognized net actuarial loss	1,676	1,657	188	165
Net amount recognized	$1,110	$ 907	$(381)	$(392)
Amounts recognized in the balance sheet consist of:				
Prepaid benefit cost	$1,327	$1,126	$ —	$ —
Accrued benefit cost	(420)	(369)	(381)	(392)
Intangible assets	10	10	—	—
Accumulated other comprehensive income	193	140	—	—
Net amount recognized	$1,110	$ 907	$(381)	$(392)

Several plans had underfunded accrued benefit obligations that exceeded their accrued benefit liabilities at December 31, 2003 and 2002. Additional minimum liabilities were established to increase the accrued benefit liabilities to the values of the underfunded accrued benefit obligations. This totaled $203 million and $150 million at December 31, 2003 and 2002, respectively, for a U.S. unfunded benefit equalization plan, a U.S. underfunded Key International Plan and for plans in the U.K., Japan, Canada and Belgium. The additional minimum liability was offset by the creation of a $10 million intangible asset and charges to other comprehensive income included in stockholders' equity of $193 million and $140 million at December 31, 2003 and 2002, respectively.

The accumulated benefit obligation for all defined benefit pension plans was $4,154 million and $3,604 million at December 31, 2003 and 2002, respectively.

Information for pension plans with accumulated benefit obligations in excess of plan assets was:

(Dollars in millions)	2003	2002
Projected benefit obligation	$918	$779
Accumulated benefit obligation	791	670
Fair value of plan assets	427	340

This is attributable primarily to an unfunded U.S. benefit equalization plan and several plans in the international markets. The unfunded U.S. benefit equalization plan provides pension benefits for employees with compensation above IRS limits and cannot be funded in a tax-advantaged manner.

Additional information pertaining to the Company's pension and postretirement plans:

(Dollars in millions)	Pension Benefits		Other Benefits	
	2003	2002	2003	2002
Increase in minimum liability included in other comprehensive income	$53	$132	$—	$—

4.26

RUDDICK CORPORATION (SEP)

Statements of Consolidated Total Non-Owner Changes in Equity

(Dollars in thousands)	2003	2002	2001
Net income (loss)	$59,882	$ 51,983	$ (727)
Other non-owner changes in equity:			
Foreign currency translation adjustment	1,957	507	(332)
Related income tax (expense) benefit	—	—	—
Minimum pension liability adjustment	(6,936)	(41,354)	(18,314)
Related income tax (expense) benefit	2,739	16,329	7,231
Total other non-owner changes in equity, net	(2,240)	(24,518)	(11,415)
Total non-owner changes in equity	$57,642	$ 27,465	$(12,142)

NOTES TO CONSOLIDATED FINANCIAL STATEMENTS

Employee Benefit Plans (In Part)

The following table sets forth the change in benefit obligation and plan assets, as well as the defined benefit plans' funded status and amounts recognized in the Company's consolidated balance sheets at September 28, 2003 and September 29, 2002 for the pension plan and the supplemental retirement plan:

	Pension Plan		Supplemental Plan	
(In thousands)	2003	2002	2003	2002
Change in benefit obligation:				
Benefit obligation at the beginning of year	$189,649	$153,625	$ 19,747	$ 19,044
Service cost	8,982	6,787	552	367
Interest cost	12,188	11,323	1,327	1,378
Plan change	—	213	—	(247)
Actuarial loss	17,754	25,399	2,921	173
Benefits paid	(8,495)	(7,698)	(1,145)	(968)
Pension benefit obligation at end of year	$220,078	$189,649	$ 23,402	$ 19,747
Change in plan assets:				
Fair value of assets at the beginning of year	$120,631	$111,985	$ —	$ —
Actual return on plan assets	15,857	(5,012)	—	—
Employer contribution	22,000	22,164	1,145	968
Benefits paid	(8,495)	(7,698)	(1,145)	(968)
Non-investment expenses	(1,044)	(808)	—	—
Fair value of assets at end of year	$148,949	$120,631	$ —	$ —
Funded status	$ (71,129)	$ (69,018)	$(23,402)	$(19,747)
Unrecognized net actuarial loss	93,631	82,917	6,762	4,043
Unrecognized prior service cost	1,384	1,552	2,023	2,154
Unrecognized transition asset	—	—	—	—
Prepaid (accrued) benefit cost	$ 23,886	$ 15,451	$(14,617)	$(13,550)
Amounts recognized in the statement of financial position consist of:				
Accrued benefit liability	$ (42,170)	$ (45,434)	$(18,571)	$(16,039)
Intangible pension asset	1,384	1,552	2,023	2,154
Accumulated other changes in non-owner equity	64,672	59,333	1,931	335

A minimum pension liability adjustment is required when the accumulated benefit obligation exceeds plan assets and accrued pension liabilities. This adjustment also requires the elimination of any previously recorded pension assets. The minimum liability adjustment, less allowable intangible assets, net of tax benefit, is reported as a component of other non-owner changes in equity. The amounts recorded in other non-owner changes in equity, net of tax, as a result of minimum pension liability adjustments for the pension and supplemental plans were $4,197,000, $25,025,000, and $11,083,000 in fiscal 2003, 2002, and 2001, respectively.

Changes in Fair Value of Derivatives

4.27

CORN PRODUCTS INTERNATIONAL, INC. (DEC)

Consolidated Statements of Comprehensive Income (Loss)

(In millions)	2003	2002	2001
Net income	$ 76	$ 63	$ 57
Comprehensive income (loss):			
Cumulative effect of adoption of SFAS 133, net of income taxes of $8 million	—	—	14
Unrealized gains (losses) on cash flow hedges, net of income tax effect of $5 million, $2 million and $11 million, respectively	9	(4)	(21)
Reclassification adjustment for losses (gains) on cash flow hedges included in net income, net of income tax effect of $5 million, $8 million and $7 million, respectively	10	14	(13)
Currency translation adjustment	58	(94)	(130)
Minimum pension liability, net of income tax effect	(2)	(1)	—
Comprehensive income (loss)	$151	$(22)	$ (93)

NOTES TO THE CONSOLIDATED FINANCIAL STATEMENTS

Note 2 (In Part): Summary of Significant Accounting Policies

Hedging Instruments

Effective January 1, 2001, the Company adopted Statement of Financial Accounting Standards No. 133, "Accounting for Derivative Instruments and Hedging Activities" ("SFAS 133"), as amended by SFAS No. 138, "Accounting for Certain Derivative Instruments and Certain Hedging Activities, an Amendment of SFAS 133" ("SFAS 138"). SFAS 133 and 138 establish standards for recognition and measurement of derivatives and hedging activities and require that all derivative instruments be recorded on the balance sheet at their respective fair values. Upon adoption, the Company recorded a cumulative effect type credit of $14 million (net of income taxes of $8 million) to other comprehensive income (loss), to recognize at fair value all derivatives that were designated as hedges of variable cash flows of certain forecasted transactions. Gains and losses on derivatives that were previously deferred as adjustments to the carrying amount of hedged items were not adjusted.

The Company uses derivative financial instruments principally to offset exposure to market risks arising from changes in commodity prices and interest rates. Derivative financial instruments currently used by the Company consist of commodity futures contracts and interest rate swap agreements. The Company enters into futures contracts, which are designated as hedges of specific volumes of commodities (corn and natural gas) that will be purchased and processed in a future month. These readily marketable exchange-traded futures contracts are recognized in the Consolidated Balance Sheets at fair value. The Company has also entered into interest rate swap agreements to take advantage of the current interest rate environment by effectively converting the interest rate on certain fixed rate debt to a variable rate.

On the date a derivative contract is entered into, the Company designates the derivative as either a hedge of variable cash flows to be paid related to certain forecasted purchases of corn or natural gas used in the manufacturing process ("a cash-flow hedge") or as a hedge of the fair value of certain fixed rate debt obligations ("a fair-value hedge"). This process includes linking all derivatives that are designated as fair-value or cash-flow hedges to specific assets and liabilities on the balance sheet or to specific firm commitments or forecasted transactions. For all hedging relationships, the Company formally documents the hedging relationships and its risk-management objective and strategy for undertaking the hedge transactions, the hedging instrument, the item, the nature of the risk being hedged, how the hedging instrument's effectiveness in offsetting the hedged risk will be assessed, and a description of the method of measuring ineffectiveness. This includes linking all derivatives that are designated as cash-flow or fair-value hedges to specific forecasted transactions or to specific assets and liabilities on the Consolidated Balance Sheet. The Company also formally assesses, both at the hedge's inception and on an ongoing basis, whether the derivatives that are used in hedging transactions are highly effective in offsetting changes in cash flows or fair values of hedged items. When it is determined that a derivative is not highly effective as a hedge or that it has ceased to be a highly effective hedge, the Company discontinues hedge accounting prospectively.

Changes in the fair value of a futures contract that is highly effective and that is designated and qualifies as a cash-flow hedge are recorded in other comprehensive income (loss), net of applicable income taxes, and recognized in the Consolidated Statement of Income when the finished goods produced using the hedged item are sold. The maximum term over which the Company hedges exposures to the variability of cash flows for commodity price risk is 36 months. Changes in the fair value of an interest rate swap agreement that is highly effective and that is designated and qualifies as a fair-value hedge, along with the loss or gain on the hedged debt obligation that is attributable to the hedged risk, are recorded in earnings. The ineffective portion of the change in fair value of a derivative instrument that qualifies as either a cash-flow hedge or a fair-value hedge is reported in earnings.

The Company discontinues hedge accounting prospectively when it is determined that the derivative is no longer effective in offsetting changes in the cash flows or fair value of the hedged item, the derivative expires or is sold, terminated or exercised, the derivative is de-designated as a hedging instrument because it is unlikely that a forecasted transaction will occur, or management determines that designation of the derivative as a hedging instrument is no longer appropriate. When hedge accounting is discontinued because it is probable that a forecasted transaction will not occur, the Company continues to carry the derivative on the Consolidated Balance Sheet at its fair value, and gains and losses that were accumulated in other comprehensive income are recognized immediately in earnings. When hedge accounting is discontinued because it is determined that the derivative no longer qualifies as an effective fair-value hedge, the Company continues to carry the derivative on the Consolidated Balance Sheet at its fair value and no longer adjusts the hedged asset or liability for changes in fair value. The adjustment of the carrying amount of the hedged asset or liability is accounted for in the same manner as other components of the carrying amount of that asset or liability. In all other situations in which hedge accounting is discontinued, the Company continues to carry the derivative at its fair value on the Consolidated Balance Sheet and recognizes any changes in its fair value in earnings.

Note 7 (In Part): Financial Instruments, Derivatives and Hedging Activities

Derivatives

The Company uses derivative financial instruments primarily to manage the exposure to price risk related to corn and natural gas purchases used in the manufacturing process and to manage its exposure to changes in interest rates on outstanding debt instruments. The Company generally does not enter into derivative instruments for any purpose other than hedging the cash flows associated with specific volumes of commodities that will be purchased and processed in a future month, and hedging the exposure related to changes in the fair value of outstanding fixed-rate debt instruments. The Company occasionally hedges commercial transactions and certain liabilities that are denominated in a currency other than the currency of the operating unit entering into the underlying transaction. The Company does not speculate using derivative instruments.

The derivative financial instruments that the Company uses in its management of commodity-price risk consist of open futures contracts and options traded through regulated commodity exchanges. The derivative financial instruments that the Company uses in its management of interest rate risk consist of interest rate swap agreements. By using derivative financial instruments to hedge exposures to changes in commodity prices and interest rates, the Company exposes itself to credit risk and market risk. Credit risk is the risk that the counterparty will fail to perform under the terms of the derivative contract. When the fair value of a derivative contract is positive, the counterparty owes the Company, which creates credit risk for the Company. When the fair value of a derivative contract is negative, the Company owes the counterparty and, therefore, it does not possess credit risk. The Company minimizes the credit risk in derivative instruments by entering into transactions only with investment grade counterparties. Market risk is the adverse effect on the value of a financial instrument that results from a change in commodity prices or interest rates. The market risk associated with commodity-price and interest rate contracts is managed by establishing and monitoring parameters that limit the types and degree of market risk that may be undertaken.

The Company maintains a commodity-price risk management strategy that uses derivative instruments to minimize significant, unanticipated earnings fluctuations caused by commodity-price volatility. For example, the manufacturing of the Company's products requires a significant volume of corn and natural gas. Price fluctuations in corn and natural gas cause market values of corn inventory to differ from its cost and the actual purchase price of corn and natural gas to differ from anticipated prices.

The Company periodically enters into futures and option contracts for a portion of its anticipated corn and natural gas usage generally over the next twelve months, in order to hedge the price risk associated with fluctuations in market prices. The contracts limit the unfavorable effect that price increases will have on corn and natural gas purchases. All of the Company's futures and option contracts have been designated as cash flow hedges.

Unrealized gains and losses associated with marking the corn and natural gas futures and option contracts to market are recorded as a component of other comprehensive income (loss) and included in the stockholders' equity section of the Consolidated Balance Sheets as part of accumulated other comprehensive income (loss). These amounts are subsequently reclassified into earnings in the month in which the related corn or natural gas is used or in the month a hedge is determined to be ineffective.

The Company assesses the effectiveness of a hedge with a corn or natural gas futures or option contract based on changes in the contract's intrinsic value. The changes in the market value of such contracts has historically been, and is expected to continue to be, highly effective at offsetting changes in the price of the hedged item. The amounts representing the ineffectiveness of these cash flow hedges are not significant.

The Company assesses its exposure to variability in interest rates by continually identifying and monitoring changes in interest rates that may adversely impact future cash flows and the fair value of existing debt instruments, and by evaluating hedging opportunities. The Company maintains risk management control systems to monitor interest rate risk attributable to both the Company's outstanding and forecasted debt obligations as well as the Company's offsetting hedge positions. The risk management control systems involve the use of analytical techniques, including sensitivity analysis, to estimate the expected impact of changes in interest rates on the fair value of the Company's outstanding and forecasted debt instruments.

The Company uses a combination of fixed and variable rate debt to finance its operations. The debt obligations with fixed cash flows expose the Company to variability in the fair value of outstanding debt instruments due to changes in interest rates. The Company has entered into interest rate swap agreements that effectively convert the interest rate on certain fixed-rate debt to a variable rate. These swaps call for the Company to receive interest at a fixed rate and to pay interest at a variable rate, thereby creating the equivalent of variable-rate debt.

The Company has designated the interest rate swap agreements as hedges of the changes in fair value of the fixed-rate debt obligation attributable to changes in interest rates. Changes in the fair value of interest rate swaps designated as hedging instruments that effectively offset the variability in the fair value of outstanding fixed-rate, long-term debt obligations are reported in earnings. These amounts offset the gain or loss (that is, the change in fair value) of the hedged fixed-rate debt instrument that is attributable to changes in interest rates (that is, the hedged risk) which is also recognized currently in earnings. The net gain or loss recognized in earnings during 2003 and 2002, representing the amount of the hedges' ineffectiveness and the component of the derivative instruments' gain or loss excluded from the assessment of hedge effectiveness, was not significant.

At December 31, 2003, the Company's accumulated other comprehensive income (loss) account included $7 million of unrealized losses, net of a $4 million tax benefit, related to derivative instruments that hedge the anticipated cash flows from future transactions, which are expected to be recognized in earnings within the next twelve months. Transactions and events expected to occur over the next twelve months that will necessitate reclassifying these derivatives losses to earnings include the sale of finished goods inventory that includes previously hedged purchases of raw corn. Cash flow hedges discontinued during the year were not material.

4.28

FLOWSERVE CORPORATION (DEC)

Consolidated Statements of Comprehensive Income/(Loss)

(Amounts in thousands)	2003	2002	2001
Net earnings (loss)	$52,888	$ 45,497	$(10,488)
Other comprehensive income (expense)			
Foreign currency translation adjustments	36,827	23,267	(40,104)
Minimum pension liability effects, net of tax effects	7,706	(42,947)	(16,223)
Cash flow hedging activity, net of tax effects			
Cumulative effect of change in accounting for hedging transactions	—	—	840
Other hedging activity	889	(161)	(4,985)
Other comprehensive income (expense)	45,422	(19,841)	(60,472)
Comprehensive income (loss)	$98,310	$ 25,656	$(70,960)

NOTES TO CONSOLIDATED FINANCIAL STATEMENTS

Note 1 (In Part): Significant Accounting Policies and Accounting Developments

Derivatives and Hedging Activities

We enter into forward contracts for purposes of hedging certain transactions denominated in foreign currencies. As part of our risk management strategy, we also enter into interest rate swap agreements for the purpose of hedging our exposure to floating interest rates on certain portions of our debt. We have a risk-management and derivatives policy statement outlining the conditions under which we can enter into hedging or forward transactions.

We employ a foreign currency hedging strategy to minimize potential losses in earnings or cash flows from unfavorable foreign currency exchange rate movements. These strategies also minimize potential gains from favorable exchange rate movements. Foreign currency exposures arise from transactions, including firm commitments and anticipated transactions, denominated in a currency other than an entity's functional currency and from foreign-denominated revenues and profits translated into U.S. dollars. The primary currencies to which we have exposure are the Euro, British pound, Canadian dollar, Mexican peso, Japanese yen, Singapore dollar, Brazilian real, Australian dollar, Argentinean peso and Venezuelan bolivar.

All derivatives are recognized on the balance sheet at their fair value. On the date that we enter into a derivative contract, we designate the derivative as (1) a hedge of (a) a forecasted transaction or (b) the variability of cash flows that are to be received or paid in connection with a recognized asset or liability (a "cash flow" hedge); or (2) a foreign currency fair value or cash flow hedge (a "foreign currency" hedge). Changes in the fair value of a derivative that is highly effective, designated and qualified as a cash flow hedge, to the extent that the hedge is effective, are recorded in other comprehensive income, until earnings are affected by the variability of cash flows of the hedged transaction. Changes in the fair value of foreign currency hedges are recorded in other comprehensive income since they satisfy the criteria for a cash flow hedge. Any hedge ineffectiveness (which represents the amount by which the changes in the fair value of the derivative do not mirror the change in the cash flow of the forecasted transaction) is recorded in current period earnings.

We formally document all relationships between hedging instruments and hedged items, as well as our risk management objective and strategy for undertaking various hedge transactions. This process includes linking all derivatives that are designated as fair value, cash flow or foreign currency hedges to (1) specific assets and liabilities on the balance sheet or (2) specific firm commitments or forecasted transactions. We also formally assess (both at the inception of the hedge and on an ongoing basis) whether the derivatives that are used in hedging transactions have been highly effective in offsetting changes in the fair value or cash flows of hedged items and whether those derivatives may be expected to remain highly effective in future periods.

We discontinue hedge accounting prospectively when:
- the derivative no longer effectively offsets changes in the fair value or cash flows of a hedged item (such as firm commitments or forecasted transactions);
- the derivative expires, terminates or is sold;
- the forecasted transaction is not probable to occur; or
- we determine that designating the derivative as a hedging instrument is no longer appropriate.

When we discontinue hedge accounting because it is no longer probable that the forecasted transaction will occur in the originally expected period, the gain or loss on the derivative remaining in accumulated other comprehensive income is reclassified into earnings. In all situations in which hedge accounting is discontinued and the derivative remains outstanding, we carry the derivative at its fair value on the balance sheet, recognizing changes in the fair value in current period earnings.

Note 8: Derivatives and Hedging Activities

We enter into forward contracts to hedge our risks associated with transactions denominated in foreign currencies. Our risk management and derivatives policy specifies the conditions under which we may enter into derivative contracts. At December 31, 2003 and 2002, we had approximately $75.1 million and $48.6 million, respectively, of notional amount in outstanding contracts with third parties. At December 31, 2003, the maximum length of any forward contract currently in place was 17 months. The fair value of outstanding forward contracts at December 31, 2003 and 2002 was an asset of $5.4 million and $3.3 million, respectively.

Also as part of our risk management program, we enter into interest rate swap agreements to hedge exposure to floating interest rates on certain portions of our debt. At December 31, 2003 and 2002, we had $215.0 million and $125.0 million, respectively, of notional amount in outstanding interest rate swaps with third parties. At December 31, 2003, the maximum length of any interest rate contract currently in place was approximately three years. At December 31, 2003 and 2002, the fair value of the interest rate swap agreements was a liability of $7.6 million and $9.8 million, respectively.

We are exposed to risk from credit-related losses resulting from nonperformance by counterparties to our financial instruments. We perform credit evaluations of our counterparties under forward contracts and interest rate swap agreements and expect all counterparties to meet their obligations. We have not experienced credit losses from our counterparties.

We adopted SFAS No. 133, "Accounting for Derivative Instruments and Hedging Activities," as amended, on January 1, 2001. In accordance with the transition provisions of SFAS 133, we recorded a net $0.8 million cumulative-effect adjustment in other comprehensive income representing the fair value of hedging instruments as of January 1, 2001 after deferred tax of $0.5 million.

Hedging related transactions, recorded to other comprehensive income (expense), net of deferred taxes, are summarized below:

(Amounts in thousands)	Other Comprehensive Income (Expense)		
	2003[1]	2002[1]	2001[1]
Recognize fair value at January 1, 2001			
Interest rate swap agreements	$ —	$ —	$(1,355)
Forward contracts	—	—	2,195
Reclassification to earnings for settlements during the year			
Interest rate swap agreements	3,014	4,336	1,205
Forward contracts	(2,074)	177	660
Change in fair value			
Interest rate swap agreements	(1,574)	(6,603)	(3,790)
Forward contracts	1,523	1,929	(3,060)
Year ended December 31	$ 889	$ (161)	$(4,145)

[1] Utilizing an income tax rate of approximately 37% comprised of the effective rates in each taxing jurisdiction.

The following amounts net of deferred taxes represent the expected recognition into earnings for our hedging contracts:

(Amounts in millions)	Interest Rate Swap	Forward Contracts	Total
2004	$(2.6)	$3.3	$ 0.7
2005	(1.4)	0.1	(1.3)
2006	(1.0)	—	(1.0)
2007	—	—	—
2008	—	—	—
Thereafter	—	—	—
Total	$(5.0)	$3.4	$(1.6)

Unrealized Losses/Gains on Certain Investments

4.29

CSP INC. (SEP)

Consolidated Statements of Shareholders' Equity and Comprehensive Income

(Amounts in thousands)	Shares	Amount	Additional Paid-In Capital	Retained Earnings	Accumulated Other Comprehensive Income	Treasury Stock	Total Shareholders' Equity	Comprehensive Income (Loss)
Balance, August 31, 2000	4,069	$41	$11,070	$19,962	$(1,079)	$(2,548)	$27,446	
Comprehensive income:								
Net loss	—	—	—	(2,885)	—	—	(2,885)	$(2,885)
Other comprehensive income (loss):								
Unrealized loss on available-for-sale securities, net of tax	—	—	—	—	(68)	—	(68)	(68)
Effect of foreign currency translation	—	—	—	—	147	—	147	147
Additional minimum pension liability	—	—	—	—	(1,472)	—	(1,472)	(1,472)
Total comprehensive loss								(4,278)
Exercise of stock options	2	—	7	—			7	
Issuance of shares under employee stock purchase plan	14	—	56	—	—	—	56	
Purchase of treasury stock	—	—	—	—	—	(313)	(313)	
Dividend distribution of shares of vertical buyer	—	—	—	(718)	—	—	(718)	
Income tax benefit related to exercise of stock options	—	—	102	—	—	—	102	
Balance August 31, 2001	4,085	41	11,235	16,359	(2,472)	(2,861)	22,302	
Comprehensive income:								
Net loss	—	—	—	(658)	—	—	(658)	(658)
Other comprehensive income (loss):								
Unrealized loss on available-for-sale securities, net of tax	—	—	—	—	(8)	—	(8)	(8)
Effect of foreign currency translation	—	—	—	—	22	—	22	22
Total comprehensive loss	—	—	—	—	—	—	—	(644)
Balance September 30, 2001	4,085	$41	$11,235	$15,701	$(2,458)	$(2,861)	$21,658	

(continued)

(Amounts in thousands)	Shares	Amount	Additional Paid-In Capital	Retained Earnings	Accumulated Other Comprehensive Income	Treasury Stock	Total Shareholders' Equity	Comprehensive Income (Loss)
Balance September 30, 2001	4,085	$41	$11,235	$15,701	$(2,458)	$(2,861)	$21,658	
Comprehensive income:								
Net loss	—	—	—	(5,663)	—	—	(5,663)	(5,663)
Other comprehensive income (loss):								
Unrealized loss on available-for-sale securities, net of tax	—	—	—	—	(22)	—	(22)	(22)
Effect of foreign currency translation	—	—	—	—	129	—	129	129
Additional minimum pension liability	—	—	—	—	(1,838)	—	(1,838)	(1,838)
Total comprehensive loss								(7,394)
Issuance of shares under employee stock purchase plan	10	—	40	—	—	—	40	
Sale of treasury stock	—	—	—	—	—	4	4	
Balance September 30, 2002	4,095	$41	$11,275	$10,038	$(4,189)	$(2,857)	$14,308	
Comprehensive income:								
Net loss	—	—	—	(1,384)	—	—	(1,384)	(1,384)
Other comprehensive income (loss):								
Unrealized loss on available-for-sale securities, net of tax	—	—	—	—	(25)	—	(25)	(25)
Effect of foreign currency translation	—	—	—	—	(725)	—	(725)	(725)
Additional minimum pension liability	—	—	—	—	(268)	—	(268)	(268)
Total comprehensive loss								$(2,402)
Issuance of shares under employee stock purchase plan	14	—	28	—	—	—	28	
Purchase of treasury stock	—	—	—	—	—	(2)	(2)	
Balance September 30, 2003	4,109	$41	$11,303	$ 8,654	$(5,207)	$(2,859)	$11,932	

NOTES TO CONSOLIDATED FINANCIAL STATEMENTS

1 (In Part): Summary of Significant Accounting Policies

Investments

The Company classifies its investments at the time of purchase as either held-to-maturity or available-for-sale. Held-to-maturity securities are those investments that the Company has the ability and intent to hold until maturity. Held-to-maturity securities are recorded at cost, adjusted for the amortization of premiums and discounts which approximates market value. Available-for-sale securities are recorded at fair value. Unrealized gains and losses net of the related tax effect on available-for-sale securities are reported in accumulated other comprehensive income, a component of stockholders' equity, until realized. The estimated fair market values of investments are based on quoted market prices as of the end of the reporting period.

Interest income is accrued as earned. Dividend income is recognized as income on the date the stock trades "ex-dividend." The cost of marketable securities sold is determined by the specific identification method and realized gains or losses are reflected in income.

3 (In Part): Investments

At September 30, 2003 and 2002, investments consisted of the following:

(Amounts in thousands)	Amortized Cost	Gross Unrealized Gains	Fair Value
September 30, 2003			
Marketable equity securities	$ 268	$ 12	$ 280
Bonds and municipal revenue notes	2,847	—	2,847
Money market funds and commercial paper	4,363	—	4,363
U.S. treasury bills	125	—	125
Total	$ 7,603	$ 12	$ 7,615
September 30, 2002			
Marketable equity securities	$ 479	$ 37	$ 516
Bonds and municipal revenue notes	6,171	—	6,171
Money market funds and commercial paper	5,304	—	5,304
U.S. treasury bills	125	—	125
Total	$12,079	$ 37	$12,116

(Amounts in thousands)	Short-Term	Long-Term	Total
September 30, 2003			
Held-to-maturity	$ 7,085	$250	$ 7,335
Available-for-sale	280	—	280
	7,365	250	$ 7,615
September 30, 2002			
Held-to-maturity	$11,512	$125	$11,637
Available-for-sale	479	—	479
	$11,991	$125	$12,116

Net unrealized gains on available-for-sale investments are reported as a separate component of stockholders' equity until realized. This change in unrealized loss amounted to ($25,000), ($22,000) and ($68,000) for the years ended September 30, 2003 and 2002 and August 31, 2001, respectively.

At September 30, 2003, the cost and estimated fair values of short-term and long-term marketable debt securities (excluding cash equivalents) by contractual maturity were as follows (in thousands):

	Cost	Fair Value
Less than one year	$6,781	$6,793
Mature in 1–2 years	127	127
Mature in 2–5 years	150	150
Mature after 5 years	545	545
Total	$7,603	$7,615

5. Accumulated Other Comprehensive Income

The components of Accumulated Other Comprehensive Income are as follows:

(Amounts in thousands)	Unrealized Gain (Loss) on Investments	Foreign Translation Adjustment	Accumulated Additional Pension Liability	Accumulated Other Comprehensive Income
Balance August 31, 2001	$ 67	$(1,067)	$(1,472)	$(2,472)
Change in period	(8)	22	—	14
Balance September 30, 2001	59	(1,045)	(1,472)	(2,458)
Change in period	(22)	129	(1,838)	(1,731)
Balance September 30, 2002	37	(916)	(3,310)	(4,189)
Change in period	(25)	(725)	(268)	(1,018)
Balance September 30, 2003	$ 12	$(1,641)	$(3,578)	$(5,207)

4.30

ELI LILLY AND COMPANY (DEC)

Consolidated Statements of Comprehensive Income

(Dollars in millions)	2003	2002	2001
Net income	$2,560.8	$2,707.9	$2,780.0
Other comprehensive income (loss)			
Foreign currency translation gains (losses)	473.0	273.6	(83.8)
Net unrealized gains (losses) on securities	72.0	(67.4)	47.7
Minimum pension liability adjustment	(9.8)	(4.6)	(95.6)
Effective portion of cash flow hedges	(2.1)	(217.9)	(42.0)
Other comprehensive income (loss) before income taxes	533.1	(16.3)	(173.7)
Provision for income taxes related to other comprehensive income (loss) items	(22.4)	93.9	36.5
Other comprehensive income (loss) (Note 14)	510.7	77.6	(137.2)
Comprehensive income	$3,071.5	$2,785.5	$2,642.8

NOTES TO CONSOLIDATED FINANCIAL STATEMENTS
(Dollars in millions)

Note 1 (In Part): Summary of Significant Accounting Policies

Investments

Substantially all debt and marketable equity securities are classified as available-for-sale. Available-for-sale securities are carried at fair value with the unrealized gains and losses, net of tax, reported in other comprehensive income. Unrealized losses considered to be other-than-temporary are recognized in earnings currently. Factors we consider in making this evaluation include company-specific drivers of the decrease in stock price, status of projects in development, near-term prospects of the issuer, the length of time the value has been depressed, and the financial condition of the industry. Realized gains and losses on sales of available-for-sale securities are computed based upon specific identification of the initial cost adjusted for any other-than-temporary declines in fair value. Investments in companies over which we have significant influence but not a controlling interest are accounted for using the equity method with our share of earnings or losses reported in other income. We own no investments that are considered to be trading securities.

Note 5 (In Part): Financial Instruments and Investments

Fair Value of Financial Instruments

A summary of our outstanding financial instruments and other investments at December 31 follows:

| | 2003 | | 2002 | |
	Carrying Amount	Fair Value	Carrying Amount	Fair Value
Short-term investments				
Debt securities	$ 957.0	$ 957.0	$1,708.8	$1,708.8
Noncurrent investments				
Marketable equity	$ 105.5	$ 105.5	$ 85.9	$ 85.9
Debt securities	3,173.1	3,173.1	2,458.6	2,458.6
Equity method and other investments	96.0	N/A	605.9	N/A
	$3,374.6		$3,150.4	
Long-term debt, including current portion	$4,867.5	$5,107.8	$4,643.6	$4,886.7

We determine fair values based on quoted market values where available or discounted cash flow analyses (principally long-term debt). The fair value of equity method investments is not readily available and disclosure is not required. The fair value and carrying amount of risk-management instruments in the aggregate were not material at December 31, 2003 and 2002. Approximately $3.6 billion of our investments in debt securities mature within five years.

A summary of the unrealized gains and losses (pretax) of our available-for-sale securities in other comprehensive income at December 31 follows:

	2003	2002
Unrealized gross gains	$72.3	$77.4
Unrealized gross losses	10.6	87.7

The net adjustment to unrealized gains and losses (net of tax) on available-for-sale securities increased (decreased) other comprehensive income by $45.4 million, ($45.0) million, and $34.3 million in 2003, 2002, and 2001, respectively. Activity related to our available-for-sale investment portfolio was as follows:

	2003	2002	2001
Proceeds from sales	$4,903.7	$3,724.2	$1,826.3
Realized gross gains on sales	72.1	57.0	14.1
Realized gross losses on sales	26.4	35.2	0.1

Note 14: Other Comprehensive Income (Loss)

The accumulated balances related to each component of other comprehensive income (loss) were as follows:

	Foreign Currency Translation	Unrealized Gains (Losses) on Securities	Minimum Pension Liability Adjustment	Effective Portion of Cash Flow Hedges	Accumulated Other Comprehensive Income (Loss)
Beginning balance at January 1, 2003	$(356.5)	$ (2.9)	$(137.8)	$(173.6)	$(670.8)
Other comprehensive income (loss)	473.2	45.4	(6.4)	(1.5)	510.7
Balance at December 31, 2003	$ 116.7	$42.5	$(144.2)	$(175.1)	$(160.1)

The amounts above are net of income taxes. The income taxes related to other comprehensive income were not significant as income taxes were generally not provided for foreign currency translation.

The unrealized gains (losses) on securities is net of reclassification adjustments of $37.4 million, $11.3 million, and $12.3 million, net of tax, in 2003, 2002, and 2001, respectively, for net realized gains on sales of securities included in net income. The effective portion of cash flow hedges is net of reclassification adjustments of $27.2 million in 2003, net of tax, for realized losses on foreign currency options and $14.2 million and $6.5 million, net of tax, in 2003 and 2002, respectively, for interest expense on interest rate swaps designated as cash flow hedges. In 2001, reclassification adjustments were $16.5 million, net of tax, for realized gains on foreign currency options.

Generally, the assets and liabilities of foreign operations are translated into U.S. dollars using the current exchange rate. For those operations, changes in exchange rates generally do not affect cash flows; therefore, resulting translation adjustments are made in shareholders' equity rather than in income.

Reclassification Adjustments

4.31

MCDERMOTT INTERNATIONAL, INC. (DEC)

Consolidated Statements of Comprehensive Income (Loss)

(In thousands)	2003	2002	2001
Net loss	$ (95,229)	$ (776,394)	$(20,022)
Other comprehensive income (loss)			
Currency translation adjustments			
Foreign currency translation adjustments	1,150	267	(4,826)
Reclassification adjustment for impairments of investments	—	18,435	—
Sales of investments in foreign entities	—	1,041	1,513
Unrealized gains (losses) on derivative financial instruments			
Unrealized gains (losses) on derivative financial instruments	673	3,858	(2,506)
Reclassification adjustment for (gains) losses included in net loss	(994)	(534)	266
Minimum pension liability adjustment			
Net of tax benefits of $1,554,000 in the year ended December 31, 2001	134,499	(451,756)	(2,849)
Unrealized gains (losses) on investments			
Unrealized gains (losses) arising during the period, net of taxes of $0, $0 and $30,000 in the years ended December 31, 2003, 2002 and 2001, respectively	(292)	371	9,286
Reclassification adjustment for net gains included in net loss, net of tax benefits of $0, $0 and $162,000 in the years ended December 31, 2003, 2002 and 2001, respectively	(405)	(997)	(3,143)
Other comprehensive income (loss)	134,631	(429,315)	(2,259)
Comprehensive income (loss)	$ 39,402	$(1,205,709)	$(22,281)

NOTES TO CONSOLIDATED FINANCIAL STATEMENTS

Note 1 (In Part): Summary of Significant Accounting Policies

Investments

Our investments, primarily government obligations and other highly liquid money market instruments, are classified as available-for-sale and are carried at fair value, with the unrealized gains and losses, net of tax, reported as a component of accumulated other comprehensive loss. We classify investments available for current operations in the balance sheet as current assets, while we classify investments held for long-term purposes as noncurrent assets. We adjust the amortized cost of debt securities for amortization of premiums and accretion of discounts to maturity. That amortization is included in interest income. We include realized gains and losses on our investments in other income (expense). The cost of securities sold is based on the specific identification method. We include interest on securities in interest income.

Derivative Financial Instruments

Our worldwide operations give rise to exposure to market risks from changes in foreign exchange rates. We use derivative financial instruments to reduce the impact of changes in foreign exchange rates on our operating results. We use these instruments primarily to hedge our exposure associated with revenues or costs on our long-term contracts that are denominated in currencies other than our operating entities' functional currencies. We record these contracts at fair value on our consolidated balance sheet. Depending on the hedge designation at the inception of the contract, the related gains and losses on these contracts are either deferred in stockholders' deficit (as a component of accumulated other comprehensive loss) until the hedged item is recognized in earnings or offset against the change in fair value of the hedged firm commitment through earnings. The ineffective portion of a derivative's change in fair value is immediately recognized in earnings. The gain or loss on a derivative financial instrument not designated as a hedging instrument is also immediately recognized in earnings. Gains and losses on derivative financial instruments that require immediate recognition are included as a component of other-net in our consolidated statement of loss.

Note 14 (In Part): Investments

The following is a summary of our available-for-sale securities at December 31, 2003:

(In thousands)	Amortized Cost	Gross Unrealized Gains	Gross Unrealized Losses	Estimated Fair Value
U.S. treasury securities and obligations of U.S. government agencies	$17,616	$8	$—	$17,624
Money market instruments	25,206	—	30	25,176
Total	$42,822	$8	$30	$42,800

At December 31, 2003, all our available-for-sale debt securities have contractual maturities of less than one year.

The following is a summary of our available-for-sale securities at December 31, 2002:

(In thousands)	Amortized Cost	Gross Unrealized Gains	Gross Unrealized Losses	Estimated Fair Value
U.S. treasury securities and obligations of U.S. government agencies	$156,365	$585	$—	$156,950
Corporate notes and bonds	10,366	95	1	10,460
Other debt securities	5,821	—	4	5,817
Total	$172,552	$680	$ 5	$173,227

Proceeds, gross realized gains and gross realized losses on sales of available-for-sale securities were as follows:

(In thousands)	Proceeds	Gross Realized Gains	Gross Realized Losses
Year ended December 31, 2003	$ 417,156	$ 405	$ —
Year ended December 31, 2002	$ 775,441	$ 997	$ —
Year ended December 31, 2001	$1,229,087	$7,614	$4,634

Note 15 (In Part): Derivative Financial Instruments

We enter into derivative financial instruments primarily as hedges of certain firm purchase and sale commitments denominated in foreign currencies. We record these contracts at fair value on our consolidated balance sheet. Depending on the hedge designation at the inception of the contract, the related gains and losses on these contracts are either deferred in stockholders' equity (as a component of accumulated other comprehensive loss) until the hedged item is recognized in earnings or offset against the change in fair value of the hedged firm commitment through earnings. The ineffective portion of a derivative's change in fair value and any portion excluded from the assessment of effectiveness are immediately recognized in earnings. The gain or loss on a derivative instrument not designated as a hedging instrument is also immediately recognized in earnings. Gains and losses on derivative financial instruments that require immediate recognition are included as a component of other-net in our consolidated statement of loss.

At December 31, 2003, we had foreign currency option contracts outstanding to purchase 9.1 million Euros at a weighted-average strike price of 1.245 with varying expiration dates through November 30, 2004. At December 31, 2002, we had forward contracts to purchase $15.5 million in foreign currencies (primarily Indonesian Rupiah and Euro) and to sell $0.9 million in foreign currencies at varying maturities through August 2003. We have designated substantially all of these contracts as cash flow hedging instruments. For the option contracts entered during 2003, the hedged risk is the risk of changes in forecasted U.S. dollar equivalent cash flows related to long-term contracts attributable to movements in the exchange rate above the strike prices. We assess effectiveness based upon total changes in cash flows of the option contracts. For forward contracts, the hedged risk is the risk of changes in functional-currency-equivalent cash flows attributable to changes in spot exchange rates of forecasted transactions related to long-term contracts. We exclude from our assessment of effectiveness the portion of the fair value of the forward contracts attributable to the difference between spot exchange rates and forward exchange rates. At December 31, 2003, we had deferred approximately $0.8 million of net gains on these derivative financial instruments, 75% of which we expect to recognize in income over the next 12 months primarily in accordance with the percentage-of-completion method of accounting. At December 31, 2002, we had deferred approximately $1.1 million of net gains on forward contracts. For the years ended December 31, 2003 and 2002, we immediately recognized net gains of approximately $0.1 million and $1.5 million, respectively. Substantially all of these net gains represent changes in the fair value of forward contracts excluded from hedge effectiveness.

4.32

VALERO ENERGY CORPORATION (DEC)

Consolidated Statements of Comprehensive Income

(Millions of dollars)	2003	2002	2001
Net income	$621.5	$ 91.5	$563.6
Other comprehensive income (loss)			
Foreign currency translation adjustment	163.0	13.2	—
Minimum pension liability adjustment, net of income tax (expense) benefit of $(2.6) and $7.7	4.9	(14.3)	—
Net gain (loss) on derivative instruments designated and qualifying as cash flow hedges			
Statement No. 133 transition adjustment, net of income tax expense of $15.2	—	—	28.3
Net gain (loss) arising during the year, net of income tax (expense) benefit of $(12.8), $(40.8) and $19.4	23.7	75.7	(36.0)
Net (gain) loss reclassified into income, net of income tax expense (benefit) of $11.3, $50.5 and $(13.9)	(20.9)	(93.8)	25.8
Net gain (loss) on cash flow hedges	2.8	(18.1)	18.1
Other comprehensive income (loss)	170.7	(19.2)	18.1
Comprehensive income	$792.2	$ 72.3	$581.7

NOTES TO CONSOLIDATED FINANCIAL STATEMENTS

1 (In Part): Summary of Significant Accounting Policies

Derivative Instruments (In Part)

All derivative instruments are recorded in the balance sheet as either assets or liabilities measured at their fair value. When Valero enters into a derivative instrument. It is designated as a fair value hedge, a cash flow hedge, an economic hedge or a trading instrument. For Valero's economic hedging relationships (hedges not designated as fair value or cash flow hedges) and for derivative instruments entered into by Valero for trading purposes, the derivative instrument is recorded at fair value and changes in the fair value of the derivative instrument are recognized currently in income. The gain or loss on a derivative instrument designated and qualifying as a fair value hedge, as well as the offsetting loss or gain on the hedged item attributable to the hedged risk, are recognized currently in income in the same period. The effective portion of the gain or loss on a derivative instrument designated and qualifying as a cash flow hedge is reported as a component of "other comprehensive income" and is reclassified into income in the same period or periods during which the hedged forecasted transaction affects income. The remaining ineffective portion of the gain or loss on the derivative instrument, if any, is recognized currently in income.

Comprehensive Income

Comprehensive income consists of net income and other gains and losses affecting stockholders' equity that, under United States generally accepted accounting principles, are excluded from net income, such as foreign currency translation adjustments, minimum pension liability adjustments and gains and losses related to certain derivative instruments.

18 (In Part): Risk Management Activities

Commodity Price Risk

Valero is exposed to market risks related to the volatility of crude oil and refined product prices, as well as volatility in the price of natural gas used in its refining operations. To reduce the impact of this price volatility, Valero uses derivative commodity instruments (swaps, futures and options) to manage its exposure to:

- changes in the fair value of a portion of its refinery feedstock and refined product inventories and a portion of its unrecognized firm commitments to purchase these inventories (fair value hedges);
- changes in cash flows of certain forecasted transactions such as forecasted feedstock purchases, natural gas purchases and refined product sales (cash flow hedges); and
- price volatility on a portion of its refined product inventories and on certain forecasted feedstock and refined product purchases that are not designated as either fair value or cash flow hedges (economic hedges).

In addition, Valero uses derivative commodity instruments for trading purposes based on its fundamental and technical analysis of market conditions.

Interest Rate Risk

Valero is exposed to market risk for changes in interest rates related to certain of its long-term debt obligations. Interest rate swap agreements are used to manage Valero's fixed to floating interest rate position by converting certain fixed-rate debt to floating-rate debt.

Foreign Currency Risk

Valero is exposed to exchange rate fluctuations on transactions related to its Canadian operations. To manage its exposure to these exchange rate fluctuations, Valero uses foreign currency exchange and purchase contracts. These contracts are not designated as hedging instruments.

Current Period Disclosures

The net gain (loss) recognized in income representing the amount of hedge ineffectiveness was as follows (in millions):

	2003	2002	2001
Fair value hedges	$4.8	$ (1.2)	$ (3.4)
Cash flow hedges	4.1	29.3	(20.8)

The above amounts were included in "cost of sales" in the consolidated statements of income. No component of the derivative instruments' gains or losses was excluded from the assessment of hedge effectiveness. No amounts were recognized in income for hedged firm commitments that no longer qualify as fair value hedges.

For cash flow hedges, gains and losses currently reported in "accumulated other comprehensive income (loss)" in the consolidated balance sheets will be reclassified into income when the forecasted transactions affect income. The estimated amount of existing net gain included in "accumulated other comprehensive income (loss)" as of December 31, 2003 that is expected to be reclassified into income within the next 12 months is $2.8 million. As of December 31, 2003, the maximum length of time over which Valero was hedging its exposure to the variability in future cash flows for forecasted transactions was one year. For the years ended December 31, 2003, 2002 and 2001, there were no amounts reclassified from "accumulated other comprehensive income (loss)" into income as a result of the discontinuance of cash flow hedge accounting.

Section 5: Stockholders' Equity

GENERAL

5.01 This section reviews the presentation of transactions, other than comprehensive income (loss) for the year, affecting stockholders' equity.

RETAINED EARNINGS

PRESENTATION OF CHANGES IN RETAINED EARNINGS

5.02 Paragraph 152 of Statement of Financial Accounting Standards (SFAS) No. 95, *Statement of Cash Flows,* states that a complete set of financial statements includes a presentation of "results of operations." Paragraph 7 of Accounting Principles Board (APB) Opinion No. 9, *Reporting the Results of Operations,* states that a statement of income and a statement of retained earnings "are designed to reflect" results of operations. As shown in Table 5-1, which summarizes the presentation formats used by the survey companies to present changes in retained earnings, changes in retained earnings are most frequently presented in a Statement of Stockholders' Equity. Examples of statements showing changes in retained earnings are presented throughout this section.

5.03

TABLE 5-1: PRESENTATION OF CHANGES IN RETAINED EARNINGS

	2003	2002	2001	2000
Statement of stockholders' equity.......	586	581	578	577
Separate statement of retained earnings...	7	9	9	7
Combined statement of income and retained earnings............................	2	3	6	10
Schedule in notes................................	5	7	7	6
Total Companies............................	**600**	**600**	**600**	**600**

DIVIDENDS

5.04 Table 5-2 shows the nature of distributions made by the survey companies to their shareholders. Approximately 58% of the survey companies paying cash dividends to common stock shareholders indicate the per share amount of such dividends in the statement of retained earnings; approximately 40% of the survey companies made a similar disclosure for cash dividends paid to preferred stock shareholders.

5.05 Stock purchase rights enable the holders of such rights to purchase additional equity in a company if an outside party acquires or tenders for a substantial minority interest in the subject Company. The one company issuing stock purchase rights during 2003, did so under a plan which replaced a plan adopted in a prior year.

5.06 Examples of distributions to shareholders follow.

5.07

TABLE 5-2: DIVIDENDS

	Number of Companies			
	2003	2002	2001	2000
Cash Dividends Paid to Common Stock Shareholders				
Per share amount disclosed in retained earnings statements..........	213	219	229	239
Per share amount not disclosed in retained earnings statements..........	157	135	156	164
Total.......................................	**370**	**354**	**385**	**403**
Cash Dividends Paid to Preferred Stock Shareholders				
Per share amount disclosed in retained earnings statements..........	22	22	17	25
Per share amount not disclosed in retained earnings statements..........	32	38	48	44
Total.......................................	**54**	**60**	**65**	**69**
Stock Dividends.............................	**4**	**6**	**4**	**12**
Dividends in Kind.............................	**7**	**10**	**14**	**7**
Stock Purchase Rights.....................	**1**	**4**	**7**	**9**

Cash Dividends

5.08

CIGNA CORPORATION (DEC)

Consolidated Statements of Comprehensive Income and Changes in Shareholders' Equity

(In millions, except per share amounts)	2003 Comprehensive Income	2003 Shareholders' Equity	2002 Comprehensive Income	2002 Shareholders' Equity	2001 Comprehensive Income	2001 Shareholders' Equity
Common stock, beginning of year		$ 68		$ 68		$ 67
Issuance of common stock for employee benefit plans		1		—		1
Common stock, end of year		$ 69		$ 68		$ 68
Additional paid-in capital, beginning of year		$ 3,212		$ 3,093		$ 2,966
Issuance of common stock for employee benefit plans		67		119		127
Additional paid-in capital, end of year		$ 3,279		$ 3,212		$ 3,093
Accumulated other comprehensive income (loss), beginning of year		$ (202)		$ 147		$ 221
Net unrealized appreciation fixed maturities	$ 98	98	$ 323	323	$ 26	26
Net unrealized appreciation (depreciation), equity securities	3	3	(24)	(24)	(80)	(80)
Net unrealized appreciation (depreciation) on securities	101		299		(54)	
Net unrealized appreciation (depreciation), derivatives	(18)	(18)	(4)	(4)	10	10
Net translation of foreign currencies	18	18	(6)	(6)	(30)	(30)
Minimum pension liability adjustment	47	47	(638)	(638)	—	—
Other comprehensive income (loss)	$148		$(349)		$ (74)	
Accumulated other comprehensive income (loss), end of year		$ (54)		$ (202)		$ 147
Retained earnings, beginning of year		$ 9,299		$ 9,882		$ 9,081
Net income (loss)	$668	668	$(398)	(398)	$989	989
Common dividends declared (per share: $1.32; $1.32; $1.28)		(185)		(185)		(188)
Retained earnings, end of year		$ 9,782		$ 9,299		$ 9,882
Treasury stock, beginning of year		$(8,510)		$(8,135)		$(6,922)
Repurchase of common stock		—		(343)		(1,139)
Other treasury stock transactions, net		(47)		(32)		(74)
Treasury stock, end of year		$(8,557)		$(8,510)		$(8,135)
Total comprehensive income (loss) and shareholders' equity	$816	$ 4,519	$(747)	$ 3,867	$915	$ 5,055

5.09

IMC GLOBAL INC. (DEC)

Consolidated Statement of Stockholders' Equity

(In millions, except per share amounts)	Outstanding Shares	Preferred Stock	Common Stock	Capital in Excess of Par Value	Accumulated Deficit	Accumulated Other Comprehensive Income (Loss)	Treasury Stock	Total Stockholders' Equity	Comprehensive Income (Loss)
Balance as of December 31, 2000	114.8	$ —	$125.2	$1,692.2	$ (790.0)	$ (58.6)	$(293.4)	$ 675.4	$(366.3)
Net loss	—	—	—	—	(66.5)	—	—	(66.5)	$ (66.5)
Foreign currency translation adjustment	—	—	—	—	—	(16.9)	—	(16.9)	(16.9)
Cumulative effect of a change in accounting principle	—	—	—	—	—	2.9	—	2.9	2.9
Net unrealized losses on derivative instruments	—	—	—	—	—	(19.5)	—	(19.5)	(19.5)
Minimum pension liability	—	—	—	—	—	(25.0)	—	(25.0)	(25.0)
Dividends ($0.08 per share)	—	—	—	—	(8.8)	—	—	(8.8)	—
Other	0.2	—	—	(11.3)	—	—	10.4	(0.9)	—
Balance as of December 31, 2001	115.0	$ —	$125.2	$1,680.9	$ (865.3)	$(117.1)	$(283.0)	$ 540.7	$(125.0)
Net loss	—	—	—	—	(110.2)	—	—	(110.2)	$(110.2)
Foreign currency translation adjustment	—	—	—	—	—	1.1	—	1.1	1.1
Net unrealized gains on derivative instruments	—	—	—	—	—	19.5	—	19.5	19.5
Minimum pension liability	—	—	—	—	—	(49.9)	—	(49.9)	(49.9)
Issuance of stock	5.4	—	5.4	62.5	—	—	—	67.9	—
Share repurchase	(5.4)	—	—	—	—	—	(79.5)	(79.5)	—
Dividends ($0.08 per share)	—	—	—	—	(9.2)	—	—	(9.2)	—
Common equity forward	—	—	—	—	—	—	9.3	9.3	—
Other	—	—	—	0.5	—	—	1.5	2.0	—
Balance as of December 31, 2002	115.0	$ —	$130.6	$1,743.9	$ (984.7)	$(146.4)	$(351.7)	$ 391.7	$(139.5)
Net loss	—	—	—	—	(135.4)	—	—	(135.4)	$(135.4)
Foreign currency translation adjustment	—	—	—	—	—	129.3	—	129.3	129.3
Net unrealized gains on derivative instruments	—	—	—	—	—	11.4	—	11.4	11.4
Minimum pension liability	—	—	—	—	—	(4.1)	—	(4.1)	(4.1)
Unrealized gain on available-for-sale securities	—	—	—	—	—	10.8	—	10.8	10.8
Issuance of preferred stock	—	2.8	—	130.3	—	—	—	133.1	—
Dividends on preferred stock ($1.8854 per share)	—	—	—	—	(5.2)	—	—	(5.2)	—
Dividends on common stock ($0.06 per share)	—	—	—	—	(6.9)	—	—	(6.9)	—
Other	0.1	—	—	(2.5)	—	—	4.4	1.9	—
Balance as of December 31, 2003	115.1	$2.8	$130.6	$1,871.7	$(1,132.2)	$ 1.0	$(347.3)	$ 526.6	$ 12.0

Dividends-in-Kind

5.10

CIRCUIT CITY STORES, INC. (FEB)

Consolidated Statements of Stockholders' Equity

(Amounts in thousands except per share data)	Shares Outstanding		Common Stock		Capital in Excess of Par Value	Retained Earnings	Total
	Circuit City	CarMax Group	Circuit City	CarMax Group			
Balance at March 1, 2000	203,868	25,614	$101,934	$ 12,807	$576,574	$1,450,859	$2,142,174
Net earnings	—	—	—	—	—	160,802	160,802
Exercise of common stock options	1,526	56	763	28	35,391	—	36,182
Shares issued under employee stock purchase plans	862	—	431	—	16,119	—	16,550
Shares issued under stock incentive plans	1,486	—	743	—	31,912	—	32,655
Tax benefit from stock issued	—	—	—	—	29,839	—	29,839
Cancellation of restricted stock	(722)	(31)	(361)	(15)	(32,774)	—	(33,150)
Unearned compensation—restricted stock	—	—	—	—	(14,223)	—	(14,223)
Cash dividends—Circuit City common stock ($0.07 per share)	—	—	—	—	—	(14,346)	(14,346)
Balance at February 28, 2001	207,020	25,639	103,510	12,820	642,838	1,597,315	2,356,483
Net earnings	—	—	—	—	—	218,795	218,795
Sale of CarMax Group common stock	—	9,517	—	4,758	134,788	—	139,546
Exercise of common stock options	541	1,941	270	971	9,669	—	10,910
Shares issued under employee stock purchase plans	867	—	434	—	11,627	—	12,061
Shares issued under stock incentive plans	1,068	2	534	1	13,605	—	14,140
Tax benefit from stock issued	—	—	—	—	2,530	—	2,530
Cancellation of restricted stock	(673)	(248)	(337)	(124)	(17,995)	—	(18,456)
Unearned compensation—restricted stock	—	—	—	—	12,985	—	12,985
Cash dividends—Circuit City common stock ($0.07 per share)	—	—	—	—	—	(14,556)	(14,556)
Balance at February 28, 2002	208,823	36,851	104,411	18,426	810,047	1,801,554	2,734,438
Net earnings	—	—	—	—	—	106,084	106,084
Exercise of common stock options	311	246	156	123	5,035	—	5,314
Shares issued under employee stock purchase plans	457	—	229	—	5,470	—	5,699
Shares issued under stock incentive plans	843	—	421	—	17,207	—	17,628
Tax benefit from stock issued	—	—	—	—	9,575	—	9,575
Cancellation of restricted stock	(479)	(8)	(240)	(4)	(8,081)	—	(8,325)
Unearned compensation—restricted stock	—	—	—	—	9,830	—	9,830
Cash dividends—Circuit City common stock ($0.07 per share)	—	—	—	—	—	(14,687)	(14,687)
Distribution of CarMax, Inc. common stock to shareholders [Note 3]	—	(37,089)	—	(18,545)	—	(533,836)	(552,381)
Special dividend from CarMax [Note 3]	—	—	—	—	—	28,400	28,400
Balance at February 28, 2003	209,955	—	$104,977	$ —	$849,083	$1,387,515	$2,341,575

NOTES TO CONSOLIDATED FINANCIAL STATEMENTS

3 (In Part): Discontinued Operations

Cash flows related to discontinued operations have been segregated on the consolidated statements of cash flows.

A) CarMax

On September 10, 2002, the company's shareholders approved the separation of the CarMax Group from Circuit City Stores, Inc. and the company's board of directors authorized the redemption of the company's CarMax Group common stock and the distribution of CarMax, Inc. common stock to effect the separation. On October 1, 2002, the separation was effective and CarMax, Inc. became an independent, separately traded public company. Each outstanding share of CarMax Group common stock was redeemed in exchange for one share of CarMax, Inc. common stock. In addition, each holder of Circuit City Group common stock received as a tax-free distribution 0.313879 of a share of CarMax, Inc. common stock for each share of Circuit City Group common stock owned as of September 16, 2002, the record date for the distribution. Following the separation, the Circuit City Group common stock was renamed Circuit City common stock. All CarMax results prior to the separation date are presented as results from discontinued operations. The company recorded no gain or loss as a result of the separation.

With the separation, CarMax paid a special dividend of $28.4 million to Circuit City Stores, Inc. in recognition of the company's continuing contingent liability on leases related to 23 CarMax locations. At February 28, 2003, the future minimum fixed lease obligations on these 23 leases totaled $480.9 million.

The relationship between the company and CarMax is governed by a transition services agreement, under which the company provides CarMax services including human resources, administrative services, special technical services, payroll processing, benefits administration, tax services, television advertising buying, computer center support and telecommunication services, with terms ranging from six to 24 months and varying renewal options. Under the agreement, CarMax pays the company the allocable portion of all direct and indirect costs of providing these services plus 10 percent. Including the 10 percent mark up, the company billed CarMax $6.7 million during fiscal 2003 for services provided after the separation. A tax allocation agreement, which generally provides that pre-separation taxes attributable to the business of each party will be borne solely by that party, also was executed upon the separation.

Net earnings from the discontinued CarMax operations were $64.5 million for the fiscal year ended February 28, 2003, representing CarMax results for the seven months prior to the separation date. Net earnings from discontinued operations were $90.8 million in fiscal 2002 and $45.6 million in fiscal 2001. Prior to the separation date, CarMax earnings were allocated to the company's Circuit City Group and CarMax Group common stocks. Circuit City Group earnings included earnings attributed to the CarMax Group shares reserved for the Circuit City Group or for issuance to Circuit City Group shareholders. The CarMax Group earnings reflected the remainder of the earnings of the CarMax business.

The assets and liabilities of the discontinued CarMax operations reflected on the consolidated balance sheet at February 28, 2002, were comprised of the following:

(Amounts in millions)	2002
Inventory	$399.1
Retained interests in securitized receivables	120.7
Accounts receivable, net	52.6
Other current assets	5.3
Total current assets	577.7
Property and equipment, net	121.0
Other assets	21.5
Total assets of discontinued CarMax operations	$720.2
Accounts payable	$ 87.2
Current installments of allocated long-term debt	78.6
Other current liabilities	57.6
Total current liabilities	223.4
Other liabilities	11.3
Total liabilities of discontinued CarMax operations	$234.7

ADJUSTMENTS TO OPENING BALANCE OF RETAINED EARNINGS

5.11 Reasons for which the opening balance of retained earnings is properly restated include certain changes in accounting principles, changes in reporting entity, and prior period adjustments. SFAS No. 16, *Prior Period Adjustments,* as amended by SFAS No. 109, *Accounting for Income Taxes*, stipulates that only corrections of errors are properly accounted for as prior period adjustments.

5.12 Table 5-3 summarizes the reasons disclosed by the survey companies as to why the opening balance of retained earnings was adjusted. Prior to 2002, a pooling of interests was the most common reason for an adjustment to retained earnings. SFAS No. 141, *Business Combinations,* issued in 2001, supersedes APB Opinion No. 16, *Business Combinations. SFAS No. 141* stipulates that the pooling-of-interests method not be used for business combinations initiated after June 30, 2001.

5.13

TABLE 5-3: ADJUSTMENTS TO OPENING BALANCE OF RETAINED EARNINGS

	Number of Companies			
	2003	2002	2001	2000
Prior period adjustments	4	6	2	5
Accounting changes	4	5	1	2
Poolings of interests	—	2	8	18
Other—described	—	1	—	—

Prior Period Adjustment

5.14

LEVI STRAUSS & CO. (NOV)

Consolidated Statements of Stockholders' Equity/(Deficit)

(Dollars in thousands)	Common Stock	Additional Paid-In Capital	Accumulated Deficit	Accumulated Other Comprehensive Income (Loss)	Stockholders' Equity (Deficit)
Balance at November 26, 2000 as originally reported	$373	$88,808	$(1,171,864)	$(15,890)	$(1,098,573)
Adjustments to opening stockholders' equity (deficit)	—	—	35,362	5,266	40,628
Balance at November 26, 2000 (restated)	373	88,808	(1,136,502)	(10,624)	(1,057,945)
Net income (restated)	—	—	93,662	—	93,662
Other comprehensive income (net of tax) (restated)	—	—	—	13,005	13,005
Total comprehensive income (restated)	—	—	93,662	13,005	106,667
Balance at November 25, 2001 (restated)	373	88,808	(1,042,840)	2,381	(951,278)
Net income (restated)	—	—	7,339	—	7,339
Other comprehensive loss (net of tax) (restated)	—	—	—	(84,390)	(84,390)
Total comprehensive loss (restated)	—	—	7,339	(84,390)	(77,051)
Balance at November 24, 2002 (restated)	373	88,808	(1,035,501)	(82,009)	(1,028,329)
Net loss	—	—	(349,317)	—	(349,317)
Other comprehensive loss (net of tax)	—	—	—	(15,526)	(15,526)
Total comprehensive loss	—	—	(349,317)	(15,526)	(364,843)
Balance at November 20, 2003	$373	$88,808	$(1,384,818)	$(97,535)	$(1,393,172)

NOTES TO CONSOLIDATED FINANCIAL STATEMENTS

Note 2: Restatements of 2001 and 2002 Financial Statements

Earlier this year, the Company determined that it had reported incorrectly on tax returns for 1998 and 1999 on the disposition of certain fixed assets, primarily a double deduction for losses related to various plant closures. These reporting errors on the Company's tax returns did not affect its results of operations for fiscal years 1998 through 2000. However, these errors did impact its results of operations for 2001 because the deferred tax liabilities for these errors were eliminated and taken into income through a 2001 reconciliation project. In preparing its third quarter financial results described in its September 10 and September 30, 2003 press releases, the Company reflected the tax effect of these errors as an adjustment to the full-year effective tax rate for 2003, in effect treating them as a change in accounting estimate that would be recorded in the third and fourth quarters of 2003. Thereafter, the Company determined that the appropriate accounting treatment for these errors is to treat them as an accounting error in 2001, the year in which the deferred tax liabilities associated with these 1998 and 1999 reporting errors were eliminated, and to restate the Company's fiscal year 2001 financial statements.

As the Company engaged in the reaudit of the 2001 financial statements, the Company identified additional errors and determined that certain other adjustments to the 2001 statements would also affect its financial statements for subsequent periods. The Company also determined that errors were made in these financial statements that were independent of the 2001 restatement items. The Company therefore decided that it would be appropriate to restate its 2002 financial statements, and to restate the financial information the Company previously reported for the first and second quarters of 2003. Unless otherwise specifically noted, the financial information in this Form 10-K reflects the 2001 restatement, the 2002 restatement and the 2003 first and second quarter restatements. In addition, we restated our financial statements for the first, second, and third quarters of 2001 and 2002. For information concerning the restatements of the quarterly results of operations, see Note 22: Quarterly Financial Data (unaudited).

Consolidated Balance Sheet Changes

	November 24, 2002		
(Dollars in thousands)	As Filed in Form 10-K on February 12, 2003	Adjustments	As Restated
Current assets			
Cash and cash equivalents	$ 96,478	$ —	$ 96,478
Restricted cash			
Trade receivables, net	660,516	(1,709)	658,807
Inventories:			
Raw materials	98,987	1,500	100,487
Work-in-process	74,048	—	74,048
Finished goods	418,679	5,178	423,857
Total inventories	591,714	6,678	598,392
Deferred tax assets	221,574	2,718	224,292
Other current assets	88,611	—	88,611
Total current assets	1,658,893	7,687	1,666,580
Property, plant and equipment, net	482,446	7,008	489,454
Goodwill		199,905	199,905
Other intangible assets	243,410	(199,905)	43,505
Non-current deferred tax assets	573,844	(1,259)	572,585
Other assets	58,691	2,200	60,891
Total assets	$3,017,284	$ 15,636	$ 3,032,920
Current liabilities			
Current maturities of long-term debt and short-term borrowings	$ 95,225	$ —	$ 95,225
Accounts payable	233,771	44,806	278,577
Restructuring reserves	65,576	(3,411)	62,165
Accrued liabilities	270,446	(45,256)	225,190
Accrued salaries, wages and employee benefits	314,385	(3,940)	310,445
Accrued taxes	105,387	6,673	112,060
Total current liabilities	1,084,790	(1,128)	1,083,662
Long-term debt, less current maturities	1,751,752	—	1,751,752
Postretirement medical benefits	548,930	—	548,930
Pension liability		228,740	228,740
Long-term employee related benefits	527,418	(228,740)	298,678
Long-term tax liabilities	66,879	28,351	95,230
Other long-term liabilities	11,558	21,158	32,716
Minority interest	21,541	—	21,541
Total liabilities	4,012,868	48,381	4,061,249
Stockholders' equity (deficit)			
Common stock—$.01 par value; 270,000,000 shares authorized;			
37,278,238 shares issued and outstanding	373	—	373
Additional paid-in capital	88,808	—	88,808
Accumulated (deficit)	(995,881)	(39,620)	1,035,501
Accumulated other comprehensive (loss)	(88,884)	6,875	(82,009)
Total stockholders' (deficit)	(995,584)	(32,745)	(1,028,329)
Total liabilities and stockholders' (deficit)	$3,017,284	$ 15,636	$ 3,032,920

Consolidated Statements of Operations Changes

(Dollars in thousands)	Year Ended November 24, 2002		
	As Filed in Form 10-K on February 12, 2003	Adjustments	As Restated
Net sales	$4,136,590	$ 9,276	$4,145,866
Cost of goods sold	2,451,785	4,406	2,456,191
Gross profit	1,684,805	4,870	1,689,675
Marketing, general and administrative expenses	1,332,798	23,327	1,356,125
Other operating (income)	(34,450)	—	(34,450)
Restructuring charges, net of reversals	124,595	(9,140)	115,455
Operating income	261,862	(9,317)	252,545
Interest expense	186,493	—	186,493
Other (income) expense, net	25,411	14,054	39,465
Income before taxes	49,958	(23,371)	26,587
Income tax expense	24,979	(5,731)	19,248
Net income	$ 24,979	$(17,640)	$ 7,339

Consolidated Balance Sheet Changes

| | November 25, 2001 | | |
| | As Filed in Form 10-K on | | |
(Dollars in thousands)	February 12, 2003	Adjustments	As Restated
Current assets			
Cash and cash equivalents	$ 102,831	$ —	$ 102,831
Restricted cash			
Trade receivables, net	621,224	(953)	620,271
Inventories:			
Raw materials	97,261	1,500	98,761
Work-in-process	50,499	—	50,499
Finished goods	462,417	17,431	479,848
Total inventories	610,177	18,931	629,108
Deferred tax assets	205,294	(2,454)	202,840
Other current assets	94,916	(3,209)	91,707
Total current assets	1,634,442	12,315	1,646,757
Property, plant and equipment, net	514,711	—	514,711
Goodwill	—	208,692	208,692
Other intangible assets	254,233	(208,692)	45,541
Non-current deferred tax assets	484,260	(8,081)	476,179
Other assets	95,840	1,317	97,157
Total assets	$ 2,983,486	$ 5,551	$ 2,989,037
Current liabilities			
Current maturities of long-term debt and short-term borrowings	$ 162,944	$ —	$ 162,944
Accounts payable	234,199	44,469	278,668
Restructuring reserves	45,220	(554)	44,666
Accrued liabilities	301,620	(63,862)	237,758
Accrued salaries, wages and employee benefits	212,728	(6,652)	206,076
Accrued taxes	26,475	7,079	33,554
Total current liabilities	983,186	(19,520)	963,666
Long-term debt, less current maturities	1,795,489	—	1,795,489
Postretirement medical benefits	544,476	—	544,476
Pension liability	—	99,246	99,246
Long-term employee related benefits	384,751	(99,246)	285,505
Long-term tax liabilities	174,978	21,860	196,838
Other long-term liabilities	16,402	18,546	34,948
Minority interest	20,147	—	20,147
Total liabilities	3,919,429	20,886	3,940,315
Stockholders' equity (deficit)			
Common stock—$.01 par value; 270,000,000 shares authorized;			
37,278,238 shares issued and outstanding	373	—	373
Additional paid-in capital	88,808	—	88,808
Accumulated (deficit)	(1,020,860)	(21,980)	(1,042,840)
Accumulated other comprehensive (loss)	(4,264)	6,645	2,381
Total stockholders' (deficit)	(935,943)	(15,335)	(951,278)
Total liabilities and stockholders' (deficit)	$ 2,983,486	$ 5,551	$ 2,989,037

Consolidated Statements of Operations Changes

	Year Ended November 25, 2001		
(Dollars in thousands)	As Filed in Form 10-K on February 12, 2003	Adjustments	As Restated
Net sales	$4,258,674	$ 17,351	$4,276,025
Cost of goods sold	2,461,198	31,077	2,492,275
Gross profit	1,797,476	(13,726)	1,783,750
Marketing, general and administrative expenses	1,355,885	25,362	1,381,247
Other operating (income)	(33,420)	—	(33,420)
Restructuring charges, net of reversals	(4,286)	(567)	(4,853)
Operating income	479,297	(38,521)	440,776
Interest expense	230,772	(10,816)	219,956
Other (income) expense, net	8,836	(10,664)	(1,828)
Income before taxes	239,689	(17,041)	222,648
Income tax expense	88,685	40,301	128,986
Net income	$ 151,004	$(57,342)	$ 93,662

The 2001 and 2002 financial statements have been restated for various adjustments that are included in one or more of the following categories:

Tax Errors and Tax Effects of Other Adjustments

As indicated above, the 2001 financial statements now reflect the correction of an error made in the Company's 2001 deferred tax reconciliation project, as a result of which the Company had erroneously credited its tax provision. That amount of $24.0 million has been reflected as an additional expense and additional liability in 2001. In addition, other errors totaling $19.0 million in recording tax provisions were made in 2001 and 2002, particularly related to providing a valuation allowance on foreign net operating losses of subsidiaries in a cumulative loss position. The Company has also tax effected the other adjustments described below.

Adjustment for Rent Expense

In the first quarter of 2003, the Company reflected $21.2 million as a pre-tax adjustment of management, general and administrative expense. This was a cumulative adjustment for prior periods to reflect the actual liability for occupancy costs and leases on a straight-line basis. Because the Company is restating these periods, it has reflected the appropriate expense in each period totaling $3.7 million in 2001 and $2.6 million in 2002, and has reversed the cumulative adjustment from the first quarter of 2003.

Timing Issues

A number of adjustments were made to the accounts relating to "out-of-period" entries. As a result of the 2001 re-audit, the Company identified a number of adjustments made by it in the 2001 and 2002 periods that were recorded in the incorrect periods.

Several of these adjustments actually related to accruals made in periods prior to fiscal 2001, including (i) over-accruals of provisions for inventory obsolescence of $35.4 million, resulting in reversals in 2001 and 2002 of $17.0 million and $6.9 million, respectively, and the remainder applied to prior periods; (ii) an over-accrual for workers' compensation expense of $10.4 million, which was reversed in 2001; (iii) an under-accrual of incentive compensation in 2000 of $8.5 million, also reversed in 2001; and

(iv) $10.9 million of improperly accrued restructuring costs, which were reversed in 2001.

The adjustments recorded by the Company represented reversals of accruals and/or reserves made in prior periods for which there was inadequate evidential support to obtain those accruals. The restated financial statements reflect these accrual reversals in the proper period.

Restructuring

The Company inappropriately applied the provisions of EITF Issue No. 94-3 and made clerical errors in the recording of restructuring accruals for our 2002 plant closures. As a result, the Company has reversed $10.4 million of the restructuring accruals taken in 2002 and reversed gains taken in 2003 when those assets were sold amounting to $6.3 million. In addition, $2.6 million of restructuring accruals for its 1999 plant closures taken in that year were reversed, and expenses are appropriately reflected for those charges in later years.

The Company also reclassified a number of items including:

- The cost for sales clerks in foreign retail stores who are its employees have been reclassified to management, general and administrative expense from a reduction against sales, in the amounts of $8.0 million in 2001 and $8.1 million in 2002.
- Foreign currency transaction effects on inventory purchases have been adjusted from other (income) expense to cost of sales and inventory in the amount of approximately $9.2 million and $4.2 million in 2001 and 2002, respectively.
- Costs related to debt issuance and other items associated with early extinguishment of debt totaling $10.8 million in 2001 have been reclassified to conform with current presentation.
- Goodwill has been reclassified in accordance with SFAS 142 out of other intangible assets for both periods ($199.9 million in 2002 and $208.7 million in 2001).
- Payables to contractors were reclassified from accrued liabilities to accounts payable ($44.8 million in 2002 and $44.5 million in 2001).

Other items to note:
- The Company reversed amortization expense recorded of $1.8 million and $0.9 million in 2002 and 2001, respectively, taken on costs improperly capitalized prior to 1999. These costs were applied to prior periods.

Change in Accounting Principle

5.15

TENET HEALTHCARE CORPORATION (DEC)

Consolidated Statements of Changes in Shareholders' Equity

(Dollars in millions, share amounts in thousands)	Shares Outstanding	Issued Par Amount	Additional Paid-In Capital	Other Comprehensive Income (Loss)	Retained Earnings	Treasury Stock	Total Shareholders' Equity
Balances, May 31, 2000	470,190	$24	$2,555	$(70)	$ 1,627	$ (70)	$ 4,066
Effect of retroactive restatement of stock-based employee compensation costs with the adoption of the fair value method of accounting for employee stock options			192		(116)		76
Restated balances, May, 31, 2000	470,190	$24	$2,747	$(70)	$ 1,511	$ (70)	$ 4,142
Net income, as restated					578		578
Other comprehensive income				26			26
Issuance of common stock	840	1	15				16
Stock options exercised, including tax benefit	17,171		293				293
Stock-based compensation expense			98				98
Restated balances, May 31, 2001	488,201	$25	$3,153	$(44)	$ 2,089	$ (70)	$ 5,153
Net income, as restated					697		697
Other comprehensive income				—			—
Issuance of common stock	692		21				21
Stock options exercised, including tax benefit	17,829	1	406				407
Stock-based compensation expense			134				134
Repurchases of common stock	(18,181)					(715)	(715)
Restated balances, May 31, 2002	488,541	$26	$3,714	$(44)	$ 2,786	$ (785)	$ 5,697
Net income, as restated					401		401
Other comprehensive income				29			29
Issuance of common stock	378	—	36				36
Stock options exercised, including tax benefit	2,901	—	74				74
Stock-based compensation expense			87				87
Repurchases of common stock	(18,082)					(500)	(500)
Restated balances, December 31, 2002	473,738	$26	$3,911	$(15)	$ 3,187	$(1,285)	$ 5,824
Net loss					(1,477)		(1,477)
Other comprehensive income				7			7
Issuance of common stock	2,994		32			2	34
Stock options exercised, including tax benefit	526		5				5
Stock-based compensation expense			176				176
Repurchases of common stock	(12,471)					(208)	(208)
Balances, December 31, 2003	464,787	$26	$4,124	$ (8)	$ 1,710	$(1,491)	$ 4,361

NOTES TO CONSOLIDATED FINANCIAL STATEMENTS

Note 1 (In Part): Basis of Presentation

Certain prior-year balances in the accompanying consolidated financial statements have been reclassified to conform to the current period's presentation of financial information. These reclassifications, primarily for the discontinued operations as described in Note 3, have no impact on total assets, liabilities, shareholders' equity, net income or cash flows. In addition, certain prior-period balances in the accompanying consolidated financial statements have been retroactively restated to reflect a change in the way we account for stock-based compensation (which we adopted during the quarter ended March 31, 2003), and are in accordance with the recognition provisions of the accounting standards authorizing the change. (See Note 7.)

Note 2 (In Part): Significant Accounting Policies

K. Stock Options

Through December 31, 2002, we applied the intrinsic-value-based method of accounting, prescribed by Accounting Principles Board Opinion No. 25, and its related interpretations (including FASB Interpretation No. 44, an interpretation of APB No. 25 issued in March 2000), to our stock-based compensation plans. In accordance with that method, no compensation cost was recognized for stock options granted to employees or directors under the plans through that date because the exercise prices for options granted were equal to the quoted market prices on the option grant dates.

In March 2003, we adopted Statement of Financial Accounting Standards No. 123. The new policy had a retroactive effective date of January 1, 2003 (the first day of our new fiscal year). The accounting standard establishes a fair-value method of accounting for stock-based compensation plans (i.e., compensation costs will be based on the fair value of stock options granted). We utilized the retroactive-restatement method to transition from the former accounting standard to the new one. As such, presentations of periods ended prior to January 1, 2003 have been restated to reflect the fair-value method of accounting, as if the change had been effective throughout those prior periods.

Note 7 (In Part): Stock Benefit Plans

In March 2003, our board of directors approved a change in accounting for stock options granted to employees and directors from the intrinsic-value method to the fair-value method recommended by SFAS No. 123, effective for the calendar year ended December 31, 2003. The transition method we chose to report this change in accounting was the retroactive-restatement method. As such, presentations of periods ended prior to January 1, 2003 have been restated to reflect the fair-value method of accounting, as if the change had been effective throughout those prior periods.

OTHER CHANGES IN RETAINED EARNINGS

5.16 In addition to opening balance adjustments, the retained earnings account is affected by direct charges and credits. The most frequent direct charges to retained earnings are net loss for the year, losses on treasury stock transactions, and cash or stock dividends. The most common direct credit to retained earnings is net income for the year. Direct charges and credits—other than net loss, net income, dividends, and stock splits—are summarized in Table 5-4. Examples of such charges and credits follow.

5.17

TABLE 5-4: OTHER CHANGES IN RETAINED EARNINGS

	Number of Companies			
	2003	2002	2001	2000
Charges				
Purchase or retirement of capital stock	69	64	87	74
Treasury stock issued for less than cost	38	32	44	41
Preferred stock accretion	4	4	5	3
Other—described	10	13	22	33
Credits				
Tax benefit on dividends paid to ESOP	9	10	9	13
Tax benefit on stock option exercise	7	3	2	N/C*
Other—described	29	28	34	33

* N/C = Not compiled. Line item was not included in table for year shown.

Treasury Stock Transactions

5.18

ELECTRONIC DATA SYSTEMS CORPORATION (DEC)

Consolidated Statements of Shareholders' Equity and Comprehensive Income (Loss)

(In millions)	Common Stock		Additional Paid-In Capital	Retained Earnings	Other Compre-hensive Loss	Treasury Stock		Share-holders' Equity
	Shares Issued	Amount				Shares Held	Amount	
Balance at December 31, 2000	493	$5	$ 949	$ 6,042	$(238)	28	$(1,619)	$ 5,139
Comprehensive income								
Net income	—	—	—	1,363	—	—	—	1,363
Currency translation adjustment	—	—	—	—	(98)	—	—	(98)
Unrealized losses on securities net of tax effect of $(1), and reclassification adjustment	—	—	—	—	(239)	—	—	(239)
Change in minimum pension liability, net of tax effect of $8	—	—	—	—	15	—	—	15
Total comprehensive income								1,041
Dividends declared	—	—	—	(283)	—	—	—	(283)
Issuance of stock purchase contracts	—	—	(118)	—	—	—	—	(118)
Stock issued for acquisition	3	—	134	—	—	1	(85)	49
Stock award transactions	—	—	(3)	—	—	(11)	621	618
Balance at December 31, 2001	496	$5	$ 962	$ 7,122	$(560)	18	$(1,083)	$ 6,446
Comprehensive income								
Net income	—	—	—	1,116	—	—	—	1,116
Currency translation adjustment	—	—	—	—	288	—	—	288
Unrealized gains on securities, net of tax effect of $1, and reclassification adjustment	—	—	—	—	6	—	—	6
Change in minimum pension liability, net of tax effect of $217	—	—	—	—	(423)	—	—	(423)
Total comprehensive income								987
Dividends declared	—	—	—	(287)	—	—	—	(287)
Stock issued for acquisition	—	—	—	—	—	(1)	85	85
Issuance of stock purchase contracts	—	—	11	—	—	—	—	11
Stock award transactions	—	—	(72)	—	—	(3)	232	160
Purchase of treasury shares	—	—	—	—	—	5	(380)	(380)
Balance at December 31, 2002	496	$5	$ 901	$ 7,951	$(689)	19	$(1,146)	$ 7,022
Comprehensive loss								
Net loss	—	—	—	(1,698)	—	—	—	(1,698)
Currency translation adjustment	—	—	—	—	466	—	—	466
Unrealized losses on securities, net of tax effect of $(1), and reclassification adjustment	—	—	—	—	(3)	—	—	(3)
Change in minimum pension liability, net of tax effect of $57	—	—	—	—	95	—	—	95
Total comprehensive loss								(1,140)
Dividends declared	—	—	—	(287)	—	—	—	(287)
Stock award transactions	—	—	16	(154)	—	(4)	257	119
Balance at December 31, 2003	496	$5	$ 917	$ 5,812	$(131)	15	$ (889)	$ 5,714

NOTES TO CONSOLIDATED FINANCIAL STATEMENTS

Note 1 (In Part): Summary of Significant Accounting Policies

Comprehensive Income (Loss) and Shareholders' Equity (In Part)

In connection with its employee stock incentive plans, the Company issued 3.7 million shares of treasury stock at a cost of $257 million during 2003. The difference between the cost and fair value at the date of issuance of such shares has been recognized as a charge to retained earnings of $154 million in the consolidated balance sheet and statement of shareholders' equity and comprehensive income (loss).

5.19

VARIAN MEDICAL SYSTEMS, INC. (SEP)

Consolidated Statements of Stockholders' Equity and Comprehensive Earnings

(In thousands, except per share amounts)	Common Stock Shares	Common Stock Amount	Capital in Excess of Par Value	Deferred Stock Compensation	Accumulated Other Comprehensive Loss	Retained Earnings	Total
Balances, fiscal year-end, 2000	63,537	$63,537	$ 19,101	$ —	$ —	$187,721	$ 270,359
Net earnings and comprehensive earnings	—	—	—	—	—	54,250	54,250
Issuance of stock under omnibus stock, stock option, and employee stock purchase plans (including tax benefit of $30,554)	3,956	3,956	69,085	—	—	—	73,041
Non-cash stock-based compensation	—	—	53	—	—	—	53
Deferred stock compensation	6	6	5,235	(5,241)	—	—	—
Amortization of deferred stock compensation	—	—	—	994	—	—	994
Repurchase of common stock	(140)	(140)	(1,314)	—	—	(2,847)	(4,301)
Balances, fiscal year-end, 2001	67,359	67,359	92,160	(4,247)	—	239,124	394,396
Net earnings	—	—	—	—	—	93,609	93,609
Minimum pension liability adjustment, net of taxes of $1,424	—	—	—	—	(2,530)	—	(2,530)
Comprehensive earnings							$ 91,079
Issuance of stock under omnibus stock, stock option, and employee stock purchase plans (including tax benefit of $17,403)	1,788	1,788	39,575	—	—	—	41,363
Amortization of deferred stock compensation	—	—	—	1,057	—	—	1,057
Repurchase of common stock	(1,357)	(1,357)	(13,457)	—	—	(40,278)	(55,092)
Balances, fiscal year-end, 2002	67,790	67,790	118,278	(3,190)	(2,530)	292,455	472,803
Net earnings	—	—	—	—	—	130,888	130,888
Minimum pension liability adjustment, net of taxes of $415	—	—	—	—	(886)	—	(886)
Comprehensive earnings							$ 130,002
Issuance of stock under omnibus stock, stock option, and employee stock purchase plans (including tax benefit of $28,142)	2,163	2,163	62,633	—	—	—	64,796
Deferred stock compensation	3	3	143	(146)	—	—	—
Amortization of deferred stock compensation	—	—	—	1,055	—	—	1,055
Non-cash stock-based compensation	—	—	119	—	—	—	119
Repurchase of common stock	(1,985)	(1,985)	(21,634)	—	—	(81,480)	(105,099)
Balances, fiscal year-end, 2003	67,971	$67,971	$159,539	$(2,281)	$(3,416)	$341,863	$ 563,676

NOTES TO THE CONSOLIDATED FINANCIAL STATEMENTS

Note 10—Stock Repurchase Program

On August 20, 2001, the Company announced that its Board of Directors had authorized the repurchase by the Company of up to one million shares (on a pre-January 15, 2002 stock split basis) of its common stock over the following twelve-month period. The time period for the repurchase was extended by the Board of Directors until February 28, 2003. On February 14, 2003, the Company's Board of Directors authorized an additional repurchase of up to two million shares of its common stock through the end of February 2004. During fiscal years 2003, 2002 and 2001, the Company paid $105.1 million, $55.1 million and $4.3 million, respectively, to repurchase 1,984,600 shares, 1,357,400 shares and 140,000 shares, respectively, of its common stock. All shares that have been repurchased have been retired. As of September 26, 2003, the Company can still purchase up to 518,000 shares.

Tax Benefit From ESOP Dividends

5.20

ROHM AND HAAS COMPANY (DEC)

Consolidated Statements of Stockholders' Equity

(In millions, except per share amounts)	Common Stock	Additional Paid-In Capital	Retained Earnings	Treasury Stock	ESOP	Accumulated Other Comprehensive Income (Loss)	Total Stockholders' Equity	Total Comprehensive Income (Loss)
Balance January 1, 2001	$605	$1,956	$1,518	$214	$119	$ (93)	$3,653	
Net earnings			395					$ 395
Transition adjustment as of January 1, 2001						6		6
Current period changes in fair value						(2)		(2)
Reclassification to earnings, net						(5)		(5)
Cumulative translation adjustment						(46)		(46)
Minimum pension liability, net of income taxes						(6)		(6)
Total comprehensive income								$ 342
Common dividends ($.80 per share)			(176)					
Tax benefit on ESOP			5					
Common stock issued								
Under bonus plan		5		(6)				
From ESOP					(6)			
Balance December 31, 2001	$605	$1,961	$1,742	$208	$113	$(146)	$3,841	

(continued)

(In millions, except per share amounts)	Common Stock	Additional Paid-In Capital	Retained Earnings	Treasury Stock	ESOP	Accumulated Other Comprehensive Income (Loss)	Total Stockholders' Equity	Total Comprehensive Income (Loss)
Balance December 31, 2001	$605	$1,961	$1,742	$208	$113	$(146)	$3,841	
Net loss			(570)					$(570)
Current period changes in fair value						5		5
Reclassification to earnings, net						(6)		(6)
Cumulative translation adjustment						53		53
Minimum pension liability, net of income taxes						(50)		(50)
Total comprehensive loss								$(568)
Common dividends ($.82 per share)			(181)					
Tax benefit on ESOP			3					
Common stock issued								
Under bonus plan		10		(8)				
From ESOP					(6)			
Balance December 31, 2002	$605	$1,971	$ 994	$200	$107	$(144)	$3,119	
Net earnings			280					$ 280
Current period changes in fair value						(5)		(5)
Reclassification to earnings, net						4		4
Cumulative translation adjustment						80		80
Minimum pension liability, net of income taxes						13		13
Total comprehensive income								$ 372
Common dividends ($.86 per share)			(191)					
Tax benefit on ESOP			4					
Common stock issued								
Under bonus plan		31		(15)				
From ESOP					(7)			
Balance December 31, 2003	$605	$2,002	$1,087	$185	$100	$ (52)	$3,357	

NOTES TO CONSOLIDATED FINANCIAL STATEMENTS

Note 21 (In Part): Stockholders' Equity

Dividends paid on ESOP shares, used as a source of funds for meeting the ESOP financing obligation, were $13 million, $13 million and $14 million in 2003, 2002 and 2001, respectively. These dividends were recorded net of the related U.S. tax benefits. The number of ESOP shares not allocated to plan members at December 31, 2003 and 2002 were 10.5 million and 11.1 million, respectively.

Tax Benefit on Stock Option Exercise

5.21

PITNEY BOWES INC. (DEC)

Consolidated Statements of Stockholders' Equity

(Dollars in thousands, except per share data)	Preferred Stock	Preference Stock	Common Stock	Capital in Excess of Par Value	Comprehensive Income	Retained Earnings	Accumulated Other Comprehensive Income	Treasury Stock at Cost
Balance, January 1, 2001	$29	$1,737	$323,338	$10,298		$3,766,995	$(139,434)	$(2,677,988)
Net income					$488,343	488,343		
Other comprehensive income								
Translation adjustments					(8,950)		(8,950)	
Net unrealized loss on derivative instruments					(6,996)		(6,996)	
Comprehensive income					$472,397			
Cash dividends								
Preferred ($2.00 per share)						(1)		
Preference ($2.12 per share)						(129)		
Common ($1.16 per share)						(285,034)		
Spin-off of Imagistics International Inc.						(311,693)		
Issuances of common stock				(5,421)				31,768
Conversions to common stock	(5)	(134)		(2,341)				2,481
Repurchase of common stock								(299,952)
Tax credits relating to stock options				4,443				
Balance, December 31, 2001	24	1,603	323,338	6,979		3,658,481	(155,380)	(2,943,691)
Net income					$475,750	475,750		
Other comprehensive income								
Translation adjustments					37,955		37,955	
Net unrealized gain on derivative instruments					167		167	
Minimum pension liability					(4,357)		(4,357)	
Comprehensive income					$509,515			
Cash dividends								
Preferred ($2.00 per share)						(1)		
Preference ($2.12 per share)						(118)		
Common ($1.18 per share)						(282,106)		
Issuances of common stock				(4,843)		(3,444)		41,591
Conversions to common stock		(171)		(3,601)				3,772
Repurchase of common stock								(300,086)
Tax credits relating to stock options				1,465				
Balance, December 31, 2002	24	1,432	323,338	—		3,848,562	(121,615)	(3,198,414)
Net income					$498,117	498,117		
Other comprehensive income								
Translation adjustments					143,158		143,158	
Net unrealized gain on derivative instruments					384		384	
Minimum pension liability					(3,864)		(3,864)	
Comprehensive income					$637,795			
Cash dividends								
Preferred ($2.00 per share)						(1)		
Preference ($2.12 per share)						(107)		
Common ($1.20 per share)						(280,762)		
Issuances of common stock						(9,448)		82,796
Conversions to common stock	(5)	(117)				(2,469)		2,591
Repurchase of common stock								(200,000)
Tax credits relating to stock options						3,762		
Balance, December 31, 2003	$19	$1,315	$323,338	$ —		$4,057,654	$ 18,063	$(3,313,027)

Redeemable Common Stock Accretion

5.22

MICRON TECHNOLOGY, INC. (AUG)

Consolidated Statements of Shareholders' Equity

(Amounts in millions)	Common Stock Number of Shares	Amount	Additional Capital	Retained Earnings	Accumulated Other Comprehensive Income (Loss)	Total Shareholders' Equity
Balance at August 31, 2000	567.3	$56.7	$2,824.2	$ 3,549.6	$ 1.5	$ 6,432.0
Comprehensive income (loss)						
Net loss				(625.0)		(625.0)
Other comprehensive income (loss)						
Net change in unrealized gain (loss) on investments, net of tax					(4.8)	(4.8)
Total comprehensive income (loss)						(629.8)
Conversion of notes to stock	24.7	2.5	682.1			684.6
Issuance of common stock warrants			480.2			480.2
Stock issued under stock plans	6.4	0.6	122.0			122.6
Tax effect of stock plans			48.3			48.3
Other			(3.1)			(3.1)
Balance at August 30, 2001	598.4	$59.8	$4,153.7	$ 2,924.6	$(3.3)	$ 7,134.8
Comprehensive income (loss)						
Net loss				(907.0)		(907.0)
Other comprehensive income (loss)						
Net change in unrealized gain (loss) on investments, net of tax					4.3	4.3
Total comprehensive income (loss)						(902.7)
Stock issued under stock plans	4.5	0.5	75.9			76.4
Stock issued in connection with purchase of DRAM assets from Toshiba Corporation	1.5					
Redeemable common stock accretion				(2.1)		(2.1)
Balance at August 29, 2002	604.4	$60.3	$4,229.6	$ 2,015.5	$ 1.0	$ 6,306.4
Comprehensive income (loss)						
Net loss				(1,273.2)		(1,273.2)
Other comprehensive income (loss)						
Net change in unrealized gain (loss) on investments, net of tax					(0.9)	(0.9)
Total comprehensive income (loss)						(1,274.1)
Stock issued under stock plans	5.7	0.5	56.9			57.4
Purchase of call spread options			(109.1)			(109.1)
Repurchase and retirement of common stock	(0.2)		(1.1)	(2.2)		(3.3)
Redeemable common stock accretion				(6.3)		(6.3)
Balance at August 28, 2003	609.9	$60.8	$4,176.3	$ 733.8	$ 0.1	$ 4,971.0

NOTES TO CONSOLIDATED FINANCIAL STATEMENTS

Redeemable Common Stock

In connection with the issuance of the 1.5 million shares of common stock for the Toshiba DRAM Acquisition, the Company granted Toshiba Corporation an option to require the Company to repurchase on October 21, 2003, all of these shares for $67.5 million in cash. Toshiba has exercised the option and the Company will redeem these shares in the first quarter of 2004. The carrying value of the redeemable common stock is accreted to its redemption amount of $67.5 million by a charge directly to retained earnings and is included in the computations of earning per share. Accretion of redeemable common stock was $6.3 million in 2003 and $2.1 million in 2002.

ADDITIONAL PAID-IN CAPITAL

PRESENTATION OF CHANGES IN ADDITIONAL PAID-IN CAPITAL

5.23 Paragraph 10 of APB Opinion No. 12, *Omnibus Opinion—1967,* states:

> 10. When both financial position and results of operations are presented, disclosure of changes in the separate accounts comprising stockholders' equity (in addition to retained earnings) and of the changes in the number of shares of equity securities during at least the most recent annual fiscal period and any subsequent interim period presented is required to make the financial statements sufficiently informative. Disclosure of such changes may take the form of separate statements or may be made in the basic financial statements or notes thereto.

5.24 Table 5-5 summarizes the presentation formats used by the survey companies to present changes in additional paid-in capital.

5.25

TABLE 5-5: PRESENTATION OF CHANGES IN ADDITIONAL PAID-IN CAPITAL

	2003	2002	2001	2000
Statement of stockholders' equity.........	515	512	497	488
Statement of additional paid-in capital..	—	—	1	3
Schedule in notes................................	11	11	11	11
No statement or schedule but changes disclosed..............................	1	2	3	4
Balance unchanged during year...........	11	11	19	21
	538	**536**	**531**	**527**
Additional paid-in capital account not presented..............................	62	64	69	73
Total Companies.................................	**600**	**600**	**600**	**600**

STOCK SPLITS

5.26 Table 5-6 shows the number of survey companies disclosing stock splits and summarizes the accounting treatments for stock splits. Examples of disclosures of stock splits follow.

5.27

TABLE 5-6: STOCK SPLITS

	2003	2002	2001	2000
Ratio				
Less than three-for-two......................	3	2	—	1
Three-for-two (50%) to two-for-one.....	4	3	6	3
Two-for-one (100%)............................	12	18	21	36
Greater than two-for-one....................	—	—	—	6
	19	**23**	**27**	**46**
Reverse Ratio				
One-for-two...	—	—	—	1
One-for-three......................................	—	1	—	—
One-for-four..	—	1	—	—
Less than one-for-four........................	—	2	4	—
Total Companies...........................	**19**	**27**	**31**	**47**
Account(s) Charged				
Additional paid-in capital.....................	7	7	8	12
Retained earnings...............................	5	1	3	2
Both additional paid-in capital and retained earnings..........................	—	1	1	N/C*
No charge...	7	18	19	33
Total Companies........................	**19**	**27**	**31**	**47**

* N/C = Not compiled. Line item was not included in table for year shown.

5.28

FEDERAL SCREW WORKS (JUN)

Statements of Stockholders' Equity

	Common Stock	Additional Capital	Retained Earnings	Accumulated Other Comprehensive Loss	Total
Balances at July 1, 2000	$1,041,661	$3,269,476	$54,233,406	$ (8,478)	$58,536,065
Net earnings for the year			4,642,924		4,642,924
Change in unrealized loss on securities available-for-sale net of taxes				(104,136)	(104,136)
Total comprehensive income					4,538,788
Purchase of 5,189 shares	(5,189)		(167,038)		(172,227)
Effect of stock split	260,415		(260,415)		—
Cash dividends declared—$1.50 per share—as restated			(2,446,924)		(2,446,924)
Balances at June 30, 2001	1,296,887	3,269,476	56,001,953	(112,614)	60,455,702
Net earnings for the year			4,505,395		4,505,395
Change in unrealized gain on securities available-for-sale, net of taxes				10,555	10,555
Total comprehensive income					4,515,950
Purchase of 62,794 shares	(62,794)		(2,201,970)		(2,264,764)
Cash dividends declared—$0.88 per share—as restated			(1,402,464)		(1,402,464)
Balances at June 30, 2002	1,234,093	3,269,476	56,902,914	(102,059)	61,304,424
Net earnings for the year			3,302,877		3,302,877
Change in unrealized gain on securities available-for-sale net of taxes				61,615	61,615
Minimum pension liability, net of $2,502,203 tax effect				(5,080,231)	(5,080,231)
Total comprehensive loss					(1,715,739)
Purchase of 78,600 shares	(78,600)		(3,003,440)		(3,082,040)
Effect of stock split	294,972		(294,972)		—
Cash dividends declared—$0.92 per share—as restated			(1,391,987)		(1,391,987)
Balances at June 30, 2003	$1,450,465	$3,269,476	$55,515,392	$(5,120,675)	$55,114,658

NOTES TO FINANCIAL STATEMENTS

Note 9—Stock Dividend

The Company declared a 5 for 4 stock split on February 14, 2003, payable as a stock dividend April 1, 2003. All per share amounts have been adjusted to retroactively give effect to the stock split.

5.29

MET-PRO CORPORATION (JAN)

Consolidated Statement of Shareholders' Equity

	Common Shares	Additional Paid-In Capital	Retained Earnings	Accumulated Other Comprehensive Income/(Loss)	Treasury Shares	Total
Balances, January 31, 2001	$720,658	$8,139,799	$51,880,800	$(491,163)	$(13,188,728)	$47,061,366
Comprehensive income:						
Net income	—	—	6,189,317	—	—	
Cumulative translation adjustment	—	—	—	(231,570)	—	
Interest rate swap, net of tax of $60,357	—	—	—	(105,004)	—	
Total comprehensive income						5,852,743
Dividends paid, $.255 per share	—	—	(1,562,968)	—	—	(1,562,968)
Dividend declared, $.0638 per share	—	—	(517,070)	—	—	(517,070)
Proceeds from issuance of common shares under dividend reinvestment plan (16,776 shares)	1,258	145,247	—	—	—	146,505
Stock option transactions	—	(405,678)	—	—	1,497,931	1,092,253
Purchase of 194,120 treasury shares	—	—	—	—	(1,793,435)	(1,793,435)
Balances, January 31, 2002	721,916	7,879,368	55,990,079	(827,737)	(13,484,232)	50,279,394
Comprehensive income:						
Net income	—	—	5,888,379	—	—	
Cumulative translation adjustment	—	—	—	617,563	—	
Interest rate swap, net of tax of $109,056	—	—	—	(202,802)	—	
Minimum pension liability adjustment, net of tax of $70,991	—	—	—	(128,983)	—	
Total comprehensive income						6,174,157
Issuance of treasury shares for acquisition of business	—	250,782	—	—	1,349,218	1,600,000
Dividends paid, $.2588 per share	—	—	(1,614,024)	—	—	(1,614,024)
Dividend declared, $.0675 per share	—	—	(559,167)	—	—	(559,167)
Proceeds from issuance of common shares under dividend reinvestment plan (9,517 shares)	714	100,801	—	—	—	101,515
Stock option transactions	—	(34,169)	—	—	387,397	353,228
Purchase of 26,588 treasury shares	—	—	—	—	(289,218)	(289,218)
Balances, January 31, 2003	722,630	8,196,782	59,705,267	(541,959)	(12,036,835)	56,045,885
Comprehensive income:						
Net income	—	—	6,346,579	—	—	
Cumulative translation adjustment	—	—	—	449,074	—	
Interest rate swap, net of tax of ($51,447)	—	—	—	78,812	—	
Minimum pension liability adjustment, net of tax of $157,492	—	—	—	(314,543)	—	
Total comprehensive income						6,559,922
Stock split four-for-three	240,866	(240,866)	—	—	—	—
Cash in lieu of fractional shares	—	(1,421)	—	—	—	(1,421)
Dividends paid, $.275 per share	—	—	(1,721,666)	—	—	(1,721,666)
Dividend declared, $.0725 per share	—	—	(602,755)	—	—	(602,755)
Stock option transactions	—	964	—	—	883,375	884,339
Purchase of 62,480 treasury shares	—	—	—	—	(893,570)	(893,570)
Balances, January 31, 2004	$963,496	$7,955,459	$63,727,425	$(328,616)	$(12,047,030)	$60,270,734

NOTES TO CONSOLIDATED FINANCIAL STATEMENTS

1 (In Part): Nature of Operations and Summary of Significant Accounting Policies

Stock Splits

On September 17, 2003, the Board of Directors declared a four-for-three stock split, effected in the form of a stock distribution, payable on October 15, 2003 to shareholders of record on October 1, 2003. The Company retained the current par value of $.10 per share for all common shares. All references in the financial statements and notes to the number of shares outstanding, per share amounts, and stock option data of the Company's common shares have been restated to reflect the effect of the stock split for all periods presented.

Shareholders' equity reflects the stock split by reclassifying from "Additional Paid-in Capital" to "Common Shares" an amount equal to the par value of the additional shares arising from the split.

5.30

PRAXAIR, INC. (DEC)

Consolidated Statements of Shareholders' Equity

(Dollar amounts in millions, except per share data, shares in thousands)	Common Stock Shares	Common Stock Amounts	Additional Paid-In Capital	Treasury Stock Shares	Treasury Stock Amounts	Retained Earnings	Accumulated Other Comprehensive Income (Loss)	Total
Balance, December 31, 2000	166,309	$2	$1,658	6,930	$(279)	$1,987	$(1,011)	$2,357
Net income						430		430
Translation adjustments							(270)	(270)
Derivative instruments, net of $2 million taxes							(4)	(4)
Minimum pension liability, net of $6 million taxes							(12)	(12)
Comprehensive income								144
Dividends on common stock ($0.34 per share)						(110)		(110)
Issuances of common stock								
For the dividend reinvestment and stock purchase plan	45		1					1
For employee savings and incentive plans	3,787		136	(619)	25			161
Purchases of common stock				1,687	(76)			(76)
Balance, December 31, 2001	170,141	$2	$1,795	7,998	$(330)	$2,307	$(1,297)	$2,477

(continued)

(Dollar amounts in millions, except per share data, shares in thousands)	Common Stock		Additional Paid-In Capital	Treasury Stock		Retained Earnings	Accumulated Other Comprehensive Income (Loss)	Total
	Shares	Amounts		Shares	Amounts			
Balance, December 31, 2001	170,141	$2	$1,795	7,998	$(330)	$2,307	$(1,297)	$2,477
Net income						409		409
Translation adjustments							(284)	(284)
Derivative instruments, net of $2 million taxes							3	3
Minimum pension liability, net of $52 million taxes							(95)	(95)
Comprehensive income								33
Dividends on common stock ($0.38 per share)						(123)		(123)
Issuances of common stock								
For the dividend reinvestment and stock purchase plan	46							—
For employee savings and incentive plans	3,763		170	(1,292)	59			229
Purchases of common stock				4,976	(276)			(276)
Balance, December 31, 2002	173,950	$2	$1,965	11,682	$(547)	$2,593	$(1,673)	$2,340
Net income						585		585
Translation adjustments							313	313
Minimum pension liability, net of $5 million taxes							8	8
Comprehensive income								906
Dividends on common stock ($0.46 per share)						(149)		(149)
Issuances of common stock								
For the dividend reinvestment and stock purchase plan	48							—
For employee savings and incentive plans	3,535		183	(1,681)	79			262
Purchases of common stock				4,614	(271)			(271)
Two-for-one stock split (Note 1)	177,418	2		14,250		(2)		—
Balance, December 31, 2003	354,951	$4	$2,148	28,865	$(739)	$3,027	$(1,352)	$3,088

NOTES TO CONSOLIDATED FINANCIAL STATEMENTS

Note 1 (In Part): Summary of Significant Accounting Policies

Stock Split

On October 28, 2003, Praxair's board of directors declared a two-for-one split of the company's common stock. The stock split was effected in the form of a stock dividend of one additional share for each share owned by stockholders of record on December 5, 2003, and each share held in treasury as of the record date. The additional shares were distributed to such holders on December 15, 2003. Information pertaining to shares, earnings per share and dividends per share has been restated in the accompanying financial statements, except for the statement of shareholders' equity, and related footnotes to reflect this split.

CHANGES IN ADDITIONAL PAID-IN CAPITAL

5.31   Table 5-7 summarizes credits and charges to additional paid-in capital. Examples of such credits and charges follow.

5.32

TABLE 5-7:   CHANGES IN ADDITIONAL PAID-IN CAPITAL

	Number of Companies			
	2003	2002	2001	2000
Credits				
Common stock issued				
Employee benefits	401	409	384	381
Business combinations	38	58	66	70
Public offerings	33	45	49	30
Debt conversions/extinguishments	12	16	18	21
Preferred stock conversions	10	20	20	14
Stock compensation tax benefits	156	159	151	127
Compensation recognized	51	31	42	N/C*
Warrants issued or exercised	7	10	11	9
Put options/warrants	1	5	3	5
Other—described	36	32	50	41
Charges				
Purchase or retirement of capital stock	99	96	110	121
Treasury stock issued for less than cost.	75	77	61	66
Restricted stock	39	22	19	22
Conversion of preferred stock	7	10	6	8
Other—described	65	73	85	69

* N/C = Not compiled. Line item was not included in the table for the year shown.

Common Stock Issued in Connection With Employee Benefit Plans

5.33

NORTHROP GRUMMAN CORPORATION (DEC)

Consolidated Statements of Changes in Shareholders' Equity

(In millions, except per share)	2003	2002	2001
Paid-in capital			
At beginning of year	$12,511	$ 4,451	$1,200
Stock issued in purchase of businesses	—	7,753	2,405
Stock issued in public offering	—	—	784
Common stock repurchased	(200)	—	—
Equity security units issuance fees and forward contract fees	—	—	(56)
Employee stock awards and options	122	307	118
At end of year	12,433	12,511	4,451
Retained earnings			
At beginning of year	2,870	3,011	2,742
Net income	866	64	427
Cash dividends	(305)	(205)	(158)
At end of year	3,431	2,870	3,011
Unearned compensation			
At beginning of year	(11)	(18)	—
Issuance of unvested stock options	—	—	(24)
Amortization of unearned compensation	5	7	6
At end of year	(6)	(11)	(18)
Accumulated other comprehensive loss			
At beginning of year	(1,048)	(53)	(23)
Change in cumulative translation adjustment	10	(1)	(3)
Change in unrealized gain on marketable securities, net of tax	1	—	—
Change in additional minimum pension liability, net of tax	964	(994)	(27)
At end of year	(73)	(1,048)	(53)
Total shareholders' equity	$15,785	$14,322	$7,391
Cash dividends per share	$ 1.60	$ 1.60	$ 1.60

NOTES TO CONSOLIDATED FINANCIAL STATEMENTS

1 (In Part): Summary of Significant Accounting Policies

Stock Compensation Plans (In Part)

The company applies Accounting Principles Board Opinion 25—*Accounting for Stock Issued to Employees* and related interpretations in accounting for awards made under stock compensation plans. When stock options are exercised, the cash proceeds received by the company are recorded as an increase to paid-in capital. No compensation expense is recognized in connection with the stock options. Compensation expense for restricted performance stock rights and restricted stock rights is estimated and accrued over the vesting period.

17. Stock Compensation Plans

At December 31, 2003, Northrop Grumman had three stock-based compensation plans: the 2001 Long-Term Incentive Stock Plan (2001 LTISP), and the 1993 Long-Term Incentive Stock Plan (1993 LTISP), both applicable to employees, and the 1995 Stock Option Plan for Non-Employee Directors (SOPND). All of these plans are approved by the company's shareholders.

Employee Plans

The 2001 LTISP and the 1993 LTISP permit grants to key employees of three general types of stock incentive awards: stock options, stock appreciation rights (SARs), and stock awards. Each stock option grant is made with an exercise price either at the closing price of the stock on the date of grant (market options) or at a premium over the closing price of the stock on the date of grant (premium options). Options generally vest in 25 percent increments one, two, three, and four years from the grant date under the 2001 LTISP and two, three, four, and five years from the grant date under the 1993 LTISP. Under both plans, options expire ten years after the grant date. No SARs have been granted under either of the LTISP's. Stock awards, in the form of restricted performance stock rights and restricted stock rights, are granted to key employees without payment to the company. Under the 2001 LTISP, recipients of restricted performance stock rights earn shares of stock based on an economic value added (EVA) metric over a three-year performance period with distributions made entirely at the end of the third year. Under the 1993 LTISP, recipients of restricted performance stock rights earn shares of stock based on a total-shareholder-return measure of performance over a five-year performance period with interim distributions three and four years after grant. If at the end of the applicable performance period objectives have not been met, unearned rights up to 100 percent of the original grant for five elected officers and the three next highest compensated employees, and up to 70 percent of the original grant for all other recipients, will be forfeited. Restricted stock rights issued under either plan vest annually, generally over three years. Termination of employment can result in forfeiture of some or all of the benefits extended under the plan. At December 31, 2003, approximately 16 million shares were available for future grants under the 2001 LTISP.

Nonemployee Plan

The SOPND permits grants of stock options to nonemployee directors. Each grant of a stock option is made at the closing market price on the date of the grant, is immediately exercisable, and expires ten years after the grant date. At December 31, 2003, 189,000 shares were available for future grants under the SOPND.

Stock Awards

Compensation expense for restricted performance stock rights is estimated and recognized over the vesting period. The fixed 30 percent minimum distribution portion is measured at the grant date fair value and the variable portion is adjusted to the fair value at the end of each accounting period. Compensation expense for restricted stock rights is measured at the grant date fair value and recognized over the vesting period. Restricted performance stock rights and restricted stock rights were granted with weighted-average grant-date fair values per share as follows: 2003—1,147,300 at $94; 2002—846,145 at $114; and 2001—812,730 at $81.

Option Conversions

In connection with the acquisition of Litton, the company converted Litton stock options to company stock options. For Litton options only, a reduction of shareholders' equity was recorded and is being amortized as compensation expense through 2005. Acquired TRW options were converted to the company's options and fully vested on the date of acquisition.

Compensation Expense

Total stock-based compensation expense was $99 million in 2003, $69 million in 2002, and $27 million in 2001.

Stock option activity for the last three years is summarized below:

	Shares Under Option	Weighted-Average Exercise Prices	Options Exercisable	Weighted-Average Exercise Prices
Outstanding at January 1, 2001	4,674,273	$ 78	2,277,341	$71
Granted, market options	2,128,810	81		
Options converted upon acquisition of Litton	1,110,485	57		
Cancelled	(215,531)	85		
Exercised	(985,424)	61		
Outstanding at December 31, 2001	6,712,613	78	2,173,779	79
Granted, market options	2,255,063	114		
Options converted upon acquisition of TRW	5,810,231	92		
Cancelled	(199,759)	78		
Exercised	(1,184,350)	76		
Outstanding at December 31, 2002	13,393,798	90	8,531,746	89
Granted, market options	2,665,489	94		
Cancelled	(228,441)	85		
Exercised	(470,829)	66		
Outstanding at December 31, 2003	15,360,017	92	9,883,528	90

At December 31, 2003, the following stock options were outstanding:

	Options Outstanding			Options Exercisable	
Range of Exercise Prices	Number Outstanding	Weighted-Average Remaining Contractual Life	Weighted-Average Exercise Prices	Number Exercisable	Weighted-Average Exercise Prices
$ 28 to 78	4,070,442	6.4 years	$ 71	2,839,109	$ 70
79 to 93	3,298,035	4.8 years	88	3,123,862	88
94 to 99	4,076,140	7.7 years	96	1,488,062	99
100 to 128	3,915,400	7.3 years	112	2,432,495	110
	15,360,017		92	9,883,528	90

5.34

OCCIDENTAL PETROLEUM CORPORATION (DEC)

Consolidated Statements of Stockholders' Equity

(In millions)	Common Stock	Additional Paid-In Capital	Retained Earnings	Accumulated Other Comprehensive Income (Loss)
Balance, December 31,2000	$74	$3,743	$1,007	$(50)
Net income	—	—	1,154	—
Other comprehensive loss, net of tax	—	—	—	(36)
Dividends on common stock	—	—	(373)	—
Issuance of common stock	—	19	—	—
Exercises of options and other, net	1	95	—	—
Balance, December 31, 2001	$75	$3,857	$1,788	$(86)
Net income	—	—	989	—
Other comprehensive income, net of tax	—	—	—	59
Dividends on common stock	—	—	(474)	—
Issuance of common stock	—	22	—	—
Exercises of options and other, net	—	88	—	—
Balance, December 31, 2002	$75	$3,967	$2,303	$(27)
Net income	—	—	1,527	—
Other comprehensive income, net of tax	—	—	—	77
Dividends on common stock	—	—	(300)	—
Issuance of common stock	—	11	—	—
Exercises of options and other, net	2	294	—	—
Balance, December 31, 2003	$77	$4,272	$3,530	$ 50

NOTES TO CONSOLIDATED FINANCIAL STATEMENTS

Note 12 (In Part): Stock Incentive Plans

Occidental applies APB No. 25 and related interpretations in accounting for its stock incentive plans (Plans), which are described below. The pro-forma effect on net income and earnings per share, had Occidental applied the fair-value recognition provisions of SFAS No. 123, are shown in Note 1.

The company has established several stock incentive plans offering certain employees and management stock options, restricted stock, stock appreciation rights and performance stock awards. These awards are granted under the 1995 and 2001 Incentive Stock Plans. The 1995 Plan was terminated, for the purposes of further award grants, upon the effective date of the 2001 Plan; however, certain 1995 Plan award grants are outstanding at December 31, 2003. An aggregate of 27,000,000 share-based awards are reserved for issuance under the 2001 Plan and at December 31, 2003, approximately 7,574,285 share-based awards were available for future awards. The company has also established the 1996 Restricted Stock Plan for non-employee directors, where non-employee directors receive awards of restricted stock as additional compensation for their services as members of the Board of Directors. A maximum of 150,000 shares of stock may be awarded under the Directors Plan and at December 31, 2003, 34,572 shares of common stock were available for future grants.

Stock Option Plans

Under the stock option plans, certain employees and executives are granted stock options with an exercise price equal to the fair value of the company's stock on the date of grant. Generally, the options vest over three years with a maximum term of ten years and one month. Under certain conditions, the option awards are forfeitable.

The following is a summary of stock option transactions during 2003, 2002 and 2001:

(Shares in thousands)	2003 Options	2003 Weighted Average Exercise Price	2002 Options	2002 Weighted Average Exercise Price	2001 Options	2001 Weighted Average Exercise Price
Beginning balance	26,972	$24.22	25,390	$23.40	18,217	$21.53
Granted or issued	5,191	$31.13	4,904	$26.43	11,039	$26.17
Exercised	(8,999)	$22.30	(3,097)	$21.12	(3,395)	$22.40
Forfeited or expired	(152)	$24.96	(225)	$22.52	(471)	$23.50
Ending balance	23,012	$26.53	26,972	$24.22	25,390	$23.40
Options exercisable at year end	12,535	$24.62	16,186	$23.33	15,023	$22.95

The following is a summary of stock options outstanding at December 31, 2003:

| | | Options Outstanding | | Options Exercisable | |
| | | Weighted Average Remaining | Weighted Average | | Weighted Average |
Range of Exercise Prices	Outstanding	Contractual Life	Exercise Price	Exercisable	Exercise Price
$14.88–$21.88	2,883,228	6.1	$20.37	2,883,228	$20.37
$23.13–$26.43	9,945,531	5.7	$25.80	6,712,650	$25.50
$26.75–$31.13	10,183,164	8.5	$29.06	2,939,602	$26.76
$14.88–$31.13	23,011,923	7.0	$26.53	12,535,480	$24.62

Business Combination

5.35

STANDARD MOTOR PRODUCTS, INC. (DEC)

Consolidated Statements of Changes in Stockholders' Equity

(In thousands)	Common Stock	Capital in Excess of Par Value	Retained Earnings	Accumulated Other Comprehensive Income (Loss)	Treasury Stock	Total
Balance at December 31, 2000	$26,649	$2,541	$190,253	$ (591)	$(24,547)	$194,305
Comprehensive loss						
Net loss			(2,485)			(2,485)
Foreign currency translation adjustment				(1,086)		(1,086)
Unrealized loss on interest rate swap agreements				(2,045)		(2,045)
Total comprehensive loss						(5,616)
Cash dividends paid			(4,236)			(4,236)
Exercise of employee stock options		(295)			768	473
Tax benefits applicable to the exercise of employee stock options		48				48
Employee Stock Ownership Plan		(417)			1,130	713
Balance at December 31, 2001	26,649	1,877	183,532	(3,722)	(22,649)	185,687
Comprehensive loss						
Net loss			(30,556)			(30,556)
Foreign currency translation adjustment				1,295		1,295
Unrealized gain on interest rate swap agreements, net of tax of $205				617		617
Minimum pension liability adjustment				(771)		(771)
Total comprehensive loss						(29,415)
Cash dividends paid			(4,290)			(4,290)
Exercise of employee stock options		(291)			880	589
Tax benefits applicable to the exercise of employee stock options		80				80
Employee Stock Ownership Plan		98			1,132	1,230
Balance at December 31, 2002	$26,649	$1,764	$148,686	$(2,581)	$(20,637)	$153,881

(continued)

(In thousands)	Common Stock	Capital in Excess of Par Value	Retained Earnings	Accumulated Other Comprehensive Income (Loss)	Treasury Stock	Total
Balance at December 31, 2002	$26,649	$ 1,764	$148,686	$(2,581)	$(20,637)	$153,881
Comprehensive loss						
Net loss			(1,518)			(1,518)
Foreign currency translation adjustment				6,162		6,162
Unrealized gain on interest rate swap agreements, net of tax of $439				1,317		1,317
Minimum pension liability adjustment				(84)		(84)
Total comprehensive loss						5,877
Cash dividends paid			(5,615)			(5,615)
Issuance of common stock related to acquisition	14,323	56,546				70,869
Exercise of employee stock options		(30)			121	91
Employee Stock Ownership Plan		(194)			1,132	938
Balance at December 31, 2003	$40,972	$58,086	$141,553	$ 4,814	$(19,384)	$226,041

NOTES TO CONSOLIDATED FINANCIAL STATEMENTS

2 (In Part): Acquisitions and Restructuring Costs

Acquisition of Dana's EMG Business (In Part)

On June 30, 2003, we completed the acquisition of substantially all of the assets and assumed substantially all of the operating liabilities of Dana Corporation's Engine Management Group ("DEM"). Prior to the sale, DEM was a leading manufacturer of aftermarket parts in the automotive industry focused exclusively on engine management.

Under the terms of the acquisition, we paid Dana Corporation $91.3 million in cash, issued an unsecured promissory note of $15.1 million, and issued 1,378,760 shares of our common stock valued at $15.1 million using an average market price of $10.97 per share. Based on the estimated final purchase price, we expect to pay in cash an additional $1.9 million. The average market price was based on the average closing price for a range of trading days preceding the closing date of the acquisition. We also incurred an estimated $7.1 million in transaction costs.

We also issued to Dana Corporation an unsecured subordinated promissory note in the aggregate principal amount of approximately $15.1 million. The promissory note bears an interest rate of 9% per annum for the first year, with such interest rate increasing by one-half of a percentage point (0.5%) on each anniversary of the date of issuance. Accrued and unpaid interest is due quarterly under the promissory note. The maturity date of the promissory note is five and a half years from the date of issuance. The promissory note may be prepaid in whole or in part at any time without penalty.

In connection with the acquisition of DEM, we completed a public equity offering of 5,750,000 shares of our common stock for net proceeds of approximately $55.7 million. The net proceeds from this equity offering were used to repay a portion of our outstanding indebtedness under our revolving credit facility with General Electric Capital Corporation. On June 30, 2003, we also completed an amendment to our revolving credit facility, which increased the amount available under the credit facility by $80 million, to $305 million, as discussed more fully in Note 7 of Notes to Consolidated Financial Statements. We then financed the cash portion of the acquisition purchase price and the costs associated with the acquisition by borrowing from our amended credit facility.

Public Offering

5.36

NEWELL RUBBERMAID INC. (DEC)

Consolidated Statements of Stockholders' Equity and Comprehensive (Loss)/Income

(In millions, except per share data)	Common Stock	Treasury Stock	Add'l Paid-In Capital	Retained Earnings	Accumulated Other Comprehensive (Loss)/Income	Total Stockholders' Equity
Balance at December 31, 2000	$282.2	$(407.5)	$215.9	$2,530.9	$(172.9)	$2,448.6
Comprehensive income/(loss)						
Net income	—	—	—	264.6	—	264.6
Foreign currency translation	—	—	—	—	(41.3)	(41.3)
Minimum pension liability adjustment, net of ($2.8) million tax	—	—	—	—	(4.5)	(4.5)
Loss on derivative instruments, net of ($7.9) million tax	—	—	—	—	(14.0)	(14.0)
Unrealized loss on securities available for sale, net of ($1.1) million tax	—	—	—	—	(2.1)	(2.1)
Reclassification adjustment for losses realized in net income, net of $1.8 million tax	—	—	—	—	3.2	3.2
Total comprehensive income						205.9
Cash dividends on common stock ($0.84 per share)	—	—	—	(224.0)	—	(224.0)
Exercise of stock options	0.2	(0.8)	3.7	—	—	3.1
Other	—	(0.2)	0.2	(0.2)	—	(0.2)
Balance at December 31, 2001	$282.4	$(408.5)	$219.8	$2,571.3	$(231.6)	$2,433.4
Comprehensive income/(loss)						
Net loss	—	—	—	(203.4)	—	(203.4)
Foreign currency translation	—	—	—	—	98.0	98.0
Minimum pension liability adjustment, net of ($43.5) million tax	—	—	—	—	(71.0)	(71.0)
Gain on derivative instruments, net of ($8.8) million tax	—	—	—	—	14.4	14.4
Total comprehensive (loss)						(162.0)
Cash dividends on common stock ($0.84 per share)	—	—	—	(224.4)	—	(224.4)
Exercise of stock options	0.7	(1.4)	17.1	—	—	16.4
Other	—	—	0.4	(0.3)	—	0.1
Balance at December 31, 2002	$283.1	$(409.9)	$237.3	$2,143.2	$(190.2)	$2,063.5
Comprehensive income/(loss)						
Net loss	—	—	—	(46.6)	—	(46.6)
Foreign currency translation	—	—	—	—	130.7	130.7
Minimum pension liability adjustment, net of ($55.5) million tax	—	—	—	—	(114.5)	(114.5)
Gain on derivative instruments, net of ($3.8) million tax	—	—	—	—	6.2	6.2
Total comprehensive loss						(24.2)
Cash dividends on common stock ($0.84 per share)	—	—	—	(230.9)	—	(230.9)
Exercise of stock options	0.3	(1.8)	7.7	—	—	6.2
Issuance of stock	6.7	—	193.4	—	—	200.1
Other	—	0.1	1.5	—	—	1.6
Balance at December 31, 2003	$290.1	$(411.6)	$439.9	$1,865.7	$(167.8)	$2,016.3

NOTES TO CONSOLIDATED FINANCIAL STATEMENTS

Footnote 11 (In Part): Stockholders' Equity

In January 2003, the Company completed the sale of 6.67 million shares of its common stock at a public offering price of $30.10 per share pursuant to an effective shelf registration statement that was previously filed with the Securities and Exchange Commission. The net proceeds of $200.1 million were used to reduce the Company's commercial paper borrowings.

Debt Conversion

5.37

D.R. HORTON, INC. (SEP)

Consolidated Statements of Stockholders' Equity

(In thousands, except common stock share data)	Common Stock	Additional Capital	Unearned Compensation	Retained Earnings	Treasury Stock	Total Stockholders' Equity
Balances at September 30, 2000 (70,074,110 shares)	$ 701	$ 537,145	$ —	$ 468,664	$(36,947)	$ 969,563
Net income	—	—	—	257,009	—	257,009
Issuances under D.R. Horton, Inc. employee benefit plans (7,450 shares)	—	125	—	—	—	125
Exercise of stock options (917,098 shares)	9	12,269	—	—	—	12,278
Cash dividends declared ($.19 per share)	—	—	—	(13,728)	—	(13,728)
Stock issued as partial consideration for acquisition (1,012,925 shares)	10	24,990	—	—	—	25,000
11% stock dividend (4,889,928 shares)	49	130,313	—	(167,309)	36,947	—
Balances at September 30, 2001 (76,901,511 shares)	$ 769	$ 704,842	$ —	$ 544,636	$ —	$1,250,247
Net income	—	—	—	404,692	—	404,692
Issuances under D.R. Horton, Inc. employee benefit plans (18,460 shares)	—	420	—	—	—	420
Exercise of stock options (756,235 shares)	8	13,559	—	—	—	13,567
Fair value of unvested stock options issued in connection with an acquisition	—	10,437	(6,009)	—	—	4,428
Amortization of unvested stock options issued in connection with an acquisition over remaining vesting period	—	—	1,556	—	—	1,556
Cash dividends declared ($.23 per share)	—	—	—	(26,107)	—	(26,107)
Stock issued as partial consideration for acquisition (20,079,532 shares)	201	620,859	—	—	—	621,060
Three-for-two stock split (48,749,353 shares)	487	(487)	—	—	—	—
Balances at September 30, 2002 (146,505,091 shares)	$1,465	$1,349,630	$(4,453)	$ 923,221	$ —	$2,269,863
Net income	—	—	—	625,955	—	625,955
Issuances under D.R. Horton, Inc. employee benefit plans (40,736 shares)	—	846	—	—	—	846
Exercise of stock options (873,353 shares)	9	11,949	—	—	—	11,958
Amortization of unvested stock options issued in connection with an acquisition over remaining vesting period	—	—	2,290	—	—	2,290
Cash dividends declared ($.27 per share)	—	—	—	(40,097)	—	(40,097)
Treasury stock purchases (2,652,800 shares)	—	—	—	—	(58,859)	(58,859)
Conversion of convertible notes (10,000,040 shares)	100	219,204	—	—	—	219,304
Balances at September 30, 2003 (154,766,420 shares)	$1,574	$1,581,629	$(2,163)	$1,509,079	$(58,859)	$3,031,260

NOTES TO CONSOLIDATED FINANCIAL STATEMENTS

Note B (In Part): Notes Payable

The Company's notes payable consist of the following (in thousands):

	2002	2003
Homebuilding		
Unsecured		
Revolving credit facility due 2006	$ —	$ —
$8\frac{3}{8}$% senior notes due 2004, net	149,339	149,736
$10\frac{1}{2}$% senior notes due 2005, net	199,559	199,691
10% senior notes due 2006, net	147,802	—
$7\frac{1}{2}$% senior notes due 2007, net	—	215,000
9% senior notes due 2008, net	102,427	—
8% senior notes due 2009, net	383,438	383,635
$9\frac{3}{8}$% senior notes due 2009, net	246,057	243,927
$9\frac{3}{4}$% senior subordinated notes due 2010, net	148,994	149,082
$7\frac{7}{8}$% senior notes due 2011, net	198,437	198,564
$9\frac{3}{8}$% senior subordinated notes due 2011, net	199,710	199,733
$10\frac{1}{2}$% senior subordinated notes due 2011, net	153,284	151,798
$8\frac{1}{2}$% senior notes due 2012, net	247,995	248,138
$6\frac{7}{8}$% senior notes due 2013, net	—	200,000
$5\frac{7}{8}$% senior notes due 2013, net	—	100,000
Zero coupon convertible senior notes due 2021, net	209,144	—
Other secured	100,790	125,841
	$2,486,976	$2,565,145
Financial services		
Mortgage warehouse facility due 2004	$ 242,355	$ 147,978
Commercial paper conduit facility due 2006	149,000	250,000
	$ 391,355	$ 397,978

● ● ● ● ● ●

On May 27, 2003, the Company called all of its zero coupon convertible senior notes due 2021 for redemption. The call for redemption gave the note holders the right to convert their notes into shares of D.R. Horton common stock or to redeem them for cash at their accreted value as of the redemption date. All of the notes were presented for conversion into D.R. Horton common stock, and accordingly the Company issued approximately 10 million shares of common stock in exchange for the notes. As a result of the conversion, common stock increased $0.1 million and additional capital increased $219.2 million.

Preferred Stock Conversion

5.38

FREEPORT-MCMORAN COPPER & GOLD INC. (DEC)

Consolidated Statements of Stockholders' Equity

(In thousands)	2003	2002	2001
Step-up convertible preferred stock			
Balance at beginning of year representing 13,999,600 shares	$ 349,990	$ 349,990	$ 349,990
Conversions to Class B common stock and redemptions	(349,990)	—	—
Balance at end of year representing 13,999,600 shares in 2002 and 2001	—	349,990	349,990
Class A common stock			
Balance at beginning of year representing 97,146,428 shares in 2002 and 97,071,944 shares in 2001	—	9,715	9,707
Issued restricted stock representing 140,665 shares in 2002 and 74,484 shares in 2001	—	14	8
Conversion to Class B common stock	—	(9,729)	—
Balance at end of year representing 97,146,428 shares in 2001	—	—	9,715
Class B common stock			
Balance at beginning of year representing 220,082,757 shares in 2003, 121,744,654 shares in 2002 and 121,687,529 shares in 2001	22,008	12,174	12,169
Step-up convertible preferred stock conversions	1,146	—	—
8¼% convertible senior notes conversions	2,176	—	—
Class A common stock conversion	—	9,729	—
Exercised stock options and issued restricted stock representing 6,702,871 shares in 2003, 1,051,010 shares in 2002 and 57,125 shares in 2001	670	105	5
Balance at end of year representing 260,001,296 shares in 2003, 220,082,757 shares in 2002 and 121,744,654 shares in 2001	26,000	22,008	12,174
Capital in excess of par value of common stock			
Balance at beginning of year	687,828	660,329	657,239
Step-up convertible preferred stock conversions	341,885	—	—
8¼% convertible senior notes conversions	303,782	—	—
Exercised stock options and other stock option amounts	106,920	14,220	899
Restricted stock grants	1,380	1,250	2,191
Reclass of redeemable preferred stock issuance costs to other assets	26,631	—	—
Tax benefit for stock option exercises	—	12,029	—
Balance at end of year	1,468,426	687,828	660,329
Retained earnings			
Balance at beginning of year	534,447	407,397	330,901
Net income	181,660	164,654	113,025
Dividends on common stock	(41,733)	—	—
Dividends on preferred stock	(27,441)	(37,604)	(36,529)
Balance at end of year	646,933	534,447	407,397
Accumulated other comprehensive income (loss)			
Balance at beginning of year	10,963	(1,184)	10,244
Other comprehensive income (loss), net of taxes			
Cumulative effect of change in accounting for derivatives	—	—	(982)
Change in unrealized derivatives' fair value	5,195	13,615	(14,920)
Reclass to earnings of net realized derivatives (gains) losses	(7,490)	(1,468)	4,474
Balance at end of year	8,668	10,963	(1,184)
Common stock held in treasury			
Balance at beginning of year representing 75,172,774 shares in 2003, 74,915,457 shares in 2002 and 74,718,076 shares in 2001	(1,338,410)	(1,333,977)	(1,332,319)
Shares purchased representing 194,000 shares in 2001	—	—	(1,620)
Tender of 1,461,430 shares in 2003, 257,317 shares in 2002 and 3,381 shares in 2001 to FCX for exercised stock options and restricted stock	(35,633)	(4,433)	(38)
Balance at end of year representing 76,634,204 shares in 2003, 75,172,774 shares in 2002 and 74,915,457 shares in 2001	(1,374,043)	(1,338,410)	(1,333,977)
Total stockholders' equity	$ 775,984	$ 266,826	$ 104,444

ATT-SEC 5.38

NOTES TO CONSOLIDATED FINANCIAL STATEMENTS

Note 6 (In Part): Stockholders' Equity

Preferred Stock

In December 2003, FCX called for redemption the deposi- tary shares representing its Step-Up Convertible Preferred Stock. Of the 14.0 million depositary shares outstanding at the time of call, 13.8 million depositary shares converted into 11.5 million shares of FCX's common stock. The remain- ing depositary shares outstanding are being redeemed for approximately $7 million in cash. These depositary shares traded on the NYSE under the symbol "FCX PrA."

Stock Option Tax Benefit

5.39

TASTY BAKING COMPANY (DEC)

Consolidated Statements of Changes in Capital Accounts

(000's)	2003 Shares	2003 Amount	2002 Shares	2002 Amount	2001 Shares	2001 Amount
Common stock						
Balance, beginning of year	9,116	$ 4,558	9,116	$ 4,558	9,116	$ 4,558
Balance, end of year	9,116	$ 4,558	9,116	$ 4,558	9,116	$ 4,558
Capital in excess of par value of stock						
Balance, beginning of year		$ 29,433		$ 29,389		$ 29,742
Issuances (terminations)						
Management stock purchase plan		(42)		17		54
Stock option plan		(7)		(25)		(600)
Conditional stock grant		—		—		(11)
Tax benefits related to management stock purchase plan and stock option plan		9		52		204
Balance, end of year		$ 29,393		$ 29,433		$ 29,389
Accumulated other comprehensive (loss)						
Balance, beginning of year		$ —		$ —		$ —
Minimum pension liability, net of taxes of $723		(1,236)		—		—
Balance, end of year		$ (1,236)		$ —		$ —
Treasury stock						
Balance, beginning of year	(1,013)	$(12,539)	(1,065)	$(13,167)	(1,271)	$(16,106)
Management stock purchase plan						
Reissued	1	17	12	159	20	270
Reacquired	(8)	(75)	(7)	(129)	(6)	(65)
Net shares reissued in connection with						
Stock option plan	—	52	47	598	156	2,141
Conditional stock grant	—	—	—	—	36	593
Balance, end of year	(1,020)	$(12,545)	(1,013)	$(12,539)	(1,065)	$(13,167)
Management stock purchase plan receivables and deferrals						
Balance, beginning of year		$ (549)		$ (554)		$ (373)
Common stock issued		(13)		(176)		(323)
Common stock repurchased		93		99		60
Note payments and amortization of deferred compensation		77		82		82
Balance, end of year		$ (392)		$ (549)		$ (554)

NOTES TO CONSOLIDATED FINANCIAL STATEMENTS
(000's, except share and per share amounts)

11. Management Stock Purchase Plan

In March of 2003, the Management Stock Purchase Plan was discontinued prospectively. The Management Stock Purchase Plan provided that common shares may be sold to management employees from time to time at prices designated by the Board of Directors (not less than 50% of the fair market value at date of grant) and under certain restrictions and obligations to resell to the company. During 2003 and 2002, 1,400 and 11,900 shares of common stock, respectively, were sold at 50% of fair market value at date of grant. The aggregate sales price of these shares was $7 and $101, respectively, for which collateral judgment notes were obtained to be paid in equal quarterly installments (not to exceed 40) with interest on the unpaid balance at 2.13% in 2003, and 2.38% in 2002. At December 27, 2003, a total of 931,567 common shares were authorized under the plan, of which 182,365 shares remained unissued.

For accounting purposes, the difference between the fair market value of the stock at the date of grant and the purchase price, $6 in 2003 and $76 in 2002, represents compensation. The compensation is deferred and, together with the notes receivable, is shown as a deduction from shareholders' equity. The deferred compensation is amortized over a ten-year period or the period the employees perform services, whichever is less. Amortization charged to income amounted to $38, $42, and $45 in 2003, 2002, and 2001, respectively.

In accordance with an Internal Revenue Service regulation, the company includes both the dividends paid on shares restricted under the plan, and the difference between the purchase price of the stock at the date of the grant and the fair market value at the date the plan restrictions lapse, as employee compensation for federal income tax purposes. The tax benefits relating to the difference between the amounts deductible for federal income taxes over the amounts charged to income for book purposes have been credited to capital in excess of par value of stock.

Compensation Recognized

5.40

NATIONAL SEMICONDUCTOR CORPORATION (MAY)

Consolidated Statements of Shareholders' Equity

(In millions)	Common Stock	Additional Paid-In Capital	Retained Earnings	Unearned Compensation	Accumulated Other Comprehensive Loss	Total
Balances at May 28, 2000	$88.8	$1,407.9	$ 186.7	$(12.6)	$ (27.5)	$1,643.3
Net income	—	—	245.7	—	—	245.7
Issuance of common stock under option, purchase, and profit sharing plans	2.2	70.0	—	—	—	72.2
Unearned compensation relating to issuance of restricted stock	0.1	7.4	—	(7.5)	—	—
Cancellation of restricted stock	—	(2.8)	—	2.0	—	(0.8)
Amortization of unearned compensation	—	—	—	4.2	—	4.2
Proceeds from sale of put warrants	—	0.4	—	—	—	0.4
Stock compensation charge	—	2.0	—	—	—	2.0
Purchase and retirement of treasury stock	(4.2)	(190.2)	—	—	—	(194.4)
Other comprehensive loss	—	—	—	—	(4.7)	(4.7)
Balances at May 27, 2001	86.9	1,294.7	432.4	(13.9)	(32.2)	1,767.9
Net loss	—	—	(121.9)	—	—	(121.9)
Issuance of common stock under option, purchase, and profit sharing plans	3.0	108.6	—	—	—	111.6
Unearned compensation relating to issuance of restricted stock	—	3.1	—	(3.1)	—	—
Cancellation of restricted stock	—	(0.9)	—	0.8	—	(0.1)
Amortization of unearned compensation	—	—	—	3.4	—	3.4
Stock compensation charge	—	0.1	—	—	—	0.1
Issuance of common stock upon conversion of convertible subordinated promissory notes	0.3	9.7	—	—	—	10.0
Other comprehensive income	—	—	—	—	10.1	10.1
Balances at May 26, 2002	90.2	1,415.3	310.5	(12.8)	(22.1)	1,781.1
Net loss	—	—	(33.3)	—	—	(33.3)
Issuance of common stock under option, purchase, and profit sharing plans	1.6	42.2	—	—	—	43.8
Unearned compensation relating to issuance of restricted stock	—	0.5	—	(0.5)	—	—
Cancellation of restricted stock	—	(1.4)	—	0.3	—	(1.1)
Amortization of unearned compensation	—	—	—	3.0	—	3.0
Effect of investee equity transactions	—	4.7	—	—	—	4.7
Other comprehensive loss	—	—	—	—	(92.2)	(92.2)
Balances at May 25, 2003	$91.8	$1,461.3	$ 277.2	$(10.0)	$(114.3)	$1,706.0

NOTES TO CONSOLIDATED FINANCIAL STATEMENTS

Note 10 (In Part): Stock-Based Compensation Plans

Other Stock Plans

We have a director stock plan, which has been approved by shareholders, that authorizes the issuance of up to 200,000 shares of common stock to eligible directors who are not employees of the company. The stock is issued automatically to eligible new directors upon their appointment to the board and to all eligible directors on their subsequent election to the board by shareholders. Directors may also elect to take their annual retainer fees for board and committee membership in stock under the plan. As of May 25, 2003, we have issued 104,176 shares under the director stock plan and have reserved 95,824 shares for future issuances.

We have a restricted stock plan, which authorizes the issuance of up to 2,000,000 shares of common stock to employees who are not officers of the company. The plan has been made available to a limited group of employees with technical expertise we consider important. We issued 30,000, 112,000 and 240,000 shares under the restricted stock plan during fiscal 2003, 2002 and 2001, respectively. Restrictions expire over time, ranging from two to six years after issuance. Based upon the market value on the dates of issuance, we recorded $0.5 million, $3.1 million and $7.5 million of unearned compensation during fiscal 2003, 2002 and 2001, respectively. This unearned compensation is included as a separate component of shareholders' equity in the financial statements and is amortized to operations ratably over the applicable restriction periods. As of May 25, 2003, we have reserved 1,049,917 shares for future issuances under the restricted stock plan. Compensation expense for fiscal 2003, 2002 and 2001 related to shares of restricted stock, was $3.0 million, $3.4 million and $3.0 million, respectively. At May 25, 2003, the weighted-average grant date fair value for all outstanding shares of restricted stock was $30.94.

5.41

RUSSELL CORPORATION (DEC)

Consolidated Statements of Stockholders' Equity

(In thousands, except share date)	Common Stock	Paid-In Capital	Retained Earnings	Treasury Stock	Accumulated Other Comprehensive Loss	Total
Balance at December 30, 2000	$414	$47,104	$716,460	$(226,470)	$(11,568)	$525,940
Comprehensive loss						
Net loss	—	—	(55,486)	—	—	(55,486)
Foreign currency translation adjustments	—	—	—	—	(1,057)	(1,057)
Cumulative effect adjustment (SFAS 133), net of tax	—	—	—	—	(578)	(578)
Losses on derivatives reclassified to earnings, net of tax of $2,850	—	—	—	—	4,529	4,529
Change in unrealized value of derivatives, net of tax of $3,241	—	—	—	—	(5,288)	(5,288)
Minimum pension liability, net of tax of $442	—	—	—	—	(720)	(720)
Comprehensive loss						(58,600)
Treasury stock acquired (8,580 shares)	—	—	—	(120)	—	(120)
Treasury stock re-issued (121,542 shares)	—	(1,712)	—	3,418	—	1,706
Cash dividends ($0.46 per share)	—	—	(14,695)	—	—	(14,695)
Balance at December 29, 2001	414	45,392	646,279	(223,172)	(14,682)	454,231
Comprehensive income						
Net income	—	—	34,306	—	—	34,306
Foreign currency translation adjustments	—	—	—	—	(997)	(997)
Losses on derivatives reclassified to earnings, net of tax of $797	—	—	—	—	1,346	1,346
Change in unrealized value of derivatives, net of tax of $696	—	—	—	—	(1,175)	(1,175)
Minimum pension liability, net of tax of $10,583	—	—	—	—	(17,865)	(17,865)
Comprehensive income	—	—	—	—	—	15,615
Treasury stock acquired (2,763 shares)	—	—	—	(30)	—	(30)
Treasury stock re-issued (180,680 shares)	—	(2,515)	—	5,089	—	2,574
Cash dividends ($0.16 per share)	—	—	(5,137)	—	—	(5,137)
Balance at January 4, 2003	414	42,877	675,448	(218,113)	(33,373)	467,253
Comprehensive income						
Net income	—	—	43,039	—	—	43,039
Foreign currency translation adjustments	—	—	—	—	5,712	5,712
Losses on derivatives reclassified to earnings, net of tax of $1,705	—	—	—	—	2,796	2,796
Change in unrealized value of derivatives, net of tax of $2,808	—	—	—	—	(4,580)	(4,580)
Minimum pension liability, net of tax of $383	—	—	—	—	(2)	(2)
Comprehensive income	—	—	—	—	—	46,965
Treasury stock acquired (73,618 shares)	—	—	—	(1,457)	—	(1,457)
Treasury stock re-issued (410,088 shares)	—	(4,785)	—	11,532	—	6,747
Cash dividends ($0.16 per share)	—	—	(5,177)	—	—	(5,177)
Compensation expense	—	533	—	—	—	533
Balance at January 3, 2004	$414	$38,625	$713,310	$(208,038)	$(29,447)	$514,864

NOTES TO CONSOLIDATED FINANCIAL STATEMENTS

Note 1 (In Part): Description of Business and Significant Accounting Policies

Stock-Based Compensation

We issue awards under incentive compensation plans as described in Note 7. On January 5, 2003, we adopted the prospective transition provisions of SFAS No. 123, *Accounting and Disclosure of Stock-Based Compensation* as amended by SFAS No. 148. SFAS No. 148 uses a fair value based method of accounting for employee stock awards. By electing the prospective transition method of SFAS No. 148, our results of operations and our financial position were not affected by stock compensation awards granted prior to January 5, 2003. For stock compensation awards granted prior to January 5, 2003, we used the intrinsic value approach under Accounting Principles Board Opinion No. 25, *Accounting for Stock Issued to Employees*.

Note 7 (In Part): Stock Rights Plan and Stock Option Plans

Our Executive Incentive Plan permits us to issue equity-based compensation awards in several forms to all officers and key employees of the Company and its subsidiaries. Under the plan, we may issue restricted stock, incentive stock options, nonqualified stock options, reload stock options, bonus shares, deferred shares, stock appreciation rights and performance shares, and performance unit awards.

Most of our salaried employees, including officers, are eligible to participate in the Russell Corporation 2000 Stock Option Plan (2000 Option Plan). Awards under the 2000 Option Plan also may be made to consultants. The 2000 Option Plan allows us to grant awards in a variety of forms, including incentive stock options, nonqualified stock options, reload stock options, restricted shares, bonus shares, deferred shares, freestanding stock appreciation rights, tandem stock appreciation rights, performance units, and performance shares.

Under the Executive Incentive Plan, the 2000 Option Plan and predecessor stock option plans, a total of 2,482,061 shares of common stock were reserved for issuance at January 3, 2004. The options are granted at a price equal to the stock's fair market value at the date of grant. All options granted prior to 1999 are exercisable two years after the date of grant and expire 10 years after the date of grant. The stock options that were granted in 1999 and later are exercisable equally over periods of either two or four years and expire 10 years after the date of grant.

The following table summarizes the status of options under the Executive Incentive Plan, 2000 Option Plan and predecessor plans:

	2003 Shares	2003 Weighted Average Exercise Price	2002 Shares	2002 Weighted Average Exercise Price	2001 Shares	2001 Weighted Average Exercise Price
Outstanding at beginning of year	4,367,793	$19.92	4,630,808	$20.11	5,102,766	$20.50
Granted at fair value	70,650	$19.48	63,658	$16.41	334,830	$17.59
Exercised	340,539	$15.28	119,047	$15.06	49,268	$15.09
Expired	85,800	$27.50	—	—	272,050	$26.38
Forfeited	316,415	$21.36	207,626	$18.03	485,470	$19.56
Outstanding at end of year	3,695,689	$20.05	4,367,793	$19.92	4,630,808	$20.11
Exercisable at end of year	3,209,053	$20.62	2,982,005	$21.58	2,550,845	$23.21

The range of exercise prices of the outstanding exercisable options are as follows at January 3, 2004:

Weighted Average Exercise Price	Number of Exercisable Shares	Number of Outstanding Shares	Weighted Average Remaining Life in Years
$11.75–$15.00	14,816	32,526	7.6
$15.01–$18.25	1,321,623	1,642,079	6.2
$18.26–$21.50	588,970	733,547	5.6
$21.51–$24.75	314,177	318,070	4.5
$24.76–$28.00	742,867	742,867	3.6
$28.01–$31.35	226,600	226,600	2.1
	3,209,053	3,695,689	

On January 5, 2003, we adopted the prospective transition provisions of SFAS No. 148, which uses a fair value based method of accounting for employee stock options and similar equity instruments. By electing the prospective transition method of SFAS No. 148, our results of operations and our financial position are not affected by stock compensation awards granted prior to January 5, 2003. We recognized approximately $0.6 million ($0.4 million after-tax) of stock-based employee compensation in fiscal 2003. For stock compensation awards granted prior to January 5, 2003, we used the intrinsic value approach under Accounting Principles Board Opinion No. 25, *Accounting for Stock Issued to Employees*. The table below presents a comparison of reported results versus pro forma results that assumes the fair value based method of accounting had been applied to all stock compensation awards granted. For the purposes of this disclosure, we estimated the fair value of employee stock options at the date of grant using the Black-Scholes option valuation model. The fair values derived for options granted during fiscal years 2003, 2002 and 2001 and key assumptions used to determine these values were as follows:

	2003	2002	2001
Risk-free interest rate	1.25%	4.50%	4.90%
Dividend yield	1.00%	1.00%	1.00%
Volatility factor	.361	.361	.397
Weighted-average expected life of options	2.0 years	7.4 years	7.8 years
Estimated fair value per option	$3.88	$6.98	$7.10

For purposes of calculating the pro forma disclosures below, the estimated fair value of the options is amortized to expense over the options' vesting period.

(In thousands, except per share data)	2003	2002	2001
Reported net income (loss)	$43,039	$34,306	$(55,486)
Stock-based employee compensation, net of tax assuming SFAS No. 148 was applied	(1,171)	(2,542)	(4,698)
Pro forma net income (loss)	$41,868	$31,764	$(60,184)
Reported net income (loss) per share—basic	$ 1.33	$ 1.07	$ (1.74)
Pro forma net income (loss) per share—basic	$ 1.29	$ 0.99	$ (1.88)
Reported net income (loss) per share—diluted	$ 1.32	$ 1.06	$ (1.74)
Pro forma net income (loss) per share—diluted	$ 1.28	$ 0.99	$ (1.88)

Warrants Issued/Exercised

5.42

AVAYA INC. (SEP)

Consolidated Statements of Changes in Stockholders' Equity

(Dollars in millions)	2003	2002	2001
Common stock			
Beginning balance	$ 4	$ 3	$ 3
Issuance of stock	—	1	—
Ending balance	$ 4	$ 4	$ 3
Additional paid-in capital			
Beginning balance	$ 1,693	$ 905	$ 825
Issuance of warrants	5	—	32
Issuance of common stock for options exercised	—	2	7
Issuance of common stock to employees under the stock purchase plan	16	18	33
Issuance of other stock unit awards	31	24	28
Issuance of common stock in connection with Warburg transactions	—	628	—
Issuance of common stock in connection with the LYONs Exchange Offer, net of tax	57		
Issuance of common stock through public offering	349	112	—
Other stock transactions	—	4	22
Adjustment to Lucent capital contribution	—	—	(42)
Ending balance	$ 2,151	$ 1,693	$ 905
Accumulated deficit			
Beginning balance	$(1,182)	$ (379)	$ —
Preferred stock accretion	—	(12)	(27)
Preferred stock conversion and exercise of warrants charge	—	(125)	—
Net loss	(88)	(666)	(352)
Ending balance	$(1,270)	$(1,182)	$(379)
Accumulated other comprehensive loss			
Beginning balance	$ (512)	$ (46)	$ (64)
Foreign currency translation	70	47	18
Minimum pension liability	(237)	(513)	—
Tax effect of minimum pension liability	93	202	—
Valuation allowance related to minimum pension liability	(93)	(202)	—
Ending balance	$ (679)	$ (512)	$ (46)
Treasury stock			
Beginning balance	$ (3)	$ (2)	$ —
Purchase of treasury stock at cost	(3)	(1)	(2)
Ending balance	$ (6)	$ (3)	$ (2)
Total stockholders' equity	$ 200	$ —	$ 481

NOTES TO CONSOLIDATED FINANCIAL STATEMENTS

11 (In Part): Convertible Participating Preferred Stock and Other Equity Transactions

Warrants to Purchase Common Stock

In consideration of their agreement to participate in the LYONs Exchange Offer, in December 2002, the Company granted the Warburg Entities series C warrants that have a four-year term and are exercisable for an aggregate of 7,355,824 shares of Avaya common stock at an exercise price of $3.50 per share. The fair value of these warrants was estimated to be $5 million and was included in additional paid-in capital. During the second quarter of fiscal 2003, upon completion of the Exchange Offer, the Company recognized the cost of these warrants as a commitment fee and recorded the amount in loss on long-term debt extinguishment, net, which is a component of other income (expense), net.

As of September 30, 2003, the Warburg Entities hold warrants to purchase the following additional shares of the Company's common stock:

Warrants	Number of Shares	Exercise Price	Expiration Date
Series A	1,143,564	$34.73	October 2, 2004
Series B	5,379,732	$34.73	October 2, 2005
Series C	7,355,824	$ 3.50	December 23, 2006
Total	13,879,120		

Stock Contribution

5.43

BARNES GROUP INC. (DEC)

Consolidated Statements of Changes in Stockholders' Equity

(Dollars in thousands)	Common Stock	Additional Paid-In Capital	Treasury Stock	Retained Earnings	Accumulated Other Non-Owner Changes to Equity	Total Stockholders' Equity
January 1, 2001	$220	$ 51,845	$(69,181)	$239,266	$(20,817)	$201,333
Comprehensive income						
Net income				19,121		19,121
Foreign currency translation adjustments, net					(1,244)	(1,244)
Unrealized losses on hedging activities, net					(662)	(662)
Comprehensive income				19,121	(1,906)	17,215
Dividends paid				(14,806)		(14,806)
Common stock repurchases			(8,798)			(8,798)
Employee stock plans		3,029	1,076	(212)		3,893
December 31, 2001	220	54,874	(76,903)	243,369	(22,723)	198,837
Comprehensive income						
Net income				27,151		27,151
Foreign currency translation adjustments, net					1,236	1,236
Unrealized losses on hedging activities, net					(502)	(502)
Minimum pension liability adjustment, net					(16,822)	(16,822)
Comprehensive income				27,151	(16,088)	11,063
Dividends paid				(15,018)		(15,018)
Stock issued for the purchase of Spectrum		(358)	3,358			3,000
Stock contribution to Barnes Foundation		(90)	488			398
Common stock repurchases			(1,147)			(1,147)
Employee stock plans		(915)	12,357	(355)		11,087
December 31, 2002	220	53,511	(61,847)	255,147	(38,811)	208,220
Comprehensive income						
Net income				33,015		33,015
Foreign currency translation adjustments, net					18,071	18,071
Unrealized gains on hedging activities, net					555	555
Minimum pension liability adjustment, net					5,710	5,710
Comprehensive income				33,015	24,336	57,351
Dividends paid				(17,564)		(17,564)
Stock issued for the purchase of Kar		(2,064)	18,561			16,497
Stock issued, equity offering	24	42,188				42,212
Stock contribution to Barnes Foundation		168	232			400
Common stock repurchases			(206)			(206)
Employee stock plans		6,789	8,608	(568)		14,829
December 31, 2003	$244	$100,592	$(34,652)	$270,030	$(14,475)	$321,739

NOTES TO CONSOLIDATED FINANCIAL STATEMENTS

12 (In Part): Common Stock

In 2003, 2002 and 2001, 704,384 shares, 414,944 shares and 290,591 shares, respectively, of common stock were issued from treasury for the exercise of stock options, various other incentive awards, purchases by the Employee Stock Purchase Plan and matching contributions to the Barnes Group Inc. Retirement Savings Plan. In 2003, 823,506 and 11,817 shares were issued from treasury in connection with the acquisition of Kar and for the payment of charitable contributions, respectively. In 2002, 119,048 shares and 17,500 shares were issued from treasury, in connection with the acquisition of Spectrum and for the payment of charitable contributions, respectively. In 2003, 2002 and 2001, the Company acquired 9,995 shares, 56,888 shares and 436,502 shares, respectively, of the Company's common stock at a cost of $206, $1,147 and $8,798, respectively. These amounts exclude shares issued and reacquired in connection with certain stock-for-stock exercises under the Company's stock option plans. These reacquired shares were placed in treasury.

Treasury Stock Purchased

5.44

AUTOZONE, INC. (AUG)

Consolidated Statements of Stockholders' Equity

(In thousands)	Common Stock	Additional Paid-In Capital	Notes Receivable	Retained Earnings	Accumulated Other Comprehensive Loss	Treasury Stock	Total
Balance at August 26, 2000	$1,543	$301,901	$(4,463)	$1,564,118	$ (5)	$(870,915)	$ 992,179
Net income				175,526			175,526
Foreign currency translation adjustment					294		294
Unrealized losses on derivatives					(5,597)		(5,597)
Comprehensive income							170,223
Repayments of notes receivable from officers			2,552				2,552
Purchase of 14,345 shares of treasury stock		5,451				(366,097)	(360,646)
Retirement of 37,000 shares of treasury stock	(370)	(71,781)		(914,448)		986,599	—
Sale of 2,061 shares of common stock under stock option and stock purchase plans	22	46,563				1,825	48,410
Tax benefit of exercise of stock options		13,495					13,495
Balance at August 25, 2001	1,195	295,629	(1,911)	825,196	(5,308)	(248,588)	866,213
Net income				428,148			428,148
Foreign currency translation adjustment					(1,447)		(1,447)
Unrealized losses on derivatives					(4,848)		(4,848)
Comprehensive income							421,853
Repayments of notes receivable from officers			1,911				1,911
Purchase of 12,591 shares of treasury stock		298				(698,983)	(698,685)
Retirement of 12,000 shares of treasury stock	(120)	(23,280)		(279,203)		302,603	—
Sale of 2,563 shares of common stock under stock option and stock purchase plans	25	55,651					55,676
Tax benefit of exercise of stock options		42,159					42,159
Balance at August 31, 2002	1,100	370,457	—	974,141	(11,603)	(644,968)	689,127
Net income				517,604			517,604
Minimum pension liability net of taxes of $(18,072)					(29,739)		(29,739)
Foreign currency translation adjustment					(8,276)		(8,276)
Net gains on outstanding derivatives net of taxes of $15,710					25,856		25,856
Net losses on terminated/matured derivatives					(20,014)		(20,014)
Reclassification of net losses on derivatives into earnings					6,479		6,479
Comprehensive income							491,910
Purchase of 12,266 shares of treasury stock		1,111				(891,095)	(889,984)
Retirement of 11,000 shares of treasury stock	(110)	(43,120)		(622,006)		665,236	—
Sale of 1,782 shares of common stock under stock option and stock purchase plans	17	45,112				174	45,303
Tax benefit of exercise of stock options		37,402					37,402
Balance at August 30, 2003	$1,007	$410,962	$ —	$ 869,739	$(37,297)	$(870,653)	$ 373,758

NOTES TO CONSOLIDATED FINANCIAL STATEMENTS

Note H—Stock Repurchase Program

As of August 30, 2003, the Board of Directors had authorized the Company to repurchase up to $3.3 billion of common stock in the open market. From January 1998 to August 30, 2003, the Company has repurchased a total of 72.1 million shares at an aggregate cost of $2.8 billion. During fiscal 2003, the Company repurchased 12.3 million shares of its common stock at an aggregate cost of $891.1 million.

At times in the past, the Company utilized equity forward agreements to facilitate its repurchase of common stock. There were no equity forward agreements for share repurchases as of August 30, 2003. At August 31, 2002, the Company held equity forward agreements, which were settled in cash during fiscal 2003, for the purchase of approximately 2.2 million shares of common stock at an average cost of $68.82 per share. Such obligations under the equity forward agreements at August 31, 2002, were not reflected on the balance sheet. During 2003, the Financial Accounting Standards Board issued Statement of Financial Accounting Standards No. 150, "Accounting for Certain Financial Instruments with Characteristics of both Liabilities and Equity" (SFAS 150). SFAS 150 applied to the Company's use of equity forward agreements to repurchase common stock and would have required the Company to record any forward purchase obligations as a liability on the balance sheet. All of the Company's outstanding forward purchase contracts were settled prior to the adoption of SFAS 150 during the fourth quarter of fiscal 2003. Accordingly, the adoption of SFAS 150 had no impact on the Company's Consolidated Financial Statements.

5.45

THE BLACK & DECKER CORPORATION (DEC)

Consolidated Statement of Stockholders' Equity

(Dollars in millions except per share data)	Outstanding Common Shares	Par Value	Capital in Excess of Par Value	Retained Earnings	Accumulated Other Comprehensive Income (Loss)	Total Stockholders' Equity
Balance at December 31, 2000	80,343,094	$40.2	$560.0	$264.0	$(171.8)	$ 692.4
Comprehensive income (loss)						
Net earnings	—	—	—	108.0	—	108.0
Cumulative effect of accounting change (net of tax)	—	—	—	—	(.7)	(.7)
Net loss on derivative instruments (net of tax)	—	—	—	—	(.2)	(.2)
Minimum pension liability adjustment (net of tax)	—	—	—	—	1.7	1.7
Foreign currency translation adjustments, less effect of hedging activities (net of tax)	—	—	—	—	(17.7)	(17.7)
Comprehensive income	—	—	—	108.0	(16.9)	91.1
Cash dividends on common stock ($.48 per share)	—	—	—	(38.8)	—	(38.8)
Purchase and retirement of common stock	(1,085,000)	(.6)	(32.9)	—	—	(33.5)
Common stock retired under equity forwards	(765,326)	(.4)	—	—	—	(.4)
Common stock issued under employee benefit plans	1,336,873	.7	39.5	—	—	40.2
Balance at December 31, 2001	79,829,641	39.9	566.6	333.2	(188.7)	751.0
Comprehensive income (loss)						
Net earnings	—	—	—	229.7	—	229.7
Net loss on derivative instruments (net of tax)	—	—	—	—	(16.4)	(16.4)
Minimum pension liability adjustment (net of tax)	—	—	—	—	(369.7)	(369.7)
Foreign currency translation adjustments, less effect of hedging activities (net of tax)	—	—	—	—	60.2	60.2
Comprehensive income (loss)	—	—	—	229.7	(325.9)	(96.2)
Cash dividends on common stock ($.48 per share)	—	—	—	(38.6)	—	(38.6)
Purchase and retirement of common stock	(1,008,101)	(.5)	(42.6)	—	—	(43.1)
Common stock issued under employee benefit plans	783,246	.4	26.1	—	—	26.5
Balance at December 31, 2002	79,604,786	39.8	550.1	524.3	(514.6)	599.6
Comprehensive income (loss)						
Net earnings	—	—	—	293.0	—	293.0
Net loss on derivative instruments (net of tax)	—	—	—	—	(15.8)	(15.8)
Minimum pension liability adjustment (net of tax)	—	—	—	—	(20.2)	(20.2)
Foreign currency translation adjustments, less effect of hedging activities (net of tax)	—	—	—	—	98.4	98.4
Comprehensive income	—	—	—	293.0	62.4	355.4
Cash dividends on common stock ($.57 per share)	—	—	—	(44.3)	—	(44.3)
Purchase and retirement of common stock	(2,011,570)	(1.0)	(76.5)	—	—	(77.5)
Common stock issued under employee benefit plans	340,248	.2	13.1	—	—	13.3
Balance at December 31, 2003	77,933,464	$39.0	$486.7	$773.0	$(452.2)	$ 846.5

NOTES TO CONSOLIDATED FINANCIAL STATEMENTS

Note 14 (In Part): Stockholders' Equity

The Corporation repurchased 2,011,570, 1,008,101, and 1,085,000 shares of its common stock during 2003, 2002, and 2001 at an aggregate cost of $77.5 million, $43.1 million, and $33.5 million, respectively.

During 1999, the Corporation executed two agreements (the Agreements) under which the Corporation could enter into forward purchase contracts on its common stock. The Agreements provided the Corporation with two purchase alternatives: a standard forward purchase contract and a forward purchase contract subject to a cap (a capped forward contract). The settlement methods generally available under the Agreements, at the Corporation's option, were net settlement, either in cash or in shares, or physical settlement.

During 2001, the Corporation terminated the capped forward contracts and standard forward purchase contracts, electing full physical settlement through its purchase of the final 525,050 shares subject to the Agreements for $25.5 million. Previously during 2001, the Corporation had received 240,276 shares of its common stock through net share settlements under the Agreements.

Treasury Stock Issued

5.46

BRIGGS & STRATTON CORPORATION (JUN)

Consolidated Statements of Shareholders' Investment

(In thousands, except per share data)	Common Stock	Additional Paid-In Capital	Retained Earnings	Accumulated Other Comprehensive Loss	Unearned Compensation on Restricted Stock	Treasury Stock	Comprehensive Income
Balances, July 2, 2000	$289	$36,478	$721,980	$(3,931)	$(226)	$(345,125)	
Comprehensive income							
Net income	—	—	48,013	—	—	—	$48,013
Foreign currency translation adjustments	—	—	—	(2,530)	—	—	(2,530)
Unrealized loss on marketable securities, net of tax of $(607)	—	—	—	(947)	—	—	(947)
Unrealized gain on derivatives	—	—	—	1,226	—	—	1,226
Total comprehensive income	—	—	—	—	—	—	$45,762
Cash dividends paid ($1.24 per share)	—	—	(26,763)	—	—	—	
Purchase of common stock for treasury	—	—	—	—	—	(6,118)	
Exercise of stock options	—	(368)	—	—	—	643	
Restricted stock issued	—	(58)	—	—	(181)	239	
Amortization of unearned compensation	—	—	—	—	102	—	
Shares issued to directors	—	(9)	—	—	—	38	
Balances, July 1, 2001	$289	$36,043	$743,230	$(6,182)	$(305)	$(350,323)	
Comprehensive income							
Net income	—	—	53,120	—	—	—	$53,120
Foreign currency translation adjustments	—	—	—	4,017	—	—	4,017
Unrealized loss on marketable securities, net of tax of $(95)	—	—	—	(148)	—	—	(148)
Unrealized loss on derivatives	—	—	—	(4,313)	—	—	(4,313)
Total comprehensive income	—	—	—	—	—	—	$52,676
Cash dividends paid ($1.26 per share)	—	—	(27,219)	—	—	—	
Exercise of stock options	—	(576)	—	—	—	1,877	
Amortization of unearned compensation	—	—	—	—	106	—	
Shares issued to directors	—	(8)	—	—	—	38	
Balances, June 30, 2002	$289	$35,459	$769,131	$(6,626)	$(199)	$(348,408)	
Comprehensive income							
Net income	—	—	80,638	—	—	—	$80,638
Foreign currency translation adjustments	—	—	—	4,454	—	—	4,454
Unrealized gain on marketable securities, net of tax of $581	—	—	—	901	—	—	901
Unrealized gain on derivatives	—	—	—	3,100	—	—	3,100
Minimum pension liability adjustment, net of tax of $(1,638)	—	—	—	(2,563)	—	—	(2,563)
Total comprehensive income	—	—	—	—	—	—	$86,530
Cash dividends paid ($1.28 per share)	—	—	(27,709)	—	—	—	
Exercise of stock options	—	(234)	—	—	—	5,835	
Restricted stock issued	—	(97)	—	—	(238)	335	
Amortization of unearned compensation	—	—	—	—	150	—	
Issuance of treasury shares	—	(44)	—	—	—	760	
Shares issued to directors	—	(10)	—	—	—	63	
Balances, June 29, 2003	$289	$35,074	$822,060	$ (734)	$(287)	$(341,415)	

Restricted Stock

5.47

HUGHES SUPPLY, INC. (JAN)

Consolidated Statements of Shareholders' Equity

(In millions, except share and per share data)	Common Stock		Capital in Excess of Par Value	Retained Earnings	Treasury Stock		Unearned Compensation	Total
	Shares	Dollars			Shares	Dollars		
Balance at January 26, 2001	24,211,485	$24.2	$228.1	$337.1	(576,783)	$(13.3)	$ (6.1)	$ 570.0
Net income	—	—	—	44.1	—	—	—	44.1
Cash dividends—$0.340 per share	—	—	—	(8.0)	—	—	—	(8.0)
Purchase of treasury stock	—	—	—	—	(394,700)	(7.5)	—	(7.5)
Shares issued under stock option plans and related tax benefits	—	—	0.3	(1.7)	265,378	5.6	—	4.2
Purchase and retirement of common shares	(91,322)	(0.1)	(0.8)	(1.1)	—	—	—	(2.0)
Retirement of treasury stock	(342,854)	(0.3)	(3.2)	(4.0)	342,854	7.5	—	—
Issuance of restricted stock, net of cancellations	(2,709)	—	0.5	1.3	339,000	7.2	(9.5)	(0.5)
Amortization of restricted stock	—	—	—	—	—	—	1.5	1.5
Cancellation of stock rights issued to bestroute.com	—	—	(7.3)	—	—	—	—	(7.3)
Balance at January 25, 2002	23,774,600	$23.8	$217.6	$367.7	(24,251)	$ (0.5)	$(14.1)	$ 594.5
Net income	—	—	—	58.1	—	—	—	58.1
Cash dividends—$0.355 per share	—	—	—	(8.5)	—	—	—	(8.5)
Purchase of treasury stock	—	—	—	—	(257,000)	(7.1)	—	(7.1)
Shares issued under stock option plans and related tax benefits	216,836	0.1	5.8	(0.1)	15,551	0.3	—	6.1
Purchase and retirement of common shares	(25,784)	—	(0.5)	(0.6)	—	—	—	(1.1)
Issuance of restricted stock net of cancellations	(29,888)	—	(0.5)	0.1	20,000	0.5	(0.1)	—
Amortization of restricted stock	—	—	—	—	—	—	2.8	2.8
Balance at January 31, 2003	23,935,764	$23.9	$222.4	$416.7	(245,700)	$ (6.8)	$(11.4)	$ 644.8
Net income	—	—	—	57.7	—	—	—	57.7
Cash dividends—$0.400 per share	—	—	—	(10.1)	—	—	—	(10.1)
Purchase of treasury stock	—	—	—	—	(258,600)	(6.0)	—	(6.0)
Shares issued under stock option plans and related tax benefits	—	—	1.2	(0.4)	199,348	5.1	—	5.9
Issuance of common stock, net	6,900,000	6.9	310.6	—	—	—	—	317.5
Purchase and retirement of common shares	(10,299)	—	(0.1)	(0.3)	—	—	—	(0.4)
Issuance of restricted stock, net of cancellations	(29,888)	—	(0.8)	1.5	88,000	2.2	(3.3)	(0.4)
Amortization of restricted stock	—	—	—	—	—	—	3.0	3.0
Balance at January 30, 2004	30,795,577	$30.8	$533.3	$465.1	(216,952)	$ (5.5)	$(11.7)	$1,012.0

NOTES TO CONSOLIDATED FINANCIAL STATEMENTS

Note 11 (In Part): Stock Option Plans

Stock Plans

In May 2002, the shareholders approved an amendment to the 1997 Stock Plan allowing the compensation committee to make grants of performance-based restricted shares to senior executives. Performance-based shares are used as an incentive to increase shareholder returns with actual awards based on various criteria, including increases in the price of our common shares, earnings per share, shareholder value and net income. Compensation expense for the number of shares issued is recognized over the vesting period. On August 21, 2002, March 18, 2003, and September 15, 2003, target awards of 125,000 shares, 35,000 shares, and 15,000 shares, respectively, were made to senior executives. These shares are to be issued in five separate tranches if the price of our common shares achieves certain price levels. During fiscal year 2004, 88,000 shares were issued with a market value at the date of grant of $3.8 million. The market value of the restricted stock at the date of grant was recorded as unearned compensation, a component of shareholders' equity, and is being charged to expense over the respective vesting periods. In fiscal year 2004 this expense totaled $0.2 million. In fiscal year 2003, none of the stock price achievement levels had been attained and accordingly, no restricted shares were issued to participants.

During fiscal year 2002, we granted certain senior executives 410,000 restricted shares in accordance with a stock performance award under the 1997 Stock Plan. The shares were awarded in five separate tranches as the price of our common shares achieved certain levels as determined by the compensation committee. At January 25, 2002, all such stock price achievement levels had been met. The shares vest five years from the award date, and are subject to certain other vesting and forfeiture provisions contained in the 1997 Stock Plan. The market value of the restricted shares was $10.7 million at the date of the grant and was recorded as unearned compensation, a component of shareholders' equity. This amount is being charged to expense over the respective vesting period and totaled $2.2 million, $2.2 million and $0.7 million in fiscal years 2004, 2003 and 2002, respectively.

During fiscal year 2003 and fiscal year 2002, we granted certain employees 20,000 shares and 11,000 shares of restricted stock, with market values at the date of grant of $0.6 million and $0.3 million, respectively. There were no non-performance shares granted to employees during fiscal year 2004. In fiscal years 2004, 2003 and 2002, we cancelled 29,888 shares, 29,888 shares and 84,709 shares, respectively, of the restricted shares granted, with market values at the date of grant of $0.5 million, $0.5 million and $1.5 million, respectively, according to the provisions of the grant. The market value of the restricted stock at the date of grant was recorded as unearned compensation, a component of shareholders' equity, and is being charged to expense over the respective vesting periods. In fiscal years 2004, 2003 and 2002, this expense totaled $0.7 million, $0.7 million and $0.8 million, respectively.

Conversion of Preferred Stock

5.48

COCA-COLA ENTERPRISES INC. (DEC)

Consolidated Statements of Shareowners' Equity

(In millions except per share data)	2003	2002	2001
Preferred stock			
Balance at beginning of year	$ 37	$ 37	$ 44
Conversion of preferred stock to common stock	(37)	—	(7)
Balance at end of year	$ —	$ 37	$ 37
Common stock			
Balance at beginning of year	$ 458	$ 453	$ 450
Exercise of employee stock options	3	4	3
Issuance of management stock performance awards	1	1	—
Balance at end of year	$ 462	$ 458	$ 453
Additional paid-in capital			
Balance at beginning of year	$2,581	$2,527	$2,673
Issuance of management stock performance awards	29	17	6
Unamortized cost of management stock performance awards	(30)	(18)	(6)
Issuance of stock under deferred compensation plans	(6)	—	2
Expense amortization of management stock performance awards	11	7	7
Exercise of employee stock options	25	28	17
Realized tax benefit on management stock performance awards	9	16	11
Conversion of preferred stock to common stock	(9)	—	2
Conversion of executive deferred compensation to equity	1	2	5
Issuance of shares to effect acquisitions	—	—	(190)
Other changes	—	2	—
Balance at end of year	$2,611	$2,581	$2,527
Reinvested earnings			
Balance at beginning of year	$ 639	$ 220	$ 613
Dividends on common stock (per share—$0.16 in 2003, 2002, and 2001)	(72)	(72)	(69)
Dividends on preferred stock	(2)	(3)	(3)
Net income (loss)	676	494	(321)
Balance at end of year	$1,241	$ 639	$ 220
Accumulated other comprehensive income (loss)			
Balance at beginning of year	$ (236)	$ (292)	$ (230)
Currency translations	572	219	40
Hedges of net investments	(86)	(77)	(24)
Gains/losses on cash flow hedges	(4)	5	—
Minimum pension liability adjustments	(106)	(105)	(78)
Gains/losses on securities	(7)	14	—
Net other comprehensive income adjustments, net of taxes	369	56	(62)
Balance at end of year	$ 133	$ (236)	$ (292)
Treasury stock			
Balance at beginning of year	$ (132)	$ (125)	$ (716)
Issuance of stock under deferred compensation plans	4	—	—
Purchase of common stock for treasury	—	—	(8)
Issuance and (refund) of shares to effect acquisitions, net	—	(7)	594
Conversion of preferred stock to common stock	46	—	5
Balance at end of year	$ (82)	$ (132)	$ (125)
Total shareowners' equity	$4,365	$3,347	$2,820

NOTES TO CONSOLIDATED FINANCIAL STATEMENTS

Note 14 (In Part): Preferred Stock

In connection with the 1998 acquisition of Great Plains Bottlers and Canners, Inc., we issued 401,528 shares of $1 par value voting convertible preferred stock (Great Plains series). The mandatory conversion date for the Great Plains series was August 7, 2003. As of December 31, 2002, 35,000 shares of the Great Plains series had been converted into 154,778 shares of common stock. During the third quarter of 2003, the remaining 366,528 outstanding preferred shares were converted into 2,119,518 shares of common stock from treasury stock. The Great Plains series shares are not included in our computation of diluted earnings per share, detailed in Note 12, in 2003, 2002, and 2001 because the effect of their inclusion would be antidilutive.

Stock Price Guarantee Settlement

5.49

MASCO CORPORATION (DEC)

Consolidated Statements of Shareholders' Equity

(In millions, except per share data)	Total	Preferred Shares ($1 Par Value)	Common Shares ($1 Par Value)	Paid-In Capital	Retained Earnings	Accumulated Other Comprehensive Income (Loss)	Restricted Stock Awards
Balance, January 1, 2001	$3,286	$—	$445	$ 631	$2,520	$(170)	$(140)
Net income	199				199		
Cumulative translation adjustments	(46)					(46)	
Unrealized gain on marketable securities, net of income tax of $16	27					27	
Total comprehensive income	180						
Shares issued	816		17	799			
Shares repurchased	(67)		(3)	(64)			
Cash dividends declared	(250)				(250)		
Stock-based compensation	(7)			15			(22)
Balance, December 31, 2001	3,958	—	459	1,381	2,469	(189)	(162)
Net income	590				590		
Cumulative translation adjustments	239					239	
Unrealized loss on marketable securities, net of income tax credit of $9	(14)					(14)	
Minimum pension liability, net of income tax credit of $34	(58)					(58)	
Total comprehensive income	757						
Shares issued	1,016		38	978			
Shares repurchased	(166)		(8)	(158)			
Cash dividends declared	(275)				(275)		
Stock-based compensation	4			6			(2)
Balance, December 31, 2002	$5,294	$—	$489	$2,207	$2,784	$ (22)	$(164)

(continued)

(In millions, except per share data)	Total	Preferred Shares ($1 Par Value)	Common Shares ($1 Par Value)	Paid-In Capital	Retained Earnings	Accumulated Other Comprehensive Income (Loss)	Restricted Stock Awards
Balance, December 31, 2002	$5,294	$—	$489	$2,207	$2,784	$ (22)	$(164)
Net income	806				806		
Cumulative translation adjustments	393					393	
Unrealized gain on marketable securities, net of income tax of $51	53					53	
Minimum pension liability, net of income tax credit of $1	(3)					(3)	
Total comprehensive income	1,249						
Shares issued	64		5	59			
Shares repurchased	(779)		(35)	(744)			
Settlement of stock-price guarantees	(67)			(67)			
Cash dividends declared	(291)				(291)		
Stock-based compensation	(14)		(1)	(12)			(1)
Balance, December 31, 2003	$5,456	$—	$458	$1,443	$3,299	$ 421	$(165)

NOTES TO CONSOLIDATED FINANCIAL STATEMENTS

C (In Part): Acquisitions

Certain recent purchase agreements provide for the payment of additional consideration in either cash or common stock, contingent upon whether certain conditions are met, including the operating performance of the acquired business and the price of the Company's common stock. Common shares that are contingently issuable at December 31, 2003 have been included in the computation of diluted earnings per common share for 2003. The Company also paid an additional $182 million of acquisition-related consideration, including amounts to satisfy share price guarantees, contingent consideration and other purchase price adjustments, in 2003, relating to previously acquired companies.

Put Option Warrant Reclassification

5.50

HASBRO, INC. (DEC)

Consolidated Statements of Shareholders' Equity

(Thousands of dollars)	Common Stock	Additional Paid-In Capital	Deferred Compensation	Retained Earnings	Accumulated Other Comprehensive Earnings	Treasury Stock	Total Shareholders' Equity
Balance, December 31, 2000	$104,847	$ 464,084	$(6,889)	$1,583,394	$(44,718)	$(773,312)	$1,327,406
Net earnings	—	—	—	59,732	—	—	59,732
Other comprehensive earnings	—	—	—	—	(23,680)	—	(23,680)
Comprehensive earnings							36,052
Stock option and warrant transactions	—	(6,004)	—	—	—	13,739	7,735
Restricted stock activity	—	(536)	3,893	—	—	(962)	2,395
Dividends declared	—	—	—	(20,724)	—	—	(20,724)
Balance, December 30, 2001	$104,847	$ 457,544	$(2,996)	$1,622,402	$(68,398)	$(760,535)	$1,352,864
Net loss	—	—	—	(170,674)	—	—	(170,674)
Other comprehensive earnings	—	—	—	—	21,584	—	21,584
Comprehensive earnings							(149,090)
Stock option and warrant transactions	—	333	—	—	—	6,267	6,600
Restricted stock activity	—	253	2,383	—	—	(866)	1,770
Dividends declared	—	—	—	(20,778)	—	—	(20,778)
Balance, December 29, 2002	$104,847	$ 458,130	$ (613)	$1,430,950	$(46,814)	$(755,134)	$1,191,366
Net earnings	—	—	—	157,664	—	—	157,664
Other comprehensive earnings	—	—	—	—	77,298	—	77,298
Comprehensive earnings							234,962
Reclass of liabilities potentially settleable in common stock	—	(107,669)	—	—	—	—	(107,669)
Stock option and warrant transactions	—	48,106	—	—	—	60,640	108,746
Restricted stock activity	—	(689)	(66)	—	—	(489)	(1,244)
Dividends declared	—	—	—	(20,921)	—	—	(20,921)
Balance, December 28, 2003	$104,847	$ 397,878	$ (679)	$1,567,693	$ 30,484	$(694,983)	$1,405,240

NOTES TO CONSOLIDATED FINANCIAL STATEMENTS
(Thousands of dollars and shares except per share data)

7) Accrued Liabilities

	2003	2002
Liabilities potentially settleable in common stock	$138,650	$ —
Royalties	110,210	131,916
Advertising	74,849	66,290
Payroll and management incentives	98,103	68,306
Accrued income taxes	66,080	56,966
Other	258,507	254,164
	$746,399	$577,642

In January 2003, the Company amended its license agreement with Lucas Licensing Ltd. ("Lucas") for the manufacture and distribution of STAR WARS toys and games. Under the amended agreement, the term was extended by ten years and is expected to run through 2018. In addition, the minimum guaranteed royalties due to Lucas were reduced by $85,000. In a separate agreement, the warrants previously granted to Lucas were also amended. The warrant amendment agreement provides the Company with a call option through October 13, 2016 to purchase all of these warrants from Lucas for a price to be paid at the Company's election of either $200,000 in cash or the equivalent of $220,000 in shares of the Company's common stock, such stock being valued at the time of the exercise of the option. Also, the warrant amendment agreement provides Lucas with a put option through January 2008 to sell all of these warrants to the Company for a price to be paid at the Company's election of either $100,000 in cash or the equivalent of $110,000 in shares of the Company's common stock, such stock being valued at the time of the exercise of the option.

On June 30, 2003, the first day of the third quarter of fiscal 2003, the Company adopted Statement of Financial Accounting Standards No. 150, "Accounting for Certain Financial Instruments with Characteristics of Liabilities and Equity," ("SFAS 150"), which establishes standards for issuers' classification as liabilities in the consolidated balance sheet of certain financial instruments that have characteristics of both liabilities and equity.

In accordance with SFAS 150, due to the put feature of the warrants, the Company reclassified the historic value of the above warrants of $107,669 from equity to current liabilities, and recorded a charge for the cumulative effect of an accounting change of $17,351, or $0.10 per diluted share, to adjust the warrants to their fair value as of that date. Under SFAS 150, the Company is required to adjust the warrants to their fair value through earnings at the end of each reporting period. In accordance with the Statement, during the last half of 2003, the Company recorded a charge to earnings of $13,630 to adjust the warrants to their fair value. This charge is included in other expense, net in the consolidated statement of operations. There is no tax benefit associated with this cumulative effect charge and fair value adjustment.

Under this warrant amendment, the term of each of the warrants issued to Lucas was extended by ten years. The increase in value of the warrants as a result of the amendment was approximately $67,900, which was recorded in the first quarter of 2003 as an intangible asset, and is being amortized over the remaining life of the licensing contract.

Should either the put or call option be required to be settled, the Company believes that it will have adequate funds available to settle them in cash if necessary. Had this option been exercised at December 28, 2003 and the Company had elected to settle this option in the Company's stock, the Company would have been required to issue 5,274 shares. If the share price of the Company's common stock were higher as of December 28, 2003 the number of shares issuable would have decreased. If the share price were lower as of December 28, 2003, the number of shares issuable would have increased.

OTHER COMPONENTS OF STOCKHOLDERS' EQUITY

5.51 Certain items such as unearned compensation expense related to stock issuances to employees, and employee stock ownership plans are presented as separate components of stockholders' equity. Other items such as foreign currency translation adjustments, unrealized gains and losses on certain investments in debt and equity securities, and minimum pension liability adjustments are considered components of other comprehensive income. *SFAS No. 130,* which is effective for fiscal years beginning after December 15, 1997, permits presentation of components of other comprehensive income and total comprehensive income in a statement of changes in stockholders' equity. In addition, the Standard allows disclosure of accumulated balances, by component, included in accumulated other comprehensive income in a statement of changes in stockholders' equity.

5.52 Examples of statements reporting changes in separate components of stockholders' equity, other than those classified as components of other comprehensive income, follow. See sections 2 and 4 for examples of presentation of other comprehensive income and related accumulated balances in statements of changes in stockholders' equity.

Unearned Compensation Expense

5.53

INTERNATIONAL MULTIFOODS CORPORATION (FEB)

Consolidated Statements of Shareholders' Equity

(In thousands)	10 Cents Par Value		Capital in Excess of Par Value	Retained Earnings	Accumulated Other Comprehensive Loss	Unearned Compensation	Total
	Common Stock	Treasury Stock					
Balance at Feb. 29, 2000	$2,184	$(68,437)	$91,888	$242,013	$(12,122)	$ (402)	$255,124
Comprehensive income	—	—	—	21,175	(5,548)	—	15,627
Dividends declared on common stock	—	—	—	(14,984)	—	—	(14,984)
9 shares purchased for treasury	—	(148)	—	—	—	—	(148)
17 shares issued for employee benefit plans	—	346	(245)	—	—	(131)	(30)
Amortization of unearned compensation	—	—	—	—	—	393	393
Balance at March 3, 2001	2,184	(68,239)	91,643	248,204	(17,670)	(140)	255,982
Comprehensive income	—	—	—	9,191	2,830	—	12,021
248 shares issued for employee benefit plans	—	5,468	829	—	—	(2,945)	3,352
Amortization of unearned compensation	—	—	—	—	—	715	715
Balance at March 2, 2002	2,184	(62,771)	92,472	257,395	(14,840)	(2,370)	272,070
Comprehensive loss	—	—	—	(46,029)	4,659	—	(41,370)
5 shares purchased for treasury	—	(107)	—	—	—	—	(107)
191 shares issued for employee benefit plans	—	4,202	1,384	—	—	(1,748)	3,838
Amortization of unearned compensation	—	—	—	—	—	1,538	1,538
Balance at March 1, 2003	$2,184	$(58,676)	$93,856	$211,366	$(10,181)	$(2,580)	$235,969

NOTES TO CONSOLIDATED FINANCIAL STATEMENTS

Note 15 (In Part): Stock Plans

Our 1989 and 1997 stock-based plans permit awards of restricted stock, incentive units and stock options to directors and key employees subject to the provisions of the plans and as determined by the Compensation and Human Resources Committee of the Board of Directors. At March 1, 2003, a total of 432,319 common shares was available for grants.

In fiscal 2003, grants of 11,424 shares of restricted stock and 59,800 restricted stock units were awarded with varying performance criteria and vesting periods. At March 1, 2003, the total number of restricted shares outstanding was 107,584. The market value of shares issued under the plans, as of the date of grant, has been recorded as unearned compensation and is shown as a separate component of shareholders' equity. Unearned compensation is expensed over the period that restrictions lapse.

5.54

KIMBERLY-CLARK CORPORATION (DEC)

Consolidated Statement of Stockholders' Equity

(Dollars in millions, shares in thousands)	Common Stock Issued Shares	Common Stock Issued Amount	Additional Paid-In Capital	Treasury Stock Shares	Treasury Stock Amount	Unearned Compensation on Restricted Stock	Retained Earnings	Accumulated Other Comprehensive Income (Loss)	Comprehensive Income
Balance at December 31, 2000	568,597	$710.8	$412.3	35,233	$(1,974.1)	$(26.1)	$ 7,982.0	$(1,337.6)	
Net income	—	—	—	—	—	—	1,609.9	—	$1,609.9
Other comprehensive income									
Unrealized translation	—	—	—	—	—	—	—	(256.7)	(256.7)
Minimum pension liability	—	—	—	—	—	—	—	(102.1)	(102.1)
Other	—	—	—	—	—	—	—	.2	.2
Total comprehensive income									$1,251.3
Options exercised and other awards	—	—	(17.5)	(2,433)	119.0	—	—	—	
Option and restricted share income tax benefits	—	—	17.7	—	—	—	—	—	
Shares repurchased	—	—	—	15,141	(909.7)	—	—	—	
Net issuance of restricted stock less amortization	—	—	3.1	(354)	16.6	(8.5)	—	—	
Dividends declared	—	—	—	—	—	—	(592.4)	—	
Balance at December 31, 2001	568,597	710.8	415.6	47,587	(2,748.2)	(34.6)	8,999.5	(1,696.2)	
Net income	—	—	—	—	—	—	1,674.6	—	$1,674.6
Other comprehensive income									
Unrealized translation	—	—	—	—	—	—	—	96.4	96.4
Minimum pension liability	—	—	—	—	—	—	—	(555.7)	(555.7)
Other	—	—	—	—	—	—	—	(2.2)	(2.2)
Total comprehensive income									$1,213.1
Options exercised and other awards	—	—	(7.7)	(1,627)	76.6	—	—	—	
Option and restricted share income tax benefits	—	—	9.9	—	—	—	—	—	
Shares repurchased	—	—	—	11,980	(683.6)	—	—	—	
Net issuance of restricted stock less amortization	—	—	1.2	(98)	4.6	9.4	—	—	
Dividends declared	—	—	—	—	—	—	(620.1)	—	
Balance at December 31, 2002	568,597	710.8	419.0	57,842	(3,350.6)	(25.2)	10,054.0	(2,157.7)	
Net income	—	—	—	—	—	—	1,694.2	—	$1,694.2
Other comprehensive income									
Unrealized translation	—	—	—	—	—	—	—	742.8	742.8
Minimum pension liability	—	—	—	—	—	—	—	(146.2)	(146.2)
Other	—	—	—	—	—	—	—	(4.3)	(4.3)
Total comprehensive income									$2,286.5
Options exercised and other awards	—	—	(18.0)	(988)	49.0	—	—	—	
Option and restricted share income tax benefits	—	—	7.4	—	—	—	—	—	
Shares repurchased	—	—	—	10,569	(537.1)	—	—	—	
Net issuance of restricted stock, less amortization	—	—	(1.5)	(415)	20.6	(1.9)	—	—	
Dividends declared	—	—	—	—	—	—	(689.0)	—	
Balance at December 31, 2003	568,597	$710.8	$406.9	67,008	$(3,818.1)	$(27.1)	$11,059.2	$(1,565.4)	

NOTES TO CONSOLIDATED FINANCIAL STATEMENTS

Note 11 (In Part): Stock Compensation Plans

Restricted Stock Awards

The Plans provide for restricted stock awards (shares or share equivalents) not to exceed 3.0 million shares. All restricted stock awards vest and become unrestricted shares in three to 10 years from the date of grant. Although participants are entitled to cash dividends and may vote such awarded shares, the sale or transfer of such shares is limited during the restricted period.

Data concerning restricted stock awards follows:

(Shares in thousands)	2003	2002	2001
Number of shares awarded	526	80	487
Weighted-average price per share	$44.54	$59.79	$55.59

The market value of the Corporation's common stock determines the value of the restricted stock, and such value is recorded at the date of the award as unearned compensation on restricted stock in a separate component of stockholders' equity. This unearned compensation is amortized to compensation expense over the periods of restriction. During 2003, 2002 and 2001, $18.2 million, $16.8 million and $13.0 million, respectively, was charged to compensation expense under the Plans. The tax effect of differences between compensation expense for financial statement and income tax purposes is recorded as additional paid-in capital.

Employee Stock Ownership Plan

5.55

THE PROCTER & GAMBLE COMPANY (JUN)

Consolidated Statements of Shareholders' Equity

(Dollars in millions/shares in thousands)	Common Shares Outstanding	Common Stock	Preferred Stock	Additional Paid-In Capital	Reserve for ESOP Debt Retirement	Accumulated Other Comprehensive Income	Retained Income	Total	Total Comprehensive Income
Balance June 30, 2000	1,305,867	$1,306	$1,737	$1,794	$(1,418)	$(1,842)	$10,710	$12,287	
Net earnings							2,922	2,922	$2,922
Other comprehensive income									
Financial statement translation						(715)		(715)	(715)
Net investment hedges, net of $276 tax						460		460	460
Other, net of tax benefit						(23)		(23)	(23)
Total comprehensive income									$2,644
Dividends to shareholders									
Common							(1,822)	(1,822)	
Preferred, net of tax benefit							(121)	(121)	
Treasury purchases	(18,238)	(18)		6			(1,238)	(1,250)	
Employee plan issuances	5,924	6		223				229	
Preferred stock conversions	2,185	2	(36)	34				—	
ESOP debt guarantee reduction					43			43	
Balance June 30, 2001	1,295,738	$1,296	$1,701	$2,057	$(1,375)	$(2,120)	$10,451	$12,010	

(continued)

(Dollars in millions/shares in thousands)	Common Shares Outstanding	Common Stock	Preferred Stock	Additional Paid-In Capital	Reserve for ESOP Debt Retirement	Accumulated Other Comprehensive Income	Retained Income	Total	Total Comprehensive Income
Balance June 30, 2001	1,295,738	$1,296	$1,701	$2,057	$(1,375)	$(2,120)	$10,451	$12,010	
Net earnings							4,352	4,352	$4,352
Other comprehensive income									
Financial statement translation						263		263	263
Net investment hedges, net of $238 tax						(397)		(397)	(397)
Other, net of tax benefits						(106)		(106)	(106)
Total comprehensive income									$4,112
Dividends to shareholders									
Common							(1,971)	(1,971)	
Preferred, net of tax benefits							(124)	(124)	
Spin-off of Jif and Crisco							(150)	(150)	
Treasury purchases	(7,681)	(8)		18			(578)	(568)	
Employee plan issuances	8,323	9		352				361	
Preferred stock conversions	4,390	4	(67)	63				—	
ESOP debt guarantee reduction					36			36	
Balance June 30, 2002	1,300,770	1,301	1,634	2,490	(1,339)	(2,360)	11,980	13,706	
Net earnings							5,186	5,186	$5,186
Other comprehensive income									
Financial statement translation						804		804	804
Net investment hedges, net of $251 tax						(418)		(418)	(418)
Other, net of tax benefits						(32)		(32)	(32)
Total comprehensive income									$5,540
Dividends to shareholders									
Common							(2,121)	(2,121)	
Preferred, net of tax benefit							(125)	(125)	
Treasury purchases	(14,138)	(14)		6			(1,228)	(1,236)	
Employee plan issuances	7,156	7		384				391	
Preferred stock conversions	3,409	3	(54)	51				—	
ESOP debt guarantee reduction					31			31	
Balance June 30, 2003	1,297,197	$1,297	$1,580	$2,931	$(1,308)	$(2,006)	$13,692	$16,186	

NOTES TO CONSOLIDATED FINANCIAL STATEMENTS

Note 9 (In Part): Postretirement Benefits and Employee Stock Ownership Plan

Defined Contribution Retirement Plans (In Part)

The Company maintains The Procter & Gamble Profit Sharing Trust (Trust) and Employee Stock Ownership Plan (ESOP) to provide funding for the U.S. defined contribution plan, as well as other retiree benefits. Operating details of the ESOP are provided at the end of this Note. The fair value of the ESOP Series A shares serves to reduce the Company's cash contribution required to fund the profit sharing plan contributions earned. Under the American Institute of Certified Public Accountants (AICPA) Statement of Position (SOP) 76-3, shares of the ESOP are allocated at original cost based on debt service requirements, net of advances made by the Company to the Trust.

Defined contribution expense pursuant to this plan was $286, $279 and $303 in 2003, 2002 and 2001, respectively, which approximates the amount funded by the Company.

Employee Stock Ownership Plan

The Company maintains the ESOP to provide funding for certain employee benefits discussed in the preceding paragraphs.

The ESOP borrowed $1,000 in 1989 and the proceeds were used to purchase Series A ESOP Convertible Class A Preferred Stock to fund a portion of the defined contribution retirement plan in the United States. Principal and interest requirements are $117 per year, paid by the Trust from dividends on the preferred shares and from cash contributions and advances from the Company. Each share is convertible at the option of the holder into one share of the Company's common stock. The liquidation value is $13.64 per share.

In 1991, the ESOP borrowed an additional $1,000. The proceeds were used to purchase Series B ESOP Convertible Class A Preferred Stock to fund a portion of retiree health care benefits. These shares are considered plan assets, net of the associated debt, of the other retiree benefits plan discussed above. Debt service requirements are $94 per year, funded by preferred stock dividends and cash contributions from the Company. Each share is convertible at the option of the holder into one share of the Company's common stock. The liquidation value is $25.92 per share.

The number of preferred shares outstanding at June 30 was as follows:

(Shares in thousands)	2003	2002	2001
Allocated	32,246	33,095	34,459
Unallocated	15,767	17,687	19,761
Total Series A	48,013	50,782	54,220
Allocated	10,324	9,869	9,267
Unallocated	25,359	26,454	27,338
Total Series B	35,683	36,323	36,605

As permitted by SOP 93-6, "Employers Accounting for Employee Stock Ownership Plans," the Company has elected, where applicable, to continue its practices, which are based on SOP 76-3, "Accounting Practices for Certain Employee Stock Ownership Plans." ESOP debt, which is guaranteed by the Company, is recorded in short-term and long-term liabilities (see Note 6). Preferred shares issued to the ESOP are offset by the reserve for ESOP debt retirement in the Consolidated Balance Sheets and the Consolidated Statements of Shareholders' Equity. Interest incurred on the ESOP debt is recorded as interest expense. Dividends on all preferred shares, net of related tax benefits, are charged to retained earnings.

The preferred shares held by the ESOP are considered outstanding from inception for purposes of calculating diluted net earnings per common share. Diluted net earnings are calculated assuming that all preferred shares are converted to common, and therefore are adjusted to reflect the incremental ESOP funding that would be required due to the difference in dividend rate between preferred and common shares.

Stock Loan Program

5.56

UNOCAL CORPORATION (DEC)

Consolidated Stockholders' Equity

(Millions of dollars except per share amounts)	2003	2002	2001
Common stock			
Balance at beginning of year	$ 269	$ 255	$ 254
Issuance of common stock for acquisition of Pure Resources' minority interest	—	13	—
Other issuance of common stock	2	1	1
Balance at end of year	271	269	255
Capital in excess of par value			
Balance at beginning of year	962	551	522
Issuance of common stock for acquisition of Pure Resources' minority interest	—	378	—
Other issuance of common stock	57	31	28
Issuance of stock options and related tax benefit	12	2	1
Balance at end of year	1,031	962	551
Unearned portion of restricted stock and options issued			
Balance at beginning of year	(20)	(29)	(21)
Issuance of restricted stock and stock options	(1)	(3)	(18)
Amortization of restricted stock and options	8	12	10
Balance at end of year	(13)	(20)	(29)
Retained earnings			
Balance at beginning of year	3,021	2,888	2,468
Net earnings for year	643	331	615
Cash dividends declared on common stock ($0.80 per share)	(208)	(198)	(195)
Balance at end of year	3,456	3,021	2,888
Treasury stock			
Balance at beginning of year	(411)	(411)	(411)
Purchased at cost	—	—	—
Balance at end of year	(411)	(411)	(411)
Notes receivable—key employees			
Balance at beginning of year	(37)	(42)	(40)
Accrued interest on loans to key employees	(2)	(2)	(2)
Principal and interest payments received from key employees	12	7	—
Balance at end of year	(27)	(37)	(42)
Accumulated other comprehensive income (loss)			
Balance at beginning of year	(486)	(88)	(53)
Foreign currency translation adjustments	145	(15)	(40)
Deferred net gains (losses) on hedging instruments	15	(49)	60
Cumulative effect of accounting change	—	—	(59)
Minimum pension liability adjustment	28	(334)	4
Balance at end of year	(298)	(486)	(88)
Total stockholders' equity	$4,009	$3,298	$3,124

NOTES TO THE CONSOLIDATED FINANCIAL STATEMENTS

Note 27—Loans to Certain Officers and Key Employees

In March 2000, the Company entered into loan agreements with ten of its officers pursuant to the Company's 2000 Executive Stock Purchase Program (the "Program"). The Program was approved by the Board of Directors of the Company and by the Company's stockholders at the Annual Stockholders meeting in May 2000. The loans were granted to the officers to enable them to purchase shares of Company stock in the open market. The loans, which except under certain limited circumstances are full recourse to the officers, mature on March 16, 2008, and bear interest at the rate of 6.8 percent per annum. The balance of the loans under this Program, including accrued interest, totaled $27 million at December 31, 2003 and $35 million at December 31, 2002, and was reflected as a reduction to stockholders' equity on the consolidated balance sheet. During 2003, accrued interest of $2 million was offset by payments from the officers of $10 million.

The Company's Pure subsidiary also had a loan program for certain of its officers and key employees, with a balance of $2 million at December 31, 2002. These loans were repaid during 2003.

_____

Section 6: Statement of Cash Flows

GENERAL

6.01 Effective for fiscal years ending after July 15, 1988, Statement of Financial Accounting Standards No. 95, *Statement of Cash Flows*, requires enterprises to present a Statement of Cash Flows which classifies cash receipts and payments by operating, investing, and financing activities. *SFAS No. 95* supersedes Accounting Principles Board (APB) Opinion No. 19, *Reporting Changes in Financial Position*, which required a statement summarizing changes in financial position.

6.02 This section reviews the format and content of the Statement of Cash Flows.

PRESENTATION IN ANNUAL REPORT

6.03 Table 6-1 shows where in relation to other financial statements a Statement of Cash Flows is presented in an annual report. As shown in Table 6-1, a Statement of Cash Flows is usually presented as the last financial statement or after the income statement and balance sheet but before the statement of changes in stockholders' equity.

6.04

TABLE 6-1: PRESENTATION IN ANNUAL REPORT

	2003	2002	2001	2000
Final statement................................	299	294	301	296
Follows income statement and balance sheet..............................	274	280	273	280
Between income statement and balance sheet..............................	26	26	26	24
First statement................................	1	—	—	—
Total Companies..........................	**600**	**600**	**600**	**600**

CASH FLOWS FROM OPERATING ACTIVITIES

6.05 Paragraphs 21–24 of *SFAS No. 95* define those transactions and events that constitute operating cash receipts and payments. *SFAS No. 95* recommends that the direct method, as defined in paragraph 27, be used to report net cash flow from operating activities. Most of the survey companies used the indirect method (reconciling net income to net cash flow from operating activities) to report net cash flow from operating activities. Regardless of whether the direct or indirect method is used, paragraph 29 of *SFAS No. 95* requires that a reconciliation of net income to net cash flow from operating activities be presented and that interest and income tax payments be disclosed.

6.06 Table 6-2 shows the methods used to report cash flows from operating activities. Companies using the direct method usually present the reconciliation of net income to net cash flow from operating activities as a schedule at the bottom of the Statement of Cash Flows or on the page adjacent to the Statement. Companies using the indirect method usually present the reconciliation within the Statement of Cash Flows.

6.07 Paragraph 29 of *SFAS No. 95* states that the reconciliation of net income to net cash flow from operating activities shall separately report all major classes of reconciling items. For example, major classes of deferrals of past operating cash receipts and payments, and accruals of expected future operating cash receipts and payments, including at a minimum changes during the period in receivables pertaining to operating activities, in inventory, and in payables pertaining to operating activities, shall be separately reported. Table 6-3 lists the major types of items used by the survey companies to reconcile net income to net cash flow from operating activities. Besides changes in trade receivables, trade payables and inventory, depreciation and amortization expense is the most frequently presented reconciling item.

6.08 Table 6-4 shows where in the financial statements interest and income tax payments are disclosed. Those survey companies disclosing the amount of interest payments in the notes to financial statements did so usually in a note discussing debt or in a note discussing details about the Statement of Cash Flows. Those survey companies disclosing the amount of income tax payments in the notes to financial statements did so usually in a note discussing income taxes or in a note discussing details about the Statement of Cash Flows.

6.09 Examples of reporting cash flows from operating activities and related interest and income tax payment disclosures follow.

6.10

TABLE 6-2: METHOD OF REPORTING CASH FLOWS FROM OPERATING ACTIVITIES

	2003	2002	2001	2000
Indirect method......................	593	593	592	593
Direct method........................	7	7	8	7
Total Companies..................	**600**	**600**	**600**	**600**

6.11

TABLE 6-3: CASH FLOWS FROM OPERATING ACTIVITIES—RECONCILING ITEMS

	2003	2002	2001
Income Statement Items			
Depreciation and/or amortization...............	600	600	600
Gain or loss on sale of property..................	203	213	195
Employee related costs.............................	190	182	157
Gain or loss on sale of assets other than property...	183	163	163
Intangible asset amortization......................	161	143	151
Equity in investee's earnings.......................	154	142	145
Restructuring..	146	140	187
Provision for bad debt...............................	142	144	134
Changes in Operating Assets and Liabilities			
Accounts receivable....................................	548	527	567
Inventories...	492	480	525
Accounts receivable combined with inventories and/or other items...............	60	79	20
Accounts payable.......................................	342	300	291
Accounts payable combined with other items..	234	270	285
Income taxes payable.................................	230	233	226
Employee related liabilities..........................	109	101	96

6.12

TABLE 6-4: INTEREST AND INCOME TAX PAYMENTS

	2003	2002	2001	2000
Interest Payments				
Notes to financial statements..............	310	312	333	315
Bottom of Statement of Cash Flows....	264	259	245	233
Within Statement of Cash Flows..........	9	8	8	20
Amount not disclosed..........................	17	21	14	32
Total Companies.............................	**600**	**600**	**600**	**600**
Income Tax Payments				
Notes to financial statements..............	310	312	331	315
Bottom of Statement of Cash Flows....	271	262	247	235
Within Statement of Cash Flows..........	12	9	11	23
Amount not disclosed..........................	7	17	11	27
Total Companies.............................	**600**	**600**	**600**	**600**

DIRECT METHOD

6.13

NORTHROP GRUMMAN CORPORATION (DEC)

(In millions)	2003	2002	2001
Operating activities			
Sources of cash—continuing operations			
Cash received from customers			
Progress payments	$ 8,575	$ 5,748	$ 3,102
Other collections	17,742	11,669	10,705
Proceeds from litigation settlement	—	220	220
Income tax refunds received	178	74	23
Interest received	17	69	17
Other cash receipts	64	34	24
Cash provided by operating activities	26,576	17,814	14,091
Uses of cash—continuing operations			
Cash paid to suppliers and employees	23,820	15,661	12,833
Interest paid	593	334	333
Income taxes paid	1,152	149	126
Payments for litigation settlements	206	—	—
Other cash payments	35	17	7
Cash used in operating activities	25,806	16,161	13,299
Cash provided by continuing operations	770	1,653	792
Cash provided by discontinued operations	28	36	25
Net cash provided by operating activities	798	1,689	817
Investing activities			
Proceeds from sale of businesses, net of cash divested	3,614	135	18
Payments for businesses purchased, net of cash acquired	(66)	181	(3,061)
Additions to property, plant, and equipment	(635)	(521)	(367)
Proceeds from sale of property, plant, and equipment	86	45	86
Proceeds from sale of investment	—	29	—
Collection of note receivable	—	—	148
Other investing activities	(45)	30	(2)
Discontinued operations	(73)	(17)	(26)
Net cash provided by (used in) investing activities	2,881	(118)	(3,204)
Financing activities			
Borrowings under lines of credit	758	504	1,173
Repayment of borrowings under lines of credit	(770)	(501)	(1,306)
Principal payments of long-term debt	(3,805)	(500)	(119)
Dividends paid	(305)	(205)	(158)
Common stock repurchases	(200)	—	—
Redemption of minority interest	(117)	—	—
Proceeds from issuance of stock	33	76	825
Proceeds from issuance of long-term debt	—	—	1,491
Proceeds from issuance of equity security units	—	—	690
Other financing activities	—	—	(64)
Discontinued operations	(343)	3	—
Net cash (used in) provided by financing activities	(4,749)	(623)	2,532
(Decrease) increase in cash and cash equivalents	(1,070)	948	145
Cash and cash equivalents, beginning of year	1,412	464	319
Cash and cash equivalents, end of year	$ 342	$ 1,412	$ 464

(In millions)	2003	2002	2001
Reconciliation of income from continuing operations before cumulative effect of accounting change to net cash provided by operating activities			
Income from continuing operations before cumulative effect of accounting change	$ 808	$ 697	$ 459
Adjustments to reconcile to net cash provided by operating activities			
Depreciation	455	332	246
Amortization of intangible assets	227	164	330
Common stock issued to employees	84	67	46
Loss (gain) on disposals of property, plant, and equipment	20	(4)	(6)
Amortization of long-term debt premium	(47)	(2)	—
Decrease (increase) in			
Accounts receivable	(5,385)	(771)	1,252
Inventoried costs	(54)	(211)	(15)
Prepaid expenses and other current assets	6	38	18
Increase (decrease) in			
Progress payments	5,264	1,109	(649)
Accounts payable and accruals	(325)	(142)	(672)
Provisions for contract losses	(24)	(135)	(65)
Deferred income taxes	1,022	(1,513)	167
Income taxes payable	(960)	1,049	(9)
Retiree benefits	(374)	943	(344)
Other noncash transactions	53	32	34
Cash provided by continuing operations	770	1,653	792
Cash provided by discontinued operations	28	36	25
Net cash provided by operating activities	$ 798	$ 1,689	$ 817
Non-cash investing and financing activities			
Sale of business			
Note receivable, net of discount	$ 455	—	—
Investment in unconsolidated affiliate	170	—	—
Purchase of businesses			
Fair value of assets acquired	$ 73	$20,206	$11,957
Cash paid, net of cash acquired	(66)	181	(3,061)
Noncash stock compensation	—	(151)	—
Common stock issued	—	(7,753)	(2,405)
Mandatorily redeemable preferred stock issued	—	—	(350)
Liabilities assumed	$ 7	$12,483	$ 6,141
Other non-cash activity			
Conversion of debt to equity	$ —	$ 3	$ —

6.14

STORAGE TECHNOLOGY CORPORATION (DEC)

(In thousands)	2003	2002	2001
Operating activities			
Cash received from customers	$ 2,258,219	$ 2,003,517	$ 2,083,280
Cash paid to suppliers and employees	(1,889,154)	(1,636,056)	(1,842,709)
Cash received from litigation and other special items	—	—	19,730
Interest received	9,912	9,956	10,189
Interest paid	(1,285)	(1,698)	(5,917)
Income tax (paid) refunded	(13,115)	(15,430)	1,522
Net cash provided by operating activities	364,577	360,289	266,095
Investing activities			
Purchase of investments	(60,959)	—	—
Proceeds from sale of investments	11,813	2,004	—
Purchase of property, plant, and equipment	(43,555)	(88,459)	(57,834)
Proceeds from sale of property, plant, and equipment	3,752	1,274	114
Other assets	4,244	(12,650)	6,417
Net cash used in investing activities	(84,705)	(97,831)	(51,303)
Financing activities			
Proceeds from employee stock plans	58,721	23,979	18,043
Repayments of credit facilities	—	(73,401)	(12,227)
Proceeds from other debt	1,325	1,625	2,305
Repayments of other debt	(2,372)	(2,577)	(9,289)
Repayment of company-owned life insurance policy loans	—	—	(30,414)
Net cash provided by (used in) financing activities	57,674	(50,374)	(31,582)
Effect of exchange rate changes on cash	6,484	(7,702)	(9,724)
Increase in cash and cash equivalents	344,030	204,382	173,486
Cash and cash equivalents at beginning of year	657,599	453,217	279,731
Cash and cash equivalents at end of year	$ 1,001,629	$ 657,599	$ 453,217
Reconciliation of net income to net cash provided by operating activities			
Net income	$ 148,912	$ 110,031	$ 67,207
Depreciation and amortization expense	87,890	90,533	107,026
Inventory writedowns	24,064	32,571	56,360
Translation (gain) loss	21,053	8,990	(23,791)
Non-cash litigation and other special items	—	—	16,471
Other non-cash adjustments to income	(22,470)	17,694	34,245
(Increase) decrease in accounts receivable	75,659	(36,098)	30,713
(Increase) decrease in inventories	959	21,403	(15,813)
(Increase) decrease in other current assets	2,297	(3,550)	(4,661)
Increase in spare parts	(16,344)	(22,998)	(11,147)
(Increase) decrease in net deferred income tax assets	(13,715)	4,622	(22,256)
Increase (decrease) in accounts payable	(7,191)	67,337	(31,646)
Increase in accrued liabilities	17,111	39,865	6,882
Increase in other current liabilities	5,020	16,869	—
Increase in income taxes payable	41,332	13,020	56,505
Net cash provided by operating activities	$ 364,577	$ 360,289	$ 266,095

INDIRECT/RECONCILIATION METHOD

6.15

LEE ENTERPRISES, INCORPORATED (SEP)

(Thousands)	2003	2002	2001
Cash provided by operating activities			
Net income	$ 78,041	$ 79,830	$ 312,470
Results of discontinued operations	20	(946)	(254,399)
Income from continuing operations	78,061	78,884	58,071
Adjustments to reconcile income from continuing operations to net cash provided by operating activities of continuing operations			
Depreciation and amortization	46,616	35,050	31,357
Stock compensation expense	4,628	3,936	3,216
Losses on sales, or expected sales, of businesses	30	339	6,233
Distributions less than earnings of associated companies	(927)	(1,338)	(552)
Change in operating assets and liabilities, net of effects from business acquisitions			
Decrease (increase) in receivables	(1,326)	2,722	(636)
Decrease (increase) in inventories and other	2,341	(6,562)	47
Decrease in accounts payable, accrued expenses and unearned revenue	(770)	(98)	(5,507)
Increase (decrease) in income taxes payable	11,450	(9,702)	6,449
Other	866	12,070	8,057
Net cash provided by operating activities	140,969	115,301	106,735
Cash required for investing activities			
Sales (purchases) of temporary cash investments, net	—	211,221	(211,221)
Purchases of property and equipment	(16,128)	(13,522)	(9,904)
Acquisitions, net	(1,073)	(753,089)	(4,518)
Proceeds from sales of businesses	—	7,509	5,341
Other	4,410	407	(3,002)
Net cash required for investing activities	(12,791)	(547,474)	(223,304)
Cash provided by (required for) financing activities			
Proceeds from (payments on) notes payable, net	(3,000)	3,000	(37,937)
Payments on long-term debt	(141,100)	(46,100)	(11,600)
Purchases of common stock	(272)	(341)	(10,050)
Proceeds from long-term debt	40,000	279,000	—
Financing costs	—	(2,442)	—
Cash dividends paid	(37,792)	(22,542)	(29,797)
Other, primarily issuance of common stock	6,400	6,588	11,358
Net cash provided by (required for) financing activities	(135,764)	217,163	(78,026)
Net cash provided by (required for) discontinued operations	4,269	(42,778)	437,337
Net increase (decrease) in cash and cash equivalents	(3,317)	(257,788)	242,742
Cash and cash equivalents			
Beginning of year	14,381	272,169	29,427
End of year	$ 11,064	$ 14,381	$ 272,169

6.16

LOCKHEED MARTIN CORPORATION (DEC)

(In millions)	2003	2002	2001
Operating activities			
Earnings from continuing operations	$ 1,053	$ 533	$ 43
Adjustments to reconcile earnings from continuing operations to net cash provided by operating activities:			
Depreciation and amortization	480	433	425
Amortization of purchased intangibles	129	125	154
Amortization of goodwill	—	—	244
Deferred federal income taxes	467	(463)	(118)
Loss from discontinued operations	—	(33)	(1,089)
Write-down of investments and other charges	42	1,127	1,051
Net charges related to discontinued operations	—	—	936
Changes in operating assets and liabilities:			
Receivables	(258)	394	(34)
Inventories	(94)	585	651
Accounts payable	330	(317)	192
Customer advances and amounts in excess of costs incurred	(285)	(460)	318
Income taxes	(16)	44	(456)
Other	(39)	320	(492)
Net cash provided by operating activities	1,809	2,288	1,825
Investing activities			
Expenditures for property, plant and equipment	(687)	(662)	(619)
Acquisition of businesses/investments in affiliated companies	(821)	(104)	(192)
Purchase of short-term investments, net	(240)	—	—
Proceeds from divestiture of affiliated companies	234	134	825
Other	53	93	125
Net cash (used for) provided by investing activities	(1,461)	(539)	139
Financing activities			
Issuances of long-term debt	1,000	—	—
Repayments of long-term debt	(2,202)	(110)	(2,508)
Long-term debt issuance and repayment costs	(175)	—	(58)
Issuances of common stock	44	436	213
Repurchases of common stock	(482)	(50)	—
Common stock dividends	(261)	(199)	(192)
Other	—	—	(12)
Net cash (used for) provided by financing activities	(2,076)	77	(2,557)
Net (decrease) increase in cash and cash equivalents	(1,728)	1,826	(593)
Cash and cash equivalents at begining of year	2,738	912	1,505
Cash and cash equivalents at end of year	$ 1,010	$2,738	$ 912

ADJUSTMENTS TO RECONCILE NET INCOME TO OPERATING CASH FLOWS

Sale of Property

6.17

SCOPE INDUSTRIES (JUN)

	2003	2002	2001
Cash flows from operating activities			
Net income (loss)	$ 3,181,267	$ 11,085,017	$(4,173,681)
Adjustments to reconcile net income (loss) to net cash flows from operating activities			
Depreciation and amortization	7,626,636	5,154,052	4,754,299
Amortization of routes and contracts	1,659,302	2,321,738	2,363,409
(Gain) on sale of investments	—	(21,080,990)	(352,160)
(Gain) on sale of property and equipment	(1,175,178)	(448,469)	(210,428)
Loss on impairment of assets	—	—	1,021,832
Unrealized loss equity investments	992,646	1,752,855	—
Deferred income taxes	19,475	(477,000)	(208,000)
Changes in operating assets and liabilities			
Accounts and notes receivable	(531,410)	(606,858)	774,946
Inventories	(61,052)	81,885	(194,114)
Prepaid expenses and other current assets	(155,281)	972,416	(811,567)
Accounts payable and accrued liabilities	(411,463)	946,875	(222,851)
Income taxes receivable or payable	(772,000)	2,417,253	(1,963,233)
Tax benefit applied to purchase of routes and contracts	365,000	560,000	560,000
Other assets	156,311	220,621	81,191
Net cash flows from operating activities	$10,894,253	$ 2,899,395	$ 1,419,643

Employee Related Costs

6.18

THE STANDARD REGISTER COMPANY (DEC)

(Dollars in thousands)	2003	2002	2001
Cash flows from operating activities			
Net income (loss)	$(39,067)	$ 32,581	$ (43,321)
Adjustments to reconcile net income (loss) to net cash provided by operating activities			
Depreciation and amortization	46,270	46,674	45,419
Asset impairments	15,910	—	41,512
Restructuring charges (reversals)	20,082	(1,837)	55,796
Pension and postretirement benefit expense (credit)	38,337	790	(3,094)
Loss (gain) on sale of assets	411	(1,999)	2,135
Unrealized loss on marketable securities	—	3,700	—
Gain on sale of other investments	—	—	(3,299)
Amortization of unearned compensation—restricted stock	2,382	1,785	686
Tax benefit from exercise of stock options	150	1,391	—
Deferred tax (benefit) expense	(26,265)	22,430	(10,635)
Changes in operating assets and liabilities, net of effects from acquisitions			
Accounts and notes receivable	29,979	34,460	70,694
Inventories	10,422	14,319	30,793
Income taxes	16,778	9,170	(13,992)
Other assets	(1,361)	(548)	1,784
Restructuring spending	(19,691)	(11,032)	(32,305)
Accounts payable and accrued expenses	(9,352)	(23,545)	3,691
Pension and postretirement obligation	(25,438)	(24,956)	(12,575)
Other deferred liabilities	5,346	(199)	4,432
Net cash provided by operating activities	$ 64,893	$103,184	$137,721

Sale of Assets Other Than Property

6.19

LYNCH CORPORATION (DEC)

(In thousands)	2003	2002	2001
Operating activities			
Net income (loss)	$ 110	$ 17,963	$(22,938)
Adjustments to reconcile net income (loss) to net cash provided by (used in) operating activities			
Gain on deconsolidation	—	(19,420)	(27,406)
Restricted operating cash	—	4,703	1,797
Loss on disposal of fixed assets	—	145	—
Loss on donation of shares	—	—	366
Asset impairment and restructuring charges	—	—	38,272
Gain realized on sale of marketable securities	(483)	—	—
Depreciation	982	1,044	4,315
Amortization of definite-lived intangible assets	257	206	244
Amortization of deferred financing charges	—	—	703
Deferred taxes	150	202	501
Recoverable income taxes	—	(532)	—
Minority interests	—	—	(4,017)
Other	(22)	—	761
Changes in operating assets and liabilities			
Receivables	(2,273)	6,294	10,861
Inventories	503	194	13,430
Accounts payable and accrued liabilities	1,617	(7,620)	(14,269)
Other assets/liabilities	(1,385)	414	4,727
Net cash provided by (used in) operating activities	$ (544)	$ 3,593	$ 7,347

Intangible Asset Amortization

6.20

THE SHERWIN-WILLIAMS COMPANY (DEC)

(Thousands of dollars)	2003	2002	2001
Operating activities			
Net income	$332,058	$127,565	$263,158
Adjustments to reconcile net income to net operating cash			
Cumulative effect of change in accounting principle	—	183,136	—
Depreciation	104,803	103,659	109,187
Amortization of intangible assets	11,761	11,989	38,911
Impairment of long-lived assets held for use	12,454	19,948	
Impairment of long-lived assets held for disposal	—	—	6,402
Provisions for qualified exit costs	14	262	5,302
Provisions for environmental-related matters	10,237	8,609	5,609
Deferred income taxes	39,872	19,747	15,677
Defined benefit pension plans net credit	(2,072)	(23,013)	(29,366)
Income tax effect of ESOP on other capital	24,665	22,380	22,902
Net increase in postretirement liability	3,904	4,086	2,990
Foreign currency related losses	1,460	8,435	2,277
Decrease in non-traded investments	20,276	9,278	—
Other	10,516	11,660	1,101
Change in working capital accounts			
(Increase) decrease in accounts receivable	(39,361)	3,588	61,497
(Increase) decrease in inventories	(153)	(229)	72,132
Increase in accounts payable	60,149	81,733	10,233
(Decrease) increase in accrued taxes	(12,117)	(5,483)	31,468
Other	(4,027)	4,778	17,035
Unusual tax-related payment	—	—	(65,677)
Costs incurred for environmental—related matters	(7,005)	(12,036)	(17,565)
Costs incurred for qualified exit costs	(1,580)	(3,663)	(3,326)
Decrease (increase) in minimum pension liability	82	(8,334)	—
Other	(7,007)	(9,178)	11,699
Net operating cash	$558,929	$558,917	$561,646

Equity Earnings/(Loss)

6.21

SUPERVALU INC. (FEB)

(In thousands)	2003	2002	2001
Cash flows from operating activities			
Net earnings	$257,042	$ 198,326	$ 72,870
Adjustments to reconcile net earnings to net cash provided by operating activities			
Depreciation and amortization	297,056	340,750	343,779
LIFO expense	4,741	143	4,991
Provision for losses on receivables	15,719	19,898	23,107
(Gain) loss on sale of property, plant and equipment	(5,564)	4,649	(1,164)
Restructure and other charges	2,918	46,300	171,264
Deferred income taxes	14,184	76,360	(38,480)
Equity in earnings of unconsolidated subsidiaries	(39,724)	(29,156)	(21,526)
Other adjustments, net	3,675	(1,228)	(3,496)
Changes in assets and liabilities			
Receivables	(46,890)	120,613	(66,482)
Inventories	(15,974)	298,150	130,657
Accounts payable	97,783	(386,504)	(13,845)
Other assets and liabilities	(11,390)	4,241	10,129
Net cash provided by operating activities	$573,576	$ 692,542	$611,804

ATT-SEC 6.20

Restructuring Charge

6.22

THE LUBRIZOL CORPORATION (DEC)

(In thousands of dollars)	2003	2002	2001
Cash provided from (used for) operating activities			
Net income	$ 90,774	$118,487	$ 94,116
Adjustments to reconcile net income to cash provided by operating activities			
Depreciation and amortization	100,423	95,831	98,832
Deferred income taxes	1,491	3,158	(2,392)
Restructuring charge	3,327	—	—
Cumulative effect of change in accounting principle	—	7,785	—
Change in current assets and liabilities net of acquisitions			
Receivables	4,726	28,984	2,217
Inventories	17,372	(10,152)	866
Accounts payable, accrued expenses and other current liabilities	(26,835)	2,566	(8,399)
Other current assets	(4,308)	(7,475)	(3,171)
	(9,045)	13,923	(8,487)
Change in noncurrent liabilities	11,648	3,636	4,740
Other items—net	(3,864)	2,048	9,029
Total operating activities	$194,754	$244,868	$195,838

Provision for Bad Debt

6.23

SEARS, ROEBUCK AND CO. (DEC)

(Millions)	2003	2002	2001
Cash flows from operating activities			
Net income	$ 3,397	$ 1,376	$ 735
Adjustments to reconcile net income to net cash provided by (used in) operating activities			
Depreciation and amortization	909	875	863
Loss on early retirement of debt	791	—	—
Cumulative effect of a change in accounting for goodwill	—	208	—
Provision for uncollectible accounts	1,747	2,261	1,866
Special charges and impairments	112	111	542
Gain on sale of businesses	(4,224)	—	—
Gain on sales of property and investments	(12)	(347)	(21)
Income tax benefit on nonqualified stock options	25	24	14
Change in (net of dispositions and acquisitions)			
Deferred income taxes	648	(203)	(190)
Retained interest in transferred credit card receivables	—	—	(759)
Credit card receivables	524	(4,833)	(810)
Merchandise inventories	(158)	45	610
Other operating assets	(496)	(56)	61
Other operating liabilities	(739)	34	(596)
Net cash provided by (used in) operating activities	$ 2,524	$ (505)	$2,315

Changes in Assets and Liabilities

6.24

R.R. DONNELLEY & SONS COMPANY (DEC)

(Thousands of dollars)	2003	2002	2001
Cash flows from operating activities			
Net income	$ 176,509	$ 142,237	$ 24,988
Restructuring and impairment charges	16,427	88,929	195,545
Reversal of tax reserves	(39,903)	(30,000)	—
(Gain) loss on sale or write-down of businesses and investments	(4,158)	(6,350)	11,895
Depreciation	276,005	288,499	315,937
Amortization	53,354	63,873	62,786
Gain on sale of assets	(4,012)	(13,824)	(8,204)
Net change in operating working capital	(159,801)	17,288	59,681
Net change in other assets and liabilities	54,730	(148,842)	(122,549)
Other	(14,966)	7,109	8,315
Net cash provided by operating activities	354,185	408,919	548,394
Cash flows from investing activities			
Capital expenditures	(202,916)	(241,597)	(273,340)
Other investments including acquisitions, net of cash acquired	(16,910)	—	(2,416)
Disposition of assets	34,847	25,471	19,346
Net cash used for investing activities	(184,979)	(216,126)	(256,410)
Cash flows from financing activities			
Repayments of long-term debt	(111,176)	(78,726)	(4,741)
Long-term borrowings	—	—	225,000
Net proceeds from (repayments of) short-term borrowings	39,905	14,591	(163,274)
Disposition of reacquired common stock	18,468	16,603	23,520
Acquisition of common stock	(2,455)	(20,029)	(273,255)
Cash dividends paid	(115,736)	(110,964)	(109,987)
Net cash used for financing activities	(170,994)	(178,525)	(302,737)
Effect of exchange rate changes on cash flows	2,082	(2,340)	(1,505)
Net increase (decrease) in cash and equivalents	294	11,928	(12,258)
Cash and equivalents at beginning of year	60,543	48,615	60,873
Cash and equivalents at end of year	$ 60,837	$ 60,543	$ 48,615
Changes in operating working capital, net of acquisitions and divestitures			
Decrease (increase) in assets			
Receivables, net	$(133,609)	$ 82,279	$ 185,413
Inventories, net	(4,143)	6,383	59,138
Prepaid expenses	9,092	(5,433)	(9,356)
Increase (decrease) in liabilities			
Accounts payable	34,514	(33,882)	(86,330)
Accrued compensation	(13,649)	(5,620)	(21,431)
Other accrued liabilities	(52,006)	(26,439)	(67,753)
Net change in operating working capital	$(159,801)	$ 17,288	$ 59,681

6.25

SCHLUMBERGER LIMITED (DEC)

(Stated in thousands)	2003	2002	2001
Cash flows from operating activities			
Income (loss) from continuing operations	$ 472,557	$(2,417,214)	$ 493,854
Adjustments to reconcile net income to net cash provided by operating activities			
Depreciation and amortization	1,570,851	1,533,406	1,875,559
Gain on the sale of Grant Prideco stock	(1,320)	—	—
Non-cash charges and gains on sale of businesses	439,976	3,196,923	271,174
Gain on sale of drilling rigs	—	(86,858)	—
Earnings of companies carried at equity, less dividends received	(74,596)	(64,280)	(61,715)
Deferred taxes	(12,286)	(48,702)	17,595
Provision for losses on accounts receivable	53,303	64,425	56,619
Change in operating assets and liabilities			
(Increase) decrease in receivables	(74,118)	542,669	(907,535)
Decrease (increase) in inventories	96,606	72,383	(259,290)
(Increase) decrease in other current assets	(47,274)	47,938	(8,048)
(Decrease) increase in accounts payable and accrued liabilities	(535,121)	(592,878)	204,751
Increase in estimated liability for taxes on income	175,857	28,470	12,626
Increase in postretirement benefits	70,394	39,659	28,417
Other—net	(21,830)	(144,158)	(162,602)
Net cash provided by operating activities	$2,112,999	$ 2,173,783	$1,561,405

INTEREST AND INCOME TAX PAYMENTS

6.26

THE DUN & BRADSTREET CORPORATION (DEC)

(Dollar amounts in millions)	2003	2002	2001
Cash flows from operating activities			
Net income	$ 174.5	$ 143.4	$ 149.9
Reconciliation of net income to net cash provided by operating activities			
Depreciation and amortization	64.0	84.2	94.5
Loss from sale of real estate	13.8	—	—
Loss (gain) from sales of businesses	2.1	(5.0)	(56.3)
Income tax benefit due to exercise of stock incentive plans	12.4	5.4	7.7
Equity (gains) losses in excess of dividends received from affiliates	(0.3)	1.7	3.5
Deferred revenue from RMS agreement	—	—	30.4
Restructuring expense, net and other asset impairments	17.4	30.9	46.6
Restructuring payments	(30.0)	(31.3)	(40.6)
Deferred income taxes	35.5	10.2	48.2
Accrued income taxes, net	10.6	59.8	(7.0)
Changes in current assets and liabilities			
(Increase) decrease in accounts receivable	(9.3)	2.0	30.7
Net (increase) decrease in other current assets	(1.2)	2.2	0.4
Net increase (decrease) in deferred revenue	3.5	(8.3)	(8.5)
Net decrease in accounts payable	—	(1.5)	(11.8)
Net decrease in accrued liabilities	(24.9)	(37.1)	(16.2)
Net increase (decrease) in other accrued and current liabilities	(7.2)	(7.3)	5.3
Changes in non-current assets and liabilities			
Increase in other long-term assets	(36.7)	(23.4)	(61.4)
Net increase (decrease) in long-term liabilities	9.4	(15.7)	0.8
Other non-cash adjustments	2.1	2.9	0.9
Net cash provided by operating activities	235.7	213.1	217.1
Cash flows from investing activities			
Cash proceeds from sales of real estate	80.2	21.5	—
Net investments in marketable securities	4.3	(4.5)	—
Cash proceeds from sales of businesses	3.6	4.8	118.2
Payments for acquisitions of businesses, net of cash acquired	(98.0)	(21.2)	(34.5)
Cash settlements of foreign currency contracts	(14.6)	(1.1)	(2.4)
Capital expenditures	(11.0)	(15.8)	(16.2)
Additions to computer software and other intangibles	(19.3)	(37.7)	(37.0)
Net assets held for sales of businesses	(9.9)	—	—
Investments in unconsolidated affiliates	(1.9)	(0.9)	(11.3)
Other	1.3	(0.3)	7.1
Net cash (used in) provided by investing activities	(65.3)	(55.2)	23.9
Cash flows from financing activities			
Payments for purchase of treasury shares	(156.1)	(117.7)	(144.9)
Net proceeds from stock plans	23.4	12.1	19.0
Decrease in commercial paper borrowings	—	—	(49.5)
Repayment of minority interest obligations	—	—	(300.0)
Increase in long-term borrowings	—	—	299.6
Other	(0.1)	0.9	(1.6)
Net cash used in financing activities	(132.8)	(104.7)	(177.4)
Effect of exchange rate changes on cash and cash equivalents	9.5	(6.6)	11.6
Increase in cash and cash equivalents	47.1	46.6	75.2
Cash and cash equivalents, beginning	191.9	145.3	70.1
Cash and cash equivalents, end	$ 239.0	$ 191.9	$ 145.3
Supplemental disclosure of cash flow information			
Cash paid			
Income taxes, net of refunds	$ 47.5	$ 28.3	$ 49.5
Interest expense	$ 17.2	$ 18.5	$ 11.1

ATT-SEC 6.26

6.27

NEWMONT MINING CORPORATION (DEC)

(In thousands)	2003	2002	2001
Operating activities			
Net income (loss)	$ 475,667	$ 158,061	$ (46,644)
Adjustments to reconcile net income (loss) to net cash provided by operating activities			
Depreciation, depletion and amortization	564,481	505,598	301,563
Accretion of accumulated reclamation obligations	22,610	—	—
Amortization of deferred stripping costs, net	(36,497)	37,195	37,410
Deferred income taxes	(36,183)	(100,290)	(91,487)
Foreign currency exchange (gain) loss	(75,670)	1,259	5,088
Minority interest, net of dividends	27,228	68,598	60,029
Equity loss (income) and impairment of affiliates, net of dividends	42,467	(35,595)	(22,275)
Write-down of inventories, stockpiles and ore on leach pads	24,945	44,439	25,105
Write-down of long-lived assets	35,260	3,652	32,711
Cumulative effect of change in accounting principle, net	34,533	(7,701)	—
Gain on investments, net	(83,166)	(47,086)	—
(Gain) loss on derivative instruments, net	(22,876)	39,805	(1,797)
Gain on extinguishment of NYOL bonds, net	(114,031)	—	—
Gain on extinguishment of NYOL derivative liability, net	(106,506)	—	—
Loss on extinguishment of debt	33,832	—	—
Loss on guarantee of OMC debt	30,000	—	—
Noncash merger and restructuring expenses	—	—	14,667
Gain on asset sales and other	(24,473)	(10,104)	(5,402)
(Increase) decrease in operating assets			
Accounts receivable	3,775	24,867	5,278
Inventories, stockpiles and ore on leach pads	(72,828)	(9,546)	35,547
Other assets	(5,052)	52,383	16,128
Increase (decrease) in operating liabilities			
Accounts payable and other current accrued liabilities	23,286	(12,216)	(15,099)
Derivative instruments	(16,318)	(33,202)	—
Early settlement of derivative instruments classified as cash flow hedges	(120,993)	(11,857)	—
Other liabilities	(14,739)	2,048	18,848
Net cash provided by operating activities	588,752	670,308	369,670
Investing activities			
Additions to property, plant and mine development	(501,400)	(300,057)	(389,964)
Receipts from (advances to) joint ventures and affiliates, net	39,321	(24,750)	(209)
Proceeds from sale of investments	232,190	500,103	—
Proceeds from the sale of TVX Newmont Americas	180,000	—	—
Proceeds from settlement of cross currency swaps	—	50,816	—
Early settlement of ineffective derivative instruments	(55,339)	(21,056)	—
Investments in affiliates	(70,072)	—	—
Cash consideration for acquisition of Newmont NFM minority interest	(11,195)	—	—
Cash consideration for Normandy shares	—	(461,717)	—
Cash received from acquisitions, net of transaction costs	—	371,417	—
Investments in marketable equity securities and other	(15,283)	(2,646)	5,146
Net cash (used in) provided by investing activities	(201,778)	112,110	(385,027)
Financing activities			
Proceeds from debt	492,841	493,371	1,021,650
Repayments of debt	(1,162,167)	(1,040,807)	(951,644)
Dividends paid on common and preferred stock	(70,759)	(49,982)	(30,972)
Decrease in restricted cash	—	—	40,000
Proceeds from stock issuances, net of issuance costs	1,286,751	67,346	7,516
Other	—	(3)	(1,464)
Net cash provided by (used in) financing activities	546,666	(530,075)	85,086
Effect of exchange rate changes on cash	(21,301)	(91)	2,144
Net change in cash and cash equivalents	912,339	252,252	71,873
Cash and cash equivalents at beginning of year	401,683	149,431	77,558
Cash and cash equivalents at end of year	$ 1,314,022	$ 401,683	$ 149,431

NOTES TO CONSOLIDATED FINANCIAL STATEMENTS

Note 25 (In Part): Supplemental Cash Flow Information

Net cash provided by operating activities included the following cash payments:

(In thousands)	2003	2002	2001
Income taxes, net of refunds	$194,297	$ 86,816	$76,020
Interest	$123,166	$137,706	$91,944

6.28

THE TIMKEN COMPANY (DEC)

(Thousands of dollars)	2003	2002	2001
Cash provided (used)			
Operating activities			
Net income (loss)	$ 36,481	$ 38,749	$ (41,666)
Adjustments to reconcile net income (loss) to net cash provided by operating activities:			
Cumulative effect of change in accounting principle	—	12,702	—
Depreciation and amortization	208,851	146,535	152,467
Loss (gain) on disposals of property, plant and equipment	4,944	5,904	(2,233)
Deferred income tax provision	4,406	17,250	23,013
Common stock issued in lieu of cash	2,744	5,217	1,441
Impairment and restructuring charges	55,967	(13,564)	41,832
Changes in operating assets and liabilities:			
Accounts receivable	(27,543)	(43,679)	44,803
Inventories	33,229	(50,611)	51,247
Other assets	(30,229)	(3,198)	(16,897)
Accounts payable and accrued expenses	(83,982)	80,761	(72,483)
Foreign currency translation (gain) loss	(2,234)	10,037	(3,886)
Net cash provided by operating activities	202,634	206,103	177,638
Investing activities			
Purchases of property, plant and equipment—net	(116,276)	(85,277)	(90,501)
Proceeds from disposals of property, plant and equipment	32,321	12,616	6,357
Proceeds from disposals of equity investments	146,335	—	—
Acquisitions	(725,120)	(6,751)	(12,957)
Net cash used by investing activities	(662,740)	(79,412)	(97,101)
Financing activities			
Cash dividends paid to shareholders	(42,078)	(31,713)	(40,166)
Purchases of treasury shares	—	—	(2,931)
Accounts receivable securitization financing borrowings	127,000	—	—
Accounts receivable securitization financing payments	(127,000)	—	—
Proceeds from issuance of common stock	54,985	—	—
Common stock issued to finance acquisition	180,010	—	—
Proceeds from issuance of long-term debt	629,800	—	80,766
Payments on long-term debt	(379,790)	(37,296)	(2,176)
Short-term debt activity—net	(41,082)	(11,498)	(90,980)
Net cash provided (used) by financing activities	401,845	(80,507)	(55,487)
Effect of exchange rate changes on cash	4,837	2,474	(2,585)
(Decrease) increase in cash and cash equivalents	(53,424)	48,658	22,465
Cash and cash equivalents at beginning of year	82,050	33,392	10,927
Cash and cash equivalents at end of year	$ 28,626	$ 82,050	$ 33,392

NOTES TO CONSOLIDATED FINANCIAL STATEMENTS
(Thousands of dollars)

5 (In Part): Financing Arrangements

Interest paid was approximately $43,000 in 2003 and $33,000 in 2002 and 2001. This differs from interest expense due to timing of payments and interest capitalized of $0 in 2003; $436 in 2002; and $1,400 in 2001 as a part of major capital additions. The weighted-average interest rate on commercial paper borrowings during the year was 1.7% in 2003, 2.1% in 2002 and 4.3% in 2001. The weighted-average interest rate on short-term debt, the majority of which related to foreign debt, was 4.1% in 2003, 4.8% in 2002 and 5.8% in 2001.

15 (In Part): Income Taxes

The company made income tax payments of approximately $13,830 in 2003, received income tax refunds of approximately $27,000 in 2002 and made income tax payments of approximately $7,210 in 2001. Taxes paid differ from current taxes provided, primarily due to the timing of payments.

CASH FLOWS FROM INVESTING ACTIVITIES

6.29 Paragraphs 15–17 of *SFAS No. 95* define those transactions and events which constitute Investing Activity cash receipts and payments. With the exception of certain transactions described in paragraphs 12 and 13 of *SFAS No. 95* and paragraph 7 of SFAS No. 104, *Statement of Cash Flows—Net Reporting of Certain Cash Receipts and Cash Payments and Classification of Cash Flows From Hedging Activities,* which amends *SFAS No. 95,* cash receipts and payments should be reported separately and not netted. Examples of reporting cash flows from Investing Activities follow.

Property Acquisitions/Disposals

6.30

LEVI STRAUSS & CO. (NOV)

(Dollars in thousands)	2003	2002	2001
Cash flows from investing activities			
Purchases of property, plant and equipment	$(68,608)	$(59,088)	$(22,541)
Proceeds from sale of property, plant and equipment	13,431	13,286	5,773
Cash (outflow) from net investment hedges	(29,307)	(13,551)	(462)
Net cash (used for) investing activities	$(84,484)	$(59,353)	$(17,230)

6.31

PATHMARK STORES, INC. (JAN)

(In millions)	2004	2003	2002
Investing activities			
Capital expenditures	$(68.8)	$ (92.6)	$(116.5)
Proceeds from sales of real estate	17.3	—	—
Lease financings	—	(12.7)	—
Cash used for investing activities	$(51.5)	$(105.3)	$(116.5)

Investments

6.32

ADMINISTAFF, INC. (DEC)

(In thousands)	2003	2002	2001
Cash flows from investing activities			
Marketable securities			
Purchases	$(25,779)	$(15,499)	$(56,604)
Proceeds from maturities	6,645	23,436	39,005
Proceeds from dispositions	9,612	25,130	8,817
Cash received (exchanged) for note receivable	2,958	(2,983)	—
Property and equipment			
Purchases	(6,771)	(36,677)	(33,232)
Investment in software development costs	(1,880)	(1,748)	(3,516)
Proceeds from dispositions	275	148	431
Proceeds from the sale of/ (investments in) other companies	457	(500)	(931)
Net cash used in investing activities	$(14,483)	$ (8,693)	$(46,030)

6.33

AETNA INC. (DEC)

(Millions)	2003	2002	2001
Cash flows from investing activities			
Proceeds from sales and investment maturities of			
Debt securities available for sale	$ 12,623.6	$ 15,679.9	$ 17,561.8
Equity securities	53.5	251.2	239.5
Mortgage loans	565.7	602.3	400.8
Investment real estate	90.4	74.3	6.3
Other investments	2,403.6	3,321.0	4,866.5
Cost of investments in			
Debt securities available for sale	(13,250.3)	(15,452.3)	(16,930.7)
Equity securities	(20.7)	(114.9)	(288.1)
Mortgage loans	(239.9)	(296.3)	(226.4)
Investment real estate	(66.8)	(47.6)	(17.9)
Other investments	(2,059.2)	(3,251.4)	(5,145.3)
Increase in property and equipment	(210.8)	(155.5)	(142.6)
Cash used for acquisition, net of cash acquired	(53.5)	—	—
Net cash (used for) provided by investing activities	$ (164.4)	$ 610.7	$ 323.9

Business Combinations

6.34

SMITH INTERNATIONAL, INC. (DEC)

(In thousands)	2003	2002	2001
Cash flows from investing activities			
Acquisition of businesses, net of cash acquired	$(101,789)	$ (60,152)	$(248,127)
Purchases of property, plant and equipment	(98,923)	(97,051)	(127,642)
Proceeds from disposal of property, plant and equipment	22,902	18,247	18,228
Purchases of stock in majority-owned subsidiary	—	(231)	(2,084)
Net cash used in investing activities	$(177,810)	$(139,187)	$(359,625)

NOTES TO CONSOLIDATED FINANCIAL STATEMENTS

3 (In Part): Business Combinations

During 2003, the Company completed three acquisitions in exchange for aggregate cash consideration of $92.1 million and the assumption of certain liabilities. In addition, cash payments of $9.7 million were made during the year to former shareholders of businesses acquired in 2002 to fund amounts due under earn-out arrangements and repay seller-financed notes. The 2003 transactions primarily consist of the following:

• On January 29, 2003, M-1 SWACO acquired certain oil-field chemical assets of Dynea International ("Dynea") in exchange for cash consideration of $77.8 million. The acquired operations, formerly based in Norway, provide a complete line of oilfield specialty chemicals used to eliminate hydrocarbon flow problems encountered during production and transportation.

• On October 1, 2003, M-1 SWACO acquired certain operating assets of Alpine Mud Products for cash consideration of $14.1 million. The acquired operations market a line of specialty fluid additives used to enhance rates of penetration in critical drilling applications, primarily to customers in the U.S. Gulf Coast region.

The following schedule summarizes investing activities related to 2003, 2002 and 2001 acquisitions included in the consolidated statements of cash flows:

(In thousands)	2003	2002	2001
Fair value of tangible and identifiable intangible assets net of cash acquired	$ 34,922	$ 57,480	$195,500
Goodwill acquired	66,147	35,616	137,100
Payments to former shareholders of businesses acquired in 2002	9,692	—	—
Total liabilities assumed	(8,972)	(32,944)	(84,473)
Cash paid for acquisition of businesses, net of cash acquired	$101,789	$ 60,152	$248,127

Sale of Discontinued Operation

6.35

UNOCAL CORPORATION (DEC)

(Millions of dollars)	2003	2002	2001
Cash flows from investing activities			
Capital expenditures (includes dry hole costs)	$(1,718)	$(1,670)	$(1,727)
Major acquisitions	—	—	(646)
Proceeds from sales of assets	642	163	81
Proceeds from sales of discontinued operations	11	3	25
Net cash used in investing activities	$(1,065)	$(1,504)	$(2,267)

NOTES TO THE CONSOLIDATED FINANCIAL STATEMENTS

Note 9—Discontinued Operations

(Millions of dollars)	2003	2002	2001
Gain on disposal before income taxes[a]	$25	$2	$27
Income taxes	9	1	10
Total earnings from discontinued operations	$16	$1	$17

[a] Gain on disposal in 2003, 2002 and 2001 is related to the former refining, marketing and transportation business.

In 2003, discontinued operations included a $25 million pre-tax gain relating to the Company's 1997 sale of its former West Coast refining, marketing and transportation assets. The sales agreement contained a provision calling for payments to the Company for price differences between California Air Resources Board Phase 2 gasoline and conventional gasoline. In 2003, the Company recorded $14 million pre-tax for this provision. The gains in 2002 and 2001 were also related to this agreement. The Company's cash proceeds related to the agreement were $11 million, $3 million and $25 million for 2003, 2002 and 2001, respectively. This provision in the agreement terminated at the end of 2003. In addition, the Company also reduced its loss provisions for the disposal of the business by $11 million pre-tax, reflecting lower than anticipated charges relating to the sold properties.

Notes Receivable

6.36

HERMAN MILLER, INC. (MAY)

(In millions)	2003	2002	2001
Cash flows from investing activities			
Notes receivable repayments	$ 189.2	$ 341.3	$ 639.4
Notes receivable issued	(190.0)	(334.4)	(628.4)
Short-term investment purchases	(4.5)	(38.9)	(113.7)
Short-term investment sales	4.2	42.3	113.0
Property and equipment additions	(29.0)	(52.4)	(105.0)
Proceeds from sales of property and equipment	20.7	0.7	0.1
Surrender of COLI policies	—	14.0	—
Other, net	2.1	1.6	(5.5)
Net cash used for investing activities	$ (7.3)	$ (25.8)	$(100.1)

NOTES TO THE CONSOLIDATED FINANCIAL STATEMENTS

Significant Accounting and Reporting Policies (In Part)

Notes Receivable

The notes receivable are primarily from certain independent contract office furniture dealers. These notes are the result of dealers in transition either through a change in ownership or general financial difficulty. The notes are collateralized by the assets of the dealers and bear interest based on the prevailing prime rate. Recorded reserves are based on historical credit experience, collateralization levels and the specific identification of other potential collection problems. Interest income relating to these notes was $0.7 million, $0.8 million, and $2.2 million in 2003, 2002, and 2001, respectively.

Capitalized Software

6.37

EMC CORPORATION (DEC)

(In thousands)	2003	2002	2001
Cash flows from investing activities			
Additions to property, plant and equipment	$ (368,545)	$ (391,076)	$ (889,309)
Capitalized software development costs	(113,427)	(126,678)	(120,724)
Purchases of short and long-term available for sale securities	(6,430,482)	(8,437,486)	(4,981,376)
Sales of short and long-term available for sale securities	5,032,720	7,199,476	4,445,271
Maturities of short and long-term available for sale securities	304,408	226,408	126,683
Business acquisitions, net of cash acquired (used)	323,930	(21,993)	(111,455)
Other	(61,801)	(25,044)	17,310
Net cash used in investing activities	$(1,313,197)	$(1,576,393)	$(1,513,600)

NOTES TO CONSOLIDATED FINANCIAL STATEMENTS

A (In Part): Summary of Significant Accounting Policies

Capitalized Software Development Costs

Research and development ("R&D") costs are expensed as incurred. Software development costs incurred subsequent to establishing technological feasibility through the general release of the software products are capitalized. Technological feasibility is demonstrated by the completion of a working model. Capitalized costs are amortized on a straight-line basis over two years which is the estimated useful life of the software product. Unamortized software development costs were $166.2 million and $143.7 million at December 31, 2003 and 2002, respectively, and are included in other assets, net. Amortization expense was $90.9 million, $128.3 million and $106.5 million in 2003, 2002 and 2001, respectively. Amounts capitalized were $113.4 million, $126.7 million and $120.7 million in 2003, 2002 and 2001, respectively.

Restricted Cash

6.38

OXFORD INDUSTRIES, INC. (MAY)

(In thousands)	2003	2002	2001
Cash flows from investing activities			
Increase in restricted cash in escrow	$(204,986)	$ —	$ —
Purchase of property, plant and equipment	(2,051)	(1,528)	(4,332)
Proceeds from sale of property, plant and equipment	947	1,097	834
Net cash used in investing activities	$(206,090)	$ (431)	$(3,498)

NOTES TO CONSOLIDATED FINANCIAL STATEMENTS

Note E. Restricted Cash

As of May 30, 2003, we had $204,986,488 in restricted cash, which was held in escrow. The cash was primarily received from our senior note offering completed on May 16, 2003 (See Note G). The proceeds from our senior note offering were restricted and could only be used to complete the acquisition of Viewpoint International, Inc. which was completed on June 13, 2003 (See Note O).

Note G. (In Part): Notes Payable and Long-Term Debt

We have $145,500,000 in uncommitted lines of credit, of which $125,000,000 is reserved exclusively for letters of credit. We do not pay any commitment fees for these available lines of credit. At May 30, 2003, there were no direct borrowings and approximately $77,000,000 in letters of credit outstanding under these lines. The weighted average interest rate on short-term borrowings during fiscal 2003 was 2.16%. These lines of credit were refinanced under our new senior credit facility which was established with the acquisition of Viewpoint International, Inc. (See Note O).

On May 16, 2003, we completed a $200,000,000 private placement of senior unsecured notes. The proceeds from the private placement were used to fund our acquisition of Viewpoint International, Inc. (See Note O). The notes bear interest at 8.875%, have an 8-year life and were sold at a discount of .713% ($1,426,000) to yield an effective interest rate of 9.0%. The terms of the notes provide certain limitations on additional indebtedness, and certain other transactions. Additionally, we are subject to certain financial covenants.

As part of the acquisition agreement, a bridge financing commitment was established to provide contingent financing in the event the placement of the senior notes was delayed. The placement of the senior unsecured notes was successful and the bridge financing commitment was terminated. The cost incurred during our fourth quarter for this commitment was approximately $1,000,000 and is included in interest expense in the accompanying statement of earnings.

A summary of debt is as follows:

(In thousands)	2003	2002
Notes payable at a fixed rate of 8.875%, due in 2011	$198,581	$ —
Industrial revenue bond at a fixed rate of 7.0% collateralized by property plant and equipment due in 2004	110	295
Capital leases due in varying installments through 2005	29	99
Less current maturities	(134)	(255)
Total long-term portion	$198,586	$ 139

Note O. (In Part): Subsequent Events

On June 13, 2003, we acquired all of the common stock of Viewpoint International, Inc. The transaction is valued at up to $325 million consisting of $240 million in cash, $10 million in Oxford common stock and up to $75 million in contingent payments, subject to the achievement by Viewpoint of certain performance targets. Viewpoint owns the Tommy Bahama lifestyle brand that is used to market a wide array of products and services including apparel, footwear, accessories, home furnishings and restaurants. Viewpoint also produces two additional collections under the Tommy Bahama label, Indigo Palms and Island Soft. It also operates over 30 Tommy Bahama retail locations across the country, six of which are retail/restaurant compounds.

We also entered into a new $275 million senior secured revolving credit facility, which has a five-year term and bears interest, at our option, at rates determined from time to time based upon (1) the higher of the federal funds rate or the applicable prime rate plus a spread or (2) LIBOR plus a spread. Borrowings under the new senior secured revolving credit facility are subject to a borrowing base calculation based on our inventories, real property and accounts receivable.

In connection with the completion of the Viewpoint acquisition, the net proceeds from our $200 million senior notes offering were released from escrow. We used the net proceeds from our senior notes offering, together with limited borrowings under our new senior secured revolving credit facility and cash on hand, to finance the cash portion of the purchase price for the Viewpoint acquisition.

Life Insurance Policies

6.39

QUANEX CORPORATION (OCT)

(In thousands)	2003	2002	2001
Investing activities			
Acquisition of Colonial Craft, net of cash and equivalents acquired	$ —	$(17,283)	$ —
Acquisition of Temroc Metals, Inc., net of cash and equivalents acquired	—	—	(17,922)
Proceeds from sale of Piper Utah property	2,832	—	—
Capital expenditures, net of retirements	(28,693)	(34,271)	(55,575)
Retired executive life insurance proceeds	6,442	26,111	—
Other, net	(3,081)	(4,365)	(3,597)
Cash used for investing activities	$(22,500)	$(29,808)	$(77,094)

NOTES TO CONSOLIDATED FINANCIAL STATEMENTS

3. Executive Life Insurance Benefit

During the fiscal year ended October 31, 2003, a former executive of the Company, on whose life the Company held life insurance policies, died. As a result, the Company received life insurance proceeds totaling $6.4 million. Estimates of the cash surrender value of these life insurance policies amount-

ing to $4.3 million were previously recognized in "Other assets" on the financial statements. The excess of the proceeds over the previously recorded cash surrender value amounting to $2.2 million was recognized as a non-taxable benefit on the income statement during the year ended October 31, 2003. The impact to the fiscal year ended October 31, 2003 basic and diluted earnings per share of this benefit was $0.13.

During the fiscal year ended October 31, 2002, another of the Company's former executives, on whose life it held life insurance policies, died. As a result, the Company received life insurance proceeds totaling $26.1 million. Estimates of the cash surrender value of these life insurance policies amounting to $15.9 million were previously recognized in "Other assets" on the financial statements. The excess of the proceeds over the previously recorded cash surrender value and the liability to the beneficiaries of the executive amounting to $9.0 million was recognized as a non-taxable benefit on the income statement during the period ended October 31, 2002. The impact on October 31, 2002 earnings per share of this benefit was $0.61 basic and $0.56 diluted.

Prepublication Costs

6.40

MCGRAW-HILL COMPANIES, INC. (DEC)

(In thousands)	2003	2002	2001
Investing activities			
Investment in prepublication costs	$(218,049)	$(249,317)	$(294,538)
Purchase of property and equipment	(114,984)	(70,019)	(116,895)
Acquisition of businesses and equity interests	(3,678)	(19,310)	(333,234)
Proceeds from disposition of property, equipment and businesses	502,665	24,304	17,876
Additions to technology projects	(28,145)	(55,477)	(28,840)
Other	—	3,299	—
Cash provided by/ (used for) investing activities	$ 137,809	$(366,520)	$(755,631)

NOTES TO CONSOLIDATED FINANCIAL STATEMENTS

1 (In Part): Accounting Policies

Prepublication Costs

Prepublication costs, principally outside preparation costs, are amortized from the year of publication over their estimated useful lives, one to five years, using either an accelerated or the straight-line method. The majority of the programs are amortized using an accelerated methodology. The Company periodically evaluates the remaining lives and recoverability of such costs, which is sometimes dependent upon program acceptance by state adoption authorities, based on expected undiscounted cash flows. If the annual prepublication amortization varied by one percentage point, the consolidated amortization expense would have increased by approximately $3.0 million.

CASH FLOWS FROM FINANCING ACTIVITIES

6.41   Paragraphs 18–20 of *SFAS No. 95* define those transactions and events which constitute financing cash receipts and payments. With the exception of certain transactions described in paragraphs 12 and 13 of *SFAS No. 95* and paragraph 7 of *SFAS No. 104*, which amends *SFAS No. 95,* cash receipts and payments should be reported separately and not netted. Examples of reporting cash flows from financing activities follow.

Debt Proceeds/Repayments

6.42

AMPHENOL CORPORATION (DEC)

(Dollars in thousands)	2003	2002	2001
Cash flow from financing activities			
Net change in borrowings under revolving credit facilities	$ 1,751	$(17,839)	$ 24,413
Decrease in borrowings under bank agreement	(150,543)	(63,205)	(30,000)
Retirement of debt			
Old bank agreement	(439,500)	—	—
Senior subordinated notes	(148,740)	—	—
Fees and expenses relating to refinancing	(9,720)	—	—
Borrowings under new bank agreement	625,000	—	—
Net change in receivables sold	10,600	(11,000)	(10,800)
Proceeds from exercise of stock options including tax benefit	35,919	5,777	—
Cash flow used by financing activities	$ (75,233)	$(86,267)	$(16,387)

NOTES TO CONSOLIDATED FINANCIAL STATEMENTS
(Dollars in thousands)

Note 2 (In Part): Long-Term Debt

Long-term debt consists of the following:

	Interest Rate at December 31, 2003	Maturity	2003	2002
Bank agreement				
Term loan—tranche A	3.2%	2006–2008	$ 90,000	$ —
Term loan—tranche B	4.0%	2010	409,000	—
Revolving credit facility		2008	—	—
Old bank agreement			—	464,043
Senior subordinated notes			—	144,000
Notes payable to foreign banks and other debt	3% to 9.5%	2004–2009	43,959	36,205
			542,959	644,248
Less current portion			10,679	78,363
Total long-term debt			$532,280	$565,885

In May 2003, the Company completed a refinancing of its senior credit facilities and redeemed all of its outstanding Senior Subordinated Notes ("Notes"). The new Bank Agreement ("Bank Agreement") consists of: (1) a $125,000 five-year Revolving Credit Facility, (2) a $125,000 Tranche A Loan (December 31, 2003 balance $90,000) and (3) a $500,000 Tranche B Loan (December 31, 2003 balance $409,000). At December 31, 2003, availability under the Revolving Credit Facility was $117,193, after a reduction of $7,807 for outstanding letters of credit. In connection with the refinancing, the Company incurred one-time expenses for the early extinguishment of debt of $10,367 (less tax effects of $3,525) or $.16 per share after tax. Such one-time expenses include the call premium on the Notes, write-off of unamortized deferred debt issuance costs and other related costs. The Company's interest rate on borrowings under the Bank Agreement is LIBOR plus 200 basis points. The Company also pays certain annual agency and commitment fees. The Bank Agreement is secured by a first priority pledge of 100% of the capital stock of the Company's direct domestic subsidiaries and 65% of the capital stock of direct material foreign subsidiaries, as defined in the Bank Agreement. In addition, if the Company's credit rating as assigned by Standard & Poor's or Moody's were to decline to BB- or Ba3, respectively, the Company would be required to perfect liens in favor of participants in the Bank Agreement in substantially all of the Company's U.S. based assets. At December 31, 2003, the Company's credit rating from Standard & Poor's was BB+ and from Moody's was Ba2. The Bank Agreement requires that the Company satisfy certain financial covenants including an interest coverage ratio (EBITDA divided by interest expense) of higher than 3X and a leverage ratio (Debt divided by EBITDA) lower than 3.8X; at December 31, 2003, such ratios as defined in the Bank Agreement were 7.82X and 2.49X, respectively. The Bank Agreement also includes limitations with respect to, among other things, (i) indebtedness in excess of $50,000 for capital leases, $200,000 for general indebtedness, $200,000 for acquisition indebtedness, (of which approximately $2,080, $0 and $0 were outstanding at December 31, 2003, respectively), (ii) restricted payments including dividends on the Company's Common Stock in excess of 50% of consolidated cumulative net income subsequent to May 2003, or approximately $38,985 at December 31, 2003, (iii) creating or incurring liens, (iv) making other investments, (v) acquiring or disposing of assets and (vi) capital expenditures.

6.43

AVNET, INC. (JUN)

(Thousands)	2003	2002	2001
Cash flows from financing activities			
Sales (reduced drawings) under accounts receivable securitization program	$(200,000)	$(150,000)	$ 350,000
Issuance of notes in public offerings, net of issuance costs (Note 7)	465,313	394,328	572,389
Repayment of notes (Note 7)	(379,197)	(528,969)	—
Repayment of commercial paper and bank debt, net	(285,795)	(517,924)	(427,227)
Payment of other debt, net	(1,686)	(4,482)	(25,983)
Cash dividends	—	(26,546)	(27,387)
Other, net	(474)	24,225	10,834
Net cash flows (used for) provided from financing activities	$(401,839)	$(809,368)	$ 452,626

NOTES TO CONSOLIDATED FINANCIAL STATEMENTS

7 (In Part): External Financing

Short-term debt consists of the following:

(Thousands)	2003	2002
Bank credit facilities	$ 11,834	$54,158
4.5% convertible notes due September 1, 2004	3,031	3,031
6.45% notes due August 15, 2003	40,859	—
8.20% notes due October 17, 2003	29,944	—
6⅞% notes due March 15, 2004	100,000	—
Other debt due within one year	1,988	2,120
Short-term debt	$187,656	$59,309

● ● ● ● ● ●

Long-term debt consists of the following:

(Thousands)	2003	2002
6.45% notes due August 15, 2003	$ —	$ 200,000
8.20% notes due October 17, 2003	—	250,000
6⅞% notes due March 15, 2004	—	100,000
7⅞% notes due February 15, 2005	360,000	360,000
8.00% notes due November 15, 2006	400,000	400,000
9¾% notes due February 15, 2008	475,000	—
Bank credit facilities	—	178,410
Commercial paper	—	63,964
Other long-term debt	7,237	6,419
Subtotal	1,242,237	1,558,793
Fair value adjustment for hedged 8.00% notes	36,162	7,043
Long-term debt	$1,278,399	$1,565,836

On February 6, 2003, the Company issued $475,000,000 of 9¾% Notes due February 15, 2008 (the "9¾% Notes"). The net proceeds from this debt issuance were approximately $465,313,000, net of underwriting fees. During 2003, the Company redeemed $159,141,000 of its 6.45% Notes due August 15, 2003 and $220,056,000 of its 8.20% Notes due October 17, 2003. Proceeds from the 9¾% Notes were used to fund the tender and early redemption of the 6.45% and 8.20% Notes with the excess proceeds held in an escrow account which will be used to repay the remaining principal on the 6.45% and 8.20% Notes at their respective maturity dates plus interest due through their maturities. The Company incurred debt extinguishment costs of $13,487,000 pre-tax, $8,152,000 after tax and $0.07 per share on a diluted basis during 2003 related primarily to premiums and other transaction costs associated with the tender and early redemption of a portion of the 6.45% and 8.20% Notes.

Capital Stock Proceeds/Payments

6.44

TEKTRONIX, INC. (MAY)

(In thousands)	2003	2002	2001
Cash flows from financing activities			
Net change in short-term debt	$ —	$ (1,018)	$ (467)
Repayment of long-term debt	(42,760)	(27,735)	(22,446)
Proceeds from employee stock plans	7,668	11,239	23,920
Repurchase of common stock	(108,363)	(42,042)	(126,160)
Net cash used in financing activities	$(143,455)	$(59,556)	$(125,153)

NOTES TO CONSOLIDATED FINANCIAL STATEMENTS

20 (In Part): Shareholders' Equity

Repurchase of Common Stock

On March 15, 2000, the Board of Directors authorized the purchase of up to $550.0 million of the Company's common stock on the open market or through negotiated transactions. This repurchase authority allows the Company, at management's discretion, to selectively repurchase its common stock from time to time in the open market or in privately negotiated transactions depending on market price and other factors. During fiscal years 2003 and 2002, the Company repurchased a total of 6.2 million and 2.1 million shares, respectively, for $108.4 million and $42.0 million, respectively. As of May 31, 2003, the Company has repurchased a total of 14.5 million shares at an average price of $21.83 per share totaling $316.5 million under this authorization. The reacquired shares were immediately retired, as required under Oregon corporate law.

6.45

WEATHERFORD INTERNATIONAL LTD. (DEC)

(In thousands)	2003	2002	2001
Cash flows from financing activities			
Proceeds (repayments) under asset securitization, net	$ 6,051	$(71,846)	$140,795
Borrowings (repayments) of short-term debt, net	(156,054)	165,104	136,364
Borrowings of long-term debt	258,351	—	347,074
Repayments on long-term debt	(12,296)	(29,738)	(12,547)
Redemption of convertible preferred debentures	(412,563)	—	—
Issuance of common shares	400,000	—	—
Purchases of treasury shares, net	(2,619)	(2,703)	(2,000)
Proceeds from stock option exercises	13,972	34,410	13,227
Other financing activities, net	(204)	(1,271)	—
Net cash provided by financing activities	$ 94,638	$ 93,956	$622,913

NOTES TO CONSOLIDATED FINANCIAL STATEMENTS

15 (In Part): Shareholders' Equity

Equity Offering

On July 3, 2003, the Company completed a public offering of ten million Common Shares in exchange for $400.0 million in cash proceeds. The Common Shares were sold through Lehman Brothers, an investment banking firm in which two directors of the Company are managing directors. The arrangements associated with this transaction were on customary terms in the industry.

Exercise of Stock Options

6.46

SPAN-AMERICA MEDICAL SYSTEMS, INC. (SEP)

	2003	2002	2001
Financing activities			
Dividends paid	$(356,268)	$(303,393)	$(301,307)
Common stock issued upon exercise of options	14,175	57,015	23,725
Net cash used for financing activities	$(342,093)	$(246,378)	$(277,582)

Dividends Paid

6.47

STEWART & STEVENSON SERVICES, INC. (JAN)

(In thousands)	2003	2002	2001
Financing activities			
Change in short-term notes payable	$ 478	$ (1,660)	$ (9,498)
Payments on long-term borrowings	(30,250)	(250)	(21,005)
Dividends paid	(9,704)	(9,681)	(9,610)
Proceeds from exercise of stock options	1,867	667	5,851
Net cash used in financing activities	$(37,609)	$(10,924)	$(34,262)

NOTES TO CONSOLIDATED FINANCIAL STATEMENTS

Note 10 (In Part): Common Stock

Cash Dividend

Cash dividends of $0.085 per common share were declared and paid in each quarter of Fiscal 2003, 2002 and 2001. Declaration and payment of dividends in the future is dependent upon the Company's earnings and liquidity position, among other factors.

Debt Issuance Costs

6.48

LSI LOGIC CORPORATION (DEC)

(In thousands)	2003	2002	2001
Financing activities			
Proceeds from borrowings	$ 350,000	$ —	$ 690,088
Repayment of debt obligations	(327)	(332)	(201,226)
Redemption/repurchase of convertible subordinated notes	(715,983)	(118,938)	—
Debt issuance costs	(10,984)	—	(16,249)
Cash paid for call spread options	(28,000)	—	—
Issuance of common stock	30,306	43,992	81,650
Net cash (used in)/provided by financing activities	$(374,988)	$ (75,278)	$ 554,263

NOTES TO CONSOLIDATED FINANCIAL STATEMENTS

Note 9 (In Part): Debt

On May 12, 2003, the Company issued $350 million of 4% Convertible Subordinated Notes (the "2003 Convertible Notes") due in 2010. The 2003 Convertible Notes are subordinated to all existing and future senior debt, are convertible at the holder's option at any time prior to the maturity date of such notes, into shares of the Company's common stock at a conversion price of $13.42 per share. The Company cannot elect to redeem the 2003 Convertible Notes prior to maturity. However, each holder of the 2003 Convertible Notes has the right to cause the Company to repurchase all of such holder's convertible notes at 100% of their principal amount plus accrued interest upon the occurrence of any fundamental change, which includes a transaction or event such as an exchange offer, liquidation, tender offer, consolidation, merger or combination. Interest is payable semiannually. The Company paid approximately $11 million in debt issuance costs that are being amortized using the interest method.

Lease Obligation Payments

6.49

GLOBALSANTAFE CORPORATION (DEC)

(In millions)	2003	2002	2001
Cash flows from financing activities			
Dividend payments	$ (36.7)	$(30.4)	$ —
Issuance of long-term debt, net of discount	249.4	—	—
Deferred financing costs	(3.6)	—	—
Lease/leaseback transaction	37.0	—	—
Payments on capitalized lease obligations	(8.3)	(1.8)	(1.8)
Ordinary shares repurchased and retired	—	(51.4)	—
Proceeds from issuance of ordinary shares	9.7	27.3	7.6
Bank overdrafts and other	6.3	8.2	—
Net cash flow provided by (used in) financing activities	$253.8	$(48.1)	$5.8

NOTES TO CONSOLIDATED FINANCIAL STATEMENTS

Note 5 (In Part): Commitments and Contingencies

In January 2003, the Company entered into a lease-leaseback arrangement with a European bank related to the Company's *Britannia* cantilevered jackup. Pursuant to this arrangement, the Company leased the *Britannia* to the bank for a five-year term for a lump-sum payment of approximately $37 million, net of origination fees of approximately $1.5 million. The bank then leased the rig back to the Company for a five-year term with an effective annual interest rate based on the 3-month British Pound Sterling LIBOR plus a margin of 0.625%, under which the Company makes annual lease payments of approximately $8.0 million, payable in advance. The Company has classified this arrangement as a capital lease.

Receivables Sold/Securitized

6.50

SEQUA CORPORATION (DEC)

(Amounts in thousands)	2003	2002	2001
Cash flows from financing activities			
Proceeds from accounts receivable sold	$ 75,000	$ 134,000	$ 125,500
Repurchases of accounts receivable sold	(155,000)	(118,000)	(179,500)
Proceeds from debt	103,235	3,248	199,230
Payments of debt	(11,555)	(11,352)	(91,006)
Payments of preferred dividends	(2,064)	(2,064)	(2,064)
Other financing activities	(824)	2,641	(136)
Net cash provided by financing activities	$ 8,792	$ 8,473	$ 52,024

NOTES TO CONSOLIDATED FINANCIAL STATEMENTS

Note 1 (In Part): Summary of Significant Accounting Policies

Basis of Presentation (In Part)

Sequa Receivables Corporation (SRC), a wholly owned special purpose corporation engaged in selling an undivided percentage ownership interest in Sequa's eligible domestic trade receivables (see Note 2 for further discussion) is a VIE. SRC's assets are available to satisfy its obligations to the bank administered multi-seller commercial paper conduit, and SRC bears the risk of loss relative to uncollectible receivables. Sequa's trade receivables are net of receivables sold under SRC's Receivables Purchase Agreement.

Note 2 (In Part): Trade Receivables, Net

Sequa Receivables Corp. (SRC), a special purpose corporation wholly owned by Sequa, has a Receivables Purchase Agreement (RPA) which was extended from its original expiration date of November 13, 2003 through November 16, 2006. Under the RPA, SRC may sell an undivided percentage ownership interest up to a maximum participation of $75,000,000 in Sequa's eligible domestic trade receivables through a bank administered multi-seller commercial paper conduit. The maximum participation under the RPA is lower than the $120,000,000 maximum provided at December 31, 2002, primarily due to the absence of receivables related to the ARC propulsion business which has been sold, a narrowing of eligible receivables to domestic customers and fewer banks participating in this market as a whole. Back-up liquidity lines provided by two banks are annually renewable at the banks' option and contain a net worth covenant applicable to Sequa. The sale of receivables through the bank administered conduit is funded through the sale of A1/P1 rated commercial paper. SRC's discount expense is 1.25% above the commercial paper rate. SRC's assets will be available to satisfy its obligations to its creditors, which have a security interest in SRC's assets, prior to distribution to Sequa. In accordance with SFAS No. 140, "Accounting for Transfers and Servicing of Financial Assets and Extinguishments of Liabilities—a Replacement of FASB Statement No. 125," transactions under the RPA qualify as a sale of receivables. At December 31, 2003, no trade receivables were sold under the RPA as Sequa repurchased the undivided percentage ownership interest previously sold using cash collections on its accounts receivable during the second quarter. At December 31, 2002, trade receivables are net of receivables sold under the RPA of $80,000,000. Other, net in the Consolidated Statement of Operations includes discount expense related to the sale of receivables of $566,000 in 2003, $1,297,000 in 2002 and $4,102,000 in 2001.

FOREIGN CURRENCY CASH FLOWS

6.51 Paragraph 25 of *SFAS No. 95* specifies the effect of exchange rate changes on cash balances held in foreign currencies be reported as a separate part of the Statement of Cash Flows. Examples of reporting foreign currency cash flows follow.

6.52

COLGATE-PALMOLIVE COMPANY (DEC)

(Dollars in millions)	2003	2002	2001
Operating activities			
Net income	$ 1,421.3	$ 1,288.3	$ 1,146.6
Adjustments to reconcile net income to net cash provided by operations			
Restructuring	53.8	—	(8.9)
Depreciation and amortization	315.5	296.5	336.2
Gain before tax on sale of non-core product lines and other investment activities	(107.2)	(5.2)	(10.8)
Voluntary contributions to benefit plans	(84.1)	(110.0)	(95.7)
Deferred income taxes	(48.8)	35.3	73.0
Cash effects of changes in			
Receivables	(14.4)	(18.0)	19.4
Inventories	(3.1)	(2.4)	(18.7)
Accounts payable and other accruals	188.7	107.7	29.8
Other non-current assets and liabilities	46.0	19.0	33.0
Net cash provided by operations	1,767.7	1,611.2	1,503.9
Investing activities			
Capital expenditures	(302.1)	(343.7)	(340.2)
Sale of non-core product lines	127.6	—	12.5
Sales (purchases) of marketable securities and investments	41.9	(10.0)	(6.2)
Other	15.0	(3.5)	10.4
Net cash used in investing activities	(117.6)	(357.2)	(323.5)
Financing activities			
Principal payments on debt	(804.0)	(763.5)	(595.9)
Proceeds from issuance of debt	229.2	964.5	887.9
Payments from outside investors	—	—	89.7
Dividends paid	(506.8)	(413.4)	(396.7)
Purchases of treasury shares	(554.9)	(1,105.2)	(1,263.3)
Proceeds from exercise of stock options	79.3	57.6	67.6
Net cash used in financing activities	(1,557.2)	(1,260.0)	(1,210.7)
Effect of exchange rate changes on cash and cash equivalents	4.5	1.2	(3.6)
Net increase (decrease) in cash and cash equivalents	97.4	(4.8)	(33.9)
Cash and cash equivalents at beginning of year	167.9	172.7	206.6
Cash and cash equivalents at end of year	$ 265.3	$ 167.9	$ 172.7

6.53

CURTISS-WRIGHT CORPORATION (DEC)

(In thousands)	2003	2002	2001
Cash flows from operating activities			
Net earnings	$ 52,268	$ 45,136	$ 62,880
Adjustments to reconcile net earnings to net cash provided by operating activities			
Depreciation and amortization	31,327	18,693	14,734
Non-cash pension income	(1,611)	(7,208)	(11,042)
Net loss (gain) on sales and disposals of real estate and equipment	359	(681)	(39,018)
Deferred income taxes	6,035	4,011	4,167
Changes in operating assets and liabilities, net of businesses acquired			
Proceeds from sales of short-term investments	—	77,050	348,911
Purchases of short-term investments	—	(35,600)	(327,761)
(Increase) decrease in receivables	(5,858)	31	(7,203)
Decrease (increase) in inventories	1,893	197	(3,232)
Increase in progress payments	1,967	3,464	4,186
Increase (decrease) in accounts payable and accrued expenses	9,343	(61)	(2,831)
Decrease in deferred revenue	(10,070)	(2,820)	(422)
Increase (decrease) in income taxes payable	3,240	(11,101)	12,694
Pension contributions	(5,729)	—	—
Increase in other current and long-term assets	(963)	(3,254)	(2,051)
Increase in other current and long-term liabilities	995	2,156	7,185
Other, net	428	(228)	63
Total adjustments	31,256	44,649	(1,620)
Net cash provided by operating activities	83,524	89,785	61,620
Cash flows from investing activities			
Proceeds from sales and disposals of real estate and equipment	1,132	2,447	45,201
Additions to property, plant, and equipment	(33,329)	(34,954)	(19,354)
Acquisition of new businesses, net of cash acquired	(71,368)	(164,661)	(58,982)
Net cash used for investing activities	(103,565)	(197,168)	(33,135)
Cash flows from financing activities			
Borrowings of debt	384,712	220,400	—
Principal payments on debt	(314,204)	(92,795)	(8,228)
Reimbursement of recapitalization expenses	—	—	1,750
Proceeds from exercise of stock options	3,868	6,226	1,804
Dividends paid	(6,520)	(6,141)	(5,443)
Net cash provided by (used for) financing activities	67,856	127,690	(10,117)
Effect of foreign currency	3,140	1,915	(1,205)
Net increase in cash and cash equivalents	50,955	22,222	16,803
Cash and cash equivalents at beginning of year	47,717	25,495	8,692
Cash and cash equivalents at end of year	$ 98,672	$ 47,717	$ 25,495

NONCASH ACTIVITIES

6.54   Paragraph 32 of *SFAS No. 95* requires the disclosure of information about noncash investing and financing activities. Examples of the disclosure of noncash activities follow.

6.55

ALBERTSON'S, INC. (JAN)

(In millions)	2004	2003	2002
Cash flows from operating activities			
Net earnings	$ 556	$ 485	$ 501
Adjustments to reconcile net earnings to net cash provided by operating activities			
Depreciation and amortization	969	943	913
Net deferred income taxes	172	100	(129)
Other noncash charges	48	21	42
Stock-based compensation	25	19	19
Goodwill amortization	—	—	56
Gain on curtailment of postretirement benefits	(36)	—	(36)
Net gain on asset sales	(24)	(9)	(54)
Restructuring (credits) charges	(8)	(16)	424
Discontinued operations noncash charges		365	54
Cumulative effect of change in accounting principle	—	94	—
Changes in operating assets and liabilities			
Receivables and prepaid expenses	(38)	21	(110)
Inventories	(62)	112	40
Accounts payable	(242)	(100)	(68)
Other current liabilities	29	(88)	287
Self-insurance	120	106	71
Unearned income	25	32	3
Other long-term liabilities	11	(25)	(4)
Net cash provided by operating activities	1,545	2,060	2,009
Cash flows from investing activities			
Capital expenditures	(1,094)	(1,359)	(1,455)
Proceeds from disposal of land, buildings and equipment	72	101	288
Proceeds from disposal of assets held for sale	119	578	118
Other	(23)	18	(31)
Net cash used in investing activities	(926)	(662)	(1,080)
Cash flows from financing activities			
Cash dividends paid	(279)	(306)	(309)
Payments on long-term borrowings	(120)	(143)	(89)
Stock purchases and retirements	(108)	(862)	—
Proceeds from long-term borrowings	9	—	623
Proceeds from stock options exercised	6	14	23
Net commercial paper activity and bank borrowings	—	—	(1,153)
Net cash used in financing activities	(492)	(1,297)	(905)
Net Increase in cash and cash equivalents	127	101	24
Cash and cash equivalents at beginning of year	162	61	37
Cash and cash equivalents at end of year	$ 289	$ 162	$ 61
Supplemental cash flow information			
Cash payments for income taxes, net of refunds	$ 231	$ 376	$ 403
Cash payments for interest, net of amounts capitalized	401	390	299
Noncash investing and financing activities			
Capitalized lease obligations incurred	62	75	79

6.56

ANHEUSER-BUSCH COMPANIES, INC. (DEC)

(In millions)	2003	2002	2001
Cash flow from operating activities			
Net income	$ 2,075.9	$ 1,933.8	$ 1,704.5
Adjustments to reconcile net income to cash provided by operating activities			
Depreciation and amortization	877.2	847.3	834.5
Deferred income taxes	129.5	160.2	(15.8)
Gain on sale of business	—	—	(17.8)
Undistributed earnings of affiliated companies	(175.7)	(305.0)	(227.6)
Other, net	31.4	(12.0)	38.2
Operating cash flow before change in working capital	2,938.3	2,624.3	2,316.0
Decrease in working capital	32.6	140.9	44.6
Cash provided by operating activities	2,970.9	2,765.2	2,360.6
Cash flow from investing activities			
Capital expenditures	(993.0)	(834.7)	(1,022.0)
New business acquisitions	(156.9)	(19.0)	(370.4)
Proceeds from sale of business	—	—	110.0
Cash used for investing activities	(1,149.9)	(853.7)	(1,282.4)
Cash flow from financing activities			
Increase in debt	1,389.0	1,151.8	1,213.4
Decrease in debt	(652.1)	(505.9)	(572.8)
Dividends paid to shareholders	(685.4)	(649.5)	(614.1)
Acquisition of treasury stock	(1,958.9)	(2,027.0)	(1,163.8)
Shares issued under stock plans	88.6	145.4	61.8
Cash used for financing activities	(1,818.8)	(1,885.2)	(1,075.5)
Net increase in cash during the year	2.2	26.3	2.7
Cash, beginning of year	188.9	162.6	159.9
Cash, end of year	$ 191.1	$ 188.9	$ 162.6

NOTES TO CONSOLIDATED FINANCIAL STATEMENTS

11. Supplemental Cash Flows Information

Accounts payable include $111.0 million and $87.4 million, respectively, of outstanding checks at December 31, 2003 and 2002.

Supplemental cash flows information for the three years ended December 31 is presented in the following table (in millions).

	2003	2002	2001
Cash paid during the year			
Interest, net of interest capitalized	$ 369.0	$ 343.0	$ 313.1
Income taxes	952.2	788.7	889.8
Excise taxes	2,169.4	2,119.5	2,052.6
Noncash investing activity			
Issuance of treasury stock related to wholesaler acquisition[1]	$ 72.6	$ —	$ —
Change in working capital			
(Increase)/decrease in current assets			
Accounts receivable	$ (39.0)	$ (9.5)	$ (20.5)
Inventories	(23.9)	28.2	16.5
Other current assets	(60.5)	53.3	4.2
Increase/(decrease) in current liabilities			
Accounts payable	107.1	41.6	4.2
Accrued salaries, wages and benefits	1.4	31.7	(20.6)
Accrued taxes	(17.9)	19.9	33.7
Other current liabilities	(21.1)	(42.0)	43.5
Derivatives fair value adjustment	77.2	17.7	(16.4)
Noncash change in working capital due to wholesaler acquisition	9.3	—	—
Net decrease in working capital	$ 32.6	$ 140.9	$ 44.6

[1] Recorded as a reduction in treasury stock for the company's average cost of the shares ($28.5), and an increase in paid-in-capital for the remainder ($44.1).

6.57

CHESAPEAKE CORPORATION (DEC)

(In millions)	2003	2002	2001
Operating activities			
Net income	$ 26.5	$ 21.9	$ 123.5
Adjustments to reconcile net income to net cash provided by (used in) operating activities			
Gain on disposal of discontinued businesses, net of taxes	—	(1.4)	(113.0)
Depreciation and amortization	54.3	48.2	71.4
Deferred income taxes	18.3	7.2	(0.5)
Non-cash restructuring	(0.4)	—	7.5
Gain on sale of business	(11.2)	—	—
Gain on sale of property, plant and equipment	(5.8)	(5.0)	(7.5)
Changes in operating assets and liabilities, net of acquisitions and dispositions			
Accounts receivable, net	18.3	1.1	(7.1)
Inventories	6.3	13.4	9.7
Other assets	1.0	2.0	2.0
Accounts payable and accrued expenses	(7.6)	(28.0)	(51.1)
Income taxes payable	(12.2)	(9.5)	(237.9)
Other	(2.1)	2.6	(3.6)
Net cash provided by (used in) operating activities	$ 85.4	$ 52.5	$(206.6)

(continued)

(In millions)	2003	2002	2001
Net cash provided by (used in) operating activities	$ 85.4	$ 52.5	$(206.6)
Investing activities			
Purchases of property, plant and equipment	(52.4)	(51.2)	(41.3)
Acquisitions	—	—	(7.2)
Proceeds from sale of businesses	—	24.9	427.1
Proceeds from sales of property, plant and equipment	14.5	14.4	18.0
Other	1.2	(0.5)	0.8
Net cash (used in) provided by investing activities	(36.7)	(12.4)	397.4
Financing activities			
Net borrowings (payments) on credit lines	15.0	(10.5)	(311.8)
Payments on long-term debt	(56.4)	(26.5)	(41.9)
Proceeds from long-term debt	2.3	6.0	172.7
Debt issuance costs	—	(0.6)	(9.2)
Dividends paid	(13.4)	(13.3)	(13.2)
Other	—	0.4	1.5
Net cash used in financing activities	(52.5)	(44.5)	(201.9)
Decrease in cash and cash equivalents	(3.8)	(4.4)	(11.1)
Cash and cash equivalents at beginning of year	15.7	20.1	31.2
Cash and cash equivalents at end of year	$ 11.9	$ 15.7	$ 20.1

NOTES TO CONSOLIDATED FINANCIAL STATEMENTS

13 (In Part): Supplemental Balance Sheet, Income Statement and Cash Flow Information

Cash Flow Information

(In millions)	2003	2002	2001
Cash paid for			
Interest (net of amounts capitalized)	$38.9	$41.6	$ 38.7
Income taxes	7.6	5.7	218.6
Supplemental investing and financing non-cash transactions			
Issuance of common stock for long-term incentive and employee benefit plans	$ 2.5	$ 0.2	$ 1.1
Dividends declared not paid	3.3	3.3	3.3
Real estate transactions (notes received)	—	17.7	—
Assets obtained by capital lease	3.5	0.4	1.7
Assets financed*	21.3	10.2	5.1

* Amounts reported as financed are recorded as purchases of property, plant and equipment in the statement of cash flows in the year paid.

6.58

WESTERN DIGITAL CORPORATION (JUN)

(In millions)	2003	2002	2001
Cash flows from operating activities			
Net income (loss)	$182.1	$ 65.4	$ (98.9)
Adjustments to reconcile net income (loss) to net cash provided by (used for) operating activities of continuing operatings			
Discontinued operations	(1.3)	(12.2)	45.2
Loss (gain) on debenture redemptions	—	0.1	(22.4)
Loss on litigation settlement	18.5	—	—
Depreciation and amortization	50.4	45.8	51.9
Non-cash interest expense	3.0	5.6	7.5
Investment gains, net	(3.4)	(4.4)	—
Non-cash adjustment to Komag investment and note	—	—	39.3
Changes in			
Accounts receivable	(25.1)	(90.5)	31.1
Inventories	(24.4)	5.4	1.8
Other assets	(0.3)	0.9	(0.1)
Accounts payable	49.3	80.0	(39.9)
Accrued expenses	23.3	(14.0)	(68.6)
Other	8.7	0.7	(5.7)
Net cash provided by (used for) continuing operations	280.8	82.8	(58.8)
Cash flows from investing activities			
Capital expenditures, net	(61.9)	(47.7)	(50.7)
Other investment activity	3.4	9.9	15.0
Net cash used for investing activities of continuing operations	(58.5)	(37.8)	(35.7)
Cash flows from financing activities			
Issuance of common stock under employee plans	44.3	10.1	7.1
Debenture redemptions and extinguishments	(88.3)	(17.6)	—
Common stock issued for cash	—	—	110.5
Other subsidiary financing activity	(5.9)	0.4	—
Net cash (used for) provided by financing activities of continuing operations	(49.9)	(7.1)	117.6
Net cash (used for) provided by discontinued operations	(2.9)	18.2	(39.5)
Net increase (decrease) in cash and cash equivalents	169.5	56.1	(16.4)
Cash and cash equivalents, beginning of year	223.7	167.6	184.0
Cash and cash equivalents, end of year	$393.2	$223.7	$167.6
Supplemental disclosure of cash flow information			
Cash paid during the period for income taxes	$ 3.5	$ 2.0	$ 1.5
Supplemental disclosure of non-cash investing and financing activities			
Common stock issued for extinguishment of convertible debentures	$ 0.2	$ 13.6	$ 95.5

CASH AND CASH EQUIVALENTS

6.59 A Statement of Cash Flows explains the change during a period in cash and cash equivalents. The amount of cash and cash equivalents reported on a Statement of Cash Flows should agree with the amount of cash and cash equivalents reported on a Statement of Financial Position. Paragraph 10 of *SFAS No. 95* requires that an entity disclose what items are treated as cash equivalents. Table 6-5 shows the descriptive terms used by the survey companies to describe a change in cash and cash equivalents. Examples of cash and cash equivalents disclosure follow.

6.60

TABLE 6-5: CASH AND CASH EQUIVALENTS

	2003	2002	2001	2000
Cash and cash equivalents.............	498	492	489	473
Cash and equivalents......................	40	44	46	45
Cash.................................	40	41	38	50
Cash and short-term investments...	9	9	10	11
Cash and short-term cash investments...............	4	6	5	5
Cash and temporary cash investments...............	3	3	4	6
Cash and temporary investments...	2	2	3	2
Cash and marketable securities......	—	—	1	1
Other descriptive captions..............	4	3	4	7
Total Companies...........................	**600**	**600**	**600**	**600**

6.61

NIKE, INC. (MAY)

Consolidated Balance Sheets

(In millions)	2003	2002
Current assets		
Cash and equivalents	$ 634.0	$ 575.5
Accounts receivable, less allowance for doubtful accounts of $87.9 and $80.4	2,101.1	1,804.1
Inventories	1,514.9	1,373.8
Deferred income taxes	163.7	140.8
Prepaid expenses and other current assets	266.2	260.5
Total current assets	$4,679.9	$4,154.7

Consolidated Statements of Cash Flows

(In millions)	2003	2002	2001
Net increase in cash and equivalents	$ 58.5	$271.5	$ 49.7
Cash and equivalents, beginning of year	575.5	304.0	254.3
Cash and equivalents, end of year	$634.0	$575.5	$304.0

NOTES TO CONSOLIDATED FINANCIAL STATEMENTS

Note 1 (In Part): Summary of Significant Accounting Policies

Cash and Equivalents

Cash and equivalents represent cash and short-term, highly liquid investments with original maturities of three months or less. The carrying amounts reflected in the consolidated balance sheet for cash and cash equivalents approximate fair value due to the short maturities.

6.62

NUCOR CORPORATION (DEC)

Consolidated Balance Sheets

	2003	2002
Current assets		
Cash and short-term investments	$ 350,332,243	$ 219,004,868
Accounts receivable	572,479,237	483,607,972
Inventories	560,395,527	588,989,548
Other current assets	137,352,901	123,759,260
Total current assets	$1,620,559,908	$1,415,361,648

Consolidated Statements of Cash Flows

	2003	2002	2001
Increase (decrease) in cash and short-term investments	$131,327,375	$(243,343,679)	$ (28,227,732)
Cash and short-term investments—beginning of year	219,004,868	462,348,547	490,576,279
Cash and short-term investments—end of year	$350,332,243	$ 219,004,868	$462,348,547

NOTES TO CONSOLIDATED FINANCIAL STATEMENTS

1 (In Part): Summary of Significant Accounting Policies

Cash and Short-Term Investments

Short-term investments are recorded at cost plus accrued interest, which approximates market, and have original maturities of three months or less at the date of purchase. Cash and short-term investments are maintained primarily with a few high-credit quality financial institutions.

6.63

OWENS-ILLINOIS, INC. (DEC)

Consolidated Balance Sheets

(Millions of dollars)	2003	2002
Current assets		
Cash, including time deposits of $85.2 ($38.6 in 2002)	$ 163.4	$ 126.4
Short-term investments	26.8	17.6
Receivables, less allowances of $52.0 ($62.5 in 2002) for losses and discounts	769.7	701.9
Inventories	1,010.1	893.5
Prepaid expenses	151.8	147.8
Total current assets	$2,121.8	$1,887.2

Consolidated Cash Flows

(Millions of dollars)	2003	2002	2001
Increase (decrease) in cash	$ 37.0	$ (29.2)	$ (74.1)
Cash at beginning of year	126.4	155.6	229.7
Cash at end of year	$163.4	$126.4	$155.6

NOTES TO CONSOLIDATED FINANCIAL STATEMENTS

1 (In Part): Significant Accounting Policies

Cash

The Company defines "cash" as cash and time deposits with maturities of three months or less when purchased. Outstanding checks in excess of funds on deposit are included in accounts payable.

6.64

SPEIZMAN INDUSTRIES, INC. (JUN)

Consolidated Balance Sheets

	2003	2002
Current assets		
Cash and cash equivalents	$ 217,000	$ 970,000
Accounts receivable	12,074,000	10,144,000
Inventories	11,329,000	13,542,000
Income tax refund	—	523,000
Deferred tax asset, current	1,432,000	1,773,000
Prepaid expenses and other current assets	964,000	1,004,000
Total current assets	$26,016,000	$27,956,000

Consolidated Statements of Cash Flows

	2003	2002	2001
Net increase (decrease) in cash and cash equivalents	$(753,000)	$970,000	$(714,000)
Cash and cash equivalents, at beginning of year	970,000	—	714,000
Cash and cash equivalents, at end of year	$ 217,000	$970,000	$ —

NOTES TO CONSOLIDATED FINANCIAL STATEMENTS

Summary of Significant Accounting Policies (In Part)

Cash and Cash Equivalents

For purposes of the statements of cash flows, the Company considers all highly liquid debt instruments with an original maturity of three months or less to be cash equivalents. The carrying amount of cash equivalents approximates fair value due to the short-term maturity of these instruments.

Section 7: Independent Auditors' Report

PRESENTATION IN ANNUAL REPORT

7.01 This section reviews the format and content of Independent Auditors' Reports appearing in the annual reports of the 600 survey companies. Statement on Auditing Standards (SAS) No. 58, *Reports on Audited Financial Statements*, and its amendments, applies to auditors' reports issued in connection with audits of historical financial statements that are intended to present financial position, results of operations, and cash flows in conformity with generally accepted accounting principles.

7.02 Commencing with auditors' reports issued or reissued on or after May 24, 2004, the format and content of independent auditors' reports appearing in the annual reports of public companies are determined by the auditing standards set by the Public Company Accounting Oversight Board (PCAOB). The Sarbanes-Oxley Act of 2002 established the PCAOB. The PCAOB is appointed by the Securities and Exchange Commission (SEC), and provides oversight for auditors of public companies. Section 103(a) of the Sarbanes-Oxley Act authorized the PCAOB to establish auditing and related professional practice standards to be used by public accounting firms registered with the PCAOB. PCAOB Rule 3100, *Compliance With Auditing and Related Professional Practice Standards*, requires auditors to comply with all applicable auditing and related professional practice standards of the PCAOB. On an initial, transitional basis, PCAOB has adopted as interim standards the generally accepted auditing standards described in the American Institute of Certified Public Accountants' (AICPA) Auditing Standards Board's SAS No. 95, *Generally Accepted Auditing Standards*, in existence on April 16, 2003, to the extent not superseded or amended by the PCAOB.

7.03 Table 7-1 shows where, in relation to the financial statements and notes thereto, the Independent Auditors' Reports were presented in the annual reports to stockholders.

7.04

TABLE 7-1: PRESENTATION IN ANNUAL REPORT

	2003	2002	2001	2000
Precedes financial statements and notes	354	343	309	296
Follows financial statements and notes	245	250	283	294
Between financial statements and notes	1	6	4	5
Other	—	1	4	5
Total Companies	**600**	**600**	**600**	**600**

TITLE

7.05 Paragraph 8a of *SAS No. 58* states that the title of an auditors' report should include the word *independent*.

7.06 All the titles of auditors' reports presented in the annual reports by the survey companies included the words *independent* and *report*. 546 titles identified the auditors as auditors, 15 as accountants, 17 as public accountants, and 19 as certified public accountants.

ADDRESSEE

7.07 Paragraph 9 of *SAS No. 58* states:

The report may be addressed to the Company whose financial statements are being audited or to its board of directors or stockholders. A report on the financial statements of an unincorporated entity should be addressed as circumstances dictate, for example, to the partners, to the general partner, or to the proprietor. Occasionally, an auditor is retained to audit the financial statements of a Company that is not his client; in such a case, the report is customarily addressed to the client and not to the directors or stockholders of the Company whose financial statements are being audited.

7.08 Table 7-2 summarizes the addressee mentioned in the auditors' reports of the survey companies.

7.09

TABLE 7-2: ADDRESSEE OF AUDITORS' REPORTS

	2003	2002	2001	2000
Board of Directors and Stockholders	509	500	462	468
Board of Directors	49	53	43	40
Stockholders	28	31	43	45
Company	8	10	47	42
Other or no addressee	6	6	5	5
Total Companies	**600**	**600**	**600**	**600**

AUDITORS' STANDARD REPORT

7.10 Paragraph 8 of *SAS No. 58* presents examples of auditors' standard reports for single-year financial statements and for comparative two-year financial statements. The examples presented in paragraph 8 of *SAS No. 58*, as amended by SAS No. 93, *Omnibus Statement on Auditing Standards—2000*, follow:

INDEPENDENT AUDITORS' REPORT

We have audited the accompanying balance sheet of X Company as of December 31, 20XX, and the related statements of income, retained earnings, and cash flows for the year then ended. These financial statements are the responsibility of the Company's management. Our responsibility is to express an opinion on these financial statements based on our audit.

We conducted our audit in accordance with auditing standards generally accepted in the United States of America. Those standards require that we plan and perform the audit to obtain reasonable assurance about whether the financial statements are free of material misstatement. An audit includes examining, on a test basis, evidence supporting the amounts and disclosures in the financial statements. An audit also includes assessing the accounting principles used and significant estimates made by management, as well as evaluating the overall financial statement presentation. We believe that our audit provides a reasonable basis for our opinion.

In our opinion, the financial statements referred to above present fairly, in all material respects, the financial position of X Company as of [at] December 31, 20XX, and the results of its operations and its cash flows for the year then ended in conformity with accounting principles generally accepted in the United States of America.

INDEPENDENT AUDITORS' REPORT

We have audited the accompanying balance sheet of X Company as of December 31, 20X2 and 20X1, and the related statements of income, retained earnings, and cash flows for the years then ended. These financial statements are the responsibility of the Company's management. Our responsibility is to express an opinion on these financial statements based on our audits.

We conducted our audits in accordance with auditing standards generally accepted in the United States of America. Those standards require that we plan and perform the audit to obtain reasonable assurance about whether the financial statements are free of material misstatement. An audit includes examining, on a test basis, evidence supporting the amounts and disclosures in the financial statements. An audit also includes assessing the accounting principles used and significant estimates made by management, as well as evaluating the overall financial statement presentation. We believe that our audits provide a reasonable basis for our opinion.

In our opinion, the financial statements referred to above present fairly, in all material respects, the financial position of X Company as of [at] December 31, 20X2 and 20X1, and the results of its operations and its cash flows for the years then ended in conformity with accounting principles generally accepted in the United States of America.

7.11 Most of the survey companies present a balance sheet for 2 years and the other basic financial statements for 3 years. Appropriate wording in this situation is stated in footnote 7 to paragraph 8 of *SAS No. 58*.

7.12 As permitted by Statement of Financial Accounting Standards No. 130, *Reporting Comprehensive Income*, 92 survey companies reported components of comprehensive income in either a separate financial statement or a combined statement of income and comprehensive income. Alternatively, *SFAS No. 130* allows components of comprehensive income to be reported in a statement of stockholders' equity. Although a Company may include the term "comprehensive income" in the title of the statement in which it is presented, *SFAS No. 130* does not require the use of the term in a Company's financial statements. *SFAS No. 130* acknowledges the use of equivalent terms. Standard auditors' reports for each situation follow.

Statement of Comprehensive Income

7.13

INDEPENDENT AUDITORS' REPORT

The Board of Directors
Swift Transportation Co., Inc.

We have audited the accompanying consolidated balance sheets of Swift Transportation Co., Inc. and subsidiaries as of December 31, 2003 and 2002, and the related consolidated statements of earnings, comprehensive income, stockholders' equity and cash flows for each of the years in the three-year period ended December 31, 2003. These consolidated financial statements are the responsibility of the Company's management. Our responsibility is to express an opinion on these consolidated financial statements based on our audits.

We conducted our audits in accordance with auditing standards generally accepted in the United States of America. Those standards require that we plan and perform the audit to obtain reasonable assurance about whether the financial statements are free of material misstatement. An audit includes, examining, on a test basis, evidence supporting the amounts and disclosures in the financial statements. An audit also includes assessing the accounting principles used and significant estimates made by management, as well as evaluating the overall financial statement presentation. We believe that our audits provide a reasonable basis for our opinion.

In our opinion, the consolidated financial statements referred to above present fairly, in all material respects, the financial position of Swift Transportation Co., Inc. and subsidiaries as of December 31, 2003 and 2002, and the results of their operations and their cash flows for each of the years in the three-year period ended December 31, 2003, in conformity with accounting principles generally accepted in the United States of America.

Statement of Operations and Comprehensive Income

7.14

REPORT OF INDEPENDENT AUDITORS

To the Stockholders of
Arden Group. Inc.

In our opinion, the accompanying consolidated balance sheets and the related consolidated statements of operations and comprehensive income, stockholders' equity and cash flows, present fairly, in all material respects, the financial position of Arden Group, Inc. and its subsidiaries at January 3, 2004 and December 28, 2002 and the results of their operations and their cash flows for each of the three years in the period ended January 3, 2004 in conformity with accounting principles generally accepted in the United States of America. These financial statements are the responsibility of the Company's management; our responsibility is to express an opinion on these financial statements based on our audits. We conducted our audits of these statements in accordance with auditing standards generally accepted in the United States of America, which require that we plan and perform the audit to obtain reasonable assurance about whether the financial statements are free of material misstatement. An audit includes examining, on a test basis, evidence supporting the amounts and disclosures in the financial statements, assessing the accounting principles used and significant estimates made by management, and evaluating the overall financial statement presentation. We believe that our audits provide a reasonable basis for our opinion.

Statement of Changes in Shareholders' Equity

7.15

INDEPENDENT AUDITORS' REPORT

The Board of Directors and Stockholders
The Home Depot, Inc.

We have audited the accompanying Consolidated Balance Sheets of The Home Depot, Inc. and subsidiaries as of February 1, 2004 and February 2, 2003 and the related Consolidated Statements of Earnings, Stockholders' Equity and Comprehensive Income, and Cash Flows for each of the fiscal years in the three-year period ended February 1, 2004. These Consolidated Financial Statements are the responsibility of the Company's management. Our responsibility is to express an opinion on these Consolidated Financial Statements based on our audits.

We conducted our audits in accordance with auditing standards generally accepted in the United States of America. Those standards require that we plan and perform the audit to obtain reasonable assurance about whether the financial statements are free of material misstatement. An audit includes examining, on a test basis, evidence supporting the amounts and disclosures in the financial statements. An audit also includes assessing the accounting principles used and significant estimates made by management, as well as evaluating the overall financial statement presentation. We believe that our audits provide a reasonable basis for our opinion.

In our opinion, the Consolidated Financial Statements referred to above present fairly, in all material respects, the financial position of The Home Depot, Inc. and subsidiaries as of February 1, 2004 and February 2, 2003, and the results of their operations and their cash flows for each of the years in the three-year period ended February 1, 2004, in conformity with accounting principles generally accepted in the United States of America.

As discussed in Note 1 to the Consolidated Financial Statements, effective February 3, 2003, the Company changed its method of accounting for cash consideration received from a vendor to conform to Emerging Issues Task Force No. 02-16 and adopted the fair value method of recording stock-based compensation expense in accordance with Statement of Financial Accounting Standards No. 123.

AUDITORS' STANDARD REPORT OF A PUBLIC COMPANY

7.16 For audits of public companies (i.e., issuers as defined by the Sarbanes-Oxley Act of 2002, and other entities when prescribed by the rules of the SEC), PCAOB Auditing Standard (AS) No. 1, *References in Auditors' Reports to the Standards of the Public Company Accounting Oversight Board*, directs auditors to state that the engagement was conducted in accordance with "the standards of the Public Company Accounting Oversight Board (United States)" whenever the auditor has performed the engagement in accordance with the PCAOB's standards. *AS No. 1* is effective for auditors' reports issued or reissued after May 24, 2004. In addition, the PCAOB adopted as interim standards the generally accepted auditing standards of the AICPA as they existed on April 16, 2003. Consequently, reference to "the standards of the Public Company Accounting Oversight Board" with respect to audits performed prior to the effective date of this standard is equivalent to the previously required reference to generally accepted auditing standards. Accordingly, upon adoption of *AS No. 1*, reference to "generally accepted auditing standards" is no longer appropriate or necessary. *AS No. 1* did not yet apply to any of the company annual reports surveyed in this edition.

7.17 An example of a standard independent registered auditor's report presented in the Appendix to *AS No. 1* follows.

*REPORT OF INDEPENDENT REGISTERED
PUBLIC ACCOUNTING FIRM*

We have audited the accompanying balance sheets of X Company as of December 31, 20X3 and 20X2, and related statements of operations, stockholders' equity, and cash flows for each of the three years in the period ended December 31, 20X3. These financial statements are the responsibility of the Company's management. Our responsibility is to express an opinion on these financial statements based on our audits.

We conducted our audits in accordance with the standards of the Public Company Accounting Oversight Board (United States). Those standards require that we plan and perform the audit to obtain reasonable assurance about whether the financial statements are free of material misstatement. An audit includes examining, on a test basis, evidence supporting the amounts and disclosures in the financial statements. An audit also includes assessing the accounting principles used and significant estimates made by management, as well as evaluating the overall financial statement presentation. We believe that our audits provide a reasonable basis for our opinion.

In our opinion, the financial statements referred to above present fairly, in all material respects, the financial position of the company as of December 31, 20X3 and 20X2, and the results of its operations and its cash flows for each of the three years in the period ended December 31, 20X3, in conformity with U.S. generally accepted accounting principles.

REFERENCE TO REPORT OF OTHER AUDITORS

7.18 When the opinion of a principal auditor is based in part on the report of another auditor, SAS No. 1, section 543, *Part of Audit Performed by Other Independent Auditors*, as amended by SAS No. 64, *Omnibus Statement on Auditing Standards—1990*, provides guidance to the principal auditor. Paragraph 7 of *section 543* states:

> When the principal auditor decides that he will make reference to the audit of the other auditor, his report should indicate clearly, in both the introductory, scope and opinion paragraphs, the division of responsibility as between that portion of the financial statements covered by his own audit and that covered by the audit of the other auditor. The report should disclose the magnitude of the portion of the financial statements audited by the other auditor. This may be done by stating the dollar amounts or percentages of one or more of the following: total assets, total revenues, or other appropriate criteria, whichever most clearly reveals the portion of the financial statements audited by the other auditor. The other auditor may be named but only with his express permission and provided his report is presented together with that of the principal auditor.

7.19 Paragraphs 12 and 13 of *SAS No. 58* reaffirm the requirements of *section 543*. Paragraph 13 presents an example of an auditors' report referring to the report of other auditors.

7.20 The auditors' report for 10 survey companies made reference to the report of other auditors. The reference to other auditors in 2 of these reports related to prior year financial statements. Examples of auditors' reports making reference to reports of other auditors follow.

7.21

INDEPENDENT AUDITORS' REPORT

To the Stockholders and Board of Directors of
Coherent, Inc.

We have audited the accompanying consolidated balance sheets of Coherent, Inc. and subsidiaries as of September 30, 2003 and 2002, and the related consolidated statements of operations, stockholders' equity, and cash flows for each of the three years in the period ended September 30, 2003. Our audits also included the consolidated financial statement schedule listed in Item 15(a)2. These financial statements and the financial statement schedule are the responsibility of Coherent's management. Our responsibility is to express an opinion on these financial statements and the financial statement schedule based on our audits. We did not audit the consolidated financial statements of Lambda Physik AG and subsidiaries (Lambda Physik) for the years ended September 30, 2003, 2002 and 2001, which statements reflect total assets constituting 22% and 19% in 2003 and 2002 and total revenues constituting 20%, 23% and 26% in 2003, 2002 and 2001, respectively, of the related consolidated totals. Those statements were audited by other auditors whose report has been furnished to us, and our opinion, insofar as it relates to the amounts included for Lambda Physik for the years ended September 30, 2003, 2002 and 2001, is based solely on the report of such other auditors.

We conducted our audits in accordance with auditing standards generally accepted in the United States of America. Those standards require that we plan and perform the audit to obtain reasonable assurance about whether the financial statements are free of material misstatement. An audit includes examining, on a test basis, evidence supporting the amounts and disclosures in the financial statements. An audit also includes assessing the accounting principles used and significant estimates made by management, as well as evaluating the overall financial statement presentation. We believe that our audits and the report of the other auditors provide a reasonable basis for our opinion.

In our opinion, based on our audits and the report of the other auditors, such consolidated financial statements present fairly, in all material respects, the financial position of Coherent, Inc. and subsidiaries as of September 30, 2003 and 2002, and the results of their operations and their cash flows for each of the three years in the period ended September 30, 2003 in conformity with accounting principles generally accepted in the United States of America. Also, in our opinion, based on our audits and the report of the other auditors, such financial statement schedule, when considered in relation to the basic consolidated financial statements taken as a whole, presents fairly in all material respects the information set therein.

7.22

REPORT OF INDEPENDENT PUBLIC ACCOUNTANTS

To the Stockholders and Board of Directors of
Waxman Industries, Inc.

We have audited the accompanying consolidated balance sheet of Waxman Industries, Inc. (a Delaware corporation) and Subsidiaries (the Company) as of June 30, 2003 and 2002, and the related consolidated statement of operations, stockholders' equity and cash flows for the years ended June 30, 2003, 2002 and 2001. These consolidated financial statements are the responsibility of the Company's management. Our responsibility is to express an opinion on these consolidated financial statements based on our audits. We did not audit the financial statements of TWI, International Taiwan, Inc. and CWI International China, Ltd. two wholly owned subsidiaries for 2003 or 2002, which statements reflect total assets of $13,578,000 and $13,895,000 as of June 30, 2003 and 2002, respectively, and total revenues of $23,223,000 and $26,832,000, respectively, for the years then ended. Those statements were audited by other auditors whose reports have been furnished to us, and our opinion, insofar as it relates to the amounts included for TWI, International Taiwan and CWI International China, Ltd., is based solely on the report of the other auditors.

We conducted our audit in accordance with auditing standards generally accepted in the United States. Those standards require that we plan and perform the audit to obtain reasonable assurance about whether the financial statements are free of material misstatement. An audit includes examining, on a test basis, evidence supporting the amounts and disclosures in the financial statements. An audit also includes assessing the accounting principles used and significant estimates made by management, as well as evaluating the overall financial statement presentation. We believe that our audits provide a reasonable basis for our opinion.

In our opinion, based on our audits and the reports of other auditors, the consolidated financial statements referred to above present fairly, in all material respects, the financial position of Waxman Industries, Inc. and Subsidiaries as of June 30, 2003 and 2002, and the results of their operations and their cash flows for the three years ended June 30, 2003, in conformity with accounting principles generally accepted in the United States.

UNCERTAINTIES

7.23 Effective for auditors' reports issued or reissued on or after February 29, 1996, SAS No. 79, *Amendment to Auditing Standards No. 58*, amends *SAS No. 58* to eliminate the requirement for an explanatory paragraph for uncertainties as defined in paragraphs 29 and 30 of amended *SAS No. 58*. *SAS No. 79* does not apply to uncertainties related to going concern situations for which SAS No. 59, *The Auditor's Consideration of an Entity's Ability to Continue as a Going Concern*, as amended, and SAS No. 85, *Management Representations*, provide guidance.

7.24 Table 7-3 summarizes the nature of uncertainties for which an explanatory paragraph was included in an auditors' report. Examples of explanatory language for a going concern situation follow.

7.25

TABLE 7-3: UNCERTAINTIES

	2003	2002	2001	2000
Going concern	11	20	21	17
Other	2	8	3	2
Total Uncertainties	**13**	**28**	**24**	**19**
Total Companies	**12**	**26**	**24**	**19**

7.26

REPORT OF INDEPENDENT AUDITORS

To the Board of Directors and Stockholders of
Acterna Corporation

In our opinion, the accompanying consolidated balance sheets and the related consolidated statements of operations, of changes in stockholders deficit, and of cash flows present fairly, in all material respects, the financial position of Acterna Corporation and its subsidiaries at March 31, 2003 and March 31, 2002, and the results of their operations and their cash flows for each of the three years in the period ended March 31, 2003 in conformity with accounting principles generally accepted in the United States of America. These financial statements are the responsibility of the Company's management; our responsibility is to express an opinion on these financial statements based on our audits. We conducted our audits of these statements in accordance with auditing standards generally accepted in the United States of America, which require that we plan and perform the audit to obtain reasonable assurance about whether the financial statements are free of material misstatement. An audit includes examining, on a test basis, evidence supporting the amounts and disclosures in the financial statements, assessing the accounting principles used and significant estimates made by management, and evaluating the overall financial statement presentation. We believe that our audits provide a reasonable basis for our opinion.

The accompanying financial statements have been prepared assuming that the Company will continue as a going concern. As discussed in Note B to the consolidated financial statements on May 6, 2003, Acterna Corporation and its United States subsidiaries filed voluntary petitions for reorganization under Chapter 11 of the United States Bankruptcy Code. As discussed in Note B to the consolidated financial statements, the Company has defaulted on its interest payments and debt covenants. These conditions raise substantial doubt about its ability to continue as a going concern. Management's plans in regard to these matters are also described in Note B. The financial statements do not include any adjustments that might result from the outcome of this uncertainty.

NOTES TO CONSOLIDATED FINANCIAL STATEMENTS

B. Voluntary Bankruptcy Filing

On May 6, 2003, (the "Filing Date") Acterna Corporation and its seven United States subsidiaries and affiliates ("the Debtors") filed voluntary petitions for reorganization under Chapter 11 of the United States Bankruptcy Code ("Chapter 11") in the United States Bankruptcy Court for the Southern District of New York (the "Bankruptcy Court") (the "Filing"). The Chapter 11 cases were consolidated for the administrative purpose of joint administration and were assigned case number 03–12837 (BRL) through 03–12843 (BRL) (the "Chapter 11 Cases"). The Company's non-U.S. subsidiaries were not included in the filing.

The filing was made in response to an ongoing decline in the communications test marketplace, which has resulted in significant operating losses and the inability of the Company to perform in accordance with its financial covenants under the Senior Secured Credit Facility, its Senior Subordinated Notes, the Convertible Notes and the Company's other debt obligations.

Under Chapter 11, the Debtors are operating their businesses as debtors-in-possession under court protection from their creditors and claimants and intend to use Chapter 11 to substantially reduce their debt obligations and implement a plan of reorganization. As a debtor-in-possession, the Debtors may not engage in any transactions outside the ordinary course of business without the approval of the Bankruptcy Court, after notice and an opportunity for a hearing.

The Company concluded, after evaluating all of its alternatives, that a federal court-supervised Chapter 11 filing provides the best forum available to restructure its debt obligations.

As a consequence of the Filing, pending litigation against the Debtors for pre-petition matters is generally stayed (subject to certain exceptions in the case of governmental authorities), and no party may take action to realize its pre-petition claims except pursuant to an order of the Bankruptcy Court, including all attempts to collect claims or enforce liens that arose prior to the commencement of the Company's Filing. Also, the debtor may assume or reject pre-petition executory contracts and unexpired leases pursuant to section 365 of the Bankruptcy Code and other parties to executory contracts or unexpired leases being rejected may assert rejection damage claims as permitted thereunder.

The Company intends to address its plan for continued operations and all other pre-petition claims in a plan of reorganization. Prior to the Filing Date, the Company negotiated the salient terms of a plan of reorganization with certain key lenders under the Senior Secured Credit Facility. The Company's current proposal for the plan of reorganization reflects:

- the conversion of the pre-petition debt held by the lenders under the Senior Secured Credit Facility into a (i) secured $75 million note and a EUR 83 million term loan and (ii) 100% of the equity of the reorganized Acterna, subject to dilution in connection with the warrants described below and a management incentive plan;
- the allocation of warrants to purchase approximately 5% of the new common stock of the reorganized Acterna to the holders of the Senior Secured Convertible Notes and the Senior Subordinated Notes in exchange for the cancellation of these Notes (these warrants will be substantially "out of the money" at the time of issuance and may never have any value within their term);
- partial payments to general unsecured creditors, subject to certain conditions; and
- no recovery with respect to the holders of the common stock.

There can be no assurance, however, that the Company's proposal will be implemented, or that the Company's creditors will not propose substantial changes to the Company's proposal.

The Debtors have received approval from the Bankruptcy Court to pay or otherwise honor certain of its pre-petition obligations in the ordinary course of business, including employee wages and benefits, customer programs, shipping charges and a limited amount of claims of essential trade creditors.

As provided by the Bankruptcy Code, the Debtors have the exclusive right to propose a plan of reorganization for a 120-day period following the Filing Date. The Debtors have the right to file an extension of their exclusivity period during which to file a plan of reorganization, but it is currently the Company's intent to file within the 120-day period. On May 20, 2003, the office of the United States Trustee appointed a creditors' committee to represent the interests of unsecured creditors. This committee will have the right to be heard on all matters that come before the Bankruptcy Court, and is likely to play an important role in the Chapter 11 Cases. The Debtors are required to bear certain of the costs incurred by the creditors' committee, including those of their counsel and financial advisors.

On June 24, 2003 the Bankruptcy Court entered an order establishing a bar date of July 31, 2003 for claims of general unsecured creditors. At this time, it is not possible to estimate the value of the claims that will ultimately be allowed by the Bankruptcy Court, due to the uncertainties of the Chapter 11 process.

Substantially all of the Debtors' pre-petition debt is in default due to the failure to meet debt covenants and pay interest on the Senior Secured Credit Facility on March 31, 2003. The accompanying Consolidated Balance Sheets as of March 31, 2003 reflect the classification of the Debtors' pre-petition debt to current because of this default. The Company has certain debt that is owed by foreign subsidiaries of the Company who are not part of the Chapter 11 filing and to the extent that this debt has a long term portion it is shown as such.

The Debtors have entered into a debtor-in-possession credit facility (the "DIP" facility) with certain members of its pre-petition bank group, for loans of up to $30 million, which has been approved by the U.S. bankruptcy court. The DIP facility is a borrowing base facility that fluctuates based on the cash on hand, amount of eligible accounts receivable and inventory. Upon the successful sale of certain non-core assets of the Company, an additional amount under the DIP facility would become available to the Debtors as well. The DIP facility also provides a sub-facility for letters of credit.

The accompanying Consolidated Financial Statements have not been prepared in accordance with Statement of Position No. 90-7 "Financial Reporting by Entities in Reorganization Under the Bankruptcy Code", ("SOP 90-7") promulgated by the American Institute of Certified Public Accountants, as the Filing Date occurred subsequent to the Company's fiscal year end. Future statements will be prepared in accordance with SOP 90-7 which requires that financial statements of debtors-in-possession be prepared on a going concern basis, which contemplates continuity of operations, realization of assets and liquidation of liabilities in the ordinary course of business. However, as a result of the Filing, the realization of certain Debtors' assets and the liquidation of certain Debtors' liabilities are subject to uncertainty. Upon implementation of SOP 90-7, the Debtors will reclassify substantially all pre-Filing liabilities to liabilities subject to compromise. This reclassification will impact the presentation of the liabilities shown on the Company's Consolidated Balance Sheet. While operating as debtors-in-possession, the Debtors may sell or otherwise dispose of assets and liquidate or settle liabilities for amounts other than those reflected in the Consolidated Financial Statements. Further, a plan of reorganization could materially change the amounts and classifications reported in the Consolidated Financial Statements, which do not currently give effect to any adjustments to the carrying value or classification of assets or liabilities that might be necessary as a consequence of a plan of reorganization.

The Company has recorded significant losses from operations and has seen a substantial reduction in revenues and operations as a result of the economic downturn and in particular the downturn within the telecommunications sector and related industries. Consequently, the Company has undertaken several restructurings during the year ended March 31, 2003 to align its cost structures and its revenues.

It is difficult to measure precisely how Chapter 11 will impact the Company's overall financial performance. There are certain added costs that will be directly attributable to operating under the Bankruptcy Code, including, but not limited to, the following: reorganization expenses, and legal, financial, and consulting fees incurred by the Company and the creditors' committee. There are numerous other indirect costs to manage the Company's Chapter 11 proceedings such as: management time devoted to Chapter 11 matters, added cost of debt capital, added costs of general business insurance, including directors and officers liability insurance, cost of restructuring professionals, and lost business and acquisition opportunities due to complexities of operating under Chapter 11. Furthermore, the Company cannot provide any assurance as to the likelihood of its plan of reorganization being accepted by the Bankruptcy Court or the creditor's committee, nor can the Company provide assurance that the plan will be successful in the event of such acceptance. All of these factors raise substantial doubt as to whether the Company can continue as a going concern.

7.27

REPORT OF INDEPENDENT AUDITORS

To the Shareholders and Board of Directors of Exide Technologies

In our opinion, the consolidated financial statements listed in the accompanying index present fairly, in all material respects, the financial position of Exide Technologies and its subsidiaries ("Exide") at March 31, 2003 and 2002, and the results of their operations and their cash flows for each of the three years in the period ended March 31, 2003 in conformity with accounting principles generally accepted in the

United States of America. In addition, in our opinion, the financial statement schedule listed in the accompanying index presents fairly, in all material respects, the information set forth therein when read in conjunction with the related consolidated financial statements. These financial statements and financial statement schedule are the responsibility of Exide's management; our responsibility is to express an opinion on these financial statements and financial statement schedule based on our audits. We conducted our audits of these statements in accordance with auditing standards generally accepted in the United States of America, which require that we plan and perform the audit to obtain reasonable assurance about whether the financial statements are free of material misstatement. An audit includes examining, on a test basis, evidence supporting the amounts and disclosures in the financial statements, assessing the accounting principles and significant estimates made by management, and evaluating the overall financial statement presentation. We believe that our audits provide a reasonable basis for our opinion.

The accompanying consolidated financial statements have been prepared assuming Exide will continue as a going concern, which contemplates continuity of Exide's operations and realization of its assets and payment of its liabilities in the ordinary course of business. As more fully described in the notes to the consolidated financial statements, on April 15, 2002, Exide filed a voluntary petition of reorganization under Chapter 11 of the United States Bankruptcy Code. The uncertainties inherent in the bankruptcy process and Exide's recurring losses from operations raise substantial doubt about Exide's ability to continue as a going concern. Exide is currently operating its business as a Debtor-in-Possession under the jurisdiction of the Bankruptcy Court, and continuation of Exide as a going concern is contingent upon, among other things, the confirmation of a Plan of Reorganization, Exide's ability to comply with all debt covenants under the existing debtor-in-possession and other ongoing financing agreements, and Exide's ability to generate sufficient cash from operations and obtain financing sources to meet its future obligations. The consolidated financial statements do not include any adjustments to reflect the possible future effects on the recoverability and classification of assets or the amount and classification of liabilities that may result from the outcome of these uncertainties.

As discussed in Notes 3, 5 and 8 to the consolidated financial statements, on April 1, 2001, Exide adopted Statement of Financial Accounting Standards (SFAS) No. 133, "Accounting for Derivative Instruments and Hedging Activities", as amended, SFAS No. 141, "Business Combinations" and SFAS No. 142, "Goodwill and Other Intangible Assets."

NOTES TO CONSOLIDATED FINANCIAL STATEMENTS

1) Basis of Presentation

The consolidated financial statements include the accounts of Exide Technologies (referred together with its subsidiaries, unless the context requires otherwise, as "Exide" or the "Company") and all of its majority-owned subsidiaries.

The accompanying Consolidated Financial Statements as of March 31, 2003 and for the year then ended have been prepared in accordance with Statement of Position 90-7 ("SOP 90-7"), "Financial Reporting by Entities in Reorganization under the Bankruptcy Code" (see Note 2). Accordingly, all pre-petition liabilities subject to compromise have been segregated in the consolidated balance sheet as of March 31, 2003, and classified as Liabilities Subject To Compromise, at the estimated amount of allowable claims. Liabilities not subject to compromise are separately classified. Additional pre-petition claims (liabilities subject to compromise) may arise due to the rejection of executory contracts or unexpired leases, or as a result of the allowance of contingent or disputed claims. Revenues, expenses, realized gains and losses and provision for losses resulting from the reorganization are reported separately as Reorganization items, net, in the consolidated statements of operations. However, because the Chapter 11 filing occurred subsequent to March 31, 2002, the accompanying Consolidated Financial Statements as of March 31, 2002, and for the fiscal years ended March 31, 2002 and 2001, have not been prepared in accordance with SOP 90-7, and may lack comparability to that extent.

These Consolidated Financial Statements have been prepared on a going concern basis, which assumes continuity of operations and realization of assets and satisfaction of liabilities in the ordinary course of business. The ability of the Company to continue as a going concern is predicated upon, among other things, confirmation of a bankruptcy reorganization plan on a timely basis, compliance with the provisions of both the debtor-in-possession financing facility ("DIP Credit Facility") and other ongoing borrowing arrangements, the ability to generate cash flows from operations and, where necessary, obtaining financing sources sufficient to satisfy the Company's future obligations, as well as certain contingencies described in Note 17. Based upon business plans updated in June 2003, the Company obtained amendments to its existing financial covenants in order to maintain compliance during fiscal 2004. The Standstill Agreement and Fifth Amendment to the Credit and Guarantee Agreement ("Standstill Agreement") expires on December 18, 2003 and the DIP Credit Facility expires 30 days prior to the expiration of the Standstill Agreement, (but no later, if the Standstill Agreement is extended, than February 15, 2004). If the Debtors do not have a plan of reorganization confirmed by the Bankruptcy Court before the expiration of these agreements, the Company will have to request extensions of such agreements. There can be no assurance that the Company will be able to have a plan confirmed by that time or obtain extensions. Failure to have a plan of reorganization confirmed by the Bankruptcy Court prior to the expiration of the Standstill Agreement or the DIP Credit Facility or to be able to obtain such extensions or failure to maintain compliance with the covenants in such agreements would result in an event of default which, absent cure within defined grace periods or obtaining appropriate waivers, would restrict the Company's access to funds necessary to maintain its operations and assist in funding of its reorganization plan. As a result of the Chapter 11 filing and consideration of various strategic alternatives, including possible asset sales, the Company would expect that any reorganization plan will result in material changes to the carrying amount of assets and liabilities in the Consolidated Financial Statements. The Consolidated Financial Statements do not, however, include adjustments, if any, to reflect the possible future effects on the recoverability and classification of recorded assets or the amounts and classifications of liabilities that may result from the outcome of these uncertainties.

Upon emergence from bankruptcy, the amounts reported in subsequent financial statements will materially change due to the restructuring of the Company's assets and liabilities as a result of any plan of reorganization and the application of the provisions of SOP 90-7 with respect to reporting upon emergence from Chapter 11 ("fresh start" accounting). Changes in accounting principles required under generally accepted accounting principles within twelve months of emerging from bankruptcy are required to be adopted at the date of emergence. Additionally, the Company may choose to make changes in accounting practices and policies at this time. For all these reasons, the financial statement for periods subsequent to emergence from Chapter 11 will not be comparable with those of prior periods.

2) Proceedings Under Chapter 11 of the Bankruptcy Code

On April 15, 2002 ("Petition Date"), Exide and three of its wholly-owned, U.S. subsidiaries (RBD Liquidation, LLC ("RBD"), Exide Delaware, LLC ("Exide Delaware") and Exide Illinois, Inc. ("Exide Illinois") filed voluntary petitions for reorganization under Chapter 11 of the federal bankruptcy laws ("Bankruptcy Code" or "Chapter 11") in the United States Bankruptcy Court for the District of Delaware ("Bankruptcy Court") under case numbers 02–11125 through 02–11128. On November 21, 2002, Refined Metals Corporation ("Refined") and Dixie Metals Company ("Dixie"), both wholly owned, non-operating subsidiaries of Exide, filed voluntary petitions for reorganization under Chapter 11 of the Bankruptcy Code in the Bankruptcy Court under case numbers 02–13449 and 02–13450. Refined and Dixie have no employees and negligible, if any, assets. RBD, Exide Delaware, Exide Illinois, Dixie and Refined, together with Exide are hereinafter referred to as the "Debtors." All of the foregoing cases are being jointly administered for procedural purposes before the Bankruptcy Court under case number 02–11125KJC.

The Debtors are currently operating their business as debtors-in-possession pursuant to the Bankruptcy Code.

The Company decided to file itself and certain of its subsidiaries for reorganization under Chapter 11, as it offered the most efficient alternative to restructure its balance sheet and access new working capital while continuing to operate in the ordinary course of business. The Company has a heavy debt burden, caused largely by a debt-financed acquisition strategy and the significant costs of integrating those acquisitions. Other factors leading to the reorganization included the impact of adverse economic conditions on the Company's markets, particularly telecommunications, ongoing competitive pressures and capital market volatility. These factors contributed to a loss of revenues and resulted in significant operating losses and negative cash flows, severely impacting the Company's financial condition and its ability to maintain compliance with debt covenants.

As debtors-in-possession under Chapter 11, the Debtors are authorized to continue to operate as an ongoing business, but may not engage in transactions outside the ordinary course of business without the approval of the Bankruptcy Court. The Company's operations outside of the U.S. are not included in the Chapter 11 proceedings. However, in connection with the Chapter 11 filing, the Company entered into a Standstill Agreement with its prepetition Senior Secured Global Credit Facility lenders, whereby those lenders have agreed to forbear collection of principal payments on foreign borrowings under the Senior Secured Global Credit Facility from non-Debtor subsidiaries until December 18, 2003, subject to earlier termination upon the occurrence of certain events. The principal events which could result in an early termination of the Standstill Agreement are:

1) non-payment of interest and principal obligations related to the European tranche of the Company's Senior Secured Global Credit Facility as and when due; 2) if any significant foreign subsidiaries commence any winding up or liquidation proceeding; 3) breach of financial and other customary negative covenants (as described with respect to the DIP Credit Facility); 4) breach of cross default provisions with respect to the European securitization agreement and 9.125% Senior Notes (Deutsche Mark denominated) agreement; and 5) breaches of representations and warranties. No such events have occurred as of March 31, 2003, or through the date of this Report.

On May 10, 2002, the Debtors received final Bankruptcy Court approval for $250,000 DIP Credit Facility. The DIP Credit Facility is being used to supplement cash flows from operations during the reorganization process including the payment of post-petition ordinary course trade and other payables, the payment of certain permitted pre-petition claims, working capital needs, letter of credit requirements and for other general corporate purposes.

Under Section 362 of the Bankruptcy Code, actions to collect pre-petition indebtedness from the Debtors, as well as most other pending pre-petition litigation, are stayed. Absent an order of the Bankruptcy Court, substantially all pre-petition liabilities are subject to settlement under a plan of reorganization to be approved by the Bankruptcy Court. As provided by the Bankruptcy Code, the Company initially had the exclusive right to solicit a plan of reorganization for 120 days. The Bankruptcy Court has extended this exclusivity period to August 7, 2003. The Company currently expects to file a plan of reorganization and related disclosure statement with the Bankruptcy Court by September 30, 2003, and plans to seek an appropriate extension of the exclusivity period from the Bankruptcy Court, if necessary. Although the Debtors expect to file a reorganization plan that provides for emergence from bankruptcy as a going concern, there can be no assurance that a reorganization plan will be proposed by the Debtors or confirmed by the Bankruptcy Court, or that any such plan will be successfully implemented.

Under the Bankruptcy Code, the Debtors may also assume or reject executory contracts, including lease obligations, subject to the approval of the Bankruptcy Court and certain other conditions. Parties affected by these rejections may file claims with the Bankruptcy Court in accordance with the reorganization process. Due to the timing of the Chapter 11 proceedings, the Company cannot currently estimate or anticipate what impact the rejection and subsequent claims of executory contracts may have on the reorganization process.

On June 14, 2002, the Company filed with the Bankruptcy Court schedules and statements of financial affairs setting forth, among other things, the assets and liabilities of the Debtors as shown by the Company's books and records on the Petition Date, subject to the assumptions contained in certain notes filed in connection therewith. All of the schedules are subject to further amendment or modification. The Bankruptcy Code provides for a claims reconciliation and resolution process. The Bankruptcy Court established April 23, 2003 as the deadline for submission of proofs of claim for general unsecured claims. A motion requesting a separate bar date for certain other claims has been filed. Pre-petition claims against the Debtors must be submitted to the Bankruptcy Court prior to the applicable bar date to be eligible to participate in any distribution of assets from the Debtors in connection with the plan of reorganization. Differences between amounts scheduled by the Debtors in filings with the Bankruptcy Court and claims by creditors will be investigated and resolved in connection with the claims resolution process. That process, however, has only recently commenced and given the number or creditors and claims filed, will take significant time to complete. As the ultimate number and amount of allowed claims is not presently known, and because any settlement terms of such allowed claims are subject to a confirmed plan of reorganization, the ultimate distribution with respect to allowed claims is not presently ascertainable.

The United States Trustee has appointed an unsecured creditors committee. The official committee and its legal representatives have a right to be heard on all matters that come before the Bankruptcy Court. The Bankruptcy Court determined that the United States Trustee should appoint an official committee of equity holders, which it has done. The Company has appealed the appointment of the equity holders committee to the United States Circuit Court of Appeals for the Third Circuit, where it is currently pending.

At this time, it is not possible to predict the effect of the Chapter 11 reorganization process on the Company's business, various creditors and security holders, or when it may be possible for the Debtors to emerge from Chapter 11. The Company's future results are dependent upon its confirming and implementing, on a timely basis, a plan of reorganization. The Company believes, however, that under any reorganization plan, the Company's common stock would likely be substantially, if not completely, diluted or cancelled as a result of the conversion of debt to equity or any other compromise of interests. Further, it is also likely that the Company's 10% senior notes and convertible senior subordinated notes will suffer substantial impairment.

The ultimate recovery, if any, by creditors, security holders and/or common shareholders will not be determined until confirmation of a plan of reorganization. No assurance can be given as to what value, if any, will be ascribed in the bankruptcy proceedings to each of these constituencies. Accordingly, Exide urges appropriate caution be exercised with respect to existing and future investments in any of these securities.

7.28

REPORT OF INDEPENDENT AUDITORS

Board of Directors
Trump Hotels & Casino Resorts, Inc.

We have audited the accompanying consolidated balance sheets of Trump Hotels & Casino Resorts, Inc. as of December 31, 2002 and 2003, and the related consolidated statements of operations, stockholders' equity and cash flows for the years then ended. Our audit also included the 2002 and 2003 financial statement schedule listed in the Index at Item 15(a). These financial statements and schedule are the responsibility of the Company's management. Our responsibility is to express an opinion on these financial statements and schedule based on our audits. The financial statements and schedule of Trump Hotels & Casino Resorts, Inc. for the year ended December 31, 2001 were audited by other auditors who have ceased operations. Those auditors expressed an unqualified opinion on those financial statements and schedule in their report dated March 13, 2002.

We conducted our audits in accordance with auditing standards generally accepted in the United States. Those standards require that we plan and perform the audit to obtain reasonable assurance about whether the financial statements are free of material misstatement. An audit includes examining, on a test basis, evidence supporting the amounts and disclosures in the financial statements. An audit also includes assessing the accounting principles used and significant estimates made by management, as well as evaluating the overall financial statement presentation. We believe that our audits provide a reasonable basis for our opinion.

In our opinion, the 2002 and 2003 financial statements referred to above present fairly, in all material respects, the consolidated financial position of Trump Hotels & Casino Resorts, Inc. at December 31, 2002 and 2003, and the consolidated results of its operations and its cash flows for the years then ended, in conformity with accounting principles generally accepted in the United States. Also in our opinion, the related financial statement schedule, when considered in relation to the basic financial statements taken as a whole, presents fairly in all material respects the information set forth therein.

The accompanying financial statements have been prepared assuming that the Company will continue as a going concern. As more fully described in Note 1, the Company has experienced increased competition, has incurred recurring operating losses and has a working capital deficit at December 31, 2003. The Company is working on various alternatives to improve the Company's financial resources which are also described in Note 1. Absent the successful completion of one of these alternatives, the Company's operating results will increasingly become uncertain. These conditions raise substantial doubt about the Company's ability to continue as a going concern; however, the financial statements do not include any adjustments to reflect the possible future effects on the recoverability and classification of assets or the amounts and classification of liabilities that may result from the outcome of this uncertainty.

January 31, 2004, except for Note 13
as to which the date is
February 12, 2004.

NOTES TO CONSOLIDATED FINANCIAL STATEMENTS

1) (In Part): Organization and Operations

The Company has incurred recurring operating losses which totaled $25.3 million, $12.0 million, and $87.3 million during the years ended December 31, 2001, 2002, and 2003, respectively and has a working capital deficit of $46.9 million at December 31, 2003. The recurring operating losses are primarily the result of substantial debt service obligations on outstanding indebtedness. In 2004, the Company's debt service obligation is approximately $225 million. Additionally, the Company has experienced increased competition and other challenges in its markets. Due to these factors, the Company has not been able to expand its operations or reinvest in the maintenance of its owned properties at desired levels. Furthermore, the Company does not currently have any short-term borrowing capacity available. Although the Company anticipates that it will have sufficient funds on hand to provide for the scheduled debt service obligations

on its outstanding indebtedness during 2004, there can be no assurances such funds will be available.

As a result of these factors, management has reviewed various financing alternatives. As discussed in Note 13, the Company announced that it has entered into an exclusivity agreement with DLJ Merchant Bankers III, L.P. ("DLJMB") in connection with a proposed $400 million equity investment by DLJMB to sponsor a comprehensive recapitalization of the Company. On the same date as the announcement of the Potential Recapitalization, certain credit agencies downgraded certain of the Company's indebtedness. The Potential Recapitalization is contingent upon a variety of factors. No assurances can be made that the Potential Recapitalization will occur, or if it does occur, that it will occur on terms acceptable to the Company to allow the Company to meet its obligations as they become due. Additionally, management has implemented programs to obtain cash flow savings and will continue to attempt to implement such programs in the upcoming year if the Potential Recapitalization does not occur. These programs include labor savings through increased automation of the Company's slot machine product on the gaming floor and the further reduction of planned capital expenditures and maintenance programs. However, there can be no assurances that these programs will be successful for any protracted period of time. Accordingly, the financial statements do not include any adjustments to reflect the possible future effects on the recoverability and classification of assets, or the amounts and classification of liabilities that may result from the outcome of this uncertainty or the comprehensive recapitalization.

13) Subsequent Event

On February 12, 2004, the Company announced that it has entered into an exclusivity agreement with DLJ Merchant Banking Partners III, L.P. ("DLJMB"), an affiliate of Credit Suisse First Boston ("CSFB"), in connection with a proposed $400 million equity investment by DLJMB to sponsor a comprehensive recapitalization of THCR. Consummation of such recapitalization is subject to a variety of conditions, as discussed below. DLJMB's proposed investment will be in the form of THCR's Common Stock and limited partnership units of THCR Holdings will, if consummated, result in a substantial deleveraging of THCR's balance sheet. DLJMB would also become the majority shareholder of THCR, with Donald J. Trump continuing as the Chairman of THCR's Board of Directors and a significant equity holder. The Potential Recapitalization, if consummated, is anticipated to, among other things, facilitate a large scale expansion of THCR's current properties. In connection with the Potential Recapitalization, THCR also intends to change its name to Trump International Corporation.

DLJMB's investment is contingent upon a number of factors, including (i) obtaining approvals from the casino gaming regulatory authorities, (ii) a restructuring of the TAC Notes ($1.3 billion outstanding at December 31, 2003) and the TCH Notes (approximately $491,842,000 outstanding at December 31, 2003) at a discount to the face amount of such notes, and (iii) agreeing upon a purchase price for THCR's Common Stock and THCR Holdings' limited partnership units with DLJMB.

Although the Company has had extensive discussions with DLJMB regarding the potential transaction, it has not entered into any definitive agreements with DLJMB or any other parties, including note holders, concerning the proposed DLJMB transaction or any other recapitalization (other than the exclusivity agreement with DLJMB and an agreement to pay DLJMB expenses in certain circumstances and a substantial fee if certain transactions occur within specified periods and DLJMB does not participate). There is no assurance that the terms of a definitive agreement concerning DLJMB's proposed investment in THCR will be reached between THCR and DLJMB, that THCR's debt will be restructured, or that any potential recapitalization will be consummated. Furthermore, the impact of the proposed recapitalization on existing security holders is uncertain. As noted above, the Potential Recapitalization is conditioned upon the holders of the TAC Notes and the TCH Notes agreeing to a reduction in the face amount of their notes.

LACK OF CONSISTENCY

7.29 Table 7-4 summarizes the accounting changes for which auditors expressed unqualified opinions but included explanatory language in their reports as required by paragraphs 16–18 of *SAS No. 58*, as amended by *SAS No. 79*. Of the 593 references to lack of consistency, 418 relate to changes made in years prior to 2003. Examples of references to lack of consistency follow.

7.30

TABLE 7-4: LACK OF CONSISTENCY

	2003	2002	2001	2000
Goodwill not amortized	358	349	4	N/C*
Asset retirement obligations	54	N/C*	N/C*	N/C*
Derivatives	47	63	83	N/C*
Stock-based compensation	36	5	8	7
Variable interest entities	30	N/C*	N/C*	N/C*
Impairment of long-lived assets	14	17	6	2
Revenue recognition	9	16	36	23
Financial instruments with liability & equity characteristics	6	N/C*	N/C*	N/C*
Early extinguishment of debt	5	N/C*	N/C*	N/C*
Sales incentives	5	10	2	N/C*
Business combinations	4	11	N/C*	N/C*
Exit/disposal activity costs	4	N/C*	N/C*	N/C*
Inventories	3	9	4	11
Guarantees	1	N/C*	N/C*	N/C*
Other—described	17	34	24	34
Total References	**593**	**514**	**167**	**77**
Total Companies	**386**	**377**	**133**	**69**

* N/C = Not compiled. Line item was not included in the table for the year shown.

Goodwill Not Amortized

7.31

REPORT OF INDEPENDENT AUDITORS

Shareholders and Board of Directors
Amcast Industrial Corporation

We have audited the accompanying consolidated statements of financial condition of Amcast Industrial Corporation and subsidiaries as of August 31, 2003 and 2002, and the related consolidated statements of operations, shareholders' equity, and cash flows for each of the three years in the period ended August 31, 2003. Our audits also included the financial statement schedule listed in the Index at item 16 (a). These financial statements and schedule are the responsibility of the Company's management. Our responsibility is to express an opinion on these financial statements and schedule based on our audits.

We conducted our audits in accordance with auditing standards generally accepted in the United States. Those standards require that we plan and perform the audit to obtain reasonable assurance about whether the financial statements are free of material misstatement. An audit includes examining, on a test basis, evidence supporting the amounts and disclosures in the financial statements. An audit also includes assessing the accounting principles used and significant estimates made by management, as well as evaluating the overall financial statement presentation. We believe that our audits provide a reasonable basis for our opinion.

In our opinion, the financial statements referred to above present fairly, in all material respects, the consolidated financial position of Amcast Industrial Corporation and subsidiaries at August 31, 2003 and 2002, and the consolidated results of their operations and their cash flows for each of the three years in the period ended August 31, 2003, in conformity with accounting principles generally accepted in the United States. Also, in our opinion, the related financial statement schedule, when considered in relation to the basic financial statements taken as a whole, presents fairly in all material respects the information set forth therein.

As discussed in "Accounting Policies" in the Notes to Consolidated Financial Statements, in 2003 the Company changed its method of accounting for goodwill and other intangible assets.

*NOTES TO CONSOLIDATED FINANCIAL STATEMENTS
($ in thousands except per share amounts)*

Accounting Policies (In Part)

Goodwill

Goodwill represents the excess of acquisition cost over the fair value of net assets acquired in business combinations. In 2002 and prior years, goodwill was amortized on the straight-line method over 40 years.

In 2003, the Company was required to adopt Statement of Financial Accounting Standards (SFAS) No. 142, "Goodwill and Other Intangible Assets." Under the adoption of SFAS No. 142, goodwill and certain other intangible assets are no longer amortized but will be reviewed annually for impairment. If, based on these reviews, the related assets are found to be impaired, their carrying value will be adjusted through a charge to earnings. Intangible assets that are not deemed to have an indefinite life will continue to be amortized over their expected useful lives and be reviewed for impairment in accordance with SFAS No. 144, "Accounting for the Impairment or Disposal of Long-Lived Assets."

Upon adoption of SFAS No. 142 in the first quarter of fiscal 2003, the Company completed its impairment review and determined that all of its goodwill, relating primarily to Speedline, was impaired. This impairment is reflected in the Company's declining stock price and the weak financial performance of the reporting units related to the impaired goodwill. As such, the Company recorded a non-cash charge of $46,536, net of tax of $464, to reduce the carrying value of its goodwill to zero. This charge is recorded as a cumulative effect of an accounting change in the accompanying consolidated financial statements.

If the Company records any goodwill related to future transactions, it will follow the accounting rules of SFAS No. 141, "Business Combinations", and will perform an impairment review annually at the beginning of the fourth fiscal quarter.

In prior years, goodwill and other long-lived assets were reviewed for impairment under SFAS No. 121, "Accounting for the Impairment of Long-Lived Assets and for Long-Lived Assets to be Disposed of", which required a review for impairment whenever events or changes in circumstances indicated that the carrying amount of an asset might not be recoverable. SFAS No. 121 required an estimation of future undiscounted cash flows expected to result from the use of the asset and its eventual disposition. SFAS No. 121 has since been superceded by SFAS No. 144.

The impact of the non-amortization provisions of Statement No. 142 is as follows:

	2003	2002	2001
Results of operations			
Reported loss from continuing operations	$ (698)	$ (4,411)	$(25,975)
Goodwill amortization	—	224	224
Adjusted loss from continuing operations	$ (698)	$ (4,187)	$(25,751)
Reported loss from discontinued operations	$ (62,447)	$(16,674)	$(11,156)
Goodwill amortization	—	1,111	1,111
Adjusted loss from discontinued operations	$ (62,447)	$(15,563)	$(10,045)
Cumulative effect of accounting change	$ (46,536)	$ —	$ —
Reported net loss	$(109,681)	$(21,085)	$(37,131)
Goodwill amortization	—	1,335	1,335
Adjusted net loss	$(109,681)	$(19,750)	$(35,796)
Basic and diluted loss per share			
Reported loss from continuing operations	$ (0.08)	$ (0.51)	$ (3.06)
Goodwill amortization	—	0.03	0.03
Adjusted loss from continuing operations	$ (0.08)	$ (0.48)	$ (3.03)
Reported loss from discontinued operations	$ (6.98)	$ (1.94)	$ (1.32)
Goodwill amortization	—	0.13	0.13
Adjusted loss from discontinued operations	$ (6.98)	$ (1.81)	$ (1.19)
Cumulative effect of accounting change	$ (5.20)	$ —	$ —
Reported net loss	$ (12.26)	$ (2.45)	$ (4.38)
Goodwill amortization	—	0.16	0.16
Adjusted net loss	$ (12.26)	$ (2.29)	$ (4.22)

7.32

REPORT OF INDEPENDENT AUDITORS

The Board of Directors and Stockholders
Quantum Corporation

We have audited the accompanying consolidated balance sheets of Quantum Corporation (the "Company") as of March 31, 2003 and 2002, and the related consolidated statements of operations, stockholders' equity and cash flows for each of the three years in the period ended March 31, 2003. Our audits also included the financial statement schedule listed in the index at Item 15a. These financial statements and

schedule are the responsibility of Quantum's management. Our responsibility is to express an opinion on these financial statements and schedule based on our audits.

We conducted our audits in accordance with auditing standards generally accepted in the United States. Those standards require that we plan and perform the audit to obtain reasonable assurance about whether the financial statements are free of material misstatement. An audit includes examining, on a test basis, evidence supporting the amounts and disclosures in the financial statements. An audit also includes assessing the accounting principles used and significant estimates made by management, as well as evaluating the overall financial statement presentation. We believe that our audits provide a reasonable basis for our opinion.

ATT-SEC 7.32

In our opinion, the financial statements referred to above present fairly, in all material respects, the consolidated financial position of Quantum Corporation at March 31, 2003 and 2002, and the consolidated results of its operations and its cash flows for each of the three years in the period ended March 31, 2003, in conformity with accounting principles generally accepted in the United States. Also, in our opinion, the related financial statement schedule, when considered in relation to the basic financial statements taken as a whole, presents fairly in all material respects the information set forth therein.

As discussed in Notes 2, 5 and 6 to the Consolidated Financial Statements, in fiscal year 2003 Quantum Corporation changed its method of accounting for goodwill and other purchased intangible assets.

NOTES TO CONSOLIDATED FINANCIAL STATEMENTS

Note 2 (In Part): Summary of Significant Accounting Policies

Intangible Assets

At March 31, 2003 the net amount of goodwill and intangible assets was $120.4 million. Goodwill and intangible assets are carried and reported at acquisition cost, net of accumulated amortization subsequent to acquisition. The acquisition cost is amortized over estimated useful lives, which range from three to ten years. Goodwill and intangible assets are reviewed for impairment whenever events or circumstances indicate impairment might exist, or at least annually, in accordance with SFAS No. 121, *Accounting for the Impairment of Long-lived assets to be Disposed of*, by comparing projected undiscounted net cash flows expected to be derived from the use of those assets against their respective net carrying amounts. Impairment, if any, is based on the excess of the carrying amount over the fair value of those assets. SFAS No. 121 was applicable to fiscal years ended March 31, 2002 and earlier.

In June 2001, the Financial Accounting Standards Board ("FASB") released SFAS No. 141, *Business Combinations* and SFAS No. 142, *Goodwill and Other Intangible Assets*, which became effective for Quantum on April 1, 2002. As a result, goodwill is no longer amortized but tested for impairment at least annually, or more often if circumstances dictate. The new rules also require business combinations initiated after June 30, 2001 to be accounted for using the purchase method of accounting, with no amortization of goodwill acquired after June 30, 2001. In October 2001, the Financial Accounting Standards Board issued SFAS No. 144, *Accounting for the Impairment or Disposal of Long-lived Assets*, which supersedes SFAS No. 121, *Accounting for the Impairment of Long-lived Assets and Assets to be Disposed of* SFAS No. 144 retains many of the provisions of SFAS No. 121 regarding the testing for impairment of acquired intangibles that are to be amortized.

Note 5: Cumulative Effect of an Accounting Change

SFAS No. 142, *Goodwill and Other Intangible Assets*, which required companies to discontinue the amortization of goodwill and certain intangible assets with an indefinite useful life, became effective for Quantum on April 1, 2002. Instead, goodwill and intangible assets deemed to have an indefinite useful life must be reviewed for impairment upon adoption of SFAS No. 142 and annually thereafter, or more frequently when indicators of impairment exist.

The assessment of impairment conducted in the first quarter of fiscal year 2003, the quarter in which Quantum adopted SFAS No. 142, required Quantum to identify its reporting units and determine the carrying value of each reporting unit by assigning the assets and liabilities, including the existing goodwill and intangible assets, to those reporting units. At the time of adoption, the Storage Solutions group was the only business unit with goodwill. The fair values of the reporting units underlying the Storage Solutions group were estimated using both a discounted cash flow and market approach methodology. The reporting units' carrying amounts exceeded their fair values, indicating that the reporting units' goodwill was impaired, therefore requiring Quantum to perform the second step of the transitional impairment test. In the second step, Quantum compared the implied fair values of the reporting units' goodwill, determined by allocating the reporting units' fair values to all of its assets (recognized and unrecognized) and liabilities in a manner similar to a purchase price allocation in accordance with SFAS No. 141, *Business Combinations*.

Upon adoption of SFAS No. 142 in the first quarter of fiscal year 2003, Quantum recorded a non-cash accounting change adjustment of $94.3 million, reflecting a reduction to the carrying value of its goodwill, as a cumulative effect of an accounting change in the accompanying consolidated statements of operations.

Note 6, *Goodwill and Intangible Assets*, provides additional discussion on the impact to Quantum's financial statements as a result of applying SFAS No. 141 and SFAS No. 142.

Note 6 (In Part): Goodwill and Intangible Assets

As a result of adopting SFAS No. 142, *Goodwill and Other Intangible Assets*, on April 1, 2002, Quantum recorded an accounting change adjustment of $94.3 million in the first quarter of fiscal year 2003 and a goodwill impairment charge of $58.7 million in the second quarter of fiscal year 2003 related to the Storage Solutions group. The impairment charge recorded in the second quarter of fiscal year 2003 was attributable to the Storage Solutions group and was primarily caused by the deterioration in the market values of comparable companies, and to a lesser extent, by a reduction in anticipated future cash flows. The fair value of the Storage Solutions group was calculated using a combination of a discounted cash flow analysis involving projected data, and a comparable market approach, which involved a comparison with companies also in the tape automation business.

As required by SFAS No. 142, intangible assets that do not meet the criteria for recognition apart from goodwill must be reclassified. In applying these criteria, Quantum transferred $2.9 million of assembled workforce from intangible assets to goodwill in the first quarter of fiscal year 2003. Also in accordance with SFAS No. 142, Quantum discontinued the amortization of goodwill effective April 1, 2002 and instead will test it for impairment annually or whenever events or changes in circumstances suggest that the carrying amount may not be recoverable, such as what occurred in the second quarter of fiscal year 2003.

On November 13, 2002, Quantum acquired Benchmark Storage Innovations Inc., resulting in an additional $28.2 million of intangible assets and $26.8 million of goodwill upon acquisition, with a further goodwill amount of $3.2 million resulting from the distribution of Quantum shares due to quarterly earn out objectives being achieved. On February 4,

2003, Quantum acquired SANlight Inc., resulting in an additional $2.7 million of intangible assets.

The following financial information reflects consolidated results adjusted as though the accounting for goodwill and intangible assets was consistent for all periods presented:

(In thousands, except per-share data)	2003	2002	2001
Reported net income (loss) before cumulative effect of an accounting change	$(264,295)	$42,502	$160,686
Add back goodwill (including assembled workforce) amortization, net of tax	—	16,053	10,812
Adjusted net income (loss)	$(264,295)	$58,555	$171,498
Adjusted basic net income per share			
Reported basic net income (loss) per share before cumulative effect of an accounting change	$ (1.63)	$ 0.27	$ 1.08
Add back goodwill (including assembled workforce) amortization, net of tax	—	0.10	0.07
Adjusted basic net income (loss) per share	$ (1.63)	$ 0.37	$ 1.15
Adjusted diluted net income per share			
Reported diluted net income (loss) before cumulative effect of an accounting change	$ (1.63)	$ 0.27	$ 1.03
Add back goodwill (including assembled workforce) amortization, net of tax	—	0.10	0.07
Adjusted diluted net income (loss) per share	$ (1.63)	$ 0.37	$ 1.10

The following table provides a summary of the carrying amount of goodwill and includes amounts originally allocated to an intangible asset representing the value of the assembled workforce:

(In thousands)	Goodwill
Balance as of March 31, 2002	$135,817
Assembled workforce reclassified to goodwill, net [1]	1,320
Cumulative effect of an accounting change [2]	(68,497)
Goodwill impairment	(58,689)
Benchmark acquisition	26,762
Additional goodwill for M4 earn out	983
Additional goodwill for Benchmark earn out	3,220
Balance as of March 31, 2003	$ 40,916

[1] Excludes $1.6 million related to the NAS business, which has been classified as discontinued operations.

[2] Excludes $25.8 million related to the NAS business, which has been classified as discontinued operations.

Asset Retirement Obligations

7.33

REPORT OF INDEPENDENT AUDITORS

To the Stockholders and the Board of Directors of ChevronTexaco Corporation

In our opinion, the consolidated financial statements listed in the index appearing under Item 15 (a)(1) on page 30 present fairly, in all material respects, the financial position of ChevronTexaco Corporation and its subsidiaries at December 31, 2003 and 2002, and the results of their operations and their cash flows for each of the three years in the period ended December 31, 2003 in conformity with accounting principles generally accepted in the United States of America. In addition, in our opinion, the financial statement

schedule listed in the index appearing under Item 15(a) (2) on page 30 presents fairly, in all material respects, the information set forth therein when read in conjunction with the related consolidated financial statements. These financial statements and the financial statement schedule are the responsibility of the Company's management; our responsibility is to express an opinion on these financial statements and the financial statement schedule based on our audits. We conducted our audits of these statements in accordance with auditing standards generally accepted in the United States of America, which require that we plan and perform the audit to obtain reasonable assurance about whether the financial statements are free of material misstatement. An audit includes examining, on a test basis, evidence supporting the amounts and disclosures in the financial statements, assessing the accounting principles used and significant estimates made by management, and evaluating the overall financial statement presentation. We believe that our audits provide a reasonable basis for our opinion.

As discussed in Note 25 on page FS-50 to the financial statements, the Company changed its method of accounting for asset retirement obligations as of January 1, 2003.

NOTES TO THE CONSOLIDATED FINANCIAL STATEMENTS
(Millions of dollars, except per-share amounts)

Note 1 (In Part): Summary of Significant Accounting Policies

Properties, Plant and Equipment (In Part)

Effective January 1, 2003, the company implemented Financial Accounting Standards Board Statement No. 143, "Accounting for Asset Retirement Obligations" (FAS 143), in which the fair value of a liability for an asset retirement obligation is recorded as an asset and a liability when there is a legal obligation associated with the retirement of a long-lived asset and the amount can be reasonably estimated. See also Note 25 on page FS-50 relating to asset retirement obligations, which includes additional information on the company's adoption of FAS 143. Previously, for oil, gas and coal producing properties, a provision was made through depreciation expense for anticipated abandonment and restoration costs at the end of the property's useful life.

Note 25. FAS 143—Asset Retirement Obligations

The company adopted Financial Accounting Standards Board Statement No. 143, "Accounting for Asset Retirement Obligations" (FAS 143), effective January 1, 2003. This accounting standard applies to the fair value of a liability for an asset retirement obligation that is recorded when there is a legal obligation associated with the retirement of a tangible long-lived asset and the liability can be reasonably estimated. Obligations associated with the retirement of these assets require recognition in certain circumstances: (1) the present value of a liability and offsetting asset for an asset retirement obligation (ARO), (2) the subsequent accretion of that liability and depreciation of the asset, and (3) the periodic review of the ARO liability estimates and discount rates. FAS 143 primarily affects the company's accounting for oil and gas producing assets and differs in several respects from previous accounting under FAS 19, "Financial Accounting and Reporting by Oil and Gas Producing Companies."

In the first quarter 2003, the company recorded a net after-tax charge of $200 for the cumulative effect of the adoption of FAS 143, including the company's share of amounts attributable to equity affiliates. The cumulative-effect adjustment also increased the following balance sheet categories: "Properties, plant and equipment," $2,568; "Accrued liabilities," $115; and "Deferred credits and other noncurrent obligations," $2,674. "Noncurrent deferred income taxes" decreased by $21.

Upon adoption, no significant legal obligations to retire refining, marketing and transportation (downstream) and chemical long-lived assets generally were recognized, as indeterminate settlement dates for the asset retirements prevented estimation of the fair value of the associated ARO. The company performs periodic reviews of its downstream and chemical long-lived assets for any changes in facts and circumstances that might require recognition of a retirement obligation.

Other than the cumulative-effect net charge, the effect of the new accounting standard on net income in 2003 was not materially different from what the result would have been under FAS 19 accounting. Included in "Depreciation, depletion and amortization" were $52 related to the depreciation of the ARO asset and $132 related to the accretion of the ARO liability.

The following table illustrates what the company's net income before extraordinary items, net income and related per share amounts would have been if the provisions of FAS 143 had been applied retroactively:

	2003	2002	2001
Proforma net income before extraordinary items	$7,430[1]	$1,137[2]	$3,933[2]
Earnings per share—basic[3]	$ 7.15	$ 1.07	$ 3.71
Earnings per share—diluted[3]	$ 7.14	$ 1.07	$ 3.70
Proforma net income	$7,430[1]	$1,137[2]	$3,290[2]
Earnings per share—basic[4]	$ 7.15	$ 1.07	$ 3.10
Earnings per share—diluted[4]	$ 7.14	$ 1.07	$ 3.09

[1] Amount excludes cumulative-effect charge of $200 ($0.18 per basic and diluted share) for the adoption of FAS 143.

[2] Includes benefit of $5 and $2 for 2002 and 2001, respectively, which represent the reversal of FAS 19 depreciation related to abandonment offset partially by proforma expenses for the depreciation and accretion of the ARO asset and liability, net of tax. There is a *de minimis* effect to net income per basic or diluted share.

[3] Reported net income before extraordinary items was $1.07 per basic and diluted share for 2002 and $3.71 per basic share ($3.70—diluted) for 2001.

[4] Reported net income was $1.07 per basic and diluted share for 2002 and $3.10 per basic share ($3.09—diluted) for 2001.

Prior to the implementation of FAS 143, the company had recorded a provision for abandonment that was part of "Accumulated depreciation, depletion and amortization." Upon implementation of FAS 143, the provision for abandonment was reversed and ARO liability was recorded. The amount of the abandonment reserve at the end of each year and the proforma ARO liability were as follows:

	2003	2002	2001
ARO liability (FAS 143) at January 1	$2,797	$2,792	$2,729
ARO liability (FAS 143) at December 31	2,856	2,797	2,792
Abandonment provision (FAS 19) at December 31	—	2,263	2,155

The following table indicates the changes to the company's before-tax asset retirement obligations in 2003:

	2003
Balance at Jan. 1—Cumulative effect of the accounting change	$2,797
Liabilities incurred	14
Liabilities settled	(128)
Accretion expense	132
Revisions in estimated cash flows	41
Balance at December 31	$2,856

Derivatives

7.34

INDEPENDENT AUDITORS' REPORT

The Stockholders and Board of Directors
ConAgra Foods, Inc.

We have audited the accompanying consolidated balance sheets of ConAgra Foods, Inc. and subsidiaries (the "company") as of May 25, 2003 and May 26, 2002, and the related consolidated statements of earnings, comprehensive income, common stockholders' equity and cash flows for each of the three years in the period ended May 25, 2003. These financial statements are the responsibility of the company's management. Our responsibility is to express an opinion on these financial statements based on our audits.

We conducted our audits in accordance with auditing standards generally accepted in the United States of America. Those standards require that we plan and perform the audit to obtain reasonable assurance about whether the financial statements are free of material misstatement. An audit includes examining, on a test basis, evidence supporting the amounts and disclosures in the financial statements. An audit also includes assessing the accounting principles used and significant estimates made by management, as well as evaluating the overall financial statement presentation. We believe that our audits provide a reasonable basis for our opinion.

In our opinion, such financial statements present fairly, in all material respects, the financial position of ConAgra Foods, Inc. and subsidiaries as of May 25, 2003 and May 26, 2002, and the results of their operations and their cash flows for each of the three years in the period ended May 25, 2003 in conformity with accounting principles generally accepted in the United States of America.

As discussed in Note 1 to the financial statements, in 2003 the company changed its method of accounting for goodwill and other intangible assets and in 2002 the company changed its method of accounting for derivative instruments and other hedging activities.

NOTES TO CONSOLIDATED FINANCIAL STATEMENTS

1 (In Part): Summary of Significant Accounting Policies

Accounting Changes (In Part)

In fiscal 2002, the company adopted SFAS No. 133, *Accounting for Derivative Financial Instruments and Hedging Activities*, and its related amendment, SFAS No. 138, *Accounting for Certain Derivative Instruments and Certain Hedging Activities* (collectively "SFAS No. 133"). The adoption of SFAS No. 133 resulted in a cumulative effect of an accounting change that reduced net income by $2.0 million, and decreased accumulated other comprehensive income by $24.6 million, net of tax, in the first quarter of fiscal 2002. Other than such cumulative effect, the effect of the change on income before cumulative effect of changes in accounting for fiscal 2002 was not material. The pro forma effect of retroactive application of SFAS No. 133, had this new standard been in effect for the prior fiscal years presented, was not material.

Stock-Based Compensation

7.35

INDEPENDENT AUDITORS' REPORT

To the Board of Directors and Shareholders

We have audited the accompanying consolidated balance sheets of Costco Wholesale Corporation and subsidiaries as of August 31, 2003 and September 1, 2002 and the related consolidated statements of income, stockholders' equity and cash flows for the 52 weeks then ended. These consolidated financial statements are the responsibility of the Company's management. Our responsibility is to express an opinion on these consolidated financial statements based on our audits. The accompanying consolidated financial statements of Costco Wholesale Corporation and subsidiaries as of September 2, 2001 were audited by other auditors who have ceased operations. Those auditors expressed an unqualified opinion on those consolidated financial statements in their report dated October 8, 2001.

We conducted our audits in accordance with auditing standards generally accepted in the United States of America. Those standards require that we plan and perform the audit to obtain reasonable assurance about whether the consolidated financial statements are free of material misstatement. An audit includes examining, on a test basis, evidence supporting the amounts and disclosures in the consolidated financial statements. An audit also includes assessing the accounting principles used and significant estimates made by management, as well as evaluating the overall consolidated financial statement presentation. We believe that our audits provide a reasonable basis for our opinion.

In our opinion, the consolidated financial statements referred to above present fairly, in all material respects, the consolidated financial position of Costco Wholesale Corporation and subsidiaries as of August 31, 2003 and September 1, 2002, and the results of their operations and their cash flows for the 52 weeks then ended in conformity with accounting principles generally accepted in the United States of America.

As discussed in Note 1 to the consolidated financial statements, the Company changed its method of accounting for stock-based compensation effective September 3, 2002.

NOTES TO CONSOLIDATED FINANCIAL STATEMENTS
(Dollars in thousands, except per share data)

Note 1 (In Part): Summary of Significant Accounting Policies

Stock-Based Compensation

The Company adopted the fair value based method of recording stock options consistent with SFAS No. 123 "Accounting for Stock-Based Compensation," for all employee stock options granted subsequent to fiscal year end 2002. Specifically, the Company adopted SFAS No. 123 using the "prospective method" with guidance provided from SFAS No. 148 "Accounting for Stock-Based Compensation—Transition and Disclosure." All employee stock option grants made in fiscal 2003 and in future years will be expensed over the stock option vesting period based on the fair value at the date the options are granted. Prior to fiscal 2003 the Company applied Accounting Principles Board Opinion (APB)

No. 25 and related interpretations in accounting for stock options. Because the Company granted stock options to employees at exercise prices equal to fair market value on the date of grant, accordingly, no compensation cost was recognized for option grants.

Had compensation costs for the Company's stock-based compensation plans been determined based on the fair value at the grant dates for awards made prior to fiscal 2003, under those plans and consistent with SFAS No. 123, the Company's net income and net income per share would have been reduced to the pro forma amounts indicated below:

	2003	2002	2001
Net income, as reported	$721,000	$699,983	$602,089
Add: Stock-based employee compensation expense included in reported net income, net of related tax effects	7,513	—	—
Deduct: Total stock-based employee compensation expense determined under fair value based methods for all awards, net of related tax effects	(70,257)	(75,743)	(65,077)
Pro-forma net income	$658,256	$624,240	$537,012
Earnings per share			
Basic—as reported	$ 1.58	$ 1.54	$ 1.34
Basic—pro-forma	$ 1.44	$ 1.38	$ 1.19
Diluted—as reported	$ 1.53	$ 1.48	$ 1.29
Diluted—pro-forma	$ 1.40	$ 1.32	$ 1.15

Recent Accounting Pronouncements (In Part)

In December 2002, the FASB issued SFAS No. 148, "Accounting for Stock-Based Compensation—Transition and Disclosure," which provides guidance for transition to the fair value based method of accounting for stock-based employee compensation and the required financial statement disclosure. Effective September 3, 2002 the Company adopted the fair value based method of accounting for stock-based compensation. See Note (1) and Note (5) of the Company's consolidated financial statements.

Note 5 (In Part): Stock Options

The Company adopted the fair value based method of recording stock options consistent with SFAS No. 123 "Accounting for Stock-Based Compensation," for all employee stock options granted subsequent to fiscal year end 2002 using the "prospective method." All employee stock option grants made in fiscal 2003 and in future years will be expensed over the stock option vesting period based on the fair value at the date the options are granted. Prior to fiscal 2003 the Company applied APB No. 25 and related interpretations in accounting for stock options. Because the Company granted stock options to employees at exercise prices equal to fair market value on the date of grant, accordingly, no compensation cost was recognized for option grants.

In fiscal 2003, the Company recognized stock compensation costs of $12,069 versus no stock compensation costs in fiscal 2002. The effects of applying SFAS No. 123 are substantially less in fiscal 2003 than the effects on net income and earnings per share expected in future periods because this is the initial year of adoption. Future years will reflect compensation expense from options granted in that year, as well as continuing recognition of expense associated with options issued in prior years as they vest. Shares granted in fiscal 2003 totaled 8,479,550 shares, with the majority of these shares being granted in the middle of the third quarter.

Total stock compensation costs on a pre-tax basis that would have been recorded had SFAS No. 123 been adopted as of its initial effective date would have totaled $112,863 in fiscal 2003 and $123,159 and $108,462 in fiscal 2002 and 2001, respectively.

The fair value of each option grant is estimated on the date of grant using the Black-Scholes option-pricing model with the following weighted average assumptions used for grants in 2003, 2002 and 2001:

	2003	2002	2001
Risk free interest rate	3.30%	4.45%	4.96%
Expected life	6 years	5 years	5 years
Expected volatility	46%	46%	43%
Expected dividend yield	0%	0%	0%

Stock option transactions relating to the aggregate of the 1993 and 2002 plans are summarized below (shares in thousands):

	2003		2002		2001	
	Shares	Price[1]	Shares	Price[1]	Shares	Price[1]
Under option at beginning of year	42,961	$31.49	39,578	$29.15	36,021	$26.09
Granted[2]	8,480	30.47	7,641	38.10	8,822	34.18
Exercised	(2,154)	16.13	(3,571)	18.77	(4,457)	14.04
Cancelled	(497)	37.14	(687)	37.12	(808)	31.35
Under option at end of year	48,790	$31.93	42,961	$31.49	39,578	$29.15

[1] Weighted-average exercise price/grant price.

[2] The weighted-average fair value based on the Black-Scholes model of options granted during fiscal 2003, 2002 and 2001, were $14.84, $17.83 and $15.47, respectively.

The following table summarizes information regarding stock options outstanding at August 31, 2003 (number of options in thousands):

	Options Outstanding			Options Exercisable	
Range of Prices	Number	Remaining Contractual Life[1]	Price[1]	Number	Price[1]
$6.66–$30.47	19,035	6.22	$22.61	11,054	$17.01
$31.55–$36.91	16,604	6.80	35.19	8,660	35.82
$38.79–$52.50	13,151	7.51	41.30	5,433	42.59
	48,790	6.77	$31.93	25,147	$29.02

[1] Weighted-average.

At September 1, 2002 and September 2, 2001, there were 19,843 and 15,500 options exercisable at weighted average exercise prices of $25.40 and $21.57, respectively.

Variable Interest Entities

7.36

REPORT OF INDEPENDENT AUDITORS

To the Shareholders
McCormick & Company, Incorporated

We have audited the accompanying consolidated balance sheets of McCormick & Company, Incorporated and subsidiaries as of November 30, 2003 and 2002 and the related consolidated statements of income, shareholders' equity and cash flows for each of the three years in the period ended November 30, 2003. These financial statements are the responsibility of the Company's management. Our responsibility is to express an opinion on these financial statements based on our audits.

We conducted our audits in accordance with auditing standards generally accepted in the United States. Those standards require that we plan and perform the audit to obtain reasonable assurance about whether the financial statements are free of material misstatement. An audit includes examining, on a test basis, evidence supporting the amounts and disclosures in the financial statements. An audit also includes assessing the accounting principles used and significant estimates made by management, as well as evaluating the overall financial statement presentation. We believe that our audits provide a reasonable basis for our opinion.

In our opinion, the financial statements referred to above present fairly, in all material respects, the consolidated financial position of McCormick & Company, Incorporated and subsidiaries at November 30, 2003 and 2002 and the consolidated results of its operations and its cash flows for each of the three years in the period ended November 30, 2003, in conformity with accounting principles generally accepted in the United States.

As discussed in note 1 of the notes to consolidated financial statements, the Company changed the manner in which it accounts for a variable interest entity upon adoption of certain provisions of Financial Accounting Standards Board Interpretation No. 46, "Consolidation of Variable Interest Entities" on September 1, 2003. Also as discussed in note 1, the Company changed the manner in which it accounts for goodwill and other intangible assets upon adoption of Statement of Financial Accounting Standard No. 142, "Goodwill and Other Intangible Assets" on December 1, 2001.

NOTES TO CONSOLIDATED FINANCIAL STATEMENTS

1 (In Part): Summary of Significant Accounting Policies

Consolidation

The consolidated financial statements include the accounts of the Company and its majority-owned subsidiaries. Significant intercompany transactions have been eliminated. Investments in unconsolidated affiliates, over which the

Company exercises significant influence, but not control, are accounted for by the equity method. Accordingly, the share of net income or loss of such unconsolidated affiliates is included in consolidated net income. The implications of the Financial Accounting Standards Board (FASB) Interpretation No. 46, "Consolidation of Variable Interest Entities" on the Company's consolidation policy are discussed later in this note.

Accounting and Disclosure Changes (In Part)

In June 2002, the FASB issued SFAS No. 146 "Accounting for Costs Associated with Exit or Disposal Activities." SFAS No. 146 generally requires companies to recognize costs associated with exit or disposal activities when they are incurred rather than at the date of a commitment to an exit or disposal plan. The Company adopted SFAS No. 146 on December 1, 2002. There was no material effect upon adoption of this statement.

In December 2002, the FASB issued Interpretation No. 45, "Guarantor's Accounting and Disclosure Requirements for Guarantees, Including Indirect Guarantees of Indebtedness of Others." Interpretation No. 45 requires that at the time a company issues a guarantee, the company must recognize an initial liability for the fair value, or market value, of the obligations it assumes under that guarantee. This interpretation is applicable on a prospective basis to guarantees issued or modified after December 31, 2002. The Company adopted FASB Interpretation No. 45 on December 1, 2002. There was no material effect upon adoption of this statement.

In January 2003, the FASB issued and subsequently revised Interpretation No. 46, "Consolidation of Variable Interest Entities." Interpretation No. 46 requires a variable interest entity to be consolidated by a company if that company is subject to a majority of the risk of loss from the variable interest entity's activities or entitled to receive a majority of the entity's residual returns or both (primary beneficiary). Currently, entities are generally consolidated by a company that has a controlling financial interest through ownership of a majority voting interest in the entity. Interpretation No. 46 is effective for companies that have interests in structures that are commonly referred to as special purpose entities for periods ending after December 15, 2003. Application for all other types of variable interest entities is required in financial statements for periods ending after March 15, 2004. During 2003, the Company concluded that it was the primary beneficiary of a variable interest entity that is the lessor of a distribution center used by the Company. The Company has elected to adopt the provisions of Interpretation No. 46 related to special purpose entities in the fourth quarter of 2003 as they apply to this lessor while deferring adoption related to other potential variable interest entities until the second quarter of 2004 as permitted by Interpretation No. 46. Effective at the beginning of the fourth quarter of 2003, the Company has consolidated the lessor of the leased distribution center and has recorded a cumulative effect of an accounting change of $2.1 million (net of income tax benefit of $1.2 million). Consolidation of this entity increased assets by $11.2 million, long-term debt by $14.0 million and minority interest by $0.5 million. Previously, this entity was not consolidated and the distribution center was accounted for as an operating lease. The effect of consolidation of this entity in prior years would have reduced net income in 2002 and 2001 by $0.3 million. The Company intends to fully adopt Interpretation No. 46 for all entities other than the lessor discussed

above beginning in the second quarter of 2004. The Company is still evaluating what effects, if any, the adoption of Interpretation No. 46 will have on other entities in which it may have a variable interest.

7.37

REPORT OF INDEPENDENT AUDITORS

To the Board of Directors and Shareholders of Xerox Corporation

In our opinion, the accompanying consolidated balance sheets and the related consolidated statements of income, cash flows and common shareholders' equity present fairly, in all material respects, the financial position of Xerox Corporation and its subsidiaries at December 31, 2003 and 2002, and the results of their operations and their cash flows for each of the three years in the period ended December 31, 2003 in conformity with accounting principles generally accepted in the United States of America. These financial statements are the responsibility of the Company's management; our responsibility is to express an opinion on these financial statements based on our audits. We conducted our audits of these statements in accordance with auditing standards generally accepted in the United States of America, which require that we plan and perform the audit to obtain reasonable assurance about whether the financial statements are free of material misstatement. An audit includes examining, on a test basis, evidence supporting the amounts and disclosures in the financial statements, assessing the accounting principles used and significant estimates made by management, and evaluating the overall financial statement presentation. We believe that our audits provide a reasonable basis for our opinion.

As discussed in Note 1, in 2003 the Company adopted the provisions of the Financial Accounting Standards Board Interpretation No. 46R, "Consolidation of Variable Interest Entities, an Interpretation of ARB 51," which changed certain consolidation policies. Additionally, as discussed in Note 1, the Company adopted the provisions of Statement of Financial Accounting Standards No. 142, "Goodwill and Other Intangible Assets" on January 1, 2002.

NOTES TO THE CONSOLIDATED FINANCIAL STATEMENTS
(Dollars in millions, except per-share data and unless otherwise indicated)

Note 1 (In Part): Summary of Significant Accounting Policies

Basis of Consolidation

The Consolidated Financial Statements include the accounts of Xerox Corporation and all of our controlled subsidiary companies. All significant intercompany accounts and transactions have been eliminated. Investments in business entities in which we do not have control, but we have the ability to exercise significant influence over operating and financial policies (generally 20 to 50 percent ownership), are accounted for using the equity method of accounting. Upon the sale of stock of a subsidiary, we recognize a gain or loss in our

Consolidated Statements of Income equal to our proportionate share of the corresponding increase or decrease in that subsidiary's equity. Operating results of acquired businesses are included in the Consolidated Statements of Income from the date of acquisition and, for variable interest entities in which we are determined to be the primary beneficiary, from the date such determination is made.

Certain reclassifications of prior year amounts have been made to conform to the current year presentation.

New Accounting Standards and Accounting Changes

Variable Interest Entities

In January 2003, the FASB issued Interpretation No. 46, "Consolidation of Variable Interest Entities, an interpretation of ARB 51" ("FIN 46"). The primary objectives of FIN 46 were to provide guidance on the identification of entities for which control is achieved through means other than through voting rights and how to determine when and which business enterprise should consolidate the variable interest entity ("VIE"). We adopted FIN 46 on July 1, 2003 and, as a result, we began consolidating our joint venture with De Lage Landen International BV ("DLL"), our vendor financing partnership in the Netherlands, effective July 1, 2003 as we were deemed to be the primary beneficiary of the joint venture's financial results. Prior to the adoption of FIN 46, we accounted for our investment with DLL under the equity method of accounting.

In December 2003, the FASB published a revision to FIN 46 ("FIN 46R"), in part, to clarify certain of its provisions. FIN 46R addressed substantive ownership provisions related to consolidation. As a result of FIN 46R, we were required to deconsolidate three of our subsidiary trusts—Capital Trust I, Capital Trust II and Capital LLC. These trusts had previously issued mandatorily redeemable preferred securities and entered into loan agreements with the Company having similar terms as the preferred securities. Specifically, FIN 46R resulted in the holders of the preferred securities being considered the primary beneficiaries of the trusts. As such, we were no longer permitted to consolidate these entities. We have therefore deconsolidated the three trusts and reflected our obligations to them within the balance sheet liability caption "Liability to subsidiary trusts issuing preferred securities." In addition to deconsolidating these subsidiary trusts, the interest on the loans, which was previously reported net of tax as a component of "Minorities' interests in earnings of subsidiaries" in our Consolidated Statements of Income, are now accounted for as interest expense within "Other expenses, net", with the tax effects presented within "Income taxes (benefits)." Accordingly, $145, $145 and $64 in interest expense on loans payable to the subsidiary trusts for the years ended December 31, 2003, 2002, and 2001, respectively, was reflected as non-financing interest expense. The related income tax effects were $56, $56 and $24, for the years ended December 31, 2003, 2002, and 2001, respectively. Financial statements for all periods presented have been revised to reflect this change. The adoption of this interpretation had no impact on the net income or earnings per share. In connection with the adoption of FIN 46R, we also reclassified prior periods for the effects of the consolidation of DLL. The impact of consolidating DLL was immaterial for all periods presented.

Note 7 (In Part): Investments in Affiliates, at Equity

Investments in corporate joint ventures and other companies in which we generally have a 20 to 50 percent ownership interest at December 31, 2003 and 2002 were as follows:

	2003	2002
Fuji Xerox	$556	$563
Investment in subsidiary trusts issuing preferred securities	69	66
Other investments	19	66
Investments in affiliates, at equity	$644	$695

Note 14—Liability to Subsidiary Trusts Issuing Preferred Securities

The Liability to Subsidiary Trusts Issuing Preferred Securities included in our Consolidated Balance Sheets reflects the obligations to our subsidiaries that have issued preferred securities. These subsidiaries are not consolidated in our financial statements because it was determined that we are not the primary beneficiary of the trusts and, therefore, are not permitted to consolidate them in accordance with FIN 46R (refer to Note 1 for further discussion). As of December 31, 2003 and 2002, the components of our liabilities to the trusts were as follows:

	2003	2002
Trust II	$1,067	$1,067
Trust I	665	665
Deferred Preferred Stock	77	61
	$1,809	$1,793

Trust II

In 2001, Xerox Capital Trust II ("Trust II") issued 20.7 million of 7.5 percent convertible trust preferred securities (the "Trust Preferred Securities") to investors for $1,035 and 0.6 million shares of common securities to us for $32. With the proceeds from these securities, Trust II purchased $1,067 of 7.5 percent convertible junior subordinated debentures due 2021 of one of our wholly-owned consolidated subsidiaries. The subsidiary purchased $1,067 aggregate principal amount of 7.5 percent convertible junior subordinated debentures due 2021 of the Company. Trust II's assets consist principally of our subsidiary's debentures and our subsidiary's assets consist principally of our debentures. On a consolidated basis, we received net proceeds of $1,004. Fees of $31 capitalized as debt issuance costs and are being amortized to interest expense over three years to the earliest put date. Interest expense was $89 in 2003 and 2002. We have effectively guaranteed, fully and unconditionally, on a subordinated basis, the payment and delivery by our subsidiary, of all amounts due on our subsidiary debentures and the payment and delivery by Trust II of all amounts due on the Trust Preferred Securities, in each case to the extent required under the terms of the securities.

The Trust Preferred Securities accrue and pay cash distributions quarterly at a rate of 7.5 percent per year of the stated amount of fifty dollars per security. Concurrently, with the initial issuance of the Trust Preferred Securities, our subsidiary used part of the proceeds received from the Company of $229 to purchase U.S. treasuries in order to secure its obligations under its debentures through the distribution payment date (November 27, 2004). The Trust Preferred Securities are convertible at any time, at the option of the investors, into 5.4795 shares of our common stock per Trust Preferred Security (equivalent share price of $9.125 per common share) ("the Conversion Ratio"). The Trust Preferred Securities are mandatorily redeemable upon the maturity of the debentures on November 27, 2021 at fifty dollars per Trust Preferred Security plus accrued and unpaid distributions. Investors may require us to cause Trust II to purchase all or a portion of the Trust Preferred Securities on December 4, 2004, and November 27, 2006, 2008, 2011 and 2016 at a price of fifty dollars per Trust Preferred Security, plus accrued and unpaid distributions. In addition, if we undergo a change in control on or before December 4, 2004, investors may require us to cause Trust II to purchase all or a portion of the Trust Preferred Securities. In either case, the purchase price for such Trust Preferred Securities may be paid in cash or our common stock, or a combination thereof. However, our liability to the trust is classified as long-term in our financial statements as we have the intent and ability to convert the obligations to equity through the issuance of common shares if put to us in 2004. If the purchase price or any portion thereof consists of common stock, investors will receive such common stock at a value of 95 percent of its then prevailing market price. Trust II may redeem all, but not part, of the Trust Preferred Securities for cash, prior to December 4, 2004, only if specified changes in tax and investment law occur, at a redemption price of 100 percent of their liquidation amount plus accrued and unpaid distributions. On or at anytime after December 4, 2004, Trust II may redeem all or a portion of the Trust Preferred Securities for cash at declining redemption prices, with an initial redemption price of 103.75 percent of their stated amount, subject to the investors' right to convert the Trust Preferred Securities into shares of our common stock at the Conversion Ratio at any time prior to any such redemption date. The Company's rights and liabilities with respect to Trust II, through our other subsidiary, contain identical conversion, put and call provisions and would be redeemed in a similar manner as the Trust Preferred Securities.

Trust I

In 1997, Xerox Capital Trust I ("Trust I") issued 650 thousand of 8.0 percent preferred securities (the "Preferred Securities") to investors for $644 ($650 liquidation value) and 20,103 shares of common securities to us for $20. With the proceeds from these securities, Trust I purchased $670 principal amount of 8.0 percent Junior Subordinated Debentures due 2027 of the Company ("the Debentures"). The Debentures represent all of the assets of Trust I. On a consolidated basis, we received net proceeds of $637 which was net of fees and discounts of $13. Interest expense, together with the amortization of debt issuance costs and discounts, amounted to $52 in 2003 and 2002. We have guaranteed (the "Guarantee"), on a subordinated basis, distributions and other payments due on the Preferred Securities. The Guarantee and our obligations under the Debentures and in the indenture pursuant to which the Debentures were issued and our obligations under the Amended and Restated Declaration of Trust governing the trust, taken together, provide a full and unconditional guarantee of amounts due on the Preferred Securities. The Preferred Securities accrue and pay cash distributions semiannually at a rate of 8 percent per year of the stated liquidation amount of one thousand dollars per

Preferred Security. The Preferred Securities are mandatorily redeemable upon the maturity of the Debentures on February 1, 2027, or earlier to the extent of any redemption by us of any Debentures. The redemption price in either such case will be one thousand dollars per share plus accrued and unpaid distributions to the date fixed for redemption.

Deferred Preferred Stock

In 1996, Xerox Capital LLC, issued 2 million deferred preferred shares for Canadian (Cdn.) $50 ($37 U.S.) to investors and all of its common shares to us for Cdn. $13 ($10 U.S.). The total proceeds of Cdn. $63 ($47 U.S.) were loaned to us. The deferred preferred shares are mandatorily redeemable on February 28, 2006 for Cdn. $90 (equivalent to $70 U.S. at December 31, 2003).

Impairment of Long-Lived Assets

7.38

REPORT OF INDEPENDENT AUDITORS

To the Shareholders and Board of Directors of Hillenbrand Industries, Inc.

In our opinion, the consolidated financial statements listed in the accompanying index present fairly, in all material respects, the financial position of Hillenbrand Industries, Inc. and its subsidiaries at September 30, 2003 and 2002, and the results of their operations and their cash flows for the fiscal year ended September 30, 2003, the ten months ended September 30, 2002 and the fiscal year ended December 1, 2001 in conformity with accounting principles generally accepted in the United States of America. In addition, in our opinion, the financial statement schedule listed in the accompanying index presents fairly, in all material respects, the information set forth therein when read in conjunction with the related consolidated financial statements. These financial statements and financial statement schedule are the responsibility of the Company's management; our responsibility is to express an opinion on these financial statements and financial statement schedule based on our audits. We conducted our audits of these statements in accordance with auditing standards generally accepted in the United States of America, which require that we plan and perform the audit to obtain reasonable assurance about whether the financial statements are free of material misstatement. An audit includes examining, on a test basis, evidence supporting the amounts and disclosures in the financial statements, assessing the accounting principles used and significant estimates made by management, and evaluating the overall financial statement presentation. We believe that our audits provide a reasonable basis for our opinion.

As discussed in Note 3 to the Consolidated Financial Statements, the Company adopted the provisions of Statement of Financial Accounting Standards No. 144, "Accounting for the Impairment or Disposal of Long-Lived Assets", as of October 1, 2002.

NOTES TO CONSOLIDATED FINANCIAL STATEMENTS
(Dollars in millions except per share data)

1 (In Part): Summary of Significant Accounting Policies

Accounting Standards (In Part)
On October 1, 2002, the Company adopted SFAS No. 144, "Accounting for the Impairment or Disposal of Long-Lived Assets". SFAS No. 144 significantly changes the criteria to be met to classify an asset as held-for-sale and what qualifies for discontinued operations treatment. The Statement also requires expected future operating losses from discontinued operations to be recorded in the period in which the losses are incurred, rather than as of the date management commits to a formal plan to dispose of a business as previously required. In addition, more dispositions will qualify for discontinued operations treatment in the income statement. The Company followed the provisions of this Statement in accounting for the divestitures of the Hill-Rom infant care and piped-medical gas businesses as discontinued operations in its Consolidated Financial Statements.

3. Discontinued Operations

In September 2003, Hill-Rom entered into definitive agreements to dispose of two non-strategic businesses.

- On September 24, 2003, Hill-Rom signed a definitive agreement to sell its piped-medical gas business to Beacon Medical Products, LLC, for an estimated $14 million, subject to adjustment for certain conditions existing at closing. The piped-medical gas business, with operations in Batesville, IN and the United Kingdom, is a leading provider of medical gas delivery and management systems in acute care facilities. Hill-Rom retained collection rights to outstanding receivables of the piped-medical gas business at the date of close of approximately $4 million.
- On September 29, 2003, Hill-Rom signed a definitive agreement to sell its Air-Shields infant care business to Dräger Medical AG & Co. KGaA for an estimated $31 million, subject to adjustment for certain conditions existing at closing. Air-Shields, based in Hatboro, PA, is a leading provider of infant care warming therapy, incubators and other infant care products. Hill-Rom retained collection rights to outstanding receivables of the infant care business at the date of close of approximately $9 million.

The divestiture of the piped-medical gas business closed in late October 2003. The sale of the Air-Shields infant care business is expected to close in the first calendar quarter of 2004, subject to required regulatory approvals. Upon the signing of the definitive sale agreements, both the infant care and piped-medical gas businesses have been treated as discontinued operations for all years provided within the Consolidated Statements of Income in accordance with the provisions of SFAS No. 144, "Accounting for the Impairment or Disposal of Long-Lived Assets". Consistent with this treatment, the operating results for each business have been removed from the individual line items comprising the Consolidated Statements of Income and presented in a separate section of the Statement of Income, for all periods. In fiscal year 2003, the results of discontinued operations also reflect an estimated loss on the disposal of the businesses of $51 million, net-of-tax, consisting of a $50 million pre-tax loss and a $1 million income tax provision. The loss on disposal

is related to $72 million of goodwill specifically assigned to the carrying value of the respective businesses. In evaluating the divestitures, it was determined that the benefits of the acquired goodwill associated with these businesses had not been realized, and would not be realized in the future, by the continuing Hill-Rom operations since they were not fully integrated. As such, all goodwill related to the previously acquired infant care and piped-medical gas businesses, other than a portion related to a retained product line that was integrated into Hill-Rom, was assigned to the respective businesses and fully considered in recognition of the estimated loss to be incurred upon completion of the divestitures. This loss was recorded as a non-cash reduction of goodwill within the Consolidated Balance Sheet, with the remaining $22 million of goodwill assigned to the businesses included in Assets of Discontinued Operations. The tax provision recorded on the loss results from the book and tax basis differentials associated with the businesses and the inability of the Company to readily utilize the capital losses expected to be generated as a result of the divestitures.

Operating results for the discontinued operations were as follows for fiscal year 2003, the ten months ended September 30, 2002 and fiscal year 2001:

	2003	2002	2001
Net revenues from discontinued operations	$101	$74	$88
Pre-tax income from discontinued operations	$ 11	$14	$ 1
Pre-tax loss on disposal of businesses	(50)	—	—
Provision for income taxes	5	6	1
(Loss) income from discontinued operations	$ (44)	$ 8	$—

Assets and liabilities of the discontinued operations, which are presented in separate line-items within the Consolidated Balance Sheet for fiscal year 2003, were as follows:

	2003
Current assets	$21
Property, plant and equipment, net	6
Goodwill	22
Assets of discontinued operations	49
Liabilities of discontinued operations	7
Net assets of discontinued operations	$42

Revenue Recognition

7.39

REPORT OF INDEPENDENT AUDITORS

To the Board of Directors and Shareholders of
The Walt Disney Company

In our opinion, the accompanying consolidated balance sheets and the related consolidated statements of income, shareholders' equity, and cash flows present fairly, in all material respects, the financial position of The Walt Disney Company and its subsidiaries (the Company) at September 30, 2003 and 2002, and the results of their operations and their cash flows for each of the three years in the period ended September 30, 2003, in conformity with accounting principles generally accepted in the United States of America. These financial statements are the responsibility of the Company's management; our responsibility is to express an opinion on these financial statements based on our audits. We conducted our audits of these statements in accordance with auditing standards generally accepted in the United States of America, which require that we plan and perform the audit to obtain reasonable assurance about whether the financial statements are free of material misstatement. An audit includes examining, on a test basis, evidence supporting the amounts and disclosures in the financial statements, assessing the accounting principles used and significant estimates made by management, and evaluating the overall financial statement presentation. We believe that our audits provide a reasonable basis for our opinion.

As discussed in Note 2, the Company adopted EITF No. 00-21, *Revenue Arrangements with Multiple Deliverables* as of October 1, 2002, changing the timing of revenue from certain contracts. Additionally, the Company adopted Statement of Financial Accounting Standards No. 142, *Goodwill and Other Intangible Assets* as of October 1, 2001 and, accordingly, ceased amortizing goodwill and indefinite lived intangible assets as of that date.

NOTES TO CONSOLIDATED FINANCIAL STATEMENTS
(Tabular dollars in millions, except per share amounts)

Note 2 (In Part): Summary of Significant Accounting Policies

Accounting Changes (In Part)

EITF 00-21

The Company adopted Emerging Issues Task Force (EITF) No. 00-21, *Revenue Arrangements with Multiple Deliverables* (EITF 00-21) in the fiscal fourth quarter of 2003. This new accounting rule addresses revenue recognition for revenues derived from a single contract that contains multiple products

or services. The rule provides additional requirements to determine when such revenues may be recorded separately for accounting purposes. Historically, the Company has recognized the NFL broadcast portion of ESPN's affiliate revenue when the NFL games were aired, as ESPN's affiliate contracts provided a basis for allocating such revenue between NFL and non-NFL programming. Since the cost of the NFL rights has also been recognized as the games were aired, the Company recognized both the NFL revenues and NFL costs in the quarters the games were aired.

Under EITF 00-21's requirements for separating the revenue elements of a single contract, the Company will no longer allocate ESPN's affiliate revenue between NFL and non-NFL programming for accounting purposes. As a consequence, the Company will no longer match all NFL revenue with NFL costs as ESPN affiliate revenue (including the NFL portion) will be recognized ratably throughout the year, while NFL contract costs will continue to be recognized in the quarters the games are aired. This accounting change impacts only the timing of revenue recognition and has no impact on cash flow. As a result of this change, the Media Networks segment will report significantly reduced revenue and profitability in the first fiscal quarter when the majority of the NFL games are aired, with commensurately increased revenues and profits in the second and third fiscal quarters.

The Company elected to adopt this new accounting rule using the cumulative effect approach. In the fiscal fourth quarter of 2003, the Company recorded an after-tax charge of $71 million for the cumulative effect of a change in accounting as of the beginning of fiscal year 2003. This amount represents the revenue recorded for NFL games in the fourth quarter of fiscal year 2002. which would have been recorded ratably over fiscal 2003 under the new accounting method. The impact in the fourth quarter reflects the recognition of the remaining $34 million of the $71 million cumulative effect, offset by the $36 million impact of not recognizing NFL revenue that, under the pre-EITF 00-21 method, the Company would have recorded in the fourth quarter of fiscal 2003 as the games were aired. This amount will be recognized during fiscal year 2004. The following table shows the quarterly effect on fiscal year 2003 of this new accounting method.

	Three Months Ended Dec. 31, 2002		Three Months Ended March 31, 2003		Three Months Ended June 30, 2003		Three Months Ended Sept. 30, 2003		Year Ended Sept. 30, 2003	
	Net Income	EPS[1]	Net Income	EPS[1]	Net Income	EPS[1]	Net Income	EPS[1]	Net Income	EPS[1]
Results prior to EITF 00-21 adoption	$ 256	$ 0.13	$229	$0.11	$400	$0.19	$417	$ 0.20	$1,302	$ 0.63
Quarterly impact of accounting change	(149)	(0.07)	85	0.04	102	0.05	(2)	(0.00)	36	0.02
	107	0.06	314	0.15	502	0.24	415	0.20	1,338	0.65
Cumulative effect of accounting change	(71)	(0.03)	—	—	—	—	—	—	(71)	(0.03)
Results subsequent to EITF 00-21 adoption	$ 36	$ 0.02	$314	$0.15	$502	$0.24	$415	$ 0.20	$1,267	$ 0.62

[1] EPS amounts are based on diluted shares outstanding and may not add due to rounding.

The following table provides a reconciliation of reported net earnings to adjusted earnings had EITF 00-21 been followed in fiscal 2002 and 2001:

| | 2002 | | 2001 | |
	Amount	Earnings Per Share	Amount	Earnings Per Share
Reported earnings attributed to Disney common stock before the cumulative effect of accounting changes	$1,236	$ 0.60	$237	$0.11
EITF 00-21 adjustment (net of tax)	(46)	(0.02)	5	–
Adjusted net income	$1,190	$ 0.58	$242	$0.11

Early Extinguishment of Debt

7.40

REPORT OF INDEPENDENT AUDITORS

To the Shareholders of
The ServiceMaster Company

We have audited the accompanying consolidated statements of financial position of The ServiceMaster Company and subsidiaries (the "Company") as of December 31, 2003 and 2002, and the related consolidated statements of operations, shareholders' equity, and cash flows for each of the three years in the period ended December 31, 2003. These financial statements are the responsibility of the Company's management. Our responsibility is to express an opinion on these financial statements based on our audits.

We conducted our audits in accordance with auditing standards generally accepted in the United States of America. Those standards require that we plan and perform the audit to obtain reasonable assurance about whether the financial statements are free of material misstatement. An audit includes examining, on a test basis, evidence supporting the amounts and disclosures in the financial statements. An audit also includes assessing the accounting principles used and significant estimates made by management, as well as evaluating the overall financial statement presentation. We believe that our audits provide a reasonable basis for our opinion.

In our opinion, such consolidated financial statements present fairly, in all material respects, the financial position of The ServiceMaster Company and subsidiaries as of December 31, 2003 and 2002, and the results of their operations and their cash flows for each of the three years in the period ended December 31, 2003, in conformity with accounting principles generally accepted in the United States of America.

As discussed in the Newly Adopted Accounting Principles note to the consolidated financial statements, effective January 1, 2003, the Company adopted Statement of Financial Accounting Standards ("SFAS") No. 145, *Rescission of FASB Statements No. 4, 44, and 64, Amendment of FASB Statement No. 13 and Technical Corrections*. Also, as discussed in the Goodwill and Intangible Assets note to the consolidated financial statements, effective January 1, 2002, the Company adopted SFAS No. 142, *Goodwill and Other Intangible Assets*.

NOTES TO CONSOLIDATED FINANCIAL STATEMENTS

Significant Accounting Policies (In Part)

Newly Adopted Accounting Principles (In Part)

In April 2002, the Financial Accounting Standards Board (FASB) issued SFAS 145, "Rescission of FASB Statements No. 4, 44, and 64, Amendment of FASB Statement No. 13, and Technical Corrections". The primary impact to the Company of this Statement is that it rescinds SFAS 4 which required all material gains and losses from the extinguishment of debt to be classified as extraordinary items. SFAS 145 requires that the more restrictive criteria of APB Opinion No. 30 will be used to determine whether such gains or losses are extraordinary. Beginning in 2003, the Company adopted the provisions of this statement and as such has reclassified the extraordinary losses in 2002 and 2001 into income from continuing operations in the accompanying Consolidated Statements of Operations. In the second quarter of 2002, the Company recorded an extraordinary loss of $.03 per diluted share ($15.4 million pre-tax, $9.2 million after-tax) from the early extinguishment of debt. In the first quarter of 2001 the Company recorded an extraordinary gain of $.02 per diluted share ($10.1 million pre-tax, $6.0 million after-tax) on the nearly extinguishment of debt. In the fourth quarter of 2001 the Company recorded an extraordinary loss of $.03 per diluted share ($16.0 million pre-tax, $9.4 million after-tax) on the early extinguishment of debt. As a result of the Company's adoption of SFAS 145 in 2003, these gains/losses have been reclassified into continuing operations as interest expense, thereby adjusting the previously reported 2002 and 2001 basic and diluted earnings per share from continuing operations by the same aforementioned amounts.

Inventories

7.41

INDEPENDENT AUDITORS' REPORT

To the Stockholders and Board of Directors of
J. C. Penney Company, Inc.

We have audited the accompanying consolidated balance sheets of J. C. Penney Company, Inc. and Subsidiaries as of January 31, 2004 and January 25, 2003, and the related consolidated statements of operations, stockholders' equity and cash flows for each of the years in the three-year period ended January 31, 2004. These consolidated financial statements are the responsibility of the Company's management. Our responsibility is to express an opinion on these consolidated financial statements based on our audits.

We conducted our audits in accordance with auditing standards generally accepted in the United States of America. Those standards require that we plan and perform the audit to obtain reasonable assurance about whether the financial statements are free of material misstatement. An audit includes examining, on a test basis, evidence supporting the amounts and disclosures in the financial statements. An audit also includes assessing the accounting principles used and significant estimates made by management, as well as evaluating the overall financial statement presentation. We believe that our audits provide a reasonable basis for our opinion.

In our opinion, the consolidated financial statements referred to above present fairly, in all material respects, the financial position of J. C. Penney Company, Inc. and Subsidiaries as of January 31, 2004 and January 25, 2003, and the results of their operations and their cash flows for each of the years in the three-year period ended January 31, 2004, in conformity with accounting principles generally accepted in the United States of America.

As discussed in Note 1 of the Notes to the Consolidated Financial Statements, the Company changed its method of determining inflation/deflation rates used in the valuation of LIFO inventories in fiscal year 2002, and the Company adopted the provisions of the Financial Accounting Standards Board's Statement of Financial Accounting Standards No. 142, "Goodwill and Other Intangible Assets," in fiscal year 2002.

NOTES TO THE CONSOLIDATED FINANCIAL STATEMENTS

1 (In Part): Summary of Significant Accounting Policies

Merchandise Inventories

Inventories are valued primarily at the lower of cost (using the last-in, first-out or "LIFO" method) or market, determined by the retail method for department stores and store support centers (SSCs) and average cost for Catalog/Internet and regional warehouses. The lower of cost or market is determined on an aggregate basis for similar types of merchandise. To estimate the effects of inflation/deflation on ending inventory, an internal index measuring price changes from the beginning to the end of the year is calculated using merchandise cost data at the item level. Prior to 2002, the internal index was based on retail prices. Retail pricing is influenced by such factors as changes in pricing strategies, competitive pricing and changes in styles and fashion, particularly in apparel merchandise. All these factors make it difficult to estimate inflation/deflation rates. Accordingly, management changed the basis of the calculation to vendor cost because it would result in a more accurate measure of inflation/deflation rates used to adjust inventory cost under the LIFO method of inventory valuation. The change resulted in a LIFO provision for 2002 of $6 million versus a credit of $17 million under the prior method. For 2002, net income was lower by $14 million and both basic and diluted EPS were lower by $0.06 as a result of this change. The cumulative effect of the accounting change and pro forma amounts for periods prior to 2002 are not determinable because cost data is not available to calculate internal indices for years prior to 2002.

The total Company LIFO (credits)/charges included in cost of goods sold were $(6) million, $6 million and $(9) million in 2003, 2002 and 2001, respectively. If the first-in, first-out or "FIFO" method of inventory valuation had been used instead of the LIFO method, inventories would have been $43 million and $49 million higher at January 31, 2004 and January 25, 2003, respectively.

EMPHASIS OF A MATTER

7.42 Paragraph 19 of *SAS No. 58*, as amended by *SAS No. 79*, states:

19. In any report on financial statements, the auditor may emphasize a matter regarding the financial statements. Such explanatory information should be presented in a separate paragraph of the auditors' report. Phrases such as "with the foregoing (following) explanation" should not be used in the opinion paragraph if an emphasis paragraph is included in the auditors' report. Emphasis paragraphs are never required; they may be added solely at the auditors' discretion. Examples of matters the auditor may wish to emphasize are–

- That the entity is a component of a larger business enterprise.
- That the entity has had significant transactions with related parties.
- Unusually important subsequent events.
- Accounting matters, other than those involving a change or changes in accounting principles, affecting the comparability of the financial statements with those of the preceding period.

7.43 The auditors' reports for 9 survey companies included explanatory information emphasizing a matter regarding the financial statements. Examples of such explanatory information follow.

7.44

INDEPENDENT AUDITORS' REPORT

To the Board of Directors and Stockholders of Albertson's, Inc.

We have audited the accompanying consolidated balance sheets of Albertson's, Inc. and subsidiaries as of January 29, 2004 and January 30, 2003 and the related consolidated statements of earnings, stockholders' equity and cash flows for each of the three years in the period ended January 29, 2004. These financial statements are the responsibility of the Company's management. Our responsibility is to express an opinion on these financial statements based on our audits.

We conducted our audits in accordance with auditing standards generally accepted in the United States of America. Those standards require that we plan and perform the audit to obtain reasonable assurance about whether the financial statements are free of material misstatement. An audit includes examining, on a test basis, evidence supporting the amounts and disclosures in the financial statements. An audit also includes assessing the accounting principles used and significant estimates made by management, as well as evaluating the overall financial statement presentation. We believe that our audits provide a reasonable basis for our opinion.

In our opinion, such consolidated financial statements present fairly, in all material respects, the financial position of Albertson's, Inc. and subsidiaries at January 29, 2004 and January 30, 2003 and the results of their operations and their cash flows for each of the three years in the period ended January 29, 2004, in conformity with accounting principles generally accepted in the United States of America.

As discussed in the notes to the consolidated financial statements, during the year ended January 30, 2003, the Company changed its methods of accounting for goodwill and for closed stores to conform to Statements of Financial Accounting Standards No. 142 and 144. Also during the year ended January 30, 2003, the Company changed its method of accounting for vendor funds to conform to Emerging Issues Task Force Issue No. 02-16.

As discussed in Note 25 to the consolidated financial statements, on March 25, 2004, the Company entered into a stock purchase agreement with J Sainsbury plc and JS USA Holdings Inc. to acquire all of the outstanding capital stock of the entities which conduct J Sainsbury plc's U.S. retail grocery business.

NOTES TO CONSOLIDATED FINANCIAL STATEMENTS
(Dollars in millions)

25 (In Part): Subsequent Events

Acquisition of Shaw's
On March 25, 2004, the Company entered into a stock purchase agreement with J Sainsbury plc and JS USA Holdings Inc. to acquire all of the outstanding capital stock of the entities which conduct J Sainsbury plc's U.S. retail grocery store business for approximately $2,100 in cash, as well as the assumption of approximately $368 in capital leases. The Company intends to use a combination of cash-on-hand and commercial paper to finance a portion of the purchase price of the acquisition. The commercial paper the Company intends to issue will be backed by the Company's existing credit facilities and/or a new senior revolving bridge facility. The Company is also contemplating various financing alternatives, including the issuance of debt and/or equity, to finance a portion of the purchase price and/or to repay some of the commercial paper.

The operations to be acquired consist of approximately 200 grocery stores in the New England area operated under the banners Shaw's and Star Markets. The operations to be acquired ("Shaw's") had sales of approximately $4,600 for the fiscal year ended February 28, 2004 and approximately $4,400 for the fiscal year ended March 1, 2003.

The acquisition is expected to close in the second quarter of 2004 following the satisfaction or waiver of certain closing conditions, including the expiration or termination of the applicable waiting period under the Hart-Scott-Rodino Act and Shaw's fiscal year ended February 28, 2004 financial statement audit reflecting a specified minimum EBITDA. Because of the goodwill that is expected to be generated as a result of the acquisition, the Company will have to obtain prospective waivers from the lenders under two of the Company's existing credit facilities in order to remain in compliance with the consolidated tangible net worth covenant contained in these agreements. No amounts were outstanding under these facilities as of January 29, 2004.

7.45

REPORT OF INDEPENDENT AUDITORS

To the Board of Directors and Shareholders of
Chiquita Brands International, Inc.

We have audited the accompanying consolidated balance sheets of Chiquita Brands International, Inc. as of December 31, 2003 and 2002 (Reorganized Company), and the related consolidated statements of income, shareholders' equity, and cash flow for the year ended December 31, 2003 (Reorganized Company), the nine months ended December 31, 2002 (Reorganized Company), the three months ended March 31, 2002 (Predecessor Company), and the year ended December 31, 2001 (Predecessor Company). These financial statements, appearing on pages 29 to 58, are the responsibility of the Company's management. Our responsibility is to express an opinion on those financial statements based on our audits.

We conducted our audits in accordance with auditing standards generally accepted in the United States. Those standards require that we plan and perform the audit to obtain reasonable assurance about whether the financial statements are free of material misstatement. An audit includes examining, on a test basis, evidence supporting the amounts and disclosures in the financial statements. An audit also includes assessing the accounting principles used and significant estimates made by management, as well as evaluating the overall financial statement presentation. We believe that our audits provide a reasonable basis for our opinion.

In our opinion, the financial statements referred to above present fairly, in all material respects, the consolidated financial position of Chiquita Brands International, Inc. at December 31, 2003 and 2002, and the consolidated results of its operations and its cash flows for the year ended December 31, 2003, the nine month period ended December 31, 2002, the three month period ended March 31, 2002, and the year ended December 31, 2001, in conformity with accounting principles generally accepted in the United States.

As more fully described in Note 16 to the Consolidated Financial Statements, effective March 19, 2002, the Company emerged from protection under Chapter 11 of the U.S. Bankruptcy Code pursuant to a Reorganization Plan that was confirmed by the Bankruptcy Court on March 8, 2002. In accordance with AICPA Statement of Position 90-7, the Company adopted "fresh start" accounting whereby its assets, liabilities and new capital structure were adjusted to reflect estimated fair value at March 31, 2002. As a result, the consolidated financial statements for the periods subsequent to March 31, 2002 reflect the Reorganized Company's new basis of accounting and are not comparable to the Predecessor Company's pre-reorganization consolidated financial statements.

Additionally, as described in Note 1 to the Consolidated Financial Statements, in 2003 the Company changed its method of accounting for employee stock options and variable interest entities, and in 2002 the Company changed its method of accounting for goodwill and other intangible assets.

NOTES TO CONSOLIDATED FINANCIAL STATEMENTS

Note 1 (In Part): Summary of Significant Accounting Policies

Basis of Presentation

On March 19, 2002, Chiquita Brands International, Inc. ("CBII"), a parent holding company without business operations of its own, completed its previously announced financial restructuring when its pre-arranged Plan of Reorganization under Chapter 11 of the U.S. Bankruptcy Code (the "Plan" or "Plan of Reorganization") became effective. For financial reporting purposes, the Company used an effective date of March 31, 2002. References in these financial statements to "Predecessor Company" refer to the Company prior to March 31, 2002. References to "Reorganized Company" refer to the Company on and after March 31, 2002, after giving effect to the issuance of new securities in exchange for the previously outstanding securities in accordance with the Plan, and implementation of fresh start accounting. In accordance with financial reporting requirements for companies emerging from a Chapter 11 restructuring, financial information for the twelve months ended December 31, 2002 is not presented in the Consolidated Financial Statements since such information would combine the results of the Predecessor Company and Reorganized Company. The securities issued pursuant to the Plan and the fresh start adjustments are described in Note 16.

Note 16. Parent Company Debt Restructuring

On March 19, 2002, CBII, a parent holding company without business operations of its own, completed its financial restructuring when its pre-arranged Plan of Reorganization under Chapter 11 of the U.S. Bankruptcy Code became effective.

Pursuant to the Plan, on March 19, 2002, $861 million of the Predecessor Company's outstanding senior notes and subordinated debentures ("Old Notes") and $102 million of accrued and unpaid interest thereon were exchanged for $250 million of 10.56% Senior Notes due 2009 ("Senior Notes") and 95.5% (38.2 million shares) of new Common Stock. Previously outstanding preferred, preference and common stock of the Predecessor Company was exchanged for 2% (0.8 million shares) of the new Common Stock as well as 7-year warrants, exercisable at $19.23 per share, to purchase up to 13.3 million additional shares of new Common Stock. In addition, as part of a management incentive program, certain executives were granted rights to receive 2.5% (1 million shares) of the new Common Stock. At December 31, 2003, 909,865 of these shares had been issued, 49,136 shares had been surrendered in satisfaction of tax withholding obligations, and 40,999 shares were held in a "rabbi trust."

No interest payments on the Old Notes were made in 2002 and 2001. The Company recorded interest expense on the Old Notes until November 28, 2001, the date the Company filed its Chapter 11 petition, but not thereafter. As a result, interest expense for the first quarter of 2002 does not include $20 million which would have been payable under the terms of the Old Notes.

The Company's emergence from Chapter 11 bankruptcy proceedings on March 19, 2002 resulted in a new reporting entity and adoption of fresh start reporting in accordance with Statement of Position ("SOP") No. 90-7, "Financial Reporting by Entities in Reorganization Under the Bankruptcy Code." The Consolidated Financial Statements as of and for the quarter ended March 31, 2002 reflect reorganization adjustments for the discharge of debt and adoption of fresh start reporting. Accordingly, the estimated reorganization value of the Company of $1,280 million, which served as the basis for the Plan approved by the bankruptcy court, was used to determine the equity value allocated to the assets and liabilities of the Reorganized Company in proportion to their relative fair values in conformity with Statement of Financial Accounting Standards No. 141, "Business Combinations." This reorganization value of $1,280 million is before consideration of indebtedness of the Company.

Financial restructuring items for the quarter ended March 31, 2002, totaling a net charge of $286 million, resulted from the following:

- Exchange of Old Notes and accrued interest for 95.5% of the new Common Stock and $250 million of Senior Notes, resulting in a gain of $154 million;
- Reduction of property, plant and equipment carrying values by $491 million, including $320 million relating to the Company's tropical farm assets and $158 million relating to the Company's shipping vessels;
- Reduction of long-term operating investments and other asset carrying values by $182 million;
- Increase in the carrying value of the Chiquita trademark of $375 million;
- Increase of $33 million in accrued pension and other employee benefits primarily associated with tropical pension/severance obligations;
- Increase in other liabilities of $16 million for unfavorable lease obligations;
- Reorganization costs of $30 million in the first quarter of 2002 primarily associated with professional fees and grants of new Common Stock to certain executives as part of the Chapter 11 restructuring agreement. Cash payments in the first quarter of 2002 associated with reorganization costs were $13 million; and
- Reduction of $63 million in long-term assets of subsidiaries that were subsequently classified as discontinued operations.

The fresh start adjustments to the carrying values of the Company's assets and liabilities were based upon the work of outside appraisers, actuaries and financial consultants, as well as internal valuation estimates using discounted cash flow analyses, to determine the relative fair values of the Company's assets and liabilities.

The following table reflects reorganization adjustments to the Company's Consolidated Balance Sheet as of March 31, 2002:

(In thousands)	Before Reorganization Adjustments	Reorganization Adjustments		After Reorganization Adjustments
		Debt Discharge	Fresh Start Adjustments	
Current assets	$ 557,380	$ —	$ —	$ 557,380
Assets of discontinued operations	383,763	—	(63,481)	320,282
Property, plant and equipment, net	861,845	—	(490,734)	371,111
Investments and other assets, net	325,128	—	(182,467)	142,661
Intangibles	11,804	—	375,781	387,585
Total assets	$2,139,920	$ —	$(360,901)	$1,779,019
Notes and loans payable	$ 25,280	$ —	$ —	$ 25,280
Long-term debt due within one year	39,650	—	—	39,650
Accounts payable and accrued liabilities	221,921	—	13,685	235,606
Liabilities of discontinued operations	194,079	—	—	194,079
Long-term debt of parent company	—	250,000	—	250,000
Long-term debt of subsidiaries	217,315	—	—	217,315
Accrued pension and other employee benefits	67,092	—	33,020	100,112
Other liabilities	87,874	—	16,350	104,224
Liabilities subject to compromise	962,820	(962,820)	—	—
Total liabilities	1,816,031	(712,820)	63,055	1,166,266
Retained earnings (deficit)	(657,016)	154,046	502,970	—
Other shareholders' equity	980,905	558,774	(926,926)	612,753*
Total liabilities and shareholders' equity	$2,139,920	$ —	$(360,901)	$1,779,019

Balance Sheet at March 31, 2002 (Unaudited)

* After deducting $654 million of indebtedness from the Company's $1,280 million estimated reorganization value, the total equity value of the Company was $626 million. Indebtedness of $654 million is composed of notes and loans payable of $25 million, long-term debt due within one year of $40 million, long-term debt of parent company of $250 million, long-term debt of subsidiaries of $217 million, and indebtedness included in liabilities of discontinued operations of $122 million. The total shareholders' equity in the March 31, 2002 Reorganized Company balance sheet excludes $13 million related to restricted management shares subject to delayed delivery, which are reflected in accounts payable and accrued liabilities above. These shares were issued in the second quarter of 2002 and are included in equity for all periods after March 31, 2002.

DEPARTURES FROM UNQUALIFIED OPINIONS

7.46 *SAS No. 58* does not require auditors to express qualified opinions as to the effects of uncertainties or as to lack of consistency. Under *SAS No. 58*, departures from unqualified opinions include opinions qualified because of a scope limitation or a departure from generally accepted accounting principles, adverse opinions, and disclaimers of opinion. Paragraphs 20–63 of *SAS No. 58*, as amended by *SAS No. 79*, discuss these departures. None of the auditors' reports issued in connection with the financial statements of the survey companies contained a departure as defined by *SAS No. 58*.

REPORTS ON COMPARATIVE FINANCIAL STATEMENTS

7.47 Paragraphs 65–74 of *SAS No. 58*, as amended by *SAS No. 79*, discuss Reports on Comparative Financial Statements. None of the auditors' reports for the survey companies expressed an opinion on prior year financial statements that differed from the opinion originally expressed.

7.48 In 2003, 9 auditor reports indicated that a change in auditors had occurred in the current year. An example of such a report follows.

7.49

REPORT OF INDEPENDENT AUDITOR

To the Board of Directors and Shareowners of
Sparton Corporation

We have audited the accompanying consolidated balance sheet of Sparton Corporation and subsidiaries as of June 30, 2003, and the related consolidated statements of income, shareowners' equity, and cash flows for the year ended June 30, 2003. Our audit also included the financial statement schedule (2003 column only) listed in the index at Item 15(a). These financial statements and schedule are the responsibility of the Company's management. Our responsibility is to express an opinion on these financial statements and schedule (2003 column only) based on our audit.

We conducted our audit in accordance with auditing standards generally accepted in the United States. Those standards require that we plan and perform the audit to obtain reasonable assurance about whether the financial statements are free of material misstatement. An audit includes examining, on a test basis, evidence supporting the amounts and disclosures in the financial statements. An audit also includes assessing the accounting principles used and significant estimates made by management, as well as evaluating the overall financial statement presentation. We believe that our audit provides a reasonable basis for our opinion.

In our opinion, the financial statements referred to above present fairly, in all material respects, the consolidated financial position of Sparton Corporation and subsidiaries at June 30, 2003, and the consolidated results of their operations and their cash flows for the year ended June 30, 2003, in conformity with accounting principles generally accepted in the United States. Also, in our opinion, the related financial statement schedule (2003 column only), when considered in relation to the basic financial statements taken as a whole, presents fairly in all material respects the information set forth therein.

REPORT OF INDEPENDENT AUDITOR

To the Board of Directors and Shareowners of
Sparton Corporation

We have audited the accompanying consolidated balance sheets of Sparton Corporation and subsidiaries as of June 30, 2002 and 2001, and the related consolidated statements of income, shareowners' equity, and cash flows for the years then ended. Our audits also included the financial statement schedule (2002 and 2001 columns only) listed in the index at Item 15(a). These financial statements and schedule are the responsibility of the Company's management. Our responsibility is to express an opinion on these financial statements and schedule (2002 and 2001 columns only) based on our audits.

We conducted our audits in accordance with auditing standards generally accepted in the United States. Those standards require that we plan and perform the audit to obtain reasonable assurance about whether the financial statements are free of material misstatement. An audit includes examining, on a test basis, evidence supporting the amounts and disclosures in the financial statements. An audit also includes assessing the accounting principles used and

significant estimates made by management, as well as evaluating the overall financial statement presentation. We believe that our audits provide a reasonable basis for our opinion.

In our opinion, the financial statements referred to above present fairly, in all material respects, the consolidated financial position of Sparton Corporation and subsidiaries at June 30, 2002 and 2001, and the consolidated results of their operations and their cash flows for the years then ended, in conformity with accounting principles generally accepted in the United States. Also, in our opinion, the related financial statement schedule (2002 and 2001 columns only), when considered in relation to the basic financial statements taken as a whole, presents fairly in all material respects the information set forth therein.

As discussed in Note 3 to the consolidated financial statements, in the year ended June 30, 2002, the Company changed its method of accounting for its investment in Cybernet Systems Corporation.

OPINION EXPRESSED ON SUPPLEMENTARY FINANCIAL INFORMATION

7.50 Many survey companies provide to stockholders a copy of the Securities and Exchange Commission Form 10-K in lieu of the annual report. The auditor's report included in the Form 10-K generally expresses an opinion on supplementary financial information to the basic financial statements, such as valuation account schedules.

7.51

INDEPENDENT AUDITORS' REPORT

To the Stockholders and Board of Directors
ABM Industries Incorporated

We have audited the accompanying consolidated balance sheets of ABM Industries Incorporated and subsidiaries as of October 31, 2003 and 2002, and the related consolidated statements of income, stockholders' equity and comprehensive income, and cash flows for each of the years in the three-year period ended October 31, 2003. In connection with our audits of the consolidated financial statements, we also have audited the related financial statement Schedule II. These consolidated financial statements and the financial statement schedule are the responsibility of the Company's management. Our responsibility is to express an opinion on these consolidated financial statements and the financial statement schedule based on our audits.

We conducted our audits in accordance with auditing standards generally accepted in the United States of America. Those standards require that we plan and perform the audit to obtain reasonable assurance about whether the financial statements are free of material misstatement. An audit includes examining, on a test basis, evidence supporting the amounts and disclosures in the financial statements. An audit also includes assessing the accounting principles used and significant estimates made by management, as well as evaluating the overall financial statement presentation. We believe that our audits provide a reasonable basis for our opinion.

In our opinion, the consolidated financial statements referred to above present fairly, in all material respects, the financial position of ABM Industries Incorporated and subsidiaries as of October 31, 2003 and 2002, and the results of their operations and their cash flows for each of the years in the three-year period ended October 31, 2003, in conformity with accounting principles generally accepted in the United States of America. Also in our opinion, the related financial statement Schedule II, when considered in relation to the basic consolidated financial statements taken as a whole, presents fairly, in all material respects, the information set forth therein.

7.52

REPORT OF INDEPENDENT PUBLIC ACCOUNTANTS

To the Stockholders and Board of Directors
Werner Enterprises, Inc.

We have audited the accompanying consolidated balance sheets of Werner Enterprises, Inc. and subsidiaries as of December 31, 2003 and 2002, and the related consolidated statements of income, stockholders' equity and comprehensive income, and cash flows for each of the years in the three-year period ended December 31, 2003. In connection with our audits of the consolidated financial statements, we have also audited the financial statement schedule for each of the years in the three-year period ended December 31, 2003, listed in Item 15(a)(2) of this Form 10-K. These consolidated financial statements and financial statement schedule are the responsibility of the Company's management. Our responsibility is to express an opinion on these consolidated financial statements and financial statement schedule based on our audits.

We conducted our audits in accordance with auditing standards generally accepted in the United States of America. Those standards require that we plan and perform the audit to obtain reasonable assurance about whether the financial statements are free of material misstatement. An audit includes examining, on a test basis, evidence supporting the amounts and disclosures in the financial statements. An audit also includes assessing the accounting principles used and significant estimates made by management, as well as evaluating the overall financial statement presentation. We believe that our audits provide a reasonable basis for our opinion.

In our opinion, the consolidated financial statements referred to above present fairly, in all material respects, the financial position of Werner Enterprises, Inc. and subsidiaries as of December 31, 2003 and 2002, and the results of their operations and their cash flows for each of the years in the three-year period ended December 31, 2003, in conformity with accounting principles generally accepted in the United States of America. In addition, in our opinion, the financial statement schedule referred to above, when considered in relation to the basic consolidated financial statements taken as a whole, presents fairly, in all material respects, the information set forth therein.

DATING OF REPORT

7.53 SAS No. 1, Section 530, *Dating of the Independent Auditor's Report*, as amended by SAS No. 7, *Communications Between Predecessor and Successor Auditors*, SAS No. 29, *Reporting on Information Accompanying the Basic Financial Statements in Auditor-Submitted Documents*, and SAS No. 98, *Omnibus Statement on Auditing Standards—2002*, discusses dating of the independent auditors' reports. Paragraphs 1 and 5 of *section 530* state:

> 1. Generally, the date of completion of the field work should be used as the date of the independent auditors' report. Paragraph .05 describes the procedure to be followed when a subsequent event occurring after the completion of the field work is disclosed in the financial statements.
>
> 5. The independent auditor has two methods available for dating the report when a subsequent event disclosed in the financial statements occurs after completion of the field work but before issuance of the related financial statements. The auditor may use "dual dating," for example, "February 16, 20XX, except for Note X, as to which the date is March 1, 20XX," or may date the report as of the later date. In the former instance, the responsibility for events occurring subsequent to the completion of field work is limited to the specific event referred to in the note (or otherwise disclosed). In the latter instance, the independent auditors' responsibility for subsequent events extends to the date of the report and, accordingly, the procedures outlined in Section 560.12 generally should be extended to that date.

7.54 Auditors' reports for 53 survey companies used dual dating. Examples of dual dating follow.

7.55

INDEPENDENT AUDITORS' REPORT

The Board of Directors and Stockholders
Alberto-Culver Company

We have audited the accompanying consolidated balance sheets of Alberto-Culver Company and Subsidiaries as of September 30, 2003 and 2002 and the related consolidated statements of earnings, cash flows and stockholders' equity for each of the years in the three-year period ended September 30, 2003. These consolidated financial statements are the responsibility of the company's management. Our responsibility is to express an opinion on these consolidated financial statements based on our audits.

We conducted our audits in accordance with auditing standards generally accepted in the United States of America. Those standards require that we plan and perform the audit to obtain reasonable assurance about whether the financial statements are free of material misstatement. An audit includes examining, on a test basis, evidence supporting the amounts and disclosures in the financial statements. An audit also includes assessing the accounting principles used and significant estimates made by management, as well as evaluating the overall financial statement presentation. We believe that our audits provide a reasonable basis for our opinion.

In our opinion, the consolidated financial statements referred to above present fairly, in all material respects, the financial position of Alberto-Culver Company and Subsidiaries as of September 30, 2003 and 2002 and the results of their operations and their cash flows for each of the years in the three-year period ended September 30, 2003, in conformity with accounting principles generally accepted in the United States of America.

As discussed in "note 1" to the consolidated financial statements, in the year ended September 30, 2002, the company changed its method of accounting for goodwill and trade names.

October 21, 2003, except as to
Note 11, which is as of
November 5, 2003.

NOTES TO THE CONSOLIDATED FINANCIAL STATEMENTS

11) Subsequent Event—Conversion of Class A Common Stock Into Class B Common Stock

On October 22, 2003, the Board of Directors approved the conversion of all of the issued shares of Class A common stock into Class B common stock on a one share-for-one share basis in accordance with the terms of the company's certificate of incorporation. Such conversion became effective after the close of business on November 5, 2003. The single class of shares continues to trade on the New York Stock Exchange under the symbol ACV. Following the conversion, all outstanding options to purchase shares of Class A common stock became options to purchase an equal number of shares of Class B common stock.

The company accounts for its stock compensation expense in accordance with APB No. 25. Under these rules, the conversion to one class of stock requires a remeasurement of the intrinsic value of all Class A stock options outstanding. As a result, the company will record a non-cash charge against pre-tax earnings of $105.9 million, of which $63.2 million will be recognized in the first quarter of fiscal year 2004, another $23.6 million will be recognized during the remainder of fiscal year 2004 and the final $19.1 million will be recognized over the following three fiscal years in diminishing amounts. The non-cash charges will reduce operating earnings, provision for income taxes, net earnings and basic and diluted net earnings per share. The balance sheet effect of the options remeasurement will increase total stockholders' equity by $22.1 million in the first quarter of fiscal year 2004 and will result in the recognition of a deferred tax asset of the same amount. Thereafter, the remaining non-cash charges will increase total stockholders' equity and result in the recognition of additional deferred tax assets of $8.3 million during the remainder of fiscal year 2004 and $6.7 million over the following three fiscal years in diminishing amounts.

In addition, on October 22, 2003, the Board of Directors authorized the company to purchase up to 1,368,300 shares of Class B common stock. This authorization replaced the Class A repurchase program disclosed in "note 4."

7.56

REPORT OF INDEPENDENT AUDITORS

To the Board of Directors and Shareholders of AMETEK, Inc.

We have audited the accompanying consolidated balance sheets of AMETEK, Inc. as of December 31, 2003 and 2002, and the related consolidated statements of income, cash flows, and stockholders' equity for each of the three years in the period ended December 31, 2003. These financial statements are the responsibility of the Company's management. Our responsibility is to express an opinion on these financial statements based on our audits.

We conducted our audits in accordance with auditing standards generally accepted in the United States. Those standards require that we plan and perform the audit to obtain reasonable assurance about whether the financial statements are free of material misstatement. An audit includes examining, on a test basis, evidence supporting the amounts and disclosures in the financial statements. An audit also includes assessing the accounting principles used and significant estimates made by management, as well as evaluating the overall financial statement presentation. We believe that our audits provide a reasonable basis for our opinion.

In our opinion, the consolidated financial statements referred to above present fairly, in all material respects, the consolidated financial position of AMETEK, Inc. at December 31, 2003 and 2002, and the consolidated results of its operations and its cash flows for each of the three years in the period ended December 31, 2003, in conformity with accounting principles generally accepted in the United States.

As discussed in Notes 1 and 6 to the consolidated financial statements, in 2002 AMETEK, Inc. changed its method of accounting for goodwill in accordance with Statement of Financial Accounting Standards No. 142 "Goodwill and Other Intangible Assets."

January 27, 2004, except for
the fourth paragraph of Note 7,
pertaining to the Company's extension
of its Revolving Credit Facility,
as to which the date is
February 25, 2004.

NOTES TO CONSOLIDATED FINANCIAL STATEMENTS

7 (In Part): Debt

The Company has an unsecured $300 million Revolving Credit Facility which had an original expiration date of September 17, 2006. On February 25, 2004, the agreement was amended to change the expiration date to February 25, 2009. Except for the new 5-year term, the Credit Facility is essentially the same as the original agreement. Interest rates on outstanding loans under the Revolving Credit Facility are either at the London Interbank Offered Rate (LIBOR) plus a negotiated spread over LIBOR, or at the U.S. prime rate plus a spread. At December 31, 2003, the Company had $36.0 million in revolving credit loans outstanding, at a blended rate of 2.4%, all of which is included in short-term borrowings. At December 31, 2003, $239.1 million was unused and available under the Revolving Credit Facility. The Company also had outstanding letters of credit totaling $24.9 million at December 31, 2003.

7.57

INDEPENDENT AUDITORS' REPORT

Board of Directors and Stockholders
Commercial Metals Company

We have audited the consolidated balance sheets of Commercial Metals Company and subsidiaries at August 31, 2003 and 2002, and the related consolidated statements of earnings, stockholders' equity, and cash flows for each of the three years in the period ended August 31, 2003. These financial statements are the responsibility of the Company's management. Our responsibility is to express an opinion on these financial statements based on our audits.

We conducted our audits in accordance with auditing standards generally accepted in the United States of America. Those standards require that we plan and perform the audit to obtain reasonable assurance about whether the financial statements are free of material misstatement. An audit includes examining, on a test basis, evidence supporting the amounts and disclosures in the financial statements. An audit also includes assessing the accounting principles used and significant estimates made by management, as well as evaluating the overall financial statement presentation. We believe that our audits provide a reasonable basis for our opinion.

In our opinion, such consolidated financial statements present fairly, in all material respects, the financial position of Commercial Metals Company and subsidiaries at August 31, 2003 and 2002, and the results of their operations and their cash flows for each of the three years in the period ended August 31, 2003 in conformity with accounting principles generally accepted in the United States of America.

November 5, 2003
(November 13, 2003, as to Note 15).

NOTES TO CONSOLIDATED FINANCIAL STATEMENTS

15. Subsequent Events

In November 2003, the Company repurchased $89 million of its 7.20% notes due in 2005. As a result of this debt repurchase, the Company will record a pre-tax charge of approximately $2.8 million.

Also, in November 2003, the Company issued $200 million of fixed rate notes due in November 2013. The interest rate is 5.625%. Interest is payable semiannually. The Company had entered into an interest rate lock, resulting in an effective rate of 5.644%.

7.58

REPORT OF INDEPENDENT AUDITORS

To the Board of Directors and Shareholders of
Eastman Kodak Company

In our opinion, the accompanying consolidated financial statements appearing on pages 40 through 78 of this Annual Report present fairly, in all material respects, the financial position of Eastman Kodak Company (the Company) at December 31, 2003 and 2002, and the results of its operations and its cash flows for each of the three years in the period ended December 31, 2003, in conformity with accounting principles generally accepted in the United States of America. These financial statements are the responsibility of the Company's management; our responsibility is to express an opinion on these financial statements based on our audits. We conducted our audits of these statements in accordance with auditing standards generally accepted in the United States of America, which require that we plan and perform the audit to obtain reasonable assurance about whether the financial statements are free of material misstatement. An audit includes examining, on a test basis, evidence supporting the amounts and disclosures in the financial statements, assessing the accounting principles used and significant estimates made by management, and evaluating the overall financial statement presentation. We believe that our audits provide a reasonable basis for our opinion.

As discussed in Note 1 to the consolidated financial statements, the Company adopted Statement of Financial Accounting Standards No. 142, "Goodwill and Other Intangible Assets," and No. 144, "Accounting for the Impairment or Disposal of Long-Lived Assets," on January 1, 2002.

February 10, 2004 except for
Note 25, as to which the date is
March 8, 2004.

NOTES TO FINANCIAL STATEMENTS

Note 25: Subsequent Events

On October 22, 2003, the Company announced that it signed a 20-year agreement with China Lucky Film Corp. On February 10, 2004, the Chinese government approved the Company's acquisition of 20 percent of Lucky Film Co. Ltd. (Lucky Film), the largest maker of photographic film in China, in exchange for approximately $100 million in cash, plus approximately $30 million in additional net cash to build and upgrade manufacturing assets, and other Kodak assets. Also, under the arrangement, the Company will provide Lucky Film with technical support, training and equipment upgrades, and Lucky Film will pay Kodak a royalty fee for the use of certain of the Company's technologies as well as dividends on the Lucky Film shares that Kodak will acquire.

On November 25, 2003, the Company announced that it had entered an agreement to acquire the assets of Scitex Digital Printing (SDP) from its parent for $250 million, net of any cash on hand at closing which totaled approximately $13 million, resulting in a net cash price of $237 million. SDP is the leading supplier of high-speed, continuous inkjet printing systems, primarily serving the commercial and transactional printing sectors. Customers use SDP's products to print utility bills, banking and credit card statements, direct mail materials, as well as invoices, financial statements and other transactional documents. The acquisition will provide the Company with additional capabilities in the transactional printing and direct mail sectors while creating another path to commercialize proprietary inkjet technology. The acquisition was completed on January 5, 2004. Kodak is in the process of obtaining a third-party valuation to assist in the purchase price allocation.

On February 9, 2004, the Company announced its intent to sell the assets and business of the Remote Sensing Systems operation, including the stock of Kodak's wholly owned subsidiary, Research Systems, Inc., collectively known as RSS, to ITT Industries for $725 million in cash. RSS, a leading provider of specialized imaging solutions to the aerospace and defense community, is part of the Company's commercial & government systems' operation within the Commercial Imaging segment and its customers include NASA, other U.S. government agencies, and aerospace and defense companies. Kodak's RSS operation had sales in 2003 of approximately $425 million. The sale of RSS is expected to result in an after-tax gain of approximately $390 million (unaudited). The after-tax gain excludes the potential impacts from any settlement or curtailment gains or losses that may be incurred in connection with the Company's pension and postretirement benefit plans, as these amounts are not currently determinable. The Company is currently evaluating whether the sale of RSS will be accounted for as a discontinued operation beginning in the first quarter of 2004 in accordance with SFAS No. 144.

On March 8, 2004, the Company announced that it had agreed with Heidelberger Druckmaschinen AG (Heidelberg) to purchase Heidelberg's 50 percent interest in NexPress, a 50/50 joint venture of Kodak and Heidelberg that makes high-end, on-demand digital color printing systems, and the equity of Heidelberg Digital LLC, a leading maker of digital black-and-white variable-data printing systems. Kodak also will acquire NexPress GmbH, a German subsidiary of Heidelberg that provides engineering and development support, and certain inventory, assets, and employees of Heidelberg's regional operations or market centers. The Company will not pay any cash at closing for the businesses being acquired. Under the terms of the acquisition, Kodak and Heidelberg agreed to use a performance-based earnout formula whereby Kodak will make periodic payments to Heidelberg over a two-year period, if certain sales goals are met. If all sales goals are met during the next two calendar years ending December 31, 2005, the Company will pay a maximum of $150 million in cash. Additional payments may also be made if certain sales goals are met during a five-year period following the closing of the transaction. This acquisition, which is expected to close in May 2004, advances the Company's strategy of diversifying its business portfolio, and accelerates its participation in the digital commercial printing industry.

7.59

INDEPENDENT AUDITORS' REPORT

To the Board of Directors and Stockholders of
Polo Ralph Lauren Corporation

We have audited the accompanying consolidated balance sheets of Polo Ralph Lauren Corporation and subsidiaries (the "Company") as of March 29, 2003 and March 30, 2002, and the related consolidated statements of income, stockholders' equity, and cash flows for each of the three years in the period ended March 29, 2003. These financial statements are the responsibility of the Company's management. Our responsibility is to express an opinion on these financial statements based on our audits.

We conducted our audits in accordance with auditing standards generally accepted in the United States of America. Those standards require that we plan and perform the audit to obtain reasonable assurance about whether the financial statements are free of material misstatement. An audit includes examining, on a test basis, evidence supporting the amounts and disclosures in the financial statements. An audit also includes assessing the accounting principles used and significant estimates made by management, as well as evaluating the overall financial statement presentation. We believe that our audits provide a reasonable basis for our opinion.

In our opinion, such consolidated financial statements present fairly, in all material respects, the financial position of the Company as of March 29, 2003 and March 30, 2002, and the results of their operations and their cash flows for each of the three years in the period ended March 29, 2003, in conformity with accounting principles generally accepted in the United States of America.

As discussed in Notes 1 and 6 to the consolidated financial statements, effective March 31, 2002 the Company changed its method of accounting for goodwill and other intangible assets to conform to Statement of Financial Accounting Standards No. 142.

As discussed in Note 1 to the consolidated financial statements, the Company eliminated the 90-day reporting lag for certain of its European subsidiaries. The results of operations of these subsidiaries for the period October 1, 2001 through December 29, 2001 are reflected as an adjustment to retained earnings in the consolidated financial statements for the year ended March 30, 2002.

May 20, 2003
(June 3, 2003 as to Note 20).

NOTES TO CONSOLIDATED FINANCIAL STATEMENTS

20. Subsequent Events

On June 3, 2003, Jones filed a lawsuit against us in the Supreme Court of the State of New York alleging among other things that we breached our agreements with Jones with respect to the "Lauren" trademark by asserting our rights pursuant to the Cross Default and Term Extension Agreement and that we induced Ms. Jackwyn Nemerov, the former President of Jones, to breach the non-compete and confidentiality clauses in Ms. Nemerov's employment agreement with Jones. Jones has indicated that it will treat the Lauren license agreements as terminated as of December 31, 2003. Jones is seeking compensatory damages of $550.0 million as well as punitive damages and to enforce the provisions of Ms. Nemerov's agreement. If Jones' lawsuit were to be determined adversely to us, it could have a material adverse effect on our results of operations and financial condition; however, we believe that the lawsuit is without merit and that we will prevail. Also on June 3, 2003, we filed a lawsuit against Jones in the Supreme Court of the State of New York seeking among other things an injunction and a declaratory judgment that the Lauren license agreements terminate as of December 31, 2003 pursuant to the terms of the Cross Default and Term Extension Agreement. The Company is preparing to begin production and marketing of the Lauren and Ralph lines with shipments beginning in January 2004.

AUDITORS' REPORT ON INTERNAL CONTROL OVER FINANCIAL REPORTING

7.60 Section 404(a) of the Sarbanes-Oxley Act of 2002 requires that management of a public company assess the effectiveness of the company's internal control over financial reporting as of the end of the company's most recent fiscal year, and to include in the company's annual report management's conclusions as to the effectiveness of the company's internal control structure and procedures. Under section 404(b) of the Sarbanes-Oxley Act of 2002, the auditor that audits the public company's financial statements included in the annual report is required to audit the company's internal control over financial reporting, and attest to and report on management's assessment of the effectiveness of internal control over financial reporting. Thus, the auditor's report on internal control over financial reporting should include two opinions: one on whether management's assessment is fairly stated, and one on the effectiveness of the internal control over financial reporting. AS No. 2, *An Audit of Internal Control Over Financial Reporting Performed in Conjunction With an Audit of Financial Statements*, establishes professional standards governing the auditor's attestation. Generally, public companies with a market capitalization exceeding $75 million are required to comply with the internal control reporting and disclosure requirements of section 404 of the Sarbanes-Oxley Act for fiscal years ending on or after November 15, 2004, with early adoption permitted. Other public companies have until fiscal years ending on or after July 15, 2005. Accordingly, independent auditors engaged to audit the financial statements of such companies also are required to audit and report on the company's internal control over financial reporting as of the end of such fiscal year. *AS No. 2* did not yet apply to any of the company annual reports surveyed in this edition.

7.61 Paragraph 169 of *AS No. 2* allows the auditor to issue a combined report (i.e., one report containing both an opinion on the financial statements and the two opinions on internal control over financial reporting), or separate reports on the company's financial statements and on internal control over financial reporting. Illustrative auditor's reports on internal control over financial reporting are included in Appendix A of *AS No. 2*. An example of a standard report on internal control over financial reporting issued separate from the report on financial statements, and a combined standard report follow.

Separate Report on Internal Control

7.62

REPORT OF INDEPENDENT REGISTERED PUBLIC ACCOUNTING FIRM

We have audited management's assessment, included in the accompanying management's report on internal control, that W Company maintained effective control over financial reporting as of December 31, 20X3, based on criteria established in *Internal Control—Integrated Framework* issued by the Committee of Sponsoring Organizations of the Treadway Commission (COSO). W Company's management is responsible for maintaining effective internal control over financial reporting and for its assessment of the effectiveness of internal control over financial reporting. Our responsibility is to express an opinion on management's assessment and an opinion on the effectiveness of the company's internal control over financial reporting based on our audit.

We conducted our audit in accordance with the standards of the Public Company Accounting Oversight Board (United States). Those standards require that we plan and perform the audit to obtain reasonable assurance about whether effective internal control over financial reporting was maintained in all material respects. Our audit included obtaining an understanding of internal control over financial reporting, evaluating management's assessment, testing and evaluating the design and operating effectiveness of internal control, and performing such other procedures as we considered necessary in the circumstances. We believe that our audit provides a reasonable basis for our opinion.

A company's internal control over financial reporting is a process designed to provide reasonable assurance regarding the reliability of financial reporting and the preparation of financial statements for external purposes in accordance with generally accepted accounting principles. A company's internal control over financial reporting includes those policies and procedures that (1) pertain to the maintenance of records that, in reasonable detail, accurately and fairly reflect the transactions and dispositions of the assets of the company; (2) provide reasonable assurance that transactions are recorded as necessary to permit preparation of financial statements in accordance with generally accepted accounting principles, and that receipts and expenditures of the company are being made only in accordance with authorizations of management and directors of the company; and (3) provide reasonable assurance regarding prevention or timely detection of unauthorized acquisition, use, or disposition of the company's assets that could have a material effect on the financial statements.

Because of its inherent limitations, internal control over financial reporting may not prevent or detect misstatements. Also, projections of any evaluation of effectiveness to future periods are subject to the risk that controls may become inadequate because of changes in conditions, or that the degree of compliance with the policies or procedures may deteriorate.

In our opinion, management's assessment that W Company maintained effective internal control over financial reporting as of December 31, 20X3, is fairly stated, in all material respects, based on criteria established in *Internal Control—Integrated Framework* issued by the Committee of Sponsoring Organizations of the Treadway Commission (COSO). Also in our opinion, W Company maintained, in all material respects, effective internal control over financial reporting as of December 31, 20X3, based on criteria established in *Internal Control—Integrated Framework* issued by the Committee of Sponsoring Organizations of the Treadway Commission (COSO).

We have also audited, in accordance with the standards of the Public Company Accounting Oversight Board (United States), the accompanying balance sheets of W Company as of December 31, 20X3 and 20X2, and the related statements of income, stockholders' equity and comprehensive income, and cash flows for each of the years in the three-year period ended December 31, 20X3 of W Company and our report dated [*date of report, which should be the same as the date of the report on the effectiveness of internal control over financial reporting*] expressed [*include nature of opinion*].

7.63 Paragraph 170 of *AS No. 2* states that when the auditor chooses to issue a separate report on internal control over financial reporting, the following paragraph should be added to the auditor's report on the financial statements.

We have also audited, in accordance with the standards of the Public Company Accounting Oversight Board (United States), the effectiveness of W Company's internal control over financial reporting as of December 31, 20X3, based on criteria established in *Internal Control—Integrated Framework* issued by the Committee of Sponsoring Organizations of the Treadway Commission (COSO) and our report dated [*date of report, which should be the same as the date of the report on the financial statements*] expressed [*include nature of opinions*].

Combined Report on Financial Statements and Internal Control

7.64

REPORT OF INDEPENDENT REGISTERED PUBLIC ACCOUNTING FIRM

We have audited the accompanying balance sheets of W Company as of December 31, 20X3 and 20X2, and related statements of income, stockholders' equity and comprehensive income, and cash flows for each of the three years in the period ended December 31, 20X3. We also have audited management's assessment, included in the accompanying management's report on internal control, that W Company maintained effective control over financial reporting as of December 31, 20X3, based on criteria established in *Internal Control—Integrated Framework* issued by the Committee of Sponsoring Organizations of the Treadway Commission (COSO). W Company's management is responsible for these financial statements, for maintaining effective internal control over financial reporting, and for its assessment of the effectiveness of internal control over financial reporting. Our responsibility is to express an opinion on these financial statements, an opinion on management's assessment, and an opinion on the effectiveness of the company's internal control over financial reporting based on our audits.

We conducted our audits in accordance with the standards of the Public Company Accounting Oversight Board (United States). Those standards require that we plan and perform the audits to obtain reasonable assurance about whether the financial statements are free of material misstatement and whether effective internal control over financial reporting was maintained in all material respects. Our audit of financial statements included examining, on a test basis, evidence supporting the amounts and disclosures in the financial statements, assessing the accounting principles used and significant estimates made by management, and evaluating the overall financial statement presentation. Our audit of internal control over financial reporting included obtaining an understanding of internal control over financial reporting, evaluating management's assessment, testing and evaluating the design and operating effectiveness of internal control, and performing such other procedures as we considered necessary in the circumstances. We believe that our audits provide a reasonable basis for our opinions.

A company's internal control over financial reporting is a process designed to provide reasonable assurance regarding the reliability of financial reporting and the preparation of financial statements for external purposes in accordance with generally accepted accounting principles. A company's internal control over financial reporting includes those policies and procedures that (1) pertain to the maintenance of records that, in reasonable detail, accurately and fairly reflect the transactions and dispositions of the assets of the company; (2) provide reasonable assurance that transactions are recorded as necessary to permit preparation of financial statements in accordance with generally accepted accounting principles, and that receipts and expenditures of the company are being made only in accordance with authorizations of management and directors of the company; and (3) provide reasonable assurance regarding prevention or timely detection of unauthorized acquisition, use, or disposition of the company's assets that could have a material effect on the financial statements.

Because of its inherent limitations, internal control over financial reporting may not prevent or detect misstatements. Also, projections of any evaluation of effectiveness to future periods are subject to the risk that controls may become inadequate because of changes in conditions, or that the degree of compliance with the policies or procedures may deteriorate.

In our opinion, the financial statements referred to above present fairly, in all material respects, the financial position of W Company as of December 31, 20X3 and 20X2, and the results of its operations and its cash flows for each of the years in the three-year period ended December 31, 20X3, in conformity with accounting principles generally accepted in the United States of America. Also in our opinion, management's assessment that W Company maintained effective internal control over financial reporting as of December 31, 20X3, is fairly stated, in all material respects, based on criteria established in *Internal Control—Integrated Framework* issued by the Committee of Sponsoring Organizations of the Treadway Commission (COSO). Furthermore, in our opinion, W Company maintained, in all material respects, effective internal control over financial reporting as of December 31, 20X3, based on criteria established in *Internal Control—Integrated Framework* issued by the Committee of Sponsoring Organizations of the Treadway Commission (COSO).

MANAGEMENT AND SPECIAL PURPOSE COMMITTEE REPORTS

7.65 There were 274 survey companies that presented a Report of Management. These reports may include:
- Description of management's responsibility for preparing the financial statements,
- Identification of independent auditors,
- Statement about management's representations to the independent auditors,
- Statement about financial records and related data made available to the independent auditors,
- Description of special purpose committees of the Board of Directors,
- General description of the company's system of internal control, and
- Description of the company's code of conduct.

Occasionally, survey companies presented a report of a special purpose committee, such as the Audit Committee or the Compensation Committee.

7.66 The Sarbanes-Oxley Act of 2002 requires management to include in its annual report an assessment of the effectiveness of the company's internal control over financial reporting. Paragraph 162 of *AS No. 2* specifies that management is required to state a direct conclusion about whether

the company's internal control over financial reporting is effective. Management's report on internal control over financial reporting is required to include the following:
- A statement of management's responsibility for establishing and maintaining adequate internal control over financial reporting for the company;
- A statement identifying the framework used by management to conduct the required assessment of the effectiveness of the company's internal control over financial reporting;
- An assessment of the effectiveness of the company's internal control over financial reporting as of the end of the company's most recent fiscal year, including an explicit statement as to whether that internal control over financial reporting is effective; and
- A statement that the registered public accounting firm that audited the financial statements included in the annual report has issued an attestation report on management's assessment of the company's internal control over financial reporting.

7.67 Examples of reports of management and certain special purpose committee reports follow. None of the survey companies made a report on internal control over financial reporting as specified by *AS No. 2*.

Reports of Management

7.68

DELPHI CORPORATION (DEC)

MANAGEMENT RESPONSIBILITY

Management is responsible for the preparation and presentation of our consolidated financial statements. These statements have been prepared in conformity with accounting principles generally accepted in the United States of America and, as such, include amounts based on management judgments and estimates. We are further responsible for maintaining an internal control structure designed to provide reasonable assurance that the books and records reflect the transactions of Delphi and that established policies and procedures are appropriately followed.

Deloitte & Touche LLP, an independent audit firm, is engaged to audit our consolidated financial statements. The audit is conducted in accordance with auditing standards generally accepted in the United States of America that comprehend the consideration of internal control and tests of transactions to the extent necessary to form an independent opinion on the consolidated financial statements prepared by management. The independent auditors' report follows this report.

The Board of Directors, through the Audit Committee (composed entirely of independent Directors) is responsible for assuring that management fulfills its responsibilities in the preparation of the consolidated financial statements. The Audit Committee selects the independent auditors (subject to shareholder ratification) and reviews the scope of the audits and the accounting principles being applied in financial reporting. The independent auditors, representatives of management, and the Vice President of Corporate Audit Services meet regularly (separately and jointly) with the Audit Committee to:

- Review the activities of each,
- Ensure that each is properly discharging its responsibilities,
- Review any audit significant findings or recommendations, and
- Assess the effectiveness of internal controls.

Each quarter, the Audit Committee meets with management and privately with the independent auditors in advance of the public release of operating results and filing of annual and quarterly reports with the Securities and Exchange Commission. It is management's conclusion that internal controls at December 31, 2003 provide reasonable assurance that the books and records reflect the transactions of Delphi and that the businesses comply with established policies and procedures. Deloitte & Touche LLP has full and free access to meet with the Audit Committee, without management representatives present, to discuss the results of the audit, the adequacy of internal control, and the quality of financial reporting.

We also have policies and procedures designed to ensure that our corporate governance practices are consistent with the corporate governance requirements of the Sarbanes-Oxley Act of 2002 and with the listing requirements of the New York Stock Exchange. These practices include:

- Clear corporate governance policies,
- A majority of our Board is independent from Delphi and its management,
- Independent members of our Board meet regularly without management,
- All of our Board Committees have charters that clearly establish roles and responsibilities,
- A formal code of ethics, "Foundation for Excellence" which applies to all of our employees, including our Board and our senior management, and
- We have an ethics "hot-line" available to all employees globally.

We are committed to clear, deliberate and sound corporate governance and business practices and transparency in our financial reporting.

Chairman, Chief Executive Officer and President

Vice Chairman and Chief Financial Officer

Chief Accounting Officer and Controller

7.69

INTERNATIONAL PAPER COMPANY (DEC)

REPORT OF MANAGEMENT ON FINANCIAL STATEMENTS

The management of International Paper Company is responsible for the fair presentation of the information contained in the financial statements in this Annual Report. The statements are prepared in accordance with accounting principles generally accepted in the United States of America and reflect management's best judgment as to our financial position, results of operations, cash flows and related disclosures.

International Paper maintains a system of internal accounting and disclosure controls designed to provide reasonable assurance: (a) that transactions are properly recorded and summarized so that reliable financial records and reports can be prepared and assets safeguarded; and (b) that information required to be disclosed by us in reports filed with the Securities and Exchange Commission (SEC) is recorded, processed, summarized and reported on a timely basis. We have formed a Disclosure Committee to oversee this process. We believe that these controls are effective and have completed all the certifications required by the Sarbanes-Oxley Act of 2002 and SEC regulations.

Our ethics program is an important part of the internal controls system. It includes long-standing principles and policies on ethical business conduct that require employees to maintain the highest ethical and legal standards in the conduct of International Paper business, that have been distributed to all employees, a toll-free telephone helpline whereby any employee may report suspected violations of law or International Paper's policy, and an office of ethics and business practice. The internal controls system further includes careful selection and training of supervisory and management personnel, appropriate delegation of authority and division of responsibility, dissemination of accounting and business policies throughout International Paper, and an extensive program of internal audits with management follow-up.

The independent auditors provide an objective, independent review of management's discharge of its responsibility for the fair presentation of our financial statements. They review our internal controls and conduct tests of procedures and accounting records to enable them to form the opinion set forth in their report.

The Board of Directors, assisted by the Audit and Finance Committee (Committee), monitors management's administration of International Paper's financial and accounting policies and practices, and the preparation of these financial statements. The Committee, which currently consists of five independent directors, meets regularly with representatives of management, the independent auditors and the Internal Auditor to review their activities. The Committee's Charter takes into account the New York Stock Exchange rules relating to Audit Committees and the SEC rules and regulations promulgated as a result of the Sarbanes-Oxley Act of 2002. A copy of the charter is available on our internet Web site at www.internationalpaper.com, or may be obtained from the Corporate Secretary at our corporate headquarters. The Committee has reviewed and discussed the consolidated financial statements for the year ended December 31, 2003, including critical accounting policies and significant management judgments, with management and the independent auditors. The Committee's report recommending the inclusion of such financial statements in this Annual Report on Form 10-K is set forth in our Proxy Statement.

The independent auditors and the Internal Auditor both have free access to the Committee and meet regularly with the Committee, with and without management representatives in attendance.

Chairman and Chief Executive Officer

Senior Vice-President and Chief Financial Officer

Audit Committee Reports

7.70

ELI LILLY AND COMPANY (DEC)

AUDIT COMMITTEE REPORT

The audit committee reviews the company's financial reporting process on behalf of the board. Management has the primary responsibility for the financial statements and the reporting process, including the systems of internal controls and disclosure controls. In this context, we have met and held discussions with management and the independent auditors. Management represented to us that the company's consolidated financial statements were prepared in accordance with generally accepted accounting principles, and we have reviewed and discussed the audited financial statements and related disclosures with management and the independent auditors, including a review of the significant management judgments underlying the financial statements and disclosures.

The independent auditors report to us and to the board. We have sole authority to appoint (subject to shareholder ratification) and to terminate the engagement of the independent auditors.

We have discussed with the independent auditors matters required to be discussed by Statement on Auditing Standards No. 61 (Communication With Audit Committees), including the quality, not just the acceptability, of the accounting principles, the reasonableness of significant judgments, and the clarity of the disclosures in the financial statements. In addition, we have received the written disclosures and the letter from the independent auditors required by the Independence Standards Board Standard No. 1 (Independence Discussions With Audit Committees) and have discussed with the independent auditors the auditors' independence from the company and its management. In concluding that the auditors are independent, we determined, among other things, that the nonaudit services provided by Ernst & Young (as described below) were compatible with their independence. Consistent with the requirements of the Sarbanes-Oxley Act of 2002, we have adopted additional policies to ensure the independence of the independent auditors, such as prior committee approval of nonaudit services and required audit partner rotation.

We discussed with the company's internal and independent auditors the overall scope and plans for their respective audits. We periodically meet with the internal and independent auditors, with and without management present, to discuss the results of their examinations, their evaluations of the company's internal controls, and the overall quality of the company's financial reporting. We also periodically meet in executive session.

In reliance on the reviews and discussions referred to above, we recommended to the board (and the board subsequently approved the recommendation) that the audited financial statements be included in the company's annual report on Form 10-K for the year ended December 31, 2003, for filing with the Securities and Exchange Commission. We have also appointed the company's independent auditors, subject to shareholder ratification.

Chair, Audit Committee

7.71

PFIZER INC (DEC)

AUDIT COMMITTEE'S REPORT

The Audit Committee reviews the Company's financial reporting process on behalf of the Board of Directors. Management has the primary responsibility for the financial statements and the reporting process, including the system of internal controls.

In this context, the Committee has met and held discussions with management and the independent auditor regarding the fair and complete presentation of the Company's results. The Committee has discussed significant accounting policies applied by the Company in its financial statements, as well as alternative treatments. Management represented to the Committee that the Company's consolidated financial statements were prepared in accordance with accounting principles generally accepted in the United States of America, and the Committee has reviewed and discussed the consolidated financial statements with management and the independent auditor. The Committee discussed with the independent auditor matters required to be discussed by Statement of Auditing Standards No. 61, *Communication With Audit Committees*.

In addition, the Committee has discussed with the independent auditor the auditor's independence from the Company and its management, including the matters in the written disclosures required by the Independence Standards Board Standard No. 1, *Independence Discussions with Audit Committees*. The Committee also has considered whether the independent auditor's provision of non-audit services to the Company is compatible with the auditor's independence. The Committee has concluded that the independent auditor is independent from the Company and its management.

The Committee discussed with the Company's internal and independent auditors the overall scope and plans for their respective audits. The Committee meets with the internal and independent auditors, with and without management present, to discuss the results of their examinations, the evaluations of the Company's internal controls, and the overall quality of the Company's financial reporting.

In reliance on the reviews and discussions referred to above, the Committee recommended to the Board of Directors, and the Board has approved, that the audited financial statements be included in the Company's Annual Report on Form 10-K for the year ended December 31, 2003, for filing with the Securities and Exchange Commission. The Committee has selected and the Board of Directors has ratified, subject to shareholder approval, the selection of the Company's independent auditor.

Chair, Audit Committee

Compensation Committee Report

7.72

MERCK & CO., INC. (DEC)

*COMPENSATION AND BENEFITS COMMITTEE'S
REPORT*

The Compensation and Benefits Committee, comprised of independent directors, approves compensation objectives and policies for all employees and sets compensation for the Company's executive officers. The Committee seeks to ensure that rewards are closely linked to Company, division, team and individual performances. The Committee also seeks to ensure that compensation and benefits are set at levels that enable Merck to attract and retain highly qualified employees. The Committee views stock ownership as a vehicle to align the interests of employees with those of the Company's stockholders. Consistent with the long-term focus inherent in the Company's R&D-based pharmaceutical business, it is the policy of the Committee to make a high proportion of executive officer compensation dependent on long-term performance and on enhancing stockholder value.

Chairperson

Appendix of 600 Companies

List of 600 Companies on Which Tabulations Are Based

In this edition, companies have been assigned the same number as in the Fifty-seventh (2003) edition. 21 companies in the 2003 edition have been eliminated and their numbers left unused. These companies were replaced by companies not previously included in any prior editions. Companies are listed in alphabetical order. An additional listing in company reference number order follows.

ALPHABETICAL LISTING

Company Name	Company Reference Number	Month of Fiscal Year End*	Company Name	Company Reference Number	Month of Fiscal Year End*
3Com Corporation	951	5	Anheuser-Busch Companies, Inc.	51	12
3M Company	379	12	Anthem, Inc.	1096	12
Abbott Laboratories	10	12	A. O. Smith Corporation	494	12
ABM Industries Incorporated	30	10	Apple Computer, Inc.	52	9
Acterna Corporation	1071	3	Applied Industrial Technologies, Inc.	955	6
Acuity Brands, Inc.	1095	8	Applied Materials, Inc.	863	10
ADC Telecommunications, Inc.	921	10	Archer Daniels Midland Company	53	6
Administaff, Inc.	988	12	Arden Group, Inc.	54	12
Adolph Coors Company	147	12	Arkansas Best Corporation	1072	12
Advanced Micro Devices, Inc.	652	12	Armstrong Holdings, Inc.	1033	12
ADVO, Inc.	861	9	Arrow Electronics, Inc.	844	12
Aetna Inc.	989	12	ArvinMeritor, Inc.	1073	9
AGCO Corporation	862	12	Ashland Inc.	60	9
Air Products and Chemicals, Inc.	16	9	AT&T Corp.	43	12
Airgas, Inc.	1030	3	Atmel Corporation	864	12
AK Steel Holding Corporation	56	12	Ault Incorporated	738	5
Alberto-Culver Company	601	9	Automatic Data Processing, Inc.	865	6
Albertson's, Inc.	17	1	AutoZone, Inc.	991	8
Alcoa Inc.	24	12	Avaya Inc.	1034	9
Allegheny Technologies Incorporated	776	12	Avery Dennison Corporation	604	12
Allergan, Inc.	796	12	Avnet, Inc.	65	6
Alliant Techsystems Inc.	777	3	Avon Products, Inc.	66	12
Allied Waste Industries, Inc.	922	12	Badger Meter, Inc.	68	12
ALLTEL Corporation	1031	12	Baker Hughes Incorporated	70	12
Altria Group, Inc.	437	12	Baldor Electric Company	778	12
Amazon.com, Inc.	953	12	Ball Corporation	71	12
Amcast Industrial Corporation	25	8	Banta Corporation	806	12
Amerada Hess Corporation	26	12	Barnes & Noble, Inc.	992	1
American Biltrite Inc.	28	12	Barnes Group Inc.	605	12
American Greetings Corporation	33	2	Bassett Furniture Industries, Incorporated	606	11
American Standard Companies Inc.	41	12			
Ameron International Corporation	44	11	Bausch & Lomb Incorporated	74	12
AMETEK, Inc.	6	12	Baxter International Inc.	75	12
Amgen Inc.	841	12	B/E Aerospace, Inc.	866	2
Amkor Technology, Inc.	954	12	Beckman Coulter, Inc.	846	12
Ampco-Pittsburgh Corporation	46	12	Becton, Dickinson and Company	78	9
Amphenol Corporation	842	12	BellSouth Corporation	958	12
Anacomp, Inc.	696	9	Bemis Company, Inc.	81	12
Anadarko Petroleum Corporation	990	12	Best Buy Co., Inc.	993	2
Analog Devices, Inc.	924	10	BJ Services Company	896	9
Analogic Corporation	48	7	The Black & Decker Corporation	85	12

*Months are numbered in calendar-year sequence, January through December (e.g., January = 1 and February = 2).

Company Name	Company Reference Number	Month of Fiscal Year End*	Company Name	Company Reference Number	Month of Fiscal Year End*
Blount International, Inc.	699	12	Convergys Corporation	1098	12
The Boeing Company	87	12	Cooper Cameron Corporation	900	12
Boise Cascade Corporation	88	12	Cooper Industries, Ltd.	146	12
Boston Scientific Corporation	867	12	Cooper Tire & Rubber Company	849	12
Bowater Incorporated	607	12	Corn Products International, Inc.	1099	12
Bowne & Co., Inc.	91	12	Corning Incorporated	149	12
Briggs & Stratton Corporation	93	6	Costco Wholesale Corporation	961	8
Brinker International, Inc.	1074	6	Courier Corporation	150	9
Bristol-Myers Squibb Company	94	12	Cox Communications, Inc.	1001	12
Brown Shoe Company, Inc.	97	1	Crane Co.	152	12
Brown-Forman Corporation	657	4	C. R. Bard, Inc.	845	12
Brunswick Corporation	99	12	Crompton Corporation	1077	12
Burlington Coat Factory Warehouse Corporation	959	5	Crown Holdings, Inc.	154	12
Burlington Resources Inc.	700	12	CSP Inc.	107	9
Cablevision Systems Corporation	994	12	CTS Corporation	701	12
Cabot Corporation	108	9	Cummins Inc.	1100	12
Caesars Entertainment, Inc.	1018	12	Curtiss-Wright Corporation	158	12
Campbell Soup Company	110	7	CVS Corporation	372	12
Caremark Rx, Inc.	995	12	Dana Corporation	161	12
Carlisle Companies Incorporated	897	12	Danaher Corporation	664	12
Carpenter Technology Corporation	610	6	Darden Restaurants, Inc.	1043	5
Caterpillar Inc.	113	12	Datascope Corp.	927	6
CDW Corporation	996	12	Dean Foods Company	166	5
Cendant Corporation	1036	12	Deere & Company	167	10
Centex Corporation	836	3	Del Monte Foods Company	962	4
CenturyTel, Inc.	1037	12	Dell Inc.	963	1
Ceridian Corporation	145	12	Delphi Corporation	1003	12
Champion Enterprises, Inc.	740	12	Deluxe Corporation	168	12
Charter Communications, Inc.	1038	12	The Dial Corporation	257	12
Chesapeake Corporation	659	12	Diebold, Incorporated	1101	12
ChevronTexaco Corporation	121	12	Dillard's, Inc.	850	1
Chiquita Brands International, Inc.	557	12	DIMON Incorporated	782	6
Ciena Corporation	1039	10	The Dixie Group, Inc.	665	12
Cigna Corporation	997	12	Dollar General Corporation	1102	1
Cintas Corporation	1040	5	Donaldson Company, Inc.	744	7
Circuit City Stores, Inc.	868	2	Dover Corporation	176	12
Cisco Systems, Inc.	869	7	The Dow Chemical Company	177	12
Citizens Communications Company	1041	12	Dow Jones & Company, Inc.	178	12
CLARCOR Inc.	658	11	D.R. Horton, Inc.	1103	9
Clear Channel Communications, Inc.	998	12	The Dun & Bradstreet Corporation	182	12
Cleveland-Cliffs Inc.	130	12	Earthlink, Inc.	1078	12
The Clorox Company	131	6	The Eastern Company	190	12
CNF Inc.	1075	12	Eastman Chemical Company	871	12
Coca-Cola Bottling Co. Consolidated	1076	12	Eastman Kodak Company	191	12
The Coca-Cola Company	133	12	Eaton Corporation	192	12
Coca-Cola Enterprises Inc.	660	12	eBay Inc.	1104	12
Coherent, Inc.	742	9	Ecolab Inc.	617	12
Colgate-Palmolive Company	135	12	E. I. du Pont de Nemours and Company	184	12
Collins Industries, Inc.	137	10	Electronic Arts Inc.	1079	3
Comcast Corporation	999	12	Electronic Data Systems Corporation	964	12
Comdisco Holding Company, Inc.	1000	9	Eli Lilly and Company	339	12
Commercial Metals Company	140	8	Elkcorp	194	6
Computer Associates International, Inc.	925	3	EMC Corporation	1005	12
Computer Sciences Corporation	848	3	EMCOR Group, Inc.	901	12
ConAgra Foods, Inc.	142	5	Emerson Electric Co.	195	9
ConocoPhillips	438	12	Enesco Group, Inc.	510	12
Constellation Brands, Inc.	1097	2	Engelhard Corporation	198	12
			Equifax Inc.	902	12

*Months are numbered in calendar-year sequence, January through December (e.g., January = 1 and February = 2).

Company Name	Company Reference Number	Month of Fiscal Year End*	Company Name	Company Reference Number	Month of Fiscal Year End*
The Estee Lauder Companies Inc.	872	6	Hecla Mining Company	273	12
Ethyl Corporation	199	12	Hercules Incorporated	276	12
Exide Technologies	873	3	Herman Miller, Inc.	377	5
Exxon Mobil Corporation	202	12	Hershey Foods Corporation	277	12
The Fairchild Corporation	656	6	Hewlett-Packard Company	278	10
Fedders Corporation	206	8	Hillenbrand Industries, Inc.	624	9
Federal Screw Works	747	6	Hilton Hotels Corporation	1011	12
Federal-Mogul Corporation	208	12	H.J. Heinz Company	275	4
Federated Department Stores, Inc.	209	1	The Home Depot, Inc.	905	1
Ferro Corporation	800	12	HON INDUSTRIES Inc.	263	12
First Data Corporation	851	12	Honeywell International Inc.	20	12
Fiserv, Inc.	1044	12	Hormel Foods Corporation	282	10
Fleetwood Enterprises, Inc.	212	4	Hubbell Incorporated	930	12
Flowers Foods, Inc.	1080	12	Hughes Supply, Inc.	283	1
Flowserve Corporation	903	12	Humana Inc.	285	12
Fluor Corporation	216	12	Hurco Companies, Inc.	287	10
FMC Corporation	203	12	IDT Corporation	1046	7
Foot Locker, Inc.	596	1	IKON Office Solutions, Inc.	18	9
Ford Motor Company	219	12	Illinois Tool Works Inc.	625	12
Fortune Brands, Inc.	29	12	IMC Global Inc.	752	12
Foster Wheeler Ltd.	221	12	Ingersoll-Rand Company Limited	292	12
Freeport-McMoRan Copper & Gold Inc.	965	12	Ingram Micro Inc.	906	12
Furniture Brands International, Inc.	296	12	Intel Corporation	295	12
Gannett Co., Inc.	228	12	InterActiveCorp	985	12
The Gap, Inc.	1008	1	Interface, Inc.	753	12
Gateway, Inc.	874	12	Intergraph Corporation	801	12
GenCorp Inc.	230	11	International Business Machines Corporation	298	12
General Dynamics Corporation	232	12			
General Electric Company	233	12	International Flavors & Fragrances Inc.	627	12
General Mills, Inc.	237	5			
General Motors Corporation	238	12	International Multifoods Corporation	301	2
Genuine Parts Company	242	12	International Paper Company	302	12
Georgia Gulf Corporation	748	12	The Interpublic Group of Companies, Inc.	837	12
Georgia-Pacific Corporation	243	12			
Giant Industries, Inc.	1081	12	Interstate Bakeries Corporation	303	5
The Gillette Company	246	12	Intuit Inc.	1106	7
GlobalSantaFe Corporation	929	12	Iomega Corporation	931	12
Golden Enterprises, Inc.	247	5	ITT Industries, Inc.	291	12
Goodrich Corporation	1045	12	Jabil Circuit, Inc.	1012	8
The Goodyear Tire & Rubber Company	249	12	Jacobs Engineering Group Inc.	754	9
The Great Atlantic & Pacific Tea Company, Inc.	254	2	Jacuzzi Brands, Inc.	948	9
			J. C. Penney Company, Inc.	428	1
Greif Bros. Corporation	256	10	JDS Uniphase Corporation	1047	6
Grey Global Group Inc.	1082	12	JLG Industries, Inc.	305	7
Griffon Corporation	1083	9	The J. M. Smucker Company	917	4
Guidant Corporation	904	12	Johnson & Johnson	308	12
Guilford Mills, Inc.	259	9	Johnson Controls, Inc.	309	9
Halliburton Company	264	12	Jones Apparel Group, Inc.	878	12
Harley-Davidson, Inc.	673	12	Jostens, Inc.	312	12
Harman International Industries, Incorporated	1105	6	Joy Global Inc.	268	10
			Juno Lighting, Inc.	712	11
Harrah's Entertainment, Inc.	829	12	Kaman Corporation	629	12
Harris Corporation	269	6	KB Home	967	11
Harsco Corporation	270	12	Kellogg Company	317	12
Hartmarx Corporation	271	11	Kellwood Company	838	1
Hasbro, Inc.	623	12	Kelly Services, Inc.	318	12
H.B. Fuller Company	621	11	Kerr-McGee Corporation	320	12
HCA Inc.	899	12	Kimball International, Inc.	853	6
Health Net, Inc.	1010	12	Kimberly-Clark Corporation	324	12

*Months are numbered in calendar-year sequence, January through December (e.g., January = 1 and February = 2).

Company Name	Company Reference Number	Month of Fiscal Year End*	Company Name	Company Reference Number	Month of Fiscal Year End*
KLA-Tencor Corporation	932	6	Micron Technology, Inc.	787	8
Kmart Holding Corporation	314	1	Microsoft Corporation	825	6
Knape & Vogt Manufacturing Company	326	6	Milacron Inc.	127	12
Knight-Ridder, Inc.	327	12	Mohawk Industries, Inc.	857	12
Kohl's Corporation	933	1	Molex Incorporated	716	6
The Kroger Co.	329	1	Monsanto Company	383	8
La-Z-Boy Incorporated	879	4	Motorola, Inc.	387	12
LaBarge, Inc.	332	6	MPS Group, Inc.	1050	12
Lafarge North America Inc.	678	12	Murphy Oil Corporation	390	12
Lam Research Corporation	880	6	NACCO Industries, Inc.	403	12
The Lamson & Sessions Co.	713	12	Nash Finch Company	1017	12
Lance, Inc.	854	12	Nashua Corporation	761	12
Land O'Lakes, Inc.	1107	12	National Presto Industries, Inc.	397	12
L. B. Foster Company	669	12	National Semiconductor		
LEAR Corporation	1013	12	Corporation	398	5
Lee Enterprises, Incorporated	336	9	Navistar International Corporation	299	10
Leggett & Platt, Incorporated	337	12	NCR Corporation	392	12
Lennar Corporation	1014	11	The New York Times Company	400	12
Levi Strauss & Co.	1108	11	Newell Rubbermaid Inc.	680	12
Lexmark International, Inc.	908	12	Newmont Mining Corporation	936	12
Liz Claiborne, Inc.	611	12	Nextel Communications, Inc.	1051	12
Lockheed Martin Corporation	341	12	NIKE, Inc.	401	5
Louisiana-Pacific Corporation	824	12	Noble Energy, Inc.	910	12
Lowe's Companies, Inc.	344	1	Nordstrom, Inc.	911	1
The L.S. Starrett Company	512	6	Northrop Grumman Corporation	405	12
LSI Logic Corporation	907	12	Novell, Inc.	839	10
The Lubrizol Corporation	345	12	Novellus Systems, Inc.	1052	12
Lucent Technologies Inc.	968	9	Nucor Corporation	633	12
Lufkin Industries, Inc.	714	12	NVR, Inc.	1110	12
Lynch Corporation	348	12	Occidental Petroleum Corporation	408	12
Lyondell Chemical Company	757	12	Office Depot, Inc.	970	12
MagneTek, Inc.	758	6	Olin Corporation	411	12
Mandalay Resort Group	898	1	Omnicom Group Inc.	682	12
The Manitowoc Company, Inc.	1084	12	Oracle Corporation	972	5
Manpower Inc.	855	12	Owens-Illinois, Inc.	416	12
Marriott International, Inc.	1015	12	Oxford Industries, Inc.	417	5
Marsh Supermarkets, Inc.	1048	3	PACCAR Inc	419	12
Masco Corporation	360	12	Pall Corporation	421	7
Mattel, Inc.	361	12	Parker Hannifin Corporation	424	6
Maxim Integrated Products, Inc.	1049	6	Pathmark Stores, Inc.	1111	1
Maxtor Corporation	1085	12	Paychex, Inc.	1053	5
MAXXAM Inc.	760	12	Peerless Mfg. Co.	790	6
The May Department Stores Company	362	1	Pentair, Inc.	684	12
Maytag Corporation	363	12	PeopleSoft, Inc.	973	12
McCormick & Company, Incorporated	364	11	The Pepsi Bottling Group, Inc.	1019	12
McDermott International, Inc.	365	12	PepsiAmericas, Inc.	288	12
McDonald's Corporation	366	12	PepsiCo, Inc.	432	12
The McGraw-Hill Companies, Inc.	368	12	PerkinElmer, Inc.	187	12
McKesson Corporation	369	3	Perot Systems Corporation	1054	12
MeadWestvaco Corporation	1109	12	Pfizer Inc	435	12
Media General, Inc.	631	12	Phelps Dodge Corporation	436	12
Medtronic, Inc.	371	4	Phillips-Van Heusen Corporation	634	1
Merck & Co., Inc.	373	12	Photo Control Corporation	686	12
Meredith Corporation	374	6	Pilgrim's Pride Corporation	913	9
Merisel, Inc.	1016	12	Pitney Bowes Inc.	441	12
Merrimac Industries, Inc.	882	12	Plains Resources Inc.	1020	12
Met-Pro Corporation	375	1	Polaris Industries Inc.	883	12
Metro-Goldwyn-Mayer Inc.	934	12	Polo Ralph Lauren Corporation	974	3
Mettler-Toledo International Inc.	1086	12	PolyOne Corporation	966	12

*Months are numbered in calendar-year sequence, January through December (e.g., January = 1 and February = 2).

ATT-APP

Company Name	Company Reference Number	Month of Fiscal Year End*	Company Name	Company Reference Number	Month of Fiscal Year End*
Potlatch Corporation	446	12	Smurfit-Stone Container Corporation	628	12
PPG Industries, Inc.	418	12	Snap-on Incorporated	496	12
Prab, Inc.	447	10	Solectron Corporation	888	8
Praxair, Inc.	828	12	Sonoco Products Company	691	12
Precision Castparts Corp.	975	3	Span-America Medical Systems, Inc.	834	9
PRIMEDIA Inc.	912	12	Sparton Corporation	498	6
The Procter & Gamble Company	451	6	Spectrum Control, Inc.	499	11
Pulte Homes, Inc.	1021	12	Speizman Industries, Inc.	721	6
QUALCOMM Incorporated	914	9	Spherion Corporation	1059	12
Quanex Corporation	455	10	Sprint Corporation	1025	12
Quantum Corporation	884	3	SPX Corporation	642	12
Quintiles Transnational Corp.	1055	12	St. Jude Medical, Inc.	1112	12
RadioShack Corporation	528	12	Standard Commercial Corporation	812	3
Raytheon Company	461	12	Standard Motor Products, Inc.	507	12
The Reader's Digest Association, Inc.	792	6	The Standard Register Company	509	12
Reebok International Ltd.	885	12	Standex International Corporation	767	6
Regal Entertainment Group	1087	12	The Stanley Works	511	12
Republic Services, Inc.	976	12	Staples, Inc.	983	1
The Reynolds and Reynolds			Starbucks Corporation	984	9
Company	939	9	Starwood Hotels & Resorts		
Rite Aid Corporation	886	2	Worldwide, Inc.	1060	12
R.J. Reynolds Tobacco Holdings, Inc.	1023	12	Steel Technologies Inc.	723	9
Robbins & Myers, Inc.	764	8	Steelcase Inc.	942	2
Robert Half International Inc.	977	12	Stewart & Stevenson Services, Inc.	768	1
Rock-Tenn Company	915	9	Storage Technology Corporation	804	12
Rockwell Automation, Inc.	469	9	Stryker Corporation	1061	12
Rockwell Collins, Inc.	1056	9	Sun Microsystems, Inc.	769	6
Rohm and Haas Company	470	12	SunGard Data Systems Inc.	1113	12
The Rowe Companies	471	11	Sunoco, Inc.	520	12
RPM International Inc.	1057	5	SUPERVALU INC.	522	2
R.R. Donnelley & Sons Company	175	12	Swift Transportation Co., Inc.	1089	12
Ruddick Corporation	811	9	Sybase, Inc.	889	12
Russell Corporation	832	12	Symbol Technologies, Inc.	1114	12
Ryder System, Inc.	1088	12	SYSCO Corporation	887	6
Ryerson Tull, Inc.	293	12	Target Corporation	165	1
Safeway Inc.	478	12	Tasty Baking Company	529	12
Sanmina-SCI Corporation	1024	9	Tech Data Corporation	1026	1
Sara Lee Corporation	479	6	Tecumseh Products Company	530	12
Saucony, Inc.	675	12	Tektronix, Inc.	794	5
SBC Communications Inc.	979	12	Tellabs, Inc.	944	12
Schering-Plough Corporation	481	12	Temple-Inland Inc.	532	12
Schlumberger Limited	482	12	Tenet Healthcare Corporation	1027	12
Science Applications International			Tenneco Automotive Inc.	534	12
Corporation	980	1	Teradyne, Inc.	890	12
Scientific Industries, Inc.	765	6	Terra Industries Inc.	676	12
Scientific-Atlanta, Inc.	1058	6	Tesoro Petroleum Corporation	535	12
Scope Industries	484	6	Texas Industries, Inc.	725	5
The Scotts Company	833	9	Texas Instruments Incorporated	537	12
Seaboard Corporation	858	12	Textron Inc.	538	12
Sears, Roebuck and Co.	486	12	Thermo Electron Corporation	813	12
Sensient Technologies Corporation	814	12	Thomas & Betts Corporation	771	12
Sequa Corporation	519	12	Thor Industries, Inc.	1090	7
Service Corporation International	487	12	Time Warner Inc.	923	12
The ServiceMaster Company	940	12	The Timken Company	542	12
The Sherwin-Williams Company	490	12	The TJX Companies, Inc.	770	1
Silicon Graphics, Inc.	981	6	The Toro Company	726	10
Skyworks Solutions, Inc.	23	9	Tower Automotive, Inc.	945	12
Smith International, Inc.	941	12	Toys"R"Us, Inc.	772	1
Smithfield Foods, Inc.	690	4	TransTechnology Corporation	727	3

*Months are numbered in calendar-year sequence, January through December (e.g., January = 1 and February = 2).

Company Name	Company Reference Number	Month of Fiscal Year End*
Tribune Company	547	12
Trinity Industries, Inc.	646	3
Trump Hotels & Casino Resorts, Inc.	1062	12
Tupperware Corporation	891	12
Twin Disc, Incorporated	728	6
Tyler Technologies, Inc.	549	12
Tyson Foods, Inc.	550	9
Unifi, Inc.	553	6
Unisys Corporation	102	12
United Rentals, Inc.	1063	12
United States Steel Corporation	561	12
United Stationers Inc.	1028	12
United Technologies Corporation	564	12
UnitedHealth Group Incorporated	859	12
Universal Corporation	566	6
Universal Forest Products, Inc.	949	12
Universal Health Services, Inc.	1064	12
Unocal Corporation	568	12
UNOVA, Inc.	947	12
USG Corporation	552	12
UST Inc.	563	12
Valero Energy Corporation	647	12
Varco International Inc.	1091	12
Varian Medical Systems, Inc.	571	9
Verizon Communications Inc.	1029	12
VF Corporation	570	12
Viacom Inc.	920	12
Viad Corp	893	12
Vishay Intertechnology, Inc.	731	12
Vulcan Materials Company	573	12
Wal-Mart Stores, Inc.	648	1
Walgreen Co.	575	8
The Walt Disney Company	174	9
The Washington Post Company	649	12
Waste Management, Inc.	580	12
Wausau•Mosinee Paper Corporation	581	12
Waxman Industries, Inc.	732	6
Weatherford International Ltd.	950	12
Wendy's International, Inc.	1115	12
Werner Enterprises, Inc.	1066	12
Western Digital Corporation	733	6
Weyerhaeuser Company	586	12
Whirlpool Corporation	588	12
WHX Corporation	587	12
The Williams Companies, Inc.	1067	12
Winn-Dixie Stores, Inc.	593	6
Winnebago Industries, Inc.	594	8
Wm. Wrigley Jr. Company	597	12
Wolverine World Wide, Inc.	734	12
Worthington Industries, Inc.	735	5
W. R. Grace & Co.	252	12
W.W. Grainger, Inc.	253	12
Wyeth	35	12
Wyndham International, Inc.	1068	12
Xerox Corporation	1093	12
Xilinx, Inc.	1069	3
XO Communications, Inc.	1070	12
York International Corporation	650	12
Yum! Brands, Inc.	1094	12

COMPANIES INCLUDED IN FIFTY-SEVENTH EDITION NOT INCLUDED IN THIS EDITION OF THE SURVEY

Company Name	Company Reference Number
Agway Inc.	952
Allen Telecom Inc.	602
Bethlehem Steel Corporation	83
BMC Industries, Inc.	67
Broadwing Inc.	1035
Burlington Industries, Inc.	818
Concord EFS, Inc.	1042
Dole Food Company, Inc.	112
El Paso Corporation	1004
Farmland Industries, Inc.	1007
National Service Industries, Inc.	399
OfficeMax, Inc.	971
The Penn Traffic Company	427
Pillowtex Corporation	938
Rouge Industries, Inc.	916
SPS Technologies, Inc.	477
Temtex Industries, Inc.	533
TRICON Global Restaurants, Inc.	943
Veritas Software Corporation	1065
Weirton Steel Corporation	835
Wiltel Communications Group, Inc.	1092

*Months are numbered in calendar-year sequence, January through December (e.g., January = 1 and February = 2).

ATT-APP

NUMERICAL LISTING

Company Reference Number	Company Name	Month of Fiscal Year End*	Company Reference Number	Company Name	Month of Fiscal Year End*
6	AMETEK, Inc.	12	142	ConAgra Foods, Inc.	5
10	Abbott Laboratories	12	145	Ceridian Corporation	12
16	Air Products and Chemicals, Inc.	9	146	Cooper Industries, Ltd.	12
17	Albertson's, Inc.	1	147	Adolph Coors Company	12
18	IKON Office Solutions, Inc.	9	149	Corning Incorporated	12
20	Honeywell International Inc.	12	150	Courier Corporation	9
23	Skyworks Solutions, Inc.	9	152	Crane Co.	12
24	Alcoa Inc.	12	154	Crown Holdings, Inc.	12
25	Amcast Industrial Corporation	8	158	Curtiss-Wright Corporation	12
26	Amerada Hess Corporation	12	161	Dana Corporation	12
28	American Biltrite Inc.	12	165	Target Corporation	1
29	Fortune Brands, Inc.	12	166	Dean Foods Company	5
30	ABM Industries Incorporated	10	167	Deere & Company	10
33	American Greetings Corporation	2	168	Deluxe Corporation	12
35	Wyeth	12	174	The Walt Disney Company	9
41	American Standard Companies Inc.	12	175	R.R. Donnelley & Sons Company	12
43	AT&T Corp.	12	176	Dover Corporation	12
44	Ameron International Corporation	11	177	The Dow Chemical Company	12
46	Ampco-Pittsburgh Corporation	12	178	Dow Jones & Company, Inc.	12
48	Analogic Corporation	7	182	The Dun & Bradstreet Corporation	12
51	Anheuser-Busch Companies, Inc.	12	184	E. I. du Pont de Nemours and Company	12
52	Apple Computer, Inc.	9	187	PerkinElmer, Inc.	12
53	Archer Daniels Midland Company	6	190	The Eastern Company	12
54	Arden Group, Inc.	12	191	Eastman Kodak Company	12
56	AK Steel Holding Corporation	12	192	Eaton Corporation	12
60	Ashland Inc.	9	194	Elkcorp	6
65	Avnet, Inc.	6	195	Emerson Electric Co.	9
66	Avon Products, Inc.	12	198	Engelhard Corporation	12
68	Badger Meter, Inc.	12	199	Ethyl Corporation	12
70	Baker Hughes Incorporated	12	202	Exxon Mobil Corporation	12
71	Ball Corporation	12	203	FMC Corporation	12
74	Bausch & Lomb Incorporated	12	206	Fedders Corporation	8
75	Baxter International Inc.	12	208	Federal-Mogul Corporation	12
78	Becton, Dickinson and Company	9	209	Federated Department Stores, Inc.	1
81	Bemis Company, Inc.	12	212	Fleetwood Enterprises, Inc.	4
85	The Black & Decker Corporation	12	216	Fluor Corporation	12
87	The Boeing Company	12	219	Ford Motor Company	12
88	Boise Cascade Corporation	12	221	Foster Wheeler Ltd.	12
91	Bowne & Co., Inc.	12	228	Gannett Co., Inc.	12
93	Briggs & Stratton Corporation	6	230	GenCorp Inc.	11
94	Bristol-Myers Squibb Company	12	232	General Dynamics Corporation	12
97	Brown Shoe Company, Inc.	1	233	General Electric Company	12
99	Brunswick Corporation	12	237	General Mills, Inc.	5
102	Unisys Corporation	12	238	General Motors Corporation	12
107	CSP Inc.	9	242	Genuine Parts Company	12
108	Cabot Corporation	9	243	Georgia-Pacific Corporation	12
110	Campbell Soup Company	7	246	The Gillette Company	12
113	Caterpillar Inc.	12	247	Golden Enterprises, Inc.	5
121	ChevronTexaco Corporation	12	249	The Goodyear Tire & Rubber Company	12
127	Milacron Inc.	12	252	W. R. Grace & Co.	12
130	Cleveland-Cliffs Inc.	12	253	W.W. Grainger, Inc.	12
131	The Clorox Company	6	254	The Great Atlantic & Pacific Tea Company, Inc.	2
133	The Coca-Cola Company	12	256	Greif Bros. Corporation	10
135	Colgate-Palmolive Company	12	257	The Dial Corporation	12
137	Collins Industries, Inc.	10	259	Guilford Mills, Inc.	9
140	Commercial Metals Company	8			

*Months are numbered in calendar-year sequence, January through December (e.g., January = 1 and February = 2).

Company Reference Number	Company Name	Month of Fiscal Year End*	Company Reference Number	Company Name	Month of Fiscal Year End*
263	HON INDUSTRIES Inc.	12	373	Merck & Co., Inc.	12
264	Halliburton Company	12	374	Meredith Corporation	6
268	Joy Global Inc.	10	375	Met-Pro Corporation	1
269	Harris Corporation	6	377	Herman Miller, Inc.	5
270	Harsco Corporation	12	379	3M Company	12
271	Hartmarx Corporation	11	383	Monsanto Company	8
273	Hecla Mining Company	12	387	Motorola, Inc.	12
275	H.J. Heinz Company	4	390	Murphy Oil Corporation	12
276	Hercules Incorporated	12	392	NCR Corporation	12
277	Hershey Foods Corporation	12	397	National Presto Industries, Inc.	12
278	Hewlett-Packard Company	10	398	National Semiconductor Corporation	5
282	Hormel Foods Corporation	10	400	The New York Times Company	12
283	Hughes Supply, Inc.	1	401	NIKE, Inc.	5
285	Humana Inc.	12	403	NACCO Industries, Inc.	12
287	Hurco Companies, Inc.	10	405	Northrop Grumman Corporation	12
288	PepsiAmericas, Inc.	12	408	Occidental Petroleum Corporation	12
291	ITT Industries, Inc.	12	411	Olin Corporation	12
292	Ingersoll-Rand Company Limited	12	416	Owens-Illinois, Inc.	12
293	Ryerson Tull, Inc.	12	417	Oxford Industries, Inc.	5
295	Intel Corporation	12	418	PPG Industries, Inc.	12
296	Furniture Brands International, Inc.	12	419	PACCAR Inc	12
298	International Business Machines Corporation	12	421	Pall Corporation	7
299	Navistar International Corporation	10	424	Parker Hannifin Corporation	6
301	International Multifoods Corporation	2	428	J. C. Penney Company, Inc.	1
302	International Paper Company	12	432	PepsiCo, Inc.	12
303	Interstate Bakeries Corporation	5	435	Pfizer Inc	12
305	JLG Industries, Inc.	7	436	Phelps Dodge Corporation	12
308	Johnson & Johnson	12	437	Altria Group, Inc.	12
309	Johnson Controls, Inc.	9	438	ConocoPhillips	12
312	Jostens, Inc.	12	441	Pitney Bowes Inc.	12
314	Kmart Holding Corporation	1	446	Potlatch Corporation	12
317	Kellogg Company	12	447	Prab, Inc.	10
318	Kelly Services, Inc.	12	451	The Procter & Gamble Company	6
320	Kerr-McGee Corporation	12	455	Quanex Corporation	10
324	Kimberly-Clark Corporation	12	461	Raytheon Company	12
326	Knape & Vogt Manufacturing Company	6	469	Rockwell Automation, Inc.	9
327	Knight-Ridder, Inc.	12	470	Rohm and Haas Company	12
329	The Kroger Co.	1	471	The Rowe Companies	11
332	LaBarge, Inc.	6	478	Safeway Inc.	12
336	Lee Enterprises, Incorporated	9	479	Sara Lee Corporation	6
337	Leggett & Platt, Incorporated	12	481	Schering-Plough Corporation	12
339	Eli Lilly and Company	12	482	Schlumberger Limited	12
341	Lockheed Martin Corporation	12	484	Scope Industries	6
344	Lowe's Companies, Inc.	1	486	Sears, Roebuck and Co.	12
345	The Lubrizol Corporation	12	487	Service Corporation International	12
348	Lynch Corporation	12	490	The Sherwin-Williams Company	12
360	Masco Corporation	12	494	A. O. Smith Corporation	12
361	Mattel, Inc.	12	496	Snap-on Incorporated	12
362	The May Department Stores Company	1	498	Sparton Corporation	6
363	Maytag Corporation	12	499	Spectrum Control, Inc.	11
364	McCormick & Company, Incorporated	11	507	Standard Motor Products, Inc.	12
365	McDermott International, Inc.	12	509	The Standard Register Company	12
366	McDonald's Corporation	12	510	Enesco Group, Inc.	12
368	The McGraw-Hill Companies, Inc.	12	511	The Stanley Works	12
369	McKesson Corporation	3	512	The L.S. Starrett Company	6
371	Medtronic, Inc.	4	519	Sequa Corporation	12
372	CVS Corporation	12	520	Sunoco, Inc.	12
			522	SUPERVALU INC.	2

*Months are numbered in calendar-year sequence, January through December (e.g., January = 1 and February = 2).

ATT-APP

Company Reference Number	Company Name	Month of Fiscal Year End*
528	RadioShack Corporation	12
529	Tasty Baking Company	12
530	Tecumseh Products Company	12
532	Temple-Inland Inc.	12
534	Tenneco Automotive Inc.	12
535	Tesoro Petroleum Corporation	12
537	Texas Instruments Incorporated	12
538	Textron Inc.	12
542	The Timken Company	12
547	Tribune Company	12
549	Tyler Technologies, Inc.	12
550	Tyson Foods, Inc.	9
552	USG Corporation	12
553	Unifi, Inc.	6
557	Chiquita Brands International, Inc.	12
561	United States Steel Corporation	12
563	UST Inc.	12
564	United Technologies Corporation	12
566	Universal Corporation	6
568	Unocal Corporation	12
570	VF Corporation	12
571	Varian Medical Systems, Inc.	9
573	Vulcan Materials Company	12
575	Walgreen Co.	8
580	Waste Management, Inc.	12
581	Wausau•Mosinee Paper Corporation	12
586	Weyerhaeuser Company	12
587	WHX Corporation	12
588	Whirlpool Corporation	12
593	Winn-Dixie Stores, Inc.	6
594	Winnebago Industries, Inc.	8
596	Foot Locker, Inc.	1
597	Wm. Wrigley Jr. Company	12

COMPANIES ADDED FOR 1987 EDITION

601	Alberto-Culver Company	9
604	Avery Dennison Corporation	12
605	Barnes Group Inc.	12
606	Bassett Furniture Industries, Incorporated	11
607	Bowater Incorporated	12
610	Carpenter Technology Corporation	6
611	Liz Claiborne, Inc.	12
617	Ecolab Inc.	12
621	H.B. Fuller Company	11
623	Hasbro, Inc.	12
624	Hillenbrand Industries, Inc.	9
625	Illinois Tool Works Inc.	12
627	International Flavors & Fragrances Inc.	12
628	Smurfit-Stone Container Corporation	12
629	Kaman Corporation	12
631	Media General, Inc.	12
633	Nucor Corporation	12
634	Phillips-Van Heusen Corporation	1
642	SPX Corporation	12
646	Trinity Industries, Inc.	3
647	Valero Energy Corporation	12
648	Wal-Mart Stores, Inc.	1

Company Reference Number	Company Name	Month of Fiscal Year End*
649	The Washington Post Company	12
650	York International Corporation	12

COMPANIES ADDED FOR 1988 EDITION

652	Advanced Micro Devices, Inc.	12
656	The Fairchild Corporation	6
657	Brown-Forman Corporation	4
658	CLARCOR Inc.	11
659	Chesapeake Corporation	12
660	Coca-Cola Enterprises Inc.	12
664	Danaher Corporation	12
665	The Dixie Group, Inc.	12
669	L. B. Foster Company	12
673	Harley-Davidson, Inc.	12
675	Saucony, Inc.	12
676	Terra Industries Inc.	12
678	Lafarge North America Inc.	12
680	Newell Rubbermaid Inc.	12
682	Omnicom Group Inc.	12
684	Pentair, Inc.	12
686	Photo Control Corporation	12
690	Smithfield Foods, Inc.	4
691	Sonoco Products Company	12

COMPANIES ADDED FOR 1989 EDITION

696	Anacomp, Inc.	9
699	Blount International, Inc.	12
700	Burlington Resources Inc.	12
701	CTS Corporation	12
712	Juno Lighting, Inc.	11
713	The Lamson & Sessions Co.	12
714	Lufkin Industries, Inc.	12
716	Molex Incorporated	6
721	Speizman Industries, Inc.	6
723	Steel Technologies Inc.	9
725	Texas Industries, Inc.	5
726	The Toro Company	10
727	TransTechnology Corporation	3
728	Twin Disc, Incorporated	6
731	Vishay Intertechnology, Inc.	12
732	Waxman Industries, Inc.	6
733	Western Digital Corporation	6
734	Wolverine World Wide, Inc.	12
735	Worthington Industries, Inc.	5

COMPANIES ADDED FOR 1990 EDITION

738	Ault Incorporated	5
740	Champion Enterprises, Inc.	12
742	Coherent, Inc.	9
744	Donaldson Company, Inc.	7
747	Federal Screw Works	6
748	Georgia Gulf Corporation	12
752	IMC Global Inc.	12
753	Interface, Inc.	12
754	Jacobs Engineering Group Inc.	9
757	Lyondell Chemical Company	12

*Months are numbered in calendar-year sequence, January through December (e.g., January = 1 and February = 2).

Company Reference Number	Company Name	Month of Fiscal Year End*
758	MagneTek, Inc.	6
760	MAXXAM Inc.	12
761	Nashua Corporation	12
764	Robbins & Myers, Inc.	8
765	Scientific Industries, Inc.	6
767	Standex International Corporation	6
768	Stewart & Stevenson Services, Inc.	1
769	Sun Microsystems, Inc.	6
770	The TJX Companies, Inc.	1
771	Thomas & Betts Corporation	12
772	Toys"R"Us, Inc.	1

COMPANIES ADDED FOR 1991 EDITION

776	Allegheny Technologies Incorporated	12
777	Alliant Techsytems Inc.	3
778	Baldor Electric Company	12
782	DIMON Incorporated	6
787	Micron Technology, Inc.	8
790	Peerless Mfg. Co.	6
792	The Reader's Digest Association, Inc.	6
794	Tektronix, Inc.	5

COMPANIES ADDED FOR 1992 EDITION

796	Allergan, Inc.	12
800	Ferro Corporation	12
801	Intergraph Corporation	12
804	Storage Technology Corporation	12

COMPANIES ADDED FOR 1993 EDITION

806	Banta Corporation	12
811	Ruddick Corporation	9
812	Standard Commercial Corporation	3
813	Thermo Electron Corporation	12
814	Sensient Technologies Corporation	12

COMPANIES ADDED FOR 1994 EDITION

824	Louisiana-Pacific Corporation	12
825	Microsoft Corporation	6
828	Praxair, Inc.	12
829	Harrah's Entertainment, Inc.	12
832	Russell Corporation	12
833	The Scotts Company	9
834	Span-America Medical Systems, Inc.	9

COMPANIES ADDED FOR 1995 EDITION

836	Centex Corporation	3
837	The Interpublic Group of Companies, Inc.	12

Company Reference Number	Company Name	Month of Fiscal Year End*
838	Kellwood Company	1
839	Novell, Inc.	10

COMPANIES ADDED FOR 1996 EDITION

841	Amgen Inc.	12
842	Amphenol Corporation	12
844	Arrow Electronics, Inc.	12
845	C. R. Bard, Inc.	12
846	Beckman Coulter, Inc.	12
848	Computer Sciences Corporation	3
849	Cooper Tire & Rubber Company	12
850	Dillard's, Inc.	1
851	First Data Corporation	12
853	Kimball International, Inc.	6
854	Lance, Inc.	12
855	Manpower Inc.	12
857	Mohawk Industries, Inc.	12
858	Seaboard Corporation	12
859	UnitedHealth Group Incorporated	12

COMPANIES ADDED FOR 1997 EDITION

861	ADVO, Inc.	9
862	AGCO Corporation	12
863	Applied Materials, Inc.	10
864	Atmel Corporation	12
865	Automatic Data Processing, Inc.	6
866	B/E Aerospace, Inc.	2
867	Boston Scientific Corporation	12
868	Circuit City Stores, Inc.	2
869	Cisco Systems, Inc.	7
871	Eastman Chemical Company	12
872	The Estee Lauder Companies Inc.	6
873	Exide Technologies	3
874	Gateway, Inc.	12
878	Jones Apparel Group, Inc.	12
879	La-Z-Boy Incorporated	4
880	Lam Research Corporation	6
882	Merrimac Industries, Inc.	12
883	Polaris Industries Inc.	12
884	Quantum Corporation	3
885	Reebok International Ltd.	12
886	Rite Aid Corporation	2
887	SYSCO Corporation	6
888	Solectron Corporation	8
889	Sybase, Inc.	12
890	Teradyne, Inc.	12
891	Tupperware Corporation	12
893	Viad Corp	12

COMPANIES ADDED FOR 1998 EDITION

896	BJ Services Company	9
897	Carlisle Companies Incorporated	12

*Months are numbered in calendar-year sequence, January through December (e.g., January = 1 and February = 2).

Company Reference Number	Company Name	Month of Fiscal Year End*	Company Reference Number	Company Name	Month of Fiscal Year End*
898	Mandalay Resort Group	1	963	Dell Inc.	1
899	HCA Inc.	12	964	Electronic Data Systems Corporation	12
900	Cooper Cameron Corporation	12	965	Freeport-McMoRan Copper & Gold Inc.	12
901	EMCOR Group, Inc.	12	966	PolyOne Corporation	12
902	Equifax Inc.	12	967	KB Home	11
903	Flowserve Corporation	12	968	Lucent Technologies Inc.	9
904	Guidant Corporation	12	970	Office Depot, Inc.	12
905	The Home Depot, Inc.	1	972	Oracle Corporation	5
906	Ingram Micro Inc.	12	973	PeopleSoft, Inc.	12
907	LSI Logic Corporation	12	974	Polo Ralph Lauren Corporation	3
908	Lexmark International, Inc.	12	975	Precision Castparts Corp.	3
910	Noble Energy, Inc.	12	976	Republic Services, Inc.	12
911	Nordstrom, Inc.	1	977	Robert Half International Inc.	12
912	PRIMEDIA Inc.	12	979	SBC Communications Inc.	12
913	Pilgrim's Pride Corporation	9	980	Science Applications International Corporation	1
914	QUALCOMM Incorporated	9	981	Silicon Graphics, Inc.	6
915	Rock-Tenn Company	9	983	Staples, Inc.	1
917	The J. M. Smucker Company	4	984	Starbucks Corporation	9
920	Viacom Inc.	12	985	InterActiveCorp	12

COMPANIES ADDED FOR 1999 EDITION

921	ADC Telecommunications, Inc.	10
922	Allied Waste Industries, Inc.	12
923	Time Warner Inc.	12
924	Analog Devices, Inc.	10
925	Computer Associates International, Inc.	3
927	Datascope Corp.	6
929	GlobalSantaFe Corporation	12
930	Hubbell Incorporated	12
931	Iomega Corporation	12
932	KLA-Tencor Corporation	6
933	Kohl's Corporation	1
934	Metro-Goldwyn-Mayer Inc.	12
936	Newmont Mining Corporation	12
939	The Reynolds and Reynolds Company	9
940	The ServiceMaster Company	12
941	Smith International, Inc.	12
942	Steelcase Inc.	2
944	Tellabs, Inc.	12
945	Tower Automotive, Inc.	12
947	UNOVA, Inc.	12
948	Jacuzzi Brands, Inc.	9
949	Universal Forest Products, Inc.	12
950	Weatherford International Ltd.	12

COMPANIES ADDED FOR 2000 EDITION

951	3Com Corporation	5
953	Amazon.com, Inc.	12
954	Amkor Technology, Inc.	12
955	Applied Industrial Technologies, Inc.	6
958	BellSouth Corporation	12
959	Burlington Coat Factory Warehouse Corporation	5
961	Costco Wholesale Corporation	8
962	Del Monte Foods Company	4

COMPANIES ADDED FOR 2001 EDITION

988	Administaff, Inc.	12
989	Aetna Inc.	12
990	Anadarko Petroleum Corporation	12
991	AutoZone, Inc.	8
992	Barnes & Noble, Inc.	1
993	Best Buy Co., Inc.	2
994	Cablevision Systems Corporation	12
995	Caremark Rx, Inc.	12
996	CDW Corporation	12
997	Cigna Corporation	12
998	Clear Channel Communications, Inc.	12
999	Comcast Corporation	12
1000	Comdisco Holding Company, Inc.	9
1001	Cox Communications, Inc.	12
1003	Delphi Corporation	12
1005	EMC Corporation	12
1008	The Gap, Inc.	1
1010	Health Net, Inc.	12
1011	Hilton Hotels Corporation	12
1012	Jabil Circuit, Inc.	8
1013	LEAR Corporation	12
1014	Lennar Corporation	11
1015	Marriott International, Inc.	12
1016	Merisel, Inc.	12
1017	Nash Finch Company	12
1018	Caesars Entertainment, Inc.	12
1019	The Pepsi Bottling Group, Inc.	12
1020	Plains Resources Inc.	12
1021	Pulte Homes, Inc.	12
1023	R.J. Reynolds Tobacco Holdings, Inc.	12
1024	Sanmina-SCI Corporation	9
1025	Sprint Corporation	12
1026	Tech Data Corporation	1
1027	Tenet Healthcare Corporation	12

*Months are numbered in calendar-year sequence, January through December (e.g., January = 1 and February = 2).

Company Reference Number	Company Name	Month of Fiscal Year End*	Company Reference Number	Company Name	Month of Fiscal Year End*
1028	United Stationers Inc.	12	1079	Electronic Arts Inc.	3
1029	Verizon Communications Inc.	12	1080	Flowers Foods, Inc.	12
			1081	Giant Industries, Inc.	12
			1082	Grey Global Group Inc.	12
			1083	Griffon Corporation	9
			1084	The Manitowoc Company, Inc.	12
			1085	Maxtor Corporation	12
			1086	Mettler-Toledo International Inc.	12
			1087	Regal Entertainment Group	12
			1088	Ryder System, Inc.	12
			1089	Swift Transportation Co., Inc.	12
			1090	Thor Industries, Inc.	7
			1091	Varco International Inc.	12
			1093	Xerox Corporation	12
			1094	Yum! Brands, Inc.	12

COMPANIES ADDED FOR 2002 EDITION

1030	Airgas, Inc.	3
1031	ALLTEL Corporation	12
1033	Armstrong Holdings, Inc.	12
1034	Avaya Inc.	9
1036	Cendant Corporation	12
1037	CenturyTel, Inc.	12
1038	Charter Communications, Inc.	12
1039	Ciena Corporation	10
1040	Cintas Corporation	5
1041	Citizens Communications Company	12
1043	Darden Restaurants, Inc.	5
1044	Fiserv, Inc.	12
1045	Goodrich Corporation	12
1046	IDT Corporation	7
1047	JDS Uniphase Corporation	6
1048	Marsh Supermarkets, Inc.	3
1049	Maxim Integrated Products, Inc.	6
1050	MPS Group, Inc.	12
1051	Nextel Communications, Inc.	12
1052	Novellus Systems, Inc.	12
1053	Paychex, Inc.	5
1054	Perot Systems Corporation	12
1055	Quintiles Transnational Corp.	12
1056	Rockwell Collins, Inc.	9
1057	RPM International Inc.	5
1058	Scientific-Atlanta, Inc.	6
1059	Spherion Corporation	12
1060	Starwood Hotels & Resorts Worldwide, Inc.	12
1061	Stryker Corporation	12
1062	Trump Hotels & Casino Resorts, Inc.	12
1063	United Rentals, Inc.	12
1064	Universal Health Services, Inc.	12
1066	Werner Enterprises, Inc.	12
1067	The Williams Companies, Inc.	12
1068	Wyndham International, Inc.	12
1069	Xilinx, Inc.	3
1070	XO Communications, Inc.	12

COMPANIES ADDED FOR 2003 EDITION

1071	Acterna Corporation	3
1072	Arkansas Best Corporation	12
1073	ArvinMeritor, Inc.	9
1074	Brinker International, Inc.	6
1075	CNF Inc.	12
1076	Coca-Cola Bottling Co. Consolidated	12
1077	Crompton Corporation	12
1078	Earthlink, Inc.	12

COMPANIES ADDED FOR 2004 EDITION

1095	Acuity Brands, Inc.	8
1096	Anthem, Inc.	12
1097	Constellation Brands, Inc.	2
1098	Convergys Corporation	12
1099	Corn Products International, Inc.	12
1100	Cummins Inc.	12
1101	Diebold, Incorporated	12
1102	Dollar General Corporation	1
1103	D.R. Horton, Inc.	9
1104	eBay Inc.	12
1105	Harman International Industries, Incorporated	6
1106	Intuit Inc.	7
1107	Land O'Lakes, Inc.	12
1108	Levi Strauss & Co.	11
1109	MeadWestvaco Corporation	12
1110	NVR, Inc.	12
1111	Pathmark Stores, Inc.	1
1112	St. Jude Medical, Inc.	12
1113	SunGard Data Systems Inc.	12
1114	Symbol Technologies, Inc.	12
1115	Wendy's International, Inc.	12

COMPANIES INCLUDED IN FIFTY-SEVENTH EDITION NOT INCLUDED IN THIS EDITION OF THE SURVEY

67	BMC Industries, Inc.	
83	Bethlehem Steel Corporation	
112	Dole Food Company, Inc.	
399	National Service Industries, Inc.	
427	The Penn Traffic Company	
477	SPS Technologies, Inc.	
533	Temtex Industries, Inc.	
602	Allen Telecom Inc.	
818	Burlington Industries, Inc.	
835	Weirton Steel Corporation	
916	Rouge Industries, Inc.	

*Months are numbered in calendar-year sequence, January through December (e.g., January = 1 and February = 2).

ATT-APP

Company
Reference
Number   *Company Name*

938	Pillowtex Corporation
943	TRICON Global Restaurants, Inc.
952	Agway Inc.
971	OfficeMax, Inc.
1004	El Paso Corporation
1007	Farmland Industries, Inc.
1035	Broadwing Inc.
1042	Concord EFS, Inc.
1065	Veritas Software Corporation
1092	Wiltel Communications Group, Inc.

Company Index

P

PACCAR Inc (Dec), 2.26, 2.168
Pall Corporation (Jul), 1.120
Pathmark Stores, Inc. (Jan), 1.40, 2.159, 6.31
Paychex, Inc. (May), 1.93, 2.104
Peerless Mfg. Co. (Jun), 2.90, 3.23
The Pepsi Bottling Group, Inc. (Dec), 1.198
PepsiAmericas, Inc. (Dec), 2.313
PerkinElmer, Inc. (Dec), 2.310
Perot Systems Corporation (Dec), 1.84
Pfizer Inc (Dec), 2.149, 7.71
Phelps Dodge Corporation (Dec), 1.103, 1.208, 3.151,
    3.160
Pilgrim's Pride Corporation (Sep), 3.30
Pitney Bowes Inc. (Dec), 3.45, 5.21
Polo Ralph Lauren Corporation (Mar), 1.187, 7.59
PolyOne Corporation (Dec), 1.123, 1.195, 3.130
Potlatch Corporation (Dec), 1.138, 2.232, 3.75
PPG Industries, Inc. (Dec), 2.218, 3.103
Praxair, Inc. (Dec), 1.144, 5.30
PRIMEDIA Inc. (Dec), 2.282, 2.298, 2.330
The Procter & Gamble Company (Jun), 3.73, 5.55
Pulte Homes, Inc. (Dec), 2.243

Q

QUALCOMM Incorporated (Sep), 2.29
Quanex Corporation (Oct), 1.181, 3.28, 6.39
Quantum Corporation (Mar), 1.31, 1.129, 7.32
Quintiles Transnational Corp. (Dec), 1.100

R

RadioShack Corporation (Dec), 3.97
Raytheon Company (Dec), 3.161
Republic Services, Inc. (Dec), 1.141, 2.81
The Reynolds and Reynolds Company (Sep), 3.18
R.J. Reynolds Tobacco Holdings, Inc. (Dec), 2.270, 3.72
Robert Half International Inc. (Dec), 2.36
Rockwell Automation, Inc. (Sep), 2.217
Rockwell Collins, Inc. (Sep), 2.208, 3.137
Rohm and Haas Company (Dec), 5.20
R.R. Donnelley & Sons Company (Dec), 6.24
Ruddick Corporation (Sep), 2.255, 4.26
Russell Corporation (Dec), 1.21, 5.41
Ryerson Tull, Inc. (Dec), 3.125

S

Safeway Inc. (Dec), 2.274
Sanmina-Sci Corporation (Sep), 3.38
Sara Lee Corporation (Jun), 1.163
Saucony, Inc. (Dec), 3.88, 3.162
Schlumberger Limited (Dec), 2.87, 6.25

Scientific-Atlanta, Inc. (Jun), 1.111, 2.157
Scope Industries (Jun), 6.17
Sears, Roebuck and Co. (Dec), 1.189, 6.23
Sequa Corporation (Dec), 6.50
The ServiceMaster Company (Dec), 2.273, 3.89, 7.40
The Sherwin-Williams Company (Dec), 6.20
Smith International, Inc. (Dec), 2.211, 6.34
Smithfield Foods, Inc. (Apr), 3.90
Snap-on Incorporated (Dec), 2.133, 2.331
Solectron Corporation (Aug), 2.237
Span-America Medical Systems, Inc. (Sep), 6.46
Sparton Corporation (Jun), 1.130, 7.49
Speizman Industries, Inc. (Jun), 6.64
Sprint Corporation (Dec), 1.17, 1.203
SPX Corporation (Dec), 1.124
Standard Commercial Corporation (Mar), 2.117
Standard Motor Products, Inc. (Dec), 2.236, 2.276, 5.35
The Standard Register Company (Dec), 4.14, 6.18
Standex International Corporation (Jun), 1.12
The Stanley Works (Dec), 2.216, 3.09, 3.98
Starwood Hotels & Resorts Worldwide, Inc. (Dec),
    3.120
Steelcase Inc. (Feb), 2.256, 2.271
Stewart & Stevenson Services, Inc. (Jan), 2.08, 6.47
Storage Technology Corporation (Dec), 6.14
Stryker Corporation (Dec), 2.86
Sun Microsystems, Inc. (Jun), 1.121, 3.52
SUPERVALU INC. (Feb), 6.21
Swift Transportation Co., Inc. (Dec), 7.13
Sybase, Inc. (Dec), 2.161
Symbol Technologies, Inc. (Dec), 1.105

T

Target Corporation (Jan), 1.68
Tasty Baking Company (Dec), 2.251, 5.39
Tecumseh Products Company (Dec), 1.167, 2.233
Tektronix, Inc. (May), 6.44
Tenet Healthcare Corporation (Dec), 1.37, 1.106, 5.15
Tenneco Automotive Inc. (Dec), 3.40, 4.12
Teradyne, Inc. (Dec), 3.19
Tesoro Petroleum Corporation (Dec), 2.252
Texas Instruments Incorporated (Dec), 2.150, 3.109
Textron Inc. (Dec), 3.43
Thor Industries, Inc. (Jul), 2.152
The Timken Company (Dec), 4.10, 6.28
Trump Hotels & Casino Resorts, Inc. (Dec), 7.28

U

United Rentals, Inc. (Dec), 2.296
United States Steel Corporation (Dec), 1.13, 1.164, 3.156
United Stationers Inc. (Dec), 2.40, 2.244
United Technologies Corporation (Dec), 1.193
Universal Corporation (Jun), 2.91, 2.332
Universal Forest Products, Inc. (Dec), 2.329
Universal Health Services, Inc. (Dec), 1.125
Unocal Corporation (Dec), 2.265, 5.56, 6.35
UNOVA, Inc. (Dec), 3.147

V

Valero Energy Corporation (Dec), 4.32
Varian Medical Systems, Inc. (Sep), 5.19
VF Corporation (Dec), 1.142, 4.17
Viacom Inc. (Dec), 2.53
Viad Corp (Dec), 1.202

W

Wal-Mart Stores, Inc. (Jan), 1.69
The Walt Disney Company (Sep), 2.169, 7.39
The Washington Post Company (Dec), 2.118
Wausau•Mosinee Paper Corporation (Dec), 3.112
Waxman Industries, Inc. (Jun), 7.22
Weatherford International Ltd. (Dec), 2.54, 6.45
Werner Enterprises, Inc. (Dec), 7.52
Western Digital Corporation (Jun), 1.175, 6.58

Whirlpool Corporation (Dec), 2.179, 2.275
WHX Corporation (Dec), 3.29
Wm. Wrigley Jr. Company (Dec), 2.314
Worthington Industries, Inc. (May), 3.22
W. R. Grace & Co. (Dec), 1.108, 2.166, 3.59
W.W. Grainger, Inc. (Dec), 3.56
Wyeth (Dec), 2.27, 2.320
Wyndham International, Inc. (Dec), 2.88

X

Xerox Corporation (Dec), 1.85, 2.193, 7.37

Y

Yum! Brands, Inc. (Dec), 1.18, 1.171, 3.25, 3.57

Pronouncement Index

All of the pronouncements cited in the narrative portions (not in the survey company illustrations) of this edition of *Accounting Trends & Techniques* have been listed below. Titles and paragraph locations have been included for ease of use and reference. Specific pronouncement location can also be found by consulting the Subject Index, which follows this section.

Accounting Trends & Techniques

Subject Index

A

B

C

F

FINANCIAL ACCOUNTING STANDARDS BOARD
INTERPRETATIONS *see* "Pronouncement Index"

FINANCIAL ACCOUNTING STANDARDS BOARD
STATEMENTS, *see* Statements of Financial
Accounting Standards (FASB)

FINANCIAL INSTRUMENTS
Accounting Changes, 1.61, 1.62
Concentration of Credit Risk, 1.172–1.175
Derivatives, 1.155–1.159, 2.89, 2.164, 2.215, 2.266, 3.24, 3.54
Fair Value Disclosures, 1.168–1.171
Financial Guarantees, 1.160–1.164
Letters of Credit, 1.165
Liability and Equity Characteristics, 1.61, 1.62
Off-Balance-Sheet, 1.160–1.167
Sale of Receivables With Recourse, 1.166, 1.167
SFAS No. 105, 1.151
SFAS No. 107, 1.151
SFAS No. 119, 1.151
SFAS No. 133, 1.151
SFAS No. 138, 1.151
SFAS No. 149, 1.151
SFAS No. 150, 1.151
Table 1-13: Financial Instruments, 1.154

FINANCIAL STATEMENTS
Comparative, 1.41–1.43, 7.47–7.49
Notes to, 1.46–1.48
Rounding of Amounts, 1.44, 1.45
Table 1-5: Rounding of Amounts, 1.45
Table 1-6: Notes to Financial Statements, 1.48

FINANCING ACTIVITIES, *see* Statement of Cash
Flows

FIRST-IN, FIRST-OUT, *see* Inventories

FISCAL PERIODS
Change in, 1.36, 1.37
Definition, 1.32, 1.38–1.40
Table 1-4: Month of Fiscal Year End, 1.35

FIVE-YEAR SUMMARY OF OPERATIONS
SEC Rule 14a-3 Requirements, 1.12, 1.13

FIXED ASSETS, *see* Property, Plant, and
Equipment

FOREIGN CURRENCY CASH FLOWS, *see* Foreign
Currency Translation

FOREIGN CURRENCY TRANSACTIONS
Gains, 3.23
Losses, 3.50

FOREIGN CURRENCY TRANSLATION
Cumulative Translation Adjustments, 4.23, 4.24
SFAS No. 95, 6.51
Statement of Cash Flows, 6.51–6.53

FORMAT
Balance Sheet, 2.03–2.05
Income Statement, 3.03–3.09
SFAS No. 94, 2.04
Table 2-2, 2.06
Table 3-2, 3.07

FORWARD-LOOKING STATEMENTS
SEC Rule 14a-3 Requirements, 1.16, 1.17

FRANCHISES
Fees, 3.25
Intangible Assets, 2.151

FUTURES, *see* Financial Instruments

G

GAIN CONTINGENCIES
Plaintiff Litigation, 1.110, 1.111
Receivables, 1.112
SFAS No. 5, 1.95
Table 1-11: Contingencies, 1.97

GAINS, *see also* Revenue
Change in Fair Value of Derivatives, 3.24
Debt Extinqiushement, 1.71, 3.29
Discontinued Operations, Adjustment From Prior
Period, 3.148
Equity in Earnings of Investee, 3.21
Foreign Currency Transactions, 3.23
Franchise Fees, 3.25
Income Statement Presentation, 3.19–3.30
Insurance Recoveries, 3.28
Interest, 3.19
Liability Accruals Reduced, 3.22
License Fees, 3.25
Litigation Settlement, 3.26
Nonrecurring Gain, 3.30
Rentals, 3.27
Royalties, 3.25
Sale of Assets, 3.20
Table 3-4: Gains, 3.14

GOODWILL
Accounting Changes, 1.72
Intangible Asset, 2.141–2.144
Lack of Consistency, 7.31, 7.32
Not Amortized, 7.31, 7.32
SFAS No. 142, 2.135

GOVERNMENT
Grants Receivable, 2.44
Investigations, Loss Contingencies, 1.105, 1.106

GUARANTEES AND WARRANTIES
Accounting Changes, 1.65
ESOP Debt, 2.328
Financial Guarantees, 1.160–1.164
Loss Contingencies, 1.109
Other Current Liabilities, 2.208
Other Noncurrent Liabilities, 2.275
Product Warranties, 2.208
Stock Price Guarantee, 5.49

H

HEDGING, *see* Derivatives; Financial Instruments

I

M

N

O

P

Q

R

T

U